Lecture Notes in Computer Science 7042

Commenced Publication in 1973
Founding and Former Series Editors:
Gerhard Goos, Juris Hartmanis, and Jan van Leeuwen

César San Martin Sang-Woon Kim (Eds.)

Progress in Pattern Recognition, Image Analysis, Computer Vision, and Applications

16th Iberoamerican Congress, CIARP 2011
Pucón, Chile, November 15-18, 2011
Proceedings

 Springer

Volume Editors

César San Martin
Universidad de La Frontera
Avda. Francisco Salazar 01145
Temuco, Chile
E-mail: cesarsanmartin@ufro.cl

Sang-Woon Kim
Myongji University
San 38-2, Namdong, Cheoingu, Yongin 449-728
Republic of Korea
E-mail: kimsw@mju.ac.kr

ISSN 0302-9743   e-ISSN 1611-3349
ISBN 978-3-642-25084-2   e-ISBN 978-3-642-25085-9
DOI 10.1007/978-3-642-25085-9
Springer Heidelberg Dordrecht London New York

Library of Congress Control Number: 2011939577

CR Subject Classification (1998): I.5, I.4, I.2.10, I.2.7, F.2.2, J.3

LNCS Sublibrary: SL 6 – Image Processing, Computer Vision, Pattern Recognition,
and Graphics

Typesetting: Camera-ready by author, data conversion by Scientific Publishing Services, Chennai, India

Printed on acid-free paper

Springer is part of Springer Science+Business Media (www.springer.com)

Preface

Nowadays, pattern recognition is a discipline that involves several areas of computer sciences such as: signal and image processing and analysis, computer vision, data mining, neural networks, artificial intelligence, clustering, statistical approaches, as well as their applications in areas like robotics, health, telecommunication, document analysis, speech processing, and natural language among others.

The Iberoamerican Congress on Pattern Recognition (CIARP) series have a relatively long tradition in the Iberoamerican research community, and have had participants from all over the world. CIARP 2011 was held in Pucón, Chile, during November 15–18, and received contributions by authors from Algeria, Argentina, Austria, Brazil, Canada, Chile, Colombia, Cuba, France, Germany, Hungary, Iran, Italy, Republic of Korea, Mexico, The Netherlands, New Zealand, Poland, Portugal, Romania, Russian Federation, Spain, Sweden, Switzerland, Tunisia, UK, USA, and Uruguay.

Previous versions of CIARP were held in Cuba in 1995, 1997, 1999, 2003, 2005, and 2008, Mexico in 1998, 2002, 2004, 2006, 2009, Portugal in 2000, Chile in 2007, and Brazil in 2001 and 2010. The conferences held in Portugal, Brazil, Cuba 2003/2005, Mexico 2004/2006/2008, Chile 2007, and Brazil 2010 were sponsored by IAPR. From the 2003 conference, the proceedings have been published by Springer in its *Lecture Notes in Computer Science* series.

The Organizing Committee of this version hopes that all scientists, researchers, engineers, and students enjoyed the conference, increased their experience and knowledge in pattern recognition fields and also enjoyed the magical environment and welcome offered by Pucón city and its people.

November 2011

César San Martín
Sang-Woon Kim

Organization

CIARP 2011 was organized by the Information Processing Laboratory (IPL) of Universidad de La Frontera (UFRO) Chile.

General Conference Co-chair

César San Martín   Universidad de La Frontera, Chile
Sang-Woon Kim   Myomgji University, South Korea

Volume Editors

César San Martín   IPL Universidad de La Frontera, Chile

Organizing Committee

César San Martín   IPL-UFRO
Gloria Millaray Curilem   UFRO
Marco Mora   Universidad Católica del Maule, Chile

CIARP Steering Committee

José Ruiz Shulcloper   (ACRP, Cuba)
Alberto Sanfeliu   (AERFAI, Spain)
Aurélio Campilho   (APRP, Portugal)
Eduardo Bayro-Corrochano   (MACVNR, Mexico)
César San Martín   (AChiRP, Chile)
Olga Belon   (SIGPR-SBC, Brazil)
Alvaro Pardo   (APRU, Uruguay)
Marta Mejail   (SARP, Argentina)
César Beltrán Castañón   (APeRP, Perú)

Scientific Committee

Marcia Aguena   Brazil
Amadeo Argulles   Mexico
Rene Alquezar   Spain
Leopoldo Altamirano   Mexico
Helder Araujo   Portugal
Jose Miguel Benedi   Spain
Isabelle Bloch   France

Dibio Borges	Brazil
Jesus Ariel Carrasco-Ochoa	Mexico
Anustup Choudhury	USA
Millaray Curilem	Chile
Pablo De Cristforis	Argentina
Ana Luisa Dine	Brazil
Ramiro Donoso	Chile
Robert P. W. Duin	The Netherlands
Jan Olof Eklundh	Sweden
Jacques Facon	Brazil
Edgardo Felipe-Riveron	Mexico
Alicia Fernndez	Uruguay
Francesc J. Ferri	Spain
Ana Fred	Portugal
Vicente Garca	Spain
Alexander Gelbukh	Mexico
Lev Goldfarb	Canada
Herman Gomes	Brazil
Francisco Gomez-Fernandez	Mexico
Norberto Goussies	Argentina
Edwin Hancock	UK
Fernando Huenupan	Chile
Martin Kampel	Austria
Sang-Woon Kim	South Koera
Reinhard Klette	New Zealand
Walter Kropatsch	Austria
Yulia Ledeneva	Mexico
Ales Leonardis	Slovenia
Miren Lopez De Ipia Pea	Spain
Itzam Lpez-Yez	Mexico
Jos Fco. Martnez-Trinidad	Mexico
Nelson Mascarenhas	Brazil
Michelle Matos Horta	Brazil
Gerard Medioni	USA
Marta Mejail	Argentina
Domingo Mery	Chile
Miguel Moctezuma	Mexico
Ramon Mollineda	Spain
Raul Montoliu	Spain
Roman Osorio	Mexico
Alvaro Pardo	Uruguay
Francisco Jose Perales	Spain
Eanes Pereira	Brazil
Maria Petrou	UK
Jorge Pezoa	Chile

Armando Pinho	Portugal
Filiberto Pla	Spain
Carlos Pon	Chile
Orion Reyes-Galaviz	Mexico
Carlos A Reyes-Garcia	Mexico
Vladimir Riazanov	Russian Federation
Roberto Rodriguez	Cuba
Arun Ross	USA
Luis Rueda	Canada
Jose Ruiz-Shulcloper	Cuba
Cesar San Martin	Chile
Joo Sanches	Portugal
Salvador Sanchez	Spain
Carlo Sansone	Italy
Humberto Sossa Azuela	Mexico
Alvaro Soto	Chile
Alessandro Verri	Italy
Xavier Vilasis	Spain
Cornelio Yez-Mrquez	Mexico
Sebastin Zambanini	Austria
Pablo Zegers	Chile
Andreas Zweng	Austria

Sponsoring Institutions

Universidad de La Frontera, Chile, (UFRO)
The International Association for Pattern Recognition (IAPR)
Asociacón Chilena de Reconocimiento de Patrones (AChiRP)
Asociación Cubana de Reconocimiento de Patrones (ACPR)
Mexican Association for Computer Vision, Neural Computing and Robotics
    (MACVNR)
Special Interest Group of the Brazilian Computer Society (SIGPR-SBC)
Asociación Española de Reconocimientos de Formas y Análisis de Imágenes
    (AERFAI)
Portuguese Association for Pattern Recognition (APRP)
Sociedad Argentina de Reconocimiento de Patrones (SARP)
Asociación de Reconocimiento de Patrones de Uruguay (APRU)
Asociación Peruana de Reconocimiento de Patrones (APeRP)

Table of Contents

Computer Vision

Clustering and Artificial Intelligence

Pattern Recognition and Classification

Applications of Pattern Recognition

Selected Topics of Chilean Workshop on Pattern Recognition

The Dissimilarity Representation
for Structural Pattern Recognition

Robert P.W. Duin[1] and Elżbieta Pękalska[2]

[1] Pattern Recognition Laboratory,
Delft University of Technology, The Netherlands
r.duin@ieee.org
[2] School of Computer Science,
University of Manchester, United Kingdom
pekalska@cs.man.ac.uk

Abstract. The patterns in collections of real world objects are often not based on a limited set of isolated properties such as features. Instead, the totality of their appearance constitutes the basis of the human recognition of patterns. Structural pattern recognition aims to find explicit procedures that mimic the learning and classification made by human experts in well-defined and restricted areas of application. This is often done by defining dissimilarity measures between objects and measuring them between training examples and new objects to be recognized.

The dissimilarity representation offers the possibility to apply the tools developed in machine learning and statistical pattern recognition to learn from structural object representations such as graphs and strings. These procedures are also applicable to the recognition of histograms, spectra, images and time sequences taking into account the connectivity of samples (bins, wavelengths, pixels or time samples).

The topic of dissimilarity representation is related to the field of non-Mercer kernels in machine learning but it covers a wider set of classifiers and applications. Recently much progress has been made in this area and many interesting applications have been studied in medical diagnosis, seismic and hyperspectral imaging, chemometrics and computer vision. This review paper offers an introduction to this field and presents a number of real world applications[1].

1 Introduction

In the totality of the world around us we are able to recognize events or objects as separate items distinguished from their surroundings. We recognize the song of a bird in the noise of the wind, an individual tree in the wood, a cup on the table, a face in the crowd or a word in the newspaper. Two steps can now be distinguished. First, the objects are detected in their totality. Second, the isolated

[1] We acknowledge financial support from the FET program within the EU FP7, under the SIMBAD project (contract 213250) as well as the Engineering and Physical Sciences Research Council in the UK.

C. San Martin and S.-W. Kim (Eds.): CIARP 2011, LNCS 7042, pp. 1–24, 2011.

object is recognized. These two steps are strongly interconnected and verified by each other. Only after a satisfactory recognition the detection takes place. It may even be questioned whether it is not artificial to make a distinction of these processes in the human recognition of interesting items in the surrounding world.

It is common to separate the two processes in the design of artificial recognition systems. This is possible and fruitful as it is known what type of objects are considered in most applications. For example, we know that the system under construction has to recognize faces and is not intended to recognize characters or objects such as cups. The detection step is thereby simplified to selectively focus on faces only, on characters only or on cups only. The recognition step, however, may now lack important information from the context: the recognition of an isolated character is more difficult than its recognition given the entire word. Recognition systems that take the context into account can become more accurate, albeit at the price of a higher complexity.

On the level of the recognition of a single object a similar observation can made. In the traditional pattern recognition approaches this is mainly done by describing objects by isolated features. These are object properties that are appropriate locally, at some position on the object, e.g. the sharpness of a corner, or by global properties that describe just a single aspect such as the weight or size of the object. After these features are determined in a first step, the class or the name of the object is determined: it is a cup and not an ashtray, or it is the character 'C' out of the character set in the alphabet. Again it can be doubted whether these steps reflect the human recognition process.

Is it really true that we consciously observe a set of features before we come to a decision? Can we really name well-defined properties that distinguish a cup from an ashtray, or John from Peter? Some experts who have thought this over for their field of expertise may come a long way. Many people, however, can perfectly perform a recognition task, but can hardly name specific features that served the purpose. It is only under pressure when they mention some features.

In general, the process of human decision making may not be based on clear arguments but on an unconscious intuition, instead. Arguments or justifications may be generated afterwards. They may even be disputed and refuted without changing the decision. This points in the direction that human recognition and decision making are global processes. These processes take the entire object or situation into account and a specification into isolated observations and arguments becomes difficult.

The above reasoning raises the question whether it is possible to constitute an automatic pattern recognition procedure that is based on the totality of an object. In this paper some steps in this direction are formulated on the basis of the dissimilarity representation. A review will be given of the research that is done by the authors and their colleagues. Although many papers and experiments will be mentioned that describe their work, it should be emphasized that the context of the research has been of significant importance. The publications and remarks by researchers such as Goldfarb [29], Bunke [44], Hancock and Wilson [40,63], Buhman and Roth [36], Haasdonk [30], Mottle [41], Edelman [25] and

Vapnik [58] have been a significant source of inspiration on this topic. It is however the aim of this paper to sketch our own line of reasoning in such a way that it may serve as inspiration for newcomers in this area. We will therefore restrict this paper to an intuitive explanation illustrated by some examples. More details can be found in the references. Parts of this paper have been extracted from a recent journal paper [20] which deals with the same topic but which is more dedicated to research results and in which less effort has been made to introduce ideas and concepts carefully.

A global description of objects, which takes their totality into account, should be based on knowledge of how all aspects of the object contribute to the way it appears to the observer. To make this knowledge explicit some structural model may be used, e.g. based on graphs. This is not a simple task and usually demands much more background knowledge of the application area than the definition of some local properties such as features. The feature-based approach is mainly an effort in measuring the properties of interest in the observations as presented by the sensors. As features describe objects just partially, objects belonging to different classes may share the same feature vectors. This overlap has to be solved by a statistical analysis. The two approaches, mentioned above, are linked to the two subfields: structural and statistical pattern recognition.

The possibility to merge the two fields has intrigued various researchers over the decades. Thereby, it has been a research topic from the early days of pattern recognition. Originally, most attempts have been made by modifying the structural approach. Watanabe [59] and especially Fu [26] pointed to several possibilities using information theoretic considerations and stochastic syntactical descriptions. In spite of their inspiring research efforts, it hardly resulted in practical applications. Around 1985 Goldfarb [29] proposed to unify the two directions by replacing the feature-based representation of individual objects by distances between structural object models. As this proposal hardly requires a change of the existing structural recognition procedures, it may be considered as an attempt to bridge the gap between the two fields by approaching it from the statistical side. Existing statistical tools might thereby become available in the domain of structural pattern recognition. This idea did not attract much attention as it was hardly recognized as a profitable approach.

After 1995, the authors of this paper started to study this proposal further. They called it the *dissimilarity representation* as it allows various non-metric, indefinite or even asymmetric measures. The first experiences were published in a monograph in 2005, [49]. An inspiration for this approach was also the above explained observation that a human observer is primary triggered by object differences (and later similarities) and that the description by features and models comes second; see [25]. The analysis of dissimilarities, mainly for visualization, was already studied in the domain of psychonomy in the 1960s, e.g. by Shepard [54] and Kruskal [35]. The emphasis of the renewed interest in dissimilarities in pattern recognition, however, was in the construction of vector spaces that are suitable for training classifiers using the extensive toolboxes available in multivariate statistics, machine learning and pattern recognition. The significance for the accessibility of these tools in structural object recognition was recognized by Bunke [55,44] and others such as Hancock and Wilson [64] and Mottle [42,41].

Before introducing the further contents, let us first summarize key advantages and drawbacks of using the dissimilarity representation in statistical learning:

- Powerful statistical pattern recognition approaches become available for structural object descriptions.
- It enables the application expert to use model knowledge in a statistical setting.
- As dissimilarities can be computed on top of a feature-based description, the dissimilarity approach may also be used to design classifiers in a feature space. These classifiers perform very well in comparative studies [23].
- As a result, structural and feature-based information can be combined.
- Insufficient performance can often be improved by more observations without changing the dissimilarity measure.
- The computational complexity during execution, i.e. the time spent on the classification of new objects, is adjustable.
- The original representation can be large and computationally complex as dissimilarities between all object pairs may have to be computed. There are ways to reduce this problem [48,39,13].

In this paper we present an intuitive introduction to dissimilarities (Sec. 2), ways to use them for representation (Sec. 3), the computation of classifiers (Sec. 4), the use of multiple dissimilarities (Sec. 5) and some applications (Sec. 6). The paper is concluded with a discussion of problems under research.

2   Dissimilarities

Suppose we are given an object to be recognized. That means: can we name it, or can we determine a class of objects of which it belongs to? Some representation is needed if we want to feed it to a computer for an automatic recognition. Recognition is based on a comparison with previous observations of objects like the one we have now. So, we have to search through some memory. It would be great if an identical object could be found there. Usually, an exact match is impossible. New objects or their observations are often at least slightly different from the ones previously seen. And this is the challenge of pattern recognition: can we recognize objects that are at most similar to the examples that we have been given before? This implies that we need at least the possibility to express the similarity between objects in a quantitative way. In addition, it is not always advantageous to look for an individual match. The generalization of classes of objects to a 'concept', or a distinction which can be expressed in a simple classification rule is often faster, demands less memory and/or can be more accurate.

It has been observed before [25], and it is in line with the above discussions, that in human recognition processes it is more natural to rely on similarities or dissimilarities between objects than to find explicit features of the objects that are used in the recognition. This points to a representation of objects based on a pairwise comparison of the new examples with examples that are already collected. This differs from the feature-based representations that constitute the basis of the traditional approaches to pattern recognition described in the well-known textbooks by Fukunaga [27], Duda, Hart and Stork [17], Devijver and Kittler [16], Ripley [53], Bishop [7],Webb [60] and Theodorides [56]. We want to point out that although the pairwise dissimilarity representation presented here is different in its foundation from the feature-based representation, many procedures described in the textbooks can be applied in a fruitful way.

We will now assume that a human recognizer, preferably an expert w.r.t. the objects of interest, is able to formulate a dissimilarity measure between objects that reflects his own perception of object differences (for now we will stick to dissimilarity measures). A dissimilarity measure $d(o_i, o_j)$ between two objects o_i and o_j out of a training set of n objects may have one or more of the following properties for all $i, j, k \leq n$.

- **Non-negativity:** $d(o_i, o_j) \geq 0$.
- **Identity of indiscernibles:** $d(o_i, o_j) = 0$ if and only if $o_i \equiv o_j$.
- **Symmetry:** $d(o_i, o_j) = d(o_j, o_i)$.
- **Triangle inequality:** $d(o_i, o_j) + d(o_j, o_k) \geq d(o_i, o_k)$.
- **Euclidean:** An $n \times n$ dissimilarity matrix D is Euclidean if there exists an isometric Euclidean embedding into a Euclidean space. In other words, a Euclidean space with n vectors can be found such that the pairwise Euclidean distances between these vectors are equal to the original distances in D.
- **Compactness:** A dissimilarity measure is defined here as compact if a sufficiently small perturbation of an object (from a set of allowed transformations) leads to an arbitrary small dissimilarity value between the disturbed object and its original. We call such a measure compact because it results in compact class descriptions for which sufficiently small disturbances will not change the class membership of objects. Note that this definition is different than compactness discussed in topological spaces.

The first two properties together produce positive definite dissimilarity measures. The first four properties coincide with the mathematical definition of a metric distance measure.

Non-negativity and symmetry seem to be obvious properties, but sometimes dissimilarity measures are defined otherwise. E.g. if we define the distance to a city as the distance to the border of that city, then a car that reaches the border from outside has a distance zero. When the car drives further into the city the distance may be counted as negative in order to keep consistency. An example of an asymmetric distance measure is the directed Hausdorff distance between two sets of points A and B: $d_H(A, B) = max_x\{min_y\{d(x, y), x \in A, y \in B\}\}$.

An important consequence of using positive definite dissimilarity measures is that classes are separable for unambiguously labeled objects (identical objects belong to the same class). This directly follows from the fact that if two objects have a distance zero they should be identical and as a consequence they belong to the same class. For such classes a zero-error classifier exists (but may still be difficult to find). See [49]. This is only true if the dissimilarity measure reflects all object differences. Dissimilarity measures based on graphs, histograms, features or other derived measurements may not be positive definite as different objects may still be described by the same graph (or histogram, or sequence) and thereby have a zero dissimilarity.

The main property is the Euclidean property. A metric distance measure in fact states that the Euclidean property holds for every set of three points while the first two properties (positive definiteness) state that the dissimilarity of every pair of points is Euclidean.

We may distinguish the properties of the dissimilarity measure itself and the way it works out for a set of objects. The first should be analyzed mathematically from the definition of the measure and the known properties of the objects. The second can be checked numerically from a given $n \times n$ dissimilarity matrix D. There might be a discrepancy between what is observed in a finite data matrix and the definition of the measure. It may occur for instance that the matrix D for a given training set of objects is perfectly Euclidean but that the dissimilarities for new objects behave differently.

The concept of compactness is important for pattern recognition. It was first used in the Russian literature around 1965, e.g. see Arkedev and Braverman [3], and also [18]. We define here that a compact class of objects consists of a finite number of subsets, such that in each subset every object can be continuously transformed (morphed) into every other object of that subset without passing through objects outside the subset. This property of compactness is slightly different from the original concept defined in [3] where it is used as a hypothesis on which classifiers are defined. It is related to the compactness used in topology. Compactness is a basis for generalization from examples. Without proof we state here that for compact classes the consequence of the no-free-lunch theorem [65] (every classifier is as good as any other classifier unless we use additional knowledge) is avoided: compactness pays the lunch. The prospect is that for the case of positive definite dissimilarity measures and unambiguously labeled objects, the classes can be separated perfectly by classifiers of a finite complexity.

3 Representation

A representation of real world objects is needed in order to be able to relate to them. It prepares the generalization step by which new, unseen objects are classified. So, the better the representation, the more accurate classifiers can be trained. The traditional representation is defined by numerical features. The use of dissimilarities is an attractive alternative, for which arguments were given in Introduction. This section provides more details by focussing on the object structure.

3.1 Structural Representations

The concept of structure is ill defined. It is related to the global connectivity of all parts of the object. An image can be described by a set of pixels organized in a square grid. This grid may be considered as the structure of the image. It is, however, independent of the content of the image. If this is taken into account then the connectivity between the pixels may be captured by weights, e.g. related to the intensity values of the neighboring pixels. We may also forget that there are pixels and determine regions in the image by a segmentation procedure. The structure may then be represented by a graph in which every node is related to an image segment and the graph edges correspond to neighboring segments. Nodes and edges may have attributes that describe properties of the segments and the borders between them.

A simpler example of a structure is the contour of an image segment or a blob: its shape. The concept of shape leads to a structure, but shapes are also characterized by features, e.g. the number of extremes or a set of moments. A structural representation of a shape is a string. This is a sequence of symbols representing small shape elements, such as straight lines (in some direction) or curves with predefined curvatures. Shapes are also found in spectra, histograms and time signals. The movement of an object or a human body may be described as a set of coordinates in a high-dimensional space as a function of time. This multi-dimensional trajectory has a shape and may be considered as a structure.

The above examples indicate that structures also have some (local) properties that are needed for their characterization. Examples of pure structures without attributes can hardly be found. Certainly, if we want to represent them in a way that facilitates comparisons, we will use attributes and relations (connections). The structural representations used here will be restricted to attributed graphs and sequences.

3.2   The Dissimilarity Representation

Dissimilarities themselves have been discussed in Sec. 2. Three sets of objects may be distinguished for constructing a representation:

- **A representation set** $R = \{r_1, \ldots, r_k\}$. These are the objects we refer to. The dissimilarities to the representation set have to be computed for training objects as well as for test objects used for evaluation, or any objects to be classified later. Sometimes the objects in the set R are called prototypes. This word may suggest that these objects are in some way typical examples of the classes. That can be the case but it is not necessary. So prototypes may be used for representation, but the representation set may also consist of other objects.
- **A training set** $T = \{o_1, \ldots, o_n\}$. These are the objects that are used to train classifiers. In many applications we use $T := R$, but R may also be just a (small) subset of T, or be entirely different from T.
- **A test set** S. These are the objects that are used to evaluate classification procedure. They should be representative for the target objects for which the classification procedure is built.

After determining these three sets of objects the dissimilarity matrices $D(T, R)$ and $D(S, R)$ have to be computed. Sometimes also $D(T, T)$ is needed, e.g. when the representation set $R \subset T$ has to be determined by a specific algorithm. The next problem is how to use these two or three matrices for training and testing. Three procedures are usually considered:

- **The k-nearest neighbor classifier.** This is the traditional way to classify new objects in the field of structural pattern recognition: assign new objects to the (majority) class of its (k) nearest neighbor(s). This procedure can directly by applied to $D(S, T)$. The dissimilarities inside the training set, $D(T, T)$ or $D(T, R)$ are not used.
- **Embedded space.** Here a vector space and a metric (usually Euclidean) are determined from $D(T, T)$ containing $n = |T|$ vectors, such that the distances between these vectors are equal to the given dissimilarities. See Sec. 3.3 for more details.
- **The dissimilarity space.** This space is postulated as a Euclidean vector space defined by the dissimilarity vectors $d(\cdot, R) = [d(\cdot, r_1), \dots, d(\cdot, r_k)]^T$ computed to the representation set R as dimensions. Effectively, the dissimilarity vectors are used as numerical features. See Sec. 3.4.

3.3   Embedding of Dissimilarities

The topic of embedding dissimilarity matrices has been studied for a long time. As mentioned in the introduction (Sec. 1), it was originally used for visualizing the results of psychonomic experiments and other experiments representing data in pairwise object comparisons [54,35]. In such visualization tasks, a reliable, usually 2D map of the data structure is of primary importance. Various nonlinear procedures have been developed over the years under the name of multi-dimensional scaling (MDS) [9].

It is difficult to reliably project new data to an existing embedded space resulting from a nonlinear embedding. Therefore, such embeddings are unsuitable for pattern recognition purposes in which a classifier trained in the embedded space needs to be applied to new objects. A second, more important drawback of the use of nonlinear MDS for embedding is that the resulting space does not reflect the original distances anymore. It usually focusses either on local or global object relations to force a 2D (or other low-dimensional) result.

For the purpose of generalization a restriction to low-dimensional spaces is not needed. Moreover, for the purpose of the projection of new objects linear procedures are preferred. Therefore, the linear MDS embedding has been studied, also known as classical scaling [9]. As the resulting Euclidean space is by its very nature not able to perfectly represent non-Euclidean dissimilarity data, see Sec. 2, a compromise has to be made. The linear Euclidean embedding procedure is based on an eigenvalue decomposition of the Gram matrix derived from the given $n \times n$ dissimilarity matrix D, see [29,49], in which some eigenvalues become negative for non-Euclidean dissimilarities. This conflicts with the construction of a Euclidean space as these eigenvalues are related to variances of the extracted features, which should be positive. This is solved in classical scaling by neglecting all 'negative' directions. The distances in this embedded space may thereby be entirely different from the original dissimilarity matrix D.

The approach followed by the pseudo-Euclidean embedding is to construct a vector space [49] in which the metric is adjusted such that the squared distance contributions of the 'negative' eigenvectors are counted as negative. The resulting pseudo-Euclidean space thereby consists out of two orthogonal Euclidean spaces of which the distances are not added (in the squared sense) but subtracted. Distances computed in this way are exactly equal to the original dissimilarities, provided that they are symmetric and self-dissimilarity is zero. Such an embedding is therefor an isometric mapping of the original D into a suitable pseudo-Euclidean space, which is an inner product space with an indefinite inner product.

The perfect representation of D in a pseudo-Euclidean embedded space is an interesting proposal, but it is not free from some disadvantages:

– Embedding relies on a square dissimilarity matrix, usually $D(T, T)$. The dissimilarities between all pairs of training objects should be taken into account. The computation of this matrix as well as the embedding procedure itself may thereby be time and memory demanding operations.
– Classifiers that obey the specific metric of the Pseudo-Euclidean space are difficult to construct or not yet well defined. Some have been studied [32,50,21], but many problems remain. For instance, it is not clear how to define a normal distribution in a pseudo-Euclidean space. Also the computation of SVM may be in trouble as the related kernel is indefinite, in general [31]. Solutions are available for specific cases. See also Sec. 4.
– There is a difficulty in a meaningful projection of new objects to an existing pseudo-Euclidean embedded space. The straightforward projection operations are simple and linear, but they may yield solutions with negative distances to other objects even though the original distances are non-negative. This usually happens when a test object is either an outlier or not well represented in the training set T (which served to define the embedded space). A possible solution is to include such objects in the embedding procedure and retrain the classifier for the new objects. For test objects this implies that they will participate in the representation. Classification may thereby improve at the cost of the retraining. This approach is also known as transductive learning [58].
– The fact that embedding strictly obeys the given dissimilarities is not always an advantage. All types of noise and approximations related to the computation of dissimilarities are expressed in the result. It may thereby be questioned whether all non-Euclidean aspects of the data are informative. In [19] it is shown that there are problems for which this is really the case.

In order to define a proper topology and metric, mathematical texts, e.g. [8], propose to work with the associated Euclidean space instead of the pseudo-Euclidean space. In this approach all 'negative' directions are treated as 'positive' ones. As a result, one can freely use all traditional classifiers in such a space. The information extracted from the dissimilarity matrix is used but the original distance information is not preserved and may even be significantly distorted. Whether this is beneficial for statistical learning depends on the problem.

3.4   The Dissimilarity Space

The dissimilarity space [46,49] postulates a Euclidean vector space defined by the dissimilarity vectors. The elements of these vectors are dissimilarities from a given object to the objects in the representation set R. The dissimilarity vectors serve as features for the objects in the training set. Consequently, such a space overcomes all problems that usually arise with the non-Euclidean dissimilarity measures, simply by neglecting the character of the dissimilarity. This approach is at least locally consistent for metric distance measures: distances in the dissimilarity space between pairs of objects characterized by small dissimilarities $d(o_i, o_j)$ will also have a small distance as their dissimilarity vectors $d(o_i, R) = [d(o_i, r_1), \ldots, d(o_i, r_k)]^T$ and $d(o_j, R) = [d(o_j, r_1), \ldots, d(o_j, r_k)]^T$ will be about equal. This may serve as a proof that the topology of a set of objects with given dissimilarities $\{d(o_i, o_j)\}_{i,j=1:n}$ is identical to the topology of this set of objects in the dissimilarity space $\{d_E(d(o_i, R), d(o_j, R))\}_{i,j=1:n}$ provided that R is sufficiently large (to avoid that different objects have, by accident, a zero distance in the dissimilarity space).

If all training objects are used for representation, the dimension of the dissimilarity space is equal to $|T|$. Although, in principle, any classifier defined for a feature space may be applied to the dissimilarity space, some of them will be ill-defined or overtrained for such a large representation set. Dimension reduction, e.g. by prototype selection may thereby be an important issue in this approach [48,39,13]. Fortunately, these studies show that if the reduction is not put to the extreme, a randomly selected representation set may do well. Here the dissimilarity space is essentially different from a traditional feature space: features may be entirely different in their nature. A random selection of R may exclude a few significant examples. The objects in a training set, however, will in expectation include many similar ones. So, a random selection is expected to sample all possible aspects of the training set, provided that the training set T as well as the selected R are sufficiently large.

If a representation set R is a subset of T and we use the complete set T in training, the resulting representation $D(T, R)$ contains some zero dissimilarities to objects in R. This is not expected to be the case for new test objects. In that sense the training objects that participate in the representation set are not representative for test objects. It might be better to exclude them. In all our experiments however we found just minor differences in the results if we used $D(T \backslash R, R)$ instead of $D(T, R)$.

Although any feature-based classifier can be used in a dissimilarity space, some fit more naturally than others. For that reason we report a number of experiments and their findings in Sec. 4.

4   Classifiers

We will discuss here a few well-known classifiers and their behavior in various spaces. This is a summary of our experiences in many studies and applications. See [49] and its references.

In making a choice between embedding and the dissimilarity space for training a classifier one should take into account the essential differences between these spaces. As already stated, embedding strictly obeys the distance characteristics of the given dissimilarities, while the dissimilarity spaces neglects this. In addition, there is a nonlinear transformation between these spaces: by computing the distances to the representation objects in the embedded space the dissimilarity space can be defined. As a consequence, a linear classifier in the embedded space is a nonlinear classifier in the dissimilarity space, and the other way around. Comparing linear classifiers computed in these spaces is thereby comparing linear and nonlinear classifiers.

It is outside the scope of this paper, but the following observation might be helpful for some readers. If the dissimilarities are not constructed by a procedure on a structural representation of objects, but are derived as Euclidean distances in a feature space, then the pseudo-Euclidean embedding effectively reconstructs the original Euclidean feature space (except for orthonormal transformations). So in that case a linear classifier in the dissimilarity space is a nonlinear classifier in the embedded space, which is the same nonlinear classifier in the feature space. Such a classifier, computed in a dissimilarity space, can perform very well [23].

4.1 Nearest Neighbor Classifier

The k-nearest neighbor (k-NN) classifier in an embedded (pseudo-)Euclidean space is based on the distances computed in this space. By definition these are the original dissimilarities (provided that the test examples are embedded together with the training objects). So without the process of embedding this classifier, can directly be applied to a given dissimilarity matrix. This is the classifier traditionally used by many researchers in the area of structural pattern recognition. The study of the dissimilarity representation arose because this classifier does not make use of the given dissimilarities in the training set. Classification is entirely based on the dissimilarities of a test object to the objects in the training (or representation) set only.

The k-NN rule computed in the dissimilarity space relies on a Euclidean distance between the dissimilarity vectors, hence the nearest neighbors are determined by using all dissimilarities of a given object to the representation objects. As explained in Sec. 3.4 for the metric case and for large sets it is expected that the distances between similar objects are small for the two spaces. So, it is expected that learning curves are asymptotically identical, but for small training sets the dissimilarity space works better as it uses more information.

4.2 Parzen Density Classifiers

The class densities computed by the Parzen kernel density procedure are based on pairwise distance computations between objects. The applicability of this classifier as well as its performance is thereby related to those of the k-NN rule. Differences are that this classifier is more smooth, depending on the choice of the smoothing parameter (kernel) and that its optimization involves the entire training set.

4.3   Normal Density Bayes Classifiers

Bayes classifiers assume that classes can be described by probability density functions. Using class priors and Bayes' rule the expected classification error is minimized. In case of normal density function either a linear classifier (Linear Discriminant Analysis, LDA) arises on the basis of equal class covariances, or a quadratic classifier is obtained for the general case (Quadratic Discriminant Analysis, QDA). These two classifiers belong to best possible in case of (close to) normal class distributions and a sufficiently large training set. As mean vectors and covariance matrices can be computed in a pseudo-Euclidean space, see [29,49], these classifiers exist there as well if we forget the starting point of normal distributions. The reason is that normal distributions are not well defined in pseudo-Euclidean spaces; it is not clear what a normal distribution is unless we refer to associated Euclidean spaces.

In a dissimilarity space the assumption of normal distributions works often very well. This is due to the fact that many cases dissimilarity measures are based on, or related to sums of numerical differences. Under certain conditions large sums of random variables tend to be normally distributed. It is not perfectly true for distances as we often get Weibull [12] or χ^2 distributions, but the approximations are sufficient for a good performance of LDA and QDA. The effect is emphasized if the classification procedure involves the computation of linear subspaces, e.g. by PCA. Thanks to projections normality is emphasized even more.

4.4   Fisher's Linear Discriminant

In a Euclidean space the Fisher linear discriminant (FLD) is defined as the linear classifier that maximizes the Fisher criterion, i.e. the ratio of the between-class variance to the within-class variance. For a two-class problem, the solution is equivalent to LDA (up to an added constant), even though no assumption is made about normal distributions. Since variance and covariance matrices are well defined in pseudo-Euclidean spaces, the Fisher criterion can be used to derive the FLD classifier there. Interestingly, FLD in a pseudo-Euclidean space coincides with FLD in the associated Euclidean space. FLD is a linear classifier in a pseudo-Euclidean space, but can be rewritten to FLD in the associated space; see also [50,32].

In a dissimilarity space, which is Euclidean by definition, FLD coincides with LDA for a two-class problem. The performance of these classifiers may differ for multi-class problems as the implementations of FLD and LDA will usually vary then. Nevertheless, FLD performs very well. Due to the nonlinearity of the dissimilarity measure, FLD in a dissimilarity space corresponds to a nonlinear classifier in the embedded pseudo-Euclidean space.

4.5   Logistic Classifier

The logistic classifier is based on a model of the class posterior probabilities as a function of the distance to the classifier [1]. The distance between a vector and a linear hyperplane in a pseudo-Euclidean space however is an unsuitable concept for classification as it can have any value $(-\infty, \infty)$ for vectors on the same side of this hyperplane. We are not aware of a definition and an implementation of the logistic classifier for pseudo-Euclidean spaces. Alternatively, the logistic classifier can be constructed in the associated Euclidean space.

In a dissimilarity space, the logistic classifier performs well, although normal density based classifiers work often better. It relaxes the demands for normality as made by LDA. It is also more robust in case of high-dimensional spaces.

4.6   Support Vector Machine (SVM)

The linear kernel in a pseudo-Euclidean space is indefinite (non-Mercer). The quadratic optimization procedure used to optimize a linear SVM may thereby fail [30]. SVM can however be constructed if the contribution of the positive subspace of the Euclidean space is much stronger than that of the negative subspace. Mathematically, it means that the measure is slightly deviating from the Euclidean behavior and the solution of SVM optimization is found in the positive definite neighborhood. Various researchers have reported good results in applying this classifier, e.g. see [11]. Although the solution is not guaranteed and the algorithm (in this case LIBSVM, [14]) does not stop in a global optimum, a good classifier can be obtained.

In case of a dissimilarity space the (linear) SVM is particularly useful for computing classifiers in the complete space for which $R := T$. The given training set defines therefore a separable problem. The SVM does not or just hardly overtrain in this case. The advantage of this procedure is that it does not demand a reduction of the representation set. A linear SVM is well defined. By normalizing the dissimilarity matrix (such that the average dissimilarity is one) we found stable and good results in many applications by setting the trade-off parameter C in the SVM procedure [15] to $C = 100$. Hereby, additional cross-validation loops are avoided to optimize this parameter. As a result, in an application one can focus on optimizing the dissimilarity measure.

4.7   Combining Classifiers

In the area of dissimilarity representations many approaches can be considered. Various strategies can be applied for the choice of the representation set, either embedded or dissimilarity spaces can be used, and various modifications can be considered, e.g. refinements or correction procedures for these spaces; see [24,21]. Instead of selecting one of the approaches, classifier combining may provide an additional value. However, as all these classifiers are based on the same dissimilarities they do not provide any additional or valuable information. Effectively, just additional procedures are considered that encode different nonlinearities. As the given square dissimilarity matrix D describes an already linearly separable set of objects (under the assumption of the positive definite dissimilarity) we do not expect that in general much can be gained by combining, although an occasional success is possible in particular problems.

5   Multiple Dissimilarities

Instead of generating sets of classifiers defined on the same dissimilarity representation also modifications of the dissimilarity measure may be considered. Another measure can emphasize other aspects of the objects. The resulting dissimilarity matrices cannot be derived from each other, in general. Consequently, they are chosen to encode different information. Combining various dissimilarity representations or classifiers derived from them is now much more of interest. These types of studies are closely related to the studies on kernel metric learning [61,68,66]. An important difference is that the study of kernels is often focussed on the use of SVM for classification, and consequently positive definite kernels obeying the Mercer conditions are the key. As the dissimilarity representation permits many classifiers this point is not relevant for dissimilarity measures. On the contrary, the unrestricted use of dissimilarity definitions is of particular significance for structural pattern recognition as there non-Euclidean measures naturally arise. See also [22].

There are a number of reasons why a set of different dissimilarities between objects arises. A few examples are:

- The same set of objects is observed multiple times under different conditions.
- The dissimilarities are computed on different samplings from the original signals (multi-scale approach).
- Different dissimilarity measures are used on the same signals.

A very interesting observation that can be made from various studies such as [33,57] is that a simple element-wise averaging of dissimilarity matrices defined by different measures often leads to a significant improvement of the classification error over the best individual measure. Attempts to improve this further by a weighted averaging is sometimes successful but often appears not to be useful. The precise value of the weights does not seem to be very significant, either.

6   Application Examples

In this section we will discuss a few examples that are typical for the possibilities of the use of dissimilarities in structural pattern recognition problems. Some have been published by us before [22] for another readership. They are repeated here as they may serve well as an illustration in this paper.

6.1   Shapes

A simple and clear example of a structural pattern recognition problem is the recognition of blobs: 2D binary structures. An example is given in Fig. 1. It is an object out of the five-class chickenpieces dataset consisting of 445 images [2]. One of the best structural recognition procedure uses a string representation of the contour described by a set of segments of the same length [10]. The string elements are the consecutive angles of these segments. The weighted edit

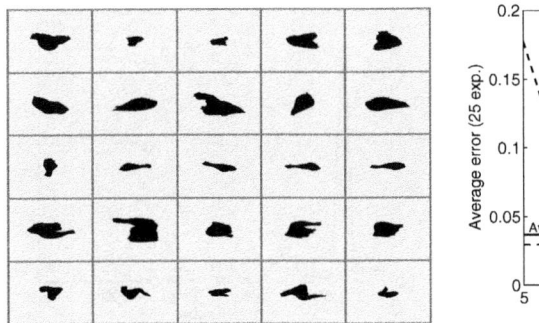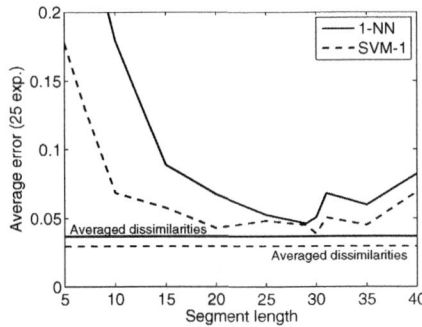

Fig. 1. Left: some examples of the chickenpieces dataset. Right: the error curves as a function of the segment length L.

distances between all pairs of contours are used to compute dissimilarities. This measure is non-Euclidean. A (γ, L) family of problems is considered depending on the specific choice for the cost of one editing operation γ as well as for the segment's length L used in the contour description. As a result, the classification performance depends on the parameters used, as shown in Fig 1, right. 10-fold cross-validation errors are shown there for the 1-NN rule directly applied on the dissimilarities as well as the results for the linear SVM computed by LIBSVM, [14], in the dissimilarity space. In addition the results are shown for the average of the 11 dissimilarity matrices. It is clearly observed that the linear classifier in the dissimilarity space (SVM-1) improves the traditional 1-NN results and that combining the dissimilarities improves the results further on.

6.2   Histograms and Spectra

Histograms and spectra offer very simple examples of data representations that are judged by human experts on their shape. In addition, also the sampling of the bins or wavelengths may serve as a useful vector representation for an automatic analysis. This is thanks to the fact that the domain is bounded and that spectra are often aligned. Below we give an example in which the dissimilarity representation outperforms the straightforward vector representation based on sampling because the first can correct for a wrong calibration (resulting in an imperfect alignment) in a pairwise fashion. Another reason to prefer dissimilarities for histograms and spectra over sampled vectorial data is that a dissimilarity measure encodes shape information. For examples see the papers by Porro [52,51].

   We will consider now a dataset of 612 FL3-A DNA flow cytometer histograms from breast cancer tissues in a resolution of 256 bins. The initial data were acquired by M. Nap and N. van Rodijnen of the Atrium Medical Center in Heerlen, The Netherlands, during 2000-2004, using the four tubes 3-6 of a DACO Galaxy flow cytometer. Histograms are labeled into three classes: aneuploid (335 patients), diploid (131) and tetraploid (146). We averaged the histograms of the four tubes thereby covering the DNA contents of about 80000 cells per patient.

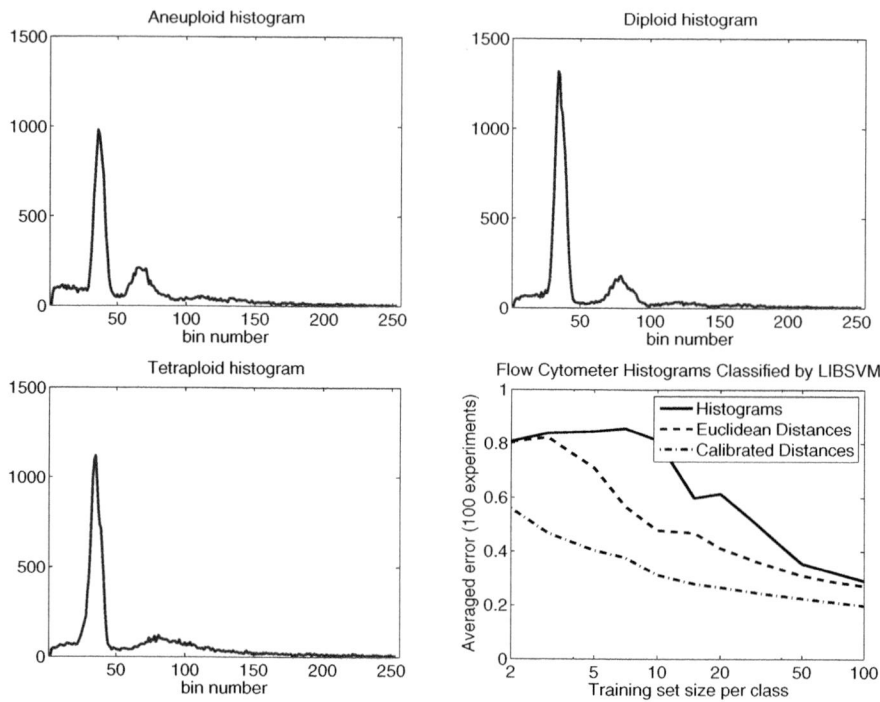

Fig. 2. Examples of some flow cytometer histograms: aneuploid, diploid and tetraploid. Bottom right shows the learning curves.

We removed the first and the last bin of every histogram as here outliers are collected, thereby obtaining 254 bins per histogram. Examples of histograms are shown in Fig. 2. The following representations are used:

Histograms. Objects (patients) are represented by the normalized values of the histograms (summed to one) described by a 254-dimensional vector. This representation is similar to the pixel representation used for images as it is based on just a sampling of the measurements.

Euclidean distances. These dissimilarities are computed as the Euclidean distances in the vector space mentioned above. Every object is represented by by a vector of distances to the objects in the training set.

Calibrated distances. As the histograms may suffer from an incorrect calibration in the horizontal direction (DNA content) for every pairwise dissimilarity we compute the multiplicative correction factor for the bin positions that minimizes their dissimilarity. Here we used the ℓ_1 distance. This representation makes use of the shape structure of the histograms and removes an invariant (the wrong original calibration).

A linear SVM with a fixed trade-off parameter C is used in learning. The learning curves for the three representations are shown in the bottom right of Fig. 2. They clearly illustrate how for this classifier the dissimilarity representation leads to

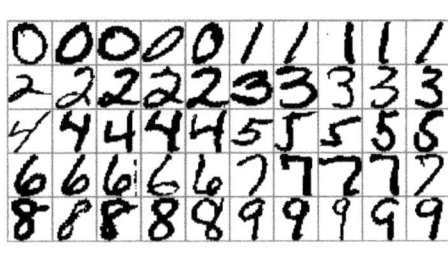

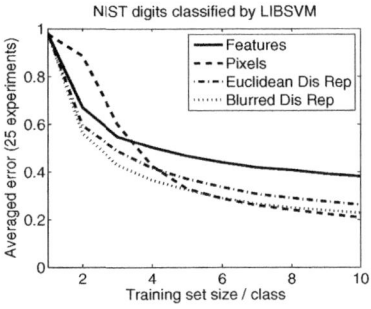

Fig. 3. Left: examples of the images used for the digit recognition experiment. Right: the learning curves.

better results than the vector representation based on the histogram sampling. The use of the background knowledge in the definition of the dissimilarity measure improves the results further.

6.3   Images

The recognition of objects on the basis of the entire image can only be done if these images are aligned. Otherwise, earlier pre-procession or segmentation is necessary. This problem is thereby a 2-dimensional extension of the histogram and spectra recognition task. We will show an example of digit recognition by using a part of the classic NIST database of handwritten numbers [62] on the basis of random subsets of 500 digits for the ten classes 0-9. The images were resampled to 32×32 pixels in such a way that the digits fit either horizontally or vertically. Fig. 3 shows a few examples: black is '1' and white is '0'. The dataset is repeatedly split into training and test sets and hold-out classification is applied. In every split the ten classes are evenly represented.

The following representations are used:

Features. We used 10 moments: the seven rotations invariant moments and the moments $[00], [01], [10]$, measuring the total number of black pixels and the centers of gravity in the horizontal and vertical directions.

Pixels. Every digit is represented by a vector of the intensity values in $32 * 32 = 1024$ dimensional vector space.

Dissimilarities to the training object. Every object is represented by the Euclidean distances to all objects in the training set.

Dissimilarities to blurred digits in the training set. As the pixels in the digit images are spatially connected blurring may emphasize this. In this way the distances between slightly rotated, shifted or locally transformed but otherwise identical digits becomes small.

The results are shown in Fig. 3 on the right. They show that the pixel representation is superior for large training sets. This is to be expected as this representation stores asymptotically the universe of possible digits. For small training sets a suitable set of features may perform better. The moments we use here are very general features. Better ones can be found for digit description. As explained before a feature-based description reduces the (information on the) object: it may be insensitive for some object modifications. For sufficiently large representation sets the dissimilarity representation may see all object differences and may thereby perform better.

6.4   Sequences

The recognition of sequences of observations is in particular difficult if the sequences of a given class vary in length, but capture the same 'story' (information) from the beginning to the end. Some may run faster, or even run faster over just a part of the story and slow down elsewhere. A possible solution is to rely on Dynamic Time Warping (DTW) that relates the sequences in a nonlinear way, yet obeys the order of the events. Once two sequences are optimally aligned, the distance between them may be computed.

An example in which the above has been applied successfully is the recognition of 3-dimensional gestures from the sign language [38] based on an statistically optimized DTW procedure [4]. We took a part of a dataset of this study: the 20 classes (signs) that were most frequently available. Each of these classes has 75 examples. The entire dataset thereby consists of a 1500×1500 matrix of DTW-based dissimilarities. The leave-one-out 1-NN error for this dataset is 0.041, which is based on the computation of 1499 DTW dissimilarities per test object. In Fig. 4, left, a scatterplot is shown of the first two PCA components showing that some classes can already be distinguished with these two features (linear combinations of dissimilarities).

We studied dissimilarity representations consisting of just one randomly drawn example per class. The resulting dissimilarity space has thereby 20 dimensions. New objects have to be compared with just these 20 objects. This space is now filled with randomly selected training sets of containing between 2 and 50 objects per class. Remaining objects are used for testing. Two classifiers are studied, the linear SVM (using the LIBSVM package [14]) with a fixed trade-off parameter $C = 100$ (we used normalized dissimilarity matrices with average dissimilarities of 100) and LDA. The experiment was repeated 25 times and the results averaged out. The learning curves in Fig. 4, right, show the constant value of the 1-NN classifier performance using the dissimilarities to the single training examples per class only, and the increasing performances of the two classifiers for a growing number of training objects. Their average errors for 50 training objects per class is 0.07. Recall that this is still based on the computation of just 20 DTW dissimilarities per object as we work in the related 20-dimensional dissimilarity space. Our experiments show that LDA reaches an error of 0.035 for a representation set of three objects per class, i.e. 60 objects in total. Again, the training set size is 50 examples per class, i.e. 1000 examples in total. For testing new objects one needs to compute a weighted sum (linear combination) of 60 dissimilarity values giving the error of 0.035 instead of computing and ordering 1500 dissimilarities to all training objects for the 1-NN classifier leading to an error of 0.041.

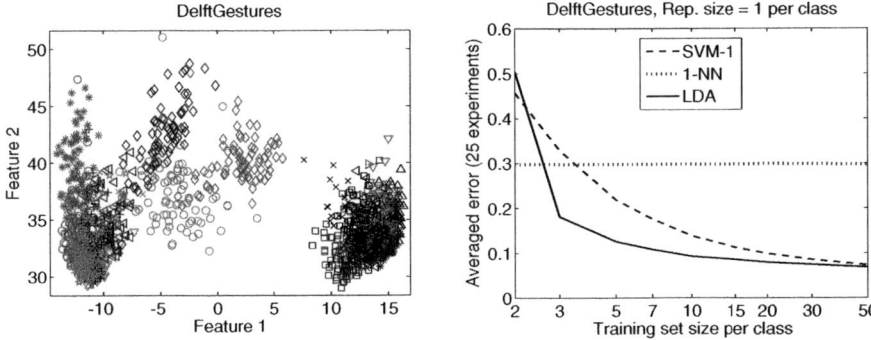

Fig. 4. PCA and learning curves for the 20-class Delft Gesture Dataset

6.5   Graphs

Graphs[2] are the main representation for describing structure in observed objects. In order to classify new objects, the pairwise differences between graphs have to be computed by using a graph matching technique. The resulting dissimilarities are usually related to the cost of matching and may be used to define a dissimilarity representation. We present here classification results obtained with a simple set of graphs describing four objects in the Coil database [43] described by 72 images for every object. The graphs are the Delaunay triangulations derived from corner points found in these images; see [67]. They are unattributed. Hence, the graphs describe the structure only. We used three dissimilarity measures:

CoilDelftSame. Dissimilarities are found in a 5D space of eigenvectors derived from the two graphs by the JoEig approach; see [37]
CoilDelftDiff. Graphs are compared in the eigenspace with a dimensionality determined by the smallest graph in every pairwise comparison by the JoEig approach; see [37]
CoilYork. Dissimilarities are found by graph matching, using the algorithm of Gold and Ranguranjan; [28]

All dissimilarity matrices are normalized such that the average dissimilarity is 1. In addition to the three dissimilarity datasets we used also their averaged dissimilarity matrix.

In a 10-fold cross-validation experiment, with $R := T$, we use four classifiers: the 1-NN rule on the given dissimilarities and the 1-NN rule in the dissimilarity space (listed as 1-NND in Table 6.5), LDA on a PCA-derived subspace covering 99% of the variance and the linear SVM with a fixed trade-off parameter $C = 1$. All experiments are repeated 25 times. Table 6.5 reports the mean classification errors and the standard deviations of these means in between brackets. Some interesting observations are:

---

[2] Results presented in this section are based on joint research with Prof. Richard Wilson, University of York, UK, and Dr. Wan-Jui Lee, Delft University of Technology, The Netherlands.

Table 1. 10-fold cross-validation errors averaged over 25 repetitions

dataset	1-NN	1-NND	PCA-LDA	SVM-1
CoilDelftDiff	0.477 (0.002)	0.441 (0.003)	0.403 (0.003)	0.395 (0.003)
CoilDelftSame	0.646 (0.002)	0.406 (0.003)	0.423 (0.003)	0.387 (0.003)
CoilYork	0.252 (0.003)	0.368 (0.004)	0.310 (0.004)	0.326 (0.003)
Averaged	0.373 (0.002)	0.217 (0.003)	0.264 (0.003)	0.238 (0.002)

- The CoilYork dissimilarity measure is apparently much better than the two CoilDelft measures.
- The classifiers in the dissimilarity space however are not useful for the CoilYork measure, but they are for the CoilDelft measures. Apparently these two ways of computing dissimilarities are essentially different.
- Averaging all three measures significantly improves the classifier performance in the resulting dissimilarity space, even outperforming the original best CoilYork result. It is striking that this does not hold for the 1-NN rule applied to the original dissimilarities.

7   Discussion

In this paper we have given a review of the arguments why the dissimilarity representation is useful for applications in structural pattern recognition. This has been illustrated by a set of examples on real world data. This all shows that using the collective information from all other objects and relating them to each other on the top of the given pairwise dissimilarities (either in the dissimilarity or embedded space), reveals an additional source of information that is otherwise unexplored.

The dissimilarity representation makes the statistical pattern recognition tools available for structural data. In addition, features are given the use of combiners may be considered or the features may be included in the dissimilarity measure. If either the chosen or optimized dissimilarity measure covers all relevant aspects of the data, then a zero dissimilarity arises if and only if the objects are identical. In that case the classes are separable in a sufficiently large dissimilarity space. Traditional statistical classification tools are designed for overlapping classes. They may still be applied, but the topic of designing proper generalization tools may be reconsidered for the case of high-dimensional separable classes. For instance, the demand that a training set should be representative for the future data to be classified in the statistical sense (i.e. they are generated from the same distributions) is not necessary anymore. These sets should just cover the same domain.

A result, not emphasized in this paper, is that for positive definite dissimilarity measures, see Sec. 2, and sufficiently complex classifiers, any measure asymptotically (for increasing training and representation sets) reaches a zero-error classifier. So, a poorly discriminative dissimilarity measure can be compensated by a large training set as long as the measure is positive definite.

An interesting experimental observation is that if several of these measures are given the average of the dissimilarity matrix offers a better representation than any of them separable. Apparently, the asymptotic convergence speeds (almost) always contribute in combinations and do not disturb each other.

One may wonder whether the dissimilarity measures used in Sec. 6 are all have the positive definite property. However, entirely different objects may be described by identical histograms or graphs. So, the users should analyze, if they need this property and whether an expert is able to label the objects unambiguously on the basis of histograms or graphs only. If not, as a way to attain a better generalization, he may try to extend the distance measure with some features, or simply add another, possibly bad measure, which is positive definite.

They area of dissimilarity representations is conceptually closely related to kernel design and kernel classifiers. It is, however, more general as it allows for indefinite measures and makes no restrictions w.r.t. the classifier [47,50]. The dissimilarity representation is essentially different from kernel design in the sense that the dissimilarity matrix is not necessarily square. This has not only strong computational advantages, but also paves the way to the use of various classifiers. As pointed out in Sec. 3.4, systematic prototype selection is mainly relevant to obtain low-dimensional dissimilarity spaces defined by a small set of prototypes. Another way to reach this goal, not discussed here due to space limit, is the use of out-of-the training set prototypes or the so-called generalized dissimilarity representation. Here prototypes are replaced by sets of prototypes, by models based on such sets, or by artificially constructed prototypes; see [5,6,45,34].

For future research in this field we recommend the study of dissimilarity measures for sets of applications such as spectra, images, etcetera. In every individual application measures may be optimized for the specific usage, but the availability of sets of measures for a broader field of structural applications may, according to our intuition, be most profitable for the field of structural pattern recognition.

References

1. Anderson, J.A.: Logistic discrimination. In: Krishnaiah, P.R., Kanal, L.N. (eds.) Handbook of Statistics 2: Classification, Pattern Recognition and Reduction of Dimensionality, pp. 169–191. North Holland, Amsterdam (1982)
2. Andreu, G., Crespo, A., Valiente, J.M.: Selecting the toroidal self-organizing feature maps (TSOFM) best organized to object recognition. In: Proceedings of ICNN 1997, International Conference on Neural Networks, vol. II, pp. 1341–1346. IEEE Service Center, Piscataway (1997)
3. Arkedev, A.G., Braverman, E.M.: Computers and Pattern Recognition. Thompson, Washington, D.C (1966)
4. Bahlmann, C., Burkhardt, H.: The writer independent online handwriting recognition system frog on hand and cluster generative statistical dynamic time warping. IEEE Trans. Pattern Anal. Mach. Intell. 26(3), 299–310 (2004)
5. Bicego, M., Cristani, M., Murino, V., Pękalska, E., Duin, R.P.W.: Clustering-based construction of hidden markov models for generative kernels. In: Cremers, D., Boykov, Y., Blake, A., Schmidt, F.R. (eds.) EMMCVPR 2009. LNCS, vol. 5681, pp. 466–479. Springer, Heidelberg (2009)

6. Bicego, M., Pękalska, E., Tax, D.M.J., Duin, R.P.W.: Component-based discriminative classification for hidden markov models. Pattern Recognition 42(11), 2637–2648 (2009)
7. Bishop, C.: Pattern Recognition and Machine Learning. Springer, Heidelberg (2006)
8. Bognár, J.: Indefinite Inner Product Spaces. Springer, Heidelberg (1974)
9. Borg, I., Groenen, P.: Modern Multidimensional Scaling. Springer, New York (1997)
10. Bunke, H., Buhler, U.: Applications of approximate string matching to 2D shape recognition. Pattern Recognition 26(12), 1797–1812 (1993)
11. Bunke, H., Riesen, K.: Graph classification on dissimilarity space embedding. In: da Vitoria Lobo, N., Kasparis, T., Roli, F., Kwok, J.T., Georgiopoulos, M., Anagnostopoulos, G.C., Loog, M. (eds.) S+SSPR 2008. LNCS, vol. 5342, p. 2. Springer, Heidelberg (2008)
12. Burghouts, G.J., Smeulders, A.W.M., Geusebroek, J.M.: The distribution family of similarity distances. In: Advances in Neural Information Processing Systems, vol. 20 (2007)
13. Calana, Y.P., Reyes, E.B.G., Orozco-Alzate, M., Duin, R.P.W.: Prototype selection for dissimilarity representation by a genetic algorithm. In: ICPR 2010, pp. 177–180 (2010)
14. Chang, C.C., Lin, C.J.: LIBSVM: a library for support vector machines (2001), software http://www.csie.ntu.edu.tw/~cjlin/libsvm
15. Cortes, C., Vapnik, V.: Support-vector networks. Machine Learning 20, 273–297 (1995)
16. Devijver, P.A., Kittler, J.V.: Pattern Recognition: A Statistical Approach. Prentice-Hall, Englewood Cliffs (1982)
17. Duda, R., Hart, P., Stork, D.: Pattern Classification, 2nd edn. John Wiley & Sons, Inc., Chichester (2001)
18. Duin, R.P.W.: Compactness and complexity of pattern recognition problems. In: Perneel, C. (ed.) Proc. Int. Symposium on Pattern Recognition 'In Memoriam Pierre Devijver', pp. 124–128. Royal Military Academy, Brussels (1999)
19. Duin, R.P.W., Pękalska, E.: Non-euclidean dissimilarities: Causes and informativeness. In: Hancock, E.R., Wilson, R.C., Windeatt, T., Ulusoy, I., Escolano, F. (eds.) SSPR&SPR 2010. LNCS, vol. 6218, pp. 324–333. Springer, Heidelberg (2010)
20. Duin, R.P.W., Pękalska, E.: The dissimilarity space: Bridging structural and statistical pattern recognition. Pattern Recognition Letters (in press, 2011)
21. Duin, R.P.W., Pękalska, E., Harol, A., Lee, W.-J., Bunke, H.: On euclidean corrections for non-euclidean dissimilarities. In: da Vitoria Lobo, N., Kasparis, T., Roli, F., Kwok, J.T., Georgiopoulos, M., Anagnostopoulos, G.C., Loog, M. (eds.) S+SSPR 2008. LNCS, vol. 5342, pp. 551–561. Springer, Heidelberg (2008)
22. Duin, R.P.W.: Non-euclidean problems in pattern recognition related to human expert knowledge. In: Filipe, J., Cordeiro, J. (eds.) ICEIS 2010. LNBIP, vol. 73, pp. 15–28. Springer, Heidelberg (2011)
23. Duin, R.P.W., Loog, M., Pękalska, E., Tax, D.M.J.: Feature-based dissimilarity space classification. In: Ünay, D., Çataltepe, Z., Aksoy, S. (eds.) ICPR 2010. LNCS, vol. 6388, pp. 46–55. Springer, Heidelberg (2010)
24. Duin, R., Pękalska, E.: On refining dissimilarity matrices for an improved nn learning. In: ICPR, pp. 1–4 (2008)
25. Edelman, S.: Representation and Recognition in Vision. MIT Press, Cambridge (1999)
26. Fu, K.: Syntactic Pattern Recognition and Applications. Prentice-Hall (1982)

27. Fukunaga, K.: Introduction to Statistical Pattern Recognition, 2nd edn. Academic Press (1990)
28. Gold, S., Rangarajan, A.: A graduated assignment algorithm for graph matching. IEEE Trans. Pattern Anal. Mach. Intell. 18(4), 377–388 (1996)
29. Goldfarb, L.: A new approach to pattern recognition. In: Kanal, L., Rosenfeld, A. (eds.) Progress in Pattern Recognition, vol. 2, pp. 241–402. Elsevier (1985)
30. Haasdonk, B.: Feature space interpretation of SVMs with indefinite kernels. IEEE TPAMI 25(5), 482–492 (2005)
31. Haasdonk, B., Burkhardt, H.: Invariant kernel functions for pattern analysis and machine learning. Machine Learning 68(1), 35–61 (2007)
32. Haasdonk, B., Pękalska, E.: Indefinite kernel fisher discriminant. In: ICPR, pp. 1–4 (2008)
33. Ibba, A., Duin, R.P.W., Lee, W.J.: A study on combining sets of differently measured dissimilarities. In: ICPR, pp. 3360–3363. IEEE (2010)
34. Kim, S.W., Duin, R.P.W.: On improving dissimilarity-based classifications using a statistical similarity measure. In: Bloch, I., Cesar Jr., R.M. (eds.) CIARP 2010. LNCS, vol. 6419, pp. 418–425. Springer, Heidelberg (2010)
35. Kruskal, J.: Multidimensional scaling by optimizing goodness of fit to a nonmetric hypothesis. Psychometrika 29, 1–27 (1964)
36. Laub, J., Roth, V., Buhmann, J.M., Müller, K.R.: On the information and representation of non-euclidean pairwise data. Pattern Recognition 39(10), 1815–1826 (2006)
37. Lee, W.J., Duin, R.P.W.: An inexact graph comparison approach in joint eigenspace. In: da Vitoria Lobo, N., Kasparis, T., Roli, F., Kwok, J.T., Georgiopoulos, M., Anagnostopoulos, G.C., Loog, M. (eds.) S+SSPR 2008. LNCS, vol. 5342, pp. 35–44. Springer, Heidelberg (2008)
38. Lichtenauer, J.F., Hendriks, E.A., Reinders, M.J.T.: Sign language recognition by combining statistical DTW and independent classification. IEEE Trans. Pattern Analysis and Machine Intelligence 30(11), 2040–2046 (2008)
39. Lozano, M., Sotoca, J.M., Sánchez, J.S., Pla, F., Pękalska, E., Duin, R.P.W.: Experimental study on prototype optimisation algorithms for prototype-based classification in vector spaces. Pattern Recognition 39(10), 1827–1838 (2006)
40. Luo, B., Wilson, R.C., Hancock, E.R.: Spectral embedding of graphs. Pattern Recognition 36(10), 2213–2230 (2003)
41. Mottl, V., Seredin, O., Dvoenko, S., Kulikowski, C.A., Muchnik, I.B.: Featureless pattern recognition in an imaginary hilbert space. In: ICPR, vol. 2, pp. 88–91 (2002)
42. Mottl, V., Dvoenko, S., Seredin, O., Kulikowski, C., Muchnik, I.: Featureless pattern recognition in an imaginary Hilbert space and its application to protein fold classification. In: Perner, P. (ed.) MLDM 2001. LNCS (LNAI), vol. 2123, pp. 322–336. Springer, Heidelberg (2001)
43. Nene, S.A., Nayar, S.K., Murase, H.: Columbia object image library (COIL-100), Columbia University (1996)
44. Neuhaus, M., Bunke, H.: Bridging the Gap Between Graph Edit Distance and Kernel Machines. World Scientific (2007)
45. Orozco-Alzate, M., Duin, R.P.W., Castellanos-Domínguez, G.: A generalization of dissimilarity representations using feature lines and feature planes. Pattern Recognition Letters 30(3), 242–254 (2009)
46. Pękalska, E., Duin, R.P.W.: Dissimilarity representations allow for building good classifiers. Pattern Recognition Letters 23(8), 943–956 (2002)

47. Pękalska, E., Duin, R.P.W.: Beyond traditional kernels: Classification in two dissimilarity-based representation spaces. IEEE Transactions on Systems, Man, and Cybernetics, Part C: Applications and Reviews 38(6), 729–744 (2008)
48. Pękalska, E., Duin, R.P.W., Paclík, P.: Prototype selection for dissimilarity-based classifiers. Pattern Recognition 39(2), 189–208 (2006)
49. Pękalska, E., Duin, R.: The Dissimilarity Representation for Pattern Recognition. World Scientific, Singapore (2005)
50. Pekalska, E., Haasdonk, B.: Kernel discriminant analysis for positive definite and indefinite kernels. IEEE Trans. Pattern Anal. Mach. Intell. 31(6), 1017–1032 (2009)
51. Porro-Muñoz, D., Duin, R.P.W., Talavera-Bustamante, I., Orozco-Alzate, M.: Classification of three-way data by the dissimilarity representation. Signal Processing 91(11), 2520–2529 (2011)
52. Porro-Muñoz, D., Talavera, I., Duin, R.P.W., Hernández, N., Orozco-Alzate, M.: Dissimilarity representation on functional spectral data for classification. Journal of Chemometrics, n/a–n/a (2011)
53. Ripley, B.D.: An introduction to statistical pattern recognition. Cambridge University Press, Cambridge (1996)
54. Shepard, R.: The analysis of proximities: Multidimensional scaling with an unknown distance function. i. Psychometrika 27, 125–140 (1962)
55. Spillmann, B., Neuhaus, M., Bunke, H., Pękalska, E.z., Duin, R.P.W.: Transforming strings to vector spaces using prototype selection. In: Yeung, D.-Y., Kwok, J.T., Fred, A., Roli, F., de Ridder, D. (eds.) SSPR 2006 and SPR 2006. LNCS, vol. 4109, pp. 287–296. Springer, Heidelberg (2006)
56. Theodoridis, S., Koutroumbas, K.: Pattern Recognition, 4th edn. Academic Press (2008)
57. Ulas, A., Duin, R.P., Castellani, U., Loog, M., Mirtuono, P., Bicego, M., Murino, V., Bellani, M., Cerruti, S., Tansella, M., Brambilla, P.: Dissimilarity-based detection of schizophrenia. International Journal of Imaging Systems and Technology 21(2), 179–192 (2011)
58. Vapnik, V.: Statistical Learning Theory. John Wiley & Sons, Inc. (1998)
59. Watanabe, S.: Pattern Recognition: Human and Mechanical. Wiley (1985)
60. Webb, A.: Statistical pattern recognition. Wiley (2002)
61. Weinberger, K.Q., Saul, L.K.: Distance metric learning for large margin nearest neighbor classification. Journal of Machine Learning Research 10, 207–244 (2009)
62. Wilson, C., Garris, M.: Handprinted character database 3. Tech. rep., National Institute of Standards and Technology (February 1992)
63. Wilson, R., Luo, B., Hancock, E.: Pattern vectors from algebraic graph theory. IEEE Trans. on PAMI 27, 1112–1124 (2005)
64. Wilson, R.C., Hancock, E.R.: Spherical embedding and classification. In: Hancock, E.R., Wilson, R.C., Windeatt, T., Ulusoy, I., Escolano, F. (eds.) SSPR&SPR 2010. LNCS, vol. 6218, pp. 589–599. Springer, Heidelberg (2010)
65. Wolpert, D.H. (ed.): The Mathematics of Generalization. Addison-Wesley, Reading (1995)
66. Woznica, A., Kalousis, A., Hilario, M.: Learning to combine distances for complex representations. In: Ghahramani, Z. (ed.) ICML. ACM International Conference Proceeding Series, pp. 1031–1038. ACM (2007)
67. Xiao, B., Hancock, E.R.: Geometric characterisation of graphs. In: Roli, F., Vitulano, S. (eds.) ICIAP 2005. LNCS, vol. 3617, pp. 471–478. Springer, Heidelberg (2005)
68. Yang, L., Jin, R., Sukthankar, R., Liu, Y.: An efficient algorithm for local distance metric learning. In: AAAI. AAAI Press (2006)

Describing When and Where in Vision*

Walter G. Kropatsch, Adrian Ion, and Nicole M. Artner

PRIP, Vienna University of Technology, Austria
krw@prip.tuwien.ac.at
http://www.prip.tuwien.ac.at/

Abstract. Different from the what and where pathways in the organization of the visual system, we address representations that describe dynamic visual events in a unified way.

Representations are an essential tool for any kind of process that operates on data, as they provide a language to describe, store and retrieve that data. They define the possible properties and aspects that are stored, and govern the levels of abstraction at which the respective properties are described. In the case of visual computing (computer vision, image processing), a representation is used to describe information obtained from visual input (e.g. an image or image sequence and the objects it may contain) as well as related prior knowledge (experience).

The ultimate goal, to make applications of visual computing be part of our daily life, requires that vision systems operate reliably, nearly anytime and anywhere. Therefore, the research community aims to solve increasingly more complex scenarios. Vision both in humans and computers is a dynamic process, thus variations (change) always appear in the spatial and the temporal dimensions. Nowadays significant research efforts are undertaken to represent variable shape and appearance, however, joint representation and processing of spatial and temporal domains is not a well-investigated topic yet. Visual computing tasks are mostly solved by a two-stage approach of frame-based processing and subsequent temporal processing. Unfortunately, this approach reaches its limits in scenes with high complexity or difficult tasks e.g. action recognition. Therefore, we focus our research on representations which jointly describe information in space and time and allow to process data of space-time volumes (several consecutive frames).

In this keynote we relate our own experience and motivations, to the current state of the art of representations of shape, of appearance, of structure, and of motion. Challenges for such representations are in applications like multiple object tracking, tracking non-rigid objects and human action recognition.

---

* Supported by the Austrian Science Fund under grants P20134-N13 and P18716-N13.

C. San Martin and S.-W. Kim (Eds.): CIARP 2011, LNCS 7042, p. 25, 2011.

Applications of Multilevel Thresholding Algorithms to Transcriptomics Data

Luis Rueda and Iman Rezaeian

School of Computer Science, University of Windsor,
401 Sunset Ave., Windsor, ON, N9B3P4, Canada
{lrueda,rezaeia}@uwindsor.ca

Abstract. Microarrays are one of the methods for analyzing the expression levels of genes in a massive and parallel way. Since any errors in early stages of the analysis affect subsequent stages, leading to possibly erroneous biological conclusions, finding the correct location of the spots in the images is extremely important for subsequent steps that include segmentation, quantification, normalization and clustering. On the other hand, genome-wide profiling of DNA-binding proteins using ChIP-seq and RNA-seq has emerged as an alternative to ChIP-chip methods. Due to the large amounts of data produced by next generation sequencing technology, ChIPseq and RNA-seq offer much higher resolution, less noise and greater coverage than its predecessor, the ChIPchip array.

Multilevel thresholding algorithms have been applied to many problems in image and signal processing. We show that these algorithms can be used for transcriptomics and genomics data analysis such as sub-grid and spot detection in DNA microarrays, and also for detecting significant regions based on next generation sequencing data. We show the advantages and disadvantages of using multilevel thresholding and other algorithms in these two applications, as well as an overview of numerical and visual results used to validate the power of the thresholding methods based on previously published data.

Keywords: microarray image gridding, image analysis, multi level thresholding, transcriptomics.

1 Introduction

Among other components, the genome contains a set of genes required for an organism to function and evolve. However, the genome is only a source of information and in order to function, the genes express themselves into proteins. The transcription of genes to produce RNA is the first stage of gene expression. The transcriptome can be seen as the complete set of RNA transcripts produced by the genome. Unlike the genome, the transcriptome is very dynamic. Despite having the same genome regardless of the type of cell or environmental conditions, the transcriptome varies considerably in differing circumstances because of the different ways the genes may express.

Transcriptomics, the field that studies the role of the transcriptome, provides a rich source of data suitable for pattern discovery and analysis. The quantity and size of these data may vary based on the model and underlying methods used for analysis. In gene

C. San Martin and S.-W. Kim (Eds.): CIARP 2011, LNCS 7042, pp. 26–37, 2011.

expression microarrays, the raw data are represented in terms of images, typically in TIFF format which are approximately 20-30MB per array. These TIFF files are processed and transformed into quantified data used for posterior analysis. In contrast, high throughput sequencing methods (e.g. ChIP-seq and RNA-seq) generate more than 1TB of data, while the sequence files (approximately 20-30GB) are typically used as a starting point for analysis [16]. Clearly, these sequence files are an order of magnitude larger than those from arrays.

1.1   DNA Microarray Image Gridding

Various technologies have been developed to measure the transcriptome, including hybridization or sequence-based approaches. Hybridization-based approaches typically involve processing fluorescently labeled DNA microarrays. Microarrays are one of the most important technologies used in molecular biology to massively explore the abilities of the genes to express themselves into proteins and other molecular machines responsible for different functions in an organism. These expressions are monitored in cells and organisms under specific conditions, and are present in many applications in medical diagnosis, pharmacology, disease treatment, among others. If we consider DNA microarrays, scanning the slides at a very high resolution produces images composed of sub-grids of spots. Image processing and analysis are two important aspects of microarrays, and involve various steps. The first task is gridding, which is quite important as errors are propagated to subsequent steps. Roughly speaking, gridding consists of determining the spot locations in a microarray image (typically, in a sub-grid). The gridding process requires the knowledge of the sub-girds in advance in order to proceed, which is not necessarily available in advance.

Many approaches have been proposed for microarray image gridding and spot detection, being the most widely known the following. The Markov random field (MRF) is one of them, which applies specific constraints and heuristic criteria [15]. Other gridding methods used for gridding include mathematical morphology [8], Bayesian model-based algorithms [1,6], the hill-climbing approach [13], a Gaussian mixture model approach [18], Radon-transform-based method [11], a genetic algorithm for separating sub-grids and spots [5], and the recently introduced maximum margin method [4]. A method that we have proposed and has been successfully used in microarray gridding is the multilevel thresholding algorithm [21], which is discussed in more detail later in the paper.

1.2   ChIP-Seq and RNA-Seq Peak Finding

Hybridization-based approaches are high throughput and relatively inexpensive, except for high-resolution tiling arrays that interrogate large genomes. However, these methods have several limitations, which include reliance upon existing knowledge about the genome, high background levels owing to cross-hybridization, and a limited dynamic range of detection owing to both background and saturation of signals [16,26]. Moreover, comparing expression levels across different experiments is often difficult and can require complicated normalization methods.

Recently, the development of novel high-throughput DNA sequencing methods has provided a new method for both mapping and quantifying transcriptomes. These methods, termed ChIP-seq (ChIP sequencing) and RNA-seq (RNA sequencing), have clear advantages over existing approaches and are emerging in such a way that eukaryotic transcriptomes are to be analyzed in a high-throughput and more efficient manner [26].

Chromatin immunoprecipitation followed by high-throughput sequencing (ChIP-seq) is a technique that provides quantitative, genome-wide mapping of target protein binding events [2,17]. In ChIP-seq, a protein is first cross-linked to DNA and the fragments subsequently sheared. Following a size selection step that enriches for fragments of specified lengths, the fragments ends are sequenced, and the resulting reads are aligned to the genome. Detecting protein binding sites from massive sequence-based datasets with millions of short reads represents a truly bioinformatics challenge that has required considerable computational innovation in spite of the availability of programs for ChIP-chip analysis [3,9,18,19].

With the increasing popularity of ChIP-seq technology, a demand for peak finding methods has emerged and it causes developing new algorithms. Although due to mapping challenges and biases in various aspects of existing protocols, identifying peaks is not a straightforward task.

Different approaches have been proposed for detecting peaks based ChIP-seq/RNA-seq mapped reads so far. Zhang et al. presents a Model-based Analysis of ChIP-seq data (MACS), which analyzes data generated by short read sequencers [28]. It models the shift size of ChIP-seq tags, and uses it to improve the spatial resolution of predicted binding sites. A two-pass strategy called PeakSeq has been presented in [20]. This strategy compensates for signal caused by open chromatin, as revealed by the inclusion of the controls. The first pass identifies putative binding sites and compensates for genomic variation in mapping the sequences. The second pass filters out sites not significantly enriched compared to the normalized control, computing precise enrichments and significance. A statistical approach for calling peaks has been recently proposed in [7], which is based on evaluating the significance of a robust statistical test that measures the extent of pile-up reads. Specifically, the shapes of putative peaks are defined and evaluated to differentiate between random and non-random fragment placements on the genome. Another algorithm for identification of binding sites is site identification from paired-end sequencing (SIPeS) [25], which can be used for identification of binding sites from short reads generated from paired-end solexa ChIP-seq technology.

In this paper, we review the application of optimal multilevel thresholding (OMT) to gridding and peak finding problems in transcriptomics. Moreover, a conceptual and practical comparison between OMT and other state-of-the-art approaches is also presented.

2   Optimal Multilevel Thresholding

Multilevel thresholding is one of the most widely-used techniques in different aspects of signal and image processing, including segmentation, classification and object discrimination. Given a histogram with frequencies or probabilities for each bin, the aim of multilevel thresholding is to divide the histogram into a number of groups (or classes) of contiguous bins in such a way that a criterion is optimized. In microarray image gridding, we compute vertical (or horizontal) running sums of pixel intensities, obtaining histograms in which each bin represents one column (or row respectively), and the running sum of intensities corresponds to the frequency of that bin. The frequencies are then normalized in order to be considered as probabilities. Each histogram is then processed (see below) to obtain the optimal thresholding that will determine the locations of the separating lines.

Consider a histogram H, an ordered set $\{1, 2, \ldots, n-1, n\}$, where the ith value corresponds to the ith bin and has a probability, p_i. Given an image, $A = \{a_{ij}\}$, H can be obtained by means of the horizontal (vertical) running sum as follows: $p_i = \sum_{j=1}^{m} a_{ij}$ ($p_j = \sum_{i=1}^{n} a_{ij}$). We also consider a threshold set T, defined as an ordered set $T = \{t_0, t_1, \ldots, t_k, t_{k+1}\}$, where $0 = t_0 < t_1 < \ldots < t_k < t_{k+1} = n$ and $t_i \in \{0\} \cup H$. The problem of multilevel thresholding consists of finding a threshold set, T^*, in such a way that a function $f : H^k \times [0,1]^n \to \mathbb{R}^+$ is maximized/minimized. Using this threshold set, H is divided into $k+1$ classes: $\zeta_1 = \{1, 2, \ldots, t_1\}, \zeta_2 = \{t_1 + 1, t_1 + 2, \ldots, t_2\}, \ldots, \zeta_k = \{t_{k-1}+1, t_{k-1}+2, \ldots, t_k\}, \zeta_{k+1} = \{t_k+1, t_k+2, \ldots, n\}$. The most important criteria for multilevel thresholding are the following [12]:

Between class variance:

$$\Psi_{\mathrm{BC}}(T) = \sum_{j=1}^{k+1} \omega_j \mu_j^2 \tag{1}$$

where $\omega_j = \sum_{i=t_{j-1}+1}^{t_j} p_i$, $\mu_j = \frac{1}{\omega_j} \sum_{i=t_{j-1}+1}^{t_j} i p_i$;

Entropy-based:

$$\Psi_{\mathrm{H}}(T) = \sum_{j=1}^{k+1} H_j \tag{2}$$

where $H_j = -\sum_{i=t_{j-1}+1}^{t_j} \frac{p_i}{\omega_j} \log \frac{p_i}{\omega_j}$;

Minimum error:

$$\Psi_{\mathrm{ME}}(T) = 1 + 2 \sum_{j=1}^{k+1} \omega_j (\log \sigma_j - \log \omega_j) \tag{3}$$

where $\sigma_j^2 = \sum_{i=t_{j-1}+1}^{t_j} \frac{p_i (i - \mu_j)^2}{\omega_j}$.

A dynamic programming algorithm for *optimal* multilevel thresholding was proposed in our previous work [12], which is an extension for irregularly sampled histograms. For this, the criterion has to be decomposed as a sum of terms as follows:

$$\Psi(T_{0,m}) = \Psi(\{t_0, t_1, \ldots, t_m\}) \triangleq \sum_{j=1}^{m} \psi_{t_{j-1}+1, t_j} , \tag{4}$$

where $1 \leq m \leq k+1$ and the function $\psi_{l,r}$, where $l \leq r$, is a real, positive function of $p_l, p_{l+1}, \ldots, p_r$, $\psi_{l,r} : H^2 \times [0,1]^{l-r+1} \to \mathbb{R}^+ \cup \{0\}$. If $m = 0$, then $\Psi(\{t_0\}) = \psi_{t_0, t_0} = \psi_{0,0} = 0$. The thresholding algorithm can be found in [12]. In the algorithm, a table C is filled in, where $C(t_j, j)$ contains the optimal solution for $T_{0,j} = t_0, t_1, \ldots, t_j$, $\Psi^*(T_{0,j})$, which is found from $\min\{t_j\} \leq t_j \leq \max\{t_j\}$. Another table, $D(t_j, j)$, contains the value of t_{j-1} for which $\Psi^*(T_{0,j})$ is optimal. The algorithm runs in $O(kn^2)$, and has been further improved to achieve linear complexity, i.e. $O(kn)$, by following the approach of [14].

2.1 Using Multi-level Thresholding for Gridding DNA Microarray Images

A DNA microarray image contains spots arranged into sub-grids. The image contains various sub-grids as well, which are found in the first stage. Once the sub-grids are found, the spots centers are to be identified. A microarray image can be considered as a matrix $A = \{a_{i,j}\}, i = 1, \ldots, n$ and $j = 1, \ldots, m$, where $a_{ij} \in \mathbb{Z}^+$, and A is a sub-grid of a DNA microarray image. The aim of sub-gridding is to obtain vectors, namely $\mathbf{h} = [h_1, \ldots h_{p-1}]^t$ and $\mathbf{v} = [v_1, \ldots v_{q-1}]^t$, that separate the sub-grids. Finding the spot locations is done analogously – more details of this, as well as those of the whole process can be found in [21]. The aim of gridding is to find the corresponding spot locations given by the horizontal and vertical adjacent vectors. Post-processing or refinement allows us to find a spot region for each spot, which is enclosed by four lines.

When producing the microarrays, based on the layout of the printer pins, the number of sub-grids or spots is known. But due to misalignments, deformations, artifacts or noise during producing the microarray images, these numbers may not be available. Thus, it is important that the gridding algorithm allows some flexibility in finding these parameters, as well as avoiding the use of other user-defined parameters. This is what the thresholding methods endeavor to do, by automatically finding the best number of thresholds (sub-grids or spots) – more details in the next section.

2.2 Using Multi-level Thresholding for Analyzing ChIP-Seq/RNA-Seq Data

In ChIP-seq and RNA-seq analysis, a protein is first cross-linked to DNA and the fragments subsequently pruned. Then, the fragments ends are sequenced, and the resulting reads are aligned to the genome. The result of read alignments produces a histogram in such a way that the x axis represents the genome coordinate and the y axis the frequency of the aligned reads in each genome coordinate. The aim is to find the significant peaks corresponding to enriched regions. For this reason, a non-overlapping moving window is used. By starting from the beginning, a dynamic window of minimum size t is being applied to the histogram and each window that could be analyzed separately. The size of the window could be different for each window to prevent truncating a peak before its end. Thus, for each window a minimum number of t bins is used and, by starting from the end of previous window, the size of window is increased until a zero value in the histogram is reached.

The aim is to obtain vectors $C_{w_i} = [c_{w_i}^1, \ldots c_{w_i}^n]^t$, where w_i is the ith window and C_{w_i} is the vector that contains n threshold coordinates which correspond to the ith window. Figure 1 depicts the process of finding the peaks corresponding to the regions of interest for the specified protein. The input to the algorithm includes the reads and the output of the whole process is the location of the detected significant peaks by using optimal multilevel thresholding combined with our recently proposed α index.

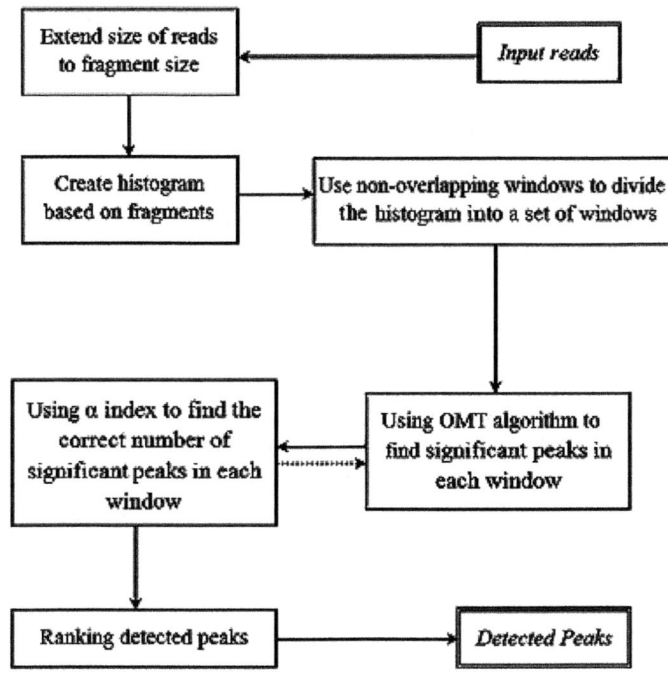

Fig. 1. Schematic representation of the process for finding significant peaks

3 Automatic Detection of the Number of Clusters

Finding the correct number of clusters (number of sub-grids or spots or the number of regions in each window in ChIP-seq/RNA-seq analysis) is one of the most challenging issues. This stage is crucial in order to fully automate the whole process. For this, we need to determine the correct number clusters or thresholds prior to applying multi-level thresholding methods. This is found by applying an index of validity (derived from clustering techniques) and testing over all possible number of clusters (or thresholds) from 2 to $\sqrt{n}$, where n is the number of bins in the histogram. We have recently proposed the $\alpha(x)$ index, which is the result of a combination of a simple index and the well-known I index [23] as follows:

$$\alpha(K) = \sqrt{K}\frac{I(K)}{A(K)} = \frac{\left(\frac{E_1}{E_K} \times D_K\right)^2}{\sqrt{K}\Sigma_{i=1}^{K}p(t_i)}. \tag{5}$$

For maximizing $I(K)$ and minimizing $A(K)$, the value of $\alpha(K)$ must be maximized. Thus, the best number of thresholds K^* based on the α index is given by:

$$K^* = \operatorname*{argmax}_{1 \le K \le \delta} \alpha(K) = \operatorname*{argmax}_{1 \le K \le \delta} \frac{\left(\frac{E_1}{E_K} \times D_K\right)^2}{\sqrt{K}\Sigma_{i=1}^{K}p(t_i)}. \tag{6}$$

4 Comparison of Transcriptomics Data Analysis Algorithms

4.1 DNA Microarray Image Gridding Algorithms Comparison

A conceptual comparison of microarray image gridding methods based on their features is shown in Table 1. The methods included in the comparison are the following: (i) Radon transform sub-gridding (RTSG) [11], (ii) Bayesian simulated annealing gridding (BSAG) [1], (iii) genetic-algorithm-based gridding (GABG) [5], (iv) hill-climbing gridding (HCG) [13], (v) maximum margin microarray gridding (M^3G) [4], and the optimal multilevel thresholding algorithm for gridding (OMT) [21]. As shown in the table, OMT does not need any number-based parameter, and hence making it much more powerful than the other methods. Although the index or thresholding criterion can be considered as a "parameter", this can be fixed by using the between class criterion. In a previous work, we have "fixed" the index of validity to the α index and the between class as the thresholding criterion. As can also be observed in the table, most algorithms and methods require the use of user-defined and subjectively fixed parameters. One example is the GABG, which needs to adjust the mutation and crossover rates, probability of maximum and minimum thresholds, among others. It is critical then to adjust these parameters for specific data, and variations may occur across images of different characteristics.

Table 1. Conceptual comparison of recently proposed DNA microarray gridding methods

Method	Parameters	Sub-grid Detection	Spot Detection	Automatic Detection No. of Spots	Rotation
Rueda07	n: Number of sub-grids	√	×	×	√
Antoniol04	α ,β: Parameters for balancing prior and posterior probability rates	×	√	√	√
Zacharia08	μ , c :Mutation and Crossover rates, p_{max}: probability of maximum threshold, p_{low}: probability of minimum threshold, f_{max} : percentage of line with low probability to be a part of grid, T_p: Refinement threshold	√	√	√	√
Rueda06	λ , σ: Distribution parameters	×	√	√	×
Bariamis10	c: Cost parameter	×	√	√	√
OMT	None[1]	√	√	√	√

[1] The only parameters that would be needed in the proposed method are the "thresholding criterion" and the "index of validity". These two "parameters" are methodological, not number-based, and hence making OMT less dependent on parameters.

4.2 Comparison of Algorithms for ChIP-Seq and RNA-Seq Analysis

A conceptual comparison between thresholding algorithms and other ChIP and RNA-Seq methods based on their features is shown in Table 2. The methods included in the comparison are the following: (i) GLobal Identifier of Target Regions (CLITR) [22], (ii)

Table 2. Conceptual comparison of recently proposed methods for ChIP-seq and RNA-seq data

Method	Peak selection criteria	Peak ranking	Parameters
GLITR	n: Classification by height and relative enrichment	Peak height and fold enrichment	Target FDR, number nearest neighbors for clustering
MACS v1.3.5	Local region Poisson p value	p value	p-value threshold, tag length, m-fold for shift estimate
PeakSeq	Local region binomial p value	q value	Target FDR
Quest v2.3	height threshold, background ratio	q value	KDE bandwidth, peaks height, sub-peak valley depth, ratio to background
SICER v1.02	p value from random background model, enrichment relative to control	q value	Window length, gap size, FDR (with control) or E-Value (no control)
SiSSRs v1.4	$N^+ - N^-$ sign change, $N^+ + N^-$ threshold in region	p value	FDR, $N^+ + N^-$ threshold
T-PIC	Local height threshold	p value	Average fragment length, significance p value, minimum length of interval
OMT	number of ChIP reads minus control reads in window	volume	Average fragment length

Model-based Analysis of ChIP-seq (MACS)[28], (iii) PeakSeq [20], (iv) quantitative enrichment of sequence tags (Quest) [24], (v) SICER [27], (vi) Site Identification from Short Sequence Reads (SiSSRs) [10], (vii) Tree shape Peak Identification for ChIP-seq (T-PIC) [7], and (viii) the optimal multilevel thresholding algorithm, OMT. As shown in the table, all algorithms require some parameters to be set by the user based on the particular data to be processed, including p-values, FDR, number os nearest neighbors, peak height, valley depth, window length, gap size, among others. OMT is the algorithm that requires almost no parameter at all. Only the average fragment length is needed, but this parameter can be easily estimated from the underlying data. In practice, if enough computational resources are available, the fragment length would not be needed, since the OMT algorithm could be run directly on the whole histogram.

5 Experimental Analysis

This section is necessarily brief and reviews some experimental results as presented in [21]. For the experiments, two different kinds of DNA microarray images have been used, which were obtained from the Stanford Microarray Database (SMD) the Gene Expression Omnibus (GEO). The images have different resolutions, number of sub-grids and spots. We have used the between-class variance as the thresholding criteria, since it is the one that delivers the best results. All the sub-grids in each image are detected with a 100% accuracy, and also spot locations in each sub-grid can be detected efficiently with an average accuracy of 96.2% for SMD dataset and 96% for GEO dataset. Figure 2 shows the detected sub-grids from the AT-20387-ch2 image (left) and the detected spots in one of sub-grids (right). As shown in the figure, the proposed method precisely detects the sub-grids location at first, and in the next stage, each sub-grid is divided precisely into the corresponding spots with the same method.

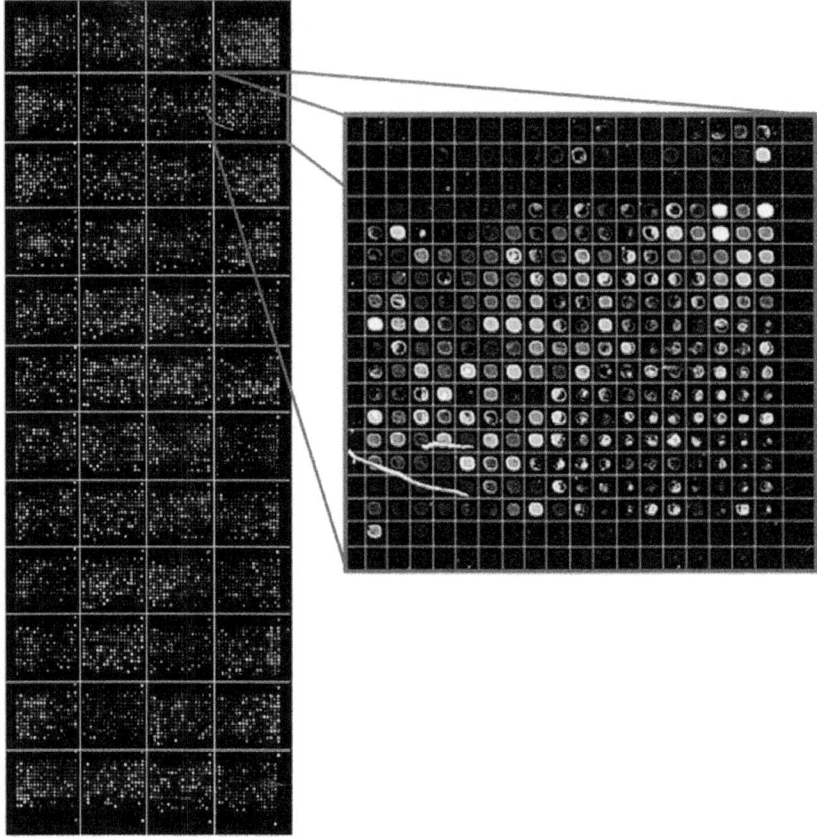

Fig. 2. Detected sub-grids in AT-20387-ch2 microarray image (left) and detected spots in one of sub-grids (right)

In addition to this, some experimental, preliminary results for testing performance of the OMT algorithm on ChIP/RNA-seq data are shown here. We have used the FoxA1 dataset [28], which contains experiment and control samples of 24 chromosomes. The experiment and control histogram were generated separately by extending each mapped position (read) into an appropriately oriented fragment, and then joining the fragments based on their genome coordinates. The final histogram was generated by subtracting the control from the experiment histogram. To find significant peaks, we used a non-overlapping window with the initial size of 3000bp. To avoid truncating peaks in boundaries, each window is extended until the value of the histogram at the end of the window becomes zero. Figure 3 shows three detected regions for chromosomes 9 and 17 and their corresponding base pair coordinates. It clear from the pictures that the peaks contain a very high number of reads, and then these regions are quite likely to represent binding sites, open reading frames or other bio-markers. A biological assessment of these bio-markers can corroborate this.

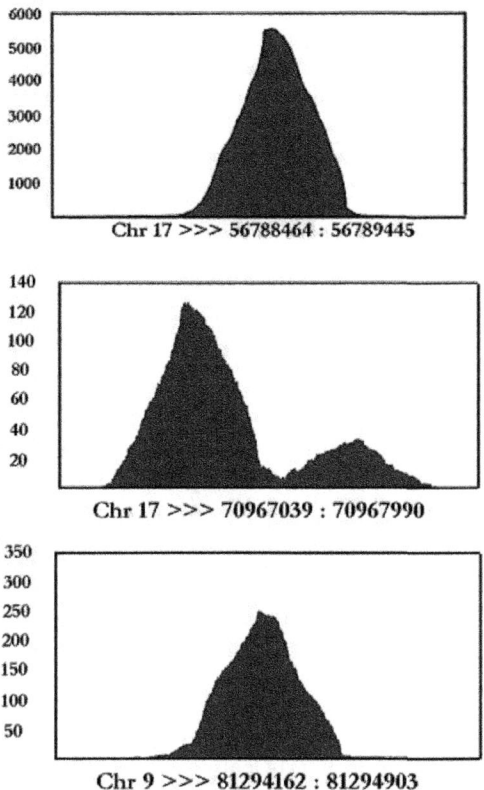

Fig. 3. Three detected regions from FoxA1 data for chromosomes 9 and 17. The x axis corresponds to the genome position in bp and the y axis corresponds to the number of reads.

6   Discussion and Conclusion

Transcriptomics provide a rich source of data suitable for pattern analysis. We have shown how multilevel thresholding algorithms can be applied to an efficient analysis of transcriptomics and genomics data by finding sub-grids and spots in microarray images, as well as significant peaks in high-throughput next generation sequencing data. OMT can be applied to a wide range of data from different sources and with different characteristics, and allows data analysis such as sub-grid and spot detection in DNA microarray image gridding and also for detecting significant regions on ChIP and RNA-seq data. OMT has been shown to be statistically sound and robust to noise in experiments and it is able to use on different approaches with a little change – this is one the most important features of this algorithm.

Thresholding algorithms, though shown to be quite useful for transcriptomics and genomics data analysis, are still emerging tools in these areas, and open the possibility for further advancement. One of the problems that deserves attention is the use of other thresholding criteria, including minimum error, entropy-based and others. For these two criteria the algorithm still runs in quadratic or n-logarithmic complexity, and which make the whole process sluggish. Processing a whole genome or even a chromosome for finding peaks in ChIP or RNA-seq is still a challenge, since it involves histograms with several million bins. This makes it virtually impossible to process a histogram at once, and so it has to be divided into several fragments. Processing the whole histograms at once is one of the open and challenging problems that deserve more investigation. Next generation sequence data analysis is an emerging and promising area for pattern discovery and analysis, which deserve the attention of the research community in the field.

Acknowledgments. This work has been partially supported by NSERC, the Natural Sciences and Engineering Research Council of Canada.

References

1. Ceccarelli, B., Antoniol, G.: A Deformable Grid-matching Approach for Microarray Images. IEEE Transactions on Image Processing 15(10), 3178–3188 (2006)
2. Barski, A., Zhao, K.: Genomic location analysis by chip-seq. Journal of Cellular Biochemistry (107), 11–18 (2009)
3. Buck, M., Nobel, A., Lieb, J.: Chipotle: a user-friendly tool for the analysis of chip-chip data. Genome Biology 6(11), R97 (2005)
4. Bariamis, D., Maroulis, D., Iakovidis, D.: M^3G: Maximum Margin Microarray Gridding. BMC Bioinformatics 11, 49 (2010)
5. Zacharia, E., Maroulis, D.: Micoarray image gridding via an evolutionary algorithm. In: IEEE International Conference on Image Processing, pp. 1444–1447 (2008)
6. Antoniol, G., Ceccarelli, M.: A Markov Random Field Approach to Microarray Image Gridding. In: Proc. of the 17th International Conference on Pattern Recognition, pp. 550–553 (2004)
7. Hower, V., Evans, S., Pachter, L.: Shape-based peak identification for chip-seq. BMC Bioinformatics 11(81) (2010)
8. Angulo, J., Serra, J.: Automatic Analysis of DNA Microarray Images Using Mathematical Morphology. Bioinformatics 19(5), 553–562 (2003)
9. Johnson, W., Li, W., Meyer, C., Gottardo, R., Carroll, J., Brown, M., Liu, X.S.: Model-based analysis of tiling-arrays for chip-chip. Proceedings of the National Academy of Sciences 103(33), 12457–12462 (2006)
10. Jothi, R., Cuddapah, S., Barski, A., Cui, K., Zhao, K.: Genome-wide identification of in vivo proteindna binding sites from chip-seq data. Nucleic Acids Research 36(16), 5221–5231 (2008)
11. Rueda, L.: Sub-grid Detection in DNA Microarray Images. In: Proceedings of the IEEE Pacific-RIM Symposium on Image and Video Technology, pp. 248–259 (2007)
12. Rueda, L.: An Efficient Algorithm for Optimal Multilevel Thresholding of Irregularly Sampled Histograms. In: Proceedings of the 7th International Workshop on Statistical Pattern Recognition, pp. 612–621 (2008)
13. Rueda, L., Vidyadharan, V.: A Hill-climbing Approach for Automatic Gridding of cDNA Microarray Images. IEEE Transactions on Computational Biology and Bioinformatics 3(1), 72–83 (2006)
14. Luessi, M., Eichmann, M., Schuster, G., Katsaggelos, A.: Framework for efficient optimal multilevel image thresholding. Journal of Electronic Imaging 18 (2009)
15. Katzer, M., Kummer, F., Sagerer, G.: A Markov Random Field Model of Microarray Gridding. In: Proceeding of the 2003 ACM Symposium on Applied Computing, pp. 72–77 (2003)

16. Malone, J., Oliver, B.: Microarrays, deep sequencing and the true measure of the transcriptome. BMC Biology 9(1), 34 (2011)
17. Park, P.J.: Chip-seq: advantages and challenges of a maturing technology. Nat. Rev. Genetics 10(10), 669–680 (2009)
18. Qi, Y., Rolfe, A., MacIsaac, K.D., Gerber, G., Pokholok, D., Zeitlinger, J., Danford, T., Dowell, R., Fraenkel, E., Jaakkola, T.S., Young, R., Gifford, D.: High-resolution computational models of genome binding events. Nat. Biotech. 24(8), 963–970 (2006)
19. Reiss, D., Facciotti, M., Baliga, N.: Model-based deconvolution of genome-wide dna binding. Bioinformatics 24(3), 396–403 (2008)
20. Rozowsky, J., Euskirchen, G., Auerbach, R., Zhang, Z., Gibson, T., Bjornson, R., Carriero, N., Snyder, M., Gerstein, M.: Peakseq enables systematic scoring of chip-seq experiments relative to controls. Nat. Biotech. 27(1), 66–75 (2009)
21. Rueda, L., Rezaeian, I.: A fully automatic gridding method for cdna microarray images. BMC Bioinformatics 12, 113 (2011)
22. Tuteja, G., White, P., Schug, J., Kaestner, K.H.: Extracting transcription factor targets from ChIP-Seq data. Nucleic Acids Res. 37(17), e113 (2009)
23. Maulik, U., Bandyopadhyay, S.: Performance Evaluation of Some Clustering Algorithms and Validity Indices. IEEE Trans. on Pattern Analysis and Machine Intelligence 24(12), 1650–1655 (2002)
24. Valouev, A., Johnson, D., Sundquist, A., Medina, C., Anton, E., Batzoglou, S., Myers, R., Sidow, A.: Genome-wide analysis of transcription factor binding sites based on ChIP-Seq data. Nat. Meth. 5(9), 829–834 (2008)
25. Wang, C., Xu, J., Zhang, D., Wilson, Z., Zhang, D.: An effective approach for identification of in vivo protein-DNA binding sites from paired-end ChIP-Seq data. BMC Bioinformatics 41(1), 117–129 (2008)
26. Wang, Z., Gerstein, M., Snyder, M.: RNA-Seq: a revolutionary tool for transcriptomics. Nat. Rev. Genet. 10(1), 57–63 (2009)
27. Zang, C., Schones, D.E., Zeng, C., Cui, K., Zhao, K., Peng, W.: A clustering approach for identification of enriched domains from histone modification ChIP-Seq data. Bioinformatics 25(15), 1952–1958 (2009)
28. Zhang, Y., Liu, T., Meyer, C., Eeckhoute, J., Johnson, D., Bernstein, B., Nusbaum, C., Myers, R., Brown, M., Li, W., Liu, X.S.: Model-based analysis of chip-seq (macs). Genome Biology 9(9), R137 (2008)

Unsupervised Fingerprint Segmentation Based on Multiscale Directional Information

Raoni F.S. Teixeira and Neucimar J. Leite

Institute of Computing, University of Campinas
Av. Albert Einstein, 1251 - Barão Geraldo - Campinas - SP CEP: 13083-852

Abstract. The segmentation task is an important step in automatic fingerprint classification and recognition. In this context, the term refers to splitting the image into two regions, namely, *foreground* and *background*. In this paper, we introduce a novel segmentation approach designed to deal with fingerprint images originated from different sensors. The method considers a multiscale directional operator and a scale-space toggle mapping used to estimate the image background information. We evaluate our approach on images of different databases, and show its improvements when compared against other well-known state-of-the-art segmentation methods discussed in literature.

Keywords: fingerprint segmentation, biometrics, mathematical morphology, scale-space image simplification.

1 Introduction

In fingerprint context, the term *segmentation* usually indicates the separation of the fingerprint area (also known as *foreground*) from the image *background* [9]. This is illustrated in Fig. 1 which shows a fingerprint image (Fig. 1a), and a boundary separating the *foreground* from the *background* (Fig. 1b) in the original image.

Fig. 1. Segmentation example of a fingerprint image

This task is a very important step in automatic fingerprint classification and recognition, since many methods for extractions features depend naturally on it. For example, in Ref. [3] the segmentation is used to dismiss *singular points* detected in the *background* and in Ref. [12] it is used to reduce the search space in the *minutiae* detection.

C. San Martin and S.-W. Kim (Eds.): CIARP 2011, LNCS 7042, pp. 38–46, 2011.

In this paper, we present an unsupervised fingerprint segmentation algorithm which explores the simplification properties of a scale-space toggle operator [4] and a multi-scale directional operator [11]. As we will see elsewhere, unlike the well-known approach in [2], which considers a supervised technique based on a learning of specific parameters for each fingerprint sensor, our unsupervised method is quite simple, general and leads to segmentation results comparable with the accurate segmentations obtained in the aforementioned work.

The rest of this paper is organized as follows. Section 2 briefly reviews some fingerprint segmentation approaches found in literature. Section 3 and 4 introduce, respectively, the morphological transformations and the directional field estimation considered in this work. Section 5 describes the proposed segmentation method and Section 6 presents some experimental results. Finally, some conclusions are drawn in Section 7.

2 Related Work

Due to its importance, several approaches for fingerprint image segmentation can be found in the literature (for a review, see, for example, [9]). Generally, these approaches can be broadly classified as *supervised* and *unsupervised*, depending on the training or execution parameters specification.

The work in Ref. [12] introduces an *unsupervised* approach where each block of an image is classified as *background* and *foreground*, according to the variance of the image gray levels, in a direction orthogonal to the ridge orientation computed by a gradient-based method. Another *unsupervised* approach is proposed in Ref. [13], which considers the foreground segmentation through a convolution of each image block with a set of eight Gabor filters [7]. In [15], an *unsupervised* algorithm for rolled fingerprint is presented. The algorithm first binarizes the fingerprint image and then computes three iterations of morphological erosion to preserve only the connected components with the largest number of pixels.

The *supervised* approach described in [16] considers 11 image features and uses a neural network to learn the correctness of the estimated gradient-based orientation of the different blocks in a fingerprint image.

Finally, the method defined in [2] computes three pixel features (coherence, mean and variance) and uses a linear classifier to label the corresponding pixels as *background* or *foreground*. A *supervised* approach is used to train the linear classifier and a final morphological post-processing is performed to eliminate holes and regularize the external silhouette of the fingerprint area. Due to its specificity with respect to the considered database (sensor), this approach yields very accurate segmentation results and is the basis of many techniques, discussed in the literature, for fingerprint image enhancement and analysis [9,5].

3 Mathematical Morphology

The segmentation introduced here is based mainly on mathematical morphological transformations, briefly discussed in this section, and on a directional field estimation approach presented in Section 4. The morphological transformations try to extract relevant structures of an image, by taking into account a small signal named structuring function [14].

Let $f : \mathcal{D} \subset \mathbf{Z}^2 \to \mathbf{Z}$ be an image function and $g : \mathcal{G} \subset \mathbf{Z}^2 \to \mathbf{Z}$ be this structuring function. The two fundamental morphological transformations, erosion and dilation, are:

Dilation : The dilation of a function $f(x, y)$ by a structuring function $g(a, b)$, $[\delta_g(f)](x, y)$, is given by: $[\delta_g(f)](x, y) = \max_{a,b \in \mathcal{G}}\{f(x + a, y + b) + g(a, b)\}$. Erosion : The erosion of the function $f(x, y)$ by a structuring function $g(a, b)$, $[\epsilon_g(f)](x, y)$, is given by: $[\epsilon_g(f)](x, y) = \min_{a,b \in \mathcal{G}}\{f(x + a, y + b) - g(a, b)\}$.

3.1   Multi-scale Morphological Transformations

The notion of scale (size) is related to the way we observe the physical world, where different features can be made explicit at different scales. In multiscale morphology, the notion of scale is achieved by scaling the structuring function $g_\sigma : \mathcal{G} \subset \mathbf{Z}^2 \to \mathbf{Z}$, such that [6]

$$g_\sigma(a, b) = \mid \sigma \mid g(\sigma^{-1}a, \sigma^{-1}b) \quad a, b \in \mathcal{G}, \forall \sigma \neq 0, \tag{1}$$

where σ conveys the notion of scale.

In this work, we consider the pyramidal structuring function, given by $g(a, b) = max\{\mid a \mid, \mid b \mid\}$, whose scaled version is $g_\sigma(a, b) = -\sigma^{-1}max\{\mid a \mid, \mid b \mid\}$.

Specifically, here we use a small 3×3 structuring function, where g_σ is zero at position $(0, 0)$ and $-\sigma^{-1}$ otherwise. As explored in [6] and [1], this non-flat structuring function possesses interesting image simplification properties including, for example, a monotonic filtering of the image extrema (its regional maxima and minima).

4   Directional Field Estimation

The directional field [9] is related to the global shape of a fingerprint and describes the local directions of the segment lines represented by a *ridge-valley* pattern. In this work, we use a multi-scale directional operator for estimating these patterns' orientation.

4.1   Multi-scale Directional Operator

The multi-scale directional operator [11] can be regarded as a generalization of the method presented in [10]. It is based on the observation that, in fingerprint images, the contrast between the direction following a ridge-valley pattern and its orthogonal orientation is greater than the contrast achieved for any other pair of directions.

Shortly, the multiscale operator estimates the orientation of each pixel (x, y) by dividing the semicircle in D discrete directions and computing the standard deviation (std) of the gray values for the set of line segments along each direction.

The coordinates (x, y) of the points in a discrete line segment with length n and direction α are computed by considering a sliding window Γ of size $n \times n$, such that

$$x = x_{center} + p \times cos(\alpha)$$
$$y = y_{center} + p \times sin(\alpha), \tag{2}$$

for all p such that $-n/2 \leq p \geq n/2$. x_{center} and y_{center} are the coordinates of the point containing the sliding window Γ centered in this location.

The set s_i^n of D discrete lines with length n and discrete direction i is computed by repeating this procedure for all D directions ($i \in \{0, 1, ... D - 1\}$), by respectively changing the value of α accordingly ($\alpha = 0$, $1 \times 180/D$, $2 \times 180/D, ..., (D - 1) \times 180/D$). The directional image d' at a finer scale is then computed as follows:

$$d'(x, y) = \begin{cases} i, & if \ std(s_i^n) < std(s_{\perp(i)}^n) \\ \perp (i), & if \ std(s_i^n) > std(s_{\perp(i)}^n) \\ v, & otherwise \end{cases} \tag{3}$$

where i and $\perp (i)$ corresponds to the pair of orthogonal directions exhibiting the highest contrast (e.g., $max_{j \in \{0, ..., D/2-1\}}\{std(j) - std(\perp (j))\}$) and v is a special differentiable value representing the result of the function in a homogeneous region, i.e., region which does not have dominant direction. In our experiments, we consider $D = 8$ and $n = 35$ in the definition of the image given by Eq. 3.

Finally, the directional field image d is obtained by considering a window $\Omega : \mathcal{D} \subset \mathbf{Z}^2 \rightarrow \mathbf{Z}$ (also known as *smoothing window*) centered at each pixel on the d' image, according to the following equation.

$$d(x, y) = mode_{a,b \in \mathcal{D}}\{d'(x + a, y + b)\}, \tag{4}$$

where $\mathcal{D}$ corresponds to the domain of the *smoothing window* and *mode* stands for the statistical mode which, in this case, computes the most frequent direction in Ω.

Note that the size of this smoothing window constitutes a scale factor in the sense that a small window yields a finer representation of the corresponding directional field, while a large one defines a coarser representation.

5   Proposed Approach

The segmentation method proposed in this paper consists of the following steps, as shows the flowchart in Fig. 2.

The *Finer directional field detection* block computes the orientation of the input image by considering the multi-scale directional operator (Section 4) with a small smoothing window, Ω_s, of size 5×5. This smoothing operation defines an orientation image w representing a fine scale of the directional field. This fine representation preserves important orientation details used in the following algorithm step, namely *Background subtraction*, which performs a subtraction of the background from the original fingerprint image. This operation separates the ridge-valley foreground regions from the rest of the image, as follows

$$f'(x,y) = f(x,y) - b(x,y),\qquad(5)$$

where f' stands for the foreground image conveying the papillary information, f indicates the original input image, and b, an estimate of the background region.

To obtain this background estimation, we define a mapping that explores some simplification properties of a scale-space toggle operation. These properties include, for example, suppression of the image extrema (regional maxima and minima) in a monotonic way, i.e, without creation of new extrema [4]. The toggle transformation corresponding to the estimation b is given by

$$b(x,y) = \begin{cases} f(x,y), \ if \ \phi_1^k(x,y) - f(x,y) <= \phi_2^k(x,y) - f(x,y), \\ \phi_3(x,y), \ otherwise, \end{cases}\qquad(6)$$

where, again, f corresponds to the input image, $\phi_1^k = [\delta_{g_\sigma}(f)]^k$ and $\phi_2^k = [\epsilon_{g_\sigma}(f)]^k$ are, respectively, the dilation and erosion of f with the scaled structuring function g_σ, k times, and $\phi_3 = [\delta_{g \perp w}(f)]$ corresponds to the linear dilation of f in the orthogonal direction of the orientation indicated by the finer directional field image w, at each location (x,y).

Informally, the toggle mapping in Eq. 6 defines as estimate for b the pixels converging to the regional maxima in a uniform or quasi-uniform region, based on the proximity of $f(x,y)$ with the dilation $\phi_1^k(x,y)$, and in the regions conveying papillary information, represented by the directional dilation $\phi_3(x,y)$ which takes into account the orientation of the ridges in the original image f. Fig. 3 illustrates the above transformations for a noisy image of the FCV2000 database. This figure corresponds to the background subtraction given by Eq. 5. It is worth noting that regions corresponding to the image background and valleys (without papillary information) converged to the regional maxima of these regions represented here in white.

Finally, the *Coarser directional field detection* block in Fig. 2 considers a large smoothing window, Ω_l, of size 45×45, in order to regionally define the dominant direction of the ridges in the foreground image f'. The outermost lines of the regions, containing the same directional field, constitute the fingerprint segmentation result depicted by the silhouettes in Fig. 4.

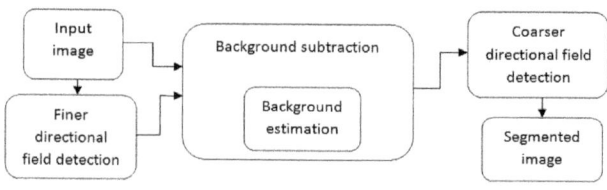

Fig. 2. Flowchart of the proposed segmentation method

Fig. 3. Segmentation example for an FCV2000 database image

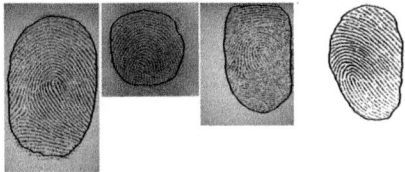

Fig. 4. Segmentation examples of different FVC database images

6   Experimental Results

In order to demonstrate the effectiveness of our approach, we compare it against two state-of-the-art methods, namely, the Bazen and Gerez's segmentation algorithm, and the one proposed by the NIST (National Institute of Standard and Technology) biometric system [15]. To do this, we consider two experiments. In the first, we take into account a set of images, typical of different types of sensors (optical, capacitive, thermal, etc), and obtained from the FVC (Fingerprint Verification Competition) databases [8]. In the second experiment, we work with the rolled fingerprint images provided by NIST and scanned from the FBI database. In the following results, the ground truth was obtained by a manual extraction of the fingerprint regions and the accuracy of the segmentation was established based on the F-measure defined as $\frac{2 \times Precision \times Recall}{Precision + Recall}$, where $Precision = \frac{tp}{tp+fp}$ and $Recall = \frac{tp}{tp+fn}$, fp, fn and tp correspond to false positives, false negatives and true positives, respectively.

6.1   FVC Databases

In this first experiment, we take into account 778 images originated from different sensors and belonging to the FVC2000 (DB1 and DB4) and FVC2002 and FVC2004 (DB1, DB2, DB3 and DB4) databases. We compare our segmentation results against the ones given by the Bazen and Gerez's algorithm, one of the most accurate method described in literature [2]. The values in Table 1 show the equivalence of our results with those of Bazen and Gerez's algorithm. Note that our approach does not suffer from the interoperability problem in the sense that it does not need any particular training related to different sensors or databases. Indeed, our method does not include any specific training and was designed to be robust enough to deal with images obtained from a variety of sensors, which means with data of different quality, resolution or gray-level.

Table 1. F-measure values for the segmentation of the FVC database images

Databases	Bazen and Gerez [2]	Our Approach
2000-DB3	0.93048	0.96165
2000-DB4	0.97909	0.95933
2002-DB1	0.96828	0.98211
2002-DB2	0.93827	0.95757
2002-DB3	0.97411	0.96044
2002-DB4	0.98215	0.97939
2004-DB1	0.98347	0.98812
2004-DB2	0.92180	0.90778
2004-DB3	0.96060	0.97837
2004-DB4	0.97727	0.96519

6.2   NIST Database

In the second experiment, we consider a set of images from the NIST database and compare the results obtained by considering the segmentation approach of the NIST system, Bazen and Gerez's algorithm, and our proposed method. These results are indicated in Table 2, which shows a better performance of our approach with respect to the baseline algorithms.

Table 2. F-measure values for the methods considered with the NIST Database

Bazen and Gerez [2]	NIST	Our Approach
0.94193	0.95565	0.95602

Finally, note that for each database we trained the linear classifier used in [2] by considering 20 images and taking into account the following parameters: epochs $= 10^4$, $\eta_0 = 10^{-4}$, $\tau = 10^4$ and Gaussian window with $\sigma = 9$. The fixed parameters obtained through experimental tests, concerned with Eq. 6, and related to our approach are as follows: number of iterations $k = 15$, scale $\sigma = 25$ of the morphological transformations (dilation and erosion), and length $|g| = 17$ of the linear structuring element of the orthogonal dilation given by Φ_3. Fig. 5 shows a segmentation example of an image of the NIST database.

Fig. 5. Segmentation examples of NIST, Bazen and Gerez and Our Approach

7   Conclusions and Future Works

In this paper, we introduced a novel segmentation method designed to deal with fingerprint images captured from different sensors. To assess the method, we have performed experiments with more than 800 images of different databases. These experiments show that the proposed method yields accurate and robust segmentation results with the great advantage of being, unlike other approaches, independent from the type of the different available sensors. Indeed, it is worth noting that most existing fingerprint segmentation algorithms are based on a prior classification of the images foreground and background, according to a certain knowledge. Further, thresholding or training techniques are used in the segmentation process, which algorithmically imply a lack of sensor interoperability. In our case, we avoid this aspect by taking into account global characteristics of a fingerprint image explored here by means of its multiscale representation and the directional field inherent to its basic structure.

References

1. Dorini, L.B., Leite, N.J.: A scale-space toggle operator for morphological segmentation. In: Proceedings of 8th Int. Symp. on Mathematical Morphology, vol. 1, pp. 101–112 (2007)
2. Bazen, A.M., Gerez, S.H.: Segmentation of fingerprint images. In: Proc. of the Workshop on Circuits Sys. and Signal Processing, pp. 276–280 (2001)
3. Bazen, A.M., Gerez, S.H.: Systematic methods for the computation of the directional fields and singular points of fingerprints. IEEE Trans. Pattern Anal. Mach. Intell. 24(7), 905–919 (2002)
4. Baldo Dorini, L., Jerônimo Leite, N.: Multiscale morphological image simplification. In: Ruiz-Shulcloper, J., Kropatsch, W.G. (eds.) CIARP 2008. LNCS, vol. 5197, pp. 413–420. Springer, Heidelberg (2008)
5. Yang, G., Zhou, G.-T., Yin, Y., Yang, X.: K-means based fingerprint segmentation with sensor interoperability. EURASIP Journal on Advances in Signal Processing, 1–12 (2010)
6. Jackway, P.T., Deriche, M.: Scale-space properties of the multiscale morphological dilation-erosion. IEEE Transactions on Pattern Analysis and Machine Intelligence 18(1), 38–51 (1996)
7. Jain, A.K., Farrokhnia, F.: Unsupervised texture segmentation using gabor filters. Pattern Recogn. 24(12), 1167–1186 (1991)
8. Maio, D., Maltoni, D., Cappelli, R., Wayman, J., Jain, A.: Fvc2000: Fingerprint verification competition. IEEE Transactions on Pattern Analysis and Machine Intelligence 24, 402–412 (2002)
9. Maltoni, D., Maio, D., Jain, A.K., Prabhakar, S.: Handbook of Fingerprint Recognition, 2nd edn. Springer, Heidelberg (2009)
10. Mehtre, B.: Fingerprint image analysis for automatic identification. Machine Vision and Applications 6, 124–139 (1993), doi:10.1007/BF01211936
11. Oliveira, M.A., Leite, N.J.: A multiscale directional operator and morphological tools for reconnecting broken ridges in fingerprint images. Pattern Recognition 41(1), 367–377 (2008)

12. Ratha, N.K.: Adaptive flow orientation based feature extraction in fingerprint images. Pattern Recognition 28, 1657–1672 (1995)
13. Shen, L., Kot, A.C., Koo, W.M.: Quality measures of fingerprint images. In: Bigun, J., Smeraldi, F. (eds.) AVBPA 2001. LNCS, vol. 2091, pp. 266–271. Springer, Heidelberg (2001)
14. Soille, P.: Morphological Image Analysis. Springer, Heidelberg (1999)
15. Watson, C.I., Garris, M.l.D., Tabassi, E., Wilson, C.L., Mccabe, R.M., Janet, S., Ko, K.: User's guide to nist biometric image software (nbis). Tech. rep., NIST Research Report (NISTIR) - 7392 (2007)
16. Zhu, E., Yin, J., Hu, C., Zhang, G.: A systematic method for fingerprint ridge orientation estimation and image segmentation. Pattern Recogn. 39(8), 1452–1472 (2006)

Thermal Noise Estimation and Removal in MRI: A Noise Cancellation Approach*

Miguel E. Soto, Jorge E. Pezoa, and Sergio N. Torres

Departamento de Ingeniería Eléctrica and Center for Optics and Photonics (CEFOP)
Universidad de Concepción, Concepción, Chile
{miguelsoto,jpezoa,sertorre}@udec.cl
http://www.cefop.cl

Abstract. In this work a closed-form, maximum-likelihood (ML) estimator for the variance of the thermal noise in magnetic resonance imaging (MRI) systems has been developed. The ML estimator was, in turn, used as *a priori* information for devising a single dimensional noise-cancellation–based image restoration algorithm. The performance of the estimator was assessed theoretically by means of the Crámer-Rao lower bound, and the effect of selecting an appropriate set of no-signal pixels on estimating the noise variance was also investigated. The effectivity of the noise-cancellation–based image restoration algorithm in compensating for the thermal noise in MRI was also evaluated. Actual MRI data from the LONI database was employed to assess the performance of both the ML estimator and the image restoration algorithm.

1 Introduction

Several methods for thermal noise variance estimation in magnetic resonance (MR) imagery have been proposed in the literature. A simple taxonomy classifies the methods in temporal, spatial, and spatio-temporal. On one hand, the temporal methods exploit the information of the same voxel at different frames in order to estimate and compensate for the noise. On the other hand, spatial methods utilize a single image and attempt to exploit the fact that uniform features must yield uniform regions in the acquired image.

Temporal filtering techniques have the advantage of not comprising the spatial resolution of the images; however, the main disadvantage of such methods is the necessity of acquiring more than one image per slice of tissue under analysis [1]. Spatial filtering techniques have the main advantage of being simple, because they exploit heuristics such as the large number of pixels that receive no signal at all, hence their output signal must be uniformly zero; the thermal noise or some statistics of it may be estimated from such no signal pixels. The main disadvantage of spatial filtering is the reduction of spatial resolution in the filtered

* Authors acknowledge the support of CEFOP and Grant CONICYT PFB-0824. Data used in this article were obtained from the ADNI database (adni.loni.ucla.edu). As such, investigators within ADNI contributed to the design and implementation of ADNI and provided data but did not participate in analysis or writing of this paper.

C. San Martin and S.-W. Kim (Eds.): CIARP 2011, LNCS 7042, pp. 47–54, 2011.

images. Examples of spatial approaches are maximum-likelihood (ML) estimators [2,3], histogram-based estimators [4], and spatial filters such as Gaussian or Hanning masks [5].

In this paper a closed-form, ML estimator for the variance of thermal noise in magnetic resonance imaging (MRI) systems has been derived by means of an algebraic trick and the knowledge on the distribution of the noise process. The estimator has been compared theoretically to other well-known noise variance estimators by means of the fundamental result called the Crámer-Rao lower bound (CRLB). The performance of the estimator has been also tested experimentally using simulated and actual MRI data, which was obtained from the Alzheimer's disease neuroimaging initiative (ADNI) project's database. Additionally, the ML estimator developed here was employed used as *a priori* information for developing a noise-cancellation–based image restoration algorithm, meaning that the images are be regarded as one dimensional signals for their processing. The image restoration algorithm is shown to be effective in rendering good-quality filtered images from a set of noisy MR data. Finally, it must be commented that the study conducted here is restricted only to the case of having: (i) magnitude-only MR images; and (ii) a single MR image.

The rest of this paper is organized as follows: in Section 2 images rendered by MRI systems are mathematically modeled and a ML estimator for the thermal additive noise corrupting the images is derived. In Section 2.4 the performance of ML estimator is assessed and compared to other classical estimator. In Section 3 an image restoration procedure based upon the technique of noise cancellation is presented as well. Finally, in Section 4 our conclusions are stated.

2   Estimation of the Noise Variance

2.1   Thermal Noise in MRI

The complex MR image, $X_r(m, n)$, rendered by an MRI system is modeled by:

$$X_r(m, n) = x(m, n) + N(m, n) ,   \tag{1}$$

where $x(m, n)$ and $N(m, n)$ are the magnetization distribution and the noisy component of the reconstructed signal, respectively. $N(m, n)$ is considered a complex white random process, whose real and imaginary parts are pairwise independent Gaussian random variables (r.v.s) with zero mean and variance σ^2. To avoid the phase errors of MRI systems or simply because the complex image may not be available to the users, the so-called magnitude image is obtained after taking the magnitude of $X_r(m, n)$, [6]. Therefore, the typical model for a pixel in an MR image is given by:

$$S(m, n) = \left((x_R(m, n) + N_R(m, n))^2 + (x_I(m, n) + N_I(m, n))^2 \right)^{1/2} ,   \tag{2}$$

where the sub indexes R and I denotes the real and imaginary parts, respectively. Equation (2) shows that $S(m, n)$ corresponds to a function of two r.v.s normally distributed. It is not hard to show that each pixel of the magnitude image is a r.v. following a Rician distribution with parameters $a_x(m,n) = |x_r(m,n)| = \sqrt{x_R^2(m,n) + x_I^2(m,n)}$ and σ^2, [6,7,4,8]. Note that when no signal is present, i.e. $x(m,n) = 0$, $S(m,n)$ follows a Rayleigh distribution [6].

2.2   Related Work: Some Thermal Noise Variance Estimators

Noise variance estimation in MRI is performed using both the uniform regions of the noisy image and heuristics on the underlying probability density function (pdf) of the noisy data. Some commonly used variance estimators are:

1. *Histrogram's maximum of background noise (HMBN) estimator* [9]: Derived based upon the fact that the maximum value of the Rayleigh distribution is attained when $s(m,n) = \sigma$. If we consider that the histogram is an estimate of the actual pdf, then the HMBN estimator is given by $\widehat{\sigma^2}_{HMBN} = \mathrm{argmax}\, \hat{f}_{S(m,n)}(s)$, with $\hat{f}_{S(m,n)}(s)$ an estimated pdf yielded using the uniform regions of an image.

2. *Total least-squares error (TLSE) of pdf fitting estimator* [10]: Derived based on minimizing the TLSE of fitting the partial histogram of a noisy image with a (scaled) Rayleigh pdf, *i.e.* $\hat{f}_{Y(m,n)}(y) = K \exp(-\lambda y)$, with $\lambda \triangleq (2\sigma^2)^{-1}$ and $K \triangleq k\lambda$ a scaling factor. Clearly the resulting estimator is $\widehat{\sigma^2}_{LS} = (2\lambda)^{-1}$.

3. *Conventional estimator.* Derived exploiting the second moment of the Rayleigh pdf. The second moment of $S(m,n)$ when no signal is present is $E\{S^2(m,n)\} = 2\sigma^2$. So, if it is estimated using the sample second moment of $S(m,n)$ over a set of ℓ independent samples of $S(m,n)$, then $\widehat{\sigma^2}_c = \frac{1}{2\ell} \sum_{i=1}^{\ell} s_i^2(m,n)$.

2.3   A Closed-Form ML Estimator for Thermal Noise in MRI Systems

In order to obtain a closed-form ML estimator for thermal noise in MRI systems we apply an algebraic trick which simplifies the derivation process. Let us define a new r.v. representing the magnitude squared of $X_r(m,n)$, i.e., $Y(m,n) \triangleq S(m,n)^2$. Since $X_r(m,n)$ follows a Rayleigh distribution (when no signal is present), then $Y(m,n)$ follows an exponential distribution with parameter σ^2. From estimation theory, a closed-form ML estimator for an exponential distribution can be obtained in a straightforward manner, [11]. More precisely, the resulting estimator is $\widehat{\sigma^2}_{ML} = \frac{1}{2\ell} \sum_{i=1}^{\ell} y_i(m,n)$, which is identical to the conventional estimator. From estimation theory, when ML estimator exists then it is unbiased and asymptotically minimum variance, thereby asymptotically achieving the CRLB, *i.e.*, it attains asymptotically the best performance.

2.4   Performance Assessment of the ML Estimator

Under the simulation scenario, the precision and accuracy of the aforementioned estimators will be assessed drawing samples from Rayleigh r.v.s with known variances. In addition, the performance will be evaluated using real MRI data. The MR data was obtained from ADNI database and comprises a sequence of

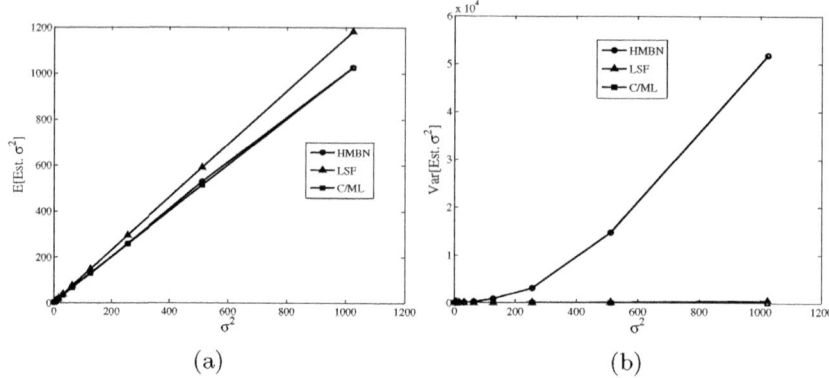

Fig. 1. Noise estimation $\widehat{\sigma^2}$ using simulated data at different values of σ^2: (a) average, (b) variance

166 proton-density–weighted images, each of them of size 256×256 pixels. The parameters used to acquire the images are: TE=1.29 s, TR=3.3 s, flip angle=2 degrees, slice thickness=1.2 mm, quantized in 12 unsigned bits. The Laboratory of Neuro Imaging (LONI) identifier of the data is 002_S_1018. From now on, we refer to the data as 002_S_1018.

Scenario 1: Simulations. We have conducted an experiment considering ten different (true) values for σ^2, namely, $\sigma^2 = \{2^0, 2^1, 2^2, \ldots, 2^{10}\}$. We have created, for each value of σ^2, a vector with 2^{16} realizations of independent and identically distributed (iid) Rayleigh r.v.s. Such an experiment was repeated 5000 times so that we can compute both the average and the variance of the estimated noise variance. Results obtained are depicted in Fig. 1, where it can be observed that the ML estimator yields, as expected, an unbiased estimate with the minimum variance. The estimator based upon the maximum value of the histogram is unbiased; however, the variance of the estimation increases as σ^2 does it. Also, the TLSE-based estimator is a biased estimator, whose bias increases as σ^2 does. In terms of accuracy, the TLSE achieves the minimum variance.

Scenario 2: Real data no-signal images. Here we have taken the first ten images from 002_S_1018. The first eight images contain slices of air, while the last two contain small areas with human body tissue. Notice that the slice thickness was taken fairly thin, so that the noise in the images was accentuated. Fig. 2 shows three images from 002_S_1018. Fig. 2(a) shows an no-signal image, and its histogram clearly shows the shape of a Rayleigh distribution. Fig. 2(b) shows almost the same phenomenon, where the small white circle at the lower center of the image represents pixels with some signal values. Due to the number of pixels having signal is small as compared with the no-signal pixels, we can say that the distribution of the image is approximately Rayleigh. Clearly, when tissue is present such as in Fig. 2(c) the assumption on a Rayleigh distribution is violated. In order to test if the parameters of the Rayleigh distribution for the

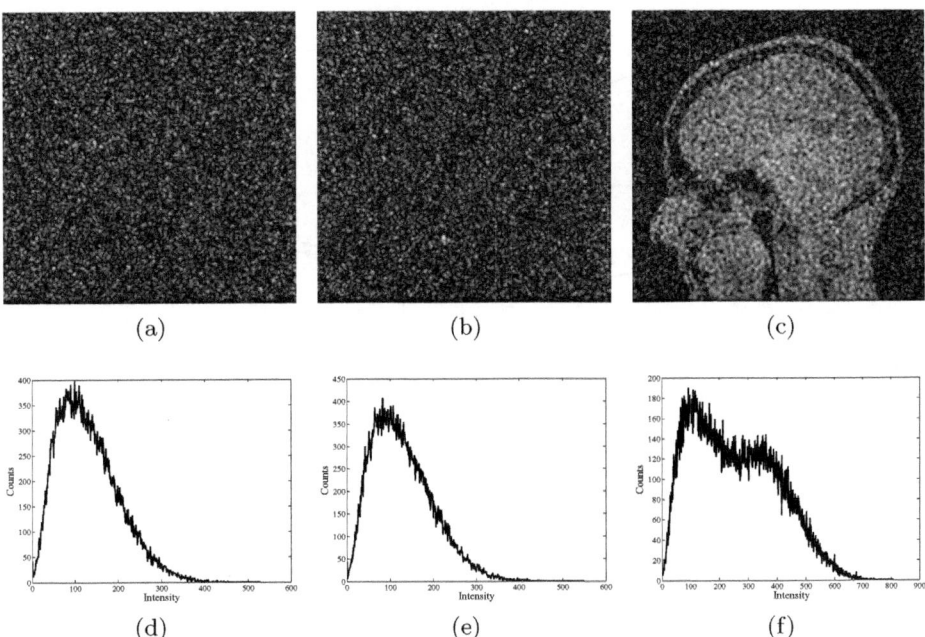

Fig. 2. Sample images and their corresponding histogram from 002_S_1018. Image: (a) 1, (b) 10 and (c) 88. Image Histogram: (d) 1, (e) 10 and (f) 88.

thermal noise are stationary during the acquisition process, the noise variance is estimated at every image of the first ten images of 002_S_1018. Fig. 3a shows the results of the estimation process. In light of these results, it can be concluded that: (i) the statistics of the thermal noise does not change during the acquisition process; and (ii) the estimate of the ML estimator appears to be consistent along the images, while the other two estimates do not.

Scenario 3: Real data noisy images. The image shown in Fig. 2(c) will be employed to estimate the noise variance. Since signal and noise are both present in the image, first we have to carefully select no-signal regions. In order to perform an automated estimation procedure we have adjusted a threshold value, τ, for the intensities in order to discriminate no-signal pixels. *A priori*, by inspecting the histogram the value $\tau = 300$ seems to be an accurate value for no-signal pixels. The results obtained for this scenario are shown in Fig. 3b. Clearly, the selection of a right τ value is crucial for achieving estimation performance. Notice that after a certain value for τ the estimate achieved by the maximum of the histogram estimator is the same. Such situation is easily explained because increasing τ introduces in the histogram pixel values with less number of counts, hence the maximum value remains the same. Note also that the results given by the TLSE fit estimator are the worst in terms of precision. Moreover, if we do not properly select τ then estimated values can be totally wrong such as the negative value for the noise variance estimated when $\tau < 250$. This is attributable to the fact that as τ increases the histogram departs from the shape of a Rayleigh pdf.

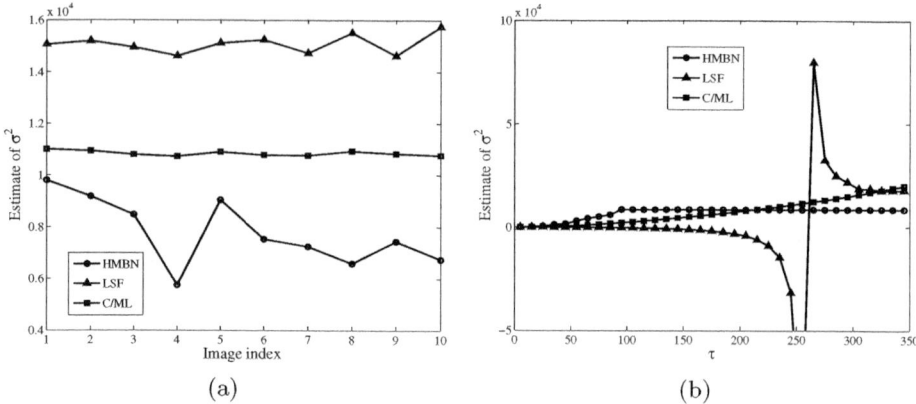

Fig. 3. The estimated noise variance, $\widehat{\sigma^2}$: (a) at the first 10 images of the 002_S_1018 LONI data (*Scenario 2*) and (b) as a function of the threshold value τ, using the no-signal pixels of the image in Fig. 2c) (*Scenario 3*)

Notice that the estimated values disagree with those obtained using a no-signal image. This is because some pixels with small signal values are regarded as no-signal pixels, and their inclusion in the histogram degrade the estimation process. To counteract for such problem, a region-of-interest–based estimation was performed. We have selected four squared regions outside of the patients head, corresponding to a 21% of the total number of pixels. Using such values the estimated noise variances are: $\widehat{\sigma^2}_{HMBN} = 5788$, $\widehat{\sigma^2}_{LS} = 16634$, and $\widehat{\sigma^2}_{ML} = 11040$. Note now that those values are consistent with the ones computed using the image in Fig. 2(a) and (b).

3   Image Restoration

Typically, when the noise variance of the thermal noise is available, signal estimators can be constructed to render restored images. A common signal estimator is obtained exploiting the second moment of a Rician distribution, [4]:

$$\widehat{a_x}(m,n) = \left(N^{-1} \sum_{i=1}^{N} y_i(m,n) - 2\widehat{\sigma^2}\right)^{1/2} . \tag{3}$$

Such estimator is valid for local regions where a common signal value was corrupted by the thermal noise.

Here, we propose a new signal estimator based upon the technique of noise cancellation, which is commonly used in signal processing when one desires to recover signals corrupted by additive noise, [12]. The main motivation for implementing image restoration via a noise cancellation is that the whole processing it is performed in a pixel-by-pixel basis; no spatial resolution is compromised.

From (2) we have that:

$$Y(m,n) = \widehat{a_x^2}(m,n) + Z(m,n) , \tag{4}$$

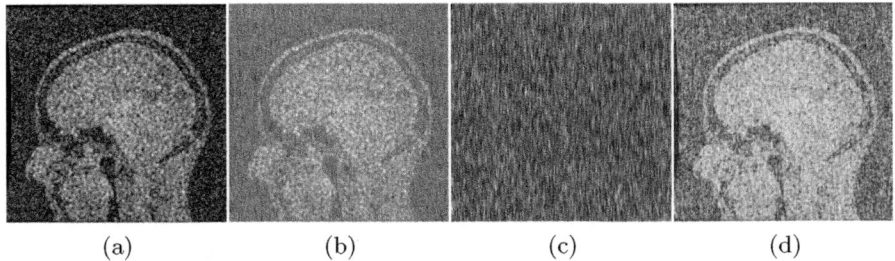

(a)   (b)   (c)   (d)

Fig. 4. A sample image from the 002_S_1018: (a) noisy image; and (b) restored version. The difference image between: (c) the squares of the noisy image and the restored image; and (d) the noisy image and the restored image.

where $\widehat{a_x^2}(m,n) \triangleq a_x^2(m,n) + 2x_R(m,n)N_R(m,n) + 2x_I(m,n)N_I(m,n)$ and $Z(m,n) \triangleq N_R^2(m,n) + N_I^2(m,n)$.

The rationale behind a noise-cancellation system is the following: If by designing an filter we are capable of producing $\hat{Z}(m,n)$, a fairly good approximation of $Z(m,n)$, then $e(m,n) \triangleq Y(m,n) - \hat{Z}(m,n) \approx \widehat{a_x^2}(m,n)$, which corresponds to a fairly good estimate of $a_x^2(m,n)$. Suppose that an finite impulse response (FIR) filter with L coefficients, denoted as $h_0, h_1, \ldots, h_{L-1}$, is designed to obtain $\hat{Z}(m,n)$. Suppose also that independent samples of an exponential distribution, with parameter $(2\sigma^2)^{-1}$ are available as well, and let us denote them as $W(m,n)$. Given that the image processing will be conducted as a single-dimensional signal processing, then Y and W correspond to stacked versions of the images $Y(m,n)$ and $W(m,n)$. Thus, according to least squares theory we calculate the mean square error (MSE) of the estimate of a_x^2 as: $\text{MSE} = \mathsf{E}\left[e^2\right] = \phi_{YY}[0] - 2\sum_{i=0}^{L-1} h_i \phi_{WY}[i] + \sum_{i=0}^{L-1}\sum_{j=0}^{L-1} h_i h_j \phi_{WW}[i-j]$, where $\phi_{YY}[n]$ and $\phi_{WW}[n]$ are the autocorrelation sequences of Y and W, respectively, and $\phi_{WY}[n]$ is the cross-correlation sequence between W and Y. By minimizing the MSE with respect to the design parameters $h_0, \ldots, h_{L-1}$ produces the system of linear equations $\mathbf{\Phi}_{WW}\mathbf{h}_L = \mathbf{\Phi}_{WY}$, whose solution is $\mathbf{h}_L^* = \mathbf{\Phi}_{WW}^{-1}\mathbf{\Phi}_{WY}$, and provides the filter coefficients h_i that minimize the estimation error of a_x^2.

Restoration of noisy images: In the restoration process, the estimated value for σ given by the ML estimator we is fed to the noise-cancellation filter, so that a sequence of iid r.v.s exponentially distributed with parameter $\lambda = (2\widehat{\sigma^2}_{ML})^{-1} = 4.55 \cdot 10^{-5}$ is drawn. The single parameter that needs to be adjusted in the image restoration method is the number of filter coefficients L. Typically, such parameter is determined after some training procedure. In our case, the best results were achieved for $L = 10$, where by best results we mean that the quality of the images seems to be the best to the naked eye. It must be noted that such subjective assessment is employed only due to the absence of reference or clean images. In Fig. 4 we show a sample original image, its restored version using the proposed method as well as the difference image between the noisy and the restored image. We clearly see that the noise level in the restored image has decreased at expense of producing a low contrast image. From the difference image we can infer that no structure should be visible when we subtract the square of the magnitude of the noisy image to the square of the magnitude of the restored image. This is expected because the noise canceling system was designed to fulfill this criterion. However, for the difference of magnitudes considerable image structure is not captured by the whole filtering process.

4   Conclusions

Thermal noise variance estimation in MRI is commonly performed using heuristics about the presence or absence of MR signal, and next, using some simple generic estimator. Among all the estimators, the closed-form ML estimator developed here is the best choice because of both its statistical efficiency and its simple implementation. In MRI working with the magnitude squared of the data greatly simplifies the algebraic manipulation of the models. Moreover, working with the magnitude squared of the signal creates a simple framework to simulate thermal noise in MRI when solely magnitude images are available. However, such algebraic manipulation cannot eliminate the inherent non-linear behavior the magnitude images, ultimately leading to restored images of reduced performance compared to those achieved when data is squared.

References

1. Vovk, U., et al.: A review of methods for correction of intensity inhomogeneity in MRI. IEEE Trans. on Medical Imaging 26(3), 405–421 (2007)
2. Sijbers, J., et al.: Maximum-likelihood estimation of rician distribution parameters. IEEE Trans. on Medical Imaging 17(3), 357–361 (1998)
3. Aja-Fernandez, S., et al.: Noise and signal estimation in magnitude MRI and rician distributed images: A lmmse approach. IEEE Trans. on Image Proc. 17(8), 1383–1398 (2008)
4. Sijbers, J., et al.: Automatic estimation of the noise variance from the histogram of a magnetic resonance image. Physics Medicine & Biology 52(5), 1335–1348 (2007)
5. Kruggel, F., et al.: Comparison of filtering methods for fMRI datasets. NeuroImage 10, 530–543 (1999)
6. Nowak, R.D.: Wavelet-based rician noise removal for magnetic resonance imaging. IEEE Trans. on Image Processing 8(10), 1408–1419 (1999)
7. Kisner, S.J., Talavage, T.M.: Testing the distribution of nonstationary mri data. Eng. in Medicine & Biology Soc. 3, 1888–1891 (2004)
8. Xu, Y., et al.: COmplex-Model-Based Estimation of thermal noise for fMRI data in the presence of artifacts. Mag. Resonance Imaging 25, 1079–1088 (2007)
9. van Kempen, G., van Vliet, L.: The influence of the background estimation on the superresolution properties of non-linear image restoration algorithms. In: Proc. SPIE Progress Biomedical Optics, vol. 3605, pp. 179–189 (1999)
10. Brummer, M.E., et al.: Automatic detection of brain contours in MRI data sets. IEEE Trans. Medical Imaging 12, 153–168 (1993)
11. Poor, H.V.: An Introduction to Signal Detection and Estimation, 2nd edn. Springer, Heidelberg (1994)
12. Proakis, J.G., Manolakis, D.G.: Digital signal processing: principles, algorithms, and applications, 4th edn. Prentice-Hall, Inc. (2006)

Spectral Model for Fixed-Pattern-Noise in Infrared Focal-Plane Arrays*

Jorge E. Pezoa and Osvaldo J. Medina

Departamento de Ingeniería Eléctrica and Center for Optics and Photonics (CEFOP)
Universidad de Concepción, Concepción, Chile
{jpezoa,osvaldomedina}@udec.cl
http://www.telecomunicaciones.udec.cl

Abstract. In this paper a novel and more realistic analytical model for the fixed-pattern noise present in infrared focal plane arrays is developed. The model captures, in the frequency domain, the spatial structure of the fixed-pattern noise yielding a suitable input/output representation for an infrared focal plane array. The theoretical and practical applicability the model is illustrated by both synthesizing fixed-pattern noise from three different infrared cameras and improving the performance of a previously reported fixed-pattern noise compensation algorithm.

1 Introduction

Infrared cameras are being used in a wide range of applications such as temperature measurement, spectral-signature analysis, night vision, and predictive machinery maintenance. Infrared cameras collect the spectral information by means of imaging sensing devices called infrared focal plane arrays (FPAs). An infrared FPA is an integrated circuit composed of either a linear or a matrix of infrared photodetectors. An image is created after reading and properly assembling the infrared information collected by all the photodetectors in the array [1]. In theory, all the photodetectors in the FPA respond in exactly the same manner when a spatially uniform spectral object is placed in front of the array. Unfortunately practical FPA do not respond in such a way when a flat infrared input impinges the array.

The fixed-pattern noise (FPN) in infrared FPAs is the nonuniform spatial response of the FPA when a spatially uniform stimulus is used as an input. The FPN is a quasi-stationary, spatially structured type of noise, which produces a grid-like pattern on top of the true images. The FPN is attributed to device manufacturing mismatches and parameter variations across the FPA, such as photodetector area and dark current [2, 3]. Since the grid-like pattern severely degrades the true images, it is mandatory to compensate for the FPN before using the imagery acquired by an infrared camera equipped with an FPA.

Surprisingly, the spatial structure of the FPN is oversimplified in the literature under the assumption that the FPN is spatially independent [4, 5, 6]. Only few

* Authors acknowledge the support of CEFOP and Grant CONICYT PFB-0824.

C. San Martin and S.-W. Kim (Eds.): CIARP 2011, LNCS 7042, pp. 55–63, 2011.

papers have considered the existence of spatial structure in the FPN [7, 8]; however, in none of these works specific models for the FPN have been developed. To the best of our knowledge, the work [9] by El Gamal *et al.* is the only paper available where a model for the FPN has been developed. Such a model was developed in the spatial domain by means of random fields and was specifically developed for modeling noise in CMOS sensors.

In this work we have tackled the necessity of supplying appropriate theoretical models for FPN. To do so, we have developed a novel analytical model for the spatial structure of FPN. The model has been developed in the frequency domain after experimentally characterizing the spectrum of several infrared FPAs. The analytic characterization models the magnitude of the FPN using a linear combination of unidimensional second-order exponential functions, while the phase of the FPN is assumed to be random and uniformly distributed. The analytic model is completed by deriving a total least-squares estimator for the FPN parameters. The main advantage of the model presented here is that it yields a more realistic input/output representation for an entire infrared FPA. The theoretical and practical applicability of our model is illustrated by both synthesizing FPN from three different IR cameras and improving the performance of a previously reported FPN compensation algorithm.

The rest of this paper is organized as follows. Section 2 presents the spectral analysis of FPN conducted using experimental data. In the same section, an analytical model for the FPN in the frequency domain is developed using simple mathematical expressions with a small number of parameters. The ability of the analytical model developed in Section 2.2 to represent the FPN is verified in Section 3 by means of simulations and experimental data. Finally, in Section 4 the conclusions of our work are outlined.

2   Analytical Model of FPN

2.1   Spectral Analysis

Theoretically speaking, the spatial output of an ideal infrared FPA to a flat input should be flat; in the frequency domain, such ideal response should be observed as a delta function. However, when an actual infrared FPA is illuminated by a blackbody source, the observed output is not flat and in the spatial frequency domain a specific shape is observed. By assuming that the FPN has only an additive component, [10, 4, 5, 6], the shape observed in the frequency domain is precisely the frequency-domain representation of the FPN. To obtain a realistic model, an experimental spectral analysis of the FPN has been conducted by collecting data from different infrared cameras illuminated with black-body radiator sources.

For instance, Fig. 1(a) shows an actual sample-frame taken with a CEDIP brand infrared camera. The size of the frame is 240×320 pixels and a black-body source at a temperature of $20°C$ was employed as an input. Note that, a grid-like pattern is observed instead of a flat image. Note also that, from basic Fourier theory, a grid-like FPN should be represented in the Fourier domain by a cross-like shape. Figure 1(b) shows the magnitude of the fast Fourier transform (FFT) of the sample frame shown in Fig. 1(a). In this figure the magnitude of the Fourier transform of both the flat input and the FPN can be observed. In the Fourier domain, the flat input corresponds to the impulse at the center of the spectrum, while the FPN has a clearly defined structure with one vertical spectral band and one horizontal spectral band. Regarding the phase representation of the FPN, in our analysis we have observed a lack of structure in the phase. Such behavior can be justified by the isotropic behavior of the FPN.

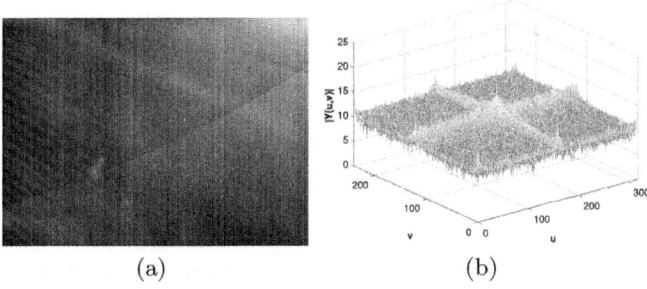

(a)   (b)

Fig. 1. (a) Sample frame of FPN. (b) Magnitude of the FFT of the sample frame.

Finally, our experience a grid-like pattern is a very common type of FPN in practical devices. Consequently, for the remaining of this paper we will assume that the FPN is in fact represented, in the Fourier domain, by one vertical and one horizontal band as those shown in Fig. 1(b). With this, we can introduce a precise analytical model for the class of all infrared sensors whose FPN manifests itself as a pattern of vertical and horizontal lines.

2.2   Spectral Analytical Model

From the analysis presented in the previous subsection we state that the magnitude of the FPN can be modeled as a lineal combination of two independent second-order exponential functions, each one of them having three parameters: the location parameter, the amplitude parameter, and the scale parameter. Regarding the phase, here we have assumed that it can be modeled as a white noise process, with uniform distribution in $[-\pi, \pi]$. Thus, given an FPA of size $2M + 1 \times 2N + 1$ pixels, the magnitude and phase of the FPN can be mathematically modeled as:

$$|Y(u,v)| = B_u \exp\left(\frac{-(u - u_0)^2}{2\sigma_u^2}\right) + B_v \exp\left(\frac{-(v - v_0)^2}{2\sigma_v^2}\right), \qquad (1)$$

$$\angle Y(u,v) \sim U[-\pi, \pi], \qquad (2)$$

where $u = -M, \ldots, M$, $v = -N, \ldots, N$, and $Y(u,v)$ is the two-dimensional Fourier transform of the FPN. The parameters u_0, B_u, and σ_u (correspondingly, v_0, B_v, and σ_v) are the location, the amplitude, and the scale, respectively, of the horizontal (correspondingly, vertical) band.

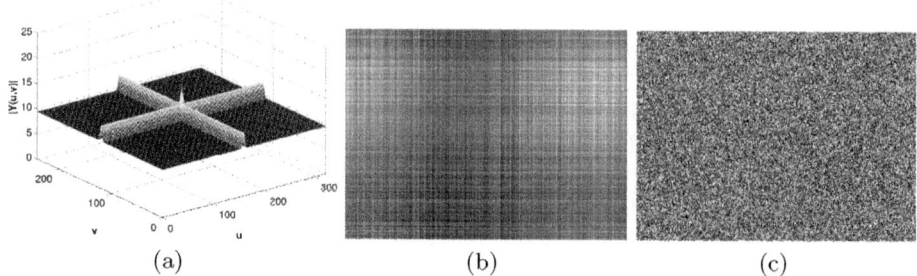

Fig. 2. Synthetic versions of the FPN shown in Fig. 1: (a) Magnitude spectrum, and (b) Spatially structured. (c) Sample frame of spatially unstructured fixed-pattern noise.

For completeness, we have developed also in this paper parameter estimators for (1). We provide only formulae for estimating u_0, B_u, and σ_u. Estimators for v_0, B_v, and σ_v can be obtained *mutatis mutandis*. First, note that the location parameter for the second-order exponential functions must be zero due to the geometry of the FPN, *i.e.* $u_0 = 0$. Next, by exploiting the total least-squares error principle and parameter estimators for B_u and σ_u are given by the following non-linear system of equations:

$$(2M + 1) \ln \hat{B}_u - \sum_{u=-M}^{M} \left(\ln(Y(u)) + (2\hat{\sigma}_u^2)^{-1}(u - u_0)^2 \right) = 0, \qquad (3)$$

$$\sum_{u=-M}^{M} (u - u_0)^4 - 2\hat{\sigma}_u^2 \sum_{u=-M}^{M} (u - u_0)^2 (\ln \hat{B}_u - \ln(Y(u))) = 0. \qquad (4)$$

3   Results

The ability of the analytical model to represent the FPN is verified in this section. We have synthesized FPN using the traditional approach taken in the literature, that is, samples of FPN are drawn from a white spatial process following an uniform distribution supported on the same dynamical range as the raw data. Such samples of unstructured FPN are compared to synthetic, spatially structured FPN generated using the model (1) and (2).

First, we aim to mimic the actual FPN of the CEDIP camera shown in Fig. 1. To do so, we use (3) and (4) and estimate that $B_u \approx \hat{B}_u = 5.2$ and $\sigma_u \approx \hat{\sigma}_u = 2.5$, and employed these values to plot the magnitude spectrum shown in Fig. 2(a). Next, we used (1) and (2) to render samples of synthetic FPN. One of such samples is shown in Fig. 2(b). A naked-eye inspection to Figs. 2(b) and (c) shows that: (i) the synthetic FPN resembles the actual FPN shown in Fig. 1(a); and (ii) the unstructured (spatially white) noise in Fig. 2(c) is clearly not a valid representation of the FPN.

Second, we objectively compare samples of actual FPN to both unstructured synthetic FPN and synthetic FPN generated using our model. The comparison has been made by means of the root mean-squared error (RMSE) between actual and synthetic samples of FPN. Figures 3(a) to (c) show samples of actual FPN from three infrared cameras. Note that in these cameras the FPN is exhibited as a horizontal and/or vertical regular pattern. Table 1 lists the RMSE in synthesizing

FPN in both the spatial and the frequency domain. These results clearly indicate that the RMSE for the structured synthetic FPN is always lower than the RMSE of the unstructured synthetic FPN. In Figs. 3(d) to (f) the magnitude spectrum of the FPN shown in Figs. 3(a) to (c) have been plotted, while in Figs. 3(g) to (h) samples of synthetic FPN, drawn the proposed model, are shown. Clearly, the spatial structure of the actual FPN can be observed in the synthetic versions of the noise.

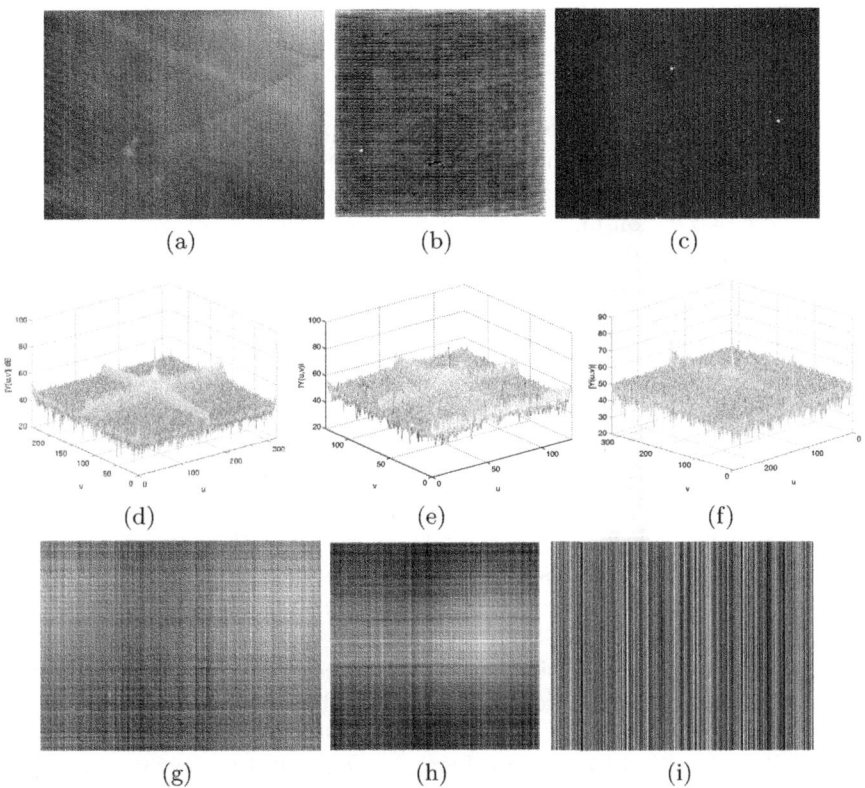

Fig. 3. FPN from different infrared cameras: (a) CEDIP. (b) Amber. (c) Quantum Dots. Magnitude spectrum of FPN: (d) CEDIP. (e) Amber. (f) Quantum Dots. A sample of ynthetic FPN: (g) CEDIP. (h) Amber. (i) Quantum Dots.

Third, in hyperspectral push-broom cameras (where a scanning procedure must be employed to create infrared images) the FPN observed as a striping pattern [11,12,13]. A sample of striping FPN in hyperspectral push-broom cameras is shown in Fig. 4(a) and its magnitude spectrum is shown in Fig. 4(b). We note that the striping noise can be considered a special case of the model for the grid-like FPN we have introduced here. In particular, the mathematical expression for the magnitude of the striping noise reduces to: $|Y(u,v)| = B_u \exp\left(\frac{-(u-u_0)^2}{2\sigma_u^2}\right)$.

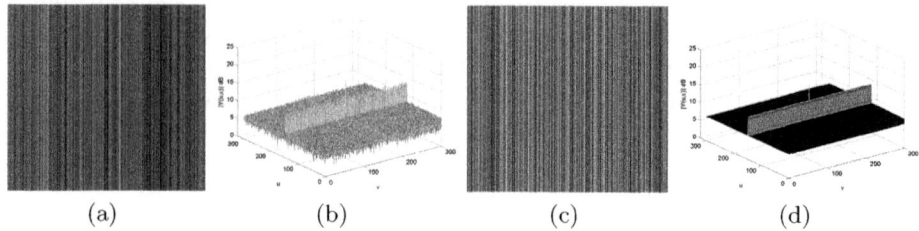

Fig. 4. (a) Actual sample of striping noise; and its (b) Magnitude spectrum. (c) Synthetic sample of striping noise; and its (d) Magnitude spectrum.

Figures 4(c) and (d) show, respectively, a sample of synthetic striping noise in the spatial domain and the magnitude spectrum of synthetic FPN.

Fourth, as a final application of our model, we have supplemented the noise-cancellation–based non-uniformity correction (NUC) algorithm developed by Godoy et al. in [10] with our analytical model, thereby obtaining an enhanced version of such NUC algorithm. In [10], Godoy et al. employed spatially white FPN as the required source of correlated noise which is essential to any noise-cancellation system. Here, we have replaced such noise source by our model of spatially structured FPN. Intuitively speaking, if the noise source is replaced by a proper FPN model, the performance of the NUC algorithm should be improved.

Figures 5(a) and (d) correspond to raw frames acquired using the Amber infrared camera. Figures 5(b) and (e) correspond to corrected versions of the raw frames obtained when the unstructured FPN is used as the source of correlated noise in the noise-cancellation–based NUC method, while Figs. 5(c) and (f) correspond to corrected versions of the raw frames obtained when the structured FPN is employed as the source of correlated noise. It can be observed from the figures that corrected frames obtained using the spatially structured FPN look better than those obtained using the unstructured FPN. This result is important because it confirms the intuition that, only by substituting the source of FPN the performance of the noise-cancellation–based NUC algorithm can be improved.

In addition to the subjective evaluation, a quantitative performance analysis between the original and the enhanced versions of the NUC algorithm was conducted by means of the so-called roughness metric. The roughness metric is employed to assess NUC methods when no reference images are available. The metric is a combination of high-pass spatial filters aiming to measure the sharp changes in

Table 1. RMSE in synthesizing FPN for different cameras

	Spatial domain		Spectral domain	
	Structured	Unstructured	Structured	Unstructured
CEDIP	0.3180	0.4248	8.6782	19.8853
Amber	0.1378	0.3028	11.0094	23.5877
Quantum Dots	0.3746	0.4485	11.3907	22.9642

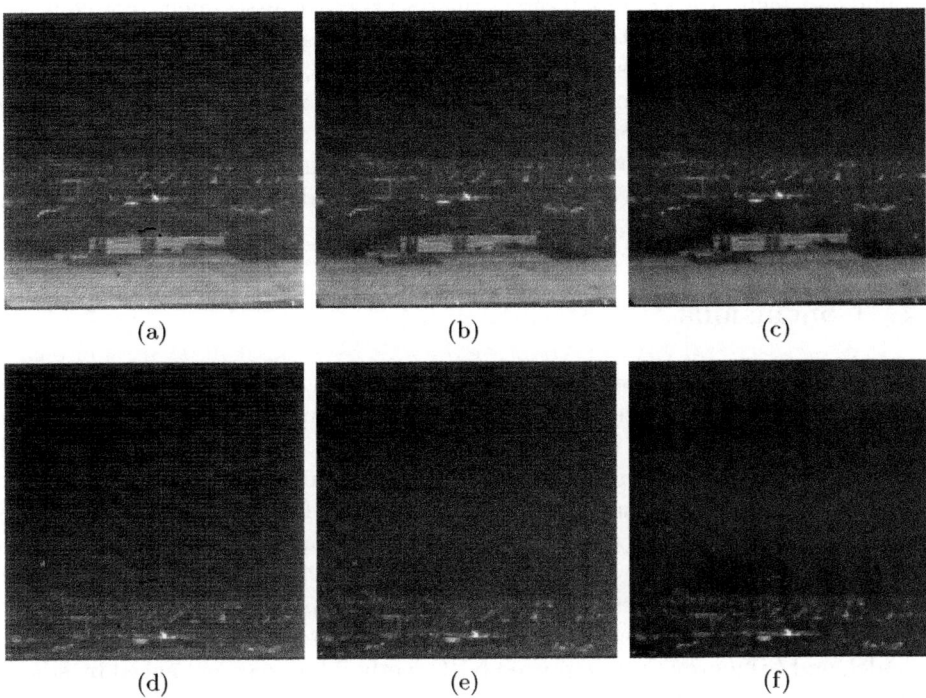

(a)   (b)   (c)

(d)   (e)   (f)

Fig. 5. (a) and (d) Sample frames corrupted by FPN. (b) and (e) Corrected versions of previous frames when unstructured FPN is employed. (c) Corrected versions of previous frames when spatially structured FPN is employed.

both the horizontal and the vertical directions. By definition, the roughness metric achieves only non-negative values, a better the performance is mapped onto values for roughness closer to zero. (The mathematical definition of the metric can be

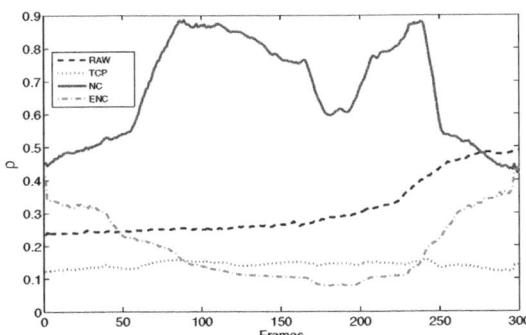

Fig. 6. Roughness comparison. RAW: Noisy frame. TPC: Two-point calibration. NC: Noise-cancellation algorithm. ENC: Noise-cancellation algorithm with structured FPN.

found elsewhere [10].) Figure 6 shows the results of the assessment. For comparison in Fig. 6 we have plotted also the worst-case scenario, labeled as RAW, corresponding to the roughness metric of the noisy images, and the best-case scenario, labeled as TPC, corresponding to a laboratory calibration [2,10]. In Fig. 6 can be observed that the FPN compensation using spatially structured noise, labeled as ENC, is indeed better than the correction obtained using unstructured FPN, labeled as NC. The improved performance is attributed to the spatially structured noise source supplied by our model.

4   Conclusions

In this work, the spatial structure of the FPN corrupting infrared FPAs has been analytically modeled in the frequency domain. Our model represents the FPN in the frequency domain by means of two components: a deterministic part, which defines the spatial structure, and a random part, which characterizes the phase. Our results have shown that: (i) samples of synthetic FPN can be easily drawn by using our model; (ii) the synthetic FPN rendered by our abstraction is objectively and subjectively a proper approximation to the actual FPN observed in infrared FPAs. Also, we have presented two interesting applications of our model: (i) striping noise in hyperspectral cameras can be regarded as a special case of our model, and (ii) a previously reported NUC method has been enhanced by simply employing our model for FPN.

References

1. Dereniak, E.L., Boreman, G.D.: Infrared Detectors and Systems, 1st edn. John Wiley & Sons, Inc. (1996)
2. Holst, G.C.: CCD Arrays, cameras, and displays. In: SPIE - International Society for Optical Engineering (1998)
3. López-Alonso, J.M., et al.: Principal-component characterization of noise for infrared images. Applied Optics 41, 320–331 (2002)
4. Zhou, H., Liu, S., Lai, R., Wang, D., Cheng, Y.: Solution for the nonuniformity correction of infrared focal plane arrays. Applied Optics 44, 2928–2932 (2005)
5. Narayanan, B., Hardie, R.C., Muse, R.A.: Scene-based nonuniformity correction technique that exploits knowledge of the focal-plane array readout architecture. App. Optics 44, 17 (2005)
6. Torres, S.N., Hayat, M.M.: Kalman filtering for adaptive nonuniformity correction in infrared focal plane arrays. JOSA-A Opt. Soc. America 20(5) (2003)
7. Qian, W., Chen, Q., Gu, G.: Space low-pass and temporal high-pass nonuniformity correction algorithm. Optical Review 17, 24–29 (2010)
8. Hardie, R.C., Douglas, R.D.: A map estimator for simultaneous superresolution and detector nonuniformity correction. EURASIP J. Advances Signal Proc. (2007)
9. El Gamal, A., Fowler, F., Min, H., Liu, X.: Modeling and estimation of FPN components in CMOS image sensors. In: Proc. SPIE, vol. 3301, pp. 168–177 (1998)
10. Godoy, S., Pezoa, J.E., Torres, S.N.: Noise-cancellation based nonuniformity correction algorithm for infrared focal-plane arrays. Applied Optics 47 (2008)

11. Gómez-Chova, L., Alonso, L., Guanter, L., Camps-Valls, G., Calpe, J., Moreno, J.: Correction of systematic spatial noise in push-broom hyperspectral sensors: application to chris/proba images. App. Optics 47(28) (2008)
12. Leathers, R., Downes, T., Priest, R.: Scene-based nonuniformity corrections for optical and SWIR pushbroom sensors. Optics Express 13(13), 5136–5150 (2005)
13. Fischer, A.D., Thomas, T.J., Leathers, R.A., Downes, T.V.: Stable scene-based non-uniformity correction coefficients for hyperspectral SWIR sensors. In: IEEE Aerospace Conference, 2007, pp. 1–14 (2007)

Blotch Detection for Film Restoration

Alvaro Pardo*

School of Engineering and Technologies
Universidad Catolica del Uruguay
apardo@ucu.edu.uy

Abstract. Blotches are one of the most common film degradations that must be detected and corrected in the process of film restoration. In this work we will address the problem of blotch detection in the context of digital film restoration. Although there are several methods for blotch detection, in the literature their evaluation is usually subjective. In this work we propose a new method for blotch detection and an objective methodology to evaluate its performance. We show that the proposed method outperforms other existing methods while using this objective metric.

1 Introduction

Digital Film Restoration is a relevant problem that has attracted the attention of the digital image processing community. Due to aging, films undergo several degradation processes, some natural and others linked to poor storing conditions or careless manipulation. The principal defects in degraded films are: dirt-dust (noise), scratches, blotches, lost or degradation of color, film grain, missing frames, etc. For details we refer to [4] and [6].

In this work we will address the problem of blotch detection. Blotches are one of the most common film degradations. They are caused by the loss of film covering (white blotches) or dirt covering (dark blotches) the surface of the film. They are localized in a frame and produce temporal discontinuities. As we will see later, blotches can be modeled as a random process.

The main goals of this paper are the following. Firstly, we propose a blotch detection method that outperforms the previous ones using an objective methodology here proposed. Second, we also propose an objective methodology to evaluate the performance of blotch detection methods. The evaluation of our proposed method will be done against a traditional method [7] and a recently proposed one [2].

The outline of the paper is as follows. In Section 2 we review the related methods in the literature and concentrate ourselves in the two methods that will be evaluated and compared with our approach. Then in Section 3 we present our proposal for blotch detection. In Section 4 we discuss the evaluation setting and present the obtained results and finally in Section 5 we conclude and discuss the results.

---

* This work was soported by STIC-AMSUD MMVPSCV-Mathematical Models for Visual Perception ans Subpixel Computer Vision and ANII-FMV-2009-1-3042.

C. San Martin and S.-W. Kim (Eds.): CIARP 2011, LNCS 7042, pp. 64–70, 2011.

2   Related Methods

Since blotches are localized temporal discontinuities most existing methods in the literature rely on motion compensation and frame differencing to detect pixels with large differences. Although most existing algorithms propose motion compensation without further consideration, it must be noted that motion compensation in noisy sequences is not an easy task. In this work we will assume that motion estimation and compensation can be performed. As we will see later, in our proposal we specially consider the fact that motion estimation can fail.

SROD [7] is a classical method for blotch detection which is very attractive for its simplicity and efficiency. Given the current frame, $F_n(x, y)$, the method computes pixel-wise differences with previous and next motion compensated frames, $F_{n-1}^c(x, y)$ and $F_{n+1}^c(x, y)$ respectively. Let (r_1, r_2, r_3) be the pixel values $(F_{n-1}^c(x, y-1), F_{n-1}^c(x, y), F_{n-1}^c(x, y+1))$. Similarly (r_4, r_5, r_6) are the pixel values in a column centered at $F_{n+1}^c(x, y)$. The SROD declares the pixel (x, y) as part of a blotch if:

$$F_n(x, y) - \max\{r_1, ..., r_6\} > T \text{ or } F_n(x, y) - \min\{r_1, ..., r_6\} < -T,$$

where T is the detection threshold of the algorithm.

In [2] the authors proposed a blotch detection method that follows the a contrario methodology [3]. Not only they present a method to detect the blotches candidates but also they embed in the same method a validation step. The Adaptive Spike Detection Index (ASDI) is defined as:

$$ASDI(x, y) = \max\{Fx(Dx^-), Fx(Dx^+)\}\text{sign}(Dx^+.Dx^-),$$

where Dx^+ and Dx^- are the average of pixel differences between the current frame and previous and next motion compensated ones across a neighborhood N centered at (x, y). $Fx(q)$ is the tail of the Gaussian distribution, $\mathcal{N}(0, \sigma_x^2/|N|)$, $|N|$ is the area of the neighborhood N and σ_x is the local standard deviation of the frame differences. For the simulations N is set as in [2] as a 3×3 neighborhood.

A pixel (x, y) is validated as a blotch if $0 \leq ASDI(x, y) \leq \epsilon/|\Omega|$, where $|\Omega|$ is the size of the frame.

3   Proposed Method

As we already mentioned, motion compensation is a challenging task in the case of noisy sequences. For degraded films the problem can be even worst due to the blotches themselves, the scratches, film grain, etc. For this reason in our method, after motion estimation and compensation, we allow some local adaptation during blotch detection.

Given the pixel (x, y) we consider a search window W centered at this pixel to define the proposed detection as:

$$D(x, y) = \min\left\{|F_n(x, y) - F_{n-1}^c(x', y')|, |F_n(x, y) - F_{n+1}^c(x', y')|/(x', y') \in W\right\}.$$

The underlying idea behind this definition is to look for the most similar pixel in an extended search window W. In this way we can cope with errors in the steps of motion estimation and compensation. Although we use pixel-wise differences the idea can be extended to compute the differences using neighborhoods around each pixel, i.e. block based distances. This is in fact the idea applied in [2].

In order to detect the blotch candidates we threshold $D(x, y)$ and compute $B(x, y) = D(x, y) > Td$. We choose a simple threshold $Td \geq 1$ and complement the detection with a validation step. Therefore, in the thresholding step we over detect to then, in the second step, validate the detections.

Our validation step is similar as the one proposed in [2] due to its probabilistic nature. However, in contrast with the validation step in [2] we validate blotches candidates and not pixels. For every connected component in the image $B(x, y)$ we compute its probability given the empirical distribution of the values in $D(x, y)$.

For every connected component C of $B(x, y)$ we compute the minimum of $D(x, y)$ for pixels in C. Let's call this value

$$dmin = \min\{D(x, y)/(x, y) \in C\}.$$

Then, using the empirical distribution of values in $D(x, y)$ we define

$$p = \text{Probability}(D(x, y) > dmin).$$

Assuming that pixels are independent[1] we define the probability of observing the connected component C as:

$$\text{Probability}(C) = p^{|C|}$$

where $|C|$ is the area of the connected component C.

We declare a blotch as valid if its probability of occurrence, given the background model obtained as the empirical distribution of values of $D(x, y)$, is very small. To do that we use a logarithmic scale and declare a connected component C as a blotch if $\log(\text{Probability}(C)) = |C| \log p < p*$. In all the experiments we set $p* = -100$.

The previous validation step favors large connected components and small well contrasted ones. In the first case, since the size of the connected component C is used as an exponent, the larger C the smaller the probability. On the other hand, if the C is well defined, i.e. large differences $D(x, y)$, its probability is also small. Both cases are the most distinguishable types of blotches as they strike from spatial and temporal neighboring pixels.

It is important to note that the only parameter in our method is the threshold, $p*$, used to validate the connected components.

4   Evaluation

Although there exists an extensive literature about blotch detection the evaluation of the different proposals is usually performed in a subjective manner or

---

[1] This is in some way a naive assumption.

using a limited number of labeled frames used as ground truth. This makes it very difficult to compare different methods in an objective way. Hence we propose a method to simulate blotches and a set of scores to compare the performance of each method.

4.1 Blotch Simulation

As stated in the introduction blotches are localized regions of temporal discontinuity. The size and shape of these regions can vary and the probability of observing a blotch in one frame does not constrain the same the observation in other frames. Based on these considerations we devised a simple method to artificially create blotches.

We start generating an image with Gaussian noise of zero mean and variance σ. Then we filter this image with an box filter of size 5×5 and then threshold it at $\sigma/4$. The result is an image with some connected components of pixels with varying size and shape. Now we have to simulate the random nature of the blotch observation and its random intensity. For that we first randomly select the blotches using an uniform distribution and then randomly select the grey level of the blotch in $[gmin, gmax]$. We simulate only dark blotches but the generation of bright ones is straight forward. Finally, once we have the image of blotches we filter with a Gaussian window to smooth its borders. In Figure 4.3 we show a sample realization of this proposal.

4.2 Evaluation Scores

For the objective evaluation we propose two set of scores; one set to measure the performance of the detection at the pixel level and the other one at the blotch level. In all cases we assume to know the number of blotches and their positions in the frame as a result of the simulation process described in previous section.

We define the following scores:

- FNp:= Number of False Negative pixels,
- FPp:= Number of False Positive pixels,
- FN:= Number of False Negative Blotches,
- FP:= Number of False Positive Blotches,
- P:= Precision at pixel level,
- R:= Recall at pixel level.

The figures in Table 1 are the average for 10 trials with different blotch simulations. To compare all the methods in equal basis in each case we report the best results with respect to the F1 score. This score measure the method accuracy averaging with the same weights precision and recall.

The best results of SROD were obtained with the parameter $T = 2$. For ASDI, as noted by the authors, we observed little differences for values of parameter ϵ in the range $[10^{-8}, 10^{-2}]$. For our proposed method the threshold was set between 1 and 3 with best results obtained for $Td = 1$.

Table 1. Evalaution Scores for the three evaluated methods. The figures were obtained averaging 10 trials with different blotch simulations.

	SROD	Proposed	ASDI
FNp	323	122	**119**
FPp	**5**	86	1447
FN	**0**	**0**	0
FP	**0**	1	544
P	**0,930**	0,894	0,397
R	0,744	0,911	**0,914**
F1	0,850	**0,886**	0,532

In all cases the motion estimation and compensation was performed with the Lucas-Kanade approach [5]. We used a pyramidal implementation developed by Bouguet [1].

4.3   Results

From the results summarized in Table 1 we can conclude the following. No method outperforms the other two in all scores. The proposed method is the one with best balance between FPp and FNp and precision very close to the one obtained by ASDI. This leads to the best F1 score among the three evaluated methods. On the other hand, the reduction of FNp comes at the expense of increasing the number of FPp. For this reason SROD gives the best result in terms of FPp but the worst in terms of FNp. ASDI suffers from a large number of FPp and FP due to the detection of a large collection of small false blotches. The FP in our method correspond to a false detection due to an error in the motion estimation-compensation step, see Figure 4.3.

Now we are going to discuss the results from the point of view of the final application. While performing film restoration we want a low number of FP. If the restoration will be assisted by a technician it is very cumbersome to have a large number of false positive. If the restoration is to some extent automatic, a large number of false positive blotches may produce the modification of the frame in too many places increasing the chances of observing the corrections in the restored film. Also, this will produce an increase in the computation cost of the restoration. Based on these considerations the best two methods are SROD and the proposed one. ASI should be improved to reduce the large number of FPp and FP. We believe this can be implemented using a post-processing step.

Regarding the quality of the blotch detection, a useful method should produce the smallest number of FNp. In this way, the restoration after detection is simplified and the chances of an undetectable restoration are increased. FNp usually concentrate at the borders of the blotches which may deteriorate the restorations steps which usually involve some kind of inpanting procedure. From this point of view the best methods are ASDI and the proposed one.

If we take all the previous comments into consideration we conclude the following. Although none of the methods clearly outperforms the other two, the proposed method is the one with highest F1 score while achieving a FNp rate close to the best obtained by ASDI. Furthermore, the FPp and FP scores of the proposed method are clearly better than ASDI. When comparing our method with SROD we can see that we reduced the number of FNp increasing the number of FPp. It must be noted that this increase is due to only one blotch (FP) produced by our method. Hence, from the application point of view our method is a good balance between SROD and ASDI. Since, all methods have their strong and weak points a combination of them could lead to a better performance. This will be part of our future work.

Fig. 1. Left: Results with SROD. Middle: Proposed Method. Right: ASDI.

Fig. 2. Sample of simmulated blotches

5 Conclusions

In this paper we addressed the problem of blotch detection in the context of digital film restoration. A new method for blotch detection together with an objective evaluation methodology of the detection performance was proposed. Based on this objective methodology we compared our proposed method for blotch detection with two other references from the literature, a classical method [7] and a recently introduced one [2]. We showed that the proposed method outperforms in some of the scores proposed the other two. Also, we argued that from an application point of view our proposed method has clear benefits. Finally, since none of the three methods outperforms the other two in all scores we believe there is room for improvement via the combination of the three methods. This will be part of our future work.

References

1. Bouguet: Pyramidal implementation of the lucas kanade feature tracker description of the algorithm. Technical report, Intel Corporation (2002)
2. Buades, A., Delon, J., Gousseau, Y., Masnou, S.: Adaptive blotches detection for film restoraion. In: ICIP 2010, pp. 3317–3320 (2010)
3. Desolneux, A., Moisan, L., Morel, J.M.: Gestalt Theory and Image Analysis. Springer, Heidelberg (2007)
4. Kokaram, A.: Motion Picture Restoration: Digital Algorithms for Artefact Suppression in Degraded Motion Picture Film and Video. Springer, Heidelberg (2001)
5. Lucas, B., Kanade, T.: An iterative image registration technique with an application to stereo vision. In: Image Understanding Workshop, pp. 674–679 (1981)
6. Pinz, A., Schallauer, P., Haas, W.: Automatic restoration algorithms for 35mm film. J. Computer Vision Research 1(3), 59–85 (1999)
7. Van Roosmalen, P.M.B.: Restoration of Archvied Film and Video. PhD thesis, Delft University (1999)

Rapid Cut Detection on Compressed Video

Jurandy Almeida, Neucimar J. Leite, and Ricardo da S. Torres⋆

Institute of Computing, University of Campinas – UNICAMP
13083-852, Campinas, SP – Brazil
{jurandy.almeida,neucimar,rtorres}@ic.unicamp.br

Abstract. The temporal segmentation of a video sequence is one of the most important aspects for video processing, analysis, indexing, and retrieval. Most of existing techniques to address the problem of identifying the boundary between consecutive shots have focused on the uncompressed domain. However, decoding and analyzing of a video sequence are two extremely time-consuming tasks. Since video data are usually available in compressed form, it is desirable to directly process video material without decoding. In this paper, we present a novel approach for video cut detection that works in the compressed domain. The proposed method is based on both exploiting visual features extracted from the video stream and on using a simple and fast algorithm to detect the video transitions. Experiments on a real-world video dataset with several genres show that our approach presents high accuracy relative to the state-of-the-art solutions and in a computational time that makes it suitable for online usage.

Keywords: video analysis, temporal segmentation, shot boundary, cut detection, compressed domain.

1 Introduction

Recent advances in technology have increased the availability of video data, creating a strong requirement for efficient systems to manage those materials.

Making efficient use of video information requires that the data be stored in an organized way. For this, it must be divided into a set of meaningful and manageable units, so that the video content remains consistent in terms of camera operations and visual events. This has been the goal of a well-known research area, called video segmentation [9].

Different techniques have been proposed in the literature to address the temporal segmentation of video sequences [5, 7, 10, 12–16]. Many of those research works have focused on the uncompressed domain. Although existing methods provide a high quality, they are extremely time-consuming and require a huge amount of space.

In this paper, we present a novel approach for temporal segmentation of video sequences that operates directly in the compressed domain. It relies on exploiting visual features extracted from the video stream and on a simple and fast algorithm to detect the video transitions. The improvement of the computational efficiency makes our technique suitable for online tasks.

⋆ Thanks to Brazilian agencies FAPESP, CNPq, and CAPES for funding.

C. San Martin and S.-W. Kim (Eds.): CIARP 2011, LNCS 7042, pp. 71–78, 2011.

We evaluate the proposed algorithm on a real-world video dataset with different video genres and compare our technique with the state-of-the-art approaches for temporal video segmentation. Results from an experimental evaluation over several types of video transitions show that our method presents high accuracy and computational speed.

The remainder of this paper is organized as follows. Section 2 describes related work. Section 3 presents our approach and shows how to apply it to segment a video sequence. Section 4 reports the results of our experiments and compares our technique with other methods. Finally, we offer our conclusions and directions for future work in Section 5.

2   Basic Concepts and Related Work

A video shot is a series of inter-related frames captured from a single camera. In the editing stage of video production, video shots are joined together to form the complete sequence. They represent a continuous action in time and space, where no changes in scene content can be perceived [8].

There are two different types of transitions that can occur between shots: abrupt (discontinuous) transitions, also referred as cuts; and gradual (continuous) transitions, which include camera movements (e.g., panning, tilting, zooming) and video editing effects (e.g., fade-in, fade-out, dissolving, wiping) [9].

A comprehensive review of methods to address the problem of identifying the boundary between consecutive shots can be found in [9, 11]. Most of existing research works have focused on the uncompressed domain. Although those techniques provide a high quality, they spend lots of time and space for decoding and analyzing a video sequence. For this reason, such approaches are unsuitable for online tasks.

The most common approach relies on the definition of similarity metrics between consecutive frames. Usual metrics are based on pixel-wise differences [16] and color histograms [13]. Tracking of image features (e.g., edges [14]) can also be used to detect the shot boundary, since they tend to disappear in a cut. In a different approach, patterns are detected in a bi-dimensional subsampling of the video, called video slice or visual rhythm [5, 7].

Since video data are usually available in compressed form, it is desirable to directly process the compressed video without decoding. It allows us to save high computational load in full decoding the video stream.

Several methods for video segmentation that directly manipulate compressed have been proposed for specific domains, such as sports, music, and news [10, 12, 15]. Focusing on a particular domain helps to reduce levels of ambiguity when analysing the content of a video by applying prior knowledge of the domain during the analysis process [9].

Different from all of the previous techniques which operate directly in the compressed domain, our approach is designed to segment generic videos and, hence, it does not use any specific information beyond the video content.

3   Our Approach

Video data have a lot of redundant information. For saving computational time, the video stream is divided into a set of meaningful and manageable units. Most video codecs (e.g., MPEG-1/2/4) are based on GOPs as basic units. The I-frame contains enough information to characterize the content of the whole GOP.

The compression of the I-frames of a MPEG video is carried out by dividing the original image into 8x8 pixel blocks and transforming the pixels values of each block into 64 DCT coefficients. The DC term $c(0,0)$ is related to the pixel values $f(i,j)$ via the following equation [15]:

$$c(0,0) = \frac{1}{8} \sum_{x=0}^{7} \sum_{y=0}^{7} f(x,y).$$

In other words, the value of the DC term is 8 times the average intensity of the pixel block. If we extract the DC term of all the pixel blocks, we can use those values to form a reduced version of the original image. This smaller image is known as the DC image [15]. Fig. 1 illustrates an original image of size 384×288 and its DC image with 48×36.

Fig. 1. Original image at 384×288 and its DC image at 48×36. Frame extracted from the video I of the test set.

Initially, we discard a lot of GOPs by computing the pairwise dissimilarity of consecutive I-frames. For this, we convert each DC image to a 256-dimensional feature vector by computing a color histogram. It is extracted as follows: the YCbCr color space is divided into 256 subspaces (colors), using 16 ranges of Y, 4 ranges of Cb, and 4 ranges of Cr. The value for each dimension of the feature vector is the density of each color in the entire DC image.

Let $\mathcal{H}^i$ be the i-th bin of the color histogram $\mathcal{H}$. We measure the dissimilarity between the I-frames by using the well-known histogram intersection, which is define as

$$d(\mathcal{H}_{t_1}, \mathcal{H}_{t_2}) = \frac{\sum_i \min(\mathcal{H}_{t_1}^i, \mathcal{H}_{t_2}^i)}{\sum_i \mathcal{H}_{t_1}^i},$$

where $\mathcal{H}_{t_1}$ and $\mathcal{H}_{t_2}$ are the color histograms extracted from the I-frames taken at the times t_1 and t_2, respectively. This function returns a real value ranging

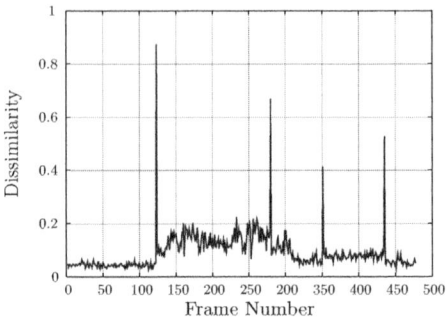

Fig. 2. Pairwise dissimilarities of between frames of the video I of the test set

from 0 for situations in which those histograms are not similar at all, to 1 for situations in which they are identical.

Fig. 2 shows an example of how those values are distributed along time. It can be observed that there are instants of time in which the dissimilarity value varies considerably (corresponding to peaks), while there are longer periods in which the variance is small (corresponding to very dense regions). Usually, peaks correspond to sudden movements in the video or to shot boundaries.

We analyze only the GOPs for which the histogram intersection is below 0.85. If they are completely intra-coded (i.e., only I-frames), we compute the normalized pixel-wise difference of the luminance (Y) between the DC-images. Then, an abrupt cut is declared every time the dissimilarity value is greater than 0.3 and the normalized pixel-wise difference is greater than 0.1. The choice of those values is detailed in Section 4.

Otherwise, we exploit the motion compensation algorithm to detect shot boundaries. For this, we examine the number of inter-coded macroblocks inside each P or B-frame. The main idea is that the motion compensation algorithm cannot find a good match in the nearest past and/or future I and/or P-frames if the GOP are in the shot boundary.

This causes most of the macroblocks of the P-frames to be intra-coded instead of inter-coded. If the ratio of the number of intra-coded macroblocks to the total number of macroblocks is greater than 0.1, there is a high probability to exist a cut in the neighborhood of this P-frame. In this case, we analyze its precedent B-frames to detect both type and location of this video transition. For GOPs that do not contain B-frames, an abrupt cut is declared if the percentage of intra-coded macroblocks in this P-frame is greater than 60%.

Three possible behaviours for the macroblocks of the B-frames are shown in Fig. 3. The width of the arrows indicate the dominant direction for the motion compensation. In this work, a B-frame has a dominant direction if the number of macroblocks with motion compensation in a given direction is the double of that in the opposite direction.

If most of the B-frames are encoded with forward motion compensation, an abrupt transition is detected between the last B-frame and its subsequent anchor frame (I or P). On the other hand, if most of the B-frames are encoded with backward motion compensation an abrupt transition is detected between the

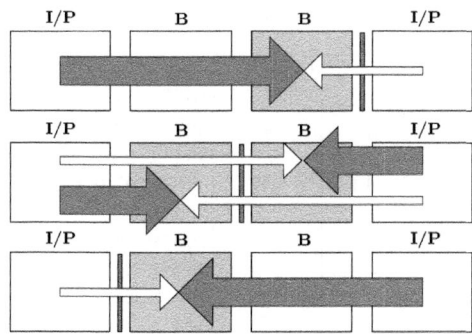

Fig. 3. The possible behaviours for the macroblocks of the B-frames

first B-frame and its precedent anchor frame (I or P). Finally, if the forward direction is dominant in the first half of the B-frames and the backward direction is dominant the last half of the B-frames, then an abrupt cut is detected in the middle of those sequence. In order to avoid false alarms, a video transition is declared only if the percentage of intra-coded macroblocks in such B-frames is greater than 50%.

If none of the above conditions is satisfied, we check if there exists a possible gradual transition. For this, we examine the variation of the percentage of inter-coded macroblocks with forward motion compensation along the frames of the GOP. In the case of gradual transitions, those values form a *plateau* (i.e., an isosceles trapezoid), as first observed by Yeo and Liu [15]. Since a gradual transition has a certain duration, at least 7 frames should be involved to declare a shot boundary.

4 Experiments and Results

Experiments were carried out on a real-world video dataset with known ground-truth data. For benchmarking purposes, we used the test set[1] presented in [14]. This benchmark contains 10 video sequences, including a variety of genres and quality levels, as shown in Table 1.

For selecting the threshold values used to detect video transitions, we computed the pairwise similarities of consecutive frames. Remember that the similarity value between the I-frames is measured using the histogram intersection, whereas for P- or B-frames the similarity value relies on the ratio of the number of inter-coded macroblocks to the total number of macroblocks.

Fig. 4 presents the probability density function (PDF) for the distribution of the similarity value of sequential and transitional frames. Notice that the PDF curves for the different types of video frames are well-separated, evidencing the high discriminating capability of our strategy.

---

[1] All the video sequences and the ground-truth data are available at
http://www.site.uottawa.ca/~laganier/videoseg/
(last accessed on 20 July 2011).

Table 1. The main characteristics of each video sequence in test set

Video	Genre	Dur. (s)	Dim.	GOP size	# Frames
A	cartoon (low quality)	21	192 × 144	6	650
B	action (motion)	38	320 × 142	6	959
C	horror (black/white)	53	384 × 288	2	1619
D	drama (high quality)	105	336 × 272	15	2632
E	science-fiction	17	384 × 288	2	536
F	commercial (effects)	7	160 × 112	15	236
G	commercial	16	384 × 288	1	500
H	comedy	205	352 × 240	12	5133
I	news	15	384 × 288	1	479
J	action	36	240 × 180	12	873

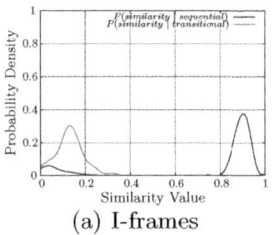
(a) I-frames

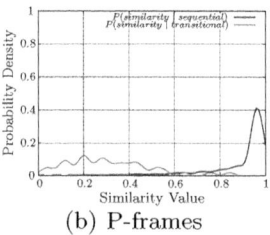
(b) P-frames

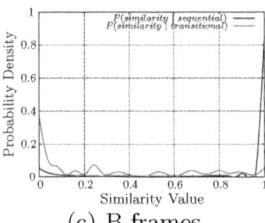
(c) B-frames

Fig. 4. The probability density function (PDF) for the distribution of the similarity value of different types of video frame

We assess the effectiveness of the proposed method using the metrics of precision and recall. Precision (P) is the ratio of the number of temporal positions correctly identified as cuts to the total number of temporal positions identified as cuts. Recall (R) is the ratio of the number of temporal positions correctly identified as cuts to the total number of cuts in the video sequence. However, there is a trade-off between precision and recall. Greater precision decreases recall and greater recall leads to decreased precision. So, we also employ the F-measure for assessing the quality of the temporal segmentation. The F-measure (F) combines both precision and recall into a single measure by a harmonic mean:

$$F = \frac{2 \times P \times R}{P + R}.$$

The experiments were performed on a machine equipped with an Intel Core 2 Quad Q6600 processor (four cores running at 2.4 GHz) and 2 GBytes of DDR3-memory. The machine run Ubuntu Linux (2.6.31 kernel) and the ext3 file system.

Table 2 compares our technique with four different approaches: (1) histogram-based method [13], (2) feature-based method with automatic threshold selection [14], (3) visual rhythm with longest common subsequence (LCS) [5], and (4) visual rhythm with clustering by k-means [7]. The average rates of each quality measure correspond to the weighted mean of individual results, whose weights are the total number of cuts in each video. In addition, the weighted standard deviations reveal the amount of dispersion with respect to those values.

Table 2. Comparison of precision (P), recall (R), and F-measure (F) achieved by different approaches for each video of the test set

Video	Our proposal (compressed)			Visual rhythm with k-means [7]			Visual rhythm with LCS [5]			Feature tracking method [14]			Histogram (MOCA) [13]		
	P	R	F	P	R	F	P	R	F	P	R	F	P	R	F
A	1.000	1.000	1.000	1.000	1.000	1.000	1.000	0.857	0.923	1.000	1.000	1.000	1.000	1.000	1.000
B	1.000	1.000	1.000	0.500	1.000	0.667	0.096	1.000	0.176	1.000	1.000	1.000	1.000	0.375	0.545
C	0.891	0.907	0.899	0.662	0.907	0.766	0.635	0.870	0.734	0.595	0.870	0.707	0.936	0.536	0.682
D	1.000	1.000	1.000	1.000	1.000	1.000	1.000	0.971	0.985	1.000	1.000	1.000	1.000	0.941	0.969
E	0.815	0.786	0.800	0.828	0.857	0.842	0.676	0.821	0.742	0.938	1.000	0.968	0.955	0.700	0.808
F	1.000	1.000	1.000	1.000	1.000	1.000	1.000	1.000	1.000	1.000	1.000	1.000	1.000	1.000	1.000
G	0.938	0.833	0.882	0.950	1.000	0.974	1.000	0.842	0.914	0.810	0.944	0.872	1.000	0.667	0.800
H	0.974	0.949	0.961	0.949	0.974	0.961	0.943	0.868	0.904	0.895	0.895	0.895	0.971	0.895	0.932
I	1.000	1.000	1.000	1.000	1.000	1.000	0.667	0.500	0.571	1.000	1.000	1.000	1.000	0.500	0.667
J	0.776	0.506	0.612	0.683	0.869	0.765	0.639	0.885	0.742	0.497	0.897	0.637	0.850	0.395	0.540
Avg.	0.882	0.786	0.825	0.793	0.923	0.848	0.745	0.878	0.789	0.730	0.924	0.803	0.932	0.621	0.730
Dev.	0.095	0.213	0.164	0.156	0.061	0.111	0.205	0.067	0.153	0.220	0.054	0.157	0.063	0.229	0.178

The results indicate that the proposed method is robust to several conditions (e.g., frame rate, frame size, total duration, etc.), showing high accuracy compared to the state-of-the-art solutions. Notice that our approach provides the best achievable F-measure for the majority of the video sequences (7 of 10).

The key advantage of our technique is its computational efficiency. Since the time required to segment video sequences is hardware dependent (with faster hardware the computational speed increases and the production time decreases) and the source codes of all the compared methods are not available, it is impossible to perform a fair comparison of performance in relation to our technique.

In order to evaluate the efficiency of our approach, we analyze the time per frame spent for processing all the steps of our algorithm, excluding the time for the partial decoding of each frame. We performed 10 replications for each video in order to guarantee statistically sound results.

According to those experiments, all the steps of our technique takes a mean time equals to 112 ± 38 microseconds per frame (confidence higher than 99.9%). For online usage, by considering a maximum waiting time of 39 seconds [6], the proposed method can be used for videos up to 349515 frames (about 194 minutes at 29.97 frames per second). It is important to recall that those values depend on the computational power of the employed hardware.

5 Conclusions

In this paper, we have presented a novel approach for video cut detection that works in the compressed domain. Our technique relies on exploiting visual features extracted from the video stream and on using a simple and fast algorithm to detect the video transitions. Such combination makes our technique suitable for online usage.

We have validated our technique using a real-world video dataset with different video genres and compared our technique with the state-of-the-art approaches for temporal video segmentation. Results from an experimental evaluation over several types of video transitions show that our method presents high accuracy and computational speed.

Future work includes the evaluation of other visual features and similarity metrics. In addition, the proposed method can be augmented to consider local features [4] and/or motion analysis [2, 3]. Finally, we want to investigate the effects of integrating our technique into a complete system for search-and-retrieval of video sequences [1].

References

1. Almeida, J., Leite, N.J., Torres, R.S.: Comparison of video sequences with histograms of motion patterns. In: Int. Conf. Image Processing (ICIP 2011) (2011)
2. Almeida, J., Minetto, R., Almeida, T.A., Torres, R.S., Leite, N.J.: Robust estimation of camera motion using optical flow models. In: Bebis, G., Boyle, R., Parvin, B., Koracin, D., Kuno, Y., Wang, J., Wang, J.-X., Wang, J., Pajarola, R., Lindstrom, P., Hinkenjann, A., Encarnação, M.L., Silva, C.T., Coming, D. (eds.) ISVC 2009. LNCS, vol. 5875, pp. 435–446. Springer, Heidelberg (2009)
3. Almeida, J., Minetto, R., Almeida, T.A., Torres, R.S., Leite, N.J.: Estimation of camera parameters in video sequences with a large amount of scene motion. In: Proc. of Int. Conf. Syst. Signals Image (IWSSIP 2010), pp. 348–351 (2010)
4. Almeida, J., Rocha, A., Torres, R.S., Goldenstein, S.: Making colors worth more than a thousand words. In: Int. Symp. Applied Comput. (ACM SAC 2008), pp. 1180–1186 (2008)
5. Bezerra, F.N., Leite, N.J.: Using string matching to detect video transitions. Pattern Anal. Appl. 10(1), 45–54 (2007)
6. Bouch, A., Kuchinsky, A., Bhatti, N.T.: Quality is in the eye of the beholder: meeting users' requirements for internet quality of service. In: Int. Conf. Human Factors Comput. Syst. (CHI 2000), pp. 297–304 (2000)
7. Guimarães, S.J.F., Patrocínio Jr., Z.K.G., Paula, H.B., Silva, H.B.: A new dissimilarity measure for cut detection using bipartite graph matching. Int. J. Semantic Computing 3(2), 155–181 (2009)
8. Hanjalic, A.: Shot-boundary detection: Unraveled and resolved? IEEE Trans. Circuits Syst. Video Techn. 12(2), 90–105 (2002)
9. Koprinska, I., Carrato, S.: Temporal video segmentation: A survey. Signal Processing: Image Communication 16(5), 477–500 (2001)
10. Lee, S.W., Kim, Y.M., Choi, S.W.: Fast scene change detection using direct feature extraction from MPEG compressed videos. IEEE Trans. Multimedia 2(4), 240–254 (2000)
11. Lienhart, R.: Reliable transition detection in videos: A survey and practitioner's guide. Int. J. Image Graphics 1(3), 469–486 (2001)
12. Pei, S.C., Chou, Y.Z.: Efficient MPEG compressed video analysis using macroblock type information. IEEE Trans. Multimedia 1(4), 321–333 (1999)
13. Pfeiffer, S., Lienhart, R., Kühne, G., Effelsberg, W.: The MoCA project - movie content analysis research at the University of Mannheim. In: GI Jahrestagung, pp. 329–338 (1998)
14. Whitehead, A., Bose, P., Laganière, R.: Feature based cut detection with automatic threshold selection. In: Enser, P.G.B., Kompatsiaris, Y., O'Connor, N.E., Smeaton, A., Smeulders, A.W.M. (eds.) CIVR 2004. LNCS, vol. 3115, pp. 410–418. Springer, Heidelberg (2004)
15. Yeo, B.L., Liu, B.: Rapid scene analysis on compressed video. IEEE Trans. Circuits Syst. Video Techn. 5(6), 533–544 (1995)
16. Zhang, H., Kankanhalli, A., Smoliar, S.W.: Automatic partitioning of full-motion video. Multimedia Syst. 1(1), 10–28 (1993)

Local Quality Method for the Iris Image Pattern

Luis Miguel Zamudio-Fuentes[1], Mireya S. García-Vázquez[1],
and Alejandro Alvaro Ramírez-Acosta[2]

[1] Centro de Investigación y Desarrollo de Tecnología Digital (CITEDI-IPN),
Avenida del Parque 1310, Tijuana, B.C. México 22510
[2] MIRAL. R&D, 1047 Palm Garden, Imperial Beach, 91932 USA
{zamudio,mgarciav}@citedi.mx, ramacos10@hotmail.com

Abstract. Recent researches on iris recognition without user cooperation have introduced video-based iris capturing approach. Indeed, it provides more information and more flexibility in the image acquisition stage for non-cooperative iris recognition systems. However, a video sequence can contain images with different level of quality. Therefore, it is necessary to select the highest quality images from each video to improve iris recognition performance. In this paper, we propose as part of a video quality assessment module, a new local quality iris image method based on spectral energy analysis. This approach does not require the iris region segmentation to determine the quality of the image such as most of existing approaches. In contrast to other methods, the proposed algorithm uses a significant portion of the iris region to measure the quality in that area. This method evaluates the energy of 1000 images which were extracted from 200 iris videos from the MBGC NIR video database. The results show that the proposed method is very effective to assess the quality of the iris information. It obtains the highest 2 images energies as the best 2 images from each video in 226 milliseconds.

Keywords: Iris recognition, biometrics, video, quality assessment.

1 Introduction

According to the literature, considerable improvement in recognition performance is possible when poor quality images are removed using image quality assessment stage in an automated biometric system [1]. Motivated by this idea, we propose as part of a video quality assessment module that our research group is currently developing [2-4, 7], a new local quality iris image method based on spectral energy analysis. The figure 1 shows how the iris video sequence is first globally analyzed to quickly determine the quality of the whole image and obtain a small quality image set [4]. Secondly, the images resulting from that analysis are used for local quality assessment to obtain the best two images from a video that are optimal to continue with the recognition module.

Existing approaches about local iris quality measures consist of extracting the iris region from the image based on segmentation algorithm, and then evaluate the quality of this area using different bands of the Mexican hat wavelet [5]. Similarly, after

C. San Martin and S.-W. Kim (Eds.): CIARP 2011, LNCS 7042, pp. 79–88, 2011.
© Springer-Verlag Berlin Heidelberg 2011

segmentation stage, other authors localize two small regions near to the limit of the pupil to measure the quality applying the third-level wavelet transformation of the two selected regions [6]. Those researches considered that the region near the edge of the pupil was the area that contained more feature information of the iris.

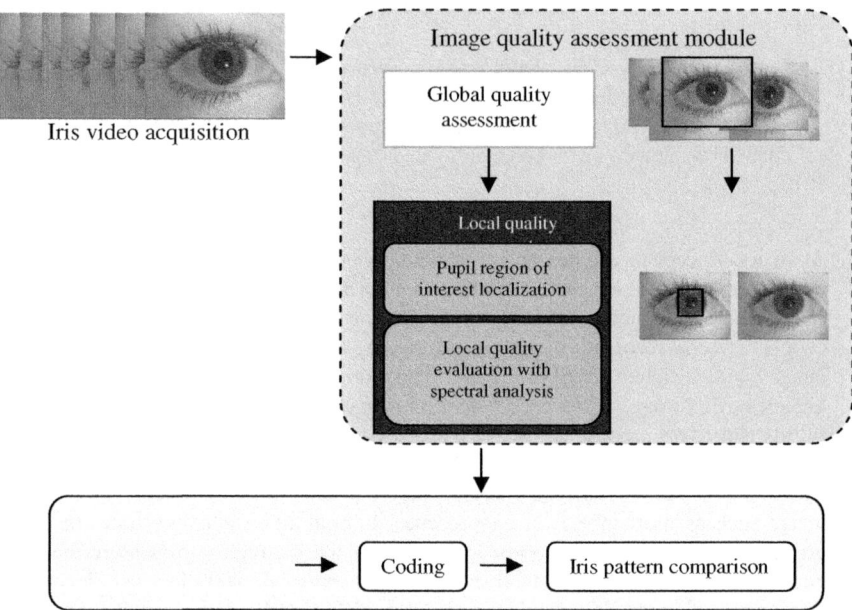

Fig. 1. Typical iris recognition system with video-based iris capturing that includes the proposed image quality assessment module

In this paper, our proposition also examines the local quality in the region near the pupil, but without iris segmentation stage. Note that in this work, the pupil region of interest (PROI) is automatically located. A square region of interest (SROI) which covers the majority features of iris information is determined from PROI central point. Then SROI is used to analyze the high and low frequencies from all pixel intensities values.

In summary, the local quality assessment stage evaluates all images coming from the global stage (previous work realized in [2, 4, 7]). In this phase, the area of PROI is first dynamically determined. Secondly, the SROI is obtained from PROI central point, and then this information is used to analyze the quality of the SROI using Kang's Kernel [1, 8, and 9]. It is important to highlight that in our previous work [7], Kang's kernel was superior to other kernels in showing less computing time and more efficiency performance.

The remainder of this paper is organized as follows. Section 2 reviews the local quality assessment. Continue in section 3 with the implementation and results. Finally, in section 4, we draw the conclusions.

2 Local Quality Stage

The main features of the iris information are located near to the boundary of the pupil. Therefore, it is important in all iris recognition systems to ensure the biometric information quality in that region. According to [7], the iris image quality is determinate by two factors: defocus and blur. These factors are considered visually similar. However, they differ in how they are generated. Defocus is an optic aberration in which an image is simply out of focus. On the other hand, blur is produced by the relative displacement between the object and the camera. These factors can be analyzed and detected through a kernel that measures the image energy. The energy of a defocused or blurred image concentrates on the lower frequency part. Hence, spectral analysis of the frequency suggests that an effective way to estimate the degree of focus is measuring its total energy at higher spatial frequencies. The quality assessment in our system begins with a global analysis of all images in an iris video, in which the whole image is evaluated with a kernel to rapidly select a set of high quality images as it is described by Colores et al in [7]. It is important to note that the global stage provides a rough good quality images. Nevertheless, in some regions of the iris texture can remain important imperfections such as blur, defocus, reflection, etc. To ensure that the iris region is free of imperfections, this paper proposes to add the stage of local quality to the image quality assessment module. In this stage, all images coming from the global stage are processed.

2a Pupil Region of Interest Localization

During the video acquisition, the position of the pupil may differ from one image to other. For that reason, it is important to dynamically localize the PROI in the image. This region is used to make different processes in iris images like: to detect and eliminate the pupil, to localize and extract the iris region and particularly local quality assessment. As it is known, the intensity of the pupil is close to zero in a grayscale [10]. Using this principle, we developed a basic histogram analysis method of grayscale levels to find the maximum and minimum intensity values. This simple method shows information about how the intensities are distributed around the image.

To dynamically determine the pupil region of interest we propose the following algorithm, which localizes the minimum and maximum values over the histogram. First, a histogram is obtained using the intensities of each image resulting from the global quality analysis (Figure 2a). Secondly, an average filter is applied to smooth the curve generated; this is in order to eliminate false peaks and valleys (Figure 2b). Thirdly the slopes of the curve are calculated to determine any positive to negative change and vice versa. The observed changes are used to locate and determine the position of the lobes or peaks and valleys of the histograms (Figure 2c).

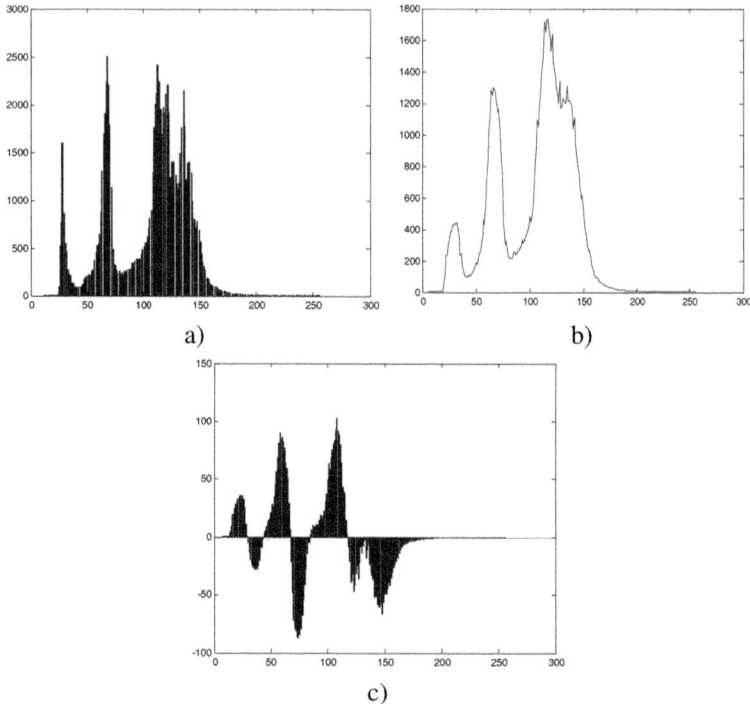

a)

b)

c)

Fig. 2. Histogram analysis

The position of the first peak value is considered as the intensity value of the pupil. To dynamically determine the PROI, the following inequality is evaluated to localize the positions of the pixels belonging to the pupil,

$$f(x,y) = \begin{cases} 255, & I(x,y) < h_1 \\ I(x,y), & otherwise. \end{cases} \quad (1)$$

where $f(x,y)$ is the resulting image, $I(x,y)$ is the intensity value of each pixel of the image and h_1 is the value of the first peak encountered in the implementation of the algorithm. The next step is to extract all x, y positions from the pixels that changed its intensity to 255. To calculate the pseudo-center of the PROI, we obtain the average positions of x and y using equation 2,

$$center_x = \frac{1}{k}\sum_{i=1}^{k} pos_x(i), \quad center_y = \frac{1}{k}\sum_{i=1}^{k} pos_y(i) \quad (2)$$

where $pos_x(i)$ and $pos_y(i)$ are the x, y positions and k is the total number of pixels that changed the intensity value. Once the pseudo-center is calculated, the algorithm determines a square area of size 160x160 pixels called square region of interest

(SROI). Figure 3 shows, two examples of this region. After localizing the dynamic search area, the next step is the assessment of the local quality with spectral analysis, which is described in the next section.

The pupil area is not considered into the local quality assessment.

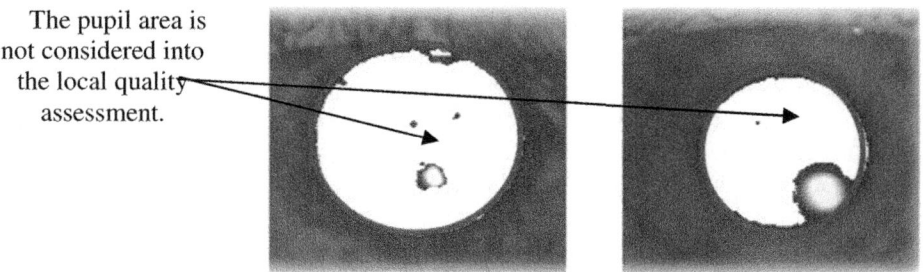

Fig. 3. Square region of interest (SROI)

2b   Local Quality Evaluation with Spectral Analysis

Once the SROI is obtained, this area is convolved with a kernel to evaluate the focus degree existing in that region. There are many kernels to perform this evaluation, the kernel of Daugman [11], Byung et al, and Kang et al [1, 8, 9]. However, to carry out the local quality assessment a Kang's kernel is conducted (Figure 4). This election was done after analyzing the results presented by Colores et al [7]. In this work, it was shown that Kang's kernel takes less time that the Daugman's kernel.

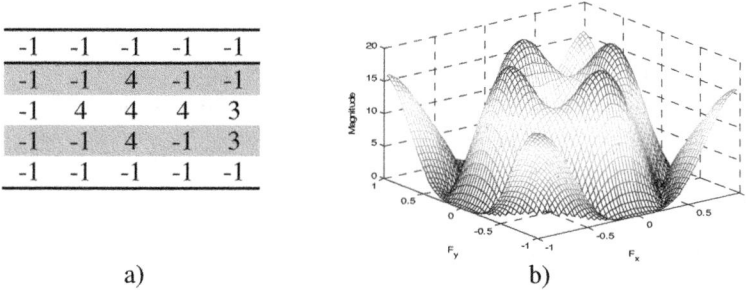

-1	-1	-1	-1	-1
-1	-1	4	-1	-1
-1	4	4	4	3
-1	-1	4	-1	3
-1	-1	-1	-1	-1

a)   b)

Fig. 4. a) 5x5 Kang's kernel. b) The frequency response of the kernel (Fourier spectrum).

To perform the local quality assessment, this kernel is convolved with the SROI according to the following equation in the space domain:

$$imfilter(x,y) = sroi(x,y) * k(x,y) = \sum_{m=0}^{M-1}\sum_{n=0}^{N-1} sroi(m,n)k(x-m,y-n) \quad (3)$$

where $imfilter(x, y)$ is the filtered image, $sroi(x, y)$ is the square region of interest, $k(x, y)$ is Kang's kernel. According to the convolution theorem [12], the convolution product reduces in the frequency domain to a simple product, as is shown in equation 4:

$$IMFILTER(u, v) = SROI(u, v) \cdot K(u, v) \qquad (4)$$

The filtered image $IMFILTER(u, v)$ is obtained by multiplying the square region of interest $SROI(u, v)$ and Kang's kernel $K(u, v)$ [1, 8-9] to estimate the degree of focus. As a result of using the mentioned theorem, the computation time is reduced in the frequency domain. After multiplication, the inverse Fourier transform is calculated and the energy of the image through Parseval's theorem using the equations 5 and 6 to obtain the spectral energy density [13] (energy). Finally, a threshold is applied to determine the quality of the square region of interest (eq.7),

$$imfilter(x, y) = F^{-1}\{IMFILTER(u, v)\} \qquad (5)$$
$$ene = |imfilter|^2 \qquad (6)$$
$$ene > T \qquad (7)$$

ene is the energy of the $SROI(u, v)$ and T is the threshold applied to determine the quality of the SROI.

3   Implementation and Results

The local quality assessment method is tested with 1000 images of 200 videos from the MBGC NIR video database [14]. The data set selected were acquired using an Iridian LG EOU 2200 camera. Each video consist of 300 to 400 eye frames with a resolution of 480 by 640 pixels in 8 bits-grayscale space (intensity values ranging from 0 to 255) at 30 frames per second (fps). For each video, 5 images are extracted using the global quality assessment image set of our previous work [2, 4, 7] (see fig. 1). These 5 images are randomly chosen by making a subset from the image quality set, and then one of these is selected for each subset.

The following describes the algorithm developed for the local quality assessment:

- Locate the pupil region of interest for the five images from each video.
- Determine the square region of interest SROI.
- Take the intensities values of the SROI and obtain the corresponding values in the frequency domain as the result of the DFT (Discrete Fourier Transform).
- Calculate the Kang's kernel value in the frequency domain using the DFT.
- Perform the convolution operation between the SROI and K, using the convolution theorem of Fourier transforms (Eq. 4).
- Use Equation 5 and calculate the inverse Discrete Fourier Transform to obtain its value in the space domain of the result $IMFILTER$.
- Calculate the energy of the result using the equation 6.

- Evaluate the inequality of equation 7 and select the highest two energies from the five energies, which are highest quality images of the video. Then continue with the pre-processing stage of the recognition system [2].

After computing the algorithm, the results are concentrated in Table 1. It shows the energy obtained in the local quality assessment for the first 30 videos of the 200 videos from the MBGC used in this evaluation. The table has twelve columns, from left to right the first column represents the video number and the next five columns are the energies by image from the first fifteen videos. The next six rows represent the rest energies of the other videos. It is observed that the majority of the energies are around 90 and 120 J/Hz that means the photon flux [15]. However, this method obtains the highest two energies which are highlighted in Table 1 to identify the best images from a video sequence. On the other hand, most of the highest energies are among images 3, 4 and 5. All results are available upon request.

Table 1. Spectral energy density for each video

Video	im1	im2	im3	im4	im5	Video	im1	im2	im3	im4	im5
1	103.17	109.61	110.23	**113.07**	**113.85**	16	116.31	115.09	**120.11**	**116.34**	111.45
2	80.16	89.18	**98.41**	93.79	**103.38**	17	**99.30**	92.99	92.44	92.58	88.60
3	101.16	109.79	**111.32**	**113.70**	109.05	18	105.63	100.80	**101.05**	98.16	**101.79**
4	77.20	**95.13**	93.88	91.42	**94.27**	19	96.06	91.95	**110.94**	**112.16**	91.04
5	95.47	97.50	**107.14**	106.15	**110.44**	20	**111.53**	**114.78**	89.74	107.95	104.94
6	87.18	96.46	**98.36**	96.65	**100.48**	21	**109.95**	**113.07**	111.99	108.71	105.60
7	99.77	96.00	**108.07**	**101.68**	100.93	22	97.23	104.02	103.39	**111.56**	**107.58**
8	91.92	91.78	**105.82**	90.13	**88.03**	23	**149.80**	136.59	140.43	**149.84**	124.70
9	103.96	107.79	111.56	**114.42**	**113.20**	24	124.37	142.21	**156.35**	**152.38**	103.39
10	98.86	**113.16**	104.10	**111.15**	109.69	25	98.84	101.68	**104.27**	**103.78**	91.15
11	92.15	99.36	**100.24**	96.26	**103.57**	26	106.33	**113.84**	**110.79**	109.67	106.16
12	102.72	96.99	**106.62**	**108.29**	102.81	27	**120.18**	**124.08**	114.04	111.64	118.90
13	**108.78**	100.70	**111.80**	99.36	98.37	28	109.61	**114.71**	97.37	102.58	**115.37**
14	111.37	**112.65**	**111.61**	109.39	108.15	29	90.20	101.27	**108.74**	104.03	**110.98**
15	91.45	**100.73**	91.98	88.49	**93.45**	30	**143.73**	110.40	**126.62**	114.30	106.33

To illustrate an example of this assessment, the video number 23 or 05303d273 as is label in the MBGC is used in Figure 5. Image 1 and image 4 show a sharp and distinguishable iris pattern. In contrast, in the images 2 and 3 the iris is not distinguishable and image 5 is not sharp enough.

In Table 2 important differences between the proposed and the existing approaches [5, 6] are pointed out. For instance, the iris information used in the existing approaches came from CASIA [16] iris database, which is acquired under controlled environment. The subject is steady at the acquisition time and the quality of the images is optimal for recognition. While in the proposed method, the iris information is extracted from the MBGC NIR video database, which is provided as a challenge, since it was acquired under unconstraint environment and the subjects were walking at the acquisition time. The proposed method uses a significant number of iris pixels to assess the local quality, in average 200% more iris texture information than Yi Chen, Yi Huang et al [5, 6], and in contrast to them, it doesn't need iris segmentation.

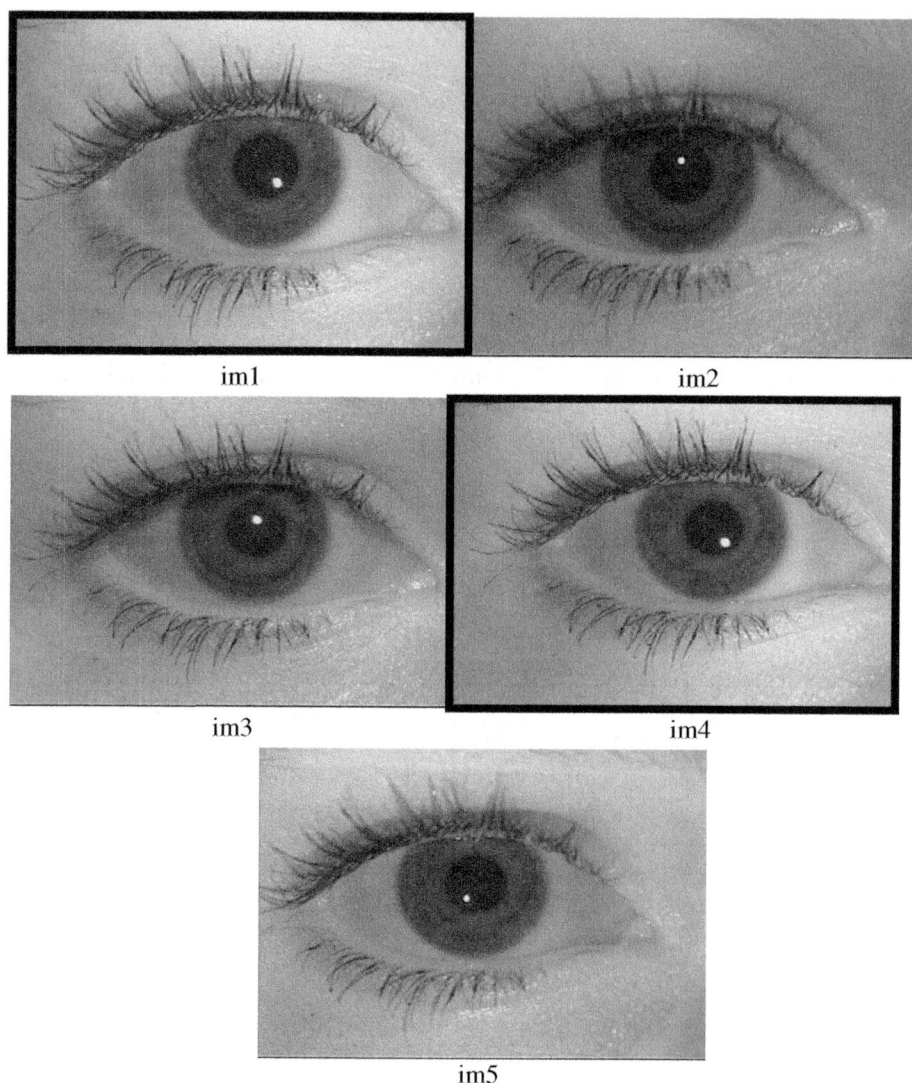

im1

im2

im3

im4

im5

Fig. 5. Example of the local quality assessment

In addition, according to [7], the Park's kernel (which is used in our proposed module to assess the quality of the iris information), is more effective in computing time and produce less FAR and FRR than Continuous Wavelet Transform. Even though our propose method is a fast quality assessment module that just takes 226 ms, we don't discard the stages added in [6] which could be optimized and included for future work to improve the module. Finally, the accuracy of the evaluated methods depends on SROI selection in the case of the proposed method, iris segmentation in [5], and the painted eyelid and eyelashes for the case [6].

Table 2. Comparison between the proposed method and existing approaches

	Proposed	Yi Chen et al [5]	Yi Huang et al [6]
Iris information from	Video	Images	Image sequence
Database	MBGC[14]	CASIA[16]	CASIA[16]
Resolution	640x480	320x280	320x280
Energy evaluation	Park's Kernel	Mexican Hat	Continuous Wavelets transform
Number of iris pixels evaluated	~ 21252	Not specified	6144
Iris segmentation	No	Yes	Yes
# video	200	No	300
# images	1000	2608	3600
Quality assess time	226 ms	Not specified	Not specified
Inaccuracy when	Bad SROI selection	Bad iris segmentation	Spectacled iris images, Iris affected by pained eyelashes or eyelid
Platform	Matlab R2008b	Not specified	Matlab 7.0ï

The proposed method was tested using Matlab R2008b in a 2.2 Ghz Pentium dual core computer with 3 Gb of ram. In addition, it is not optimized to work in real time. However, the computing time that will take to assess the local quality for video sequence is in average 226 milliseconds. Therefore, it could be optimized for real time automatic iris recognition systems.

4   Conclusions

In this paper, we propose and evaluate an algorithm for local quality assessment as part of a video quality assessment module. In contrast to other methods, it uses approximately 200% more significant portion of the iris region to determine the quality in that area. This method does not need the segmentation of the iris region to determine the quality of the image. In addition, the proposed method is suitable for real time optimization in automatic iris recognition systems. It takes just only 226 ms to access the local quality for each video sequence. In the MBGC video database, according Table 1, most of the highest energies are among images 3, 4 and 5. It means that in the acquisition step, the first images that were acquired are not in the focus plane. The results showed that the proposed algorithm is fast and very effective to identify whether the iris region is out of focus or not. Furthermore, it obtains two images of the highest quality from a video sequence. These two images provide more reliable information which is useful to further stage of the recognition system. With the conjunction of the video quality assessment module through the global and the local quality assessment we are ensuring that the iris region is focused. Consequently, the accuracy and the robustness of the system will increase by minimizing the false reject rate (FRR) and false acceptation rate (FAR). On the other hand, the accuracy of this method depends on the automatically selection of the SROI. For future improvement, we are going to analyze other quality factor as pupil dilatation, segmentation accuracy, iris information ratio and obtain the relation between FRR and FAR.

Acknowledgment. This research was supported by grant SIP20110032 from IPN-CITEDI.

References

[1] Kang, B.J., Park, K.R.: A study on fast iris restoration based on focus checking. In: Perales, F.J., Fisher, R.B. (eds.) AMDO 2006. LNCS, vol. 4069, pp. 19–28. Springer, Heidelberg (2006)

[2] Zamudio-Fuentes, L.M., García-Vázquez, M.S., Ramírez-Acosta, A.A.: Iris Segmentation Using a Statistical Approach. In: Martínez-Trinidad, J.F., Carrasco-Ochoa, J.A., Kittler, J. (eds.) MCPR 2010. LNCS, vol. 6256, pp. 164–170. Springer, Heidelberg (2010)

[3] García-Vázquez, M., Ramírez-Acosta, A.: Person verification process using iris information. Research in Computing Science 44, 97–104 (2009)

[4] Zamudio, L.M.: Reconocimiento del iris como identificación biométrica utilizando el video. MSc thesis, IPN (January 2011)

[5] Chen, Y., Dass, S.C., Jain, A.K.: Localized iris image quality using 2-d wavelets. In: ICB 2006 (2006)

[6] Huang, Y., Ma, Z., Xie, M.: Rapid and effective method of quality assessment on sequence iris image. In: MIPPR 2007. Proc. of SPIE, vol. 6786 (2007)

[7] Colores-Vargas, J.M., García-Vázquez, M.S., Ramírez-Acosta, A.A.: Measurement of defocus level in iris images using different convolution kernel methods. In: Martínez-Trinidad, J.F., Carrasco-Ochoa, J.A., Kittler, J. (eds.) MCPR 2010. LNCS, vol. 6256, pp. 125–133. Springer, Heidelberg (2010)

[8] Kang, B.J., Park, K.R.: Real-time image restoration for iris recognition Systems. IEEE Trans. on Systems 37(6), 1555–1566 (2007)

[9] Kang, B.J., Park, K.R.: A study on restoration of iris images with motion-and-optical blur on mobile iris recognition devices. Wiley Periodicals (2009)

[10] Lee, Y., Phillips, P.J., Micheals, R.J.: An Automated Video-Based System for Iris Recognition. In: Tistarelli, M., Nixon, M.S. (eds.) ICB 2009. LNCS, vol. 5558, pp. 1160–1169. Springer, Heidelberg (2009)

[11] Daugman, J.G.: How iris recognition works. IEEE Trans. Circ. Syst. Video Tech. 14(1), 21–30 (2004)

[12] Gonzalez, R.C., Woods, R.: Digital image processing. Addison-Wesley (1996)

[13] Correlation and Spectral Density,
http://www.ensc.sfu.ca/~jiel/courses/327/bin/pdf/Pre_15_Rxx.pdf

[14] Multi Biometric Grand Challenge, http://face.nist.gov/mbgc

[15] Image formation,
http://www.cs.toronto.edu/~fleet/courses/2503/fall10/Handouts/imageFormation.pdf

[16] Chinese Academy of Sciences, Institute of Automation (CASIA),
http://figment.cse.usf.edu/~sfefilat/data/papers/WeBCT9.29.pdf

Assessment of SAR Image Filtering Using Adaptive Stack Filters

María E. Buemi[1], Marta Mejail[1], Julio Jacobo[1],
Alejandro C. Frery[2], and Heitor S. Ramos[2]

[1] Departamento de Computación
Facultad de Ciencias Exactas y Naturales
Universidad de Buenos Aires
[2] LCCV & CPMAT
Instituto de Computação
Universidade Federal de Alagoas

Abstract. Stack filters are a special case of non-linear filters. They have a good performance for filtering images with different types of noise while preserving edges and details. A stack filter decomposes an input image into several binary images according to a set of thresholds. Each binary image is then filtered by a Boolean function, which characterizes the filter. Adaptive stack filters can be designed to be optimal; they are computed from a pair of images consisting of an ideal noiseless image and its noisy version. In this work we study the performance of adaptive stack filters when they are applied to Synthetic Aperture Radar (SAR) images. This is done by evaluating the quality of the filtered images through the use of suitable image quality indexes and by measuring the classification accuracy of the resulting images.

Keywords: Non-linear filters, speckle noise, stack filters, SAR image filtering.

1 Introduction

SAR images are generated by a coherent illumination system and are affected by the coherent interference of the signal from the terrain [1]. This interference causes fluctuations of the detected intensity which varies from pixel to pixel, an effect called speckle noise, that also appears in ultrasound-B, laser and sonar imagery. Speckle noise, unlike noise in optical images, is neither Gaussian nor additive; it follows other distributions and is multiplicative. Classical techniques, therefore, lead to suboptimal results when applied to this kind of imagery. The physics of image formation leads to the following model: the observed data can be described by the random field Z, defined as the product of two independent random fields: X, the backscatter, and Y, the speckle noise. The backscatter is a physical magnitude that depends on the geometry and water content of the surface being imaged, as well as on the angle of incidence, frequency and polarization of the electromagnetic radiation emitted by the radar. It is the main

C. San Martin and S.-W. Kim (Eds.): CIARP 2011, LNCS 7042, pp. 89–96, 2011.
© Springer-Verlag Berlin Heidelberg 2011

source of information sought in SAR data. Different statistical distributions have been proposed in the literature for describing speckled data. In this work, since we are dealing with intensity format, we use the Gamma distribution, denoted by Γ, for the speckle, and the reciprocal of Gamma distribution, denoted by Γ^{-1}, for the backscatter. These assumptions, and the independence between the fields, result in the intensity $\mathcal{G}^0$ law for the return [2]. This family of distributions is indexed by three parameters: roughness α, scale γ, and the number of looks n, and it has been validated as an universal model for several types of targets. Speckle has a major impact on the accuracy of classification procedures, since it introduces a low signal-to-noise ratio. The effectiveness of techniques for combating speckle can be measured, among other quantities, through the accuracy of simple classification methods. The most widespread statistical classification technique is the Gaussian maximum likelihood classifator. Stack filters are a special case of non-linear filters. They have a good performance for filtering images with different types of noise while preserving edges and details. Some authors have studied these filters, and many methods have been developed for their construction and applicaton as in [3]. These filters decompose the input image, by thresholds, in binary slices. Each binary image is then filtered using a Boolean function evaluated on a sliding window. The resulting image is obtained summing up all the filtered binary images. The main drawback in using stack filters is the need to compute optimal Boolean functions. Direct computation on the set of all Boolean functions is unfeasible, so most techniques rely on the use of a pair of images: the ideal and corrupted one. The functions are sought to provide the best estimator of the former using the latter as input. The stack filter design method used in this work is based on an algorithm proposed by Yoo *et al.* [4].

We study the application of this type of filter to SAR images, assessing its performance by evaluating the quality of the filtered images through the use of image quality indexes like the universal image quality index and the correlation measure index and by measuring the classification accuracy of the resulting images using maximum likelihood Gaussian classification.

The structure of this paper is as follows: In Section 2 we summarise the $\mathcal{G}^0$ model for speckled data. Section 3 gives an introduction to stack filters, and describes the filter design method used in this work. In Section 4 we discuss the results of filtering through image quality assesment and classification performance. Finally, in Section 5 we present the conclusions.

2   The Multiplicative Model

Following [5], we will only present the univariate intensity case. Other formats (amplitude and complex) are treated in detail in [2].

The intensity $\mathcal{G}^0$ distribution that describes speckled return is characterized by the following density:

$$f(z) = \frac{L^L \Gamma(L - \alpha)}{\gamma^\alpha \Gamma(L) \Gamma(-\alpha)} \frac{z^{L-1}}{(\gamma + Lz)^{L-\alpha}},$$

where $-\alpha, \gamma, z > 0$, $L \geq 1$, denoted $\mathcal{G}^0(\alpha, \gamma, L)$.

The α parameter corresponds to image roughness (or heterogenity). It adopts negative values, varying from $-\infty$ to 0. If α is near 0, then the image data are extremely heterogeneous (for example: urban areas), and if α is far from the origin then the data correspond to a homogeneous region (for example: pasture areas). The values for forests lay in-between.

Many filters have been proposed in the literature for combating speckle noise, among them the ones by Lee and by Frost. These filters will be applied to speckled data, along with the filter proposed in this work. For quality performance the comparision will be done between the stack filter and the Lee filter. Classification performance will be assessed by classifying data filtered with the Lee, Frost and stack filters using a Gaussian maximum likelihood approach.

3   Stack Filters

This section is dedicated to a brief synthesis of stack filter definitions and design. For more details on this subject, see [4,6,7].

Consider images of the form $X\colon S \rightarrow \{0,\dots,M\}$, with S the support and $\{0,\dots,M\}$ the set of admissible values. The threshold is the set of operators $T^m\colon \{0,\dots,M\} \rightarrow \{0,1\}$ given by

$$T^m(x) = \begin{cases} 1 \text{ if } x \geq m, \\ 0 \text{ if } x < m. \end{cases}$$

We will use the notation $X^m = T^m(x)$. According to this definition, the value of a non-negative integer number $x \in \{0,\dots,M\}$ can be reconstructed making the summation of its thresholded values between 0 and M. Let $X = (x_0,\dots,x_{n-1})$ and $Y = (y_0,\dots,y_{n-1})$ be binary vectors of length n, define an order relation given by $X \leq Y$ if and only if holds that $x_i \leq y_i$ for every i. This relation is reflexive, anti-symmetric and transitive, generating therefore a partial ordering on the set of binary vectors of fixed length. A boolean function $f\colon \{0,1\}^n \rightarrow \{0,1\}$, where n is the length of the input vectors, has the stacking property if and only if

$$\forall X, Y \in \{0,1\}^n, \ X \leq Y \Rightarrow f(X) \leq f(Y).$$

We say that f is a positive boolean function if and only if it can be written by means of an expression that contains only non-complemented input variables. That is, $f(x_1, x_2, \dots, x_n) = \bigvee_{i=1}^{K} \bigwedge_{j \in P_i} x_j$, where n is the number of arguments of the function, K is the number of terms of the expression and P_i is a subset of the interval $\{1,\dots,N\}$. '$\bigvee$' and '$\bigwedge$' are the AND and OR Boolean operators. It is possible to proof that this type of functions has the stacking property.

A stack filter is defined by the function $S_f\colon \{0,\dots,M\}^n \rightarrow \{0,\dots,M\}$, corresponding to the Positive Boolean function $f(x_1, x_2, \dots, x_n)$ expressed in the given form by (3). The function S_f can be expressed by means of $S_f(X) = \sum_{m=1}^{M} f(T^m(X))$.

In this work we applied the stack filter generated with the fast algorithm described in [4].

Stack filters are built by a training process that generates a positive boolean function that preserves the stacking property. Originally, this training is performed providing two complete images on S, one degraded and one noiseless. The algorithm seeks the operator that best estimates the later using the former as input, and as a means of measuring error.

The implementation developed for this work supports the application of the stack filter many times. Our approach consists of using a set of regions of interest, much smaller than the whole data set, and relying on the analysis the user makes of these information. Graphical and quantitative analyses are presented. The user is prompted with the mean value of each region as the default desired value, but he/she can choose other from a menu (including the median, the lower and upper quartiles and a free specification). This freedom of choice is particularly useful when dealing with non-Gaussian degradation as is the case of, for instance, impulsive noise.

4   Results

In this section, we present the results of building stack filters by training. These filters are applied to both simulated and real data. The stack filters obtained are compared to SAR image filters. This comparision is done by assessing smoothing and edge preservation through image quality indexes and by evaluating the influence of filtering on classification performance.

4.1   Image Quality Assesment

The indexes used to evaluate the quality of the filtered images are the universal image quality index [8] and the correlation measure β. The universal image quality index Q is given byequation (1)

$$Q = \frac{\sigma_{XY}}{\sigma_X \sigma_Y} \frac{2\overline{XY}}{\overline{X}^2 + \overline{Y}^2} \frac{2\sigma_X \sigma_Y}{\sigma_X^2 + \sigma_Y^2}, \tag{1}$$

where $\sigma_X^2 = (N-1)^{-1} \Sigma_{i=1}^N (X_i - \overline{X})^2$, $\sigma_Y^2 = (N-1)^{-1} \Sigma_{i=1}^N (Y_i - \overline{Y})^2$, $\overline{X} = N^{-1} \Sigma_{i=1}^N X_i$ and $\overline{Y} = N^{-1} \Sigma_{i=1}^N Y_i$. The dynamic range of index Q is $[-1, 1]$, being 1 the best value. To evaluate the index of the whole image, local indexes Q_i are calculated for each pixel using a suitable square window, and then these results are averaged to yield the total image quality Q. The correlation measure is given by

$$\beta = \frac{\sigma_{\nabla^2 X \nabla^2 Y}}{\sigma_{\nabla^2 X}^2 \sigma_{\nabla^2 Y}^2}, \tag{2}$$

where $\nabla^2 X$ and $\nabla^2 Y$ are the Laplacians of images X and Y, respectively.

In Table 1 the correlation measure β and the quality index Q are shown. The comparison is made between Lee filtered and stack filtered SAR images. To this

Table 1. Statistics from image quality indexes

contrast	β index				Q index			
	Stack filter		Lee filter		Stack filter		Lee filter	
	$\overline{\beta}$	s_β	$\overline{\beta}$	s_β	$\overline{Q}$	s_Q	$\overline{Q}$	s_Q
10:1	0.1245	0.0156	0.0833	0.0086	0.0159	0.0005	0.0156	0.0004
10:2	0.0964	0.0151	0.0663	0.0079	0.0154	0.0005	0.0148	0.0004
10:4	0.0267	0.0119	0.0421	0.0064	0.0124	0.0008	0.0120	0.0006
10:8	−0.0008	0.0099	0.0124	0.0064	0.0041	0.0013	0.0021	0.0006

end, a Monte Carlo experiment was performed, generating 1000 independent replications of synthetic 1-look SAR images for each of four contrast ratios. The generated images consist of two regions separated by a vertical straight border. Each sample corresponds to a different contrast ratio, wich ranges from 10:1 to 10:8. This was done in order to study the effect of the contrast ratio in the quality indexes considered.

It can be seen that, according to the results obtained for the β index, the stack filter exhibits a better performance at high contrast ratios, namely 10:1 and 10:2, while the Lee filter shows the opposite behavior. The results for the Q index show slightly better results for the stack filter all over the range of contrast ratios. It is remarkable the small variance of these estimations, compared to the mean values obtained.

Fig. 1 shows the boxplots of the observations summarized in Table 1. From the plots for the β index, it can be seen that, the Lee filter has a lower degree of variability with contrast and that both are almost symmetric. The plots of the Q index show a better performance for the stack filter for all the contrast ratios considered.

4.2 Classification Performance

The quality of the classification results are obtained by calculating the confusion matrix, after Gaussian Maximum Likelihood Classification (GMLC).

Fig. 2(a), left, presents an image 128×128 pixels, simulated with two regions: samples from the $\mathcal{G}^0(-1.5, \gamma^*_{-1.5,1}, 1)$ and from the $\mathcal{G}^0(-10, \gamma^*_{-10,1}, 1)$ laws form the left and right halves, respectively, where $\gamma^*_{\alpha,n}$ denotes the scale parameter that, for a given roghness α and number of looks n yields an unitary mean law. In this manner, Fig. 2(a) presents data that are hard to classify: extremely heterogeneous and homogeneous areas with the same mean, with the lowest possible signal-to-noise ratio ($n = 1$). The mean value of the dashed area was used as the "ideal" image. Fig. 2(b) and 2(c), left, show the result of applying the resulting filter once and 95 times, respectively. The right side of Fig. 2(a), Fig. 2(b) and Fig. 2(c) present the GMLC of each image. Not only the pointwise improvement is notorious, but the edge presevation is also noteworthy, specially in Fig. 2(c), right, where the straight border has been completely retrieved.

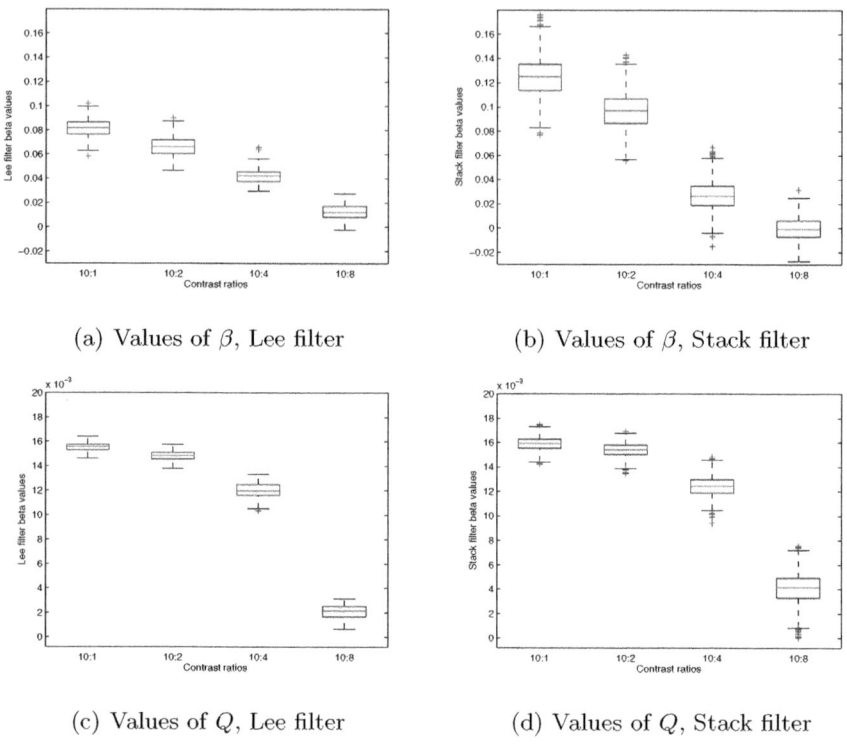

(a) Values of β, Lee filter

(b) Values of β, Stack filter

(c) Values of Q, Lee filter

(d) Values of Q, Stack filter

Fig. 1. Boxplots of the quality indexes

Fig. 3 compares the performance of the proposed stack filter with respect to two widely used SAR filters: Lee and Kuan. Fig. 3(a) presents the original data, and the regions of interest used for estimating the Boolean function. In this case, again, the mean on each region was used as the 'ideal' image. Fig. 3(b), Fig.3(c) and Fig. 3(d) present the result of applying the Frost, Lee and Stack filters (one and 22 iterations) to the original SAR data. The right side of previous figures present the corresponding GMLC. The stack filter produces better results than classical despeckling techniques.

Table 2 presents the main results from the confusion matrices of all the GMLC, including the results presented in [9] which used the classical stack filter estimation with whole images. It shows the percentage of pixels that was labeled by the user as from region R_i that was correctly classified as belonging to region R_i, for $1 \leq i \leq 3$. "None" denotes the results on the original, unfiltered, data, "Sample Stack k" denotes our proposal of building stack filters with samples, applied k times, "Stack k" the classical construction applied k times, and "Frost" and "Lee" the classical speckle reduction filters.

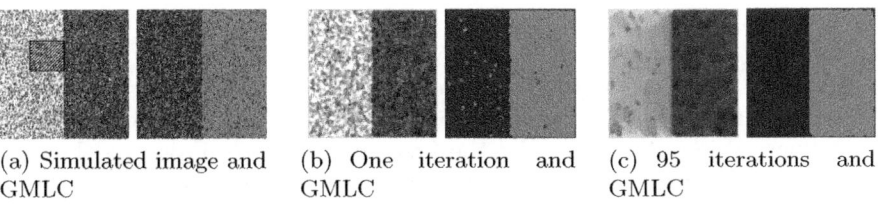

(a) Simulated image and GMLC

(b) One iteration and GMLC

(c) 95 iterations and GMLC

Fig. 2. Training by region of interest: simulated data

(a) Image, samples and GMLC

(b) Frost and GMLC

(c) Lee and GMLC

(d) Stack Filter 20 and GMLC

Fig. 3. Training by region of interest: real image

Table 2. Statistics from the confusion matrices

Filter	R_1/R_1	R_2/R_2	R_3/R_3
None	13.40	48.16	88.90
Sample Stack 1	9.38	65.00	93.19
Sample Stack 22	**63.52**	**74.87**	**96.5**
Stack 1	14.35	64.65	90.86
Stack 40	62.81	89.09	94.11
Stack 95	**63.01**	**93.20**	**94.04**
Frost	16.55	55.54	90.17
Lee	16.38	52.72	89.21

It is clear the superior performance of stack filters (both classical and by training) over speckle filters, though the stack filter by training requires more than a single iteration to outperform the last ones.

Stack filters by training require about two orders of time less than classical stack filters to be built, and they produce comparable results. Using regions of interest is, therefore, a competitive approach.

5   Conclusions

In this work, the effect of adaptive stack filtering on SAR images was assessed. Two viewpoints were considered: a classification performance viewpoint and a quality perception viewpoint. For the first approach, the Frost and Lee filters were compared with the iterated stack filter using a metric extracted from the confusion matrix. A real SAR image was used in this case. For the second approach, a Monte Carlo experience was carried out in which 1-look synthetic SAR, i.e., the noisiest images, were generated. In this case, the Lee filter and a one pass stack filter were compared for various degrees of contrast. The β and the Q indexes were used as measures of perceptual quality. The results of the β index shows that the stack filter performs better in cases of high contrast. The results of the Q index show slightly better performance of the stack filter over the Lee filter. This quality assessment is not conclusive but indicates the potential of stack filters in SAR image processing for visual analysis. The classification results and the quality perception results suggest that stack filters are promising tools in SAR image processing and analysis.

References

1. Oliver, C., Quegan, S.: Understanding Synthetic Aperture Radar Images. Artech House (1998)
2. Frery, A.C., Müller, H.-J., Yanasse, C.C.F., Sant'Anna, S.J.S.: A model for extremely heterogeneous clutter. IEEE Transactions on Geoscience and Remote Sensing 35(3), 648–659 (1996)
3. Prasad, M.K.: Stack filter design using selection probabilities. IEEE Transactions on Signal Processing 53(3), 1025–1037 (2005)
4. Yoo, J., Fong, K.L., Huang, J.-J., Coyle, E.J., Adams III, G.B.: A fast algorithm for designing stack filters. IEEE Transactions on Image Processing 8(8), 772–781 (1999)
5. Moschetti, E., Palacio, M.G., Picco, M., Bustos, O.H., Frery, A.C.: On the use of Lee's protocol for speckle-reducing techniques. Latin American Applied Research 36(2), 115–121 (2006)
6. Astola, J., Kuosmanen, P.: Fundamentals of Nonlinear Digital Filtering. CRC Press, Boca Raton (1997)
7. Lin, J.-H., Kim, Y.T.: Fast algorithms for training stack filters. IEEE Transactions on Signal Processing 42(3), 772–781 (1994)
8. Wang, Z., Bovik, A.C.: A universal image quality index. IEEE Signal Processing Letters 9(3), 81–84 (2002)
9. Buemi, M.E., Mejail, M.E., Jacobo-Berlles, J., Gambini, J.: Improvement in SAR image classification using adaptive stack filters. In: Proceedings XX Brazilian Symposium on Computer Graphics and Image Processing (SIBGRAPI), pp. 263–270. IEEE Computer Press (2007)

Subcutaneous Adipose Tissue Segmentation in Whole-Body MRI of Children[*]

Geoffroy Fouquier[1], Jérémie Anquez[1], Isabelle Bloch[1],
Céline Falip[2], and Catherine Adamsbaum[2,3]

[1] Telecom ParisTech, CNRS LTCI, and Whist Lab, Paris, France
[2] Service de radiologie pédiatrique, Hôpital Saint Vincent de Paul, Paris, France
[3] Université Paris Descartes, faculté de médecine, Paris, France

Abstract. In this paper, we propose a new method to segment the subcutaneous adipose tissue (SAT) in whole-body (WB) magnetic resonance images of children. The method is based on an automated learning of radiometric characteristics, which is adaptive for each individual case, a decomposition of the body according to its main parts, and a minimal surface approach. The method aims at contributing to the creation of WB anatomical models of children, for applications such as numerical dosimetry simulations or medical applications such as obesity follow-up. Promising results are obtained on data from 20 children at various ages. Segmentations are validated with 4 manual segmentations.

1 Introduction

This paper is a first step towards the development of semi-automatic approaches for WB magnetic resonance images (MRI) segmentation and designing 3D models of the anatomy of children. These models are meant for dosimetry studies, to assess the children exposure to electromagnetic fields. We propose to build a set of models representing children at different ages, and suitable for deformations in order to test different postures during dosimetry studies, and hence generating a larger set of models from an existing set.

Our purpose is thus the realistic modeling of the human body in a semi-automatic way, since manual processing of the data is time consuming and cannot ensure to obtain topologically correct and smooth structures due to slice by slice processing. The process relies first on identifying the main body subparts by analyzing the body silhouette. Then, we propose to decompose the subject anatomy by segmenting SAT, the muscles and the bones, which represent about 80% of the subject body mass. In this article we describe the first step of this approach and SAT segmentation. In the context of realistic modeling, accuracy is not the main expected feature of the method since the segmentation is not aimed at providing an exact individual model of each patient. What is important is that the fat is well located, topologically correct, and approximately fits the

---

[*] This work was partially supported by the French National Research Agency (ANR) within the KidPocket project. G. Fouquier is now with eXenSa, Paris and J. Anquez with Theraclion, Paris.

C. San Martin and S.-W. Kim (Eds.): CIARP 2011, LNCS 7042, pp. 97–104, 2011.

actual thickness (an approximate thickness is sufficient, since it will be prone to modifications during deformations).

WB MRI consists of an important amount of data and semi-automated segmentation methods are desirable to process them. However, only few works have been dedicated to this task since it is an emerging modality. Most approaches rely on low level methods and were developed for adults' images. For instance, T1-weighted MRI data are thresholded, and SAT is identified through region growing in the early work presented in [3]. A fuzzy c-means following intensity correction is used in [10] to identified AT and an active contour model allows to separate SAT and VAT (visceral adipose tissues) afterwards. Data acquired with the DIXON sequence are processed by means of thresholding, mathematical morphology tools and connected component extraction in [9]. The most sophisticated method is proposed in [6], where anatomical landmarks such as the spine are identified to constrain the segmentation of both SAT and VAT. However, this work only focuses on the abdominal region of the subject's anatomy. This approach has later been adapted to the case of children (5 years old) in [7] where the reduced amount of fat is challenging. Whole-body images are considered but only the abdominal region is segmented.

Here a patient-adaptive method for the WB SAT segmentation is proposed. Our contribution is to propose a method to segment SAT in the whole-body at once. Furthermore, the proposed approach does not require data homogenization thanks to the regularization. The study concerns images of children between 10 and 17 years old and the proposed method is therefore the first one dealing with SAT in WB children images.

2   MRI Database

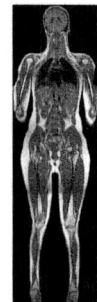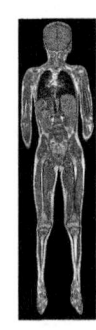

WB MRI images of children have been acquired thanks to collaborating hospital, within protocols dedicated to the exploration of suspected autoinflammatory diseases such as chronic recurrent multifocal osteomyelitis (CRMO). These acquisitions are emerging thanks to shorter sequence durations. A set of 20 images has been acquired with the same Siemens scanner (1.5T) using T1 ($TR = 675ms$, $TE = 11ms$) sequence, using multiple coils. Examples of images are displayed in Figure 1. The table stops at each station. Depending on the patient, around 32 coronal slices are acquired with a slice thickness of $6mm$. The reconstructed voxel size for all images is $1.3 \times 1.3 \times 7.2\ mm^3$. The total scan time is 97s for $T1$ acquisitions. Due to the strong anisotropy, the data exhibit a lot of partial volume effect. Due to the use of multiple coils, images actually result from the composition of 4 or 5 images (depending on the patient height), and some artifacts may appear such as missing parts due to field size or lower intensity at the transition between two images. An example of the latter can be seen at the arms level in Figure 1 on the left.

Fig. 1. Slices of WB images of two patients

3   SAT Segmentation

The proposed method for SAT segmentation is based on a minimal surface approach. To make the method automatically adaptive to each patient, the grey level histogram is first analyzed to separate the background. Then a key feature of the method consists in using prior spatial information on the SAT location to define two regions, included in SAT and in the rest of the body, respectively: each voxel on the surface of the body is considered as fat and each voxel far enough from the surface is considered as belonging to the other class. A minimal surface approach is finally applied to estimate the best boundary between these two initial regions. Note that the hypothesis that the fat is the first tissue on the surface of the body is an approximation which is justified by the resolution of the images and their anisotropy, which make the skin not visible (its $1mm$ thickness cannot be properly imaged with a voxel of $1.3 \times 1.3 \times 7.2mm^3$).

3.1   Identification of the Body Silhouette

Figure 2(a) presents the histogram of the image displayed in Figure 1(a). Similar histograms are observed on the whole database. Values corresponding to the background form a peak which decreases quickly. A second peak corresponds to the intensities of the muscles and the soft tissues (such as abdominal organs). The background mask is obtained by thresholding the original image. The selected threshold corresponds to the lowest value between the two identified peaks, and is determined automatically as the first valley of a filtered version of the histogram. The result (Figure 2(b)) separates the body from the

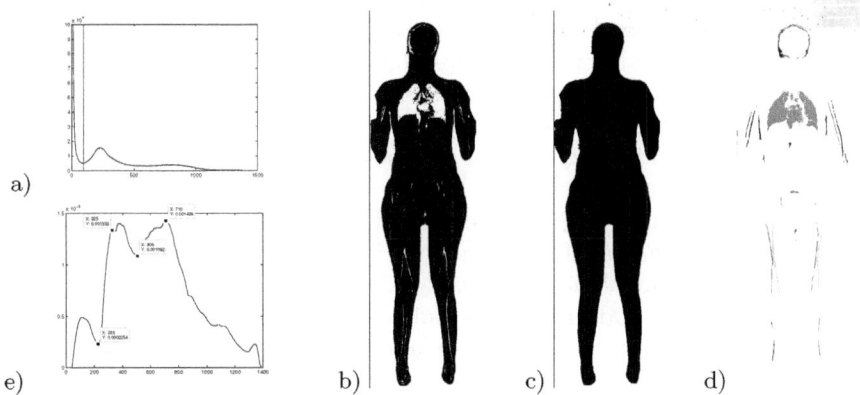

a)

e)

b)

c)

d)

Fig. 2. Automatic method to extract the body silhouette. The threshold is obtained from histogram analysis. (a) Histogram of a WB T1 MRI and threshold value (in red). (b) The thresholding result separates the background and some internal parts of the body, such as air-filled organs like lungs (in white). (c) Identification of the body silhouette. (d) The remaining dark components in the body. (e) Analysis of the silhouette of the body from the head to the feet: Each point represents the surface of the corresponding axial slice of the binary mask. The marked points correspond to the neck, the armpit, the waist and the hips.

background, except components filled with air, liquid, or bones corticals (LCR, cortical bones, airways, lungs, part of the stomach, the heart and the intestine). A hole filling applied to the body allows us to add some of these components but a few others such as airways are directly connected to the background and thus cannot be filled. These components are disconnected using a morphological closing of the body component. A result is presented in Figure 2(c). The radius of the structuring element has been manually set and the same value is used for all images ($5mm$). This operation adds unwanted parts in the mask such as fine space between the arms and the abdomen. Among the remaining components in the body (Figure 2(d)), the lungs may be identified as the biggest one (both lungs are generally connected in these images).

3.2   Separation of the Main Parts of the Body

As mentioned above, it is possible to consider that each voxel on the surface of the body belongs to SAT. To identify the body surface, the body mask alone is not sufficient since during the acquisitions the patient's hands lie on the thighs, the arms are sometimes in contact with the abdomen, and thigh fat may be in contact. Therefore, we propose to roughly separate the body into its main parts, namely head, thorax, abdomen, shoulders, arms, forearms, hips, thighs and legs. This identification allows us to cope with unwanted connections and to guarantee that different parts that should be separated are actually so.

The information on the image orientation is used to analyze the silhouette of the body, following a central axis from the top of the head to the feet. For each axial slice orthogonal to this axis, the area inside the body is computed. Figure 2.e presents the curve of these values. Reference points are then identified: the first peak corresponds to the middle of the head, the first valley to the neck. The shoulders (second peak), the hips (highest remaining peak) and the waist (lowest valley between shoulder and hips) are also identified. Peaks and valleys are detected on a filtered version of the curve (using a simple median filter). The curve is similar for all images in our database, which allows us to automate this step for all images.

A first automatic body parts identification is achieved using these reference points and results in a labeling of the main body parts illustrated in Figure 3(b). The shoulders region labeling also uses the segmentation of the lungs and more local analysis of the body mask. The initial labeling is then manually corrected to separate the arms from the abdomen and the thighs (see Figure 3(c,d)). Other errors are corrected at the same time. This connection step is the only manual step in our approach.

3.3   Initialization of SAT Segmentation

The minimal surface approach used for the final segmentation is optimized using a graph-cut method, and is based on two hard constraining regions, one included

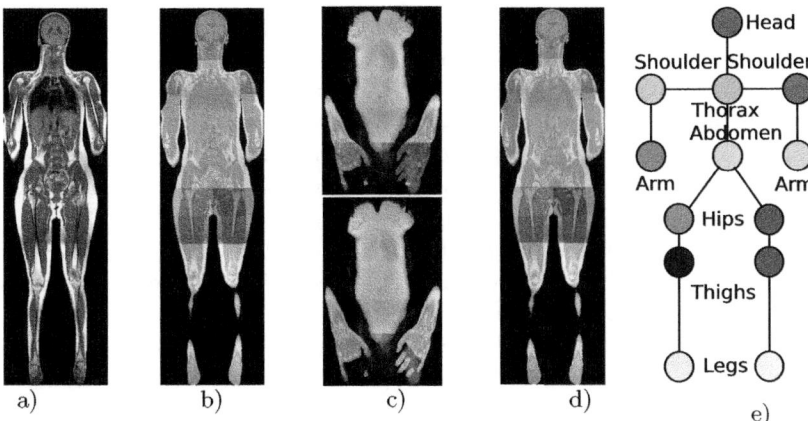

Fig. 3. (a) A slice of an image. (b) Automatic labeling: the arms have the same label as the thorax and the abdomen. The hands have the labels of hips. (c) Separation of the hands from the thighs. (d) Corrected labeling. Each forearm (including the hand) has its own label. (e) Connections between body parts.

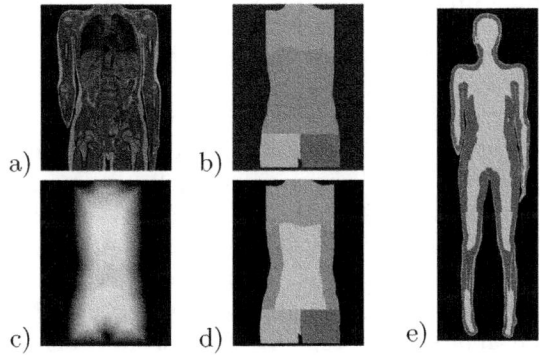

Fig. 4. Initialization derived from the labeling. Each voxel on the surface of the body is marked as SAT. Voxels far enough from the surface are marked as non-fat. (a) Here the arms are in contact with the abdomen. Each body part given by the previous step is processed independently. (b) The abdomen is merged with anatomically neighboring body parts (such as thorax or hips, but not arms). (c) Distance map from the background. (d) Extraction of border and inside classes for the selected body part. (e) Results from each part are merged to provide the initialization: each voxel in green belongs surely to SAT while each voxel in brown belongs to the inside class. The remaining voxels (in red) are not classified yet.

in SAT and one included in non-fat regions, called "inside region". These two regions will be the seeds of the graph model and constitute the initialization of segmentation.

For SAT, each boundary voxel of the body is considered as part of it, as explained before. The previous body part identification allows us to detect the body surface by considering each part independently. For each voxel of the border of a region, there are three possibilities: (i) it has a neighbor in the background, (ii) it is connected to an authorized label and thus the voxel is considered inside the body, (iii) it is connected to a non-authorized label and thus the voxel is on the surface of the body. For example a voxel which is in the arm and neighbor of a background voxel is

always on the surface of the body. If a voxel of the arm is neighbor of an abdomen voxel, then this voxel is also on the surface of the body. But if a voxel of
the arm is neighbor of a shoulder voxel, then it is not on the surface of the body.

For the inside class, each region is considered again and merged with the
neighbor regions having an authorized connection (as defined above). Figure 4(b)
shows the merging of the abdomen and its neighbors (thorax and hips). A distance map to the background is computed (Figure 4(c)) and used to perform an
erosion whose size depends on the body part: sequential erosions are performed
with an unitary ball until a given ratio of the initial body part volume is kept.
For elongated body parts such as legs, the structuring element is a disk in the
axial plane and not a ball. The eroded region is then masked by the original
region mask to provide the inside class (for the abdomen in our example). This
is repeated for each body part. The obtained initialization is illustrated in Figure 4(e) where voxels in green belong surely to fat and voxels in light brown
belong to the inside class. Voxels in red are not assigned yet to any class, and
the aim of the segmentation will be to find the best segmentation surface within
this red region.

3.4   Segmentation by Minimal-Surface Approach

The final segmentation is performed using a minimal-surface method, minimizing
the following energy function: $E(l) = \sum_p D(p, l_p) + \beta \sum_{p,q} V(p, q)$ with p and
q two points, l_p a label, $D()$ a data fidelity term, β a fixed coefficient and V
a regularization term. The data fidelity term is defined for each voxel except
for the background using the a priori information previously defined. For each
unclassified voxel, the probability for this voxel to belong to each class is given
by a Gaussian distribution of the intensity of each class (muscles and tissues
on the one hand, AT and bone narrow on the other hand) previously computed
on the whole image. The minimal surface is computed generally between these
two classes and the regularization allows us to separate SAT from other AT
or bones.

The regularization term is defined as follows: $V(p, q) = \frac{1}{\max\{(1.0 - grad_{pq}), \varepsilon\}} |l_p -
l_q|$ with $grad_{pq}$ an estimation of the normalized gradient between p and q which
takes into account the image anisotropy. The parameter ε is set to 10^{-6} in our
experiments. The parameter β is also fixed in our experiments and the same
value is used for all images (0.75).

This energy is minimized using the graph-cut approach described in [1,5,2]
using the α-expansion algorithm until convergence.

4   Results and Discussion

Experiments have been conducted on our MRI database. Figure 5 present results
on three cases, where the manual segmentation appears in green, the SAT segmentation appears in blue, and 3D reconstructions of the two classes are shown
as well. The first patient is a 10 year old girl, the second one a 13 year old

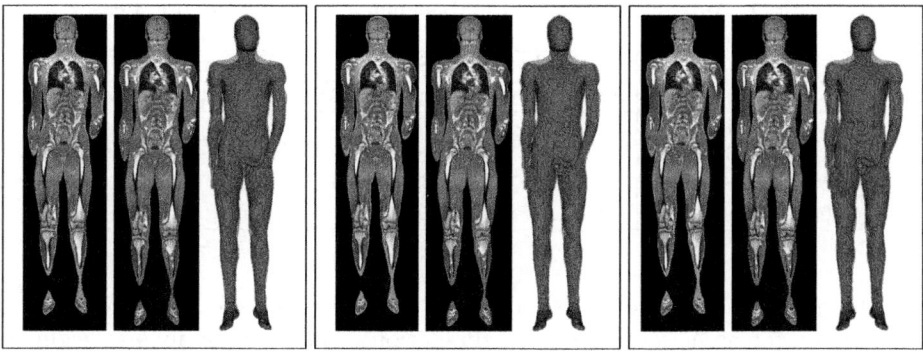

Fig. 5. Manual segmentation (in green), SAT segmentation (in blue): 10 year old girl (left) and overweighted 13 year old girl (right)

overweighted girl. The last one is a 17 year boy with very little fat. The results have been reviewed by radiologists, who confirmed their good quality, and the correct detection of all SAT locations. Moreover, the obtained results answer the needs raised by the foreseen applications: SAT is generally well recognized, it has the required topology (by construction, since the approach guarantees the topology of an empty sphere), and the fat thickness is approximately preserved. Some errors are inherent to the method: each voxel on the surface of the body is marked as fat, therefore small extremities such as fingers or ears are entirely considered as fat. Note that this will be corrected in a further step, since a skin layer will then be introduced on higher resolution reconstructions, before dosimetry simulations. Other errors are due to the poor resolution of the images in the coronal direction, making the transition between fat and bone sometimes unclear. Therefore some parts of the tibias are often marked as fat. Parts of the clavicles are also often classified as fat.

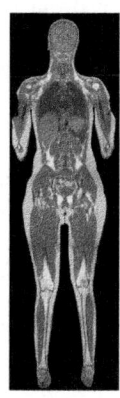

A quantitative evaluation of the segmentation was achieved thanks to 4 manual segmentations of SAT on the whole-body, including the 3 cases presented in Figure 5. Each segmentation has been achieved by an expert user and takes approximately 4h per image. Manual segmentations have been reviewed by other radiologists. Table 1 presents the mean distance between the automated segmentation and the manual one for each of the 4 cases, as well as the similarity index. The best results are for the over-weight girl and the lowest for the skinny boy. The very low amount of fat in this case along with the partial volume effect make the manual segmentation challenging even for an expert. The resulting segmentation guarantees the topology, even if there is no fat to show. This may be a limitation of the method. When considering only the abdomen and the hips, results are better. The results on the 16 other images of our database show a similar quality, according to a visual inspection performed by medical experts.

Fig. 6. 14 years old girl model

Table 1. Automated segmentation vs manual segmentation for 4 cases

	details		Whole Body SAT		Abdominal SAT	
	Corpulence	Age	Mean dist (vox)	Similarity	Mean Dist (vox)	Similarity
p1	normal	13	1.18	87.40%	0.99	92.67%
p12	over-weight	13	1.28	88.11%	1.06	92.71%
p15	skinny	17	1.94	65.44%	1.22	77.42%
p16	normal	10	1.12	82.46%	1.54	88.14%

These results are a useful first step towards the design of realistic WB models of children for numerical dosimetry simulations. Future work aims at segmenting more tissues and organs to complete these models. An illustration of one of these models is presented in Figure 6. Beside the primary goal of dosimetry simulations, interesting medical outcome could be derived from this segmentation. As pointed out in [4], the body fat distribution could be studied to analyze the body mass index and monitor therapy for obesity, or evaluate its change according to pathologies. Differentiating SAT from VAT is then important. Also body fat automatic segmentation allows fat distributions comparison in studies such as in [8].

References

1. Boykov, Y., Kolmogorov, V.: An experimental comparison of min-cut/max-flow algorithms for energy minimization in vision. IEEE PAMI 26(9) (2004)
2. Boykov, Y., Veksler, O., Zabih, R.: Efficient approximate energy minimization via graph cuts. IEEE PAMI 20(12), 1222–1239 (2001)
3. Brennan, D., Whelan, P., Robinson, K., Ghita, O., O'Brien, J., Sadleir, R., Eustace, S.: Rapid automated measurement of body fat distribution from whole-body MRI. Am. J. of Roentgenology 185(2), 418–423 (2005)
4. Darge, K., Jaramillo, D., Siegel, M.: Whole-body MRI in children: current status and future applications. Eur. J. Radiol. 68(2), 289–298 (2008)
5. Kolmogorov, V., Zabih, R.: What energy functions can be minimized via graph cuts? IEEE PAMI 26(2), 147–159 (2004)
6. Kullberg, J., Johansson, L., Ahlström, H., Courivaud, F., Koken, P., Eggers, H., Börnert, P.: Automated assessment of whole-body adipose tissue depots from continuously moving bed MRI: A feasibility study. J. Magnetic Resonance Imaging 30(1), 185–193 (2009)
7. Kullberg, J., Karlsson, A.K., Stokland, E., Svensson, P.A., Dahlgren, J.: Adipose tissue distribution in children: Automated quantification using water and fat MRI. J. Magnetic Resonance Imaging 32(1), 204–210 (2010)
8. Machann, J., et al.: Standardized assessment of whole body adipose tissue topography by MRI. J. Magnetic Resonance Imaging 21(4), 455–462 (2005)
9. Martinez-Moller, et al.: Tissue classification as a potential approach for attenuation correction in whole-body PET/MRI: evaluation with PET/CT data. J. Nuclear Medicine 50(4), 520–526 (2009)
10. Sussman, D., Yao, J., Summers, R.: Automated measurement and segmentation of abdominal adipose tissue in MRI. In: IEEE ISBI, pp. 936–939. IEEE (2010)

Infrared Focal Plane Array Imaging System Characterization by Means of a Blackbody Radiator

Francisca Parra[1,2,3], Pablo Meza[1,2], Carlos Toro[1,2], and Sergio Torres[1,2]

[1] Departamento de Ingeniería Eléctrica, Universidad de Concepción, Casilla 160-C,
Concepción, Chile
[2] Center for Optics and Photonics, Universidad de Concepción, Concepción
[3] Aeronautical Polytechnic Academy Chilean Air Force Santiago, Chile

Abstract. Infrared (IR) Focal plane array (IRFPA) cameras are nowadays both, more accessible and with a broad variety in terms of detectors design. In many cases, the IRFPA characterization is not completely given by the manufacturer. In this paper a long wave 8-12 [μm] microbolometer IRFPA is characterized by means of calculating the Noise Equivalent Temperature Difference (NETD) and the Correctability performance parameters. The Correctability parameter has been evaluated by using a black body radiator and Two-Points calibration technique. Also, the Transfer Function of the microbolometer IR camera has been experimentally obtained as well as the NETD by the evaluation of radiometric data from a blackbody radiator. The obtained parameters are the key for any successful application of IR imaging pattern recognition.

1 Introduction

Currently, the development of IR imaging sensors have been such that the market has been flooded with different types of IR cameras, each one with different features as presented in [1]. The main difference between these cameras is in the sensor type used for detecting the infrared radiation.

Depending on the interaction nature between the detector material and the IR radiation, the photo-detectors are classified on intrinsic, extrinsic, photo-emissive, and quantum well detectors [2]. The second class of IR detectors is composed by thermal detectors, where the incident radiation is absorbed and it changes the material temperature, that change modifies some physical properties as resistivity to generate an electrical signal output.

In contrast to photo-detectors, the thermal detectors typically operate at room temperature. One of the most popular thermal detectors is the amorphous silicon (a-Si) microbolometer as presented in [3] and as any detector, they are affected by many type of noise sources.

In spite of the the first bolometer was designed in 1880, according to [4], the development release to this technology was under classify military contacts, so

C. San Martin and S.-W. Kim (Eds.): CIARP 2011, LNCS 7042, pp. 105–112, 2011.
© Springer-Verlag Berlin Heidelberg 2011

the public according to this in 1992 were surprising in the worldwide infrared community, and they are still object to several research.

To apply a IR microbolometer camera to IR imaging application a fully characterization of the detector noise is needed. Inherent to this kind of equipments is the Fixed Pattern Noise (FPN); it can be defined as a fixed noise superimposed over the IR image. The FPN is generated by the nonuniform response of the neighbors detectors for the same integrated IR irradiance. Several methods have been developed to eliminate this undesired effect, with different results and operations conditions, some of them are compared in [5].

In [6] and [7] it is shown the importance to have a good understanding of the detectors response. This can be achieve by using a thermal reference known as a blackbody [8], which is a laboratory equipment capable of delivering a flat input temperature. Having this in consideration, many FPA parameter such that radiometric curves, NETD, Correctability, etc., can be calculated using this equipment, as it is presented in [9] and [10].

The present study deals with three laboratory characterization parameters evaluated for a CEDIP Jade Uncooled (UC) camera, long wave 8-12 [μm] microbolometer IRFPA. This paper is organized as follows: In section 2, the radiometric curve, the NETD, and the Correctability parameters are defined. In section 3 the experimental technique to perform an evaluation of such parameters is described and the main results are shown. Finally, the most important conclusions are detailed on section 4.

2   Parameters

In this section, the three parameters under analysis are presented. They are able to represent different characteristics of an IR imaging system. Note that they are interdependent, because as it will be shown, the radiometric analysis gives the basis to perform the NETD and the Correctability analysis.

2.1   Radiometric Transfer Function

For measurements of radiometric parameters, the experimental setup use a blackbody calibration source, whose temperatures radiance can be accurately calculated, and the IRFPA imaging system to be evaluated. The blackbody is composed by a plate with a roughened surface covered with a high emissivity painting. The uniform temperature surface can be stabilized in a time lower than 10 minutes with an emissivity average of 0.95.

This equipment is essential to perform the IRFPA System Transfer Function (SiTF). It is estimated by the measure of several flat inputs at different temperature radiation, which are controlled by the blackbody source. The data acquired can be represented as a Data Cube, because there exists information on three dimensions, two spatial axes and one temporal axe. The measures resulted must be averaged, and then the SiTF is determined [11]. It is typically represented in response units of voltage, digital counts, etc. vs units of the source such as temperature, flux, etc. Therefore, any digital value can be associated to a specific input temperature.

According to this behavior, at a frame n^{th}, a general model for each ij detector in the FPA is often described by a linear relationship between the incoming irradiance $X_{i,j}(n)$ and the readout data $Y_{i,j}(n)$ as follows:

$$Y_{i,j} = A_{i,j} X_{i,j} + B_{i,j} \tag{1}$$

The SiTF, can be used also to determine how is increased the signal detected regarding the input, and to determine the sections in which it can be approached to the first order model described in the equation 1. In a Two-Point or Multipoint correction method, this is particularly important because it will indicate the range for which the method is more accurate to apply.

2.2 Noise Equivalent Temperature Difference, NETD

The NETD is a performance metrics to measure the IRFPA thermal resolution, as it is mentioned in [12], it is the smallest difference in a uniform temperature scene that the FPA can detect. According to [13], the typical value for a microbolometer is on the order of 100 [mK]. Note that the knowledge of such parameter is crucial for IR pattern recognition. Further, the NETD parameter measures the system's ability to perceive targets with a low thermal contrast with the imaging background. It can be defined as the ratio between the noise rms inherent on the system and the SiTF, then:

$$NETD = \frac{N_{rms}[volts]}{SITF_{Slope}[volts/K]} \tag{2}$$

2.3 Correctability

There are several methods to calibrate IR imaging system. The foregoing, has generated the need of IR image quality indexes to evaluate the quality of the applied correction method.

The Correctability figure of merit is based on the use of a thermal reference (blackbody source). Further, the Correctability is able to evaluate the mitigation of the FPN after calibration. Moreover this parameter magnitude is proportional to the rate within the total noise and the temporal noise. Mathematically, it is defined by:

$$c = \sqrt{\frac{\sigma_{total}^2}{\sigma_v^2} - 1} \tag{3}$$

where σ_{total}^2 is the spatial variance given by:

$$\sigma_{total}^2 = \frac{\sum_{j=1}^{n}(Y_j^c - \overline{Y})^2}{n-1} \tag{4}$$

Y_j^c is the jth corrected pixel value, $\overline{Y}$ is the spatial sample mean of the un-corrected frame, and n is the number of pixels on the FPA.

Note that a Correctability value $c = 0$ indicates that the FPN has been completely removed, which is highly desired. If the value is $c = 1$, the FPN after the correction equals the temporal noise. When the level of correction is poor, the residual FPN exceeds the values of the temporal noise, achieving c values greater than 1.

3   Experimental Setup and Data Processing

To measure, experimentally, the IR imaging parameters outlined above, a labora-tory set up has been implemented. This is composed by a CEDIP Jade UC FPA Camera with a spatial resolution of 240×320 pixels, a spectral response between 8-12 $[\mu m]$, 14 bits digital output. Further, detector material is an uncooled a-Si microbolometer. For this system, the manufacturer guaranties a NETD lower than 100 $[mK]$. The reference IR source used is a blackbody radiator, which operates between 0-150 $[°C]$ and with a thermal resolution of 0.1 $[°C]$.

Fig. 1. Laboratory Setup

3.1   Radiometric Procedure

To measure the SiTF, 300 IR imaging frames where captured for each blackbody setup temperature. Furthermore, the integration time of the IR imaging system is fixed at 60 μs. Therefore, the dimensions for each data cube are $240 \times 320 \times 300$. In this case, there have been implemented measures between 0 and 150$[°C]$ with 5°$[C]$ incremental between the IR imaging frames. The average of each data cube was plotted and it is represented by the Fig. 2.

Note that on Fig. 2 the standard deviation of each data cube decreases as long as the temperature increases.

With the experimental data a linear regression, in the least squares sense, was performed over all the image's dynamic range. However because of the nonlinear-ity of the imaging system response to the blackbody radiator, a linear regression by sections is required. Further, the dynamic range has been separated on three

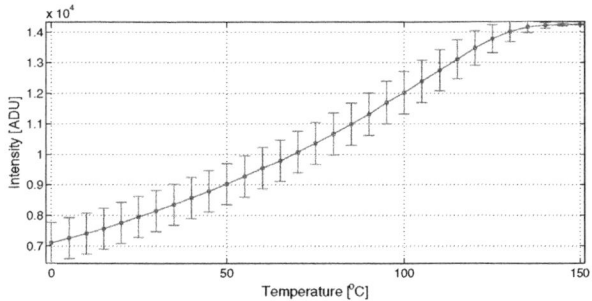

Fig. 2. Transfer Function CEDIP Camera

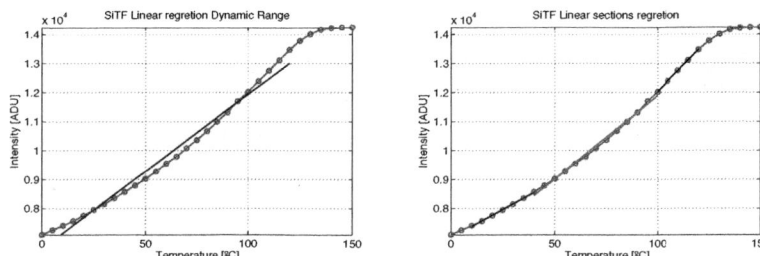

Fig. 3. SiTF Linear regression

sections representing the low, medium and high temperature values. The above procedure can be seen in Fig. 3.

It can be seen in Table 1 the First-Order parameter obtained after the linear regression for each range. Note that the slope is growing from the first section to the third one.

Table 1. First-Order parameter of the radiometric procedure

[T. Range [°C]	$\overline{A_{i,j}}$ [ADU/°C]	$\overline{B_{i,j}}$ [ADU]
[10 , 40]	39.1	6973.7
[40 , 100]	57.5	6128.8
[100 , 120]	72.7	4741.3

3.2 NETD Experimental Procedure

The NETD must be calculated at different levels of temperature, because the slope obtained by linear regression is growing along with the temperature levels. Therefore, the steps to perform the NETD can be numbered as follows:

1. A temporal noise estimation is calculated for each specific temperature in the linear range.

2. A temporal IR imaging frame average at each temperature is calculated.
3. To isolate the temporal component in one frame, the difference between the particular frame and the previous averaged frame is obtained. This procedure is repeated for each frame in the chosen data cube.
4. Now it is calculated the rms value of the previous obtained frame.
5. Calculate the standard deviation for each pixel along the temporal axis and then the final frame is averaged, see Fig. 4 for a best understanding.

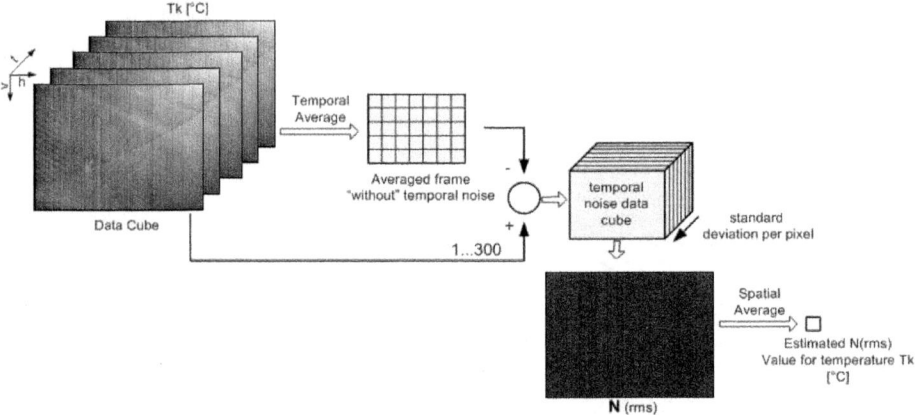

Fig. 4. Temporal Noise Procedure

The results are detailed on Table 2. It is appreciated a NETD value decrease as the temperature is higher. Furthermore, it shows that the NETD is not constant for all the temperatures. According to this, it is possible to say that the thermal resolution is better when the target temperature is higher.

Table 2. NETD experimental result at different temperature ranges

T. Range [°C]	T. Selected [°C]	SiTF [a.u/mK]	N(rms)[a.u.]	NETD [mK]
[10 , 40]	20	39.1	3.71	95.0
[40 , 100]	70	57.5	4.08	70.9
[100 , 120]	110	72.7	4.77	65.6

3.3   Correctability Experimental Procedure

To evaluate the Correctability IR imaging performance parameter, it is necessary to perform a FPN correction on the raw IR imaging obtained by using the experimental setup shown in Fig. 1. A Two-Point correction has been implemented, retrieving the correction parameters for different ranges of temperature $[T_{min}, T_{max}]$. The corrupted video set is selected by taking a temperature image between the $[T_{min}, T_{max}]$.

The procedure steps to calculate the Correctability can be enumerated as follow:

1. Select the raw IR frame and its corresponding calibrated frame over which the Correctability will be calculated.
2. Calculate the spatial sample variance σ_{total}^2, given by the equation 4, over the two previous frames.
3. Calculate the temporal variance σ_v^2.
4. Finally, apply the equation 3 to evaluate the Correctability parameter.

Note that this steps can be replicated to any FPN calibration method. The results shown in Table 3 indicate that the correction with the poorest performance happened for the widest temperature range. This result is expected due to the low accuracy of the linear approximation in broad ranges.

Table 3. Correctability performance parameters at six different temperatures, each one tested with a different Two-Point correction

$[T_{min}, T_{max}]$°C at T°C	Correctability
[25 , 45] measured at 35	0.6581
[60 , 80] measured at 70	0.6733
[95 , 115] measured at 105	23.4465
[20 , 30] measured at 25	0.5858
[10 , 140] measured at 75	94.2718

4   Conclusions

In this paper, three IR imaging system parameters have been analyzed by means of a laboratory characterization. This has been achieved by using a CEDIP Jade UC IRFPA camera and a Mikron blackbody radiator.

The radiometric transfer function coming out to be nonlinear up to 100 [°C] and down to 20 [°C]. Further, the linear operation range was determined to be between the previous values. Such linear range justifies the potential to apply the JADE camera to most of the imaging applications in the field of human biometrics.

The calculated NETD values are consistences with the ones delivered by the manufacturer. Further, the best NETD obtained was 65 [mK], which is a acceptable value for human biometrics IR pattern recognition.

Finally, the IR Correctability performance values obtained for two-points correction method, corroborate the figure of merit behavior according to the accuracy of the correction. The best value obtained was 0.59, which represent a correction below the electronic temporal noise.

As a general conclusion, it is necessary to say that the IR microbolometer technology is very noisy for IR pattern recognition and special performance parameters computations are necessary for any particular application.

Acknowledgements. This work was partially supported by Programa de Financiamiento Basal grant PFB08024. Pablo Meza and Carlos Toro are supported by a CONICYT PhD Scholarship. Sergio Torres is supported by Fondo Nacional de Desarrollo Científico y Tecnológico (FONDECYT) 1100522. Francisca Parra is also supported by the Aeronautical Polytechnic Academy Chilean Air Force.

References

1. Scribner, D.A., Kruer, M.R., Killiany, J.M.: Infrared focal plane array technology. Proceedings of the IEEE 79, 66–85 (1991)
2. Rogalski, A.: Infrared detectors: an overview. Infrared Physics and Technology 43, 187–210 (2002)
3. Vedel, C., Martin, J.L., Ouvrier-Buffet, J.L., Tissot, J.L., Vilain, M., Yon, J.J.: Amorphous silicon based uncooled microbolometer IRFPA. In: SPIE Conference on Infrared Technology and Applications XXV, Orlando, vol. 3698 (1999)
4. Rogalski, A.: Infrared Detectors, 2nd edn. Taylor & Francis, Boca Raton (2011)
5. Vera, E., Meza, P., Torres, S.: Total variation approach for adaptive nonuniformity correction in focal-plane arrays. Opt. Lett. 36, 172–174 (2011)
6. Dantes, D.: Characterization of infrared detectors for space applications. In: SPIE Detectors, Focal Plane Arrays, and Applications, vol. 2894, pp. 180–186 (1996)
7. Yon, J.J., Mottin, E., Biancardini, L., Letellier, L., Tissot, J.L.: Infrared microbolometer sensors and their application in automotive safety. In: Advanced Microsystems for Automotive Applications, pp. 137–157 (2003)
8. Mikron Infrared: Calibration Sources,
   http://www.mikroninfrared.com/EN/products/calibration-sources/
9. Schulz, M., Caldwell, L.: Nonuniformity correction and correctability of infrared focal plane arrays. Infrared Physics and Technology 36, 763–777 (1995)
10. Torres, S., Hayat, M., Armstrong, E.: On the Performance Analysis of a Recent statistical algorithm for non-uniformity correction in focal-plane arrays. In: Proc. CISST, vol. 3703 (2000)
11. Perconti, P., Zeibel, J., Pellegrino, J., Driggers, R.: Medical Infrared Imaging, pp. 4-1–4-10 (July 2007)
12. Vandervelde, T.E., Lenz, M.C., Varley, E., Barve, A., Shao, J., Shenoi, R.V., Ramirez, D.A., Jan, W., Sharma, Y.D., Krishna, S.: Quantum Dots-in-a-Well Focal Plane Arrays. IEEE Journal of Selected Topics in Quantum Electronics 14(4), 1150–1161 (2010)
13. Laveigne, J., Franks, G., Sparkman, K., Prewarski, M., Nehring, B., McHugh, S.: LWIR NUC Using an Uncooled Microbolometer Camera. In: Technologies for Synthetic Environments: Hardware-in-the-Loop Testing XV. Proceedings of the SPIE, vol. 7663 (2010)

An Adaptive Color Similarity Function for Color Image Segmentation

Rodolfo Alvarado-Cervantes and Edgardo M. Felipe-Riveron[*]

Center for Computing Research, National Polytechnic Institute, Juan de Dios Batiz w/n, Col.
Nueva Industrial Vallejo, P.O. 07738, Mexico
ateramex@gmail.com, edgardo@cic.ipn.mx

Abstract. In this paper an interactive, semiautomatic image segmentation method is presented which, processes the color information of each pixel as a unit, thus avoiding color information scattering. The process has only two steps: 1) The manual selection of few sample pixels of the color to be segmented in the image; and 2) The automatic generation of the so called *Color Similarity Image* (CSI), which is just a gray level image with all the tonalities of the selected colors. The color information of every pixel is integrated in the segmented image by an adaptive color similarity function designed for direct color comparisons. The color integrating technique is direct, simple, and computationally inexpensive and it has also good performance in gray level and low contrast images.

Keywords: Color image segmentation, Adaptive color similarity function, HSI parameter distances.

1 Introduction

Image segmentation consists of partitioning an entire image into different regions, which are similar in some preestablished manner. Segmentation is an important feature of human visual perception, which manifests itself spontaneously and naturally. It is also one of the most important and difficult tasks in image analysis and processing. All subsequent steps, such as feature extraction and objects recognition depend on the quality of segmentation. Without a good segmentation algorithm, objects of interest in a complex image are difficult (often impossible) to recognize using automated techniques. At present, several segmentation techniques are available for color images, but most of them are just monochromatic methods applied on the individual planes in different color spaces where the results are combined later in different ways [5]. A common problem arises when the color components of a particular pixel are processed separately; the color information is so scattered in its components and most of the color information is lost [2] [5] [7].

In this work, an interactive, semiautomatic image segmentation method is presented which uses the color information for each pixel as a whole, thus avoiding color information scattering. In our method, the three color components (RGB) of every pixel transformed to the HSI color model are integrated in two steps: in the definitions

---

[*] Corresponding author.

C. San Martin and S.-W. Kim (Eds.): CIARP 2011, LNCS 7042, pp. 113–124, 2011.

of distances in hue, saturation and intensity planes $[\Delta_h, \Delta_s, \Delta_i]$ and in the construction of an adaptive color similarity function that combines these three distances assuming normal probability distributions.

To obtain a consistent color model for direct color comparisons, some simple but important modifications to the classical HSI color space were necessary. These modifications eliminated the discontinuities occurring in the red hue (in 0 and 360 degrees) and all the problems associated with them.

The segmentation method proposed basically relies on the calculation of an adaptive color similarity function for every pixel in a RGB 24-bit true color image. As the results in Section 4 show, the method offers a useful and efficient alternative for the segmentation of objects with different colors in relatively complex color images with good performance in the presence of the unavoidable additive noise. It has also good performance in gray level and low contrast images.

2   Previous Work

There has been a considerable amount of research dedicated to the problem of color image segmentation due to its importance and potential, and because color is an effective and robust visual cue for differentiating between objects in an image. The current available techniques and approaches vary widely from extensions of classical monochromatic techniques to mathematical morphology [2], clustering schemes [4] [10], wavelets [3] and quaternions [9], among others. Until recently, the majority of published approaches were based on monochromatic techniques applied to each color component image in different color spaces, and in different ways to produce a color composite [5].

Some color similarity measures and distances are presented in [8]. All these measures compare color pixels as units. They are all based in three dimensional vector representations of color in which each vector component corresponds to the RGB color channels components.

A technique that combines geometrical and color features for segmentation extending concepts of mathematical morphology (for gray images) is developed in [2] to process color images. The final segmentation is obtained by fusing a hierarchical partition image and a text/graphic finely detailed image. In [7], the authors argue that the common polar color spaces such as HLS, HSV, HSI, and so on are unsuited to image processing and analysis tasks. After presenting three prerequisites for 3D-polar coordinate color spaces well-suited to image processing, they derive a coordinate representation which satisfies their prerequisites that they called Improved HLS (IHLS) space. In the technique presented in [9] the color information for every pixel is represented and analyzed as a unit in the form of quaternions for which every component of the RGB color pixel corresponds to the i, j and k imaginary bases accordingly. This representation of color is shown to be effective only in the context of segmenting color images into regions of similar color texture.

The CIE L*a*b* and the CIE L*u*v* color spaces were developed expressly to represent perceptual uniformity and therefore meet the psychophysical need for a human observer. The difference between two colors can be calculated as the Euclidian distance between two color points in these spaces, an important characteristic in image segmentation [5] [8].

3 Description of the Method

The method basically relies on the calculation of a color similarity function for every pixel in a RGB 24-bit true color image to form what we call a *Color Similarity Image* (CSI), which is a gray level image. A true color image usually contains millions of colors and many thousands of them represent the same perceived color of a single object due to the presence of additive noise, lack of definition between color borders and regions, shadows in the scene, etc. [1] [6] [8]. The color similarity function allows the clustering of the many thousands colors representing the same perceived color in a single gray output image. The generation of a CSI image only requires calculating Eq. 1 for every pixel in the RGB input image. Thus the complexity is linear with respect to the number of pixels of the source image.

Firstly, we compute the color centroid and color standard deviation of a small sample consisting of few pixels. The computed centroid represents the desired color to be segmented using the technique we designed for that purpose.

Then, our color similarity function uses the color standard deviation calculated from the pixel sample to adapt the level of color scattering in the comparisons [13]. The result of a particular similarity function calculation for every pixel and the color centroid (meaning the similarity measure between the pixel and the color representative value) generates the CSI. The generation of this image is the basis of our method and preserves the information of the color selected from the original color image. This CSI is a digital representation of a continuous function $\in [0 - 1]$ extended to the range of $[0 - 255]$ which can also be viewed as a fuzzy variable of the membership function of every pixel related to a given selected color. In CSI is possible to appreciate not only the color after segmentation but also all the minimal variations in its tonalities when it is multiplied by the original image.

As can be visually observed from the experiments of section 4, the majority of CSI contain some information that is lost during the thresholding step.

The CSI can be thresholded with any non supervised method like Otsu's [11], which was the method used to obtain the results presented in this work.

To generate a CSI we need: (1) a color image in RGB 24-bit true color format and (2) a small set of arbitrarily located pixels forming a sample of the color desired to be segmented. From this sample of pixels we calculate the statistical indicators according to our HSI modified color model [13]. This information is necessary to adapt the color similarity function in order to obtain good results. To obtain the CSI we calculate for every pixel (i, j) in the image the following color similarity function S :

$$S_{i,j} = e^{\left(\frac{-\Delta_h^2}{2\sigma_h^2}\right)} * e^{\left(\frac{-\Delta_s^2}{2\sigma_s^2}\right)} * e^{\left(\frac{-\Delta_i^2}{2\sigma_i^2}\right)} \tag{1}$$

where Δ_h is the hue distance between $hue(i, j)$ and the $average\_hue$; Δ_s is the saturation distance between $saturation(i, j)$ and the $average\_saturation$; Δ_i is the intensity distance between $intensity(i, j)$ and the $average\_intensity$; σ_h is the hue standard deviation of the sample; σ_s is the Saturation standard deviation of the sample; σ_i is the Intensity standard deviation of the sample. In Eq. (1) the color information is integrated giving high importance to perceptual small changes in hue, as well as giving wide or narrow tolerance to the intensity and saturation values depending on the initial sample, which is representative to the desired color to be segmented.

The common disadvantages attributed to the cylindrical color spaces such as the irremovable singularities of hue in very low saturations or in its periodical nature [5] (which is lost in its standard representation as an $angle \in [0°, 360°]$) are overcome in our technique using vector representation in $\Re^2$, in the separation of chromatic and achromatic regions, and in the definition of the Δ_h, Δ_s and Δ_i distances.

Among the different options using the same hue and saturation attributes common in the cylindrical spaces like HSI, HSV, HLS, IHLS, etc., we use the intensity value but this choice is of minor importance because the achromatic information is much less important to discriminate colors than the chromatic one (mainly the hue). So the use of all this different spaces should give approximately the same results. The use of Gaussians in the definition of $S_{i,j}$ (Eq. 1) reflects our belief that the color model modifications proposed in this paper takes into account normal distributions of the color attributes in the modified HSI space.

3.1 Pixel Sample Selection

The pixel sample is a representation of the desired color(s) to be segmented from a color image. From this pixel sample we obtain two necessary values to feed our segmentation algorithm: the color centroid and a measure of the dispersion from this centroid, in our case the standard deviation. These two values are represented accordingly to our modified HSI model.

If we take only one pixel, its color would represent the color centroid, and would produce dispersion equal to zero, giving in the calculation of Eq. (1) a Dirac delta. This means that the similarity function would be strictly discriminative to the pixel color. This is not the general intention of segmenting color images where usually a lot of colors are present in the image, many thousands of them representing the same perceived color of a single object or region due to additive noise.

If we additionally take another pixel, we obtain then the centroid from both and the standard deviation of each one of them to feed our algorithm. So when we look for this additional pixel, we should take it from a region which was not (or poorly) segmented when we used only the first pixel.

If we continue adding more and more pixels to the sample we find that the corresponding centroid of the area to be segmented increases in accuracy. Here we may have a relatively minimum representative sample of the color area to segment. Beyond this point, increasing the number of pixels does not affect sensibly the segmentation quality because adding more pixels to the sample of the same perceived color does not affect the statistical estimators to feed the algorithm.

3.2 The Achromatic Zone G

The achromatic zone G is the region in the HSI color space where no hue is perceived. This means that color is perceived only as a gray level because the color saturation is very low or intensity is either too low or too high.

Given the three-dimensional HSI color space, we define the achromatic zone G as the union of the points inside the cylinder defined by $Saturation < 10\%$ of MAX and the two cones $Intensity < 10\%$ of MAX and $Intensity > 90\%$ of MAX, were MAX is the maximum possible value as presented in [8]. Pixels inside this region are perceived as gray levels.

3.3 Calculating the Average Hue

In order to obtain the average of the hue (H_m) of several pixels from a sample, we take advantage of the vector representation in $\Re^2$. Vectors that represent the hue values of individual pixels are combined using vector addition. From the resulting vector we obtain the average hue corresponding to the angle of this vector with respect to the red axis. Thus H_m is calculated in the following manner:

For every pixel $P(x, y)$ in the sample the following $\Re^3$ to $\Re^2$ transformation is applied:

$$V_1(P) = \begin{bmatrix} 1 & -\cos(\pi/3) & -\cos(\pi/3) \\ 0 & \sin(\pi/3) & -\sin(\pi/3) \end{bmatrix} * \begin{bmatrix} R \\ G \\ B \end{bmatrix} = \begin{bmatrix} x \\ y \end{bmatrix} \qquad \text{If } P \notin G \qquad (2)$$

and $V(P) = V_1(P)/\|V_1(P)\|$;

In other case:

$$V(P) = \begin{bmatrix} 0 \\ 0 \end{bmatrix} \qquad\qquad \text{If } P \in G$$

where $V(P)$ is the normalized projection of the RGB coordinates of the pixel P to the perpendicular plane to the Intensity axis of the RGB cube when the x axis is collinear to the Red axis of the chromatic circle. On the other hand G (see Section 3.2) represents the achromatic zone in the HSI space and $[RGB]^t$ is a vector with the color components of the pixel in the RGB color space.

3.4 Calculating the Hue Distance Δ_h

Using the vector representation of Hue obtained by the $\Re^3$ to $\Re^2$ transformation of RGB space points expressed in Eq. (2), we can calculate the hue distance Δ_h between two colors pixels or color centroids C_1 and C_2, as follows:

$$\Delta_h(C_1,C_2) = |V_1 - V_2| \qquad \text{If } C_1 \text{ and } C_2 \notin G$$

$$= 0 \qquad \text{If } C_1 \text{ or } C_2 \in G$$

where G is the achromatic region, and V_1 and V_2 are the vectors in $\Re^2$ calculated with the transformation on C_1 and C_2 given in Eq. (2).

3.5 Saturation Distance and Intensity Distance

We can calculate them by using the standard conversions for saturation and intensity from RGB to HIS space [8], normalized in the range [0, 1]:

$$saturation(P) = 1 - \left[\frac{3}{R+G+B} \min(R,G,B) \right] \qquad (3)$$

$$intensity(P) = \frac{1}{3}(R+G+B)$$

In expression (3), we defined the saturation equal zero in case of the black color.

We use the Euclidean distance to define saturation distance Δ_s and intensity distance Δ_i between two pixels or color centroids.

The CSI is a gray level image, so it can be dealt with any mathematical morphology technique used for gray level images. Filters, operators, thresholds, etc. can be applied directly to the CSI when geometrical characteristics are considered. The common intensity image can be processed too as a complementary information source. The generation of a CSI only requires calculating Eq. 1 for every pixel in the RGB input image. Thus the complexity is linear with respect to the number of pixels of the source image.

4 Results and Discussion

In this section we present the results of our segmentation method applied to three difficult to segment images: a classical complex color image, a gray level infrared image and a low contrast color image. These experiments consisted of segmentation color regions according to the following two steps:

1) Selection of the pixel sample. This is the only step to be left up to the user. In order to have a helping direction for this task the following considerations may be useful to select the number of pixels of the sample: If the color of the desired area to segment is solid (without additive noise) it is only necessary to have one pixel sample from the desired area. However, if we want to take in account the color lack of definition happening in the borders, we have to take a sample of the new colors that appear in that area due to the above condition. The pixels of the samples from the original images can be selected arbitrarily, that is, in any order, in any number and physically adjacent or not.

2)   CSI calculation. This step is automatic; its output is a gray image showing the similarity of each pixel of the RGB true color image to the color centroid formed with the chosen pixel sample taken from the region of interest to be segmented, being white for 100% of similarity and black for 0%.

The user can threshold now the CSI. This step could be necessary to obtain a template for a final segmentation of the desired color from the region of interest; it could be arranged as an automatic step by using, for example, the non-supervised Otsu's thresholding method [11]. This guarantees than the colors segmented be the real ones. During the thresholding of the CSI some information may be lost what could not be convenient. If the CSI itself is used as a template, then we get better segmented areas (without loss of pixels), one for each selected color, but then they are altered in some measure due to the intrinsically gray levels that conform the CSI.

Figure 1 shows an RGB color image (sized 301 x 226 pixels and 27146 different colors) of tissue stained with hemotoxylin and eosin (H&E), which is a very popular staining method in histology and the most widely used stain in medical diagnosis. This staining method helps pathologists to distinguish different tissue types [12].

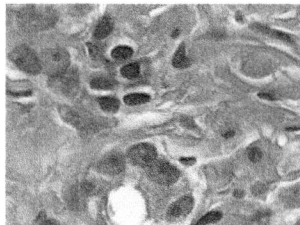
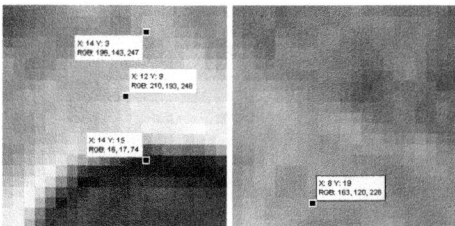

Fig. 1. Stained tissue   **Fig. 2.** Sample composed by 4 pixels located in two zones with blue color

In this image we can see three main hues of colors despite the thousands (more than 27,000 colors) of actual RGB values to represent them: blue, pink and white. Different pixel tonalities in the image depend on their particular saturation and on the unavoidable presence of additive noise. The proposed color segmentation method is practically immune to these conditions, although obviously some solutions could be used to improve the quality of the segmented regions, as for example, preprocessing the image for smoothing noises of different types, applying some morphological method to reduce objects with given characteristics, and so on.

In this experiment we took a sample composed by 4 pixels located in two zones with blue color. They are selected from an enlarged 21 x 21 pixels region as shown in Fig. 2.

From this sample we calculated the color centroid and the standard deviation in our modified HSI space; with these two values we use the Eq. 1 to calculate for every pixel the pixel values of the CSI shown in Fig. 3.

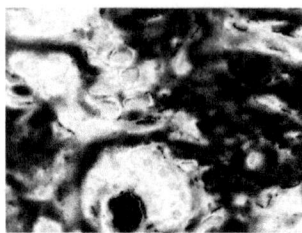
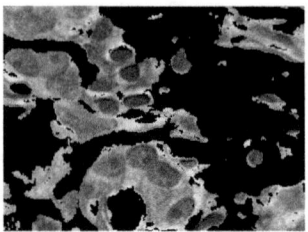

Fig. 3. The Color Similarity Image (CSI) of blue

Fig. 4. Zones of the segmented blue color

After applying Otsu's thresholding method we obtained the color segmentation shown in Fig. 4.

For the pink area we repeated the same process. Figure 5 shows the pixels sample (from 4 pixels), its corresponding CSI is shown in Fig. 6 and the final segmentation of the pink zone is shown in Fig. 7.

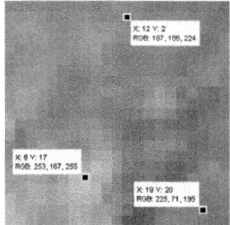

Fig. 5. Pixels sample of 4 points for the pink color

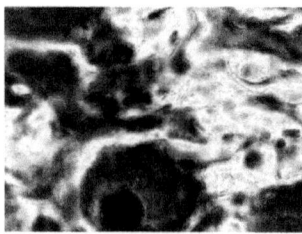
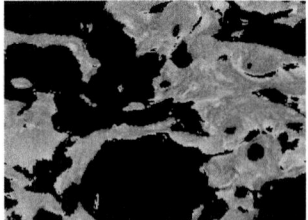

Fig. 6. CSI of the pink color

Fig. 7. Zones of the segmented pink color

Repeating the above process in Fig. 8 we show the pixel sample and in Fig. 9 the CSI (left) and the final segmentation of white color areas (right).

In Figure 10 (right) we show a composite image of Fig. 4, Fig. 7, and Fig. 9 (right) using consecutively the logical XOR operation. We use this operation instead of the OR one to guarantee that in the composite image a given pixel appear only in one color segmented zone, as it is expected in all segmentation task. The black pixels

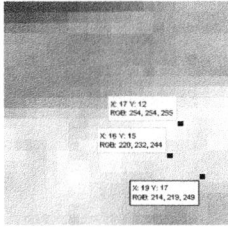 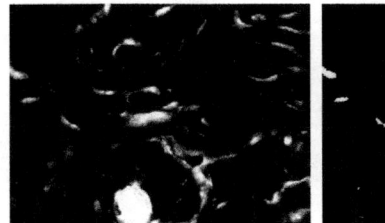 

Fig. 8. Pixel sample for the white color

Fig. 9. CSI of the white color (left) and zones of the segmented white color (right)

represent those colors that were not segmented by any of the three color choices or, on the contrary, when the pixel appeared with the same value (1 or 0) in two binary images (they were made black by the consecutive XOR operation). In this example, non-segmented pixels were 4546 pixels from a total of 68026 pixels, which is only 6.6% (4546/68026) of the total number of pixels of the original image. It can be observed in Fig 10 (right) that a good amount of the black pixels belongs to borders between regions of different colors where they are clearly undefined.

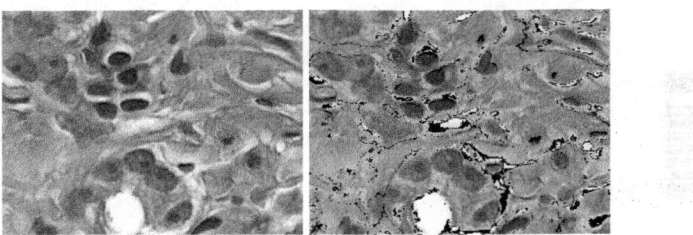

Fig. 10. Original image (left) and composite image (right)

Comparing both images in Fig. 10 demonstrates the accuracy of the blue, pink and white segmented zones obtained by the method, not only from the point of view of the number of segmented pixels but from the point of view also of the quality of the tonalities of the colors that appear in the original image. These results were obtained with as few as only 12 pixels belonging to only three samples, one associated to each color blue, pink and white. The composite image shown in Fig. 10 (right) was created through the selection of samples with a maximum of 4 pixels for each color considered to be segmented. The size and/or shape of the segmented regions of different colors depend on the number, the distribution and quantity of pixels that makes up each sample, as well as if two or more samples have pixels with the same or very similar color. With samples well selected the method guarantee very good color segmentation.

It is possible with the proposed color segmentation method to divide a region having a particular color (i. e. blue region in Fig. 4) in two or more sub-regions having the same basic color (blue) but having two different saturation (darker nuclei with clearer zones surrounding them). Figure 11 shows the seven pixels sample selected from two different zones belonging to the darker blue nuclei.

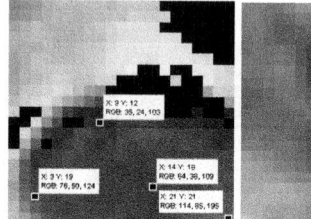

Fig. 11. Sample of 7 pixels corresponding to the blue nuclei

Figure 12 shows the CSI of dark blue nuclei, and Fig. 13 shows the final segmented image. Figure 14 shows the well-differentiated nuclei (colored in green) surrounded by clearer blue zones. The possibilities of the method are many, requiring only a few well-selected samples from well-distributed zones and having the suitable number of pixels each.

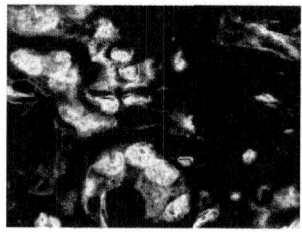 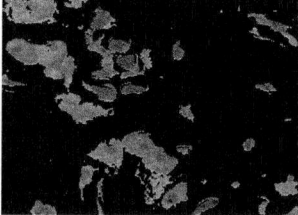 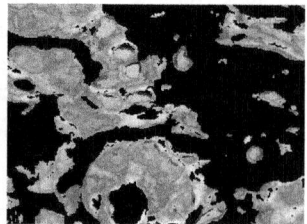

Fig. 12. CSI of blue nuclei   **Fig. 13.** Segmented darker blue nuclei   **Fig. 14.** Well differentiated green nuclei surrounded by clearer blue zones

We will show the good results obtained by our method applied to gray images and low contrast color images in the following two examples. Figure 15 shows a gray level image obtained with an infrared camera; we took a small pixel sample (of 4 pixels) from the face area and obtain its correspondent CSI shown in Figure 16. The segmented face appears in figure 17 after thresholding with Otsu method.

In Figure 18 a fossil inserted in a rock is shown, we took a small pixel sample of the fossil area from which we obtained its corresponding CSI (Fig 19). Figure 20 shows the resulting image after thresholding with Otsu method.

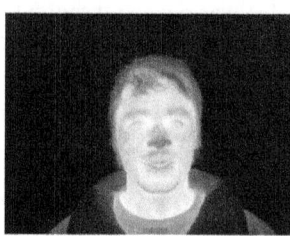  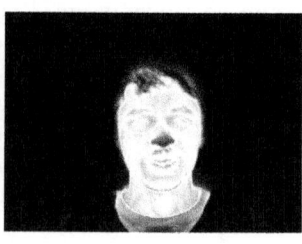 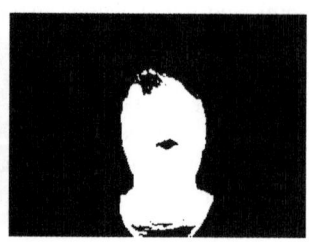

Fig. 15. Infrared image   **Fig. 16.** CSI of face   **Fig. 17.** Segmented face

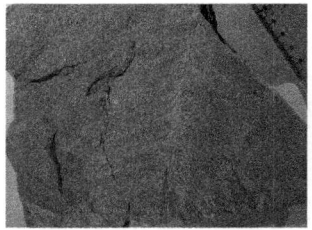 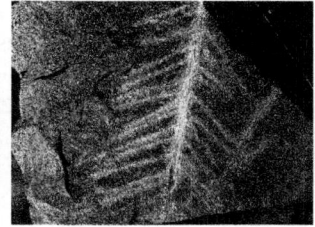 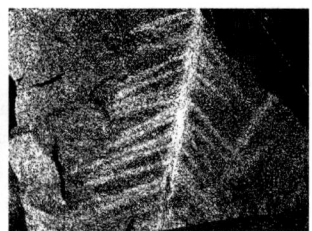

Fig. 18. Leaf fossil in rock   **Fig. 19.** CSI of fossil   **Fig. 20.** Threshold by Otsu

5 Conclusions

The results in the previous section demonstrate that the color segmentation method presented in this paper offers a useful and efficient alternative for the segmentation of objects with different colors in relatively complex color images with good performance in the presence of the unavoidable additive noise, in images with low contrast and also in gray level images.

The steps required to obtain a good segmentation of regions with different colors by using the proposed methodology are usually straightforward, simple and repetitive. If color (or a given gray level) is a discriminative characteristic, only the selection of a given threshold to the color similarity function CSI is needed to obtain a good segmentation result. From many experiments we have observed that colors were obtained in a straightforward way only by thresholding the Color Similarity Image.

In our method, the three RGB color components of every pixel transformed to the HSI color model are integrated in two steps: in the definitions of distances $[\Delta_h, \Delta_s, \Delta_i]$ in hue, saturation and intensity planes and in the construction of an adaptive color similarity function that combines these three distances assuming normal probability distributions. Thus the complexity is linear ($O[n]$) with respect to the number of pixels n of the source image. The method discriminates whichever type of different color objects independently on their shapes and tonalities in a very straightforward way.

Acknowledgements. The authors of this paper thank the Computing Research Center (CIC), Mexico, Research and Postgraduate Secretary (SIP), Mexico, and National Polytechnic Institute (IPN), Mexico, for their support.

References

1. Alvarado-Cervantes R.: Segmentación de patrones lineales topológicamente diferentes, mediante agrupamientos en el espacio de color HSI. M. Sc. Thesis, Center for Computing Research, National Polytechnic Institute, Mexico (2006)
2. Angulo, J., Serra, J.: Mathematical morphology in color spaces applied to the analysis of cartographic images. In: Proceedings of International Congress GEOPRO, México (2003)

3. Bourbakis, N., Yuan, P., Makrogiannis, S.: Object recognition using wavelets, L-G graphs and synthesis of regions. Pattern Recognition 40, 2077–2096 (2007)
4. Chang, H., Yeung, D.Y.: Robust path-based spectral clustering. Pattern Recognition 41, 191–203 (2008)
5. Cheng, H., Jiang, X., Sun, Y., Wang, J.: Color image segmentation: Advances and prospects. Pattern Recognition 34(12), 2259–2281 (2001)
6. Gonzalez, R.C., Woods, R.E.: Digital Image Processing, 3rd edn. Prentice Hall, USA (2008)
7. Hanbury, A., Serra, J.A.: 3D-polar coordinate colour representation suitable for image analysis. Technical Report PRIP-TR-77, Austria (2002)
8. Plataniotis, K.N., Venetsanopoulos, A.N.: Color Image Processing and Applications, 1st edn. Springer, Germany (2000)
9. Shi, L., Funt, B.: Quaternion color texture segmentation. Computer Vision and Image Understanding 107, 88–96 (2007)
10. Van den Broek, E.L., Schouten, T.E., Kisters, P.M.F.: Modelling human color categorization. Pattern Recognition Letters (2007)
11. Otsu, N.: A threshold selection method from gray-level histograms. IEEE Trans. Sys., Man., Cyber. 9, 62–66 (1979)
12. Matlab v 7.4.0.287: Image Processing Toolbox, Color-Based Segmentation Using K-Means Clustering (R2007a)
13. Alvarado-Cervantes, R., Felipe-Riveron, E.M., Sanchez-Fernandez, L.P.: Color Image Segmentation by Means of a Similarity Function. In: Bloch, I., Cesar Jr., R.M. (eds.) CIARP 2010. LNCS, vol. 6419, pp. 319–328. Springer, Heidelberg (2010)

A New Prior Shape Model for Level Set Segmentation

Poay Hoon Lim[1], Ulas Bagci[2], and Li Bai[1]

[1] School of Computer Science, University of Nottingham, Nottingham, NG8 1BB
`phl@cs.nott.ac.uk, bai@cs.nott.ac.uk`
[2] Radiology and Imaging Science Department, NIH, MD 20892
`ulas.bagci@nih.gov`

Abstract. Level set methods are effective for image segmentation problems. However, the methods suffer from limitations such as slow convergence and leaking problems. As such, over the past two decades, the original level set method has been evolved in many directions, including integration of prior shape models into the segmentation framework. In this paper, we introduce a new prior shape model for level set segmentation. With a shape model represented implicitly by a signed distance function, we incorporate a local shape parameter to the shape model. This parameter helps to regulate the model fitting process. Based on this local parameter of the shape model, we define a shape energy to drive the level set evolution for image segmentation. The shape energy is coupled with a Gaussian kernel, which acts as a weight distribution on the shape model. This Gaussian effect not only allows evolution of level set to deform around the shape model, but also provides a smoothing effect along the edges. Our approach presents a new dimension to extract local shape parameter directly from the shape model, which is different from previous work that focused on an indirect manner of feature extractions. Experimental results on synthetic, optical and MR images demonstrate the feasibility of this new shape model and shape energy.

Keywords: image segmentation, level set method, prior shape model, shape energy.

1 Introduction

Image segmentation is fundamental to image understanding. Although region and boundary-based segmentation methods have been implemented successfully in many physical applications, these classical methods still not fully utilize the image information to achieve their purposes, for example, in clinical applications. Since its introduction by Osher and Sethian [10], the level set methods have been widely used for image segmentation. For highly challenging segmentation tasks such as tracking moving objects, segmenting occluded scenes and objects of interest from medical images, level set methods have achieved promising results when coupled with prior knowledge or prior shape models [6],[7],[12],[14],[16]. When information such as gradient is missing from images, the prior shape

C. San Martin and S.-W. Kim (Eds.): CIARP 2011, LNCS 7042, pp. 125–132, 2011.
© Springer-Verlag Berlin Heidelberg 2011

helps level set evolve toward the desired region of interest. The segmentation is determined by a dissimilarity measure between the evolving level set function and the prior shape. Different shape models and shape representations have been proposed to couple with the level set methods over the past 10 years. For example, Leventon et al. [9] suggested the representation of a set of training shapes by the principal component of their signed distance function; Tsai [16] proposed to carry out optimization directly within the subspace of the first few eigenmodes. Other examples of shape models for level set can be found in Rousson and Paragios [12],[13]. However, these models suffer from shortcomings such as the predefined statistical data distribution might be invalid because it differs from the actual data distribution [5], or modeling non-linear variability of the data with linear methods may not be admissible etc. A more comprehensive review on statistical approaches on integrating shape for level set segmentation is discussed by Cremer et al [8].

In this paper, we introduce a new shape model and an associated shape energy for level set segmentation. Our inspirations come from the work presented by Rousson and Paragios [14]. While Rousson introduces a confidence map to identify the reliability of shape fitting process during level set evolution, we focus on extracting local statistical properties from the shape model to enhance the level set evolution. Our segmentation framework consists of two new features: a local shape variance and a kernel weighted functional.

2   The Segmentation Framework

2.1   Level Set Method

The level set technique, also known as the implicit deformable model, is by embedding the interface in a higher dimensional scalar function. The interface is represented implicitly as a level set (usually the zero-th level set) of the introduced scalar function. The rest of the scalar function is defined as the signed distance function from the interface, i.e., the level set.

Suppose that the level set $\phi(x)$ is evolving in time, i.e., $\phi(x(t), t) = 0$. Taking derivative of the last equation with respect to t yields

$$\frac{\partial \phi}{\partial t} + \nabla \phi(x(t), t) \cdot x'(t) = 0.$$

As the rate of change of $x(t)$ is in the normal direction of the surface, $\boldsymbol{n} = \frac{\nabla \phi}{|\nabla \phi|}$, one can rewrite the equation as

$$\frac{\partial \phi}{\partial t} + F|\nabla \phi| = 0,$$

where $F = x'(t) \cdot \frac{\nabla \phi}{|\nabla \phi|}$ represents the speed function. In recent development of level set function, the "variational level set method" is introduced: An energy $E(\phi)$ is defined in relation to the the speed function. The minimization of such energy which generates the Euler-Lagrange equation, provides the evolution equation through the calculus of variation:

$$\frac{\partial \phi}{\partial t} = -\frac{\partial E(\phi)}{\partial \phi}.$$

Our purpose is to integrate shape energy into this evolution equation, i.e., to define a speed function for level set evolution with the introduction of local parameter from a shape model.

2.2   Prior Shape Model

Inspired by Rousson and Paragios [14], our prior shape model is constructed from a set of training samples represented implicitly by signed distance functions $\{\phi_1, \phi_2, \ldots, \phi_N\}$. An initial shape model is obtained by taking the average from these signed distance functions. A re-initialization algorithm [15] is then applied to this initial shape model to approximate a signed distance function, ϕ_m, which becomes the shape model. In our case, ϕ_m forms a global parameter of the shape model. In order to better represent the local information of the shape model, we use a locally enhance, neighboring dependent variance to capture the local shape features:

$$\sigma_l^2 = \sum_{x \in \{\phi=0\}} \sum_{x_i \in U_x} \frac{(\phi_m(x_i) - \phi_m(x))^2}{|U_x|},$$

where $U_x \subset \phi_m$ is a local window surrounding x. This local shape parameter not only maintains the smoothness of the shape model, but also incorporates the local features of the shape. The local variance taken around a pixel-wise neighborhood in the shape model provides an insight into the localized properties on the signed distance function: larger variance indicates a larger average distance difference, i.e., a steeper change in the level set function. This has a better physical representation in comparison to the variance obtained for voxel-wise approach in the training samples.

2.3   The Shape Energy

Global variance and variance for shape model were used in various work in the past. However, these variances might not reflect the desired shape model information accurately due to variations such as ill alignment of the training samples, wide range of scaling etc. Under certain extreme circumstances, such variations might jeopardize the accuracy of level set evolution. Bear in mind of these limitations, we propose a regularized factor to accompany the energy that incorporates local statistical features. This regularized term is extracted from the prior shape model by taking into account the local average of signed distance function. To achieve our purpose, we use a pixel-wise local statistical variance from the shape model, σ_l^2. This is in line with the localization of the shape model whereby information is integrating from local neighborhood. The localization along the level set shall enhance the control of the edge based stopping functional.

To formulate the shape energy, we adopt the symmetric dissimilarity measure between two shapes proposed by Chan and Zhu [3], Riklin-Raviv [11], Charpiat [4]:

$$D(\phi, \phi_m) = \int_\Omega \frac{1}{2} \left(H(\phi) - H(\phi_m) \right)^2 dx,$$

where $H(\phi)$ is the Heaviside function. This is then incorporated with an external energy that drive the zero level set towards the object boundary [1]:

$$E_1(\phi) = \lambda \int_\Omega g\delta(\phi)|\nabla\phi|\, dx,$$

where g is the edge indicator function $g = \frac{1}{1+|\nabla G_\sigma * I|^2}$, and G_σ is the Gaussian kernel with standard deviation σ.

The total energy is thus

$$\begin{aligned} E(\phi) &= D(\phi, \phi_m) + E_1(\phi) \\ &= \int_\Omega \frac{1}{2} \left(H(\phi) - H(\phi_m) \right)^2 dx + \lambda \int_\Omega g\delta(\phi)|\nabla\phi|\, dx. \end{aligned}$$

By taking the Gâteaux derivative of $E(\phi)$, followed by the gradient decent flow that minimizes the functional

$$\frac{\partial\phi}{\partial t} = -\frac{\partial E}{\partial\phi},$$

we obtain the standard evolution equation

$$\frac{\partial\phi}{\partial t} = -\left(H(\phi) - H(\phi_m) \right)\delta(\phi) - \lambda\delta(\phi)div\left(g\frac{\nabla\phi}{|\nabla\phi|} \right).$$

Now, to incorporate the regularizing effect from shape model's local parameter into the level set evolution, we consider a variation of the above evolution equation by multiplying it with a weighted constraint:

$$w(\phi) = \frac{1}{2\sigma_l^2} e^{-(H(\phi)-H(\phi_m))^2/2\sigma_l^2},$$

where σ_l^2 is the local variance along the level set. Note that $w(\phi)$ acts as a "weighing" function giving the evolution term $(H(\phi) - H(\phi_m))\delta(\phi)$ higher influence when the difference between the level set and the shape model is larger. Hence, our level set evolution equation is

$$\frac{\partial\phi}{\partial t} = -\frac{1}{2\sigma_l^2} e^{-(H(\phi)-H(\phi_m))^2/2\sigma_l^2} \left((H(\phi) - H(\phi_m))\delta(\phi) + \lambda\delta(\phi)div\left(g\frac{\nabla\phi}{|\nabla\phi|} \right) \right).$$

3   Experimental Results

We implement the proposed framework on synthetic noisy images and optical images with partial blurring effect as well as MR images of spine. For synthetic images, we created five synthetic images of various sizes and aspect ratios as training samples while for optical and MR images, we use four and six training samples respectively. The classical edge based [1] and region based methods [2] are used to compare and to highlight the effectiveness of our approach.

In Fig. 1, we show the shape model and local shape variance of the sample images. The zero level set or shape contour are outlined from the signed distance function images to show the shape model used in our experiments. The contour of training samples are plotted on the extracted local shape parameter images. Images of voxel-wise variance on the shape models are illustrated here for the purpose of comparison with our proposed local variance information. Unlike the

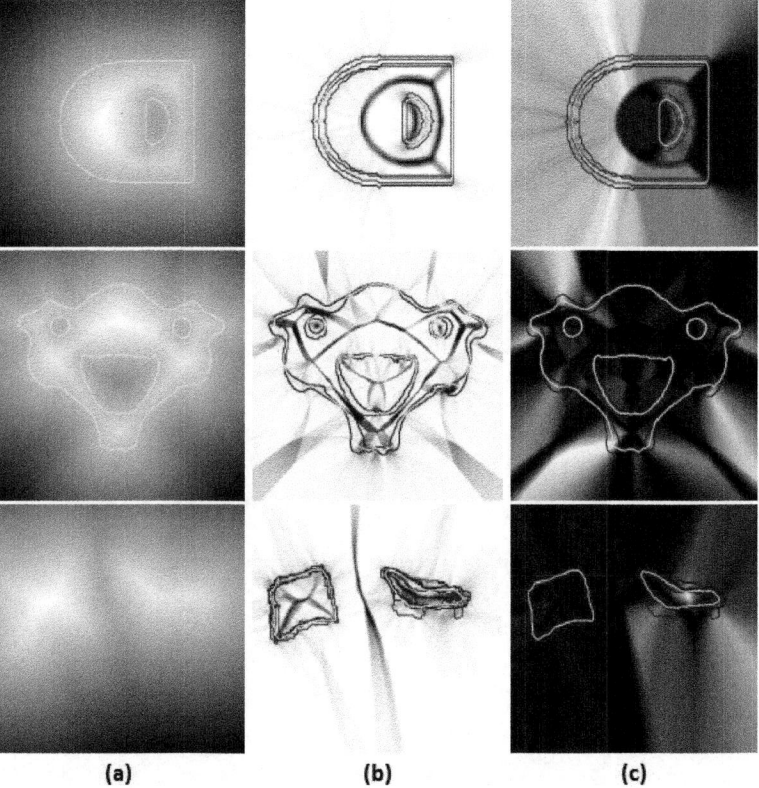

(a)   (b)   (c)

Fig. 1. The shape model is outlined in red while the training samples are outlined in blue. (a) The shape model and (b) variance local used in our proposed prior shape model for synthetic image (top), optical image (middle) and MR image of spine (bottom) respectively. (c) The voxel-wise variance are shown as comparison to our proposed local shape parameter.

voxel-wise variance, this local shape parameter highlights the local variations of shape model without creating unwanted excessive variation effects outside the shape model neighborhoods, which happens to the voxel-wise variance. The absence of these excessive side effect helps to ensure the stability of this local shape parameter when applying to level set evolutions.

Fig. 2 demonstrates results obtained from the edge based, region based and shape based approaches respectively. A well known fact on the edge based approach is its sensitivity to initial contour placement, this can be observed from the MR image sample, where part of the image contour is badly located when the initial contour is placed across the edge of region of interest. In addition, even when the initial contour is placed inside the region of interest, the segmentation result is still not as accurate comparing to the results from our proposed shape based approach. Obviously the segmentation for synthetic and optical images by edge based method are not effective because the method cannot handle blurring edges. Although the region based is not sensitive to initial contour placement, the inhomogeneity of image intensities has caused the mal performance of the method on MR image and it is not accurate on blurring edges, as

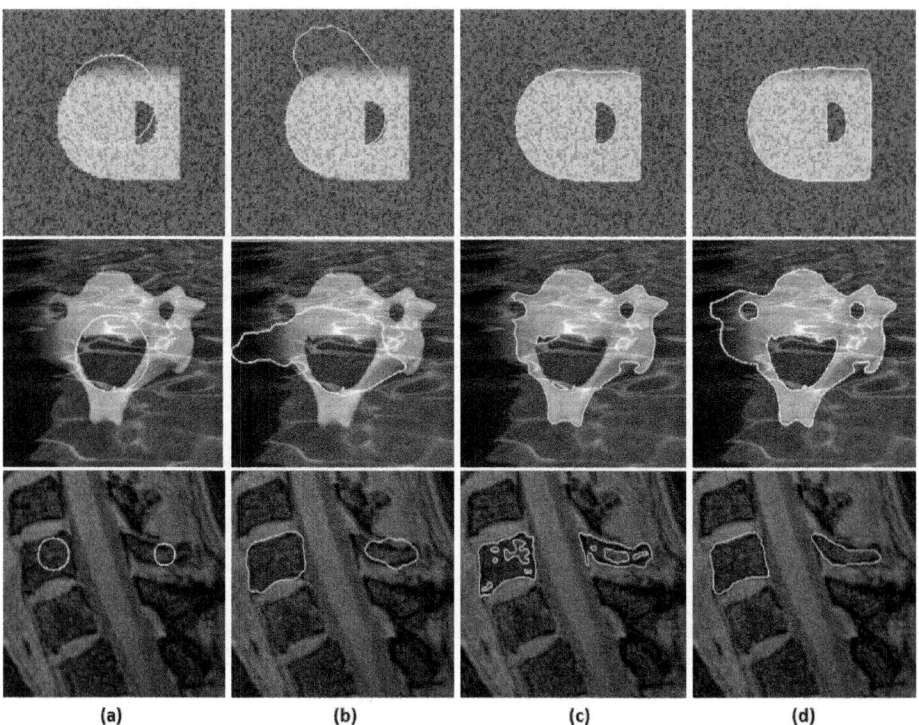

(a)   (b)   (c)   (d)

Fig. 2. (a) The initial contour placement used by all the methods for segmentation. Results obtained by (b) edge based method, (c) region based method and (d) our proposed shape prior based method for synthetic image (top), optical image (middle) and MR image of spine (bottom).

seen on synthetic and optical images. Whereas results from our shape based approach clearly highlight the region of interest in all sample images and achieved an average accuracy of 93% when tested on fifteen sample images.

4   Conclusion

We have proposed a new image segmentation framework encompassing area dissimilarity, shape model and local variance. Our shape model guides the level set evolution through the introduction of a local shape parameter, together with a new shape energy. The shape parameter provides localized information that acts as a moderator for the shape model and in the level set evolution process. Although our work is inspired by by Rousson and Paragios [14], we take a different path in our approach. Unlike their work whereby emphasis is on capturing the shape model reliability and alignment during level set evolution, we look closer into the local property of shape model and to incorporate it into the segmentation process. In particular, we focus on integrating the local variance of shape model into the level set evolution for regularizing purposes. The proposed segmentation framework has been tested on synthetic images with added noise and blurring effect, as well as on MR images of spine. Experimental results on these images are promising. We merely use one local feature for this work, i.e., the local variance of shape model. Future work is to explore and encompass more information from the shape model, for example, the local geometrical features and to couple it into the level set segmentation framework. Although similar work has been carried out in the past, somehow the information is extracted in an indirect manner, i.e., through the principal component analysis of shape model, and the extracted information are mostly in global sense. With a more direct approach in acquiring information from shape model, we anticipate to obtain better shape parameters for level set segmentation.

Acknowledgments. The authors would like to thank Professor Jayaram K. Udupa of Department of Radiology, University of Pennsylvania for the medical data and advice.

References

1. Caselles, V., Kimmel, R., Sapiro, G.: Geodesic active contours. International Journal of Computer Vision 22(1), 61–79 (1997)
2. Chan, T.F., Vese, L.A.: Active contours without edges. IEEE Transactionson Image Processing 10(2), 266–277 (2001)
3. Chan, T., Zhu, W.: Level set based shape prior segmentation. Technical Report 03-66, Computational Applied Mathematics, UCLA, Los Angeles, USA (2003)
4. Charpiat, G., Faugreas, O., Keriven, R.: Approximations of shape metrics and application to shape warping and empirical shape statistics. Journal of Foundations of Computational Mathematics 5(1), 1–58 (2005)
5. Cremers, D., Kohlberger, T., Schnorr, C.: Shape Statistics in Kernel Space for Variational Image Segmentation. Pattern Recognition 36(9), 1929–1943 (2003)

6. Cremers, D., Osher, S.J., Soatto, S.: Kernel Density Estimation and Intrinsic Alignment for Shape Priors in Level Set Segmentation. International Journal of Computer Vision 69(3), 335–351 (2006)
7. Cremers, D.: Dynamical statistical shape priors for level set based tracking. IEEE Transaction on Pattern Analysis and Machine Intelligence 28(8), 1262–1273 (2006)
8. Cremers, D., Rousson, M., Deriche, R.: A Review of Statistical Approaches to Level Set Segmentation: Integrating Color, Texture, Motion and Shape. International Journal of Computer Vision 72(2), 195–215 (2007)
9. Leventon, M., Grimson, E., Faugeras, O.: Level set based segmentation with intensity and curvature priors. IEEE Mathematical Methods in Biomedical Image Analysis, 4–11 (2000)
10. Osher, S., Sethian, J.A.: Fronts propagating with curvature-dependent speed: Algorithms based on Hamilton-Jacobi formulations. Journal of Computational Physics 79(1), 12–49 (1988)
11. Riklin-Raviv, T., Kiryati, N., Sochen, N.: Unlevel-sets: Geometry and prior-based segmentation. In: Pajdla, T., Matas, J(G.) (eds.) ECCV 2004, Part IV. LNCS, vol. 3024, pp. 50–61. Springer, Heidelberg (2004)
12. Rousson, M., Paragios, N.: Shape priors for level set representations. In: Heyden, A., Sparr, G., Nielsen, M., Johansen, P. (eds.) ECCV 2002, Part II. LNCS, vol. 2351, pp. 78–92. Springer, Heidelberg (2002)
13. Rousson, M., Paragios, N., Deriche, R.: Implicit active shape models for 3d segmentation in MRI imaging. In: Barillot, C., Haynor, D.R., Hellier, P. (eds.) MICCAI 2004, Part I. LNCS, vol. 3216, pp. 209–216. Springer, Heidelberg (2004)
14. Rousson, M., Paragios, N.: Prior Knowledge, Level Set Representations & Visual Grouping. Int. J. Comput. Vis. 76, 231–243 (2008)
15. Sussman, M., Smereka, P., Osher, S.: A level Set Approach for Computing Solutions to Incompresible Two-Phase Flow. Journal of Computational Physics 114, 146–159 (2002)
16. Tsai, A., Yezzi Jr., A., Wells, W., Tempany, C., Tucker, D., Fan, A., Grimson, W., Willsky, A.: A Shape-Based Approach to The Segmentation of Medical Imagery Using Level Sets. IEEE Trans. on Medical Imaging 22(2), 137–154 (2003)

Efficient 3D Curve Skeleton Extraction from Large Objects*

László Szilágyi, Sándor Miklós Szilágyi, David Iclănzan, and Lehel Szabó

Sapientia - Hungarian Science University of Transylvania,
Faculty of Technical and Human Science, Tîrgu-Mureş, Romania
lalo@ms.sapientia.ro

Abstract. Curve skeletons are used for linear representation of 3D objects in a wide variety of engineering and medical applications. The outstandingly robust and flexible curve skeleton extraction algorithm, based on generalized potential fields, suffers from seriously heavy computational burden. In this paper we propose and evaluate a hierarchical formulation of the algorithm, which reduces the space where the skeleton is searched, by excluding areas that are unlikely to contain relevant skeleton branches. The algorithm was evaluated using dozens of object volumes. Tests revealed that the computational load of the skeleton extraction can be reduced up to 100 times, while the accuracy doesn't suffer relevant damage.

Keywords: 3D curve skeleton, potential fields, hierarchical algorithm, parallel computation, graphical processing units.

1 Introduction

In the two dimensional case, the medial axis of an object is the collection of points that have at least two closest points to the boundary of the object. On the other hand, the skeleton is defined as the locus of centers of maximal circles inscribed within the object. A circle C is considered maximal, if there is no other circle inscribed in the object that entirely contains C. In two dimensions, the medial axis and the skeleton are practically the same.

In three dimensions, the medial surface is the term that corresponds to 2D medial axis. The medial surface also contains linear curves in places where there are at least three surfaces at the same distance. Figure 1(left) shows the medial surface of an object. There are several 3D computer graphics applications, where 3D objects are desired to be represented as a collection of linear curves. For example, the inverse kinematics, which is very practical and thus quite popular in animations, demands such a representation. However, the 3D skeleton of an object does not have a mathematical definition. We could say that the 3D curve skeleton (3DCS) is a subset of the medial surface, a collection of curves which is centered within the object, but that is not a rigorous definition. Figure 1(right) the desired shape of the 3DCS of an object.

---

* This work was supported by the Sapientia Institute for Research Programs.

C. San Martin and S.-W. Kim (Eds.): CIARP 2011, LNCS 7042, pp. 133–140, 2011.

There are several 3DCS extraction algorithms, which approximate this curve collection based on different physical approaches. All of them give an approximation of the 3DCS. As we will see later, the segments of the skeleton shown in Fig. 1(right) will be slightly bent in the proximity of bifurcation points.

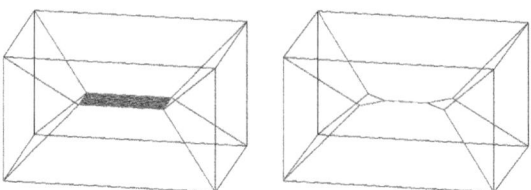

Fig. 1. Medial surface (left) and 3D curve skeleton (right) of a deformed cube

The most important properties the 3DCSs share are:

1. Homotopic: the curve skeleton is required to be topologically equivalent to the original object, that is, the number of connected components, tunnels and cavities should be the same [11].
2. Invariant to isometric transformations: this is important in applications where the skeleton is used as shape descriptor.
3. Thin: curve skeletons are one dimensional. In discrete applications they can be either single voxel wide lines, or zero width lines described by points having real valued coordinates.
4. Centered: the curve skeleton lays within the medial surface of the objects, and is centered within the surface patches it belongs to [12].
5. Curve skeletons are reliable if all surface points are visible from some place on the skeleton [9].
6. A curve skeleton extraction method is robust, if the resulting skeleton is not sensitive to small variations of the boundary.

In the discrete case, 2D skeleton extraction is traditionally performed by thinning via hit-or-miss transform, by applying the L mask family from Golay's alphabet. Most of the algorithms developed for 3DCS extraction also work in 2D. They will be enumerated in the followings. The literature of 3D curve skeleton extraction consists of several various approaches:

1. Thinning and boundary propagation methods iteratively remove so-called *simple points* from the objects, which by definition, do not influence the topology of the object [3]. Methods vary according to the criteria they apply to find simple points.
2. Distance field based methods apply the distance transform with a selected chamfer metric, for each internal point of the object, and extract the skeleton from the distance field data [4].
3. Geometric methods are generally applied to objects described as triangular or polygonal meshes. The most popular algorithmic scheme in this family is mesh contraction [2].

4. General field based methods were first introduced in 2D formulation [1,8]. 3D solutions use potential fields [5,6], repulsive force fields [13,14], or radial basis functions [10] to create a general field. The skeleton is extracted afterwards based on some special points (complete extinguishment and saddle points) within the field.

2   Generalized Potential Field

According to the theory of electrostatics, every electrical charge generates a potential field. This means that whenever another charged object approaches the initial one, it will be attracted or repelled according to the sign of both charges. The magnitude of the force is computed as: $F = kq_1q_2/d^2$, where k is a constant, d is the distance between the two charged objects, while q_A an q_B are the two charges. In case of the generalized potential field applied in computer graphics, the constant k is neglected, the charges are considered unitary and of same polarity, while the distance is treated in a generalized way, in the sense that the magnitude of the force is equal to the $-\alpha$'th power of the distance: $F = d^{-\alpha}$. In other words, the force vector that applies to charged object B, because of the presence of charged object A, is: $\boldsymbol{F} = \boldsymbol{d}_{AB}|\boldsymbol{d}_{AB}|^{-(\alpha+1)}$, where $\boldsymbol{d}_{AB}$ represents the distance vector between the objects. Expressed in 3D Euclidean coordinates, the components of the above force vectors are:

$$F_x = \frac{x_B - x_A}{|\boldsymbol{d}_{AB}|^{\alpha+1}} \qquad F_y = \frac{y_B - y_A}{|\boldsymbol{d}_{AB}|^{\alpha+1}} \qquad F_z = \frac{z_B - z_A}{|\boldsymbol{d}_{AB}|^{\alpha+1}} \;, \qquad (1)$$

where A and B represent the points where the charges are placed, and the length of the vector $\boldsymbol{d}_{AB}$ is $|\boldsymbol{d}_{AB}| = \sqrt{(x_B - x_A)^2 + (y_B - y_A)^2 + (z_B - z_A)^2}$.

The generalized potential field is applied as follows. At first, electrical charge is placed and uniformly distributed upon the outer surface of the object. In the following step, the generalized potential field is computed in every internal grid point of the object. Or in other words, a small object with unit charge virtually marches over every internal grid point, and the electrostatic force vector that applies to the object is computed for each position.

The formula of the GPF is deduced by summing all its components. All external point charges may have their effect to the electrostatic field in any internal point, so we need to sum up all vectors:

$$\mathcal{F}(I) = \sum_{P \in \Omega} F_x(I, P) \times \boldsymbol{i} + \sum_{P \in \Omega} F_y(I, P) \times \boldsymbol{j} + \sum_{P \in \Omega} F_z(I, P) \times \boldsymbol{k} \;, \qquad (2)$$

where $\boldsymbol{i}$, $\boldsymbol{j}$, $\boldsymbol{k}$ represent the unit vectors in the three main axial directions, and Ω is the set of surface points that hold the external charges. The above formula is a good approximation of the GPF in internal point I, but is not exact. As it was already pointed out (but not applied) in [7], only those external points should be included in Ω, from which the internal point I is visible. Visibility can be described mathematically with the following expression:

$$I \text{ is visible from } P \Leftrightarrow \lambda I + (1 - \lambda)P \text{ is an internal point } \forall 0 < \lambda \leq 1 \;. \qquad (3)$$

The identification of the curve skeleton from the computed GPF is produced in several steps:

1. Find the critical points, where GPF is a zero vector. These will generally be points where two or more branches of the skeleton meet, or in other words, points where the skeleton bifurcates. They usually will not fall in exact grid points, but we can easily locate the unit sized cube volume where they are situated. We need to look for those cubes where all three vector components $\mathcal{F}_x$, $\mathcal{F}_y$, and $\mathcal{F}_z$ change their sign.
2. At the time when critical points are located, we can also check, which are the cubes where not all three, but at least one of the three components change their sign. These cubes will contain so-called saddle points, which will also contribute to the curve skeleton.
3. Compute the exact coordinates of critical points using trilinear interpolation.
4. Locate the segments of the first order curve skeleton. Each such segment must have critical points at both ends, and all such segment should cross only such cubes where saddle points are located. The segments are identified using a backtracking algorithm. The small number of possible ways assures the quick performance of the backtracking algorithm.
5. The exact coordinates of saddle points participating in the skeleton are established along the following two considerations. Those components that change their sign within the saddle point's cube, precisely define one or two exact coordinates via linear or bilinear interpolation. The other coordinates can be established such a way, that saddle points are uniformly distributed along the skeleton, and the curve of the skeleton remains smooth.
6. The second order curve skeleton will additionally contain branches, which connect critical points with high curvature surface points of the object. In this order, a set of high curvature surface points is searched for. Curvature is easily represented by the number of inner neighbors of the surface point. The less inner neighbors a surface point has, the higher its curvature value is. Further on, only those high curvature points are kept within the set, which have a locally maximal curvature value.
7. Secondary branches of the curve skeleton are located again using backtracking, crossing only cubes that contain saddle points.
8. The GPF based curve skeleton extraction algorithm also gives the possibility to neglect some of the irrelevant secondary branches. This is performed via ordering the branches according their divergence, and keeping only those which have a lower value than a predefined threshold, or keeping a predefined percentage that have low divergence values.

3   The Proposed Hierarchical Approach

The GPF based curve skeleton extraction algorithm given in [6] reports a very long execution time in case of objects containing over $N = 10^5$ voxels. The approximate length of such an object is of $n = \sqrt[3]{N}$ units.

The most time consuming part of the algorithm is the computation of the GPF in each grid point, as each couple formed by an internal point and a surface point has to be taken into consideration. As the number of internal points has the order of $\mathcal{O}(n^3)$, and the surface points count up to the order of $\mathcal{O}(n^2)$, the complexity of GPF computation will be of order $\mathcal{O}(n^5)$. This is an enormous load in case of large objects.

Cornea tried to reduce the duration of GPF computation by suppressing the set of external points considered for each internal point. Those external points were neglected, which according to their z coordinate, were guaranteed to be too far from the currently processed internal point. This modification reduces some of the computational complexity, but also may cause deformations of the skeleton. In this paper we propose a hierarchical approach for 3DCS extraction of large objects. The general idea is to reduce the number of internal points where the GPF is computed. This is achieved along the following terms:

Let us resize the object, reduce its size μ times in every direction. For the case of simplicity, let us consider now $\mu = 2$. This practically reduces the number of internal voxels μ^3 times and the number of surface voxels μ^2 times. If we extract the skeleton of this reduced object, it will have approximately the same shape as the skeleton of the original, large object, just it will be reduced in size μ times.

Now let us turn back to the original large object. We magnify the skeleton of the small object μ times and place it into the large object. Only those internal voxels, which are situated closer to the magnified skeleton, than a predefined threshold distance δ will be considered for the time consuming process of GPF computation. Such a way, the $\mathcal{O}(n^5)$-complexity operation is executed with a μ times smaller n, while in the big object, GPF computation will have the complexity of $\mathcal{O}(n^3)$.

This hierarchical size reduction can be performed in more than one steps, too, achieving thus μ^2 or μ^3 times size reduction, and an even more convenient computational load.

The reduction of the object can be performed as long as it does not influence the topology of the object. Further on, it is limited by the fact, that the reduced object must be at least two pixels wide everywhere. The recommended threshold value is: $\delta = (1.5 - 2.0)\mu$ voxels.

4   Efficient Implementation Using GPU

Modern GPU's can efficiently handle large matrices and can perform quick computations on large amounts of data. That is why, if we wish to accelerate the computation of GPF using a GPU, we need to organize our data into matrices. Let us write the coordinates of surface points into a matrix denoted by $\mathcal{S}$:

$$\mathcal{S} = \begin{pmatrix} x_1 & y_1 & z_1 \\ x_2 & y_2 & z_2 \\ \dots\dots\dots \\ x_\omega & y_\omega & z_\omega \end{pmatrix},$$

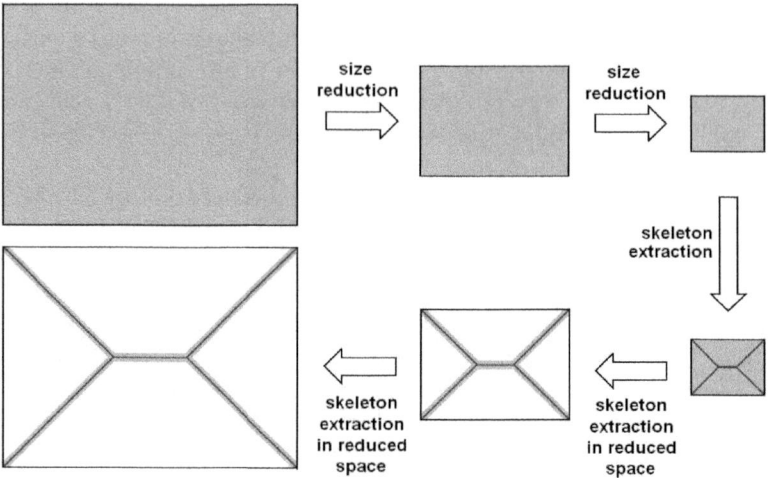

Fig. 2. Hierarchical size reduction exhibited in 2D, in two steps. Red lines indicate the extracted skeleton, while gray areas are the regions where the skeleton is looked for. White areas are excluded from the computations as they are not likely to contain any part of the skeleton.

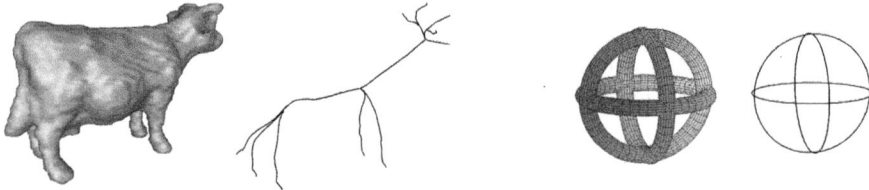

Fig. 3. Some examples of extracted skeletons

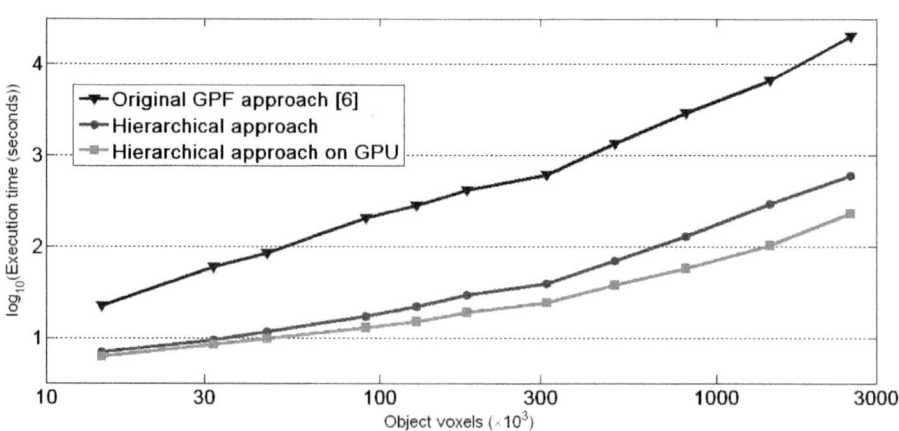

Fig. 4. Execution times for various object volumes, obtained by the original GPF-based skeleton extraction method, and the proposed hierarchical approaches

where ω represents the cardinality of the set of surface points Ω. We keep the coordinates of the current internal point in a vector $I = [x_I, y_I, z_I]$. We need to perform the following steps. First, we subtract I from each row of S, and compute the square of each element in the matrix. Compute the sum of the three columns of the matrix, and denote this single column by D. Raise each element of D to the power $(1 + \alpha)/2$. Use an odd integer for α to make the exponent an integer. Build an ω-row 3-column matrix M by placing ω identical rows $[x_I, y_I, z_I]$ under each other. Subtract the original S from this matrix M, and denote the result by Q. Divide each row of Q with the corresponding element in D, and finally sum up all columns of the matrix. The resulting 3-element vector will contain the three directional components of the GPF in the point I, namely $[\mathcal{F}_x(I), \mathcal{F}_y(I), \mathcal{F}_z(I)]$. In a GPU, the above computations can be organized to perform the above operations on several internal points in parallel.

5   Results and Discussion

The algorithm has been implemented in c++ programming language, using the JAMA and TNT packages for matrix operations. GPU implementation relies on AMD's FireStream SDK, and an ATI HD 5750 video card.

Several tests have been performed using artificially created object volumes of different sizes. The main evaluation criteria were: accuracy – how much the hierarchical formulation influences the correctness of the extracted skeleton, and efficiency – how many times quicker the proposed approach extracts the skeleton, compared to the speed of the original formulation.

The most simple skeleton extracted by the GPF based algorithms is the core skeleton, which is formed of critical points and first order branches only. The presence of secondary branches is controlled by the divergence threshold. These secondary branches are rarely useful in computer graphics applications, so the divergence threshold has to be kept at a low value. Another reason for this low threshold value could be the possible sensitivity to the noise present on the boundary of the object.

Parameter α controls the variation of the potential field's strength with distance. The optimal value of this parameter we found $\alpha = 5$: this assures good stability of the algorithm, while the computational load is not raised too high.

The hierarchical size reduction of the object has a damaging effect upon accuracy only if the size reduction changes the object's topology. The preservation of topology should limit the maximum applied size reduction factor.

From the point of view of efficiency, we found that the proposed approach can reduce the computational load of the algorithm $5 - 50$ times, depending on the chosen size reduction ratio. Figure 4 shows some execution times obtained on various object volumes. At the skeleton extraction of larger objects, it is more likely to obtain a higher speedup ratios. Involving a GPU for GPF computation can produce a further speedup factor of 2 to 5.

6   Conclusions and Future Work

In this paper we have proposed a hierarchical formulation of the general potential field based 3D curve skeleton extraction algorithm. The proposed method proved accurate as long as the executed size reduction did not change the topology of the object. The computational efficiency of the proposed method is outstanding, a 5-50 times speedup ratio is achievable, depending on the size of the object. Implementing the proposed hierarchical formulation of GPU's can rise the speedup factor well above 100.

As a future work, we would like to implement a different computation method of the GPF field, which will take into consideration the visibility problem, thus improving the accuracy as well.

References

1. Ahuja, N., Chuang, J.: Shape representation using a generalized potential field model. IEEE Trans. Patt. Anal. Mach. Intell. 19, 169–176 (1997)
2. Au, O.K.C., Tai, C.L., Chu, H.K., Cohen-Or, D., Lee, T.Y.: Skeleton extraction by mesh contraction. ACM Trans. Graph. 27(3), article 44, 1–10 (2008)
3. Bertrand, G., Malandain, G.: A new charactrization of three-dimensional simple points. Patt. Recogn. Lett. 15, 169–175 (1994)
4. Bitter, I., Kaufman, A.E., Sato, M.: Penalized-distance volumetric skeleton algorithm. IEEE Trans. Vis. Comp. Graph. 7, 195–206 (2001)
5. Chuang, J., Tsai, C., Ko, M.C.: Skeletonization of three- dimensional objects using generalized potential field. IEEE Trans. Patt. Anal. Mach. Intell. 22, 1241–1251 (2000)
6. Cornea, N.D., Silver, D., Yuan, X., Balasubramanian, R.: Computing hierarchical curve-skeletons of 3D objects. The Visual Computer 21, 945–955 (2005)
7. Cornea, N.D., Silver, D., Min, P.: Curve-skeleton properties, applications, and algorithms. IEEE Trans. Vis. Comp. Graph. 13, 530–548 (2007)
8. Grigorishin, T., Yang, Y.H.: Skeletonization: an electrostatic field-based approach. Patt. Anal. Appl. 1, 163–177 (1998)
9. He, T., Hong, L., Chen, D., Liang, Z.: Reliable path for virtual endoscopy: ensuring complete examination of human organs. IEEE Trans. Vis. Comp. Graph. 7, 333–342 (2001)
10. Ma, W.C., Wu, F.C., Ouhyoung, M.: Skeleton extraction of 3D objects with radial basis functions. In: Proc. IEEE Int'l Conf. Shape Modeling and Applications, pp. 1–10 (2003)
11. Saha, P.K., Chaudhuri, B.B.: 3D digital topology under binary transformation with applications. Comp. Vis. Image Understand. 63, 418–429 (1996)
12. Sanniti di Baja, G., Svensson, S.: A new shape descriptor for surfaces in 3D images. Patt. Recogn. Lett. 23, 703–711 (2002)
13. Wang, Y.S., Lee, T.Y.: Curve-skeleton extraction using iterative least squares optimization. IEEE Trans. Vis. Comp. Graph. 14, 926–936 (2008)
14. Wu, F.C., Ma, W.C., Liou, P., Liang, R.H., Ouhyoung, M.: Skeleton extraction of 3D objects with visible repulsive force. In: Proc. Eurographics Symp. Geometry Processing, pp. 1–7 (2003)

Improving Tracking Algorithms Using Saliency

Cristobal Undurraga[1] and Domingo Mery[2]

Computer Science Department, Pontificia Universidad Católica de Chile
Av.Vicuña Mackenna 4860, Santiago, Chile
`caundurr@uc.cl, dmery@ing.puc.cl`

Abstract. One of the challenges of computer vision is to improve the automatic systems for the recognition and tracking of objects in a set of images. One approach that has recently gained importance is based on extracting descriptors, such as the covariance descriptor, because they manage to remain invariant in the regions of these images despite changes of translation, rotation and scale. In this work we propose, using the Covariance Descriptor, a novel saliency system able to find the most relevant regions in an image, which can be used for recognition and tracking objects. Our method is based on the amount of information from each point in the image, and allows us to adapt the regions to maximize the difference of information between the region and its environment. The results show that this tool's improvements can boost trackers precision up to 90% (with initial precision of 50%) without compromising the recall.

Keywords: Saliency, Edge Detector, Tracking, Object Recognition, Covariance Descriptor.

1 Introduction

When recognizing objects in an image there are several approaches to define them. It can be done by: points of interest, descriptors with relevant information [9]; bags of words, areas that define the object [10]; features of a region, variance of the features of the region [11]; local appearence, attention operators based on symetry [7]; among others. One of the methods that has shown good results in object recognition and tracking is based on regions characterized by the *covariance descriptor* proposed by Porikli et al. [11]. This descriptor represents a region or window by a covariance matrix formed from the image's features. Our approach was inspired by the good results obtained in different applications that use this descriptor [2], [12], [14].

One of the problems from tracking algorithms that use one of the descriptors previously described, is chosing the correct window that gives sgnificant information for the recognition. To determine this region, one has to take into consideration the final use of the system. By example, for people tracking, one would choose a face detector such as Voila-Jones [13] or a people detector such as Felzenszwalb [5]. Several trackers and detectors use a rectangular region, from which arises the problem that within the chosen region is the described

C. San Martin and S.-W. Kim (Eds.): CIARP 2011, LNCS 7042, pp. 141–148, 2011.

object and also the background of the image. This causes that a large amount of information of the region is not from the object, causing a low performance of the tracker. Therefore if the object has little significant infomation and the background has many, the trackers will get confused by considering that the background is more important than the object.

We searched to solve this problem through the quantification of the image's information. This would be acheived by adapting the target region to reduce the noise caused by the background, maximizing the information's contrast between the window and its neighborhood. Currently, to determine if an area or a point contains relevant information, we use saliency systems. Itti et al. [6] present a model for saliency detection, which searches for saliencies in three diferents layers: a color layer, an intensity layer and an orientation layer. Then it linearly combines the zones found by the three layers to obtain the saliency map of the image. On the other hand, Achanta et al [1] present a method to determine salient regions in images using low-level features of luminance and color.

Our saliency method, unlike the method of Itti et al. [6], searches for saliency zones by integrating the color, intensity and orientation layers, and evaluating their covariance on a point through its neighborhood. With this information, we quantify the amount of variation in a pixel allowing us to form a system of saliency. From this we retrieve the saliency map and we define a better region to initialize the tracker, obtaining a high improvement in the precision, from a 50% to a 90%.

In this paper, we present a novel system for the improvement of recognition and tracking algorithms through the quantification of a pixel's information. It's simple and fast. Using the properties of the covariance descriptor to establish the variance of diferents features in a pixel, we found the areas containing the largest amount of information. This article is organized as follows: in section 2 we present the mathematical bases, the hypothesis and the implementation of the problem; in section 3, we present the methodology and the results; finally, in section 4 we present the conclusions and future works.

2 Proposed Method

2.1 Covariance Descriptor

The covariance descriptor for one point proposed by Porikli et al. [11], is formally defined as:

$$F(x, y, i) = \phi_i(I, x, y) \qquad (1)$$

where: I is an image which can be in RGB, grayscale, infrared, etc.; x and y are ther coordinates of a pixel; F is a $W \times H \times d$ matrix, where W is the width of the image, H the height and d is the number of features used; and ϕ_i is the function that relates the image to the i-th feature; i.e. the function to get the i-th feature from de image I. The proposed method uses a 11 characteristic tensor F, which is defined by:

$$F(x, y, i) = [x \; y \; R \; G \; B \; |I_x| \; |I_y| \; \sqrt{|I_x|^2 + |I_y|^2} \; |I_{xx}| \; |I_{yy}| \; \sqrt{|I_{xx}|^2 + |I_{yy}|^2}] \quad (2)$$

For further analysis in the selection of features for the covariance descriptor and the method of calculation of the covariance matrix, we encourage the reader to take a look on the work of Cortez et al. [4].

2.2 Saliency Model

In order to establish the amount of information contained in a pixel, we build the matrix F from (1). The idea is to get the amount of information for a pixel, that's why we define the region of the descriptor as the neighborhood of the pixel. But we need a metric to evaluate the covariance matrix. In our experiments we tested with the largest singular value, with the infinity norm, the determinant and the logarithm of the absolute value of the determinant. The latter gave the best results. Therefore, we define the magnitude of the obtained matrix C_R as the logarithm of the absolute value of the determinant of the matrix. Thus, we define the amount of information I for a pixel (x, y) with a neigborhood N as:

$$S(x, y) = \log(|\det(C_{R(N)})| + 1) \tag{3}$$

2.3 Saliency Region Detector

With the saliency map already obtained, we determined the window where the higher amount of information was concentrated. For this we created an algorithm that reduces the size of a window to maximize the information within it. For a fast calculation we used the same method to calculate the covariance matrix: first, we created the integral matrix of the saliency map I_S; and then, we calculated the information in a region with:

$$I_{S(R)} = I_S(x, y) + I_S(x', y') - I_S(x', y) - I_S(x, y') \tag{4}$$

We defined a line as a rectangle with a side of one pixel long. Then we set the window as the entire image and begun to reduce it. We set a stopping point: defining what percentage of the image's information we wanted to be inside the window. Then, for each side, we calculated how much information they gave. The one that gave less information was reduced, and so on until the region contained the percentage of information previously defined.

2.4 Effectiveness Score

To evaluate tracking algorithms there are two widely used metrics: precision and recall. But having two scores that are almost as important, is a problem. Here is where an other score is needed, that combines both metrics, as it does the F-score. However, for a further analysis on the tracked path, the precision is more important than the recall, so a $F_{0.5}$-score is advised. Using a variable parameter tends to cause conflict because of the variability of the results when the parameter is altered. So to measure the performance of the tracking algorithms we propose a new score called effective score defined as:

$$E - score = \sqrt[3]{precision^2 * recall} \qquad (5)$$

This new score gives us a powerfull tool for choosing the best percentage of information taking into account the precision and the recall. This score was not used to compare us with other methods, but to determine the best percentage for a set of images.

2.5   Automatic Determination of the Percentage of Information

We have discussed an algorithm to choose a better initial region, however, we have to set the parameter of the percentage of information. If we want this to work automatically then we have to establish a method that sets the value of the parameter. For this task we have chosen a bayesian network where the set of variables are: the percentage of information (A_i); the training videos (B_k); the most similar training video (C); and the success for tracking (E). From the joint distribution we have:

$$\arg\max_{i} P(E|A_iC) \qquad (6)$$

After a few arithmetics operations and considering the law of total probabilty we have:

$$\arg\max_{i} \sum_{k=1}^{m} [P(E|A_iB_k)P(B_k)] \sum_{j=1}^{n} [P(E|A_jC)] \qquad (7)$$

where: A_i is a given percentage; and B_k is a video of the training set, where $P(B_k)$ is the probability of the test region to be like the training region given theirs covariance matrices similarities.

3   Experiments and Results

The aim of the experiments described below is to show the main aspects of our method and then to show a successful application for the improvement of monitoring systems.

3.1   Saliency Region Detector

The goal of this algorithm is to determine if a point is salient or not. For each point of the image, we assign the square region of five pixels as its neighborhood. From this we obtain a map of saliency using the variation of the features that form the covariance matrix. In comparison with other algorithms, our map is much more visually understandable, since the saliency is for each point and not for an area (Figure 1).

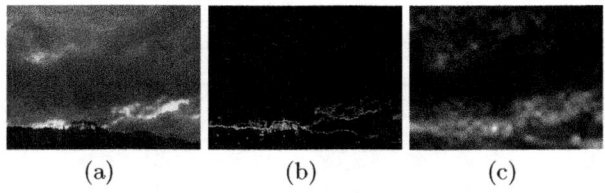

(a)   (b)   (c)

Fig. 1. Example of the saliency map obtained through the Covariance matrix: (a) original image; (b) our proposed saliency map; (c) Itti's saliency map [6]

In reality, indoor backgrounds are complex and have too much information. That's why we use a similar process, minimizing the information within the window. Thus, we leave most of the background information outside, which produces noise and errors when tracking. By eliminating the sides that contain higher amount of information we reduce the window, which decreases the information within it and maximises the contrast of information between the region and its neighborhood (Figure 2).

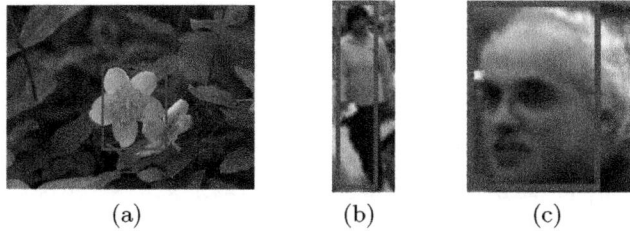

(a)   (b)   (c)

Fig. 2. Example of windows obtained removing sides that contain higher amount of information and leaving 66 percent of it within de window: (a) region obtained from full image; (b) region obtained from image cropped whith a pedestrian detector [5]; (c) region obtained from image cropped whith a face detector [13]

3.2   Improvement of Tracking Algorithms

The application to which we tested our saliency model was tracking algorithms. We experimented with twenty videos obtained from a supermarket, hoping to verify if there was an improvement by applying it at the beginning of a tracking system. In scenarios like the supermarket, where everything is done to attract the customer's attention, the saliency algorithms select the background as points of interest and not the person, who tends to have more uniform colors.

As tracking algortihms we used two state of the art methods: the on-line naive bayes nearest neighbor (ONBNN) for covariance descriptors [3], and the TLD real-time algorithm [8]. As initial region we used two different methods: ground truth of a person, to analyse how important is a small amount of background for a tracking system; and a people detector [5], to determine the benefits of the method in a full tracking system. Finally, as saliency algorithms we used three methods: our method, center surround by Achante et al. [1] and Itti et Al algorithm [6].

Fig. 3. Results obtained on images with lots of information in the background. First row corresponds to the reference result obtained using the ONBNN [3]. The second row is the result where the initial region was modified with our algorithm.

Table 1. Average percentage from twenty videos with initial region ground truth and a people detector, after using a saliency model to adapt the region (100 % means no saliency algorithm was used and *a*uto the autoselection of percentage using the E-Score as the tracking success).

	(%)	Ground Truth						Felzenszwalb					
Tracker		ONBNN			LTD			ONBNN			LTD		
Saliency		Us	C.S.	Itti's	Us	C.S.	Itti's	Us	C.S.	Itti's	Us	C.S.	Itti's
Precision	10	**95.6**	85.9	5.9	46.2	39.6	0.0	**84.7**	82.6	8.7	12.8	15.7	0.0
	20	**92.9**	91.8	10.6	43.7	51.0	0.0	90.4	**91.1**	14.0	25.2	19.9	0.0
	30	**94.3**	92.6	24.7	64.4	52.7	5.9	**88.0**	79.0	22.5	25.8	27.1	0.0
	40	89.0	**92.5**	44.8	68.7	51.5	2.2	**86.6**	78.1	31.8	26.6	58.6	0.0
	50	**88.5**	87.5	53.4	67.1	68.4	18.0	74.4	**79.2**	45.5	23.3	63.4	0.0
	60	85.2	**87.0**	58.7	65.6	67.5	22.3	**72.0**	66.1	50.0	22.6	65.1	0.0
	70	**87.7**	76.7	73.5	62.5	61.3	27.2	70.3	**71.9**	67.7	42.2	69.2	0.0
	80	76.3	74.6	**82.5**	54.7	61.5	28.8	65.4	67.8	**79.7**	57.9	64.2	0.0
	90	78.1	76.1	**84.5**	59.0	59.1	31.9	65.4	62.8	**88.8**	64.8	57.7	0.0
	100	57.1			51.3			60.4			59.2		
	Auto	94.4	-	-	79.6	-	-	85.7	-	-	72.9	-	-
Recall	10	**21.2**	16.0	0.0	15.4	9.8	0.0	**18.3**	16.7	0.0	4.8	3.4	0.0
	20	**26.4**	21.7	0.7	16.0	17.5	0.0	**26.2**	24.5	0.1	9.6	6.1	0.0
	30	**34.0**	30.4	1.2	25.5	19.2	0.0	**31.9**	30.1	0.5	9.4	10.6	0.0
	40	**38.7**	37.6	2.0	30.2	24.5	0.1	**37.0**	34.7	0.9	13.2	18.6	0.0
	50	**44.1**	39.2	3.4	30.9	28.0	1.4	38.4	**38.7**	1.8	13.7	26.7	0.0
	60	43.8	**45.2**	6.3	34.3	36.8	2.4	**40.6**	36.5	3.1	19.6	28.8	0.0
	70	**47.9**	43.5	8.1	33.5	33.0	3.1	**41.7**	41.7	5.5	28.9	32.8	0.0
	80	45.3	**46.7**	12.7	34.8	32.7	3.1	41.5	**43.3**	8.2	41.1	33.4	0.0
	90	**49.1**	48.2	16.2	34.4	32.7	3.7	**44.2**	41.3	12.8	52.3	32.5	0.0
	100	45.9			38.1			45.6			48.2		
	Auto	50.4	-	-	40.2	-	-	52.4	-	-	42.2	-	-

Table 2. Average percentage using the bayesian network to automatically select the best percentage of information. We compare the use of Precision, Recall, F-Score and E-Score as succes of the ONBNN tracker using ground truth for initial region.

	Ground Truth				Felzenszwalb			
	Precision	Recall	F-Score	E-Score	Precision	Recall	F-Score	E-Score
Normal	57.1	45.9	50.0	52.2	60.4	45.6	55.9	54.5
Precision	98.2	29.0	61.3	62.9	92.9	27.8	61.0	61.1
Recall	85.2	56.5	74.1	72.5	81.3	54.4	72.3	70.2
F-Score	95.0	49.2	78.1	75.3	85.7	52.4	74.2	71.8
E-Score	94.4	50.4	77.9	75.4	85.7	52.4	74.2	71.8

The results show that saliency algorithms increase the precision of tracking algorithms, however, in some cases, they tend to sacrifice the recall (Table 1). Our method gets higher results in precision without compromising to much recall, or even increasing it. This allows us to obtain better F-Score and E-Score and through an analysis of these scores, we found that better results for ground truth are found using a 70% of the information and for felzenszwalb are found using a 40% of the information. Using better regions, we can prevent that a region gets stuck in the initial position because it doesn't get confused with the background (Figure 3).

Finally, using our bayesian network and choosing the precision as the success of the tracker, we can improve the precision of the ONBNN tracker from a 57.1% to a 98.2% but decreasing the recall. Inversely, if we choose the recall as the success of the tracker we can improve it from a 45.9% to a 56.5% while also increasing the precision to 85.2 %. However, using a Score as the success, we increase the precision to an average of 97.7% while increasing the recall to an average of 49.8% (Table 2). This shows that scores give us powerful information for the improvement of tracking algoritms. They improve the precision and the recall at the same time, reaching high precision levels.

4 Conclusions

To improve the tracking systems we have developed a novel saliency model that uses the covariance descriptor. This saliency system allows us to determine whether an object will be easy or difficult to follow in a video, given that the background contains more- or less- information than the object, and to extract enough information to improve recognition and tracking systems.

We could also improve the initial regions coming from detectors, thus reducing the noise produced by the backgrounds. Although we do not always see improvements in the tracking systems, we could improve the results in cases where they may have failed, keeping the same performance in other cases.

We also propose the use of a bayesian network to efficiently select the best initial region. This allows us to choose if we use, or not, saliency to improve the tracker. We noticed, that bigger regions have less problems to be tracked so, it's more efficient not to use the saliency. However, smaller regions has several problems to be tracked so, it's highly recommended to perform our saliency algorithm to improve the tracking results.

Acknowledgements. The authors would like to thank Fernando Betteley from Cencosud S.A. for facilitate the adquisition of videos in one of Santa Isabel's Supermarkets. Part of this work was done while C.U. was at The National Institute of Astrophysics, Optics and Electronics supported by the LACCIR Short Stays Program. This research was supported in part by LACCIR project #S1009LAC006. This work was supported in part by The School of Engineering, Pontificia Universidad Catolica de Chile, Grant FIA.

References

1. Achanta, R., Estrada, F., Wils, P., Süsstrunk, S.: Salient region detection and segmentation. In: Gasteratos, A., Vincze, M., Tsotsos, J.K. (eds.) ICVS 2008. LNCS, vol. 5008, pp. 66–75. Springer, Heidelberg (2008)
2. Batista, J.: A region covariance embedded in a particle filter for multi-objects tracking. Update (2008)
3. Cortez, P., Mery, D., Sucar, L.: Object Tracking Based on Covariance Descriptors and On-Line Naive Bayes Nearest Neighbor Classifier. In: 2010 Fourth Pacific-Rim Symposium on Image and Video Technology, pp. 139–144. IEEE (2010)
4. Cortez, P., Undurraga, C., Mery, D., Soto, A.: Performance evaluation of the Covariance descriptor for target detection. In: 2009 International Conference of the Chilean Computer Science Society, pp. 133–141. IEEE (2009)
5. Felzenszwalb, P.F., Girshick, R.B., McAllester, D., Ramanan, D.: Object detection with discriminatively trained part-based models. IEEE Transactions on Pattern Analysis and Machine Intelligence 32(9), 1627–1645 (2010)
6. Itti, L., Koch, C., Niebur, E.: A Model of Saliency-Based Visual Attention for Rapid Scene Analysis. Colorectal disease: The Official Journal of the Association of Coloproctology of Great Britain and Ireland 4(2), 147–149 (2002)
7. Jugessur, D., Dudek, G.: Local appearance for robust object recognition. CVPR (2000)
8. Kalal, Z., Matas, J., Mikolajczyk, K.: Online learning of robust object detectors during unstable tracking. In: 2009 IEEE 12th International Conference on Computer Vision Workshops, ICCV Workshops, pp. 1417–1424 (September 2009)
9. Lowe, D.: Object recognition from local scale-invariant features. In: Proceedings of the Seventh IEEE International Conference on Computer Vision, vol. 2, pp. 1150–1157 (1999)
10. Nowak, E., Jurie, F., Triggs, B.: Sampling strategies for bag-of-features image classification. In: Leonardis, A., Bischof, H., Pinz, A. (eds.) ECCV 2006, Part IV. LNCS, vol. 3954, pp. 490–503. Springer, Heidelberg (2006)
11. Tuzel, O., Porikli, F., Meer, P.: Region covariance: A fast descriptor for detection and classification. In: Leonardis, A., Bischof, H., Pinz, A. (eds.) ECCV 2006, Part II. LNCS, vol. 3952, pp. 589–600. Springer, Heidelberg (2006)
12. Tuzel, O., Porikli, F., Meer, P.: Pedestrian detection via classification on Riemannian manifolds. IEEE Transactions on Pattern Analysis and Machine Intelligence 30(10), 1713–1727 (2008)
13. Viola, P., Jones, M.: Robust real-time object detection. International Journal of Computer Vision (2002)
14. Yao, J., Odobez, J.m., Parc, C.: Fast Human Detection from Videos Using Covariance Features. Learning (2008)

Using Adaptive Run Length Smoothing Algorithm for Accurate Text Localization in Images

Martin Rais, Norberto A. Goussies, and Marta Mejail

Departamento de Computación, Facultad de Ciencias Exactas y Naturales,
Universidad de Buenos Aires, Buenos Aires, Argentina

Abstract. Text information in images and videos is frequently a key factor for information indexing and retrieval systems. However, text detection in images is a difficult task since it is often embedded in complex backgrounds. In this paper, we propose an accurate text detection and localization method in images based on stroke information and the Adaptive Run Lenght Smoothing Algorithm. Experimental results show that the proposed approach is accurate, has high recall and is robust to various text sizes, fonts, colors and languages.

1 Introduction

The tremendous increase of multimedia content has raised the need for automatic semantic information indexing and retrieval systems. Text information present in images and videos are an important source of high-level semantics.

Large variations in text fonts, colors, styles, and sizes, as well as the low contrast between the text and the often complicated background, make text detection and localization extremely challenging. Frequently, image compression tends to deteriorate image quality resulting in even harder to recognize texts.

Textual information extraction (TIE) is usually split into five steps: detection, localization, verification, segmentation and recognition. Text detection is used to separate text regions from non-text regions. Text localization is used to localize text lines using rectangular bounding boxes (BBs). During text verification, all localized text lines are verified in order to eliminate false positives. Text segmentation is performed to compute the foreground of the text and finally, text recognition is where the detected text image is converted into plain text.

In this work, we present a method that accurately detects, localizes and verifies text in images and video frames. Inspired by [7], stroke information and a machine learning approach is used to detect text with high recall rates and very good precision. To obtain the initial bounding boxes (BBs), we propose a combined Adaptive Run Lenght Smoothing Algorithm (ARLSA) and Connected Components Analysis (CCA) based algorithm that localizes text more accurately than Li et al [7]. After a refinement phase, an innovative ARLSA-based verification is proposed followed by a final SVM verification step using its output scores to further check results.

C. San Martin and S.-W. Kim (Eds.): CIARP 2011, LNCS 7042, pp. 149–156, 2011.
© Springer-Verlag Berlin Heidelberg 2011

This paper is organized as follows: In section 2 we present current state-of-the-art methods, in section 3 our method will be described in detail, in section 4 we will discuss about experimental results and finally, in section 5 we will draw our conclusions regarding this topic.

2   Related Work

Text detection and localization methods are usually clasified into four distinct categories. The first category uses connected component analysis (CCA) [14] in which regions with maximum homogeneity are obtained from an image and then non-text connected components (CCs) are filtered out based on geometrical constrains. CCA-based methods are robust against font size, however, they are sensible to noise and tend to fail when texts are not homogeneous. The second category uses an edge-based approach to detect and localize text [9]. Techniques within this category detect text based on strength, density or distribution information from edges, and assumes high contrast differences between the text and the background. Edge-based methods are fast and have high recall rates, however, the large amount of false alarms is usually its main problem. Also, it fails when text is not contrasted enough with the background. The third category is based on textures [11], and makes use of the fact that texts have specific texture patterns that allows us to distinguish them from the background. Texture-based methods are robust to noise and low quality images, however they are time-consuming and tend to fail when the background is cluttered with text. Recently, pattern clasiffication methods have been addressed to detect and localize text in images based on elaborately selected features [3]. For more information about textual information extraction in videos and images, the reader should refer to the survey paper [5].

Using stroke information to detect and localize text was first introduced by [8]. Since then, several text localization methods have used stroke information to detect and localize text in images such as [7]. In those works, it has been proven that stroke information can be used to succesfully detect and localize text in images since it captures the intrinsic characteristics of text itself.

3   Methodology

As shown in Fig. 1, the proposed algorithm has three distinct stages for text localization: coarse text detection, a refinement stage followed by text verification.

During the Coarse Text Detection stage, we perform a fast morphology-based coarse text detection using a Multi-Scale Wavelet edge map. Then, stroke filter is performed over the original image using the results from the first detection as a mask to improve performance. We later apply a sliding window algorithm in which we perform SVM classification to generate the initial bounding boxes based on the Adaptive Run Length Smoothing Algorithm (ARLSA) [10].

During the refinement stage, we first apply a Zero Crossing projection profile technique to split multiple line bounding boxes, followed by an Expand method to improve precission.

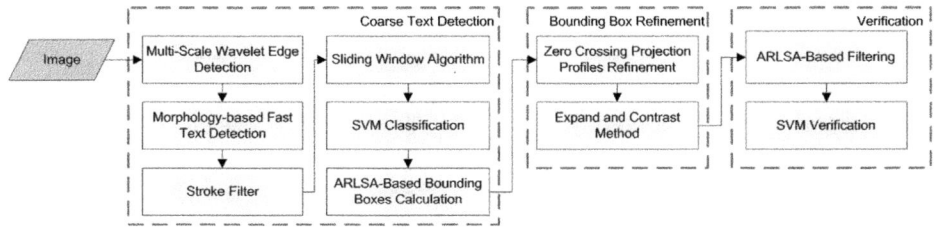

Fig. 1. Flowchart of the proposed algorithm

Finally, in the verification stage, we introduce an ARLSA-based filtering method followed by an SVM verification to further improve precission.

3.1   Coarse Text Detection

Wavelet Multi-Scale Edge Detection. We use the method in [6] for fast multi-scale edge detection. The scale of the method controls the threshold for which edges are detected. A large scale tends to remove small signal fluctuations, filtering background edges from the results. However, text edges with small signal fluctuations may also be removed if the scale is too large. In our work, we use 3 as the scale of the algorithm.

Initial text region detection. We first convert the input image into grayscale. Then we calculate stroke information using the stroke filter from [8] but only on text areas from the morphology-based text detection. Using the stroke information, we employ the sliding window algorithm from [7] to detect text regions.

A Support Vector Machine (SVM) [2] classifier is used in this work since, as stated in [12], compared with other classifiers such as neural networks and decision trees, SVM is easier to train, needs fewer training samples and has better generalization ability. The SVM was trained on a dataset containing 368 text samples and 611 non-text samples using the same feature set as [7]. The sliding window in this case moves $W/4$ horizontally and $H/4$ vertically. Fig. 3b gives an example of the output result after the stage.

CC Analysis and ARLSA. The authors of [7] used a fixed set of computation steps that heuristically obtain initial bounding boxes partitioning the connected polygons that result from the sliding window procedure mentioned above. However this have several drawbacks, specially the fact that it frequently split text lines in two bounding boxes as in Fig. 2b.

Because of this, we take a new and more effective way in order to obtain the initial bounding boxes. We first calculate a saliency map as in [1]. For every window that is classified as a text line, all the values of its pixels are incremented in the saliency map by one. Meanwhile, we calculate another map that represents the number of visits by a sliding window for each pixel. After the whole image is classified and the sliding window algorithm is over, we use this second map to normalize the saliency map from 0 to 1. The results of this can be seen in

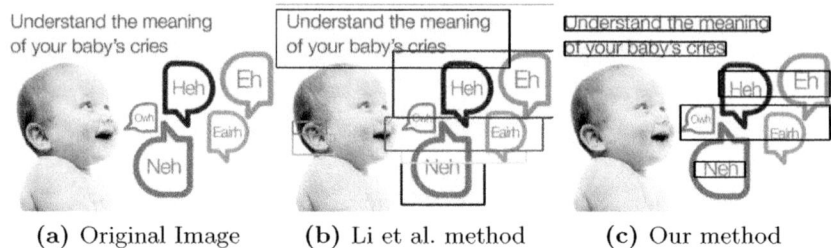

(a) Original Image   (b) Li et al. method   (c) Our method

Fig. 2. Initial Bounding Boxes comparison

the Fig. 3b. Then, we generate a binary detection map using the method in [1]. Example of the binary detection map is shown in the Fig. 3c.

We later use this binary detection as a mask for the edges map, removing all edges that are not text-related. We use this new map as the input of the horizontal ARLSA algorithm detailed in [10] generating what can be seen in Fig. 3d. The purpose of the ARLSA algorithm, as used in [13], is to join all characters among the same line, implying that all isolated edges cannot belong to text so we remove them by performing a morphological opening leading to Fig. 3e. Then, we generate the bounding boxes based on the connected components as in Fig. 3f. Finally, we put together all pairs of rectangles based on the following conditions:

- The relation between their heights is lower than a certain threshold T_{height}.
- Their vertical distance is lower than a certain threshold T_{vdist}.
- Their horizontal distance is lower than a certain threshold T_{hdist}.

In this paper, we set $T_{height} = 2.5$, T_{vdist} as the maximum of both heights divided by 2 and T_{hdist} as the minimum of both heights. This will lead to Fig. 3g and Fig. 3h.

3.2   Localization

After we obtain the initial BBs, a text line refinement is performed. First, a projection profiles based method is used to split BBs with more than one line and shrink them to better adapt to text areas. This is followed by an expand method to further improve precission of the algorithm.

Zero Crossing and Projection Profiles refinement. We use the zero crossing technique from [11] to refine text BBs.

After applying this method, we perform a conventional vertical projection profile method. For each column, the pixel values are summed and if the sum is lower than a certain threshold, the column is deleted. In order to avoid splitting two words of the same text line, we require that the number of concurrent columns marked to be deleted equals a certain threshold.

In our work, both methods are applied sequentially, and will be repeated until no further changes are made to the bounding boxes after an iteration.

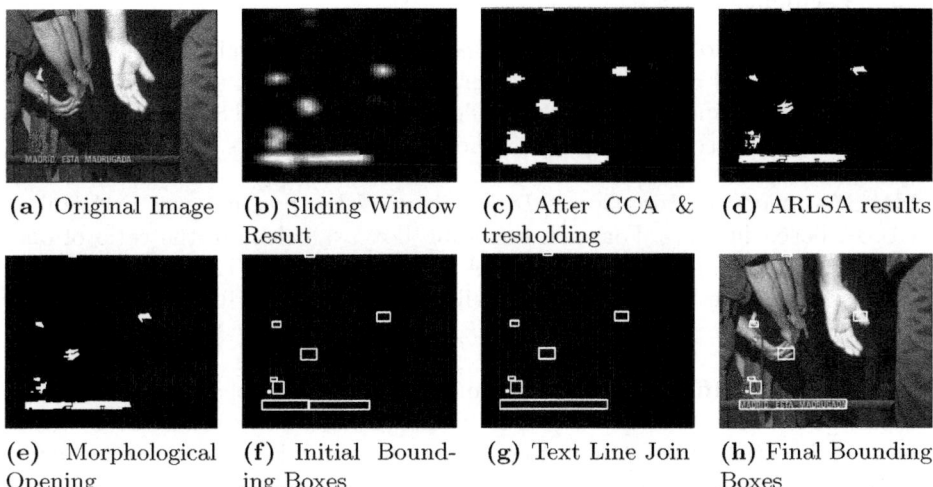

(a) Original Image   **(b)** Sliding Window Result   **(c)** After CCA & tresholding   **(d)** ARLSA results

(e) Morphological Opening   **(f)** Initial Bounding Boxes   **(g)** Text Line Join   **(h)** Final Bounding Boxes

Fig. 3. ARLSA-based bounding boxes calculation

Expand. It may happen that the Zero Crossing technique shrinks a BB supressing any of both horizontal borders of a text region (top or bottom). Also, it could happen that during the coarse detection, a BB missed any border of a text region. Thus, it is neccesary to expand the BBs in order to obtain better localization recall and precission.

For this purpose, we multiply the image resulting from the sliding window such as Fig. 3b by the multi-scale wavelet edge detection and we use this image as the input of our expand procedure.

To expand, we first take the next horizontal line above the top edge of the BB and calculate its sum. We expand bounding box B horizontally until threshold T_h is not met. We do the same with the next horizontal line below the bottom edge. We then make the same procedure vertically until treshold T_v is not verified. Treshold T_h is obtained in the following way:

$$T_h(B) = (Avg_h(B) - Min_h(B)) * k_e \qquad (1)$$

where k_e is a constant and

$$Avg_h(B) = \frac{1}{H} \sum_i^H \sum_j^W B(j, i) \qquad (2)$$

and $Min_h(B)$ stands for the minimum value of the horizontal projection profiles of the bounding box B while W and H are their respectives width and height. $k_e = 0.75$ is used for this work. The vertical treshold T_v is obtained the same as T_h but vertically.

3.3   Verification

Once the localization stage has refined the rectangles, some false positives bounding boxes may still be part of the answer. Therefore, we first apply an innovative ARLSA-based verification procedure followed by a combined SVM approach that uses SVM output scores to verify candidate bounding boxes.

ARLSA-based verification. To eliminate false positive, we perform an ARLSA-based filtering. For each bounding box, we calculate the ratio of ones among the bounding box on the ARLSA image, such as in Fig. 3d. If this ratio is below a certain treshold k_{ARLSA}, we will classify the bounding box as non-text and remove it. For this work, we used $k_{ARLSA} = 0.7$.

SVM-based verification. In order to perform an SVM-based verification, we employ two SVMs. Our first SVM is trained using the same feature set as in the text detection stage, but in this case, using variable sized bounding boxes. We consider the prediction score obtained from this SVM and if it is within a predefined range $[-k_{SVM}, k_{SVM}]$ where $k_{SVM} \leq 1$, it implies that the prediction is not certain. Thus, in those cases, we further verify the bounding box using a third SVM. The feature set used in this case includes the 6 features used in the second SVM of [7] plus one new feature to achieve better recognition accuracy. The new feature introduced is the mean of the image map that results from the ARLSA algorithm in the bounding box. This is discriminative since, as shown in Fig. 3d, the ARLSA map of a text region must have most of their pixels marked.

4   Results

In order to detect bigger font sizes, we employ a multiresolution approach performing our three stages of textual information extraction to an image in different resolutions and finally results are combined to the original resolution. To avoid combining overlapping bounding boxes of different resolutions, the approach from [1] is used eliminating the edges in the current resolution of the already detected characters in the previous resolutions.

As explained in [1], most authors use box-based or pixel-based recall, precision and accuracy measures that in general, fail to reflect the true quality of the results. Very few works deal with the problem of evaluation methods.

Our evaluation method was proposed in Anthimopoulos et al. [1], and is character oriented, meaning it will base its results on the quantity of characters recognized/missed. They conclude that the number of characters in a text line is proportional to its ratio width to height. Based on that, let GB_i be the ith ground truth bounding box with $1 \leq i \leq N$ and hg_i its height while DB_j be the jth detected bounding box with $1 \leq j \leq M$ and hd_j its height, they propose to calculate the recall and precision as:

$$\textbf{Recall} = \frac{\sum_{i=1}^{N} \frac{|GDI_i|}{hg_i^2}}{\sum_{i=1}^{N} \frac{|GB_i|}{hg_i^2}} \tag{3}$$

$$\textbf{Precision} = \frac{\sum_{i=1}^{M} \frac{|DGI_i|}{hd_i^2}}{\sum_{i=1}^{M} \frac{|DB_i|}{hd_i^2}} \tag{4}$$

where GDI_i and DGI_i are the corresponding intersections:

$$GDI_i = \begin{cases} GB_i, & \text{if } \frac{GB_i \cap \left(\bigcup_{i=1}^{M} DB_i\right)}{GB_i} \geq th \\ GB_i \cap \left(\bigcup_{i=1}^{M} DB_i\right), & \text{otherwise} \end{cases} \tag{5}$$

$$DGI_i = \begin{cases} DB_i, & \text{if } \frac{DB_i \cap \left(\bigcup_{i=1}^{N} GB_i\right)}{DB_i} \geq th \\ DB_i \cap \left(\bigcup_{i=1}^{N} GB_i\right), & \text{otherwise} \end{cases} \tag{6}$$

and $th = 0.75$ is a treshold that avoids penalizing minor inconsistencies.

To test our algorithm, we used the Microsoft common test set from [4]. As can be seen in Table 1, our method outperforms previous methods. Some sample results are shown in Fig. 4.

Table 1. Performance Comparison

Method	Recall (%)	Precision (%)	F-Measure (%)
Our approach	**93.34%**	**96.7%**	**94.99%**
Li et al. [7]	91.1%	95.8%	93.39%
Liu et al. [8][1]	91.3%	92.4%	91.85%
Ye et al. [12][1]	90.8%	90.3%	90.55%

(a)   (b)   (c)

Fig. 4. Sample text localization results using the proposed method

5   Conclusion

In this paper, we proposed an effective text detection and localization method based on stroke information. To overcome speed issues, we first perform a fast morphological text detection that we later use as a mask for calculating the stroke filter. We then detect text using a machine-learning approach and obtain

---

[1] As reported in [7].

initial bounding boxes by a mixed CCA and an ARLSA approach. To further refine the bounding boxes, we employ a zero-crossing projection profile technique followed by a expand technique to gain better recall. Finally, the text regions are verified by an SVM approach using their output scores to further check the results.

Experimental results show that the proposed text detection and localization method is robust to noise, text size, color and text language. It does also outperform other stroke-based methods such as [7].

References

[1] Anthimopoulos, M., Gatos, B., Pratikakis, I.: A two-stage scheme for text detection in video images. Image Vision Comput. 28, 1413–1426 (2010)
[2] Cortes, C., Vapnik, V.: Support-vector networks. Machine Learning 20(3), 273–297 (1995)
[3] Herv, D., Chen, D., Bourlard, H.: Text Identification in Complex Background Using SVM. In: Proc. of IEEE Conference on Computer Vision and Pattern Recognition, vol. 2, pp. 621–626 (2001)
[4] Hua, X., Wenyin, L., Zhang, H.: An Automatic Performance Evaluation Protocol for Video Text Detection Algorithms. IEEE Transactions on Circuits and Systems for Video Technology 14, 498–507 (2004)
[5] Jung, K.: Text information extraction in images and video: a survey. Pattern Recognition 37(5), 977–997 (2004)
[6] Li, J.: A Wavelet Approach to Edge Detection. Master's thesis, Sam Houston State University, Huntsville, Texas (August 2003)
[7] Li, X., Wang, W., Jiang, S., Huang, Q., Gao, W.: Fast and Effective Text Detection. In: International Congress in Image Processing 2008 (2008)
[8] Liu, Q., Jung, C., Kim, S., Moon, Y., Kim, J.: Stroke Filter for Text Localization in Video Images, pp. 1473–1476 (October 2006)
[9] Lyu, M.R., Song, J., Cai, M.: A comprehensive method for multilingual video text detection, localization, and extraction. IEEE Transactions on Circuits and Systems for Video Technology 15(2), 243–255 (2005)
[10] Nikolaou, N., Makridis, M., Gatos, B., Stamatopoulos, N., Papamarkos, N.: Segmentation of historical machine-printed documents using Adaptive Run Length Smoothing and skeleton segmentation paths. Image Vision Comput. 28, 590–604 (2010)
[11] Shivakumara, P., Phan, T.Q., Tan, C.L.: A Gradient Difference Based Technique for Video Text Detection, pp. 156–160 (2009)
[12] Ye, Q., Huang, Q., Gao, W., Zhao, D.: Fast and robust text detection in images and video frames. Image and Vision Computing 23(6), 565–576 (2005)
[13] Zhao, M., Li, S., Kwok, J.: Text detection in images using sparse representation with discriminative dictionaries. Image and Vision Computing 28(12), 1590–1599 (2010)
[14] Zhong, Y., Karu, K., Jain, A.K.: Locating text in complex color images. In: Proceedings of the Third International Conference on Document Analysis and Recognition, ICDAR 1995, vol. 1. IEEE Computer Society, Washington, DC, USA (1995)

Fast Rotation-Invariant Video Caption Detection Based on Visual Rhythm

Felipe Braunger Valio, Helio Pedrini, and Neucimar Jeronimo Leite

Institute of Computing - University of Campinas
Campinas, SP, Brazil, 13084-971

Abstract. Text detection in images has been studied and improved for decades. There are many works that extend the existing methods for analyzing videos, however, few of them create or adapt approaches that consider inherent characteristics of videos, such as temporal information. This work proposes a very fast method for identifying video frames that contain text through a special data structure called visual rhythm. The method is robust to detect video captions with respect to font styles, color intensity, and text orientation. A data set was built in our experiments to compare and evaluate the effectiveness of the proposed method.

1 Introduction

Several video-based applications are becoming more common, driven by factors such as popularization of digital television, increase of bandwidth for data transmission via Internet, evolution of augmented reality research, and the development of mobile equipments for multimedia purpose.

Texts in video provide relevant information of a scene content. For instance, a portion of the video is commonly used in news to exhibit information such as weather forecast, sport scores, text alerts, financial market overview. Captions are employed in TV documentaries to describe a location, a person, a title or an event. Almost all commercials use a certain type of subtitle to provide more information of products, since their exhibition time is restricted to only few seconds. In movies, subtitles are used to inform their cast and credits, or an introductory story. Systems have also become more practical for text translation, navigation based on textual content, indexing of multimedia libraries, detection of events such as appearance of commercials, blocks of news, among others.

Since videos concentrate a large amount of information, their analysis is a task of high computational cost. A way to speed up the caption detection process is to eliminate frames that certainly are not subtitled.

This paper describes and evaluates a fast method for detecting video frames containing captions based on a data structure called visual rhythm. The captions can be written in different languages and orientations. The visual rhythm can be generated in multiple scales by means of a space-filling curve. Regions of interest are segmented from the visual rhythm and then classified as captions or non-captions according to a small number of rules.

C. San Martin and S.-W. Kim (Eds.): CIARP 2011, LNCS 7042, pp. 157–164, 2011.
© Springer-Verlag Berlin Heidelberg 2011

The text is organized as follows. Section 2 describes some related work available in the literature. The definitions of visual rhythm and video caption are introduced in Sections 3 and 4, respectively. In Section 5, the proposed method is presented and discussed. Experimental results obtained are shown in Section 6. Finally, Section 7 concludes with some final remarks.

2   Related Work

Most works related to caption detection are based on approaches used to identify texts in still images, where temporal information is also considered.

Some works consider the pre-calculated MPEG DCT coefficients to speed up the detection process. The work in [2] performs the closed caption detection in sports videos by filtering group of images not supposed to have subtitles. In [12], DCT coefficients are taken into account to extract contrast and regularity information, which can be used to detect the existence of captions in video frames. Both considered only the I-frames in MPEG video streams. The work in [13] also detects captions on the I-frames of a MPEG sequence. In this case, the DCT coefficients are filtered based on texture analysis. These three strategies fail to detect the exact frames from the beginning and end of the subtitle.

The work in [5] considers an SVM classifier in the discrimination of features derived from a wavelet transform. The frame rate is reduced to 1 *fps* to speed up the method, so it cannot precisely define the range of frames conveying the corresponding caption information.

A set of morphological operators is used in [10] to detect candidate regions in each frame. Further, statistical moment and linear projections are considered in the textual classification of the image components. In order to emphasize contrast, a convolution filter is introduced in [1], followed by the analysis of edge density and connected components in each sub-region of a frame. Both works perform a frame-by-frame detection, showing that they are costly operations.

In [3], the authors consider the visual rhythm to locate potential frames with subtitles. A Prewitt filter is used to extract horizontal edges. Each edge, after a size filtering, is considered a potential caption. This strategy proved to generate many false positives. The used visual rhythm corresponds to the union of the vertical, diagonal, and reverse diagonal lines.

Finally, the work in [6] analyzes an initial set of frames and try to refine the obtained results, for the next frames, through the assumption that the previously detected captions should last for a certain period of time.

3   Visual Rhythm

A video slice is defined as a set of pixels of an image linearly arranged in a 1D signal. The *visual rhythm* is then represented by the slices of all frames of a video sequence, kept together in a certain manner. Equation 1 defines a 1D slice, f, of a frame F with M rows and N columns.

$$f[i] = \sum_{p=k-j}^{k+j} \alpha_p F(i, p) \tag{1}$$

where $0 \leq i < M$, $0 \leq p < M$, $k = M/2$, and $\sum \alpha_p = 1$. When $j = 0$, pixels in the middle column of F are taken to form the corresponding slice. Here, to guarantee a certain contrast homogeneity of the slices we consider $j = 1$ and perform a maximum filter in Equation 1, such that

$$f[i] = \max\left[\alpha_{p-1}F(i, p-1), \alpha_p F(i, p), \alpha_{p+1}F(i, p+1)\right] \tag{2}$$

By putting these slides together over time, we define a 2D image which constitutes the visual rhythm representation [8]. Independently from the way the slices are formed, each slice is disposed vertically to generate the corresponding visual rhythm whose width depends on the number of frames in the whole video.

Figure 1 shows the visual rhythm for a sequence of captioned frames in a video. Several features can be clearly observed from the figure, such as scene transitions. The captions, in particular, are easily identifiable, represented by the white rectangular bands in the lower image area.

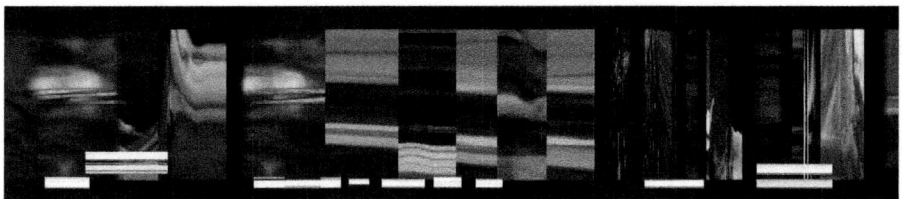

Fig. 1. Visual rhythm generated from captioned video frames

To improve the caption detection process, more detailed curves can be used to extract pixels more evenly distributed along the frames compared to a vertical slice, as defined in Equation 1. Although the use of space-filling curves [9], such as Hilbert, Peano, or zig-zag scans, increases the visual rhythm height and, consequently, execution time, the results of the caption detection process are more precise, as reported in Section 6.

4   Caption Features

In this work, we consider the following basic aspects of the subtitled texts in a video sequence: (i) they are superimposed to the images by an editing technique, and (ii) there is no caption motion during a certain range of time.

The work in [4] describes important features related to subtitling practices in image sequences, which include duration and height of captions. Some of these issues are taken into account in our work to establish some caption filters. One of them considers that, except for extreme cases, the lowest line of the caption should be at least 1/12 of the screen height just above the bottom of the screen.

According to the aforementioned work, the minimum duration of a single-word subtitle should be 3/2 seconds. For the spectator to clearly perceive a caption transition, at least 1/4 of a second needs to be inserted between two consecutive subtitles.

5   Proposed Methodology

The main steps of the proposed methodology are illustrated in Figure 2, which are described in more details in the following subsections.

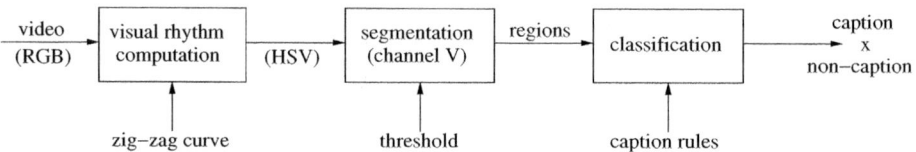

Fig. 2. Diagram of the proposed method

5.1   Visual Rhythm Calculation

Initially, each frame of the video sequence, in RGB format, is scanned by a certain curve to produce a slice. The zig-zag curve, shown in Figure 3, was chosen since it is simple and capable of passing across captions in arbitrary orientations. This curve can be parameterized at multiple scales by varying its number of diagonal lines. The greater the curve length, the larger the size of the visual rhythm, such that a proper scale should be obtained to balance efficiency and accuracy. Results are shown in Section 6.

To avoid a caption not being detected during the curve traversal by passing, for instance, exactly between two words, a morphological dilation operation is applied to each color band of the original frame. A way of speeding up this process is to apply the dilation only to pixels passing through the curve. Each frame can also be partitioned into a number of blocks with uniform size. For

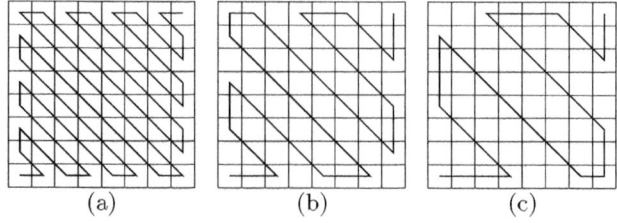

Fig. 3. Examples of zig-zag curves in three different scales

instance, when frames are divided into 5 × 5 blocks, coarser or finer scale curves could be used in each block to produce portions of slices. The resulting visual rhythm is obtained by the union of these 25 partial slices and converted into HSV color space.

The proposed segmentation and classification approaches are described in the following subsections, as shown in Figure 2. These two steps should be quite simple in order to improve computational time.

5.2 Segmentation

The visual rhythm segmentation is basically the extraction of candidate caption regions in the V channel of HSV format. A threshold is applied to the visual rhythm image to separate the regions from the background. It is worth mentioning that captions are embedded into the video frames, assuring a proper contrast with the foreground.

As a result of the segmentation process, connected regions are formed by a set of pixels with low gradient. Figure 4 gives an example of segmented image from a portion of the visual rhythm shown in Figure 1.

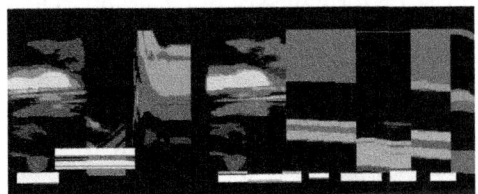

Fig. 4. Result of segmentation process for a portion of the visual rhythm shown in Figure 1

5.3 Classification

The classification step labels the segmented regions as caption or non-captions. As mentioned before, captions will form rectangular areas. Ideally, each caption in the visual rhythm generates a single connected region after the segmentation.

The classification has three steps. Initially, regions that do not meet certain requirements for caption dimensions are discarded. Captions should be at least 45 pixels wide and at most 1/12 of the frame height, as discussed in Section 4. Second, a measure of rectangularity, defined as the ratio between the area of a segmented region and the area of its bounding box, should be within a tolerance value. Third, a thinning algorithm [11] is applied to each region, which will generate a horizontal line if the region is a rectangle. Regions that do not form horizontal lines are discarded.

6   Results

Results for a number of video sequences are reported in this section. The data set is formed by a collection of videos of various categories, containing captions in different languages (western, eastern and middle eastern) and orientations. Due to the difficulty in finding videos with captions in any orientation, subtitles rotated by 10°and 20°were embedded into some videos. The beginning and end frame numbers in which captions appear in the tested videos were manually identified to be used as ground truth. All videos are in a resolution of about 480×270 pixels. The data set used in our experiments is available in [7]. The method has been implemented in C++ on a PC with 2.3 GHz Pentium IV CPU and 1GB RAM memory.

The visual rhythm was adequately generated by using a zig-zag curve with three lines. Each frame can be partitioned into 3×3 regions. A threshold value of 40 was used to separate the candidate caption regions, whereas a rectangularity measure of 0.95 was used to classify the regions as captions or non-captions.

The proposed methodology was applied to the video sequences and compared against three different approaches. The F-measure, computed through precision and recall rates, as well as the number of frames per second during the execution, are used to evaluate the performance of our method. The F-measure is defined as

$$\text{F-Measure} = 2 * \frac{\text{precision} * \text{recall}}{\text{precision} + \text{recall}} \tag{3}$$

where $\text{precision} = \dfrac{\text{tp}}{\text{tp} + \text{fp}}$, $\text{recall} = \dfrac{\text{tp}}{\text{tp} + \text{fn}}$, and fp, fn and tp correspond to false positives, false negatives and true positives, respectively.

Table 1 presents the results obtained with the tested methods. Even with simple segmentation and classification approaches, it is possible to see that the proposed method produces superior results for the majority of the video sequences, including captions written in Japanese and Arabic languages, as well as rotated captions.

Table 2 shows the average number of video frames analyzed per second (FPS). It can be observed that the use of visual rhythm is much faster than the frame-by-frame approaches. Although the proposed method slightly looses in performance when compared with [3], it is possible to speed up the process in detriment of certain accuracy level.

The plot, shown in Figure 5, presents the F-measure for the proposed method, varying the number of frame partitions (1×1, 3×3 or 5×5 blocks) and the number of diagonal lines (1, 3, 5 or 7) used to build the zig-zag curve. It can be observed that it is not advantageous to divide the video frames into 5×5 blocks. The best result was obtained when no fragmentation (1×1) was applied, however, this requires a more detailed curve (5 lines), costing more processing time. On the other hand, the video fragmentation into 3×3 blocks and the use of 3 lines produce a nearly identical result, justifying the choice of this setting in our experiments. A very detailed curve (7 lines) has a significant drop in the plot due to the increase of the number of false positives.

Table 1. Video data sets and performance of the tested approaches

Method	Measures (%)	News	Movies	Commercial	Japanese	Arabic	Rotated
Proposed	Precision	76.7	78.5	79.0	94.7	96.6	79.6
	Recall	97.6	93.8	100.0	99.7	95.8	99.6
	F-Measure	**85.9**	84.7	**88.2**	**97.1**	**96.2**	**88.5**
Wu et al. [10]	Precision	73.5	77.4	61.4	88.0	69.0	65.4
	Recall	99.5	94.8	98.5	99.5	99.0	100.0
	F-Measure	84.6	**85.0**	75.7	93.4	81.3	79.1
Agnihotri and	Precision	90.0	85.3	65.5	79.6	68.0	75.1
Dimitrova [1]	Recall	73.6	66.7	57.1	33.3	18.0	56.3
	F-Measure	81.0	74.8	61.0	46.9	28.5	64.3
Chun et al. [3]	Precision	41.7	33.8	73.1	24.8	14.0	73.9
	Recall	99.8	88.3	92.9	94.1	92.1	60.4
	F-Measure	58.9	47.4	81.8	39.2	24.3	66.4
Number of frames		6285	15589	900	11140	6875	650

Table 2. Average number of frames analyzed per second for each tested approach

Method	FPS
Proposed	93.10
Wu et al. [10]	0.84
Agnihotri and Dimitrova [1]	2.52
Chun et al. [3]	109.24

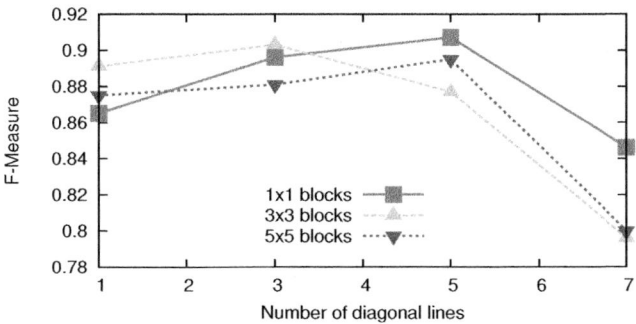

Fig. 5. Results for F-Measure obtained by varying the number of diagonal lines in the zig-zag curve and the number of frame blocks for the proposed method

7   Conclusions and Future Work

A new video caption detection method is described in this work. A data structure, called visual rhythm, is created by sub-sampling each video frame with a multi-scale curve. The captions are detected from the visual rhythm through a set of simple rules.

The method is robust to detect captions located in any position and orientation in the video frames, as well as unknown text layout common in different languages. Experimental results demonstrated the effectiveness of the proposed method compared to three other approaches.

As future work, we plan to investigate more effective techniques for segmenting and classifying the visual rhythm, which may significantly improve the results of the proposed method in terms of precision and recall rates.

Acknowledgments. The authors are thankful to FAPESP, CNPq and CAPES for the financial support.

References

1. Agnihotri, L., Dimitrova, N.: Text Detection for Video Analysis. In: IEEE Workshop on Content-Based Access of Image and Video Libraries, pp. 109–113 (1999)
2. Chen, D.Y., Hsiao, M.H., Lee, S.Y.: Automatic Closed Caption Detection and Font Size Differentiation in MPEG Video. In: Chang, S.-K., Chen, Z., Lee, S.-Y. (eds.) VISUAL 2002. LNCS, vol. 2314, pp. 276–287. Springer, Heidelberg (2002)
3. Chun, S.S., Hyeokman, K., Jung-Rim, K., Sangwook, O., Sanghoon, S.: Fast text caption localization on video using visual rhythm. In: Chang, S.-K., Chen, Z., Lee, S.-Y. (eds.) VISUAL 2002. LNCS, vol. 2314, pp. 259–268. Springer, Heidelberg (2002)
4. Karamitroglou, F.: A Proposed Set of Subtitling Standards in Europe. Translation Journal 2(2) (February 2007)
5. Lee, C.C., Chiang, Y.C., Huang, H.M., Tsai, C.L.: A Fast Caption Localization and Detection for News Videos. In: International Conference on Innovative Computing, Information and Control, Los Alamitos, CA, USA, pp. 226–229 (September 2007)
6. Lienhart, R., Wernicke, A.: Localizing and Segmenting Text in Images and Videos. IEEE Transactions on Circuits and Systems for Video Technology 12(4), 256–268 (2002)
7. LIV: Video Sequences (2010),
   http://www.liv.ic.unicamp.br/~felipebvalio/base.zip
8. Ngo, C., Pong, T., Chin, R.: Detection of Gradual Transitions through Temporal Slice Analysis. In: IEEE Conference on Computer Vision and Pattern Recognition, pp. 36–41 (1999)
9. Sagan, H.: Space-Filling Curves. Springer, New York (1994)
10. Wu, J.-C., Hsieh, J.-W., Chen, Y.-S.: Morphology-based Text Line Extraction. Machine Vision and Applications 19(3), 195–207 (2008)
11. Zhang, T.Y., Suen, C.Y.: A fast parallel algorithm for thinning digital patterns. Communications of the ACM 27, 236–239 (1984)
12. Zhang, Y., Chua, T.S.: Detection of Text Captions in Compressed Domain Video. In: ACM Multimedia, Los Angeles, CA, USA, pp. 201–204 (2000)
13. Zhong, Y., Zhang, H., Jain, A.: Automatic Caption Localization in Compressed Video. IEEE Transactions on Pattern Analysis and Machine Intelligence 22(4), 385–392 (2000)

Morphology Based Spatial Relationships between Local Primitives in Line Drawings

Naeem A. Bhatti[1,*] and Allan Hanbury[2]

[1] Institute of Computer Aided Automation, Vienna University of Technology,
Favoritenstrasse. 9/183-2, 1040 Vienna, Austria
bhatti@caa.tuwien.ac.at
[2] Institute of Software Technology and Interactive Systems,
Vienna University of Technology,
Favoritenstrasse. 9/188, 1040 Vienna, Austria
hanbury@ifs.tuwien.ac.at

Abstract. Local primitives and their spatial relationships are useful in the analysis, recognition and retrieval of document and patent binary images. In this paper, a morphology based approach is proposed to establish the connections between the local primitives found at the optimally detected junction points and end points. The grayscale geodesic dilation is employed as the basic technique by taking a marker image with gray values at the local primitives and the skeleton of the original image as the mask image. The geodesic paths along the skeleton between the local primitives are traversed and their points of contact are protected by updating the mask image after each geodesic dilation iteration. By scanning the final marker image for the contact points of the traversed geodesic paths, connections between the local primitives are established. The proposed approach is robust and scale invariant.

Keywords: local primitives, spatial relationships, grayscale geodesic dilation.

1 Introduction

Binary images such as technical drawings, diagrams, flowcharts etc. are found in patents and scientific documents. They are composed of lines intersecting each other in different directions. The local pattern formed by the composition of intersecting or crossing lines at a junction point and end point of lines is called a local primitive. Local primitives and their spatial arrangement are useful in the analysis, recognition and retrieval of binary images. To capture the content of binary images found in patents, different geometric shapes and their spatial relationships have been the target information to be explored in the literature.

In an attempt to capture the topological information in drawings, the spatial relationships between shape primitives have been modeled at inclusion, adjacency and disjoint levels in [8] and at inclusion and adjacency levels in [14].

---

* This research work was supported by Higher Education Commission (HEC) Pakistan under the "Pakistan Overseas Scholarship Program for PhD in Selected Fields".

C. San Martin and S.-W. Kim (Eds.): CIARP 2011, LNCS 7042, pp. 165–172, 2011.

Targeting the retrieval of hand drawn sketches, Leung et al. [12] and Parker et al. [15] estimate shape types from each stroke using heuristics and exploit spatial relationship at only inclusion level with the geometrical relationship between multiple strokes. Fonseca et al. [7] capture the topological information of the drawing by isolating polygons and modeling the spatial relationships of polygons in the form of a topology graph. Liu et al. [13] detect the lines and curves in a line drawing and capture the local neighborhood structure of a local patch in the drawing by considering a primitive as a reference and using four geometric cues such as relative minimum distance (the minimum distance between the neighbor and the reference primitives divided by the length of the reference), relative distance, relative length and relative angle to describe the spatial relationships between the reference and neighboring primitives. Huet et al. [11] extract line patterns in skeleton images obtained by Voronoi Skeletonization of patent images and create line segments from the extracted line patterns by a polygonization technique. The relational features of a line segment in relation to another line segment such as relational angle and relational position are used to capture the geometric structure of the image. In an attempt to generate an approximate formal ground truth similar to the ground truth binary map (silhouette) created by a human from the input map of an image, Bergevin et al. [2] use six criteria for grouping the constant-curvature contour primitives in a pairwise fashion based on the Gestalt grouping laws [6]. A grouping criterion is decided based upon the distance of the two primitives in pixels. Santosh et al. [16] presented an approach to unify the topological and spatial relations between two objects by finding a unique reference point set based on their minimum bounding rectangle topology. Forstner [9] emphasizes that the neighborhood relations derived from a Voronoi diagram exhibit uncertainty when the common sides of two Voronoi cells are comparably short. The author proposed the concept of fuzzy Delaunay triangulation which takes into account the uncertainty in neighborhood relations between point fields based on a Voronoi diagram or planar Delaunay triangulation [18].

For the natural images, the local features lying at an arbitrary distance (Euclidean) to a specific local feature inside its circular neighborhood of arbitrary radius are assumed to be spatially related to each other [1], [3]. In binary line drawing images, the technique of an arbitrary circular neighborhood around a local primitive establishes the spatial relationship between two local primitives which may not be geodesically related to each other. In a line drawing image, two local primitives with a geodesic path (skeletal line connection) between them that does not pass through any other primitives are said to have a *geodesic spatial neighborhood relationship*.

To establish the geodesic spatial relationships between the local primitives, a novel mathematical morphology based approach is proposed in this paper. The main contributions are: (1) establishment of connections between local primitives based on the geodesic paths (skeletal line connections between them), (2) adaptation of the mask image after each geodesic dilation iteration to protect the points of contact of the traversed geodesic paths between the local primitives, (3) extraction of adjacency relations (connections) between local primitives based on the image generated by infinite geodesic dilations by the proposed algorithm. The proposed approach is robust in establishing the spatial relationships between all the local primitives found in a line drawing image and is explained in Section 3. The detection and classification of local primitives is explained in Section 2. The results for the proposed approach are presented and discussed in Section 4 and a conclusion is drawn in Section 5.

2   Detection and Classification of Local Primitives

At first, a homotopic skeleton of the original image is obtained by performing a series of sequential morphological thinning operations [17]. Template based matching [17] is used to detect junction points and end points in the homotopic skeleton which gives rise to false detections due to the false skeletal lines introduced during the thinning process of the image as can be seen in Figure 1(a). A morphological spurring operation [17] removes the parasitic skeletal lines in the skeleton image by the number of iterations it is performed. An intersection of the skeleton image containing detections with an iteratively morphological spurred image eradicates the false detections. To determine an optimum number of iterations for the morphological spurring operation, the proposed approach takes into account the average thickness of lines L_{th} obtained by taking a weighted average of the pattern spectrum [17] $PS_k(I)$ obtained from the granulometry of the original image, given as:

$$L_{th} = \frac{\sum_k PS_k(I) * k}{\sum_k PS_k(I)} \tag{1}$$

where $PS_k(I)$ is the value of bin k of the $PS_k(I)$ and is obtained by taking the discrete derivative of the granulometric curve of the original image. To remove the noisy detections, an optimum number of spurring iterations for EPs are computed as $GI_{EP} = \lceil L_{th}/2 \rceil$ and for JPs as $GI_{JP} = \lfloor L_{th} \rfloor$ (the values for L_{th} obtained are floating point) [5]. An optimum detection for JPs and EPs is shown in the Figures 1(b) and 1(c) respectively. The combined optimum detection of EPs and JPs is shown in Figure 2(l) superimposed as green plus marks on the ground truth marked as red.

The local primitives (EPPs and JPPs) are classified into primitive classes by taking into account their composition in an 8-directional space using a distance based approach [4]. Lines in regions around junction and end points are quantized into 8 directions, which are represented in a binary vector similar to the approach used in the Local Binary Pattern (LBP) [10]. There are 8 end point primitive classes and 244 junction point primitive classes (not 248 because the junction point primitives composed of lines having an angular difference of exactly 180° with each other do not fulfill the definition of a junction point primitive and would be 4 in number in 8-directional space). As a result of this process, each EPP and JPP has a class number associated with it. It is also possible to quantize into 4 directions instead of 8, resulting in only 14 classes (4 for EPPs and 10 for JPPs).

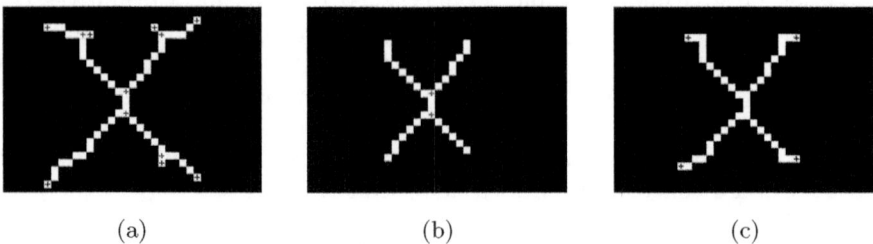

(a)   (b)   (c)

Fig. 1. (a) Noisy thinned image with JPs and EPs detected (b) The GI_{JP} times spurred skeletal image with JPs detection.(c) EPs detection in GI_{EP} times spurred skeletal image.

3   Geodesic Spatial Relationships between Local Primitives

To establish the geodesic spatial neighborhood relationship between such local primitives, the proposed approach intends to traverse the existing geodesic path between them. By establishing the geodesic spatial relationships between the local primitives found in a line drawing, the pair-wise co-occurrence of local primitives can be captured. To traverse the geodesic paths between all the local primitives, the proposed approach constructs a gray scale image G by placing unique gray value pixels at the positions of the local primitives and a gray scale skeleton image S by assigning a gray value $G_m = \max(G) + 1$ to the non-zero pixels in the binary skeleton image obtained by GI_{EP} spurring iterations in Section 2. To establish the geodesic spatial relationships between the local primitives, a morphology based approach using successive gray scale geodesic dilations is adopted. Considering S as the mask image and G as the marker image, the proposed approach performs successive gray scale geodesic dilations [17]. At the nth grayscale geodesic dilation, a grayscale marker image I_{d_n} and the grayscale mask image I_{m_n} are obtained by:

$$I_{d_n} = \delta \left(I_{d_{n-1}} \right) \wedge I_{m_{n-1}} \tag{2}$$

$$I_{m_n} = I_{m_{n-1}} \wedge f_{0 \to G_m} \left(I_{d_n} \right) \tag{3}$$

where $n = 1, 2, \dots$ and $I_{d_0} = G$, $I_{m_0} = S$ are the initial grayscale marker and mask images as shown in Figures 2 (a) and (d) respectively for an example image. The function $f_{0 \to G_m}$ converts all zero-pixels in I_{d_n} to G_m. Successive gray scale geodesic dilations are performed until $I_{d_n} = I_{d_{n-1}}$ where each dilation operation δ is performed by a unit structuring element. When applying the above process, at each successive geodesic dilation operation, geodesic paths emerging from each local primitive towards their spatially connected local primitives are traversed by converting one non-zero pixel of each geodesic path (skeletal line connection) to the corresponding gray value of the local primitive. A geodesic path consisting of n pixels between two local primitives takes $n/2$ successive dilation operations to be traversed from each local primitive. In this way, geodesic

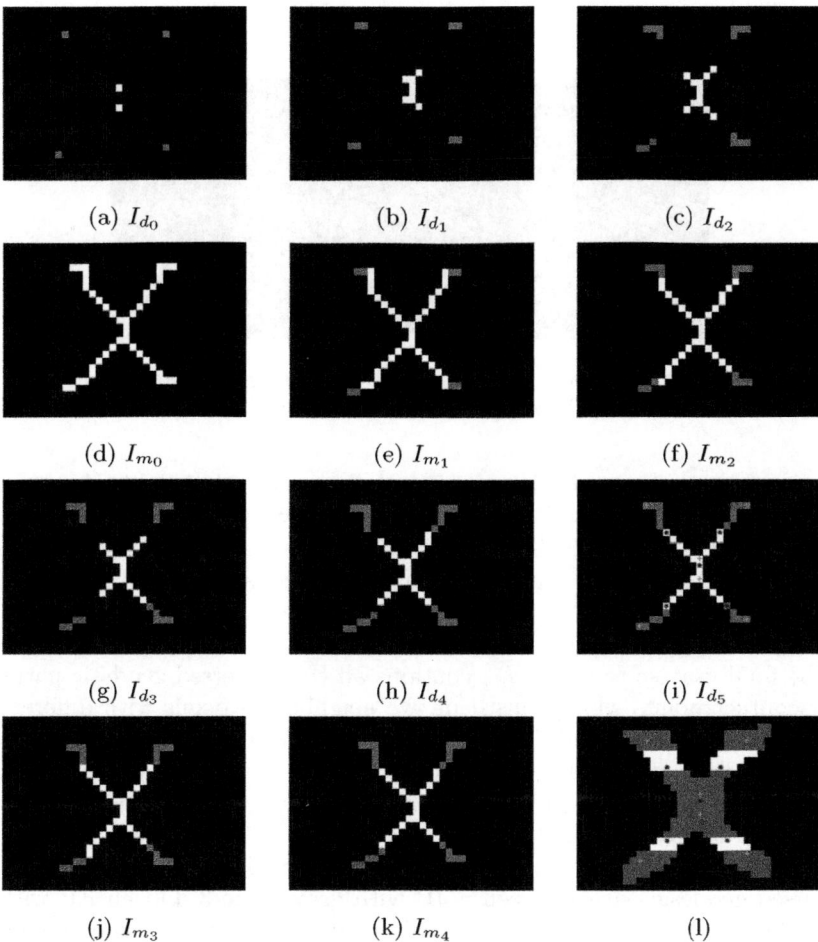

Fig. 2. (a)-(c) and (g)-(i) show the successive grayscale marker images at each successive grayscale geodesic dilation. $I_{d_0} = G$ is the initial gray scale marker image and I_{d_5} is the final grayscale image for the example image containing points of contact shown with blue asterisk marks and locations of local primitives with green plus marks. (d)-(f) and (j), (k) show the corresponding grayscale mask images at successive geodesic dilation. $I_{m_0} = S$ is the initial mask image obtained by assigning gray value G_m to non-zero pixels to the skeleton image $SSI_{GI_{EP}}$. The original example image with red ground truth for JPs and EPs, superimposed detection of JPs and EPs in green plus marks and their contact points for geodesic spatial relationships in blue asterisk marks determined by the proposed method is shown in (l).

paths of short length are traversed before than the long ones. Continuing the path traversing procedure overruns the contact points of already traversed paths of short lengths. To protect the contact points, the mask image I_{m_n} is updated after each successive dilation operation as given by Equation 3. The successive

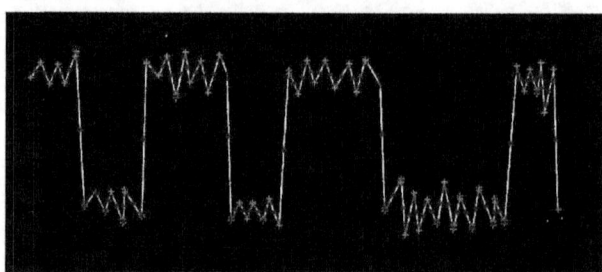

Fig. 3. One of the ten images with ground truth points (red) and superimposed detected EPs and JPs (green) with contact points of traversed geodesic paths (blue)

steps involved in the establishment of geodesic spatial relationships between local primitives by the proposed approach are shown visually for an example image in the Figure 2. Figures 2 (b), (c), (g), (h) and (i) show the images obtained by the successive gray scale geodesic dilation operations given by Equation 2. The corresponding I_{m_n} mask images for the I_{d_n} marker images are shown in Figures 2 (d), (e), (f), (j) and (k).

The final gray scale image I_{d_n} contains all the traversed geodesic paths with their contact points which consist of two neighboring pixels with different gray values indicating the spatially connected local primitives. Local primitives which have geodesic spatial relationships between them are found by scanning I_{d_n} for the neighboring different gray value pixels and their neighborhood relations are established by locating their corresponding locations in the original image using the initial grayscale image e.g. the neighboring pixels at a contact point of the traversed geodesic path between a JP with gray value 3 and an EP with gray value 20 indicates that JP 3 is spatially connected to EP 20 and the geodesic

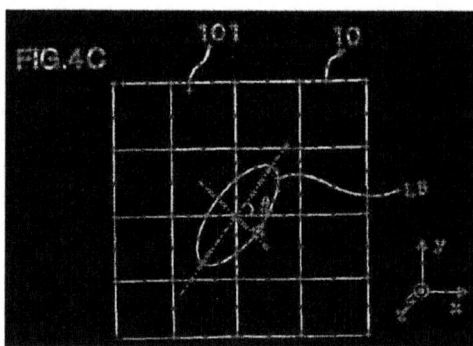

Fig. 4. One of the ten images with ground truth points (red) and superimposed detected EPs and JPs (green) with contact points of traversed geodesic paths (blue)

spatial relationship between the corresponding local primitives of these gray values is established in the original image. The established geodesic spatial relationships between the local primitives (EPPs and JPPs) by the proposed approach are shown superimposed on the final I_{d_n} (which is I_{d_5} for this image) and original example image with ground truth of junction and end points (marked as red) in Figures 2 (i) and (l). The green points mark the JPs and EPs and the blue points mark the contact points of the geodesic paths traversed from each point towards other neighboring points.

4   Results and Discussion

To evaluate the performance of the proposed approach ten images are selected from a publically available patent image database[1]. The visual results for two out of the ten selected images are shown in Figures 3 and 4. It can be seen that the proposed approach successfully establishes the geodesic spatial relationships between all the local primitives found at the detected junction and end points. Having established the geodesic neighborhood relations of the local primitives by the developed method, the pairwise co-occurrences of the local primitives in addition to their independent occurrences can be captured. In an occurrence histogram each bin represents the occurrence frequency of a local primitive, whereas each bin of co-occurrence histogram represents the occurrence frequency of a pair of local primitives. The representation of line drawing images in terms of the occurrence and co-occurrence histograms of local primitives are useful in the recognition, analysis and retrieval of these images. It is noted that the establishment of geodesic spatial relationships is highly dependent on the detection of EPs and JPs which is a first step in the proposed approach. Due to the false EPs and JPs detections, geodesic spatial relationships can be established between a true and a false local primitive, which can be overcome by eradicating the false detections. The proposed approach takes $n/2$ iterations to establish the spatial relationships between two primitives which are n pixels apart. So, the computational complexity of the approach depends upon the longest distance (in terms of pixels) of any two primitives in an image and scale of the image as well.

5   Conclusion

A novel mathematical morphology based approach employing the grayscale geodesic dilation is proposed to establish the spatial relationships between the local primitives found at the junction and end points in binary line drawing images. The proposed approach is robust and successfully established the geodesic spatial relationships between all the local primitives. As the detection and classification of local primitives found at the junction points and end points is the first step, the establishment of geodesic spatial relationships depends upon the detection of these points. By establishing the geodesic spatial relationships between

---

[1] http://mklab.iti.gr/content/patent-database

local primitives, their pairwise co-occurrences in addition to the independent occurrences can be captured in the form of histograms which are useful in the recognition, retrieval and classification of drawing images.

References

1. Amores, J., Sebe, N., Radeva, P.: Context-based object-class recognition and retrieval by generalized correlograms. IEEE Transactions on Pattern Analysis and Machine Intelligence 29, 1818–1833 (2007)
2. Bergevin, R., Filiatrault, A.: Enhancing Contour Primitives by Pairwise Grouping and Relaxation. In: Kamel, M.S., Campilho, A. (eds.) ICIAR 2007. LNCS, vol. 4633, pp. 222–233. Springer, Heidelberg (2007)
3. Bhatti, N.A., Hanbury, A.: Co-occurrence bag of words for object recognition. In: Proceedings of the 15th Computer Vision Winter Workshop, pp. 21–28 (2010)
4. Bhatti, N.A., Hanbury, A.: Detection and classification of local primitives in line drawings. In: Proceedings of the 35th Austrian Association for Pattern Recognition (2011)
5. Bhatti, N.A., Hanbury, A.: Granulometry based detection of junction and end points in patent drawings. In: Proceedings of the 7th International Symposium on Image and Signal Processing and Analysis, ISPA (2011)
6. Desolneux, A., Moisan, L., Morel, J.-M.: Seeing, Thinking and Knowing. In: Carsetti, A. (ed.) Kluwer Academic Publishers, Dordrecht (2004)
7. Fonseca, M.J., Ferreira, A., Jorge, J.A.: Content-based retrieval of technical drawings. Special Issue of International Journal of Computer Applications in Technology, IJCAT (2004)
8. Fonseca, M.J., Ferreira, A., Jorge, J.A.: Sketch-based retrieval of complex drawings using hierarchical topology and geometry. Computer Aided Design 41(12), 1067–1081 (2009)
9. Förstner, W.: Uncertain neighborhood relations of point sets and fuzzy delaunay triangulation. In: Mustererkennung 1999, 21. DAGM-Symposium, pp. 213–222 (1999)
10. Heikkila, M., Pietikainen, M., Schmid, C.: Description of interest regions with local binary patterns. Pattern Recognition 42(3), 425–436 (2009)
11. Huet, B., Guarascio, G., Kern, N.J., Mérialdo, B.: Relational skeletons for retrieval in patent drawings. In: ICIP, pp. 737–740 (2001)
12. Leung, W.H., Chen, T.: User-independent retrieval of free-form hand-drawn sketches. In: Proc. of the IEEE ICASSP 2002, pp. 2029–2032. IEEE Press (2002)
13. Liu, R., Wang, Y., Baba, T., Masumoto, D.: Shape detection from line drawings with local neighborhood structure. Pattern Recognition 43(5), 1907–1916 (2010)
14. Park, J.H., Um, B.S.: A new approach to similarity retrieval of 2-d graphic objects based on dominant shapes. Pattern Recogn. Lett. 20(6), 591–616 (1999)
15. Parker, C., Chen, T.: Hierarchical matching for retrieval of hand-drawn sketches. In: ICME, pp. 29–32. IEEE Computer Society, Washington, DC, USA (2003)
16. Santosh, K.C., Wendling, L., Lamiroy, B.: Unified Pairwise Spatial Relations: An Application to Graphical Symbol Retrieval. In: Ogier, J.-M., Liu, W., Lladós, J. (eds.) GREC 2009. LNCS, vol. 6020, pp. 163–174. Springer, Heidelberg (2010)
17. Soille, P.: Morphological Image Analysis: Principles and Applications, 2nd edn. Springer, Heidelberg (2003)
18. Forstner, W., Heuel, S.: A dual, scalable and hierarchical representation for. perceptual organization of binary images. In: Workshop on Perceptual Organization in Computer Vision. IEEE Computer Society (1998)

Fully Automatic Methodology for Human Action Recognition Incorporating Dynamic Information

Ana González, Marcos Ortega Hortas, and Manuel G. Penedo

University of A Coruña, VARPA group, A Coruña 15071, Spain
{ana.gonzalez,mortega,mgpenedo}@udc.es

Abstract. In this paper, a star-skeleton-based methodology is described for analyzing the motion of a human target in a video sequence. Star skeleton is a fast skeletonization technique by connecting centroid of target object to its contour extremes. We represent the skeleton as a five-dimensional vector, which includes information about the positions of head and four limbs of a human shape in a given frame. In this manner, an action is composed of a sequence of star skeletons. With the purpose of use an HMM which allows model the actions, a posture codebook is built integrating star skeleton and motion information. With this last information we can distinct better between actions. Supervised (manual) and No-supervised methods (clustering-based methodology) have been used to create the posture codebook. The codebook is dependently of the actions to represent (We choose four actions as example: walk, jump, wave and jack). Obtained results show, firstly, including motion information is important to get a correctly differentiation between actions. On the other hand, using a clustering methodology to create the codebook causes a substantial improvement in results.

Keywords: Human action recognition, Star skeleton, Clustering, Hidden Markov Models.

1 Introduction

Vision-based human action recognition is currently a significant research topic, since it can be useful for a wide variety of applications, such as video indexing and browsing, virtual or augmented reality.

Several human action recognition methods were proposed in the past few years: model-based methods, eigenspace technique and Hidden Markov Model. HMM has been used successfully in speech recognition and is a training based recognition technique. HMM transforms the problem of action recognition into the problem of pattern recognition. Yamato et al. [6] are the first researchers who applied HMM for action recognition. Some of the recent works [1], [2], [4] and [7] have shown that HMM performs well in human action recognition as well.

This paper [1] proposes an action recognition method based on HMM using star skeleton as the recognition feature, with a symbol codebook built using

C. San Martin and S.-W. Kim (Eds.): CIARP 2011, LNCS 7042, pp. 173–180, 2011.

clustering-based methodology, in an automatic way. In addition, each symbol of our codebook includes information of the motion direction of the target in order to consider dynamic information.

The paper is organized as follows. In section 2, we make a review of the system proposed by [1] and [2]. In section 3 we introduce the automatic generation of the codebook. We also introduce the need of including dynamic information (direction vector) in the posture of a human in base to complete the description of each symbol and improve the action recognition. Section 4 shows some experimental results and, finally, section 5 offers final conclusions and future work discussion.

2   Action Recognition Using Star Skeletonization

The system architecture consists of three parts: feature extraction, mapping features to symbols and action recognition.

A frame is processed to extract the contours from a human silhouette. Then, the associated star skeleton is obtained according to a distance defined in the skeleton space. A posture codebook is built containing representative star skeletons (symbols) of each action. When the system gets a new star skeleton, it is mapped to the most similar symbol in the codebook. HMMs are used to model the different actions. They receive a symbol sequence and give a probability value associated to the action each HMM is trained for.

2.1   Feature Extraction

Obviously, there is no perfect motion detection algorithm. In this approach, a very simple method is used: background subtraction. There will be spurious pixels detected and other anomalies, so a preprocessing step is needed. The difference between the background image and the current frame is binarized and morphological dilation and erosion are used to extract a high quality border contour.

The method proposed by [2] provides a real-time method for detecting extremal points on the boundary of the target to get the star skeleton. This structure consists of the head and four limbs of a human joined to its centroid. This is described as follows:

- Considering (x_i, y_i) points from border contour and N_b the total number of these points, the centroid (x_c, y_c) of the target is determined by:

$$x_c = \frac{1}{N_b} \sum_{i=1}^{N_b} x_i \quad y_c = \frac{1}{N_b} \sum_{i=1}^{N_b} y_i \qquad (1)$$

- The distances d_i (d_i is expressed as a one dimensional signal $d(i) = d_i$) from each border point to centroid are calculated:

$$d_i = \sqrt{(x_i - x_c)^2 + (y_i - y_c)^2} \qquad (2)$$

- d_i is smoothed (d_i') to reduce noise using a smoothing filter.
- The extremal points come by the local maxima of (d_i'). The star structure is built connecting them to the target centroid.
- In order to make the process valid independently of the person characteristics, normalization should be made to get relative distribution of the feature vectors. This is achieved dividing vectors by human dimensions (width and height).

Figure 1 shows examples of different skeletons obtained from person contours.

Fig. 1. Star skeletons obtained for distinct human targets

2.2   Mapping Features to Symbols

Once we have the star skeleton, we must define the concept of distance between feature vectors. The star skeleton is made up of five sub-vectors, so star distance between two feature vectors U and V ($d^*(U, V)$) could be defined as the sum of the Euclidean distances of the five sub-vectors.

$$d^*(U, V) = \sum_{i=1}^{5} ||U_i - V_i|| \qquad (3)$$

However, it is necessary to consider that the particular position of each human extremal is unknown, so a greedy mapping is needed to compare two feature vectors. The star distance is defined by minimal sum of the five sub-vectors in U in all permutations, where K is the total number of possible permutations and U_i^p is the sub-vector i in the permutation p in the feature vector U:

$$d^*(U, V) = \arg\min_p \sum_{i=1}^{5} ||U_i^p - V_i|| \quad p \in 1..K \qquad (4)$$

With the star distance defined, we can build a codebook with the most representative star skeletons for all the actions considered. Star skeletons obtained of each frame will be mapped to a symbol in the codebook to make the action recognition possible. Using a finite set of symbols the codebook is built manually: they choose subjectively symbols are subjectively chosen to be representative in a visual way.

2.3   Action Recognition

In order to achieve the action recognition, one HMM is designed for each action to be considered. The number of states was empirically determined. Once we have each action model trained (with symbols from the codebook), we calculate the probability of each model of generate the observation posture sequence. Considering the set of h HMMs of the model (where P_i is the HMM for action i) and a given symbol sequence s, the action associated to s will be calculated as:

$$\arg \max_i P_i(s), i = 1..h \tag{5}$$

where $P_i(s)$ is the probability of s in P_i. Also, it is required that the given sequence ends in a final state of P_i

3   Automatic Generation of Codebook

The process of constructing the codebook is manual in the current model. It carries some disadvantages, such as the subjective selection of symbols by a human, as well as the fact that symbols may not be representative enough in the codebook. Also, in a manual selection the time of the processing is high and tedious.

All these limitations can be improved choosing the most representative star skeletons, using an automatic method. In this paper we propose a way of building the codebook using a clustering-based method to automatically select the components in the codebook.

The method used to get the codebook symbols is the K-means, where the number of clusters is prefixed before the clustering. This number was chosen in base of the number of symbols used by [1] and considering a sufficient number to modeling the actions successfully. However, K-means algorithm has some limitations. In this case, the main inconvenient is the initialization-dependency inherent to the algorithm. This may lead to bad results, because in the training set there could be symbols more frequent than others. If in the initialization step, many clusters are assigned to very similar symbols, at the end of the process, some clusters will not have any symbol of the training set assigned. In addition, the rest of the clusters will not represent successfully all the possible symbols.

In order to find a solution for the problem of the K-means initialization, we introduce a modification at this point. First clusters must be really representative of the training set. The variance in the group is considered in order to extract the most different symbols from the set, so clusters are initialized as follows:

1. We choose cluster c as the symbol from the training set which minimizes the variance in the symbols group $G - c$:

$$\arg \min_c \text{Var}(G - c), c \in G \tag{6}$$

2. We compare each symbol in the training set with the first cluster using (4). Symbols $c' \in G$ too similar to the first cluster (up to a threshold λ, i.e. $|c - c'| \leq \lambda$) are eliminated from the training set: $G' = G - c'$.

3. If $|C \cup c| < n$ and $|G'| > 0$ then $G = G'$ and go to step 1; else $n = |C|$.

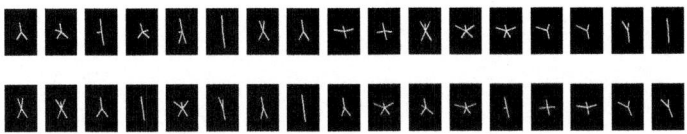

Fig. 2. 17-cluster codebook generated using manual method (above) and K-means algorithm (below) with initial $n = 20$ and $\lambda = 0.95$

Fig. 3. Sequence of star skeletons for action *walk* (left) and *jump* (right)

The main problem in this step is choose λ to discriminate the similarity between symbols. λ was selected empirically. High values of λ make elimination process too aggressive, leaving some clusters with no symbols assigned. This situation is also possible if the variance between symbols is very low. In these cases, the final number of clusters is automatically reduced by K-means. Figure 2 shows examples of codebooks, manual and K-means-generated by. Pattern recognition techniques present problems to distinguish very similar patterns. In our case, some symbols in the codebook are shared by many actions; even a sequence of an action can be a subsequence in another one, as Figure 3 shows. If we want to differentiate them, it is necessary to represent them in a different way. Using position each human extremal to represent a posture is not enough, so we add dynamic information to the symbols in the codebook. This information includes the direction of motion of the human target between consecutive frames. In this way, we can know if the star skeleton calculated in a frame is displaced respect the star skeleton in the previous.

The most important is to know the variation respect Y-axis: this can be a difference between the symbols in jump and walk sequence. It is also important know if the human target is still or moving, but system must work independently if he is moving left or right in the scene. Motions are accordingly transformed from left to right in any case.

The displacement of a human target is defined as the variation of the center of human target in the Y-axis over the X-axis during a sequence of frames. For an easier processing, we work with the angle of variation (measured in degrees) to evaluate the magnitude and direction of motion. This angle α of motion in the frame i respect to previous frame is computed as:

$$\alpha = \arctan((y_i - y_{i-1})/(x_i - x_{i-1})) \tag{7}$$

Where x_i and y_i are the pixels representing the mean point of human target dimensions in the frame i. The motion direction in function of α is shown in Figure 4. A color-coding is used to represent it in the skeleton figures. This dynamic component must be added to each symbol in the codebook, so the final

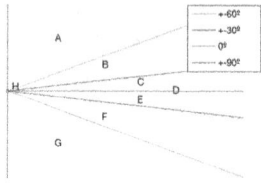

Legend	Angle of motion(Degrees)
▨	$90 \leq \alpha > 60$
▨	$60 \geq \alpha > 30$
▨	$30 \geq \alpha > 0$
■	$\alpha = 0$
■	$-30 \leq \alpha < 0$
■	$-60 \leq \alpha < -30$
■	$-90 \leq \alpha < -60$
☐	No motion

Fig. 4. Left: Diagram with the different types of possible direction in motion sequences. Right: Coding of the different directions of motion.

codebook will be the Cartesian product of the star skeletons (symbols obtained by K-means method) with all possible directions of displacement A calculated as (7) shows. A symbol s in the codebook is now defined as (8). When a new star skeleton comes we look for the most similar symbol in the new codebook, which is now a Cartesian product of skeleton symbols and direction symbols.

$$s = (c, \alpha) \quad c \in C, \alpha \in A \tag{8}$$

4   Results

Video sequences used in training and test phases have been token from [8] database, some frames of them are shown as example in Figure 5. Many sequences are extracted from each video and The number of sequences in the training set for each considered action is 206 (walk), 172 (jump), 98 (wave) and 104 (jack). Table 1 shows the confusion matrix of testing data. The left side is the ground truth of action types and the upper side is the recognition action types. It is possible to know in which type of action the system misclassifies sequences. From Table 1, left and center, we can see that a 91% of sequences are classified successfully with the manual method, while, with the K-means-based methodology this rate is over 97%. K-means achieved a significant improvement.

Empirically, we observed that if a sequence mapped to codebook symbols has an odd or not frequent symbol, the associated HMM can produce a high probability but, in some cases, it does not have to finish in a Markov final state. If the rest HMMs produce very low probability, we can use a threshold t to discriminate when it is neccesary to take the HMM with highest probability even if it had not finished in a final state. Thus, we follow the criterion given by (5) but introducing a new constraint: even in the case that model P_i does not end processing the sequence in a final state, the sequence is assigned to P_i if

$$P_i(s) \geq P_i^{'}(s) + t \qquad i = 1..h, \ \ t \in [0, 1] \tag{9}$$

Fig. 5. Examples of action video sequences from used database

Table 1. Confusion matrix for recognition of testing data using manual codebook (left) and K-means codebook (center). Confusion matrix for recognition of testing data using K-means codebook and HMMs with $t = 0.65$ (right).

	Walk	Jump	Wave	Jack
Walk	27	1	0	3
Jump	0	26	0	0
Wave	0	7	63	0
Jack	0	2	0	20

	Walk	Jump	Wave	Jack
Walk	28	2	0	1
Jump	0	26	0	0
Wave	0	0	70	0
Jack	0	1	0	21

	Walk	Jump	Wave	Jack
Walk	30	1	0	0
Jump	0	26	0	0
Wave	0	0	70	0
Jack	0	0	0	22

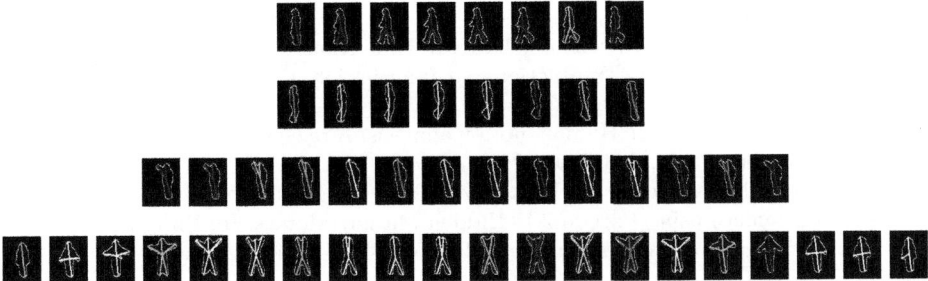

Fig. 6. Stars skeleton mapped to walk, jump, wave and jack action sequences

Adding this constraint improves the performance rendered by our HMMs, as shown in table 1, right. Finally, Figure 6 presents examples of sequences for different actions. It shows the contour of human targets and the symbols in the codebook matched with them. The direction obtained is also indicated in the skeletons with the color coding shown in Figure 4. It is simple to see that, although the sequences share many symbols, specially jump ones, the direction associated is different in each action and problems of shared symbols and subsequences are solved.

5   Conclusions and Future Work

In this paper improvements on action recognition based in star skeleton has been presented. Codebook selection is fully automatic, avoiding human intervention and its subjectivity. In addition, manual method chooses clusters among a finite symbols set, while the proposed clustering-based methodology chooses a optimal representation of the symbols, independently of set size and its variety.

K-means-method chooses initial clusters considering the variance in the symbols set, so the symbols chosen are the most representative. The number of clusters is enough to represent successfully all the actions presented as example.

Other methodologies can also be used to build the codebook in an automatic fashion, as Neural Networks. With this methodology more complex actions than those presented here could be considered. For more realistic applications it would be possible the continued recognition of successive sequences with different actions using dynamic HMM.

Acknowledgements. This paper has been partly funded by the Xunta de Galicia through the 10TIC009CT and 10/CSA918054PR grant contracts.

References

1. Chen, H.-S., Chen, H.-T., Chen, Y.-W., Lee, S.-Y.: Human Action Recognition Using Star Skeleton. In: Proc. VSSN 2006, Santa Barbara, CA, USA, pp. 171–178 (October 2006)
2. Fujiyoshi, H., Lipton, J., Kanade, T.: Real-Time Human Motion Analysis by Image Skeletonization. IEICE Transactions on Information and Systems E87-d(1), 113–119 (2004)
3. Aggarwal, J.K., Cai, Q.: Human motion analysis: A review. Computer Vision Image Understanding 73(3), 428–440 (1999)
4. Aloysius, L.H.W., Dong, G., Huang, Z., Tan, T.: Human Posture Recognition in Video Sequence using Pseudo 2-D Hidden Markov Models. In: Proc. International Conference on Control, Automation, Robotics and Vision Conference, vol. 1, pp. 712–716 (2004)
5. Kellokumpu, V., Pietikäinen, M., Heikkilä, J.: Human Activity Recognition Using Sequences of Postures. In: Proc. IAPR Conference on Machine Vision Application, pp. 570–573 (2005)
6. Yamato, J., Ohya, J., Ishii, K.: Recognizing Human Action in Time-Sequential Images using Hidden Markov Model. In: Proc. IEEE International Conference on Computer Vision and Pattern Recognition, pp. 379–385 (1992)
7. Cucchiara, R., Grana, C., Prati, A., Vezzani, R.: Probabilistic posture classification for Human-behavior analysis. IEEE Transactions on Systems, Man and Cybernetics 35(1), 42–54 (2005)
8. Classification Database (2005),
   http://www.wisdom.weizmann.ac.il/~vision/SpaceTimeActions.html

Local Response Context Applied to Pedestrian Detection

William Robson Schwartz[1], Larry S. Davis[2], and Helio Pedrini[1]

[1] University of Campinas, Institute of Computing, Campinas, SP, 13084-971, Brazil
[2] University of Maryland, Dept. of Computer Science, College Park, MD, 20742, USA
{schwartz,helio}@ic.unicamp.br, lsd@umiacs.umd.edu

Abstract. Appearing as an important task in computer vision, pedestrian detection has been widely investigated in the recent years. To design a robust detector, we propose a feature descriptor called Local Response Context (LRC). This descriptor captures discriminative information regarding the surrounding of the person's location by sampling the response map obtained by a generic sliding window detector. A partial least squares regression model using LRC descriptors is learned and employed as a second classification stage (after the execution of the generic detector to obtain the response map). Experiments based on the ETHZ pedestrian dataset show that the proposed approach improves significantly the results achieved by the generic detector alone and is comparable to the state-of-the-art methods.

Keywords: pedestrian detection, local response context, partial least squares regression.

1   Introduction

Pedestrian detection is of fundamental importance in computer vision due to the use of people's location for tasks such as person recognition, tracking, pose estimation, and action recognition. To reduce the amount of noise (false detections) input to these tasks, it is important to maintain a low miss-detection rate while reducing as much as possible the number of false alarms, which can only be achieved with the use of robust detection algorithms.

The main challenges faced to locate people in images are related to pose variation, illumination changes, blur, and partial occlusions. To deal with such conditions, most pedestrian detectors are either holistic or part-based [14]. While the latter, which employs a generative process to combine detected parts to a prior human model, is more suitable to handle conditions such as pose variation and partial occlusions, the former is able to collect more discriminative information by performing a statistical analysis to combine a set of low-level features within a detection window due to the larger size of the whole body, compared to the size of the parts.

To be able to locate all humans in an image, a holistic detector employs an image sweeping based on a sliding window which considers multiple scales and small strides. A consequence resulting of this approach is the existence of multiple

C. San Martin and S.-W. Kim (Eds.): CIARP 2011, LNCS 7042, pp. 181–188, 2011.

decreasing responses around the person's location. These multiple responses are normally removed by non-maximum suppression.

The evaluation of the response provided by a single detection window (as done when non-maximum suppression is applied) may generate ambiguities since that peak response can be caused by false alarms such as trees or poles, which present shapes similar to pedestrians. Nevertheless, the analysis of the spatial distribution of responses around detection windows (context) might reduce or even remove such ambiguities because the behavior of detector responses may vary according to the type of object.

The contribution of the context around the person's location for detection has been observed in the work of Dalal and Triggs [2] with the addition of a number of background pixels on the four sides of the detection window. Therefore, one way of incorporating more context is to increase even more the detection window size to add more background information. However, there is the consequence that the feature space becomes extremely high dimensional since robust detection is better achieved through feature combination [11].

The addition of more descriptors to capture extra background information, besides increasing the feature space dimensionality, does not incorporate information regarding the object being detected (pedestrians) because descriptors are general and only add such information after a learning process. On the other hand, if detection responses are considered, some information regarding the problems is already incorporated since the responses depend on the object class, and the dimensionality of the feature space for the detector is not changed.

This work proposes the use of local response context to improve pedestrian detection. The process works as follows. After the execution of a holistic detector and the composition of the response map for an image, responses around each detection window are sampled to compose a feature vector, referred as to *Local Response Context* (LRC). In the training phase, feature vectors located around detection windows containing pedestrian and detection windows with background are used to learn a regression model. Therefore, the responses are used as a new set of descriptors. Finally, during the classification, LRC feature vectors are projected onto the model and classified as pedestrian or background.

2   Related Work

Dalal and Triggs [2] proposed the use of histogram of oriented gradient (HOG) as feature descriptor for human detection, whose results outperformed other features. Zhu et al. [20] presented a method that significantly speeds up human detection by combining HOG descriptors with a cascade of rejectors. Variable size blocks are used in their method, such that larger blocks allow rejection of the majority of detection windows in the early few stages of the cascade. Zhang et al. [19] described a multiple resolution framework for object detection based on HOG to reduce computational cost, where lower resolution features are firstly used to reject most of the negative windows, then expensive higher resolution features are used to obtain more precise detection. Begard et al. [1] developed two learning algorithms for real-time pedestrian detection using different implementations of AdaBoost to optimize the use of the local descriptors.

A human detection method using covariance matrices as feature descriptors and a learning algorithm based on a Riemannian manifold was presented by Tuzel et al. [15]. Their method produced superior results when compared with the methods proposed by Dalal and Triggs [2] and Zhu et al. [20]. Mu et al. [10] developed a human detection method based on two variants of local binary patterns (LBP), comparing the results against the use of covariance matrix and HOG descriptors. Wu and Nevatia [17] proposed a cascade-based framework to integrate heterogeneous features for object detection, such as edgelet, HOG and covariance descriptors. Maji et al. [8] proposed features based on a multi-level version of HOG and histogram intersection kernel support vector machines (IKSVM) to obtain a good balance between performance and accuracy in pedestrian detection.

Part-based representations have also been used for human detection. Shet and Davis [13] employed a logical reasoning approach to utilizing contextual information and knowledge about human interactions, extending the output of different low-level detectors for human detection. Lin and Davis [7] proposed a pose-invariant feature descriptor for human detection and pose segmentation. Tran and Forsyth [14] developed a two-step pedestrian detection strategy, where the configuration of the best person within each detection window is firstly estimated, then features are extracted for each part resulting from this estimation and passed to a support vector machine classifier to make the final decision.

Context information has been used to increase accuracy of the human detection process. Gualdi et al. [6] exploited context information through a relevance feedback strategy, which enhances the pedestrian detection step by using training on positive and negative samples, and a weak scene calibration, which estimates the scene perspective to discard outliers. Statistical relationship between objects and people, modeled by Markov logic networks, was used by Wu et al. [18] to incorporate user activities as context information for object recognition. Morency [9] described co-occurrence graphs for modeling relations between visual head gestures and contextual cues, such as spoken words or pauses, to select relevant contextual features in multiparty interactions.

3   Proposed Method

In this section, we describe the proposed method for incorporating local response context for pedestrian detection. Since the addition of feature descriptors extracted from surrounding regions of a detection window would result in an extremely high dimensional space (millions of descriptors to describe a single detection window), we use detection responses of a local neighborhood to build a new classifier to improve the discrimination between human and non-human samples.

A holistic sliding-window detector (referred as to *generic detector*) extracts feature descriptors for each detection window, then presents the resulting feature vector to a classification method, which results in a response value used as

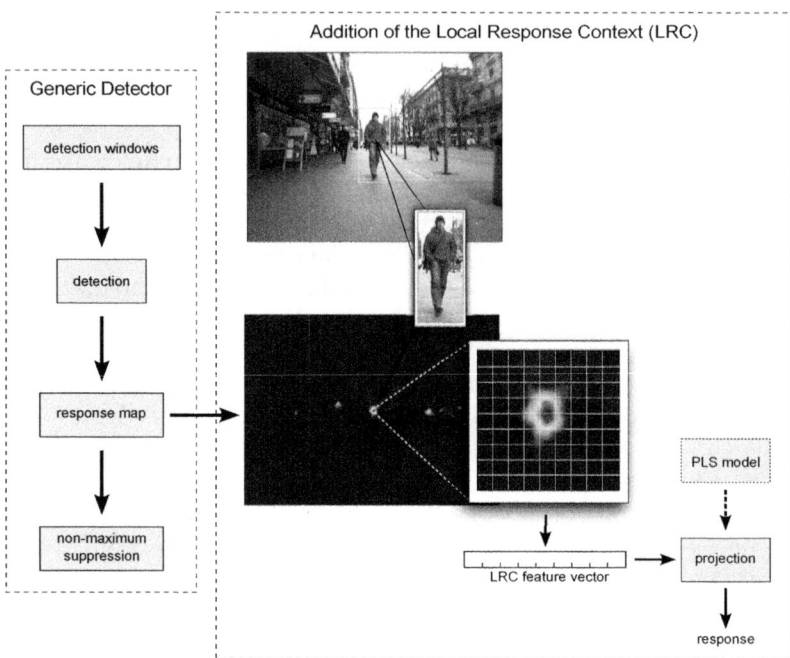

Fig. 1. Proposed method. The left-hand side shows the detection process performed by a generic pedestrian detector. The right-hand side shows the incremented detection process with the addition of the local response context descriptor. Using the resulting response map, LRC descriptors are extracted for each detection window and projected onto a PLS model, resulting in a more accurate classification between humans and non-humans.

confidence to separate humans from background. A response map, $R(x, y)$ with the image size, is built using the resulting set of responses (a response is placed at the centroid of the location of its corresponding detection window). Finally, a non-maximum suppression procedure is executed to maintain only detection windows with the highest responses. This process is illustrated on the left-hand side of Figure 1.

In contrast to the generic detector, which applies the non-maximum suppression after building the response map, we use this map to sample responses in the neighborhood of each detection window to extract the *local response context* descriptor, which will be used for a second and more accurate detection process, as illustrated on the right-hand side of Figure 1. The complete procedure is composed of feature extraction, training and classification.

The feature extraction works as follows. Let d_i be a detection window with centroid located at (x, y) and its local neighborhood defined by a square with left-most corner at $(x - \Delta, y - \Delta)$ and right-most corner $(x + \Delta, y + \Delta)$, where Δ is a value defined experimentally. The responses $R(x', y')$ inside this region are sampled and linearized to compose the feature vector $\boldsymbol{v}_{\mathrm{LRC}}$, used to describe d_i during its classification.

For the training, a generic pedestrian detector is executed for a previously labeled image sequence, resulting in a set of response maps. For each detection window, a feature vector based on LRC is extracted. Then, the detection windows are separated according to their classes (humans or non-humans) given by the ground-truth locations. Finally, a Partial Least Squares (PLS) model [12] is built to classify samples using labels +1 for human and −1 for non-human.

Partial least squares is a method for modeling relations between sets of observed variables in a latent space. It constructs new predictors as linear combinations of the original variables summarized in a matrix X of descriptor variables (matrix with feature vectors) and a vector y of responses (class labels). PLS decomposes the input variables as

$$X = TP^T + E$$
$$y = Uq^T + f$$

where T and U are $n \times p$ matrices containing p extracted latent vectors, the $(m \times p)$ matrix P and the $(1 \times p)$ vector q represent the loadings and the $n \times m$ matrix E and the $n \times 1$ vector f are the residuals. The PLS method, using the nonlinear iterative partial least squares (NIPALS) algorithm [16], constructs a matrix of weights W indicating the importance of each descriptor. Using these weights, the regression coefficients $\beta_{m \times 1}$ can be estimated by

$$\beta = W(P^T W)^{-1} T^T y. \tag{1}$$

Then, the regression response, y_v, for a feature vector v_{LRC} is obtained by

$$y_v = \overline{y} + \beta^T v_{\mathrm{LRC}} \tag{2}$$

where $\overline{y}$ is the sample mean of y.

Once the PLS model has been estimated in the training process, it is stored to be used during the classification, when test sequences are presented. The classification is illustrated on the right-hand side of Figure 1 and works as follows. First, for each image, a generic pedestrian detector is executed to obtain the response map. Then, the feature vector v_{LRC} is extracted for a detection window d_i and projected onto the PLS model using Equation 2. The higher the response, the more likely is that d_i contains a human (due to the class labeling used). Finally, using the response map generated by this classification process, the non-maximum suppression can be performed to locate pedestrians individually.

4   Experimental Results

This section presents and compares results obtained with local response context. First, we present a brief summary of the human detector used to obtain the response maps. Then, we describe the parameter choice considered and, finally, we compare detection results achieved when LRC is incorporated to results obtained by state-of-the-art approaches.

The PLS Human Detector. As generic detector, used to obtain responses for each detection window to build the response map, we employed the human detection method proposed by Schwartz et al. [11], which is available for download. This is a holistic detector based on a combination of descriptors focusing on shape (histograms of oriented gradients), texture (co-occurrence matrices), and color (color frequency) that uses PLS to reduce the dimensionality of the feature space and provide discriminability between the two classes.

The detection is performed as follows. Each detection window is decomposed into overlapping blocks and feature descriptors are extracted and concatenated in a feature vector. This feature vector is then projected onto a PLS model and the resulting latent variables are classified as either a human or non-human by a quadratic classifier. Finally, a response map is output for each image.

Experimental Setup. To evaluate our method, we use the ETHZ pedestrian dataset [3], which is composed of three video sequences collected from a moving platform. These sequences contain frames of size 640×480 pixels. For all the experiments, the detection is performed over 16 scales to consider humans with heights between 60 and 500 pixels, with strides of 4 pixels in the x-axis and 8 pixels in the y-axis. This setup results in 64,292 detection windows per frame.

To learn the PLS model with the local response context, the initial 50 frames of the training sequence #0 from the ETHZ pedestrian dataset is used. From these frames, 163 human exemplars and 750 counter-examples (15 per frame chosen in decreasing order according to the response of the corresponding detection windows) are sampled. The PLS model is built considering a latent space of 10 dimensions. In addition, $\Delta = 19$ is used for the neighborhood, resulting in a feature vector with 1521 descriptors. These parameters were chosen empirically during the training and kept fixed during the classification stage.

Comparisons. Figure 2 shows curves comparing the proposed method (referred as to *local response context*) in the three ETHZ sequences to other methods of the literature. In these plots, the x-axis shows the number of false positive per image (FPPI) and the y-axis shows the recall, which is the fraction of detected pedestrian samples among all pedestrians in the video sequence.

Curves shown in Figure 2 compare our method to four state-of-the-art approaches in the literature. The most important comparison is to the PLS human detector [11] since the proposed method uses the response map generated by it. Therefore, any gain in performance compared to that method is due to the addition of the LRC. The other approaches in the comparison were proposed by Ess et al. [3,4,5]. These methods employ not only low-level descriptors, as in the proposed method, but also scene information such as depth maps, ground-plane estimation, occlusion reasoning, and tracking to detect pedestrians.

Discussion. According to the results displayed in Figure 2, there are significant improvements on the recall when compared to the use of the the PLS human detector [11], which shows a clear contribution of the LRC. In addition, even though the other methods in the comparison use extra information, the proposed method presents very similar or better results in all video sequences. Therefore,

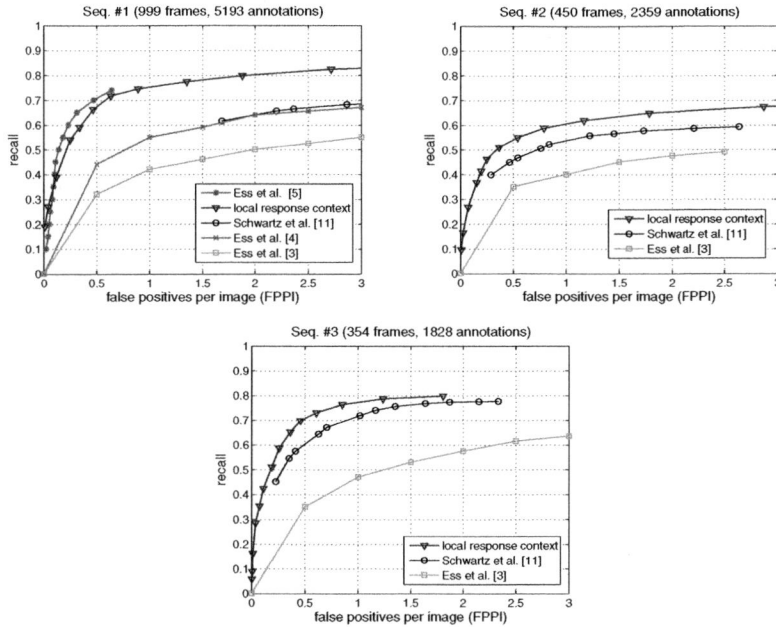

Fig. 2. Comparisons using three video sequences of the ETHZ pedestrian dataset. The proposed method is referred as to local response context.

the use of extra information such as ground-plane estimation and tracking might be exploited to achieve further improvements in the future.

One of the advantages of using LRC descriptors instead of considering low-level descriptors extracted from the neighborhood is the fairly low dimensionality of the feature vectors (1521 descriptors for a neighborhood with 19 pixels). If the detection window of the PLS human detector [11] were increased to consider a local neighborhood, the number of descriptors in the feature vector would be easily higher than one million, which might prevent the method from running due to the extremely high memory consumption and computation.

5   Conclusions

This work presented a pedestrian detection approach based on the local response context. This method uses response maps computed by a generic pedestrian detector (PLS Human Detector for this work) to extract feature descriptors that are used to build a PLS model employed to classify detection windows as humans or non-humans. Experimental results presented improvements on detection rates on the ETHZ dataset when compared to the PLS Human Detector. In addition, the proposed detector achieved results comparable to state-of-the-art methods.

Acknowledgements. The authors are thankful to FAPESP, CNPq and CAPES for the financial support. Larry Davis acknowledges the support of the Office of

Naval Research under a subcontract from Carnegie Mellon University on the MURI grant "Rich Representations With Exposed Semantics for Deep Visual Analysis."

References

1. Begard, J., Allezard, N., Sayd, P.: Real-time human detection in urban scenes: Local descriptors and classifiers selection with adaboost-like algorithms. In: CVPR Workshops (2008)
2. Dalal, N., Triggs, B.: Histograms of Oriented Gradients for Human Detection. In: CVPR (2005)
3. Ess, A., Leibe, B., Gool, L.V.: Depth and Appearance for Mobile Scene Analysis. In: ICCV (2007)
4. Ess, A., Leibe, B., Schindler, K., van Gool, L.: A Mobile Vision System for Robust Multi-Person Tracking. In: CVPR (2008)
5. Ess, A., Leibe, B., Schindler, K., Gool, L.V.: Moving Obstacle Detection in Highly Dynamic Scenes. In: ICRA (2009)
6. Gualdi, G., Prati, A., Cucchiara, R.: Contextual Information and Covariance Descriptors for People Surveillance: An Application for Safety of Construction Workers. EURASIP Journal on Image and Video Processing (2011)
7. Lin, Z., Davis, L.S.: A pose-invariant descriptor for human detection and segmentation. In: Forsyth, D., Torr, P., Zisserman, A. (eds.) ECCV 2008, Part IV. LNCS, vol. 5305, pp. 423–436. Springer, Heidelberg (2008)
8. Maji, S., Berg, A., Malik, J.: Classification using intersection kernel support vector machines is efficient. In: CVPR (2008)
9. Morency, L.P.: Co-occurrence graphs: contextual representation for head gesture recognition during multi-party interactions. In: WUCVP (2009)
10. Mu, Y., Yan, S., Liu, Y., Huang, T., Zhou, B.: Discriminative local binary patterns for human detection in personal album. In: CVPR (2008)
11. Schwartz, W.R., Kembhavi, A., Harwood, D., Davis, L.S.: Human Detection Using Partial Least Squares Analysis. In: ICCV (2009)
12. Schwartz, W., Guo, H., Davis, L.: A Robust and Scalable Approach to Face Identification. In: Daniilidis, K., Maragos, P., Paragios, N. (eds.) ECCV 2010, Part VI. LNCS, vol. 6316, pp. 476–489. Springer, Heidelberg (2010)
13. Shet, V., Neuman, J., Ramesh, V., Davis, L.: Bilattice-based logical reasoning for human detection. In: CVPR (2007)
14. Tran, D., Forsyth, D.: Configuration estimates improve pedestrian finding. In: NIPS (2007)
15. Tuzel, O., Porikli, F., Meer, P.: Human Detection via Classification on Riemannian Manifolds. In: CVPR (2007)
16. Wold, H.: Partial least squares. In: Kotz, S., Johnson, N. (eds.) Encyclopedia of Statistical Sciences, vol. 6, pp. 581–591. Wiley, New York (1985)
17. Wu, B., Nevatia, R.: Optimizing discrimination-efficiency tradeoff in integrating heterogeneous local features for object detection. In: CVPR (2008)
18. Wu, C., Aghajan, H.: Using context with statistical relational models: object recognition from observing user activity in home environment. In: WUCVP (2009)
19. Zhang, W., Zelinsky, G., Samaras, D.: Real-time accurate object detection using multiple resolutions. In: ICCV (2007)
20. Zhu, Q., Yeh, M.C., Cheng, K.T., Avidan, S.: Fast human detection using a cascade of histograms of oriented gradients. In: CVPR (2006)

Fast Finsler Active Contours and Shape Prior Descriptor

Foued Derraz[1,2,4], Abdelmalik Taleb-Ahmed[2], Laurent Peyrodie[3],
Gerard Forzy[1,4], and Christina Boydev

[1] Faculté Libre de Médecine, 46 Port de Lille, Lille France
[2] LAMIH FRE CNRS 3036, Le Mont Houy, 59313 Valenciennes Université de Valenciennes,
Valenciennes, France
[3] HEI - Hautes Etudes d'Ingénieur, Lille, France
[4] Groupe Hospitalier de l'Institut Catholique de Lille, Lille, France
foued.derraz@icl-lille.fr,
taleb@univ-valenciennes.fr, laurent.peyrodie@hei.fr,
gerard.forzy@ghcl.net

Abstract. In this paper we proposed a new segmentation method based Fast Finsler Active Contours (FFAC). The FFAC is formulated in the Total Variation (TV) framework incorporating both region and shape descriptors. In the Finsler metrics, the anisotropic boundary descriptor favorites strong edge locations and suitable directions aligned with dark to bright image gradients. Strong edges are not required everywhere along. We prove the existence of a solution to the new binary Finsler active contours model and we propose a fast and easy algorithm in characteristic function framework. Finally, we show results on some MR challenging images to illustrate accurate.

Keywords: Finsler Active contours, Wulff Shape, characteristic function, Shape prior, Primal dual.

1 Introduction

The Finsler Active Contours (FAC) has been proposed as natural way for adding directionality to the Active Contours [1, 2, 10]. The utilization of general Finsler metrics instead of Riemannian metrics allows the boundary descriptor to favor appropriate locations and suitable directions [10, 12]. The boundary descriptor is weighted by some position and direction-dependent local image information. The local image information can be obtained from a direction-a learned dependent pattern detector. In order to obtain fast and optimal segmentation we proposed both to use local information such anisotropic boundary descriptor [11] and global information such as statistic and geometric shape prior knowledge in the formulation of FAC. The formulation of FAC in Total Variation framework [4, 7], allows the convert non-convex segmentation problem into a convex problem segmentation. The goal is to use an anisotropic boundary descriptor that forces attracting AC at distinct specific positions with particular orientations. Integration position and orientation leads to TV primal dual formulation of segmentation problem. The formulation of the segmentation problem in the characteristic function leads to a fast globally segmentation procedure. We demonstrate the powerful of the proposed segmentation method on some challenging MR images.

C. San Martin and S.-W. Kim (Eds.): CIARP 2011, LNCS 7042, pp. 189–196, 2011.
© Springer-Verlag Berlin Heidelberg 2011

2   Review of Finsler Active Contours

In this work, we are interested in a fast segmentation based Finsler Active Contours (FAC) model. We proposed to reformulate traditional FAC in characteristic function framework($\chi \in [0,1]$)as combination of finsler, region and shape descriptors in Total variation framework:

$$
\begin{cases}
E(\chi) = \underbrace{\int_{\Omega} k_f (\mathbf{x}, \mathbf{p}_\perp) |\nabla \chi(\mathbf{x})| d\mathbf{x}}_{E_b(\partial\Omega)} \\
+ \lambda_1 \underbrace{\int_{\Omega} k_r (\mathbf{x}, \Omega) \chi(\mathbf{x}) d\mathbf{x}}_{E_{data}(\mathbf{x},\Omega)} + \lambda_2 \underbrace{\int_{\Omega} k_s (\mathbf{x}, \Omega_{ref}) \chi(\mathbf{x}) d\mathbf{x}}_{E_{shape}(\mathbf{x},\Omega_{ref})} \\
\chi = 1_{\{\mathbf{x}:\lambda_1 k_r (\mathbf{x},\Omega) + \lambda_2 k_s (\mathbf{x},\Omega_{ref})<0,: \lambda_1,\lambda_2 \in \Box^{*+}\}}
\end{cases}
\tag{1}
$$

where λ_1, λ_2 are the calibration factors, k_b is the boundary descriptor, k_r is the regions descriptor defined in the same manner as in [9] and k_s is the shape prior descriptor defined as in [13] and Ω_{ref} the reference shape. In Finsler metrics [10], the traditional isotropic descriptor $k_b(\cdot)$ is replaced by an anisotropic Finsler descriptor $k_f(\mathbf{x},\mathbf{p})$ by adding the directionality to the traditional boundary descriptor:

$$
\begin{cases}
k_f (\mathbf{x},\mathbf{p}) = k_b (\mathbf{x},\mathbf{p}_\perp) \max\left(\left| \mathbf{p}_\parallel^1 - \mathbf{p}_\parallel^2 \right|_2, \left| \mathbf{p}_\parallel^1 - \mathbf{p}_\parallel^2 \right|_2 \right)^{m=1 or 2} \\
\mathbf{p} = \left[\mathbf{p}_\perp, \mathbf{p}_\parallel \right]
\end{cases}
\tag{2}
$$

where $\mathbf{p}_\parallel = \left[\mathbf{p}_\parallel^1, \mathbf{p}_\parallel^2 \right]'$ denote the tangential direction to the curve $\partial\Omega$ and $\mathbf{p}_\perp = \left[\mathbf{p}_\perp^1, \mathbf{p}_\perp^2 \right]$ denote the normal direction to the curve $\partial\Omega$. Since the desired result is a curve in higher dimensions, a dynamic programming approach is used to determine the implicit convex minimizer of FAC energy [10]. In the next section we are interested in a definition of new convex Finsler descriptor in the TV framework ensuring a globally and optimal segmentation. When other convex or non-convex descriptors such as regions or shape prior descriptors are incorporated within Finsler descriptor, the solution is also implicitly convex.

3   Finsler Active Contours in the Total Variation Framework

In this section, we replace the isotropic boundary descriptor in (1) by anisotropic descriptor in TV framework [4, 6, 8, 12]. More formally, let $(\psi_\mathbf{x})_{\mathbf{x} \in \Omega}$ be a family of weighted anisotropic, positively 1-homogeneous functions, the segmentation problem can be formulated as:

$$E_{FAC}(\chi) = \underbrace{\int_\Omega \psi_x (\nabla \chi) dx}_{E_{finsler}(\ )} + \lambda_1 \underbrace{\int_\Omega k_r (\mathbf{x},\Omega) \chi(\mathbf{x}) dx}_{E_{data}(\mathbf{x},\Omega)} + \lambda_2 \underbrace{\int_\Omega k_s (\mathbf{x},\Omega_{ref}) \chi(\mathbf{x}) dx}_{E_{shape}(\mathbf{x},\Omega_{ref})} \tag{3}$$

Where ψ is induced by potential shapes noted as Wulff shapes W_ψ [6, 8, 11].

Definition

Let $\psi : \Box^2 \to \Box$ be a convex, positively 1-homogeneous function $\psi(\lambda \nabla \chi) = \lambda \psi(\nabla \chi)$, for $\lambda > 0$.

The Wulff shape W_ψ convex, bounded and closed set $(0 \in W_\psi)$ is defined as:

$$W_\psi = \left\{ \forall \mathbf{x} \in \Omega \subset \Box^2, \ \nabla \chi \in \Box^2 : \langle \mathbf{p}, \nabla \chi \rangle \le \psi(\nabla \chi) \right\}$$

$$such \ W_\psi = \left\{ -\mathbf{p} : \mathbf{p} \in W_\psi \right\} \tag{4}$$

$$and \ \psi(\nabla \chi) = \max_{\mathbf{p} \in -W_\psi} \left(\langle \mathbf{p}, \nabla \chi \rangle \right) = \max_{\mathbf{p} \in W_\psi} \left(\langle -\mathbf{p}, \nabla \chi \rangle \right)$$

where $\langle , \rangle$ denote the inner product in $\Box^2$.

The nature of solution of (3) was already shown for the TV [4, 6, 11] by rewriting the anisotropic TV in terms of characteristic function and extended to general families Wulff shape.

Lemma

Let ψ be a positively 1-homogeneous function, and the descriptors k_r and k_s. Then any global minimizer of (3) can be considered as a global minimize.

Proof: Assume $\chi^* : \Omega \to [0,1]$ is a global minimizer of (3). The corresponding characteristic function $\hat{\chi}$ is then defined as:

$$\hat{\chi}(\mathbf{x}) = \begin{cases} 1 & if \ \chi^*(\mathbf{x}) \ge 0 \\ 0 & if \ \chi^*(\mathbf{x}) < 0 \end{cases} \tag{5}$$

If $\nabla \hat{\chi} \ne 0$ has the same direction as $\nabla \chi^*$, then we can write $\nabla \hat{\chi} = c \nabla \chi^*$, $c \in \Box^{*+}$. The dual energy of (3) is given by:

$$E_{FAC}(\mathbf{p}) = \int_\Omega \min \left(0, div(\mathbf{p}) + \lambda_1 k_r (\mathbf{x},\Omega) + \lambda_2 k_s (\mathbf{x},\Omega_{ref}) \right) dx \tag{6}$$

which is maximized with respect to a vector field $\mathbf{p}$ subject to $-\mathbf{p} \in W_{\psi_x}$. By inserting the respective constraints on χ and $\mathbf{p}$ using the dirac function δ, the primal (3) and dual (6) energies can be stated as:

$$E^*(\chi) = E_{FAC}(\chi) + \int_\Omega \delta_{[0,1]}(\chi(\mathbf{x})) dx \tag{7}$$

and we can expressed the dual energy as:

$$E_{FAC}^{*}\left(\mathbf{p}\right)=E_{FAC}\left(\mathbf{p}\right)-\int_{\Omega}\delta_{W_{\psi}}\left(-\mathbf{p}\right)d\mathbf{x} \tag{8}$$

We use the Karush-Kuhn-Tucker (KKT) conditions to prove the optimality of $\hat{\chi}$ [3]. Let $\mathbf{p}^{*}$ be the corresponding dual solution for χ^{*}. The KKT conditions stated as:

$$\nabla\chi^{*}\in\partial\int\delta_{W_{\psi}}\left(-\mathbf{p}^{*}\right)-div\left(\mathbf{p}^{*}\right)\in\lambda_{1}\partial\int k_{r}\left(\mathbf{x},\Omega\right)\chi^{*}d\mathbf{x}+\lambda_{2}\partial\int k_{s}\left(\mathbf{x},\Omega_{ref}\right)\chi^{*}d\mathbf{x}+\delta_{[0,1]}\left(\chi^{*}\right) \tag{9}$$

Hence the KKT conditions can be applied point-wise. Therefore, $\left(\chi^{*},\mathbf{p}^{*}\right)$ are minimizers of the primal energy (7) and its corresponding dual energy (8) if and only if:

$$\nabla\chi^{*}\in\delta_{W_{\psi}}\left(-\mathbf{p}^{*}\right)-div\left(\mathbf{p}^{*}\right)\in\lambda_{1}k_{r}\left(\mathbf{x}\right)\chi^{*}+\lambda_{2}k_{s}\left(\mathbf{x},\Omega_{ref}\right)\chi^{*}+\delta_{[0,1]}\left(\chi^{*}\right) \tag{10}$$

Then, we established that $\nabla\hat{\chi}$ is sub gradient of $\delta_{W_{\psi}}\left(-\mathbf{p}^{*}\right)$:

$$\delta_{W_{\psi}}\left(-\mathbf{p}^{*}\right)+\left(\nabla\hat{\chi}\right)^{T}\left(\mathbf{p}-\mathbf{p}^{*}\right)\leq\delta_{W_{\psi}}\left(-\mathbf{p}\right) \tag{11}$$

Since $-\mathbf{p}^{*}\in W_{\psi}$ and $-\mathbf{p}\in W_{\psi}\Rightarrow\delta_{W\psi}\left(-\mathbf{p}^{*}\right)=0$ and $\delta_{W\psi}\left(-\mathbf{p}\right)=0$ and we can write:

$$\left(\nabla\hat{\chi}\right)^{T}\left(\mathbf{p}-\mathbf{p}^{*}\right)=c\left(\nabla\chi^{*}\right)^{T}\left(\mathbf{p}-\mathbf{p}^{*}\right)\leq0,c\in\square^{+} \tag{12}$$

We can establish that $\nabla\hat{\chi}\in\delta_{W_{\psi}}\left(-\mathbf{p}^{*}\right)$.

To establish that $-div\left(\mathbf{p}^{*}\right)$ is sub gradient [3] in (12), we consider two cases. In the first case χ^{*} is already either 0 or 1, then $\hat{\chi}=\chi^{*}$. The second case χ^{*} is in the open interval $]0,1[$, then $\partial\delta_{[0,1]}\left(\chi^{*}\right)=0$, since $\delta_{[0,1]}\left(\cdot\right)$ is constant in $[0,1]$:

$$\delta_{[0,1]}\left(\hat{\chi}\right)\leq\delta_{[0,1]}\left(\chi\right)+div\left(\mathbf{p}^{*}\right)\left(\chi-\hat{\chi}\right) \tag{13}$$

Then $-div\left(\mathbf{p}^{*}\right)\in\lambda_{1}k_{r}\left(\mathbf{x},\Omega\right)\hat{\chi}+\lambda_{2}k_{s}\left(\mathbf{x},\Omega_{ref}\right)\hat{\chi}+\delta_{[0,1]}\left(\hat{\chi}\right)$, thus $\left(\hat{\chi},\mathbf{p}^{*}\right)$ also satisfies the KKT conditions and $\hat{\chi}$ is therefore a global binary minimizer.

4   Finsler Active Contours in the TV Framework

In this section, we consider that $\psi\left(\nabla\chi\right)=\max_{\mathbf{p}\in W_{\psi}}\left(-\mathbf{p}^{T}\nabla\chi\right)$, the energy in (7) and (8) can be formulated in a primal-dual setting as:

$$E(\chi,\mathbf{p}) = \int_{\Omega} \underbrace{\max_{-\mathbf{p}\in W_{\psi}} \langle \mathbf{p}, \nabla\chi(\mathbf{x}) \rangle}_{\psi_{\mathbf{x}}(\chi)} dx + \int_{\Omega} \left\{ \begin{array}{c} \lambda_1 k_r(\mathbf{x},\Omega) \\ + \lambda_2 k_s(\mathbf{x},\Omega_{ref}) \end{array} \right\} \chi(\mathbf{x}) dx \tag{14}$$

and the respective gradient descent (for χ) and ascent (for $\mathbf{p}$) equations are:

$$\begin{cases} \dfrac{\partial\chi(\mathbf{x},\tau)}{\partial\tau} = div(\mathbf{p}) - \lambda_1 k_r(\mathbf{x},\Omega) - \lambda_2 k_s(\mathbf{x},\Omega_{ref}), \quad \chi(.,\tau=0) = \mathbf{1}_{\min(dist(\mathbf{x},\partial\Omega_0))} \\ \dfrac{\partial\mathbf{p}}{\partial\tau} = -\nabla\chi(\mathbf{x},\tau), \quad \mathbf{p}_0 = design\ as\ in\ \sec t 5.2 \end{cases} \tag{15}$$

where τ is an artificial time parameter, $\partial\Omega_0$ is the initial contour curve. Enforcing the constraints on χ and $\mathbf{p}$ is both done by clamping $[0,1]$, and reprojecting $\mathbf{p}$ onto the feasible set $W_{\psi_{\mathbf{x}}}$.

The Energy based region term is usually defined as a domain integral of the region descriptor k_r:

$$E_{data}(I,\Omega) = \int_{\Omega} \sqrt{p(I|\Omega) p(I|\Omega\setminus\Omega_i)} dx \tag{16}$$

Where the region descriptor based on Bhattachryya distance [9] is calculated using the gradient shape tool [5]:

$$k_r(\mathbf{x},\Omega) = \frac{1}{2} \left\{ \begin{array}{l} \sqrt{p_{in}(I(\mathbf{x}),\Omega) p_{out}(I,\Omega)} \left(\dfrac{1}{|\Omega_{in}|} - \dfrac{1}{|\Omega_{out}|} \right) + \\ \int_{R^+} \dfrac{1}{|\Omega_{out}|} \sqrt{\dfrac{p_{in}(I,\Omega)}{p_{ref}(I,\Omega)}} \cdot \left(G_{\sigma_{ker}}(I - I(\Omega)) - \sqrt{p_{out}(I,\Omega)} \right) dI \\ - \int_{R^+} \dfrac{1}{|\Omega_{in}|} \sqrt{\dfrac{p_{out}(I,\Omega)}{p_{in}(I,\Omega)}} \cdot \left(G_{\sigma_{ker}}(I - I(\Omega)) - \sqrt{p_{in}(I,\Omega)} \right) dI \end{array} \right\} \tag{17}$$

We therefore estimate density by Parzen kernel, which can better describe the regions. This method estimates the probability density function based on the histograms, using a smoothed Gaussian kernel:

$$p(I,\Omega_i) = \frac{1}{|\Omega_i|} \int_{\Omega_i} G_{\sigma}(I - I(\Omega_i)) dx \tag{18}$$

where G_{σ} denote the Gaussian kernel and σ^2 the variance.

The shape prior descriptor is defined as the Euclidean distance between the evolving Legendre moment region $\eta(\Omega)$ and the reference shapes $\{\chi_{ref}^i, i = 1,...,N\}$:

$$E_{shape}(\mathbf{x},\Omega_{ref}) = \int_{\Omega} k_{shape}(\mathbf{x},\chi_{ref}^i) dx = \sum_{p,q}^{p+q\le N} |\eta_{pq}(\chi) - \eta_{pq}(\chi_{ref}^i)|^2 \tag{19}$$

where the η_{pq} are defined as follows, using the geometric moments M_{pq} and the coefficients a_{pq} of the Legendre polynomials [13]:

$$\eta_{pq} = \frac{(2p+1)(2q+1)}{4} \sum_{u=0}^{p} \sum_{v=0}^{q} a_{pu} a_{qv} M_{uv} \tag{20}$$

Where $M_{pq}(\chi) = \frac{1}{\chi^{\frac{p+q+2}{2}}} \int_{\Omega} (x-\overline{x})^{p} (y-\overline{y})^{q} \, dxdy$ and $(\overline{x}, \overline{y})$ are the shape barycenter coordinates. In the next section we established our based fast FAC segmentation method.

5   Results

5.1   Data and Protocol

In this section, we provide prostate segmentation results for two data sets obtained from Saint Philibert Hospital Lille France. The MR images are pre-processed through the following pipeline: 1) spatial registration, 2) noise removal and 3) intensity standardization. We use the T1 weighted and T2 weighted MR sequences. The image sizes are 256x256 pixels, each slice thickness is 3.5mm with spacing between slices of 3.9 mm.

5.2   Finsler Shape Design

There is a wide spread of the possibilities to design ψ_x. In Fig. 1(a), the Wulff shape is composed by a half-circle with radius 1 and a circular segment combining gradient direction with gradient magnitude. Designing ψ_x in such manner allows straightforward reprojection for the vector field after the gradient ascent update (15).

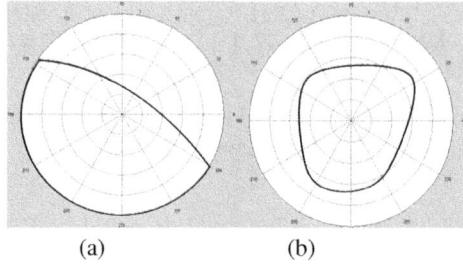

(a)   (b)

a) Wulff Shape for TV FAC Wullf b) Shape for Traditional FAC

Fig. 1. Construction of Wulff shape for Finsler Active Contours

5.3   Learned Shapes

The prostate learned shapes are designed by an expert using manual segmentation. In the figure 2, the object shape is segmented using 20 learned shapes and the segmentation is done using statistical and geometric shape prior.

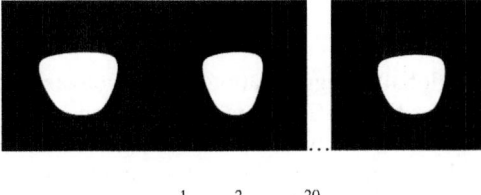

$$\chi_{ref}^1 , \chi_{ref}^2 , ..., \chi_{ref}^{20}$$

Fig. 2. Construction of Wulff shape for Finsler Active Contours

In the next section we introduced our interactive user term used to suitability segmentation method.

5.4 Segmentation Results

To quantify the accuracy of the segmentation, we measured the Dice Similarity Coefficient (DSC) between the manually segmented prostate and our segmentation method. We provide not only qualitative results (Fig. 3), but also give quantitative results in the form of the DSC to illustrate the viability of the proposed method in the context of prostate segmentation (see Table. 1).

Table 1. Quantitative evaluation of the segmentation

Patient no	DSC of FAC	DSC of FAC TV
Patient no 01	80,02%	85,63%
Patient no 02	79,1%	82,69%
Patient no 03	75,06%	79,23%
Patient no 04	77,21%	79,75%
Patient no 05	75,7%	79,30%

To quantify the accuracy of the segmentation, we measured the overlap between the segmented prostate areas defined by manual segmentation and our segmentation method.

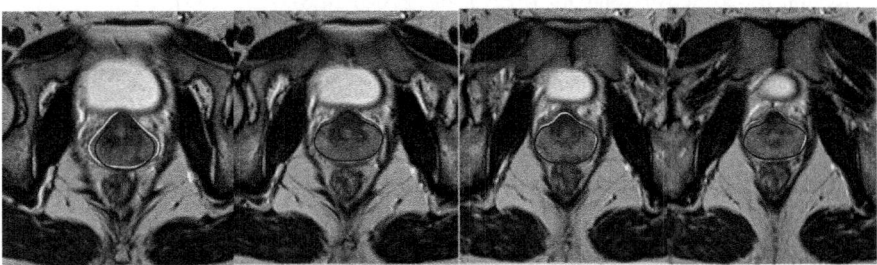

Fig. 3. Segmentation by TV FAC. In blue color traditional FAC, red color segmentation results of our method and in yellow color manual segmentation.

6 Conclusion

We developed a fast globally segmentation based convex Finsler active contours model for binary segmentation in TV framework incorporating statistical and shape prior knowledge. The position and orientation are dependent on prior for the boundary segmentation in Finsler metrics. Finsler active contours provide an alternative approach to integrating image-based priors on the location and orientation of the traditional boundary descriptor. Future work will address extending other classes of energies [9] that can be optimized in TV framework.

References

1. Chan, T.F., Vese, L.: Active contours without edges. IEEE Trans. IP 10(2), 266–277 (2001)
2. Appleton, B., Talbot, H.: Globally minimal surfaces by continuous maximal flows. IEEE Trans. PAMI 28(1), 106–118 (2006)
3. Borwein, J.M., Lewis, A.S.: Convex analysis and nonlinear optimization: theory and examples, 2nd edn. Canadian Mathematical Society (2000)
4. Bresson, X., Esedoglu, S., Vandergheynst, P., Thiran, J., Osher, S.: Fast Global Minimization of the Active Contour/Snake Model. JMIV 28(2) (2007)
5. Herbulot, A., Besson, S.J., Duffiner, S., Barlaud, M., Aubert, G.: Segmentation of vectorial image features using shape gradients and information measures. JMIV 25(3), 365–386 (2006)
6. Caselles, V., Chambolle, A.: Anisotropic curvature-driven flow of convex sets. Nonlinear Analysis 65(8), 1547–1577 (2006)
7. Rousson, M., Paragios, N.: Prior Knowledge, Level Set Representations and Visual Grouping. IJCV 76(3), 231–243 (2008)
8. Peng, D., Osher, S., Merriman, B., Zhao, H.: The Geometry of Wulff Crystal Shapes and Its Relations with Riemann Problems. In: Nonlinear PDE' 1998, pp. 251–303 (1998)
9. Michailovich, O., Rathi, Y., Tannenbaum, A.: Image Segmentation Using Active Contours Driven by the Bhattacharyya Gradient Flow. IEEE Trans. IP 16(11), 2787–2801 (2007)
10. Melonakos, J., Pichon, E., Angenent, S., Tannenbaum, A.: Finsler active contours. IEEE Trans. PAMI 30(3), 412–423 (2008)
11. Chan, T.F., Esedoglu, S.: Aspects of total variation regularized L1 function approximation. SIAM JAM 65(5), 1817–1837 (2005)
12. Chern, S., Shen, Z.: Riemann-Finsler Geometry. World Scientific (2005)
13. Foulonneau, A., Charbonnier, P., Heitz, F.: Affine-Invariant Geometric Shape Priors for Region-Based Active Contours. IEEE Trans. PAMI 28(8), 1352–1357 (2006)
14. Zhang, X., Burger, M., Osher, S.: A Unified Primal-Dual Algorithm Framework Based on Bregman Iteration. J. Sci. Comput. 46(1), 20–46 (2010)
15. Lellmann, J., Breitenreicher, D., Schnörr, C.: Fast and Exact Primal-Dual Iterations for Variational Problems in Computer Vision. In: Daniilidis, K., Maragos, P., Paragios, N. (eds.) ECCV 2010, Part II. LNCS, vol. 6312, pp. 494–505. Springer, Heidelberg (2010)

NURBS Skeleton: A New Shape Representation Scheme Using Skeletonization and NURBS Curves Modeling

Mohamed Naouai[1,2], Atef Hammouda[1], Sawssen Jalel[1], and Christiane Weber[2]

[1] Faculty of Science of Tunis, University campus el Manar DSI 2092 Tunis
Belvdaire-Tunisia Research unit Urpah
naouai@polytech.unice.fr, atef_hammouda@yahoo.fr, sawssen.jalel@gmail.com
[2] Laboratory Image and Ville UMR7011-CNRS-University Strasbourg 3rue de
l'Argonne F-67000 Strasbourg
naouai@polytech.unice.fr, christiane.weber@lorraine.u-strasbg.fr

Abstract. The representation and description of shapes or regions that have been segmented out of an image are early steps in the operation of most Computer vision systems; they serve as a precursor to several possible higher level tasks such as object/character recognition. In this context, skeletons have good properties for data reduction and representation. In this paper we present a novel shape representation scheme, named "NURBS Skeleton", based on the thinning medial axis method, the pruning process and the Non Uniform Rational B-Spline (NURBS) curves approximation for the modeling step.

Keywords: Skeleton, shape description, Medial Axis Transform (MAT), NURBS curves.

1 Introduction

Shape representation is one of the most important problems in pattern recognition and computer vision, and is an issue related to both data reduction and data description. Skeletons or Medial Axis Transform (MAT), as the shape descriptor, were described as having good properties for data reduction [1], [2].

There are two well-known paradigms for skeletonization methods: The first is that of "peeling an onion", i.e. iterative thinning of the original image until no pixel can be removed without altering the topological and morphological properties of the shape [5]. These methods require only a small number of lines in an image buffer at any time, which can be an advantage when dealing with large images. But on the other hand, multiple passes are necessary before reaching the final result, so that computation time may become quite high.

The second definition used for a skeleton is that of the ridge lines formed by the centers of all maximal disks included in the original shape, connected to preserve connectivity. This leads directly to the use of distance transforms or similar measures [13], [14], [15], which can be computed in only two passes on the image.

C. San Martin and S.-W. Kim (Eds.): CIARP 2011, LNCS 7042, pp. 197–205, 2011.

The main drawback of traditional skeletons is their high sensitivity to noise in contour. Many methods have been proposed to stabilize the skeleton extraction, mostly by pruning "false" branches that are believed to be caused by noise in the outline [3], [4]. A different approach based on self-similarity of a smooth outline curve was presented in [9].

An efficient shape representation scheme using voronoi skeletons is described in [10]. This scheme possesses the important properties of connectivity as well as Euclidien metrics. Redundant skeletal edges are deleted in a pruning step which guarantees that connectivity of the skeleton will be preserved.

According to OGNIEWICZ and KUBLER [11], a robust and time-efficient skeletonization of a shape, which is connectivity preserving and based on Euclidian metrics, can be achieved by first regularizing the voronoi diagram (VD) of a shape's boundary points, i.e. by removal of noise sensitive parts of the tessellation and then by establishing a hierarchic organization of skeleton constituents. Each component of the VD is attributed with a measure of prominence which exhibits the expected invariance under geometric transformations and noise.

Couprie et al. [12], proposed a new definition and an algorithm for the discrete bisector function, which is an important tool for analyzing and filtering Euclidian skeletons. They introduced a new thinning algorithm which produces homotopic discrete skeletons. These algorithms, which are valid both in 2D and 3D, are integrated in a skeletonization method which is based on exact transformations and allows the filtering of skeletons.

This paper is organized as follows. Section 2 presents NURBS curves. The proposed "NURBS Skeleton" is detailed in section 3. Working examples are illustrated in section 4. Finally we summarize our research in Section 5.

2   NURBS Curves

We recall that a NURBS curve of degree p is defined by:

$$C(u) = \frac{\sum_{i=0}^{n} N_{i,p}(u) w_i P_i}{\sum_{i=0}^{n} N_{i,p}(u) w_i} \tag{1}$$

Where $\{P_i\}$ are control points, $\{w_i\}$ are the weights associated with these points. Indeed, each w_i determines the influence of point P_i on the curve. And the $\{N_{i,p}(u)\}$ are the B-spline basis functions of degree p defined on the non-periodic and non-uniform knot vector U, recursively by:

$$N_{i,p}(u) = \frac{u - u_i}{u_{i+p} - u_i} N_{i,p-1}(u) + \frac{u_{i+p+1} - u}{u_{i+p+1} - u_{i+1}} N_{i+1,p-1}(u) \tag{2}$$

Where

$$N_{i,0}(u) = \begin{cases} 1 & \text{si } u_i \leq u < u_{i+1} \\ 0 & \text{sinon} \end{cases}$$

The non-periodic knot vector is defined by $U = \{a, ..., a, u_{p+1}, ..., u_{mp-1}, b, ..., b\}$ with a multiplicity of a and b which is equal to the order of the curve. This constraint ensures the passage of the curve by the two endpoints. Throughout this paper, we assume that the parameter lies in the range $u \in [0, 1]$ and the weight w_i is set to 1. For a detailed presentation of NURBS and its properties, we refer the reader to reference [6]. However, the main properties interesting for us in NURBS curves can be summarized into four points:

- Interpolation of extreme points.
- Affine invariance (translation, rotation, homothety)
- Convex hull: curve is still in the convex hull of its control points.
- Local modification: if a parameter (point, weight) is changed, curve is changed only within a certain interval.

3 NURBS Skeleton

3.1 Skeleton Extraction

The alternative approach we follow consists in creating a version of the object that is as thin as possible, i.e. thinning the object to a set of idealized thin lines. The resulting thin lines are called the skeleton or medial axis, of the input pattern and they are the thinnest representation of the original object that preserves the topology aiding synthesis and understanding. The methods to accomplish this, are called thinning or skeletonization.

In this first phase of our approach, skeleton of the considered shape is extracted using the algorithm described in [5]. Fig. 1 shows the result after applying skeleton's extraction algorithm.

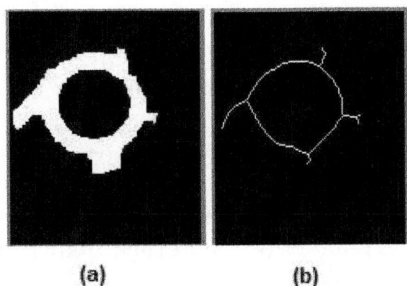

(a)   **(b)**

Fig. 1. (a) Initial shape. (b) Skeleton extraction.

3.2 Interest Points Detection

The detection of end points, junction points and curve points of medial axis is important for a structural description that captures the topological information embedded in the skeleton. The thin lines can be converted into a graph associating the curve points with the edges, the end and the junction points with the vertices. Such a skeletal graph can then be used as an input to graph matching

$$\begin{bmatrix}0&1&0\\0&1&0\\0&0&0\end{bmatrix}\ \begin{bmatrix}0&0&1\\0&1&0\\0&0&0\end{bmatrix}\ \begin{bmatrix}0&0&0\\0&1&1\\0&0&0\end{bmatrix}\ \begin{bmatrix}0&0&0\\0&1&0\\0&0&1\end{bmatrix}\ \begin{bmatrix}0&0&0\\0&1&0\\0&1&0\end{bmatrix}\ \begin{bmatrix}0&0&0\\0&1&0\\1&0&0\end{bmatrix}\ \begin{bmatrix}0&0&0\\1&1&0\\0&0&0\end{bmatrix}\ \begin{bmatrix}1&0&0\\0&1&0\\0&0&0\end{bmatrix}$$

Fig. 2. SEs for the end points: the fundamental A and its rotations (Θ_1(A),Θ_2(A),...,Θ_7(A)) in order

algorithms [7], [8]. In this paper, we introduce algorithms for detecting interest points or skeletons characteristic points (see Fig. 4) (end points, junction points and curve points) based on a morphological approach.Formally we define the end points, the junction points as follows:

Definition 1: A point of one-pixel width digital curve is an end point if it has a single pixel among its 3×3 neighborhood.

Definition 2: A point of one-pixel width digital curve is defined as a junction point if it has more than two curve pixels among its 3×3 neighborhood.

We propose another, purely morphological, method to detect end points and junction points from a skeleton as follows. To extract the end points, we perform erosion transform with the complement of each SE defining an end point $\overline{A}$, and its rotations $\Theta_i(\overline{A})$. On the complement of X ($\overline{X}$), we take the union of all the results and then we intersect the union with X.

$$ENDPOINTS(X) = \left[\bigcup_i \varepsilon_{\Theta_i(\overline{A})}(\overline{X})\right] \bigcap X \tag{3}$$

where $\varepsilon_{\Theta_i(\overline{A})}(\overline{X})$ denotes the erosion of $\overline{X}$ by $\Theta_i(\overline{A})$.

According to the definition of junction points, only curve pixels are considered in the neighboring configuration. In the eight-connected square grid, we can have two fundamental configurations corresponding to a junction point, B and C, and their seven rotations of 45° (Fig. 3). Thus, the extraction of the junction points from a skeleton is obtained by performing erosion transforms with each SE(B, C) and their rotations $\Theta_i(B)$ and $\Theta_i(C)$. and then taking the union of the results:

$$JUNCTIONPOINTS(X) = \left[\bigcup_i \varepsilon_{\Theta_i(B)}(X)\right] \cup \left[\bigcup_i \varepsilon_{\Theta_i(C)}(X)\right] \tag{4}$$

All the curve points are trivially obtained by removing the end points and the junction points from the skeleton.

3.3 Edges Extraction and Pruning Process

Skeletal pixels are classified into three sets which are the junction set (JS), the end set (ES) and the curve set (CS). Evidently, if S is the universal set corresponding to the skeleton, then:

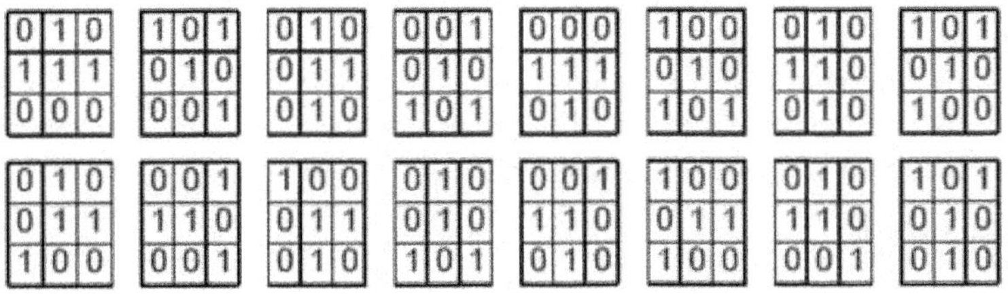

$$
\begin{array}{ccc} 0&1&0\\ 1&1&1\\ 0&0&0 \end{array} \quad
\begin{array}{ccc} 1&0&1\\ 0&1&0\\ 0&0&1 \end{array} \quad
\begin{array}{ccc} 0&1&0\\ 0&1&1\\ 0&1&0 \end{array} \quad
\begin{array}{ccc} 0&0&1\\ 0&1&0\\ 1&0&1 \end{array} \quad
\begin{array}{ccc} 0&0&0\\ 1&1&1\\ 0&1&0 \end{array} \quad
\begin{array}{ccc} 1&0&0\\ 0&1&0\\ 1&0&1 \end{array} \quad
\begin{array}{ccc} 0&1&0\\ 1&1&0\\ 0&1&0 \end{array} \quad
\begin{array}{ccc} 1&0&1\\ 0&1&0\\ 1&0&0 \end{array}
$$

$$
\begin{array}{ccc} 0&1&0\\ 0&1&1\\ 1&0&0 \end{array} \quad
\begin{array}{ccc} 0&0&1\\ 1&1&0\\ 0&0&1 \end{array} \quad
\begin{array}{ccc} 1&0&0\\ 0&1&1\\ 0&1&0 \end{array} \quad
\begin{array}{ccc} 0&1&0\\ 0&1&0\\ 1&0&1 \end{array} \quad
\begin{array}{ccc} 0&0&1\\ 1&1&0\\ 0&1&0 \end{array} \quad
\begin{array}{ccc} 1&0&0\\ 1&1&0\\ 1&0&0 \end{array} \quad
\begin{array}{ccc} 0&1&0\\ 0&1&1\\ 0&0&1 \end{array} \quad
\begin{array}{ccc} 1&0&1\\ 0&1&0\\ 0&1&0 \end{array}
$$

Fig. 3. SEs for the junction points: B and its rotations $(\Theta_1(B),\Theta_2(B),...,\Theta_7(B))$ and C and its rotations $(\Theta_1(C),\Theta_2(C),...,\Theta_7(C))$

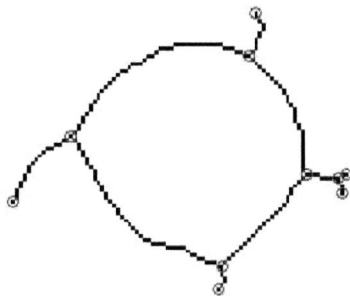

Fig. 4. Interest points detection

$$S = JS \oplus ES \oplus CS \tag{5}$$

Considering these sets, skeleton can be converted into a graph associating the curve points with the edges, the end and the junction points with the nodes. Thus, an edge is defined as the set of adjacent pixels which is limited between two nodes. Consequently, three types of edges can be considered, according to the type of their extreme nodes. They are:

External edges: both extreme nodes are end nodes.
Internal edges: both extreme nodes are junction nodes.
Branches: one node is an end node and the other one is a junction node.

Following the edge definition, an automatic search of skeletal edges is executed. Simultaneously, short skeletal branches which are not significant are removed. This latter is called the pruning process. Hence, skeleton is reduced and data is updated which requires to rerun the interest points detection process and the edges extraction process in order to save only significant edges.

3.4   NURBS Curves Approximation

In the previous step, the skeleton of the shape is partitioned in edges. The goal of this phase is to construct these objects by using NURBS curves approximation. We recall that to construct a NURBS curve of degree p, it is necessary to define n+1 control points to approximate. Each point is identified by its coordinates in the plane and by its weight.

Therefore, the selection of control points and the scheduling of these points are inevitable to construct a NURBS curve. Our algorithm operates edge by edge, according to the following instructions:

1. Selects an edge E.
2. Determines the controls points of E.
3. Sets the NURBS curve parameters (degree p, knot vector U, weights W).
4. Generates the corresponding NURBS curve.

Depending on the size of the considered edge, a threshold value has to be introduced in order to subsample the edge's pixels set. In fact, this value must be, obviously, strictly less than the edge's size.

More the threshold value decreases, more the number of subsampled values increases. In our work, we set this value to 5 for the edges of sizes greater than 15. Otherwise, it is fixed at 2.

In addition to these subsampled values, edge's extreme nodes are included in the set of control points. This ensures the continuity between different edges. Thus, for each edge, we define the set of controls points P as:

$$P = \{Extreme\,Nodes\} \bigcup \{Subsampled\,Values\} \tag{6}$$

4   Experimental Results

The experimental results of the NURBS Skeleton are shown in the following figures. In fact our method produces smooth curves representing the shape's skeleton where non significant information is deleted unlike the Thinning medial axis method [5] and the voronoi medial axis method [1].

In Fig. 7, the Fig. 7(a) presents the original binary image. Fig. 7(b) is the skeleton obtained by the Thinning medial axis method and Fig. 7(c) is the result of the NURBS Skeleton method. In this example five branches have been erased.

In Fig. 8, two branches have been erased. These latter corresponds to the goat's feet and are significant in this shape representation. Hence, by increasing the threshold value for the pruning process, we risk losing useful information. Nevertheless, the shape obtained by our method is more smooth with few inflection points.

Fig. 9 shows an example of an airplane with some small salient subparts. Fig. 9(b) is the skeleton generated by the Thinning medial axis method and does not look like an airplane. Fig. 9(c) is the skeleton generated by our method that some small subparts were removed. The skeleton can be recognized easily as an airplane.

The experimental results are very promising both in shape representation and shape reduction. In fact, Table. 1 presents reduction factors of tested shapes. This factor is calculated as:

$$RF = \frac{Interest\,points\,number\,obtained\,by\,Thinning\,Medial\,Axis}{Interest\,points\,number\,obtained\,by\,NURBS\,Skeleton} \tag{7}$$

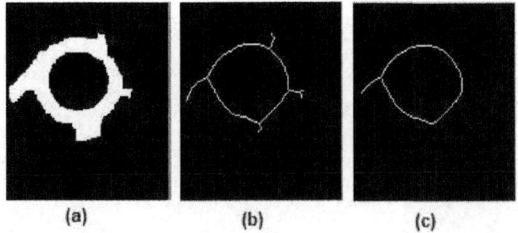

Fig. 5. Example of closed shape: (a) Original shape. (b) Thinning medial axis. (c) NURBS Skeleton.

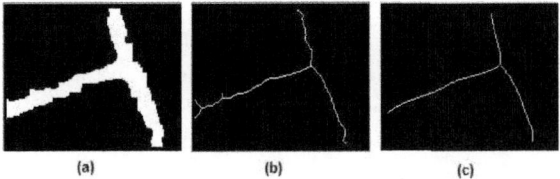

Fig. 6. Example of T shape: (a) Original shape. (b) Thinning medial axis. (c) NURBS Skeleton.

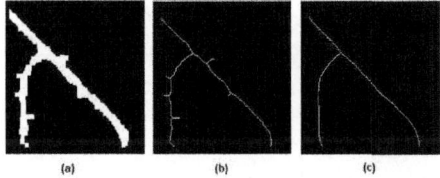

Fig. 7. Example of Y shape: (a) Original shape. (b) Thinning medial axis. (c) NURBS Skeleton.

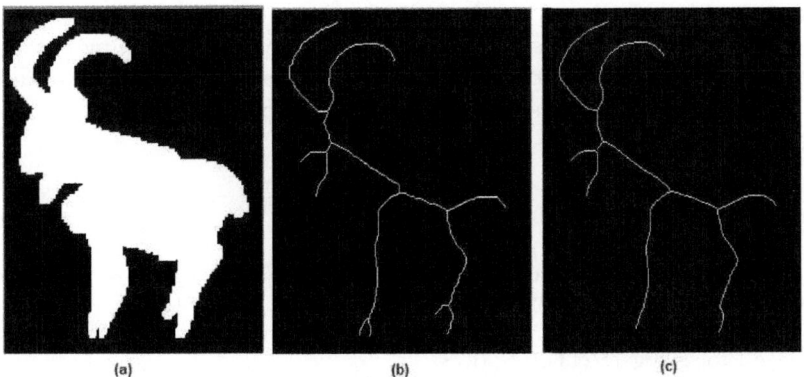

Fig. 8. Example of a goat: (a) Original shape. (b) Thinning medial axis. (c) NURBS Skeleton.

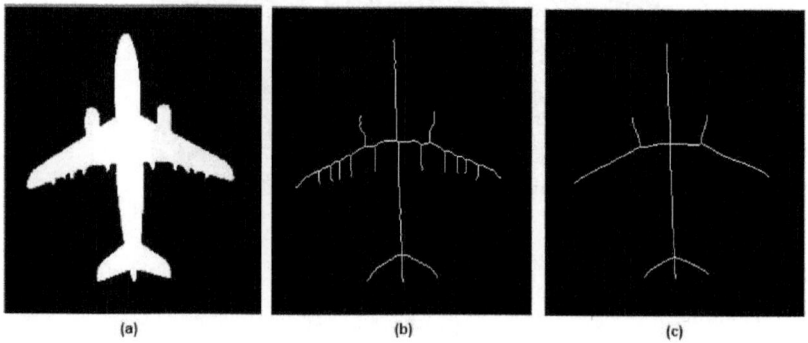

(a)   (b)   (c)

Fig. 9. Example of an airplane: (a) Original shape. (b) Thinning medial axis. (c) NURBS Skeleton.

Table 1. Interest points number and reduction factor

Images	Thinning Medial Axis	NURBS Skeleton	Reduction factor (RF)
Closed shape	10	2	5
T shape	8	4	2
Y shape	14	4	3.5
Goat	16	12	1.3
Airplane	32	12	2.6

5   Conclusion

We describe in this paper a novel skeleton extraction algorithm in binary images for shape representation. This algorithm named "NURBS Skeleton" is based on the thinning medial axis method, the pruning process and the Non Uniform Rational B-Spline (NURBS) curves approximation for the modeling step. This novel method has produced good results for data reduction by the use of pruning process.However, increasing the threshold value for the pruning process may cause losing useful information. Good results are also obtained for data representation by emphasizing the wealth of NURBS modeling in the field of pattern recognition.

References

1. Mang, C., Yun-cai, L.: Connection Skeleton Extraction Based on Contour Connectedness. Shanghai Jiaotong Univ. (Sci.) 13(5), 521–527 (2008)
2. Pavaldis, T.: A review of algorithms for shape analysis. Computer Graphics and Image Processing 7, 243–258 (1978)
3. Kimmel, R.: Skeletonization via distance maps and level sets. Computer Vision and Image Understanding 62(3), 382–391 (1995)
4. Brandt, J.W., Algazi, V.R.: Continuous skeleton computation by voronoi diagram. CVGIP: Image Understanding 55, 329–338 (1994)

5. Lam, L., Lee, S.-W., Suen, C.Y.: Thinning Methodologies-A Comprehensive Survey. IEEE Transactions on Pattern Analysis and Machine Intelligence 14(9), 879 (1992)
6. Piegl, L., Tiller, W.: The NURBS Book. 2nd edn.
7. Messmer, B.T., Bunke, H.: EFcient subgraph isomorphism detection: a decomposition approach. IEEE Trans. Knowledge Data Eng. 12(2), 307–323 (2000)
8. Ruberto, D., Rodriguez, G., Casta, L.: Recognition of shapes bymorphological attributed relational graphs. In: Atti dellVIII Convegno AIIA 2002, Siena, Italy (2002); Messmer, B.T., Bunke, H.: EFcient subgraph isomorphism
9. Liu, T.L., Geiger, D., Kohn, R.V.: Representation and self similarity of shape. In: Proceedings of the Sixth International Conference on Computer Vision, pp. 1129–1135. IEEE Computer Society, Washington (1999)
10. Niranjan, M., Rajan, V.T.: An efficient shape representation scheme using Voronoi skeletons. Pattern Recognition Letters 16, 147–160 (1995)
11. Ogniewicz, R.L., Kbler, O.: Hierarchic Voronoi Skeletons. Pattern Recognition 28(3), 343–359 (1995)
12. Couprie, M., Coeurjolly, D., Zrour, R.: Discrete bisector function and Euclidian skeleton in 2D and 3D. Image and Vision Computing 25, 1543–1556 (2007)
13. Borgefors, G.: Distance Transforms in Digital Images. Computer Vision, Graphics and Image Processing 34, 344–371 (1986)
14. Chiang, J.Y., Tue, S.C., Leu, Y.C.: A New Algorithm for Line Image Vectorization. Pattern Recognition 31(10), 1541–1549 (1998)
15. Niblack, C.W., Gibbons, P.B., Capson, D.W.: Generating Skeletons and Centerlines from the Distance Transform. CVGIP: Graphical Models and Image Processing 54(5), 420–437 (1992)

Multiple Manifold Learning by Nonlinear Dimensionality Reduction

Juliana Valencia-Aguirre[1], Andrés Álvarez-Meza[1], Genaro Daza-Santacoloma[2], Carlos Acosta-Medina[1,3], and César Germán Castellanos-Domínguez[1]

[1] Signal Processing and Recognition Group, Universidad Nacional de Colombia, Manizales, Colombia
[2] Faculty of Electronic Engineering, Universidad Antonio Nariño, Bogotá, Colombia
[3] Scientific Computing and Mathematical Modeling Group, Universidad Nacional de Colombia, Manizales, Colombia
{jvalenciaag,amalvarezme,gdazas,cdacostam,cgcastellanosd}@unal.edu.co

Abstract. Methods for nonlinear dimensionality reduction have been widely used for different purposes, but they are constrained to single manifold datasets. Considering that in real world applications, like video and image analysis, datasets with multiple manifolds are common, we propose a framework to find a low-dimensional embedding for data lying on multiple manifolds. Our approach is inspired on the manifold learning algorithm Laplacian Eigenmaps - LEM, computing the relationships among samples of different datasets based on an intra manifold comparison to unfold properly the data underlying structure. According to the results, our approach shows meaningful embeddings that outperform the results obtained by the conventional LEM algorithm and a previous close related work that analyzes multiple manifolds.

Keywords: Manifold learning, multiple manifolds, laplacian eigenmaps, video analysis.

1 Introduction

Often, in machine learning and pattern recognition literature, the nonlinear dimensionality reduction (NLDR) techniques are reviewed as learning methods for discovering an underlying low-dimensional structure from a set of high-dimensional input samples, that is, NLDR techniques unfold a non-linear manifold embedded within a higher-dimensional space. Nevertheless, most of the NLDR algorithms are constrained to deal with a single manifold, attaining unappropriate low-dimensional representations when input data lie on multiple manifolds, because the inter-manifold distance is usually much larger than the intra-manifold distance [1], moving apart each manifold from the others, regardless of whether the behavior among them is similar.

To our best knowledge, some few works [2,3,1] have proposed the application of the NLDR techniques to the analysis of multiple manifold datasets. Particularly, in [1] a framework to learn an embedded manifold representation from multiple

C. San Martin and S.-W. Kim (Eds.): CIARP 2011, LNCS 7042, pp. 206–213, 2011.
© Springer-Verlag Berlin Heidelberg 2011

data sets called *Learning a Joint Manifold* (LJM) is presented, which finds a common manifold among the different data sets, without assuming some kind of correspondence between the different manifolds. However, the main drawback of this approach is that for obtaining suitable low dimensional representations, the input samples must be similar in appearance. When the multiple manifolds do not have a close resemblance among them, the LJM method fails to embed the data. On the other hand, the approach presented in [3] actually requires the use of correspondence labels among the samples in order align the data sets, in such case the complexity of the challenge is lower than when no one correspondence is assumed. A similar solution is proposed in [4].

Unlike these mentioned works for dealing with multiple manifolds, our work makes possible to analyze dissimilar objects/subjects in appearance but with a common behavior (similar motion), moreover our methodology allows to employ objects/subjects with different input dimensions and number of samples among manifolds. These features of our work are the major contribution to the state of the art. Our approach is inspired on the manifold learning algorithm Laplacian Eigenmaps - LEM [5], because its optimization problem has an analytic solution avoiding local minima, and few free parameters need to be fixed by user. Our approach can be employed to visually identify in a low-dimensional space the dynamics of a given activity, learning it from a variety of datasets. We test the method on two real-world databases, changing the number of samples and input dimensions per manifold. Our proposal is compared against both the conventional Laplacian Eigenmaps (LEM) [2] and the closest work found in the state of the art for multiple-manifold learning (LJM) [1]. Overall, our methodology achieves meaningful low dimensional representations, visually outperforming the results obtained by the other methods. This work is organized as follows. In Section 2, a brief description about LEM algorithm is presented. Section 3 introduces the proposed methodology for multiple manifold dimensionality reduction. In Section 4 the experimental results are described and discussed. Finally, in Section 5, we conclude about the obtained results.

2   Laplacian Eigenmaps – LEM

Laplacian Eigenmaps (LEM) is a NLDR technique based on preserving the intrinsic geometric structure of a manifold. Let $\mathbf{X} \in \mathbb{R}^{n \times p}$ the input data matrix with row vectors $\mathbf{x}_i$ ($i = 1, \ldots, n$). The LEM transformation finds a low-dimensional Euclidean space $\mathbf{Y} \in \mathbb{R}^{n \times m}$, with row vectors $\mathbf{y}_i$ ($m \ll p$). This algorithm has three main steps. First, an undirected weighted graph G with n nodes (one for each $\mathbf{x}_i$) is built. Nodes i and j are connected by an edge $E_{ij} = 1$, if i is one of the k nearest neighbors of j (or viceversa) according to the Euclidean distance [2]. In the second step, a weight matrix $\mathbf{W} \in \mathbb{R}^{n \times n}$ is calculated. For this purpose two alternatives variants can be considered: heat kernel or simple minded. In the heat kernel variant, if nodes i and j are connected, then $W_{ij} = \kappa(\mathbf{x}_i, \mathbf{x}_j)$, being $\kappa(\cdot, \cdot)$ a kernel function, otherwise, $W_{ij} = 0$. For the simple minded option, $W_{ij} = 1$ if vertices i and j are connected by an edge, otherwise, $W_{ij} = 0$. Then, the $\mathbf{L} \in \mathbb{R}^{n \times n}$ Laplacian graph is given by $\mathbf{L} = \mathbf{D} - \mathbf{W}$, where $\mathbf{D} \in \mathbb{R}^{n \times n}$ is a diagonal matrix with elements $D_{ii} = \sum_j W_{ji}$. In the third step, the following objective function is minimized

$$\sum_{ij} (\mathbf{y}_i - \mathbf{y}_j)^2 W_{ij}, \tag{1}$$

which implies a penalty if neighboring points $\mathbf{x}_i$ and $\mathbf{x}_j$ are mapped far apart. Finally, the LEM problem can be accomplished solving the generalized eigenvalue problem $\mathbf{LY}_{:,l} = \lambda_l \mathbf{DY}_{:,l}$; where λ_l is the eigenvalue corresponding to the $\mathbf{Y}_{:,l}$ eigenvector, with $l = 1, \ldots, n$. First eigenvector is the unit vector with all equal components, while the remaining m eigenvectors form the embedded space.

3   Multiple Manifold Learning – MML

The NLDR techniques based on manifold learning fail when they look for a common low-dimensional representation for data lying on multiple manifolds. In this sense, we propose relate each input sample $\mathbf{x}_i$ with C different manifolds that share a similar underlying structure. Let $\boldsymbol{\Psi} = \{\mathbf{X}^c\}_{c=1}^C$ an input manifold set, where $\mathbf{X}^c \in \mathbb{R}^{n_c \times p_c}$. Our goal is to find a mapping from $\boldsymbol{\Psi}$ to a low-dimensional space $\mathbf{Y} \in \mathbb{R}^{n \times m}$ (with $m \ll p_c$, and $n = \sum_{c=1}^C n_c$), which reveals both the intra manifold structure (relationships within manifold), and the inter manifold structure (relationships among manifolds). Consequently, a weight matrix $\mathbf{A}$, that takes into account both structures, can be computed as

$$\mathbf{A} = \begin{bmatrix} \mathbf{W}^1 & \mathbf{M}^{12} & \cdots & \mathbf{M}^{1c} & \cdots & \mathbf{M}^{1C} \\ \mathbf{M}^{21} & \mathbf{W}^2 & \cdots & \mathbf{M}^{2c} & \cdots & \mathbf{M}^{2C} \\ \vdots & \vdots & \ddots & \vdots & \ddots & \vdots \\ \mathbf{M}^{c1} & \mathbf{M}^{c2} & \cdots & \mathbf{W}^c & \cdots & \mathbf{M}^{cC} \\ \vdots & \vdots & \ddots & \vdots & \ddots & \vdots \\ \mathbf{M}^{C1} & \mathbf{M}^{C2} & \cdots & \mathbf{M}^{Cc} & \cdots & \mathbf{W}^C \end{bmatrix}, \tag{2}$$

where each $\mathbf{W}^c \in \mathbb{R}^{n_c \times n_c}$ is the traditional LEM intra manifold weight matrix for each $\mathbf{X}^c$ [1]. Furthermore, each $\mathbf{M}^{cb} \in \mathbb{R}^{n_c \times n_b}$ ($b = 1, \ldots, C$) block is a soft correspondence matrix between $\mathbf{X}^c$ and $\mathbf{X}^b$.

In [1] a methodology called Learning a Joint Manifold Representation (LJM) is proposed to unfold the data underlying structure from multiple manifolds, which calculates the matrix $\mathbf{A}$ (equation (2)), computing the intra manifold structure matrices $\mathbf{W}^c$ as in traditional LEM, and the inter manifold structure matrices $\mathbf{M}^{cb}$ by solving a permutation matrix $\mathbf{P}$, which allows to find a maximum weight matching by permuting the rows of $\mathbf{U}^{cb} \in \mathbb{R}^{n_c \times n_b}$, $U_{qr}^{cb} = \kappa(\mathbf{x}_q, \mathbf{x}_r)$, $\mathbf{x}_q \in \mathbf{X}^c$, and $\mathbf{x}_r \in \mathbf{X}^b$ ($q = 1, \ldots, n_c$; $r = 1, \ldots, n_b$). Nonetheless, LJM is quite sensitive to feature variability between samples of different manifolds, due to $\mathbf{U}^{cb}$ is inferred in the high-dimensional space. Moreover, LJM is limited to analyze input matrices $\mathbf{X}^c$ which belong to the same input dimension ($p_1 = p_2 = \cdots = p_c = \cdots = p_C$), as can be seen in the calculation of each $\mathbf{U}^{cb}$.

In this work, we propose to identify the correspondence among data points from different manifolds without making a high-dimensional sample comparison. In other words, the similarities among observations of different manifolds are not directly calculated in each pair $\mathbf{X}^c$ and $\mathbf{X}^b$. Therefore, we compute each soft correspondence matrix $\mathbf{M}^{cb}$ in (2) as

$$M_{qr}^{cb} = \frac{\left\langle \mathbf{w}_q^c, \mathbf{w}_r^b \right\rangle}{\left\| \mathbf{w}_q^c \right\| \left\| \mathbf{w}_r^b \right\|}, \tag{3}$$

where $\mathbf{w}_q^c \in \mathbb{R}^{1 \times n_c}$ and $\mathbf{w}_r^b \in \mathbb{R}^{1 \times n_b}$ are row vectors of $\mathbf{W}^c$ and $\mathbf{W}^b$, respectively. It is important to note that equation (3) is not well defined when $n_c \neq n_b$, thereby, we use a conventional interpolation method based on cubic splines for oversampling the lowest size vector to properly compute the inner product between $\mathbf{w}_q^c$ and $\mathbf{w}_r^b$. Our approach for Multiple Manifold Learning (MML) aims to calculate the relationships among samples of different manifolds, comparing the intra manifold similarities contained in each $\mathbf{W}^c$ (equation (3)). Finally, given the weight matrix $\mathbf{A}$, we minimize the following objective function

$$\sum_{ij} (\mathbf{y}_i - \mathbf{y}_j)^2 A_{ij}. \tag{4}$$

Solving equation (4) as in traditional LEM algorithm allows us to find a low-dimensional space $\mathbf{Y}$ for data lying on multiple manifolds.

4   Experimental Results

We tested the conventional LEM algorithm [2], the LJM technique [1], and our proposed methodology MML on two real-world databases, in order to find a 2D low-dimensional representation ($m = 2$) for data lying on multiple manifolds. The first database, the Columbia Object Image Library (COIL-100) [6], contains 72 RGB-color images, for each one of the 100 objects, in PNG format, which were taken at pose intervals of 5 degrees while the object is rotated 360 degrees. In this work, the following objects are used: Car, Frog and Duck. The image size is 128×128, which are transformed to gray scale. The second database is the CMU motion of body (Mobo) [7], which holds 25 individuals walking a treadmill. All subjects are captured using six high resolution color cameras distributed evenly around the treadmill. For concrete testing, we used the silhouette sequences of one gait cycle for slow walk of three persons, which are captured from a side view. The images are resized to 80×61. The Figure 1 shows some images samples of COIL-100 and Mobo databases.

Three types of experiments are performed. Firstly, we use the selected objects of COIL-100 with a same amount of observations per set ($n_1 = n_2 = n_3 = 72$), and equal input dimensions ($p_1 = p_2 = p_3 = 16384$). In this case, the number of nearest neighbors is fixed as $k = 3$. For the second experiment, we use the Mobo database, which leads input samples per manifold of different sizes: $n_1 = 36$, $n_2 = 40$, $n_3 = 38$ and $p_1 = p_2 = p_3 = 4880$. The number of neighbors is set to $k = 2$. In order to test the algorithms on a dataset that contains

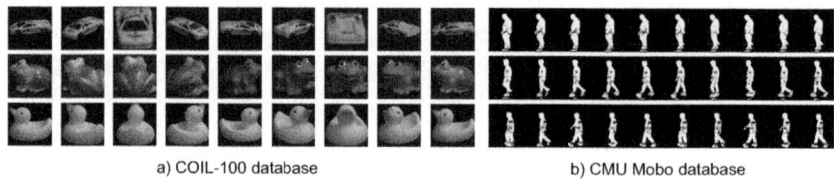

a) COIL-100 database   b) CMU Mobo database

Fig. 1. Databases examples

multiple manifolds with high-variability in the input sample sizes, we use the COIL-100 but performing an uniform sampling of the observations, obtaining input spaces with $n_1 = 72$, $n_2 = 36$, $n_3 = 18$ and $p_1 = p_2 = p_3 = 16384$. Here, the number of nearest neighbors are fixed as $k_1 = 4$, $k_2 = 2$, $k_3 = 1$. Finally, the third experiment aims to validate the proposed methodology for analyzing datasets with different amount of observations and input dimensions (image resolution). For this purpose, we employ the COIL-100 performing an uniform sampling of the observations, and resizing the images. Thence, the obtained input spaces have the following characteristics: $n_1 = 72$, $n_2 = 36$, $n_3 = 18$ and $p_1 = 16384$, $p_2 = 8100$, $p_3 = 2784$.

According to the results presented in Figures 2(a), 3(a) and 4(a), traditional LEM is not able to find the correspondence among different datasets which are related to a common underlying data structure. For all the provided

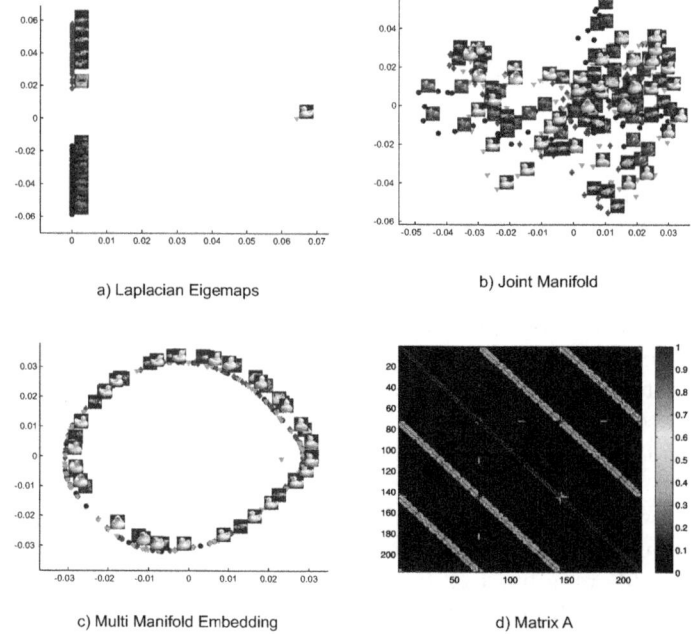

a) Laplacian Eigemaps   b) Joint Manifold

c) Multi Manifold Embedding   d) Matrix A

Fig. 2. Three objects, equal amount of observations

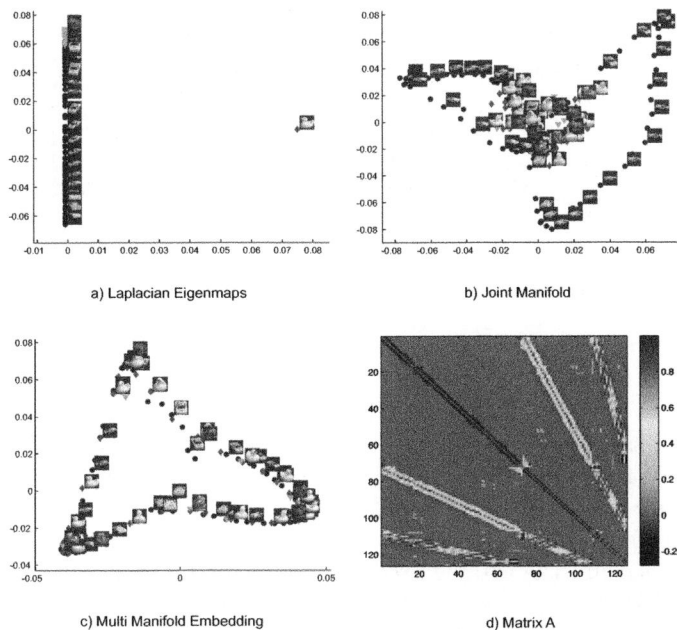

Fig. 3. Three objects, different amount of observations

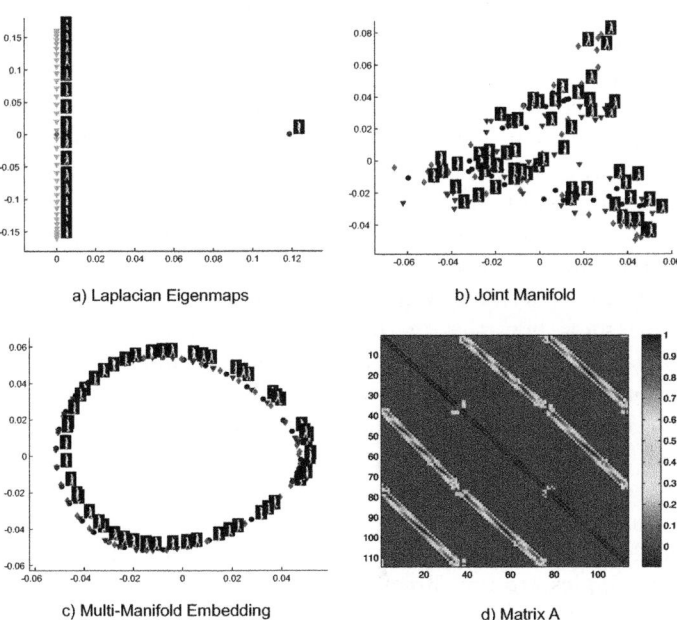

Fig. 4. Three Gait subjects, different amount of observations

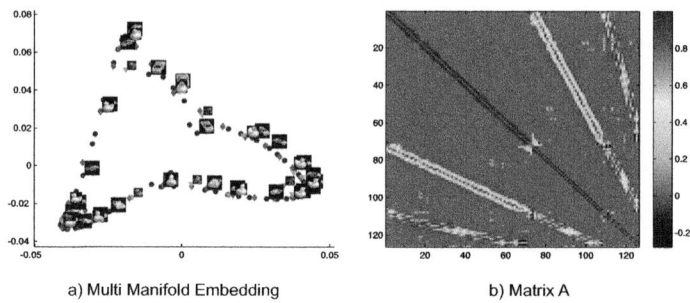

a) Multi Manifold Embedding   b) Matrix A

Fig. 5. Different amount of observations and input dimensions (image resolution)

experiments, LEM performs a clustering of points for each manifold. That algorithm can not find a low-dimensional representation that unfolds the underlying data structure from multiple manifolds, due to the weight matrix $\mathbf{W}$ in LEM is computed only considering pixel intensity similarities among frames. Again, taking into the account the attained results with the LJM technique (Figures 2(b), 3(b), and 4(b)), it can be seen how it attempts to find a correspondence among datasets but losing the intrinsic geometry data structure of the phenomenon (object motion). More precisely, for the COIL-100 database, the dynamic of the rotation is not reflected in the embedded space. Similar results are obtained for gait analysis in the Mobo database, although LJM tries to reveal the elliptical motion shape, it is not able to conserve a soft correspondence among samples. Note that the application of LJM technique is limited to analyze frames of video sharing a similar geometry, due to $\mathbf{U}^{cb}$ is inferred in the high-dimensional space (pixels frame comparison). Overall, the LJM method can not properly learns the relationships among objects performing the same activity, it just develops well when the analyzed manifolds are similar in appearance.

Finally, the results obtained with the proposed methodology MML, demonstrate that the computed low-dimensional space exhibits the appropriated dynamic of a given activity, learning it from multiple datasets. Figures 2(c), 3(c), 4(c), and 5(a) show how this method learns the relationships among frames of videos related to a similar activity, unfolding the underlying data structure. The low-dimensional representations found by MML reflects the activity dynamics and the soft correspondence among points of different datasets. Furthermore, our approach identifies a soft correspondence among videos even when they do not share a common similarity appearance, number of observations, and/or resolution. This can be explained because the relationships among samples of different datasets are computed based on an intra manifold comparison (equation (3)) the samples are not directly compared on the high dimensional input space, instead of that, the samples are compared by means of their own similarity representations, which is the similarity between a sample an each one of the other samples on the same manifold. The Figures 2(d), 3(d), 4(d), and 5(b) confirm it.

5 Conclusion

In this paper a new NLDR methodology for finding a common low-dimensional representation from multiple datasets is presented. We proposed to calculate an unique embedding space in order to visually identify the dynamics of a given activity performed by a variety of objects/subjects. In other words, different manifolds that share a similar underlying structure are mapped to the same low-dimensional space. Our methodology is inspired on the manifold learning algorithm LEM, computing the relationships among samples of different datasets based on an intra manifold comparison to properly unfold the data underlying structure. According to the obtained results, our approach outperformed the original LEM method, and a previous similar work called LJM [1] that analyzes multiple manifolds. The main advantage of this proposed methodology is the possibility for analyzing dissimilar objects/subjects in appearance but with a common behavior (similar motion). Moreover our methodology allows to employ objects/subjects with different input dimensions and number of samples among manifolds. As future work, we are interested in apply our methodology to support human motion classification and identification of impairments, as well as for computer animation.

Acknowledgments. Research funded by ARTICA, the project 20201006570 and a M.sc. scholarship by UNAL, and the project 20201006594 funded by U. de Caldas and UNAL. GDS was supported by the project 20110108 - PI/UAN-2011-505gb UAN.

References

1. Torki, M., Elgammal, A., Lee, C.S.: Learning a joint manifold representation from multiple data sets. In: ICPR, pp. 1068–1071 (2010)
2. Belkin, M., Niyogi, P.: Laplacian eigenmaps for dimensionality reduction and data representation. Neural Computation 15(6) (2003)
3. Liu, X., Lu, H., Li, W.: Multi-manifold modeling for head pose estimation. In: 17th IEEE International Conference on Image Processing, ICIP, pp. 3277–3280 (2010)
4. Ham, J.H., Lee, D.D., Saul, L.K.: Learning high dimensional correspondences from low dimensional manifolds. In: Workshop on The Continuum from Labeled to Unlabeled Data in Machine Learning and Data Mining, pp. 34–41 (2003)
5. Belkin, M., Niyogi, P.: Laplacian eigenmaps and spectral techniques for embedding and clustering. In: NIPS, pp. 585–591 (2001)
6. Nene, S.A., Nayar, S.K., Murase, H.: Columbia object image library: Coil-100. Technical report, Department of Computer Science, Columbia University (1996)
7. Gross, R., Shi, J.: The cmu motion of body (mobo) database, tech. report cmu-ri-tr-01-18. Technical report, Robotics Institute, Carnegie Mellon University (2001)

Modeling Distance Nonlinearity in ToF Cameras and Correction Based on Integration Time Offsets

Claudio Uriarte[1], Bernd Scholz-Reiter[1], Sheshu Kalaparambathu Ramanandan[1,2], and Dieter Kraus[2]

[1] Bremer Institut für Produktion und Logistik, BIBA, Bremen, Germany
{uri,bsr,kaa}@biba.uni-bremen.de
[2] Institute of Water-Acoustics, Sonar-Engineering and Signal-Theory,
University of Applied Sciences Bremen, Bremen, Germany
Dieter.Kraus@hs-bremen.de

Abstract. Time of Flight (ToF) cameras capture the depth images based on a new sensor technology allowing them to process the whole 3D scenario at once. These cameras deliver the intensity as well as the amplitude information. Due to difference in travel time of the rays reaching the sensor array, the captured distance information is affected by non linearities. In this paper, the authors propose three models (the monostatic, bistatic and optimized) for correcting the distance non linearity. The thermal characteristic of the sensor is studied in real time and analysis for integration time offsets for different reflectivity boards are carried out. The correction results are demonstrated for different reflectivity targets based on our models and analyzed integration offsets.

Keywords: Photonic-Mixer-Device, calibration, integration time, ToF camera, bistatic modeling, monostatic modeling.

1 Introduction

The PMD cameras work with the Time-of-Flight principle. A light source mounted on the camera emits modulated light that travels to the target. The reflected light travels back to the pixel array in the sensor, where it is correlated. The correlation result is a measure of the distance to the target. This distance measure is affected by non linearities due to different travel time of the rays. Ideally the travel time is approximated to be a constant in the measurement principle, but in practice this introduces distance non linearities in the captured image. Another major problem with the ToF cameras is that the amount of reflected light strongly depends on the reflectivity of the objects which leads to erroneous distance calculations. The exact reason is not discovered yet. A black target placed at the exactly the same distance to the camera as a white one shows differences in distance measurements dependent on integration time. In this paper, a method is proposed for correcting the distance non linearities as well as the integration time offsets for different reflectivity. Chapter 2 outlines the experimental setup used for the measurements. Chapter 3 outlines the thermal characteristics of the camera and chapter 4 presents the three models proposed by the authors. Chapter 5 outlines the real test results carried out for black

C. San Martin and S.-W. Kim (Eds.): CIARP 2011, LNCS 7042, pp. 214–222, 2011.

and white boards for various integration times. Chapter 6 presents the non linear as well as integration time offset correction results for a checkered board. Finally chapter 7 concludes this paper.

2   Experimental Setup

The setup consists on a CamCube 2.0 PMD camera from PMDTechnologies [1] mounted on a sled on a linear motion table allowing a perpendicular motion towards and away from a board on which the paper targets are fixed. The sled is driven by a stepper motor allowing a maximum travelling distance of 7800mm. The roll, pitch and yaw of the camera can be manually adjusted with the camera mount. To simplify the time-consuming measurements, the data acquisition was fully automated using a PC running Windows XP SP3. A Matlab script was used both to communicate with the motor controller as well as to acquire the data.

Fig. 1. Experimental setup with a computer controlled motion table

The measurements were done in the dark, with only the integrated LED-array as light source. To prevent the effects of unwanted reflection from objects near the setup, a zig-zag shader was built to cover the metal guide, as proposed by [2]. In the same manner a wall cardboard boxes was built along the side the linear motion table. All other exposed surfaces were covered with a low reflection black cloth. The experimental setup is shown in Figure 1.

For the characterization measurements only the center pixel (103,103) of the sensor was used and the camera was held perpendicular to the target. To adjust the pitch and yaw, the camera was placed at 1000mm from the board and several measurements of the target board were performed and averaged. The pixel having the shortest distance was identified and the rotation of the camera adjusted in that direction. This procedure was repeated several times for the pitch and yaw until the center pixel showed the shortest average distance to the target.

3 Warm-Up Drift of the CamCube 2.0

Thermal drift is a major issue with sensors, as it affects their measuring accuracy until the operating temperature is reached. PMD cameras face a similar problem. In this experiment the thermal drift was determined. For this, a white target was placed at 3000 mm from the camera. After turn on readings were taken continuously for 8 hours for different integration times (50ms, 25ms and 5ms). The warm-up curves for the different integration times can be seen in figure 2. During the initial minutes of operation an unsteady behavior is noticed and the measurements are stabilized after approximately 60 minutes. In order to avoid any deviation errors due to warm-up, all the experiments mentioned in this paper are taken after a safe 60 minutes capturing time. The statistics for the experiment is shown in Table 1.

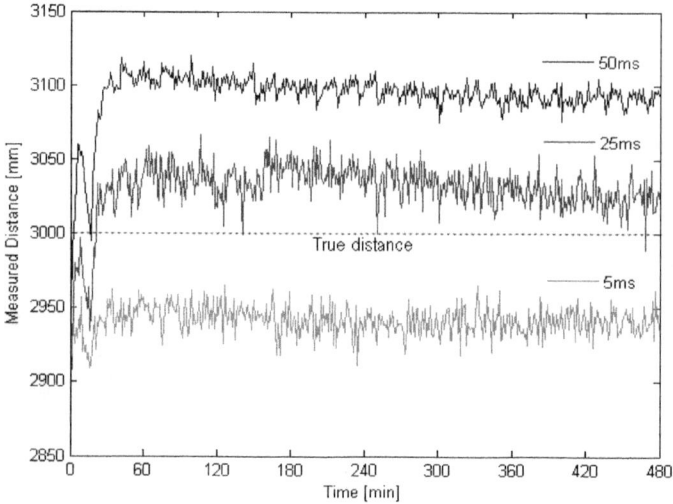

Fig. 2. Measured distances for a period of 8 hours of a white target placed at 3000mm

Table 1. Mean and standard deviation of the measurements of Figure 2

Integration time [ms]	Mean [mm]	Standard deviation [mm]
5	2941.4	6.6
25	3033.1	8.2
50	3096.7	4.8

4 Non Linear Distortion Modeling

Since the source and the receiver are spatially separated due to structural reasons, most of the ToF cameras exhibit a bistatic constellation. A preliminary investigation into such a constellation is outlined in [3]. The distance formula for any ToF Camera is given by:

$$D = c \cdot t_d / 2 \tag{1}$$

(where D – distance between the camera and the observation point, c – speed of light and t_d – the time of flight of the transmitted signal). This equation is an approximation as t_d is assumed to be constant and hence is only valid for larger distances between the camera and the observation point. In practice, distance information for each pixel is altered according to the travel time of the rays impinging on it. The strength of the received signal is affected by the level of backscattering as well as the losses inside the medium. Some signal distortion models have been presented in [4] and [5]. The bistatic constellation modifies the travel time for different rays which introduces a nonlinear distance variation throughout the distance image. This distance variation can often be seen as a curvature when imaging objects perpendicular to the camera. If not accounted, this imaging non linearity can affect the whole system calibration procedure and can even affect all the post processing stages. In this paper a solution is presented by modeling the traversal paths by initially employing an ideal monostatic approach and then extending it to the practical scenario of bistatic constellation.

For our experiment, a plain perpendicular matted black board kept at 750 mm away is illuminated and imaged by the camera. The image formation is approximated to that of a pin hole camera model and the illustrations are shown in Figure 3.

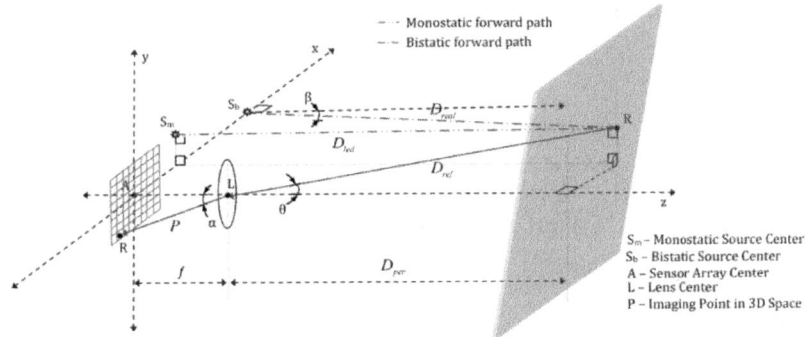

Fig. 3. Monostatic and bistatic models for distance correction

The distance measured by the PMD camera can be modeled as demonstrated in Figure 3. From the true monostatic model where the source and the receiver is at the same point, we introduce a small variation by assuming that the source is ideal rectangular and each imaging point on the 3D space is illuminated by a point source on x-y plane perpendicular to it. The light from the source hits the board at the point R, reflects back to the lens center at L and is focused on the sensor array. Ideally each light ray traverses a constant path length of D_{led}, variable path length of D_{ref} as well as a variable path length P according to the field of view of the camera (related to θ) and the focusing angle α. But practically D_{led} varies for each 3D point due to the spherical wavefront and interference. For the bistatic model, we assume that the source is kept at S_b imaging the point R in 3D space with the ray path length D_{real} making an angle β with the line parallel to z axis passing through S_b and perpendicular to x-y plane. Here the non linearities in the distance image are corrected by modeling the travel path of the reflected and transmitted rays. The correction required for each pixel is calculated by computing the true perpendicular distance D_{per} traversed by each ray from the board to the lens. All the following discussion includes the sensor to camera coordinates back projection [6] to find the angles θ, α and β given by the equations

$$x = f \cdot X_c / Z_c = (x_{im} - O_x) S_x . \tag{2}$$

$$y = f \cdot Y_c / Z_c = (y_{im} - O_y) S_y . \tag{3}$$

(where x, y – coordinates of sensor array; f – focal length ; X_c, Y_c – coordinates of the board; Z_c – distance from the camera to the board; O_x, O_y – principal point; x_{im}, y_{im} – image coordinates and S_x, S_y – size of the sensor pixel in both directions). Since the exact position of the board from the camera as well as the distance from the sensor array centre to the light source centre is known, the angles θ, α and β can be calculated geometrically. The CamCube 2.0 PMD camera has a focal length of 12.8mm and a pixel size of 40µm in both the sensor directions according to PMD Technologies [1]. Assuming that the indices (i,j,k) correspond to the coordinates of the imaged point R in 3D space, the measured distance D_{mes} can be rewritten from (1) as

$$D_{mes\,(i,j,k)} = (D_{led\,(i,j,k)} + D_{ref\,(i,j,k)} + P_{(i,j,k)}) / 2 . \tag{4}$$

From the mentioned monostatic model, the measured distance and the path length D_{led} can be approximated as

$$D_{mes\,(i,j,k)} = (D_{ref\,(i,j,k)} \cdot \cos(\theta_{(i,j,k)}) + f + D_{ref\,(i,j,k)} + P_{(i,j,k)}) / 2 . \tag{5}$$

$$D_{led\,(i,j,k)} = D_{ref\,(i,j,k)} \cdot \cos(\theta_{(i,j,k)}) + f . \tag{6}$$

The reflected ray is then given by (7). Hence the perpendicular distance to the lens from any imaged 3D point is given by (8) and thereby the corrected distance for monostatic model can be expressed as (9).

$$D_{ref\,(i,j,k)} = (2 \cdot D_{mes\,(i,j,k)} - f - P_{(i,j,k)}) / (1 + \cos(\theta_{(i,j,k)})) . \tag{7}$$

$$D_{per\,(i,j,k)} = D_{ref\,(i,j,k)} \cdot \cos(\theta_{(i,j,k)}) . \tag{8}$$

$$D_{cor(i,j,k)} = D_{per\,(i,j,k)} + f . \tag{9}$$

Modeling the bistatic constellation considering the angle β (from Figure 3), the reflected distance can be expressed similarly as

$$D_{ref\,(i,j,k)} = (2 \cdot D_{mes\,(i,j,k)} - (f / \cos(\beta_{(i,j,k)})) - P_{(i,j,k)}) / (1 + (\cos(\theta_{(i,j,k)}) / \cos(\beta_{(i,j,k)}))) . \tag{10}$$

The bistatic model uses this reflected distance to calculate the correction results from (8) and (9). Now an optimization method is presented for the previous monostatic model considering the path length of the reflected ray obtained from (7). The perpendicular distance to each 3D point calculated from (8) is used to find the optimized angular path traversed by the rays from the source to the board with the knowledge of β (from Figure 3). This optimized angular path can be given by

$$D_{opt\,(i,j,k)} = (D_{per\,(i,j,k)} + f) / \cos(\beta_{(i,j,k)}) . \tag{11}$$

The optimized path length is then applied in (4) to get the non linear correction from (7), (8) and (9). Results for the three approaches are presented in Figure 4 and 5.

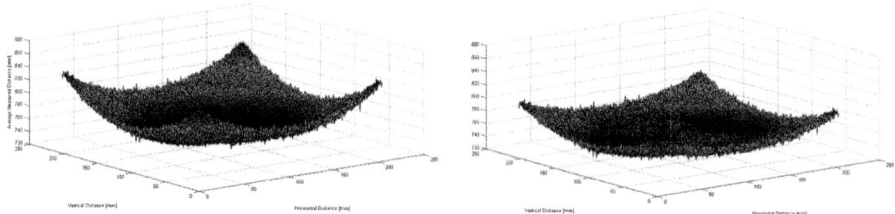

Fig. 4. Results of the measurement of a white target at 750mm from the camera; left: uncorrected distances; right: corrected distances using the monostatic model

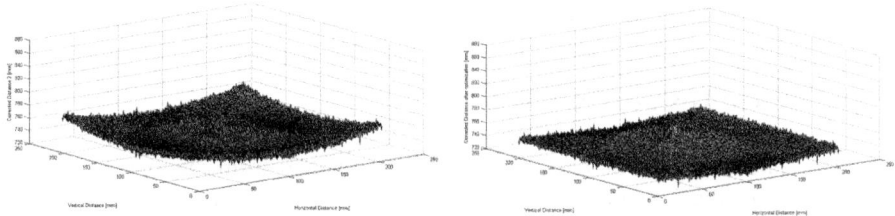

Fig. 5. Results of the measurement of a white target at 750mm from the camera; left: correction using the bistatic model; right: correction using the optimized model

5   Reflectivity Based Integration Time Offset Analysis

Preliminary results for distance correction based on the amplitude images have been published in [7]. Here, the problem is extended for a wide range of integration time. The experiment consists of imaging a black as well as a white board kept at true distances from 500 to 7000mm. The camera is moved in steps of 500mm. Each step measures the distance and amplitude for 16 different integration times varying from 1 to 46ms in steps of 3ms each. 500 samples of each integration time corresponding to a true distance are averaged to analyze the distance and amplitude variation for the centre pixel. The obtained 3D curve for measured distance and that for measured amplitude is plotted in Figures 6 and 7. A difference in amplitude as well as measured distance between the

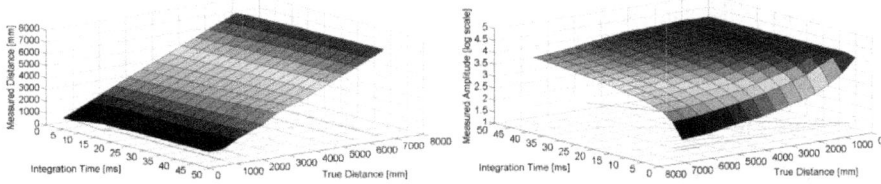

Fig. 6. Measured distance for different true distances and integration times for black target

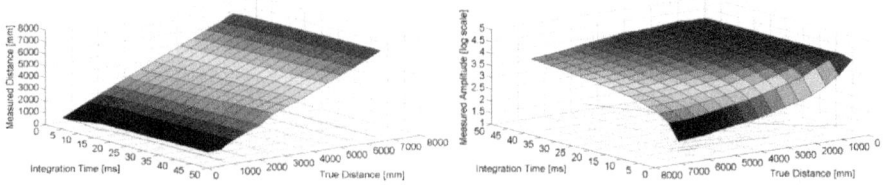

Fig. 7. Measured distance for different true distances and integration times for white target

black and white targets is observed and it is attributed to the differences in reflectivity. Distance and amplitude deviations due to different reflectivity are currently under research and preliminary results have been published in [8].

6   Combined Distance Correction

The black and white region can be clearly distinguished from the amplitude curves with respect to the integration time. Here an experimental demonstration is made for correcting a black and white checkered board based on both the prescribed non linear models as well as the integration time offsets. A multi dimensional LUT based approach is employed similar to [9] for distance offset correction. For the experiment, a black and white checkered board with a dimension of 420x297mm is mounted on the centre of an imaging board and is analyzed at a distance of 1000mm. The pattern consists of 5 black and 4 white checks arranged alternately. The integration time of the camera is set at 7ms. The distance images captured by the camera are back projected from (2) and (3) in Figure 8. The distance non linearities are corrected according to the bistatic and the optimization models presented in chapter 4.

A distance offset correction of 80mm is observed from the LUTs for the white board for the implemented integration time. The offset correction is done to the white checkered regions distinguished by the amplitude LUT. The final correction results are shown in Figure 9 and in Figure 10. Considerable improvements in the mean and standard deviation for a true distance of 1000mm were achieved (Table 2).

Table 2. Mean and standard deviation for the correction results for a true distance of 1000mm

Model	Mean [mm]	Standard deviation [mm]
Uncorrected	1046.6	27.5
Bistatic with Offset Correction	1008.7	9.7
Optimized with Offset Correction	996.5	9.5

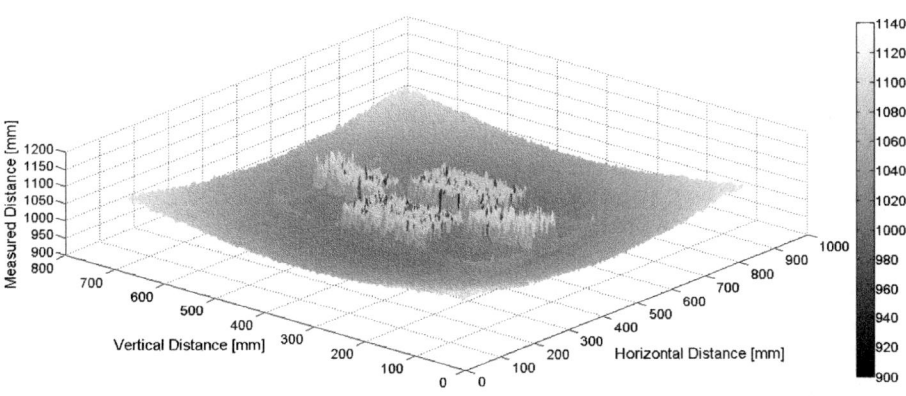

Fig. 8. Uncorrected distance measurement of a checkered target at a true distance of 1000mm

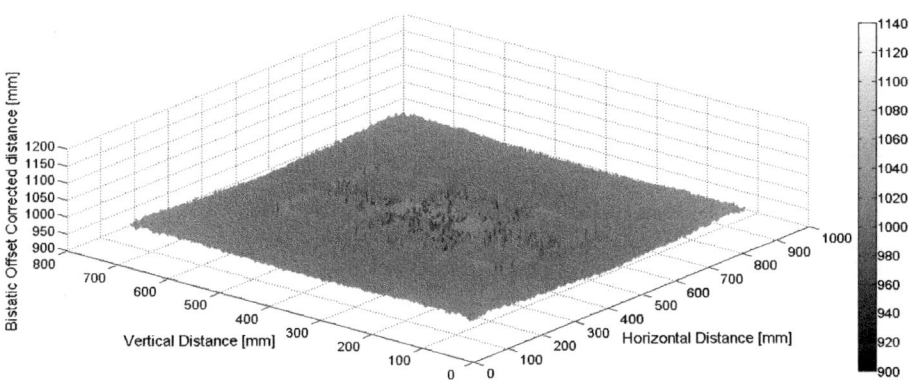

Fig. 9. Corrected distance using the bistatic model and distance offset

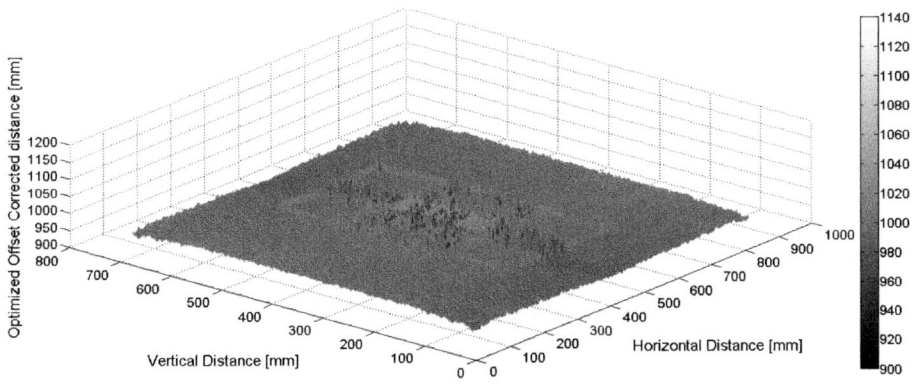

Fig. 10. Corrected distance using the optimized model and distance offset

7 Conclusion

In this paper the nonlinearities in the captured distance information of CamCube 2.0 is studied. Three models have been described in order to correct these non linear distance distortions. Characterization of the camera is performed and 60 minutes of warm up time is experimentally demonstrated. LUT based distance offset correction is demonstrated for different integration time and reflectivities. Finally the distance distortion in a black and white checkered pattern is corrected by combining the non linear distortion models as well as integration time offsets.

Further work will be done in the correction of the distance using a bistatic model considering the interference of the light sources of the camera. Sensor response to targets other than black and white will be determined in order to improve the calibration method.

Acknowledgement. The authors gratefully acknowledge the financial support by German Federal Ministry of Economics and Technology (BMWi) for the ROBOCON project.

References

1. PMD Technologies GmbH, http://www.pmdtec.com/
2. Rapp, H.: Experimental and Theoretical Investigation of Correlating TOF-Camera Systems. Diploma Thesis, University of Heidelberg, Heidelberg (2007)
3. Peters, V., Loffeld, O.: A Bistatic Simulation Approach for a High Resolution 3D PMD-Camera'. International Journal of Intelligent Systems Technologies and Applications 5(3/4) (2008)
4. Jamtsho, S., Lichti, D.: Modelling Scattering Distortion in 3D Range Camera. International Archives of Photogrammetry, Remote Sensing and Spatial Information Sciences, Newcastle, vol. XXXVIII (2010)
5. Mure-Dubois, J., Hugli, H.: Optimized Scattering Compensation for Time-of-Flight Camera. In: Proceedings of the SPIE Three-Dimensional Methodes for Inspection and Metrology V, Boston, vol. 6762 (2007)
6. Zhang, Z.: A Flexible New Technique for Camera Calibration. IEEE Transactions on Pattern Analysis and Machine Intelligence 22 (2000)
7. Oprisescu, S., Falie, D., Ciuc, M., Buzuloiu, V.: Measurements with ToF Cameras and their necessary corrections. In: Proceedings of the IEEE International Symposium on Signals, Circuits & Systems (ISSCS), Iasi, vol. 1, pp. 221–224 (2007)
8. Lindner, M., Schiller, I., Kolb, A., Koch, R.: Time-of-Flight sensor calibration for accurate range sensing. Computer Vision and Image Understanding 114(12), 1318–1328 (2010)
9. Kahlmann, T., Ingensand, H.: Calibration and Development for Increased Accuracy of 3D Range Imaging Cameras. In: Proceedings of the ISPRS Com., Dresden (2006)

A Measure for Accuracy Disparity Maps Evaluation

Ivan Cabezas, Victor Padilla, and Maria Trujillo

Escuela de Ingeniería de Sistemas y Computación, Universidad del Valle,
Ciudadela Universitaria Melendez, Cali, Colombia
{ivan.cabezas,victor.padilla,maria.trujillo}@correounivalle.edu.co

Abstract. The quantitative evaluation of disparity maps is based on error measures. Among the existing measures, the percentage of Bad Matched Pixels (BMP) is widely adopted. Nevertheless, the BMP does not consider the magnitude of the errors and the inherent error of stereo systems, in regard to the inverse relation between depth and disparity. Consequently, different disparity maps, with quite similar percentages of BMP, may produce 3D reconstructions of largely different qualities. In this paper, a ground-truth based measure of errors in estimated disparity maps is presented. It offers advantages over the BMP, since it takes into account the magnitude of the errors and the inverse relation between depth and disparity. Experimental validations of the proposed measure are conducted by using two state-of-the-art quantitative evaluation methodologies. Obtained results show that the proposed measure is more suited than BMP to evaluate the depth accuracy of the estimated disparity map.

Keywords: Computer vision, corresponding points, disparity maps, quantitative evaluation, error measures.

1 Introduction

A stereo image set captures a 3D scene from slightly different viewpoints. A disparity estimation algorithm takes as input a stereo image set, and produces a set of disparity maps (DM) as output. Disparity is the shift between stereo corresponding points. The 3D structure of the captured scene can be recovered based on estimated disparities. The estimation of DM is a fundamental problem in computer vision, which has to be addressed in several applications domains, such as: robotics, unmanned vehicles, entertainment and telecommunications, among others [6], [12], [16]. The evaluation of DM, in terms of estimation accuracy, is quite important since small inaccuracies may have a large impact on the results of the 3D final reconstruction. Moreover, the objective comparison of different disparity estimation algorithms is based on the quantitative evaluation of DM [10], [15]. This evaluation allows also for the tuning of parameters of an algorithm within a particular context [7], determining the impact of specific components and procedures [5], and decision taking for researchers and practitioners

C. San Martin and S.-W. Kim (Eds.): CIARP 2011, LNCS 7042, pp. 223–231, 2011.

among others. In fact, a quantitative evaluation approach must be supported by a quantitative evaluation methodology [2]. Among the different components that a quantitative evaluation methodology may involve, the set of error measures is a fundamental one.

In some scenarios, the quantitative evaluation of DM has to be conducted in the absence of ground-truth data. In this case, a prediction error approach can be used to perform the evaluation [14]. This approach consists in comparing a set of third views of the scene, against a set of rendered views computed from reference images and their associated DM.

Image quality measures such as the Mean Squared Error (MSE), the Root Median Squared Error (RMSE), the Peak Signal-to-Noise Ratio (PSNR), and the Structural Similarity Index Measure (SSIM) [19] can be used for quantitative evaluation under a prediction error approach [15]. Although, the MSE, the RMSE, and the PSNR are widely adopted and have a clear physical meaning, they are not closely related to the perceived visual quality by the human visual system [18], [19].

The disparity gradient and the disparity acceleration indices are presented in [20] to measure the smoothness of the DM. These indices require the use of thresholds. However, no information is provided about how the threshold can be fixed. Moreover, the capability of these indices to distinguish between an inaccurate estimation and a true depth discontinuity is not discussed. On the other hand, the fact that the DM may vary smoothly but, at the same time, they may be totally inaccurate is ignored.

The comparison of results using the SSIM and the PSNR measures on noisy DM by adding salt and pepper is addressed in [13]. Although it is concluded in [13] that obtained PSNR values are closer to the scores assigned by subjective evaluation, this conclusion does not coincide with the well-known drawback of the PSNR [18], [19]. Additionally, there is not a clear relation between the type and the level of noise introduced, and the artifacts that a disparity estimation algorithm may produce. Consequently, the considered evaluation scenario lacks of realism.

Ground-truth based error measures can be computed by comparing estimated DM against disparity ground-truth data. Measures such as, the Mean Absolute Error (MAE), the MSE, and the RMSE are considered in [10], [16] for ground-truth based evaluation. A modification of SSIM, termed R-SSIM, and designed for range images, is proposed in [8]. The modification consists in the introduction of the capability to handle missing data in both, the ground-truth disparity map, and in the estimated DM. It is shown in [8] that there exists a strong linear association between the BMP and the R-SSIM.

A modification of the Mean Absolute Percentage Error (MAPE) is presented in [16]. The modification consists in the capability to handle the absence of estimations in the evaluated DM. Although MAPE considers the inverse relation between depth and disparity, it is designed in the context of forecasting [3]. Additionally, the use of the mean, which is sensitive to outliers, may introduce bias in the evaluation.

The BMP, was introduced in [10] as a component of the Middlebury's evaluation methodology [9], [11]. It is formulated in Equation (1).

$$\text{BMP} = \frac{1}{N} \sum_{(x,y)} \varepsilon(x,y); \quad \varepsilon(x,y) = \begin{cases} 1 & \text{if } |D_{true}(x,y) - D_{estimated}(x,y)| > \delta \\ 0 & \text{if } |D_{true}(x,y) - D_{estimated}(x,y)| \le \delta \end{cases} ,(1)$$

where, D_{true} is the disparity ground-truth data, $D_{estimated}$ is the disparity map under evaluation, and δ is the error tolerance threshold (commonly, $\delta = 1$).

The error tolerance threshold δ is considered by the BMP in order to determine if there is a disparity estimation error. The BMP can be gathered on different image regions, related to different image phenomena, such as occluded, near to depth discontinuities, and areas lacking of texture, among others [10].

Among the existing quantitative measures, the BMP is widely used. However, it is a measure of the quantity of errors occurring in DM. Moreover, such a quantity may do not indicate how accurately a particular disparity map fulfils the task for which it was estimated: to recover the depth of the scene captured in the stereo image set [4]. In fact, the BMP can be seen as a binary function by the using of a threshold, which selection may impact on the evaluation results.

In this paper, a ground-truth based measure is presented. The proposed measure is supported by the inverse relation between depth and disparity. It computes a global error measure with a physical interpretation and without thresholds intervention.

2   Problem Statement

The BMP is commonly used as a measure of disparity errors evaluation. Nevertheless, in practice, the estimation of the DM is an intermediate step on a process, which the ultimate goal is to achieve depth accuracy. In fact, the BMP has drawbacks such as: it may be sensitive to the selection of δ, since small changes on this value, may lead to obtain significantly different percentages. Moreover, the magnitude of the difference between the estimated disparity and the ground-truth value is ignored. Thus, the BMP may conceal disparity estimation errors of large magnitude, and at the same time, it may penalise errors of low impact on the final 3D reconstruction. On the other hand, disparity estimation errors of the same magnitude may cause depth errors of different magnitude. However, the BMP does not consider this fact. Consequently, the BMP measure is not suited to measure the depth accuracy of a disparity estimation process.

The DM of the Tsukuba, Venus, Teddy and Cones stereo images [10], [11] are used in Fig. 1 for illustrating the stated problem. These maps are varying smoothly, and their percentages of BMP are equals to zero. However, Table 1 shows that the values of other ground-truth based measures, as well as image quality values of rendered views, computed from the DM, are contradicting to the values reported by the BMP. It can be observed, that although the BMP is reporting a perfect accuracy on the entire image, the other ground-truth based error measures, the MSE and the MAPE, are indicating error presence. Additionally, the MSSIM, the MSE and the PSNR of rendered views are indicating

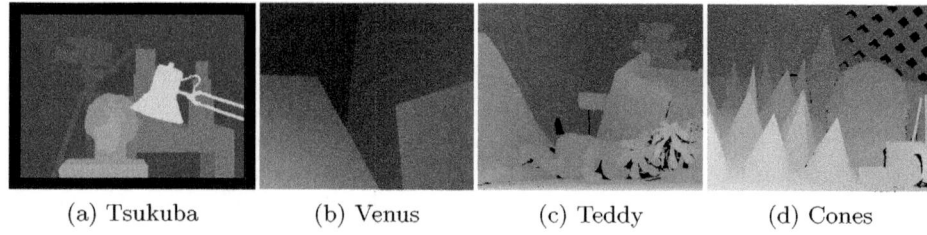

| (a) Tsukuba | (b) Venus | (c) Teddy | (d) Cones |

Fig. 1. DM, varying smoothly but being totally wrong

Table 1. Obtained values of the BMP ($\delta = 1$), the MSE, the MAPE, based on ground-truth; and obtained values of the MSSIM, the MSE and the PSNR, based on rendered views, by using the DM in Fig. 1

Disparity Map	BMP all	MSE all	MAPE all	MSSIM	MSE	PSNR
Fig. 1(a)	0.000	1.000	16.474	0.758	187.091	25.410
Fig. 1(b)	0.000	1.000	14.316	0.792	173.636	25.734
Fig. 1(c)	0.000	1.000	4.117	0.831	128.543	27.040
Fig. 1(d)	0.000	1.000	3.380	0.744	184.313	25.475

a low quality. This exemplifies the sensitivity of the BMP to the selection of δ, and the fact that obtaining a low percentage of BMP does not imply, necessarily, that the DM under evaluation are accurate in terms of 3D scene reconstruction.

3   The Sigma-Z-Error

The proposed measure in this paper is termed Sigma-Z-Error (SZE). It is based on the inverse relation between depth and disparity using the error magnitude. In this sense, it aims to measure the final impact of a disparity estimation error, which depends on the true distance between the stereo camera system and the captured point, and on the disparity error magnitude. The SZE is described as follows.

The distance between a point of the captured scene and the camera system can be computed, without loss of generality, based on the information of the stereo rig and the estimated disparity as is formulated in Equation (2).

$$Z_{true} = \frac{f * B}{d_{true}} , \qquad (2)$$

where f is the focal length in pixels, B is the baseline in meters (i.e. the distance between optical centres), d_{true} is the true disparity value in pixels, and Z_{true} is the distance along the camera Z axis in meters.

However, in practice, an inaccurate Z distance is generated due to a disparity estimation error, as is formulated in Equation (3).

$$Z_{false} = \frac{f * B}{d_{false}} \, , \tag{3}$$

where Z_{false} is the inaccurate distance estimation, and d_{false} is the falsely estimated disparity.

The proposed SZE measure consists in summing the difference between Z_{true} and Z_{false}, over the entire estimated disparity map (or in a particular image region) based on the information provided by disparity ground-truth data. The SZE is formulated in Equation (4).

$$SZE = \sum_{(x,y)} \left| \frac{f * B}{D_{true}(x,y) + \mu} - \frac{f * B}{D_{estimated}(x,y) + \mu} \right| \, , \tag{4}$$

where, μ is a small constant which avoids the instability caused by missing disparity estimations. The SZE fulfils the properties of a metric. However, it is unbounded.

Table 2 shows the values of the SZE and the BMP, as well as the PSNR and the MSSIM of the rendered views using different DM (i.e. the ground-truth, an inaccurate map varying smoothly, and a map containing streaking artefacts) of the Cones stereo image. It can be observed that despite of the low values of the MSSIM and the PSNR, the BMP values are indicating that there is no estimation error.

Table 3 shows obtained values of the BMP, the MAE, the MSE, and the MAPE, based on disparity ground-truth data by three different disparity estimation algorithms [9], and using the Venus stereo image. It can be observed that the values of the BMP are quite similar. On the other hand, the values of the SZE and the MAPE are indicating that there exists a difference in the accuracy of the considered algorithms.

Fig. 2 illustrates estimated DM calculated using the Tsukuba stereo image, and four disparity estimation algorithms [9], which have similar results of the percentage of the BMP on the non-occluded region. Table 4 shows obtained values on the non-occluded region, in relation to DM in Fig. 2, of the SZE, the BMP, the MAE, the MSE, and the MAPE, as well as the MSSIM using rendered views. In this case, the obtained values of the SZE are consistent with

Table 2. Obtained ground-truth based error measures and rendered image quality measures considering DM of the Cones stereo image

Disparity Map	SZE nonocc	SZE all	SZE disc	BMP nonocc	BMP all	BMP disc	PSNR	MSSIM
Ground-truth	0.000	0.000	0.000	0.000	0.000	0.000	29.948	0.903
Inaccurate	193.703	218.905	66.945	0.000	0.000	0.000	25.475	0.774
Artefacts	11.088	11.800	3.524	0.000	0.000	0.000	24.639	0.729

Table 3. Obtained values of the SZE, the BMP, the MAE, the MSE and the MAPE, considering different algorithms, and using the Venus image

Algorithm	SZE all	BMP all	MAE all	MSE all	MAPE all
CoopRegion	552.274	0.206	0.106	0.076	1.849
Undr+OvrSeg	735.384	0.224	0.199	0.097	2.815
AdaptingBP	929.368	0.212	0.165	0.104	3.069

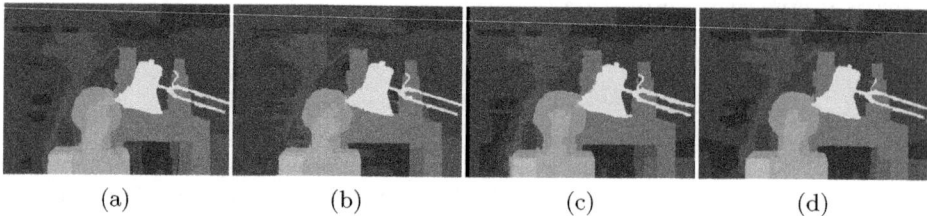

(a)   (b)   (c)   (d)

Fig. 2. Disparity maps of the Tsukuba image, estimated by: (a) DoubleBP, (b) CoopRegion, (c) GlobalGCP, (d) OutlierConf

Table 4. Obtained ground-truth based error measures and rendered image quality measures for disparity maps in Fig. 2

Algorithm	SZE nonocc	BMP nonocc	MAE nonocc	MSE nonocc	MAPE nonocc	MSSIM
DoubleBP	658.867	0.880	0.223	0.475	3.764	0.908
CoopRegion	662.485	0.872	0.228	0.507	3.780	0.905
GlobalGCP	817.656	0.868	0.263	0.530	4.560	0.908
OutlierConf	915.254	0.879	0.284	0.550	4.921	0.908

the obtained values of the MAE, the MSE, and the MAPE, and contradictories with the percentage of the BMP. On the other hand, the MSSIM values may be indicating that the quality of the rendered views may appear quite similar for a human observer.

4   Experimental Evaluation

In order to assess the impact of the proposal on evaluation results, the SZE and the BMP are considered as the error measures during an evaluation process. The top fifteen ranked algorithms in [9] (May, 2011) are selected as the algorithms under evaluation, and Tsukuba, Venus, Teddy and Cones stereo images are selected as the test-bed [11].

Two evaluation methodologies are used: the Middlebury methodology [9], [10], [11], and the **A*** methodology [2]. The **A*** methodology is a non-linear evaluation

Table 5. Quantitative evaluation of algorithms considering the SZE and the BMP as error measures, using the Middlebury and the $\mathbf{A}^*$ evaluation methodologies, respectively

Algorithm	SZE Avg. Rank	SZE Rank	SZE Algorithm $\in A^*_{(SZE)}$	BMP Avg. Rank	BMP Rank	BMP Algorithm $\in A^*_{(BMP)}$
GC+SegmBorder	1.17	1	Yes	9.58	11	Yes
SubPixDoubleBP	5.25	2	No	8.50	9	Yes
CoopRegion	5.92	3	No	5.33	3	Yes
SurfaceStereo	7.00	4	No	8.00	8	Yes
FeatureGC	7.67	5	Yes	8.75	10	Yes
CostFilter	7.83	6	No	11.25	15	No
ObjectStereo	8.08	7	No	7.92	7	Yes
AdaptingBP	8.42	8	No	4.83	2	Yes
Undr+OvrSeg	8.50	9	No	10.08	13	Yes
DoubleBP	8.83	10	Yes	6.33	4	Yes
WarpMat	9.75	11	No	9.75	12	Yes
GlobalGCP	9.83	12	No	10.92	14	Yes
OutlierConf	10.00	13	No	7.25	5	Yes
RDP	10.42	14	No	7.42	6	Yes
ADCensus	11.33	15	No	4.08	1	Yes

methodology. It computes the Pareto optimal set (denoted as A^*) from the set of algorithms under evaluation (denoted as A), by considering vectors of error measures [1], [17]. In this way, the set A^* contains those algorithms of comparable performance among them, and at the same time, of superior performance to $A \backslash A^*$.

Table 5 shows evaluation results of the error measures and the evaluation methodologies considered. It can be observed that using the SZE the evaluation results are significantly different, in both methodologies, to the results obtained by using the BMP as the error measure. Moreover, the smaller cardinality of the set A^*, when the SZE measure is used, can be attributed to a larger uniformity in the error measurements.

5   Conclusions

In this paper, the SZE is introduced as a measure for evaluating quantitatively estimated DM. It is based on the inverse relation between depth and disparity. The SZE offers advantages over the BMP, since it is focused on the impact of disparity estimation errors in terms of distance along the Z axis. In this way, it is related to an error value with a physical interpretation and meaning. Moreover, the SZE does not require the use of thresholds, which may introduce bias to the evaluation results. The analysis of different estimated DM shows that, under different circumstances, the BMP may not reflect properly the accuracy, in terms of depth, of the estimated disparity map. On the other hand, the SZE is consistent with other measures.

Innovative results in relation to algorithms evaluation were obtained when the SZE was used to support the quantitative evaluation, since it leads to a different ranking, by using the Middlebury evaluation methodology and a different composition of the set A^* by using the $\mathbf{A}^*$ evaluation methodology. Thus, the algorithms that are reported as achieving the most accurate DM, based on the BMP measure, may not necessarily correspond to those allowing the most accurate 3D reconstruction.

References

1. Ben Said, L., Bechikn, S., Ghedira, K.: The r-Dominance: A New Dominance Relation for Interactive Evolution Multi-criteria Decision Making. IEEE Trans. On Evolutionary Computation 14(5), 801–818 (2010)
2. Cabezas, I., Trujillo, M.: A Non-linear Quantitative Evaluation Approach for Disparity Estimation. In: Proc. Intl. Joint Conf. on Computer Vision and Computer Graphics Theory and Applications, pp. 704–709 (2011)
3. Chen, H., Wu, L.: A New Measure of Forecast Accuracy. In: Intl. Conf. on Information and Financial Engineering, pp. 710–712 (2010)
4. Gallup, D., Frahm, J., Mordohai, P., Pollefeys, M.: Variable Baseline/Resolution Stereo. In: Proc. Computer Vision and Pattern Recognition, pp. 1–8 (2008)
5. Hirschmuller, H., Scharstein, D.: Evaluation of Stereo Matching Costs on Images with Radiometric Differences. IEEE Trans. Pattern Analysis and Machine Intelligence, 1582–1599 (2009)
6. Isgro, F., Trucco, E., Xu, L.: Towards Teleconferencing by View Synthesis and Large-Baseline Stereo. In: Proc. Conf. on Image Processing, pp. 198–203 (2001)
7. Kostliva, J., Cech, J., Sara, R.: Feasibility Boundary in Dense and Semi-Dense Stereo Matching. In: Conf. on Comp. Vision and Pattern Recognition, pp. 1–8 (2007)
8. Malpica, W., Bovick, A.: Range Image Quality Assessment by Structural Similarity. In: IEEE Conf. on Acoustics, Speech and Signal Processing, pp. 1149–1152 (2009)
9. Scharstein,   D.:   Middlebury   Stereo   Evaluation, http://vision.middlebury.edu/stereo/
10. Scharstein, D., Szeliski, R.: A Taxonomy and Evaluation of Dense Two-Frame Stereo Correspondence Algorithms. Intl. Journal of Computer Vision 47, 7–42 (2002)
11. Scharstein, D., Szeliski, R.: High-accuracy Stereo Depth Maps using Structured Light. In: Computer Vision and Pattern Recognition, pp. 195–202 (2003)
12. Schreer, O., Fehn, C., Atzpadin, N., Muller, M., Smolic, A., Tanger, R., Kauff, P.: A Flexible 3D TV System for Different Multi-Baseline geometries. In: Proc. Conf. on Multimedia and Expo, pp. 1877–1880 (2006)
13. Shen, Y., Chaohui, L., Xu P., Xu, L.: Objective Quality Assessment of Noised Stereoscopic Image. In: Proc. Third Intl Conf. on Measuring Technology and Mechatronics Automation, pp. 745–747 (2011)
14. Szeliski, R.: Prediction Error as a Quality Metric for Motion and Stereo. In: Proc. Intl. Conf. on Computer Vision, vol. 2, pp. 781–788 (1999)

15. Szeliski, R., Zabih, R.: An Experimental Comparison of Stereo Algorithms. In: Triggs, B., Zisserman, A., Szeliski, R. (eds.) ICCV-WS 1999. LNCS, vol. 1883, pp. 1–19. Springer, Heidelberg (2000)
16. Van der Mark, W., Gavrila, D.: Real-time Dense Stereo for Intelligent Vehicles. IEEE Trans. on Intelligent Transportation Systems 7(1), 38–50 (2006)
17. Van Veldhuizen, D., Zydallis, D., Lamont, G.: Considerations in Engineering Parallel Multiobjective Evolutionary Algorithms. IEEE Trans. Evolutionary Computation 7(2), 144–173 (2003)
18. Wang, D., Ding, W., Man, Y., Cui, L.: A Joint Image Quality Assessment Method Based on Global Phase Coherence and Structural Similarity. In: Proc. Intl. Congress on Image and Signal Processing, pp. 2307–2311 (2010)
19. Wang, Z., Bovik, A., Sheikn, H., Simocell, E.: Image Quality Assessment: From Error visibility to Structural Similarity. IEEE Trans. on Image Processing 13(4), 600–612 (2004)
20. Zhang, Z., Hou, C., Shen, L., Yang, J.: An Objective Evaluation for Disparity map Based on the Disparity Gradient and Disparity Acceleration. In: Proc. Intl. Conf. on Information Technology and Computer Science, pp. 452–455 (2009)

Mixing Hierarchical Contexts for Object Recognition

Billy Peralta and Alvaro Soto

Pontificia Universidad Católica de Chile
bmperalt@uc.cl, asoto@ing.puc.cl

Abstract. Robust category-level object recognition is currently a major goal for the Computer Vision community. Intra-class and pose variations, as well as, background clutter and partial occlusions are some of the main difficulties to achieve this goal. Contextual information in the form of object co-ocurrences and spatial contraints has been successfully applied to reduce the inherent uncertainty of the visual world. Recently, Choi et al. [5] propose the use of a tree-structured graphical model to capture contextual relations among objects. Under this model there is only one possible fixed contextual relation among subsets of objects. In this work we extent Choi et al. approach by using a mixture model to consider the case that contextual relations among objects depend on scene type. Our experiments highlight the advantages of our proposal, showing that the adaptive specialization of contextual relations improves object recognition and object detection performances.

1 Introduction

Humans have the remarkable ability to quickly recognize objects in images even though the objects might have different sizes, rotations, and poses. This ability is still a main challenge for artificial vision systems. In particular, several works in robotics [2],[8] and [15] have shown the relevance of using visual object recognition modules to interact with the world, but there is still a need for more robust and flexible object recognition techniques.

In the literature of object recognition, there are significant milestones, such as [16], which proposes a new feature that is invariant to rotation and scaling, and [24], which proposes a real time object detector. Machine learning techniques have also been successfully used in the computer vision area, such as [13], [11] and [12]. In general, the most recent progress in the area of object recognition has been closely related to the sinergistic combination of tool from computer vision and machine learning.

Currently, object detectors are mainly trained using images from single object categories, as we can see in datasets such as Pascal [10], Caltech [13] and MIT-CSAIL [1]. As a consequence, typical approaches do not consider contextual relations among objects and scenes. These types of relations are highly relevant to reduce some of the ambiguities of the visual world. For example, in Figure 1,

C. San Martin and S.-W. Kim (Eds.): CIARP 2011, LNCS 7042, pp. 232–239, 2011.

(a) Grass and building relations   (b) Road and tree relations

Fig. 1. In real images, particular objects usually tend to co-occur and have positional relationships among them

we can see cases of outdoor scenes where particular objects usually tend to co-occur and have positional relationships among them.

An interesting option to improve the performance of single object detectors is to include in the models contextual relations among objects [14], such as co-ocurrences, or mutual spatial or scale constrains. In [19] spatial context is modelled using a variant of a boosting algorithm. In a seminal work, [22] uses contextual relations based on the statistics of low-level features in terms of the global scene and the objects in it. Recently, Hoi et al. [5] model inter-object relations using a tree-structured Bayesian network.

The works mentioned above assume that there is only one possible fixed contextual relation among objects. We believe that a richer representation should include the typical variations that occur among object relationships under different scenarios. For example, if we analyze the relation between a person and a dog, this is not fixed but it changes according to different scenarios. In the case of a park scene, person and dog objects co-occurs frequently, but in an office scene they hardly co-occur.

Our idea is to learn conditional relationships among objects according to each latent scene. In particular, we present an extension to the work in [5], where we use mixture models to capture a richer set of adaptive relations among objects and scenes. This paper is organized as follows. Section 2 describes previous work. Section 3 introduces the method proposed in this paper. Section 4 presents and discusses our main results. Finally, Section 5 shows our main conclusions and some future avenues of research.

2 Background

2.1 Related Work

In the case of object recognition considering context, we can divide the related work in two levels: global and local context [14]. In the case of global context, most works exploit scene configuration as an complementary information source. This configuration is represented using a statistics of the complete image. Ulrich and Nourbakhsh introduce color histograms as the representation of an image and a k-nearest neighbors scheme for classification [23]. They apply their method to topological localization of an indoor mobile robot, but retraining is needed for each specific indoor environment. Torralba proposes an image representation based on global features that represent dimensions in a space that they call Gist feature [22]. To construct it, an image is passed through a Gabor filter bank using 4 scales and 8 orientations, then the image is divided into a 4x4 non-overlapping grid, and finally the output energy of each filter is averaged within each grid cell. Chang et al. use low-level global features that are used to estimat a belief or confidence function over the available scene labels [3]. They build one classifier for each available scene category.

In the case of local context, contextual information is derived from specific blocks or local areas around object positions. Sinha and Torralba [20] improve face detection using local contextual regions. Torralba et al. [21] introduce a Boosting approach in combination with a Conditional Random Field (CRF) to recognize objects. They apply their method to recognize objects and structures in office and street scenes. Shotton et al. [19] combine layouts of textures and context to recognize objects. He uses a CRF to learn model of objects and a boosting algorithm to combine the texture information and the object model. Galleguillos et al. [14] use a CRF to maximize the true labeling of objects inside one scene constrained by co-ocurrence and location relations. Hoi et al. [5] model inter-object relations using a tree-structured Bayesian network. By using a tree, they avoid the combinatorial explosion in the number of possible relations. Another advantage of this tree-representation is the efficiency for making inference over data. Aditionally, Rabinovich et al. [18] show that textual data from Web is an useful source to estimate co-ocurrence between objects.

3   Our Model

We learn scene types using a classical clustering algorithm: *K-Means*. The use of an unsupervised method to find scene types is due to the absence of scenes labels. We execute the clustering on the space of the global feature Gist G_G [5]. We use the clusters provided by K-Means to build a Gaussian Mixture Model with variances and weigths of components equal to one. Accordingly, we modify the graphical model proposed by Choi et al. [5] by adding a mixture element, as shown in Figure 2. We describe next each of the elements of this model.

3.1   Specification of the Model

In what follows, the subindex i refers to object class i and the subindex k refers to the ranking of the detection. This ranking comes from the order of the scores of the multiple detections of the object detector of Felzenszwalb [12].

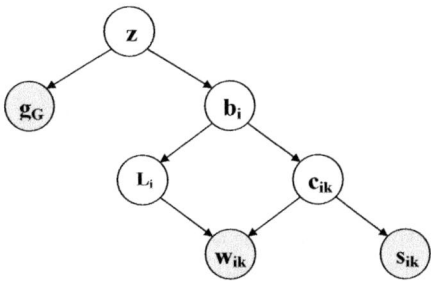

Fig. 2. Proposed graphical model

Location of window (W). The location of a detection window $w_{ik} = (L_y,$ $\log L_z)$, where L_y is the vertical location of the window and L_z is the scale of the window. We model the location distribution as a Gaussian. It is conditional on c_{ik}, a binary variable that indicates if a detection is correct, and also the expected mean of the location of objects L_i; where we consider the true appearances, L_i, and the false appearances, $\bar{L}_i$. The covariance for the true positive cases is given by Λ_i and for the false positives by $\bar{\Lambda}_i$. We define **(i)** $p(w_{ik}|c_{ik} = 1, L_i) = Normal(w_{ik}; L_i, \Lambda_i)$ and **(ii)** $p(w_{ik}|c_{ik} = 0, L_i) = Normal(w_{ik}; \bar{L}_i, \bar{\Lambda}_i)$. In case that there is not object, we assume a Uniform distribution.

Score (S). The score of classifier $s_{ik} \in \Re$. We model the score as a distribution that depends on whether the window is a correct detection or a false positive. Using Bayes rule, we have $p(s_{ik}|c_{ik}) = p(c_{ik}|s_{ik})p(s_{ik})|p(c_{ik})$. The logistic regressors are used to model $p(c_{ik}|s_{ik})$. This allow us to increase robustness, since there are few samples with $c_{ik} = 1$.

In the case that there is not a positive case in the partition, we add an artificial detection with score slightly greater than the maximum value of the current scores. This is because the logistic regresor requires at least two classes.

Correct detection (C). The correct detections $c_{ik} \in 0, 1$, where 0 means a false positive and 1, a true positive. We model the correct detection as depending on the presence of objects b: **(i)** $p(c_{ik} = 1|b_i = 1)$ equal to frequencies from training set when object i appears; and **(ii)** $p(c_{ik} = 1|b_i = 0)$ equal to zero.

Parameter of location (L). We model the distribution of locations as depending of presence of objects b: $p(L|b) = p(L_{root}|b_{root}) \prod_i p(L_i|L_{pa(i)}, b_i, b_{pa(i)})$, where L_i is the median of all instances of object i, and it is composed by $(L_y, \log L_z)$. Its components are L_y, the vertical position in the image, and L_z, the scale of detection. The use of logarithm has been shown suitable in previous work [5].

In the case of conditional components, we use Gaussians for the location of object i, using the following expressions for the respectives cases: **(i)** if $b_i = 1$ and $b_{pa(i)} = 1$, we use the location of object $pa(i)$; **(ii)** if $b_i = 1$ and $b_{pa(i)} = 0$, we use the location of object i; and finally **(iii)** if $b_i = 0$, we use the location of all objects in all images. In case of objects that do not appear in a partition, again we use a Uniform distribution.

Presence of object (B). The presence of object $b_i \in 0, 1$. We model object presence as a function of the learned tree model and the partition z. We have: $p(b|z) = p(b_{root}|z) \prod_i p(b_i|b_{pa(i)}, z)$.

We learn the tree from data using the Chow-Liu algorithm on each partition [6]. There is a restriction for the case of objects that do not appear in a particular partition. For these objects we consider a mutual information equal to zero, and we add them as children of the last added node to the tree. In this way, we diminish the influence of these variables.

Global Gist (g_G). We model the global Gist feature [22] as depending on partition z, so we have $p(g_G = g|z) = Normal(g; u_z, \Sigma_z)$. We consider the variance and weights equal to one. It helps to simplify the distant metric.

In the model of Choi et al. [5], g_G is used as a direct prior of the individual objects. However, it is independent of the context-hierarchical model, as we want to evaluate the goodness of the context model, we do not use this information for both techniques in order to make a fair comparison.

Partition (z). The partition $z \in 0, |Z|$, where $|Z|$ is the number of scences. This partition represents the latent scenes for the database. In this case, we obtain its value for a particular image according to the model of clustering.

It is important to mention that due to the computational complexity, we do not apply a joint optimization over partitions and local models. Instead, we first apply a clustering of images, and afterwards we learn the local models.

3.2 Inference

The inference is straightforward because we separate each tree in its own partition. We make an inference using message passing algorithms for each tree ($p(b, c, L/g, W, s, z)$) [17]. Then we obtain the final score by combining the scores of each component with its respective parameters.

$$\hat{b}, \hat{c}, \hat{L} = argmax_{b,c,L} \sum_z p(z) * p(b, c, L/g, W, s, z)$$

Similarly to [5], we use the following iterative procedure to detect objects: first we make an inference without consider the locations ($\hat{b}_0, \hat{c}_0 \propto p(b, c|g, s)$) , then we infer the locations ($\hat{L} \propto argmax_L p(L|\hat{b}_0, \hat{c}_0, W)$), and finally we infer the presence of each object ($\hat{b}, \hat{c} \propto p(b, c|s, g, \hat{L}, W)$).

4 Experiments

In our experiments, we use the dataset created by Choi et al. [4]. This dataset has 111 classes, 4.367 training images, and 4.317 test images. In general, the

Table 1. APR for Choi-database

	Baseline	Tree	MT						
#Trees	-	1	2	3	4	5	6	7
Recognition	6.82	7.08	7.28	7.39	**7.59**	7.30	7.47	7.53
Detection	13.31	17.74	18.08	18.16	**18.28**	18.14	18.11	17.94

detection of the objects in these images is highly challenging, including a variety of poses, scales, rotations, and scene types. As a baseline technique, we use the object detector proposed by Felzenszwalb et al. [12], which is based on the mixture of multiscale deformable part models and a variant of SVM. In average, this detector provides approximately 500 detections for each image. We use as a performance metric of our model the average precision-recall metric (APR) [7]. This metric corresponds to the area under the precision-recall curve.

In order to test the method, we define the detection and recognition tasks. The detection for an object Γ is defined as the procedure where we determine if the object Γ appears or not in the entire image; in this case, we only use the detection for object Γ with top likelihood. In the recognition task for object Γ, we check if each detection of object Γ inside the image is a true positive.

Table 1 shows the results using the baseline technique [12] (*BaseLine*), the method proposed by Choi et al. [5] based on a single tree (*Tree*), and our proposed method based on a mixture model (*MT*).

In table 1, we show the average of the APR for the 111 object categories. We note that our method improves performance for both tasks, recognition and

Fig. 3. Sample detections for the proposed method

detection. The best number of trees in this dataset is 4. When we compare this result to [5], we find a favourable difference of 0.51 for APR recognition and 0.54 for APR detection.

Figure 3 shows the six most confident detections provided by the proposed method for some test images[1]. As an example, we can see in the first figure of the second row how our method correctly recognizes three cars, one person, one tree, and the sky.

5   Conclusions

In this work, we present an extension of the model of Choi et al. based on a mixture of trees that combines conditional contextual relations among objects. Our experiments using a standard dataset indicate that the proposed model improves the results of a state-of-art technique in terms of object detection and recognition according to the APR metric. These improvements provide evidence that an adaptive modelling of the interactions among object help recognition.

As future work, we plan to enhance our model using a more informative clustering process, such as including explicit latent models or a discriminative clustering technique. We also plan to include adaptive policies to control the execution of object classifiers, such as the method proposed in [9].

Acknowledgements. This work was partially funded by FONDECYT grant 1095140.

References

1. Murphy, K., Torralba, A., Freeman, W.T.: The mit-csail database of objects and scenes (2010), http://web.mit.edu/torralba/www/database.html
2. Bartlett, M.S., Littlewort, G., Fasel, I., Chenu, J., Ishiguro, H., Movellan, J.R.: Towards social robots: Automatic evaluation of human-robot interaction by face detection and expression classification. In: Advances in Neural Information. MIT Press (2003)
3. Chang, E., Goh, K., Sychay, G., Wu, G.: Cbsa: Content-based soft annotation for multimodal image retrieval using bayes point machines. IEEE Transactions on Circuits and Systems for Video Technology 13, 26–38 (2003)
4. Choi, M.: Large database of object categories (2010), http://web.mit.edu/~myungjin/www/HContext.html
5. Choi, M.J., Lim, J.J., Torralba, A., Willsky, A.S.: Exploiting hierarchical context on a large database of object categories. In: IEEE Conference on Computer VIsion and Pattern Recognition, CVPR (2010)
6. Chow, C.I., Liu, C.N.: Approximating discrete probability distributions with dependence trees. IEEE Transactions on Information Theory 14, 462–467 (1968)
7. Davis, J., Goadrich, M.: The relationship between precision-recall and roc curves. In: ICML 2006: Proceedings of the 23rd International Conference on Machine Learning, pp. 233–240. ACM Press (2006)

---

[1] We suggest to see these images in color.

8. Ekvall, S., Kragic, D., Jensfelt, P.: Object detection and mapping for service robot tasks. Robotica 25(2), 175–187 (2007)
9. Espinace, P., Kollar, T., Soto, A., Roy, N.: Indoor scene recognition through object detection. In: Proc. of IEEE Int. Conf. on Robotics and Automation, ICRA (2010)
10. Everingham, M., Van Gool, L., Williams, C.K.I., Winn, J., Zisserman, A.: The PASCAL Visual Object Classes (VOC) challenge. International Journal of Computer Vision 88(2), 303–338 (2010)
11. Fei-Fei, L.: A bayesian hierarchical model for learning natural scene categories. In: CVPR, vol. 2, pp. 524–531 (2005)
12. Felzenszwalb, P.F., McAllester, D.A., Ramanan, D.: A discriminatively trained, multiscale, deformable part model. In: Proc. IEEE Conference on Computer Vision and Pattern Recognition (2008)
13. Fergus, R., Perona, P., Zisserman, A.: Object class recognition by unsupervised scale-invariant learning. In: CVPR, pp. 264–271 (2003)
14. Galleguillos, C., Belongie, S.: Context based object categorization: A critical survey. Computer Vision and Image Understanding 114(6), 712–722 (2010); special Issue on Multi-Camera and Multi-Modal Sensor Fusion
15. Huebner, K., Björkman, M., Rasolzadeh, B., Schmidt, M., Kragic, D.: Integration of Visual and Shape Attributes for Object Action Complexes. In: Gasteratos, A., Vincze, M., Tsotsos, J.K. (eds.) ICVS 2008. LNCS, vol. 5008, pp. 13–22. Springer, Heidelberg (2008)
16. Lowe, D.: Object recognition from local scale-invariant features, pp. 1150–1157 (1999)
17. Pearl, J.: Reverend Bayes on inference engines: A distributed hierarchical approach. In: Proceedings of the American Association of Artificial Intelligence National Conference on AI, Pittsburgh, PA, pp. 133–136 (1982)
18. Rabinovich, A., Vedaldi, A., Galleguillos, C., Wiewiora, E., Belongie, S.: Objects in context. In: ICCV 2007, pp. 1–8 (2007)
19. Shotton, J., Winn, J., Rother, C., Criminisi, A.: Textonboost for image understanding: Multi-class object recognition and segmentation by jointly modeling texture, layout, and context (2007)
20. Sinha, P., Torralba, A.: Detecting faces in impoverished images. Journal of Vision 2(7), 601 (2002)
21. Torralba, A., Murphy, K.P., Freeman, W.T.: Contextual models for object detection using boosted random fields. In: Advances in Neural Information Processing Systems 17 (NIPS), pp. 1401–1408 (2005)
22. Torralba, A.: Contextual priming for object detection. IJCV 53 (2003)
23. Ulrich, I., Nourbakhsh, I.: Appearance-based place recognition for topological localization. In: Proceedings of IEEE International Conference on Robotics and Automation, ICRA 2000, vol. 2, pp. 1023–1029 (2000)
24. Viola, P., Jones, M.: Rapid object detection using a boosted cascade of simple features, pp. 511–518 (2001)

Encoding Spatial Arrangement of Visual Words

Otávio A.B. Penatti, Eduardo Valle, and Ricardo da S. Torres*

Recod Lab, Institute of Computing, University of Campinas (Unicamp),
Campinas, Brazil
penatti@ic.unicamp.br, mail@eduardovalle.com, rtorres@ic.unicamp.br

Abstract. This paper presents a new approach to encode spatial-relationship information of visual words in the well-known visual dictionary model. The current most popular approach to describe images based on visual words is by means of bags-of-words which do not encode any spatial information. We propose a graceful way to capture spatial-relationship information of visual words that encodes the spatial arrangement of every visual word in an image. Our experiments show the importance of the spatial information of visual words for image classification and show the gain in classification accuracy when using the new method. The proposed approach creates opportunities for further improvements in image description under the visual dictionary model.

Keywords: spatial-relationship, visual words, visual dictionaries.

1 Introduction

Automatically understanding the content of multimedia data has become very important since there is an exponential growth of multimedia information available recently. The scientific and industrial communities have reached many advances in this field in the latest years. A very popular and effective technique for multimedia information description is by using visual dictionaries [14], which are mainly used in tasks of scene and object categorization.

The main idea of using visual dictionaries is to consider that the visual patterns present in images are similar to textual words present in textual documents. Therefore, an image is composed by visual words as a textual document is composed by textual words.

The process to generate visual dictionaries takes several steps. To obtain the visual words of images, usually interest point detectors, like Hessian-Affine and Harris-Laplace [9] detectors are used; the detected points are described by descriptors like SIFT [8]; and the points in feature space are then clustered to create the visual words. The words thus obtained are more general than the low level descriptors, since the clustering step will tend to quantize the descriptor space into "similar looking" regions.

---

* Authors thank CNPq, Capes, and Fapesp (2009/10554-8, 2009/05951-8, 2009/18438-7) for the financial support.

C. San Martin and S.-W. Kim (Eds.): CIARP 2011, LNCS 7042, pp. 240–247, 2011.

When the visual dictionary is created, an image can be described by their visual patterns (visual words). The most traditional image descriptor based on visual words is the *bag-of-words*. It is simply a histogram of the visual words in the image. Therefore, when using visual dictionaries we can still have only one feature vector per image, even capturing local information.

The use of visual dictionaries is very popular and new approaches for improving the use and generation of them constantly appear in the literature [1,3,12]. As the traditional bag-of-words descriptor does not encode spatial information of images, some works try to overcome this weakness [2,5,7]

This paper presents an approach to encode the spatial information of visual words into the feature vector. Our approach captures the spatial arrangement of every visual word in an image. Its basic model is at the same time very simple and easily adaptable, opening the opportunity for a whole family of methods to represent the spatial relationship of visual words.

The remainder of the paper is organized as follows: Section 2 shows the importance of spatial information of visual words for image description. Section 3 presents our approach to encode the spatial arrangement of visual words. Section 4 shows the experiments and results. Section 5 concludes the paper.

2   Spatial-Relationship Information in Visual Dictionaries

Spatial information of visual words is very important for the characterization of images and objects. Different objects and scenes may be composed by the same visual appearances in different spatial compositions, making that spatial distribution critical to their discrimination.

The traditional bag-of-words descriptor used to describe images based on visual words does not encode spatial information. The need to encode the spatial information of visual words has motivated the creation of some new approaches to tackle the problem. One of the most popular is the spatial pyramid [7] which splits the image into hierarchical cells and computes bags-of-words for each cell, concatenating the results at the end. Other approaches employ the co-occurrence of pairs of visual words [14] or correlograms of visual words [13]. The method presented in [2] proposes image splitting by linear and circular projections, generating one bag for each projection. Most of these approaches suffer from the problem of generating huge amounts of data.

Although the spatial information of visual words is important for visual characterization, their frequency of occurrence, which is captured by the bag, is also very important, as observed in many applications [1,6,11]. Therefore, combining frequency of occurrence and spatial information of visual words should be a promising direction for further improvements.

3   Proposed Approach

Our approach to encode spatial-relationship information of visual words is based on the idea of dividing the image space into quadrants [10] using each point as

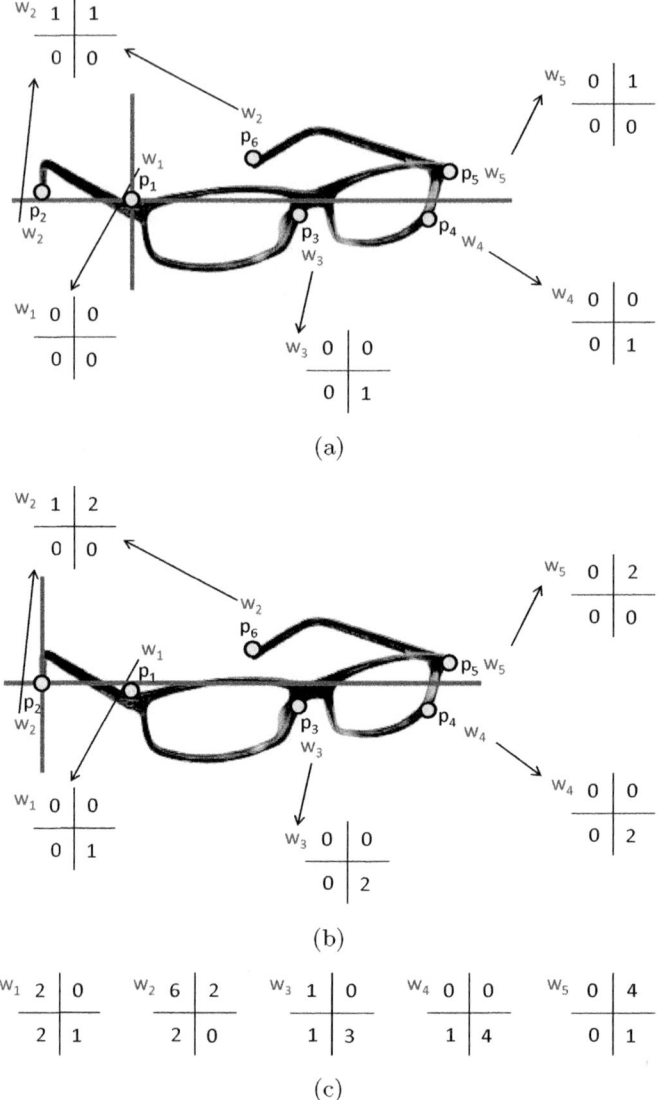

Fig. 1. Example of partitioning and counting. The small circles are the detected points, tagged by their associated visual words (w_i's). We start in (a), putting the quadrant's origin in p_1 and counting in the visual word associated with each other point, where it is in relation to p_1. On the second step (b) the quadrant is at p_2; we add again the counters of the words associated with each other point in the position corresponding to their position in relation to p_2. We proceeded until the quadrant has visited every point in the image. Final counter values are shown in (c).

the origin of the quadrants and counting the number of words that appear in each quadrant. We count how many times a visual word w_i appears in each quadrant in relation to all other points in an specific image. This counting will tell us the *spatial arrangement* of the visual word w_i. Intuitively, the counting will measure the word's positioning in relation to the other points in the image. It reveals that a word w_i tends to be below, at right, or surrounded by other points, for example.

The image space is divided as follows: for each point p_i detected in the image, we divide the space into 4 quadrants, putting the point p_i in the quadrant's origin; then, for every other detected point p_j, we increment the counting of the visual word associated with p_j in the position that corresponds to the position of p_j in relation to p_i. For example, if w_j is the visual word associated with p_j and p_j is at top-left from p_i, the counter for top-left position of w_j is incremented. After all points are analyzed in relation to p_i, the quadrant's origin goes to the next point p_{i+1}, and the counting in relation to p_{i+1} begins. When all points have already been the quadrant's origin, the counting finishes. Figure 1 shows an example of partitioning the image space and counting.

Every word will be associated with 4 numbers. Those numbers tell the spatial arrangement of every visual word in the image. The same visual word can appear in several different locations in an image, however, there is only one set of 4 counters associated with it. The complexity of this method is $O(k^2)$, while the traditional bag is $O(k)$, where k is the dictionary size.

When the counting is finished, each 4-tuple is normalized by its sum. If the word w_i has non-zero values only in its bottom-right counter, for instance, we can say that w_i is a bottom-right word, that is, it appears always at bottom-right position in relation to other points. If w_i has top-left and top-right counters with high values, we can say that w_i is a word that usually appears above other points. If all counters of w_i are equally distributed, w_i is surrounded by other points (middle-word) or it is a word that repeatedly surrounds other points (border-word).

Another advantage of our method is that we do not need to tune parameters for better performance, as no parametrization is necessary.

4   Experiments

The experiments were conducted on the challenging Caltech-256 database [4], including the *clutter* class (257). The visual dictionary was generated using some of the most common parameters in the literature [1]: Hessian-Affine detector, SIFT descriptor, and 1000 aleatory centers. The visual words were hard assigned to the detected points [1]. The training and classification was performed by SVM with RBF kernel.

We compared our method with the traditional bag-of-words descriptor (BoW), which has only the frequency of occurrence of the words in the image. Our method is here called as WSA (words spatial arrangement). In our method, the feature vector also contains the frequency of occurrence of the words in the image, like BoW. Therefore, the feature vector of WSA is composed by 5 values per visual word. We also compared BoW to a variation of WSA that does not contain the word frequency of occurrence (WSA-noBag).

The validation was performed by increasing the number of training samples per class. The training samples were randomly selected. All samples that were not in the training set were used in the testing set. Each experiment was repeated 10 times (varying randomly the training set). Figure 2 summarizes the results, showing the average accuracies obtained.

The curves show that WSA is superior to BoW in classification accuracy. This superiority is clear from training sets larger than 5 samples per class. The larger the training set, the larger the difference in favor of WSA. This indicates that the spatial arrangement of visual words aggregates important information to distinguish images and object categories. The results for WSA-noBag are below BoW showing that the frequency of occurrence of visual words is a little more important than only their spatial arrangement. However, the spatial arrangement is almost as discriminant as the frequency of occurrence of a visual word, demonstrating the importance of encoding spatial information of visual words. The superior performance of WSA indicates that combining frequency of occurrence and spatial arrangement of visual words is effective.

To better understand how the spatial information affects recognition results, we have performed a detailed (per class) analysis of classification accuracy considering a training set size of 30 samples per class. Table 4 shows the results obtained for the classes where the differences between BoW and WSA is large (greater than or equal to 0.1). Comparing BoW and WSA, we notice how promising is the use of spatial information together with frequency of occurrence information. WSA is superior in most of the classes and, in some of them, the spatial arrangement makes a large difference (more than 0.1 in absolute improvement of classification rate).

It is worth noting that for a few classes the spatial information was so important that even WSA-noBag (without frequency information) had performances remarkably superior to BoW. It was the case, for example, of classes 15 (bonsai), 25 (cactus), 44 (comet), 137 (mars), 156 (paper-shredder), 234 (tweezer), and 252 (car-side). This shows, in itself, the discriminating power of words spatial configurations.

For a few classes, interestingly, adding spatial information actually perturbs the classification. Those classes were few enough to be enumerated: 3 (backpack), 20 (brain), 24 (butterfly), 26 (cake), 103 (hibiscus), 129 (leopards), 142 (microwave), 241 (waterfall) and 250 (zebra). We are still investigating this phenomenon, but we believe that in some situations of very stereotyped textures (waterfalls, leopards, zebras, butterflies) with lots of detected points, the spatial configuration might confuse the descriptor.

In general, the spatial arrangement of visual words aggregates important discriminant information to the traditional bag-of-words.

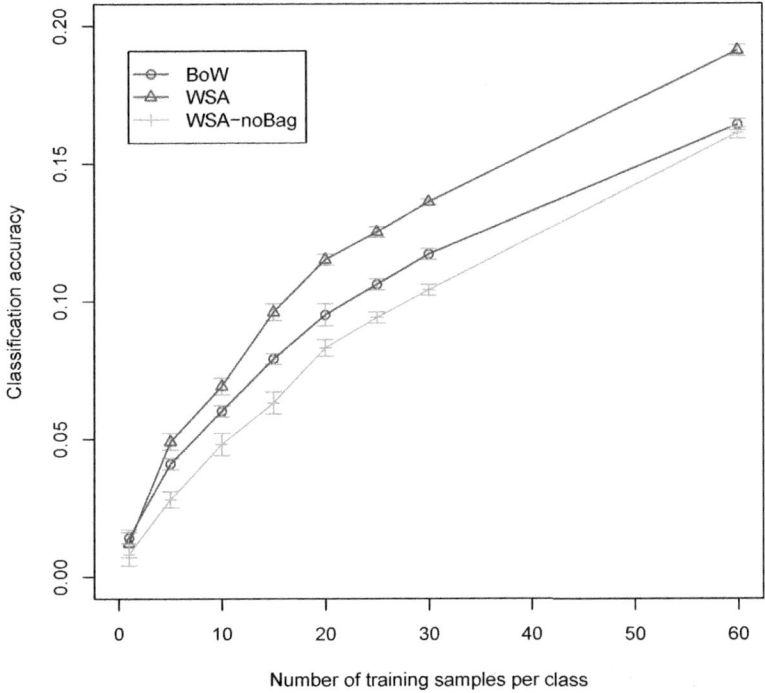

Fig. 2. Overall classification accuracy of the methods in Caltech-256. Each data point is the average for 10 runs, and the error bars are confidence intervals for alpha=0.05.

5   Discussion

This paper presents a simple and effective approach to encode spatial-relationship information of visual words. Our approach is based on the partition of the image space and in the counting of the occurrences of the visual words in relation to the other visual words positions. It is able to capture the spatial arrangement of every visual word in an image. Experiments show that aggregating the spatial arrangement of visual words to the traditional bag-of-words increases classification accuracy.

Our approach is also promising in the sense that the encoded information can be used in different ways. In this paper we directly use the spatial arrangement of words, however, more elaborated ideas can be applied over this spatial information. For example, the encoded information can categorize visual words spatially, like top-word, right-word, etc. The categorization can be used in many different ways, like, for instance, computing one bag for each category of visual word. We are already investigating the use of one bag for interior-words and other for border-words.

Table 1. Classes of Caltech-256 where the differences in accuracy between the different methods tested were large

Class	Class name	WSA-noBag	BoW	WSA
2	american-flag	0.13	0.12	**0.21**
3	backpack	0.07	**0.22**	0.08
15	bonsai	0.25	0.15	**0.25**
20	brain	0.15	**0.30**	0.14
21	breadmaker	0.04	0.06	**0.33**
24	butterfly	0.19	**0.39**	0.20
25	cactus	**0.27**	0.09	0.18
26	cake	0.04	**0.23**	0.07
44	comet	**0.53**	0.33	0.48
53	desk-globe	0.13	0.10	**0.26**
67	eyeglasses	0.40	0.34	**0.48**
75	floppy-disk	0.18	0.13	**0.36**
100	hawksbill	0.24	0.16	**0.30**
103	hibiscus	0.20	**0.42**	0.22
112	human-skeleton	0.09	0.05	**0.16**
123	ketch	0.22	0.15	**0.34**
127	laptop	0.14	0.10	**0.22**
129	leopards	0.62	**0.87**	0.60
137	mars	0.56	0.46	**0.61**
142	microwave	0.07	**0.23**	0.08
146	mountain-bike	0.29	0.24	**0.40**
156	paper-shredder	**0.25**	0.06	0.22
177	saturn	0.47	0.52	**0.62**
182	self-p.lawn-mower	0.27	0.26	**0.45**
234	tweezer	**0.86**	0.38	0.54
238	video-projector	0.06	0.13	**0.25**
241	waterfall	0.08	**0.38**	0.17
248	yarmulke	0.04	0.15	**0.26**
250	zebra	0.09	**0.25**	0.15
251	airplanes	0.34	0.30	**0.57**
252	car-side	0.50	0.38	**0.51**

Other improvements in the encoding of the spatial arrangement are also under investigation. A prior investigation is being made in the following scenario. We have the same object in different locations in two different images with clutter background. As the current counting schema considers all points in the image, in this case, the counting will change considerably from one image to another. To avoid this, we are investigating the use of windows around the point when counting. Other improvements are being tested, like a change in the partitioning schema. Instead of using 4 quadrants, we are trying to partition the space horizontally and vertically independently. This way of partitioning is more robust to rotation. Another possibility of use of our approach is for segmentation purposes, like, for instance, using the middle-words as seeds for some segmentation methods.

References

1. Boureau, Y.L., Bach, F., LeCun, Y., Ponce, J.: Learning mid-level features for recognition. In: CVPR, pp. 2559–2566 (2010)
2. Cao, Y., Wang, C., Li, Z., Zhang, L., Zhang, L.: Spatial-bag-of-features. In: CVPR, pp. 3352–3359 (2010)
3. van Gemert, J.C., Veenman, C.J., Smeulders, A.W.M., Geusebroek, J.M.: Visual word ambiguity. TPAMI 32(7), 1271–1283 (2010)
4. Griffin, G., Holub, A., Perona, P.: Caltech-256 object category dataset. Tech. Rep. 7694, California Institute of Technology (2007)
5. Hoíng, N.V., Gouet-Brunet, V., Rukoz, M., Manouvrier, M.: Embedding spatial information into image content description for scene retrieval. Pattern Recognition 43(9), 3013–3024 (2010)
6. Wenjun, L., Min, W.: Multimedia forensic hash based on visual words. In: ICIP, pp. 989–992 (2010)
7. Lazebnik, S., Schmid, C., Ponce, J.: Beyond bags of features: Spatial pyramid matching for recognizing natural scene categories. In: CVPR, vol. 2, pp. 2169–2178 (2006)
8. Lowe, D.G.: Distinctive image features from scale-invariant keypoints. Int. Journal of Comp. Vis. 60(2), 91–110 (2004)
9. Mikolajczyk, K., Schmid, C.: Scale and affine invariant interest point detectors. Int. Journal of Comp. Vis. 60, 63–86 (2004)
10. Penatti, O.A.B., Torres, R.da.S.: Spatial relationship descriptor based on partitions. REIC 7(3) (2007) (in Portuguese)
11. Philbin, J., Chum, O., Isard, M., Sivic, J., Zisserman, A.: Lost in quantization: Improving particular object retrieval in large scale image databases. In: CVPR (2008)
12. Jianzhao, Q., Yung, N.: Category-specific incremental visual codebook training for scene categorization. In: ICIP, pp. 1501–1504 (2010)
13. Savarese, S., Winn, J., Criminisi, A.: Discriminative object class models of appearance and shape by correlatons. In: CVPR, vol. 2, pp. 2033–2040 (2006)
14. Sivic, J., Russell, B.C., Efros, A.A., Zisserman, A., Freeman, W.T.: Discovering objects and their location in images. In: ICCV, vol. 1, pp. 370–377 (2005)

Color-Aware Local Spatiotemporal Features for Action Recognition

Fillipe Souza[1], Eduardo Valle[2], Guillermo Chávez[3], and Arnaldo de A. Araújo[1]

[1] NPDI Lab, DCC/UFMG, Belo Horizonte/MG, Brazil
[2] RECOD Lab, IC/Unicamp, Campinas/SP, Brazil
[3] ICEB/UFOP, Ouro Preto/MG, Brazil
fdms18@gmail.com, mail@eduardovalle.com,
gcamarac@gmail.com, arnaldo@dcc.ufmg.br

Abstract. Despite the recent developments in spatiotemporal local features for action recognition in video sequences, local color information has so far been ignored. However, color has been proved an important element to the success of automated recognition of objects and scenes. In this paper we extend the space-time interest point descriptor STIP to take into account the color information on the features' neighborhood. We compare the performance of our color-aware version of STIP (which we have called HueSTIP) with the original one.

Keywords: Color invariance, spatiotemporal local features, human action recognition.

1 Introduction

In this work we provide a discussion on the role of spatiotemporal color features for human action recognition in realistic settings. Color is a prominent feature of the real world scenes and objects. Not surprisingly, it has become a powerful tool in automated object recognition [1] [2] [3]. However, color has not yet been given its deserved importance in the universe of unconstrained action recognition.

Several spatiotemporal local feature descriptors and detectors have been proposed and evaluated in action recognition. Detectors rely commonly on a measure function (or response function) to locate interest regions. Those local regions (also called patches) can be described in terms, for example, of histograms of gradient orientations and optical flow. Laptev [4] presented a spatiotemporal extension of the Harris-Laplace corner detector proposed by Mikolajczyk and Schmid [5]. Spatiotemporal corners are found when strong intensity variations over the spatial and temporal domains occur simultaneously. This method has proved efficient for action recognition in controlled datasets such as the KTH dataset [6]. Dollár et al. [7] proposed a spatiotemporal detector based on temporal Gabor filters that considers only local variations having periodic frequency components. Another spatiotemporal interest point detector was designed in [8] by Willems et al. This detector uses the Hessian determinant as a saliency measure and 3D convolution approximations by box-filters in order to find regions

C. San Martin and S.-W. Kim (Eds.): CIARP 2011, LNCS 7042, pp. 248–255, 2011.
© Springer-Verlag Berlin Heidelberg 2011

of interest. Here we will only provide a formal discussion of the spatiotemporal local feature detector used in this work, the one proposed in [4].

To improve the discriminative power and illumination invariance of local features to object recognition and image categorization, a set of color descriptors for spatial local features was proposed in [3] by van de Sande et al. for static images. The distictiveness of their color descriptors was evaluated experimentally and their invariant properties under illuminations changes were analyzed. They derived different color descriptors, including combinations with the intensity-based shape descriptor SIFT [9]. Van de Weijer et al. [2] had already proposed color histograms providing robustness to photometric and geometrical changes, photometric stability and generality. Their work was the basis for some of the descriptors developed in [3], including our own.

The most important contribution of this work is the combination of the work by van de Weijer et al. [2] and Laptev [4] to propose the use of color descriptors to describe local spatiotemporal interest points (features). To this end, we have produced preliminary results on the matter, such that only information from the hue channel (of the HSI color system) is evaluated as the source of color data for the description of space-time interest points. The second contribution is an analysis of the proposal on the prevailing application of automated recognition of human actions (on a challenging dataset, the Hollywood2 [10]). We make a performance comparison between which has been considered as standard in the literature and our proposal. We then discuss the results clarifying the cases of success and failure brought by the addition of color information.

The rest of this paper is organized as follows. In section 2 we are concerned with the formal description of the spatiotemporal interest point detector used. Further, the details on the color descriptors are presented in section 3. The experiments and their results are discussed in section 4 and section 5 concludes the work.

2   Spatiotemporal Interest Points

Laptev [4] proposed a differential operator that checks for local extremas over spatial and temporal scales at the same time. Extrema in specific space-time locations refer to particular patterns of events. This method is built on the Harris [11] and Förstner [12] interest point operators, but extended to the temporal space. Essentially, as a corner moves across an image sequence, at the change of its direction an interest point is identified. Other typical situations are when image structures are either split or unified. For being one of the major elements in this work, a few details and mathematical considerations on the detector design are presented next.

Many interest events in videos are characterized by motion variations of image structures over time. In order to retain those important information, the concept of spatial interest points is extended to the spatio-temporal domain. This way, the local regions around the interest points are described with respect to derivatives in both directions (space and time).

At first, the selection of interest point in the spatial domain is described. The linear scale-space representation of an image can be mathematically defined as $L^{sp} : R^2 \times R_+ \mapsto R$, which is the convolution of f^{sp} with g^{sp}, where $f^{sp} : R^2 \mapsto R$ represents a simple model of an image and g^{sp} is the Gaussian kernel of variance σ_l^2. Then,

$$L^{sp}(x, y; \sigma_l^2) = g^{sp}(x, y; \sigma_l^2) * f^{sp}(x, y), \qquad (1)$$

and

$$g^{sp}(x, y; \sigma_l^2) = \frac{1}{2\pi\sigma_l^2} \exp(-(x^2 + y^2)/2\sigma_l^2). \qquad (2)$$

Localizing interest points means to find strong variations of image intensities along the two directions of the image. To determine those local regions, the second moment matrix is integrated over a Gaussian window having variance σ_i^2, for different scales of observation σ_l^2, which is written as the equation:

$$\mu^{sp}(.; \sigma_l^2, \sigma_i^2) = g^{sp}(.; \sigma_i^2) * ((\nabla L(.; \sigma_l^2))(\nabla L(.; \sigma_l^2))^T)$$
$$= g^{sp}(.; \sigma_i^2) * \begin{pmatrix} (L_x^{sp})^2 & L_x^{sp} L_y^{sp} \\ L_x^{sp} L_y^{sp} & (L_y^{sp})^2. \end{pmatrix} \qquad (3)$$

The descriptors of variations along the dimensions of f^{sp} are the eigenvalues of Equation 3: λ_1 and λ_2, with $\lambda_1 \leq \lambda_2$. Higher values of those eigenvalues are a sign of an interest point and generally lead to positive local maxima of the Harris corner function, provided that the ratio $\alpha = \lambda_2/\lambda_1$ is high and satisfies the constraint $k \leq \alpha/(1+\alpha)^2$:

$$H^{sp} = \det(\mu^{sp}) - k.trace^2(\mu^{sp})$$
$$= \lambda_1\lambda_2 - k(\lambda_1 + \lambda_2)^2. \qquad (4)$$

Analogously, the procedure to detect interest points in the scape-time domain is derived by rewriting the equations to consider the temporal dimension. Thus, having an image sequence modeled as $f : R^2 \times R \mapsto R$, its linear representation becomes $L : R^2 \times R \times R_+^2 \mapsto R$, but over two independent variances σ_l^2 (spatial) and τ_l^2 (temporal) using an anisotropic Gaussian kernel $g(.; \sigma_l^2, \tau_l^2)$. Therefore, the complete set of equations for detecting interest points described in [4] is the following.

$$L(.; \sigma_l^2, \tau_l^2) = g(.; \sigma_l^2, \tau_l^2) * f(.), \qquad (5)$$

$$g(x, y, t; \sigma_l^2, \tau_l^2) = \frac{1}{\sqrt{(2\pi)^3 \sigma_l^4 \tau_l^2}}$$
$$\times \exp(-(x^2 + y^2)/2\sigma_l^2 - t^2/\tau_l^2), \qquad (6)$$

$$\mu = g(.; \sigma_i^2, \tau_i^2) * \begin{pmatrix} L_x^2 & L_x L_y & L_x L_t \\ L_x L_y & L_y^2 & L_y L_t \\ L_x L_t & L_y L_t & L_t^2. \end{pmatrix} \qquad (7)$$

$$H = \det(\mu) - k.trace^3(\mu)$$
$$= \lambda_1\lambda_2\lambda_3 - k(\lambda_1 + \lambda_2 + \lambda_3)^3, \tag{8}$$

restricted to $H \geq 0$, with $\alpha = \lambda_2/\lambda_1$ and $\beta = \lambda_3/\lambda_1$, and subject to $k \leq \alpha\beta/(1 + \alpha + \beta)^3$

3 Local Features

Given a local interest region denoted by a spatiotemporal interest point, 3D local features accounting for appearance (histograms of oriented gradient) and motion (histograms of optical flow) are computed by using information from the neighborhood at (x, y, t). A spatiotemporal volume is sliced into $n_x \times n_y \times n_t$ 3D cells, in particular, $n_x = n_y = 3$ and $n_t = 2$. For each cell 4-bin histograms of gradient orientations (**HoG**) and 5-bin histograms of optical flow (**HoF**) are calculated, normalized and concatenated (**HoGHoF**, used by STIP [4]).

3.1 Color Descriptor

In this section, the hue histogram based color descriptor is roughly described. From the work in [2], the hue calculation has the form:

$$hue = \arctan\left(\frac{\sqrt{3}(R - G)}{R + G - 2B}\right). \tag{9}$$

It is known that, in the HSI color space, the hue value becomes unstable as it approaches the grey axis. In attempt to atenuate this problem, van de Weijer et al. [2] analyzed the error propagation in the hue transformation and verified the inverse proportionality of the hue certainty to the saturation. This way, the authors demonstrated that the hue color model achieves robustness by weighing the hue sample by the corresponding saturation, which is given by Equation 10:

$$sat = \sqrt{\frac{2(R^2 + G^2 + B^2 - RG - RB - GB)}{3}}. \tag{10}$$

To construct the hue histogram, we calculate the bin number to which the hue value (of the spatiotemporal volume) belongs with $bin = hue * 36/2\pi$. Then, at the position bin of the histogram the saturation value is accumulated. Before incrementing the histogram bin with a given amount of saturation, the saturation is weighed by a corresponding value of a Gaussian mask having the size of the spatiotemporal volume. The size and values forming the spatiotemporal Gaussian mask will vary according to the spatial and temporal scales of the interest point. The computed hue histogram will be further concatenated to the HoGHoF feature vector and this combination will be called **HueSTIP**.

4 Experiments

In our experiments, we investigated the power of the spatiotemporal local features containing color information for action recognition. This section describes the experimental setup followed by the analysis of the obtained results.

4.1   Dataset

We wanted to evaluate the performance of the descriptors for human action recognition in natural scenarios. Therefore, the Hollywood2 dataset [10] was a natural choice. This dataset is composed of 12 action classes: answering phone, driving car, eating, fighting, getting out of the car, hand shaking, hugging, kissing, running, sitting down, sitting up, standing up (see Figure 1). Videos were collected from a set of 69 different Hollywood movies, where 33 were used to generate the training set and 36 the test set. Action video clips were divided in three separate subsets, namely an automatic (noisy) training set, a (clean) training set and the test set. We only used the clean training set containing 823 samples and the test set containing 884 samples.

Fig. 1. Illustration of the Hollywood2 dataset containing human action from Hollywood movies

4.2   Bag-of-Features Video Representation

When spatiotemporal local features are extracted, they only provide a very local and disconnected representation of the video clips. One way to give a more meaningful representation is to use the *bag-of-features* (**BoF**) approach, which has been successfully applied to many applications of video analysis [3] [13]. Using BoF requires the construction of a vocabulary of features (or visual vocabulary). Although this is commonly accomplished by using k-means, it is well known that for very high-dimensional spaces, simple clustering algorithms perform badly, and thus a reasonable and efficient choice is just to select a random sample to form the visual vocabulary: this saves computational time and achieves comparable results [14]. The vocabulary size was set to 4000 since this number has empirically demonstrated good results and is consistent with the literature [13] [10]. At this point, spatiotemporal local features of a video clip are assigned to the closest visual word of the vocabulary (we use Euclidean distance function), producing a histogram of visual words. This histogram of visual word frequencies now accounts for the new video representation.

4.3   Classification

To classify the videos, we have used Support Vector Machines (SVM), using the LibSVM [15] implementation. Since our aim is to highlight the performance of the descriptors, we have chosen to simplify the classifier by using linear kernels (experiments with more complex kernels were performed with comparable results). SVM being a binary classifier, LibSVM implements multi-classification by the one-to-one method, which creates $n(n-1)/2$ binary classifiers (where n is the number of classes) and applies a majority voting scheme to assign the class of an unknown element.

4.4   Experimental Protocol

1. Extract local features of the whole dataset (using both descriptors, HueSTIP and STIP),
2. Build the visual vocabularies, one for each feature type (HueSTIP or STIP),
3. Assemble the histograms of visual words representing each video clips of the dataset,
4. Learn the classifiers (one for each feature type) of the clean training set using SVM, in which the training and test samples are already separately available, as described in 4.1,
5. Classify the samples of the test dataset.

4.5   Results and Discussion

Table 1 evaluates the performance of both descriptors, STIP and HueSTIP, for the human action recognition task. It shows that there exists a gain in using color information for the classification of specific actions. Especially, half of the classes had the best performance achieved by HueSTIP, namely *AnswerPhone*, *FightPerson*, *HugPerson*, *Run*, *SitDown*, and *StandUp*. This increased performance brought by HueSTIP may have come either from information retrieved from parts of the objects of interest in the foreground or the background scenarios that is usually ignored by traditional shape or motion descriptors but gains meaning as the color description is considered.

Performance improvements achieved by HueSTIP for the *AnswerPhone* class can be justified by the color information from the background describing the indoor scenario in which this action usually takes place (see Figure 2 A) for an illustration of this fact), which are very similar among videos of this type of action. This is also the case for the *SitDown* class, as can be seen in Figure 2 B). For the *FightPerson* class, we have that in situations involving aggressive behaviors, the presence of blood can be expected, which can be an important aspect of the scene if color information is taken into account. Also, it is clear by the images in Figure 2 C) that features extracted from the scenes of violence acts where the camera mainly focuses on the abrupt moving of faces and arms of the actors will hold information of skin color in their descriptions, which together with features of optical flow and gradients may help to narrow the meaning of fight video's feature vectors. Regarding the class *Run* and *StandUp*, color information from the outdoor scenario might be useful.

However, for many other classes, the addition of color information actually results in losses. This is somewhat intuitive in *DriveCar* and *GetOutCar*, where the color variablity of cars acts more as a confusion than a help. The huge loss in

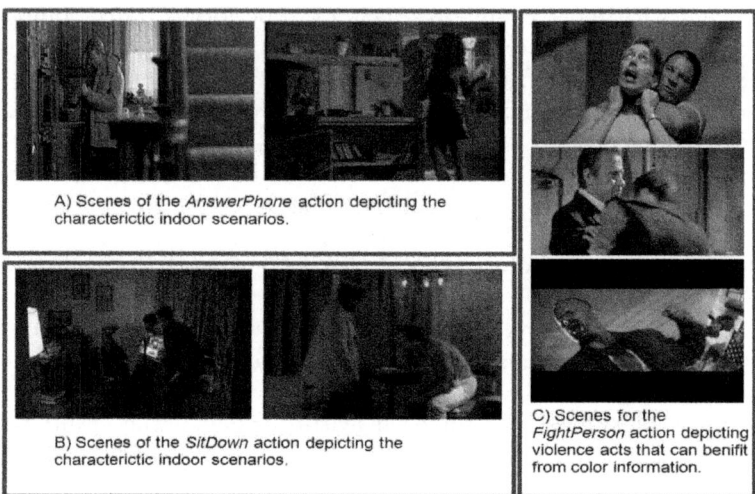

A) Scenes of the *AnswerPhone* action depicting the characterictic indoor scenarios.

B) Scenes of the *SitDown* action depicting the characterictic indoor scenarios.

C) Scenes for the *FightPerson* action depicting violence acts that can benifit from color information.

Fig. 2. Samples of scenes depicting situations that explain some of the results

Table 1. This table reports the accuracy rates given by each feature algorithm at the recognition of the twelve human actions depicted by videos of the Hollywood2 dataset

Action	HueSTIP	STIP	Action	HueSTIP	STIP
AnswerPhone	**12.5%**	9.4%	*HugPerson*	**18.2%**	12.1%
DriveCar	71.6%	**76.5%**	*Kiss*	38.8%	**49.5%**
Eat	45.5%	**57.6%**	*Run*	**58.9%**	57.5%
FightPerson	**68.6%**	62.9%	*SitDown*	**45.4%**	41.7%
GetOutCar	8.8%	**19.3%**	*SitUp*	0.0%	0.0%
HandShake	6.7%	**8.9%**	*StandUp*	**54.1%**	51.4%

performance in classes like *Eat* and *Kiss*, however was somewhat unexpected and reveal the weakness of using the same neighborhood for extracting the optical flow and color information. It is important to note that the lower performance in those cases (using HueSTIP) might have been caused by the difference in the density of points if compared with STIP, which had a greater number of points extracted due to a different parametrization.

5   Conclusion

We consider that HueSTIP has shown promising results for a preliminary work: the experiments show it can improve classification rates of actions, but that this improvement tends to be very class-dependent.

We are currently working on some of its interesting issues, especially the reasons why its performance is so unexpectedly low in a few classes. We suspect that using the same feature detector for STIP and HueSTIP might give the former an unfair advantage for the classes where the interesting color phenomena happens at different scales than interesting grayscale phenomena.

Acknowledgments. We would like to thank CNPq, CAPES, FAPEMIG and FAPESP, Brazilian agencies, for the financial support to this work.

References

1. Gevers, T., Stokman, H.: Robust histogram construction from color invariants for object recognition. PAMI 26, 113–117 (2004)
2. van de Weijer, J., Schmid, C.: Coloring local feature extraction. In: Leonardis, A., Bischof, H., Pinz, A. (eds.) ECCV 2006, Part II. LNCS, vol. 3952, pp. 334–348. Springer, Heidelberg (2006)
3. van de Sande, K.E.A., Gevers, T., Snoek, C.G.M.: Evaluating color descriptors for object and scene recognition. PAMI 32(9), 1582–1596 (2010)
4. Laptev, I.: On space-time interest points. IJCV 64(2-3), 107–123 (2005)
5. Mikolajczyk, K., Schmid, C.: Scale and affine invariant interest point detectors. IJCV 60(1), 63–86 (2004)
6. Wang, H., Ullah, M.M., Kläser, A., Laptev, I., Schmid, C.: Evaluation of local spatio-temporal features for action recognition. In: BMVC, p. 127 (September 2009)
7. Dollár, P., Rabaud, V., Cottrell, G., Belongie, S.: Behavior recognition via sparse spatio-temporal features. In: VS-PETS (October 2005)
8. Willems, G., Tuytelaars, T., Van Gool, L.: An efficient dense and scale-invariant spatio-temporal interest point detector. In: Forsyth, D., Torr, P., Zisserman, A. (eds.) ECCV 2008, Part II. LNCS, vol. 5303, pp. 650–663. Springer, Heidelberg (2008)
9. Lowe, D.G.: Distinctive image features from scale-invariant keypoints. IJCV 60(2), 91–110 (2004)
10. Marszałek, M., Laptev, I., Schmid, C.: Actions in context. In: CVPR (2009)
11. Harris, C., Stephens, M.: A combined corner and edge detector. In: 4th Alvey Vision Conf., pp. 147–152 (1988)
12. Forstner, W., Gulch, E.: A fast operator for detection and precise location of distinct points, corners and centres of circular features. In: ISPRS, pp. 281–305 (1987)
13. Laptev, I., Marszałek, M., Schmid, C., Rozenfeld, B.: Learning realistic human actions from movies. In: CVPR (June 2008)
14. Viitaniemi, V., Laaksonen, J.: Experiments on selection of codebooks for local image feature histograms. In: Sebillo, M., Vitiello, G., Schaefer, G. (eds.) VISUAL 2008. LNCS, vol. 5188, pp. 126–137. Springer, Heidelberg (2008)
15. Chang, C.C., Lin, C.J.: LIBSVM: a library for support vector machines (2001), software http://www.csie.ntu.edu.tw/~cjlin/libsvm

On the Flame Spectrum Recovery by Using a Low-Spectral Resolution Sensor

Luis Arias* and Sergio Torres

Department of Electrical Engineering, University of Concepcio Casilla 160-C,
Concepcion, Chile,
Center for Optics and Photonics CEFOP, University of Concepcion,
Casilla 4016, Concepcion, Chile

Abstract. In this paper, the Maloney-Wandell and Imai-Berns recovering spectrum techniques are evaluated to extract the continuous flame spectrum, by using three principal components from training matrices constructed from a flame's spectrum database. Six different sizes of training matrices were considered in the evaluation. To simulate the Maloney-Wandell and Imai-Bern methods, a commercial camera sensitivity was used as a base in the extraction process. The GFC (Goodness-of-fit coefficient) and RMSE (Root-mean-square error) quality metrics were used to compare the performance in the recovering process. The simulation results shown a better performance by using the Maloney-Wandell method in the recovering process, with small sizes of training matrices. The achieved results make of the recovering-spectral techniques a very attractive tools for designing advanced monitoring strategies for combustion processes.

Keywords: recovering techniques, flame spectrum, optical sensors.

1 Introduction

It is known that the flame spectrum conveys important information about the combustion state. Thus, optical sensing of flame spectral emission by using non-intrusive methods is nowadays an important field of development which has been tackled by using several active/passive optical sensors (like lasers, CCD cameras, photodiodes, photomultipliers, radiometers, among another) [1, 2].

However, the sensors/techniques mentioned above are limited in the extraction of spatial-spectral information from flames simultaneously. For example, the use of CCD cameras in combustion process monitoring, is based mainly in the correlation between spatial flame's morphology with combustion parameters like the air excess [3]. However, the spectral information of such flame it can not be extracted, until now, with this device, due to the low spectral-resolution (normally, three channels R, G and B).

---

* Corresponding author. luis.arias@cefop.udec.cl

C. San Martin and S.-W. Kim (Eds.): CIARP 2011, LNCS 7042, pp. 256–263, 2011.

It is known that if we want to measure the spatial distribution along the flame of such spectral information, it should be strictly necessary to use an hyperspectral camera system, because both the spatial and spectral information are extracted simultaneously [4,5]. However, the main disadvantage of these systems is the low-time of image acquisition, making impossible to use this system in sensing the spectral information in real-time from the flame.

In this paper a first approach in the continuous flame's spectrum extraction by using the sensitivity of a trichromatic RGB camera is evaluated by using the Maloney-Wandell and Imai-Berns estimation methods [6,7], owing to the accurate results they provide. That is, the idea is to extract a high spectral resolution spectrum by using the data given by a low-spectral resolution sensor, like a camera. These methods are based on a priori knowledge of the kind of spectra we want to recover, which can be performed by using principal components analysis (PCA), nonnegative matrix factorization (NMF) or independent component analysis (ICA). This is accomplished through the construction of a training matrix containing previously database spectral measurements, which can be linearly combined to reconstruct an unknown spectrum from the sensor's array signals. That is, any spectrum can be expressed by:

$$E_{N \times 1} = V_{N \times n} \cdot \epsilon_{n \times 1} \tag{1}$$

where V is a matrix containing the n *representative* spectrums extracted from the training matrix at N wavelengths and the vector ϵ contains the coefficient of the linear combination. The n *representative* spectrums should maintain much of the original *information* of the original spectrum. The recovering-spectrum process start assuming that the optical sensor's array have a linear response. Thus, and in absent of noise, the optical sensor's response can be modeled as:

$$ck_{k \times 1} = \omega^t_{k \times N} \cdot E_{N \times 1} \tag{2}$$

where ck is the optical sensor response of the k channel (in a RGB camera, for example, the array is composed by k = 1, 2 and 3), ω^t is the transposed of the matrix containing the spectral sensitivity (responsivity and filters transmissions) of the sensors, and E is the spectrum impinging in the optical array. In the following, a brief description of the below algorithms is given.

2   Brief Descriptions of Recovering-Spectrum Algorithms to be Evaluated

In this section, a brief description of the Maloney-Wandell and Imai-Berns estimation methods is given.

2.1   Maloney-Wandell Recovering-Method

The recovering process of E (that is $\hat{E}$, at N wavelength samples) is achieved by found a matrix which transform the sensor's array responses ck in the coefficient of the linear combination, ϵ. This is performed by replacing the Eq. (1) into Eq. (2):

$$ck_{k\times 1} = w^t_{k\times N} \cdot V_{N\times n} \cdot \epsilon_{n\times 1} \tag{3}$$

$$ck_{k\times 1} = \Lambda_{k\times n} \cdot \epsilon_{n\times 1} \tag{4}$$

that is, the pseudoinverse of Λ (Λ^+) directly transform the sensor's array response in the coefficient needed for the linear estimate of the spectrum from the sensor's response. Therefore, and replacing on Eq. (1), the estimated (recovered) spectrum can be calculated as:

$$\hat{E}_{N\times 1} = V_{N\times n} \cdot \Lambda^+_{n\times k} \cdot ck_{k\times 1} \tag{5}$$

Note that the spectral-dimensionality (wavelength resolution) of the recovered spectrum depends on the spectral-dimensionality of the training matrix. On the other hand, the recovered spectrum directly depends on the spectral sensitivity of the optical system (inserted on Λ^+), and therefore the optimum spectral characteristics of the optical system (i.e responsivity and filters transmission) should be estimated at different applications.

2.2   Imai-Berns Recovering-Method

The main difference between this method versus the above described (Maloney-Wandell) is which in this case it is not necessary to know the spectral responsivity of the sensors, but sacrificing accuracy in the recovered process. This method is based directly on found empirically a relationship between the sensor's response c_k for each spectrum m contained in the training matrix and the coefficients ϵ from the principal components. That is, for each m spectrum it is measured the sensor's responses, which can be combined with the respective coefficients like:

$$\epsilon_{n\times m} = G_{n\times k} \cdot ck_{k\times m} \tag{6}$$

In this case, the information provided by the training matrix is included on G. Therefore, by pseudoinverting the sensor's response matrix ($ck^+_{k\times m}$) we can found the matrix G which allow us to estimate (to recover) the spectrum from:

$$\hat{E}_{N\times 1} = V_{N\times n} \cdot G_{n\times k} \cdot ck_{k\times 1} \tag{7}$$

3   Metrics for Quality Evaluation in the Recovering Spectrum Process

Different metrics to quantify the quality in the reconstruction process have been traditionally used [8, 9], like the root-mean-square error (RMSE) and the goodness-of-fit coefficient (GFC). The GFC metric is based on the Schwartz's inequality [10], and is defined as:

$$GFC = \frac{\left| \sum_j E(\lambda_j) \hat{E}(\lambda_j) \right|}{\left[\left| \sum_j [E(\lambda_j)]^2 \right| \left| \sum_j \left[\hat{E}(\lambda_j) \right]^2 \right| \right]^{1/2}} \tag{8}$$

where E is the original measured sample data at the wavelength λ_j and $\hat{E}$ is the recover spectrum at the wavelength λ_j. Accurate estimation require GFC> 0.995. GFC > 0.999 mean quite good spectral matches, and GFC> 0.9999 an excellent spectral match.

4   Recovering Continuous Flame Spectrum Using Simulated Camera Responses

Both, Maloney-Wandell and Imai-Berns recovering-methods have been implemented to simulate a first approach in recover continuous flame spectrum, based on a flame spectrum's data base taken in our laboratories since 2005 with a previously calibrated USB2000 radiometer (with spectral resolution of 2048 from 339.38-1025.09 nm). Eight different training-matrices TM (with sizes of 4, 5, 6, 7, 8, 9, 20 and 40) have been constructed from where extract the respective matrix V (Eq. (1)). In order to evaluate the differences on the recovered results, the above described metrics GFC and RMSE have been calculated.

Like is mentioned in [11], three PCA basis vectors are enough to recover skylight spectra with acceptable accuracy. Assuming that the continuous flame spectrum have similar spectral-characteristics like skylight, three PCA has been extracted from the training matrices. Therefore, three spectral sensitivities bases have been selected, simulating the spectral response of a Basler A602-fc RGB camera provided by the manufacturer (Fig. 1(a)) in order to construct the matrix Λ^+ (Eq. (4)). Five calibrated spectrums (test spectrums) measured at different flame temperatures were used to be recovered (Fig. 1(b)) in the range 380-700nm.

4.1   Computational Results

In Fig. 2 it is depicted fourth different TM's which have been used in the simulation. From this TM's are extracted the respective three PCA's used to construct

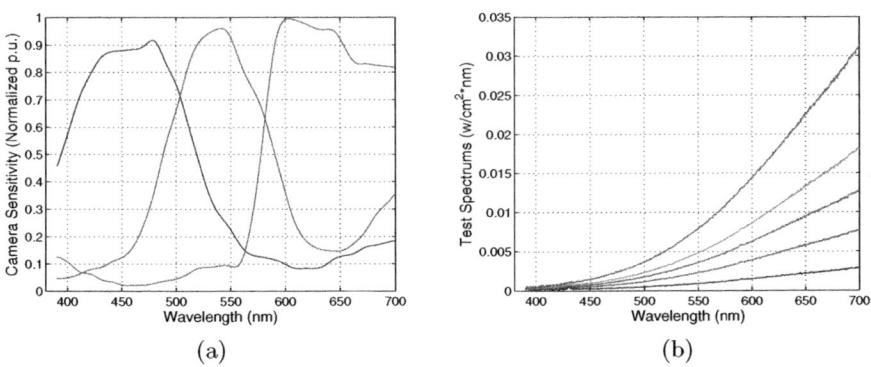

(a)   (b)

Fig. 1. (a) Spectral sensitivity of the Basler A602-fc camera, (b) Flame's spectrums samples at different temperatures measured with the USB2000 radiometer

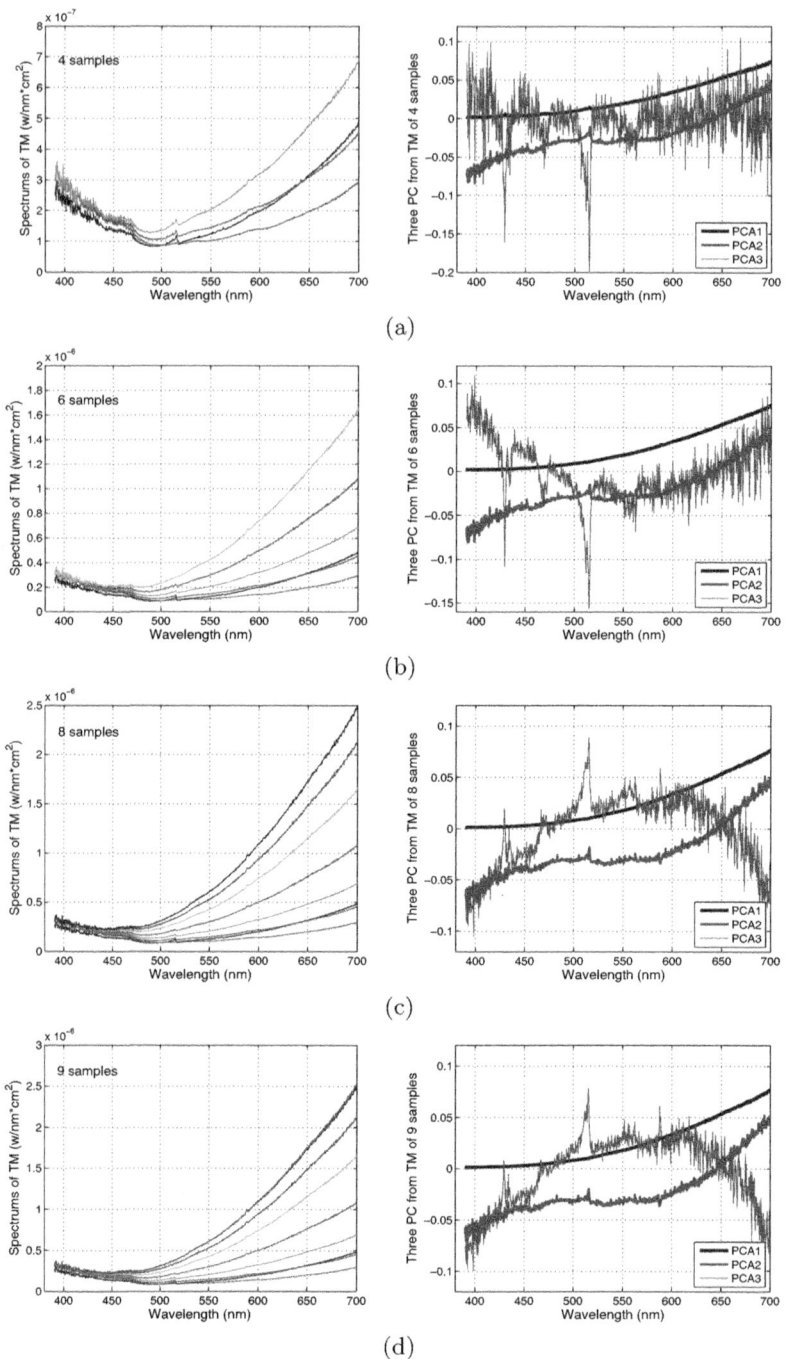

Fig. 2. Constructed training matrices TM and the respective three principal components PC , considering (a) 4 samples, (b) 6 samples, (c) 8 samples and (d) 9 samples

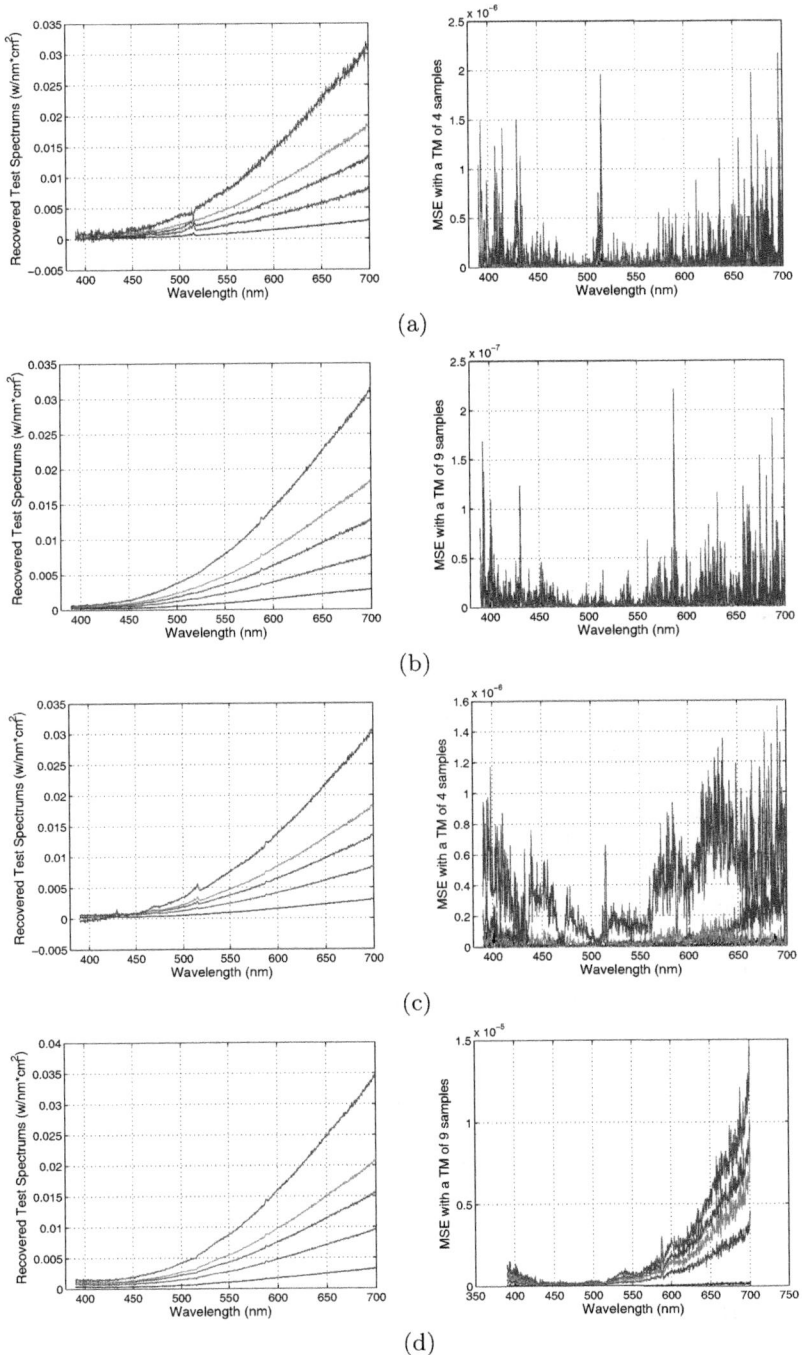

Fig. 3. Examples of recovered spectrum and the respective MSE by using Maloney-Wandell method with (a) with 4 samples and (b) 9 samples in the TM and by using the Imai-Bern method with (c) 4 samples and (d) 9 samples in the TM

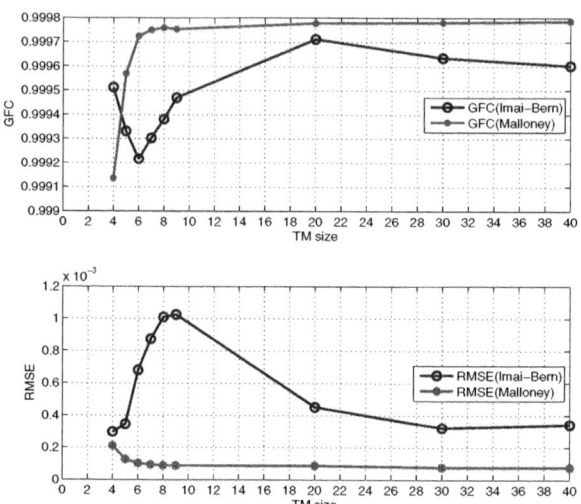

Fig. 4. Evolution of the mean values of GFC and RMSE quality metrics calculated from 5 test samples, for different size of m (training matrix)

the respective matrix V. It can be observed with the 2 first PCA (PCA1 and PCA2) exhibit a similar behavior when the size of the training matrix increase. Therefore, it can be concluded that the third PCA (PCA3) not provide significatively information from the constructed TM's.

In Fig. 3 it is depicted the recovered spectrums and the calculated Mean-Square Error (MSE) by using the Maloney-Wandell method (Fig. 4(a) and (b)) and the Imai-Bern method (Fig. 4(c) and (d)), by using a TM of 6 and 9. It can be seen that the performance of Maloney-Wandell method in the recovering process of the continuous flame spectrum is better than the Imai-Bern method.

The evolution of the quality metrics GFC and RMSE, calculated as the mean of the metrics calculated from the test spectrums (five spectrums) it is depicted in Fig. 4 versus an increment in the size of the TM. It can be corroborated that the Maloney-Wandell method exhibit an accurate results than the Imai-Bern method, but however it can be seen that the GFC metric is not significatively enhanced with an increment in the size of the training matrix. This result can be explained because the third PCA3 tends to stabilization with an increment of the TM (Fig. 2(c) and (d)).

5   Conclusion

We have shown the performance of the Maloney-Wandell and Imai-Bern methods in the process of recover continuous flames spectrums by simulating the use of a low-spectral resolution camera and a data base of flame's spectrums. Three principal components were extracted from different computed training matrices, where it has been observed with the 2 first PCA (PCA1 and PCA2) exhibit a similar behavior when the size of the training matrix increase. The third PCA3 not provide significatively information from the constructed TM's but however tends to stabilization with an increment of the TM.

The Maloney-Wandell method has shown a better spectral recovering process than the Imai-Bern method, by evaluating both, GFC and RMSE quality metrics, but however the performance in the recovering process not depend significatively on the size of the training matrix.

The performance achieved by using the Maloney-Wandell simulating the use of a low-spectral resolution sensor and with an appropriated training matrix of flame's spectrums makes of these techniques a very attractive tools for designing advanced monitoring strategies for combustion processes.

Acknowledgement. The authors thanks the support of Thermofluids laboratory, University of Concepcion and the Basal Project Found FB024.

References

1. Docquier, N., Candel, S.: Combustion control and sensors: a review. Progress in Energy and Combustion Science 28, 107–150 (2001)
2. Arias, L., Torres, S., Sbarbaro, D., Farias, O.: Photodiode-based sensor for flame sensing and combustion-process monitoring. Appl. Opt. 47, 66–77 (2008)
3. Hernandez, R., Ballester, J.: Flame imaging as a diagnostic tools for industrial combustion. Combustion and Flame 155, 509–528 (2008)
4. Manolakis, D., Marden, D., Shaw, G.A.: Hyperspectral image processing for automatic target detection applications. Lincoln Laboratory J. 14(1), 79–116 (2003)
5. Landgrebe, D.: Hyperspectral image data analysis. IEEE Signal Processing Magazine 19(1), 17–28 (2002)
6. Maloney, L.T., Wandell, B.A.: Color constancy: a method for recovering surface spectral reflectance, vol. 3, pp. 29–33 (1986)
7. Imai, F.H., Berns, R.S.: Spectral estimation using trichromatic digital cameras, vol. 3, pp. 42–48 (1999)
8. Imai, F., Rosen, M., Berns, R.: Comparative study of metrics for spectral match quality, pp. 492–496 (2002)
9. Lopez, M., Hernández, J., Valero, E., Nieves, J.: Colorimetric and spectral combined metric for the optimization of multispectral systems, pp. 1685–1688 (2005)
10. Nieves, J.L., Valero, E.M., Hernandez, J., Romero, J.: Recovering fluorescent spectra with an RGB digital camera and color filters using different matrix factorizations, vol. 46, pp. 4144–4154 (2007)
11. Lopez, M., Hernandez, J., Valero, E., Romero, J.: Selecting algorithms, sensors, and linear bases for optimum spectral recovery of skylight, vol. 24, pp. 942–956 (2007)

On the Importance of Multi-dimensional Information in Gender Estimation from Face Images

Juan Bekios-Calfa[1], José M. Buenaposada[2], and Luis Baumela[3]

[1] Dept. de Ingeniería de Sistemas y Computación, Universidad Católica del Norte
Av. Angamos 0610, Antofagasta, Chile
juan.bekios@ucn.cl
[2] Dept. de Ciencias de la Computación, Universidad Rey Juan Carlos
Calle Tulipán s/n, 28933, Móstoles, Spain
josemiguel.buenaposada@urjc.es
[3] Dept. de Inteligencia Artificial, Universidad Politécnica de Madrid
Campus Montegancedo s/n, 28660 Boadilla del Monte, Spain
lbaumela@fi.upm.es

Abstract. Estimating human face demography from images is a problem that has recently been extensively studied because of its relevant applications. We review state-of-the-art approaches to gender classification and confirm that their performance drops significantly when classifying young or elderly faces. We hypothesize that this is caused by the existence of dependencies among the demographic variables that were not considered in traditional gender classifiers. In the paper we confirm experimentally the existence of such dependencies between age and gender variables. We also prove that the performance of gender classifiers can be improved by considering the dependencies with age in a multi-dimensional approach. The performance improvement is most prominent for young and elderly faces.

1 Introduction

By demographic classification we denote the problem of extracting personal attributes from face images [2,9], voice [12], clothing [16], names [2] or even gait [10]. This is a problem that has received very much attention recently because of its applications in human computer interaction, video indexing and video analytics for business intelligence [9]. The main demographic variables are gender, ethnicity and age. There is nevertheless a plethora of other interesting variables such as hairstyle, hair color, facial expression, wear glasses or not, have mustache or not, etc. We will concentrate on the gender attribute and its relation with age on near frontal face images.

Gender is perhaps the most widely studied facial demographic attribute in the Computer Vision field [14,3,11,4]. The state-of-the-art recognition rate in the Color FERET database [15] involving frontal faces with frontal illumination and 5 fold cross-validation is around 93% using either a Support Vector Machine

C. San Martin and S.-W. Kim (Eds.): CIARP 2011, LNCS 7042, pp. 264–271, 2011.

with Radial Basis function [14], pair-wise comparison of pixel values within a boosting framework [3] or linear discriminant techniques [4]. This performance drops significantly if classifiers are trained and tested on different databases. For example, if we train our classifier with the FERET database and test it with images from PAL [13], the performance drops to roughly 70% success rate [4]. This is mainly due to the different demographic distributions in both databases. FERET is a database with mostly Caucasian adult subjects whereas PAL includes people from more ethnic groups and with a broader range of ages. In general, when a gender classifier is trained with a data set with limited demography and tested with a data set with more general samples the classification rate drops significantly. This suggest the existence of a dependency between gender and other demographic variable.

In this paper we will study the dependencies between gender and age given the facial appearance. Dependencies among demographic variables have also been previously considered in the literature. Gao and Ai [19] showed experimentally that by exploiting the relation between ethnicity and gender a boost of 4-5% in gender classification accuracy can be obtained for mongoloid and African faces. Guo and Mu [8], in experiments with the MORPH-II database, found that age estimation can have large errors if the influence of gender and ethnicity is no considered. Finally, Guo et al. [7] considered the dependencies between age and gender. They found that gender recognition accuracy was 10% higher in adult faces than in young and senior faces and studied the influence of different image features (LBP, HOG and BIF) in estimating gender. In this paper we also consider the influence of age in the estimation of gender, but from a completely different perspective. We will study whether the accuracy in gender can be improved by jointly estimating age and gender.

2   Exploiting the Dependencies between Gender and Age

In this section we study the dependencies between the age and gender demographic variables given the facial apperance. First we will prove experimentally that those dependencies exist. Secondly we will exploit them to improve the accuracy of gender classification.

2.1   Are There Any Dependencies between Age and Gender?

If we assume that in any age range there is equal number of men and women and for any gender the distribution of population in ages is similar, then we are implicitly assuming that age and gender demographic variables are statistically independent. That is, $P(A, G) = P(A)P(G)$, were A and G denote respectively age and gender variables and P the probability of an event.

To confirm whether A and G are independent variables we have trained a gender classifier as explained in Section 2.2 with the data in the GROUPS database (see 3 for a description) and tested it on PAL. The classifier has been trained with all men and women images in GROUPS but we compute the accuracy

Table 1. Accuracy in GROUPS/PAL experiment. First row shows results for a gender classifier trained with images from all age ranges. Second row displays results of four gender classifiers each one trained only with face images from a given age range. First four columns display results of four age ranges. Last column shows average results for all age ranges.

Experiment/Age category	13-19	20-36	37-65	66+	Global
Gender	65.62%	75.56%	65.04%	64.53%	68.73
Gender | Age	65.62%	76.47%	73.98%	74.87%	74.78

stratified into four age groups. In the first row of Table 1 we show the results of this experiment. Gender estimation for the range 20–36 are above the state-of-the-art in [4] whereas the results for the other age ranges are clearly below. This results indicates that the performance of the classifier depends on the age range. Moreover, to confirm the existence of a dependency between age and gender we have trained four gender classifiers, one per age range, in GROUPS and tested it on data from the same age range in PAL. This experiment provides information on the performance of a gender classifier that knows the age range of the subject. As we can see in the second row in Table 1, the classifier performance increases, most notably for elderly. This experiment clearly shows the existence of a dependency between age, A and gender G, given the facial appearance, represented by the classifier discriminating variables X.

In summary, if the appearance of a face, X, depends on the gender, G, and age, A, of the subject, then age and gender are conditionally dependent, given the appearance of the face X, i.e. $P(A, G|X) \neq P(A|X)P(G|X)$.

2.2   Multi-dimensional Classification of Gender and Age

We will simultaneously estimate gender and age using a multi-dimensional approach. The term *Multi-dimensional Classification* was introduced first by Gaag and Waal [5] to represent classification problems in which there are several class variables. This problem is a generalization of the multi-label problem [1]. In the multi-dimensional case each label is transformed into a dimension, which can have more than two values, in opposition to a label, which can only have two values.

Let be $D = \{d_1, \ldots, d_M\}$ the set of M dimensions of a given multi-dimensional problem and let be $V_i = \{c_1^i, \ldots, c_{N_i}^i\}$ the set of possible values for dimension d_i where $N_i = |V_i|$. Let be $D_\times = V_1 \times V_2 \times \ldots \times V_d$ the Cartesian product of all V_i dimension values sets. The output of a multi-dimensional classifier for an input instance, $\mathbf{x}$, is a vector $\mathbf{z} \in D_\times$. In the demography classification problem, one of the possible multi-dimensional formulations could be to have three dimensions, $D = \{age, gender, ethnicity\}$ and the corresponding values $V_{age} = \{young, adult, senior\}$, $V_{gender} = \{male, female\}$ and $V_{ethnicity} = \{Caucasian, African, mongoloid\}$.

One of the baseline approaches to multi-label classification is a problem transformation method: Label Powerset (LP) [17]. The LP approach explores all possible label combinations. LP interprets every possible subset of labels (a combination of labels) appearing on the multi-label training set as a single class in a multi-class problem. The Label Powerset (LP) approach has an extension for the multi-dimensional case. The Dimension Powerset (DP) interprets every element in $D_\times$ as a single class in a multi-class classification problem. For each new instance the DP classifier outputs the estimated class that in fact represents a valid combination of dimensions values in the original multi-dimensional problem. The number of classes in the DP transformed problem is bounded by the minimum of N, number of training samples, and $|D_\times|$. Learning is difficult on the DP method with a low number of training samples in any combination of dimensions values (e.g. in demography classification the combination of Caucasian, male and young). In our case, we have 2 gender values and seven age categories, then we will have a 14 classes in the transformed (from a multi-dimensional one) multi-class classification problem. As the number of dimensions grows, it is very likely to find a combination of dimensions values with very low or no training data at all. To avoid such a problem we remove classes with few data.

In our approach we train the multi-class classifier for $D_\times$ in the PCA+LDA transformed subspace (LDA after Principal Components Analysis projection). In our experiments we use a K-Nearest Neighbor (KNN) classifier in the PCA+LDA transformed subspace. However, any multi-class classifier could be used within our framework. Depending on the amount of training data, the performance of the classifier built on PCA+LDA subspace decreases when retaining all PCA eigenvectors associated with non-zero eigenvalues. We select the dimension of the subspace resulting from the PCA step. We sort PCA eigenvectors in descending eigenvalue order. We then perform cross-validation and select the dimension with the best performance for the classification in the PCA+LDA subspace. This cross-validation driven feature selection (wrapper) approach is essential to correctly train a PCA+LDA procedure [4]. In the same cross-validation procedure we look for the dimension for the PCA initial step and the number of neighbors, k, that accounts for the best performance.

3 Experiments

In this section we evaluate the performance of the multi-dimensional framework estimating the combination of gender and age dimensions. We use the Images of Groups Dataset [6] (GROUPS database) and the Productive Aging Lab Face (PAL) database [13] for training and testing. We crop and re-size images to a base size of 25×25 pixels using OpenCV's[1] 2.1.0 face detector, which is based on [18]. Then we equalize the histogram to gain some independence from illumination changes. Finally, we also apply an oval mask to prevent the background from influencing our results.

---

[1] http://opencv.willowgarage.com

3.1 Face Databases

The Images of Groups Dataset[2] (in the following GROUPS database), consists of 28,231 faces labeled with age and gender extracted from 5,800 pictures of people groups. Most faces were automatically detected. The seven age categories used are: 0-2, 3-7, 8-12, 13-19, 20-36, 37-65, and 66+. In this database age labels are discrete. In our experiments we use those face detections from the GROUPS database that have at least 60×60 pixels (13,051 out of a total of 28,231 faces). See Fig. 1 for some examples of faces from this database. In Table 2 we give information on the number of images per age category.

Fig. 1. Some of the images from GROUPS database

The PAL Database consists of frontal pictures of 576 individuals. There is only one frontal face image per subject although 3 individuals have two pictures in the database. Therefore, we use 579 images in our PAL experiments. The right profile and some facial expressions are also available for some subjects. There are 219 male and 357 female subjects divided into four groups depending on their age. In this database, the actual continuous face age is available for each image. In our experiments we only use frontal images and only one image per subject. See some sample images in Fig. 2. Again, the number of images per age category in this database is shown in Table 2.

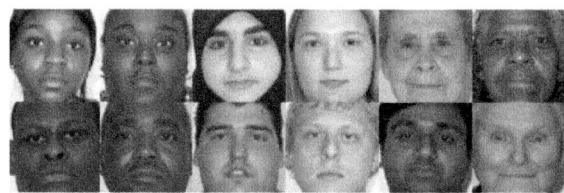

Fig. 2. Some cropped images after face detection, from the PAL database

3.2 Gender Estimation Results

To evaluate the performance of a gender estimation algorithm we are interested in the algorithm's generalization capabilities. To this end we train our algorithm using one database and test it on a different one. We train our algorithms

---

[2] http://chenlab.ece.cornell.edu/people/Andy/ImagesOfGroups.html

Table 2. Number of image per age category

Database/Age Range	0-2	3-7	8-12	13-19	20-36	37-65	66+	Total
GROUPS	460	807	368	777	6972	3109	558	13051
PAL	-	-	-	32	221	123	203	579

Table 3. Multi-dimensional gender accuracy in GROUPS/PAL experiment

Experiment/Age category	13-19	20-36	37-65	66+	Global
Gender×Age	68.75%	76.01%	65.85%	71.92%	72.01%

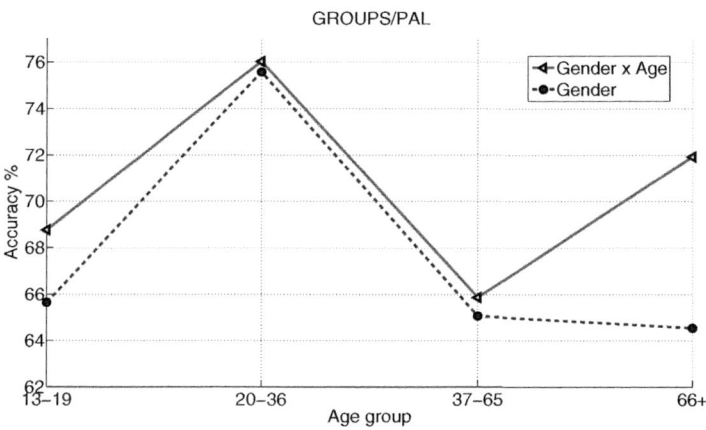

Fig. 3. GROUPS/PAL experiment comparison between uni-dimensional and multi-dimensional approaches

with GROUPS and test them with PAL (GROUPS/PAL experiment). We use GROUPS for training because it is large (≈13000 data) and it has a broad demography with realistic acquisition conditions. On the other hand, we use PAL for testing because it is a difficult database for gender recognition mostly due to the broad demography [4].

As already said in Section 2 we use a PCA+LDA dimensionality reduction procedure and a KNN classifier. We use a five-fold cross-validation scheme to estimate the classifier parameters (number of retained eigenvectors and number of neighbors in KNN). We have performed two experiments, one using only the *Gender* dimension (see Table 1) and another using *Gender×Age* dimension powerset (see Table 3). Note that in PAL there are no faces in the 0 to 12 years age ranges. The global accuracy (computed by weighted mean of the per age category accuracy using the proportion of data on each category) of the multi-dimensional approach (*Gender×Age*) is better than the uni-dimensional one (only Gender) by 3%. Most interestingly, the multi-dimensional approach outperforms the uni-dimensional one in Table 1 for all age categories (see also Fig. 3). Moreover, the most difficult categories for the uni-dimensional classifier, 13-19 and 66+, are those for which the improvement is highest, 3.13% and 7.39% respectively. This shows that the multi-dimensional procedure is able to exploit the dimension combination and improve the gender estimation accuracy.

4   Conclusions

In the paper we have reviewed the state-of-the-art in gender recognition from near frontal face images. We have confirmed previous results reporting the existence of dependencies between age and gender. Our approach explores the combination of various demographic variables and proves the interest of exploiting variable combination to improve classifier performance. In future research lines it would be interesting to use both better visual descriptors, as used in [7] within the multi-dimensional approach.

Acknowledgment. The authors gratefully acknowledge funding from the Spanish *Ministerio de Ciencia e Innovación* under contracts TIN2010-19654 and the *Consolider Ingenio* program contract CSD2007-00018.

References

1. de Carvalho, A., Freitas, A.A.: A tutorial on multi-label classification techniques. Foundations of Computational Intelligence. Function Approximation and Classification, vol. 5. Springer, Heidelberg (2009)
2. Gallagher, A.C., Chen, T.: Estimating age, gender and identity using first name priors. In: Proc. of CVPR (2008)
3. Baluja, S., Rowley, H.A.: Boosting sex identification performance. International Journal of Computer Vision 71(1) (January 2007)
4. Bekios-Calfa, J., Buenaposada, J.M., Baumela, L.: Revisiting linear discriminant techniques in gender recognition. IEEE Transactions on Pattern Analysis and Machine Intelligence 33(4), 858–864 (2011)
5. van der Gaag, L.C., de Waal, P.R.: Multi-dimensional bayesian network classifiers. In: European Conference on Probabilistic Graphical Models, pp. 107–114 (2006)
6. Gallagher, A.C., Chen, T.: Understanding images of groups of people. In: Proc. of CVPR, pp. 256–263 (2009)
7. Guo, G., Dyer, C.R., Fu, Y., Huang, T.S.: Is gender recognition affected by age? In: Proc. of IEEE International Workshop on Human-Computer Interaction (HCI 2009), pp. 2032–2039 (2009)
8. Guo, G., Mu, G.: A study of large-scale ethnicity estimation with gender and age variations. In: IEEE Int. Workshop on Analysis and Modeling of Faces and Gestures (AMFG 2010), pp. 79–86 (2010)
9. Kumar, N., Berg, A.C., Belhumeur, P.N., Nayar, S.K.: Attribute and Simile Classifiers for Face Verification. In: Proc. of ICCV (October 2009)
10. Li, X., Maybank, S., Yan, S., Tao, D., Xu, D.: Gait components and their application to gender recognition. IEEE Transactions on Systems, Man, and Cybernetics, Part C: Applications and Reviews 38(2), 145–155 (2008)

11. Mäkinen, E., Raisamo, R.: Evaluation of gender classification methods with automatically detected and aligned faces. IEEE Transactions on Pattern Analysis and Machine Intelligence 30(3), 541–547 (2008)
12. Metze, F., Ajmera, J., Englert, R., Bub, U., Burkhardt, F., Stegmann, J., Muller, C., Huber, R., Andrassy, B., Bauer, J., Littel, B.: Comparison of four approaches to age and gender recognition for telephone applications. In: Proc. of the IEEE International Conference on Acoustics, Speech and Signal Processing, ICASSP 2007, vol. 4, pp. 1089–1092 (2007)
13. Minear, M., Park, D.C.: A lifespan database of adult facial stimuli. Behavior Research Methods, Instruments and Computers 36, 630–633 (2004)
14. Moghaddam, B., Yang, M.H.: Learning gender with support faces. IEEE Transactions on Pattern Analysis and Machine Intelligence 24(5), 707–711 (2002)
15. Phillips, P., Moon, H., Rauss, P., Rizvi, S.: The feret evaluation methodology for face recognition algorithms. IEEE Transactions on Pattern Analysis and Machine Intelligence 22(10), 1090–1104 (2000)
16. Sivic, J., Zitnick, C.L., Szeliski, R.: Finding people in repeated shots of the same scene. In: Proc. BMVC (2006)
17. Tsoumakas, G., Katakis, I., Vlahavas, I.: Random k-labelsets for multi-label classification. IEEE Transactions on Konwledge and Data Engineering (2010)
18. Viola, P., Jones, M.J.: Robust real-time face detection. International Journal of Computer Vision 57(2), 137–154 (2004)
19. Gao, W., Ai, H.: Face gender classification on consumer images in a multiethnic environment. In: Tistarelli, M., Nixon, M.S. (eds.) ICB 2009. LNCS, vol. 5558, pp. 169–178. Springer, Heidelberg (2009)

Pattern Classification Using Radial Basis Function Neural Networks Enhanced with the Rvachev Function Method

Mark S. Varvak

NAWCTSD, 12350 Research Parkway,
Orlando, Florida, 32826, USA
mark.varvak@navy.mil

Abstract. The proposed method for classifying clusters of patterns in complex non-convex, disconnected domains using Radial Basis Function Neural Networks (RBFNNs) enhanced with the Rvachev Function Method (RFM) is presented with numerical examples. R-functions are used to construct complex pattern cluster domain, parameters of which are applied to RBFNNs to establish boundaries for classification. The error functional is a convex quadratic one with respect to weight functions which take weight values on the discrete connectors between neurons. Activation function of neurons of RBFNNs is the $\mathbf{sgn}(\cdot)$ function and, therefore, the error function is non-smooth. The delta learning rule during training phase is applied. The sub-gradient of the discretized error function is used rather than its gradient, because it is not smooth. The application of the RFM allows for the creation, implementation, and resolution of large heterogeneous NNs capable to solving diverse sets of classification problems with greater accuracy.

Keywords: Rvachev Function Method (RFM), clustering, classification, Radial Basis Functions (RBFs), Artificial Neural Networks (ANNs).

1 Introduction

The Vector Quantization clustering method for classifying clusters of vectors uses a covariance matrix and standard deviation or a Euclidian distance between the cluster centroid and a tested vector for classifying the tested vector for inclusion in that cluster [3,4]. This technique is applicable only to compact, simply connected, convex domains. A more powerful and robust clustering method is needed to classify vectors into pattern clusters in the more general types of geometrical domains.

This paper describes a new method for pattern cluster classification applying R-functions, developed by V.L.Rvachev in [8], and used in combination with RBFNNs. These R-functions depict a cluster's shell, i.e., boundaries of convex as well as non-convex, and connected as well as disjoint domains in $\mathbb{R}^n$ in closed functional form.

C. San Martin and S.-W. Kim (Eds.): CIARP 2011, LNCS 7042, pp. 272–279, 2011.

The proposed method applies the R-functions as factors to the Radial Basis Functions (RBFs) in RBFNNs that ensure improved cluster classification with, consequently, improved accuracy of class representations and simplified NNs cluster classification algorithms.

Support Vector Machines (SVMs) with Bayes decision rules are also used in multi-category classification [5], but the statistics upon which these classification methods are based does not support classification of clusters in a complex domain.

RBFNNs are often used in the classification of scattered data because they can describe cluster property of the data via parameters [2,3]. However, the description of data's cluster properties can be improved using the Rvachev Function Method (RFM) with parameterized R-functions. In addition, implementing the RFM allows creating and applying large heterogeneous neural networks to diverse sets of classification problems with greater accuracy.

Traditional Neural Network techniques are also used in solving data classification problems [4]. But, the acceptable results require large amounts of computational power and the classification accuracy is often insufficient for practical applications. For example, it is impossible to classify clusters by a perceptron whose inputs are taken from regions of limited diameter [7]. The proposed clustering method, based upon the application of R-functions in the construction of general type cluster domains together with the RBFNNs approach copes with this constraint.

2   The Rvachev Function Method and R-Functions

R-functions possess the property of almost differentiability in $\mathbb{R}^n$ and inherit some sort of boolean properties such as being positive or negative in some specific regions according to the boolean functions from which they were constructed. R-functions are composed from real almost differentiable functions by "boolean operators" represented by their counterparts of operators over real functions. This means that for each "boolean operation" over real functions, there is a combination of functional operators over real functions. The resulting function has a single analytical expression in the sense that it is represented by closed form formulas of almost differentiable functions. An R-function is an implicit real function whose sign is determined solely by the signs of its arguments [8]. An R-function and its arguments are real-valued, but by interpreting positive values as *true* and negative values as *false*, an R-function is transformed into equivalent boolean function. Boolean functions and corresponding R-functions are termed "friends". An R-function is defined mathematically as a mapping $f(\boldsymbol{x}) : \mathbb{R}^n \mapsto \mathbb{B}$, where $\mathbb{R}^n$ is an n-dimensional space of real values and $\mathbb{B}$ is the boolean bipolar space $\{-1, 1\}$. The function $f(\boldsymbol{x})$ is implicitly defined in $\mathbb{R}^n$ as almost differentiable a finite number of times.

For the purpose of demonstrating the strengths of boolean closed form implicit real functions and the RFM, the examples of the constructed boolean closed form implicit real function in 2-dimensional domains Ω are presented below.

274   M.S. Varvak

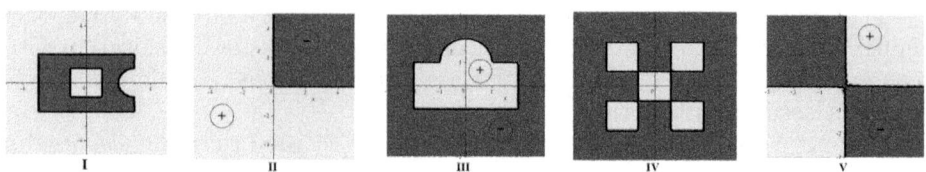

Fig. 1. i) **R**-function "Drawing" given in work [8, page 77].   ii) **R**-function "NAND" given by (1).   iii) **R**-function "Rectangle + Half Circle" given in work [8, page 66]. iv) **R**-function "Tic Tac Toe" given in work [8, page 71].   v) **R**-function "XNOR" given by (2).

1. Closed functional expression [8, page 77] for "Drawing" domain shown on the position (i) of Figure 1.
2. Closed functional expression for "NAND" domain shown on the position (ii) of Figure 1.

$$\omega_2(x,y) = \frac{1}{2} \times (|y - x| - x - y) > 0. \tag{1}$$

3. Closed functional expression [8, page 66] for "Rectangle + Half Circle" domain shown on the position (iii) of Figure 1.
4. Closed functional expression [8, page 71] for "Tic Tac Toe" domain shown on the position (iv) of Figure 1.
5. Closed functional expression for "XNOR" domain shown on the position (v) of Figure 1.

$$\omega_5(x,y) = xy > 0. \tag{2}$$

Thus, this demonstrates capabilities of boolean analytical closed form functions in construction of versatile geometrical objects.

3   Discrete-Continuous NNs and **R**-Functions

The application of NNs as classifiers has a sufficiently long history and many established results reflected in articles and summarized in monographs [3,4]. Nonetheless, there are situations where the regular NN method does not work well and may lead to errors in classification of patterns of clusters. To improve and avoid such misclassifications many authors propose different types of computationally complex techniques: additional layers of nodes, new activation functions, changing network topology with connectors, modification of learning rules, new target optimal functions, and then substantiate these techniques with numerical experiments. For rigorous users these methods cause somewhat feelings of dissatisfaction and lack of confidence in the results of these computational experiments even though there are some asymptotical and probabilistic error estimations of misclassification.

The approach presented here with applications of R-functions and NNs can be viewed as a generalization or modification of Radial Basis Functions (RBFs) with NNs when optimizing parameters include not only weights of nodes' connectors but also parameters of outlining shells of clusters, and tends to increase confidence in the numerical results.

At first, we describe regular NNs to be used for classification of clusters of pattern and then we will show the proposed modification aimed to improve the quality of classification even in difficult cases such as: non-convex, and disjoint domains of clusters of patterns. In NNs literature this situation has been termed *meshed and/or general type* domains [6].

For typical linear node of a NNs we have the activation function ϕ which provides linear separation of clusters of patterns on scalar product of vectors of weights w_i and inputs x_i.

$$y = \phi\left(\sum_i^n w_i x_i - \theta\right), \tag{3}$$

where w_i are weights of connectors, x_i are input values, $\phi(\cdot)$ is an activation function, which in this article particularly is $\mathbf{sgn}(\cdot)$, and θ is the threshold.

We consider incoming into neuron values x_i subject to Lebesgue - Stiltijes integration with integrand including an R-function ω_i, and Radial Basis Functions f_i with a differential of Lebesgue measurable weight function $W(s)$ in the field S. We use the following definition of Radial Basis Function (RBF):
A function $f : \mathbb{R}^d \to \mathbb{R}$ is said to be radial if there exists a function $\psi : [0, \infty] \to \mathbb{R}$ such that $f(x) = \psi(\|x\|_2), \forall x \in \mathbb{R}^d$ [9].

$$y = \mathbf{sgn}\left(\int_S \omega(\bar{\mathbf{x}})(f(\|\bar{\mathbf{x}} - \bar{\mathbf{r}}\|_2) - \theta)dW(s)\right) \tag{4}$$

$$= \begin{cases} \mathbf{sgn}\left(\int_S \omega(\bar{\mathbf{x}})(f(\|\bar{\mathbf{x}} - \bar{\mathbf{r}}\|_2) - \theta)w(s)ds\right) & \text{if } W(s) \text{ is Riemann integrable} \\ \mathbf{sgn}\left(\sum_i \omega(\bar{\mathbf{x}})(f_i(\|\bar{\mathbf{x}} - \bar{\mathbf{r_i}}\|_2) - \theta)w_i\right) & \text{if } W(s) \text{ is discrete.} \end{cases}$$

Thus, we consider a neuron immersed into a continuous field with discrete connectors between neurons. The continuous part of so called neuron field may resemble any known physical field like electrical, gravitational, etc. Properties of such field has to be defined phenomenologically. This functional may contain aging and stochastic parameters. In the given form (4), it expresses energy of stimulus factors $\bar{\mathbf{x}}$ on the density of a neuron field $w(s)$. Based on the similarities in operations between R-functions and traditional neurons: see section 2, (3),(4), a heterogeneous NNs can be constructed whilst it is not exploring here.

4   Error Functions for Classification in RBFNNs Training

We consider Sum-of-Squares Error SSE function, which is given by a sum over all patterns $\bar{\mathbf{x}}$ in the training set, over all k outputs of vector $\bar{\mathbf{y}} = (y_1, y_2, \dots, y_k)$, and a corresponding vector field of weights $\bar{\mathbf{W}}$, with a regularization factor λ in the form

$$SSE(\bar{\mathbf{W}}) = \|\bar{\mathbf{y}}(\bar{\mathbf{x}}) - \mathbf{sgn}\left(\int_S \omega(\bar{\mathbf{x}})(f(\|\bar{\mathbf{x}} - \bar{\mathbf{r}}\|_2) - \theta)d\bar{\mathbf{W}}(s)\right)\|_2^2 + \lambda\|\bar{\mathbf{w}}\|_2^2. \tag{5}$$

For only discrete connections between neurons, Lebesgue-Stiltijes integration is converted from (5) into summation, shown in (6), over weighted w_i connection values for each output $y_j, j = \overline{1, k}$. Thus, in the absence of a field of interactions, and only for the discrete case we have for SSE

$$SSE(\bar{\mathbf{w}}) = \|\bar{\mathbf{y}}(\bar{\mathbf{x}}) - \mathbf{sgn}\left(\sum_{i=1}^{k} \omega(\bar{\mathbf{x}})(f(\|\bar{\mathbf{x}} - \bar{\mathbf{r}}\|_2) - \theta)w_i\right)\|_2^2 + \lambda\|\bar{\mathbf{w}}\|_2^2. \quad (6)$$

4.1 Problem Formulation

To solve classification problem of finding discriminant expression separating clusters of different classes in a NNs form, we need to find

$$\mathbf{w}^* \in W^* = argmin\{SSE(\mathbf{w}) : w \in W, |\omega(\bar{x})| \neq 0\}. \quad (7)$$

It is assumed that the optimal set of weights W^* is not empty and is bounded. To find a minimum of (7) the gradient method is used. Since the objective function (7) is not everywhere differentiable and functionally complex, we use finite differences. The calculation of finite differences can be done numerically by perturbing each weight sequentially. Our activation function is the $\mathbf{sgn}(\cdot)$ which is differentiable only in a generalized sense and, therefore, can be estimated as some value $g(\bar{\mathbf{x}}_k; w_i)$ for error on the pattern $\bar{\mathbf{x}}_k$. Thus, we have for the batch learning delta rule

$$\Delta w_i = -\eta \sum_k w_{kj}(\mathbf{y}(\bar{\mathbf{x}}_k) - \mathbf{o}(\bar{\mathbf{x}}_k))g(\bar{\mathbf{x}}_k; w_i). \quad (8)$$

We denote $\mathbf{o}(\bar{\mathbf{x}}_k)$ as vector node output corresponding to input vector pattern $\bar{\mathbf{x}}_k$, $\mathbf{y}(\bar{\mathbf{x}}_k)$ as the target vector corresponding to the same input vector pattern, $g(\bar{\mathbf{x}}_k; w_i)$ as the sub-gradient of the optimization problem, and η as learning rate.

4.2 RBFs and R-Functions for Representation of Cluster of Patterns

Radial Basis Functions (RBFs) are used widely in neural networks and it is known that interpolating properties of RBFs are insensitive to their precise form, but the quality of interpolation depends on parameters of interpolating RBFs. RBFs are smoothing and averaging outputs of noisy and scattered data and, therefore, decently represent clusters of data (patterns). Mid-layer of RBFNNs serves for unsupervised training to determine parameters for cluster representation [1]. Adding to these functions a multiplier in the form of R-functions we enhance the capability to describe clusters of patterns for classification procedure.

Let $\omega(x, y)$ be an R-function which describes some domain of patterns. This geometrical description might not precisely outline boundaries of clusters. Performing some transformations, we can adjust the description of boundaries. We restrict ourselves only to linear transformation in order to substantiate concept on numerical experiments, namely : translation, rotation, scaling, and shearing.

An R-function $\omega(x, y; a, b, \theta, \gamma_1, \gamma_2, s_1, s_2)$ with transformational parameters $a, b, \theta, \gamma_1, \gamma_2, s_1, s_2$ can be adjusted to given clusters in such a way that the clusters will fit better into the boundaries of domains. A general form of transformation including scaling, shearing, rotation, and translation has the expression

$$x' = s_1 x \cos\theta - \gamma_1 y \sin\theta + a$$
$$y' = \gamma_2 x \sin\theta + s_2 y \cos\theta + b, \tag{9}$$

where a, b are components of a translational vector, s_1, s_2 are scaling parameters in the direction of x, y respectively, γ_1, γ_2 are shearing parameters, and θ is the rotational parameter.

5   Numerical Explorations: Substantiation of Concepts

To substantiate concepts of this new method for cluster classification, we select clusters for numerical experiments shown in Figures 2 and 3.

For each form of clusters we present equation of boundary with transformational parameters. For case "STRIP" with transformational parameters $a, b, \gamma_1, \gamma_2, \theta$

$$\omega_{strip}(x, y) = 0.25 - (s_1 x \cos(\theta) - \gamma_1 y \sin(\theta) - a)^2. \tag{10}$$

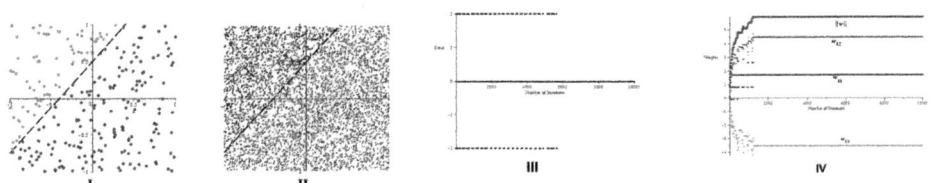

Fig. 2. i) RBFNNs training on 250 patterns in 2 clusters separated by (12).   ii) Error of testing 0.4% on 5000 patterns in 2 clusters separated by RBFNNs corresponding to (12).   iii) Error of training on 250 patterns in 2 clusters separated by (12).   iv) Weights after training on 250 patterns in 2 clusters separated by (12).

Fig. 3. i) RBFNNs training on 250 patterns in 2 clusters separated by (10).   ii) Error of testing 0.1% on 5000 patterns in 2 clusters separated by RBFNNs corresponding to (10).   iii) RBFNNs training on 250 patterns in 2 clusters separated by (11).   iv) Error of testing 0.32% on 5000 patterns in 2 clusters separated by RBFNNs corresponding to (11).

For case "TRIANGLE"

$$\omega_{triangle}(x, y) = 8. - \gamma_2 x \sin(\theta) - s_2 y \cos(\theta) + b -$$
$$\frac{8}{3} \times |-s_1 x \cos(\theta) + \gamma_1 y \sin(\theta) + a| - |8. - 3\gamma_2 x \sin(\theta) -$$
$$3 s_2 y \cos(\theta) + 3b - \frac{8}{3} \times |-s_1 x \cos(\theta) + \gamma_1 y \sin(\theta) + a||, \tag{11}$$

and case "LINE"

$$\omega_{line}(x, y) = 1.25 s_1 x + 1.25 \gamma_1 y - 1.25a -$$
$$\gamma_2 x - s_2 y + b + .5. \tag{12}$$

As Radial Basis Functions for hidden layer in the RBFNNs we take system of functions

$$\psi_j(x, y; r_{j1}, r_{j2}) = \exp[-(x - r_{j1})^2 - (y - r_{j2})^2], j = 1, 2, 3. \tag{13}$$

For the proposed numerical experiments, we construct perceptron with two input nodes for patterns x, y, three nodes of hidden layer, and one output node in output layer. Thus, our output function for classification has the form

$$z(x, y) = \mathbf{sgn}\left[\sum_{j=1}^{3} w_j \omega_{cluster}(x, y; a_j, b_j, \gamma_{1j}, \gamma_{2j}, \theta_j, s_{1j}, s_{2j})\psi_j(x, y; r_{j1}, r_{j2})\right].$$

For example, for clusters separated by a line $\omega_{line}(x, y)$, we reached error of classification on 250 patterns equal to zero after 6000 iterations. RBFNNs weight parameters stabilized, shown on Figure 2, and testing the trained RBFNN for pattern classifications on 5000 patterns showed error of 0.4%. Analogous results for clusters in cases: "STRIP", "TRIANGLE" were received with the difference found only with the values where error of classification tend to zero and parameters of RBFNNs become stabilized on 250 patterns. Results of checking of classification of significantly bigger number of patterns (5000 patterns) shown on the corresponding figures and further substantiate the concept of the new method numerically.

6   Summary

The proposed method for classification of clusters of patterns enables classification of pattern clusters in complex domains, such as: non-convex, non-connected domains on presented numerical examples.

   R-functions used to construct complex domain containing pattern clusters perform clustering role together with RBFs in the RBFNNs method. Parameters of RBFs define centers of pattern clusters and parameters of R-functions tune clusters within their boundaries.

The error functional is a convex quadratic one with respect to weight functions which takes weighted values at the discrete connections between neurons. As a generalization of traditional neural networks, a neuron continuous field can be considered; and scalar product between the stimulus patterns and the weights of connections represents energy delivered to a neuron.

The activation function of neurons is the **sgn**($\cdot$) function, and therefore, the error functional is non-smooth. For numerical examples the continuous part of neural fields is neglected and only the discrete part is used.

For neural networks learning, the delta rule is applied where instead of the gradient factor, the sub-gradient of the discretized error function is used because the error function is not smooth.

In case of multiple classes of pattern cluster classification, the RBFNNs together with R-functions must have k outputs such that this neural network can distinguish up to 2^k classes.

The application of the RFM allows for the creation, implementation, and resolution of large heterogeneous NNs capable to solving diverse sets of classification problems with greater accuracy in principle. In this case, the proposed clustering method copes with the classification of clusters by a perceptron whose inputs are taken from regions of limited diameter [7].

References

1. Bishop, C.M.: Neural Network for Pattern Recognition. Oxford University Press (1995)
2. Buhmann, M.: Radial Basis Functions. Theory and Implementation. Cambridge University Press (2003)
3. Duda, R.E., Hart, P.E., Stork, D.G.: Pattern Classification. Wiley Inerscience (2000)
4. Hassoun, M.H.: Fundamentals of Artificial Neural Networks. The MIT Press (1995)
5. Lee, Y., Lin, Y., Wahba, G.: Multicategory Support Vector Machines: Theory and Application to the Classification of Microarray Data and Satellite Radiance Data. J. of the American Statistical Association 99(465), 67–81 (2004)
6. Lippman, R.P.: An Introduction to Computing with Neural Nets. In: Lau, C. (ed.) Neural Networks. Theoretical Foundation and Analysis. IEEE Press (1992)
7. Minsky, M.L., Papert, S.A.: Perceptrons. MIT Press, Cambridge (1990)
8. Rvachev, V.L.: Geometric Applications of Logic Algebra. Naukova Dumka, Kiev (1967) (in Russian)
9. Wendland, H.: Scattered data approximation. Cambridge University Press (2010)

Micro-Doppler Classification for Ground Surveillance Radar Using Speech Recognition Tools

Dalila Yessad[1], Abderrahmane Amrouche[1], Mohamed Debyeche[1],
and Mustapha Djeddou[2]

[1] Speech Communication and Signal Processing Laboratory,
Faculty of Electronics and Computer Sciences, USTHB,
P.O. Box 32, El Alia, Bab Ezzouar, 16111, Algiers, Algeria
[2] Communication Systems Laboratory, Ecole Militaire
Polytechnique, BEB, Algiers, Algeria
namrouche@usthb.dz,
{yessad.dalila,mdebyeche,djeddou.mustapha}@gmail.com

Abstract. Among the applications of a radar system, target classification for ground surveillance is one of the most widely used. This paper deals with micro-Doppler Signature (μ-DS) based radar Automatic Target Recognition (ATR). The main goal for performing μ-DS classification using speech processing tools was to investigate whether automatic speech recognition (ASR) techniques are suitable methods for radar ATR. In this work, extracted features from micro-Doppler echoes signal, using MFCC, LPC and LPCC, are used to estimate models for target classification. In classification stage, two parametric models based on Gaussian Mixture Model (GMM) and Greedy GMM were successively investigated for echo target modeling. Maximum a posteriori (MAP) and Majority-voting post-processing (MV) decision schemes are applied. Thus, ASR techniques based on GMM and GMM Greedy classifiers have been successfully used to distinguish different classes of targets echoes (humans, truck, vehicle and clutter) recorded by a low-resolution ground surveillance Doppler radar. Experimental results show that MV post processing improves target recognition and the performances reach to $99,08\%$ correct classification on the testing set.

Keywords: Automatic Target Recognition (ATR), micro-Doppler Signatures (μ-DS), Automatic Speech Recognition (ASR), Gaussian Mixture Model (GMM), Greedy GMM, Maximum a Posteriori (MAP), Majority Vote (MV).

1 Introduction

Target classification using radar signatures has potential applications in air/marine traffic and ground surveillance radar. The goal for any target recognition system is to give the most accurate interpretation of what a target is at any given point in time. ATR is a crucial task for both military and civil applications.

C. San Martin and S.-W. Kim (Eds.): CIARP 2011, LNCS 7042, pp. 280–287, 2011.

In the acquisition stage, each target is illuminated with a frequency stepped signal and the returned echoes are then received. The radar operator identifies targets from the audio representation of the echoes signal. Mechanical vibration or rotation of a target may induce additional frequency modulations on the returned radar signal. This phenomenon, known as the micro-Doppler effect, generates sidebands at the target Doppler frequency.

Techniques based on micro-Doppler signatures [1], [2] are used to divide targets into several macro groups such as aircrafts, vehicles, creatures, etc. An effective tool to extract information from this signature is the time-frequency transform [3]. The time-varying trajectories of the different micro-Doppler components are quite revealing, especially when viewed in the joint time-frequency space [4]. Anderson [5] used micro-Doppler features to distinguish among humans, animals and vehicles. In [6], analysis of radar micro-Doppler signature with time-frequency transform was discussed. The time-frequency signature of the micro-Doppler provides additional time information and shows micro-Doppler frequency variations. Thus, additional information about vibration rate or rotation rate is available for target recognition. Gaussian mixture model (GMM)-based classification methods are widely applied to automatic speech and speaker recognition [7]. Mixture models form a common technique for probability density estimation. In [8], it was proved that any density can be estimated using finite Gaussian mixture. A Greedy learning of GMM based target classification for ground surveillance Doppler radar, recently proposed in [9], overcomes the drawbacks of the Expectation Minimization (EM) algorithm. The greedy learning algorithm does not require prior knowledge of the number of components in the mixture, because it inherently estimates the model order.

In this paper, we investigate the micro-Doppler radar signatures in order to obtain best classification performances. The classification algorithms are implemented using three kinds of features; Mel-Frequency Cepstral Coefficients (MFCC), Linear Prediction Coding (LPC) and Cepstrum Coefficient feature sets (LPCC), extracted from echoes signals recorded by Doppler radar. These features are fed respectively to GMM and greedy GMM parametric and statistical classifier approaches for multi-hypotheses problem. The classification tasks include the determination of the statistical modeling of extracted features distribution and the application of Maximum a posteriori (MAP) rule. As a post-processing enhancement method, a majority vote technique is proposed.

This paper is organized as follows: in section 2, features extractions and classification schemes are presented. In Section 3, we describe the experimental framework including the data collection. Experimental results are drawn in section 4.

2   Classification Scheme

In this paper, a supervised classification process was performed and two decision methods were implemented.

2.1 Feature Extraction

In practical case, a human operator listen to the audio Doppler output from the surveillance radar for detecting and may be identifying targets. In fact, human operators classify the targets using an audio representation of the micro-Doppler effect, caused by the target motion. As in speech processing a set of operations are taken during pre-processing step to take in count the human ear characteristics. Features are numerical measurements used in computation to discriminate between classes. In this work, we investigated three classes of features namely, LPC, LPCC, and MFCC.

Linear Prediction Coding (LPC). Linear prediction is the process of predicting future sample values of a digital signal from a linear system. It is therefore about predicting the signal $x(n)$ at instant n from p previous samples as in (1).

$$x(n) = \sum_{k=1}^{p} a_k x(n-k) + e(n) \tag{1}$$

So the coding by linear prediction consists in determining coefficients a_k that minimize the error $e(n)$. LPC are expected to give very accurate formant information of acoustic signals. We considered the LPC up to the 16th order (excluding the zero coefficient) and applied it directly to the radar signal.

Cepstral Linear Prediction Coding (LPCC). The cepstrum coefficients $\{ceps_q\}_{q=0}^{Q}$ can be estimated from the LPC coefficients $\{a_q\}_{q=1}^{p}$ using a recursion procedure:

$$ceps_q = \begin{cases} ln(G), & q=0 \\ a_q + \sum_{k=1}^{q-1} \frac{k-q}{q} a_k ceps_{q-k}, & 1 \leqslant q \leqslant p \\ \sum_{k=1}^{p} \frac{k-q}{q} a_k ceps_{q-k}, & p < q \leqslant Q \end{cases} \tag{2}$$

Where G is the gain term in the LPC model, p the LPC model order, and $Q+1$ the number of cepstrum coefficients.

Mel Frequency Cepstral Coefficients (MFCC). The most commonly used feature vector in speech recognition is composed of Mel-Frequency Cepstral Coefficients (MFCC). Fig.1 is a block diagram of the MFCC generation process from micro-Doppler signal. The MFCC extraction is done in three steps:

1. Step 1-a: Cut up the signal in several overlapping windows;

2. Step 1-b: To decrease the spectral distortion a Hamming windowing is applied to signal frames;

$$W(n) = 0.54 - 0.46 * cos(\frac{2\pi n}{N-1}) \tag{3}$$

Where N is the window size.

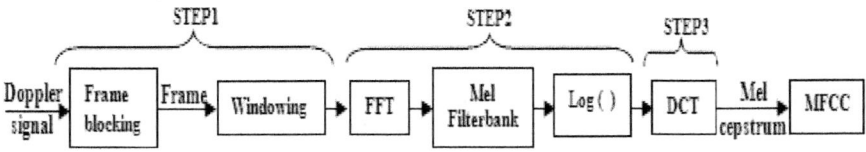

Fig. 1. MFCC generation

3. Step 2-a: Apply the FFT ;

4. Step 2-b: The Mel-frequency scale is applied to obtain an appropriate signal representation In fact psychophysical studies have shown that human perception of the frequency content of sounds does not follow a linear scale. The recognition model thus reflects the behaviour of the brain in this respect and is equally applicable to both speech and radar Doppler. We use the following transformation formula;

$$mel(f) = 2595 * log10(1 + \frac{f}{700}) \tag{4}$$

5. Step 2-c: Apply the logarithm after the Mel scale;

6. Step 3: Finally, obtain the discrete cosine transform (DCT) of the output signal.

2.2 Modelisation

In the present work, each target class is represented by two parametric models; GMM and Greedy GMM.

Gaussian mixture model (GMM). Gaussian mixture model (GMM) is a mixture of several Gaussian distributions. The probability density function is defined as a weighted sum of Gaussians:

$$p(x; \theta) = \sum_{c=1}^{C} \alpha_c N(x; \mu_c, \Sigma_c) \tag{5}$$

Where α_c is the weight of the component c, $0 < \alpha_c < 1$ for all components, and $\sum_{c+1}^{C} \alpha_c = 1$. μ_c is the mean of components and Σ_c is the covariance matrix. We define the parameter vector θ:

$$\theta = \{\alpha_1, \mu_1, \Sigma_1, ..., \alpha_c, \mu_c, \Sigma_c\} \tag{6}$$

Estimating the Gaussian mixture parameters for one class can be considered as an unsupervised learning in the case where samples are generated by individual components of the mixture distribution. The expectation maximization (EM) algorithm is an iterative method for calculating maximum likelihood distribution parameter. This algorithm starts from an initial guess θ^0 for the distribution parameters and the log-likelihood is guaranteed to increase at each iteration until it converges. The initialization is one of the crucial problems of the EM algorithm. The selection of θ^0 determines where the algorithm converges or hits the boundary of the parameter space producing singular, meaningless results. An elegant solution for the initialization problem is provided by the greedy learning of GMM [10].

Greedy Gaussian mixture model (Greedy GMM). The greedy algorithm starts with a single component and then adds components into the mixture one by one. The optimal starting component for a Gaussian mixture is trivially computed, optimal meaning the highest training data likelihood. The algorithm repeats two steps: insert a component into the mixture, and run EM until convergence. Inserting a component that increases the likelihood the most is thought to be an easier problem than initializing a whole near-optimal distribution. Component insertion involves searching for the parameters for only one component at a time. Recall that EM finds a local optimum for the distribution parameters, not necessarily the global optimum which makes it initialization dependent method [10].

2.3   Classifiers

A classifier is a function that defines the decision boundary between different patterns (classes). Each classifier must be trained with a training dataset before being used to recognize new patterns, such that it generalizes training dataset into classification rules. Two decision methods were examined. The first one suggests the maximum a posteriori probability (MAP) and the second uses the majority vote (MV) post-processing after classifier decision.

Decision. If we have a group of targets represented by the GMM models: $\lambda_1, \lambda_2, ..., \lambda_\xi$, The classification decision is done using the posteriori probability (MAP):

$$\hat{S} = \arg \underline{\xi} \max p(\lambda_s | X) \tag{7}$$

According to Bayesian rule:

$$\hat{S} = \arg \max \frac{p(X|\lambda_s)p(\lambda_s)}{p(X)} \tag{8}$$

X: is the observed sequence.

Assuming that each class has the same a priori probability ($p(\lambda_s) = 1/\xi$) and the probability of apparition of the sequence is the same for all targets the classification rule of Bayes becomes:

$$\hat{S} = \arg \max p(X|\lambda_s) \tag{9}$$

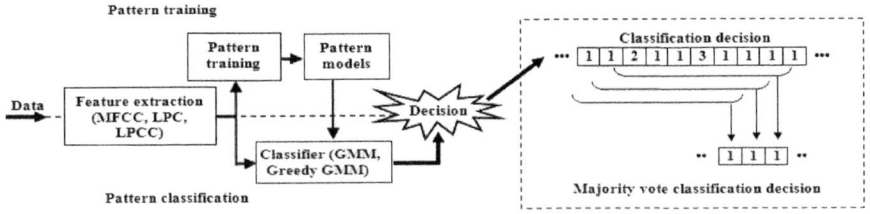

Fig. 2. Majority vote post-processing after classifier decision

Majority Vote. The majority vote (MV) post-processing can be employed after classifier decision. It uses the current classification result, along with the previous classification results and makes a classification decision based on the class that appears most often. A plot of the classification by MV (post-processing) after classifier decision is shown in Fig.2.

3   Measurements and Data Collection

Data were obtained using records of a low-resolution ground surveillance radar. The target was detected and tracked automatically by the radar, allowing continuous target echo records from the following targets: 1, 2, and 3 persons, vehicle, truck and clutter. We first collected the Doppler signatures from the echoes of six different targets in movements namely, one, two, and three persons, vehicle, truck and vegetation clutter. The target was detected and tracked automatically by a low-power Doppler radar operating at 9.72 GHz, sweep in azimuth 30 at 270 and emission power is 100mW. When the radar transmits an electromagnetic signal in the surveillance area, this signal interacts with the target and then returns to the radar. After demodulation and analog to digital conversion,

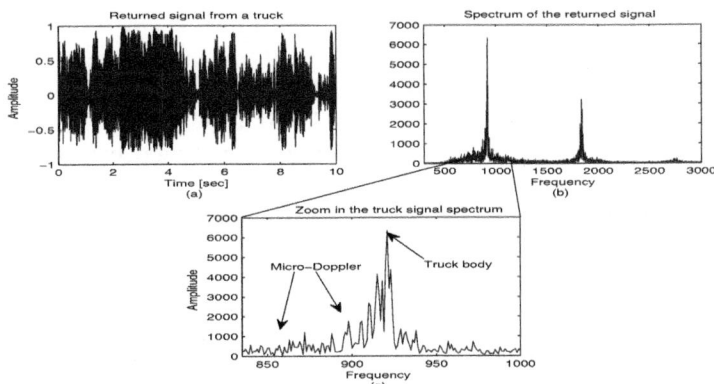

Fig. 3. (a)Returned signal from a truck (b) Spectrum of the returned signal (c) Zoom in the truck signal spectrum

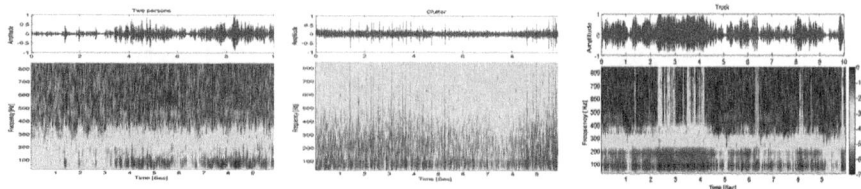

Fig. 4. Radar echo samples and the typical spectrograms of three moving targets; a) Two persons, b) Clutter, c) Truck

the received echoes are recorded in wav audio format; each record has a duration of 10 seconds. By taking the Fourier transform of the recorded signal, the micro-Doppler frequency shift may be observed in the frequency domain. An illustration of a measurement and its spectrum is shown in Fig.3. The change of the properties of the returned signal reflects the characteristics of the target. When the target is moving, the carrier frequency of the returned signal will be shifted due to Doppler effect. The Doppler frequency shift can be used to determine the radial velocity of the moving target. If the target or any structure on the target is vibrating or rotating in addition to target translation, it will induce frequency modulation on the returned signal that generates sidebands about the target's Doppler frequency. This modulation is called the micro-Doppler (μ-DS) phenomenon. The μ-DS phenomenon can be regarded as a characteristic of the interaction between the vibrating or rotating structures and the target body. Fig.4 (a)-(c) show the temporal representation and the typical spectrograms of three targets for two persons, clutter and truck. Each target class has unique time-frequency characteristic which can be used for classification. These particular plots are obtained by taking a succession of FFTs and using a sampling rate of 8 KHz, FFT size of 256 points, overlap of 128, and a hamming window.

4   Results

In this work, target class pdfs were modeled by GMMs using both greedy and EM estimation algorithms. MFCC, LPCC and LPC coefficients were used as classification features. The MAP and the majority voting decision concepts were

Table 1. Confusion matrix of Greedy GMM-based classifier with MFCC coefficients and MV post-processing after MAP decision rule for six-class problem

Class / Decision	1Person	2Persons	3Persons	Vehicle	Truck	Clutter
1Person	96.30	1.85	0	1.85	0	0
2Persons	0	100	0	0	0	0
3Persons	0	0	100	0	0	0
Vehicle	1.85	0	0	98.15	0	0
Truck	0	0	0	0	100	0
Clutter	0	0	0	0	0	100

examined. Table 1 presents the confusion matrix of Greedy GMM based classifier with MFCC coefficients and MV post-processing after MAP decision for six class problem. Greedy GMM outperform GMM classifier. To improve classification accuracy, majority vote post-processing can be employed. The resulting effect is a smooth operation that removes spurious misclassification. Indeed, the classification rate improves to 99.08% for Greedy GMM after MAP decision following majority vote post-processing, 97.93% for GMM after MV decision.

5 Conclusion

Acoustics features like LPC, LPCC and MFCC are used to exploit the micro-Doppler signatures issued from moving target in order to provide separation among the target classes like humans, vehicles, trucks and clutter. Speech recognition techniques, using GMM and Greedy GMM including the MAP decision rules, have been successfully applied for ground surveillance radar. Experimental results show that the Greedy GMM using MFCC features gives the best classification performances. However, it fails to avoid all classification errors, which we are bound to eradicate through MV-post processing which guarantees a 99.08% classification rate for six-class problem presented in this work.

References

1. Thayaparan, T., Abrol, S., Riseborough, E., Stankovic, L., Lamothe, D., Duff, D.: Analysis of radar micro-Doppler signatures from experimental helicopter and human data. IEE Proc. Radar Sonar Navigation 1(4), 288–299 (2007)
2. Natecz, M., Rytel-Andrianik, R., Wojtkiewicz, A.: Micro-Doppler analysis of signal received by FMCW radar. In: International Radar Symposium, Germany (2003)
3. Boashash, B.: Time frequency signal analysis and processing, 1st edn. Elsevier Ltd. (2003)
4. Chen, V.C., Ling, H.: Time frequency transforms for radar imaging and signal analysis. Artech House, Boston (2002)
5. Anderson, M., Rogers, R.: Micro-Doppler analysis of multiple frequency continuous wave radar signatures. In: SPIE Proc. Radar Sensor Technology, vol. 654 (2007)
6. Chen, V.C.: Analysis of radar micro-Doppler signature with time-frequency transform. In: Proc. Tenth IEEE Workshop on Statistical Signal and Array Processing, pp. 463–466 (2000)
7. Reynolds, D.A., Quatieri, T.F., Dunn, R.B.: Speaker verification using adapted Gaussian mixture models. Digit. Signal Process. 10, 19–41 (2000)
8. Li, J.Q., Barron, A.R.: Mixture density estimation. In: Advances in Neural Information Processing Systems, vol. 12. MIT Press, Cambridge (2000)
9. Bilik, I., Tabrikian, J., Cohen, A.: GMM-based target classification for ground surveillance Doppler radar. IEEE Trans. on Aerospace and Electronic Systems 42(1), 267–278 (2006)
10. Verbeek, J.J., Vlassis, N., Krose, B.: Efficient greedy learning of Gaussian mixture models. Neural Computation 5(2), 469–485 (2003)

Semantic Integration of Heterogeneous Recognition Systems

Paweł L. Kaczmarek and Piotr Raszkowski

Gdańsk University of Technology,
Faculty of Electronics, Telecommunications and Informatics,
Narutowicza 11/12 Str., 80-233 Gdańsk, Poland
{pawel.kaczmarek,piotr.raszkowski}@eti.pg.gda.pl
http://www.eti.pg.gda.pl

Abstract. Computer perception of real-life situations is performed using a variety of recognition techniques, including video-based computer vision, biometric systems, RFID devices and others. The proliferation of recognition modules enables development of complex systems by integration of existing components, analogously to the Service Oriented Architecture technology. In the paper, we propose a method that enables integration of information from existing modules to calculate results that are more accurate and complete. The method uses semantic description of concepts and reasoning to manage syntactic differences between information returned by modules. The semantic description is based on existing real-world concepts in video recognition and ubiquitous systems. We propose helper functionalities such as: module credibility rating, confidence level declaration and selection of communication protocol. Two integration modes are defined: voting of matching concepts and aggregation of complementing concepts.

Keywords: integration, ontology, computer perception, monitoring.

1 Introduction

Video-based computer vision is a typical method of computer perception of real-life situations. In a wider context, computer perception may be realized using biometric systems, RFID devices, environment condition sensors, and others. The techniques differ in the contents of input data and recognition algorithms, which determines their quality and the scope of application. Despite the differences, the systems have many similarities as all of them attempt to recognize concepts encountered in real-life.

The proliferation of computer perception systems [13] [2] [11] results in their overlapping functionality such as face recognition, people counting, car identification and others. Consequently, there exist many alternative components realizing similar functionality. It becomes possible to apply the Service Oriented Architecture (SOA) approach in this area and develop complex systems by integration of existing components. During the process, the developer selects from alternative components those that supply most desired attributes, for example low

C. San Martin and S.-W. Kim (Eds.): CIARP 2011, LNCS 7042, pp. 288–295, 2011.

price, high accuracy and high performance. The approach reduces development cost and time, but requires resolution of integration problems. The problems cover all layer of computer system, from the communication layer to semantic understanding of data [14] [6].

In the paper, we propose a method of integration of existing recognition modules in order to achieve results that are more accurate and more complete. We assume, that different modules supply information about the same situation, although the systems may recognize different elements of the situation and use incompatible descriptions. Our method integrates results from different sources and performs semantic reasoning to calculate a coherent description of a situation. We base our solution on ontological description of concepts that occur in the environment and reasoning rules that are applied to input data.

We propose two alternative integration modes in the method: voting and aggregation. The voting mode assumes that integrated modules recognize the same concept and the calculation aims at achieving a more accurate result. The aggregation mode, in turn, assumes that a complex information is composed from partial information returned by modules. Fig. 1 shows a concept diagram of integration by voting.

The rest of the paper is organized as follows. The next section describes related work and gives background about techniques used in our research. Sect. 3 describes main functionality of the solution. Sect. 4 describes system implementation. Finally, Sect. 5 concludes the paper.

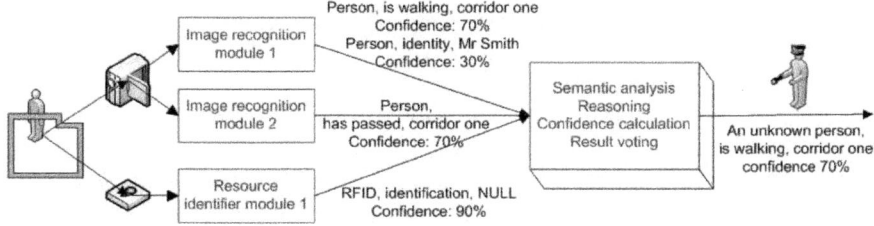

Fig. 1. General overview of module integration using semantic reasoning

2   Background and Related Work

Ontologies and semantic description of concepts are commonly used in computer vision systems in different aspects of the process. [8][5][10] propose ontology-based image retrieval, in which ontologies are used to describe both low-level visual properties, such as color, shape and texture, and high-level concepts regarding image contents, such as person, building and car. The SOUPA ontology [4] is a mature ontology designed to describe situations in ubiquitous and pervasive environments. The ontology contains concepts such as time, place, person, which largely overlaps with concepts encountered in image recognition systems.

[1] describes VERL (A Video Event Representation Language) - a formal language for describing an ontology of events that occur in real-life, and VEML (Video Event Markup Language) - used to annotate instances of the events described in VERL. The languages were designed as a part of the ARDA "Challenge Project on Video Event Taxonomy" project. The results supply formal mechanisms to describe events that can be identified during video analysis. [3] describes a similar approach, in which an ontology describes concepts related to video events. Two main types of concepts are distinguished: physical objects observed in a scene and video events occurring in a scene. In further work, we use selected concepts from existing ontologies to uniformly describe information retrieved by alternative modules.

Image retrieval is applied in a wide range of systems. For example, ubiquitous systems augment reality with computer-driven intelligence that automates every-day tasks and dynamically adapts to changing conditions [13]. The systems use devices and mechanisms of real-world perception such as move sensors, biometric systems, RFID devices. Monitoring systems use image retrieval to identify events that violate security restrictions and require appropriate actions. The systems use both video-based computer vision and non-video sensors for reality perception, analogously to ubiquitous environments [15] [9]. In our work, we propose a method of integration of existing real-world perception systems, rather than new methods of image and video processing.

Integration of components requires resolution of dependability and interoperability issues. The work [7] describes problems encountered during development of dependable applications out of undependable components. Authors propose a classification of component attributes and their rating. Typically, dependability is achieved using a variety of redundancy techniques [12]. The use of redundancy seems especially suited for SOA-based development, as there exist many modules supplying a similar functionality. Interoperability is another important issue in SOA-based applications. [6,14] overview existing definitions and metrics of interoperability. Metrics describe various levels of module integration, ranging from low-level communication protocol compatibility to high-level integration of information. Semantic understanding and ontological description of data concepts are important elements of high-level interoperability.

3   System Infrastructure and Operation

The proposed method assumes that there exist alternative computer perception modules supplying the same functionality. We integrate information from the alternative modules and calculate aggregated results to increase recognition accuracy and reliability. The method requires the following metadata information:

- A registry of integrated modules.
- An ontology of considered concepts.

The registry stores information about known recognition modules together with their credibility rating. Credibility ratings (denoted *cred*) are defined by administrator on module registration and adjusted during system operation. Initially, system operator defines relative rating of modules that are integrated with the system. During operation, the integration system monitors module results and calculates simple correlation between data received from modules. If the correlation of results for some modules fall below a specified threshold, the system informs administrator. The administrator is expected to adjust the ratings either manually or automatically by specifying feedback information about correctness of results returned from modules.

The ontology contains concepts encountered in real-life situations, analogously to ontologies like SOUPA [4], VERL [1] and WordNet. We anticipate confidence level (denoted $conf$) for input information and for output results, which allows application of fuzzy reasoning. Result confidence is calculated from confidence of input and credibility of the sending module as described in detail later.

3.1   Reasoning Rules

The system uses two alternative modes for integration of knowledge from recognition systems:

– voting mode,
– aggregation mode.

The voting mode attempts to detect a single concept and generate a result with higher accuracy. It is assumed that recognition systems supply alternative descriptions of the same situation, although they have limited functionality and may return imprecise results. For example, results from different face recognition systems are voted to determine the identity of a recognized person with higher accuracy.

The aggregation mode attempts to reason about a complex situation on the basis of detailed information. In this mode, we assume that integrated modules recognize the same scene, although they have complementing (rather than alternative) functionality. For example, alternative image recognition systems detect that a scene contains doors, windows and people, which enables us to reason that the scene contains a building in a public place. The concepts are aggregated and the system reasons about a possible complex situation.

The ontology is enriched with appropriate reasoning rules for both voting and aggregation modes. The voting mode requires mainly processing of the class structure to detect subclasses and superclasses of recognized concepts. The aggregation mode, in turn, requires rather analysis of concept relationships, such as "consists of", "contains", "stores".

Although modules should send information compatible with concepts defined in the common ontology, it may happen that unknown concepts are sent. In this case, the system applies a simple syntactic comparison of input data. In the approach, it is required that concepts supplied by different modules match exactly, that is if two modules recognize the same concept, they use the same word for description.

3.2   Information Processing Steps

Assuming that appropriate metadata has been configured and integration mode (voting, aggregation) has been selected, information processing in the system is done in the following main steps as shown in Algorithm 1.

Algorithm 1. Main steps of information processing in the integration system
---
input: data (d) sent from recognition modules $(R = (r_1, r_2, ..., r_N))$
output: compound result

1: **for all** Received data **do**
2:     Create appropriate object structure for SPARQL processing.
3:     Search the ontology for received concepts.
4:     **if** Received concepts (in d) are found in the ontology **then**
5:        **if** There exist d_i, d_j that contain syntactically different data **then**
6:           Apply ontology-based reasoning
7:           Calculate sums of $cred * conf$ for inputs that are syntactically identical among R
8:           Select a reference input Ref as the input with highest value of $\sum cred * conf$
9:           Query ontology for semantic understanding of data (for example: Mr Smith, Mr John)
10:          Calculate a common base of concepts taking Ref as reference (for example: person)
11:       **end if**
12:       Apply voting weighted with relative conficence $(cred * conf)$.
13:       Calculate confidence level of the result from module credibility and input data confidence.
14:       $Confidence = \frac{\sum_N cred * conf}{\sum_N cred}$
15:       Calculate correlation of results from modules to adjust credibility rating.
16:    **else**
17:       Received concepts are not matched
18:       Calculate relative confidence of each input $cred * conf$.
19:       Apply syntactic, majority voting weighted with relative confidence.
20:    **end if**
21:    Return compound result and confidence to the end user.
22: **end for**

---

4   System Implementation

As a part of the research, we develop a system that realizes the proposed method. The system supplies a web-based user interface that enables initial configuration and monitoring of operation. The current work covers registration of integrated recognition modules together with their credibility description as a major element of system configuration. Additionally, detailed configuration options are set, including, among others, specification of: integration modes (aggregation, voting), dictionary and ontology processing, time constraints for communication.

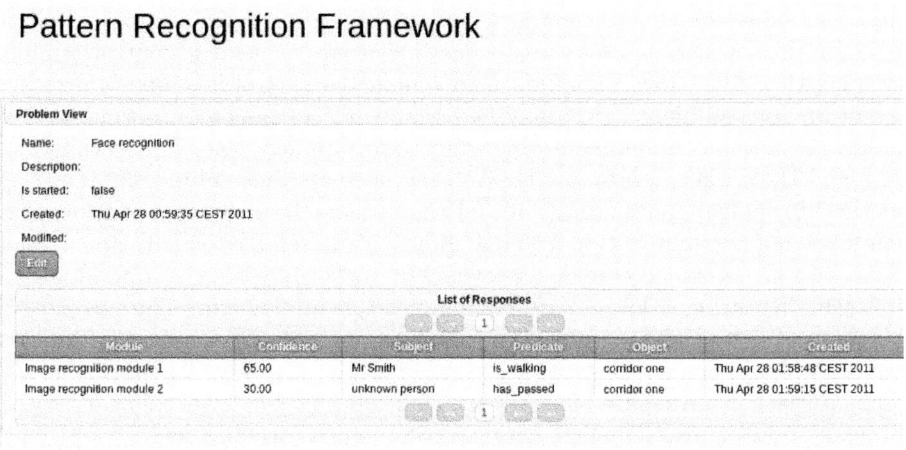

Pattern Recognition Framework

Problem View

Name:	Face recognition
Description:	
Is started:	false
Created:	Thu Apr 28 00:59:35 CEST 2011
Modified:	

[Edit]

List of Responses

[ ] [ ] 1 [ ] [ ]

Module	Confidence	Subject	Predicate	Object	Created
Image recognition module 1	65.00	Mr Smith	is_walking	corridor one	Thu Apr 28 01:58:48 CEST 2011
Image recognition module 2	30.00	unknown person	has_passed	corridor one	Thu Apr 28 01:59:15 CEST 2011

[ ] [ ] 1 [ ] [ ]

Fig. 2. Exemplary screenshot of the implemented system

The system is implemented in the Java 6 EE language using NetBeans IDE environment. We used the PrimeFaces Java framework to design a user-friendly web-based interface. Glassfish v3 Application Server is used as the deployment platform for the system MySQL 5 database is used as persistent storage. Fig. 2 shows an exemplary screenshot of the implemented system.

4.1   Ontology Processing in the System

We use Protégé as the editor for the ontology stored in the system. Our work focuses on defining concepts related to office area. This includes classes such as person, room, action, device, and appropriate individuals, for example Mr Smith, Mr Jones, Room100, Room200 etc.

Runtime ontology processing is performed using Jena OWL API and the Sparql processing engine. Sparql queries aim at retrieving information from the ontology that will be useful for common understanding of received data. As as example, consider the figure from the Introduction section (Fig. 1). The first module detected that a person is walking (confidence 70%) and the person is Mr Smith (confidence 30%). The second module detected that a person has passed (confidence 70%). The RFID system informs that is has not received any identification (confidence 90%). Therefore, we conclude that someone is walking the area, but it is not necessarily Mr Smith. Therefore, the reasoning should return information that an unknown person is walking the area, while the confidence of the information is 70%, assuming that modules have equal credibility.

4.2   Communication Protocol

The system requires that recognition modules send knowledge organized analogously to N-triples, containing the subject, the predicate and the object.

The communication format enables relatively simple processing on the recognition module side. The communication protocol anticipates grouping of triples into one logical set. In this case, a module needs to send a control triple informing that following communication should be merged into one information. Additionally, confidence level may be assigned to transmitted information.

Two concrete communication interfaces are supplied: the Web services interface and the socket interface. The Web services interface defines the sendTriple method for single communication and the registerResponse method for grouping following communication into one information. sendExtendedTriple enriches data with the assigned confidence level. The socket interface supplies analogous functionality using a lower level communication mechanism. The interface enables transmission of integer operation codes and character arrays of information, for example: 31 - start of triple, 32 - end of triple, 41 - start of extended triple. The interface is anticipated for systems that focus on low-level solutions and are difficult to integrate with Web services communication libraries.

5   Conclusions and Future Work

The proposed method intends to integrate information from independent recognition modules in order to achieve more accurate and complete results. The approach is driven by the SOA technology, in which applications are developed from existing, alternative modules. The use of open communication standards will promote interoperability and easy integration of modules. The current implementation work enables us to refine and adjust the method to concrete cases.

Integration of concrete recognition modules will be the main scope of future work. We plan to integrate both our proprietary implementations and existing modules, which requires minor adjustment of modules to integration system requirements. The adjustment covers two main areas: (i) implementation of appropriate network interface for data transmission and (ii) use of common concepts for description of recognized elements. During method design, we intended to minimize the work that is required to integrate recognition modules.

Adjustment of reasoning rules and ontological description of concepts is another interesting area of future work, as currently we analyze a limited number of rules and concepts. Extension of the knowledge base enables application of the system in a wide range of areas. Existing knowledge bases, such as WordNet or SOUPA ontology, supply virtually unlimited possibilities of concept definition and processing. We hope that the method will increase accuracy of recognition systems in the future and will promote application of existing systems in new areas.

Acknowledgments. The work was supported in part by the Polish Ministry of Science and Higher Education under research projects N N519 172337 and N N519 432338.

References

1. Bolles, B., Nevatia, R.: A hierarchical video event ontology in owl. Tech. rep., 2004 ARDA Challenge Project (2004)
2. Bradski, G., Kaehler, A.: Learning OpenCV: Computer Vision with the OpenCV Library. O'Reilly Media (2008)
3. Bremond, F., Maillot, N., Thonnat, M., Vu, V.T.: Ontologies for video events. Tech. rep., Institut National de Recherche en Informatique et en Automatique (2004)
4. Chen, H., Perich, F., Finin, T., Joshi, A.: Soupa: Standard ontology for ubiquitous and pervasive applications. In: International Conference on Mobile and Ubiquitous Systems: Networking and Services (2004)
5. Dasiopoulou, S., Papastathis, V.K., Mezaris, V., Kompatsiaris, I., Strintzis, M.G.: An ontology framework for knowledge-assisted semantic video analysis and annotation. In: 3rd International Semantic Web Conference (2004)
6. Ford, T., Colombi, J., Graham, S., Jacques, D.: A survey on interoperability measurement. In: 12th ICCRTS Adapting C2 to the 21st Century
7. Gorbenko, A., Kharchenko, V., Popov, P., Romanovsky, A., Boyarchuk, A.: Development of dependable web services out of undependable web components. Tech. Rep. CS-TR-863, University of Newcastle upon Tyne (2004)
8. Hois, J., Wünstel, M., Bateman, J., Röfer, T.: Dialog-based 3d-image recognition using a domain ontology. LNCS (2007)
9. Kaczmarek, P.L., Zielonka, P.: A video monitoring system using ontology-driven identification of threats. In: International Conference on Human System Interaction (2009)
10. Maillot, N., Thonnat, M., Boucher, A.: Towards ontology-based cognitive vision. Machine Vision and Applications, Special issue on ICVS (2003)
11. Szeliski, R.: Computer Vision: Algorithms and Applications. Springer, Heidelberg (2010), http://szeliski.org/Book/
12. ReSIST: Resilience for Survivability in IST, A European Network of Excellence: Resilience-Building Technologies: State of Knowledge (2006)
13. Poslad, S.: Ubiquitous Computing: Smart Devices, Environments and Interactions. Wiley Publishing (2009)
14. Tolk, A.: Beyond technical interoperability - introducing a reference model for measures of merit for coalition interoperability. In: 8th International Command and Control Research and Technology Symposium, Washington, D.C. (2003)
15. Tyrer, J.: Dtect - the vehicle monitoring system. Loughborough University, Vehicle Occupancy Ltd (2007)

A New Distributed Approach for Range Image Segmentation

Smaine Mazouzi[1] and Zahia Guessoum[2]

[1] Dép. d'informatique, Université de Skikda, BP 26, Route ElHadaik, 21000, Algeria
smazouzi@univ-skikda.dz
[2] LIP6, Université de Paris 6, 104, av. du Président Kennedy, 75016, Paris, France
zahia.guessoum@lip6.fr

Abstract. In this paper we introduce a new distributed approach for image segmentation based on multi-agent systems. Several agents are placed randomly in the image, then each of them starts a region growing around its position. Several agents can be within the same homogeneous region. So, they must exchange information to better labeling pixels reached by these agents. Every labeled pixel is smoothed by replacing its parameters by those of the pixel in the center of the region seed. A set of real range images from the ABW image base was used to evaluate the proposed approach. Experimental results show the potential of the approach to provide an accurate and efficient image segmentation.

Keywords: Image segmentation, Multi-agent systems, Region growing.

1 Introduction

Segmenting an image is necessary to perform several tasks in image analysis and object recognition. Based on some similarity criterion, it consists in participating pixels of an image in homogeneous and contiguous sets, called regions. Mostly, image segmentation methods are divided in two categories: Edge-based methods, and region-based methods. In the first category, pixels corresponding to discontinuities in image information are selected [4,6]. After, the obtained pixels are chained and partitioned into disjoint sets to form boundaries of image regions. Edge-based methods are characterized by a low computational cost, suitable for real-time applications. However, they are sensitive to noise and distortions in images. Region-based methods use some homogeneity creterion in order to gather pixels in homogeneous and contiguous regions [3,1]. Contrary to edge-based methods, region-based ones are time and memory costly, and their performances depend on the selection of the region seeds. Nevertheless, they provide better results even in presence of noise and distortions.

Most of authors having proposed multi-agent systems for image segmentation have opted for supervised approaches [2,9,10,11,7], where the number or the shape of the regions are beforehand fixed. So, these systems can be used only with images for that they were conceived. We propose through this work an unsupervised and distributed method, modeled as a multi-agent system, for image

C. San Martin and S.-W. Kim (Eds.): CIARP 2011, LNCS 7042, pp. 296–303, 2011.

segmentation. We do not make any assumption on the number of the regions in considered images. The principle of the system consists in placing randomly in the image a high number of autonomous and situated agents. Each one of them proceeds for a region growing from a given seed, selected according to a quality criterion. So, many agents can coexist within the same region. In this case, they must exchange some informations in order to better label shared pixels. A given image region is successively smoothed by several agents which are situated within. This allow good surface fitting, that allow in its turn accurate region extraction. Moreover, in our case agents are weakly coupled, allowing the implementation of the proposed system on massively parallel computers.

The reminder of the paper is organized as follows: in Section 2 we start by introducing how surfaces are modeled in range images. The reminder of the Section 2 is devoted to the proposed approach. We introduce in this section the principle of the multi-agent system, and agent behavior, modeled as an Alive method within the agent. Experimental results and comparison are introduced through Section 3, in which we show the parameter selection, and the obtained results. Finally, a conclusion summarizes our paper, and underlines perspective work.

2   Multi-agent Image Segmentation

2.1   Surface Modeling in Range Images

In this work we have used range images for experimental purpose. However, the proposed approach can be used with any type of images, including 2-D and 3-D images. In a range image, each pixel (x, y) memorizes the depth $d(x, y)$ spacing the range finder plane and the corresponding point of the scene. In order to define a homogeneity criterion allowing region growing, we use a new representation (d^*) of the row image, where $d^*(x, y)$ represents the tangent plane to the surface at (x, y). The tangent plane at (x, y) is obtained by the multiple regression method using the set of neighboring pixels situated within a 3×3 window centred at (x, y), and whose depths are close, according to a given threshold (Tr_h). The plane equation in a 3-D coordinate system may be expressed as follows:

$$z = ax + by + c \tag{1}$$

where $(a, b, -1)^T$ is a normal vector to the plane, and $|c|/\sqrt{a^2 + b^2 + 1}$ is the orthogonal distance between the plane and the coordinate origin. We consider that a pixel belongs to a planar region, given its plane equation, if the distance (h) between the respective planes is less than (Tr_h), and the angle (ϕ) between the respective normals is less than Tr_ϕ, where Tr_h and Tr_ϕ are respectively the distance and the angle thresholds. The quality of plane estimation $q(x, y)$ at (x, y) according to the regression model is also computed. The latter is used to accept or reject a region seed when an agent is initialized at a random position in the image.

2.2   Agent Behavior

A population of 1500 situated agents are randomly placed in the image. Each agent performs a region growing starting from its position. Contrary to classical region growing, where pixels are labeled as certainly homogeneous pixels, each pixel in our case is labeled as homogeneous pixel with certainly degree. This latter is expressed by the angle between the normal vector at the pixel in question, and the normal vector at the center of the region seed. The agent writes also its identifier at the current pixel. So, each homogenous pixel memorizes the identifier of the last agent having included the pixel into its homogeneous region.

At the creation of an agent, this latter examines its neighborhood in order to decides if it can be a region seed, from where it starts a region growing. For this, the agent calculates the estimation quality (q) according to the multiple regression model.

$$q = \frac{\sum_{i \in Seed} (\widehat{z_i} - \overline{z})^2}{\sum_{i \in Seed} (z_i - \overline{z})^2} \tag{2}$$

where $\widehat{z_i}$ and z_i are respectively the estimated and the measured range value of the pixel i in the seed.

If the estimation quality q is greater than a given threshold Q, the agent performs a region growing from the given seed, by iteratively including the homogeneous pixels at the current borders of the region in growth. At each homogeneous reached pixels which is not yet labeled (by any other agent), the agent writes its identifier, the angle ϕ between the normal vector to the surface at the current pixel and the normal vector to the surface at the seed center. However, if the reached pixel has been labeled before, the agent, lets called A, initiates a communication with the agent, lets called B, whom has last labeled the pixel. The agent A requests needed informations form the agent B in order decide if the label of the pixel must be set, or left as it is (Fig. 1). The information needed consists in the size of the region corresponding to the agent B.

The agent A makes decision according to several parameters which are : sizes of the two regions $(Size_A, Size_B)$ and the angles between respectively the normal surface vectors at the pixel and the region seeds (ϕ_A, ϕ_B). So, the label which it was (B) is set to (A) if :

$$\phi_A + \eta \times Size_A < \phi_B + \eta \times Size_B \tag{3}$$

with η a constant parameter set at the parameter selection (see Section 3.1). In this case the angle ϕ_B, memorized at the position of the pixel, is set to ϕ_A.

At each reached homogeneous pixel, the image is smoothed by replacing the parameters (a, b, c) of the plane at the pixel with those of the region seed center.

The method *Alive*, introduced below, represents the behavior of a given agent. The job on an agent can be interrupted by an information request. In this case the interrupted agent responds by sending the current region size via the *IncomingRequest* event. Then, it returns to continue with the *Alive* thread.

The agent environnement is formed by the Image array (d^*) and a second array called *Labels*, both of $ImageSize^2$ elements. Each element in *Labels* array

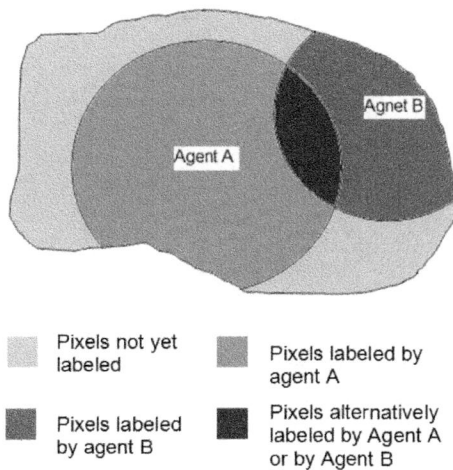

Fig. 1. Two agents growing the same region. Pixels are labeled A by Agent A, or B by Agent B according to region sizes and to angles between normal vectors.

memorizes an agent identifier (the last has labeled the pixel), and the angle between the normal vector at the pixel and the normal vector at the seed center. At any time an agent can receive a request for information, as an event. It then responds the sender by sending its current region size.

According to this behavior of agents, a given planar region is smoothed and labeled by several agents (belonging all to the same region). The way by which pixels are smoothed allows a smart image denoising, given the fact that pixels of the same homogeneous region are smoothed by considering the best region seed.

3   Experimentation

Most of authors having dealt with range images [6,8,3,1] have used a dedicated framework for performance evaluation of range image segmentation algorithms, proposed by Hoover et al. [5].

According to this framework a machine-generated segmentation (MS) is compared to an ideal segmentation, which represents a ground truth (GT). An extracted region can be classified as a correct detection, an over-segmentation, an under-segmentation, a missed region, or a noise region. A compare tool tolerance T; $50\% < T \leq 100\%$ is used to express the strictness of the classification. The 40 real images of ABW set are divided into two subsets: 10 training images, and 30 test images. Four methods, namely USF, WSU, UB and UE, cited in [5] are involved in the result comparison.

3.1   Parameter Selection

The set of training images with their ground truth segmentation is used according to a supervised learning approach, in order to select optimal values of

---

Algorithm 1. Method *Alive()*

---

repeat
    $(x_c, y_c) \leftarrow (random(ImageSize); random(ImageSize))$
until $SurfaceQualityAt(x_c, y_c) \geq Q$
$(x_{seed}, y_{seed}) \leftarrow (x_c, y_c)$
$RegionSize \leftarrow 0$
$PushOnStake(x_c, y_c)$
while Not(StakeEmpty) **do**
  $PopFromStake(x, y)$
  $\phi_A \leftarrow Calculate\phi(x, y)$
  if $Labels(x, y).Agent = 0$ **then**
    $Labels(x, y).Agent \leftarrow Self$
    $Labels(x, y).\phi \leftarrow \phi_A$
    $RegionSize \leftarrow RegionSize + 1$
  else
    $\phi_B \leftarrow Labels(x, y).\phi$
    $RegionSizeB \leftarrow RequestInfos(Labels(x, y).Agent)$
    if $\phi_A + \eta * RegionSize > \phi_B + \eta * RegionSize_B$ **then**
      $Labels(x, y).Agent \leftarrow Self$
      $Labels(x, y).\phi \leftarrow \phi_A$
      $RegionSize \leftarrow RegionSize + 1$
    end if
  end if
  $Image(x, y) \leftarrow Image(x_{seed}, y_{seed})$
  for $x_c \leftarrow x - 1\ To\ x + 1$ **do**
    for $y_c \leftarrow y - 1\ To\ y + 1$ **do**
      if $Labels(x_c, y_c).Agent \neq Self\ And\ Homogeneous(x_c, y_c)$ **then**
        $PushOnStake(x_c, y_c)$
      end if
    end for
  end for
end while

Algorithm 2. Event *IncomingRequest(AGENT Sender)*

$SendInfos(Sender, RegionSize)$

---

the involved parameters. Optimal parameter values correspond to the maximum of regions correctly detected, according to a ground truth (GT), with T set to 80% [5].

Our method, named MABIS for Multi-Agent-Based Image Segmentation uses four parameters, for which optimal values must be set. Namely they are Tr_ϕ, Tr_h, Q, and η (see Section 2). The value of η is simply set to $1/RSA$, where RSA is the average of sizes of all regions in the training set. For the reminder of parameters, 64 combinations namely $(Tr_\phi, Tr_h, Q) \in \{12°, 15°, 18°, 21°\} \times \{12, 16, 20, 24\} \times \{0.90, 0.95, 0.97, 0.99\}$, were run on the training set. Obtained optimal values of the parameters, which correspond to the maximum correct detection for the overall training set of range images, are as follows: $Tr_\phi = 18°$, $Tr_h = 16$, and $Q = 0.95$.

3.2 Experimental Results

We use an example of a range image to illustrate detailed results and to compare them to those obtained by other authors. Latter, we introduce the results of correct detection using the overall set of test images. The test image named abw.test.8 was considered, by several authors [5,6,8,3,1] as a typical image in order to show visual results of segmentation, and to compare the involved methods. Obtained results with this image are presented in Fig. 2. Fig. 2a shows the rendered range image. Fig. 2b, 2c 2d and 2e show image segmentation of respectively USF, WSU, UB and UE methods. Fig. 2f presents the segmentation result obtained by our method.

Table 1. Comparison results with abw.test.8 image for $T=80\%$

Method	GT region	Correct detection	Over-segmentation	Under-segmentation	Missed	Noise
USF	21	17	0	0	4	3
WSU	21	12	1	1	6	4
UB	21	16	2	0	3	6
UE	21	18	1	0	2	2
MABIS	21	17	1	0	1	1

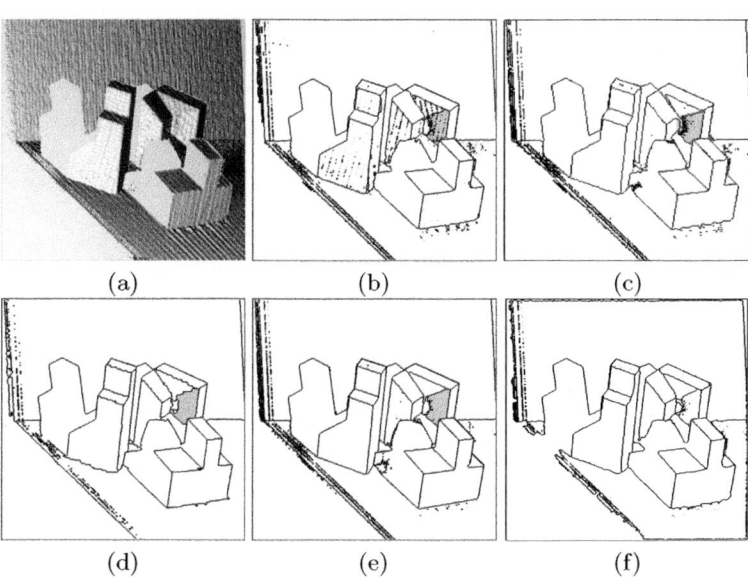

(a)   (b)   (c)

(d)   (e)   (f)

Fig. 2. Segmentation results of abw.test.8 image. (a) Rendered Range image; (b) USF result; (c) WSU result; (d) UB result; (e) UE result; (f) MABIS result.

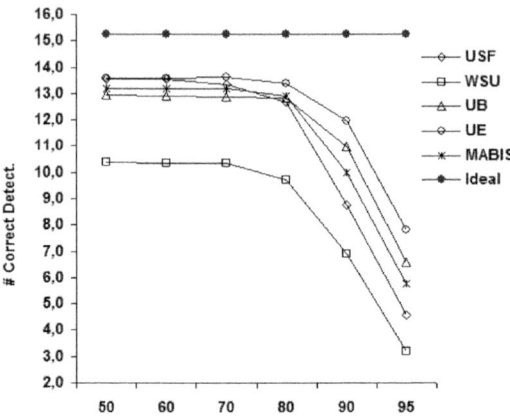

Fig. 3. Average results of correctly detected regions of all methods, according to the compare tool tolerance T ; $0.5 < T \leq 1.0$

We can see in Table 1 that the number of correct detected regions is equivalent to those obtained with the UE and USF algorithms, that scored better than UB and WSU. Our results for all incorrect detected regions are better than those corresponding to all the involved algorithms.

For the overall set of test images, Fig. 3 shows the average numbers of correctly detected regions, according to the compare tool tolerance T; $T \in \{51\%,$ $60\%, 70\%, 80\%, 90\%, 95\%\}$. Results show that the number of correctly detected regions by our method is in average equivalent to UE and USF algorithms, and better than those of UB and WSU ones. It scored higher than WSU for all the values of the compare tool tolerance T. It scored higher than USF for $T > 70\%$, and better than UB for $T < 90\%$.

4   Conclusion

In this paper we have presented an unsupervised and distributed approach for image segmentation, with application to range images. The distributed entities were modeled as autonomous and situated agents. Each agent performs region growing and image smoothing starting from a region seed, selected according to a quality criterion. Agents can share pixels, and thus must exchange information in order to better label pixels. Several tests and comparisons were performed using real images. Obtained experimental results has allowed to validate the proposed approach which provides an efficient region-based range image segmentation. In futur work, we plan to test the approach with other types of images, including range images containing curved objects, 2D grey-level, and color images.

References

1. Bab Hadiashar, A., Gheissari, N.: Range image segmentation using surface selection criterion. IEEE Transactions on Image Processing 15(7), 2006–2018 (2006)
2. Ballet, P., Rodin, V., Tisseau, J.: Edge detection using a multiagent system. In: 10th Scandinavian Conference on Image Analysis, Lapeenranta, Finland, pp. 621–626 (1997)
3. Ding, Y., Ping, X., Hu, M., Wang, D.: Range image segmentation based on randomized hough transform. Pattern Recognition Letters 26(13), 2033–2041 (2005)
4. Fan, T.J., Medioni, G.G., Nevatia, R.: Segmented description of 3-D surfaces. IEEE Journal of Robotics and Automation 3(6), 527–538 (1987)
5. Hoover, A., Jean-Baptiste, G., Jiang, X., Flynn, P.J., Bunke, H., Goldgof, D.B., Bowyer, K.W., Eggert, D.W., Fitzgibbon, A.W., Fisher, R.B.: An experimental comparison of range image segmentation algorithms. IEEE Transactions on Pattern Analysis and Machine Intelligence 18(7), 673–689 (1996)
6. Jiang, X., Bunke, H.: Edge detection in range images based on Scan Line approximation. Computer Vision and Image Understanding 73(2), 183–199 (1999)
7. Jones, J., Saeed, M.: Image enhancement, an emergent pattern formation approach via decentralised multi-agent systems. Multiagent and Grid Systems Journal (ISO Press) Special Issue on Nature inspired systems for parallel, asynchronous and decentralised environments 3(1), 105–140 (2007)
8. Li, S., Zhao, D.: Gradient-based polyhedral segmentation for range images. Pattern Recognition Letters 24(12), 2069–2077 (2003)
9. Liu, J., Tang, Y.Y.: Adaptive image segmentation with distributed behavior-based agents. IEEE Transactions on Pattern Analysis and Machine Intelligence 21(6), 544–551 (1999)
10. Richard, N., Dojat, M., Garbay, C.: Automated segmentation of human brain MR images using a multi-agent approach. Artificial Intelligence in Medicine 30(2), 153–176 (2004)
11. Rodin, V., Benzinou, A., Guillaud, A., Ballet, P., Harrouet, F., Tisseau, J., Le Bihan, J.: An immune oriented multi-agent system for biological image processing. Pattern Recognition 37(4), 631–645 (2004)

Embedded Feature Selection for Support Vector Machines: State-of-the-Art and Future Challenges

Sebastián Maldonado[1] and Richard Weber[2]

[1] Universidad de los Andes, Faculty of Engineering and Applied Sciences
Av. San Carlos de Apoquindo 2200, Las Condes, Santiago, Chile
[2] Department of Industrial Engineering, University of Chile

Abstract. Recently, databases have incremented their size in all areas of knowledge, considering both the number of instances and attributes. Current data sets may handle hundreds of thousands of variables with a high level of redundancy and/or irrelevancy. This amount of data may cause several problems to many data mining algorithms in terms of performance and scalability. In this work we present the state-of-the-art the for embedded feature selection using the classification method Support Vector Machine (SVM), presenting two additional works that can handle the new challenges in this area, such as simultaneous feature and model selection and highly imbalanced binary classification. We compare our approaches with other state-of-the-art algorithms to demonstrate their effectiveness and efficiency.

Keywords: Embedded methods, Feature selection, SVM.

1 Introduction

Feature selection is an important topic in pattern recognition, especially in high-dimensional applications. A low-dimensional representation of the data reduces the risk of *overfitting* [3,5], improving model generalization. Feature selection is a combinatorial problem in the number of original features [3], and finding the optimal subset of variables is considered NP-hard.

Support Vector Machine (SVM) [10] is an effective classification method with significant advantages such as the absence of local minima, an adequate generalization to new objects, and a representation that depends on few parameters [5,10]. This method, however, does not directly determine the importance of the features used [5,6].

Several feature selection approaches for SVM have been proposed in the literature. An excellent review has been published by Guyon et al. [3]. Since then, several trends have arisen in concordance with the new challenges: First, given the increasing size of data sets, data mining methods are required to be more efficient in terms of training time and scalability. Data sets with millions of instances and a high level of irrelevant variables are more and more common for

C. San Martin and S.-W. Kim (Eds.): CIARP 2011, LNCS 7042, pp. 304–311, 2011.
© Springer-Verlag Berlin Heidelberg 2011

new data mining applications, such as e. g. social network mining, and pattern recognition methods must adapt to the new challenges. In the same direction, model selection, meaning the process of fitting adjustable parameters to build the model, and feature selection are usually considered as different tasks. The advantages of developing a model selection framework that simultaneously performs feature selection and parameter fitting are the reduction of computational effort and avoiding the risk of overfitting [4]. Finally, several pattern recognition tasks involve classification with highly imbalanced data sets, and feature selection methods should be adapted to this challenge. In this paper we present two embedded methods for feature selection using SVM, comparing both approaches with well-known feature selection strategies and analyzing them in terms of the three challenges presented.

This paper is structured as follows. In Section 2 we provide a general overview of the different feature selection approaches. Section 3 introduces SVM for classification. Recent developments for embedded feature selection using SVM are reviewed in Section 4, providing experimental results using two real-world data sets. A summary of this paper can be found in Section 5, where we provide its main conclusions and address future challenges.

2   Feature Selection

Three main directions have been developed for feature selection: filter, wrapper, and embedded methods [3]. The first scheme (*filter methods*) uses statistical properties of the features to filter out irrelevant ones. This is usually done before applying any classification algorithm. Common filter methods are the Fisher Criterion Score, which is based on Fisher's Linear Discriminant Analysis (LDA), or entropy measures such as Information Gain [3]. This strategy has advantages, such as its simplicity, scalability and a reduced computational effort; but it ignores the interactions between the variables and the relationship between them and the classification algorithm.

Wrapper methods are computationally demanding, but generally provide more accurate results than filter methods. A wrapper algorithm explores the whole feature space to score feature subsets according to their predictive power. Since the exhaustive search for an optimal subset of features grows exponentially with the number of original variables, heuristic approaches have been suggested [3]. Commonly used wrapper strategies are the Sequential forward selection (SFS) and the Sequential backward elimination (SBE) [3]. In the first case, each candidate variable is included into the current set, and the resulting is evaluated. The variable whose inclusion resulted in the best evaluation is inserted in the current set. Subsequently, SBE starts with the variable set that consists of all the candidate variables, and the variable whose exclusion resulted in the best evaluation is considered to be eliminated from the current set. Advantages of wrapper methods include the interaction between subset of variables and the model. The main disadvantage is the high computational cost and the risk of overfitting [3]. Greedy strategies may also get stuck in a local optimum, leading to an unsatisfactory subset of features. To overcome this problem, several random search strategies have been proposed [3].

Embedded methods attempt to find an optimal subset of features in the process of model building. These methods depend directly on the nature of the classification method used. In general, embedded methods present important advantages in terms of variable and model interaction, capturing accurately the dependencies between variables, being computationally less demanding than wrapper methods. [3]. However, these techniques are conceptually more complex, and modifications to the classification algorithm may lead to a poor performance. In Section 4 several embedded approaches for SVM will be presented.

3   Support Vector Machine for Binary Classification

This section introduces SVM for binary classification as developed by Vapnik [10]. Given training vectors $\mathbf{x}_i \in \Re^n$, $i = 1, ..., m$ and a vector of labels $\mathbf{y} \in \Re^m$, $y_i \in \{-1, +1\}$, SVM provides the optimal hyperplane $f(\mathbf{x}) = \mathbf{w}^T \cdot \mathbf{x} + b$ to separate the training classes. For a linearly separable problem, this hyperplane maximizes the sum of the distances to the closest positive and negative training instances, which is called *margin*. In order to maximize this margin, we need to classify correctly the vectors $\mathbf{x}_i$ of the training set into two different classes y_i, using the smallest norm of coefficients $\mathbf{w}$ [10]. For a non-linear classifier, SVM maps the data points into a higher dimensional space $\mathcal{H}$, where a separating hyperplane with maximal margin is constructed. The dual formulation of SVM can be stated as follows:

$$\underset{\boldsymbol{\alpha}}{\text{Max}} \quad \sum_{i=1}^{m} \alpha_i - \frac{1}{2} \sum_{i,s=1}^{m} \alpha_i \alpha_s y_i y_s K(\mathbf{x}_i, \mathbf{x}_s) \tag{1}$$

subject to

$$\sum_{i=1}^{m} \alpha_i y_i = 0$$

$$0 \leq \alpha_i \leq C \qquad i = 1, ..., m.$$

The mapping is performed by a kernel function $K(\mathbf{x}, \mathbf{y})$ which defines an inner product in $\mathcal{H}$. From a variety of available kernel functions, the polynomial and the Gaussian kernel are chosen in many applications [4,5]:

1. Polynomial function: $K(\mathbf{x}_i, \mathbf{x}_s) = (\mathbf{x}_i \cdot \mathbf{x}_s + 1)^d$, where $d \in \mathbb{N}$ is the degree of the polynomial.
2. Radial basis function: $K(\mathbf{x}_i, \mathbf{x}_s) = \exp\left(-\frac{||\mathbf{x}_i - \mathbf{x}_s||^2}{2\rho^2}\right)$, where $\rho > 0$ is the parameter controlling the width of the kernel.

The selection of the best Kernel function is still a matter of research [6]. Empirically, we have achieved best classification performance with the Gaussian Kernel [5,6].

4   Embedded Feature Selection for SVM

According to the emerging challenges related to feature selection as identified in the introduction, we present recently developed algorithms and show how they can contribute to the future trends. Section 4.1 presents state-of-the-art embedded methods for SVM. Section 4.2 presents our previously developed approaches, which address the mentioned trends. Finally, Section 4.3 presents numerical results for two well-known benchmark data sets.

4.1   Related Work and Analysis

There are different strategies for embedded feature selection. First, feature selection can be seen as an optimization problem. For example, the methods presented in Neumann et al. [7] add an extra term that penalizes the cardinality of the selected feature subset to the standard cost function of SVM. By optimizing this modified cost function features are selected simultaneously to model construction. Another embedded approach is the Feature Selection ConcaVe (FSV) [1], based on the minimization of the "zero norm" : $\|\mathbf{w}\|_0 = |\{i : w_i \neq 0\}|$. Note that $\|\cdot\|_0$ is not a norm because the triangle inequality does not hold [1], unlike l_p-norms with $p > 0$. Since l_0-"norm" is non-smooth, it was approximated by a concave function:

$$\|\mathbf{w}\|_0 \approx \mathbf{e}^T(\mathbf{e} - \exp(-\beta|\mathbf{w}|)) \tag{2}$$

with an approximation parameter $\beta \in \Re_+$ and $\mathbf{e} = (1, ..., 1)^{\mathbf{T}}$. The problem is finally solved by using an iterative method called Successive Linearization Algorithm (SLA) for FSV [1]. Weston et al. [12] proposed an alternative approach for zero-"norm" minimization (l_0-SVM) by iteratively scaling the variables, multiplying them by the absolute value of the weight vector $\mathbf{w}$. Perkins et al. consider simultaneously the three objectives goodness-of-fit, a regularization parameter for structural risk minimization, and feature penalization, considering a secuencial forward selection strategy [8]. An important drawback of these methods is that they are limited to linear classification functions [3,5].

Several embedded approaches consider backward feature elimination in order to establish a ranking of features, using SVM-based contribution measures to evaluate their relevance. One popular method is known as Recursive Feature Elimination (SVM-RFE) [4]. The goal of this approach is to find a subset of size r among n variables ($r < n$) which maximizes the classifier's performance. The feature to be removed in each iteration is the one whose removal minimizes the variation of $W^2(\boldsymbol{\alpha})$:

$$W^2(\boldsymbol{\alpha}) = \sum_{i,s=1}^{m} \alpha_i \alpha_s y_i y_s K(\mathbf{x}_i, \mathbf{x}_s) \tag{3}$$

The scalar $W^2(\boldsymbol{\alpha})$ is a measure of the model's predictive ability and is inversely proportional to the margin. Features are eliminated applying the following procedure:

1. Given a solution α, for each feature p calculate:

$$W_{(-p)}^2(\alpha) = \sum_{i,s=1}^{m} \alpha_i \alpha_s y_i y_s K(x_i^{(-p)}, x_s^{(-p)}) \qquad (4)$$

where $x_i^{(-p)}$ represents the training object i with feature p removed.

2. Eliminate the feature with smallest value of $|W^2(\alpha) - W_{(-p)}^2(\alpha)|$.

Another ranking method that allows kernel functions was proposed by Rako-tomamonjy [9], which considers a *leave-one-out* error bound for SVM, the *radius margin bound*[10] $LOO \leq 4R^2||w||^2$, where R denotes the radius of the smallest sphere that contains the training data. This bound is also used in Weston et al. [11] through the *scaling factors* strategy. Feature selection is performed by scaling the input parameters by a vector $\sigma \in [0,1]^n$. Large values of σ_j indicate more useful features. The problem consists in choosing the best kernel of the form:

$$K_\sigma(x_i, x_s) \equiv K(\sigma * x_i, \sigma * x_s) \qquad (5)$$

where $*$ is the component-wise multiplication operator. the method presented by Weston et al. considers the gradient descent algorithm for updating σ. Canu and Grandvalet [2] propose to limit the use of the attributes by constraining the scaling factors using a parameter σ_0, which controls the norm of σ.

4.2   Proposed Methods for Embedded Feature Selection

We consider two approaches that attempt to perform feature selection and model selection (hyperparameter setting) in the same algorithm. The main idea is to define a procedure that simultaneously defines both the classifier and the se-lected features, instead of the standard two-step methodology that first selects features and then constructs the classifier via model selection for a given subset of variables. The first approach is a ranking method called Holdout SVM (HO-SVM) [5], which defines a new contribution measure based on the number of errors in a validation subset. Then, a backward feature elimination procedure is performed, pruning those features whose removal keeps this contribution mea-sure small, until an explicit stopping criterion is reached: when the elimination of variables lead to a degradation of the predictive performance, i.e. the number of errors in the validation set grows by removing any feature. Algorithm 1 formally presents this approach.

   The second approach, called Kernel-Penalized SVM (KP-SVM) [6], uses the scaling factors principle to penalize the use of features in the dual formulation of SVM (1). This penalization is performed by considering an additional term that penalizes the zero norm of the scaling factors, in a similar way as in (2). The respective optimization procedure is done by updating the scaling factors using a variation of the gradient descent approach, as presented in Algorithm 2.

Algorithm 1. HO-SVM Algorithm for Feature Selection

---

1. Initial Model selection: set C and kernel parameter ρ, $\boldsymbol{\sigma} = (1, ..., 1)$
2. **repeat**
   (a) Random split of the training data in subsets $TRAIN$ and VAL
   (b) SVM Training (Formulation (1))using $TRAIN$ for a given subset of features $\boldsymbol{\sigma}$, kernel of the form presented in (5).
   (c) **for** each feature p with $\sigma_p = 1$, **do** determine $E_{(-p)}(\boldsymbol{\alpha}, \boldsymbol{\sigma})$, the number of classification errors when feature p is removed.
   (d) remove feature j with the smallest value of $E_{(-p)}(\boldsymbol{\alpha}, \boldsymbol{\sigma})$:

$$E_{(-p)}(\boldsymbol{\alpha}, \boldsymbol{\sigma}) = \sum_{l \in VAL} \left| y_l^v - sign \left(\sum_{i \in TRAIN} \alpha_i y_i K_{\boldsymbol{\sigma}}(\mathbf{x}_i^{(-p)}, \mathbf{x}_l^{v(-p)}) + b \right) \right| \quad (6)$$

   where VAL is the Validation subset and $\mathbf{x}_l^v$ and y_l^v are the objects and labels of this subset, respectively. $\mathbf{x}_i^{(-p)}$ ($\mathbf{x}_l^{v(-p)}$) means training object i (validation object l) with feature p removed.
3. **until** the smallest value of $E_{(-p)}(\boldsymbol{\alpha}, \boldsymbol{\sigma})$ is greater than $E(\boldsymbol{\alpha}, \boldsymbol{\sigma})$, which is the number of errors in the Validation subset using all features as indicated by the current vector $\boldsymbol{\sigma}$, i.e. without removing any further feature.

Algorithm 2. Kernel Width Updating and Feature Elimination

---

1. Initial Model selection: set C and kernel parameter $\boldsymbol{\sigma} = \rho \cdot \mathbf{e}$;
2. cont=true; t=0;
3. **while**(cont==true) **do**
4.   train SVM (Formulation (1), kernel of the form presented in (5)) for a given $\boldsymbol{\sigma}$;
5. $\boldsymbol{\sigma}^{t+1} = \boldsymbol{\sigma}^t - \gamma \Delta F(\boldsymbol{\sigma}^t)$;
   where γ is the gradient descent parameter. For a given feature j, the gradient for kernel updating $\Delta_j F(\boldsymbol{\sigma})$ is:

$$\Delta_j F(\boldsymbol{\sigma}) = \sum_{i,s=1}^{m} \sigma_j (x_{i,j} - x_{s,j})^2 \alpha_i \alpha_s y_i y_s K(\mathbf{x}_i, \mathbf{x}_s, \boldsymbol{\sigma}) + C_2 \beta exp(-\beta \sigma_j) \quad (7)$$

6.   **for all** $(\sigma_j^{t+1} < \epsilon)$ **do**
7. $\sigma_j^{t+1} = 0$;
8.   **end for**
   where ϵ is the threshold for feature selection: when a kernel variable σ_j in the iteration $t+1$ is below a threshold ϵ, we consider this feature irrelevant, and we eliminate it by setting $\sigma_j = 0$.
9.   **if** $(\boldsymbol{\sigma}^{t+1} == \boldsymbol{\sigma}^t)$ **then**
10.   cont=false;
11.   **end if**
12. $t = t + 1$;
13. **end while**;

4.3   Experimental Results

We applied the proposed approaches for feature selection and the alternative embedded methods FSV and SVM-RFE on two well-known benchmark data sets: A real-world data set from the UCI data repository, and a DNA microarray data set. Wisconsin Breast Cancer data set (WBC) contains 569 observations described by 30 continuous features, while Colorectal Microarray data set (CRMA) contains the expression of the 2000 genes with highest minimal intensity across 62 tissues. Results in terms of mean classification accuracy over 100 realizations using the test subset are shown in Table 1, where the first two rows consider the stopping criterion for HO-SVM and the latter two rows the stopping criterion for KP-SVM. From this table we obtain that the proposed approaches outperform the alternative methods in terms of classification performance for a given number of selected features, while KP-SVM is particularly effective for high-dimensional data sets, such as CRMA, obtaining significantly better results for a small number of attributes. For the method KP-SVM, convergence is achieved in 25 iterations for WBC and 75 iterations for CRMA. Therefore, this method is more efficient than backward approaches, since the number of iterations to reach convergence is smaller than the number of original variables.

Table 1. Comparison of four embedded methods for SVM

	n	FSV	RFE-SVM	HO-SVM	KP-SVM
WBC	12	94.70±1.3	95.47±1.1	**97.69±0.9**	*
CRMA	100	91.17±6.7	95.61±5.4	**96.36±5.3**	*
WBC	15	95.23±1.1	95.25±1.0	*	**97.55±0.9**
CRMA	20	92.03±7.7	92.52±7.2	*	**96.57±5.6**

5   Conclusions and Future Challenges

In this paper we present two embedded methods for feature selection using SVM. A comparison with other embedded techniques shows the advantages of our approach in terms of effectiveness and dimensionality reduction. We also present three different challenges regarding the future of feature selection. The first trend is the importance of considering the process of model selection as a whole, including both feature selection and hyperparameter setting [4]. Several embedded methods attempt to establish a ranking of features from a training set, being necessary a second step that finally leads to the intended model, defining the adequate number of ranked variables. This second step, usually done via cross-validation, is both time consuming and may lead to overfitting, especially when the feature ranking is done using non-linear functions. Both methods presented, HO-SVM and KP-SVM, performs the model selection as a whole, determining the selected number of features in the same algorithm. Alternative approaches, such as FSV and SVM-RFE, require the mentioned additional step, and can be compared with the proposed approaches only using their stopping criterion.

The second presented trend is the increasing size of the data sets, making too complex methods less tractable for large scale pattern recognition. The main benefit of KP-SVM is that we can reach convergence in a small number of iterations, even if the number of variables is very high, making it computationally less intensive. An additional advantage is that ranking methods based on greedy search present difficulties when data sets are high dimensional.

The third and last presented trend is the extension to highly imbalanced data sets, a very relevant topic in pattern recognition. The proposed approaches can be easily adapted to this task. For example, HO-SVM may consider a cost function $C_{(-p)}(\alpha, \sigma)$ instead of the number of errors, establishing asymmetric costs for the Type I and Type II errors. For KP-SVM, the proposed formulation could consider different costs of errors by penalizing the vector ξ differently, depending on the label of the instance i. As future work, we consider the implementation of these models to compensate for the undesired effects caused by imbalanced data sets in model construction; an issue which occurs for example in the domains of Spam filtering, microarray analysis and fraud detection.

Acknowledgments. Support from the Chilean "Instituto Sistemas Complejos de Ingeniería" (ICM: P-05-004-F, CONICYT: FB016) is greatly acknowledged (www.sistemasdeingenieria.cl).

References

1. Bradley, P., Mangasarian, O.: Feature selection vía concave minimization and support vector machines. In: Int. Conference on Machine Learning, pp. 82–90 (1998)
2. Canu, S., Grandvalet, Y.: Adaptive scaling for feature selection in SVMs. In: Advances in NIPS, vol. 15, pp. 553–560. MIT Press, Cambridge (2002)
3. Guyon, I., Gunn, S., Nikravesh, M., Zadeh, L.A.: Feature extraction, foundations and applications. Springer, Berlin (2006)
4. Guyon, I., Saffari, A., Dror, G., Cawley, G.: Model selection: Beyond the Bayesian frequentist divide. JMLR 11, 61–87 (2009)
5. Maldonado, S., Weber, R.: A wrapper method for feature selection using Support Vector Machines. Information Sciences 179(13), 2208–2217 (2009)
6. Maldonado, S., Weber, R., Basak, J.: Kernel-Penalized SVM for Feature Selection. Information Sciences 181(1), 115–128 (2011)
7. Neumann, J., Schnörr, C., Steidl, G.: Combined SVM-Based Feature Selection and Classification. Machine Learning 61(1-3), 129–150 (2005)
8. Perkins, S., Lacker, K., Theiler, J.: Grafting: Fast incremental feature selection by gradient descent in function space. JMLR 3, 1333–1356 (2003)
9. Rakotomamonjy, A.: Variable Selection Using SVM-based Criteria. JMLR 3, 1357–1370 (2003)
10. Vapnik, V.: Statistical Learning Theory. John Wiley and Sons, New York (1998)
11. Weston, J., Mukherjee, S., Chapelle, O., Ponntil, M., Poggio, T., Vapnik, V.: Feature selection for SVMs. In: Advances in NIPS, vol. 13. MIT Press, Cambridge (2001)
12. Weston, J., Elisseeff, A., Schölkopf, B., Tipping, M.: The use of zero-norm with linear models and kernel methods. JMLR 3, 1439–1461 (2003)

An Efficient Approach to Intensity Inhomogeneity Compensation Using c-Means Clustering Models*

László Szilágyi, David Iclănzan, Lehel Crăciun, and Sándor Miklós Szilágyi

Sapientia - Hungarian Science University of Transylvania,
Faculty of Technical and Human Science, Tîrgu-Mureş, Romania
lalo@ms.sapientia.ro

Abstract. Intensity inhomogeneity or intensity non-uniformity (INU) is an undesired phenomenon that represents the main obstacle for magnetic resonance (MR) image segmentation and registration methods. Various techniques have been proposed to eliminate or compensate the INU, most of which are embedded into clustering algorithms, and they generally have difficulties when INU reaches high amplitudes. This study reformulates the design of c-means clustering based INU compensation techniques by identifying and separating those globally working computationally costly operations that can be applied to gray intensity levels instead of individual pixels. The theoretical assumptions are demonstrated using the fuzzy c-means algorithm, but the proposed modification is compatible with a various range of c-means clustering based techniques. Experiments using synthetic phantoms and real MR images indicate that the proposed approach produces practically the same segmentation accuracy as the conventional formulation, but 20-30 times faster.

Keywords: image segmentation, magnetic resonance imaging, intensity inhomogeneity, c-means clustering, histogram.

1 Introduction

Magnetic resonance imaging (MRI) is popular due to its high resolution and good contrast. However, the automatic segmentation of such images is not trivial because of the noise that may be present. Intensity inhomogeneity or intensity non-uniformity (INU) represents an undesired phenomenon in MRI, manifested as a slowly varying bias field with possibly high magnitude, making pixels belonging to the same tissue be observed with different intensities. INU is the main obstacle for intensity based segmentation methods: several efficient and accurate removal techniques exist for high frequency noise [13], but the segmentation in the presence of inhomogeneities represents a significant computational load [16].

Inhomogeneities in magnetic resonance (MR) images are usually categorized by their origin. Device related INU artifacts can be efficiently compensated via

---

* This research was funded by CNCSIS UEFISCDI, project no. PD_667, under contract no. 28/05.08.2010.

C. San Martin and S.-W. Kim (Eds.): CIARP 2011, LNCS 7042, pp. 312–319, 2011.

calibration methods based on prior information obtained by using a uniform phantom. Alternately, INU artifacts related to the shape, position, structure and orientation of the patient, are much more difficult to handle [16]. Several retrospective INU compensation approaches have been reported, which include homomorphic filtering [5], polynomial or B-spline surface fitting [14], segmentation based techniques via maximum likelihood estimation [9], Markov random fields [17], fuzzy c-means clustering [1,8,10], or nonparametric estimation [3]. Further INU compensation procedures based on histogram involve high-frequency maximization [11], information maximization [15], or histogram matching [12]. The most complete review of INU compensation techniques can be found in [16].

Probably the most widely used compensation tool is the fuzzy c-means (FCM) algorithm [2], having several adaptations for INU estimation and being combined with a series of further techniques. Pham and Prince introduced a modified objective function producing bias field estimation and containing extra terms that force INU vary smoothly [8]. Liew and Hong created a log bias field estimation technique that models the INU with smoothing B-spline surfaces [6]. Ahmed et al. established a regularization operator that allowed the labeling of a pixel to be influenced by its immediate neighbors [1]. This approach reduced some of the complexity of its ancestors, but the zero gradient condition that was used for bias field estimation leads to several misclassifications [10].

The compensation of INU artifacts is a computationally costly problem, which demands highly efficient design and implementation. This paper demonstrates that the INU compensation on a single-channel intensity image via c-means clustering can be performed much more efficiently than it was reported in previous formulations. The operations performed during the iterations of the alternating optimization (AO) scheme are separated into globally working ones and locally applied ones, and their execution is optimized according to their necessities: global criteria are applied to gray intensities instead of individual pixels, which makes a drastic reduction of the computational load. Using this novel formulation, and applying it to improved clustering models (e.g. [7,13]) combined with multi-stage INU compensation, can make c-means clustering more attractive on the combined scales of accuracy and efficiency. Improving the accuracy is not in the scope of this paper. Our main goal is to reduce the execution time without damaging the accuracy.

2   Background Works

The conventional FCM algorithm optimally partitions a set of object data into a previously set number of c clusters based on the iterative minimization of a quadratic objective function. When applied to segment gray-scale images, FCM clusters the intensity value of pixels x_k, $k = 1 \ldots n$. The objective function

$$J_{\mathrm{FCM}} = \sum_{i=1}^{c} \sum_{k=1}^{n} u_{ik}^{m} (x_k - v_i)^2 \ , \tag{1}$$

is optimized under the so-called probability constraint $\sum_{i=1}^{c} u_{ik} = 1$, $k = 1 \ldots n$, where $u_{ik} \in [0,1]$ is the fuzzy membership function indicating the degree to which pixel k is assigned to cluster i, v_i represents the centroid or prototype of the i-th cluster, and $m > 1$ is the fuzzy exponent. The minimization of the cost function is reached by alternately applying the optimization of J_{FCM} over $\{u_{ik}\}$, $i = 1 \ldots c$, $k = 1 \ldots n$ with v_i fixed, and the optimization of J_{FCM} over $\{v_i\}$, $i = 1 \ldots c$, with u_{ik} fixed [2].

In real data processing, the observed data $\{y_k\}$ differs from the actual one $\{x_k\}$. In this paper we only assume to handle the INU artifacts, by compensating during segmentation. Literature recommends three different data variation models for intensity inhomogeneity. If we consider the INU as a bias field, for any pixel k, we will have $y_k = x_k + b_k$, where b_k represents the bias value at pixel k [1,8,10]. In case of gain field modeling [13], there will be a gain value g_k for each pixel k, such that $y_k = g_k x_k$. Finally, the so-called log bias approach in fact is a gain field estimation reduced to bias computation using the logarithmic formula $\log y_k = \log g_k + \log x_k$ [6]. Regardless of the used compensation model, the variation of the intensity between neighbor pixels has to be slow. The zero gradient conditions derived from FCM's objective function does not fulfil this demand. Consequently, a smoothing operation is necessary to assure this slow variation of the estimated bias or gain field.

In the INU compensation problem, the conventional FCM based approach optimizes the objective function:

$$J_{\text{FCM}-b} = \sum_{i=1}^{c} \sum_{k=1}^{n} u_{ik}^m (y_k - b_k - v_i)^2 \ . \tag{2}$$

Zero gradient conditions and Lagrange multipliers lead to the following optimization formulas. The fuzzy partition is obtained as:

$$u_{ik}^{\star} = \frac{(y_k - b_k - v_i)^{-2/(m-1)}}{\sum_{j=1}^{c}(y_k - b_k - v_j)^{-2/(m-1)}} \qquad \forall k = 1 \ldots n, \quad \forall i = 1 \ldots c \ . \tag{3}$$

Cluster prototypes are updated as:

$$v_i^{\star} = \frac{\sum_{k=1}^{n} u_{ik}^m (y_k - b_k)}{\sum_{k=1}^{n} u_{ik}^m} \qquad \forall i = 1 \ldots c \ . \tag{4}$$

The bias field for the pixel x_k is estimated as:

$$b_k^{\star} = y_k - \frac{\sum_{i=1}^{c} u_{ik}^m v_i}{\sum_{i=1}^{c} u_{ik}^m} \qquad \forall k = 1 \ldots n \ . \tag{5}$$

3   Methodology

When a clustering algorithm is required to perform quickly on a large set of input data, the aggregation of similar input values is an easily implementable choice. It is well known, that the FCM algorithm in image processing belongs to the segmentation methods that work with global information. This means that pixels will be assigned to clusters based on their own intensity (color), without regard to their position in the image. Consequently, pixels with same intensity will belong to the same clusters with the same membership degrees. Based on this assumption, it is obvious that the FCM-based segmentation of single-channel intensity image can be performed based on the histogram, by clustering the colors instead of individual pixels [13].

Table 1. The proposed accelerated algorithm

---

01 $t = 0$

02 Set initial bias field $b_k^{(t=0)} = 0$, $\forall k = 1 \ldots n$

03 Choose initial cluster prototypes $v_i^{(t=0)}$

04 Repeat

05     $t \leftarrow t + 1$

06   Compute new histogram $h_l^{(t)}$, $\forall l \in \Omega^{(t)}$

07   Compute new fuzzy partition $u_{il}^{(t)}$, $\forall i = 1 \ldots c$ and $\forall l \in \Omega^{(t)}$, using Eq. (7)

08   Compute new cluster prototypes $v_i^{(t)}$, $\forall i = 1 \ldots c$, using Eq. (8)

09   Compute auxiliary lookup table values $q_l^{(t)}$, $\forall l \in \Omega^{(t)}$, using Eq. (9)

10   Compute new estimated bias field $b_k^{(t)}$, $\forall k = 1 \ldots n$, using Eq. (10)

11   Smoothen the estimated bias field using the chosen filter

12 Until convergence occurs, that is $\sum_{i=1}^{c} |v_i^{(t)} - v_i^{(t-1)}| < \varepsilon$

13 Assign pixel k ($k = 1 \ldots n$) to the cluster with index $\arg \max_i \{u_{i,y_k - b_k}, i = 1 \ldots c\}$

When INU artifacts are present, local conditions must be involved into the compensation process, in order to assure the smooth variation of the estimated inhomogeneity. Consequently, pixels of similar or same observed intensity cannot be collected and handled together. In the followings, we will demonstrate that most operations of the INU compensation algorithm can be executed using global information, which will lead to a drastic reduction of the computational load.

Let us consider the cost function of the bias estimation approach, given in Eq. (2). The input image contains pixels in order of 10^4-10^5, and intensity levels in order of 10^2-10^3. In every iteration of the AO algorithm, we need to aggregate those pixels, which bear the same intensity after having the current estimated bias subtracted. That is why, we investigate the distribution of the composite variable $y_k - b_k$, which varies from iteration to iteration. Let us denote by $h_l^{(t)}$ the number of pixels for which the compensated intensity in iteration t satisfies $y_k - b_k = l$. Obviously, if we denote by $\Omega^{(t)}$ the range of possible values of $y_k - b_k$, we will have $\sum_{l \in \Omega^{(t)}} h_l^{(t)} = n$. As the matter of fact, $h_l^{(t)}$ with $l \in \Omega^{(t)}$ represents the intensity histogram of the compensated image in iteration t.

Using the above notations, we can aggregate equal values of $y_k - b_k$ in the cost function, which in iteration t will become:

$$J_{\text{FCM-qb}} = \sum_{i=1}^{c} \sum_{l \in \Omega^{(t)}} h_l^{(t)} u_{il}^m (l - v_i)^2 \ . \tag{6}$$

Zero gradient conditions and Lagrange multipliers lead to the following optimization formulas. Fuzzy memberships are established as

$$u_{il}^{\star} = \frac{(l - v_i)^{-2/(m-1)}}{\sum_{j=1}^{c} (l - v_j)^{-2/(m-1)}} \qquad \forall l \in \Omega^{(t)} \quad \forall i = 1 \ldots c \ . \tag{7}$$

One evaluation of the above formula computes the fuzzy labels of $h_l^{(t)}$ pixels at the same time. Cluster prototypes are updated as:

$$v_i^{\star} = \frac{\sum_{l \in \Omega^{(t)}} h_l^{(t)} u_{il}^m l}{\sum_{l \in \Omega^{(t)}} h_l^{(t)} u_{il}^m} \qquad \forall i = 1 \ldots c \ . \tag{8}$$

This formula is evaluated c times in every iteration, like in case of conventional FCM-b, but here both the denominator and divisor of the fraction sum up much fewer terms. Obviously the estimated bias field has to treat each pixel separately. But even here we can simplify the computations by introducing some auxiliary variables and organizing them into a lookup table. In this order, let

$$q_l = \frac{\sum_{i=1}^{c} u_{il}^m v_i}{\sum_{i=1}^{c} u_{il}^m} \qquad \forall l \in \Omega^{(t)} \ , \tag{9}$$

and subsequently, for any pixel with index $k = 1 \ldots n$, we get the estimated bias:

$$b_k^{\star} = y_k - q_{l_k} \quad \text{with} \quad l_k = y_k - b_k^{(t-1)} \ . \tag{10}$$

The proposed accelerated algorithm is summarized in Table 1.

4   Results and Discussions

The theoretical time complexity of the conventional and accelerated approach is compared in Table 2, where ω stands for the cardinality of the set Ω or the number of different intensity values in the current compensated image. Considering the fact that the number of present gray intensities (ω) is less than the number of pixels (n) in the image by minimum two orders of magnitude, we can state that the time consuming first three steps of the conventional algorithm are replaced with much quicker solutions in the proposed algorithm.

Both the conventional and proposed approaches were tested on 24 artificial phantoms and 40 real MR images. Artificial phantoms were created by adding slowly varying INU noise to single-channel intensity images that contained two easily separable regions of constant intensity. Real MR images were taken from the Internet Brain Segmentation Repository [4]. All benchmark results were obtained on a PC with Athlon64 processor running at 2GHz frequency.

Figure 1(a) summarizes the benchmark results of both algorithms that were executed on artificial phantoms of various sizes. In case of two classes, the proposed algorithm accelerates the execution about 15-25 times. It is also visible that the speed-up ratio slightly rises if we increase the size of the input phantom

Table 2. Computational complexity of algorithmic steps

Algorithmic step	Conventional (FCM-b)	Accelerated (FCM-qb)
Partition updating	$\mathcal{O}(nc^2)$	$\mathcal{O}(\omega c^2)$
Cluster prototype updating	$\mathcal{O}(nc)$	$\mathcal{O}(\omega c)$
Bias estimation	$\mathcal{O}(nc)$	$\mathcal{O}(n + \omega c)$
Bias smoothing	$\mathcal{O}(n)$	$\mathcal{O}(n)$
Histogram updating	$-$	$\mathcal{O}(n)$

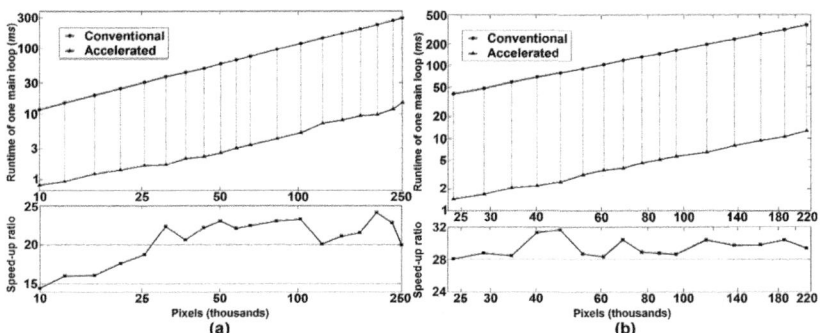

Fig. 1. Runtime of one main loop, using the conventional and accelerated approach (up), and the resulting speed-up ratio (down), all represented against the number of pixels in the image: (a) phantom images, segmented into $c = 2$ classes; (b) real MR images, segmented into $c = 3$ classes

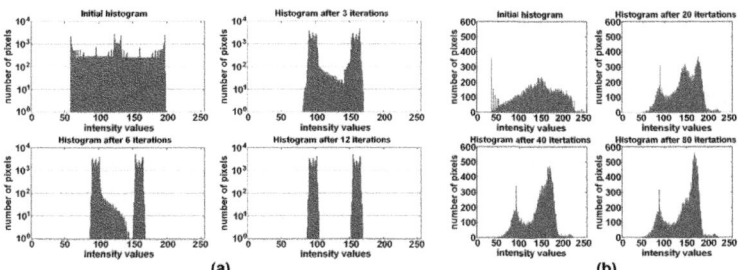

Fig. 2. (a) The evolution of the histogram of an INU contaminated two-class phantom image, during the iteration cycles; (b) The evolution of the intensity distribution of an INU contaminated real MR image during the iteration cycles

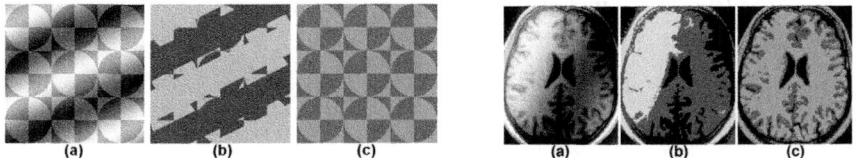

Fig. 3. Segmentation of phantoms (left) and real MR images (right): (a) original image, (b) failed segmentation without INU compensation, (c) successful segmentation with INU compensation

image. Real MR brain images of different sizes, artificially contaminated with inhomogeneity were also fed to both algorithms. These images were segmented into $c = 3$ classes corresponding to white matter (WM), gray matter (GM), and cerebro-spinal fluid (CSF), respectively. Benchmark results are exhibited in Fig. 1(b). The speed-up ratio is even higher: it varies between 28 and 32.

Figure 2(a) shows the variation of the histogram of a phantom image during the iterative compensation. The two classes are perfectly separated after 10-12 iteration cycles. The regions the compensation produces are not piecewise constant, but they are easily separable, so the classification can be 100% accurate. Figure 2(b) shows the variation of the histogram of a brain MRI image segmented into three clusters, during the iterative compensation. Here convergence requires 30-80 iterations. As the WM and GM have their intensities close to each other, in the presence of noise their histograms overlap, so their distributions cannot be completely separated by INU compensation. This is a primary source of misclassifications, equally present in both the conventional and proposed approaches.

Figure 3 exhibits the segmentation and INU compensation of a two-class phantom, and a real MR image. Without compensation the segmentation fails, but compensation makes the classes perfectly separable. The beneficial effect of INU compensation is also visible in real MR images, but here tissues are not perfectly separable due to their overlapping intensity ranges.

As $c \ll \omega \ll n$, the theoretical complexity values exhibited in Table 2 suggest that the running time of the accelerated algorithm hardly depends on the number of clusters. To confirm this hypothesis, we have fed various images to the algorithm, setting the number of clusters c to values ranging from 2 to 8. The obtained speed-up ratios linearly grew together with c, reaching 65 at $c = 8$.

Both approaches theoretically perform the same computations, so the accelerated approach should have exactly the same accuracy as the conventional one. However, in practice, there is a secondary source of errors in the proposed approach due to the quantification error of the bias field. In our tests, bias quantification never increased the number of misclassifications more than 1%.

The proposed method is also compatible with other INU modeling schemes: in case of modeling INU as gain field, or in the log-bias approach, the partition and cluster prototypes can be computed using the histogram, just as we have shown in the bias field formulation. The proposed approach is insensitive to the chosen bias smoothing procedure: the user has the freedom to apply for example the mean spread filtering [10]. Further on, the formulation of the proposed solution is adaptable to other c-means clustering algorithms [13].

5   Conclusion

In this paper, we have reformulated the c-means clustering based approach of INU compensation and segmentation of magnetic resonance images, in order to drastically reduce the processing time. We have shown that the most time consuming parts of the conventional algorithm's iteration cycle can be applied to individual gray intensities instead of individual pixels. We achieved an approach that performs the segmentation of brain MR images 20-30 times faster, without causing relevant change in terms of accuracy. The proposed algorithm is highly compatible with various reported c-means clustering based INU compensation techniques. With this increased execution speed, c-means clustering may receive a significantly higher popularity in the domain of MR image segmentation.

References

1. Ahmed, M.N., Yamany, S.M., Mohamed, N., Farag, A.A., Moriarty, T.: A modified fuzzy c-means algorithm for bias field estimation and segmentation of MRI data. IEEE Trans. Med. Imag. 21(3), 193–199 (2002)
2. Bezdek, J.C.: Pattern recognition with fuzzy objective function algorithms. Plenum, New York (1981)
3. Derganc, J., Likar, B., Pernuš, F.: Nonparametric segmentation of multispectral MR images incorporating spatial and intensity information. Progr. Biomed. Opt. Imag. 3(1), 391–400 (2002)
4. Internet Brain Segmentation Repository, http://www.cma.mgh.harvard.edu/ibsr
5. Johnston, B., Atkins, M.S., Mackiewich, B., Anderson, M.: Segmentation of multiple sclerosis lesions in intensity corrected multispectral MRI. IEEE Trans. Med. Imag. 15(2), 154–169 (1996)
6. Liew, A.W.C., Hong, Y.: An adaptive spatial fuzzy clustering algorithm for 3-D MR image segmentation. IEEE Trans. Med. Imag. 22(9), 1063–1075 (2003)
7. Pal, N.R., Pal, K., Keller, J.M., Bezdek, J.C.: A possibilistic fuzzy c-means clustering algorithms. IEEE Trans. Fuzzy Syst. 13(4), 517–530 (2005)
8. Pham, D.L., Prince, J.L.: Adaptive fuzzy segmentation of magnetic resonance images. IEEE Trans. Med. Imag. 18(9), 737–752 (1999)
9. Rajapakse, J.C., Kruggel, J.C.: Segmentation of MR images with intensity inhomogeneities. Image Vis. Comput. 16(3), 165–180 (1998)
10. Siyal, M.Y., Yu, L.: An intelligent modified fuzzy c-means based algorithm for bias field estimation and segmentation of brain MRI. Patt. Recogn. Lett. 26(13), 2052–2062 (2005)
11. Sled, J.G., Zijdenbos, A.P., Evans, A.C.: A nonparamtertic method for automatic correction of intensity nonuniformities. IEEE Trans. Med. Imag. 17(1), 87–97 (1998)
12. Styner, M., Brechbuchler, C., Székely, G., Gerig, G.: Parametric estimate of intensity inhomogeneities applied to MRI. IEEE Trans. Med. Imag. 19(3), 153–165 (2000)
13. Szilágyi, L., Szilágyi, S.M., Benyó, B., Benyó, Z.: Intensity inhomogeneity compensation and segmentation of MR brain images using hybrid c-means clustering models. Biomed. Sign. Proc. Contr. 6(1), 3–12 (2011)
14. Vemuri, P., Kholmovski, E.G., Parker, D.L., Chapman, B.E.: Coil sensitivity estimation for optimal SNR reconstruction and intensity inhomogeneity correction in phased array MR imaging. In: Christensen, G.E., Sonka, M. (eds.) IPMI 2005. LNCS, vol. 3565, pp. 603–614. Springer, Heidelberg (2005)
15. Vovk, U., Pernuš, F., Likar, B.: MRI intensity inhomogeneity correction by combining intensity and spatial information. Phys. Med. Biol. 49(17), 4119–4133 (2004)
16. Vovk, U., Pernuš, F., Likar, B.: A review of methods for correction of intensity inhomogeneity in MRI. IEEE Trans. Med. Imag. 26(3), 405–421 (2007)
17. Zhang, Y., Brady, M., Smith, S.: Segmentation of brain MR images through a hidden Markov random field model and the expectation-maximization algorithm. IEEE Trans. Med. Imag. 20(1), 45–57 (2001)

A New Asymmetric Criterion for Cluster Validation

Hosein Alizadeh, Behrouz Minaei-Bidgoli, and Hamid Parvin

Islamic Azad University, Mahdishahr Branch, Mahdishahr, Iran
{halizadeh,b_minaei,parvin}@iust.ac.ir

Abstract. In this paper a new criterion for clusters validation is proposed. Many stability measures to validate a cluster have been proposed such as Normalized Mutual Information. We propose a new criterion for clusters validation. The drawback of the common approach is discussed in this paper and then a new asymmetric criterion is proposed to assess the association between a cluster and a partition which is called Alizadeh-Parvin-Minaei criterion, APM. The APM criterion compensates the drawback of the common Normalized Mutual Information (NMI) measure. Then we employ this criterion to select the more robust clusters in the final ensemble. We also propose a new method named Extended Evidence Accumulation Clustering, EEAC, to construct the matrix of similarity from these selected clusters. Finally, we apply a hierarchical method over the obtained matrix to extract the final partition. The empirical studies show that the proposed method outperforms other ones.

Keywords: Clustering Ensemble, Stability Measure, Cluster Evaluation.

1 Introduction

Data clustering or unsupervised learning is an important and very difficult problem. The objective of clustering is to partition a set of unlabeled objects into homogeneous groups or clusters [6]. Clustering techniques require the definition of a similarity measure between patterns. Since there is no prior knowledge about cluster shapes, choosing a specific clustering method is not easy [17]. Studies in the last few years have tended to combinational methods. Cluster ensemble methods attempt to find better and more robust clustering solutions by fusing information from several primary data partitionings [11].

Fern and Lin [7] have suggested a clustering ensemble approach which selects a subset of solutions to form a smaller but better-performing cluster ensemble than using all primary solutions. The ensemble selection method is designed based on quality and diversity, the two factors that have been shown to influence cluster ensemble performance. This method attempts to select a subset of primary partitions which simultaneously has both the highest quality and diversity. The Sum of Normalized Mutual Information, SNMI [8]-[10] and [18] is used to measure the quality of an individual partition with respect to other partitions. Also, the Normalized Mutual Information, NMI, is employed for measuring the diversity among partitions. Although the ensemble size in this method is relatively small, this method achieves significant performance improvement over full ensembles. Law et al. proposed a

C. San Martin and S.-W. Kim (Eds.): CIARP 2011, LNCS 7042, pp. 320–330, 2011.
© Springer-Verlag Berlin Heidelberg 2011

multi objective data clustering method based on the selection of individual clusters produced by several clustering algorithms through an optimization procedure [14]. This technique chooses the best set of objective functions for different parts of the feature space from the results of base clustering algorithms. Fred and Jain [10] have offered a new clustering ensemble method which learns the pairwise similarity between points in order to facilitate a proper partitioning of the data without the a priori knowledge of the number of clusters and of the shape of these clusters. This method which is based on cluster stability evaluates the primary clustering results instead of final clustering.

Moller and Radke [16] have introduced an approach to validate a clustering results based on partition stability. This method uses a perturbation which is produced by adding some noise to the data. An empirical study robustly indicates that the perturbation usually outperforms bootstrapping and subsampling. Whereas the empirical choice of the subsampling size is often difficult [5], the choosing of the perturbation strength is not so crucial. This method uses a Nearest Neighbor Resampling approach (NNR) that offers a solution to both problems of information loss and empirical control of the change degree made to the original data. The NNR techniques were first used for time series analysis [3]. Inokuchi et al. [12] have proposed a kernelized validity measures where a kernel means the kernel function used in support vector machines. Two measures are considered in this measure. One is the sum of the traces of the fuzzy covariances within clusters and the second is a kernelized Xie-Beni's measure [19]. This validity measure is applied to the determination of the number of clusters and also the evaluation of robustness of different partitionings. Das and Sil [4] have proposed a method to determine the number of clusters which validates the clusters using splitting and merging technique in order to obtain optimal set of clusters.

We discuss the drawbacks of the common approaches and then have proposed a new asymmetric criterion to assess the association between a cluster and a partition which is called Alizadeh-Parvin-Minaei criterion, APM. The APM criterion compensates the drawbacks of the common method. Also, a clustering ensemble method is proposed which is based on aggregating a subset of primary clusters. This method uses the Average APM as fitness measure to select a number of clusters. The clusters which satisfy a predefined threshold of the mentioned measure are selected to participate in the clustering ensemble. To combine the chosen clusters, a co-association based consensus function is employed.

2 Proposed Method

In this section, first the proposed clustering ensemble method is briefly outlined, and then its phases are described in the subsequent subsections in more detail.

The main idea of the proposed clustering ensemble method is to utilize a subset of the best performing primary clusters in the ensemble instead of all of them. It seems that every cluster does not have a good quality. So, in this method just those clusters which satisfy enough stability to participate in the combination are chosen. The cluster selection is done based on cluster stability which is defined according to Normalized Mutual Information, NMI.

The manner of computing stability is described in the following sections in detail. As seen in Fig 1, a subset of the most stable clusters is first selected for combination. This is simply done by applying a stability-threshold to each cluster. In the next step, the selected clusters are used to construct the co-association matrix. Several methods have been proposed for combination of the primary results [2] and [18]. In our work, some clusters in the primary partitions may be absent (having been eliminated by the stability criterion). Since the original EAC method [8] cannot truly identify the pairwise similarity while there is only a subset of clusters, we present a new method for constructing the co-association matrix. We call this method: Extended Evidence Accumulation Clustering method, EEAC. Finally, we use the hierarchical single-link clustering to extract the final clusters from this matrix.

Since goodness of a cluster is determined by all the data points, the goodness function $g_j(C_i,D)$ depends on both the cluster C_i and the entire dataset D, instead of C_i alone. The stability as measure of cluster goodness is used in [13]. Cluster stability reflects the variation in the clustering results under perturbation of the data by resampling. A stable cluster is one that has a high likelihood of recurrence across multiple applications of the clustering method. Stable clusters are usually preferable, since they are robust with respect to minor changes in the dataset [14].

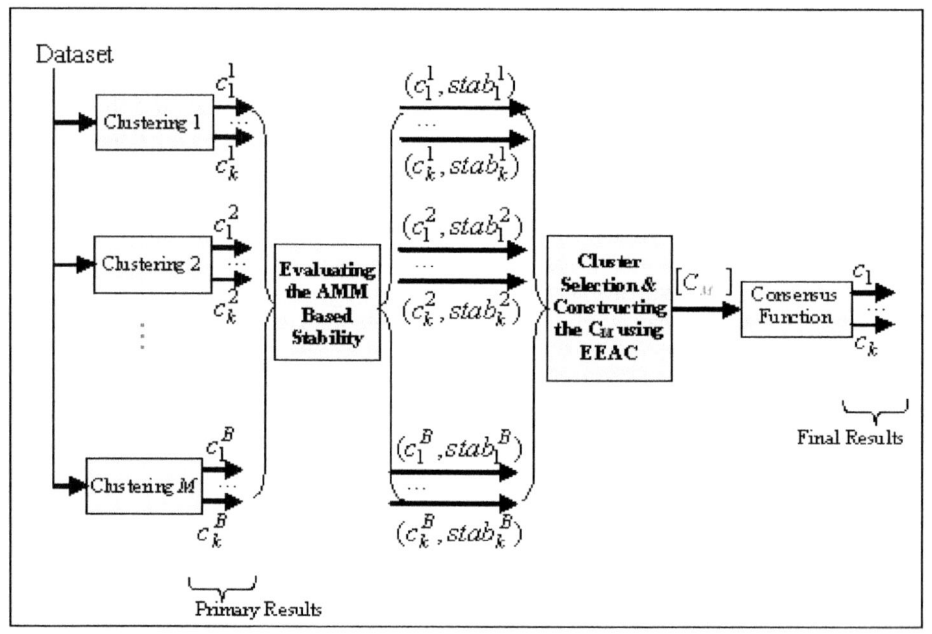

Fig. 1. Training phase of the Bagging method

Now assume that we want to compute the stability of cluster C_i. In this method first a set of partitionings over resampled datasets is provided which is called the reference set. In this notation D is resampled data and $P(D)$ is a partitioning over D. Now, the problem is: "How many times is the cluster C_i repeated in the reference partitions?"

Denote by NMI(C_i,$P(D)$), the Normalized Mutual Information between the cluster C_i and a reference partition $P(D)$. Most previous works only compare a *partition with another partition* [18]. However, the stability used in [14] evaluates the similarity between a *cluster and a partition* by transforming the cluster C_i to a partition and employing common partition to partition methods. To illustrate this method let $P_1 = P^a = \{C_i, D/C_i\}$ be a partition with two clusters, where D/C_i denotes the set of data points in D that are not in C_i. Then we may compute a second partition $P_2 = P^b = \{C^*, D/C^*\}$, where C^* denotes the union of all "positive" clusters in $P(D)$ and others are in D/C^*. A cluster C_j in $P(D)$ is positive if more than half of its data points are in C_i. Now, define NMI(C_i,$P(D)$) by NMI(P^a,P^b) which is calculated as [9]:

$$NMI(P^a, P^b) = \frac{-2\sum_{i=1}^{k_a}\sum_{j=1}^{k_b} n_{ij}^{ab} \log\left(\frac{n_{ij}^{ab}.n}{n_i^a.n_j^b}\right)}{\sum_{i=1}^{k_a} n_i^a \log\left(\frac{n_i^a}{n}\right) + \sum_{j=1}^{k_b} n_j^b \log\left(\frac{n_j^b}{n}\right)} \tag{1}$$

where n is the total number of samples and n_{ij}^{ab} denotes the number of shared patterns between clusters $C_i^a \in P^a$ and $C_j^b \in P^b$; n_i^a is the number of patterns in the cluster i of partition a; also n_j^b are the number of patterns in the cluster j of partition b.

This computation is done between the cluster C_i and all partitions available in the reference set. Fig. 2 shows this method.

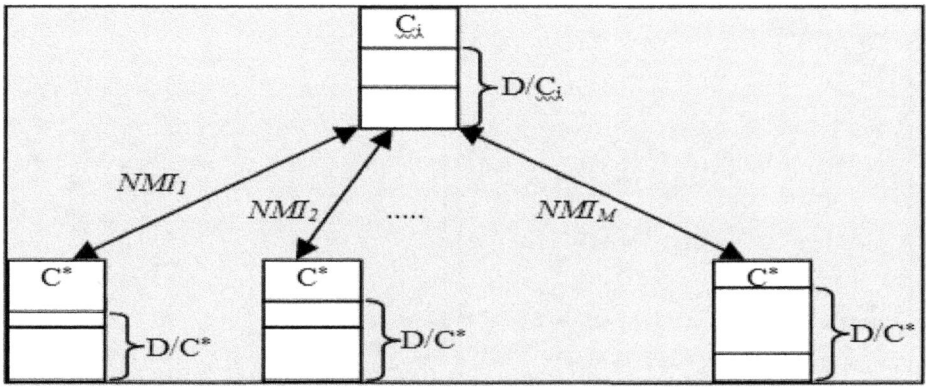

Fig. 2. Computing the Stability of Cluster C_i

NMI_i in Fig. 2 shows the stability of cluster C_i with respect to the i-th partition in reference set. The total stability of cluster C_i is defined as:

$$Stability(C_i) = \frac{1}{M}\sum_{i=1}^{M} NMI_i \tag{2}$$

where M is the number of partitions available in reference set. This procedure is applied for each cluster of every primary partition.

Here a drawback of computing stability is introduced and an alternative approach is suggested which is named Max method. Fig. 3 shows two primary partitions for which the stability of each cluster is evaluated. In this example K-means is applied as the base clustering algorithm with K=3. For this example the number of all partitions in the reference set is 40. In 36 partitions the result is relatively similar to Fig 3a, but there are four partitions in which the top left cluster is divided into two clusters, as shown in Fig 3b. Fig 3a shows a true clustering. Since the well separated cluster in the top left corner is repeated several times (90% repetition) in partitionings of the reference set, it has to acquire a great stability value (but not equal to 1), however it acquires the stability value of 1. Because the two clusters in right hand of Fig 3a are relatively joined and sometimes they are not recognized in the reference set as well, they have less stability value. Fig. 3.b shows a spurious clustering which the two right clusters are incorrectly merged. Since a fixed number of clusters are forced in the base algorithm, the top left cluster is divided into two clusters. Here the drawback of the stability measure is apparent rarely. Although it is obvious that this partition and the corresponding large cluster on the right reference set (10% repetition), the stability of this cluster is evaluated equal to 1. Since the NMI is a symmetric equation, the stability of the top left cluster in fig 3.a is exactly equal to the large right cluster in fig 3.b; however they are repeated 90% and 10%, respectively. In other words, when two clusters are complements of each other, their stabilities are always equal. This drawback is seen when the number of positive clusters in the considered partition of reference set is greater than 1. It means when the cluster C* is obtained by merging two or more clusters, undesirable stability effects occur.

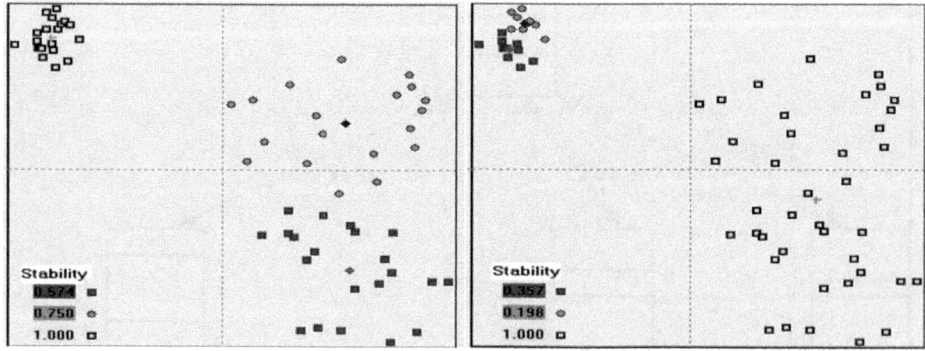

Fig. 3. Two primary partitions with k=3. (a) True clustering. (b) Spurious clustering.

Here, a new criterion is proposed which can solve this problem. Assume that the problem is evaluating the APM criterion for cluster C_l in Fig. 4a with respect to clustering obtained in Fig. 4b.

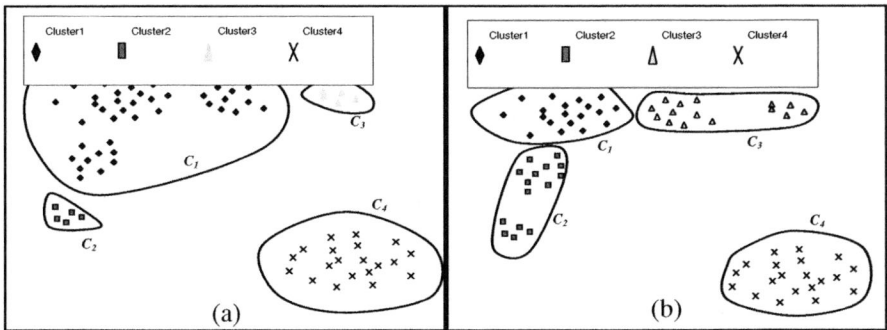

Fig. 4. evaluating the APM criterion for cluster C_1 from clustering (a) with respect to clustering (b), with $k=4$

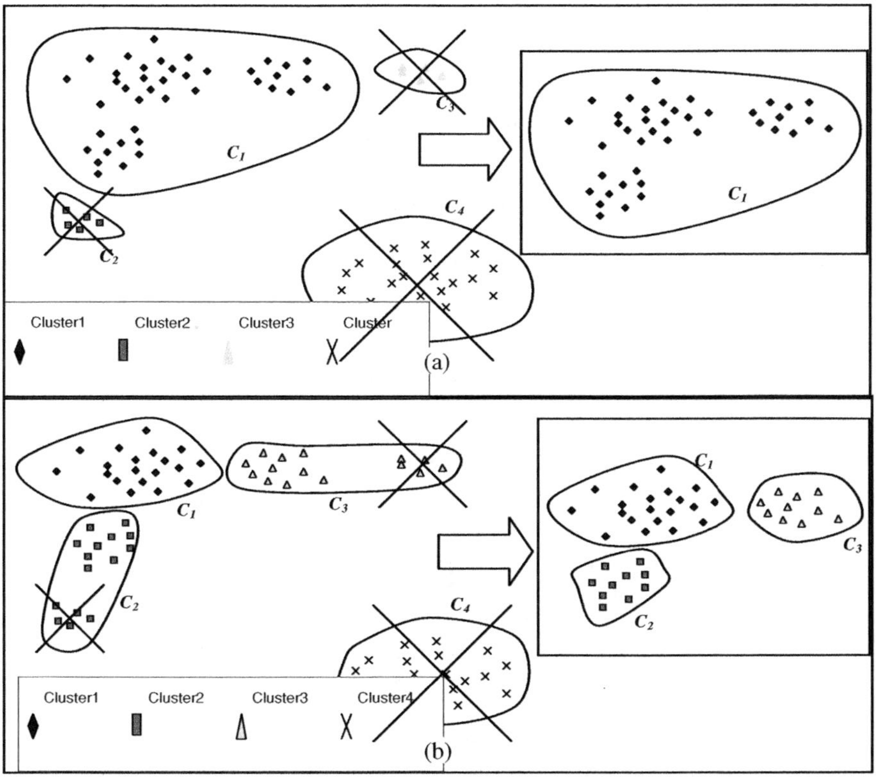

Fig. 5. Providing data for evaluating the APM criterion. (a) Deleting all other clusters except C_1 from P^a. (b) deriving P^{b*}, the corresponding samples of C_1 in P^b

The main idea in this method is to eliminate the symmetricalness which exists in NMI equation. In this approach, except the cluster C_1 all other clusters in P^a are taken out. Also, all clusters in P^b which are not included the samples of this cluster are eliminated. In the next step, the other samples which are not in C_1 of P^a, are removed from clusters in P^b (from the clusters which include some of these samples). This process is depicted in Fig. 5.

Now, the entropy between remained clusters in two partitions P^a and P^b is computed (see Fig. 6). On account of the other involved samples are eliminated, this criterion is not symmetric.

All the previous works are based on the NMI definition as equation 1. Even for evaluating the occurrence of a cluster in a partition, the problem is modified in some way to become the comparing problem between two partitions and then the NMI equation is used. In this paper, the problem is not changed according to definition of NMI; instead, the NMI equation is modified so that the occurrence of a cluster in a partition is computed. It is done by evaluating the entropy between the considered cluster and other pseudo clusters in the corresponding partition. In this paper the Alizadeh-Parvin-Moshki-Minaei criterion, APM, is defined between a cluster C_i from P^a and the partition P^{b*} from P^b, as below equation:

$$APMM(C_i^a, P^{b*}) = \frac{-2\log\left(\frac{n}{n_i^a}\right)\sum_{j=1}^{k_{b*}} n_j^{b*}}{n_i^a \log\left(\frac{n_i^a}{n}\right) + \sum_{j=1}^{k_{b*}} n_j^{b*} \log\left(\frac{n_j^{b*}}{n}\right)} \qquad (3)$$

where n is number of samples available in the cluster C_i and n_{ij}^{ab*} denotes the number of shared samples between the clusters $C_i^a \in P^a$ and $C_j^{b*} \in P^{b*}$. Also k_{b*} is the number of clusters in P^{b*}.

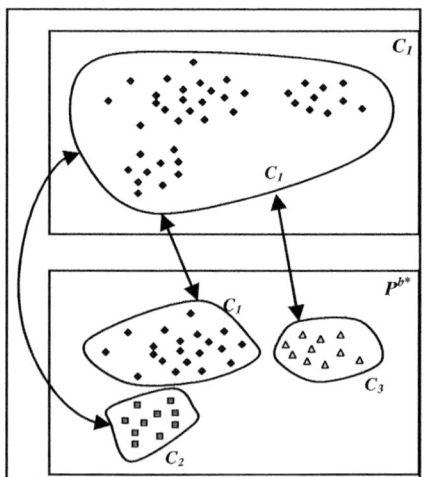

Fig. 6. Computing the entropy between the cluster C_1 from P^a and P^{b*} from P^b

Here, the Average APM, AAPM is proposed as a measure of stability of a primary cluster C_i with respect to the partitions available in the reference set as equation 4:

$$AAPMM(C_i) = \frac{1}{M} \sum_{j=1}^{M} APMM(C_i^a, P_j^{b*}) \tag{4}$$

where P_j^{b*} is from j-th partition of the reference set.

In the following step, the selected clusters are used to construct the co-association matrix. In the EAC method the m primary results from resampled data are accumulated in an $n \times n$ co-association matrix. Each entry in this matrix is computed from this equation:

$$C(i, j) = \frac{n_{i,j}}{m_{i,j}} \tag{5}$$

where n_{ij} counts the number of clusters shared by objects with indices i and j in the partitions over the primary B clusterings. Also m_{ij} is the number of partitions where this pair of objects is simultaneously present. There are only a fraction of all primary clusters available, after thresholding. So, the common EAC method cannot truly recognize the pairwise similarity for computing the co-association matrix. In our novel method (Extended Evidence Accumulation Clustering, or EEAC) each entry of the co-association matrix is computed by:

$$C(i, j) = \frac{n_{i,j}}{\max(n_i, n_j)} \tag{6}$$

where n_i and n_j are the number present in remaining (after stability thresholding) clusters for the i-th and j-th data points, respectively. Also, n_{ij} counts the number of remaining clusters which are shared by both data points indexed by i and j, respectively.

3   Experimental Results

This section reports and discusses the empirical studies. The proposed method is examined over 5 different standard datasets. It is tried for datasets to be diverse in their number of true classes, features and samples. A large variety in used datasets can more validate the obtained results. Brief information about the used datasets is available in Table 1. More information is available in [15].

Table 1. Brief information about the used datasets

	Class	Features	Samples
Glass	6	9	214
Breast-C	2	9	683
Wine	3	13	178
Bupa	2	6	345
Yeast	10	8	1484

All experiments are done over the normalized features. It means each feature is normalized with mean of 0 and variance of 1, N(0, 1). All of them are reported over means of 10 independent runs of algorithm. The final performance of the clustering algorithms is evaluated by re-labeling between obtained clusters and the ground truth labels and then counting the percentage of the true classified samples. Table 2 shows the performance of the proposed method comparing with most common base and ensemble methods.

Table 2. Experimental results

Dataset	Simple Methods (%)				Ensemble Methods (%)			
	Single Linkage	Average Linkage	Complete Linkage	Kmeans	Kmeans Ensemble	Full Ensemble	Cluster Selection by NMI Method	Cluster Selection by max Method
Wine	37.64	38.76	83.71	96.63	96.63	97.08	97.75	**98.31**
Breast-C	65.15	70.13	94.73	95.37	95.46	95.10	95.75	**98.33**
Yeast	34.38	35.11	38.91	40.20	45.46	47.17	**47.17**	**47.17**
Glass	36.45	37.85	40.65	45.28	47.01	47.83	48.13	**50.47**
Bupa	57.68	57.10	55.94	54.64	54.49	55.83	58.09	**58.40**

The first four columns of Table 2 are the results of some base clustering algorithms. The results show that although each of these algorithms can obtain a good result over a specific dataset, it does not perform well over other datasets. For example, according to Table 2 the K-means algorithm has a good clustering result over Wine dataset in comparison with linkage methods. But, it has lower performance in comparison to linkage methods in the case of Bupa dataset. Also, the complete linkage has a good performance in Breast-Cancer dataset in comparison with others; however it is not in the case of all datasets. The four last columns show the performance of some ensemble methods in comparison with the proposed one. Taking a glance at the last four columns in comparison with the first four columns shows that the ensemble methods do better than the simple based algorithms in the case of performance and robustness along with different datasets. The first column of the ensemble methods is the results of an ensemble of 100 K-means which is fused by EAC method. The 90% sampling from dataset is used for creating diversity in primary results. The sub-sampling (without replacement) is used as the sampling method. Also the random initialization of the seed points of K-means algorithm helps them to be more diverse. The single linkage algorithm is applied as consensus function for deriving the final clusters from co-association matrix. The second column from ensemble methods is the full ensemble which uses several clustering algorithms for generating the primary results. Here, 70 K-means with the above mentioned parameters in addition to 30 linkage methods provide the primary results. The third column of *Ensemble Methods* is consensus partitioning using EEAC algorithm of top 33% stable clusters, employing NMI method as measure of stability. The fourth column of the ensemble methods is also consensus partitioning using EEAC algorithm of top 33% stable clusters, employing max method as measure of stability.

4   Conclusion and Future Works

In this paper a new clustering ensemble method is proposed which is based on a subset of total primary spurious clusters. Since the quality of the primary clusters are not equal and presence of some of them can even yield to lower performance, here a method to select a subset of more effective clusters is proposed. A common cluster validity criterion which is needed to derive this subset is based on normalized mutual information. In this paper some drawbacks of this criterion is discussed and an alternative criterion is suggested which is named Alizadeh-Parvin-Moshki-Minaei, APM. The experiments show that the APM criterion does slightly better than NMI criterion generally; however it significantly outperforms the NMI criterion in the case of synthetic data sets. Because of the symmetry which is concealed in NMI criterion and also in NMI based stability, it yields to lower performance whenever symmetry is also appeared in the data set. Another innovation of this paper is a method for constructing the co-association matrix where some of clusters and respectively some of samples do not exist in partitions. This new method is called Extended Evidence Accumulation Clustering, EEAC. The empirical studies over several data sets robustly show that the quality of the proposed method is usually better than other ones.

References

1. Alizadeh, H., Minaei-Bidgoli, B., Parvin, H., Mohsen, M.: An Asymmetric Criterion for Cluster Validation. In: International Conference on Industrial, Engineering and Other Applications of Applied Intelligent Systems (IEA/AIE 2011). LNCS. Springer, Heidelberg (in press, 2011) ISSN: 0302-9743
2. Ayad, H., Kamel, M.S.: Cumulative Voting Consensus Method for Partitions with a Variable Number of Clusters. IEEE Trans. on Pattern Analysis and Machine Intelligence 30(1), 160–173 (2008)
3. Brandsma, T., Buishand, T.A.: Simulation of extreme precipitation in the Rhine basin by nearest-neighbour resampling. Hydrology and Earth System Sciences 2, 195–209 (1998)
4. Das, A.K., Sil, J.: Cluster Validation using Splitting and Merging Technique. In: Int. Conf. on Computational Intelligence and Multimedia Applications, ICCIMA (2007)
5. Davison, A.C., Hinkley, D.V., Young, G.A.: Recent developments in bootstrap methodology. Statistical Science 18, 141–157 (2003)
6. Faceli, K., Marcilio, C.P., Souto, D.: Multi-objective Clustering Ensemble. In: Proceedings of the Sixth International Conference on Hybrid Intelligent Systems (HIS 2006) (2006)
7. Fern, X.Z., Lin, W.: Cluster Ensemble Selection. In: SIAM International Conference on Data Mining, SDM 2008 (2008)
8. Fred, A., Jain, A.K.: Data Clustering Using Evidence Accumulation. In: Proc. of the 16th Intl. Conf. on Pattern Recognition, ICPR 2002, Quebec City, pp. 276–280 (2002)
9. Fred, A., Jain, A.K.: Combining Multiple Clusterings Using Evidence Accumulation. IEEE Trans. on Pattern Analysis and Machine Intelligence 27(6), 835–850 (2005)
10. Fred, A., Jain, A.K.: Learning Pairwise Similarity for Data Clustering. In: Proc. of the 18th Int. Conf. on Pattern Recognition (ICPR 2006) (2006)
11. Fred, A., Lourenco, A.: Cluster Ensemble Methods: from Single Clusterings to Combined Solutions. Studies in Computational Intelligence (SCI), vol. 126, pp. 3–30 (2008)
12. Inokuchi, R., Nakamura, T., Miyamoto, S.: Kernelized Cluster Validity Measures and Application to Evaluation of Different Clustering Algorithms. In: IEEE Int. Conf. on Fuzzy Systems, Canada (July 16-21, 2006)
13. Lange, T., Braun, M.L., Roth, V., Buhmann, J.M.: Stability-based model selection. In: Advances in Neural Information Processing Systems, vol. 15. MIT Press (2003)

14. Law, M.H.C., Topchy, A.P., Jain, A.K.: Multiobjective data clustering. In: Proc. of IEEE Conference on Computer Vision and Pattern Recognition, vol. 2, pp. 424–430 (2004)
15. Newman, C.B.D.J., Hettich, S., Merz, C.: UCI repository of machine learning databases (1998), http://www.ics.uci.edu/~mlearn/MLSummary.html
16. Möller, U., Radke, D.: Performance of data resampling methods based on clustering. Intelligent Data Analysis 10(2) (2006)
17. Roth, V., Lange, T., Braun, M., Buhmann, J.: A Resampling Approach to Cluster Validation. In: Intl. Conf. on Computational Statistics, COMPSTAT (2002)
18. Strehl, A., Ghosh, J.: Cluster ensembles - a knowledge reuse framework for combining multiple partitions. Journal of Machine Learning Research 3, 583–617 (2002)
19. Xie, X.L., Beni, G.: A Validity measure for Fuzzy Clustering. IEEE Trans. on Pattern Analysis and Machine Intelligence 13(4), 841–846 (1991)

Semi-supervised Classification by Probabilistic Relaxation*

Adolfo Martínez-Usó, Filiberto Pla, José Martínez Sotoca, and Henry Anaya-Sánchez

Institute of New Imaging Technologies - Dept. of Computer Languages and Systems
Universitat Jaume I, 12071 Castellón, Spain

Abstract. In this paper, a semi-supervised approach based on probabilistic relaxation theory is presented. It combines two desirable properties; firstly, a very small number of labelled samples is needed and, secondly, the assignment of labels is consistently performed according to our contextual information constraints. The proposed technique has been successfully applied to pattern recognition problems, obtaining promising preliminary results in database classification and image segmentation. Our methodology has also been evaluated against a recent state-of-the-art algorithm for semi-supervised learning, obtaining generally comparable or better results.

Keywords: Semi-supervised, Probabilistic Relaxation, Classification.

1 Introduction

Unsupervised learning assumes that all the observations are caused by latent variables that can be somehow modelled. However, there exist many tasks that are generally too specialised to use unsupervised techniques and, at the same time, too time-consuming for an expert if every single case should be solved manually, spending a large amount of time isolating the most interesting parts of the images. These tasks are especially common, for instance in remote sensing or medical imaging applications. Therefore, a process that is able to do this work in an accurate way without too much participation of an expert has become a very demanding task on these fields.

Semi-supervised learning has received an increasing attention for the last years and has been widely extended to many fields [1]. Semi-supervised approaches arise from the idea of using together a large amount of unlabelled data, which is often cheap and easy, and few labelled data, which is hard to obtain since it requires human experts or special devices. The important point here is to manage a better classifier (or clustering result) than from the unlabelled data alone.

Relaxation methods find numerical solutions for a wide range of problems in physics and engineering and, more concretely, probabilistic relaxation has demonstrated to be very useful for pattern recognition [3]. A general framework for the theoretical foundations of relaxation processes can be found in [5]. This general relaxation structure has

---

* This work was supported by the Spanish Ministry of Science and Innovation under the projects Consolider Ingenio 2010 CSD2007-00018, AYA2008-05965-C04-04/ESP, TIN2009-14103-C03-01 and by Caixa-Castelló foundation under the projects P1 1B2009-45.

C. San Martin and S.-W. Kim (Eds.): CIARP 2011, LNCS 7042, pp. 331–338, 2011.

attracted important interest, being often refined in a number of ways by means of *ad hoc* or heuristic choices [11].

Relaxation approaches are *iterative* processes that are used for reducing ambiguities in assigning symbolic labels to a set of nodes (clusters, objects, etc.) which is often known as equilibrating or *relaxing* a system. Relaxation methods involve *contextual information* that describes relations between single components [5], defining a neighbourhood in accordance with the properties of the system. The contextual information is generally introduced into the process from our *a priori* knowledge of the problem. Therefore, these approaches present two interesting features; the use of the context of the problem and the expected good performance to obtain a robust solution [7].

A semi-supervised approach based on probabilistic relaxation is presented in this paper. Using few labelled samples introduced by an expert (contextual information), the proposed method is able to propagate this information to the whole system. Experimental evidences of the robustness of the methodology will be also offered by means of applying the presented technique to several pattern recognition fields such as database classification or image segmentation.

2   Probabilistic Relaxation Methodology

A probabilistic relaxation method is an iterative process that assigns consistent labels to a initial set of nodes on the basis of the contextual information, which is also introduced into the model. A node is a point in a graph that represents objects, clusters, regions, etc. whereas the contextual information is generally related to the relationship among those nodes, that is, arcs among the nodes in the graph.

In the proposed approach, an initial Gaussian mixture that models the input data is assumed. Let us consider that each mode of the Gaussian mixture is a node of a fully connected graph. Therefore, let us suppose a set of nodes $\mathcal{N} = \{n_1, n_2, \ldots, n_N\}$, a set of class labels $\mathcal{L} = \{\omega_1, \omega_2, \ldots, \omega_L\}$ and a *support* function $Q^s(n_i \leftarrow \omega_k)$ representing that the node n_i would be labelled with ω_k. This support function results from each binary relation with the set $\overline{\mathcal{N}}_i$ of neighbouring nodes of n_i at the step s^{th} of the iterative process,

$$Q^{s+1}(n_i \leftarrow \omega_k) = Q^s(n_i \leftarrow \omega_k) + \frac{1}{|\overline{\mathcal{N}}_i|} \sum_{j \in \overline{\mathcal{N}}_i} \mathcal{C}_{ij} \; P^s(\omega_k \mid n_j) \qquad (1)$$

where $\mathcal{C}_{ij}$ are the coefficients representing the *strength of interaction* between nodes n_i and n_j. These coefficients are independent of the estimated posterior probabilities (P) and can be computed ahead of time, remaining constant during the entire process. Coefficients $\mathcal{C}_{ij}$ satisfy that $\sum_{j=1}^{N} \mathcal{C}_{ij} = 1$. Our approach defines these coefficients as:

$$\mathcal{C}_{ij} = \frac{\mathcal{D}(i,j)}{\sum_l \mathcal{D}(i,l)}, \;\; \text{being} \;\; \mathcal{D}(i,j) = exp\left(\frac{c_{ij}}{\kappa}\right) \;\; \text{where} \;\; \kappa = min\,(c_{mn}) \;\; \forall m, n \in \mathcal{N}.$$
$$(2)$$

Coefficients $c_{ij} = \frac{\alpha_{ij}}{d(i,j)}$ for nodes i, j represent the relationship between the relative density α_{ij} and the distance $d(i,j)$ between the nodes. Note that $\mathcal{D}(i,j)$ is a potential term that acts as a relative measure of potential similarity function. It will be high for the neighbouring node with the best rate for coefficient c_{ij} and very low for the rest of the nodes.

Coefficients α have been worked out using the d-dimensional volumes that form each node, being d the dimension of the data. That is, since each node represents a mode of a Gaussian mixture, the radius of each dimension of the ellipse formed by the mode can be derived from the covariance matrix of the mixture mode. In our case, radius is approximated as 3 times the standard deviation. Therefore, if we have d radius for each mode, say $\langle r_1, r_2, \ldots, r_d \rangle$, the d-dimensional ellipsoid volume $\mathcal{V}$ and the density ρ for mode m are calculated as

$$\mathcal{V}(m) = \frac{\pi^{\frac{d}{2}}}{\Gamma(\frac{d}{2} + 1)} \prod_i^d r_i \qquad \rho(m) = \frac{card(m)}{\mathcal{V}(m)} \qquad (3)$$

where Γ is the gamma function and $card(\cdot)$ provides the number of samples of the mode. In this sense, each sample belongs to the ellipsoid where it is contained, assigning to the nearest ellipse centroid those samples that could belong to several ellipsoids (intersections).

Therefore, using these equations, the coefficient α between the modes i and j is calculated as $\alpha_{ij} = \frac{\rho(i,j)}{\rho(i)+\rho(j)}$, where density $\rho(i,j)$ is worked out considering the possible mode formed by the samples of both modes i and j.

The updating formula for calculating the posterior probability $P^s(\omega_k \mid n_i)$ for label ω_k given the node n_i is:

$$P^{s+1}(\omega_k \mid n_i) = \frac{P^s(\omega_k \mid n_i) Q^s(n_i \leftarrow \omega_k)}{K} \qquad (4)$$

where $K = \sum_{l=1}^{|\mathcal{L}|} P^s(\omega_l \mid n_i) Q^s(n_i \leftarrow \omega_l)$ is a normalising factor.

The system (P^0) is initialised on the basis of the *a priori* information of the problem statement, also setting $Q^0 = P^0$ in this initialisation. The number of neighbouring nodes ($\overline{\mathcal{N}}$) is set up to the number of classes of the problem.

2.1 The Algorithm

The algorithm here presented for a semi-supervised probabilistic relaxation (**semi-PR**) has three input sources: the number of classes, the labelled data and unlabelled data. The unlabelled data is divided into two subsets for training and test. Multiple initial probability distributions (modes) per class are considered, being the number of modes of each class estimated in the initialisation stage. Thus, **semi-PR** generates a Gaussian mixture model of the data where each initial mode is a node of the graph used for the probabilistic relaxation described in Sect. 2. Each node of the graph has its initial probabilities according to the contextual information provided by the user and the strength of interaction between nodes is used in the edges of the graph.

Initialising the mixture. The initialisation stage provides the preliminary Gaussian mixture that models the whole dataset as a reduced description of the data. Several techniques have been taken into account [9,10] to learn this initial mixture. However, the more robust behaviour has been found using a vector quantization design [6] for estimating the N centroids that cover the whole dataset and then assigning each sample to the nearest centroid found by the vector quantizer. Thus, the training data is divided into N modes where the mean and covariance of each mode is estimated. Figure 1 shows several examples of this initialisation stage in its second row.

The initialisation stage is finished by a final refinement of the initial mixture, where modes with a high *compatibility* (α coefficients) are merged into one. That is, given a pair of modes i, j, if the α_{ij} value is higher than certain threshold T, these modes are considered together as a single mode. Figure 1 shows examples of this refinement process in its third row.

It is worth saying that both the initial N and the refinement threshold T have been set up to values that are safe enough for not creating any mode with instances from different classes. The experimental part of this work describes these values.

Semi-supervised Probabilistic Relaxation Algorithm. The Gaussian modes found in the initialisation stage are used as initial nodes for our proposed Semi-supervised Probabilistic Relaxation Algorithm. The initial probabilities (P^0) for each node are based on the *a priori* information that stems from our problem, that is, from initial modes found in the initialisation stage and from the supervised samples. These supervised samples allow us to label some of the initial nodes/modes to certain classes. The probabilities of the modes where no *a priori* information is available are equally distributed for each class before starting the relaxation process.

The objective of the **semi-PR** algorithm is to iteratively optimise Equation (4) until all the initial nodes would be consistently labelled for each class. For this optimisation, Equation (1) must be also calculated at each iteration, providing the *level of agreement* for each node and their possible labels. Distance $d(i,j)$ in coefficients c_{ij} is worked out using the Mahalanobis distance between the nodes n_i and n_j.

The process stops when, for each node of the system, one of the class probabilities exceeds $1 - \epsilon_1$, being $\epsilon_1 \ll 1$. As the literature suggests [2], if the whole changes in the system do not exceed certain threshold ϵ_2, the system is supposed relaxed enough and the process also stops in this case. Note that the process needs to keep iterating until the previous stopping conditions are reached, even so, from the first iterations the propagation of information is channelled through the probabilistic relaxation model. Therefore, parameters ϵ_1 and ϵ_2 are not critical, although they can probably be considered application-dependent.

3   Experimental Results

The experimental part of this work shows the preliminary results obtained by our proposal in several applications. Experiments are divided into the results obtained using several synthetic toy datasets (Sect. 3.1) and the results obtained in colour image segmentation (Sect. 3.2).

Initial mixtures in all the cases have heuristically been set up to 40 modes ($N = 40$), having a refinement threshold $T = 0.5$. In addition, unless otherwise stated, only two supervised samples per class are used, which have randomly been selected from the training set. The position of these labelled samples is drawn in the resulting labelled dataset as black-square spots. Samples of the test set are eventually classified performing their maximum class conditional likelihood according to the resulting Gaussian mixture model associated with each class.

3.1   Results on $2D$-Datasets

Figure 1 shows the results obtained on synthetic $2D$-datasets with two classes. These toy datasets are frequently used in the literature as illustrative examples to show the robustness of a technique. **Semi-PR** algorithm shows very consistent results with a classification accuracy higher than 95% in all the cases.

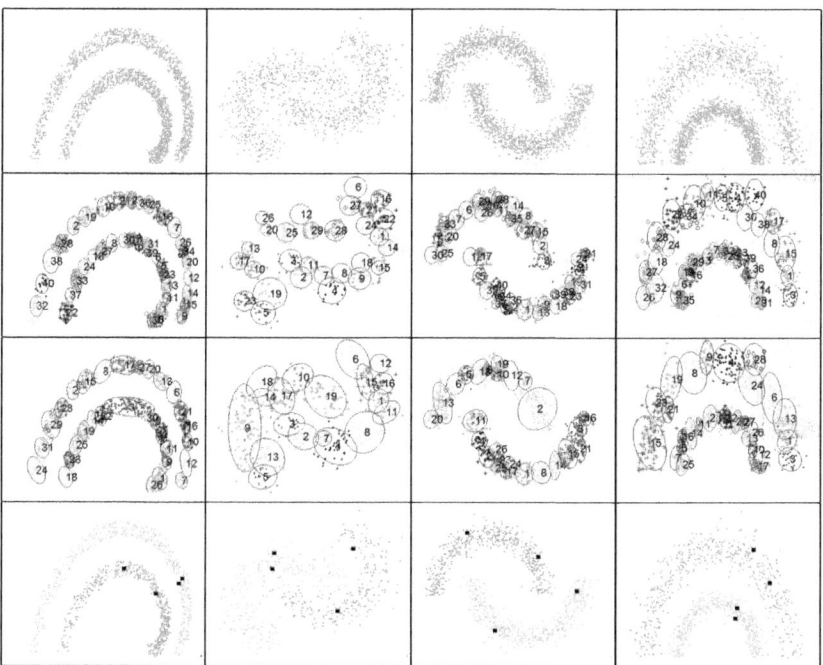

Fig. 1. Experiments on synthetic 2D-datasets with two classes. From top to bottom in rows, input data, preliminary initialisation, initialisation refinement and results of the presented technique.

Figure 2 shows the results obtained on synthetic $2D$-datasets in a multi-class schema. The first row of the figure shows the input datasets from which, although these datasets are provided unlabelled, is easy to have an idea of which should be the ideal clustering solution. These datasets, let us name DS1, DS2 and DS3[1] from left to right in columns,

---

[1] DS2 and DS3 datasets are available from CLUTO - Software for Clustering High-Dimensional Datasets at *http://glaros.dtc.umn.edu/gkhome/cluto/cluto/download*.

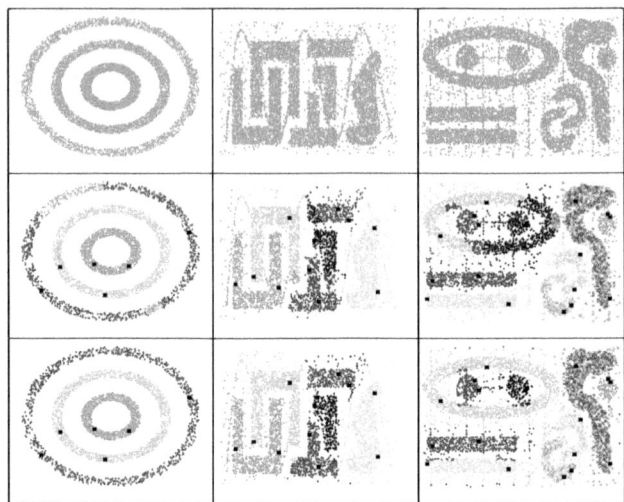

Fig. 2. Experiments on synthetic 2D-datasets multi-class. From top to bottom in rows, input data, results obtained by **Semi-LGC** and results obtained by the presented technique (**Semi-PR**).

have been used not only for testing our proposal but for comparing our results with the semi-supervised algorithm proposed by Zhou *et al.* in [12], hereafter called **Semi-LGC**. This algorithm is a very well-known work and representative of graph based semi-supervised learning approaches. Parameters for the **Semi-LGC** algorithm have been estimated in a similar way to [8], being the kernel parameter σ conveniently defined as the third part of the average distance between each point and its nearest neighbour.

Figure 2 shows in its second row the results obtained by **Semi-LGC** algorithm whereas the results obtained by our proposal are shown in the third row. As it can be seen, **Semi-PR** has found more consistent solutions than **Semi-LGC** for these datasets, solving perfectly DS1 and obtaining an acceptable labelling result for DS2 and DS3. Since **Semi-LGC** algorithm works in a transductive way, for this experiment no division into training and test sets has been done. The same two supervised samples per class (randomly selected) have been used for **Semi-PR** and **Semi-LGC** algorithms.

Finally, it is also important to compare the performance of the two semi-supervised approaches in terms of the classification accuracy for different number of labelled samples. We have used the datasets shown in Figure 1 to this end. Let us name TOY1, TOY2, TOY3 and TOY4 to each column (dataset) of the figure. Again, no division into training and test set has been done and the same supervised samples, randomly selected, per class have been used in both algorithms. Figure 3 shows the classification rate (y-axis) for each semi-supervised method related to the number of labelled samples provided per class (x-axis). Each method has been carried out 10 times in order to reduce the influence of the stochasticity in the experiment.

As it can be seen, both algorithms perform very similar in datasets TOY1, TOY2 and TOY3. However, our proposal clearly outperforms the classification accuracy obtained by **Semi-LGC** in TOY4.

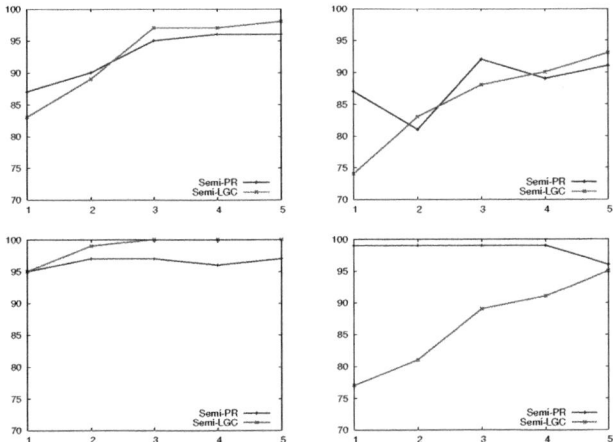

Fig. 3. Performance obtained for **Semi-LGC** algorithm and our proposal (**Semi-PR**) related to the number of supervised samples per class used. From left to right and top to bottom, classification accuracy for TOY1, TOY2, TOY3 and TOY4 datasets.

3.2   Results on Colour Image Segmentation

The proposed technique has also been used for segmenting colour images. The total amount of pixels is equally divided into two sets, one for training and another for test. From each image, the number of classes is known and only two labelled pixels per class are provided to the algorithm, which have randomly been taken from the training set. Each sample is a $2D$-vector representing the chroma of a pixel in the $L^*a^*b^*$ colour space, that is, the a^*b^* dimensions.

Figure 4 shows the image segmentation results obtained for the well-known images of *house* and *toys*. As it can be seen, the segmentation results are quite robust, especially in the case of the *house* image. The segmentation result for *toys* image, although acceptable, shows some important mistakes mainly due to the effect of shadows and brightness. Note that there are some isolated pixels that are badly labelled. This is due to the fact that there is no spatial constraint in the process, but some spatial regularisation could be applied as in [4].

Fig. 4. Image segmentation results. From left to right, source image *house* (5 classes), segmentation result, source image *toys* (12 classes) and its segmentation result.

4   Conclusions

The main objective of this work is to develop a robust semi-supervised algorithm using probabilistic relaxation that can be applied to several application problems. Our methodology satisfies the use of few labelled samples and the assignment of labels according to the contextual constraints.

This work supports the increasing attention that the semi-supervised learning is receiving during the last years. The presented approach has demonstrated an effective use of labelled and unlabelled data in experiments including classification in toy data problems and image segmentation. For a classification problem, the accuracy obtained has been comparable to a recent semi-supervised approach from the literature, being capable to reach the highest classification rates with very few labelled samples. For an image segmentation problem, the methodology has demonstrated some promising results in classic images from the literature.

The promising results obtained in terms of the amount of supervised information needed to finish the task allow our proposal to be very suitable for partial annotation. Therefore, in order to extend this work, further actions will include testing the algorithm from a practical point of view in interactive image segmentation or applications in remote sensing or medical imaging. Future work will also include testing the algorithm in other problems *i)* with higher dimensionality, *ii)* in presence of noise and *iii)* with a higher level of overlapping among the classes.

References

1. Chapelle, O., Scholkopf, B., Zien, A. (eds.): Semi-supervised Learning. MIT Press (2006)
2. Christmas, W.J.: Structural matching in computer vision using probabilistic reasoning. PhD thesis, CVSSP, University of Surrey (1995)
3. Christmas, W.J., Kittler, J., Petrou, M.: Structural matching in computer vision using probabilistic relaxation. IEEE Trans. on PAMI 17(8), 749–764 (1995)
4. Diplaros, A., Vlassis, N., Gevers, T.: A spatially constrained generative model and an EM algorithm for image segmentation. IEEE Trans. on Neural Networks 18(3), 798–808 (2007)
5. Faber, P.: A theoretical framework for relaxation processes in pattern recognition: Application to robust nonparametric contour generalization. IEEE Trans. on PAMI 25(8), 1021–1027 (2003)
6. Gersho, A., Gray, R.M.: Vector quantization and signal compression. Kluwer Academic Publishers, Norwell (1992)
7. Haralick, R.M.: Decision making in context. IEEE Trans. on PAMI 5(4), 417–428 (1983)
8. Liu, Q., Liao, X., Li, H., Stack, J.R., Carin, L.: Semisupervised multitask learning. IEEE Trans. on PAMI 31(6), 1074–1086 (2009)
9. Martinez-Uso, A., Pla, F., Sotoca, J.M.: A semi-supervised gaussian mixture model for image segmentation. In: ICPR, pp. 2941–2944 (2010)
10. Shi, T., Belkin, M., Yu, B.: Data spectroscopy: Learning mixture models using eigenspaces of convolution operators. In: ICML 2008, pp. 936–943 (2008)
11. Wang, H., Hancock, E.R.: Probabilistic relaxation using the heat equation. In: ICPR, vol. 2, pp. 666–669 (2006)
12. Zhou, D., Bousquet, O., Lal, T.N., Weston, J., Schölkopf, B.: Learning with local and global consistency. In: Advances in Neural Information Processing Systems, vol. 16, pp. 321–328. MIT Press (2004)

Identification of the Root Canal from Dental Micro-CT Records[*]

László Szilágyi[1,2], Csaba Dobó-Nagy[3], and Balázs Benyó[1]

[1] Budapest University of Technology and Economics, Department of Control
Engineering and Information Technology, Budapest, Hungary
[2] Sapientia - Hungarian Science University of Transylvania,
Faculty of Technical and Human Science, Tîrgu-Mureş, Romania
lalo@ms.sapientia.ro
[3] Semmelweis University, Independent Section of Radiology, Budapest, Hungary

Abstract. This paper presents a novel semi-automated image processing procedure dedicated to the identification and characterization of the
dental root canal, based on high-resolution micro-CT records. After the
necessary image enhancement, parallel slices are individually segmented
via histogram based quick fuzzy c-means clustering. The 3D model of
root canal is built up from the segmented cross sections using the reconstruction of the inner surface, and the medial line is extracted by a 3D
curve skeletonization algorithm. The central line of the root canal can
finally be approximated as a 3D spline curve. The proposed procedure
may support the planning of several kinds of endodontic interventions.

Keywords: image processing, skeleton extraction, micro computed tomography, fuzzy c-means algorithm.

1 Introduction

The ability to localize all canals within a tooth is essential for rendering successful endodontic treatment and for ensuring long term successful outcome. In
the process, it is necessary to minimize risks and untoward sequelae associated
with treatment of challenging teeth. For example, severely curved or multiple
curved canals may pose diagnostic and treatment challenge. The new imaging
technologies such as CBCT show great promise to ascertain, before endodontic
treatment is commenced. Since this novel modality provides digitized images in
3D, this raw data of the set of voxels serves as a basis of further analysis. In order
to make the system more efficient and effective, the work of our interdisciplinary
research group focuses on the automatic recognition of the root and root canals
and mathematical description of root canal curvatures, as well. The integration
of these steps of image processing in novel systems may significantly improve the

---

[*] This project is supported in part by the New Széchenyi Plan (Project ID: TÁMOP-
4.2.1/B-09/1/KMR-2010-0002), and the Hungarian National Scientific Research
Foundation, Grants No. T80316 and T82066. The work of L. Szilágyi was supported
by János Bolyai Fellowship Program of the Hungarian Academy of Sciences.

C. San Martin and S.-W. Kim (Eds.): CIARP 2011, LNCS 7042, pp. 339–346, 2011.

endodontic practice in the near future. Also, the attempt to automatically locate and classify the root canals may result in significantly decreased chair time for both the patient and the practitioner.

Root canals differ from individual to individual and from tooth to tooth. That is why whenever an endodontic intervention is planned, the shape of that given root canal needs to be accurately detected. Modern medical imaging devices make it possible to record high resolution cross sections of the teeth, which can be fed to image processing techniques to extract the shape of the root canal. This problem has been solved several different ways, based on recorded data originating from various imaging tools.

Analui et al [1] elaborated a geometric approach for modeling and measurement of root canal of human dentition based on stereo digital radiography. Hong et al [6] used both 2D radiographic and endoscopic images to build up a 3D tooth model, while Endo et al [4] turned to ultrasonic imaging and implemented a fuzzy logic based root canal detection. Lee et al [7] used micro CT images and a 3D reconstruction software to measure the three-dimensional canal curvature in maxillary first molars via mathematical modeling.

Recently, several other 3D dental structure reconstruction systems were elaborated, including Willerhausen et al [11] who used X-ray images, and Van Soest et al [8], who applied optical coherence tomography records for 3D structure reconstruction. Germans et al [5] presented an imaging system based on virtual reality that can navigate through the reconstructed 3D structure and make measurements concerning the curvature of the root canal. An excellent review of current researches based on micro-CT data can be found in [9].

In this paper we introduce a complete image processing procedure, which starts with the enhancement of input micro CT slices, continues with 2D image segmentation based on an enhanced fuzzy c-means clustering [10], identification of the root center in 2D slices via a region growing method. At this point the algorithm can bifurcate: we can interpolate the 3D shape of the root canal's medial axis from the centers detected in 2D, or we can build a 3D tubular shape model and extract the medial axis using 3D morphological operations.

2   Background Works: 3D Curve Skeleton Extraction

In two dimensions, the skeleton of an object is defined as the union of locations that possess at least two closest points on the boundary of the object. These places are usually localized using the grass-fire algorithm or the method of largest circles. The straightforward extension of these algorithms to 3D objects produces skeletons consisting of medially placed curves and surfaces. As several computer graphics applications demanded the concise representation of 3D objects with curve arcs, the notion of 3D curve skeleton was introduced, having no mathematical definition, but sharing a series of specific properties [3].

In the followings, we will shortly introduce the 3D curve skeleton extraction methods and discuss only those specific properties, which are relevant in our application. Methods based on thinning or boundary propagation iteratively remove so-called simple points (whose presence does not affect the topology), from the surface of the object. This is generally achieved using a hit-or-miss transform extended to three dimensions. Approaches based on distance fields define and compute the minimum distance of each discrete interior point to the surface of the object, an approximate the curve skeleton with the ridges of this distance field. Geometric models generally use a graph-based representation the approximation of the medial surface or curve of the object. Generalized potential field methods define an internal potential field that differs from the distance field (e.g. electrostatic field generated by placing point charges to all discrete boundary locations [2]), and extract a hierarchical structure composed of critical and saddle points of the field.

Being a straightforward extension of 2D skeletons, 3D curve skeletons are also composed of loci having at least two closest points on the boundary of the object. This property makes curve skeletons suitable to approximate the center line of the root canal. Curve skeletons preserve the topology of the object, and embody the hierarchy of its components, which is relevant at the detection of bifurcations. In order to suit the needs of our application, we have to choose the approach that yields the smoothest curve and performs the least sensitive to slight changes of the object boundary. As we will see later, these latter conditions are most suited by the potential field approach.

For further details on the topic of 3D curve skeletons, the reader is referred to [3], which is an excellent repository of such methods and their properties.

3   Methods

Dental micro CT records consist of single channel intensity images, representing high-resolution (1500-3000dpi) scans of parallel cross sections of a certain tooth. A set of images may contain several hundreds of scanned horizontal planes, which usually are linearly distributed along an axis that is orthogonal to the scanned planes. The distribution of pixel intensity levels varies from slice to slice, but there are a few rules which most slices obey. In this order, the anatomical structure is reflected by pixel intensities. In normal cases, cross sections contain a light gray spot corresponding to the dentin, usually lighter at its edges (that is because the enamel) with circularly distributed texture due to imaging artifacts, possibly surrounding one or more darker regions, which represent the root canal containing soft tissues. The cementum, when visible, is usually somewhat lighter than the dentin.

The main goal of our image processing procedure is to identify the 3D structure of the root canal that we can build up from the inner darker regions identified from all cross sections. Afterwards, we need to track the spatial curve that corresponds to the central line. The detected central line must follow the topology of the root canal, by reflecting its curves and bifurcations.

Figure 1(left) exhibits the diagram of the image processing procedure. The following paragraphs discuss the functionality of each box of the diagram.

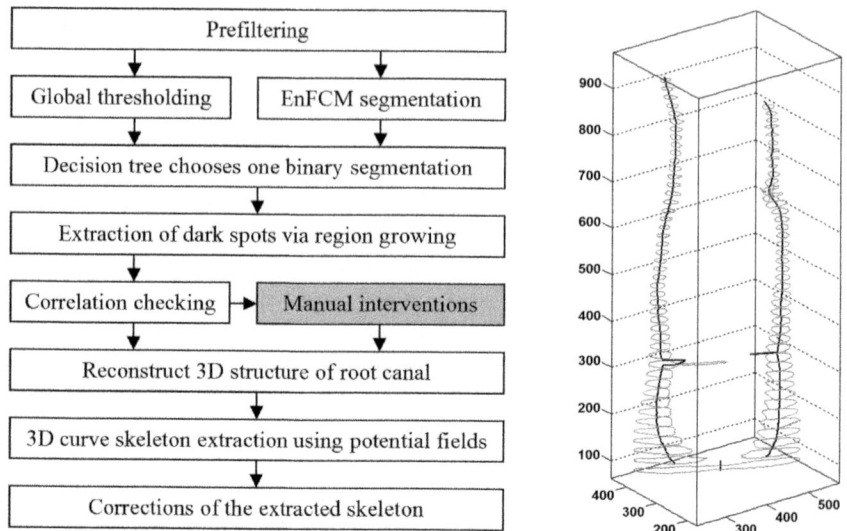

Fig. 1. (left) The steps of the proposed algorithm; (right) Checking the correlation of dark spot centers in neighbor slices reveal the presence of bifurcations (around slice 70) and the need for manual interaction (around slice 310). Both events can be localized and identified automatically.

Preprocessing. The automatic image segmentation must be preceded by some image enhancement steps. In our application, the following preprocessing steps are employed: (1) A simple median filter, which reduces the high frequency noise that is most visible in the dentin's texture; (2) Establishing the region of interest (ROI) by trimming the image: this way we get rid of the dark areas that represent outer space. It is necessary to store the exact coordinates of the ROI; (3) Some basic morphological operators are used to remove texts from the original image and regularize the boundary of the root canal.

Segmentation in 2D. The final result of the planar segmentation should be a binary image. Even if the image enhancement techniques have already suppressed the disturbing textures, in order to assure high quality segmentation, we need to apply a double partitioning and combine their outcome.

In this order, this phase produces two different partitions that are both obtained using the enhanced FCM (EnFCM) clustering algorithm [10]. The first partition is achieved by performing EnFCM on the ROI of the slice, setting the number of clusters to $c = 4$. In the followings, this partition will be referred to as local partition, as it is computed from the local data of the slice. The second partition is produced by a simple thresholding operation, using a previously computed threshold τ_{global} that was obtained by EnFCM from the whole dataset, using $c = 2$ clusters. This latter partition is called global partition of the slice, because it uses the global threshold extracted from the data of all slices. As the matter of fact, not all slices contribute to the global threshold: only a representative selection of slices is taken into consideration, in order to reduce computation time. The global threshold produces a binary image at once. The local partition contains 4 different colors, corresponding to the prototypes of the 4 clusters, v_1 to v_4. Let us suppose the intensity values are ordered increasingly, that is, $v_{i+1} > v_i$, $\forall i = 1 \ldots c - 1$. The 4 clusters are then separated in two classes, using the threshold $\eta_{local} = (v_{i+1} - v_i)/2$, where $i = \arg \max_j \{v_{j+1} - v_j, j = 1 \ldots c - 1\}$. In most cases, both binary images are good quality partitions, but there are exceptions, when one of these algorithms fails. In these cases we need to select the correct partition.

Decision making. In order to provide an intelligent selection of the correct binary partition, we have built up a decision tree, based on 250 slices representing above mentioned exceptions. The decision is made in a four dimensional search space, corresponding to parameters: τ_{global}, and $\tau_i = (v_{i+1} - v_i)/2$, where $i = 1 \ldots 3$. The output of the tree is the decision whether the local or the global binary partition is the correct one. During the training process, we employed the entropy minimization technique until all leaves of the tree became homogeneous. After having the decision tree trained, the decision can be made quickly. Finally we obtain a binary image, where the inner dark regions have to be localized.

Region growing and selection. The identification of dark spots situated within the light area of the binary image, is performed by an iterative region growing method. As long as there are dark pixels in the segmented image, a dark pixel is arbitrarily chosen and a region is grown around it. Outer space (which is also dark) is obviously discarded, and the detected dark spots are separately stored. Each branch of the root canal, which is present in the cross section, should normally be represented by a single dark region within the slice. Unfortunately, mostly because of imaging artifacts or complex shaped canals, there are some cases, when a single canal branch is manifested by more than one dark region. These cases can be detected automatically, but their treatment sometimes requires manual interventions.

Each dark spot has its center point, which we can compute two different ways: as the center of gravity of the spot, or by the means of morphological thinning. The center of gravity is easier to compute, but sometimes it falls outside the spot. Morphological thinning always gives a quasi centrally located center point, but it brings more computational load.

The automatic selection of detected spots can be performed by several different protocols, which are: P1 – always extracts the largest dark spot from the slice; P2 – also extracts the second/third/fourth largest spot if it is present and is larger than a small threshold size; P3 – adaptive, which may extract any number of spots, according to some predefined rules that concern the size of different spots. Protocol P1 can be used in cases of incisor teeth only, when a priori anatomical information makes the presence of a single spot highly probable.

Automatic shape regularization. Due to the artifacts present in the original microCT records, the dark spot detected in certain slices may contain irregularities. There are several kinds of such cases: some can be treated by automatic regularization techniques, while there are also cases that require manual interaction. For example, a light "island" within the dark spot is easily removable. Strange shaped "peninsulas" can be treated by large masked median filter or morphological opening/closing. There are also cases where the real root canal is detected as several separate dark spots situated very close from each other, which need to be unified. Automatic unification is possible using morphological operations or distance transform.

Correlation checking. The accurate segmentation of the microCT images may demand manual intervention. Luckily, the necessity of such steps is visible from the correlation of detected dark spots within adjacent cross sections, or in other words, there cannot be a relevant change in the structure found within neighbor slices. Wherever there is a large distance between the center points detected in neighbor slices, either we have a bifurcation, or some intervention is likely to be beneficial. In case of bifurcation, the number of dark spots in the neighbor slices should differ, but correlate with the other neighbors of each.

Manual interactions to improve accuracy. The user has the opportunity to change the result of the automatic segmentation within any of the slices. As it was justified in the previous section, the user is advised where the interaction is required. The implemented manual interventions are: M1 – overrule the decision dictated by the decision tree; M2 – Change the local threshold to any desired value; M3 – discard some of the automatically detected dark spots; M4 – unify several dark spots using a parametric active contour model (snake).

Reconstruct the spatial shape of the root canal. The inner dark spots localized within each slice are put together in space to form a three dimensional object that describes the shape of the root canal. The center line of this object will be searched for using a procedure based on 3D curve skeleton extraction.

3D curve skeleton extraction. As mentioned in [3], there are various approximation algorithms for the 3D curve skeleton of voxelized objects. We need to employ such an approach which provides a smooth curve with low amount of branches, and extremely insensitive to zigzagged surfaces. This sort of curve skeleton is reportedly produced by potential field methods. We have successfully implemented the method proposed in [2], and applied it to extract the skeletons of the root canal object.

Corrections of the extracted skeleton. The 3D curve skeleton accurately handles critical cases like root canal bifurcations, or slices that are far from being orthogonal to the root canal's direction. Under such circumstances, the curve skeleton is an excellent approximation of the center line. However, at all endings of the root canal, the curve skeleton is either shorter than it should be as the iterative thinning has its effect from every direction, or it has several short branches connected to high curvature points of the surface of the reconstructed 3D object. In order to produce an accurate center line with the skeleton extraction algorithm, we need to choose the divergence parameter of Cornea's potential field approach low enough, so that the endings of the skeleton towards superficial high curvature points are not present. Further on, in order to avoid the shortened endings of the skeleton, we need to virtually lengthen all endings of the reconstructed tubular 3D object with as many slices (identical to the peripheral one) as necessary. The number of such virtually added slices is well approximated as the shortest radius of the dark spot in the peripheral slice.

Most steps of the algorithm summarized in Fig. 1(left) are performed automatically. The only box having gray background represents a step that requires manual interaction. This step is not mandatory in simple cases, e.g. incisor teeth on images with low amount of artifacts.

4   Results and Discussion

The proposed algorithm can automatically process more than 95% of the recorded image sets, while the rest of the cases need manual interaction. Using a Pentium4 PC, the processing of a slice in 2D lasts 0.3-0.5 seconds, while a central canal reconstruction is interpolated in less than a second. The accuracy of the detected medial axis also depends on the number of slices involved. An accuracy that is suitable to guide medical intervention can be obtained from carefully selected subsets of at least 50 slices.

Figure 2(left) exhibits the intermediary results provided by the 2D segmentation. Three cases of various difficulties are presented in the three rows of the image. The first row presents a simple case involving a slice with two dark spots representing two different, easily detectable root canals (there was a bifurcation several slices away from this one). The slice in the middle row manifests an odd shaped dark region, which was successfully detected. The slice presented in the

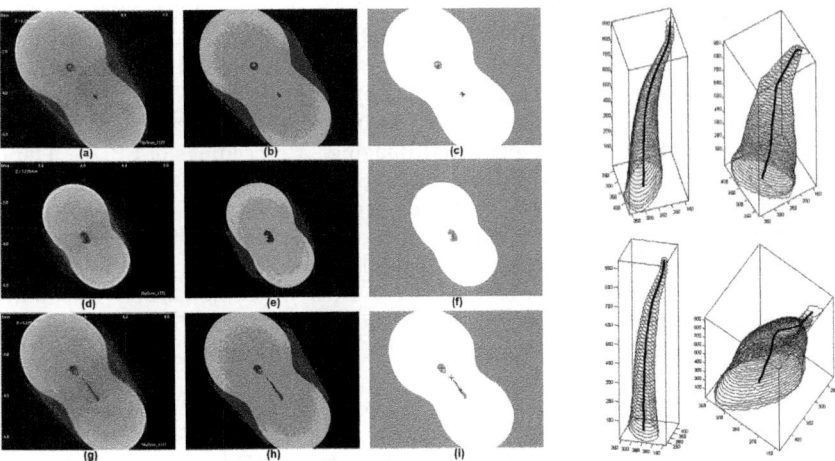

Fig. 2. (left) Detailed view of image segmentation in 2D: each row represents a different slice. First column shows the original recorded images; second column presents the clustered images (4 clusters); last column indicates the segmented binary images with detected center points; (right) 3D views of a root canal, with the extracted medial line. Numbers indicate pixels, which are easily convertible to millimeters.

third row shows a difficult case: three different dark spots are present in the segmented images, but they belong to only two different canal branches. This is the case which requires correlation test with neighbors or decision overruling performed by the ANN.

Figure 2(right) shows four different 3D views of a root canal, together with its detected medial axis. The central line was produced from 944 equidistant slices, segmented in 2D with binary separation using the global optimal threshold.

5   Conclusions

We have proposed and implemented a complex image processing procedure for the detection of the center line from dental micro CT records. In most cases the algorithm performs automatically, but there are still a few nodes in the decision tree where the decision has to be made interactively. Thus we have created an imaging system that can efficiently assist certain medical interventions.

References

1. Analoui, M., Krisnamurthy, S., Brown, C.: Modeling and measurement of root canal using stereo digital radiography. In: Proceedings of SPIE - The International Society for Optical Engineering, vol. 3976, pp. 306–314 (2000)
2. Cornea, N.D., Silver, D., Yuan, X., Balasubramanian, R.: Computing hierarchical curve-skeletons of 3D objects. The Visual Computer 21, 945–955 (2005)
3. Cornea, N.D., Silver, D., Min, P.: Curve-skeleton properties, applications, and algorithms. IEEE Trans. Vis. Comp. Graph. 13, 530–548 (2007)
4. Endo, M., Kobashi, S., Kondo, K., Hata, Y.: Dentistry support ultrasonic system for root canal treatment aided by fuzzy logic. In: Proceedings of IEEE International Conference on Systems, Man and Cybernetics, vol. 2, pp. 1494–1499 (2005)
5. Germans, D.M., Spoelder, H.J.W., Renambot, L., Bal, H.E., van Daatselaar, S., van der Stelt, P.: Measuring in virtual reality: a case study in dentistry. IEEE Trans. Instrum. Meas. 57, 1177–1184 (2008)
6. Hong, S.Y., Dong, J.: 3-D root canal modeling for advanced endodontic treatment. In: Progress in Biomedical Optics and Imaging - Proceedings of SPIE - The International Society for Optical Engineering, vol. 4702, pp. 321–330 (2002)
7. Lee, J.K., Ha, B.H., Choi, J.H., Perinpanayagam, H.: Quantitative three-dimensional analysis of root canal curvature in maxillary first molars using micro-computed tomography. J. Endodontics 32, 941–945 (2006)
8. van Soest, G., Shemesh, H., Wu, M.K., van der Sluis, L.W.M., Wesselink, P.R.: Optical coherence tomography for endodontic imaging. In: Progress in Biomedical Optics and Imaging - Proceedings of SPIE 6843, vol. 6843, art. no. 68430F, pp. 1–8 (2008)
9. Swain, M.V., Xue, J.: State of the art of micro-CT applications in dental research. Int. J. Oral. Sci. 1, 177–188 (2009)
10. Szilágyi, L., Benyó, Z., Szilágyi, S.M., Adam, H.S.: MR brain image segmentation using an enhanced fuzzy c-means algorithm. In: 25th Annual Int'l. Conference of IEEE Engineering in Medicine and Biology Society, pp. 724–726 (2003)
11. Willershausen, B., Kasaj, A., Röhrig, B., Marroquin, B.B.: Radiographic investigation of frequency and location of root canal curvatures in human mandibular anterior incisors in vitro. J. Endodontics 34, 152–156 (2008)

Semi-supervised Constrained Clustering with Cluster Outlier Filtering

Cristián Bravo and Richard Weber

Department of Industrial Engineering
Universidad de Chile
{cbravo,rweber}@dii.uchile.cl

Abstrcat. Constrained clustering addresses the problem of creating minimum variance clusters with the added complexity that there is a set of constraints that must be fulfilled by the elements in the cluster. Research in this area has focused on "must-link" and "cannot-link" constraints, in which pairs of elements must be in the same or in different clusters, respectively. In this work we present a heuristic procedure to perform clustering in two classes when the restrictions affect all the elements of the two clusters in such a way that they depend on the elements present in the cluster. This problem is highly susceptible to outliers in each cluster (extreme values that create infeasible solutions), so the procedure eliminates elements with extreme values in both clusters, and achieves adequate performance measures at the same time. The experiments performed on a company database allow to discover a great deal of information, with results that are more readily interpretable when compared to classical k-means clustering.

1   Introduction

Among all methods for unsupervised pattern recognition, clustering [9] is possibly the most widely used technique. One of the research areas that has been receiving increasing attention in the last decade is the use of additional information regarding the problem, incorporated to the problem by using constraints that the elements must satisfy. This area is called "constrained clustering" [3], and has been applied to a wide range of fields [1,6,7].

The methods of constrained clustering present a semi-supervised approach to obtain segments of a dataset incorporating certain restrictions that the members of one cluster, the members of different clusters, or the general structure of the clusters must fulfill. The term "semi-supervised" refers to the incorporation of knowledge that is not directly present in the data, or that is known only for a limited number of cases, in order to improve the results on the entire domain.

In this paper, a method to perform semi-supervised clustering with two classes is presented, that differs from the usual formulation in a key aspect: the constraints have to be satisfied by all the elements present in a cluster, against all the elements in the other cluster, clearly a challenge since simply changing one element from one cluster to another changes the whole set of constraints.

C. San Martin and S.-W. Kim (Eds.): CIARP 2011, LNCS 7042, pp. 347–354, 2011.

Such application is common in social phenomena, where it is expected that the members of one group are, in some aspects, different than all the elements of the other cluster. One example is clustering customers whose client value is different, or segmenting groups with a defined utility.

In order to solve this problem, a heuristic method that takes into account the structure of the problem will be presented, to then test the proposed approach against classical k-means clustering, using a database of unreturned (defaulted) loans.

This work is structured as follows: Section 2 provides a brief overview of semi-supervised clustering, to then present the proposed algorithm in section 3. An application of the method and its results are presented in section 4, and finally conclusions are drawn in section 5.

2   Constrained Clustering and Semi-supervised Methods

There are two different approaches reported in the literature for constrained clustering, as noted for example in [4], and both are based on the concept of "Must-Link" and "Cannot-Link" restrictions. The first set of constraints indicates that two elements must always belong to the same cluster, whereas the second one does not permit the presence of two elements in the same cluster.

The methods that can be constructed from these pairwise constraints have been studied in depth, and usually differ in the role of the respective constraints: in the first case the algorithm fulfills an objective or distance function using the information from restrictions, the best known application of this work appearing in [2], which uses Hidden Markov Random Fields to estimate the probability of belonging to each cluster.

In the second type of models, the constraints limit the presence of elements in one cluster or the other, using some heuristic approach to change and alter the clusters and converging to a new solution. One example of this type of procedures is [8] where the authors propose to alter the k-means procedure and iteratively construct clusters. A similar approach is followed in this paper adapting it to the new problem: each of the elements of one cluster must satisfy the restrictions against most of the elements of the other cluster. The inclusion of these constraints for each instance has not received such extensive study so far, with some attempts to select only relevant constraints to, for example, make the problem more tractable and select the information that is more relevant [10].

There are several issues that must be addressed in the problem stated above. First, each time an element is changed from a cluster many restrictions have to be recalculated and re-checked. Second, the high number of restrictions can make the problem intractable. And finally, if there is an element with an extreme value in one of the clusters, that is, an element whose variables make the value of the constraints too high or too low, the problem can easily become infeasible. To approach this, in the next section we will present a heuristic approach to solve the problem efficiently.

3   Iterative Procedure for Constrained Clustering with Extreme Value Elimination

The procedure presented here differs from previous works in that it filters outliers in each iteration, checking for the best solution in terms of violations and cluster robustness. In each iteration the results are not necessarily feasible, because such search is an NP-hard problem and it would make the algorithm impractical [4]. With this modification, the procedure is very fast, as it is necessary when clustering medium to large datasets.

If we assume a dataset X with N elements, and a partition of the dataset into two clusters, such that each one (X_1 and X_2) is formed by elements $x_i^1 \in X_1$, $i \in \{1, \ldots, I_1\}$ and $x_j^2 \in X_2$, $j \in \{1, \ldots, I_2\}$, with centroids c_1 and c_2, the problem is to solve the following optimization problem, adapted from a common formulation [5]:

$$\min_{M, c_1, c_2, \text{ext}_1, \text{ext}_2} \quad \sum_{i=1}^{N} \sum_{k=1}^{2} \|x_i - c_k\|^2 \cdot m_i$$

$$
\begin{aligned}
s.t. \quad & M \in \{0, 1\}^N \\
& R_1 \cdot x_i^1 (\geq \vee \leq) \text{ext}_1 \quad \forall x_i^1 \mid m_i = 1 \\
& R_2 \cdot x_j^2 (\geq \vee \leq) \text{ext}_2 \quad \forall x_j^2 \mid m_i = 0 \\
& \text{ext}_1 (\geq \vee \leq) b_2 \cdot x_i^2 \quad \forall x_i^1 \mid m_i = 0 \\
& \text{ext}_2 (\geq \vee \leq) b_1 \cdot x_j^1 \quad \forall x_j^2 \mid m_i = 1
\end{aligned}
\tag{1}
$$

Where R_1 and R_2 are the set of parameters associated with the constraints that each case must satisfy, against all the other functions of the values in the other cluster, represented by vectors b_1 and b_2 and extreme values ext_1 and ext_2. Vector M indicates the cluster to which element i belongs, taking a value of 1 if the element belongs to cluster 1 and of 0 if it is not. This formulation is a reduced form used to illustrate the complexity of the problem, since the variable m_i is present in the definition of the restrictions. A more explicit version would have $N \times N$ restrictions, one for each element and cluster, since *a priori* it is not known in which cluster each element is, nor the centroids of each cluster.

In order to solve this problem, we propose a heuristic procedure that takes into account the constraints that must be satisfied and takes advantage of the fact that the linear restrictions are bound to possess a maximum or minimum value in the dataset, that is, that given a fixed distribution of elements in the cluster, only the values ext_1 and ext_2 have to be checked against the elements of the cluster. The procedure starts with random centroids, and in each iteration the elements in the cluster are compared to the extreme value of the other cluster, i.e., if the element is in cluster 1, then it is checked whether restriction $R_1 \cdot x_i^1 (\geq \vee \leq) \text{ext}_1$ is satisfied with the largest or smallest element present in cluster 2, according to what is necessary. In case at the end of the movements the conditions are not fulfilled by all cases, then the extreme values in both clusters are removed from the analysis and the process is repeated. The algorithm continues until

---

Algorithm 1. CCF(Dataset X, R_1, R_2, b_1, b_2)

1: $C = (C_1, C_2) \leftarrow$ Random(size(2))
2: Flag $\leftarrow 1^N$ {*If element is used or outlier*}
3: **while** Movement in $C > \epsilon$ **do**
4:     Assign elements to closest cluster
5:     $M1 \leftarrow X$(cluster $= 1$)
6:     $M2 \leftarrow X$(cluster $= 2$)
7:     Calculate ext_1 and ext_2 from vectors $M2 \cdot b_2$ and $M1 \cdot b_2$
8:     Violations $\leftarrow 0$, Eliminated $\leftarrow 0$
9:     **while** Eliminated $< 0.01N$ **or** Violations $> \epsilon N$ **do**
10:        **for** $i = 1$ **to** N **do**
11:            **if** Flag(i) $= 0$ **then**
12:                Skip i
13:            **end if**
14:            **if** Cluster(x_i) $= 1$ **then**
15:                $R \leftarrow R_1 \cdot x_i$
16:            **else**
17:                $R \leftarrow R_2 \cdot x_i$
18:            **end if**
19:            **if** Element i violates conditions **then**
20:                Change cluster of element
21:                Violations $\leftarrow$ Violations $+ 1$
22:            **end if**
23:        **end for**
24:        **if** Violations $> \epsilon$ **then**
25:            Flag($I(\text{ext}_2)$) $\leftarrow 0$, Flag($I(\text{ext}_1)$) $\leftarrow 0$
26:            Eliminated $\leftarrow$ Eliminated $+ 2$
27:        **end if**
28:        Recalculate($M1, M2, \text{ext}_1, \text{ext}_2$)
29:     **end while**
30:     Recalculate(C)
31: **end while**

---

both the violations are below a threshold and the values of the centroids do not move more than a given tolerance. The algorithm for constrained clustering with filtering (CCF) is described in Algorithm 1.

The elements in each cluster have to satisfy the restrictions against most of the elements in the other cluster, and this is accomplished by eliminating a small number of extreme cases in each iteration and seeking that all other satisfy the constraints. At each step the minimum variance cluster is approximated (by assigning elements to the closest cluster), and is this solution the one that is perturbed by moving the elements according to the constraints. The convergence of the algorithm is ensured, since at worst case (infeasible problem) only two elements will remain and the method will stop with one element per cluster.

4   Experimental Results

To test the presented methodology, a dataset consisting of 24,500 loans granted to mass-market is available, all of which were not returned. The database originates from a Chilean organization, and comprises a 10 year period, from 1997 to 2007. Each loan is described by the following variables, which are associated to the customer or to the loan itself:

- Collaterals: The collaterals are described by two variables. The first is a dummy variable that indicates whether the customer secured the loan or not (With_Collaterals), The second one represents the value of the collateral (Value_Collateral_UF), in UF, the Chilean inflation-adjusted monetary unit.
- Amount and Rate: The amount of the loan, in UF, and the total annual interest rate charged for the loan.
- Arrears and Cancellations: The total sum of days the installments of the loan were in arrear before defaulting is included in variable Days_Arrear. Also, sometimes the institution will cancel the payment of punishments and excess interest that arises from arrear. This event is resumed into two different variables, considering the number of times this happened in the loan lifetime (Num_Cond), and the amount that was reduced (Amount_Cond). Additionally if some of the interests due to be paid are also discounted from the installments, this value is annotated in variable Interest_Low.
- Extensions: Sometimes the company will extend the period of an installment. The number of times a customer applies to this benefit appears in variable Num_Post, and the amount adjusted appears in Amount_Adjust, and, since the adjustment can be positive or negative, the total amount of negative adjustments is incorporated into Negative_Adj.

4.1   Constraints

In this case, a set of constraints is created from the economical behavior expected between the customers. In particular, the set R of restrictions characterizes the rationality of not paying back the loan for two reasons: failure in capacity of repayment (class G), and failure in willingness of repayment (class W). In this setting, customers request an amount x_G or x_W of money, are charged a rate r, and discount their income using discount rates of δ_W and δ_G. The lender has requested a collateral valued at C_i for each customer i, and discounted by the company by a value of 40%, that is $\alpha = 0.6$, which is a known value, and discounts its income by a value of $\delta_C = 0.93$. There is an external chance of losing income (which translates into failure in paying back the loan) given by $q = 0.15$, extracted from the long term default rate of the institution, and an *a priori* belief that the customer is of class W given by $\theta = 0.55$, arising from internal estimations of the company, as well as parameters δ_G and δ_W which were fixed to values of 0.75 and 0.5 respectively.Under this setting, and assuming linear utilities, it is possible to estimate the amounts that should be requested such that rationality is achieved. The restrictions that are proposed are:

$$x_{G1}(1 - \delta_G(1 - q)(1 + r)) + \delta_G x_{G2}(1 - q)\cdot$$
$$(1 - \delta_G(1 - q)(1 + r)) - \delta_G q C_1 - \delta_G^2(1 - q)q C_2 \geq 0 \tag{2}$$
$$\theta x_{G1}(-1 + \delta_C(1 - q)(1 + r)) - (1 - \theta)x_{W1} + x_{G2}\delta_C\theta\cdot$$
$$(-1 + \delta_C(1 - q)(1 + r)) + C_1\alpha\delta_C(1 - \theta(1 - q)) + \theta(1 - q)q\delta_C^2\alpha C_2 \geq 0 \tag{3}$$
$$x_{W1} \geq C_1\delta_W q \tag{4}$$

These restrictions come from assuming that customers in class G desire a second loan, while customers in class W do not. The extensive formulation of this game-theory problem is not relevant to the clustering procedure itself, so it will be omitted in this work.

4.2   Results

The experiments are run on the normalized database, and then the results are de-normalized to better reflect the differences obtained, the method was implemented using MATLAB and the code is available upon request. The method eliminates only 2% of the total cases, and converges in two minutes which, given that the database is medium sized, it is a very good convergence time. To test the stability of the method, the procedure was run 10 times from different random starting points, all converging to roughly the same result as is to be expected.

To study the information that the model brings the centroids of the cluster must be studied. Table 1 (left) presents the obtained results.From the clustering procedure it arises that the differences in collaterals are important but have to be interpreted carefully, since the collateral value is used in the constraints. More relevant is that the percentage of customers with a collateral is not really meaningful between the clusters, so the conclusion is that is not the presence of a collateral the relevant information, but its value. Also, customers in class G request a far larger amount for their loans, which would be consistent with a default based on the capacity of payment. Considering the total number of days in arrear, class G accumulates 170+ days more than class W before defaulting, indicating that they make a greater effort of paying back the loan than class W. The procedure also shows that they apply for a larger number of renegotiations (0.74 per customer in average), get greater adjustments and debt reliefs, and are more prone to receive a discount on their due interests (1.32 UF per customer in average, versus 0.31). Finally, they pay almost one full installment more than the customers in class W.

The values of the variables hint that there is indeed a different behavior detected, but to shed light on whether this procedure brings indeed more information than classic K-Means clustering, Table 1 (right) presents the results of a K-Means clustering procedure that will be used for comparison. Stability comparisons, such as Davis-Bouldin index, are not relevant, since obviously the constrained algorithm will have a greater standard deviation than the unconstrained problem.

Table 1. De-normalized centroids for semi-supervised clustering procedure (left) and k-means procedure (right)

Variable	Class G	Class W	Variable	Cluster 1	Cluster 1
With_Collaterals	0.41	0.33	With_Collaterals	0.35	0.34
Amount	52.94	14.82	Amount	21.78	22.57
Days_Arrear	895.78	719.82	Days_Arrear	1242.10	337.93
Num_Cond	0.27	0.36	Num_Cond	0.56	0.15
Num_Post	0.85	0.46	Num_Post	0.42	0.64
Num_Reneg	0.72	0.45	Num_Reneg	0.68	0.35
Amount_Adjust	-0.27	-0.08	Amount_Adjunt	-0.15	-0.05
Amount_Cond	4.23	2.44	Amount_Cond	4.63	1.21
Negative_Adj	0.41	0.09	Negative_Adj	0.26	0.06
Interest_Low	1.32	0.31	Interest_Low	1.06	0.04
Payments	2.81	2.42	Payments	2.25	2.70
Value_Coll_UF	71.37	7.93	Value_Coll_UF	18.55	21.64
Rate	1.10	1.10	Rate	1.10	1.10

The two tables show the advantages of incorporating additional information in the form of constraints, since the k-means procedure focuses on two variables: days in arrear and reduction in rate (Interest_Low). All the other variables present only minor differences or equivalent results to the proposed method. The conclusion that can be extracted from the k-means procedure is that there are indeed two groups with some difference in their payments behavior, but the information that can be deduced does not permit a more meaningful interpretation. This is contrasted with the much richer information that the semi-supervised clustering procedure brings, where the differences between these variables are also present, but are also complemented with a series of other, more subtle, differences that arise from the restrictions imposed.

5   Conclusions

A procedure to estimate the centroids of a two-class constrained clustering problem was presented. The main difference between this procedure and the ones presented previously in the literature is that the constraints are associated to all elements in each cluster, as well as allowing intra-cluster restrictions. This problem is much harder to solve than traditional constrained clustering with must-link and cannot-link constraints, since each time an object changes its cluster, all the constraints have to be re-checked. Additionally, since all the objects must be checked with respect to all restrictions, it is usually not possible to satisfy the constraints for all elements.

The proposed method is a heuristic procedure based on first obtaining minimum variance clusters and then adjusting the constraints and filtering outliers. The experimental results show that it performs fast and reliably, presents few eliminated cases, and shows a reasonable convergence time.

However, the most important feature of the method is that the results use correctly the additional information that is considered through the constraints. When applying the method to a database of defaulted loans, the results from a classical K-Means algorithm are greatly enriched, presenting more subtle differences between the classes and profiling two different segments of defaulters using only expected rational behavior.

It can be concluded that the model is useful for the presented problem, and that the results show the benefits of including external information in clustering procedures. Future work in this line is to use these results to improve classification in credit risk problems.

Acknowledgments. The first author would like to acknowledge CONICYT for the grants that finance this research, to the Ph.D. program in Engineering Systems for their support in the development of this work, and to C. Mora for her aid in editing this paper. Also, support from the Institute on Complex Engineering Systems (ICM: P-05-004-F, CONICYT: FBO16) (www.sistemasdeingenieria.cl) is acknowledged.

References

1. Bard, J.F., Jarrah, A.: Large-scale constrained clustering for rationalizing pickup and delivery operations. Transportation Research Part B: Methodological 43(5), 542–561 (2009)
2. Basu, S., Bilenko, M., Mooney, R.J.: A probabilistic framework for semi-supervised clustering. In: Proceedings of the Tenth ACM SIGKDD International Conference on Knowledge Discovery and Data Mining, KDD 2004, pp. 59–68. ACM, New York (2004)
3. Basu, S., Davidson, I., Wagstaff, K.: Constrained Clustering: Advances in Algorithms, Theory, and Applications. Chapman & Hall/CRC (2008)
4. Davidson, I., Ravi, S.S.: Clustering with constraints: Feasibility issues and the k-means algorithm. In: Proceedings of the SIAM International Conference on Data Mining (SDM 2005) (2005)
5. Dogan, H., Guzelis, C.: Gradient networks for clustering. In: Gknar, Ä.C., Sevgi, L. (eds.) Complex Computing-Networks. Springer Proceedings Physics, vol. 104, pp. 275–278. Springer, Heidelberg (2006)
6. Levy, M., Sandler, M.: Structural segmentation of musical audio by constrained clustering. IEEE Transactions on Audio, Speech, and Language Processing 16(2), 318–326 (2008)
7. Patil, G., Modarres, R., Myers, W., Patankar, P.: Spatially constrained clustering and upper level set scan hotspot detection in surveillance geoinformatics. Environmental and Ecological Statistics 13, 365–377 (2006)
8. Wagstaff, K., Cardie, C., Rogers, S., Schroedl, S.: Constrained k-means clustering with background knowledge. In: Proceedings of the Eighteenth International Conference on Machine Learning, pp. 577–584. Morgan Kaufmann (2001)
9. Xu, R., Wunsch, D.: Clustering. Wiley-IEEE Press (2008)
10. Zhao, W., He, Q., Ma, H., Shi, Z.: Effective semi-supervised document clustering via active learning with instance-level constraints. Knowledge and Information Systems 1, 1–19 (2011)

New Results on Minimum Error Entropy Decision Trees

Joaquim P. Marques de Sá[1], Raquel Sebastião[2], João Gama[2], and Tânia Fontes[1]

[1] INEB-Instituto de Engenharia Biomédica, FEUP, Universidade do Porto,
Rua Dr. Roberto Frias, s/n, 4200-465 Porto, Portugal
{jmsa,trfontes}@fe.up.pt
[2] LIAAD - INESC Porto, L.A., Rua de Ceuta, 118, 6
4050-190 Porto, Portugal
{raquel,jgama}@liaad.up.pt

Abstract. We present new results on the performance of Minimum Error Entropy (MEE) decision trees, which use a novel node split criterion. The results
were obtained in a comparive study with popular alternative algorithms, on 42
real world datasets. Carefull validation and statistical methods were used. The
evidence gathered from this body of results show that the error performance of
MEE trees compares well with alternative algorithms. An important aspect to
emphasize is that MEE trees generalize better on average without sacrifing error
performance.

Keywords: decision trees, entropy-of-error, node split criteria.

1 Introduction

Binary decision trees, based on univariate node splits, are popular tools in pattern recognition applications, given the semantic interpretation often assignable to nodal decision rules and fast computation. Available design algorithms for these trees are based
on greedy construction of locally optimal nodes using some node split criterion. All
node split criteria proposed until today are based, as far as we know, on estimates of
class conditional input distributions at each node. A recent KDnuggets Poll
(www.kdnuggets.com) disclosed that the most used analytic software were Rapid-
Miner, R, and KNIME (freeware tools) and SPSS, SAS and Matlab (commercial
tools). The decision tree algorithms in all these tools use "classic" split criteria
(known since the seminal works on decision trees; for a survey see e.g. [1]): Gini,
Information Gain and Twoing splitting rules.

In a recent paper [2] we proposed a new type of node split criterion that is not a
"randomness measure" of class conditional distributions; instead, it is a "randomness
measure" of nodal error distribution, concretely its entropy. We showed how to use
this concept in the construction of "Minimum Error Entropy" (MEE) trees.

In the present paper we provide further comparative results on the application to
real world datasets of MEE tree and competing tree design algorithms, using more
datasets and sound validation and analysis methods, allowing, therefore, to reach a
body of well-grounded conclusions concerning the advantages of using MEE trees.

C. San Martin and S.-W. Kim (Eds.): CIARP 2011, LNCS 7042, pp. 355–362, 2011.
© Springer-Verlag Berlin Heidelberg 2011

2 MEE Trees

MEE trees are built by selecting, at each node a pair (x, ω), where x is a data feature and ω a class label, minimizing the error entropy. Consider a candidate split between a class $\omega_k \in \Omega$ and its complement $\overline{\omega}_k = \cup_{i \neq k} \omega_i$ using a rule y based on the values of x (e.g., $x < \Delta$). For any x, the rule y produces a class assignment $\omega_y(x) \in \{\omega_k, \overline{\omega}_k\}$ which is compared to the true class label $\omega(x)$; an "error" variable $\omega(x) - \omega_y(x)$ is then defined. Denoting T and Y the random variables (r.v.) for a convenient coding of $\omega(x)$ and $\omega_y(x)$ (say, assigning 1 if $\omega = \omega_k$ and 0 otherwise), we then also have an r.v. of the "errors" (deviations), $E = T - Y$, taking value in $\{-1, 0, 1\}$, such that:

- $P(E = 1) = P(T = 1, Y = 0) \equiv P_{10}$ is the misclassification probability of ω_k;
- $P(E = -1) = P(T = 0, Y = 1) \equiv P_{01}$ is the misclassification probability of $\overline{\omega}_k$;
- $P(E = 0) = 1 - P_{01} - P_{10}$ is the correct classification probability.

The MEE split rule consists of finding y minimizing the error (Shannon) entropy:

$$EE \equiv EE(P_{01}, P_{10}) = -P_{01} \ln P_{01} - P_{10} \ln P_{10} - (1 - P_{01} - P_{10}) \ln(1 - P_{01} - P_{10}).$$

The motivation for using MEE splits in decision trees stems from two main facts: by minimizing EE one is, in general, for not too overlapped distributions, favoring error distributions concentrated at the origin, with split points corresponding to the minimum probability of error; MEE will not work for largely overlapped $P(x|\omega_k)$ and $P(x|\overline{\omega}_k)$ distributions [3], providing a natural way when to stop tree growing, therefore inherently limiting the model complexity.

Details on the practical application of these principles to the construction of MEE trees are given in [2], showing that MEE trees can be applied to data described by either numerical or nominal features, and to any number of classes. The MEE tree algorithm written in Matlab, together with its description, is available at http:// gno-mo.fe.up.pt/~nnig/. The main steps of the MEE tree algorithm are as follows (further details in [2]):

1. At each tree node we are given an $n \times f$ (n cases, f features) matrix X and an $n \times c$ (n cases, c classes) matrix T, filled with zeros and ones. A univariate split y minimizing EE is searched for in the $f \times c$-dimensional space.
2. For that purpose, the error rates $P_{10} = n_{10}/n$, $P_{01} = n_{01}/n$ ($n_{tt'}$: number of class t cases classified as t') are computed for each candidate class label t.
3. The rule minimizing (the empirical) EE is assigned to the node and if a stopping criterion is satisfied the node becomes a leaf. Otherwise, the left and right node sets are generated and steps 1 and 2 iterated.

A leaf is reached whenever a lower bound on the number of instances is reached or $minEE$ occurs at interval ends, corresponding to the large distribution overlap case.

An important aspect shown in [2] is that MEE trees are quite insensitive to pruning; i.e., in general, the tree built without pruning is the same or almost the same as the one to which pruning was applied. This is a consequence of what was said above:

for largely overlapped $P(x \mid \omega_k)$ and $P(x \mid \overline{\omega}_k)$ distributions one is able to detect an invalid MEE point and stop node splitting. Therefore, MEE enforces simple models with good generalization ability.

3 Materials and Methods

3.1 Real World Datasets and Experimental Setup

The MEE algorithm was applied to the 42 datasets presented in Table 1, and the results confronted with those obtained using the CART-Gini, CART-Information-Gain and CART-Twoing algorithms (available in Matlab) and the popular C4.5 algorithm (available in Weka). All algorithms were run with unit misclassification costs, estimated priors and the same minimum number of instances at a node: 5.

All datasets are from the well-known UCI repository [4], except the colon, central nervous system and leukemia datasets which are from the Kent Ridge Biomedical Dataset (http://datam.i2r.a-star.edu.sg/datasets/krbd).

The CART and MEE algorithms were run with Cost-Complexity Pruning (CCP) with the 'min' criterion and 10-fold cross-validation. The C4.5 algorithm was run with Pessimistic Error Pruning (PEP) at 25% confidence level [1].

Table 1. Datasets. The number of categorical features is given inside parentheses.

	Arrythmya	Balance	Car	Clev. HD2	Clev.HD5	CNS	Colon
No. cases	452	625	1278	297	297	60	62
No. features	274 (54)	4 (4)	6 (6)	13 (8)	13 (8)	7129 (0)	2000 (0)
No. classes	9	3	4	2	5	2	2
	Cork stop.	Credit	CTG	Dermatol.	E-coli	Flags	H. surv
No. cases	150	653	2126	358	327	194	306
No. features	10 (0)	15 (9)	21 (0)	34 (33)	5 (0)	26 (20)	3 (0)
No. classes	3	2	10	6	5	7	2
	Heart	Image Seg.	Landsat	Led	Leukemia	LRS	Lymphog.
No. cases	270	2310	6435	200	72	531	148
No. features	13 (8)	18 (0)	36 (0)	7 (7)	7129 (0)	101 (1)	18 (17)
No. classes	2	7	6	10	2	6	3
	Mammog.	Monk	Mushrrom	Ozone	Page blks	Parkinsons	Pen Digits
No. cases	830	556	8214	1847	5473	195	10992
No. features	4 (3)	6 (6)	21 (21)	72 (0)	10 (0)	22 (0)	16 (0)
No. classes	2	2	2	2	5	2	10
	P. Diabetes	P. Gene	Robot-1	Spect-Heart	Spectf-Heart	Swiss HD	Synth. Chart
No. cases	768	106	88	267	267	120	600
No. features	8 (0)	57 (57)	90 (0)	22 (22)	44 (0)	7 (4)	60 (0)
No. classes	2	2	4	2	2	5	6
	Thyroid	VA HD	Wdbc	Wpbc	Wine	Yeast	Zoo
No. cases	215	186	569	194	178	1479	101
No. features	5 (0)	6 (4)	30 (0)	32 (0)	13 (0)	6 (0)	16 (16)
No. classes	3	5	2	2	3	9	7

3.2 Statistical Methods

Ten-fold crossvalidation (CV10) was applied to all datasets and tree design algorithms. According to the theoretical analysis of crossvalidation [5], ten is a sensible choice for the number of folds. A more recent work, [6], also confirmed the good performance of CV10 when compared with alternative validation methods.

Besides average test error estimates we also computed average design (resubstitution) error estimates, allowing us to evaluate generalization. Statistics regarding tree sizes in the cross-validation experiments were also computed.

All results obtained for the five methods were evaluated following recommendations in [7-10], by namely performing: counts of wins and losses with chi-square test; multiple sign test comparing each method against MEE; Friedman test; post-hoc Dunn-Sidak test for multiple comparison; post-hoc Finner test for comparison of each method against MEE. The post-hoc tests are only performed when a significant Friedman $p < 0.05$ is found. The Finner test for post-hoc comparisons of a proposed method against another was analyzed in [8] and found to be more powerful than competing tests.

4   Results

4.1   Error Rates

Table 2 presents the cross-validation estimates of the error rate, with the best MEE solution found for class unions up to [$c/2$]. The total number of wins (smallest error) and losses are also shown in Table 2 with the chi-square test p: no significant difference is found relative to the equal distribution hypothesis.

The Friedman test did not detect significant differences ($p = 0.453$) for these 42 datasets. The mean ranks for the five methods (following from now on Table 2 order) are: 2.98, 3.16, 3.27, 2.68 and 2.92.

The comparison between MEE vs any of the other algorithms, with the signs used in the multiple sign test [8], was also performed. Denoting by e the error rate, the null hypothesis of the test is H_0: $e_j \leq e_{\text{MEE}}$, where j is any algorithm MEE is compared with. H_0 is rejected whenever the sum of minuses is below a certain critical value, which is in this case 16 at $p = 0.05$. Since all sums of minuses (resp. 19, 17, 17, 23) are above the critical value, we conclude that MEE performs similarly to any of the other algorithms.

4.2   Generalization

Denoting by e_R and e_{CV} respectively the mean training set error rate and the mean test set (CV10) error rate, we computed $D = |e_R - e_{CV}|/\bar{s}$, using the pooled standard deviation $\bar{s}$. D reflects the generalization ability of the classifiers. The Friedman test found a significant difference ($p \approx 0$) of the methods for the D values (mean ranks: 2.69, 2.91, 3.01, 4.22 and 2.16); the post-hoc Dunn-Sidak test revealing a significant difference between MEE vs C4.5 and Twoing (see Fig. 1). The post-hoc Finner test found, in fact, significantly better generalization of MEE vs *any* of the other methods.

Table 2. CV10 estimates of test set Pe-(std) with wins (bold) and losses (italic)

	Arrythmya	Balance	Car	Clev. HD2	Clev.HD5	CNS
Gini	0.3518 (0.022)	**0.1952 (0.016)**	0.0434 (0.005)	0.2357 (0.025)	*0.4680 (0.029)*	0.3500 (0.062)
Info Gain	0.3606 (0.023)	0.2528 (0.017)	0.0457 (0.005)	0.2593 (0.025)	**0.4512 (0.029)**	**0.3000 (0.059)**
Twoing	0.3628 (0.023)	0.2176 (0.017)	**0.0405 (0.005)**	*0.2761 (0.026)*	0.4613 (0.029)	0.3167 (0.060)
C4.5	*0.3934 (0.023)*	0.2192 (0.017)	0.0434 (0.005)	**0.1987 (0.023)**	0.4577 (0.029)	*0.4833 (0.065)*
MEE	**0.3208 (0.022)**	*0.3120 (0.019)*	*0.0718 (0.006)*	0.2222 (0.024)	0.4646 (0.029)	0.3667 (0.062)

	Colon	Cork stop.	Credit	CTG	Dermatol.	E-coli
Gini	*0.2581 (0.056)*	**0.1133 (0.028)**	0.1363 (0.013)	0.1689 (0.008)	**0.0531 (0.012)**	*0.1927 (0.022)*
Info Gain	*0.2581 (0.056)*	*0.1400 (0.028)*	0.1363 (0.013)	0.1877 (0.008)	0.0587 (0.012)	0.1896 (0.022)
Twoing	0.2419 (0.054)	0.1267 (0.027)	0.1363 (0.013)	0.1811 (0.008)	0.0670 (0.013)	0.1682 (0.021)
C4.5	0.2419 (0.054)	**0.1133 (0.026)**	**0.1332 (0.013)**	**0.1731 (0.008)**	*0.0991 (0.016)*	0.1713 (0.021)
MEE	**0.1935 (0.050)**	0.1200 (0.027)	*0.1424 (0.014)*	*0.1891 (0.008)*	0.0559 (0.012)	**0.1315 (0.019)**

	Flags	H. surv	Heart	Image Seg.	Landsat	Led
Gini	0.4794 (0.036)	0.2680 (0.025)	0.2037 (0.025)	0.0403 (0.004)	**0.1294 (0.004)**	0.3100 (0.033)
Info Gain	0.4639 (0.036)	**0.2647 (0.025)**	0.2444 (0.026)	0.0368 (0.004)	0.1361 (0.004)	0.3050 (0.033)
Twoing	*0.4845 (0.036)*	0.2745 (0.026)	*0.2481 (0.026)*	0.0485 (0.004)	0.1406 (0.004)	0.3200 (0.033)
C4.5	**0.4022 (0.035)**	*0.3070 (0.026)*	**0.2000 (0.024)**	0.0385 (0.004)	0.1324 (0.004)	*0.5869 (0.035)*
MEE	0.4691 (0.036)	**0.2647 (0.025)**	0.2444 (0.026)	*0.0589 (0.005)*	*0.1566 (0.005)*	**0.3000 (0.032)**

	Leukemia	LRS	Lymphog.	Mammog.	Monk	Mushrrom
Gini	0.1806 (0.045)	0.1450 (0.015)	*0.2754 (0.037)*	0.2084 (0.014)	0.1007 (0.013)	0.0004 (0.000)
Info Gain	*0.1944 (0.047)*	0.1450 (0.015)	*0.2754 (0.037)*	0.2157 (0.014)	0.1187 (0.014)	**0.0000 (0.000)**
Twoing	0.1667 (0.044)	**0.1431 (0.015)**	**0.2061 (0.033)**	0.2072 (0.014)	*0.1331 (0.014)*	**0.0000 (0.000)**
C4.5	**0.1389 (0.041)**	*0.2917 (0.020)*	0.2528 (0.036)	**0.2000 (0.014)**	0.1115 (0.013)	**0.0000 (0.000)**
MEE	0.1667 (0.044)	0.1638 (0.016)	0.2500 (0.036)	*0.2386 (0.015)*	**0.0989 (0.013)**	*0.0009 (0.000)*

	Ozone	Page blks	Parkinsons	Pen Digits	P. Diabetes	P. Gene
Gini	**0.0693 (0.006)**	0.0342 (0.002)	*0.1590 (0.026)*	0.0418 (0.002)	**0.2487 (0.016)**	0.2547 (0.042)
Info Gain	**0.0693 (0.006)**	0.0347 (0.002)	0.1487 (0.025)	**0.0357 (0.002)**	0.2695 (0.016)	*0.3208 (0.045)*
Twoing	0.0731 (0.006)	*0.0365 (0.003)*	0.1487 (0.025)	0.0378 (0.002)	0.2695 (0.016)	0.2642 (0.043)
C4.5	*0.0785 (0.006)*	**0.0281 (0.002)**	**0.1242 (0.024)**	0.0418 (0.002)	0.2578 (0.016)	0.2547 (0.042)
MEE	0.0704 (0.006)	0.0347 (0.002)	0.1436 (0.025)	*0.0666 (0.002)*	*0.3216 (0.017)*	**0.1698 (0.036)**

	Robot-1	Spect-Heart	Spectf-Heart	Swiss HD	Synth. Chart	Thyroid
Gini	0.2727 (0.047)	0.2022 (0.025)	0.2097 (0.025)	0.6117 (0.044)	0.1150 (0.013)	0.0844 (0.019)
Info Gain	0.2841 (0.048)	0.2060 (0.023)	**0.2060 (0.025)**	0.6083 (0.045)	0.0817 (0.011)	*0.1023 (0.021)*
Twoing	**0.1932 (0.042)**	*0.2210 (0.025)*	*0.2172 (0.025)*	*0.6250 (0.044)*	*0.1200 (0.013)*	0.0977 (0.020)
C4.5	*0.3500 (0.051)*	**0.1873 (0.024)**	0.2135 (0.025)	**0.5847 (0.045)**	0.0833 (0.011)	**0.0558 (0.016)**
MEE	0.2614 (0.047)	0.1985 (0.024)	**0.2060 (0.025)**	0.6083 (0.045)	**0.0617 (0.010)**	0.0977 (0.020)

	VA HD	Wdbc	Wpbc	Wine	Yeast	Zoo
Gini	*0.7527 (0.032)*	0.0650 (0.010)	**0.2371 (0.031)**	0.1067 (0.023)	0.4219 (0.013)	0.1683 (0.037)
Info Gain	*0.7527 (0.032)*	*0.0721 (0.011)*	0.2474 (0.031)	**0.0562 (0.017)**	0.4206 (0.013)	0.1683 (0.037)
Twoing	0.7419 (0.032)	0.0685 (0.011)	**0.2371 (0.031)**	0.0787 (0.020)	0.4381 (0.013)	0.1386 (0.034)
C4.5	0.7366 (0.032)	0.0650 (0.010)	*0.3144 (0.031)*	0.0899 (0.021)	**0.4077 (0.013)**	*0.3069 (0.046)*
MEE	**0.7097 (0.033)**	**0.0615 (0.010)**	**0.2371 (0.031)**	*0.1180 (0.024)*	*0.5335 (0.013)*	**0.1089 (0.031)**

	Gini	Info Gain	Twoing	C4.5	MEE	p
Wins	7	9	6	14	13	0.27
Losses	6	8	9	10	12	0.70

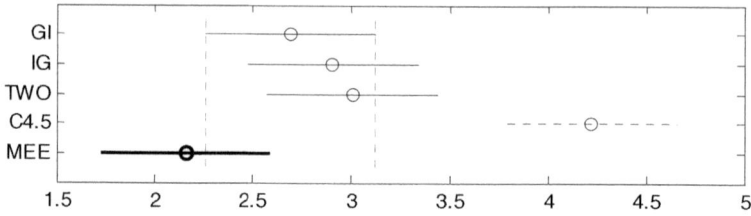

Fig. 1. Dunn-Sidak comparison intervals for the D scores

4.3 Tree Sizes

Table 3 shows the averages and ranges of tree sizes achieved in the cross-validation experiments by all algorithms. The total number of wins (smallest average tree size) and losses are also shown in Table 3 with the chi-square p. A significant difference is found relative to the equal distribution hypothesis. Performing the multiple sign test as in the preceding section, we found a significant difference of MEE vs C4.5: smaller trees on average for MEE. The Friedman test also found a significant difference ($p \approx 0$) with mean ranks 2.51, 2.43, 2.80, 4.35 and 2.92. The post-hoc comparisons tests confirmed the conclusions of the multiple sign test (see Fig. 2).

We re-analyzed the test set error rates and the D scores for the 20 datasets where MEE found the smallest average tree size. We arrived essentially to the same conclusions as in 4.1 and 4.2.

We also analyzed the tree size ranges (see Table 3), since a significantly smaller range of tree sizes is a symptom of a more stable algorithm [11-12]. We didn't find any statistically significant diference of the tree size ranges, either for the Friedmann ($p = 0.3$) or the multiple sign test.

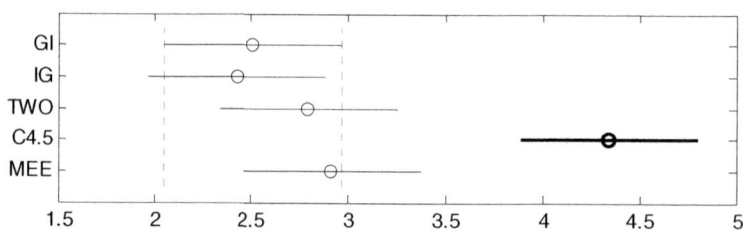

Fig. 2. Dunn-Sidak comparison intervals for the average tree size

Table 3. Average-(ranges) of tree sizes with wins (bold) and losses (italic)

	Arrythmya	Balance	Car	Clev. HD2	Clev.HD5	CNS
Gini	12.2 (10)	**26.6 (10)**	66.2 (38)	**6.8 (8)**	**5.6 (16)**	**1.6 (2)**
Info Gain	12.8 (8)	26.6 (20)	58.0 (34)	7.8 (8)	6.8 (8)	2.0 (2)
Twoing	**11.6 (14)**	27.6 (8)	66.0 (26)	8.8 (10)	5.8 (12)	2.4 (2)
C4.5	*37.8 (24)*	43.6 (12)	71.4 (12)	*19.2 (10)*	*34.8 (16)*	6.2 (4)
MEE	36.2 (10)	*90.6 (52)*	*115.0 (48)*	18.8 (12)	22.0 (42)	3.2 (4)
	Colon	Cork stop.	Credit	CTG	Dermatol.	E-coli
Gini	**3.0 (0)**	**5.0 (0)**	**3.0 (0)**	74.6 (46)	13.4 (6)	10.8 (12)
Info Gain	**3.0 (6)**	**5.0 (0)**	**3.0 (0)**	70.2 (52)	15.8 (6)	10.2 (14)
Twoing	**3.0 (4)**	**5.0 (0)**	**3.0 (0)**	*60.0 (30)*	*16.2 (2)*	11.0 (14)
C4.5	5.8 (2)	5.8 (6)	24.8 (20)	136 (26)	**13.0 (0)**	*17.2 (8)*
MEE	3.2 (2)	**5.0 (0)**	12.4 (24)	**56.8 (16)**	14.1 (2)	**9.4 (2)**
	Flags	H. surv	Heart	Image Seg.	Landsat	Led
Gini	12.8 (12)	*4.2 (28)*	11.2 (12)	79.8 (58)	**108.8 (80)**	22.0 (24)
Info Gain	**10.0 (14)**	**1.0 (0)**	10.8 (32)	55.2 (36)	131.2 (98)	**20.6 (8)**
Twoing	10.6 (20)	2.6 (8)	**8.4 (10)**	70.4 (74)	110.4 (98)	25.6 (20)
C4.5	*27.8 (6)*	4.2 (6)	17.2 (8)	59.8 (18)	*331.6 (58)*	22.0 (6)
MEE	20.0 (36)	**1.0 (0)**	*19.4 (14)*	**32.4 (8)**	125.6 (56)	23.0 (14)
	Leukemia	LRS	Lymphog.	Mammog.	Monk	Mushrrom
Gini	**3.0 (0)**	11.6 (4)	**6.0 (4)**	**5.8 (14)**	28.8 (28)	18.2 (8)
Info Gain	**3.0 (0)**	11.8 (6)	**6.0 (4)**	6.2 (6)	30.0 (24)	**16.2 (2)**
Twoing	**3.0 (0)**	**11.2 (2)**	6.4 (4)	6.2 (6)	**27.0 (24)**	18.8 (2)
C4.5	*3.8 (2)*	*28.8 (12)*	13.8 (8)	16.8 (4)	31.0 (14)	23.0 (0)
MEE	**3.0 (0)**	24.2 (6)	*17.6 (22)*	24.6 (12)	33.6 (28)	*42.6 (16)*
	Ozone	Page blks	Parkinsons	Pen Digits	P. Diabetes	P. Gene
Gini	**1.0 (0)**	23.4 (28)	5.4 (8)	336.8 (184)	6.0 (4)	7.8 (10)
Info Gain	**1.0 (0)**	23.4 (22)	7.6 (10)	327.6 (216)	6.6 (14)	**5.6 (8)**
Twoing	3.4 (24)	22.6 (24)	8.8 (18)	*371.2 (152)*	8.4 (36)	7.0 (8)
C4.5	*54.0 (34)*	54.8 (16)	15.0 (4)	271.4 (32)	30.6 (28)	*11.4 (6)*
MEE	**1.0 (2)**	20.8 (6)	**3.0 (0)**	**233.0 (60)**	2.2 (4)	8.6 (8)
	Robot-1	Spect-Heart	Spectf-Heart	Swiss HD	Synth. Chart	Thyroid
Gini	**8.2 (4)**	6.0 (14)	1.6 (6)	1.8 (8)	24.8 (20)	8.0 (6)
Info Gain	8.8 (4)	13.4 (24)	**1.0 (0)**	**1.0 (0)**	37.4 (18)	7.4 (8)
Twoing	9.4 (2)	**5.8 (20)**	2.2 (12)	1.6 (6)	*39.2 (24)*	*9.2 (12)*
C4.5	*10.4 (4)*	13.6 (4)	*28.4 (12)*	*17.8 (16)*	28.8 (6)	9.0 (4)
MEE	**8.2 (2)**	23.2 (28)	**1.0 (0)**	**1.0 (0)**	22.0 (2)	5.0 (0)
	VA HD	Wdbc	Wpbc	Wine	Yeast	Zoo
Gini	**5.8 (18)**	10.2 (14)	**1.0 (0)**	*11.8 (16)*	22.4 (22)	10.6 (6)
Info Gain	10.0 (18)	10.2 (14)	1.6 (6)	8.4 (2)	**22.0 (16)**	10.8 (4)
Twoing	8.6 (28)	11.0 (20)	**1.0 (0)**	7.8 (4)	17.8 (12)	**10.4 (2)**
C4.5	*26.0 (20)*	15.4 (10)	13.8 (26)	8.8 (2)	*135.2 (40)*	*11.0 (0)*
MEE	23.4 (12)	**5.2 (2)**	**1.0 (0)**	**6.6 (4)**	25.4 (10)	*11.0 (0)*

	Gini	Info Gain	Twoing	C4.5	MEE	p
Wins	15	15	11	1	20	0.00
Losses	3	0	5	27	9	0.00

5 Conclusions

The present work provided a substantial body of results concerning classification experiments carried out in 42 real-world datasets, with varied number of cases, classes and features, by trees designed using the MEE approach and the popular CART-Gini, CART-Information-Gain, CART-Twoing and C4.5 algorithms. The statistical analysis of the test set (CV10) error rates, obtained in these experiments showed that the MEE algorithm competes well with the other algorithms.

Moreover, we have obtained in the present work statistically significant evidence that the MEE algorithm produces, on average, smaller trees than the popular C4.5 algorithm.

As to the generalization issue, MEE trees were found to generalize better than those produced by the other algorithms without sacrifice on performance.

These features of the MEE tree design, particularly the better generalization of MEE tree solutions, together with their relative insensibility to pruning shown elsewhere [2], are of importance in many pattern recognition applications.

Aknowledgement. The work of Raquel Sebastião is supported by the Portuguese Foundation for Science and Technology (FCT) under the PhD Grant SFRH/BD/41569/2007.

References

1. Rokach, L., Maimon, O.: Decision Trees. In: Maimon, O., Rokach, L. (eds.) Data Mining and Knowledge Discovery Handbook. Springer, Heidelberg (2005)
2. Marques de Sá, J.P., Sebastião, R., Gama, J.: Tree Classifiers Based on Minimum Error Entropy Decisions. Can. J. Artif. Intell., Patt. Rec. and Mach. Learning (in press, 2011)
3. Silva, L., Felgueiras, C.S., Alexandre, L., Marques de Sá, J.: Error Entropy in Classification Problems: A Univariate Data Analysis. Neural Computation 18, 2036–2061 (2006)
4. Asuncion, A., Newman, D.J.: UCI Machine Learning Repository. University of California, School of Information and Computer Science, Irvine, CA (2010),
   `http://www.ics.uci.edu/~mlearn/MLRepository.html`
5. Kearns, M.: A Bound on the Error of Cross Validation Using the Approximation and Estimation Rates, with Consequences for the Training-Test Split. Neural Computation 9, 1143–1161 (1997)
6. Molinaro, A.M., Simon, R., Pfeiffer, R.M.: Prediction Error Estimation: A Comparison of Resampling Methods. Bioinformatics 21, 3301–3307 (2005)
7. Demšar, J.: Statistical Comparisons of Classifiers over Multiple Data Sets. J. of Machine Learning Research 7, 1–30 (2006)
8. García, S., Fernández, A., Luengo, J., Herrera, F.: Advanced Nonparametric Tests for Multiple Comparisons in the Design of Experiments in Computational Intelligence and Data Mining: Experimental Analysis of Power. Information Sciences 180, 2044–2064 (2010)
9. Hochberg, Y., Tamhane, A.C.: Multiple Comparison Procedures. John Wiley & Sons, Inc. (1987)
10. Salzberg, S.L.: On Comparing Classifiers: Pitfalls to Avoid and a Recommended Approach. Data Mining and Knowledge Discovery 1, 317–328 (1997)
11. Jensen, D., Oates, T., Cohen, P.R.: Building Simple Models: A Case Study with Decision Trees. In: Liu, X., Cohen, P., Berthold, M. (eds.) IDA 1997. LNCS, vol. 1280, pp. 211–222. Springer, Heidelberg (1997)
12. Li, R.-H., Belford, G.G.: Instability of Decision Tree Classification Algorithms. In: Proc. 8th ACM SIGKDD International Conference on Knowledge Discovery and Data Mining, pp. 570–575 (2002)

Section-Wise Similarities for Classification of Subjective-Data on Time Series

Isaac Martín de Diego, Oscar S. Siordia, Cristina Conde,
and Enrique Cabello

Face Recognition and Artificial Vision Group,
Universidad Rey Juan Carlos,
C. Tulipán, S/N, 28934, Móstoles, España
{isaac.martin,oscar.siordia,cristina.conde,enrique.cabello}@urjc.es

Abstract. The aim of this paper is to present a novelty methodology to develop similarity measures for classification of time series. First, a linear segmentation algorithm to obtain a section-wise representation of the series is presented. Then, two similarity measures are defined from the differences between the behavior of the series and the level of the series, respectively. The method is applied to subjective-data on time series generated through the evaluations of the driving risk from a group of traffic safety experts. These series are classified using the proposed similarities as kernels for the training of a Support Vector Machine. The results are compared with other classifiers using our similarities, their linear combination and the raw data. The proposed methodology has been successfully evaluated on several databases.

Keywords: Similarity, Kernel Method, Classification, Time Series, Data Segmentation.

1 Introduction

Similarity measures between time series is a common issue that has been treated in several ways. Usually, the statistical models fitted to the series are compared. Nevertheless, subjective-data time series are rarely taked into account. This kind of data corresponds to information collected from human opinions over a period of time. In this case, it is not possible to successfully fit a unique model to all the data set since the changes on the level of the series usually respond to a great variety of factors. In the particular case of driving risk evaluations from human experts, these factors are related to driver's responses to vehicle or road variations (speed, aceleration, road conditions, etc). The driver's distraction study is a very difficult problem due to the high number of factors involved in the distraction-related accidents [1]. However, these distractions can be reduced with the development of a system that can automatically evaluate the driver's behavior. CABINTEC ("Intelligent cabin truck for road transport") is an ongoing project focused on risk reduction for traffic safety [2]. One of the main objectives of the project is to identify driver's unsuitable behavior and lacks of attention. For that purpose, a system for automatic driving risk evaluation is

C. San Martin and S.-W. Kim (Eds.): CIARP 2011, LNCS 7042, pp. 363–371, 2011.

being developed using time series information from several traffic safety experts. Further, a previous selection of experts is needed in order to detect unpracticed experts whose opinions should not be considered. For this purpose, it is necessary to measure the similarity between experts risk evaluations time series.

Most of the known similarity measures between time series are concerned with the distance between series levels. However, for subjective data, it is necessary to define a measure that considers the similarity in the behavior (trend of data) as well as the similarity in the level. For this purpose, a proper representation of the time series is needed. The same idea for signal matching has a long history in cardiac signal analysis (see, for instance, [3]). However, most of these representations imply sensitivity to noise, lack of intuitiveness, and the need to fine-tune many parameters [4]. In this paper, an alternative representation based on a linear segmentation of the time series is proposed. The segmented representation allows the definition of two similarity measures considering the behavior of the series and the series level, respectively. The defined similarities were used as kernels to train a Support Vector Machine (SVM) and a k-NN (k-Nearest Neighbor) classifier. The proposed methodology, main contribution of this paper, was applied for the classification of a group of traffic safety experts labeled according to their professional experience. The data acquisition process was made as follows: a driving simulation exercise of ten minutes was recorded from a truck cabin simulator from the Centro de Estudios e Investigaciones Técnicas de Gipuzkoa (CEIT) [2]. Then, a group of 47 traffic safety experts were asked to evaluate the driving risk of the simulated exercise. For that purpose, the simulation reproduction tool Virtual Co-driver was used [5]. To collect the experts evaluations, a Visual Analog Scale (VAS) was employed. This method has been considered the best for subjective measurements (see, for instance, [6]). The considered VAS ranges from 0 to 100, where 100 refers to the highest driving risk level. Finally, to know some aspects of experts experience in the traffic safety field, a personal quiz was applied.

The rest of the paper is organized as follows. Section 2 presents our algorithm for the linear segmentation of time series. In Section 3, the section-wise similarities are defined. Several experiments on real databases are considered in Section 4 to evaluate the relative performance of the proposed similarities. Section 5 concludes this paper.

2   Linear Segmentation Algorithm

In order to define a similarity between time series, small oscillations out of the main trend could be uninformative and generate noise. In this case, these oscillations should be removed. This happens, for instance, when dealing with subjective-data time series, where a linear behavior along a temporary period of time is expected. A variety of algorithms have been proposed to obtain proper representations of time series (see, for instance, [7] and [8]). In this paper, an algorithm to reduce the complexity of the data through the fit of regression lines in local sections of the series has been developed. The linear model was selected

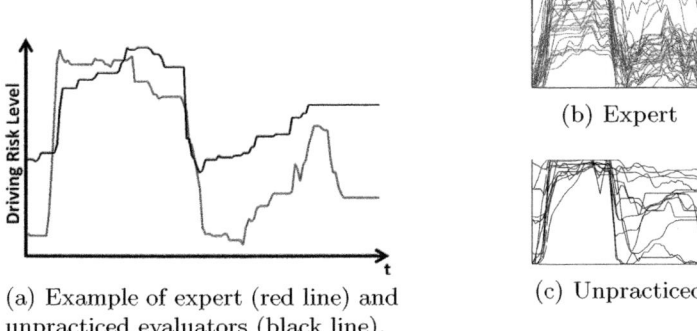

(b) Expert

(a) Example of expert (red line) and
unpracticed evaluators (black line).

(c) Unpracticed

Fig. 1. Labeled CABINTEC time series in accordance with the traffic safety experience
of the human evaluator: (a) example series of an expert and an unpracticed evaluator,
(b) series of the experts evaluations, and (c) series of the unpracticed evaluators

due to its low computational cost. To illustrate the algorithm an example of the
CABINTEC time series will be used (Figure 1(a)). The key idea of the algorithm
is to represent the time series into a section-wise linear approximation losing
the least amount of usefull information. The output will be a set of estimated
regression lines, one per section. A scheme of the algorithm is presented in
Algorithm 1.

Algorithm 1. Linear segmentation of the curve f

Input: Curve f, n-Order Tangent f^n, R^2_{min}, ρ (reduction parameter), $T = length(f)$
Output: $Y = \{y_s\}^S_{s=1}$, set of S lines estimated by linear regression, one per section.
    Initialize: $ini = 1$
    1. Set: $\tau = max(f^n)$
    2. Select end **as the first** t^* **in** $ini + 1 : T$ **such that**
        $f^n(t^*) \geq max(\ \tau,\ f^n(t^* + 1),\ f^n(t^* - 1))$
    3. Estimate the line y_s **in section** $[ini, end]$
    if $(R^2(y_s) > R^2_{min})$ **or** $(\tau < min(f^n))$ **then**
        $y_s \in Y$ **(store the regression parameters of the estimated line)**
        $ini = i$ **(change to next section)**
        go to 1
    else
        $\tau = \rho\tau$ **(reduce the threshold)**
        go to 2
    end if

The start and end points of each section must denote a change on the trend of
the serie. For that purpose the tangent of the time serie at each point needs to
be defined. Let $f(t)$ be the value of curve f evaluated in time $t = \{1, \ldots, T\}$.
Let $f^n(t)$ the value of its tangent of order n, calculated as:

Table 1. Linear Segmentation Algorithm on CABINTEC data

R^2_{min}	0.40	0.70	0.80	0.90	1.00	Original Data
Number of Sections	2	10	18	23	130	131 registers
Segmented Graph Result						

$$f^n(t) = hf(t) - \sum_{i=-n,\ i\neq 0}^{n} h_i f(t+i), \tag{1}$$

where $h_i = 1/(2|i|)$, and h is the sum of all h_i.

Notice that the weight (h_i) assigned to the i-th neighbor of the point t is inversely proportional to the distance between them.

The basis of this time series segmentation algorithm is to look for strong changes in the trend of data. This aim is achieved by the search of local maxima of f^n. When a point is selected in step 2 of Algorithm 1, a section s in the serie is defined, and a regression line is fitted to the data in that section. Let $R^2_{y_s}$ be the square of the sample correlation coefficient of the regression line. If the fitted model explains much of the variability of the section, the calculated parameters of the regression line are stored and the algorithm iterates. In other case, no linear behavior is expected. Therefore, the section needs to be subdivided.

An example of the algorithm performance is presented in Table 1. The segmented graphical result and the number of sections generated by the algorithm were calculated for different selections of R^2_{min}, the minimum fit (or one minus the maximum error) allowed. For this example a tangent of order 5 was used. When $R^2_{min} = 0.40$, only two sections were generated. It is clear that the unique cut point was given by the global maximum of the 5-order tangent. Notice that the higher the R^2_{min} was, the higher the number of sections were obtained. In the case of $R^2_{min} = 1$, a section is generated for each pair of points. To choose the optimal linear representation of the database we consider a trade-off between the global linear error and the complexity of the representation as follows:

$$\alpha(1 - R^2) + (1 - \alpha)\frac{\text{number of sections}}{T - 1}. \tag{2}$$

In the example, $R^2_{min} = 0.90$ minimizes expression (2) (trade-off parameter $\alpha = 0.5$, which implies similar relevance for both terms).

3   Section-Wise Similarities

Given a set of segmented time series, it is possible to calculate several section-wise similarities between them. Next, we propose one similarity measure based

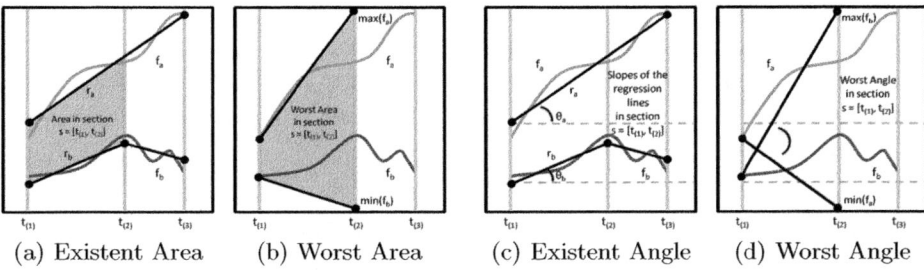

(a) Existent Area   (b) Worst Area   (c) Existent Angle   (d) Worst Angle

Fig. 2. Level and Angle based section-wise similarities of the time series f_a and f_b, in the section between the points $t_{(1)}$ and $t_{(2)}$

on the differences between the level of the sections lines, and one similarity measure based on the differences between the angles of the sections lines.

Let f_a and f_b be two different time series. Let $\{A\}$ and $\{B\}$ be the set of initial and final points that defined the sections obtained for f_a and f_b, respectively, from Algorithm 1. The similarity measures will be built on sections defined from the union of sets $\{A\}$ and $\{B\}$. That is, every initial or final point of a section from f_a or f_b will be used.

3.1   Level Based Similarity

Let $s = [t_{(1)}, t_{(2)}]$ be the section where $t_{(1)}$ and $t_{(2)} \in \{A\} \cup \{B\}$. Let r_a and r_b be the regression lines obtained from Algorithm 1 for f_a and f_b, respectively, in s (see Figure 2(a)). Consider the area L bounded by r_a and r_b calculated as:

$$L = \frac{1}{2}[(r_a(t_{(1)}) - r_b(t_{(1)})) + (r_a(t_{(2)}) - r_b(t_{(2)}))] * (t_{(2)} - t_{(1)}), \qquad (3)$$

where $r_i(t_{(j)})$ denotes the value of the regression line r_i in the point $t_{(j)}$.

Notice that $(t_{(2)} - t_{(1)})$ is the width (number of points) of section s. The level based similarity calculated in the section s, denoted by $s_{OS}(s)$, is obtained as the relation between the area in (3) and the worst possible area $\check{L}$ as follows: $s_{OS}(s) = 1 - L/\check{L}$. Notice that in this way, the proposed similarity measure is in $[0, 1]$. The worst area $\check{L}$ is calculated from the maximum possible change in the analyzed section. For that purpose, a line from $f_b(t_{(1)})$ to $min(f_b)$ and a line from $f_a(t_{(1)})$ to $max(f_a)$ are considered, as shown in Figure 2(b). Finally, the overall level based section-wise similarity for the time series f_a and f_b is calculated as the weighted sum of all the sectional similarities as follows:

$$S_{OS}(f_a, f_b) = \frac{\sum_{s=1}^{S} w(s) \, s_{OS}(s)}{\sum_{s=1}^{S} w(s)}, \qquad (4)$$

where $w(s)$ is the time width of section $s = 1, \ldots, S$.

3.2 Angle Based similarity

The angle based section-wise similarity considers the angle formed by the regression lines r_a and r_b defined in the section s. Let θ_a and θ_b be the slopes of r_a and r_b, respectively (see Figure 2(c)). The angle between the regression lines is calculated as:

$$\theta_{ab} = |\theta_a - \theta_b| \,. \tag{5}$$

The angle based similarity calculated in the section s, denoted by $s_{1S}(s)$, is obtained as the relation between the angle θ_{ab} and the worst possible angle $\breve{\theta}$: $s_{1S}(s) = 1 - \theta_{ab}/\breve{\theta}$. The worst angle $\breve{\theta}$ is calculated with the crossed maximum possible change in the analyzed section. That is, a line from $f_b(t_{(1)})$ to $max(f_b)$ and a line from $f_a(t_{(1)})$ to $min(f_a)$ as shown in Figure 2(d) are considered. Finally, the overall angle based section-wise similarity for the time series f_a and f_b is calculated as the weighted sum of all the sectional similarities as follows:

$$S_{1S}(f_a, f_b) = \frac{\sum_{s=1}^{S} w(s)\, s_{1S}(s)}{\sum_{s=1}^{S} w(s)}\,, \tag{6}$$

where $w(s)$ is the time width of section $s = 1, \ldots, S$.

4 Experiments

The CABINTEC time series (Figure 1), were labeled in accordance with the experience in traffic safety of each human evaluator. Each evaluator was labeled as expert or unpracticed depending on their profession and years of experience in the field (Figure 1(b) and Figure 1(c)). This information was obtained from personal quizzes applied to each evaluator before the knowledge acquisition experiments.

In order to test the accuracy and utility of similarities defined in Section 3, several classification experiments were performed. These similarities were used as kernel to train a SVM following [9] ($C = 100$). Further, the similarity matrices were applied to a 1-Nearest Neighbor classifier. In addition, for benchmarking, two similarities based on the Euclidean distance were considered. Let f_a and f_b be two time series. S_{0P} denotes a point-wise similarity based on the Euclidean

Table 2. Summary of the databases considered in the classification experiments

Database Name	Number of Classes	Number of series	Time Series Length	Train set %
CABINTEC	2	47	313	50
Gun Point	2	200	150	25
ECG200	2	200	96	50
Coffee	2	56	286	50
Growth	2	93	31	64

Table 3. Error rate and (standard deviation) of the classification experiments using section-wise similarities (single and combined), point-wise similarities (single and combined), SVM on raw data and NFDA on raw data

Classification Algorithm	Similarity Applied	CABINTEC		Gun Point		ECG200		Coffee		Growth	
SVM	S_{0S}	18.8	(0.21)	**5.0**	**(0.07)**	12.6	(0.10)	19.6	(0.25)	5.8	(0.11)
	S_{1S}	29.4	(0.25)	14.3	(0.10)	20.6	(0.11)	2.9	(0.09)	6.0	(0.10)
	$\frac{S_{0S}+S_{1S}}{2}$	**10.2**	**(0.21)**	6.9	(0.08)	16.0	(0.10)	3.2	(0.12)	5.0	(0.10)
	S_{0P}	19.5	(0.20)	6.8	(0.10)	11.8	(0.10)	8.8	(0.22)	4.9	(0.10)
	S_{1P}	32.4	(0.23)	6.7	(0.11)	19.6	(0.11)	5.2	(0.15)	6.6	(0.12)
	$\frac{S_{0P}+S_{1P}}{2}$	15.5	(0.20)	6.0	(0.10)	13.7	(0.10)	3.1	(0.15)	4.5	(0.09)
K-NN	S_{0S}	20.2	(0.22)	9.1	(0.09)	**9.7**	**(0.09)**	22.9	(0.25)	7.8	(0.12)
	S_{1S}	25.4	(0.24)	10.0	(0.09)	15.9	(0.11)	6.6	(0.14)	7.2	(0.12)
	$\frac{S_{0S}+S_{1S}}{2}$	15.3	(0.20)	7.4	(0.09)	11.1	(0.09)	14.2	(0.21)	**3.3**	**(0.10)**
	S_{0P}	19.9	(0.21)	11.7	(0.10)	11.6	(0.09)	18.9	(0.25)	7.2	(0.11)
	S_{1P}	36.6	(0.23)	10.8	(0.10)	17.5	(0.11)	22.2	(0.25)	8.8	(0.15)
	$\frac{S_{0P}+S_{1P}}{2}$	18.1	(0.21)	10.4	(0.10)	12.9	(0.10)	8.8	(0.19)	6.8	(0.12)
SVM	Raw Data	21.5	(0.07)	6.1	(0.03)	11.5	(0.32)	11.1	(0.08)	7.4	(0.36)
NFDA	Raw Data	19.1	(0.07)	19.8	(0.05)	16.4	(0.38)	**0.5**	**(0.01)**	5.1	(0.03)

distance in the raw data: $\sqrt{\sum_{i=1}^{T}(f_a(i)-f_b(i))^2}$. Similarly, S_{1P} denotes a point-wise similarity based on the Euclidean distance in the angle gived by the n-order tangent (f^n): $\sqrt{\sum_{i=1}^{T}(f_a^n(i)-f_b^n(i))^2}$. Further, for the section-wise and point-wise similarities, linear combinations denoted by $\frac{S_{0S}+S_{1S}}{2}$ and $\frac{S_{0P}+S_{1P}}{2}$ were considered. Additionally to CABINTEC dataset, several well-known databases, out of the driving risk problem, were employed: the Gun Point, ECG200, Coffee, and Growth databases. A summary of these databases is shown in Table 2 (see [10] and [11] for a complete description). The linear segmentation algorithm proposed in Section 2 was applied to all the series.

In order to use Algorithm 1, the reduction parameter ρ and the order of the tangent n were established as 0.90 and 5 respectively in all cases. The parameter R_{min}^2 was selected by the minimization of (2) using train data. Two additional classifiers were considered and applied to the raw data: a SVM with a RBF kernel, and a classifier based in functional data representation (NFDA) [12]. Notice that k-NN applied to the point-wise similarity S_{0P}, corresponds to the k-NN evaluation on raw data. To compare the performance of the methods, the average classification results obtained in the test sets over 1 000 runs were calculated. The mean error rate and its standard deviation in the test sets are presented in Table 3. In our case study, the CABINTEC database, the best global result was achieved by the combination of the section-wise similarities used as kernel for the SVM. The error reduction obtained by this combination regarding the individual similarities (10.2% vs. 29.4% and 18.8%) shows their complementarities in this database. Likewise, the combination of the point-wise similarities reached an error reduction. Similar results were obtained with the K-NN classifier. As a summary, in almost all the databases, the section-wise similarities or their combination achieved the best results. These results show the capacity of our method to reduce the complexity of the data, preserving the usefull information for classification purposes.

5   Conclusions

The main contribution of this paper, is a novelty methodology for the similarity measurement and classification of time series. A linear segmentation algorithm for the proper representation of subjective-data time series has been developed. Then, two similarity measures have been defined from the differences between the level of the series and the angle of the series, respectively. These similarities have been used as kernels to train a SVM. The application of the methodology to the CABINTEC database achieves outstanding results in the classification of traffic safety experts according to their experience. Moreover, very competitive results were achieved even in databases out of our study case. The results of the classification experiments show that the angle based similarities contain relevant information for classification purposes. This information, based on the behavior of the data, shows to be complementary to the information collected by the level based similarities. In this work, the section similarities were averaged over the total number of sections. In the future, the use of the individual similarities calculated in each section will be considered. In addition, the section-wise similarities could be used to detect clusters of experts when no label information is available.

Acknowledgments. Supported by the Minister for Science and Innovation of Spain: CABINTEC (PSE-37010-2007-2) and VULCANO (TEC2009-10639-C04-04). Thanks to CONACYT and CONCYTEY for supporting the project through their scholarship programs.

References

1. Zhang, H., Schreiner, C., Zhang, K., Torkkola, K.: Naturalistic use of cell phones in driving and context-based user assistance. In: Proc. of the 9th Int. Conf. on Human Computer Interaction with Mobile Devices and Services, pp. 273–276 (2007)
2. Brazalez, A., et al.: CABINTEC: Cabina inteligente para el transporte por carretera. In: Proc. of the Congreso Español de Sistemas Inteligentes de Transporte (2008)
3. Tamil, E.M., et al.: A review on feature extraction & classification techniques for biosignal processing (Part I: Electrocardiogram). In: Proc. of the 4th Kuala Lumpur Int. Conference on Biomedical Engineering 2008, vol. 21, pp. 117–121 (2008)
4. Keogh, E., Pazzani, M.: An enhanced representation of time series which allows fast and accurate classification, clustering and relevance feedback. In: KDD, pp. 239–243 (1998)

5. Siordia, O.S., Martín, I., Conde, C., Reyes, G., Cabello, E.: Driving risk classification based on experts evaluation. In: Proceedings of the 2010 IEEE Intelligent Vehicles Symposium (IV 2010), pp. 1098–1103 (2010)
6. Randall, C., et al.: A comparison of the verbal rating scale and the visual analog scale for pain assessment. Technical Report 1, Int. Journal of Anesthesiology (2004)
7. Keogh, E., Chu, S., Hart, D., Pazzani, M.: Segmenting time series: A survey and novel approach. In: Data Mining in Time Series Databases, pp. 1–22 (1993)
8. Lachaud, J.-O., Vialard, A., de Vieilleville, F.: Analysis and comparative evaluation of discrete tangent estimators. In: Andrès, É., Damiand, G., Lienhardt, P. (eds.) DGCI 2005. LNCS, vol. 3429, pp. 240–251. Springer, Heidelberg (2005)
9. Martín, I., Muñoz, A., Moguerza, J.: Methods for the combination of kernel matrices within a support vector framework. Mach. Learn. 78, 137–174 (2010)
10. Keogh, E., Xi, X., Wei, L., Ratanamahatana, A.: The ucr time series classification/clustering (2006), http://www.cs.ucr.edu/~eamonn/time_series_data/
11. Ramsay, J., Silverman, B.: Functional Data Analysis. Springer Series in Statistics, Secaucus, NJ, USA (2005)
12. Ferraty, F., Vieu, P.: Nonparametric Functional Data Analysis: Theory and Practice. Springer Series in Statistics (2006)

Some Imputation Algorithms for Restoration of Missing Data

Vladimir Ryazanov

Institution of Russian Academy of Sciences Dorodnicyn Computing Centre of RAS,
Vavilov st. 40, 119333 Moscow, Russia
http://www.ccas.ru

Abstract. The problem of reconstructing the feature values in samples of objects given in terms of numerical features is considered. The three approaches, not involving the use of probability models and a priori information, are considered. The first approach is based on the organization of the iterative procedure for successive elaboration of missing values of attributes. In this case, the analysis of local information for each object with missing data is fulfilled. The second approach is based on solving an optimization problem. We calculate such previously unknown feature values for which there is maximum correspondence of metric relations between objects in subspaces of known partial values and found full descriptions. The third approach is based on solving a series of recognition tasks for each missing value. Comparisons of these approaches on simulated and real problems are presented.

Keywords: missing data, imputation, feature, pattern recognition, feature values restoration.

1 Introduction

Many problems in data mining can be written in the standard form. Let be given a sample $\{z_i, \bar{x}_i\}, i = 1, 2, ..., m$, $\bar{x}_i = (x_{i1}, x_{i2}, ..., x_{in})$ is the feature description of some object, $z_i, x_{ij} \in R$. We assume scalar z_i is defined by vector $\bar{x}_i$. It is necessary to calculate $z = f(\bar{x})$ by some vector $\bar{x}$. Here $z, x_j \in R$.

Here we can distinguish three specific tasks:

1. $z \in \{1, 2, ..., l\}, z_i, i = 1, 2, ..., m$, are known (supervised classification or recognition task);
2. $z \in \{1, 2, ..., l\}$, but the values $z_i, i = 1, 2, ..., m$, (and may be l) are unknown (unsupervised classification or clustering task);
3. $z \in (a, b)$, $z_i, i = 1, 2, ..., m$ are known (task of regression reconstruction).

In this paper we consider the case of missing data for some features (unknown feature values are denoted by Δ).

There are various approaches: taking into account the type of tasks (clustering, classification or regression), cases of training or classification , taking

C. San Martin and S.-W. Kim (Eds.): CIARP 2011, LNCS 7042, pp. 372–379, 2011.

into account additional a priori knowledge and hypotheses, the direct solution of problems with missing data or their decision after a preliminary gaps reconstruction . We consider the case when the problems are solved in the following two steps. First signs of recovering missing values in object descriptions. In the second phase is addressing these problems for a complete description, which already uses the standard well-known algorithms.

There are different approaches to solve the problem of reconstruction of missing feature values that are commonly referred to as marginalisation, imputation, and projection. In the case of marginalization or skipping incomplete objects, the incomplete objects in the dataset are discarded simply in order to create a new complete dataset [1]. In this case, you may lose a large amount of information. In the case of *Imputation approaches,* a value from the entire dataset to fill the missing attribute is estimated. The well-known imputation techniques are the mean of known values of the same feature in other instances, median, random [1, 2], the nearest neighbour method [3]. In [4], a partial imputation technique has been proposed. It consists of the imputation of missing data using complete objects in a small neighborhood of the incomplete ones. In [5], a new approach is proposed , using the entropy to estimate the missing values.

The *Projection methods* (or imputation by regression) realize the next idea. The feature space is reduced to one dimension less for each missing attribute. So, it is necessary to compute a special classifier or regression function in the reduced space. Usually, complete objects of the training set are used to build the optimal classifier\regression. In [6], the imputation technique using support vector regressions (SVR) is studied and compared with some well-known ones. The results showed the high precision obtained by SVR technique with regards to the mean, median, of the nearest neighbor techniques.

It is well known and reliable algorithm for filling gaps by maximum likelihood (EM algorithm) [1, 2]. A disadvantage is the low rate of convergence, if missed a lot of data. Probably, there are a lot of local optimal solutions. It is assumed a reasonable probabilistic model of classification or regression.

In this article we propose three algorithms for the restoration feature values according to the training samples, based on attempts to implement the following principles:

– use all the objects of training sample, regardless of the number of existing gaps;
– do not use any probabilistic assumptions about the data set;
– background information is only sample data;
– features in general are not independent.

Initial information is training sample of objects $X = \{\bar{x}_1, \bar{x}_2, ..., \bar{x}_m\}$. We assume that $x_{ij} \in \{M_j, \Delta\}, M_j \subseteq R$. Unknown feature values x_{ij} are denoted as Δ. Let the set of pairs of indexes J specifies all unknown values of attributes of the objects of training sample $J = \{\langle i, j \rangle : x_{ij} = \Delta\}$. Region $M_j, j = 1, 2, ..., n$, of permissible values of each feature is a finite set, which is determined by a given sample.

The task of reconstruction of unknown feature values is to find a sample $X^* = \{\bar{x}_1^*, \bar{x}_2^*, ..., \bar{x}_m^*\}$ of complete descriptions $\bar{x}_i^* = (x_{i1}^*, x_{i2}^*, ..., x_{in}^*)$, $x_{ij}^* = \begin{cases} x_{ij}, & x_{ij} \neq \Delta, \\ \in M_j, & x_{ij} = \Delta, \end{cases}$, "the most corresponding" sample given a partial descriptions X. This "best match" can be defined explicitly or not explicitly. We consider the following three approaches and specific algorithms.

2   Local Method for Reconstructing Feature Values

First, all the unknown feature values are filled with random numbers from the range of admissible values of variable $x_{ij} \in M_j, j = 1, 2, ..., n$. Next, the unknown values sequentially modified by a combination of method k-nearest neighbor and shift procedure. Let be given the metric in the space of the feature descriptions.

Step 0. Initializing random $x_{ij}^{(0)} \in M_j, \forall \langle i, j \rangle \in J$. Obtain the full descriptions. If $\langle i, j \rangle \in J$, let $x_{ij}^{(0)*}$ is an average value of feature j over the k nearest neighbors of $\bar{x}_i$. Then define $x_{ij}^1 = x_{ij}^{(0)} + \theta(x_{ij}^{(0)*} - x_{ij}^{(0)}), \forall \langle i, j \rangle \in J, x_{ij}^{(1)} = x_{ij}^{(0)}, \forall \langle i, j \rangle \notin J$. Here $0 < \theta \leq 1$.

Step t=1,2,.... We have $\bar{x}_i^{(t-1)} = (x_{i1}^{(t-1)}, ..., x_{in}^{(t-1)})$. For each pair $\langle i, j \rangle \in J$, the $x_{ij}^{(t-1)*}$ is calculated as the average value of feature j over the k- nearest neighbors of the object $x_i^{(t-1)}$. Then define $x_{ij}^{(t)} = x_{ij}^{(t-1)} + \theta(x_{ij}^{(t-1)*} - x_{ij}^{(t-1)})$, $\forall \langle i, j \rangle \in J$, $x_{ij}^{(t)} = x_{ij}^{(t-1)}, \forall \langle i, j \rangle \notin J$. Step is repeated, if not satisfied the stopping criterion. Otherwise, the restoration of gaps is finished.

Stopping   criterion: the   maximum   number   of   iterations N, $\sum_{\langle i,j \rangle \in J} \left| x_{ij}^{(t)} - x_{ij}^{(t-1)} \right|^2 \leq \varepsilon$, etc. Finally, we put $x_{ij}^{(final)}, \forall \langle i, j \rangle \in J$ the nearest value from M_j.

3   Optimization Method for Reconstructing Feature Values

The essence of this approach is that missing values should take such values for which the metric relationships between objects in space of "full descriptions" as would correspond to metric relations in the subspaces of known "partial descriptions".

Let $\bar{x}_i, \bar{x}_j$ is a pair of training objects. We introduce the notation: $\Omega_i^0 = \{t : x_{it} \neq \Delta\}$, $\Omega_i^1 = \{t : x_{it} = \Delta\}$. Let $\Omega_{ij}^{00} = \Omega_i^0 \cap \Omega_j^0$, $\Omega_{ij}^{01} = \Omega_i^0 \cap \Omega_j^1$, $\Omega_{ij}^{10} = \Omega_i^1 \cap \Omega_j^0$, $\Omega_{ij}^{11} = \Omega_i^1 \cap \Omega_j^1$. We will use the Euclidean metric $\rho^2(\bar{x}_i, \bar{x}_j) = \left(\sum_{t \in \Omega_{ij}^{00}} (x_{it} - x_{jt})^2 + \sum_{t \in \Omega_{ij}^{01}} (x_{it} - y_{jt})^2 + \sum_{t \in \Omega_{ij}^{10}} (y_{it} - x_{jt})^2 + \sum_{t \in \Omega_{ij}^{11}} (y_{it} - y_{jt})^2 \right)$. Here and below, for convenience, the unknown values of features x_{it} are replaced by the parameters y_{it}: $\{\langle i, j \rangle \in J\}$ for all pairs of indexes.

We will consider the next distances in the feature subspaces.

$\rho^+(\bar{x}_i, \bar{x}_j) = \left(\sum_{t\in\Omega_{ij}^{00}}(x_{it} - x_{jt})^2\right)^{\frac{1}{2}}$ is a distance in the subspace in which the values of the features of both objects are known.

$\rho^{++}(\bar{x}_i, \bar{x}_j) = \left(\sum_{t\in\Omega_{ij}^{00}}(x_{it} - x_{jt})^2 + \sum_{t\in\Omega_{ij}^{01}}(x_{it} - y_{jt})^2 + \sum_{t\in\Omega_{ij}^{10}}(y_{it} - x_{jt})^2\right)^{\frac{1}{2}}$ is a distance in the subspace, in which the feature values are known at least for one object.

We consider the following two criteria of filling gaps quality as a function of the unknown values of features:

$$\Phi(\langle y_{ij}\rangle) = \sum_{\substack{i,j=1 \\ i>j}}^{m}(\rho(\bar{x}_i, \bar{x}_j) - N_{ij}^+\rho^+(\bar{x}_i, \bar{x}_j))^2,$$

$$F(\langle y_{ij}\rangle) = \sum_{\substack{i,j=1 \\ i>j}}^{m}(\rho(\bar{x}_i, \bar{x}_j) - N_{ij}^{++}\rho^{++}(\bar{x}_i, \bar{x}_j))^2.$$

Here N_{ij}^+, N_{ij}^{++} are chosen according to one of the following ways:

1.a $N_{ij}^+ = 1$, 1.b. $N_{ij}^+ = \frac{n}{|\Omega_{ij}^{00}|}$ (if $|\Omega_{ij}^{00}| = 0$ put $\rho(\bar{x}_i, \bar{x}_j) - N_{ij}^+\rho^+(\bar{x}_i, \bar{x}_j) = 0$).

2.a. $N_{ij}^{++} = 1$, 2.b. $N_{ij}^{++} = \frac{n}{|\Omega_{ij}^{00}+\Omega_{ij}^{01}+\Omega_{ij}^{10}|}$

(if $|\Omega_{ij}^{00} + \Omega_{ij}^{01} + \Omega_{ij}^{10}| = 0$ put $\rho(\bar{x}_i, \bar{x}_j) - N_{ij}^{++}\rho^{++}(\bar{x}_i, \bar{x}_j) = 0$).

Gradient of the first criterion is as follows

$$\frac{\partial\Phi(\langle y_{ij}\rangle)}{\partial y_{\alpha\beta}} = 2\sum_{\substack{i\neq\alpha, \\ \rho^+(\bar{x}_i, \bar{x}_\alpha)>0}}\frac{(\rho(\bar{x}_i, \bar{x}_\alpha) - N_{i\alpha}^+\rho^+(\bar{x}_i, \bar{x}_\alpha))}{\rho(\bar{x}_i, \bar{x}_\alpha)}(y_{\alpha\beta} - x_{i\beta}),$$

Gradient for $F(\langle y_{ij}\rangle)$ is the analogy one.

Then we apply the method of steepest descent with constraints

$y_{ij} \in [\min_{t=1,2,...,m} x_{tj}, \max_{t=1,2,...,m} x_{tj}]$.

In the local and optimization approaches, we do not distinguish between numeric and discrete features. After restoring the values of features, we put

$x_{ij}^* = a_{sj} : a_{sj} \in M_j, \left|a_{sj} - x_{ij}^{(final)}\right| = \min_{\substack{t=1,2,...,m \\ <t,j>\notin J}} \left|a_{tj} - x_{ij}^{(final)}\right|$. In the case

of two possible solutions, we take one from them which has a higher frequency on the training data.

4   Restoration of Feature Values as the Solution of Recognition Problem

Meaningful task is to assign these numerical values for objects with a gaps, which are the most "agreed" with known features of the object. The reconstruction problem is solved sequentially for each pair $\langle i, j \rangle \in J$ as a special recognition task. Let for an object $\bar{x}_i$ from the sample X value x_{ij} is unknown. For simplicity, we further denote $\bar{y} = \bar{x}_i, \bar{y} = (y_1, y_2, ..., y_n), \Omega_i = \{j_1, j_2, ...j_\tau\}, \Theta_i = \{k_1, k_2, ..., k_\sigma\} = \{1, 2, ..., n\} \backslash \Omega_i, x_{ij} = \Delta, \forall j \in \Omega_i$. Denote $M_j = \{a_1, a_2, ..., a_N\}$ as the set of all possible values of j−th feature. It is calculated by known data. Let $a = a_1 < a_2 < ... < a_N = b$.

The general algorithm consists in solving of $[\log_2 N] + 1$ dichotomous recognition tasks. It was used the estimation calculation algorithm, based on voting over support sets of a given power [7]. This algorithm reflects the correlation properties between features and doesn't use any training.

1. There is a set of numbers $a = a_1 < a_2 < ... < a_N = b$. We consider two classes: $K_1 = \{\bar{x} | a \leq x_j \leq a_{[\frac{N}{2}]}\}, \tilde{K}_1 = K_1 \bigcap X, K_2 = \{\bar{x} | a_{[\frac{N}{2}]} < x_j \leq b\}, \tilde{K}_2 = K_2 \bigcap X$.

2. Estimate $\Gamma_t(\bar{y}) = \sum_{\bar{x}_\lambda \in \tilde{K}_t} C^k_{d(\bar{x}_\lambda, \bar{y})}$ for class $K_t, t = 1, 2$ (degree of membership of an object $\bar{y}$ to class $K_t, t = 1, 2$) is computed. Here $d(\bar{x}_\lambda, \bar{y}) = |\{\beta : |y_\beta - x_{\lambda\beta}| \leq \varepsilon_\beta\}, \beta \in \Theta_i \bigcap \Theta_\lambda|, 1 \leq k \leq n$ is an integer (control input parameter), $\varepsilon_\beta = \frac{2}{|h_\beta|(|h_\beta|-1)} \sum_{\bar{x}_u, \bar{x}_v \in \tilde{K}_1 \bigcup \tilde{K}_2, u > v, x_{u\beta}, x_{v\beta} \neq \Delta} |x_{u\beta} - x_{v\beta}|$, $h_\beta = \left| \{\bar{x}_a \in \tilde{K}_1 \bigcup \tilde{K}_2 : x_{a\beta} \neq \Delta\} \right|$.

3. If $\Gamma_1(\bar{y}) \geq \Gamma_2(\bar{y})$ put $\bar{y} \in K_1$, otherwise $\bar{y} \in K_2$.

4. If, the class to which $\bar{y}$ is assigned contains only one element $\bar{x}_a$, then we put $y_j = x_{aj}$. The task of restoring the value x_{ij} is considered to be resolved. Otherwise, the transition at point 1 and process is repeated with respect to the set $a_1 < a_2 < ... < a_{[\frac{N}{2}]}$ (if $\bar{y}$ assigned in class K_1) or relative to the set $a_{[\frac{N}{2}]+1} < a_{[\frac{N}{2}]+2} < ... < a_N$ (if $\bar{y}$ assigned in class K_2). It is clear that no more than $[\log_2 N] + 1$ steps, we obtain the first situation 4.

To calculate estimates for the classes one can use other ways of calculating estimates [7].

5   The Results of Numerical Experiments

This section presents the initial results of the application and comparison of some different feature values restoration techniques. Two models of the creation of data gaps have been considered.

In the first model in each training object $\alpha\%$ of feature values were considered missing. This selection was performed randomly in a uniform distribution law. In the second model, $\alpha\%$ of elements of training set were considered as missing. The choice of these pairs "object-feature" also was performed randomly according uniform distribution law. Experiments were carried out as follows. According to the original training set, the training samples with gaps were formed by the first or second model. The samples of incomplete feature descriptions were restored by the algorithm mean substitution, and the algorithms proposed in this paper. After that, for all tables were solved the supervised classification (recognition) problems using different algorithms. We used the implementation of algorithms in a software system " Recognition" [8]. Experiments were conducted with model data and with one practical problem.

As a model task, a mixture of two normal distributions has been considered. Training and the control data consisted of 200 vectors, 100 ones from each class. The vectors consisted of values of 10 independent features. Features of the first (second) class are normally distributed according normal distributions with parameters $a = 0, \sigma^2 = 9$ (respectively $a = 5, \sigma^2 = 9$), where the a is an expectation, σ^2 is a variance. Transformations of training and control data in the samples with gaps were run with $\alpha= 35$. Restoration of training and control samples were carried out independently. Fig. 1 shows the visualization of control sample. Black and gray dots correspond to the first and second classes, respectively. They are displaying objects from a R^{10} on a plane with maximum preservation of metric relations between objects in R^{10} [9].

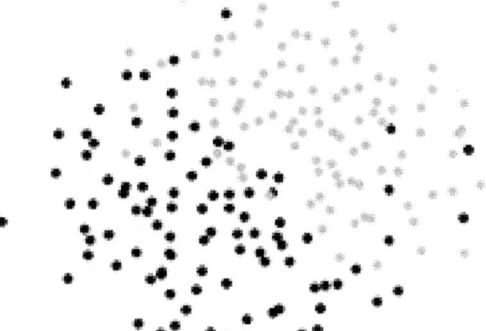

Fig. 1. Visualization of the control sample in a simple model task

Tables 1 and 2 present the recognition results to a control sample and its modifications by various algorithms.

Recognition accuracy was estimated as the percentage of correctly recognized objects of control sample. When training of the various algorithms used standard values of their control parameters. The task of choosing the optimal parameters of the algorithms for training was not considered. So, the results of different algorithms for solving same tasks are very different. The rows of tables presents the results of recognition of different algorithms: LM – "linear machine" [9], k –neighbors – "k-nearest neighbors" [9], AEC – "estimation calculation algorithms" [7], LDF – "Fisher linear discriminator"[9], LR - "voting algorithm over sets of logical regularities of classes [10].

Each column of the table presents the results of recognition of different modifications of the original checklist: the source table, the method of mean substitution, applications of methods 1, 2, 3, that denote the local, optimization and based on pattern recognition tasks solving methods. In the local method we used the values of parameters $\theta = 0.8$, $N = 50$, $k = 5$, in an optimization algorithm has been used functional $\Phi(\langle y_{ij}\rangle)$ for $N_{ij}^+ = 1$.

Table 1. Recognition of simulated data for the first model of gaps creation

recogn. method \ table	source table	mean substitution	method 1	method 2	method 3
LM	84.5	85.0	84.5	86.0	84.5
k neighbors	−87.0	82.0	82.5	83.0	81.5
AEC	86.0	73.0	79.5	75.5	80.0
LDF	86.0	81.0	82.5	81.5	77.5
LR	85.0	72.5	81.0	78.5	78.0

Table 2. Recognition of simulated data for the second model of gaps creation

recogn. method \ table	source table	mean substitution	method 1	method 2	method 3
LM	84.5	85.5	81.5	86.0	84.5
k neighbors	−87.0	82.5	85.5	81.5	85.0
AEC	86.0	75.0	78.0	78.5	83.0
LDF	86.0	79.0	81.5	79.5	82.0
LR	85.0	69.9	77.5	79.5	81.5

6   Conclusion

There was considered a model task that has been created on the basis of three normal distributions having linearly inseparable centers of the classes. Besides, here were used some other recognition algorithms (neural network with back propagation training [11], binary decision trees [9], SVM [12], multiplicative neural network [13]). As a test task,we examined a sample of patients with complaints of chest pain from Heart Disease Databases (Hungarian Institute of Cardiology. Budapest: Andras Janosi, M.D., University Hospital, Zurich, Switzerland: William Steinbrunn, M.D., University Hospital, Basel, Switzerland: Matthias Pfisterer, M.D., V.A. Medical Center, Long Beach and Cleveland Clinic Foundation: Robert Detrano, M.D., Ph.D.). The results were similar to those of considered earlier.

For a more accurate evaluation of the proposed approaches and their comparison necessary to carry out a large series of experiments both on real and simulated data, and various models of missing data modelling. Nevertheless, these preliminary calculations confirm some a priori expectations. Local averaging of characteristics (method 1) is better than the average for the full sample. Method 2 showed good results, but apparently it will be inefficient for problems with a large number of gaps. In method 3 is used an algorithm AEC. The calculation of the degree of affiliation $\Gamma_t(\bar{y})$ for object $\bar{y}$ to a certain class K_t is based on a comparison $\bar{y}$ with each $\bar{x}_\lambda \in \bar{K}_t$. Comparison takes place on different subsets of features in the maximum feature subspace where $\bar{y}$ and $\bar{x}_\lambda$ have no gaps. This expresses the fact of existance of dependencies between features (see [7]).

The total ratio of the first places of compared methods is 4:7:16:9. Methods 1-3 show generally higher results. In any case, the creation of new algorithms for reconstruction of unknown feature values is important. Having a set of different recovery algorithms, we improve the chances of a more exact solution of classification problems.

Acknowledgments. This work was supported by RAS Presidium programs number 14 and "Basic Sciences - Medicine, Program number 2 of Department of Mathematical Sciences of RAS, RFBR 09-01-00409, 10-01-90015 Bel_a, 10-01-90419 Ukr_a.

References

1. Little, R.J.A., Rubin, D.B.: Statistical Analysis with Missing Data. Wiley, New York (1987)
2. Zloba, E.: Statistical methods of reproducing of missing data. J. Computer Modelling & New Technologies 6(1), 51–61 (2002)
3. Morin, R.L., Raeside, D.E.: A reappraisal of distance-weighted k-nearest neighbor classification for pattern recognition with missing data. IEEE Transactions on Systems, Man and Cybernetics, 241–243 (1981)
4. Zhang, S.: Parimputation: From imputation and null-imputation to partially imputation. IEEE Intelligent Informatics Bulletin 9(1), 32–38 (2008)
5. Delavallade, T., Dang, T.H.: Using Entropy to Impute Missing Data in a Classification Task. In: IEEE International Conference on Fuzzy Systems, London, pp. 1–6 (2007)
6. Honghai, F., Guoshun, C., Cheng, Y., Bingru, Y., Yumei, C.: A SVM Regression Based Approach to Filling in Missing Values. In: Khosla, R., Howlett, R.J., Jain, L.C. (eds.) KES 2005. LNCS (LNAI), vol. 3683, pp. 581–587. Springer, Heidelberg (2005)
7. Zhuravlev, Y.I., Nikiforov, V.V.: Recognition Algorithms based on Estimate Evaluation. J. Kibernetika 3, 1–11 (1971) (in Russian)
8. Zhuravlev, Y.I., Ryazanov, V.V., Senko, O.V.: Recognition. Mathematical methods. Programm. System. Applications, Fazis, Moscow (2006) (in Russian)
9. Duda, R.O., Hart, P.E., Stork, D.G.: Pattern Classification, 2nd edn. Wiley interscience (2001)
10. Ryazanov, V.V.: Logical Regularities in Pattern Recognition (Parametric Approach). Computational Mathematics and Mathematical Physics 47(10), 1720–1735 (2007); ©Pleiades Publishing, Ltd., Original Russian Text ©V.V. Ryazanov, published in Zhurnal Vychislitel'noi Matematiki i Matematicheskoi Fiziki 47(10), 1793–1808 (2007)
11. Fausett, L.: Fundamentals of Neural Networks. Prentice-Hall (1994)
12. Vapnik, V.: The Nature of Statistical Learning Theory. Springer, Heidelberg (1995)
13. Ishodzhanov, T.R., Ryazanov, V.V.: A gradient search for logical regularities of classes with a linear dependence. In: 14th All-Russian Conference on Mathematical Methods for Pattern Recognition: 14 All-Russian Conference, pp. 123–124. MAKS Press, Vladimir region (2009)

A Scalable Heuristic Classifier for Huge Datasets: A Theoretical Approach

Hamid Parvin, Behrouz Minaei-Bidgoli, and Sajad Parvin

Islamic Azad University, Nourabad Mamasani Branch, Nourabad Mamasani, Iran
{parvin,b_minaei,s.parvin}@iust.ac.ir

Abstract. This paper proposes a heuristic classifier ensemble to improve the performance of learning in multiclass problems. Although the more accurate classifier leads to a better performance, there is another approach to use many inaccurate classifiers while each one is specialized for a few data in the problem space and using their consensus vote as the classifier. In this paper, some ensembles of classifiers are first created. The classifiers of each of these ensembles jointly work using majority weighting votes. The results of these ensembles are combined to decide the final vote in a weighted manner. Finally the outputs of these ensembles are heuristically aggregated. The proposed framework is evaluated on a very large scale Persian digit handwritten dataset and the experimental results show the effectiveness of the algorithm.

Keywords: Genetic Algorithm, Optical Character Recognition, Pairwise Classifier, Multiclass Classification.

1 Introduction

In practice, there may be problems that one single classifier can not deliver a satisfactory performance [7], [8] and [9]. In such situations, employing ensemble of classifying learners instead of single classifier can lead to a better learning [6]. Although obtaining the more accurate classifier is often targeted, there is an alternative way to obtain it. Indeed one can use many inaccurate classifiers each of which is specialized for a few dataitems in the problem space and then employ their consensus vote as the classification. This can lead to better performance due to reinforcement of the classifier in error-prone problem spaces.

In General, it is ever-true sentence that "combining the diverse classifiers which are better than random results in a better classification performance" [2], [6] and [10]. Diversity is always considered as a very important concept in classifier ensemble methodology. It refers to being as much different as possible for a typical ensemble. Assume an example dataset with two classes. Indeed the diversity concept for an ensemble of two classifiers refers to the probability that they produce dissimilar results for an arbitrary input sample. The diversity concept for an ensemble of three classifiers refers to the probability that one of them produces dissimilar result from the two others for an arbitrary input sample. It is worthy to mention that the diversity can converge to 0.5 and 0.66 in the ensembles of two and three classifiers respectively. Although reaching the

C. San Martin and S.-W. Kim (Eds.): CIARP 2011, LNCS 7042, pp. 380–390, 2011.

more diverse ensemble of classifiers is generally handful, it is harmful in boundary limit. It is very important dilemma in classifier ensemble field: the ensemble of accurate-diverse classifiers can be the best. It means that although the more diverse classifiers, the better ensemble, it is provided that the classifiers are better than random.

An Artificial Neural Network (ANN) is a model which is to be configured to be able to produce the desired set of outputs, given an arbitrary set of inputs. An ANN generally composed of two basic elements: (a) neurons and (b) connections. Indeed each ANN is a set of neurons with some connections between them. From another perspective an ANN contains two distinct views: (a) topology and (b) learning. The topology of an ANN is about the existence or nonexistence of a connection. The learning in an ANN is to determine the strengths of the topology connections. One of the most representatives of ANNs is MultiLayer Perceptron. Various methods of setting the strength of connections in an MLP exist. One way is to set the weights explicitly, using a prior knowledge. Another way is to 'train' the MLP, feeding it by teaching patterns and then letting it change its weights according to some learning rule. In this paper the MLP is used as one of the base classifiers.

Decision Tree (DT) is considered as one of the most versatile classifiers in the machine learning field. DT is considered as one of unstable classifiers. It means that it can converge to different solutions in successive trainings on same dataset with same initializations. It uses a tree-like graph or model of decisions. The kind of its knowledge representation is appropriate for experts to understand what it does [11].

Its intrinsic instability can be employed as a source of the diversity which is needed in classifier ensemble. The ensemble of a number of DTs is a well-known algorithm called Random Forest (RF) which is considered as one of the most powerful ensemble algorithms. The algorithm of RF was first developed by Breiman [1].

In a previous work, Parvin et al. have only dealt with the reducing the size of classifier ensemble [9]. They have shown that one can reduce the size of an ensemble of pairwise classifiers. Indeed they propose a method for reducing the ensemble size in the best meaningful manner. Here we inspire from their method, we propose a framework based on that a set of classifier ensembles are produced that its size order is not important. Indeed we propose an ensemble of binary classifier ensembles that has the order of c, where c is number of classes.

This paper proposes a framework to develop combinational classifiers. In this new paradigm, a multiclass classifier in addition to a few ensembles of pairwise classifiers creates a classifier ensemble. At last, to produce final consensus vote, different votes (or outputs) are gathered, after that a heuristic classifier ensemble algorithm is employed to aggregate them.

This paper focuses on Persian handwritten digit recognition (PHDR), especially on Hoda dataset [4]. Although there are well works on PHDR, it is not rational to compare them with each other, because there was no standard dataset in the PHDR field until 2006 [4]. The contribution is only compared with those used the same dataset used in this paper, i.e. Hoda dataset.

2   Artificial Neural Network

A first wave of interest in ANN (also known as 'connectionist models' or 'parallel distributed processing') emerged after the introduction of simplified neurons by McCulloch and Pitts in 1943. These neurons were presented as models of biological neurons and as conceptual components for circuits that could perform computational tasks. Each unit of an ANN performs a relatively simple job: receive input from neighbors or external sources and use this to compute an output signal which is propagated to other units. Apart from this processing, a second task is the adjustment of the weights. The system is inherently parallel in the sense that many units can carry out their computations at the same time. Within neural systems it is useful to distinguish three types of units: input units (indicated by an index i) which receive data from outside the ANN, output units (indicated by an index o) which send data out of the ANN, and hidden units (indicated by an index h) whose input and output signals remain within the ANN. During operation, units can be updated either synchronously or asynchronously. With synchronous updating, all units update their activation simultaneously; with asynchronous updating, each unit has a (usually fixed) probability of updating its activation at a time t, and usually only one unit will be able to do this at a time. In some cases the latter model has some advantages.

An ANN has to be configured such that the application of a set of inputs produces the desired set of outputs. Various methods to set the strengths of the connections exist. One way is to set the weights explicitly, using a priori knowledge. Another way is to 'train' the ANN by feeding it teaching patterns and letting it change its weights according to some learning rule. For example, the weights are updated according to the gradient of the error function. For further study the reader must refer to an ANN book such as Haykin's book on theory of ANN [3].

Tid	Refund	Marital Status	Taxable Income	Cheat
1	Yes	Single	125K	No
2	No	Married	100K	No
3	No	Single	70K	No
4	Yes	Married	120K	No
5	No	Divorced	95K	Yes
6	No	Married	60K	No
7	Yes	Divorced	220K	No
8	No	Single	85K	Yes
9	No	Married	75K	No
10	No	Single	90K	Yes

Fig. 1. An exemplary raw data

3   Decision Tree Learning

DT as a machine learning tool uses a tree-like graph or model to operate deciding on a specific goal. DT learning is a data mining technique which creates a model to predict the value of the *goal* or *class* based on input variables. Interior nodes are the representative of the input variables and the leaves are the representative of the target value. By splitting the source set into subsets based on their values, DT can be learned. Learning process is done for each subset by recursive partitioning. This process continues until all remain features in subset has the same value for our goal or until there is no improvement in *Entropy*. Entropy is a measure of the uncertainty associated with a random variable.

Data comes in records of the form: $(x,Y) = (x_1, x_2, x_3,..., x_n ,Y)$. The dependent variable, Y, is the target variable that we are trying to understand, classify or generalize. The vector **x** is composed of the input variables, x_1, x_2, x_3 etc., that are used for that task. To clarify that what the DT learning is, consider Fig.1. Fig.1 has 3 *attributes Refund, Marital Status* and *Taxable Income* and our goal is cheat status. We should recognize if someone cheats by the help of our 3 attributes. To do learn process, attributes split into subsets. Fig.2 shows the process tendency. First, we split our source by the *Refund* and then *MarSt* and *TaxInc*.

For making rules from a decision tree, we must go upward from leaves as our antecedent to root as our consequent. For example consider Fig.2. Rules such as following are apprehensible. We can use these rules such as what we have in Association Rule Mining.

- Refund=Yes⇒cheat=No
- TaxInc<80, MarSt= (Single or Divorce), Refund=No⇒cheat=No
- TaxInc>80, MarSt= (Single or Divorce), Refund=No⇒cheat=Yes
- Refund=No, MarSt=Married⇒cheat=No

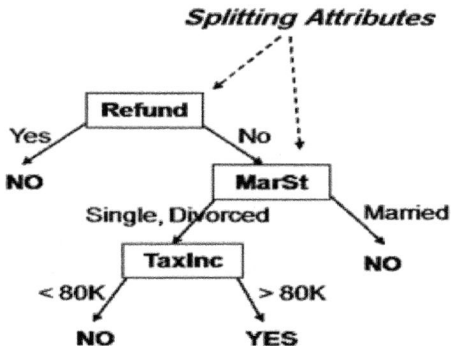

Fig. 2. The process tendency for Fig.1

4 Proposed Algorithm

The main idea behind the proposed method is to use a number of pairwise classifiers to reinforce the main classifier in the error-prone regions of the problem space. Fig.3 depicts the training phase of the proposed method schematically.

In the proposed algorithm, a multiclass classifier is first trained. Its duty is to produce a confusion matrix over the validation set. Note that this classifier is trained over the total train set. At next step, the pair-classes which are mostly confused with each other and are also mostly error-prone are detected. After that, a number of pairwise classifiers are employed to reinforce the drawbacks of the main classifier in those error-prone regions. A simple heuristic is used to aggregate their outputs.

At the first step, a multiclass classifier is trained on all train data. Then, using the results of this classifier on the validation data, confusion matrix is obtained. This matrix contains important information about the functionalities of classifiers in the dataset localities. The close and Error-Prone Pair-Classes (EPPC) can be detected using this matrix. Indeed, confusion matrix determines the between-class error distributions. Assume that this matrix is denoted by a. Item a_{ij} of this matrix determines how many instances of class c_j have been misclassified as class c_i.

Table 1 shows the confusion matrix obtained from the base multiclass classifier. As you can see, digit 5 (or equivalently class 6) is incorrectly recognized as digit 0 fifteen times (or equivalently class 1), and also digit 0 is incorrectly recognized as digit 5 fourteen times. It means 29 misclassifications have totally occurred in recognition of these two digits (classes). The mostly erroneous pair-classes are respectively (2, 3), (0, 5), (3, 4), (1, 4), (6, 9) and so on according to this matrix. Assume that the i-th mostly EPPC is denoted by $EPPC_i$. So $EPPC_1$ will be (2, 3). Also assume that the number of selected EPPC is denoted by k.

After determining the mostly erroneous pair-classes, or EPPCs, a set of m ensembles of binary classifiers is to be trained to jointly, as an ensemble of binary classifiers, reinforce the main multiclass classifier in the region of each EPPC. So as it can be inferred, it is necessary to train k ensembles of m binary classifiers. Assume that the ensemble which is to reinforce the main multiclass classifier in the region of $EPPC_i$ is denoted by PWC_i. Each binary classifier contained in PWC_i, is trained over a bag of train data like RF. The bags of train data contain only b percept of the randomly selected of train data. It is worthy to be mentioned that pairwise classifiers which are to participate in PWC_i are trained only on those instances which belongs to $EPPC_i$. Assume that the j-th classifier binary classifier of PWC_i is denoted by $PWC_{i,j}$. Because there exists m classifiers in each of PWC_i and also there exists k EPPC, so there will be $k*m$ binary classifiers totally. For example in the Table 1 the EPPC (2, 3) can be considered as an erroneous pair-class. So a classifier is necessary to be trained for that EPPC using those dataitems of train data that belongs to class 2 or class 3. As mentioned before, this method is flexible, so we can add arbitrary number of PWC_i to the base primary classifiers. It is expected that the performance of the proposed framework outperforms the primary base classifier. It is worthy to note that the accuracies of $PWC_{i,j}$ can easily be approximated using the train set. Because $PWC_{i,j}$ is trained only on b percept of the train set with labels belong to $EPPC_i$, provided that b is very small rate, then the accuracy of $PWC_{i,j}$ on the train set with labels belong to $EPPC_i$ can be considered as its approximated accuracy. Assume that the mentioned approximated accuracy of $PWC_{i,j}$ is denoted by $P_{i,j}$.

It is important to note that each of PWC_i acts as a binary classifier. As it mentioned each PWC_i contains m binary classifiers with an accuracy vector, P_i. It means of these binary ensemble can take a decision with weighed sum algorithm illustrated in [5]. So we can combine their results according to weighs computed by the equation 1.

$$w_{i,j} = \log(\frac{p_{i,j}}{1 - p_{i,j}})$$ 1

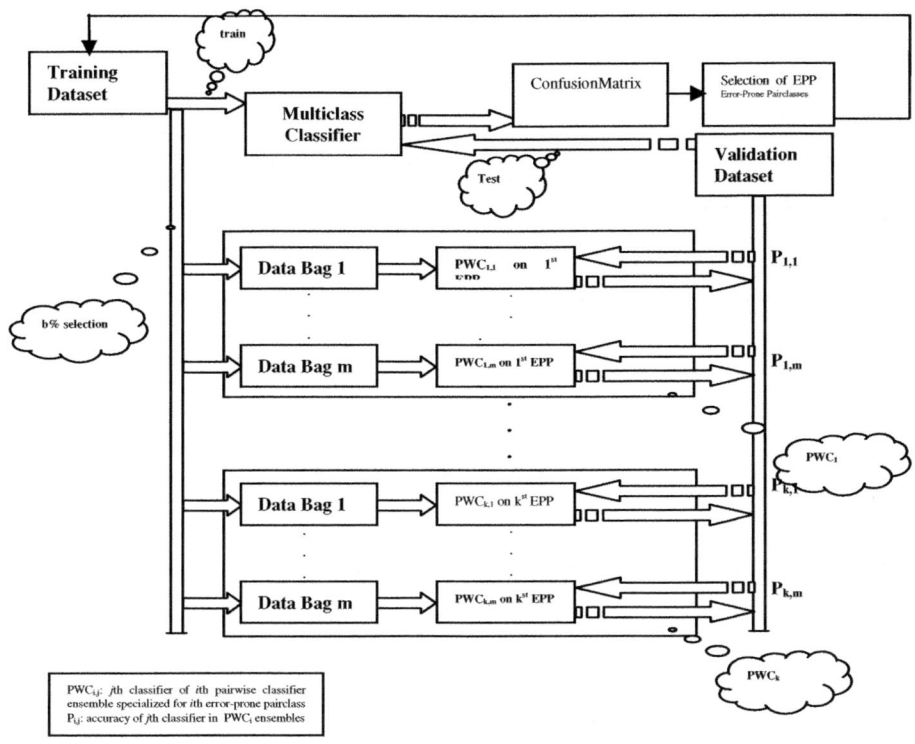

Fig. 3. The first training phase of the proposed method

where $w_{i,j}$ is the accuracy of j-th classifier in the i-th binary ensemble. It is proved that the weights obtained according to the equation 1 are optimal weights in theory. Now the two outputs of each PWC_i are computed as equation 2.

$$PWC_i(x \mid h) = \sum_{j=1}^{m} w_{i,j} * PWC_{i,j}(x \mid h) \quad , \quad h \in EPPC_i \qquad 2$$

where x is a test data.

The last step of the proposed framework is to combine the results of the main multiclass classifier and those of PWC_i. It is worthy to note that there are $2*k$ outputs from the binary ensembles plus c outputs of the main multiclass classifier. So the problem is to map a $2*k+c$ intermediate space to a c space each of which corresponds to a class. The results of all these classifiers are fed as inputs in the aggregators. The Output i of aggregator is the final joint output for class i. Here, the aggregation is done using a special heuristic method. This process is done using a heuristic based ensemble which is illustrated in the Fig.4. As the Fig.4 shows, after producing the intermediate space, the outputs of i-th ensemble of binary classifier are multiplied in a q_i number. This q_i number is equal to the sum of the main multiclass classifier's confidences for the classes belong to $EPPC_i$. Assume that the results of the multiplication of q_i by the outputs of PWC_i are denoted by $MPWC_i$. It is important to note that $MPWC_i$ is a vector of two confidences; the confidences of the classifier framework to the classes belonging to PWC_i.

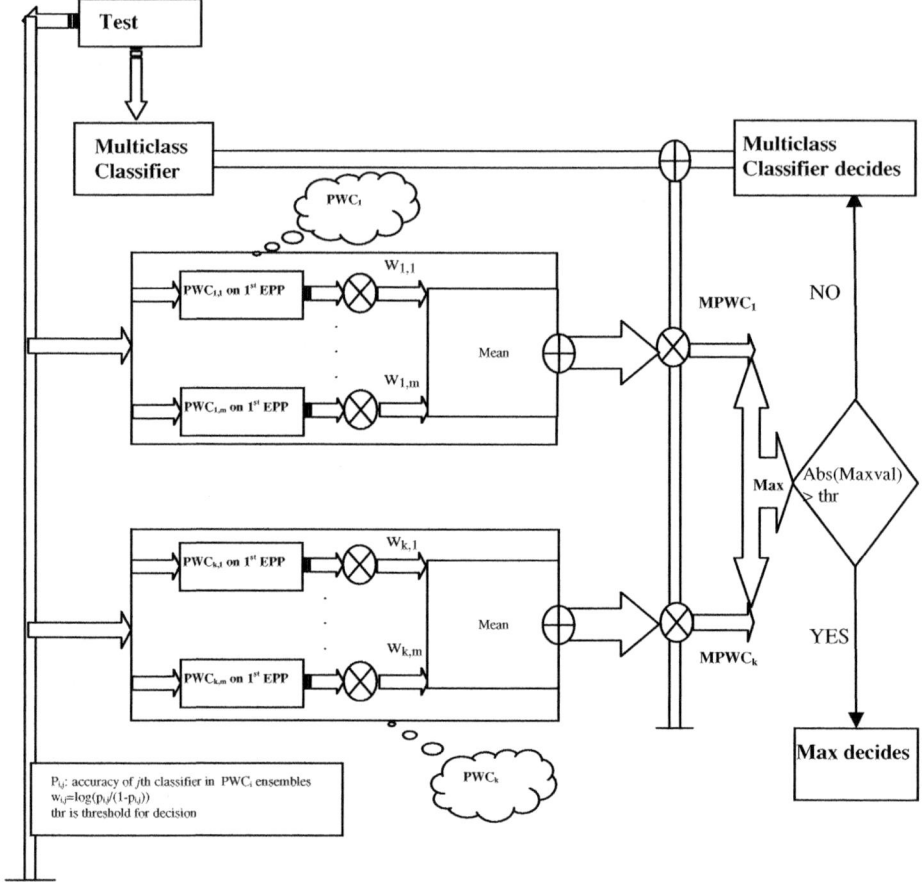

Fig. 4. Heuristic test phase of the proposed method test

After calculating the $MPWC_i$, the max value is selected between all of them. If the framework's confidence for the most confident class is satisfactory for a test data, then it is selected for final decision of framework, else the main multiclass classifier decides for the data. It means that the final decision is taken by equation 3.

$$Decision(x) = \begin{cases} MaxDecision(x) & \max_{h \in EPPC_{sc}} (MPWC_{sc}(h \mid x)) > thr \\ \max_{h \in \{1,\dots,c\}} (MCC(h \mid x)) & otherwise \end{cases} \qquad 3$$

where $MCC(h|x)$ is the confidence of the main multiclass classifier for the class h given a test data x. $MPWC_{sc}(h|x)$ is the confidence of the sc-th ensemble of binary classifiers for the class h given a test data x. MaxDecision is calculated according to equation 4.

$$MaxDecision(x) = \arg \max_{h \in EPPC_{sc}} (MPWC_{sc}(h \mid x)) \qquad 4$$

where sc is:

$$sc(x) = \arg\max_{i} \left(\max_{h \in EPPC_i} (MPWC_i(h \mid x)) \right) \qquad 5$$

Because of the reinforcement of the main classifier by some ensembles in erroneous regions, it is expected that the accuracy of this method outperforms a simple MLP or unweighted ensemble. Fig.3 along with Fig.4 stands as the structure of the ensemble framework.

5   Why the Proposed Method Works Results

As we presume in the paper, it is aimed to add as many as pairwise classifiers to compensate a predefined error rate, $PDER*EF(MCL,DValidation)$, where $PDER$ is a predefined error rate and $EF(MCL,DValidation)$ is error frequency of multiclass classifier, MCL, over the validation data, $DValidation$. Assume we add $|EPS|$ pairwise classifiers to the main MLC. It is as in the equation below.

$$\sum_{i=1}^{|eps|} (p(\hat{w} = EPPC_i.x \mid w = EPPC_i.y, x) + p(\hat{w} = EPPC_i.y \mid w = EPPC_i.x, x)) \qquad 6$$
$$= PDER * EF(MCL, DValidation, DTrain)$$

Now assume that a data instance x which belongs really to class q is to be classified by the proposed algorithm; it has the error rate which can be obtain by equation 12. First assume p^p_{max} is probability for the proposed classifier ensemble to take decision by one of its binary classifiers that is able to distinguish two classes: q and p. Also assume p^{pr}_{max} is probability for the proposed classifier ensemble to take decision by one of its binary classifiers that is able to distinguish two classes: r and p. They can be is obtained by equation 7 and 8 respectively.

$$p^{pr}_{max}(EPPC=(p,r) \mid x \in q) = (MCC(p \mid x) + MCC(r \mid x)) * \max(PWC(p \mid x), PWC(r \mid x)) \qquad 7$$

$$p^{p}_{max}(EPPC=(p,q) \mid x \in q) = (MCC(p \mid x) + MCC(q \mid x)) * \max(PWC(p \mid x), PWC(q \mid x)) \qquad 8$$

We can assume equation 9 without losing generality.

$$\forall r \neq q \mid \max(PWC(p \mid x \in q), PWC(r \mid x \in q)) \cong \mu << \max(PWC(p \mid x \in q), PWC(q \mid x \in q)) = \lambda \qquad 9$$

where μ is a fixed value and then we have:

$$p^{pr}_{max}(EPPC = (p,r) \mid x \in q) \cong (MCC(p \mid x) + MCC(r \mid x)) \times \mu \propto (b_{p.q} + b_{r.q}) \times \mu \qquad 10$$

$$p^{p}_{max}(EPPC = (p,q) \mid x \in q) = (MCC(p \mid x) + MCC(q \mid x)) \times \lambda = (b_{p.q} + b_{q.q}) \times \lambda \qquad 11$$

As it is inferred from the algorithm in the same condition, its error can be formulated as follow.

$$error(x \mid w = q) = \sum_{EPPC=(p,q)} p_{\max}^{p}(EPPC \mid x) * p_{pair}(p \mid x) +$$

$$\sum_{EPPC=(p,r)} p_{\max}^{pr}(EPPC \mid x) + (1 - p_{\max}^{p} - p_{\max}^{pr})(1 - b_{q,q}) \qquad 12$$

where p_{pair} is probability of taking correct decision by binary classifier and $b_{j,q}$ is defined as follow.

$$b_{j,p} = \frac{confusion_{j,p}}{\sum_{i=1}^{c} confusion_{i,p}} \qquad 13$$

So we can reformulate equation 12 as follow:

$$error(x \mid w = q) = \sum_{EPPC=(p,q)} p_{\max}^{p}(EPPC \mid x) * p_{pair}(p \mid x) + \sum_{EPPC=(p,r)} p_{\max}^{pr}(EPPC \mid x)$$

$$+ (1 - p_{\max}^{p} - p_{\max}^{pr})(1 - b_{q,q}) \cong \sum_{EPPC=(p,q)} p_{\max}^{p}(EPPC \mid x) * p_{pair}(p \mid x) + \qquad 14$$

$$(1 - p_{\max}^{p} - p_{\max}^{pr})(1 - b_{q,q})$$

Note that in equation 14 if $p^{pr}{}_{max}$ and $p'{}_{max}$ are zero for an exemplary input the error of
classification will be still equal to the main multiclass classifier. If they are not zero
for an exemplary input the misclassification rate will still be reduced because of reduction in second part of equation 14. Although the first part increases the error in
equation 14, but if we assume that the binary classifiers are more accurate than the
multiclass classifier, then the increase is nullified by the decrease part.

6   Experimental Results

This section evaluates the results of applying the proposed framework on a Persian
handwritten digit dataset named Hoda [4]. This dataset contains 102,364 instances of
digits 0-9. Dataset is divided into 3 parts: train, evaluation and test sets. Train set
contains 60,000 instances. Evaluation and test datasets are contained 20,000 and
22,364 instances. The 106 features from each of them have been extracted which are
described in [4].

In this paper, MLP and DT are used as base primary classifier. We use MLPs with
2 hidden layers including respectively 10 and 5 neurons in the hidden layer 1 and 2, as
the base Multiclass classifier and base simple classifiers. Confusion matrix is obtained
from its output. Also DT's measure of decision is taken as Gini measure. The classifiers' parameters are kept fixed during all of their experiments. It is important to take a
note that all classifiers in the algorithm are kept unchanged. It means that all classifiers are considered as MLP in the first experiments. After that the same experiments
are taken by substituting all MLPs whit DTs.

Table 1. Unsoft confusion matrix pertaining to the Persian handwritten OCR

	0	1	2	3	4	5	6	7	8	9
0	969	0	0	4	1	14	2	0	0	1
1	4	992	1	0	2	4	1	1	1	15
2	1	1	974	18	9	1	4	4	0	1
3	0	0	13	957	12	0	3	2	0	1
4	5	0	3	17	973	3	2	2	0	3
5	15	0	0	0	0	977	1	0	0	0
6	2	6	2	1	3	0	974	5	1	3
7	3	0	3	1	0	1	1	986	0	0
8	0	1	0	1	0	0	2	0	995	0
9	1	0	4	1	0	0	10	0	3	976

The parameter k is set to 11. So, the number of pairwise ensembles of binary classifiers added equals to 11 in the experiments. The parameter m is also set to 9. So, the number of binary classifiers per each EPPC equals to 9 in the experiments. It means that 99 binary classifiers are trained for the pair-classes that have considerable error rates. Assume that the error number of each pair-class is available. For choosing the most erroneous pair-classes, it is sufficient to sort error numbers of pair-classes. Then we can select an arbitrary number of them. This arbitrary number can be determined by try and error which it is set to 11 in the experiments.

As mentioned 9*11=99 pairwise classifiers are added to main multiclass classifier. As the parameter b is selected 20, so each of these classifiers is trained on only b precepts of corresponding train data. It means each of them is trained over 20 percept of the train set with the corresponding classes. The cardinality of this set is calculated by equation 15.

$$Car = \|train\| * 2 * b / c = 60000 * 2 * 0.2 / 10 = 2400 \qquad 15$$

It means that each binary classifier is trained on 2400 datapoints with 2 class labels. Table 2 shows the experimental results comparatively. As it is inferred the framework is outperforms the previous works and the simple classifiers in the case of employing decision tree as the base classifier.

Table 2. The accuracies of different settings of the proposed framework

Methods	DT	ANN
A simple multiclass classifier	96.57	97.83
Parvin et al. [9]	97.93	98.89
Weighed fusion	99.01	98.46

7 Conclusion

In this paper, a new method is proposed to improve the performance of multiclass classification system. We also propose a framework based on that a set of classifier ensembles are produced that its size order is not important. Indeed we propose an ensemble of binary classifier ensembles that has the order of c, where c is number of classes. So first an arbitrary number of binary classifier ensembles are added to main classifier. Then results of all these classifier are given to a set of a heuristic based ensemble. Usage of confusion matrix make proposed method a flexible one. The number of all possible pairwise classifiers is $c*(c-1)/2$ that it is $O(c^2)$. Using this method without giving up a considerable accuracy, we decrease its order to $O(1)$. This feature of our proposed method makes it applicable for problems with a large number of classes. The experiments show the effectiveness of this method. Also we reached to very good results in Persian handwritten digit recognition which is a very large dataset.

References

1. Breiman, L.: Bagging Predictors. Journal of Machine Learning 24(2), 123–140 (1996)
2. Gunter, S., Bunke, H.: Creation of classifier ensembles for handwritten word recognition using feature selection algorithms. In: IWFHR 2002 (January 15, 2002)
3. Haykin, S.: Neural Networks, a comprehensive foundation, 2nd edn. Prentice Hall International, Inc. (1999) ISBN: 0-13-908385-5
4. Khosravi, H., Kabir, E.: Introducing a very large dataset of handwritten Farsi digits and a study on the variety of handwriting styles. Pattern Recognition Letters 28(10), 1133–1141 (2007)
5. Kuncheva, L.I.: Combining Pattern Classifiers, Methods and Algorithms. Wiley, New York (2005)
6. Minaei-Bidgoli, B., Punch, W.F.: Using Genetic Algorithms for Data Mining Optimization in an Educational Web-based System. In: GECCO (2003)
7. Parvin, H., Alizadeh, H., Minaei-Bidgoli, B.: A New Approach to Improve the Vote-Based Classifier Selection. In: International Conference on Networked Computing and Advanced Information Management (NCM 2008), Korea (2008)
8. Parvin, H., Alizadeh, H., Fathi, M., Minaei-Bidgoli, B.: Improved Face Detection Using Spatial Histogram Features. In: The 2008 Int. Conf. on Image Processing, Computer Vision, and Pattern Recognition (IPCV 2008), Las Vegas, Nevada, USA (July 14-17, 2008)
9. Parvin, H., Alizadeh, H., Minaei-Bidgoli, B., Analoui, M.: An Scalable Method for Improving the Performance of Classifiers in Multiclass Applications by Pairwise Classifiers and GA. In: International Conference on Networked Computing and advanced Information Management (NCM 2008), Korea (2008)
10. Saberi, A., Vahidi, M., Minaei-Bidgoli, B.: Learn to Detect Phishing Scams Using Learning and Ensemble Methods. In: IEEE/WIC/ACM International Conference on Intelligent Agent Technology, Workshops (IAT 2007), Silicon Valley, USA, November 2-5, pp. 311–314 (2007)
11. Yang, T.: Computational Verb Decision Trees. International Journal of Computational Cognition, 34–46 (2006)

Improving Persian Text Classification Using Persian Thesaurus

Hamid Parvin, Behrouz Minaei-Bidgoli, and Atousa Dahbashi

School of Computer Engineering,
Iran University of Science and Technology (IUST), Tehran, Iran
{parvin,b_minaei,dahbashi}@iust.ac.ir

Abstract. This paper proposes an innovative approach to improve the performance of Persian text classification. The proposed method uses a thesaurus as a helpful knowledge to obtain the real frequencies of words in the corpus. Three types of relationships are considered in our thesaurus. This is the first attempt to use a Persian thesaurus in the field of Persian information retrieval. Experimental results show a significant improvement in the case of employing Persian thesaurus rather common methods.

Keywords: Persian Text, Persian Thesaurus, Semantic-Based Text Classification.

1 Introduction

In the current century Information Technology is considered as one of the most important fields (if not the most important field) among the researchers. Because the information is growing in a significant rapid way, its appropriate management and usage are inevitable. Indeed proper responding to the user queries is crucial in the Information Technology [1]. One of the most challenging problems in the field of Information Technology is how to do text retrieval and how to employ efficient algorithm on the mass of information.

In this direction, usage of keywords is very promising way for researchers to handle the job. A very important desire for researchers is to find the best representative keywords in the field of information retrieval. One of the most straightforward ways is based on frequency based keywords. Although this method is a very handful solution, the between word relationships are ignored there. It means while two synonym words are counted by the algorithm as two different words, it is better for the algorithm to count them as a single word and for its frequency to be equal to sum of frequencies of those two words.

To response queries of users relevantly, indexing is necessary. In general each context is consisted of two main parts: (a) external part and (b) body part. In library indexing based on first part is *descriptive cataloging* and based on second part is *subject cataloging*. Indexing needs the cognition of context. If indexing is done by computer, this will be automated indexing [2].

In text retrieval systems, indexing can be produced completely automatically. Research on creating or improving indexing methods and the automatic search for

C. San Martin and S.-W. Kim (Eds.): CIARP 2011, LNCS 7042, pp. 391–398, 2011.

information in texts for different languages has always been hot. The most sensitive and difficult step in the process during indexing should be automatically selection of the words that are used for index construction. In practice, indexing based on all words contained in the context has very high overhead. It is worthy to mention that indexing based on all the words is unnecessary.

In information processing, many systems were established. These systems are categorized in five main groups, which include: (I) Management Information System, (II) Data Base Management System, (III) Decision Support System, (VI) Question Answering System and (V) Information Retrieval System.

Text retrieval systems belong to information retrieval systems. Since a lot of similarities between information retrieval systems and database management systems, somebody may confuse the two systems with each other.

While data processing operations are performed on documents and duty of the systems is to store documents, provide and create access to documents or their representatives. In text retrieval systems, data input is natural language text (full text or selections, or abstract full text) [3]. In information retrieval systems, output in response to a search query is in the form of a set of references. These references show information about system user favorite items to them [4]. The duty of a database management system is the storage, the preservation and the retrieval system in a system, i.e. the information in this system is not natural language text; it is in the form of certain data elements that are stored in tables.

This paper has been to use existing relationships between words to help build a suitable technique for automatic thesaurus-based indexing in the Persian language.

Rest of this paper is organized as follows. Section 2 is related works. In section 3, we explain the proposed method. Section 4 demonstrates results of our proposed method against traditional comparatively. Finally, we conclude in section 5.

2   Related Work

In 1999, Turney showed that keyword extraction is one of the most important factors accelerate and facilitate information retrieval applications, but until then there is no attempt to improve quality of extracted keywords [5].

Then simultaneously in 1999, Frank et al. who worked in the field of artificial intelligence, while they were presenting machine processing algorithm, they tried to improve the quality of extracted keywords. Their work was based on Simple Bayes algorithm. Their system is named "KEA". In this method, although the quality of the extracted words significantly increased, linguistic issues were not considered [6]. The general process for extracting keywords was introduced by Liu in 2005. They elected the first candidate keywords, and then assigned a weight to each word and finally extracted the keywords with the highest weights [7]. Franz in 2002 combined statistical analysis and linguistic analysis [8]. He believed that without considering information about linguistic knowledge, statistical analysis considers disadvantageous and non-key words [8].

In direction of previous researches in 2005, to solve the drawbacks of the extraction of disadvantageous and non-key words, Freitas et al. modeled the process of keyword extraction as a classification problem [9]. Zhang et al. used a decision tree as classifier to recognize the keywords [10]. Halt used n-gram in the context of information retrieval [11]. In the first attempt, Deegan used thesaurus in 2004 [12] to improve information retrieval efficacy. After that Hyun tried to specialized thesaurus for a special query [13]. There are some successive works, tried to improve information retrieval efficacy after them [14]-[16].

Some of the work done in the field of Persian language is as follows [17]-[21]. While there are many methods in the Persian language, there is a lack of employing thesaurus in the Persian so far.

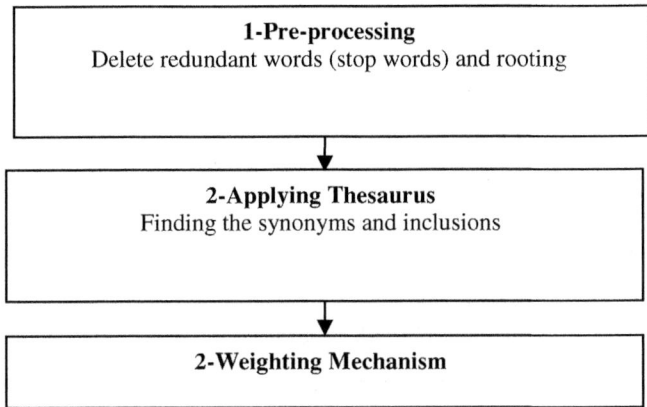

Fig. 1. Proposed Indexing framework

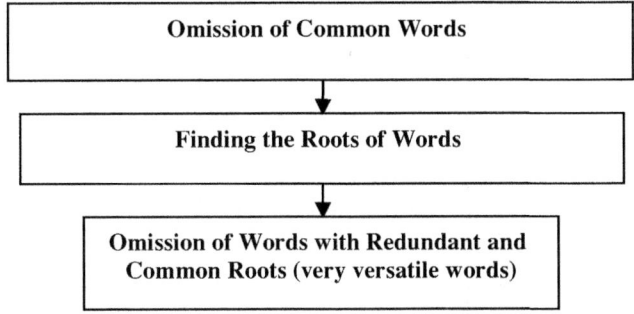

Fig. 2. Pre-processing phase of proposed framework

3 Proposed Framework

Fig. 1 depicts the proposed framework. The first step of the Fig. 1 is expanded in the Fig. 2. As seen in Fig. 2, in preprocessing step, Persian texts are refined to extract useful texts along with keywords to be ready for indexing stage. Indeed the pre-processing phase of proposed framework consists of three sub-parts. First the common words like prepositions are omitted. Then the root of each word is found. Third the common roots, like "*be*", are omitted.

In the Fig. 3 assume that the word1, word2 and word3 are synonyms. Using thesaurus these three words are converted to first word, i.e. the frequency of word1 is considered as 3.

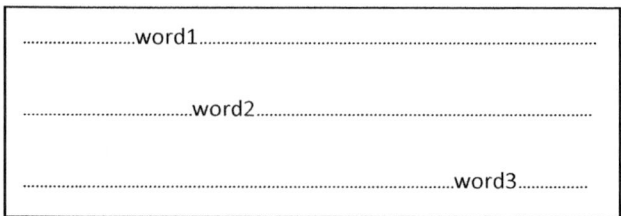

Fig. 3. A typical text with three words that are synonyms

So a table is produced from Fig. 3 that the frequencies of words are like Table 1.

Table 1. Table with frequencies of words of Fig. 3

word	#	
. . .		
word1	3	head
word2	3	
word3	3	
. . .		

So in the table of words frequencies synonym relationship is considered by a weight equals to 1, i.e. emerging the synonym of a word is equal to emerging that word. Another relationship that is taken into consideration is inclusion. For example a word an *animal* includes a *wolf*. So if in a text first *animal* is emerged, emerging a word *wolf* is equal to emerging animal with weight α, where α is less than one and vice versa. It means if an inclusion word has been emerged so far, emerging an included word is to emerge the included word by weight one, and including word by a weight below one. For example consider text of Fig. 4. Assume that *word5* is a special kind of *word4* and *word4* is special kind of *word3*. As before, *word1*, *word2* and *word3* are synonyms.

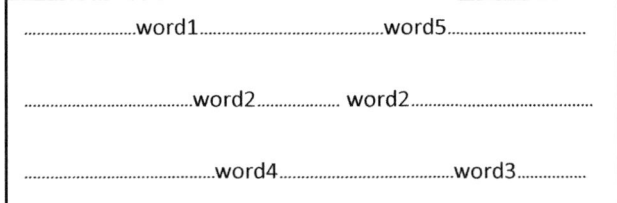

Fig. 4. A typical text with three words that are synonyms

Now a table is produced from Fig. 3 that the frequencies of words are like Table 2. For simplicity assume that α is 1/4.

Table 2. Table with frequencies of words of Fig. 4

word	#	
. . .	. . .	. . .
word1	4+1/4+1/4*1/4	head
word2	4+1/4+1/4*1/4	
word3	4+1/4+1/4*1/4	
word4	1+4*1/4+1/4	head
word5	1+1/4+4*1/4*1/4	head
. . .	. . .	. . .

In the table 2 *word1* is the head for three words, *word1*, *word2* and *word3*. Because the words, *word1*, *word2* and *word3*, are emerged 4 times, their frequencies are considered 4 at least. Besides due to emerging the *word4* that is a special kind of *word3*, a 1/4 is added to their frequencies. Due to emerging the *word5* that is a special kind of *word4*, a 1/4*1/4 is added to their frequencies. From another side, the frequency of the *word4* is at least 1, due to its appearance. Because of four appearances of the *word1*, 4 times 1/4 is added by its one appearance. Besides because of one appearance of *word5* another 1/4 is added to its frequency. This scenario is valid for *word5*. It means that one appearance of word5, plus 1/4 due to appearance of *word4* plus 4 appearances of *word1* that has inclusion relationship with length 2, i.e. 4*1/4*1/4, is considered as frequency of *word5*.

4   Experimental Results

In order to test the proposed method five different categories has been collected from Hamshahri [22] newspaper. The detail of the dataset is presented in the Table 3.

Table 3. Details of used dataset

Row	Topic	# of articles	Average # of words
1	Sport	146	204
2	Economic	154	199
3	Rural	171	123
4	Adventure	89	160
5	Foreign	130	177

After refinement of dataset, the average number of words in each category is reduced as the Table 4.

Table 4. Dataset after refinement

Row	Topic	Average # of words	Average # of words after refinement phase
1	Sport	204	149
2	Economic	199	135
3	Rural	123	76
4	Adventure	160	115
5	Foreign	177	124

After applying refinement phase, we produce a feature space as illustrated in the Table 5.

Table 5. Dataset after refinement

	Head Word1	Head Word2	Head Word1	....	Head Wordn
Article1					
Article2					
00000					
Articlem					

In Table 5, parameter n is the number of all Head Word which is a head word in an article at least. The entity jth column of ith row in Table 5 is equal to frequency value of head word j in the ith article.

By filling the Table 5 values by using thesaurus and without using thesaurus we obtain two different datasets. By 4-fold cross validation and 1-neareast neighbour classifier, we reach the results in the Table 6.

Table 6. Accuracy of 1NN classifier with and without thesaurus

	Without thesaurus	With thesaurus
Accuracy of classification	68.3%	78.4%

5   Conclusion and Future Works

In this paper, we have proposed a new method to improve the performance of Persian text classification. The proposed method uses a Persian thesaurus to reinforce the frequencies of words. With a simple classifier, it is shown that using thesaurus can improve the classification of Persian texts. We consider two relationships: synonyms and inclusion. We use a hierarchical inclusion weighting, and linear synonym weighting.

As a future work, one can turn to research on the different weighting methods.

Acknowledgments. This research is supported by Iran Communication Research Center, Tehran, Iran.

References

1. American Society of Indexers, Frequently Asked Questions Indexing. Index review in Books, Ireland (1994), http://www.asindexing.org/site/indfaq.shtml
2. Maron, M.E.: Automatic indexing: an experimental enquiry. Journal of the ACM 8, 404–417 (1961)
3. Montgomery, C.A.: Linguistics and information science. Journal of the American Society for Information Science 23, 195–219 (1972)
4. Brooks, H.M.: Expert Systems and Intelligent Information Retrieval. Information Processing and Management 23(4), 367–382 (1987)
5. Turney, P.D.: Learning Algorithms for Keyphrase Extraction. Information Retrieval 2(4), 306–336 (1999)
6. Frank, E.: Domain-Based Extraction of Technical Keyphrases. In: 6th International Joint Conference on Artificial Intelligence, India (1999)
7. Liu, Y., Ciliax, B.J., Borges, K., Dasigi, V., Ram, A., Navathe, S.B., Ingledine, R.: Comparison of two schemes for automatic keyword extraction from MEDLINE for functional gene clustering. In: 4th IEEE Computational Systems Bioinformatics Conference (CSB 2004), Stanford (2005)
8. Frantzi, K., Ananiadou, S., Mima, H.: Automatic Recognition of Multi-word Terms: the C-value/NC-value Method. Digital Libraries 3(2), 115–130 (2002)
9. Freitas, N., Kaestner, A.: Automatic text summarization using a machine learning approach. In: 16th Brazilian Symposium on Artificial Intelligence (SBIA), Brazil (2005)

10. Zhang, Y., Heywood, N.Z., Milios, E.: World Wide Web Site Summarization Web Intelligence and Agent Systems. Technical Report, CS-2002-8 (2006)
11. Hult, A.: Improved automatic keyword extraction given more linguistic knowledge. In: 8th Conference on Empirical Methods in Natural Language Processing (EMNLP), Japan (2003)
12. Deegan, M.: Keyword Extraction with Thesauri and Content Analysis,
    `http://www.rlg.org/en/page.php?Page_ID=17068`
13. Hyun, D.: Automatic Keyword Extraction Using Category Correlation of Data, Heidelberg, pp. 224–230 (2006)
14. Witten, W., Medley, I.H.: Thesaurus based automatic keyphrase indexing. In: 6th ACM/IEEE-CS JCDL 2006 (Joint Conference on Digital Libraries) (2006)
15. Klein, M., Steenbergen, W.V.: Thesaurus-based Retrieval of Case Law. In: 19th International JURIX Conference, Paris (2006)
16. Martinez, J.L.: Automatic Keyword Extraction for News Finder, Heidelberg, pp. 405–427 (2008)
17. Shahabi, A.M.: Abstract construction in Persian literature. In: Second International Conference on Cognitive Science, Tehran, p. 56 (1381) (in Persian)
18. Bahar, M.T.: Persian Grammar, ch. IV, p. 111 (1342) (in Persian)
19. Khalouei, M.: Indexing Machine. Journal Books 6(3) (in Persian)
20. Karimi, Z., Shamsfard, M.: Automatic summarization systems Persian literature. In: 12th International Conference of Computer Society of Iran (1385) (in Persian)
21. Yousefi, A.: Principles and methods for computerized indexing. Journal Books 9(2) (in Persian)
22. Hamshahri newspaper, `http://www.hamshahrionline.ir`

An Accumulative Points/Votes Based Approach for Feature Selection

Hamid Parvin, Behrouz Minaei-Bidgoli, and Sajad Parvin

Islamic Azad University, Nourabad Mamasani Branch, Nourabad Mamasani, Iran
{parvin,b_minaei,s.parvin}@iust.ac.ir

Abstract. This paper proposes an ensemble based approach for feature selection. We aim at overcoming the problem of parameter sensitivity of feature selection approaches. To do this we employ ensemble method. We get the results per different possible threshold values automatically in our algorithm. For each threshold value, we get a subset of features. We give a score to each feature in these subsets. Finally by use of ensemble method, we select the features which have the highest scores. This method is not a parameter sensitive one, and also it has been shown that using the method based on the fuzzy entropy results in more reliable selected features than the previous methods'. Empirical results show that although the efficacy of the method is not considerably decreased in most of cases, the method becomes free from setting of any parameter.

Keywords: Feature Selection, Ensemble Methods, Fuzzy Entropy.

1 Introduction

We have to use features of a dataset to classify data points in pattern recognition and data mining. Some datasets have a large number of features. Processing these datasets is not possible or is very difficult. To solve this problem, the dimensionalities of these datasets should be reduced. To do this, some of the redundant or irrelevant features should be eliminated. By eliminating the redundant and irrelevant features, the classification performance over them will be improved. Three different approaches are available for feature selection mechanism [1]. The first ones are embedded approaches. In these algorithms, feature selection is done as a part of the data algorithm. The second ones are filter approaches. These algorithm selected features before the data mining algorithm is run. The last ones are wrapper approaches. In these algorithms the target data mining algorithm is used to get the best subset of features.

A lot of methods for feature subset selection have been presented, such as similarity measures [2], gainentropies [3], the relevance of features [4], the genetic algorithms method [5], the overall feature evaluation index (OFEI) [6], the feature quality index (FQI) [6], the mutual information-based feature selector (MIFS) [7], classifiability measures [8], neuro-fuzzy approaches [9, 10], fuzzy entropy measures[11], etc.

This paper is based on Shie-and-Chen's method [11]. In Shie-and-Chen's method by use of the previous fuzzy entropy measurements and also by explaining some new definitions, the authors present a new algorithm for feature selection problem. This algorithm can select appropriate features more accurately than the other

C. San Martin and S.-W. Kim (Eds.): CIARP 2011, LNCS 7042, pp. 399–408, 2011.

algorithms. The new definitions are explained in the following section. This method uses boundary samples instead of the full set of samples. Boundary samples are some kinds of samples which are incorrectly classified samples of previously selected features. It uses two different threshold values to calculate the entropies. The most important weakness of the algorithm is raises from its sensitiveness to user-defined threshold values. User has to test different threshold values, and finally selects ones which cause the best performance. In other words this algorithm is a kind of the parameter sensitive algorithms. For a new dataset a lot of different values for two threshold values must be tested and then the best ones are selected.

In this paper we try to improve Shie-and-Chen's method. We try to solve the drawback of parameter sensitivity. To do this we use ensemble method. We get the results for different threshold values. For each threshold values, we get a subset of features. We give a score to each feature in these subsets. Finally by use of ensemble concept, we select the features which have the highest scores. This method is not a parameter sensitive one, and also it has been shown that using the method based on the fuzzy entropy results in more reliable selected features than the previous methods'.

Our contributions are three-folded.

1. We propose a novel ensemble approach in the feature selection.
2. We propose a novel method to be got rid of the drawback of parameter sensitivity for feature selection.
3. We will show empirically that the ensemble-based approach for feature selection is fully automated and parameterless, also it outperforms the original version.

2 Proposed Algorithm

The algorithm which is presented Fig. 1 is parameter sensitive. So if these parameters change, the result of algorithm can be changed significantly. When these parameters are given by the user, the quality of algorithm results will be even weaker. Because user selects the parameters randomly and experimentally, so it is possible that they are not proper values for an exemplary dataset. So the result of algorithm is not trustable. Also the proper values are not available for some datasets which are not used in this algorithm. So to find the best result we need to test the algorithm for a lot of possible threshold values. Then we must select the threshold values which cause the best results. To solve this problem we use ensemble method.

We do not select threshold values experimentally in our algorithm. Our algorithm test different possible values for thresholds and then by doing some steps, it selects the subset of features. This algorithm has 5 steps. We employ Shie-and-Chen's method by a little change in our algorithm. The result of their algorithm is a subset of features. But we get a sequence of features instead of a subset. Actually the order of feature appearance is important in our algorithm.

First step runs Shie-and-Chen's method for each pair of (T_r, T_c). The result of algorithm at this step is a table of feature sequences which are selected for each pair of threshold values. For example the result of our algorithm for Iris is shown in Table 1. We obtained this result for 5 different values for T_c and T_r. Each element in this table is a feature sequence selected by the algorithm of Fig. 1 with a different pair of threshold values. The first step of the algorithm is as Fig. 2.

FSeq= Shie-and-Chen's Algorithm(T_r, T_c)

F is a set of candidate feature, FS is the selected feature subset

FSeq is the selected feature sequence.

Step 1:

For each $f \in F$ do

$$Let \quad EM_f = \begin{bmatrix} \mu_{v1}(r_{1f}) & \cdots & \mu_{vm}(r_{1f}) \\ \vdots & \vdots & \vdots \\ \mu_{v1}(r_{nf}) & \cdots & \mu_{vm}(r_{nf}) \end{bmatrix}_{n \times m}$$

Let $E(f) = FFE(f)$

Step 2:

Let $i = 1$

Let $\hat{f} = arg\ min_{f \in F}\ E(f)$

Let $E_{FS} = E(\hat{f})$

Let $FS = FS \cup \{\hat{f}\}$

Let $FSeq(i) = f$

Let $i = i + 1$

Let $F = F - \{\hat{f}\}$

Step 3:

repeat

   for each $f \in F$ do

      Let $EM_{temp} = CEM(FS,f,T_r)$

      Let $E(f) = BSFFE(FS,f)$

   Let $\hat{f} = arg\ min_{f \in F}\ E(f)$

   Let $FS = FS \cup \{\hat{f}\}$

   Let $FSeq(i) = f$

   Let $i = i + 1$

   Let $F = F - \{\hat{f}\}$

   Let $D = E_{FS} - E(\hat{f})$

   Let $E_{FS} = E(\hat{f})$

until $(FFE(FS) = 0$ or $D \leq 0$ or $F = \phi)$

Let FS be the selected feature subset and FSeq be the selected feature sequence.

Fig. 1. Shie-and-Chen's Algorithm with a simple modification

For $T_r = base\_t_r$: $step\_t_r$:1

   For $T_c = base\_t_c$: $step\_t_c$:1

      AllFSeq(T_r, T_c) = Shie-and-Chen's algorithm(T_r, T_c);

Fig. 2. Pseudo code of the first step of algorithm

It has two loops. One of them slides over T_r and the other one slides over T_c. Two parameters *base_t_r* and *base_t_c* are the minimum values used for T_r and T_c respectively. Two parameters *step_t_r* and *step_t_c* determine the distance between two consecutive threshold values of parameters T_r and T_c respectively. *FSeq* is a two dimensional matrix whose elements are features sequences obtained by the algorithm of Fig. 3 with each possible tested pair of threshold values.

As it is inferred from Table 1, at the first and the last rows of each column we have some similar results for some threshold values. There is a similar discussion about the first and the last columns of each row. The results of algorithm for the first and the last columns of each row and the first and the last rows of each column are not trustable to reach some proper threshold values. Since these results have strongly negative effect on the final evaluation, at the second step we have to remove these repetitions. This step has two parts. The first part removes the repetitions of columns and the second part removes the repetitions of rows. First part keeps only the results at the beginning and ending of each column to reach a dissimilar result at the beginning and ending of each column. And the second part keeps only the results at the beginning and ending of a row to reach a dissimilar result at the beginning or ending of each row. In other words, we use only one of the same results at the beginning and ending parts of each row and each column in final evaluation. The following pseudo code is the first part of second step of the algorithm.

```
New_AllFSeq = AllFSeq
For    T_r = base_t_r: step_t_r :1
       q = base_ t_c
       While (true)
                q = q + step_ t_c
                if        is_same ( AllFSeq ( T_r , base_t_c ) , AllFSeq ( T_r, q ))
                          New_AllFseq ( Tr , q ) = EmptySeq
                else
                          break
       q = last_ t_c
       While (true)
                q = q - step_ t_c;
                if        is_same ( AllFSeq ( T_r , last_t_c ) , AllFSeq ( T_r, q ))
                          New_AllFseq ( T_r , q ) = EmptySeq
                else
                          break
```

Fig. 3. Pseudo code of the first part of the second step of the algorithm

Table 1. Feature subsets selected for some pairs of threshold values over Iris dataset

Tc, Tr	0.01	0.21	0.41	0.61	0.81
0.01	4, 3	3, 4	3, 4	3, 4	3, 4
0.21	4, 3	4, 3	3, 4	3, 4	3, 4
0.41	3, 4	4, 3	3, 4	3, 4	3, 4
0.61	4, 1	4, 2	3, 1	3, 1	3, 1
0.81	3, 1	4, 3, 1	3, 4	3, 4	3, 4

Equation 1 is a function that checks the similarity of its inputs. It has two input parameters which can be two sequences of features. If they are similar, the output will be 1 and if they are not similar the output is 0.

$$is\_same\ (a\,,b) = \begin{cases} 1, & if\ x = y \\ 0, & otherwise \end{cases} \qquad 1$$

It checks the similarity between the first sequence of a column and the consecutive sequences of that column. By reaching the first dissimilar sequence at the beginning or ending of a column, this part of algorithm is done for each column. Output for Iris example of doing the first part of the second step of the algorithm is available in Table 2 by horizontal shading (+ sings). The second part of the second step of the algorithm is as the algorithm of Fig. 4. It is like the first part of the second step. It checks the similarity between the first sequence of a row and the other sequences in that column. By reaching the first dissimilar sequence at the beginning or ending of a row, this part of algorithm is done for each row.

For $T_c = base\_t_c$: $step\_t_c$:1
  $q = base\_t_r$
  While (true)
      $q = q + step\_t_r$
      if   *is_same (AllFSeq (T_c , base_t_r) , AllFSeq (T_c, q))*
              New_AllFseq (T_c , q) = EmptySeq
      else
              break;
  $q = last\_t_r$
  While (true)
      $q = q - step\_t_r$
      if   *is_same (AllFSeq (T_c , last_t_r) , AllFSeq (T_c, q))*
              New_AllFseq (T_c , q) = EmptySeq
      else
              break
  AllFseq=New_AllFseq

Fig. 4. Pseudo code of the second part of the second step of the algorithm

Result of doing the second part of the second step of the algorithm over the Iris dataset which is obtained from the first step is shown in Table 2 by vertical shading (* sings).

Table 2. Delete repetitions in columns of Table 1 then delete repetitions in rows of Table 1

Tc, Tr	0.01	0.21	0.41	0.61	0.81
0.01	4, 3	*	*	*	3, 4
0.21	+	+*	+*	+*	+
0.41	3, 4	4, 3	+*	+*	+
0.61	4, 1	4, 2	*	*	3, 1
0.81	3, 1	4, 3, 1	*	*	3, 4

Third step uses majority voting to reach the best subset of features. We have to give a score to each feature. There is a subset of selected features for each pair of T_r and T_c. We change this subset to a sequence of features by their ranks of appearing at the first step. In other words each feature that appears sooner has more effect on output, so it is given a higher score. Then we sum all given scores to features for each pair of threshold values. We define the score of each feature as equation 2.

After obtaining Table 2 for each dataset, we give a score to each of its features according to equation 2. In the equation 2, we give the higher weight to the first feature which appears sooner, and we give the lower weight to the last feature which appears at the end of the sequence. For example if there are 10 features, the weight of the first feature is considered 10, and the weight of the last feature is considered 1.

$Score\ (f) =$

$$\sum_{T_r} \sum_{T_c} \sum_{i=1}^{MaxSF} isequal(\ AllFSeq\ (T_r, T_c)(i), f) * (\ |AllFSeq| - i + 1) \qquad 2$$

where MaxSF is obtained by equation 3.

$$MaxSF = max_{T_r, T_c, i}(|AllFSeq\ (T_r, T_c)(i)|) \qquad 3$$

Finally we sum all the weighted scores obtained by the algorithm for different pairs of threshold values. For example, in the Iris example the *MaxFS* is 3. In the example we get these results: Score (3) = 21, Score (4) = 21, Score (1) = 7 and Score (2) = 2.

Then we sort all features by their scores. After that we select the features with maximum scores. We select the same number of features as the Shie-and-Chen's method. In Iris example the subset of {3, 4} features is selected as final selected subset, because these features have the highest scores, and Shie-and-Chen's method selected two features for this example.

3   Experimental Results

In [11] they tested their algorithm in two stages. Their first experiment is compared with some previous methods in Table 3. These methods are OFFSS, OFEI, FQI and MIFS. This table shows the feature subsets selected by some methods. They use four datasets in this stage. These data sets are Iris, Breast Cancer Diagnostic, Pima Diabetes and Mile Per Gallon (MPG).

Table 3. Comparison of feature subsets selected by previous methods [11]

Data set	Feature subsets selected by different methods				
	Shie-and-Chen's	MIFS	FQI	OFEI	OFFSS
Iris	{4, 3}	{4, 3}	{4, 3}	{4, 3}	{4, 3}
Breast Cancer	{6, 2, 1, 8, 5, 3}	{6, 3, 2, 7}	{6, 1, 8, 3}	{6, 1, 3, 2}	{6, 3, 1, 2}
Pima Diabetes	{2, 6, 8, 7}	{2, 6, 8}	{8, 2, 1}	{2, 3, 6}	{2, 6, 7}
MPG	{4, 6, 3}	{4, 6, 2, 1}	{4, 6, 3, 2}	{4, 5, 6, 2}	{6, 2, 5, 4}

Table 4 shows the accuracies of different classifiers on the selected features obtained by the methods used in Table 3. It shows that the different classifiers on the selected features obtained by Shie-and-Chen's method have better accuracies than the other methods. It uses four classifiers to compare these methods. These classifiers are LMT, Naive Bayes, SMO and C4.5.

Table 4. Comparison between average classification accuracy rates of previous methods [11]

Data sets	Classifiers	Average classification accuracy rates of different methods				
		OFFSS	OFEI	FQI	MIFS	Shie-and-Chen's method
Iris	LMT	94.67 ± 4.27%	94.67 ± 4.27%	94.67 ± 4.27%	94.67 ± 4.27%	94.67 ± 4.27%
	Naive Bayes	96.00 4.00%	96.00 4.00%	96.00 4.00%	96.00 4.00%	96.00 4.00%
	SMO	96.00 4.00%	96.00 4.00%	96.00 4.00%	96.00 4.00%	96.00 4.00%
	C4.5	96.00 5.33%	96.00 5.33%	96.00 5.33%	96.00 5.33%	96.00 5.33%
Breast cancer	LMT	95.90 2.15%	95.90 2.15%	96.49 2.09%	95.46 1.79%	96.49 2.08%
	Naive Bayes	96.19 2.56%	96.19 2.56%	96.49 1.88%	95.31 1.58%	96.63 1.97%
	SMO	96.34 2.19%	96.34 2.19%	97.07 1.85%	96.05 2.62%	97.07 2.27%
	C4.5	95.61 2.70%	95.61 2.70%	96.93 1.90%	95.16 2.86%	96.02 2.57%
Pima diabetes	LMT	76.83 3.79%	76.04 3.63%	73.56 4.68%	75.53 4.39%	77.22 4.52%
	Naive Bayes	76.57 3.65%	76.83 4.36%	74.09 5.43%	76.44 5.50%	77.47 4.93%
	SMO	75.91 4.96%	75.91 3.80%	75.39 4.93%	75.91 4.97%	77.08 5.06%
	C4.5	75.01 3.72%	74.36 4.27%	71.74 3.18%	74.61 4.86%	74.88 5.89%
MPG	LMT	81.13 5.67%	81.13 5.67%	82.38 7.28%	84.17 7.26%	81.87 6.74%
	Naive Bayes	78.31 7.63%	78.31 7.63%	79.59 6.79%	76.28 8.25%	80.60 7.01%
	SMO	80.58 7.21%	80.58 7.21%	81.61 6.99%	76.77 4.12%	81.86 8.25%
	C4.5	79.83 7.84%	79.83 7.84%	79.58 8.24%	81.37 9.05%	79.93 7.78%

The second experiment is on five datasets and three problems. These datasets are Pima Diabetes, Cleve, Correlated, M of N-3-7-10 and Crx datasets, also Monk-1, Monk-2 and Monk-3 problems. They compare their method with Dong and Kothari's method. Table 5 shows the feature subsets which are selected by these algorithms.

Table 5. Feature subsets selected by Dong-and-Kothari's method and Shie-and-Chen's method

Data sets	Feature subsets selected by different methods	
	Dong-and-Kothari's method	Shie-and-Chen's method
Pima diabetes data set	{2, 8, 1}	{2, 6, 8, 7}
Cleve data set	{10, 13, 12, 3, 9}	{13, 3, 12, 11, 1, 10, 2, 5, 6}
Correlated data set	{6, 1, 2, 3, 4}	{6, 1, 2, 3, 4}
M of N-3-7-10 data set	{4, 9, 5, 8, 3, 6, 7}	{4, 9, 8, 5, 3, 6, 7}
Crx data set	{8, 9, 13, 10}	{9}
Monk-1 data set	{5, 1, 2}	{5, 1, 2}
Monk-2 data set	{3, 6, 1, 2, 4, 5}	{5}
Monk-3 data set	{2, 5, 4, 1}	{5, 2, 4}

Table 6 shows the accuracies of two methods using the same classifier employed for Table 3.

Table 6. Comparison between average classification accuracy rates of Dong-and-Kothari's method and Shie-and-Chen's method

Data sets	Classifiers	Average classification accuracy rates of different methods	
		Dong-and-Kothari's method	Shie-and-Chen's method
Pima diabetes data set	LMT	73.56 ± 4.68%	77.22 ± 4.52%
	Naive Bayes	73.43 ± 1.57%	77.47 ± 4.93%
	SMO	75.39 ± 4.93%	77.08 ± 5.06%
	C4.5	71.74 ± 3.18%	74.88 ± 5.89%

Table 6. (*Continued*)

Cleve data set	LMT	83.17 ± 4.24%	82.87 ± 6.23%
	Naive Bayes	84.17 ± 1.82%	84.48 ± 3.93%
	SMO	84.47 ± 5.59%	83.51± 6.09%
	C4.5	76.90 ± 8.71%	76.90 ± 8.40%
Correlated data set	LMT	100.00 ± 0.00%	100.00 ± 0.00%
	Naive Bayes	86.03 ± 3.75%	86.03 ± 3.75%
	SMO	89.87 ± 6.88%	89.87 ± 6.88%
	C4.5	94.62 ± 4.54%	94.62 ± 4.54%
M of N-3-7-10 data set	LMT	100.00 ± 0.00%	100.00 ± 0.00%
	Naive Bayes	89.33 ± 1.56%	89.33 ± 1.56%
	SMO	100.00 ± 0.00%	100.00 ± 0.00%
	C4.5	100.00 ± 0.00%	100.00 ± 0.00%
Crx data set	LMT	85.22 ± 4.04%	85.22 ± 4.04%
	Naive Bayes	84.06 ± 1.33%	85.51 ± 4.25%
	SMO	85.80 ± 3.71%	85.80 ± 3.71%
	C4.5	85.36 ± 4.12%	85.51 ± 4.25%
Monk-1 data set	LMT	100.00 ± 0.00%	100.00 ± 0.00%
	Naive Bayes	74.97 ± 1.95%	74.97 ± 1.95%
	SMO	75.02 ± 5.66%	75.02 ± 5.66%
	C4.5	100.00 ± 0.00%	100.00 ± 0.00%
Monk-2 data set	LMT	67.36 ± 1.17%	67.36 ± 1.17%
	Naive Bayes	66.22 ± 2.80%	67.14 ± 0.61%
	SMO	67.14 ± 0.61%	67.14 ± 0.61%
	C4.5	67.14 ± 0.61%	67.14 ± 0.61%
Monk-3 data set	LMT	99.77 ± 0.10%	99.77 ± 0.10%
	Naive Bayes	97.22 ± 0.47%	97.21 ± 2.71%
	SMO	100.00 ± 0.00%	100.00 ± 0.00%
	C4.5	100.00 ± 0.00%	100.00 ± 0.00%

We have implemented our feature selection algorithm in Matlab. We use weka to evaluate the mapped datasets into the selected features obtained by our feature selection algorithms. We compare the feature subsets selected by our method with those selected by Shie-and-Chen's method in Table 7 for all of datasets which are used to compare in [11].

Table 7. Comparison between feature subsets selected by our and Shie-and-Chen's methods

Data sets	Feature subsets selected by two methods	
	Shie-and-Chen's method	Our method
Iris	{4,3}	{4,3}
Breast cancer data set	{6, 2, 1, 8, 5, 3}	{6, 2, 3, 1, 9, 5}
Pima	{2, 6, 8, 7}	{2, 4, 6, 3}
MPG data set	{4, 6, 3}	{2, 4, 1}
Cleve data set	{13, 3, 12, 11, 1, 10, 2, 5, 6}	{13, 1, 12, 3, 9}
Crx data set	{9}	{9}
Monk-1 data set	{5, 1, 2}	{5, 1, 2}
Monk-2 data set	{5}	{5}
Monk-3 data set	{5, 2, 4}	{2,5,1}

Also Table 8 shows that the obtained accuracies of different classifiers on the selected features obtained by proposed method are better that the obtained accuracies of the same classifiers on the selected features obtained by Shie-and-Chen's algorithms the most datasets.

Table 8. Comparison between average classification accuracy rates of our and Shie-and-Chen's methods

Data sets	Classifiers	Average classification accuracy rates of different methods	
		Our method	Shie-and-Chen's method
Pima diabetes data set	LMT	76.30 ±4.84%	77.22 ± 4.52%
	Naive Bayes	76.30 ±4.84%	77.47 ± 4.93%
	SMO	75.65 ±5.61%	77.08 ± 5.06%
	C4.5	94.62 ±2.12%	74.88 ± 5.89%
Cleve data set	LMT	82.42 ± 5.34%	82.87 ± 6.23%
	Naive Bayes	80.41 ± 3.95%	84.48 ± 3.93%
	SMO	80.00 ± 5.99%	83.51 ± 6.09%
	C4.5	76.90 ± 8.40%	76.90 ± 8.40%
Correlated data set	LMT	100.00 ± 0.00%	100.00 ± 0.00%
	Naive Bayes	86.03 ± 3.75%	86.03 ± 3.75%
	SMO	89.87 ± 6.88%	89.87 ± 6.88%
	C4.5	94.62 ± 4.54%	94.62 ± 4.54%
M of N-3-7-10 data set	LMT	100.00 ± 0.00%	100.00 ± 0.00%
	Naive Bayes	89.33 ± 1.56%	89.33 ± 1.56%
	SMO	100.00 ± 0.00%	100.00 ± 0.00%
	C4.5	100.00 ± 0.00%	100.00 ± 0.00%
Crx data set	LMT	86.53 ±3.87%	85.22 ± 4.04%
	Naive Bayes	86.53 ±3.87%	85.51 ± 4.25%
	SMO	86.53 ±3.87%	85.80 ± 3.71%
	C4.5	85.36 ± 4.12%	85.51 ± 4.25%
Monk-1 data set	LMT	100 ± 0.00%	100.00 ± 0.00%
	Naive Bayes	72.22 ± 6.33%	74.97 ± 1.95%
	SMO	72.22 ± 6.33%	75.02 ± 5.66%
	C4.5	100.00 ± 0.00%	100.00 ± 0.00%
Monk-2 data set	LMT	67.14 ± 0.61%	67.36 ± 1.17%
	Naive Bayes	67.14 ± 0.61%	67.14 ± 0.61%
	SMO	67.14 ± 0.61%	67.14 ± 0.61%
	C4.5	67.14± 0.61 %	67.14 ± 0.61%
Monk-3 data set	LMT	97.22 ± 0.47%	99.77 ± 0.10%
	Naive Bayes	97.21 ± 2.71%	97.21 ± 2.71%
	SMO	97.22 ± 0.47%	100.00 ± 0.00%
	C4.5	100.00 ± 0.00%	100.00 ± 0.00%

4   Conclusion

In this paper we improved one of the existing feature selection algorithms, Shie-and-Chen's method. This feature selection algorithm uses fuzzy entropy concept. The problem of Shie-and-Chen's method is that it is a parameter sensitive algorithm. User should select threshold values in that algorithm experimentally. The result of algorithm for some threshold values is very weak and it is not trustable. To solve this problem we use ensemble method. Our paper runs Shie-and-Chen's algorithm for different values as thresholds and then gives a weight to each selected features according its rank. Finally by using one of the ensemble methods, majority voting, it selects the best features which have the highest scores. So this algorithm does not need any input parameter. Also the obtained accuracies of different classifiers on the selected features obtained by proposed method are better that the obtained accuracies of the same classifiers on the selected features obtained by Shie-and-Chen's algorithms.

References

1. Tan, P.N., Steinbach, M., Kumar, V.: Introduction to Data Mining, 1st edn. Addison-Wesley Longman Publishing Co. Inc. (2005)
2. Tsang, E.C.C., Yeung, D.S., Wang, X.Z.: OFFSS: optimal fuzzyvalued feature subset selection. IEEE Trans. Fuzzy Syst. 11(2), 202–213 (2003)
3. Caruana, R., Freitag, D.: Greedy attribute selection. In: Proceedings of International Conference on Machine Learning, New Brunswick, NJ, pp. 28–33 (1994)
4. Baim, P.W.: A method for attribute selection in inductive learning systems. IEEE Trans. Pattern. Anal. Mach. Intell. 10(6), 888–896 (1988)
5. Chaikla, N., Qi, Y.: Genetic algorithms in feature selection. In: Proceedings of the 1999 IEEE International Conference on Systems, Man, and Cybernetics, Tokyo, Japan, vol. 5, pp. 538–540 (1999)
6. De, R.K., Basak, J., Pal, S.K.: Neuro-fuzzy feature evaluation with theoretical analysis. Neural Netw. 12(10), 1429–1455 (1999)
7. Battiti, R.: Using mutual information for selecting features in supervised neural net learning. IEEE Trans. Neural Netw. 5(4), 537–550 (1994)
8. Dong, M., Kothari, R.: Feature subset selection using a new definition of classi-fiability. Pattern Recognit. Lett. 24(9), 1215–1225 (2003)
9. De, R.K., Pal, N.R., Pal, S.K.: Feature analysis: neural network and fuzzy set theoretic approaches. Pattern Recognit. 30(10), 1579–1590 (1997)
10. Platt, J.C.: Using analytic QP and sparseness to speed training of support vector machines. In: Proceedings of the Thirteenth Annual Conference on Neural Information Processing Systems, Denver, CO, pp. 557–563 (1999)
11. Shie, J.D., Chen, S.M.: Feature subset selection based on fuzzy entropy measures for handling classification problems. Springer Science+Business Media (2007)

Sentiment-Preserving Reduction for Social Media Analysis

Sergio Hernández[1] and Philip Sallis[2]

[1] Laboratorio de Procesamiento de Información Geoespacial,
Universidad Católica del Maule, Talca, Chile
[2] Geoinformatics Research Centre,
Auckland University of Technology, Auckland, New Zealand

Abstract. In this paper, we address the problem of opinion analysis using a probabilistic approach to the underlying structure of different types of opinions or sentiments around a certain object. In our approach, an opinion is partitioned according to whether there is a direct relevance to a latent topic or sentiment. Opinions are then expressed as a mixture of sentiment-related parameters and the noise is regarded as data stream errors or spam. We propose an entropy-based approach using a value-weighted matrix for word relevance matching which is also used to compute document scores. By using a bootstrap technique with sampling proportions given by the word scores, we show that a lower dimensionality matrix can be achieved. The resulting noise-reduced data is regarded as a sentiment-preserving reduction layer, where terms of direct relevance to the initial parameter values are stored

1 Introduction

Social networks have become ubiquitous and are used throughout the world for interpersonal communication. This form of discourse can be related to personal matters but is also about common interests, especially products and services. In particular these discussions about products and services give rise to a massive source of valuable information. In this paper, focused as it is on text communications on the web, it centers on online discussions, tweets and social networks, which are subjective in nature and therefore not easy to classify. Mostly, these communications/conversations concern the quality of a particular product.

Sentiment analysis is used in information retrieval and text mining for discovering the attitude or the subjective judgment of the writer about a particular matter. For example, it is used in social media to make judgments about certain products and services that are of interest to them. The massive amount of data that is generated by this media can be used to optimize the commodities, by analyzing the overall sentiment towards expressed about them [8].

In general, sentiment can be expressed as a quantity (e.g. a score) or as a textual opinion. The latter might reveal a polarity that can be unveiled by using data analytics [4]. In the context of data mining and knowledge discovery we can distinguish two main approaches, supervised and unsupervised learning, as being

C. San Martin and S.-W. Kim (Eds.): CIARP 2011, LNCS 7042, pp. 409–416, 2011.

possible ways to recognize patterns in the text based discourse being analyzed. Sentiment analysis or hidden meaning can be regarded as being unsupervised, because when triggered by an associated polarity, the hidden meaning is revealed.

Likes and dislikes are often concealed in words where the meaning less than obvious and in some cases, criticism can be encapsulated in a cynical or somewhat ambiguous phrase. Linguistic markers such as the identification of particular words from a list or table on the assumption that may mean something in particular could lead to a completely different meaning from the one intended [5].

For example, when analyzing sentiments about the iPad©we can find phrases containing a sentiment, such as:

```
I can't believe how fast twitter works on my iPad
```

In the other hand, phrases like

```
Free iPad 2! How awesome is that? You HAVE to join!
```

doesn't contain any sentiment information so they can be considered as spam. Moreover, we are also confronted with the reality that individual words, while having some meaning, are not richly enough preserved until they appear alongside other words in terms and phrases. In our approach, there is no prior knowledge of the sentiment or polarity of a phrase. Alternatively, an entropy-based criteria based on a non-uniform prior distribution on words can be used to gather sentiment-preserving information. We present a worked example using a *bag-of-words* representation, but the proposed approach can be generalized to other representations based on multiple correlated words [1].

This paper is organized as follows. Section 2 discusses the general framework for sentiment analysis and similar approaches in the literature. In Section 3, we describe the proposed methodology for sentiment-preserving reduction and finally, Section 4 provides a worked example using Twitter.[1]

2   Latent Topic Opinion Mining

Probabilistic models such as *topic models* can be used to discover the hidden or latent description or the topic of a group of opinions using a particular combination of words [11]. In topic modeling, a *document-term matrix* X is extracted from a text corpora. This matrix describes the occurrences of terms in documents and is composed the frequency on each one of the phrases, so each element x_{ij} contains the frequency of the word w_i in the document or opinion o_j.

A probabilistic model could consider each word as a mixture of single or multiple words (n-grams) and each opinion o being generated by first choosing a topic z and then sampling N words according to the conditional distribution $p(o)$ of words given the topic:

---

[1] http://twitter.com

$$p(o) = \sum_z p(z) \prod_{n=1}^{N} (p(w_n|z)) \tag{1}$$

If we now let each opinion to exhibit not only one but multiple topics (e.g. words having more than one meaning), the resulting generative model for a word is a mixture of multinomial random variables representing the different topics.

$$p(o, w_n) = p(o) \sum_z p(z)p(w_n|z)p(z|o) \tag{2}$$

Each opinion is then represented as a list of mixture proportions representing its membership to any particular topic. Due to the bag-of-words assumption, there is no particular order for the words w_n so the probabilistic approach is simplified. However, the frequency of counts approach might not be enough to capture the structure of the opinions and because of the large number of parameters required is also likely to pose over-fitting issues. This is especially problematic in opinion mining where the number of number of words is usually smaller than the standard documents considered in topic modeling.

Latent Dirichlet Allocation (LDA) extends the probabilistic approach based on mixtures of unigrams by considering exchangeable partition of the set $\{z_1, \ldots, z_N\}$. In LDA, words are generated by conditionally independent and identically distributed topics, so the probability of a sequence of words and topics can be written as the product:

$$p(w, z) = \int p(\theta) \Big(\prod_{n=1}^{N} p(z_n|\theta)p(w_n|z_n) \Big) d\theta \tag{3}$$

The parameter θ is used for the multinomial distribution for each topic. Now, using Dirichlet prior distributions with hyper-parameters α and β for the topics and words respectively, leaves the following generative process:

Choose $\theta \sim Dir(\alpha)$
for $n = 1$ TO N do
    Choose a topic $z_n \sim M(\theta)$
    Choose a word w_n from the conditional distribution of the word given the chosen topic $p(w_n|z_n, \beta)$
end for

2.1   Related Work

A Joint Sentiment/Topic (JST) model was proposed in [7]. In their approach, sentiment polarity is treated as an unsupervised learning problem where sentiment and topic are jointly detected from text using LDA. Given the fact that sentiment can be expressed in a more subtle way than a topic, the authors proposed to incorporate prior information by using a subjectivity lexicon with aggregated words displaying positive or negative polarity.

More recently, the JST approach has been extended into a weakly-supervised approach in [6], and the authors reported improved classification accuracy when compared to semi-supervised alternatives. Also, in the context of micro-blogging, qualitative and quantitative experiments on topic modeling using short text messages was studied in [3].

More closely related to this work, a sentiment-preserving dimension reduction methodology has been presented in [10]. The authors proposed an inverse projection from word frequencies into sentiment, where prior knowledge of the conditional distribution is used for the inverse regression of text. This approach requires labeled data and was tested in richer text corpora, such as political speeches and restaurant reviews. Instead, in our approach we analyze data from micro-blogging environments which is not labeled, so there is no prior knowledge of the sentiment of the documents. A previous article also describes the proposed methodology [2].

3   Sentiment Preserving Reduction

In order to perform opinion spam detection we would like to find a matrix $\hat{X}$ with lower dimensionality than the original matrix X. A signal denoising algorithm based on entropy can be then used to eliminate columns with non useful phrases leaving only text meaning vectors. This requires us to process a large quantity of data in order to identify errors in the signal stream and thereby, generate the matrix of non-noisy items.

For a particular set of M opinions and N_d words, the entropy is given by:

$$p(O_M) = \exp\left(- \frac{\sum_{d=1}^{M} \log p(w_d)}{\sum_{d=1}^{M} N_d} \right) \tag{4}$$

Because the number of opinions M is usually large, a brute force implementation for spam detection is not feasible. However, we can take a sample from a bootstrap sample and then compare the information gain from the entropy of the LDA model having a term matrix X_{test}. This procedure can be repeated until some criteria of convergence is achieved.

The following algorithm shows this methodology:

repeat
    Find a subset $O_J \subset O_M$ with $J < M$.
    if $P(O_J) < P(O_M)$ **then**
        Let $O_M = O_J$
    end if
until Convergence

4   Example

In this Section, we test the proposed approach with a corpus obtained using a custom development using the Twitter Application Programming Interface (API). The generated dataset contains 10.000 tweets related to the iPad during the months of March and April 2011. Using a tag cloud depiction of the dataset (see Figure 1), we can infer that most of the frequent terms cannot be associated to any sentiment or polarity. Most frequent terms like 'free' or 'win' are associated with spam. Therefore, removing terms based on sparsity could only remove the interesting patterns from the data.

Fig. 1. Tag cloud representation of tweets around the iPad

Specific toolboxes for topic modeling in the R statistical software [9] were used to produce the document-term matrices and fit the models to the data. The following data processing steps where taken :

1. Using the Twitter API, a comma-delimited text file is aggregated every 30 mins with the search topic *iPad.*.
2. Each tweet is stored on a per-row basis. Extra white spaces, numbers, common English words and punctuation are removed.
3. A document-term matrix with term and document frequency-weighting (TFIDF) is created and then sparse items with factor 0.99% are removed.
4. A Gibbs sampler is used to train the LDA model.

Choosing the number of topics is another issue in topic modeling. Here, we perform a Bayes factor test using $K = 2$ to $K = 100$ topics and the resulting number of topics $K = 3$ model is finally used. Fitting an LDA model with this dataset leaves the following posterior topic probabilities shown in Figure 2.

Table 1 shows the five most frequent terms per topic for the complete model.

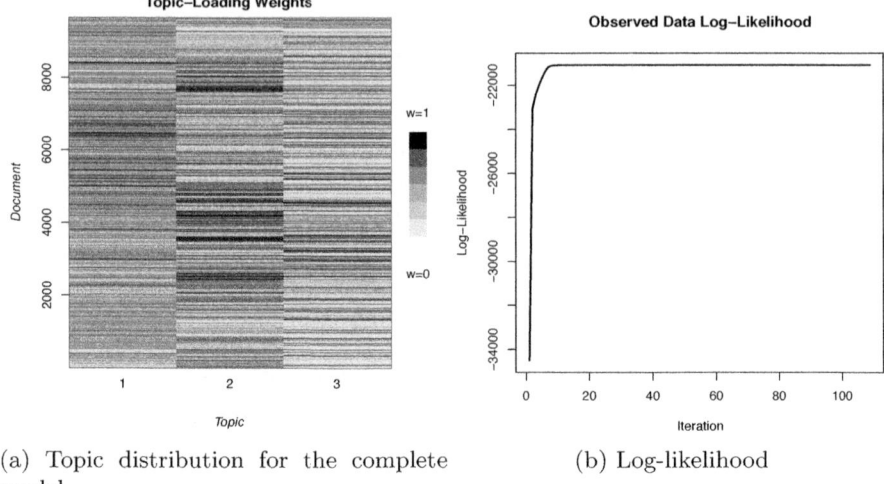

(a) Topic distribution for the complete model

(b) Log-likelihood

Fig. 2. Posterior distribution of the complete model

Table 1. Top five terms in the complete model

Topic 1	Topic 2	Topic 3
app	free	iphone
apple	apple	ipod
apps	win	join
tablet	amp	link
via	copy	click

Now, we concentrate on the sentiment-preserving algorithm. In order to sample a portion of the documents, we use a non-symmetric Dirichlet word distribution for the sentiment-preserving dimensionality reduction algorithm. The following terms were considered as relevant to the sentiment analysis task:

"love", "free","waste","compatibility","compatibility","cheesy",
"great","obscure","fantastic","low","fine","cost","speed"

Using the sentiment-preserving algorithm, a vector-valued weight function is then applied to sample a portion of the original dataset that has better entropy than the complete dataset. The posterior probabilities using the sentiment-preserving reduction are shown in Figure 3.

The five most frequent terms of the reduced model are also shown in Table 2 and the summary statistics of each model is shown in Table 3.

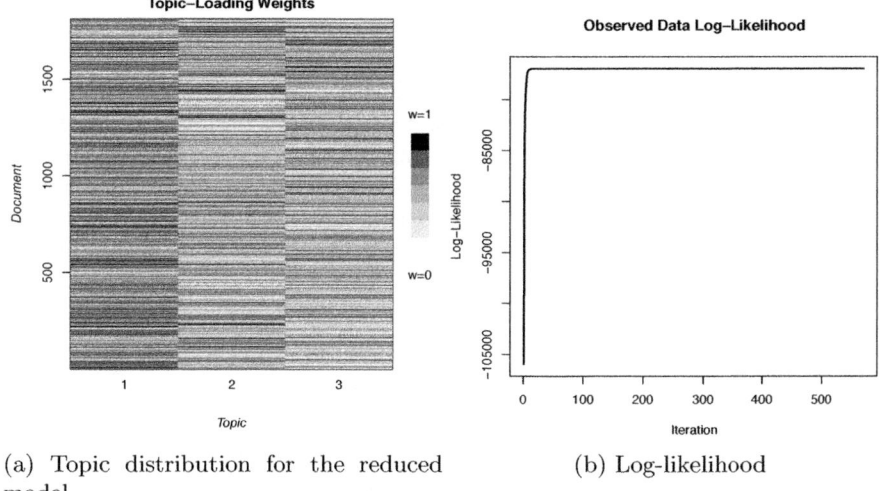

(a) Topic distribution for the reduced model

(b) Log-likelihood

Fig. 3. Posterior distribution of the reduced model

Table 2. Top 5 terms in the reduced model

Topic 1	Topic 2	Topic 3
handing	ipad	ipad
broken	tweets	giving
bugging	increase	entry
howdy	app	win
giving	free	free

Table 3. Summary statistics of the complete and the reduced model

	complete model	reduced model
Entropy	44.56	33.32
# of documents	9643	1811
Sparsity	95%	96%

5   Conclusion

Opinions are usually populated with words and phrases having subjective meanings. Probabilistic topic models can represent sentiment in opinions by modeling the uncertainty of words and topics. In this regard, sentiment becomes a signal yet to be discovered through multiple and hidden topics. However, the amount of spam in social media can lead to deceitful results.

Here, we have presented an unsupervised sentiment-preserving data reduction method. The method is based on the standard Latent Dirichlet Allocation methodology; thus not requiring any classification of polarity in the opinions. Similar to the previously proposed Joint Sentiment-Topic model, our method is also based on a manually selected subjectivity lexicon. However, we only use it as a proxy to a bootstrapping technique that gathers sentiment-rich opinions. We have demonstrated that the resulting reduction has better entropy than the model using the complete dataset, indicating better generalization performance.

Since our method is completely unsupervised, there is no direct interpretation of the sentiment over topics. Further research in semi-supervised and instrumental regression techniques will be conducted for the sentiment detection problem.

References

1. Blei, D.M., Ng, A.Y., Jordan, M.I.: Latent Dirichlet allocation. J. Mach. Learn. Res. 3, 993–1022 (2003)
2. Hernandez, S., Garden, K.L., Sallis, P.J.: A signal denoising method for text meaning vectors. In: Proceedings of the Fifth Asia Modelling Symposium (to appear, 2011)
3. Hong, L., Davison, B.D.: Empirical study of topic modeling in twitter. In: Proceedings of the First Workshop on Social Media Analytics, SOMA 2010, pp. 80–88. ACM, New York (2010)
4. Hu, M., Liu, B.: Opinion extraction and summarization on the web. In: Proceedings of the 21st National Conference on Artificial Intelligence, vol. 2, pp. 1621–1624. AAAI Press (2006)
5. Jindal, N., Liu, B.: Opinion spam and analysis. In: Proceedings of the International Conference on Web Search and Web Data Mining, WSDM 2008, pp. 219–230. ACM, New York (2008)
6. Lin, C., He, Y., Everson, R., Ruger, S.: Weakly-supervised joint sentiment-topic detection from text. IEEE Transactions on Knowledge and Data Engineering PP(99), 1 (2011)
7. Lin, C., He, Y.: Joint sentiment/topic model for sentiment analysis. In: Proceeding of the 18th ACM Conference on Information and Knowledge Management, CIKM 2009, pp. 375–384. ACM, New York (2009)
8. Pang, B., Lee, L.: Opinion mining and sentiment analysis. Found. Trends Inf. Retr. 2, 1–135 (2008)
9. R Development Core Team: R: A Language and Environment for Statistical Computing. R Foundation for Statistical Computing, Vienna, Austria (2011), http://www.R-project.org/, ISBN 3-900051-07-0
10. Taddy, M.A.: Inverse Regression for Analysis of Sentiment in Text. ArXiv e-prints (December 2010)
11. Wallach, H.M.: Topic modeling: beyond bag-of-words. In: Proceedings of the 23rd International Conference on Machine Learning, ICML 2006, pp. 977–984. ACM, New York (2006)

A Minority Class Feature Selection Method

German Cuaya, Angélica Muñoz-Meléndez, and Eduardo F. Morales

National Institute of Astrophysics, Optics and Electronics,
Computer Science Department,
Luis Enrique Erro 1, 72840 Tonantzintla, México
{germancs,munoz,emorales}@inaoep.mx
http://ccc.inaoep.mx

Abstract. In many classification problems, and in particular in medical domains, it is common to have an unbalanced class distribution. This pose problems to classifiers as they tend to perform poorly in the minority class which is often the class of interest. One commonly used strategy that to improve the classification performance is to select a subset of relevant features. Feature selection algorithms, however, have not been designed to favour the classification performance of the minority class. In this paper, we present a novel filter feature selection algorithm, called FSMC, for unbalanced data sets. FSMC selects attributes that have minority class distributions significantly different from the majority class distributions. FSMC is fast, simple, selects a small number of features and outperforms in most cases other feature selection algorithms in terms of global accuracy and in terms of performance measures for the minority class such as precision, recall, F-measure and ROC values.

Keywords: feature selection, unbalanced data set, medical domain.

1 Introduction

With the rapid advances in computer and database technologies, data sets with hundreds and thousands of variables or features are now present in pattern recognition, data mining, and machine learning applications [1–4]. Processing such huge data sets is a challenging task because traditional machine learning techniques usually work well only on small data sets. Feature selection addresses this problem by removing irrelevant, redundant, or noisy data. It improves the performance of the learning algorithm, reduces its computational cost and provides better understandings of the produced models [5].

Feature selection algorithms can be widely categorized into two groups: filter and wrapper methods [2, 4, 6–8]. Filter methods evaluate the goodness of the feature subset by using the intrinsic features of the data. They are computationally inexpensive since they do not rely on any induction algorithm. Wrapper methods, on the contrary, directly use the induction algorithm to evaluate the feature subsets. They generally outperform filter methods in terms of prediction accuracy, but are computationally more intensive.

C. San Martin and S.-W. Kim (Eds.): CIARP 2011, LNCS 7042, pp. 417–424, 2011.

The development of our work was motivated by an application in a medical domain with a relatively large number of attributes and a very unbalanced class distribution, that is common to other medical domains, and that poses problems to traditional classification algorithms and to feature selection algorithms that tend not to favour the minority class [9, 10].

There is large number of feature selection algorithms, however, very few research has been targeted particularly towards unbalanced class distributions. In particular [11], the authors propose a performance measure using ROC curves for feature selection. The main disadvantage of this work is that it uses a wrapper approach requiring repetitive and expensive model training during the feature selection process. In [12], the authors modify the ReliefF feature selection algorithm and present three filter-based feature selection techniques to attack unbalanced data sets, namely, give more weight to the instances of the minority class, oversample the minority class or undersample the majority class. The work presented in [13] is more closely related to our work. In that work the authors aproximate the probability density function (PDF) of each feature independently in an unsupervised manner and then removing those features for which their PDFs have higher covering areas with the PDFs of other features which are known as redundant features, it is important to mention that the authors used both majority and minority class data to calculate the PDFs.

In this paper, we propose a novel filter feature selection algorithm named *Feature Selection for Minority Class* (FSMC) that uses the difference between the expected value of the majority class and the expected value of minority class of each attribute to identify the relevant features for the minority class.

We evaluate the efficiency of FSMC by comparing our method to some well-known *filters* and *wrappers* feature selection strategies, applied with five different types of classifiers in several medical data sets from the UCI repository [14] and on a real data set of gait analysis. The results show that FSMC is competitive and in many cases outperforms other features selection algorithms in terms of classification accuracy, precision, recall, F-measure and ROC values for the minority class as well as selected feature size.

The rest of this paper is organized as follows. Section 2 describes the FSMC algorithm. In Section 3 the experimental results are presented, and finally, Section 4 concludes and provides future research directions.

2   FSMC

In this section we introduce a Feature Selection for Minority Class (FSMC) algorithm. The goal of FSMC is to measure the difference between the expected value of the majority class and the expected value of the minority class to select relevant features for classifying the minority class. The rationale behind our proposal is to select those features whose values are particularly different from the values of the majority class and that could help to classify instances from the minority class. The algorithm boils down to obtain the mean and standard deviation of each variable for the majority class and the mean of the same variables for the minority class. If the mean value of the minority class is at least two standard deviations away from the mean value of the majority class, then that feature is selected as relevant. This is a very simple and easy to implement criterion that to our knowledge has not been used before in the literature and, as shown in Section 3, is very competitive with respect to other feature selection algorithms. A description of FSMC is summarized in Algorithm1.

Algorithm 1. The FSMC algorithm

1: **begin**
2: Let Y a given set of attributes
3: Let $Maj(y)$ the majority class data of attribute $y \in Y$
4: Let $Min(y)$ the minority class data of attribute $y \in Y$
5: Let $RelAtt = \emptyset$ the output set of relevant attributes calculated by FSMC
6: **for all** $y \in Y$ **do**
7:    Compute the mean $(\mu_{Maj(y)})$ and standard deviation $(\sigma_{Maj(y)})$ of y in $Maj(y)$
8:    Compute the mean $(\mu_{Min(y)})$ of y in $Min(y)$
9:    **if** $(\mu_{Min(y)} > (\mu_{Maj(y)} + 2*\sigma_{Maj(y)})) \vee (\mu_{Min(y)} < (\mu_{Maj(y)} - 2*\sigma_{Maj(y)}))$ **then**
10:       Let $RelAtt \leftarrow RelAtt \cup \{y\}$
11:    **end if**
12: **end for**
13: Return $RelAtt$
14: **end**

---

3   Experimental Results and Discussion

In order to evaluate the performance of our algorithm FSMC, we used five medical data sets from the UCI ML repository, namely, arrhythmia, ozone, Pima Indians diabetes, diabetes and cardio [14]. Additionally, we used information from gait analysis involving elderly subjects provided by researchers of the National Institute of Rehabilitation of Mexico and which motivated the development of this research. In all cases we used a binary class problem.

We used five different classifiers to obtain performance measures over these data sets for the minority class, namely, precision, recall, F-measure and ROC values and also to obtain information from the global accuracy. The selected classifiers were taken from *Weka* [15] and involved different classification strategies with their default parameters: (i) PART (a decision list that uses separate-and-conquer strategy that builds a partial C4.5 decision tree in each iteration and makes the "best" leaf into a rule), (ii) J48 (C4.5 decision tree algorithm), (iii) Bagging (with 10 decision trees classifiers), (iv) BayesLogicRegresion (Bayesian network learning algorithm that estimates the parameters of $P(Y|X)$ using Logistic Regression), and (v) SMO (John Platt's sequential minimal optimization algorithm for training a support vector classifier).

We compared FSMC against seven feature selection algorithms also taken from Weka[15] with their default parameters, namely, CFsSubsetEval (evaluates a subset of features), FilteredSubsetEval (evaluates a subset of features that has been passed through a filter strategy), SVMattributeEval (evaluates the worth of an attribute using a SVM classifier), Wrapersubseteval (a wrapper feature selection strategy), PrincipalComponents (performs a PCA analysis), InfoGainAttributeEval (uses information gain to select attributes), and Relief-FAttributeEval (implements the ReliefF algorithm).

Table 1 shows in the header row the general characteristics of the different data sets used in these experiments, such as the total number of instances and attributes, as well as the number of instances in the majority and minority classes. This table summarizes also the number of relevant attributes selected by each feature selection algorithms when applied to the different data sets.

Note that FSMC selects fewer relevant attributes than the rest of algorithms in most data sets, with the exception of the human gait data set. This is convenient in problems involving a large number of variables and a few number of instances.

Table 1. Number of variables selected by eight feature selection methods including FSMC

	Datasets					
	Arrhythmia	Ozone	Pima Indians Diabetes	Diabetes	Gait	Cardio
Instances	273	1876	569	768	270	1831
Attributes	135	72	8	9	31	21
No. Maj. instances	237	1819	500	500	143	1655
No. Min. instances	36	57	69	268	127	176
Feature Selection Algorithms						
CFsSubsetEval	19	18	3	4	2	6
Filteredsubseteval	18	18	3	3	2	3
SVMattributeEval	All	All	All	All	All	All
Wrapersubseteval	None	None	None	None	None	None
PrincipalComponents	50	19	7	All	9	14
InfoGainAttributeEval	All	All	All	All	All	All
ReliefFAttributeEval	All	All	All	All	All	All
FSMC	4	8	1	1	3	1

The global accuracies obtained using the different classifiers in the data sets are shown in Table 2. In this case, we only show the performance of the three best feature selection algorithms. In all the experiments we used 10-fold cross validation.

The results presented in Table 2 show that the classifiers have, in general, better performance with the features selected by FSMC.

Table 3 shows the number of times that the classification of the minority and majority classes of all data sets was better by the different classifiers using the different subsets of attributes. Again the set variables selected by FSMC has in general better performance.

Table 2. Classification accuracy of different data sets with different classifiers based on different set of variables selected by five methods of feature selection including FSMC

Classifier	All	CFsSubsetEval	Filteredsubseteval	PrincipalComponents	FSMC
			Arrhythmia		
PART	89.74	91.58	91.58	86.08	**92.67**
J48	90.84	89.38	89.38	84.25	**92.31**
Bagging	**92.67**	91.94	91.58	90.11	91.94
BayesLogicRegresion	91.58	87.18	87.91	86.81	**92.67**
SMO	86.81	86.81	86.81	86.81	**92.31**
Average	90.33	89.38	89.45	86.81	**92.38**
			Ozone		
PART	95.36	96.54	96.54	96.48	**96.64**
J48	95.63	95.52	95.52	95.95	**96.48**
Bagging	96.86	96.86	96.86	**96.96**	96.80
BayesLogicRegresion	84.22	88.91	88.91	83.69	**90.03**
SMO	**96.96**	**96.96**	**96.96**	**96.96**	**96.96**
Average	93.81	94.96	94.96	94.01	**95.38**
			Gait Analysis		
PART	64.81	77.41	77.41	70.74	**82.22**
J48	69.26	78.15	78.15	78.52	**81.85**
Bagging	69.26	79.63	79.63	74.07	**80.37**
BayesLogicRegresion	**65.93**	53.33	53.33	57.41	59.63
SMO	52.22	**63.70**	**63.70**	54.44	54.44
Average	64.30	70.44	70.44	67.04	**71.70**
			Pima Indians Diabetes		
PART	87.70	88.23	88.23	89.10	**89.63**
J48	88.40	88.93	88.93	88.05	**89.63**
Bagging	87.17	88.23	88.23	88.40	**88.93**
BayesLogicRegresion	87.87	87.87	87.87	87.87	87.87
SMO	87.87	87.87	87.87	87.87	**88.75**
Average	87.80	88.22	88.22	88.26	**88.96**
			Diabetes		
PART	73.05	72.27	**73.31**	73.05	72.01
J48	71.48	73.44	**75.26**	71.48	72.01
Bagging	**76.69**	75.52	75.00	**76.69**	71.88
BayesLogicRegresion	**65.76**	63.93	64.06	**65.76**	65.10
SMO	65.10	62.89	63.54	65.10	**69.27**
Average	**70.42**	69.61	70.23	**70.42**	70.05
			Cardio		
PART	**98.74**	98.31	97.00	98.69	93.99
J48	98.53	**98.74**	97.27	98.03	93.99
Bagging	98.47	**98.53**	97.21	98.03	93.99
BayesLogicRegresion	93.56	91.43	93.17	91.86	**93.99**
SMO	91.59	92.41	**95.79**	93.66	93.99
Average	**96.18**	95.88	96.09	96.06	93.99

Table 3. Times that the classification of majority and minority class was better using different set of variables

	ALL	CfsSubsetEval	Filteredsubseteval	PrincipalComponents	FSMC
Wins in Accur. Min. class	8	12	8	6	**13**
Wins in Accur. Maj. class	6	8	6	11	**20**

Table 4. Times that the Precision, Recall, F-Measure, and ROC measures are better for the different feature selection algorithms

	Measure	ALL Win	ALL Tie	ALL Lose	C5sSubsetEval Win	C5sSubsetEval Tie	C5sSubsetEval Lose	Filteredsubseteval Win	Filteredsubseteval Tie	Filteredsubseteval Lose	PrincipalComponents Win	PrincipalComponents Tie	PrincipalComponents Lose	SFMC Win	SFMC Tie	SFMC Lose
Arrhythmia	Precision	2	0	3	0	0	5	0	0	5	0	0	5	3	0	2
	Recall	1	1	3	0	2	3	0	1	4	0	0	5	2	1	2
	F-Measure	2	0	3	0	1	4	0	1	4	0	0	5	2	0	3
	ROC	1	0	4	1	1	3	0	1	4	0	0	5	2	0	3
	Sum	6	1	13	1	4	15	0	3	17	0	0	20	**9**	1	10
	Perc.	30.00%	5.00%	65.00%	5.00%	20.00%	75.00%	0.00%	15.00%	85.00%	0.00%	0.00%	100.00%	**45.00%**	5.00%	50.00%
Ozone	Precision	0	2	3	0	5	0	0	5	0	0	2	3	0	2	3
	Recall	1	2	2	0	4	1	0	4	1	0	2	3	0	2	3
	F-Measure	1	2	2	0	4	1	0	4	1	0	2	3	0	2	3
	ROC	0	1	4	0	3	2	0	3	2	1	1	3	1	1	3
	Sum	**2**	7	11	0	16	4	0	16	4	1	7	12	1	7	12
	Perc.	10.00%	35.00%	55.00%	0.00%	80.00%	20.00%	0.00%	80.00%	20.00%	5.00%	35.00%	60.00%	5.00%	35.00%	60.00%
Gait	Precision	0	0	5	0	2	3	0	2	3	0	0	5	3	0	2
	Recall	1	0	4	0	1	4	0	1	4	0	0	5	3	0	2
	F-Measure	1	0	4	0	1	4	0	1	4	0	0	5	3	0	2
	ROC	1	0	4	0	2	3	0	2	3	0	0	5	2	0	3
	Sum	3	0	17	0	6	14	0	6	14	0	0	20	**11**	0	9
	Perc.	15.00%	0.00%	85.00%	0.00%	30.00%	70.00%	0.00%	30.00%	70.00%	0.00%	0.00%	100.00%	**55.00%**	0.00%	45.00%
Pima Indians Diabetes	Precision	0	1	4	0	2	3	0	1	4	0	1	4	4	1	0
	Recall	0	1	4	0	2	3	0	2	3	1	1	3	2	1	2
	F-Measure	0	1	4	0	1	4	0	2	3	1	1	3	2	1	2
	ROC	2	1	2	0	1	4	0	1	4	0	1	4	2	1	2
	Sum	2	4	14	0	6	14	0	6	14	2	4	14	**10**	4	6
	Perc.	10.00%	20.00%	70.00%	0.00%	30.00%	70.00%	0.00%	30.00%	70.00%	10.00%	20.00%	70.00%	**50.00%**	20.00%	30.00%
Diabetes	Precision	0	2	3	0	2	3	0	1	4	0	2	3	2	1	2
	Recall	0	2	3	2	0	3	0	0	5	0	2	3	1	0	4
	F-Measure	0	2	3	1	0	4	1	0	4	0	2	3	1	0	4
	ROC	0	3	2	1	0	4	0	0	5	0	3	2	1	0	4
	Sum	0	9	11	4	2	14	1	1	18	0	9	11	**5**	1	14
	Perc.	0.00%	45.00%	55.00%	20.00%	10.00%	70.00%	5.00%	5.00%	90.00%	0.00%	45.00%	55.00%	**25.00%**	5.00%	70.00%
Cardio	Precision	0	1	4	0	2	3	0	0	5	0	1	4	3	2	0
	Recall	0	0	5	2	0	3	1	0	4	1	0	4	1	0	4
	F-Measure	0	0	5	2	0	3	1	0	4	1	0	4	1	0	4
	ROC	0	0	5	2	0	3	1	0	4	1	0	4	1	0	4
	Sum	0	1	19	6	2	12	3	0	17	3	1	16	**6**	2	12
	Perc.	0.00%	5.00%	95.00%	30.00%	10.00%	60.00%	15.00%	0.00%	85.00%	15.00%	5.00%	80.00%	**30.00%**	10.00%	60.00%

Table 5. Summary of winners of Table 4

	ALL	CfsSubsetEval	Filteredsubseteval	PrincipalComponents	FSMC
Precision	2	0	0	0	**15**
Recall	3	4	1	2	**9**
F-Measure	4	3	2	2	**9**
ROC	4	4	1	2	**9**

Finally, Table 4 shows complementary information about the effectiveness of FSMC on the minority class on the six data sets. This table show how many times the precision, recall, F-measure and ROC values were better on these measures for the minority class with the classifiers used with specific set of variables. Table 5 shows the summary of how many times each feature selection algorithm won over the other algorithms in the different performance measures shown in Table 4. Again, FSMC outperforms the other feature selection algorithms in all of these measures.

4   Conclusions and Future Work

In this paper, we have presented a novel feature selection algorithm useful for unbalanced data sets. Its main feature selection strategy is based on selecting those features whose values are particularly different from the values of the majority class and that could help to classify instances from the minority class.

The experimental results show that the proposed method tends to select fewer attributes than other feature selection methods and, at the same time, outperforms most of the time such algorithms in different performance measures when tested on several data sets and with different classification algorithms.

As part of the future work we would like to extend the selection strategy to nominal attributes. We would also like to extend the selection strategy to real-valued data that do not follow a Gaussian distribution.

References

1. Jain, A., Zongker, D.: Feature Selection: Evaluation, Application, and Small Sample Performance. IEEE Trans. Pattern Analysis and Machine Intelligence 19(2), 153–158 (1997)
2. Dash, M., Liu, H.: Feature Selection for Classification. Intelligent Data Analysis 1(3), 131–156 (1997)
3. Dash, M., Liu, H.: Consistency-based Search in Feature Selection. Artificial Intelligence 151(1-2), 155–176 (2003)
4. Kohavi, R., John, G.H.: Wrapper for Feature Subset Selection. Artificial Intelligence 97(1-2), 273–324 (1997)
5. Liu, H., Motoda, H.: Feature Selection for Knowledge Discovery and Data Mining. Kluwer Academic Publishers, Norwell (1998)
6. Robnic-Sikonja, M., Kononenko, I.: Theoretical and Empirical Analysis of ReliefF and RReliefF. Machine Learning 53(1-2), 23–69 (2003)

7. Mao, K.Z.: Feature Subset Selection for Support Vector Machines Through Discriminative Function Pruning Analysis. IEEE Transactions on System, Man and Cybernetics, Part B 34(1), 60–67 (2004)
8. Hsu, C.N., Huang, H.J., Dietrich, S.: The ANNIGMA-Wrapper Approach to Fast Feature Selection for Neural Nets. IEEE Transactions on System, Man and Cybernetics, Part B 32(2), 207–212 (2004)
9. Japkowicz, N., Stephen, S.: The Class Imbalance Problem: A Systematic Study. Intelligent Data Analysis 6(5), 429–449 (2002)
10. Weiss, G.M., Provost, F.: The effect of class distribution on classifier learning: an empirical study. Technical report, Department of Computer Science, Rutgers University, New Jersey (2001)
11. Chen, X., Wasikowski, M.: FAST: A ROC-based feature selection metric for small samples and imbalanced data classification problems. In: 14th ACM SIGKDD Conference on Knowledge Discovery and Data Mining, pp. 124–132 (2008)
12. Kamal, A.H.M., Zhu, X., Pandya, A.S., Hsu, S., Narayanan, R.: Feature Selection for Datasets with Imbalanced Class Distributions. International Journal of Software Engineering and Knowledge Engineering 20(2), 113–137 (2010)
13. Alibeigi, M., Hashemi, S., Hamzeh, A.: Unsupervised Feature Selection Based on the Distribution of Features Attributed to Imbalanced Data Sets. International Journal of Artificial Intelligence and Expert Systems 2(1), 133–144 (2011)
14. Frank, A., Asuncion, A.: UCI Machine Learning Repository. University of California, School of Information and Computer Science, Irvine, CA (2010), http://archive.ics.uci.edu/ml
15. Witten, I.H., Frank, E.: Data Mining: Practical machine learning tools and techniques, 2nd edn. Morgan Kaufmann, San Francisco (2005)

Dissimilarity-Based Classifications in Eigenspaces*

Sang-Woon Kim[1] and Robert P.W. Duin[2]

[1] Dept. of Computer Science and Engineering, Myongji University,
Yongin, 449-728 South Korea
kimsw@mju.ac.kr
[2] Faculty of Electrical Engineering, Mathematics and Computer Science,
Delft University of Technology, The Netherlands
r.p.w.duin@tudelft.nl

Abstract. This paper presents an empirical evaluation on a dissimilarity measure strategy by which dissimilarity-based classifications (DBCs) [10] can be efficiently implemented. In DBCs, classifiers are not based on the feature measurements of individual objects, but rather on a suitable dissimilarity measure among the objects. In image classification tasks, however, one of the most intractable problems to measure the dissimilarity is the distortion and lack of information caused by the differences in illumination and directions and outlier data. To overcome this problem, in this paper, we study a new way of performing DBCs in eigenspaces spanned, one for each class, by the subset of principal eigenvectors, extracted from the training data set through a principal component analysis. Our experimental results, obtained with well-known benchmark databases, demonstrate that when the dimensionality of the eigenspaces has been appropriately chosen, the DBCs can be improved in terms of classification accuracies.

1 Introduction

Dissimilarity-based classifications (DBCs) [10] are a way of defining classifiers among the classes. The process is not based on the feature measurements of individual objects, but rather on a suitable dissimilarity measure among the objects. The problem with this strategy is that we need to measure the inter-pattern dissimilarities for all the training data to ensure there is no zero distance between objects of different classes. Thus, the classification performance of DBCs relies heavily on how well the dissimilarity matrix is constructed. To improve the performance, therefore, we need to ensure that the dissimilarity matrix is well designed.

With regard to solving this problem, investigations have focused on measuring the appropriate dissimilarity by using various l_p norms and traditional measures, such as those used in template matching and correlation-based analysis [10]. In image classification tasks, however, one of the most intractable problems that we encountered when employing these measuring systems is the distortion and lack of information caused by the environmental differences in computation. In face recognition, for example, there

---

* We acknowledge financial support from the FET programme within the EU FP7, under the SIMBAD project (contract 213250). This work was generously supported by the National Research Foundation of Korea funded by the Korean Government (NRF-2011-0002517).

C. San Martin and S.-W. Kim (Eds.): CIARP 2011, LNCS 7042, pp. 425–432, 2011.

are many kinds of variations based on such factors as pose (direction), expression, illumination, and distance [1], [4].

To address this problem, several strategies, including a generalization of dissimilarity representations [2], [9], a dynamic programming technique [5], a statistical similarity measuring method [6], and classification of regions of interest (ROIs) [13], have been developed and evaluated in the literature. On the other hand, subspace methods of pattern recognition are a technique in which the object classes are not primarily defined as bounded regions in a feature space, but rather given in terms of linear subspaces defined by the principal component analysis (PCA), one for each class [8].

For example, in Eigenface [1], [7], a well-known PCA approach to face recognition, face images are first decomposed into a small set of eigenvectors (i.e., eigenfaces) using a PCA. Then, each individual face is represented in terms of a linear combination of the eigenfaces. Here, the eigenvalues are equal to the variance of the projection of the image data set onto the corresponding eigenvector. Thus, the eigenvectors associated with the higher valued eigenvalues encode the larger variations in the data set, while the eigenvectors associated with the lower valued ones encode smaller variations in the set. Since the latter features encode smaller variations, it is commonly assumed that they represent noise in the data set. From this point of view, when performing DBCs in eigenspaces spanned by the principal eigenvectors, we can expect that the noise could be excluded from the dissimilarity representation.

The major task of our study is to deal with how the dissimilarity measure can be effectively computed. The goal of this paper is to demonstrate that the classification performance of DBCs can be improved by measuring the dissimilarity in the eigenspaces after constructing them by class. In particular, this goal can be achieved by appropriately projecting the data set on the eigenspaces and effectively measuring the distance between the projected points[1]. However, there is an essential difference between what we do in this paper and what Oja [8] (and also O-Alzate, et al. [9]) does. We characterize objects with distances *in the subspace*, while they use the distances *to the subspace*.

The remainder of the paper is organized as follows: In Section 2, after providing a brief introduction to DBCs, we present an explanation of the dissimilarity measure used in the eigenspaces and an improved DBC. In Section 3, we present the experimental results obtained with four benchmark image databases and UCI real-life data sets. In Section 4, we present our concluding remarks.

2   DBCs in Eigenspaces

Dissimilarity-based classifications (DBCs): A dissimilarity representation of a set of samples, $T = \{x_i\}_{i=1}^n \in \mathbb{R}^d$, is based on pairwise comparisons and is expressed, for example, as an $n \times m$ dissimilarity matrix, $D_{T,P}[\cdot, \cdot]$, where $P = \{p_j\}_{j=1}^m \in \mathbb{R}^d$, a prototype set, is extracted from T, and the subscripts of D represent the set of elements on which the dissimilarities are evaluated. Thus, each entry, $D_{T,P}[i, j]$, corresponds to

---

[1] To make it less sensitive to noisy samples, a pseudo-Euclidean embedding method is proposed in [10], where distances are isometrically embedded in a pseudo-Euclidean space and DBCs are performed. The details of the embedding are omitted here, but can be found in [10].

the dissimilarity between the pairs of objects, $\boldsymbol{x}_i$ and $\boldsymbol{p}_j$, where $\boldsymbol{x}_i \in T$ and $\boldsymbol{p}_j \in P$. Consequently, an object, $\boldsymbol{x}_i$, is represented as a column vector, $\delta(\boldsymbol{x}_i, P)$, as follows:

$$\delta(\boldsymbol{x}_i, P) = [d(\boldsymbol{x}_i, \boldsymbol{p}_1), d(\boldsymbol{x}_i, \boldsymbol{p}_2), \cdots, d(\boldsymbol{x}_i, \boldsymbol{p}_m)]^T, \ 1 \leq i \leq n. \tag{1}$$

Here, the dissimilarity matrix, $D_{T,P}[\cdot, \cdot]$, defines vectors in a *dissimilarity space* on which the d-dimensional object, $\boldsymbol{x}$, is represented as an m-dimensional vector, $\delta(\boldsymbol{x})$.

A conventional algorithm for DBCs is summarized in the following:

1. Select the prototype subset, P, from the training set, T, by using one of the selection methods described in the literature [10].

2. Using Eq. (1), compute the dissimilarity matrix, $D_{T,P}[\cdot, \cdot]$, in which each dissimilarity is computed on the basis of the measures described in the literature [10].

3. For a testing sample, z, compute a dissimilarity column vector, $\delta(z)$, by using the same measure used in Step 2.

4. Achieve the classification by invoking a classifier built in the dissimilarity space and operating it on the dissimilarity vector $\delta(z)$.

Here, we can see that the performance of DBCs relies heavily on how well the dissimilarity space, which is determined by the dissimilarity matrix, is constructed. To improve the performance, we need to ensure that the matrix is well designed.

Distance Measures in Eigenspaces [7]: The data set, T, can be decomposed into subsets, T_i, as follows [2]: $T = \bigcup_{i=1}^{c} T_i$, $T_i = \{\boldsymbol{x}_j\}_{j=1}^{n_i} \in \mathbb{R}^d$, with $n = \sum_{i=1}^{c} n_i$, $T_i \cap T_j = \phi, \forall i \neq j$. Our goal is to design a DBC in an appropriate eigenspace constructed with this *training data* set, T, and to classify a new sample into an appropriate class. To achieve this, for each T_i, we first find eigenvectors and eigenvalues, $\boldsymbol{\mu}_{ih}$ and λ_{ih}, $(h = 1, \cdots, d)$, of the covariance matrix, Σ_i, using $\Sigma_i \boldsymbol{\mu}_{ih} = \lambda_{ih} \boldsymbol{\mu}_{ih}$, and sort them in decreasing order according to the corresponding eigenvalues, i.e., $\lambda_{i1} \geq, \cdots, \geq \lambda_{id}$. Next, these eigenvectors are selected to form the row vectors of a transformation matrix, $A_i = \{\boldsymbol{\mu}_{ih}\}_{h=1}^{q} \in \mathbb{R}^d$. We then project the data samples, $\boldsymbol{x}_j$, $(j = 1, \cdots, n_i)$, into c q-dimensional subspaces, called eigenspaces, spanned by the arranged principal eigenvectors, using a transformation formula for each class as follows:

$$\boldsymbol{y}_{ij} = A_i^T (\boldsymbol{x}_j - \boldsymbol{m}_i), \ 1 \leq i \leq c, \tag{2}$$

where $\boldsymbol{y}_{ij} = (y_{ij1}, \cdots, y_{ijq})^T$ and $\boldsymbol{m}_i = \frac{1}{n_i} \sum_{j=1}^{n_i} \boldsymbol{x}_j$, where $\boldsymbol{x}_j \in T_i$.

Let $\boldsymbol{y}_{ij} \in T_i$ and $\boldsymbol{y}_{kl} \in T_k$ be q-dimensional feature vectors defined in the eigenspace. Many measures exist for $\boldsymbol{y}_{ij}$ and $\boldsymbol{y}_{kl}$, mostly constructed in an additive way after counting the differences for each feature separately. The basic measures come from the family of $l_p(p \geq 1)$ distance, $\|\boldsymbol{y}_{ij} - \boldsymbol{y}_{kl}\|_p = (\sum_{h=1}^{q} (y_{ijh} - y_{klh})^p)^{1/p}$, called Minkowski distance. Based on this distance, various measures can be defined as follows:

1. Manhattan distance (l_1 metrics): $d_{Manh}(\boldsymbol{y}_{ij}, \boldsymbol{y}_{kl}) = \sum_{h=1}^{q} |y_{ijh} - y_{klh}|$,
2. Euclidean distance (l_2 metrics): $d_{Eucli}(\boldsymbol{y}_{ij}, \boldsymbol{y}_{kl}) = \sqrt{\sum_{h=1}^{q} (y_{ijh} - y_{klh})^2}$,
3. Sum square error (SSE) distance: $d_{SSE}(\boldsymbol{y}_{ij}, \boldsymbol{y}_{kl}) = \sum_{h=1}^{q} (y_{ijh} - y_{klh})^2$,
4. Canberra distance: $d_{Canbe}(\boldsymbol{y}_{ij}, \boldsymbol{y}_{kl}) = \sum_{h=1}^{q} \frac{|y_{ijh} - y_{klh}|}{|y_{ijh}| + |y_{klh}|}$.

---

[2] The subsets have been chosen as the classes here, but clusters could also be used.

Here, the dimensionality of the eigenspace, q, can be selected based on the criteria, such as a heuristic selection [7], a cumulative proportion [8], and an intra-set distance [3]. A criterion associated with the intra-set distance is defined as follow: For an arbitrary sample, $x_j \in T_i$, the mean of $d(x_j, T_i - \{x_j\})$ over T_i is called the *intra-set distance* of T_i and is denoted by $D^2(T_i) = \frac{1}{n_i} \sum_{j=1}^{n_i} d^2(x_j, T_i - \{x_j\})$. By conveniently rearranging the elements in the summation of $D^2(T_i)$, the intra-set distance can be expressed in terms of the unbiased variances of components of the given samples like: $D^2(T_i) = 2 \sum_{k=1}^{d} \sigma_k^2$, where $\sigma_k^2 = \frac{n_i}{n_i - 1} \left(\overline{x_k^2} - (\bar{x}_k)^2 \right)$ for all $x_j \in T_i$. This is the rationale of the scheme for employing the intra-set distance as a criterion to select the dimensionality of the eigenspace. The details of the other criteria are omitted in the interest of compactness, but can be found in the related literature.

Proposed Dissimilarity-Based Classification: To overcome the limitation caused by the variations in illumination and the outlier data, in this paper, we measure the dissimilarities in a transformed subspace, rather than in the input-feature space. The basic strategy of the technique is to solve the classification problem by first mapping the input-feature space to an eigenspace, and then constructing a dissimilarity matrix with the distance measures in the eigenspace; finally, DBCs are performed on the dissimilarity space to reduce the classification error rates. The proposed approach, which is referred to as an eigenspace DBC (EDBC), is summarized in the following:

1. Select the entire training set T as the prototype subset P.
2. After computing A_i and m_i for each class, T_i, $(i = 1, \cdots, c)$, transform the input-feature vector, x_j, $(j = 1, \cdots, n_i)$, into the feature vectors, y_{ij}, using Eq. (2).
3. Using Eq. (1), compute $D_{T,T}[\cdot, \cdot]$, in which each dissimilarity, $d(x_j, x_k)$, is measured with $d(y_{ij}, y_{lk})$, where the class of the samples $\{x_k, y_{ij}, y_{lk}\}$ is the same.
4. This step is the same as Step 3 in the conventional DBC.
5. This step is the same as Step 4 in the conventional DBC.

The time complexities of the above algorithm, EDBC, can be analyzed as follows: As in the case of DBC, almost all the processing CPU-time of EDBC is consumed in computing the transformation matrix and the dissimilarity matrices. More specifically, in DBC, Step 2 of computing the $n \times n$ dissimilarity matrix requires $O(dn^2)$ time. On the other hand, the computation of that of EDBC needs $O(d^3 + dn^2 + cn^2)$ time in executing Steps 2 and 3.

3   Experimental Results

Experimental Data: The proposed method has been tested and compared with the conventional ones. This was done by performing experiments on well-known benchmark databases, namely, Kimia2 (1024/216/2) [11], Yale (1024/165/15) [4], Nist38 (256/200/2) [14], and CMU-PIE (256/1365/65) [12], and other multivariate data sets cited from UCI Machine Learning Repository[3]. Here, three numbers in brackets represent the numbers of dimensions d, samples n, and classes c, respectively. Also, Kimia2 and Nist38 are of binary images, while Yale and CMU-PIE are of gray scale images.

---

[3] http://www.ics.uci.edu/~mlearn/MLRepository.html

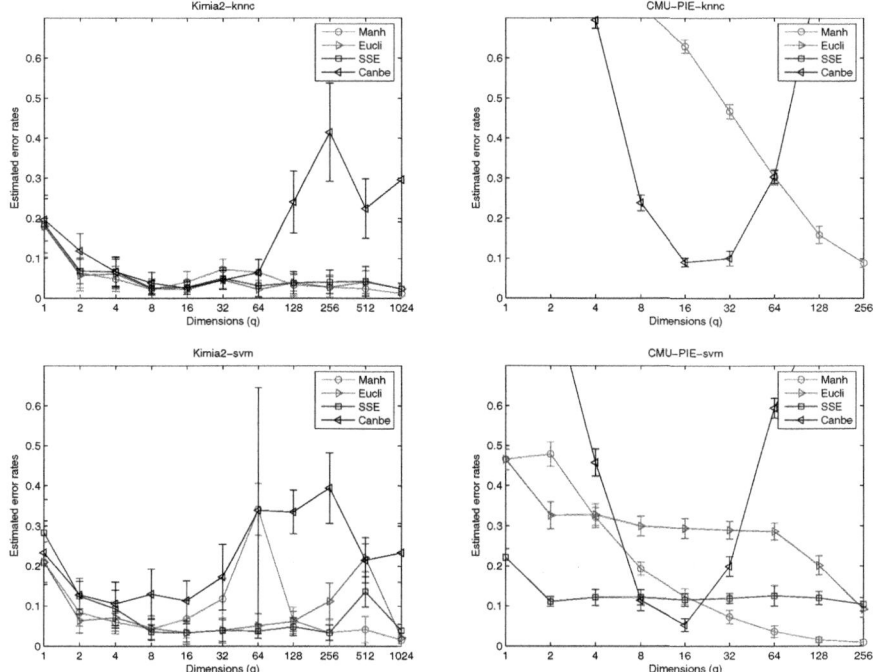

Fig. 1. A comparison of the estimated error rates of *knnc* and *libsvm* designed in the eigenspaces: (a) top left, (b) top right, (c) bottom left, and (d) bottom right; (a) and (b) are of *knnc*, (c) and (d) are of *libsvm*, obtained with Kimia2 and CMU-PIE using the four distance measures

Experimental Method: In this experiment, first, data sets are randomly split into training sets and test sets in the ratio of 75 : 25. Then, the training and testing procedures are repeated 10 times and the results obtained are averaged. To evaluate the classification accuracies of DBCs designed in the input-feature spaces and the principal eigenspaces, different classifiers, such as k-nearest neighbor classifiers and support vector machines, are employed and implemented with PRTools [4], and will be denoted as *knnc* and *libsvm*, respectively, in subsequent sections.

Experimental Results: First, the experimental results obtained in the eigenspaces for Kimia2, Yale, Nist38, and CMU-PIE were probed into. Fig. 1 shows a comparison of the error rates of *knnc* and *libsvm* designed in the dissimilarity matrices constructed with the four distance measures in the eigenspaces for the Kimia2 and CMU-PIE databases.

The observations obtained from the figures are the following ones:

- The reader first should observe that the classification accuracy of DBCs can be improved by means of appropriately choosing the distance measures in eigenspaces when the dimensionality of the subspaces is appropriately chosen.

- It should also be pointed out that the error rate of d_{Canbe}, marked with $\triangleleft$ symbol, decreases at first as the dimension increases, but rapidly increases. This overtraining

---

[4] PRTools is a Matlab toolbox for pattern recognition (refer to http://prtools.org/).

Table 1. A numerical comparison of the error rates (standard deviations) for the four databases

data sets	distance	$knnc$		$libsvm$	
$(d\,/\,n\,/\,c)$	measures	DBCs	EDBCs	DBCs	EDBCs
Kimia2 (1024/216/2)	Manh	0.0241 (0.0232)	0.0111 (0.0129)	0.0463 (0.0235)	0.0148 (0.0146)
	Eucli	0.0185 (0.0175)	0.0241 (0.0125)	0.0204 (0.0204)	0.0204 (0.0137)
	SSE	0.0241 (0.0232)	0.0241 (0.0152)	0.0463 (0.0235)	0.0389 (0.0162)
	Canbe	0.0241 (0.0232)	0.0648 (0.0330)	0.0463 (0.0235)	0.3389 (0.3068)
Yale (1024/165/15)	Manh	0.2267 (0.0953)	0.1500 (0.0393)	0.2233 (0.0668)	0.1500 (0.0451)
	Eucli	0.2100 (0.0903)	0.1800 (0.0592)	0.2033 (0.0936)	0.1867 (0.0450)
	SSE	0.2433 (0.0969)	0.2067 (0.0466)	0.2133 (0.0789)	0.1667 (0.0351)
	Canbe	0.2200 (0.0757)	0.2633 (0.0618)	0.2200 (0.0670)	0.2333 (0.0588)
Nist38 (256/200/2)	Manh	0.0420 (0.0305)	0.0120 (0.0103)	0.0520 (0.0368)	0.0120 (0.0103)
	Eucli	0.0360 (0.0295)	0.0400 (0.0249)	0.0380 (0.0358)	0.0420 (0.0220)
	SSE	0.0420 (0.0305)	0.0540 (0.0267)	0.0520 (0.0368)	0.0440 (0.0280)
	Canbe	0.0420 (0.0305)	0.1480 (0.0634)	0.0520 (0.0368)	0.2340 (0.0626)
CMU-PIE (256/1365/65)	Manh	0.7782 (0.0148)	0.0877 (0.0105)	0.1218 (0.0177)	0.0086 (0.0066)
	Eucli	0.7403 (0.0125)	0.7388 (0.0096)	0.0923 (0.0169)	0.0911 (0.0201)
	SSE	0.8283 (0.0035)	0.8311 (0.0169)	0.1114 (0.0283)	0.1037 (0.0165)
	Canbe	0.7055 (0.0115)	0.2385 (0.0195)	0.1317 (0.0188)	0.1145 (0.0262)

observed is the result of the normalization. If many eigenvectors are used, also the ones with small eigenvalues are included. Their contributions are close to the origin and as a result they get large weights: noise is emphasized.

- For the experiment of Kimia2 (and Nist38), which are relatively well represented data sets, the error rates of *libsvm* show the *peaking effect* before arriving at the lowest values (refer to Fig. 1 (c)). On the other hand, the error rates of CMU-PIE (and Yale), which are an example of small sample size (SSS) problems, do not show the phenomenon (refer to Figs. 1 (b) and (d)).

- For the experiment of CMU-PIE, in which the face images have been resized into 16×16 pixels of having only facial components, the error rates obtained with d_{Canbe} and d_{Manh} are completely different; the error rates of the latter measure steadily decrease, while those of the former sharply decrease till an optimal or near optimal dimension, but abruptly increase after passing that point (refer to Figs. 1 (b) and (d)). Also, in Fig. 1(b), the error rates of d_{Eucli} and d_{SSE} do not appear, which means that the two distance measures did not work well for the database. The similar characteristics could also be observed in the Yale and Nist38 databases.

Second, to investigate the difference of DBCs and EDBCs, the experiment (of estimating error rates) was repeated in the two spaces. In this experiment, the dissimilarity matrices were constructed with the four distance measures, where the dimensionality of the matrices was determined as follows: The dimensions of the feature spaces for all DBCs and the d_{Manh}, d_{Eucli}, and d_{SSE} measures of EDBCs are the same as d. However, for the d_{Canbe} measure, it was selected based on the criterion value of the intra-set distance (because of the characteristics shown in Fig. 1). The selected dimensions for Kimia2, Yale, Nist38, and CMU-PIE are 64, 8, 64, and 8, respectively. Table 1 shows a numerical comparison of the error rates of *knnc* and *libsvm* for the four databases.

Table 2. A numerical comparison of the error rates (standard deviations) obtained with d_{Manh} for UCI data. The results of the other measures are omitted here in the interest of compactness.

data sets	parameters (d / n / c)	knnc		libsvm	
		DBCs	EDBCs	DBCs	EDBCs
Nist	(256/2000/10)	0.0704 (0.0086)	<u>0.0420</u> (0.0098)	0.0666 (0.0092)	<u>0.0428</u> (0.0105)
Sonar	(60/208/2)	0.1980 (0.0397)	0.1451 (0.0533)	0.1667 (0.0455)	0.1588 (0.0438)
Dermatology	(34/366/6)	0.0945 (0.0260)	0.0714 (0.0209)	0.0418 (0.0253)	0.0374 (0.0221)
Wine	(13/178/3)	0.2372 (0.0512)	0.2163 (0.0640)	0.0837 (0.0745)	0.0744 (0.0628)
Malaysia	(8/291/20)	0.4627 (0.0480)	0.4610 (0.0398)	0.5695 (0.0409)	0.5881 (0.0582)

We observed the same characteristics in Table 1 as in Fig. 1. The table clearly shows that the classification accuracies of DBCs can be improved when d_{Manh} is used to measure the dissimilarity in the eigenspace (see the underlined numbers). However, for d_{Eucli}, d_{SSE}, and d_{Canbe}, the error rates of DBCs and EDBCs are *almost* the same, which means the increase and/or decrease of the error rates is not significant. Formally, d_{Eucli} should not change after an eigenvalue decomposition that involves all eigenvectors. The space is just rotated. Then, d_{Eucli} and d_{SSE} are also rotation independent. However, the values between DBC and EDBC are still slightly different; these might be caused by different training/test set splits in the experiments.

To further investigate the advantage of using the proposed scheme, and, especially, to find out which kinds of significant data set are more suitable for the scheme, we repeated the experiment with a few of UCI data sets. Table 2 shows a numerical comparison of the error rates obtained with d_{Manh} for the UCI data sets. From the table, it should be observed that the classification accuracy of the proposed scheme can be improved when applied to high-dimensional image data. However, the scheme does not work satisfactorily with low-dimensional data sets.

Additionally, it is interesting to note that PCA was applied separately to each subset T_i, ($i = 1, \cdots, c$), of the training data, not the entire set. In order to compare two ways of using an eigenspace for each class and a single eigenspace obtained with all training data, we performed two EDBCs for UCI data sets in Table 2. From the experiment, it was observed that the error rates of the latter are generally higher than those of the former. For example, the error rates of the latter knnc and libsvm are 0.0894 and 0.0562 for Nist and 0.2235 and 0.1804 for Sonar, respectively.

In review, it is not easy to crown one particular measuring method with superiority over the others in terms of solving the dissimilarity measuring problem. However, in terms of classification accuracies, the Manhattan distance measured in eigenspaces seems to be more useful for certain kinds of significant data sets than the Euclidean one does. This observation is very interesting. It deserves further discussion and exploration.

4   Conclusions

In order to improve the classification performance of DBCs, we studied a distance measuring technique based on eigenspaces of data. To achieve this improvement of DBCs, we first computed eigenvectors and eigenvalues of the training data, one for each class.

We then performed DBCs in the eigenspaces spanned by the subset of principal eigenvectors, where the dissimilarity was measured with a Manhattan distance. This measuring technique has been employed to solve the distortion and lack of information caused by the differences in illumination and directions. The proposed scheme was tested on four image databases and some UCI data sets. Our experimental results demonstrate that the classification accuracies of DBCs were improved when the dimensionality of the eigenspaces has been appropriately chosen. Although we have shown that the performance of DBCs can be improved by employing the Manhattan distance in eigenspaces, many tasks remain unchallenged. One of them is to further investigate the result that the improvement can be achieved only when using the Manhattan distance. Also, it is not yet clear which kinds of significant data sets are more suitable for the scheme.

References

1. Belhumeur, P.N., Hespanha, J.P., Kriegman, D.J.: Eigenfaces vs. Fisherfaces: Recognition using class specific linear projection. IEEE Trans. Pattern Anal. and Machine Intell. 19(7), 711–720 (1997)
2. Bicego, M., Murino, V., Figueiredo, M.A.T.: Similarity-based classification of sequences using hidden Markov models. Pattern Recognition 37, 2281–2291 (2004)
3. Friedman, M., Kandel, A.: Introduction to Pattern Recognition - Statistical, Structural, Neural and Fuzzy Logic Approaches. World Scientific, New Jersey (1999)
4. Georghiades, A.S., Belhumeur, P.N., Kriegman, D.J.: From few to many: Illumination cone models for face recognition under variable lighting and pose. IEEE Trans. Pattern Anal. and Machine Intell. 23(6), 643–660 (2001)
5. Kim, S.-W., Gao, J.: A Dynamic Programming Technique for Optimizing Dissimilarity-Based Classifiers. In: da Vitoria Lobo, N., Kasparis, T., Roli, F., Kwok, J.T., Georgiopoulos, M., Anagnostopoulos, G.C., Loog, M. (eds.) S+SSPR 2008. LNCS, vol. 5342, pp. 654–663. Springer, Heidelberg (2008)
6. Kim, S.-W., Duin, R.P.W.: On improving dissimilarity-based classifications using a statistical similarity measure. In: Bloch, I., Cesar Jr., R.M. (eds.) CIARP 2010. LNCS, vol. 6419, pp. 418–425. Springer, Heidelberg (2010)
7. Moon, H., Phillips, P.J.: Computational and performance aspects of PCA-based face-recognition algorithms. Perception 30, 303–321 (2001)
8. Oja, E.: Subspace Methods of Pattern Recognition. Research Studies Press (1983)
9. Orozco-Alzate, M., Duin, R.P.W., Castellanos-Dominguez, G.: A generalization of dissimilarity representations using feature lines and feature planes. Pattern Recognition Letters 30, 242–254 (2009)
10. Pekalska, E., Duin, R.P.W.: The Dissimilarity Representation for Pattern Recognition: Foundations and Applications. World Scientific Publishing, Singapore (2005)
11. Sebastian, T.B., Klein, P.N., Kimia, B.B.: Recognition of shapes by editing shock graphs. In: Proc. of the 8th IEEE Int'l Conf. on Computer Vision, Vancouver, Canada, pp. 755–762 (2001)
12. Sim, T., Baker, S., Bsat, M.: The CMU pose, illumination, and expression (PIE) database of human faces, Technical Report RI-TR-01-02, Carnegie Mellon Univ., Pittsburgh, PA (2001)
13. Sørensen, L., Loog, M., Lo, P., Ashraf, H., Dirksen, A., Duin, R.P.W., de Bruijne, M.: Image dissimilarity-based quantification of lung disease from CT. In: Jiang, T., Navab, N., Pluim, J.P.W., Viergever, M.A. (eds.) MICCAI 2010. LNCS, vol. 6361, pp. 37–44. Springer, Heidelberg (2010)
14. Wilson, C.L., Garris, M.D.: Handprinted Character Database 3. Technical Report, National Institute of Standards and Technology, Gaithersburg, Maryland (1992)

Dynamic Signature Recognition
Based on Fisher Discriminant

Teodoro Schmidt, Vladimir Riffo, and Domingo Mery

Pontificia Universidad Catolica de Chile, PUC
{theo,vriffo1}@uc.cl, dmery@ing.puc.cl

Abstract. Biometric technologies are the primary tools for certifying identity of individuals. But cost of sensing hardware plus degree of physical invasion required to obtain reasonable success are considered major drawbacks. Nevertheless, the signature is generally accepted as one means of identification. We present an approach on signature recognition using face recognition algorithms to obtain class descriptors and then use a simple classifier to recognize signatures. We also present an algorithm to store the *writing direction* of a signature, applying a linear transformation to encode this data as a gray scale pattern into the image. The signatures are processed applying Principal Components Analysis and Linear Discriminant Analysis creating descriptors that can be identified using a *KNN* classifier. Results revealed an accuracy performance rate of 97.47% under cross-validation over binary images and an improvement of 98.60% of accuracy by encoding simulated dynamic parameters. The encoding of real dynamic data boosted the performance rate from 90.21% to 94.70% showing that this technique can be a serious contender to other signature recognition methods.

Keywords: signature recognition, on-line signatures, off-line signatures, fishersignatures.

1 Introduction

In modern world trust between individuals has become a key factor in every activity. This enforces the need of authentication for all individuals involved in any given transaction. To accomplish the latter, biometric recognition employs two strategies: physical based characteristics and behavioral based characteristics [1]. Within the latter, the signature outstands for its social acceptance and relatively low implementation costs [2]. Even legal regulations on most countries accept signature as a key discriminant factor. Hence, correct signature identification is crucial to guarantee the suitability of any transaction taking place. This paper presents a signature's analysis technique to determine whether or not it belongs to a given person, analyzing the signature's image against the results of a previous training process. Given its importance, signatures are subject to counterfeiting. Against this, the automatic signature recognition faces two main problems: the need to identify intrinsic static characteristics of the

C. San Martin and S.-W. Kim (Eds.): CIARP 2011, LNCS 7042, pp. 433–442, 2011.

signature in question, such as its geometry (process known as off-line), and the need to identify graphological characteristics of the individual's signature, such as unique patterns of hand movements, speed and direction of writing, known as on-line analysis [3]. Thus, the problem of identifying people lies in finding efficient algorithms to analyze static and dynamic signature characteristics, and then compare those analyses results in real time against a knowledge base of signatures, previously generated. This document is organized as follows: section II describes the state of the art of signatures recognition. Section III describes the proposed method based on principal component analysis (PCA) and linear discriminant analysis (LDA). This section also details the equations used to represent the signature's writing direction. Section IV presents the experimental development, including results analysis. Finally, Section V presents conclusions and scope of this paper plus future work of this research.

2   Related Work

The two most common approaches current investigations explore are: signature changes analysis in time domain and shape analysis of signature stroke morphology. Relevant works on the first approach are [4],[5] where temporal signature evolution is analyzed using multi-section vector quantization. On the second approach, work [6] analyzes gravity, eccentricity, skewness, with good accuracy results. *Ad hoc* selection of features can be used to increase accuracy [7]. This concept is extended by sub pattern analysis of signature's stroke [8] and the analysis of humans' perception of stroke segments [9]. An issue here is the amount of data to be analyzed. One approach is to reduce the dimensionality of the feature space while maintaining discrimination between classes. A relevant work is [10] where LDA is used for dimensionality reduction and Neural Networks for classification. The drawback is that NN are hard to conceptualize due to their black box nature [11]. Nonetheless, as the potential of dimensionality reduction is obvious, a recognition method should have a simpler classifier and better feature extraction. A special note deserves the idea in [12] where a color scheme is used, based on signature changes. This creates a unique color-based fingerprint for every signature, though these fingerprints are based on morphology changes rather than dynamic features. Our method uses dimensionality reduction as face recognition methods do, that is, by using PCA [13] and LDA to create feature vectors like EigenFaces [14], and FisherFaces [15], and a simple *KNN* algorithm as classifier. We strengthen the capture process by creating a gray scale color based algorithm to encode dynamic features on to signature images.

3   Proposed Method

The action of signing is unique and exclusive for each individual. This is based not only in its geometry but on the existence of characteristics of the signature process itself, such as speed and direction of the signing action [16]. Given this, it

is very difficult to replicate the static characteristics [17] and dynamic characteristics of another individual's signature, without committing errors in the process.
The hypothesis that it is possible to recognize the subject issuer of a signature
using algorithms that belong to the face recognition problem [18] opens the
possibility of using dynamic characteristics to encode extra information within
the signatures images while capturing them. Nonetheless, the feature extraction
process can theoretically be also applied to static characteristics. Based on the
latter, our model proposes static analysis of vector of characteristics specific
to signatures captured off-line, creating Fishersignatures, which correspond to
principal component analysis and linear discriminator applied over the images.
The whole recognition process is divided in two sections: i) training using Fishersignatures method over a set of images, and ii) testing using a new image as
input for comparison against the already trained matrix of weights resulting from
the section i). Additionally, we propose an algorithm to acquire dynamic characteristics when capturing the signatures. This method encodes the data into
the original signature image, strengthening the features extraction process. The
complete signature recognition system used is shown schematically in Figure 1.

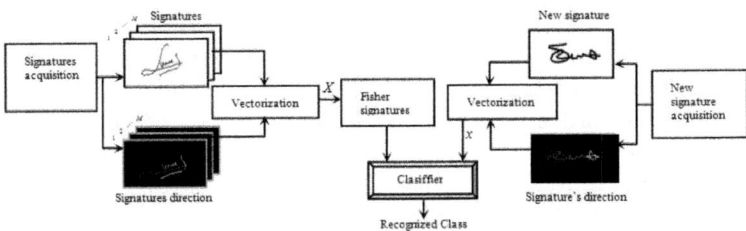

Fig. 1. Block diagram of the system proposed

3.1 Fishersignatures Training Method

Our technique for signatures recognition is based on the Eigenfaces matrix used
in face recognition to project images onto a lower dimensional space, reducing
computational complexity of features extraction. Given a set of signature images
per class $\{I_j(x,y),\ j = 1, 2, ..., M\}$, being I_j a matrix of order $N = m \times n$, the
images are column-stacked vectorized (rasterized) and named x_j, $j = 1, 2, , M$.

The vectorized training set is $X = [X_1 X_2 \ldots X_c]$ with $X_k = [x_1^k x_2^k \ldots x_M^k]$,
$k = 1, 2, ..., c$, where x_j^k is the vectorized image j for class k. The order of X is
$N \times D$, with $D = M \times c$

The *inter-class* average of the images is a vector of N elements:

$$\mu_k = \frac{1}{M} \sum_{j=1}^{M} x_j^k \quad , k = 1, 2, ..., c \tag{1}$$

The class average is a vector with N elements:

$$\mu = \frac{1}{(M \times c)} \sum_{k=1}^{c} \sum_{j}^{M} x_j^k \tag{2}$$

The difference between each image and the class average is $A = [A_1 A_2 \ldots A_D]$ where A_d, with $d = 1, 2, \ldots, D$, are in turn:

$$A_d = x_j^k - \mu \quad , d = 1, 2, \ldots, D \tag{3}$$

The covariance matrix is defined as:

$$S_T = AA^T \tag{4}$$

Next is the calculation of the Eigen vectors of AA^T, defined as u_i. The trick here is to find the v_i Eigen vectors of a new matrix $A^T A$, with λ_i being the Eigen vectors of both AA^T and $A^T A$, related through the following equality:

$$u_i = Av_i \tag{5}$$

The search for the v_i Eigen vectors is carried out using the Jacobi method [19], where all v_i are placed in descending order, following the order of the Eigen values λ_i. After normalizing $\|u_i\| = 1$, all u_i Eigen vectors are concatenated to form a U matrix of order $N \times D$, where $U = [u_1 u_2 \ldots u_i]$, $i = 1, 2, \ldots, D$. Finally, the W_E projection matrix gets defined as:

$$W_E = U^T A \tag{6}$$

Fisher discriminant increases the separation between classes preserving a low discrimination inside every class. Fisher is considered an implementation of LDA over PCA space. With this, the dimensionality of U can be reduced to $N \times D_p$, with $D_p = (M \cdot c) - c$, by redefining U as a new matrix W_{pca}. The new data projection on the reduced PCA space gets defined by W_{EF} of order $D_p \times D$:

$$W_{EF} = W_{pca}^T X \tag{7}$$

More in detail, $W_{EF} = [w_1^k w_2^k \ldots w_M^k]$. The above reduction redefines the class average with a new equation where w_j^k is the j projected vectorized image of class k:

$$\eta_k = \frac{1}{M} \sum_{j=1}^{M} w_j^k \quad , k = 1, 2, \ldots, c \tag{8}$$

Following the above transformation, the new equation for the *inter-class* average is:

$$\eta = \frac{1}{(M \times c)} \sum_{k=1}^{c} \sum_{j}^{M} w_j^k \tag{9}$$

In the same way, the class dispersion matrix gets determined by:

$$S_B = \sum_{k=1}^{c} (\eta_k - \eta)(\eta_k - \eta)^T \tag{10}$$

And the *inter-class* dispersion matrix gets determined by:

$$S_W = \sum_{k=1}^{c} \sum_{j=1}^{M} (w_j^k - \eta)(w_j^k - \eta)^T \tag{11}$$

It's interesting to note that S_B and S_W are square matrices of order $D_p \times D_p$. In order to ensure that S_B and S_W are related by $S_B W_{fld} = S_W W_{fld} \lambda$, the W_{fld} Eigen vectors and λ Eigen values are calculated defining what we call Fishersignatures, with the following equation:

$$P = W_{pca} W_{fld} \tag{12}$$

Finally, the new W_E projection matrix of Fishersignatures gets defined as:

$$W_E = P^T A \tag{13}$$

3.2   Testing Method

To classify a new signature, a *KNN* search against the closest neighbor is performed, with the following steps:

a.- Testing signature I is vectorized in to vector x of order $N \times 1$ with $N = m \times n$
b.- *Inter-class* average O is obtained from equation $O = x - \mu$
c.- LDA projection W_P is carried out using P and O: $W_P = P^T O$
d.- Euclidean   distance   from W_E to W_P denotes   a   distance   vector $\sqrt{\sum |W_E - W_P|^2}$ in which the lowest value corresponds to the signature's identified class.

3.3   Signature's Writing Direction Encoding Method

In order to capture dynamic information, such as the signature's *writing direction*, a data encoding method was developed. This method strengthens the feature extraction process by visually encoding extra information into the image, at capture time. A gray value is assigned to each pixel of the signature's track being captured. The background of the captured image is set to zero to give more contrast. The gray value for first pixel t_1 of the signature's track is 0.1, to distinguish it from the background. The gray value for last pixel of the signature's track is 1.

Let $T(x,y) = t_1(x_1, y_1), t_2(x_2, y_2), ..., t_i(x_i, y_i), ..., t_n(x_n, y_n)$ be a Cartesian coordinates vector representing the signature's track, with $t_1(x_1, y_1)$ being the first pixel written, and $t_n(x_n, y_n)$ being the last written. Each t_i pixel of vector T is assigned a gray level value given by the linear equation:

$$t_i = 0.9\frac{i-1}{n-1} + 0.1 \tag{14}$$

The background of binary captured signatures is usually set to 1 and signature's track to 0, but the above transformation captures the signature's track with a black-to-white gradient denoting the direction in which the signature was written, starting from pixel t_1 (lowest gray value), to last pixel t_n (highest value). This effect is shown in Figure 2.

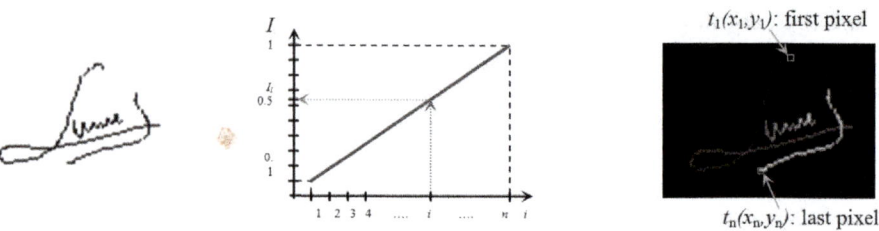

Fig. 2. Binary captured signature (*left*). Transformation to encode direction of signature (*center*). Result of visually encoded direction (*right*).

Simple visual inspection clearly shows that the image containing the signature's direction encoded in gray scale delivers more information than the binary one, even though they both share the same geometrical information, hence a Fishersignatures training and classification process using these gray scale images should deliver better performance results than their corresponding binary counterparts.

4   Experiments and Results

The database used for this work was GPDS960signature [20], with 960 classes, 24 images per class, in variable sizes. All images were normalized and resized to 102x64 pixels. These values come from the size of a tablet device used in a previous work to create a custom signature db. We preserved the resolution for comparison reasons.

Our implementation of Eigen values and vectors search rely on singular value decomposition, requiring a lot of RAM for big matrices. To solve this issue, the algorithms were tested over a smaller data set, split in 3 groups, keeping 20 signatures per class in each group: one set with 100 classes; another set with 200 classes; and a third set with 300 classes. No counterfeit signatures were used as the nature of this work was to verify performance of Fishersignatures idea using cross-validation. These signatures were not originally captured using the encoding process proposed in section 3.3. In order to verify the strengthening capability of such an algorithm, *writing direction* simulations were applied over the original b/w images. The accuracy performance of the *original* Fishersignatures classification (created with the original b/w images) was compared to new

Fishersignatures classification (created with simulated writing direction encoded onto the same images). Four different *writing direction* simulations were applied to each of the 3 data sets: first 40% of the images of a data set were applied a black-to-white (gray) gradient from left to right. Next 20% of the images of the same data set were applied the gradient from right to left. Next 20% of the images of the same data set were applied a top-down gradient. Final 20% of the images of the same data set were applied a bottom-up gray gradient. These percentages were arbitrarily chosen, based on the fact that people in western countries write from left to right, hence, simulation of this direction takes the biggest proportion. All other simulations equally share the remaining 60%. In order to maintain simplicity, the classifier used for all tests was *KNN* matching the first neighbor found for each class.

 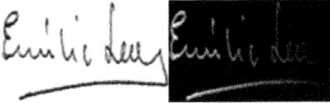

Fig. 3. Examples of simulated writing direction using a black-to-white gradient. Binary captured signature and *left-to-right direction simulation* (*left*). Binary captured signature and *right-to-left direction simulation* (*right*).

Performance results were evaluated through stratified cross validation using 5% of the data to test and the remaining 95% for training. Stratification ensures the representation of each class in the test sets. The overall performance of the method proposed is the average of 20 performances obtained. The average performance is shown in Table 1.

To fully test the proposed data encoding algorithm, a second experiment was executed. This time, the *writing direction* (dynamic data) was encoded in real time during the acquisition process. The resulting db is SRM-SDB [18] with 45 classes, 10 signatures per class, and all images acquired using the method described in 3.3 (each signature's *writing direction* encoded in gray scale). A b/w version of the images was also created for later use, where signature track's

Table 1. Accuracy performance results using cross-validation over 3 sets of images. Tests were carried out twice over each data set, one over binary images, and the next run over images with an encoded *writing direction* simulation.

Data Set	Image type	Accuracy %
100 individuals	Binary	92.20%
100 individuals	Encoded simulation	95.15%
200 individuals	Binary	97.00%
200 individuals	Encoded simulation	97.58%
300 individuals	Binary	97.47%
300 individuals	Encoded simulation	98.60%

Table 2. Accuracy performance results using cross-validation over signatures with real *writing direction* data encoded in gray scale and binary versions of same images

Data Set	Image type	Accuracy %
45 individuals	Binary (no gradient)	90.21%
45 individuals	Encoded real *writing direction*	94.70%

gray values were replaced by 0 (black) and background values were replaces by 255 (white). The accuracy of Fishersignatures created using the original *gray scale acquired* images was compared to Fishersignatures created using binarized images. The classifier was *KNN* matching the first neighbor found per class. Performance results were evaluated using stratified cross validation with 10% of data to test and 90% for training. The average performance is shown in Table 2.

5 Conclusions

In this paper we propose two contributions for an improved signature recognition technique: One contribution is the implementation of Fisher discriminant based feature vectors, we called Fishersignatures, *a la* face recognition method. The second contribution is our feature strengthening method of encoding dynamic parameters while acquiring signatures, particularly the signature's *writing direction*.

The first contribution shows that our Fishersignatures implementation creates good class separation. Even if applied over black and white images, the use of a simple classifier, such as *KNN*, to identify signatures delivers an accuracy of 97.47% in the best b/w case.

The second contribution shows that the signature acquisition process can be greatly improved by encoding extra information into a signature, without modifying its morphological characteristics, and still allow the processing of images using Fishersignatures plus a simple *KNN* classifier. This statement gets validated by two different successful experiments:

I) Encoding of simulated *writing direction* over *binary-acquired* signatures: the best accuracy rate achieved under binary analysis (97.47%) was superseded by an accuracy of 98.60% when encoding simulated dynamic information into the images.

II) Encoding of real *writing direction* at acquisition time: the proposed encoding method tested in a *real-life* scenario delivered an accuracy rate of 94.70%, which is far superior than 90.21% of accuracy obtained using a b/w version of the same images.

Although both experiments are obviously not comparable between them (given the nature of data acquisition of each experiment plus number of classes, samples, folds, etc.), it can be observed that Fishersignatures classification always delivered an accuracy of over 90% in all cases, and also that the proposed encoding method raised this accuracy in both experiments. The accuracy rate of other techniques is: 93% obtained by Karouni et al. [6], 94% obtained by Al-Mayyan et al. when using PCA [7], 93% obtained by Radhika et al. [8]. A further comparison of the best accuracy performance obtained in the first experiment (98.60%) against these other techniques shows that Fishersignatures classification delivers excellent performance, even though the *KNN* classifier seems weaker than others. Finally, accuracy results obtained denote that the combination of our two contributions can become a serious contender to other signature recognition methods.

An extension of the encoding algorithm is planned for future work, where other dynamic parameters will be encoded, such as *writing speed*. The replacement of the classifier for a stronger one, plus the analysis of a higher volume of signatures are also in our research roadmap.

Acknowledgments. This work was supported in part by School of Engineering, Pontificia Universidad Catolica de Chile, Grant FIA.

References

1. Jain, A.K., Ross, A., Prabhakar, S.: An introduction to biometric recognition. IEEE Transactions on Circuits and Systems for Video Technology 14, 4–20 (2004)
2. Prabhakar, S., Pankanti, S., Jain, A.K.: Biometric recognition: security and privacy concerns. IEEE Security & Privacy 1, 33–42 (2003)
3. Faundez-Zanuy, M.: On-line signature recognition based on VQ-DTW. Pattern Recognition 40, 981–992 (2007)
4. Pascual-Gaspar, J.M., Faundez-Zanuy, M., Vivaracho, C.: Fast on-line signature recognition based on VQ with time modeling. Engineering Applications of Artificial Intelligence 24(2), 368–377 (2011)
5. Pascual-Gaspar, J.M., Faundez-Zanuy, M., Vivaracho, C.: Efficient on-line signature recognition based on multi-section vector quantization. Pattern Analysis & Applications 14(1), 37–45 (2010)
6. Karouni, A., Daya, B., Bahlak, S.: Offline signature recognition using neural networks approach. In: Procedia Computer Science, World Conference on Information Technology, vol. 3, pp. 155–161 (2011)
7. Al-Mayyan, W., Own, H.S., Zedan, H.: Rough set approach to online signature identification. Digital Signal Processing 21(3), 477–485 (2011)
8. Radhika, K.R., Venkatesha, M.K., Sekhar, G.N.: Signature authentication based on subpattern analysis. Applied Soft Computing 11(3), 3218–3228 (2011)
9. Ebrahimpour, R, Amiri, A., Nazari, M., Hajiany, A.: Robust Model for Signature Recognition Based on Biological Inspired Features. International Journal of Computer and Electrical Engineering 2(4) (August 2010)
10. Meshoul, S., Batouche, M.: A novel approach for online signature verification using fisher based probabilistic neural networks. In: Proceedings - IEEE Symposium on Computers and Communications, pp. 314–319 (2010)
11. Tu, J.V.: Advantages and disadvantages of using artificial neural networks versus logistic regression for predicting medical outcomes. Journal of Clinical Epidemiology 49(11), 1225–1231 (1996)
12. Kulkarni, V.B.: A Colour Code Algorithm for Signature Recognition. Electronic Letters on Computer Vision and Image Analysis 6, 1–12 (2007)

13. Turk, M., Pentland, A.: Eigenfaces for Recognition. Journal of Cognitive Neuroscience 3, 71–86 (1991)
14. Turk, M., Pentland, A.: Face recognition using eigenfaces. In: Proceedings of Computer Vision & Pattern Recognition, CVPR 1991, IEEE Computer Society Conference, pp. 586–591 (1991)
15. Belhumeur, P., Hespanha, J., Kriegman, D.: Eigenfaces vs. Fisherfaces: recognition using class specific linear projection. IEEE Transactions on Pattern Analysis and Machine Intelligence 19, 711–720 (1997)
16. Vivaracho-Pascual, C., Faundez-Zanuy, M., Pascual, J.M.: An efficient low cost approach for on-line signature recognition based on length normalization and fractional distances. Pattern Recognition 42, 183–193 (2009)
17. Erkmen, B., Kahraman, N., Vural, R., Yildirim, T.: CSFNN optimization of signature recognition problem for a special VLSI NN chip. In: 3rd International Symposium on Communications, Control and Signal Processing, ISCCSP 2008, pp. 1082–1085 (2008)
18. Riffo, V., Schmidt, T., Mery, D.: Propuesta Novedosa de Reconocimiento Dinmico de Firmas. In: Proceeding of First Chilean Workshop on Pattern Recognition: Theory and Applications, pp. 44–51 (2009)
19. Hari, V.: Accelerating the SVD Block-Jacobi Method. Computing 75, 27–53 (2005)
20. Blumenstein, M., Ferrer Miguel, A., Vargas, J.F.: The 4NSigComp2010 off-line signature verification competition: Scenario 2. In: Proceedings of 12th International Conference on Frontiers in Handwriting Recognition, Kolkata, India, November 16-18, pp. 721–726 (2010) ISSBN: 978-0-7695-4221-8

A Multi-style License Plate Recognition System Based on Tree of Shapes for Character Segmentation

Francisco Gómez Fernández[1], Pablo Negri[2], Marta Mejail[1], and Julio Jacobo[1]

[1] Universidad de Buenos Aires
[2] PLADEMA, Universidad Nacional del Centro de la Provincia de Buenos Aires

Abstract. The aim of this work is to develop a multi-style license plate recognition (LPR) system. Most of the LPR systems are country-dependent and take advantage of it. Here, a new character extraction algorithm is proposed, based on the tree of shapes of the image. This method is well adapted to work with different styles of license plates, does not require skew or rotation correction and is parameterless. Also, it has invariance under changes in scale, contrast, or affine changes in illumination. We tested our LPR system on two different datasets and achieved high performance rates: above 90 % in license plate detection and character recognition steps, and up to 98.17 % in the character segmentation step.

1 Introduction

License Plate Recognition (LPR) is a very popular research area because of its immediate applications in real life. Security control and traffic safety applications, such identification of stolen cars or speed limit enforcement, have become very important application areas where the license plate (LP) analysis plays a fundamental role [1].

An LPR system can be divided in three steps: LP detection, character segmentation and character recognition. Character recognition success strongly depends on the quality of the bounding boxes, obtained by the segmentation step. Therefore, we considered that segmentation is a very important step in an LPR system. An extensive review for LPR can be found in [1]. However, the problem of LPR systems able to handle license plates from different countries and with different styles (shape, foreground-background colors, etc.) is currently an open research area. Several works implement LPR tasks achieving high performance rates, but most of them are country dependent.

In [6,10,11] LPR with multi-style analyses is addressed. Also, [6] and [11] use a similar procedure to search for LP regions, and added a recognition feedback to improve the detection step when the recognition fails. The character extraction step, is usually performed by binarization methods and a connected component analysis [10,11]. The choice of binarization-thresholds is a hard task; if it is not chosen properly, we will easily get redundant detections or miss some

C. San Martin and S.-W. Kim (Eds.): CIARP 2011, LNCS 7042, pp. 443–450, 2011.

detections too. An interesting work which handled detection and segmentation simultaneously is presented in [4].

In [11], the recognition step is carried out by a statistical approach using Fourier descriptors, and a structural approach using the Reeb Graph to distinguish ambiguous characters. In addition, for better character recognition, in [6] a three-layer artificial neural network over fixed sub-blocks from previously extracted characters, is computed.

In this work we develop a LPR System on still images adaptable to different countries. Our focus is in the segmentation step which is considered to be very important in an LPR system A new character extraction method is proposed based on the tree of shapes of an image. This method is well adapted to work under different LP styles, does not require rotation or skew correction and is parameterless. Also, it has invariance under changes in scale, contrast, or affine changes in illumination. These properties are derived by the properties of the tree of shapes [8]. The system was tested on two datasets (see examples in Fig. 1) obtaining high performance rates.

Fig. 1. Examples from two datasets used to test our system. First row shows cars images from USA. Second row shows Argentinean truck images.

This paper is organized as follows. Section 2 details the implementation of the LPR system and its steps. Experimental results over the datasets are given in section 3. Finally, section 4 presents the conclusions and future work.

2   License Plate Recognition System

In this section we introduce the three steps of the LPR system: license plate detection, character segmentation and character recognition (Fig. 2).

The initial task of any LPR system is to find the location of the LP in the image. Thus, our LP detection process starts generating several regions of interest (RoI) using morphological filters. To validate the RoIs $R_i, i = 1, \ldots, N$ and choose the most probable LP region, more exhaustive analyses are applied to give a score to each region using template matching and feature extraction [9]. Then, the system passes the region with the highest score to the segmentation step and validates its result if it has encountered more than three bounding boxes ($|\text{bbx}| > 3$ in Fig. 2) . Finally, the bounding boxes are used as an input to the character recognition step and it is validated as described in section 2.3. Following [11], if the analysis fails in the character segmentation or character recognition steps, the second most probable region will be evaluated, and so on, until the R_N region is reached. In such situation, the system returns no detection.

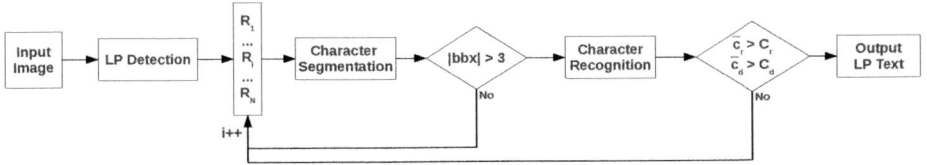

Fig. 2. LPR system diagram. Diamond shaped blocks represent validation steps.

2.1 License Plate Detection

In this section we discuss the analysis done for every region in order to give them a confidence value.

ROI generation. A morphological top-hat filtering is applied to the input image to enhance the contrast in regions with great difference in intensity values. Then, vertical contours are calculated using the Sobel filter, and successive morphological operations are then applied to connect the edges in the potential LP regions. These operations are a simple and rapid way to provide several potential RoIs. This is a critical step in the LPR system: if the LP is not detected by the morphological filters, it will be lost.

ROI evaluation. Each RoI R_i, $i = 1, ..., N$ is evaluated by two methods: template matching and text detection [5]. Then, we define four evaluation vectors of length N: **pcv** for template matching, and **mgd**, **nts** and **tbr** for text detection, where **pcv**(i) is the pattern correlation value obtained by cumulating the correlation values inside the boundaries of R_i, and **mgd**(i), **nts**(i), **tbr**(i) are the maximum gradient difference, the number of text segments and the text block ratio, inside R_i. We need to merge their information in order to decide which of the N regions is the most probable to be a license plate. To do so, we create four sorting index vectors: **pcv^{si}**, **mgd^{si}**, **nts^{si}** and **tbr^{si}**. These vectors give an index to each R_i that depends on an ascending sorting of the evaluation vectors. The R_i with the lowest value in the feature vector gets index 1, and the R_i with the highest value gets index N. Then, we define a vector **votes** of length N:

$$\textbf{votes}(i) = \textbf{pcv}^{si}(i) + \textbf{mgd}^{si}(i) + \textbf{nts}^{si}(i) + \textbf{tbr}^{si}(i)$$

The region R_m, with $m = \arg\max_{1 \leq i \leq N} \textbf{votes}(i)$ is retained as the LP.

Adapting the thresholds. The detection step can be applied to different datasets. However, the thresholds must be adapted to detect the LP in images obtained from different cameras or environments. To do this, the first images of the dataset are analyzed. As the position of each license plate is labeled in each image of the dataset, this information is used in order to fix the thresholds of the detection method. These thresholds are chosen to validate 95 % of all text segments inside the first five well recognized LPs. Also, the LP used as correlation pattern is set to the first image of the dataset.

2.2   Character Segmentation

To extract the characters in the LP we propose a new algorithm, which processes the tree of shapes of an image [8] to search for groups of characters. The tree of shapes is a complete representation of an image, i.e. the original image can be reconstructed from it. Also, the shapes in the tree are consistent with what we expect to be "objects" in the image. For instance, a character in an image will be represented by a shape (or a set of shapes) in the tree. The goal of this procedure is to state properties shared by every LP with no restrictions on the style of the plate.

Tree of shapes. A shape is defined as a connected component of a level set whose holes are "filled" (see [8] for a formal definition). Then, upper and lower level sets, at level λ, of an image u are defined as $\mathcal{X}_\lambda u = \{x \mid u(x) \geq \lambda\}$ and $\mathcal{X}^\lambda u = \{x \mid u(x) < \lambda\}$, respectively. It is known that connected components of level sets can be arranged in an inclusion tree ordered by λ, their gray level [8]. Moreover, the shapes extracted from an image can be ordered by geometrical inclusion (a shape is a child of another shape if it is included in its interior) to build the tree of shapes.

Char-grouping algorithm. This algorithm uses the fact that characters in license plates have properties in common, such as same foreground-background contrast, alignment and minimum overlap of bounding boxes, and similar width and height. The steps of this algorithm can be summarized as follows. The RoI R_m, returned by the detection step, is used to compute the tree of shapes. Then, all the nodes (shapes) in the tree are pairwise compared, linking the similar shapes, with a given criterion. Finally, the bounding boxes of the most linked node and its neighbors are returned as the result. Algorithm 1 shows the pseudo-code of the proposed algorithm.

   In order to avoid performing comparison of shapes included in other shapes or in already linked shapes, the tree of shapes is traversed taking advantage of its structure: nodes are visited top-down, and a node is never compared with a descendant of it or with a descendant of a node linked to it (line 4). This is a proper traverse, i.e. there are no repeated nor missing comparisons, due to the inclusion property of the tree of shapes, and to the fact that any two shapes are either disjoint or nested (see [8] for an explanation).

Character comparison. A feature vector is built for each node in the tree. This feature vector bears information about the bounding box and the type (upper or lower) of its associated shape. The comparison of the feature vectors (line 2) is carried out by the predicate SIMILARCHARS(n, m), which returns *true* if nodes n and m have the same type, and the distance between the corresponding shapes Φ is above a fixed threshold, and returns *false* otherwise. The distance Φ is given by

$$\Phi(n, m) = \frac{\min\big(\mathcal{W}(n),\mathcal{W}(m)\big)}{\max\big(\mathcal{W}(n),\mathcal{W}(m)\big)} + \frac{\min\big(\mathcal{H}(n),\mathcal{H}(m)\big)}{\max\big(\mathcal{H}(n),\mathcal{H}(m)\big)} + \frac{y(n) \cap y(m)}{\min\big(\mathcal{H}(n),\mathcal{H}(m)\big)} + 1 - \frac{\chi(n) \cap \chi(m)}{\min\big(\mathcal{W}(n),\mathcal{W}(m)\big)}$$

where functions $\mathcal{W}(\cdot)$ and $\mathcal{H}(\cdot)$ return width and height of the corresponding bounding boxes of n and m, respectively. Also, terms $\chi(n) \cap \chi(m)$ and $y(n) \cap y(m)$ represent the bounding box overlapping in x and y directions, respectively. In addition, shapes which lack vertical rectangularity, or which are too small, or too big or too distant, are discarded before performing the comparison.

Algorithm 1. char-grouping algorithm

Input: Tree of shapes $\mathcal{T}$
Output: Set of bounding boxes $\mathcal{S}$
1: **for all** $n, m \in \mathcal{T}$ **do**
2:     **if** SIMILARCHARS(n, m) **then**
3:         LINK(n, m)
4:         Skip n's children and m's children
5: Let n_{max} the maximum linked node
6: **for all** $n \in \mathcal{T}$ **do**
7:     **if** LINKED(n, n_{max}) **then**
8:         $\mathcal{S} \leftarrow \mathcal{S} \cup \{$ BOUNDINGBOX(n) $\}$
9: **return** $\mathcal{S}$

Fig. 3 shows examples of the bounding boxes computed by the *char-grouping algorithm*. As it can be seen, characters of LPs of very different styles are detected without modifying the algorithm. The first column shows examples of cluttered images where the detected text region is highly over-sized but the segmentation step still succeeds. The second column shows segmentation examples with different foreground-background color combination (top and middle: dark foreground and bright background, bottom: bright foreground and dark background). The third column shows how the contrast invariance property of the tree of shapes gives the advantage to work under several and nonuniform illumination conditions of image acquisition. The fourth column shows segmentations for LPs not in the tested datasets.

As we can see, the *char-grouping algorithm* has no need of rotation or skew correction, it is style independent and furthermore it is parameterless. Also, it works under changes in the scale of the license plate and under changes in contrast or illumination conditions. These properties are achieved without constraints on the style of license plate or a priori information.

Fig. 3. Examples of character segmentation using *char-grouping algorithm*

2.3   Character Recognition

A Support Vector Machine (SVM) based classifier is trained using the Histogram of Gradient (HoG) as features.

Histogram of Gradient. This feature uses gradient magnitude and orientation around a point of interest or in a region of the image to construct a histogram. The HoG feature space is composed of histograms obtained from rectangular regions shifted by one pixel inside the pattern, defined as follows.

Once a character is segmented, it is resized to a 16x12 pixels pattern and then applied a 3x3 Sobel filter. The gradient orientation of each pixel is quantized to integer values between 0 and 5 using modulo π instead of modulo 2π. In this way, dark on bright characters give the same orientation than bright on dark characters. For each pixel p in the pattern, we considered nine regions with p as top-left corner and sizes MxM, Mx2M, 2MxM, M $\in \{4, 6, 8\}$ to build the histograms. Then, the histograms are normalized to obtain their sum equals to 1.

Support vector machine. In this work, we train a SVM using *libsvm* library [2]. The strategy for the classification is the *One Against All* approach. The training characters are extracted from images labeled as non-deteriorated (see section 3) which are not included in the test dataset. We construct 35 binary (O and 0 are in the same class) SVM classifiers, each of which separates one character from the rest. To get the k-th SVM classifier the training dataset is composed as follows: the positive set correspond to samples from k-th class, and the negative set correspond to samples of other classes. In the testing phase, an input character (resized and normalized) is the input of each classifier. Then, it will be classified as the class that classifier produces the highest value.

Character recognition validation. The character recognition results are tested following the strategy developed in [11]. Two confidence values are estimated from the SVM classifiers outputs: c_r and c_d, that indicate classifier performance and discriminability, respectively. For each character, these values are calculated and the total performance is obtained performing the mean of these results, obtaining $\bar{c}_r$ and $\bar{c}_d$. If $\bar{c}_r < C_r$ and $\bar{c}_d < C_d$, all the operation is invalidated and the region is rejected. The thresholds C_d and C_d are estimated to validate the 99 % of the training dataset.

3   Experimental Results

We tested our LPR system performance on two datasets (see examples in Fig. 1). The first dataset, from now on called the USA dataset, is composed of 158 images tagged as non-deteriorated from the UCSD/Calit2 database [3]. These images were captured from outdoor parked cars and the license plates have different styles, containing alphanumeric characters without an established configuration. The second dataset, from now on called the ARG dataset[1], is composed of 439 truck images from Argentina. These images were acquired by an infrared camera placed at a truck entrance gate. All the images have the same style, but this style is not used to tune up the system. Both datasets were manually tagged with plate text, plate location and character bounding box. An extra label is added indicating if the image is deteriorated or non-deteriorated, where deteriorated images are those with a license plate which is too noisy, broken or incomplete. To validate a detection we check if the detected region intersects more than the half of the tagged region. In an analogous way, we validate the character segmentation. Also, character recognition is evaluated using the Levenshtein distance.

Additionally, we tested our system using Maximally Stable Extremal Regions (MSER) [7] in the segmentation step. The MSER has been widely used in many applications, including license plate recognition [4]. Two variants of MSER can be computed denoted as MSER+ and MSER-. The first detects bright regions with darker boundary, and the second detects dark regions with brighter boundary. For the purpose of character extraction, we set the sensitivity parameter $\Delta = 10$ and we filter out unstable or repeated regions.

Detection, segmentation and recognition rates for ARG and USA datasets are show in Table 1. The LPR system with *char-grouping algorithm* (CGA) and MSER, achieved similar detection performance rates as expected because the detection step is the same. However, the CGA outperforms MSER in 3 % in the segmentation step and therefore in recognition too, because character recognition strongly depends on the quality of the bounding boxes obtained by the segmentation step. Moreover, the MSER procedure needs information about the foreground-background contrast, e.g. MSER+ for ARG dataset and MSER- for USA dataset, resulting in a loss of the multi-style characteristic of the system. Also, CGA and MSER have better performance on the ARG dataset than on the USA database because of the difference in image acquisition conditions between both datasets.

---

[1] Available at http://www-2.dc.uba.ar/grupinv/imagenes/~fgomezf/lpr

Table 1. Detection, segmentation and recognition rates, using *char-grouping algorithm* (CGA) and Maximally Extremal Stable Regions (MSER+ and MSER-)

(a) ARG dataset

	Det	Seg	Rec
CGA	97.27	98.17	95.08
MSER+	97.04	95.54	92.18

(b) USA dataset

	Det	Seg	Rec
CGA	90.51	93.76	92.45
MSER-	89.12	90.47	89.27

4   Conclusions and Future Work

This work introduced a novel LPR system for multi-style license plates, which proposed a new algorithm for character extraction. This algorithm does not requires rotation or skew correction and is parameterless. Also, it has invariance under changes in scale, contrast, or affine changes in illumination. The quantitative and qualitative results shown in the previous sections, support the mentioned properties. Further work has to be done to study the adaptation of the detection thresholds without any a priori information. Also, we think that adding features to the nodes of the tree of shapes, like pixel distribution inside a bounding box, will enhance the comparison. Moreover, the need to extend the system to handle two-row LP is an important task to tackle in further studies.

References

1. Anagnostopoulos, C., Anagnostopoulos, I., Psoroulas, I., Loumos, V., Kayafas, E.: License plate recognition from still images and video sequences: A survey. IEEE Inteligent Transportation Systems 9(3), 377–391 (2008)
2. Chang, C.C., Lin, C.J.: LIBSVM: a library for support vector machines (2001), software http://www.csie.ntu.edu.tw/~cjlin/libsvm
3. Dlagnekov, L., Belongie, S.: Ucsd/calit2 car license plate, make and model database (2005), http://vision.ucsd.edu/car_data.html
4. Donoser, M., Arth, C., Bischof, H.: Detecting, tracking and recognizing license plates. In: Yagi, Y., Kang, S.B., Kweon, I.S., Zha, H. (eds.) ACCV 2007, Part II. LNCS, vol. 4844, pp. 447–456. Springer, Heidelberg (2007)
5. Wong, E.K., Chen, M.: A new robust algorithm for video text extraction. Pattern Recognition 36, 1397–1406 (2003)
6. Jiao, J., Ye, Q., Huang, Q.: A configurable method for multi-style license plate recognition. Pattern Recognition 42(3), 358–369 (2009)
7. Matas, J., Chum, O., Martin, U., Pajdla, T.: Robust wide baseline stereo from maximally stable extremal regions. BMVC 1, 384–393 (2002)
8. Monasse, P.: Morphological representation of digital images and application to registration. Ph.D. thesis, Université Paris IX-Dauphine (June 2000)
9. Negri, P., Tepper, M., Acevedo, D., Jacobo, J., Mejail, M.: Multiple clues for license plate detection and recognition. In: Bloch, I., Cesar Jr., R.M. (eds.) CIARP 2010. LNCS, vol. 6419, pp. 269–276. Springer, Heidelberg (2010)
10. Shapiro, V., Gluhchev, G., Dimov, D.: Towards a multinational car license plate recognition system. MVA 17, 173–183 (2006)
11. Thome, N., Vacavant, A., Robinault, L., Miguet, S.: A cognitive and video-based approach for multinational license plate recognition. MVA 21 (2010)

Feature and Dissimilarity Representations for the Sound-Based Recognition of Bird Species

José Francisco Ruiz-Muñoz[1], Mauricio Orozco-Alzate[1,2,*],
and César Germán Castellanos-Domínguez[1]

[1] Signal Processing and Recognition Group, Universidad Nacional de Colombia Sede
Manizales, km 7 vía al aeropuerto, Manizales (Caldas), Colombia
{jfruizmu,morozcoa,cgcastellanosd}@unal.edu.co
[2] Departamento de Informática y Computación, Universidad Nacional de Colombia
Sede Manizales, km 7 vía al aeropuerto, Manizales (Caldas), Colombia

Abstract. Pattern recognition and digital signal processing techniques
allow the design of automated systems for avian monitoring. They are a
non-intrusive and cost-effective way to perform surveys of bird populations and assessments of biological diversity. In this study, a number of
representation approaches for bird sounds are compared; namely, feature
and dissimilarity representations. In order to take into account the non-
stationary nature of the audio signals and to build robust dissimilarity
representations, the application of the Earth Mover's Distance (EMD) to
time-varying measurements is proposed. Measures of the leave-one-out
1-NN performance are used as comparison criteria. Results show that,
overall, the Mel-ceptrum coefficients are the best alternative; specially
when computed by frames and used in combination with EMD to generate dissimilarity representations.

Keywords: Automated avian monitoring, bird sounds, dissimilarity representations, feature representations.

1 Introduction

Advances in pattern recognition and digital signal processing allow the identification of bird species by their emitted sounds and, thereby, the design of
automated systems for avian monitoring. In spite of those advances, biodiversity
assessments have typically been carried out by visual inspection, which requires
human involvement and, therefore, may be expensive and have a limited coverage. In contrast, automatic acoustic monitoring is a non-intrusive and cost-
effective alternative that may provide good temporal and spatial coverages.

The simplest sounds in a bird song are called *elements* or *notes*. Several notes
together in a regular pattern in a song constitute a *syllable* and, in turn, several syllables are a *song phrase* [1]. Previous studies [2–4] have shown that the
sound-based recognition of bird species is suitable when considering syllables as

---

* Mauricio Orozco-Alzate is a member of Sociedad Caldense de Ornitología (SCO), a
regional ornithological society from Caldas, Colombia: http://rnoa.org/sco/

C. San Martin and S.-W. Kim (Eds.): CIARP 2011, LNCS 7042, pp. 451–458, 2011.

elementary units. Raw measurements corresponding to those elementary units have to be represented in vector spaces where classification rules can afterwards be applied. Representations for bioacoustic signals have traditionally been built by feature extraction; however, we advocate that dissimilarity representations are also a feasible option to face this problem. Furthermore, dissimilarities have the potential to build either simpler or richer representations; the later case, a richer representation, when considering for instance time-varying measurements that take into account non-stationarity. In this study, we evaluate different types of representations, including feature-based and dissimilarity-based ones, for bird sounds segmented into syllables.

Considered feature representations include the so-called *standard features* and a so-called *coarse representation of segment structure*; both of them include the syllable duration as well as features related to particular frequencies and maximum values in the frequency domain [2]. Besides, we evaluate a set of acoustical features, named in [3] and here as *descriptive features*, and the *Mel-cepstrum representation*, which is based on a linear cosine transform of a log power spectrum on a nonlinear Mel scale of frequency. Spectral analyses such as as the *Fast Fourier Transform* (FFT) and the *Parametric estimation of the Power spectral Density* (PSD) are simple initial representations to find dissimilarities between syllables. Such options to build dissimilarity representations are also considered. In addition, we calculate dissimilarities with richer spectral estimates, namely time-varying ones, that consist in dividing segments into frames and mapping each one into two-dimensional spectral or feature representations. The computation of dissimilarities between time-varying initial representations is carried out by using the *Earth Mover's Distance* (EMD), due to its usefulness to compare distributions.

The goodness of a particular representation can be roughly assessed by using measures of the leave-one-out nearest-neighbor (1-NN) performance. Such measures are commonly used as criteria when selecting features or prototypes for a representation [5]. We use them here as comparison values between the evaluated representations.

2   Methods

The design of a bird sound recognition system includes, at least, the following three stages: preprocessing, representation and performance evaluation. The first one consists in the segmentation of continuous records, whose objective is to detect intervals —according to the energy signal— where there are sounds emitted by birds. Consequently, it is assumed that bird sounds are located in signal regions with high energy levels. Steps of the segmentation stage are: computation of the energy signal, estimation of an energy threshold, search of syllables (regions having energies above a threshold), and the application of a criterion of deletion and merging of very short segments.

Regarding the second stage —representation— several methods of feature-based representations, commonly used in bioacoustics and bird sound classification, are compared in this paper. In addition, the dissimilarity-based approach is proposed as an alternative for representation. The last stage —performance evaluation— is carried out, as indicated at the end of Sec. 1, i.e. by using the leave-one-out 1-NN performance.

2.1 Feature Representations

Standard features: Segments are characterized by using four features as proposed in [2]; namely minimum and maximum frequencies, temporal duration and maximum power.

Coarse representation of segment structure: The following eleven variables, originally proposed in [2], are used as features for each segment: minimum and maximum frequencies, temporal duration and frequency of maximum power in eight non-overlapping frames.

Descriptive features: This set includes both temporal and spectral features. Segments are divided into overlapping frames of 256 samples with 50% overlap. For each frame, the following features are estimated: spectral centroid, signal bandwidth, spectral roll-off frequency, spectral flux, spectral flatness, zero crossing rate and short time energy. Feature vectors for classification are composed by mean and variance values of the feature trajectories along the frames. Frequency range (minimum and maximum frequencies), segment temporal duration and modulation spectrum (position and magnitude of the maximum peak in the modulation spectrum) are calculated from the entire segment. Therefore, 19 features are calculated with this method as proposed in [3].

Mel-cepstrum representation: Mel-frequency cepstral coefficients (MFCCs) are a feature representation method commonly used in many audio classification problems, e.g. in speech recognition. Mel-frequency scale is derived from the human perceptual system. Such systems in birds are not the same but exhibit similar characteristics; therefore, MFCCs have also been used in birdsong recognition [3, 4]. The first 12 MFCCs, the log-energy and the so-called delta and delta-delta coefficients are obtained for each frame. Their mean values along the frames are used as features, as proposed in [3].

2.2 Dissimilarity Representations

A dissimilarity representation consists in building vectorial spaces where coordinate axes represent dissimilarities —typically distance measures— to prototypes. In these spaces, classifiers can be built. In a full dissimilarity matrix, prototypes are all the elements available in a particular dataset. The matrix is often symmetric and must be real and have zero diagonal. "Dissimilarity representations can be derived in many ways, e.g. from raw (sensor) measurements such as images, histograms or spectra or, from an initial representation by features, strings or graphs" [5]. Considering that the analysis of signal properties is usually done in the frequency domain, we have calculated the spectrum for each signal by using two different approaches: FFT and PSD. Dissimilarity representations have been then computed by pointwise distances between spectra.

Dissimilarity representations, derived as described above, suppose that spectral behavior is similar in the entire segment. In order to obviate such an assumption, we also use representations that change over time (time-varying). In such a way, the acoustic space for each sound segment is efficiently covered [6]. Time-varying representations are computed by dividing sound segments into frames and converting each one to either a spectral or a feature representation. Feature sets measured for each frame were: 1) spectrogram, also known as *short time Fourier transform* (SFT); 2) PSD by using the Yule Walker method; 3) selected descriptive features (spectral centroid, signal bandwidth, spectral roll-off frequency, spectral flux, spectral flatness, zero crossing rate and short time energy); and 4) the Mel-cepstrum representation as explained in Sec. 2.1. Sets 3) and 4) must be standardized because features are not in same scale.

Measuring dissimilarities between representations: In the case of equally-sized representations (e.g. FFT or PSD) a classical measure, as the Euclidean distance, can be used. Conversely, the Euclidean distance can not be directly applied to time-varying representations. To overcome this difficulty, in this study we have used the EMD. Due to space constraints, we are not able to provide a description for this distance measure; see [7] and [6] for further implementation details.

3   Experimental Results

We performed a set of experiments on a dataset of raw field recordings taken at *Reserva Natural Río Blanco* in Manizales, Colombia. The sampling frequency of the recordings is 44.1 kHz. The dataset is composed by a total of 595 syllables distributed per species as follows[1]: *Grallaria ruficapilla* (GR, 33), *Henicorhina leucophrys* (HL, 64), *Mimus gilvus* (MG, 66), *Myadestes ralloides* (MR, 58), *Pitangus sulphuratus* (PS, 53), *Pyrrhomyias cinnamomea* (PC, 36), *Troglodytes aedon* (TA, 33), *Turdus ignobilis* (TI, 74), *Turdus serranus* (TS, 78), *Xiphocolaptes promeropirhynchus* (XP, 46) and *Zonotrichia capensis* (ZC, 54).

Evaluation for each representation was assessed by using measures of the leave-one-out 1-NN performance. For each representation, a confusion matrix is reported. In addition, the following performance measures per class are presented: True Positive rate (TP), False Positive rate (FP), Accuracy (ACC) and F1 score. Results are shown in Tables 1-4.

---

[1] Scientific names are indicated together with a pair (Abbreviation, Number of syllables).

Table 1. Results for feature representations

(a) Standard features

	GR	HL	MG	MR	PS	PC	TA	TI	TS	XP	ZC	Total	TP	FP	ACC	F1
GR	21	0	0	3	1	3	0	0	1	4	0	33	63.64	1.60	96.47	66.67
HL	1	35	8	2	4	0	7	1	2	3	1	64	54.69	4.33	91.26	57.38
MG	0	6	28	4	10	4	5	2	3	1	3	66	42.42	5.67	88.57	45.16
MR	1	1	3	39	3	5	0	3	3	0	0	58	67.24	2.98	94.12	69.03
PS	0	2	4	2	36	1	2	1	3	2	0	53	67.92	4.98	92.61	62.07
PC	2	1	4	2	0	24	0	0	0	3	0	36	66.67	2.50	95.63	64.86
TA	0	6	3	0	2	0	21	0	0	0	1	33	63.64	3.02	95.13	59.15
TI	0	0	1	1	0	0	1	67	3	1	0	74	90.54	2.30	96.81	87.58
TS	1	5	5	2	4	1	0	4	52	1	3	78	66.67	3.87	92.27	69.33
XP	2	1	1	0	1	0	0	0	1	39	1	46	84.78	2.91	96.13	77.23
ZC	2	1	1	0	2	0	2	1	4	1	40	54	74.07	1.66	96.13	77.67
Total	30	58	58	55	63	38	38	79	72	55	49	595				

Total accuracy = 67.56%

(b) Coarse representation of segment structure

	GR	HL	MG	MR	PS	PC	TA	TI	TS	XP	ZC	Total	TP	FP	ACC	F1
GR	27	0	3	0	0	0	0	0	3	0	0	33	81.82	0.71	98.32	84.38
HL	1	45	2	2	3	0	4	1	2	3	1	64	70.31	2.07	94.96	75.00
MG	0	1	43	2	2	3	1	0	11	2	1	66	65.15	4.73	91.93	64.18
MR	0	0	1	41	1	6	0	1	7	1	0	58	70.69	2.98	94.45	71.30
PS	2	0	6	1	40	0	0	0	4	0	0	53	75.47	2.21	95.80	76.19
PC	0	0	1	6	0	25	1	0	1	1	1	36	69.44	2.50	95.80	66.67
TA	0	5	1	0	3	1	22	0	0	0	1	33	66.67	1.78	96.47	67.69
TI	0	1	2	1	0	0	0	65	3	2	0	74	87.84	0.77	97.82	90.91
TS	0	2	6	2	0	3	1	2	60	1	1	78	76.92	5.61	92.10	71.86
XP	0	0	1	1	1	0	0	0	1	42	0	46	91.30	2.37	97.14	83.17
ZC	1	2	2	1	2	1	3	0	1	0	41	54	75.93	1.11	96.81	81.19
Total	31	56	68	57	52	39	32	69	89	55	47	595				

Total accuracy = 75.80%

(c) Descriptive features

	GR	HL	MG	MR	PS	PC	TA	TI	TS	XP	ZC	Total	TP	FP	ACC	F1
GR	33	0	0	0	0	0	0	0	0	0	0	33	100.00	0.36	99.66	97.06
HL	0	54	1	0	0	0	7	1	1	0	0	64	84.38	1.88	96.64	84.38
MG	1	2	58	1	3	0	0	0	1	0	0	66	87.88	1.51	97.31	87.88
MR	0	0	2	54	0	0	0	1	0	0	1	58	93.10	0.93	98.49	92.31
PS	0	0	0	0	52	0	0	0	1	0	0	53	98.11	0.74	99.16	95.41
PC	0	0	0	1	0	34	1	0	0	0	0	36	94.44	0.00	99.66	97.14
TA	0	5	2	0	0	0	26	0	0	0	0	33	78.79	1.42	97.48	77.61
TI	0	0	1	0	0	0	0	72	1	0	0	74	97.30	0.38	99.33	97.30
TS	0	3	1	1	1	0	0	0	70	1	0	78	89.74	0.77	97.98	92.11
XP	0	0	0	0	0	0	0	0	0	46	0	46	100.00	0.18	99.83	98.92
ZC	1	0	1	2	0	0	0	0	0	0	50	54	92.59	0.37	98.99	94.34
Total	32	64	65	59	56	34	34	74	74	47	52	595				

Total accuracy = 92.27%

(d) Mel-cepstrum representation

	GR	HL	MG	MR	PS	PC	TA	TI	TS	XP	ZC	Total	TP	FP	ACC	F1
GR	33	0	0	0	0	0	0	0	0	0	0	33	100.00	0.00	100.00	100.00
HL	0	58	0	0	0	0	5	0	0	1	0	64	90.63	1.69	97.48	88.55
MG	0	0	66	0	0	0	0	0	0	0	0	66	100.00	0.38	99.66	98.51
MR	0	1	0	54	1	0	0	0	0	0	1	58	93.10	0.19	99.16	95.58
PS	0	0	0	0	53	0	0	0	0	0	0	53	100.00	0.37	99.66	98.15
PC	0	0	0	1	0	34	0	0	0	0	0	36	94.44	0.18	99.50	95.77
TA	0	5	0	0	0	0	28	0	0	0	0	33	84.85	1.25	97.98	82.35
TI	0	0	1	0	0	0	1	70	0	2	0	74	94.59	0.38	98.99	95.89
TS	0	3	1	0	0	1	0	2	69	1	1	78	88.46	0.58	97.98	92.00
XP	0	0	0	0	1	0	0	0	2	43	0	46	100.00	0.18	99.83	98.92
ZC	0	0	0	0	0	0	0	0	0	0	54	54	100.00	0.37	99.66	98.18
Total	33	67	68	55	55	35	35	72	72	47	56	595				

Total accuracy = 94.45%

Table 2. Results for dissimilarity representations computed from 1-D spectra

(a) Spectra computed by FFT

				Predicted								Total	TP	FP	ACC	F1
	GR	HL	MG	MR	PS	PC	TA	TI	TS	XP	ZC					
GR	20	4	1	0	1	0	1	1	1	0	4	33	60.61	1.42	96.47	65.57
HL	0	28	6	3	1	4	7	6	3	1	5	64	43.75	7.91	86.89	41.79
MG	1	5	35	1	7	1	0	7	4	4	1	66	53.03	7.18	88.40	50.36
MR	0	2	0	33	2	0	1	6	5	0	9	58	56.90	5.03	91.26	55.93
PS	1	1	3	5	35	1	0	4	2	0	1	53	66.04	3.87	93.45	64.22
PC	1	6	1	1	0	17	1	1	6	0	2	36	47.22	3.76	93.28	45.95
TA	1	6	4	0	2	1	13	0	1	2	3	33	39.39	1.78	94.96	46.43
TI	1	5	7	3	1	3	0	40	10	3	1	74	54.05	7.49	87.73	52.29
TS	2	5	8	4	5	7	0	10	29	5	3	78	37.18	8.12	84.71	38.93
XP	0	5	8	0	1	1	0	2	6	21	2	46	45.65	2.73	93.28	51.22
ZC	1	3	0	10	1	3	0	2	4	0	30	54	55.56	5.73	90.76	52.17
Total	28	70	73	60	56	38	23	79	71	36	61	595				

Total accuracy = 50.58%

(b) Spectra computed by PSD

				Predicted								Total	TP	FP	ACC	F1
	GR	HL	MG	MR	PS	PC	TA	TI	TS	XP	ZC					
GR	31	0	1	0	0	0	0	0	0	1	0	33	93.94	0.18	99.50	95.38
HL	0	48	3	1	1	0	5	0	1	1	4	64	75.00	3.39	94.29	73.85
MG	0	4	44	1	2	0	1	3	6	5	0	66	66.67	2.65	93.95	70.97
MR	0	1	0	46	1	2	0	2	5	0	1	58	79.31	0.93	97.14	84.40
PS	0	1	0	0	41	2	0	1	3	4	1	53	77.36	2.03	96.13	78.10
PC	0	0	0	0	0	34	1	0	1	0	0	36	94.44	0.89	98.82	90.67
TA	0	6	2	1	0	0	23	1	0	0	0	33	69.70	1.60	96.81	70.77
TI	0	0	1	1	1	0	0	71	0	0	0	74	95.95	2.11	97.65	91.03
TS	0	2	2	1	4	1	0	3	58	7	0	78	74.36	3.29	93.78	75.82
XP	1	2	5	0	2	0	1	1	1	33	0	46	71.74	3.28	94.79	68.04
ZC	0	2	0	0	0	1	0	0	0	0	51	54	94.44	1.11	98.49	91.89
Total	32	66	58	51	52	39	32	82	75	51	57	595				

Total accuracy = 80.67%

Table 3. Results for dissimilarity representations derived from:

(a) SFT

				Predicted								Total	TP	FP	ACC	F1
	GR	HL	MG	MR	PS	PC	TA	TI	TS	XP	ZC					
GR	33	0	0	0	0	0	0	0	0	0	0	33	100.00	0.00	100.00	100.00
HL	0	58	1	0	0	0	5	0	0	0	0	64	90.62	1.51	97.65	89.23
MG	0	2	59	0	0	0	1	3	1	3	0	66	89.39	0.76	98.15	91.47
MR	0	1	0	52	0	0	1	0	4	0	0	58	89.66	0.00	98.99	94.55
PS	0	0	0	0	50	0	1	0	1	1	0	53	94.34	0.18	99.33	96.15
PC	0	0	0	0	0	36	0	0	0	0	0	36	100.00	0.00	99.83	98.63
TA	0	5	0	0	0	0	26	0	1	1	0	33	78.79	1.60	97.31	76.47
TI	0	0	1	0	0	0	1	72	0	0	0	74	97.30	0.19	99.50	97.96
TS	0	0	0	0	0	1	0	0	76	1	0	78	97.44	1.74	98.15	93.25
XP	0	0	2	0	0	0	0	0	2	44	0	46	95.65	0.73	98.99	93.62
ZC	0	0	0	0	1	0	1	0	0	0	52	54	96.30	0.00	99.66	98.11
Total	33	66	63	52	51	37	35	73	85	48	52	595				

Total accuracy = 93.78%

(b) Time-varying PSD

				Predicted								Total	TP	FP	ACC	F1
	GR	HL	MG	MR	PS	PC	TA	TI	TS	XP	ZC					
GR	33	0	0	0	0	0	0	0	0	0	0	33	100.00	0.00	100.00	100.00
HL	0	53	2	0	0	0	7	0	2	0	0	64	82.81	3.01	95.46	79.70
MG	0	1	56	0	0	0	4	0	4	0	1	66	84.85	1.89	96.64	84.85
MR	0	2	0	47	1	0	2	0	5	0	1	58	81.03	0.37	97.82	87.85
PS	0	1	1	0	45	0	0	1	3	2	0	53	84.91	0.55	98.15	89.11
PC	0	1	0	0	0	33	1	0	1	0	0	36	91.67	0.54	98.99	91.67
TA	0	5	0	0	0	0	27	0	0	1	0	33	81.82	1.96	97.14	76.06
TI	0	0	2	1	1	0	0	68	1	0	0	74	91.89	0.77	98.32	93.15
TS	0	1	2	1	0	1	0	3	64	6	0	78	82.05	3.68	94.45	79.50
XP	0	1	3	0	0	0	0	2	40	0	0	46	86.96	2.37	96.81	80.81
ZC	0	4	0	0	1	1	0	0	1	0	47	54	87.04	0.18	98.66	92.16
Total	33	69	66	49	48	36	38	72	83	53	48	595				

Total accuracy = 86.22%

Table 4. Results for dissimilarity representations derived for frame-based:

(a) Descriptive features

	GR	HL	MG	MR	PS	PC	TA	TI	TS	XP	ZC	Total	TP	FP	ACC	F1
GR	33	0	0	0	0	0	0	0	0	0	0	33	100.00	0.00	100.00	100.00
HL	0	56	0	0	0	0	5	0	3	0	0	64	87.50	1.13	97.65	88.89
MG	0	0	65	0	1	0	0	0	0	0	0	66	98.48	0.57	99.33	97.01
MR	0	0	0	55	0	0	0	0	0	1	2	58	94.83	0.19	99.33	96.49
PS	0	0	0	0	53	0	0	0	0	0	0	53	100.00	0.18	99.83	99.07
PC	0	0	0	0	0	35	0	0	1	0	0	36	97.22	0.00	99.83	98.59
TA	0	5	0	0	0	0	28	0	0	0	0	33	84.85	0.89	98.32	84.85
TI	0	0	1	0	0	0	0	72	1	0	0	74	97.30	0.19	99.50	97.96
TS	0	0	2	0	0	0	0	1	74	0	1	78	94.87	1.35	98.15	93.08
XP	0	0	0	0	0	0	0	0	0	46	0	46	100.00	0.18	99.83	98.92
ZC	0	1	0	1	0	0	0	0	2	0	50	54	92.59	0.55	98.82	93.46
Total	33	62	68	56	54	35	33	73	81	47	53	595				

Total accuracy = 95.29%

(b) Mel-Cepstrum

	GR	HL	MG	MR	PS	PC	TA	TI	TS	XP	ZC	Total	TP	FP	ACC	F1
GR	33	0	0	0	0	0	0	0	0	0	0	33	100.00	0.00	100.00	100.00
HL	0	59	0	0	0	0	5	0	0	0	0	64	92.19	0.94	98.32	92.19
MG	0	0	66	0	0	0	0	0	0	0	0	66	100.00	0.00	100.00	100.00
MR	0	0	0	58	0	0	0	0	0	0	0	58	100.00	0.19	99.83	99.15
PS	0	0	0	0	53	0	0	0	0	0	0	53	100.00	0.00	100.00	100.00
PC	0	0	0	0	0	36	0	0	0	0	0	36	100.00	0.00	100.00	100.00
TA	0	5	0	0	0	0	28	0	0	0	0	33	84.85	0.89	98.32	84.85
TI	0	0	0	1	0	0	0	73	0	0	0	74	98.95	0.00	99.83	99.32
TS	0	0	0	0	0	0	0	0	78	0	0	78	100.00	0.19	98.83	99.36
XP	0	0	0	0	0	0	0	0	0	46	0	46	100.00	0.00	100.00	100.00
ZC	0	0	0	0	0	0	0	0	1	0	53	54	98.15	0.00	99.83	99.07
Total	33	64	66	59	53	36	33	73	79	46	53	595				

Total accuracy = 97.98%

In order to obtain an overall impression of the one-against-all subproblems, the above-reported confusion matrices were summed across all the representations. As a result, the following observations can be made: In ascending order, the total number of syllables that were erroneously assigned to each class (FP) were: 24 (GR), 59 (PC), 60 (ZC), 74 (MR), 76 (TI), 82 (PS), 85 (XP), 91 (TA), 134 (MG), 148 (HL) and 151 (TS). Similarly, the number of syllables that were erroneously assigned to other classes (FN), in ascending order, were: 33 (GR), 52 (PC), 60 (XP), 70 (TI), 72 (PS), 72 (ZC), 88 (TA), 101 (MR), 140 (MG), 146 (HL) and 150 (TS). In consequence, the easiest identification corresponds to GR and the most difficult ones are HL, MG and MR. Notice also that the most frequent confusions are those between HL and TA.

4   Discussion

In this paper, three approaches for representing bird sounds have been analyzed: 1) feature representations, 2) dissimilarity representations for signals in the frequency domain and 3) dissimilarity representations for time-varying signal transforms. Representations —for each approach— with the highest accuracies were Mel-cepstrum representation (Table 1(d)), dissimilarity representation for PSDs (Table 2(b)) and dissimilarity representations for time-varying Mel-cepstrum (Table 4(b)); respectively. The last one was the representation with the overall highest total accuracy. In general, all representations have good accuracies per class; however, in this case, accuracy is not a reliable performance measure due to the unbalanced nature of the multiclass problem, i.e. the sample size of a class is much smaller than the combined sample size of the rest of the classes. In this case, the F1 score gives more confident results.

Mel-cepstrum and descriptive features showed a good performance in both feature and dissimilarity representations, as expected because those representations are specifically designed for audio recognition. The dissimilarity representation for PSDs, in spite of being a rather simple representation, yielded an acceptable performance with a total accuracy of 80.67%. Performances of dissimilarity representations for time-varying signal transforms are remarkable. This fact reveals the importance of taking into account the non-stationarity; which is observable by comparing results of dissimilarity representations computed for FFTs, the poorest ones with a total accuracy of 50.58%, and results of the dissimilarity representations for time-varying FFTs (SFTs) that had a total accuracy of 93.78%. In the case of PSDs, the performance also increased when deriving dissimilarities for time-varying transforms but in less proportion, with a total accuracy of 86.22%.

In summary, we conclude that Mel-cepstrum coefficients are suitable for bird sound representation, even more when dissimilarities are computed from them; i.e. when non-stationarity is taken into account. Furthemore, classifying in dissimilarity spaces derived from time-varying representations was found to be preferable instead of doing so in the corresponding 1-D representations.

Acknowledgments. This research is supported by "Programa Jóvenes Investigadores e Innovadores 2010, Convenio Interadministrativo Especial de Cooperación No. 146 de enero 24 de 2011 entre COLCIENCIAS y la Universidad Nacional de Colombia Sede Manizales" and the research program "Fortalecimiento de capacidades conjuntas para el procesamiento y análisis de información ambiental" (code Hermes-12677) funded by Universidad Nacional de Colombia.

References

1. Brenowitz, E., Margoliash, D., Nordeen, K.: An introduction to birdsong and the avian song system. Journal of Neurobiology 33(5), 495–500 (1997)
2. Acevedo, M.A., Corrada-Bravo, C.J., Corrada-Bravo, H., Villanueva-Rivera, L.J., Aide, T.M.: Automated classification of bird and amphibian calls using machine learning: A comparison of methods. Ecological Informatics 4(4), 206–214 (2009)
3. Fagerlund, S.: Bird species recognition using support vector machines. EURASIP Journal on Advances in Signal Processing 2007(1), 64–64 (2007)
4. Chou, C., Liu, P., Cai, B.: On the Studies of Syllable Segmentation and Improving MFCCs for Automatic Birdsong Recognition. In: Asia-Pacific Services Computing Conference, APSCC 2008, pp. 745–750. IEEE (2009)
5. Pękalska, E., Duin, R.P.W., Paclík, P.: Prototype selection for dissimilarity-based classifiers. Pattern Recognition 39(2), 189–208 (2006)
6. Logan, B., Salomon, A.: A music similarity function based on signal analysis. In: IEEE International Conference on Multimedia and Expo, ICME 2001, pp. 745–748 (August 2001)
7. Rubner, Y., Tomasi, C., Guibas, L.: The Earth Mover's Distance as a Metric for Image Retrieval. International Journal of Computer Vision 40(2), 99–121 (2000)

Environmental Sounds Classification Based on Visual Features

Sameh Souli[1] and Zied Lachiri[1,2]

[1] Signal, Image and pattern recognition research unit
Dept. of Genie Electrique, ENIT
BP 37, 1002, Le Belvédère, Tunisia
soulisameh@yahoo.fr
[2] Dept. of Physique and Instrumentation, INSAT
BP 676, 1080, Centre Urbain, Tunisia
zied.lachiri@enit.rnu.tn

Abstract. This paper presents a method aimed at classification of the environmental sounds in the visual domain by using the scale and translation invariance. We present a new approach that extracts visual features from sound spectrograms. We suggest to apply support vector machines (SVM's) in order to address sound classification. Indeed, in the proposed method we explore sound spectrograms as texture images, and extracts the time-frequency structures by using a translation-invariant wavelet transform and a patch transform alternated with local maximum and global maximum to pursuit scale and translation invariance. We illustrate the performance of this method on an audio database, which composed of 10 sounds classes. The obtained recognition rate is of the order 91.82 % with the multiclass decomposition method: One-Against-One.

Keywords: Environmental sounds, Visual features, Translation-invariant wavelet transform, Spectrogram, SVM Multiclass.

1 Introduction

The environmental sound classification has for purpose the identification of some everyday life sound classes. It is about an elementary task participant in the conception of remote monitoring systems for the securing urban transport, the assistance to the old persons, etc.

For a long time, choosing suitable features for environmental sounds is a basic problem in audio signal processing. The environmental sound classification system can achieve important results for surveillance and security applications. Many previous works [9], [10] and [11] have concentrated on classification of environmental sound, which used in extraction phase an audio feature vector with a very limited components number like Line Spectral Frequencies (LSF's), spectral energy distribution, Linear-Frequencies Cepstral Coefficients (LFCCs). Many other studies [1] and [2], used a combination of audio features such as wavelet-based features, MFCCs, individual temporal and frequency features. The majority of these

C. San Martin and S.-W. Kim (Eds.): CIARP 2011, LNCS 7042, pp. 459–466, 2011.
© Springer-Verlag Berlin Heidelberg 2011

studies focus on the acoustic features derived from linear models of sound production. Indeed, this work presents a classification of the environmental sounds in the visual domain by processing the time-frequency representation sounds as texture images. In the time-frequency plan the descriptors extraction method is based on using the wavelet technique followed by a local maximum application of the obtained wavelet coefficients. A patch transform is then applied to group together the similar time-frequency geometries, followed by a research for a global maximum to select a representative time-frequency structure. The classification phase is realized by using SVM's with the multiclass One-Against-One and One-Against-Rest methods.

This paper is organized in four parts. Section 2 presents the advantage of using sound environmental spectrogram, describes the visual feature extraction method and depicts the classification algorithm. Classification results are given in Section 3. Finally conclusions are presented in Section 4.

2   Description of the Classification System

In this paper, first we apply a time-frequency transformation on the signal to obtain the spectrogram. Then, we pass into the phase of characteristics extraction from the resulting spectrogram. This extraction uses the scale and translation invariance [3]. Finally, we adopt the SVM's for the classification phase.

2.1   Visual Features Extraction

A spectrogram is an energy representation of signal, obtained by Short-time Fourier transform, it displays several distinctive characteristics [12]. Therefore, a spectrogram is compact and the most efficient representation to observe the complete spectrum of environmental sounds and to express sound by combining the merit of time and frequency domains [13]. Furthermore, we can easily identify the spectrograms of environmental sounds by their contrast, since they are considered as different textures [14]. These observations show that the spectrograms contain characteristics that can be used to differentiate between different classes of environmental sounds [15].

After the signal spectrogram calculation [14], we extracted visual features based on translation-invariant wavelet transform, followed by a particular patch transform and a global selection operation [16].

In this paper, the algorithm is based on the following steps:

Step 1 : Translation-invariant wavelet transform. Let $S[x, y]$ be a spectrogram of the size $N_1 \times N_2$. We used the translation-invariant wavelet transform. The resulting wavelet coefficients will be defined by:

$$Wf(u, v, j, k) = \sum_{x=1}^{N_1} \sum_{y=1}^{N_2} S[x, y] \frac{1}{2^j} \psi^k (\frac{x-u, y-v}{2^j}) . \tag{1}$$

Where $k = 1,2,3$ is the orientation (horizontal, vertical, diagonal), $\psi^k(x, y)$ is the wavelet function. Indeed, to build a translation- invariant wavelet representation, the scale is made discrete but not the translation parameter. The scale is sampled on a dyadic analysis $\left\{2^{j}\right\}_{j\in Z}$. The use of the translation-invariant wavelet transform creates a redundancy of information that allows keeping the translation-invariance at all levels of factorization [7]. The scale invariance is carried out by normalization, using the following formula:

$$S_1(u,v,j,k) = \frac{\left|Wf(u,v,j,k)\right|}{\|S\|^2_{\sup p\left(\psi_j^k\right)}}. \qquad (2)$$

Where $\|S\|^2_{\sup p\left(\psi_j^k\right)}$ is the energy of detail wavelet coefficients of a spectrogram.

Step 2 : Local Maximum. The continuation of translation invariance [3] and [16], is done by calculating the local maximum of S_1 :

$$C_1(u,v,,j,k) = \max_{u'\in\left[2^j(u-1)+1,2^j u\right),v'\in\left[2^j(v-1)+1,2^j v\right)} S_1(u',v',j,k). \qquad (3)$$

The C_1 section is obtained by a subsampling of S_1 using a cell grid of the $2^j \times 2^j$ size   that is then followed by the local maximum. Generally, the maximum being taken at each j scale and k direction of a spatial neighborhood of a size that is proportional to $2^j \times 2^j$. The resulting C_1 at the j scale and the k direction is therefore of the $N_1/2^j \times N_2/2^j$ size, where $j = 1,2,3$.

Step 3 : Patch Transform. The idea consists of selecting N prototypes P_i of C_1, then the scalar product is calculated between the prototypes P_i and the C_1 coefficients, then followed by a sum [11] . For every patch, we get only one scalar at the end.

$$S_2(u,v,j,i) = \sum_{u'=1}^{N_1/2^j} \sum_{v'=1}^{N_2/2^j} \sum_{k=1}^{3} C_1(u',v',j,k)P_i(u'-u,v'-v,k). \qquad (4)$$

Where P_i of size $M_i \times M_i \times 3$ are the patch functions that group 3 wavelet orientations. The patch functions are extracted by a simple sampling at a random scale and a random position of the C_1 coefficients of a spectrogram [3], for instance a P_0 patch of the $M_0 \times M_0$ size contains $M_0 \times M_0 \times 3$ elements, M_0 may take the following values $(M_0 = 4,8,12)$.

Step 4: Global Maximum. The C_2 coefficients are obtained by the application of the max function on S_2 :

$$C_2(i) = \max_{u,v,j} S_2(u,v,j,i) .$$ (5)

In this work, the obtained result is a vector of NC_2 values, where N corresponds to the number of extracted patches. In this way, the C_2 obtained coefficients constitute the parameter vector for the classification.

2.2 SVM Classification

The classification is performed using a new technique of statistic learning: Support Vector Machines. The SVM's is a tool for creating practical algorithms for estimating multidimensional functions [4].

Let a set of data $(x_1, y_1),...,(x_m, y_m) \in \Re^d \times \{\pm 1\}$ where $X = \{x_1,...,x_m\}$ a dataset in $\Re^d$ where each x_i is the feature vector of a signal. In the nonlinear case, the idea is to use a kernel function $k(x_i, x_j)$, where $k(x_i, x_j)$ satisfies the Mercer conditions [5]. Here, we used a Gaussian RBF kernel whose formula is:

$$k(x, x') = \exp\left[-\|x - x'\|^2 / 2\gamma^2 \right] .$$ (6)

Where $\|.\|$ indicates the Euclidean norm in $\Re^d$.

Let Ω be a nonlinear function which transforms the space of entry $\Re^d$ to an intern space H called a feature space. Ω allows to perform a mapping to a large space in which the linear separation of data is possible [8].

$$\Omega : \Re^d \rightarrow H$$
$$(x_i, x_j) \mapsto \Omega(x_i)\Omega(x_j) = k(x_i, x_j)$$ (7)

The H space is a reproducing kernel Hilbert space (RKHS).

Thus, the dual problem is presented by a Lagrangian formulation as follows:

$$\max W(\alpha) = \sum_{i=0}^{m} \alpha_i - \frac{1}{2} \sum_{i,j=1}^{m} y_i y_j \alpha_i \alpha_j k(x_i, x_j), i = 1,...,m .$$ (8)

Under the following constraints:

$$\sum_{i=1}^{m} \alpha_i y_i = 0, \ 0 \le \alpha_i \le C .$$ (9)

They α_i are called Lagrange multipliers and C is a regularization parameter which is used to allow classification errors. The decision function will be formulated as follows:

$$f(x) = \text{sgn}(\sum_{i=1}^{m} \alpha_i y_i k(x, x_i) + b). \tag{10}$$

We hence adopted two approaches of multiclass classification: One-against-the-Rest and One-against-One. The first method one-against-the-rest builds K models of binary SVM. The SVM model assigns the label '1' for the class C_k and the supplementary label '-1' to all the remaining classes. The second method one-against-one, consists of creating a binary classification of each possible combination of classes, the result for K classes $K(K-1)/2$. The classification is then carried out in accordance with the majority voting scheme [6].

3 Experimental Results

Our corpus of sounds comes from commercial CDs [18]. Among the sounds of the corpus we find: explosions, broken glass, door slamming, gunshot, etc. We used 10 classes of environmental sounds as shown in Table 1.

All signals have a resolution of 16 bits and a sampling frequency of 44100 Hz that is characterized by a good temporal resolution and a wide frequency band. Most of the signals are impulsive, we took 2/3 for the training and 1/3 for the test. Each spectrogram is segmented into 8 non-overlapping segments. Each segment is composed of 64 samples.

For each signal, firstly we apply a time-frequency transformation, then the resultant spectrogram passes by the various stages of the proposed-visual characteristic extraction method. Finally, the obtained feature vector passed for the classification phase by using SVM's. Among the big problems met during the classification by the SVM's is the choice of the values of the kernel parameter γ and the constant of regularization C. To resolve this problem we used the cross-validation method. Indeed, according to [17], this method consists in setting up a grid-search for γ and C. For the implementation of this grid, it is necessary to proceed

Table 1. Classes of sounds and number of samples in the database used for performance evaluation

Classes	Train	Test	Total number
Door slams	208	104	312
Explosions	38	18	56
Class breaking	38	18	56
Dog barks	32	16	48
Phone rings	32	16	48
Children voices	54	26	80
Gunshots	150	74	224
Human screams	48	24	72
Machines	38	18	56
Cymbals	32	16	48
Total	670	330	1000

iteratively, by creating a couple of values γ and C. In this work, we use the following couples C, γ : C=[$2^{(0)}$, $2^{(1)}$, ..., $2^{(16)}$] et γ=[$2^{(15)}$, $2^{(-14)}$, ..., $2^{(2)}$].

In Table 2, we present the results obtained with various classes of sound and different C, γ settings of Gaussian RBF kernel. After learning phase, we test firstly the train data then the test data. We remark that the classification rate is different from one class to another. We were able to achieve an averaged accuracy rate of the order 91.82% in ten classes with one-against-one approach. There are seven classes that have a classification rate higher than 90%. But with one-against-all approach we obtained an averaged accuracy rate of the order 87.90%.

The obtained results by our classification system in nine classes of environmental sounds, with one-against-one approach, is satisfactory. Indeed, we reached a recognition

Table 2. Recognition rates for visual feature applied to one-vs-all and one-vs-one SVMs based classifiers

Classes	Kernel	Parameters (C,γ)	Multiclass Approach	Classification rate(%)		Execution Time(s)
				Train	Test	
Door slams	Gaussien	$(2^{(1)}, 2^{(-7)})$	One-vs-all	91.42	85.71	147.45
	RBF	$(2^{(1)}, 2^{(-7)})$	One-vs-One	94.28	90.47	7.91
Explosions	Gaussien	$(2^{(-5)}, 2^{(-15)})$	One-vs-all	91.28	90.47	113.19
	RBF	$(2^{(3)}, 2^{(-5)})$	One-vs-One	94.28	95.23	7.96
Class breaking	Gaussien	$(2^{(1)}, 2^{(-9)})$	One-vs-all	98,46	97,43	147.94
	RBF	$(2^{(1)}, 2^{(-7)})$	One-vs-One	97.94	97.43	7.96
Dog barks	Gaussien	$(2^{(0)}, 2^{(-8)})$	One-vs-all	90.00	83.33	113.02
	RBF	$(2^{(1)}, 2^{(-7)})$	One-vs-One	93.33	88.88	7.91
Phone rings	Gaussien	$(2^{(0)}, 2^{(-6)})$	One-vs-all	90.00	77.77	111.01
	RBF	$(2^{(2)}, 2^{(-6)})$	One-vs-One	93.33	83.33	8.01
Children voices	Gaussien	$(2^{(3)}, 2^{(-7)})$	One-vs-all	94.00	90.00	112.57
	RBF	$(2^{(1)}, 2^{(-7)})$	One-vs-One	96.00	93.33	7.88
Gunshots	Gaussien	$(2^{(5)}, 2^{(-5)})$	One-vs-all	97,85	96,42	112.77
	RBF	$(2^{(0)}, 2^{(-15)})$	One-vs-One	98.57	97.61	7.97
Human screams	Gaussien	$(2^{(0)}, 2^{(-4)})$	One-vs-all	93.33	88.88	141.32
	RBF	$(2^{(1)}, 2^{(-7)})$	One-vs-One	95.55	92.59	7.69
Machines	Gaussien	$(2^{(12)}, 2^{(2)})$	One-vs-all	91.42	85.71	112.35
	RBF	$(2^{(5)}, 2^{(-3)})$	One-vs-One	94.28	90.47	7.80
Cymbals	Gaussien	$(2^{(8)}, 2^{(-2)})$	One-vs-all	90.00	83.33	122.20
	RBF	$(2^{(2)}, 2^{(-6)})$	One-vs-One	93.33	88.88	8.56

rate of the order 92.14% with visual descriptors, but in [2] the obtained classification rate is of 90.23%, whose method is to extract from the signal the following descriptors: MFCCs, Energy and Log energy. Furthermore, by combining wavelet-based features, MFCCs, individual temporal and frequency features, "Rabaoui, et al " [2] have attained a recognition rate of the order 93.22% with the same classes and the same classification approach that we have adopted. It proves that our result is efficient compared to the number of the used characteristics parameters.

The adjustment of the extraction method of visual features, used in image processing, to the special characteristics of the environmental sounds has given satisfactory and improved classification results. Furthermore, the used feature vector represent all relevant time-frequency information in the signals to recognize.

4   Conclusion

This paper presents a new approach for environmental sound classification in the visual domain by processing spectrogram as texture images. Indeed this approach is based on the use of wavelet technique followed by a local maximum then a patch transform, and finally by a global maximum. The obtained results are very satisfactory (91.82 % with the method one-against-one and 87.90 % with the method one-against-all). The proposed approach can be improved while digging deeply into the visual domain.

Acknowledgments. We are grateful to G. Yu for many discussions by mail.

References

1. Chu, S., Narayanan, S., Kuo, C.C.J.: Environmental Sound Recognition with Time-Frequency Audio Features. IEEE Trans. on Speech, Audio, and Language Processing 17, 1142–1158 (2009)
2. Rabaoui, A., Davy, M., Rossignol, S., Ellouze, N.: Using One-Class SVMs and Wavelets for Audio Surveillance. IEEE Transactions on Information Forensics and Security 3, 763–775 (2008)
3. Schulz-Mir, H., Serre, T., Wolf, L., Bileschi, S., Riesenhuber, M., Poggio, T.: Robust Object Recognition with Cortex-Like Mechanisms. IEEE Transactions Pattern Analysis and Machine Intelligence 29, 411–426 (2007)
4. Vladimir, V., Vapnik, N.: An Overview of Statistical Learning Theory. IEEE Transactions on Neural Networks 10, 988–999 (1999)
5. Vapnik, V., Chapelle, O.: Bounds on error expectation for support vector machines. Neural Computation 12 (2000)
6. Hsu, C.-W., Lin, C.-J.: A comparison of methods for multi-class support vector machines. IEEE Transactions on Neural Networks 13, 415–425 (2002)
7. Mallat, S.: A Wavelet Tour of Signal Processing, 2nd edn. Academic Press (1999)
8. Scholkopf, B., Smola, A.: Learning with Kernels. MIT Press (2001)
9. El-Maleh, K., Samouelian, A., Kabal, P.: Frame-Level Noise Classification in Mobile Environments. In: Proc. ICASSP, Phoenix, AZ, pp. 237–240 (1999)

10. Dufaux, A., Besacier, L., Ansorge, M., Pellandini, F.: Automatic Sound Detection and Recognition For Noisy Environment. In: Proceedings of European Signal Processing Conference (EUSIPCO), Tampere, FI, pp. 1033–1036 (2000)
11. Fleury, A., Noury, N., Vacher, M., Glasson, H., Serigna, J.-F.: Sound and Speech Detection and classification in a Health Smart Home. In: 30th Annual Int. Conf. IEEE, Engineering in Medicine and Biology Society (EMBS), Canada, pp. 4644–4647 (2008)
12. He, L., Lech, M., Maddage, N.: Stress and Emotion Recognition Using Log-Gabor Filter Analysis of Speech Spectrograms. In: 3rd Int. Conf. Affective Computing and Intelligent Interaction and Workshops, ACII, Amsterdam, pp. 1–6 (2009)
13. Xinyi, Z., Jianxiao, Y., Qiang, H.: Research of STRAIGHT Spectrogram and Difference Subspace Algorithm for Speech Recognition. In: Int. Congress on Image and Signal Processing (CISP 2009), IEEE DOI Link 0910, pp. 1–4 (2009)
14. Yu, G., Slotine, J.J.: Audio Classification from Time-Frequency Texture. In: Proc. IEEE Int. Conf. on Acoustics, Speech and Signal Processing (ICASSP), Taipei, pp. 1677–1680 (2009)
15. He, L., Lech, M., Maddage, N.C., Allen, N.: Stress Detection Using Speech Spectrograms and Sigma-pi Neuron Units. In: Fifth Int. Conf. on Natural Computation, pp. 260–264 (2009)
16. Yu, G., Sloine, J.J.: Fast Wavelet-based Visual Classification. In: Proc. IEEE ICPR, Tampa (2008)
17. Hsu, C.-W., Chang, C-C., Lin, C-J.: A practical Guide to Support Vector Classification. Department of Computer Science and Information Engineering National, Taipei, Taiwan (2009)
18. Leonardo Software, Santa Monica, CA 90401, http://www.leonardosoft.com

Quaternion Correlation Filters for Illumination Invariant Face Recognition

Dayron Rizo-Rodriguez[1], Heydi Méndez-Vázquez[1], Edel García[1],
César San Martín[2], and Pablo Meza[3]

[1] Advanced Technologies Application Center. 7a # 21812 b/ 218 and 222,
Rpto. Siboney, Playa, P.C. 12200, Havana, Cuba
{drizo,hmendez,egarcia}@cenatav.co.cu
[2] Center for Optics and Photonics, University of La Frontera,
Casilla 54-D, Temuco, Chile
cesarsanmartin@ufro.cl
[3] Center for Optics and Photonics, University of Concepción,
Casilla 160-C, Concepción, Chile
pablomeza@udec.cl

Abstract. Illumination variations is one of the factors that causes the degradation of face recognition systems performance. The representation of face image features using the structure of quaternion numbers is a novel way to alleviate the illumination effects on face images. In this paper a comparison of different quaternion representations, based on verification and identification experiments, is presented. Four different face features approaches are used to construct quaternion representations. A quaternion correlation filter is used as similarity measure, allowing to process together all the information encapsulated in quaternion components. The experiment results confirms that using quaternion algebra together with existing face recognition techniques permits to obtain more discriminative and illumination invariant methods.

1 Introduction

Variations in lighting conditions is one of the principal factors causing the deterioration of face recognition systems performance [1]. Several methods have been proposed to cope with the problem of face recognition under illumination variation [2]. Among them, in [3] taking into account the benefits of the use of quaternion algebra in image processing [4], an illumination invariant face image representation based on quaternion number structure was presented. Two representations, a complex and a quaternion one, based on image image differentiation, were constructed and compared regarding their illumination invariant properties. Both representations are transformed into frequency domain and cartesian and polar expressions are obtained. The most illumination invariant component of each representation is selected and used as face image descriptor. A simple normalized correlation is used as similarity measure. In that work [3], experimental results showed that quaternion representation is better

C. San Martin and S.-W. Kim (Eds.): CIARP 2011, LNCS 7042, pp. 467–474, 2011.
© Springer-Verlag Berlin Heidelberg 2011

than the complex one, regarding illumination invariant and discriminative properties. However, only one component of quaternion representation is used as face image descriptor, discarding the remaining ones, where valuable discriminative information could be encapsulated. On the other hand, using the normalized correlation as similarity measure only permits to process one component at a time. More powerful tools are needed in order to use together all the components of quaternion representation to analyze face images.

Quaternion correlation filters have been specially designed for face recognition [5]. In [5], a multi-band processing analysis is performed, using discrete wavelet decomposition, to obtain the quaternion representation. The wavelet decomposition is used because directly provides a multi-resolution analysis of the image, however other face image extraction techniques can be used in order to obtain more illumination invariant and discriminative representations.

The aim of this work, is to compare the performance of quaternion correlation filters based on different face images representations, when dealing with illumination variations. Besides image differentiation and discrete wavelet decomposition, used in previous works for extracting the multi-band information of face images from which the quaternion representation is constructed, discrete cosine transform (DCT) and local binary patterns (LBP) are selected among different face images descriptors, because of the well known behavior of these methods in front of illumination variations [6,7]. The unconstrained optimal tradeoff quaternion filter (UOTQF) presented in [5], based on the traditional unconstrained optimal tradeoff filter (UOTF), is used to perform the cross-correlation based on each quaternion representation.

Verification and identification experiments were conducted in XM2VTS and Extended Yale B databases respectively. The quaternion representation constructed from LBP features showed the best performance in both face recognition experiments. The paper is organized as follows. In Section 2, face image decomposition to construct the quaternion frequency domain representation are described. In Section 3, the construction of quaternion correlation filter and its use in the recognition process is explained. The experimental results are drawn in Section 4. Finally, Section 5 gives the conclusions of the paper.

2   Face Images Quaternion Representation

Quaternion algebra was the first hypercomplex number system to be discovered, introduced by Hamilton in 1843 [8]. The cartesian representation of quaternion numbers is usually defined as follows:

$$q = a + b\mathbf{i} + c\mathbf{j} + d\mathbf{k} \qquad (1)$$

where a, b, c, d are real and $\mathbf{i}$, $\mathbf{j}$, $\mathbf{k}$ are orthogonal imaginary operators.

Based on Eq.(1), a general expression for face images quaternion representation, at pixel (x, y), can be defined as:

$$q(x, y) = Q_1(x, y) + Q_2(x, y)i + Q_3(x, y)j + Q_4(x, y)k \qquad (2)$$

where $Q_1(x, y)$, $Q_2(x, y)$, $Q_3(x, y)$ and $Q_4(x, y)$ would be four descriptions of the image at (x,y) coordinate, using some face feature extraction method.

Then, to construct the face image quaternion description, the first step is to decompose the image in four bands of information. For this purpose, different feature extraction methods are evaluated in this work: image differentiation, discrete wavelet decomposition, discrete cosine transform and local binary patterns.

Image differentiation (DIF) has shown to be a face image descriptor less sensitive to illumination effects [9]. In [9], first order derivatives of the images, in x and y directions, are used to assemble a complex representation of face images. Calculating again first order derivatives, in x and y directions, over each one of these components, results in four descriptions of the images which actually are the second order derivatives of the image: $\nabla^2_{xx}I(x, y)$, $\nabla^2_{xy}I(x, y)$, $\nabla^2_{yx}I(x, y)$ and $\nabla^2_{yy}I(x, y)$. In this way, the quaternion representation based on image differentiation, can be expressed as:

$$q_{DIF}(x, y) = \nabla^2_{xx}I(x, y) + \nabla^2_{xy}I(x, y)\mathbf{i} + \nabla^2_{yx}I(x, y)\mathbf{j} + \nabla^2_{yy}I(x, y)\mathbf{k} \quad (3)$$

In practice, image differentiation is implemented by convolving the signal with some form of linear filter that approximates derivative operator. In our case a Sobel filter, the one applied in [9], was used. In Figure 1(a), the above DIF decomposition process is graphically illustrated.

The wavelet transform can be used to decompose an image into different scales and resolutions. When applying the discrete wavelet decomposition (DWT), the face image is passed through a low pass filter and a high pass filter to get the low and high frequency components of the original image. This process is applied iteratively to the low and high frequency bands in order to obtain the representation at different scales and resolutions. The implementation of this process is made by projecting the original image to the wavelet basis function. In [5] the Daubechies family of wavelets is used to decompose the face images into four subbands: *low-low*(LL), *low-high*(LH), *high-low*(HL) and *high-high*(HH), which are encoded in the quaternion representation as in Eq.(4). The illustration of this process can be found on Figure 1(b).

$$q_{DWT}(x, y) = W_{LL}(x, y) + W_{LH}(x, y)\mathbf{i} + W_{HL}(x, y)\mathbf{j} + W_{HH}(x, y)\mathbf{k} \quad (4)$$

The discrete cosine transform (DCT) has been very used in face recognition. In [7], a method using the DCT to compensate for illumination variations was presented. The illumination variations are compensated, setting to zero the low-frequency DCT coefficients of an image in the logarithm domain and reconstructing a normalized image applying the inverse DCT. Varying the low-frequency coefficients used for the illumination compensation, a multi-resolution representation can be obtained, discarding and retaining different information of the face image each time. In Figure 1(c), four face images obtained by applying this process with different low-frequency DCT coefficients each time, are shown. The quaternion representation using this method can be expressed as:

$$q_{DCT}(x, y) = DCT_{L1}(x, y) + DCT_{L2}(x, y)\mathbf{i} + DCT_{L3}(x, y)\mathbf{j} + DCT_{L4}(x, y)\mathbf{k} \quad (5)$$

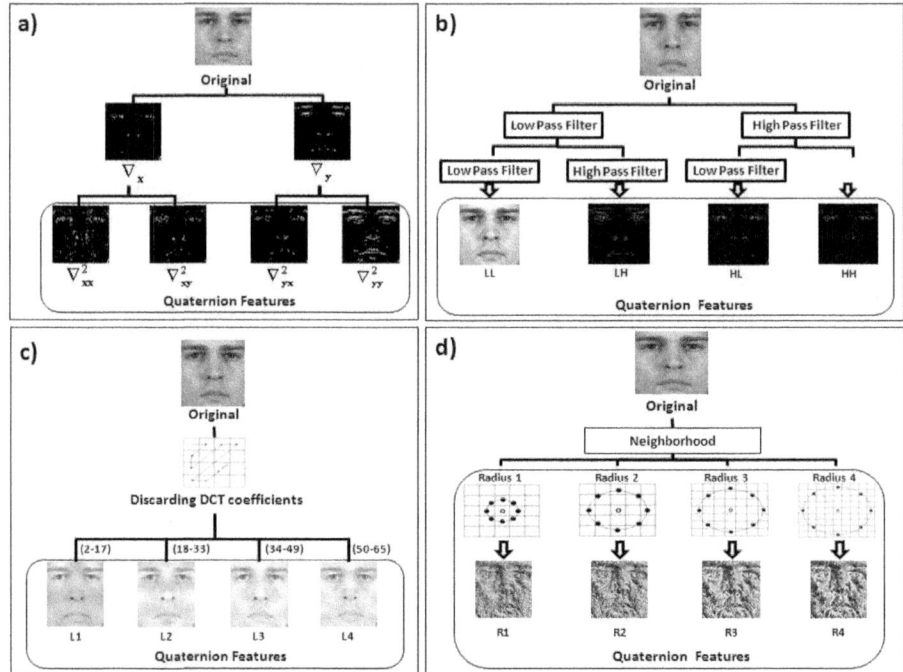

Fig. 1. Illustration of the processes of obtaining the four bands of information needed for quaternion representation, using each one of the face feature extraction method described: a) DIF, b) DWT, c) DCT and d) LBP

The local binary patterns operator (LBP) is a texture descriptor which has been very used in face analysis based on the idea that faces are composed by micro-patterns which can be well described by this operator [6]. The original LBP operator labels each pixel of an image with a value called LBP code, which corresponds to a binary number that represents its relation with the 3x3-local neighborhood. Different extensions of the original operator have been proposed. Among them, the multi-scale LBP [10], permits to codify the LBP operators at different neighborhood sizes, providing a multi-resolution analysis of face images. For the assembling of quaternion representation in Eq.(6), the LBP operator at four different radii are computed as it is shown in Figure 1(d).

$$q_{LBP}(x,y) = LBP_{R1}(x,y) + LBP_{R2}(x,y)\mathbf{i} + LBP_{R3}(x,y)\mathbf{j} + LBP_{R4}(x,y)\mathbf{k} \quad (6)$$

3   Quaternion Correlation Filters

The use of quaternion correlation filters in face recognition involves enrollment and recognition stages. During enrollment, the first step is to transform the quaternion description of training images, obtained with some of the processes described above, to the frequency domain.

The quaternion descriptions are transformed to the frequency domain, using Quaternion Discrete Fourier Transform (QDFT) [11] defined as:

$$Q(p, s) = \sum_{m=0}^{M-1} \sum_{n=0}^{N-1} e^{-\mu 2\pi((pm/M)+(sn/M))} q(m, n) \tag{7}$$

where μ is any unit pure quaternion and q is the training face images quaternion representation in the form of Eq.(2).

The quaternion correlation filter is designed based on the QDFT of the training images. The unconstrained optimal tradeoff quaternion filter (UOTQF), proposed in [5], is used for this purpose. The derivation of this filter is similar to the one of the traditional unconstrained optimal tradeoff filter (UOTF) [12], and has the following closed form solution:

$$h = \gamma(\alpha D + C)^{-1} m \tag{8}$$

where h is the designed frequency domain filter represented in the vector form, m represents the frequency domain training image in the vector form, α and γ are tradeoff parameters, which can be tuned to obtain the optimal tradeoff between maximizing the discrimination ability and minimizing the output noise variance of the filter h. D is a diagonal matrix, where the main diagonal is the average power spectrum of the training images and C is also a diagonal matrix, representing the noise power spectral density (psd). Typically a white noise model is assumed, thus C takes the form of an identity matrix. In this formulation of the UOTQF filter, all vector and matrix terms are quaternion number arrays, while for the UOTF filters they are all complex number arrays.

The UOTQF are computed and stored for each subject on the training set. Then, at recognition stage, each testing image is transformed into quaternion frequency domain by applying Eq.(7) and it is cross-correlated with every UOTQF obtained at training.

Following [5], the specialized 2-D quaternion correlation (QC), is used for the cross-correlation computation. From the magnitude value of each quaternion correlation output, a similarity score is computed. A large peak value in correlation output plane is yielded in case of a genuine identity and no discernible peaks for an impostor. The fitness measure of the peak sharpness is calculated using the peak-to-sidelobe-ratio (PSR), defined in [5].

4   Experimental Evaluation

In order to compare the behavior of the quaternion representations based on the four selected face descriptors, verification and identification experiments were conducted in XM2VTS [13] and Extended Yale B [14] databases respectively.

4.1   Verification Experiment

Configuration I of the Lausanne protocol [13], designed for experiments on XM2VTS database, was used to compare the performance of the different representations on a face verification setting. Under this configuration, the 2360 face

Table 1. Verification Results in terms of TER (%)

	Eval.	Test	Dark
Q1 DIF	33.67	29.24	51.48
DWT	32.60	27.05	49.87
DIF	23.55	20.64	41.54
DCT	58.33	55.68	75.90
LBP	22.00	18.56	40.68

Table 2. Recognition Rates (%) obtained in Identification Experiment

	S1	S2	S3	S4	S5
Q1 DIF	100.0	100.0	93.14	38.60	06.05
DWT	98.22	100.0	73.71	44.73	11.92
DIF	100.0	100.0	99.24	97.15	59.07
DCT	59.11	58.33	19.42	16.66	30.60
LBP	99.56	100.0	97.71	95.83	82.92

images of 295 subject on the database, are divided into a Training, an Evaluation and a Test sets, composed of images under controlled illumination conditions used as clients and imposters. An additional set (Dark) which contains images of every subject under non regular lighting conditions is used to test the behavior of the methods in the presence of this kind of variations.

In a verification setup, the False Rejection Rate (FRR) and the False Acceptance Rate (FAR) are used as a measure of algorithms performance. The Equal Error Rate (EER), is the point where FRR = FAR. Under the selected protocol, the similarity value obtained by the classification method at this point in the Evaluation set is used as a threshold for the decision of acceptance or rejection in the Test and Dark sets.

The Total Error Rate (TER), which is the sum of FRR and FAR, is computed for each set of the database when applying the quaternion correlation filters using the four alternatives described in previous sections. The obtained results are shown in Table 1. The first row of the table corresponds to the results obtained in [3], where only one component of the quaternion representation based on DIF is selected and used as face descriptor.

It can be appreciated in the table, that quaternion correlation filters based on DIF and LBP outperform the one proposed in [5] based on DWT whether images are affected by illumination variations (Dark set) or not (Evaluation and Test sets). On the other hand, these results are also superior to use only one component of the quaternion representation. In general, the LBP method exhibits the best results in all sets of the database, while DCT achieved the worst results.

4.2   Identification Experiment

The Extended Yale B [14] database was used to conducted the identification experiments. It contains images of 28 subjects under 64 different illumination conditions. This database is usually divided into 6 subsets according to the angle of the incident illumination. Face images with frontal lighting are used as gallery and subsets S1, S2, S3, S4 and S5 grouped the images in a way that S1 contains the ones with minor variations and S5 the most affected images.

The recognition rates obtained in each subset of the database using the correlation filters based on the four representations are shown in Table 2. Also in this case, the results obtained with only one component of the quaternion

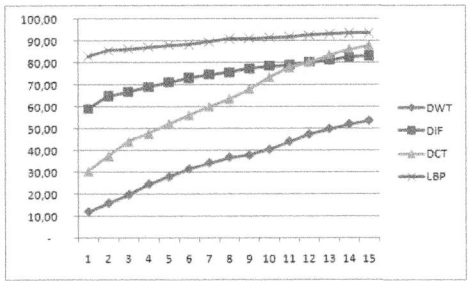

Fig. 2. Cumulative match score vs. rank curve in S5

is included in the first row of the table. Besides, in Figure 2, which represents the cumulative match score vs. rank curve, is illustrated the behavior of the four quaternion correlation filters in S5, the most difficult one respect to the illumination variations.

From the table, the quaternion filter based on DIF presents the best results in subsets S1, S2 S3 and S4, following by the one based on LBP for a little margin. However in S5, where the illumination variations are the greatest, the LBP method perform much better, which is corroborated in Figure 2, being the only method achieving more than 90% of correct classification in this subset. In this case, both LBP and DIF representation, and even the one based on DCT, perform significantly better than the one based on DWT and the use of the normalize cross-correlation of only one component of the quaternion.

5   Discussion and Conclusions

This paper presents a comparison of quaternion correlation filters based on different face images representations. Quaternion representations based on DIF, DWT, DCT and LBP are constructed and cross-correlated using the unconstrained optimal tradeoff quaternion filter (UOTQF).

The obtained results in verification and identification, confirm the hypothesis that using jointly the multi-band information encoded in a quaternion representation permits to retain more discriminative information of face images than only one component even though this is the most invariant one. On the other hand, selecting adequate face image descriptors, it is possible to improve the face recognition results on an specific problem.

In this case, the LBP method was selected because of its well known behavior dealing with the illumination problem on face recognition [6]. As was expected, the quaternion representation based on this face descriptor achieves the better results in the conducted experiments. Surprisingly, the DCT method, which has been also very used for illumination invariant face recognition [7], achieved the worst result. We think that the multi-resolution analysis based on this method and the way in which the DCT coefficients are discarded to form the quaternion need to be improved.

It can be concluded that quaternion algebra is a powerful mathematical tool that can lead to excellent results in face recognition problems, specially because of the possibility of encapsulating and processing together the multi-band information. For the continuity of this work, it is necessary to obtain better face descriptors and to analyze other correlation filters on quaternion domain, in order to improve the recognition results.

References

1. Adini, Y., Moses, Y., Ullman, S.: Face recognition: The problem of compensating for changes in illumination direction. IEEE Transactions on Pattern Analysis and Machine Intelligence 19(7) (1997)
2. Zou, X., Kittler, J., Messer, K.: Illumination invariant face recognition: A survey. In: BTAS 2007 (September 2007)
3. Rizo-Rodríguez, D., Méndez-Vázquez, H., García-Reyes, E.: Illumination Invariant Face Image Representation Using Quaternions. In: Bloch, I., Cesar Jr., R.M. (eds.) CIARP 2010. LNCS, vol. 6419, pp. 434–441. Springer, Heidelberg (2010)
4. Bayro, E.: Geometric Computing for Perception Action Systems, pp. 115–136. Springer, New York (2001)
5. Chunyan, X., Savvides, M., Vijayakumar, B.: Quaternion correlation filters for face recognition in wavelet domain. In: Proc. IEEE Int. Conf. on Acoustics, Speech, and Signal Processing (2005)
6. Marcel, S., Rodriguez, Y., Heusch, G.: On the recent use of local binary patterns for face authentication. International Journal on Image and Video Processing Special Issue on Facial Image Processing (2007) IDIAP-RR 06-34
7. Chen, W., Er, M.J., Wu, S.: Illumination compensation and normalization for robust face recognition using discrete cosine transform in logarithm domain. IEEE Transactions on Systems, Man and Cybernetics, Part B 36(2), 458–466 (2006)
8. Hamilton, W.: Elements of Quaternions. Longmans, Green, London, UK (1866)
9. Garea, E., Kittler, J., Messer, K., Mendez, H.: An illumination insensitive representation for face verification in the frequency domain. In: IEEE Computer Society, ICPR 2006, pp. 215–218 (2006)
10. Ojala, T., Pietikäinen, M., Mäenpää, T.: Multiresolution gray-scale and rotation invariant texture classification with local binary patterns. IEEE Transactions on Pattern Analysis and Machine Intelligence 24(7), 971–987 (2002)
11. Moxey, C., Sangwine, S., Ell, T.: Hypercomplex correlation techniques for vector images. IEEE Transaction on Signal Processing 51, 1941–1953 (2003)
12. Vijayakumar, B., Savvides, K., Venkataramani, K., Xie, C.: Spatial frequency domain image processing for biometric recognition. In: IEEE International Conference on Image Processing, pp. 53–56 (2002)
13. Messer, K., Matas, J., Kittler, J., Jonsson, K.: Xm2vtsdb: The extended m2vts database. In: Second International Conference on Audio and Video-based Biometric Person Authentication, pp. 72–77 (1999)
14. Lee, K.C., Ho, J., Kriegman, D.J.: Acquiring linear subspaces for face recognition under variable lighting. IEEE Transactions on Pattern Analysis and Machine Intelligence 27(5), 684–698 (2005)

Language Modelization and Categorization for Voice-Activated QA

Joan Pastor, Lluís-F. Hurtado, Encarna Segarra, and Emilio Sanchis

Grup d'Enginyeria del Llenguatge Natural i Reconeixement de Formes,
Department de Sistemes Informàtics i Computació,
Universitat Politècnica de València, València, Spain
{jpastor,lhurtado,esegarra,esanchis}@dsic.upv.es
http://dsic.upv.es/users/elirf

Abstract. The interest of the incorporation of voice interfaces to the
Question Answering systems has increased in recent years. In this work,
we present an approach to the Automatic Speech Recognition component
of a Voice-Activated Question Answering system, focusing our interest in
building a language model able to include as many relevant words from
the document repository as possible, but also representing the general
syntactic structure of typical questions. We have applied these technique
to the recognition of questions of the CLEF QA 2003-2006 contests.

Keywords: Voice-Activated Question Answering, Automatic Speech
Recognition, Language Models, Named Entities Recognition.

1 Introduction

In recent years the interest in the development of applications for accessing to
large non structured repositories of information of different types, such as text,
audio, video, or images has increased. Evaluation conferences, such as TREC[1]
and CLEF[2], organize multiple tracks in order to compare the behavior of the
different approaches proposed. One of these tracks is Question Answering (QA),
which goal is to access to information repositories, accepting questions in natural
language.

At this moment, most of the QA systems accept written sentences as input,
but in the last years the interest in using voice to ask the questions has increased
[10,8], as well as in accessing to large audio repositories. In order to develop
real world applications, it would be interesting to design speech-driven systems
providing access to information from mobile telephones, tablets or other speech
interfaces. The Automatic Speech Recognition (ASR) component of this kind of
systems has to present some specific features: to be able to deal with a large
vocabulary, to provide a good language model that characterizes the type of
questions, and to be prepared to correctly recognize some relevant words that

---

[1] http://trec.nist.gov
[2] http://www.clef-campaign.org

C. San Martin and S.-W. Kim (Eds.): CIARP 2011, LNCS 7042, pp. 475–482, 2011.
© Springer-Verlag Berlin Heidelberg 2011

have a great influence in the posterior answer searching process. In particular, the recognition of Named Entities (NE) is one of the main problems to be faced in question answering applications with speech input. NEs are key elements for the search process [5], so misrecognition of a spoken NE can produce serious errors in the search results. Some works related to the NE recognition problem are [1,7,6].

In the literature it has shown that, in general, better results in NE recognition [5] imply better performance of the Voice-activated QA system. In a previous work in our laboratory, some experiments were carried out with the QUASAR QA system [11] with the aim of studying the effect on the QA system accuracy of the word error rate introduced by the ASR system, especially from the perspective of the recognition of NEs. The experiments with simulated speech input (i.e., errors in the input questions -200 questions of the CLEF 2005 Spanish monolingual test set- were introduced) showed that when recognition errors do not affect NEs, the QA system performance is still good, even with a WER of 25%. Error rates greater than 30% made the system behavior deteriorate quickly.

In this work, we present an approach to the ASR component of a QA system, focusing our interest in the language modelization for questions, and in the influence of categorization of relevant words, such as NEs, in the system performance. The language modelization proposed is based on keeping the specific characteristics of the syntax of questions, but adding to the ASR vocabulary different sets of relevant words in order to increase the coverage. In order to determine what are the relevant word candidates to be included in the ASR vocabulary, we have used a Part-of-Speech (POS) tagging tool [9] to find NEs and common nouns in the document repository. Based on their frequency we built different sets of relevant words to study the behavior of the recognition process.

We have applied these technique to the recognition of questions of the CLEF QA 2003-2006 contests. The corpus consist of a set of questions and the target collection (the set of documents to be searched in order to find the answer) composed by documents of the EFE (Spanish news agency) of the years 1994 and 1995. Due to the correlation of the performance of the ASR system and the performance of the whole Voice-Activated QA system, we have decided to give the results in terms of the performance of the ASR system. The experimentation carried out shows that the categorized language models outperform the language model learned only with training questions.

This article is organized as follows, Section 2 presents the adaption in the vocabulary and language model of the ASR system for spoken question recognition. Section 3 presents the experimental set-up. Section 4 presents the results of the evaluation of the performance of the ASR depending on the language model and the amount of the relevant words in the vocabulary. Finally, some conclusions are presented in Section 5.

2   Language Model Estimation

In this section, we are going to describe our proposal for language model estimation for Voice-Activated QA. In this work, we have focused on the data pre-processing for training a suitable language model in order to achieve better performance in Voice-Activated QA. The main idea is to build a language model able to include as many NEs and other relevant words from the document repository as possible, but also representing the general syntactic structure of typical questions extracted from training data (*eg. Who is...?, When did... ? What is... ?*). To do that, it is necessary to build a categorized language model where the categories are related to the concepts that could be asked by the user.

Figure 1 shows how the language model for the ASR has been built. We use two different corpora to train the language model. One of them is the set including the training questions, from which the syntactic structure is estimated, and the other one is the document repository, from which the additional information to generalize the categorized language model is obtained. It is interesting to note that not all training *queries* are formulated in an interrogative way (*e.g. What is the capital of France?*) but some are in a declarative way (*e.g. Name some tennis players.*), so our model has to be aware of this in order to have a better recognition performance.

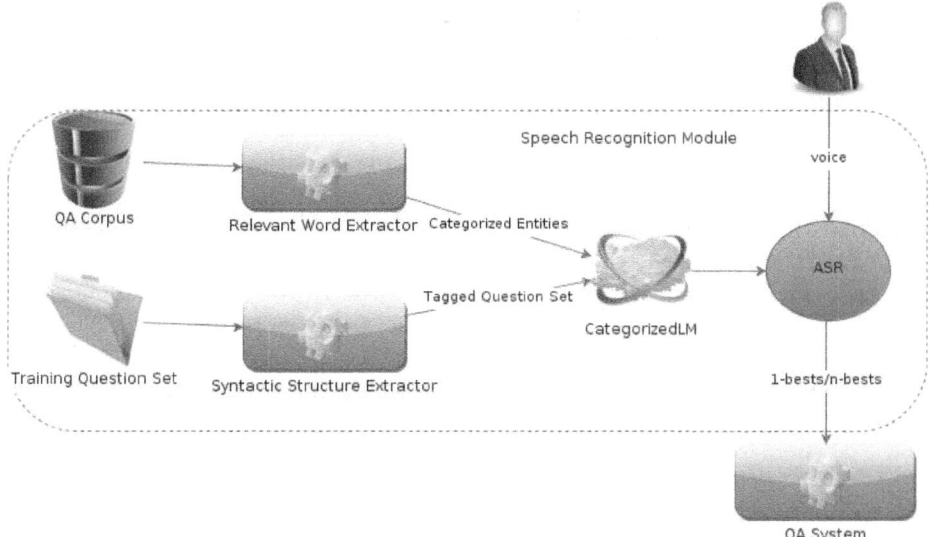

Fig. 1. Speech Recognition Module

2.1   Categorized Language Model

In order to incorporate relevant information to the language model, we have to select which relevant words can be categorized. To do that, after deciding which categories must been selected a POS tagging process is applied in order to obtain the instances of the different categories from the document repository. The key point of our experimentation concerns the amount of relevant words to be included in the language model. The categories used in our language model are:

- Named Entities: usually is the main concept which has been asked by the user.
- Dates and numbers: not all possible combinations of dates (year, month and day) and numbers are included in the training set.
- Common Nouns (CNs): in some cases NEs are not the main concept of the question, or simply there are not in the question. In other cases not only the NE but also some common nouns provides the relevant information to find the answer (e.g Who is the *president* of France?).
- The rest of the words, where, formally, each word belongs to its own class (*i.e.* one class per word).

2.2   Category Members Selection

First, for retrieving the categorized data, we use FreeLing POS Tagging feature [9,2,3]. The words belonging to any of the categories previously described are replaced by their specific tag in the training question set.

Second, we perform the same POS tagging process to the document repository (the target collection where the information has to be retrieved) and we extract the frequency sorted lists of NEs and CNs. The NE list includes more than one million of different elements. Analyzing this set, we have checked that most of these NEs appear just a few times, sometimes due to orthographic mistakes. If we filter out all the NEs that appear less than 10 times, the number of remaining NEs is around 80, 000 and if the threshold is 20 times then the amount of NEs is reduced to around 48, 000. We can assume that the most common NEs in the corpus are the most likely to appear in a question, so they would be added to our NE set, which will be provided as an input to the ASR component. Something similar occurs with the CNs; in this case, the 4, 000 more frequent CNs cover more than the 85% of the CNs present in the training questions.

Each word tagged as NEs or CNs during the tagging process has a confidence score of belonging to that category. Figure 2 shows how the coverage of NEs and CNs increases as more items are included in each category considering only those words with a score of belonging to the category higher than a threshold. It can be seen that the use of different threshold has no influence on the coverage of NEs. Regarding CNs, the more permissive you are the more coverage you get.

2.3   Orthographic Entity Merging

The document repository is a heterogeneous collection of documents that includes all the news published by the EFE agency along two years. For this reason, there are some NEs that appears written in different ways. Usually, these NEs have several orthographic transcriptions with the same phonetic transcription (*e.g, Korea and Corea, Qatar and Catar*).

To avoid this problem, we have merged the entities with the same phonetic transcription keeping the orthographic transcription of the most frequent one. To do that, we have used the Grapheme-to-phoneme tool Ort2Fon [4].

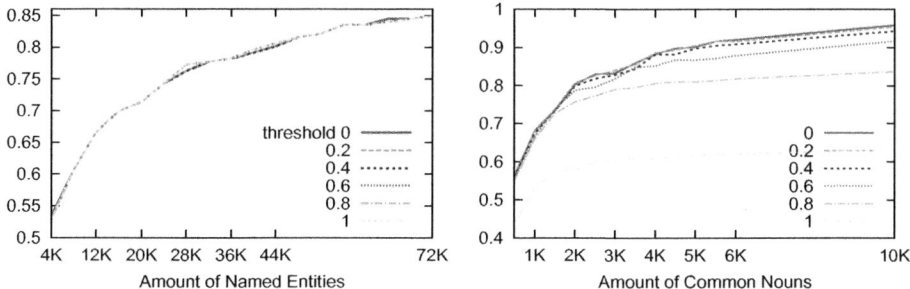

Fig. 2. NE/CN Coverage

There are some especial cases where two different entities has the same phonetic transcription (*e.g Baldi and Valdi*). In this case, due to the fact that the ASR is unable to discriminate between them, the most frequent one is used.

3 Experimentation

3.1 Evaluation Metrics

The most commonly used parameter to measure the performance of ASR is the Word Error Rate (*WER*). Another criterion which indicates the performance of the language model regardless of the ASR used is the percentage of Out-of-Vocabulary words (*OOV*). In addition to WER and OOV, we have defined some other measures related to the recognition of relevant words:

- *NE_ACC*: Named Entities accuracy. A good indicator of the performance of the global Voice-Activated QA system would be determine the set of test NEs properly recognized by the ASR.
- *CN_ACC*: Common Nouns accuracy. In the way that NEs accuracy, CNs accuracy would be a good indicator of the performance of the Voice-Activated QA system.
- *WER_SW*: WER without considering stop words. Usually, stop words are not taken into account by the QA systems.

3.2 Experimental Setup

In our experiments, we have used the questions from the CLEF QA 2003-2006 contests in Spanish. The document repository (the set of documents to be searched in order to find the answer) is composed by documents of the EFE

(Spanish news agency) of the years 1994 and 1995. The set of questions amounts to $1,800$ questions divided in two subsets: $1,600$ for training and 200 for test. The 200 test questions were acquired by an specific user and are used as input of the ASR.

For the experimentation, three different language models were applied:

- *Single NEs model*: using an incremental number of NE between $4,000$ and $48,000$ in order to check how an increase of the amount of NE affects to the performance of the recognizer.
- *NEs Modified model*: using the same number of entities as in the previous model, but including the phonetic approach described in section 2.3.
- *NEs/CNs Modified model*: using the same entities as in the *NE Model Modified Model* and including an amount of $4,000$ CNs.

4   Results

Table 1 presents the results of the experimentation, It is also included, as a baseline, the language model trained only with the training questions without either categorization nor generalization (*Plane training model*). This Table only shows the best results for each one of the language models. Figure 3 shows, for each model, how the number of relevant words in the model affects the different proposed measures.

Table 1. Experimental results summary

	WER	NE_ACC	CN_ACC	WER_SW	OOV
Plane Training model	0.384	0.420	0.768	0.449	0.222
Single NEs Model (best)	0.326	0.551	0.825	0.402	0.133
NEs Modified Model (best)	0.315	0.546	0.817	0.389	0.127
NEs/CNs Modified Model (best)	0.290	0.537	0.871	0.350	0.089

It can be seen that, for all models, WER and WER without stop words (WER_SW) measures gets worse when a few amount of entities is included. While the WER remains stable for *Single NEs model* and *NEs Modified model*, the performance slightly improves for the *NEs/CNs Modified model*. It is important to see that each improvement has a good impact in all system measures.

Figure 3 shows that in the *Single NE model* the NE accuracy decreases significantly until $20,000$ NEs, while in the other models it remains stable. This occurs because some entities, which are well recognized in previous experiments, are confused when the amount of NEs is increased. The *NEs/CNs Modified model* provides a more flexible language model which avoids this problem. Even in the *NEs/CNs Modified model*, the accuracy increases when more NEs are added.

It is interesting to see how the *Single NEs model* has the best Named Entity accuracy with the smallest NEs set ($4,000$), also the other recognition measures work better with the *NE/CNs Modified Model* while the amount of NE/NCs increases.

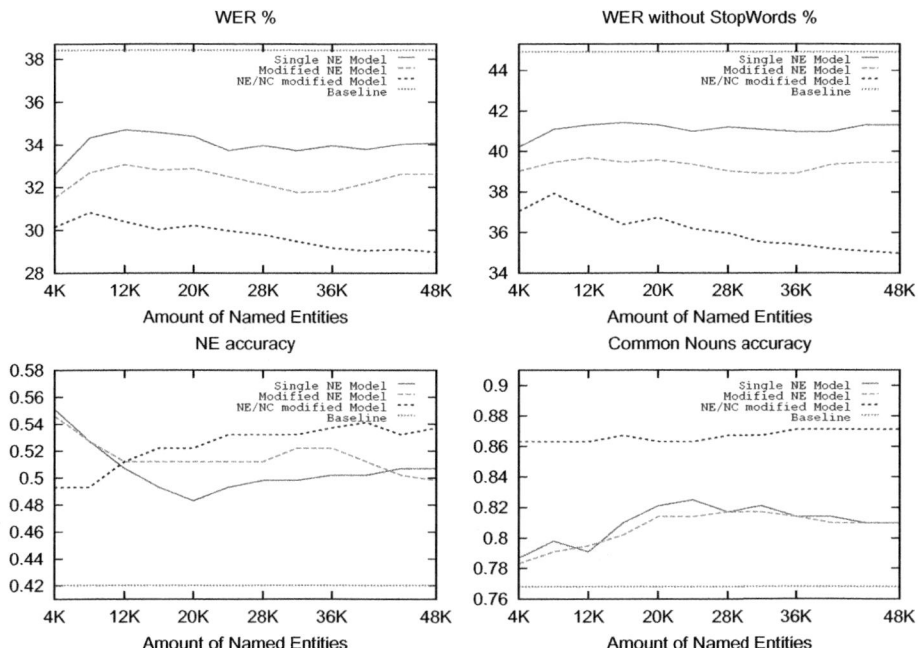

Fig. 3. Language Models results

5   Conclusion and Future Work

In this paper, we have presented an approach to the Automatic Speech Recognition component of a Voice-Activated Question Answering system. We have focused out interest in building a language model able to include as many relevant words from the document repository as possible, but also representing the general syntactic structure of typical questions.

The proposed language models, in which relevant words from the document repository are included, present better results in all the evaluation measures than the language model learned only with training questions (*Plane Training model*).

As future work, we propose first, to take into account non-Spanish Named Entities and their phonetics. Second, we propose to create an interaction mechanism which provides the user with a list of possible NEs to be chosen.

Acknowledgements. Work partially supported by the Spanish MICINN under contract TIN2008-06856-C05-02, and by the Vicerrectorat d'Investigació, Desenvolupament i Innovació of the Universitat Politècnica de València under contract 20100982.

References

1. Akiba, T., Itou, K., Fujii, A.: Language model adaptation for fixed phrases by amplifying partial n-gram sequences. Systems and Computers in Japan 38(4), 63–73 (2007)
2. Atserias, J., Casas, B., Comelles, E., Gónzalez, M., Padró, L., Padró, M.: Freeling 1.3: Five years of open-source language processing tools. In: Proceedings of the 5th International Conference on Language Resources and Evaluation (2006)
3. Carreras, X., Chao, I., Padró, L., Padró, M.: Freeling: An open-source suite of language analyzers. In: Proceedings of the 4th Language Resources and Evaluation Conference (2004)
4. Castro-Bleda, M.J., España-Boquera, S., Marzal, A., Salvador, I.: Grapheme-to-phoneme conversion for the spanish language. In: Pattern Recognition and Image Analysis. Proceedings of the IX Spanish Symposium on Pattern Recognition and Image Analysis, pp. 397–402. Asociación Española de Reconocimiento de Formas y Análisis de Imágenes, Benicàssim (2001)
5. Chu-Carroll, J., Prager, J.: An experimental study of the impact of information extraction accuracy on semantic search performance. In: Proceedings of the Sixteenth ACM Conference on Information and Knowledge Management, CIKM 2007, pp. 505–514. ACM (2007)
6. Harabagiu, S., Moldovan, D., Picone, J.: Open-domain voice-activated question answering. In: Proceedings of the 19th International Conference on Computational Linguistics, COLING 2002, vol. 1, pp. 1–7. Association for Computational Linguistics (2002)
7. Kim, D., Furui, S., Isozaki, H.: Language models and dialogue strategy for a voice QA system. In: 18th International Congress on Acoustics, Kyoto, Japan, pp. 3705–3708 (2004)
8. Mishra, T., Bangalore, S.: Speech-driven query retrieval for question-answering. In: 2010 IEEE International Conference on Acoustics Speech and Signal Processing (ICASSP), pp. 5318–5321. IEEE (2010)
9. Padró, L., Collado, M., Reese, S., Lloberes, M., Castellón, I.: Freeling 2.1: Five years of open-source language processing tools. In: Proceedings of 7th Language Resources and Evaluation Conference (2010)
10. Rosso, P., Hurtado, L.F., Segarra, E., Sanchis, E.: On the voice-activated question answering. IEEE Transactions on Systems, Man, and Cybernetics, Part C: Applications and Reviews PP(99), 1–11 (2010)
11. Sanchis, E., Buscaldi, D., Grau, S., Hurtado, L., Griol, D.: Spoken QA based on a Passage Retrieval engine. In: IEEE-ACL Workshop on Spoken Language Technology, Aruba, pp. 62–65 (2006)

On the Computation of the Geodesic Distance with an Application to Dimensionality Reduction in a Neuro-Oncology Problem

Raúl Cruz-Barbosa[1], David Bautista-Villavicencio[1], and Alfredo Vellido[2]

[1] Universidad Tecnológica de la Mixteca, 69000, Huajuapan, Oaxaca, México
{rcruz,dbautista}@mixteco.utm.mx
[2] Universitat Politècnica de Catalunya, 08034, Barcelona, Spain
avellido@lsi.upc.edu

Abstract. Manifold learning models attempt to parsimoniously describe multivariate data through a low-dimensional manifold embedded in data space. Similarities between points along this manifold are often expressed as Euclidean distances. Previous research has shown that these similarities are better expressed as geodesic distances. Some problems concerning the computation of geodesic distances along the manifold have to do with time and storage restrictions related to the graph representation of the manifold. This paper provides different approaches to the computation of the geodesic distance and the implementation of Dijkstra's shortest path algorithm, comparing their performances. The optimized procedures are bundled into a software module that is embedded in a dimensionality reduction method, which is applied to MRS data from human brain tumours. The experimental results show that the proposed implementation explains a high proportion of the data variance with a very small number of extracted features, which should ease the medical interpretation of subsequent results obtained from the reduced datasets.

1 Introduction

The choice of a type of distance as a similarity measure is relevant in many supervised, unsupervised and semi-supervised machine learning tasks [1]. For real-valued data, the Euclidean distance is the most common choice due to its intuitive understanding and the simplicity of its computation. In manifold learning, though, the Euclidean distance has been shown not always to be the most adequate choice to measure the (dis)similarity between two data points [2,3,4]. This is most relevant when working with data that reside in a high-dimensional space of which we ignore the intrinsic geometry, a common situation in biomedicine or bioinformatics.

An alternative distance function that may alleviate the previously mentioned problem is the geodesic distance, since it measures similarity along the embedded manifold, instead of doing it through the embedding space. Unlike the Euclidean distance, the geodesic one follows the geometry of the manifold that models the

C. San Martin and S.-W. Kim (Eds.): CIARP 2011, LNCS 7042, pp. 483–490, 2011.

data. In this way, it may help to avoid some of the distortions (such as breaches of topology preservation) that the use of a Euclidean metric may introduce when learning the manifold (due to undesired manifold curvature effects).

Manifold learning methods that use geodesic distances can be categorized, according to their main task, as unsupervised [2,4,5] and semi-supervised. The first semi-supervised methods used for classification task were reported in [6] and [7]. These methods, as well as many others that involve the geodesic distance [8], are known as graph-based methods. Most of them compute the data point pairwise distance of a graph using the basic Dijkstra algorithm, as well as use a full data matrix representation for finding the shortest path between them. This may lead to computational time and storage problems. The current study provides different approaches to the computation of the geodesic distance and the implementation of Dijkstra's shortest path algorithm, comparing their performances.

The best performing methods are bundled in a software module that is inserted in a nonlinear dimensionality reduction (NLDR) method, namely ISOMAP [2], which is then applied to the analysis of magnetic resonance spectroscopy (MRS) data from human brain tumours. The performance of the proposed method is compared to that of the original ISOMAP implementation.

2   Geodesic Distances

The explicit calculation of geodesic distances can be computational impractical. This metric, though, can be approximated by graph distances [9], so that instead of finding the minimum arc-length between two data points lying on a manifold, we would set to find the shortest path between them, where such path is built by connecting the closest successive data points. In this paper, this is done using the K-rule, which allows connecting the K-nearest neighbours. A weighted graph is then constructed by using the data and the set of allowed connections. The data are the vertices, the allowed connections are the edges, and the edge labels are the Euclidean distances between the corresponding vertices. If the resulting graph is disconnected, some edges are added using a minimum spanning tree procedure in order to connect it. Finally, the distance matrix of the weighted undirected graph is obtained by repeatedly applying Dijkstra's algorithm [10], which computes the shortest path between all data samples. For illustration, this process is graphically represented in Fig. 1.

2.1   Computation of the Geodesic (Graph) Distance

There are different implementation alternatives for some of the stages involved in the geodesic distance computation (see Fig. 1). This computation is constrained by the type of graph representation of the dataset and by the chosen shortest path algorithm. Two alternatives for graph representation are the *adjacency matrix* and the *adjacency list*. The former consists in a n by n matrix structure, where n is the number of vertices in the graph. If there is an edge from a vertex

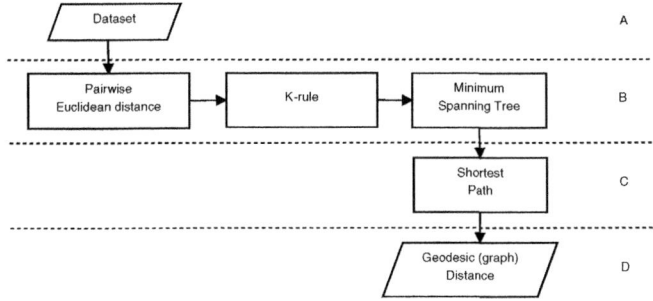

Fig. 1. Graph distance procedure scheme. Stage (A) represents the input data. Stage (B) is for building the weighted, undirected, connected graph. Stage (C) is for computing the geodesic (graph) distance, which is returned in Stage (D).

i to a vertex j, then the element a_{ij} is 1, otherwise it is 0. This kind of structure provides faster access for some applications but can consume huge amounts of memory. The latter considers that each vertex has a list of which vertices it is adjacent to. This structure is often preferred for sparse graphs as it has smaller memory requirements.

On the other hand, three options (of several) for the shortest path algorithm are: (basic) Dijkstra, Dijkstra using a Fibonacci heap (F-heap) and Floyd-Warshall. All of them assume that the graph is a weighted, connected graph. The time complexity of the simplest implementation of Dijkstra's algorithm is $O(|V|^2)$, using the Big-O notation. For some applications where the obtained graph is a sparse graph, Dijkstra's algorithm can save memory resources by storing the graph in the form of adjacency list and using an F-heap as a priority queue to implement extracting minimum efficiently. In this way, the time complexity of the algorithm can be improved to $O(|E| + |V|log|V|)$.

An F-heap is a binary tree with the property that, for every subtree, the root is the minimum item. This data structure is widely used as priority queue [11]. The priority queues are used to keep a dynamic list of different priorities jobs. An F-heap allows several operations as, for instance, ***Insert()***, which adds a new job to the queue and ***ExtractMin()***, which extracts the highest priority task.

Another approach for computing the shortest path is provided by the Floyd-Warshall algorithm, which is an example of dynamic programming. It finds the lengths of the shortest paths between all pairs of vertices. Unlike Dijkstra's algorithm which assumes that all weights are positive, this algorithm can deal with positive or negative edge weights. Its complexity is $O(|V|^3)$.

3   Experiments

The goal of the experiments herein reported is twofold. Firstly, we aim to assess which combination of graph representation and shortest path algorithm produces the best time performance for computing the geodesic distance for datasets with increasing numbers of items. Secondly, the software implementation of the best found solution is inserted in the NLDR ISOMAP algorithm. Its performance is compared to that of the original Tenenbaum's implementation (basic and land-mark versions) and to standard Principal Component Analysis (PCA), in terms of the amount of explained variance as a function of the number of new features extracted. We hypothesize that the connected graph built through the proposed procedure adds more geometric information to ISOMAP than the largest connected component found by the original version.

The experiments were carried out setting the K parameter to a value of 10, in order to get a connected graph when the K-rule is applied. After that, K was set to 1 for gauging the time performance of the geodesic distance computation when graph is sparse and unconnected. All experiments were performed using a dual-processor 2.3 Ghz BE-2400 desk PC with 2.7Gb RAM.

3.1 UCI Datasets and MRS Brain Tumour Database

Five datasets from the UCI machine learning repository [12], with increasing number of items, were used for the experiments. They are: *Ecoli* (336 7-dimensional points belonging to 8 classes representing protein location sites); *German* (1000 24-dimensional data points belonging to good or bad credit risks; *Segmentation* (2,310 19-dimensional items representing several measurements of image characteristics belonging to seven different classes); *Pageblocks* (5,473 items described by 10 attributes, concerning block measurements of distinct documents corresponding to five classes); and *Pendigits* (10,992 16-dimensional items corresponding to (x, y) tablet coordinate information measurements, which belong to ten digits).

We also experiment with MRS data acquired at different echo times (short -STE- and long -LTE-), as well as with a combination of both. Data belong to a multi-center, international database [13], and consist of: (1) 217 STE spectra, including 58 meningiomas (mm), 86 glioblastomas (gl), 38 metastases (me), 22 astrocytomas grade II (a2), 6 oligoastrocytomas grade II (oa), and 7 oligodendrogliomas grade II (od); (2) 195 LTE spectra, including 55 mm, 78 gl, 31 me, 20 a2, 6 oa, and 5 od. (3) 195 items built by combination (through direct concatenation) of the STE and LTE spectra for the same patients. Only the clinically relevant regions of the spectra were analyzed. They consist of 195 frequency intensity values (measured in parts per million (ppm), an adimensional unit of relative frequency position in the data vector), starting at 4.25 ppm. These frequencies become the observed data features.

3.2 Results and Discussion

The time performance results for computing geodesic (graph) distances, using $K = 10$, are shown in Table 1. Here, a combination of adjacency matrix for graph representation and basic Dijkstra as the choice for shortest path algorithm outperformed the other combinations, except for *Pageblocks*. This is due to the faster access to elements in an adjacency matrix when basic Dijkstra's

Table 1. Time performance results for the computation of geodesic (graph) distances (assuming a connected graph by setting $K = 10$) for several UCI datasets and different settings. The '–' symbol indicates that the memory limit was exceeded.

Dataset (# items)	Shortest path	Representation	Time (s)
Ecoli (336)	Dijkstra	Adjacency Matrix	0.43
	Dijkstra+F-heaps	Adjacency Matrix	1.19
	Floyd-Warshall	Adjacency Matrix	0.53
	Dijkstra	Adjacency List	0.67
	Dijkstra+F-heaps	Adjacency List	1.59
	Floyd-Warshall	Adjacency List	0.42
German (1000)	Dijkstra	Adjacency Matrix	12.43
	Dijkstra+F-heaps	Adjacency Matrix	25.03
	Floyd-Warshall	Adjacency Matrix	23.67
	Dijkstra	Adjacency List	16.18
	Dijkstra+F-heaps	Adjacency List	38.39
	Floyd-Warshall	Adjacency List	18.71
Segmentation (2310)	Dijkstra	Adjacency Matrix	185.57
	Dijkstra+F-heaps	Adjacency Matrix	297.31
	Floyd-Warshall	Adjacency Matrix	347.16
	Dijkstra	Adjacency List	229.83
	Dijkstra+F-heaps	Adjacency List	511.59
	Floyd-Warshall	Adjacency List	292.89
Pageblocks (5473)	Dijkstra	Adjacency Matrix	3621.90
	Dijkstra+F-heaps	Adjacency Matrix	4031.93
	Floyd-Warshall	Adjacency Matrix	18369.84
	Dijkstra	Adjacency List	3585.92
	Dijkstra+F-heaps	Adjacency List	8039.92
	Floyd-Warshall	Adjacency List	10409.90
Pendigits (10992)	Dijkstra	Adjacency Matrix	– –
	Dijkstra+F-heaps	Adjacency Matrix	– –
	Floyd-Warshall	Adjacency Matrix	– –
	Dijkstra	Adjacency List	124363.18
	Dijkstra+F-heaps	Adjacency List	66105.34
	Floyd-Warshall	Adjacency List	204604.99

algorithm required them. It is worth noting how the time performance for the adjacency list representation and Dijkstra is better for larger datasets. This effect is pronounced for *Pendigits*, with which the matrix representation can not deal due to the storage restrictions of the operating system (it dedicates approximately 700 Mb for each process). In this case, the best combination is the adjacency list and Dijkstra using F-heaps. Now, using the matrix representation, and if time results are compared for Dijkstra and Dijkstra using F-heaps algorithms, we observe that the time proportion decreases when number of items increases; this difference is more pronounced for Dijkstra implemented with F-heaps. This tendency is not maintained for the list representation using small and medium datasets, but it is notably low for large datasets as *Pendigits*. Thus, it can be inferred that, for large datasets, the best time performance for computing geodesic distances would be provided by an adjacency list (or matrix, when storage restrictions are discarded) representation and Dijkstra using F-heaps. The opposite occurs for the Floyd-Warshall algorithm independently from the graph representation. Its performance is good only for small sets.

Now, the K parameter for the K-rule is set to 1, in order to show the time performance when the procedure is dealing with an unconnected and sparse graph (see Table 2). The pattern found in the results reported in Table 1 is

Table 2. Time performance results for the computation of geodesic (graph) distances (assuming an unconnected, sparse graph by setting $K = 1$) for several UCI datasets and different settings. The '–' symbol indicates that the memory limit was exceeded.

Dataset (# items)	Shortest path	Representation	Time (s)
Ecoli (336)	Dijkstra	Adjacency Matrix	0.47
	Dijkstra+F-heaps	Adjacency Matrix	1.21
	Floyd-Warshall	Adjacency Matrix	0.6
	Dijkstra	Adjacency List	0.67
	Dijkstra+F-heaps	Adjacency List	1.57
	Floyd-Warshall	Adjacency List	0.44
German (1000)	Dijkstra	Adjacency Matrix	12.85
	Dijkstra+F-heaps	Adjacency Matrix	25.72
	Floyd-Warshall	Adjacency Matrix	23.32
	Dijkstra	Adjacency List	16.18
	Dijkstra+F-heaps	Adjacency List	37.89
	Floyd-Warshall	Adjacency List	19.27
Segmentation (2310)	Dijkstra	Adjacency Matrix	186.55
	Dijkstra+F-heaps	Adjacency Matrix	294.22
	Floyd-Warshall	Adjacency Matrix	345.38
	Dijkstra	Adjacency List	228.47
	Dijkstra+F-heaps	Adjacency List	507.53
	Floyd-Warshall	Adjacency List	192.38
Pageblocks (5473)	Dijkstra	Adjacency Matrix	3483.08
	Dijkstra+F-heaps	Adjacency Matrix	3955.05
	Floyd-Warshall	Adjacency Matrix	10867.04
	Dijkstra	Adjacency List	5549.91
	Dijkstra+F-heaps	Adjacency List	7678.91
	Floyd-Warshall	Adjacency List	10179.90
Pendigits (10992)	Dijkstra	Adjacency Matrix	– –
	Dijkstra+F-heaps	Adjacency Matrix	– –
	Floyd-Warshall	Adjacency Matrix	– –
	Dijkstra	Adjacency List	131085.17
	Dijkstra+F-heaps	Adjacency List	67312.69
	Floyd-Warshall	Adjacency List	193720.78

maintained. In general, it is observed that the modified minimum spanning tree procedure to connect the graph does influence the time results. The larger the dataset, the less affected the Dijkstra+F-heaps connection algorithm is.

Finally, the optimized geodesic distance calculation software module, developed in C++, was embedded in the NLDR ISOMAP algorithm, herein named ISOMAP gMod. Its performance was compared to that of Tenenbaum's ISOMAP implementation and PCA. The corresponding results are shown in Table 3. It can be observed that using ISOMAP gMod helps to explain a large percentage of the data variance with far fewer extracted features than the alternative implementations. For the LTE set (195 features corresponding to spectral frequencies), even just the first extracted feature explains 80% of the data variance. Moreover, for the high-dimensional SLTE set (390 features), two extracted features suffice to explain nearly 90% of the data variance. Overall, the ISOMAP gMod implementation outperforms all alternatives according to this evaluation measure. Further experiments were conducted with versions of the datasets reduced to 20 features through prior selection. Results are reported in Table 4 and they are consistent with those in Table 3.

Table 3. Explained variance as a function of the number of extracted features. ISOMAP variants: Standard, Landmark (Land) and with the proposed optimized module (gMod). NEF stands for *number of extracted features*.

Dataset (itemXdim)	DR method	% of variance explained by NEF										#Var > 80%	% (#Var)
		1	2	3	4	5	6	7	8	9	10		
LTE	PCA	57.82	9.89	8.32	5.36	4.97	3.54	3.25	2.61	2.16	2.09	4	81.39
(195 × 195)	ISOMAP	58.31	12.08	9.88	4.52	3.96	2.72	2.45	2.18	2.05	1.85	3	80.28
	ISOMAP Land	58.82	10.49	7.35	4.46	4.11	3.61	3.21	3.00	2.62	2.33	4	81.11
	ISOMAP gMod	80.50	9.06	3.50	2.25	1.19	1.02	0.76	0.66	0.59	0.46	1	80.50
STE	PCA	66.88	7.68	6.58	5.74	3.71	2.64	2.18	1.80	1.41	1.38	3	81.14
(217 × 195)	ISOMAP	67.05	8.38	7.86	4.70	3.12	2.30	2.00	1.65	1.55	1.39	3	83.29
	ISOMAP Land	66.42	7.42	6.58	4.26	3.16	2.92	2.70	2.45	2.18	1.92	3	80.42
	ISOMAP gMod	78.15	8.10	3.75	3.06	2.14	1.35	1.04	0.90	0.81	0.70	2	86.24
SLTE	PCA	61.61	8.28	7.10	6.02	4.16	3.40	2.77	2.58	2.14	1.94	4	83.01
(195 × 390)	ISOMAP	65.26	9.73	7.01	3.97	3.0	2.83	2.55	2.09	1.88	1.67	3	82.00
	ISOMAP Land	66.27	9.48	4.48	4.26	3.51	3.22	2.57	2.40	1.98	1.85	3	80.23
	ISOMAP gMod	75.28	13.22	4.53	1.76	1.32	1.00	0.88	0.77	0.68	0.55	2	88.50

Table 4. Summary of the explained variance as a function of the first 20 extracted features. Legend as in Table 3

Dataset (item× dim)	DR method	#Var> 80%	% (#Var)
LTE	PCA	6	80.85
(195 × 195)	ISOMAP	6	80.84
	ISOMAP Land	8	81.73
	ISOMAP gMod	2	87.23
STE	PCA	4	81.52
(217 × 195)	ISOMAP	4	80.20
	ISOMAP Land	6	80.78
	ISOMAP gMod	2	83.19
SLTE	PCA	6	80.64
(195 × 390)	ISOMAP	6	82.17
	ISOMAP Land	6	80.27
	ISOMAP gMod	2	85.71

4   Conclusion

The use of the geodesic metric has been shown to be relevant in NLDR manifold learning models. Its implementation, though, is not trivial and usually requires graph approximations. The characteristics of the software implementation of such approximations may have a considerably impact on the computational requirements, but also on the final results. Experimental results have shown that the combined use of an adjacency matrix and Dijkstra algoritm is recommendable for computing geodesic distances in small and medium datasets. For larger datasets, though, the use of an adjacency list representation becomes crucial.

The NLDR ISOMAP algorithm was implemented using the proposed optimized procedures and it was used to analyze a data set of small size but high dimensionality of MRS spectra corresponding to human brain tumours. In problems concerning the diagnosis and prognosis of such tumours, the interpretability of the results is paramount. Such interpretability can be helped by dimensionality reduction procedures. The ISOMAP gMod implementation has been shown to outperform several alternatives in terms of explaining a large percentage of the variance of these data through an extremely reduced number of features. Future research will investigate the use of this data reduction results in brain tumour diagnostic classification tasks. A comparison of ISOMAP variants with the original Euclidean model of them, metric MDS, should also be included.

Acknowledgments. Partial funding for this research was provided by the Mexican SEP PROMEP/103.5/10/5058 and the Spanish MICINN TIN2009-13895-C02-01 research projects. Authors gratefully acknowledge the former INTERPRET European project partners. Data providers: Dr. C. Majós (IDI), Dr. À. Moreno-Torres (CDP), Dr. F.A. Howe and Prof. J. Griffiths (SGUL), Prof. A. Heerschap (RU), Prof. L. Stefanczyk and Dr J. Fortuniak (MUL) and Dr. J. Calvar (FLENI); data curators: Dr. M. Julià-Sapé, Dr. A.P. Candiota, Dr. I. Olier, Ms. T. Delgado, Ms. J. Martín and Mr. A. Pérez (all from GABRMN-UAB). GABRMN coordinator: Prof. C. Arús.

References

1. Cruz-Barbosa, R., Vellido, A.: Semi-supervised analysis of human brain tumours from partially labeled MRS information, using manifold learning models. International Journal of Neural Systems 21, 17–29 (2011)
2. Tenenbaum, J.B., de Silva, V., Langford, J.C.: A global geometric framework for nonlinear dimensionality reduction. Science 290, 2319–2323 (2000)
3. de Silva, V., Tenenbaum, J.: Global versus local methods in nonlinear dimensionality reduction. In: Becker, S., Thrun, S., Obermayer, K. (eds.) Advances in Neural Information Processing Systems, vol. 15. The MIT Press (2003)
4. Belkin, M., Niyogi, P.: Laplacian eigenmaps for dimensionality reduction and data representation. Neural Computation 15(6), 1373–1396 (2003)
5. Roweis, S.T., Lawrence, K.S.: Nonlinear dimensionality reduction by locally linear embedding. Science (290), 2323–2326 (2000)
6. Zhu, X., Ghahramani, Z.: Learning from labeled and unlabeled data with label propagation. Technical report, CMU-CALD-02-107, Carnegie Mellon University (2002)
7. Belkin, M., Niyogi, P.: Using manifold structure for partially labelled classification. In: Advances in Neural Information Processing Systems (NIPS), vol. 15. MIT Press (2003)
8. Cruz-Barbosa, R., Vellido, A.: Semi-supervised geodesic generative topographic mapping. Pattern Recognition Letters 31(3), 202–209 (2010)
9. Bernstein, M., de Silva, V., Langford, J.C., Tenenbaum, J.B.: Graph approximations to geodesics on embedded manifolds. Technical report, Stanford University, CA, USA (2000)
10. Dijkstra, E.W.: A note on two problems in connexion with graphs. Numerische Mathematik 1, 269–271 (1959)
11. Fredman, M.L., Tarjan, R.E.: Fibonacci heaps and their uses in improved network optimization algorithms. J. ACM 34(3), 596–615 (1987)
12. Asuncion, A., Newman, D.: UCI machine learning repository, University of California, Irvine, School of Information and Computer Sciences (2007), http://www.ics.uci.edu/~mlearn/MLRepository.html
13. Julià-Sapé, M., et al.: A multi-centre, web-accessible and quality control-checked database of *in vivo* MR spectra of brain tumour patients. Magn. Reson. Mater. Phys. MAGMA 19, 22–33 (2006)

Multimodal Schizophrenia Detection by Multiclassification Analysis

Aydın Ulaş[1,*], Umberto Castellani[1], Pasquale Mirtuono[1], Manuele Bicego[1,2],
Vittorio Murino[1,2], Stefania Cerruti[3], Marcella Bellani[3], Manfredo Atzori[4],
Gianluca Rambaldelli[3], Michele Tansella[3], and Paolo Brambilla[4,5]

[1] University of Verona, Department of Computer Science, Verona, Italy
[2] Istituto Italiano di Tecnologia (IIT), Genova, Italy
[3] Department of Public Health and Community Medicine,
Section of Psychiatry and Clinical Psychology, Inter-University Centre for
Behavioural Neurosciences, University of Verona, Verona, Italy
[4] IRCCS "E. Medea" Scientific Institute, Udine, Italy
[5] DISM, Inter-University Centre for Behavioural Neurosciences, University of Udine,
Udine, Italy

Abstract. We propose a multiclassification analysis to evaluate the relevance of different factors in schizophrenia detection. Several Magnetic Resonance Imaging (MRI) scans of brains are acquired from two sensors: morphological and diffusion MRI. Moreover, 14 Region Of Interests (ROIs) are available to focus the analysis on specific brain subparts. All information is combined to train three types of classifiers to distinguish between healthy and unhealthy subjects. Our contribution is threefold: (i) the classification accuracy improves when multiple factors are taken into account; (ii) proposed procedure allows the selection of a reduced subset of ROIs, and highlights the synergy between the two modalities; (iii) correlation analysis is performed for every ROI and modality to measure the information overlap using the correlation coefficient in the context of schizophrenia classification. We see that we achieve 85.96 % accuracy when we combine classifiers from both modalities, whereas the highest performance of a single modality is 78.95 %.

Keywords: Machine learning algorithms, Magnetic resonance imaging, Support vector machines, Correlation.

1 Introduction

Computational neuroanatomy using magnetic resonance imaging (MRI) is a growing research field that employs image analysis methods to quantify morphological characteristics of different brains [5]. The ultimate goal is to identify structural brain abnormalities by comparing normal subjects (controls) with patients affected by a certain disease. Advanced computer vision and pattern

---

* Corresponding author.

C. San Martin and S.-W. Kim (Eds.): CIARP 2011, LNCS 7042, pp. 491–498, 2011.

recognition techniques may deeply help the understanding of brain characteristics and functionalities and there are several studies where these techniques are applied [4,3]. In this paper we work on schizophrenia on which a substantial body of research demonstrates numerous structural and functional brain abnormalities in patients [11,9]. [1] is an excellent review on the use of MR for psychiatric diseases for the interested readers.

In this paper, we propose an image-based analysis starting from a rather wide set of brain scans acquired by two sensors: i) 3D Morphological (SMRI), which highlight morphological properties, and ii) Diffusion Weighted Imaging (DWI), which show the microstructure of the tissues. For each brain, a set of Region of Interests (ROIs) are available in order to concentrate the analysis only on brain subparts which are in relation with the disease [2].

The main contribution of the paper is the exploitation in a multiclassification scenario of both morphological and diffusion data for schizophrenia detection; moreover we show also the effect of combining different classifiers and ROIs. In particular, we evaluate several strategies for combining several aspects [6]: ROIs, data modalities, and type of classifiers. As a second contribution, we observe the correlations[1] between the classifiers trained on different ROIs and modalities to measure the level of overlap of information contained among the ROIs and modalities.

In the following, we describe the selected data set and the experimental setup in Sect. 2 and 3, respectively. Subsequently, we report the results combining several types of data and processing strategies in Sect. 4, and finally, last remarks are discussed in Sect. 5.

2   Data Set

We used a data set of 59 patients and 55 healthy subjects for both 3D SMRI and DWI modalities (Figure 1). SMRI data are more often used for human brain research. Data are quite accurate with respect to noise and the volume-data is represented with high resolution. Conversely, DWI data are more noisy and suitable for evidencing the microstructure of the tissues aiming at analyzing the integrity of the brain. It is worth noting that DWI data are less used for human brain research, and only few work have been done in schizophrenia. Several ROIs have been traced from SMRI data by drawing contours enclosing the intended region. For each ROI, the tracing has been carried out by a trained expert following a specific protocol [3]. In Fig. 2, we show a sample of the right superior temporal gyrus: the volume is composed of 35 slices of size 41×40 (ordered from left to right, top to bottom).

In order to obtain the ROIs also on the DWI-space, we apply a nonrigid registration between diffusion and morphological images using the 3DSlicer (Available at http://www.slicer.org/) in accordance with a standard medical procedure. According with our previous work [3], we generate a histogram of properly normalized intensity values for each ROI and subject for SMRI. For DWI we extract

---

[1] The idea of using the correlations for information extraction is adapted from [13].

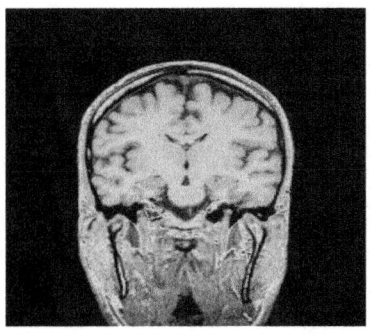 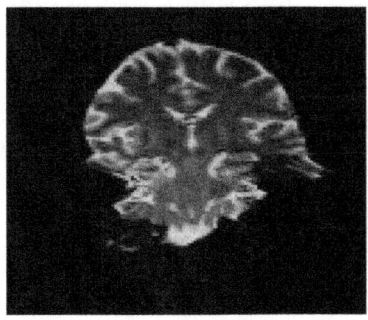

Fig. 1. Two slices acquired by 3D Morphological (SMRI) (left) and Diffusion Weighting Imaging DWI (right) techniques

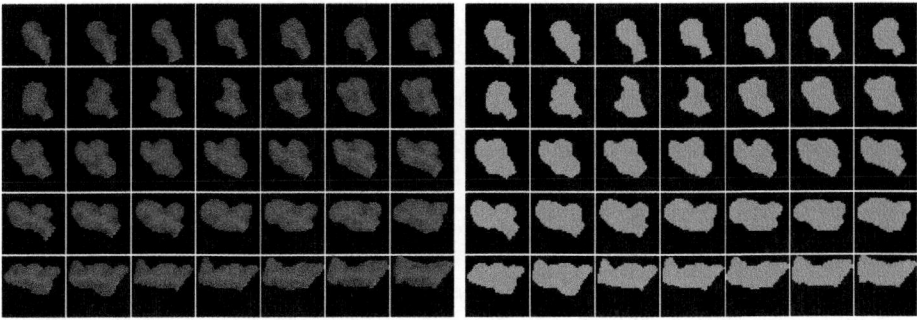

Fig. 2. Montage of the slices in the ROI volume ($41 \times 40 \times 35$) of *rstg* for subject 11. On the left, the MRI values; on the right, the corresponding binary masks.

the histograms of Apparent Diffusion Coefficient (ADC) values. Such histogram representations are the feature vectors which are evaluated by the classifiers.

3   Experimental Setup

In order to summarize the experimental setup, two issues should be highlighted, which are reported in the following.

3.1   Factor Combination

We propose to combine the following factors: i) three classifiers: k-nearest neighbor with $k = 1$ (*1nn*), support vector machine with a linear kernel (*svl*), and support vector machine with a radial basis kernel (*svr*), ii) seven ROIs × two hemispheres: Amygdala (*lamyg* and *ramyg*), Dorso-lateral PreFrontal Cortex (*ldlpfc* and *rdlpfc*), Entorhinal Cortex (*lec* and *rec*), Heschl's Gyrus (*lhg* and *rhg*), Hippocampus (*lhippo* and *rhippo*), Superior Temporal Gyrus (*lstg* and *rstg*), and Thalamus (*lthal* and *rthal*), and iii) two modalities: SMRI data, and DWI data.

3.2   Validation Criteria and Decision Rule

For every factor combination, we use leave-one-out (LOO) methodology to train the models and assess the accuracy. Instead of using a binary decision rule, we record the posterior probability outputs of each model and use them for constructing ensembles using the mean combiner (i.e. SUM rule in classifier combination).

We also add another representation which is the concatenation of SMRI and DWI data, which we call CON. Therefore, each trained basic model consists of one modality, one ROI, and one classifier (i.e., SMRI-*lamyg-1nn*). The modality, the ROI or the classifier will be omitted throughout the text when the context is clear.

3.3   Correlation of Base Classifiers

We use the posterior probability outputs of the *svr* classifier to calculate the correlation coefficient between ROIs and modalities. It's known that for ensembles to have better accuracy, we need to have diverse base classifiers. Various measures of diversity exist [7], but in general, diversity can be defined as the classifiers responding differently to the same input. Correlations of base classifiers are also used when creating ensembles, and in this paper we used the correlation coefficient proposed by Petrakos *et al.* [8] which was studied empirically in the context of decision fusion. We apply the correlation computation to see how the ROIs and modalities are correlated. In principle, one would use a validation set to compute the correlation of the classification algorithms and then form the ensemble according to this information [7]. Instead, what we do in this study is to calculate the correlation of pairwise ROIs and modalities on the test set to *observe* the overlap of information contained in different ROIs [13].

The correlation between two classifiers is calculated as in [8]:

$$\rho_2 = \frac{2 \times N_{00}}{N_{01} + N_{10} + 2 \times N_{00}}$$

where N_{ij} shows the number of subjects (N_{00}: incorrectly classified by both classifiers, N_{11}: correctly classified by both classifiers, N_{01} incorrectly classified by the first and correctly classified by the second, and N_{10}: correctly classified by the first, and incorrectly classified by the second).

4   Results and Discussions

In this section, we evaluate different strategies to combine classifiers, ROIs, and data modalities.

4.1   Exp 1: Single Classifier per ROI

In the first experiment, we compare classification performances by training a single classifier per ROI and modality. In the left part of Table 1, one can see the best LOO accuracies among the three different types of classifiers. Please, note that the best accuracy is 71.93 when we use SMRI-*ldlpfc*. The best accuracy of DWI is 62.28 when we use *lec* which is interesting because it is one of the only three ROIs where DWI is more accurate than SMRI. In half of the ROIs the accuracy improves when the feature concatenation approach is applied.

The right part of Table 1 shows instead the integration of the three types of classifiers using the mean combiner for each ROI and modality. Also this combination strategy does not yield better accuracies, sometimes makes it worse.

Table 1. Best and mean combiner (MC) accuracies using a single classifier per ROI and modality (in %)

	BEST			MC		
	SMRI	DWI	CON	SMRI	DWI	CON
lamyg	64.91	59.65	**71.93**	63.16	57.02	**69.30**
ramyg	64.91	53.51	52.63	63.16	47.37	56.14
ldlpfc	**71.93**	50.88	57.02	64.91	51.75	54.39
rdlpfc	61.40	51.75	64.91	63.16	48.25	59.65
lec	57.02	**62.28**	69.30	50.00	62.28	59.65
rec	63.16	54.39	63.16	**65.79**	53.51	55.26
lhg	55.26	58.77	62.28	52.63	57.89	58.77
rhg	57.02	57.02	58.77	51.75	51.75	54.39
lhippo	70.18	61.40	66.67	64.04	**64.04**	66.67
rhippo	57.89	60.53	57.02	55.26	46.49	47.37
lstg	62.28	57.89	64.04	59.65	57.02	62.28
rstg	62.28	51.75	64.91	58.77	49.12	66.67
lthal	63.16	52.63	57.02	60.53	50.00	57.89
rthal	61.40	57.02	58.77	58.77	53.51	57.02

4.2   Exp 2: Integration of ROIs

In the second experiment, we fix modalities and classifiers; and combine the ROIs (Table 2, upper part) using the mean combiner. One can see that the best accuracy of CON is improved from 71.93 % to 74.56 %. It's known that combining a subset of models may lead to better accuracies than using all the models [10,12]. Bearing this in mind, we have performed another experiment where we selected the best seven ROIs. We can see from Table 2 (middle) that the accuracies increase 5%, 14 % and 3% respectively when we use the *svr* classifiers and the best 7 ROIs. Using this selection strategy, we can have 76.32 accuracy when we use the morphological data. Even better is the result of the concatenation: 78.07 %. This experiment suggests that the best integration strategy is obtained when we combine a subset of different ROIs for any modality. Therefore, we design an exhaustive experiment to select automatically such subset of ROIs. We first have performed the analysis for the three modalities separately. Then, we allow the combination between all the ROIs of both the sensors at the same time. In these experiments, we use *svr*, because it has the best performace. The results can be seen in Table 2 (bottom). The optimum accuracy is 78.95 when a single modality is used, and 83.33 when we use the concatenation of both modalities whereas when both modalities are jointly combined the accuracy improves to 85.96. Another interesting fact is that optimal ROIs combination for

Table 2. Combination accuracies for combining all ROIs and a selection of ROIs (in %)

	1nn	*svl*	*svr*
SMRI	60.53	64.91	71.05
DWI	63.16	56.14	57.02
CON	57.89	67.54	**74.56**
Best7-SMRI	59.65	68.42	76.32
Best7-DWI	53.51	51.75	71.05
Best7-CON	52.63	67.54	**78.07**
opt-SMRI	-	-	78.95
opt-DWI	-	-	74.56
opt-CON	-	-	83.33
opt-JOINT	-	-	**85.96**

SMRI includes five ROIs which are not the best five. The optimum combination for DWI selects four ROIs which are again in the best seven but not the best four. This shows us that different classifiers may perform well in classifying different parts of the input space, and even though they have low single accuracies, they may bring a relevant improvement when combined with other parts.

Another interesting aspect of this evaluation is that the optimum combination including both the modalities selects five ROIs from SMRI and three ROIs from DWI which again differ from those selected for the single modality evaluation. It is worth to note that this combination strategy not only provides the best performance in detecting schizophrenic subjects, but also allows us to localize the most discriminative brain subparts.

4.3   Exp 3: Correlations of Classifiers

In the above experiments we analyze that it is good to combine multiple ROIs in order to get better ensemble accuracy. The better method is to combine the outputs of classifiers coming from different modalities which our exhaustive analysis pointed out. One could also use the correlations to come up with such ensembles, but since we exhaustively searched all the solution space, instead of showing how to build an ensemble using correlation, we will observe the pairwise correlations among ROIs and modalities. Most of the correlations are below 0.50 (note that ρ^2 gets values in the range $[0, 1]$) and the correlations above this value are unevenly distributed amongst ROIs and the two modalities. The highest correlation is 0.61 between SMRI-*lthal* and SMRI-*ldlpfc*. This shows us that the correlations between these classifiers are low and combining them to construct ensembles would lead better ensemble accuracy which was also shown by our experiments above. This also has an important medical interpretation. It shows us that the information contained in each of these ROIs and across these two modalities are different (also complementary as we show above) and we should combine the information in these ROIs and modalities to get better ensemble accuracy. Table 3 shows the correlations across modalities and hemispheres. The first part of the table shows the correlations across the two modalities using the same ROI. We can see that the highest correlation is 0.56 which is observed on *rhippo*. The second part of the table shows the correlations across the brain hemispheres. This time we can see that the highest correlation is 0.63 and between *stg* of SMRI. We can see that correlations inside ROIs are higher than cross-modality correlations which shows us that it may be a good idea to combine the two modalities which was confirmed by our combination experiments. Analyzing the table, we can also say the following: In the context of schizophrenia detection (using these features), the hemispheres of the brain are more similar in terms of morphology than function. Also we can see that the correlations between the right hemisphere of the two modalities are higher (except *stg*) than the correlations between the left hemispheres which shows that they are more similar in terms of discriminative power.

Table 3. Correlation of modalities and hemispheres. *l-* shows the left hemisphere and *r-* shows the right hemisphere.

	amyg	dlpfc	ec	hg	hippo	stg	thal
l-SMRI vs. *l*-DWI	0.37	0.41	0.39	0.39	0.44	0.49	0.44
r-SMRI vs. *r*-DWI	0.44	0.55	0.46	0.45	**0.56**	0.48	0.47
l-SMRI vs. *r*-SMRI	0.53	0.47	0.49	0.46	0.49	**0.63**	0.56
l-DWI vs. *r*-DWI	0.45	0.58	0.46	0.42	0.43	0.51	0.52

5   Conclusions

In this work, we evaluate the effectiveness of different classifier combination strategies in the context of schizophrenia detection. Even if the question "Can schizophrenia be detected just by analyzing MRI images?" is still unsolved, this study provides novel useful insights on the combined effect of two data modalities: in particular we have considered morphological and diffusion data, extracted from 14 ROIs associated to brain subparts, and classified using three types of classifiers. We have seen that neither concatenating the two modalities, nor combining different types of classifiers on the same ROI, provides the expected effect of increasing ensemble accuracy. Such effect may be found when we use a carefully selected subset of ROIs, which are combined using the mean combiner strategy. The best increase in accuracy occurs when we combine also the two data modalities (JOINT). This highlights that the information encoded in the morphological and diffusion data are different, and their contributions to the classification are complementary. We also showed this using correlation coefficients between classifiers. Using the correlation coefficients, we have seen that the classifiers trained using different modalities are more diverse. Also we have seen that in terms of schizophrenia detection, the two hemispheres are more similar in terms of morphology than in terms of function. As a future work, we will exploit the use of other classifier combination algorithms to improve the ensemble accuracies.

Acknowledgements. We acknowledge financial support from the FET programme (EU FP7), under the SIMBAD project (contract 213250).

References

1. Agarwal, N., Port, J.D., Bazzocchi, M., Renshaw, P.F.: Update on the use of MR for assessment and diagnosis of psychiatric diseases. Radiology 255(1), 23–41 (2010)
2. Bellani, M., Brambilla, P.: The use and meaning of the continuous performance test in schizophrenia. Epidemiologia e Psichiatria Sociale 17(3), 188–191 (2008)
3. Cheng, D.S., Bicego, M., Castellani, U., Cerruti, S., Bellani, M., Rambaldelli, G., Atzori, M., Brambilla, P., Murino, V.: Schizophrenia classification using regions of interest in brain mri. In: Proceedings of Intelligent Data Analysis in Biomedicine and Pharmacology, IDAMAP 2009, pp. 47–52 (2009)
4. Davatzikos, C.: Why voxel-based morphometric analysis should be used with great caution when characterizing group differences. NeuroImage 23(1), 17–20 (2004)
5. Giuliani, N.R., Calhouna, V.D., Pearlson, G.D., Francis, A., Buchanan, R.W.: Voxel-based morphometry versus region of interest: a comparison of two methods for analyzing gray matter differences in schizophrenia. Schizophrenia Research 74(2-3), 135–147 (2005)
6. Kuncheva, L.I.: Combining pattern classifiers: methods and algorithms. Wiley-Interscience (2004)
7. Kuncheva, L.I., Whitaker, C.J.: Measures of diversity in classifier ensembles and their relationship with the ensemble accuracy. Machine Learning 51(2), 181–207 (2003)
8. Petrakos, M., Kannelopoulos, I., Benediktsson, J.A., Pesaresi, M.: The effect of correlation on the accuracy of the combined classifier in decision level fusion. In: Proceedings of the IEEE International Geo-science and Remote Sensing Symposium, IGARSS 2000, vol. 6, pp. 2623–2625 (2000)
9. Rujescu, D., Collier, D.A.: Dissecting the many genetic faces of schizophrenia. Epidemiologia e Psichiatria Sociale 18(2), 91–95 (2009)
10. Ruta, D., Gabrys, B.: Classifier selection for majority voting. Information Fusion 6(1), 63–81 (2005)
11. Shenton, M.E., Dickey, C.C., Frumin, M., McCarley, R.W.: A review of mri findings in schizophrenia. Schizophrenia Research 49(1-2), 1–52 (2001)
12. Ulaş, A., Semerci, M., Yıldız, O.T., Alpaydın, E.: Incremental construction of classifier and discriminant ensembles. Information Sciences 179(9), 1298–1318 (2009)
13. Ulaş, A., Yıldız, O.T., Alpaydın, E.: Eigenclassifiers for combining correlated classifiers. Information Sciences (accepted, 2011)

Online Signature Verification Method Based on the Acceleration Signals of Handwriting Samples

Horst Bunke[1], János Csirik[2], Zoltán Gingl[2], and Erika Griechisch[2]

[1] Institute of Informatics and Applied Mathematics
Neubrückstrasse 10, CH-3012 Bern, Switzerland
bunke@iam.unibe.ch
[2] Department of Informatics, University of Szeged
Árpád tér 2., H-6720, Szeged, Hungary
{csirik,gingl,grerika}@inf.u-szeged.hu

Abstract. Here we present a method for online signature verification treated as a two-class pattern recognition problem. The method is based on the acceleration signals obtained from signing sessions using a special pen device. We applied a DTW (dynamic time warping) metric to measure any dissimilarity between the acceleration signals and represented our results in terms of a distance metric.

Keywords: online signature, biometrics, signature verification.

1 Introduction

Several types of biometric authentication exist. Some of them have appeared in the last few decades, such as DNA and iris recognition and they provide more accurate results than the earlier methods did (e.g. fingerprint, signature). Hence they are more difficult to forge. However, a signature is still the most widely accepted method for identification (in contracts, bank transfers, etc.). This is why studies tackle the problem of signature verification and examine the process in detail. Usually their aim is to study the mechanics of the process and learn what features are hard to counterfeit.

There are two basic approaches of recognising signatures; namely the offline and the online. Offline signature recognition is based on the image of the signature, while the online case uses data concerning the dynamics of the signing process (pressure, velocity, etc.). The main problem with the offline approach is that it gives higher false accept and false reject errors, but the dynamic approach requires much more sophisticated techniques.

The online signature recognition systems differ in their feature selection and decision methods. Some studies analyse the consistency of the features [1], while others concentrate on the template feature selection [2]; some combine local and global features [3].

C. San Martin and S.-W. Kim (Eds.): CIARP 2011, LNCS 7042, pp. 499–506, 2011.
© Springer-Verlag Berlin Heidelberg 2011

An important step in signature recognition was the First International Signature Verification Competition [4]. Reviews of automatic signature verification were written by Leclerc and Plamondon [5,6].

Many signals and therefore many different devices can be used in signature verification. Different types of pen tablets have been used in several studies, as in [7,8]; the F-Tablet was described in [9] and the Genius 4x3 PenWizard was used in [10]. In several studies (like ours), a special device (pen) was designed to measure the dynamic characteristics of the signing process.

In [11], the authors considered the problem of measuring the acceleration produced by signing with a device fitted with 4 small embedded accelerometers and a pressure transducer. It mainly focused on the technical background of signal recording. In [12], they described the mathematical background of motion recovery techniques for a special pen with an embedded accelerometer.

Bashir and Kempf in [13] used a Novel Pen Device and DTW for handwriting recognition and compared the acceleration, grip pressure, longitudinal and vertical axis of the pen. Their main purpose was to recognise characters and PIN words, not signatures. Rohlik et al. [14,15] employed a similar device to ours to measure acceleration. Theirs was able to measure 2-axis accelerations, in contrast to ours which can measure 3-axis accelerations. However, our pen cannot measure pressure like theirs. The other difference is the method of data processing. In [14] they had two aims, namely signature verification and author identification, while in [15] the aim was just signature verification. Both made use of neural networks.

Many studies have their own database [8,9], but generally they are unavailable for testing purposes. However some large databases are available, like the MCYT biometric database [16] and the database of the SVC2004 competition[1] [4].

In this paper we propose an online signature recognition method that is based on a comparison of the 3-axis acceleration of the handwriting process. We created our database with genuine signatures and unskilled forgeries, and used the dynamic time warping method to measure the dissimilarities between signatures. The novelty of our approach is a detailed investigation of the contribution of acceleration information in the signature verification process.

2   Proposed Method

2.1   Technical Background

We used a ballpoint pen fitted with a three-axis accelerometer to follow the movements of handwriting sessions. Accelerometers can be placed at multiple positions of the pen, such as close to the bottom and/or close to the top of the pen [11,13]. Sometimes grip pressure sensors are also included to get a comprehensive set of signals describing the movements of the pen, finger forces and gesture movements. In our study we focused on the signature-writing task, so we placed the accelerometer very close to the tip of the pen to track the movements as accurately as possible (see Figure 1).

---

[1] Available at http://www.cse.ust.hk/svc2004/download.html

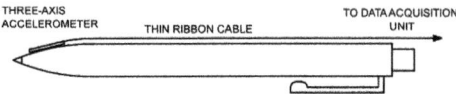

Fig. 1. The three-axis accelerometer is mounted close to the tip of the pen

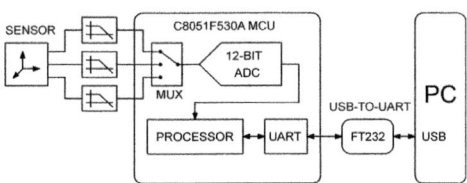

Fig. 2. Block diagram of the data acquisition system

In our design we chose the LIS352AX accelerometer chip because of its signal range, high accuracy, impressively low noise and ease-of-use. The accelerometer was soldered onto a very small printed circuit board (PCB) and this board was glued about 10mm from the writing tip of the pen. Only the accelerometer, the decoupling and filtering chip capacitors were placed on the assembled PCB. A thin five-wire thin ribbon cable was used to power the circuit and carry the three acceleration signals from the accelerometer to the data acquisition unit. The cable was thin and long enough so as not to disturb the subject when s/he provided a handwriting sample. Our tiny general purpose three-channel data acquisition unit served as a sensor-to-USB interface [17].

The unit has three unipolar inputs with signal range of 0 to 3.3V, and it also supplied the necessary 3.3V to power it. The heart of the unit is a mixed-signal microcontroller called C8051F530A that incorporates a precision multichannel 12-bit analogue-to-digital converter. The microcontroller runs a data logging program that allows easy communication with the host computer via an FT232RL-based USB-to-UART interface. The general purpose data acquisition program running on the PC was written in C#, and it allowed the real-time monitoring of signals. Both the hardware and software developments are fully open-source [18]. The block diagram of the measurement setup is shown in Figure 2.

The bandwidth of the signals was set to 10Hz in order to remove unwanted high frequency components and prevent aliasing. Moreover, the sample rate was set to 1000Hz. The signal range was closely matched to the input range of the data acquisition unit, hence a clean, low noise output was obtained. The acquired signals were then saved to a file for offline processing and analysis.

2.2   Database

The signature samples were collected from 40 subjects. Each subject supplied 10 genuine signatures and 5 unskilled forgeries, so we had a total $40 \cdot 15 = 600$

502   H. Bunke et al.

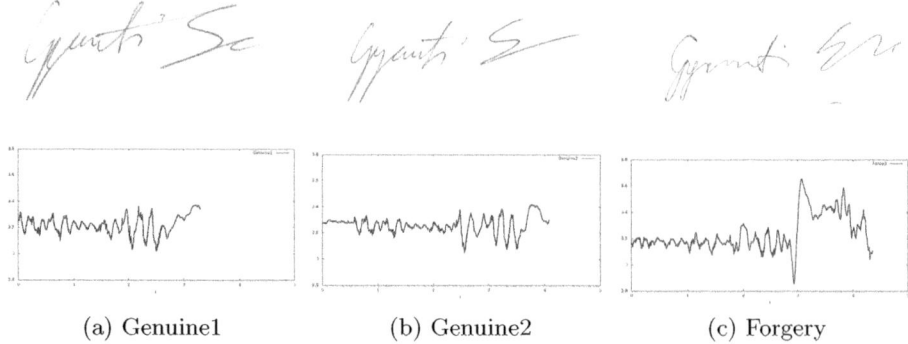

(a) Genuine1   (b) Genuine2   (c) Forgery

Fig. 3. The images and acceleration signals of two genuine signatures and one forged signature

signatures in total. The signature forgers were asked to produce 5 signatures of another person participating in the study. Each participant supplied forged samples and genuine samples.

In order to make the signing process as natural as possible, there were no constraints on how the person should sign. This led to some problems in the analysis because it was hard to compare the 3 pairs of curves (two signatures). During a signing session, the orientation of the pen can vary somewhat (e.g. a rotation with a small angle causes big differences for each axis). That was why we chose to reduce the 3 dimensional signals to 1 dimensional signals and we only compared the magnitudes of the acceleration vector data.

Figure 3 shows the acceleration signals of 2 genuine signatures and 1 forged signature. Figures 3a and 3b belong to the same author, and they appear quite similar. Figure 3c is a corresponding forged signature, which differs significantly from the first two.

2.3   Distance between Time Series

An elastic distance measure was applied to determine dissimilarities between the data. The dynamic time warping (DTW) approach is a commonly used method to compare time series. The DTW algorithm finds the best non-linear alignment of two vectors such that the overall distance between them is minimised. The DTW distance between the $u = (u_1, \ldots, u_n)$ and $v = (v_1, \ldots, v_m)$ vectors (in our case, the acceleration vector data of the signatures) can be calculated in $\mathcal{O}(n \cdot m)$ time.

We can construct, iteratively, a $C \in \mathbb{R}^{(n+1) \times (m+1)}$ matrix in the following way:

$$C_{0,0} = 0, C_{i,0} = +\infty, C_{0,j} = +\infty, \quad i = 1, \ldots, n, j = 1, \ldots, m$$
$$C_{i,j} = |u_i - v_j| + \min\left(C_{i-1,j}, C_{i,j-1}, C_{i-1,j-1}\right),$$
$$i = 1, \ldots, n, j = 1, \ldots, m.$$

After we get the $C_{n,m}$ which tells us the DTW distance between the vectors u and v. Thus

$$d_{\text{DTW}}(u,v) = C_{n,m}.$$

The DTW algorithm has several versions (e.g. weighted DTW and bounded DTW), but we decided to use the simple version above, where $|u_i - v_j|$ denotes the absolute difference between the coordinate i of vector u and coordinate j of vector v.

Since the order of the sizes of n and m are around $10^3 - 10^4$, our implementation does not store the whole C matrix, whose size is about $n \times m \approx 10^6 - 10^8$. Instead, for each iteration, just the last two rows of the matrix were stored.

Table 1. Sample distance matrix

DTW	AE00	AE01	AE02	AE03	AE04	AE05	AE06	AE07	AE08	AE09	ME10	ME11	ME12	ME13	ME14
AE00	0	62	97	122	115	63	114	103	75	223	342	277	236	316	709
AE01		0	63	70	65	113	81	67	65	160	238	232	176	258	676
AE02			0	103	66	134	75	76	63	82	252	251	175	258	695
AE03				0	99	163	127	111	108	165	278	283	228	301	712
AE04					0	156	70	70	58	78	385	445	254	409	874
AE05						0	155	146	104	308	527	450	347	490	851
AE06							0	60	36	155	331	401	221	332	793
AE07								0	49	138	199	239	178	220	669
AE08									0	116	233	247	157	225	683
AE09										0	362	484	303	365	950
ME10											0	133	70	49	258
ME11												0	107	83	197
ME12													0	67	394
ME13														0	267
ME14															0

A distance matrix is shown in Table 1. The intersection of the first 10 columns and 10 rows shows the distance values between the genuine signatures (got from the same person). The intersection of the first 10 rows and the last 5 columns tells us the distances between genuine and the corresponding forged signatures. The rest (the intersection of the last 5 rows and last 5 columns) shows the distances between the forged signatures.

The distance between the genuine signatures varies from 60 to 308 (with average distance of 95), but between a genuine and a forged signature it varies from 157 to 950 (with average distance of 390).

The distance matrices are similar to that given above. In some cases the distance between genuine and forged signatures can be easily delimited, but in other cases we cannot define a strict line.

3 Results

The performance of a signature verification algorithm can be measured by the rate of Type I error (false reject), when a genuine signature is marked as forged and Type II error (false accept), when a forged signature is marked as genuine.

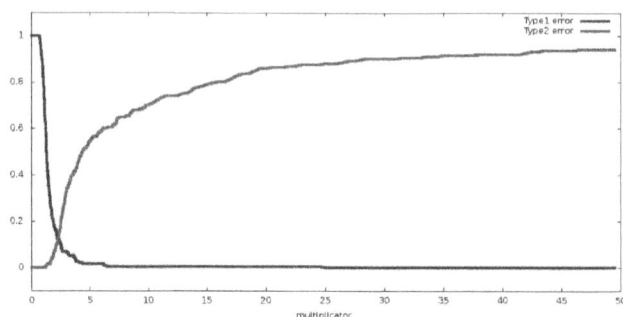

Fig. 4. False reject and false accept rates depending on the constant multiplier

For each person, 5 genuine signatures were chosen randomly as references, so they belonged to the training set. All the other signatures of this person and unskilled forgeries of their signature were used for testing. Thus the test set contained 5 genuine and 5 unskilled forged signatures for each person.

We first computed the average distance between the five elements of the training set $(D_{\mathbf{avg}})$. Then, for each signature in the test set, the average distance of the signature from the training set's five signatures was found $(D_{\mathbf{dis}})$. Now, if for some t in the set

$$D_{\mathbf{dis}} < m \cdot D_{\mathbf{avg}}$$

then t was accepted as a true signature, otherwise it was rejected.

Figures 4 shows the false reject and false accept rates depending on the constant multiplier m of the minimum distance got from the training dataset. We can see that we get a zero FA rate around $m = 7$. The curve decreases quite quickly while the increase of the FR is less marked.

Besides the average we also used two other metrics, namely the maximum and minimum distances. These were calculated from the training set via

$$D_{max}(R) = \max_{i,j=1,\ldots,|R|,i\neq j} d_{\mathrm{DTW}}(r_i, r_j) \text{ and } D_{min}(R) = \min_{i,j=1,\ldots,|R|,i\neq j} d_{\mathrm{DTW}}(r_i, r_j),$$

where the set R is the training data set, $|R|$ denotes the cardinality of R and r_i is the signature i in the training set.

We can use the same definitions to compute the distance between a test signature and a training set.

Table 2 shows the false accept and false reject errors in percentage terms. The Equal Error rate (EER) is the percentage where the false acceptance and the false rejection rates are equal. We see that we get the best results (the lowest EER), when we use $d_{\min}$ both for the training and the test set.

Table 2. Equal Error rates (EER) depending on the chosen distance on the reference set and the chosen distance between references and the sample. The values in brackets are the corresponding multipliers.

		Test distance		
		average	**maximum**	**minimum**
Training	**average**	14.50% (1.36)	23.50% (0.56)	18.00% (3.34)
	maximum	17.25% (2.02)	29.50% (0.84)	23.25% (4.82)
	minimum	15.50% (0.98)	23.25% (0.38)	13.00% (2.28)

4   Summary, Discussion and Conclusions

In this paper an online signature verification method was proposed for verifying human signatures. The proposed procedure was implemented and then tested. A test dataset was created using a special device fitted with an accelerometer. The dataset contained 600 signatures, where 400 signatures were genuine and 200 were forged. In the study we found we had to limit the 3d acceleration vector data to 1d acceleration vector data so as to make the verification task more manageable. Using a time series approach and various metrics we were able to place signature samples into two classes, namely those that are genuine and those that are forged. The results we got were instructive and the method looks promising.

The method outlined in [15], which used a similar device and neural networks to verify signatures, attained an overall accuracy ratio between 82.3% and 94.3%, depending on the author of the signatures (with an average of 87.88%). We attained an 88.50% overall accuracy ratio in the case of the minimum distance and choosing $m = 2.2$ as a multiplier. Thus our results compared to the above mentioned previous study is slightly better, despite the fact we used less data, as we did not use pressure data.

There are several ways that the work described here could be extended. First, other metrics than DTW could be included and the results compared. Second, our method just uses the magnitude of the acceleration, not the direction. Thus our verification method could be improved by extracting more useful information from the 3 dimensional signals. Third, we could compare other features (e.g. velocity, which can be computed from the acceleration data values) to learn which features are the most important in the signature verification process. A normalisation of the acceleration signals may be helpful too. Finally, we could adapt other sensors to make our signature-verifying tool more robust.

Acknowledgment. This work was supported by the Project "TÁMOP-4.2.1/B-09/1/KONV-2010-0005 - Creating the Center of Excellence at the University of Szeged", supported by the European Union and co-financed by the European Regional Development Fund.

References

1. Lei, H., Govindaraju, V.: A comparative study on the consistency of features in on-line signature verification. Pattern Rec. Letters 26, 2483–2489 (2005)
2. Richiardi, J., Ketabdar, H., Drygajlo, A.: Local and global feature selection for on-line signature verification. In: Proc. IAPR 8th International Conference on Document Analysis and Recognition (ICDAR 2005), pp. 625–629 (2005)
3. Nanni, L., Maiorana, E., Lumini, A., Campisi, P.: Combining local, regional and global matchers for a template protected on-line signature verification system. Expert Syst. Appl. 37, 3676–3684 (2010)
4. Yeung, D.Y., Chang, H., Xiong, Y., George, S., Kashi, R., Matsumoto, T., Rigoll, G.: SVC2004: First International Signature Verification Competition. In: Zhang, D., Jain, A.K. (eds.) ICBA 2004. LNCS, vol. 3072, pp. 16–22. Springer, Heidelberg (2004)
5. Plamondon, R., Lorette, G.: Automatic signature verification and writer identification - the state of the art. Pattern Rec. 22(2), 107–131 (1989)
6. Leclerc, F., Plamondon, R.: Automatic Signature Verification. In: Progress in Automatic Signature Verification
7. Daramola, S., Ibiyemi, T.: An efficient on-line signature verification system. International Journal of Engineering and Technology 10(4) (2010)
8. Kholmatov, A., Yanikoglu, B.: Identity authentication using an improved online signature verification method. Pattern Rec. Letters 26, 2400–2408 (2005)
9. Fang, P., Wu, Z., Shen, F., Ge, Y., Fang, B.: Improved dtw algorithm for online signature verification based on writing forces. In: Huang, D.-S., Zhang, X.-P., Huang, G.-B. (eds.) ICIC 2005. LNCS, vol. 3644, pp. 631–640. Springer, Heidelberg (2005)
10. Mailah, M., Lim, B.H.: Biometric signature verification using pen position, time, velocity and pressure parameters. Jurnal Teknologi A 48A, 35–54 (2008)
11. Baron, R., Plamondon, R.: Acceleration measurement with an instrumented pen for signature verification and handwriting analysis. IEEE Transactions on Instrumentation and Measurement 38, 1132–1138 (1989)
12. Lew, J.S.: Optimal accelerometer layouts for data recovery in signature verification. IBM J. Res. Dev. 24, 496–511 (1980)
13. Bashir, M., Kempf, J.: Reduced dynamic time warping for handwriting recognition based on multi-dimensional time series of a novel pen device. World Academy of Science, Engineering and Technology 45, 382–388 (2008)
14. Rohlik, O., Mautner, P., Matousek, V., Kempf, J.: A new approach to signature verification: digital data acquisition pen. Neural Network World 11(5), 493–501 (2001)
15. Mautner, P., Rohlik, O., Matousek, V., Kempf, J.: Signature verification using art-2 neural network. In: Proceedings of the 9th International Conference on Neural Information Processing, ICONIP 2002, vol. 2, pp. 636–639 (November 2002)
16. Ortega-Garcia, J., Fierrez-Aguilar, J., Simon, D., Gonzalez, J., Faundez-Zanuy, M., Espinosa, V., Satue, A., Hernaez, I., Igarza, J.J., Vivaracho, C., Escudero, D., Moro, Q.I.: MCYT baseline corpus: a bimodal biometric database. IEE Proceedings of Vision, Image and Signal Processing 150(6), 395–401 (2003)
17. Kopasz, K., Makra, P., Gingl, Z.: Edaq530: A transparent, open-end and open-source measurement solution in natural science education. Eur. J. Phys. 32, 491–504 (2011)
18. http://www.noise.physx.u-szeged.hu/edudev/edaq530

Dynamic Zoning Selection for Handwritten Character Recognition

Luciane Y. Hirabara[1], Simone B.K. Aires[1], Cinthia O.A. Freitas[1],
Alceu S. Britto Jr.[1], and Robert Sabourin[2]

[1] PUCPR-Pontificia Universidade Católica do Paraná
[2] ETS-Ecole de Technologie Supérieure
{luciane,cinthia,alceu,simone}@ppgia.pucpr.br,
robert.sabourin@etsmtl.ca

Abstract. This paper presents a two-level based character recognition method in which a dynamically selection of the most promising zoning scheme for feature extraction allows us to obtain interesting results for character recognition. The first level consists of a conventional neural network and a look-up-table that is used to suggest the best zoning scheme for a given unknown character. The information provided by the first level drives the second level in the selection of the appropriate feature extraction method and the corresponding class-modular neural network. The experimental protocol has shown significant recognition rates for handwritten characters (from 80.82% to 88.13%).

Keywords: dynamic selection, zoning mechanism, handwritten character, recognition.

1 Introduction

An important subject of research in the field of document analysis and recognition is still the recognition of handwritten characters. The motivation is that even after many research efforts there is still a gap between human reading capabilities and the recognition systems. Over the years researchers have applied different techniques and methods to reduce this gap. In this direction, several authors have presented different schemes based on zoning mechanisms or regional decomposition methods. Zoning is a simple way to obtain local information and it has been used for extraction of topological information from patterns [1]. The goal of the zoning is to obtain local characteristics instead of global characteristics. This is possible, since a zoning scheme consists in partitioning the pattern bounding box in regions or zones. The resulting partitions allow us to determine the position of specific features of the pattern to be recognized [2]. However, the major problem related to zoning mechanisms is to choose the best zoning scheme to solve the recognition problem of different classes of characters.

Thus, depending on the domain of application or the experience of the researcher the zoning can be carried out exclusively on the basis of intuitive motivations [1] or based on the easier manner, i.e. fixed or symmetrical zoning [3-5]. Different zoning approaches for characters recognition can be found in the literature. By using

C. San Martin and S.-W. Kim (Eds.): CIARP 2011, LNCS 7042, pp. 507–514, 2011.

IRONOFF handwritten database, the authors in [3] report recognition rates of 87.1% and 77.8% for uppercase and lowercase characters respectively, handling directly 2D pattern avoiding the subtle stage of the extraction of relevant and applying MLP-NN (Multiple Layer Perceptron - Neural Network). Other interesting results were reported in [5], where the recognition rate for lowercase characters was 80.75% and for uppercase characters was 89.21%; applying Class-Modular MLP-NN and a feature set based on directional and curvature histograms for the contour image and a zoning mechanism into Z = 16 (4 x 4) or Z = 20 (4 x 5) regions. Using the isolated French word images from IRONOFF database, the authors in [4] describes a system based on sliding window segmentation and 140 geometrical features are extracted from each frame. The classification stage is based on conventional discrete Hidden Markov Models (HMM) using Vector Quantization (VQ). This paper reported 83.1% of recognition rate for handwritten words.

The author in [6] uses a regular zoning scheme based on 4 symmetrical regions and reported 92.3% and 84.6% for upper and lowercase characters from NIST database. Using the same database, the work described in [7] uses an implicit zoning scheme based on row and columns discrete HMMs and reached 90.0%, and 84.0% for upper and lowercase characters, respectively. Finally, the work presented in [8] describes an automatic approach to define the zoning for offline handwritten digit recognition, using Multi-Objective Evolutionary Algorithms (MOEAs). The authors pointed out that their proposal provides a self adaptive methodology to define the zoning strategy with Z non-overlapping zones and an acceptable error rate, with no need of human intervention during the search stage. The best result was obtained using six zones composed by three symmetrical rows (horizontal: 2/6, 2/6, 2/6) and three non-symmetrical columns (vertical: 1/6, 3/6, 2/6) using a random subset from the NIST SD-19 hsf-0123 handwritten digit database with 50,000 samples for the training set, and another 10,000 for the validation set to evaluate the individual's error rate. The error rate applying this zoning strategy was 5%. However, the authors left an open problem: since, it is very difficult to find an unique and best zoning for all classes, is it possible to dynamically select the best zoning scheme for an unknown pattern?

To answer this question, this paper presents a dynamic zoning selection applied in a two-level method for character recognition. In the first level, a conventional Neural Network and a traditional zoning scheme based on four equal zones (Z=4) is used to predict the top 3 recognition results for an unknown pattern. In fact, the idea is to predict the best zoning scheme from the different options shown in Figure 1. The second level uses the selected zoning to extract the features for a feedforward MLP-NN using a Class-Modular architecture [9] that decides the final recognition result.

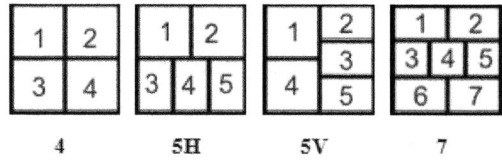

Fig. 1. Zoning Mechanisms: Z=4, 5H, 5V and 7

The paper is organized as follows. Section 2 presents the baseline system and how the dynamic zoning selection is proposed. Section 3 presents the experimental results. Section 4 discusses the experimental results and points the future works.

2 Baseline System

The proposed method uses as input a 256 grey-level image. Then, a preprocessing step is applied, which is composed of binarization (OTSU algorithm [10]) and bounding box definition. The feature set is based on Concavities/Convexities deficiencies [11]. This feature set puts on evidence the topological and geometrical properties of the shape to be recognized and is computed by labeling the background pixels of the input images. The basic idea of concavity/convexity deficiencies is the following: for each background pixel in the image we search in four-directions: North, South, East, and West - Fig. 2. When black pixels are reached in all directions, we branch out in four auxiliary directions in order to confirm if the current white pixel is really inside a closed contour. Figure 2 shows the obtained result after the labeling process. The entire and definitive alphabet has 24 different symbols ($S = 24$) [2].

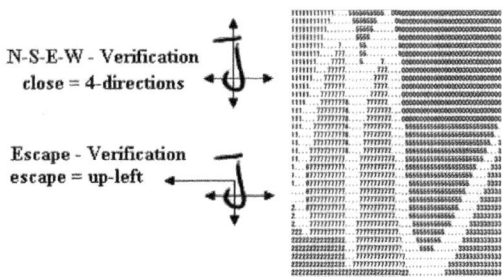

Fig. 2. Feature extraction: character *"n"*

These global features are extracted considering the following zoning strategies: $Z = 4$, 5H, 5V and 7 regions, as presented and defined by [2]. This hybrid feature extraction provided to the system a global and local description of the shape to be recognized.

The proposed classification method is based on two levels; (a) dynamic zoning selection (DZS) and (b) character recognition (CR), as depicted in Figure 3. The first level is composed of a conventional Neural Network classifier. Given an unknown character, the feature extraction is done using a classical zoning ($Z = 4$). The main objective of the first level is to provide the best zoning scheme for the second level. So, for this purpose, we previously calculate the confusion matrices of the class-modular Neural Networks trained based on the different zoning options: $Z = 4$, 5H, 5V and 7 regions as presented in Figure 1. Thus, the best zoning scheme is selected by looking for the confusion matrix that present the smaller number of confusions among the corresponding character classes involved in the Top 3 recognition result. The zoning scheme corresponding to the found matrix is selected for the feature extraction of the second level. However, in case of a tie when comparing the number of confusions, the best zoning scheme is chosen by considering only the Top 1 recognition result. In this case, the confusion matrix that presents the best recognition result for the Top 1 result is selected for feature extraction of the next level.

The second level of proposed method is based on a feedforward MLP-NN using Class-Modular architecture [9]. In Class-Modular architecture a single task is decomposed into multiple subtasks and each subtask is allocated to an expert network. In this paper, as well as in [9] the K-classification problem is decomposed into K 2-classication subproblems, one for each of the K classes. A 2-classification subproblem is solved by the 2-classifier specifically designed for the corresponding class. The 2-classifier is only responsible for one specific class and discriminates that class from the other K-1 classes. In the class-modular framework, K 2-classifiers solve the original K-classification problem cooperatively, and the class decision module integrates the outputs from the K 2-classifiers.

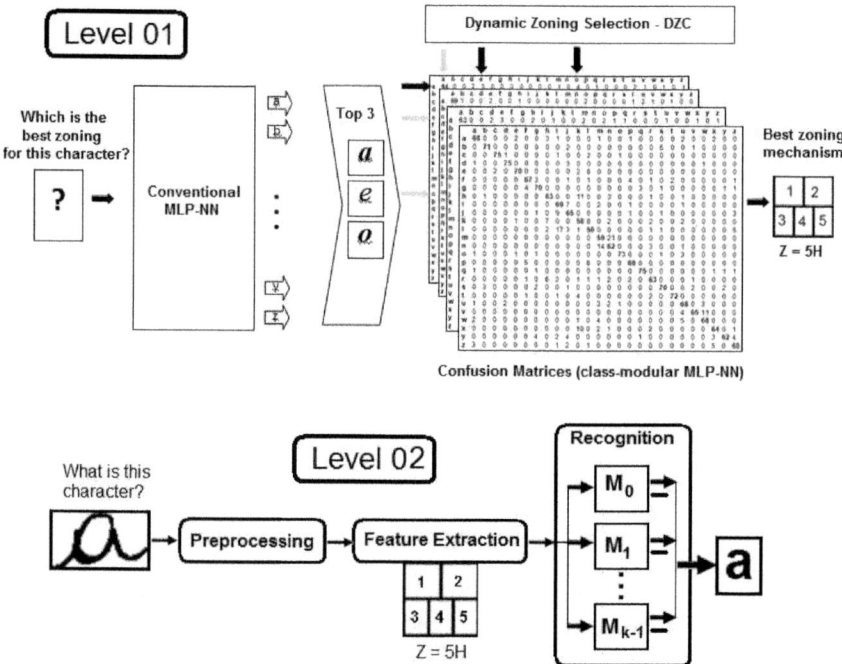

Fig. 3. Baseline system overview: Level 01(Dynamic Zoning Selection - DZS) and Level 02 (Character Recognition - CR)

At this level, the feature extraction is dynamic and depends on the zoning scheme selected in the first level.

3   Experimental Results

This section presents the main results undertaken during the development of the proposed method. The description of the used database and the results of the first and second levels of the proposed method are described.

3.1 Database

The experiments were carried out using the lowercase handwritten character database from IRESTE/University of Nantes (France), called IRONOFF (IRESTE ON/OFF Dual Database), which is composed of isolated digits, isolated lowercase and uppercase characters and, isolated words from a 197 word lexicon. The IRONOFF database was selected because it is fully cursive. It was collected from about 700 writers, mainly of French nationality. The experiments were carried out using three subsets, nominated as the training, validation and testing sets. Their compositions are as follows: 60%, 20% and 20% for training, validation, and testing, respectively. The database sums up 10,400 images of lowercase handwritten characters [12].

3.2 Conventional MLP-NN

As described before, the first level of the proposed method consists of a conventional neural network classifier, which is composed of $N = 96$ (24 x Z, where $Z = 4$) nodes in the input layer, a 59 number of nodes in the hidden layer, and an output layer with 26 nodes. Validation sets were employed in order to avoid overtraining and to make possible a Cross-Validation process. All the classes were trained together.

The proposed method considers the three major outputs (Top 3) for each sample of character class in the test database. We have experimentally evaluated different numbers of neurons in the hidden layer and the best results were achieved with 59 neurons. Firstly, the experiments consider the global feature extraction, without applying the zoning mechanism (Z-Global). Then, the classifier was experimented with the zoning schemes presented in Figure 1. We observed in Table 1 that there is an increase recognition rate when applying the $Z = 4$ as strategy of zoning, as well as an increase when compared from $Z = 4$ to $Z = 7$. At this point is possible to define the best zoning mechanism for each class of character. This information is used to construct a kind of a look-up-table used in the first level of our method. In fact, the look-up-table consists in the confusion matrices derived from the use of the different zoning strategies and the class-modular MLP-NN. Thus, by analyzing the confusion among the three major outputs (TOP3), it is possible to define the more appropriated strategy of zoning. Thereby the zoning that had the small number of confusion among the Top 3 outputs is assigned to be used in the second level of the proposed method. As explained before, in case of a tie the zoning scheme of the top 1 recognition result is selected.

3.3 Class Modular MLP-NN

The second level of the proposed method is based on a Class-Modular MLP-NN, where each of K 2-classifiers is trained independently of the other classes using the training and validation set. To train 2-classifiers for each character class ($K = 26$), we re-organize the samples in the original training and validation set into K-two groups, Z0 and Z1, such that Z0 contains the samples from the current class and Z1 all the others, taking into account the *a priori* probability for each class. To recognize the input character patterns, the class decision module takes only the values of O_0 and uses the simple winner-takes-all scheme to determine the final class. Table 1 presents the recognition rate obtained for each zoning mechanism. All these results confirm that the class-modular network is superior in terms of convergence over the conventional network (according to the monitoring of the MSE—mean-square error) and in terms of recognition capability than the conventional network, as presented by [5] [9].

Table 1. Conventional NN and Class-Modular MLP-NN

Characters	Conventional NN Recognition Rate (%)					Class-Modular MLP-NN Recognition Rate (%)			
	ZGlobal	Z4	Z5H	Z5V	Z7	Z4	Z5H	Z5V	Z7
a	68.75	83.75	82.50	80.00	83.75	80.00	86.25	78.75	85.00
b	61.25	82.50	86.25	83.75	86.25	88.75	88.75	90.00	88.75
c	71.25	95.00	97.50	93.75	95.00	93.75	95.00	88.75	93.75
d	42.50	92.50	90.00	91.25	86.25	93.75	91.25	81.25	93.75
e	76.25	83.75	83.75	77.50	63.75	82.50	83.75	77.50	87.50
f	26.25	38.75	67.50	67.50	65.00	80.00	68.75	80.00	83.75
g	40.00	65.00	71.25	67.50	61.25	63.75	65.00	73.75	87.50
h	37.50	76.25	72.50	67.50	68.75	76.25	80.00	70.00	78.75
i	80.00	81.25	82.50	82.50	77.50	86.25	88.75	86.25	86.25
j	70.00	77.50	78.75	73.75	81.25	81.25	77.50	81.25	81.25
k	61.25	66.25	73.75	62.50	76.25	65.00	72.50	72.50	72.50
l	53.75	70.00	58.75	66.25	68.75	70.00	62.50	72.50	62.50
m	13.75	48.75	71.25	60.00	61.25	50.00	53.75	85.00	73.75
n	82.50	81.25	65.00	63.75	77.50	76.25	65.00	82.50	77.50
o	82.50	88.75	90.00	93.75	91.25	88.75	87.50	90.00	91.25
p	76.25	81.25	87.50	82.50	87.50	76.25	87.50	88.75	86.25
q	87.50	95.00	93.75	98.75	97.50	95.00	92.50	88.75	93.75
r	65.00	71.25	67.50	72.50	73.75	77.50	72.50	66.25	78.75
s	76.25	85.00	77.50	81.25	86.25	88.75	78.75	81.25	87.50
t	86.25	91.25	78.75	91.25	87.50	87.50	88.75	87.50	90.00
u	50.00	83.75	83.75	78.75	82.50	87.50	83.75	68.75	85.00
v	62.50	71.25	81.25	83.75	83.75	80.00	82.50	80.00	81.25
w	83.75	88.75	92.50	87.50	90.00	83.75	87.50	90.00	85.00
x	82.50	88.75	82.50	86.25	86.25	83.75	86.25	85.00	80.00
y	90.00	92.50	90.00	92.50	87.50	90.00	90.00	87.50	77.50
z	88.75	87.50	86.25	88.75	95.00	82.50	85.00	88.75	85.00
Average	66.01	79.52	80.48	79.81	**80.82**	81.11	80.82	81.63	**83.61**

3.4 Dynamic Zoning Selection

The conventional Neural Network classifier in the first level provides the top 3 recognition result and the most promising zoning scheme based on the confusion matrices previously created by considering different zoning schemes. The second level uses such information for feature extraction and selection of the appropriated Class-Modular MLP-NN. By applying the dynamic zoning selection - DZC (first level based on class-modular MLP-NN) and character recognition – CR (second level based on class-modular MLP-NN) the system reached 88.13% of average rate. Table 2 presents the recognition rates for each class of handwritten characters.

3.5 Related Works

Table 3 presents the results of some related works that uses the IRONOFF database. Comparing results is not easy since the works refers to different sets, feature extraction and classification strategies. Taking into consideration these differences, the results indicate that the dynamic zoning selection (DZS) is promising and the recognition rates are comparable to the literature.

Table 2. DZS (Level 01) + Character Recognition (Level 02)

Character	Rec. Rate (%)	Character	Rec. Rate (%)
a	85.00	o	92.50
b	91.25	p	92.50
c	96.25	q	95.00
d	93.75	r	82.50
e	87.50	s	95.00
f	86.25	t	92.50
g	88.75	u	91.25
h	83.75	v	86.25
i	90.00	w	90.00
j	78.75	x	87.50
k	80.00	y	91.25
l	80.00	z	88.75
m	82.50	Average	**88.13**
n	82.50		

Table 3. Related works (IRONOFF databases)

Method	Tr	V	Ts	Rec. (%)
[4] – IRONOFF - words				83.1
[3] – IRONOFF uppercase lowercase	7,953 7,952	-- --	3,926 3,916	87.1 77.8
[2] – IRONOFF uppercase (Z = 4) uppercase (Z = 7)	6,240 6,240	2,080 2,080	2,080 2,080	83.0 84.7
[16] – IRONOFF - lowercase	--	--	--	80.7
Proposed Method - lowercase	6,240	2,080	2,080	88.1

4 Conclusion and Future Works

This paper presented a two-level based character recognition method in which a dynamically zoning selection (DZS) scheme for feature extraction allows us to obtain promising results for character recognition. In the first level a conventional MLP-NN and the analysis of confusion matrices are used to determine the most promising zoning scheme for a given unknown character. The information provided by the first level drives the second level in the selection of the appropriate feature extraction method and the corresponding class-modular neural network. The experimental results have shown some significant improvement in the recognition rates for lowercase handwritten characters from 80.82% (Conventional MLP-NN – Z = 7) to 88.13% (DZS + CR).

References

1. Lecce, V., Dimauro, G., Guerriero, A., Impedovo, S., Pirlo, G., Salzo, A.: Zoning design for handwritten numerical recogniotion. In: 7th Int. Workshop on Frontiers in Handwriting Recognition, pp. 583–588 (2000)
2. Freitas, C.O.A., Oliveira, L.E.S., Bortolozzi, F., Aires, S.B.K.: Handwritten Character Recognition using Non-Symmetrical Percpetual Zoning. International Journal of Pattern Recognition and Artificial Intelligence (IJPRAI) 21(1), 1–21 (2007)
3. Poisson, E., Viard-Gaudin, C., Lallican, P.M.: Multi-Modular architecture based on convolutional Neural networks for online handwritten character recognition. In: International Conference on Neural Information Processing, vol. 5, pp. 2444–2448 (2002)
4. Tay, Y.H., Lallican, P.M, Khalid, M., Gaudin, C.V, Knerr, S.: An Offline Cursive Handwritten Word Recognition System. In: IEEE Region 10 Conference, TENCON, Singapore, pp. 19–22 (2001)
5. de Avila, S., Matos, L., Freitas, C., de Carvalho, J.M.: Evaluating a Zoning Mechanism and Class-Modular Architecture for Handwritten Characters Recognition. In: Rueda, L., Mery, D., Kittler, J. (eds.) CIARP 2007. LNCS, vol. 4756, pp. 515–524. Springer, Heidelberg (2007)
6. Koerich, A.L.: Large Vocabulary Off-Line Handwritten Word Recognition, PhD thesis, École de Technologie Supérieure, Montreal-Canada (August 2002)
7. Britto Jr., A.S., Sabourin, R., Bortolozzi, F., Suen, C.Y.: Foreground and background information in an HMM-Based method for recognition of isolated characters and numeral strings. In: 9th Int. Workshop on Frontiers in Handwriting Recognition (IWFHR-9), Tokio Japan, pp. 371–376 (2004)
8. Radtke, P.V.W., Oliveira, L.S., Sabourin, R., Wong, T.: Intelligent zoning design using multi-objective evolutionary algorithms. In: 7th Int. Conf. Document Analysis and Recognition ICDAR, pp. 824–828 (2003)
9. Oh, I.-S., Suen, C.Y.: A class-modular feedforward neural network for handwriting recognition. Pattern Recognition 35, 229–244 (2002)
10. Otsu, N.: A threshold selection method from gray-level histograms. IEEE Trans. Syst. Man. Cybern. 9(1), 63–66 (1979)
11. Parker, J.R.: Algorithms for Image Processing and Computer Vision. John Wiley (1997)
12. Viard-Gaudin, C.: The ironoff user manual, IRESTE, University of Nantes, France (1999)

Forecasting Cash Demand in ATM Using Neural Networks and Least Square Support Vector Machine

Cristián Ramírez and Gonzalo Acuña

Universidad de Santiago de Chile, USACH, Departamento de Ingeniería Informática.
Av Libertador Bernardo OHiggins 1363, Santiago, Chile
cristian.ramirez@gestran.cl,
gonzalo.acuna@usach.cl

Abstract. In this work we forecast the daily ATM cash demand using dynamic models of type Nonlinear Autoregressive Exogenous inputs (NARX) and Nonlinear Autoreggressive Moving Average with Exogeneous Inputs (NARMAX) performed by Neural Networks (NN) and Least Square Support Vector Machine (LS-SVM) and used to predict one step (OSA) or multistep (MPO). The aim is to compare which model perform better results. We found that the Multilayer Perceptron NN presented the best index of agreement with an average of 0.87 in NARX-OSA and 0.85 in NARX-MPO. After, Radial Basis Function NN was 0.82 for both cases. Finally, LS-SVM obtained the worst results with 0.78 for NARX-OSA and 0.70 for NARX-MPO. No significant differences between NARX and NARMAX structures were found. Our contribution would have obtained the 2nd place in the NN5 competition of computational methods.

Keywords: MLP, RBF, LS-SVM, NARX, NARMAX, OSA, MPO, NN5, IA, SMAPE.

1 Introduction

Automatic teller machines (ATMs) are devices financed and managed by financial institutions that made available to customers a simple method for conducting financial transactions in a public space with almost no human intervention. According to estimates developed by ATMIA (ATM Industry Association) the number of ATMs worldwide for 2007 exceeded 1.6 million units [1].

Some banks tend to keep an excess of up to 40% more cash in their terminals (ATM) of what they really need. In this regard, many experts believe that excess of cash is near to 15% to 20%.

Costs related to keeping cash at an ATM represent from 35% to 60% of total maintenance costs [2]. Through improvements in administration and management of cash, banks can avoid falling into losses in new business opportunities

C. San Martin and S.-W. Kim (Eds.): CIARP 2011, LNCS 7042, pp. 515–522, 2011.

due to having high cash assets. This is why it is necessary to develop new methods and advanced ways of estimating the demand for money at an ATM, so that financial institutions can lower their operating costs.

On the other hand, banks and financial services assume that the demand for cash can be associated with certain variables that can have substantial effects on the level of demand for cash. Some of these variables that we must consider are the following [3]:

1. ATM Location
2. Seasonal factors such as weekends, holidays, etc.
3. Historical data from the ATM.

At present the tools and technological processes have become more complex, so it is necessary to develop methods and applications that succeed in improving these tasks. One way to address this problem adequately is to model the system dynamics using system identification [4].

System identification [5] has had great relevance in different areas of knowledge such as physics, chemistry, biology, economics, etc because dynamical systems -those in which the output value depends not only on the values of its inputs at the same moment, but also of its past values- abound in our environment and that is the reason why models are required for their analysis, forecasting, simulation, design and control. These models need to simulate the real behavior of the systems in cases when there is limited prior knowledge of its structure [4].

Our contribution consists in performing a comparative analysis of different model structures (Non Linear Regressive with Exogeneous Input, NARX and/or Non Linear Regressive Moving Average with Exogeneous Input NARMAX) using NN (Multilayer Perceptron, MLP and Radial Basis Function, RBF) and Least Square-Support Vector Machine (LS-SVM) for One-Step-Ahead (OSA) and Model Predictive Output (MPO) cash demand in ATM.

This document is configured as follows: after the Introduction, in Section 2 data processing is developed, followed by the methodology used (Section 3). In Section 4 results are shown and finally in Section 5 we will present the conclusions obtained in this work.

2   Data Processing

Data comes from the NN5 competition [6] and correspond to a set of 30 series of ATM's withdrawals used for training purposes. In addition, 11 series of the same characteristics that are called reduced dataset NN5, serve as a benchmark for comparison between the results here obtained and the general ranking of the competition.

NN5 time series competition includes a time series of cash withdrawals on a daily basis from ATMs located in different parts of England. All series show a strong cyclical component of 7 days, as well as some recurring seasonal periods such as summer holidays or Christmas. Almost all series contain empty values (missing values) and some of these series show long-term trends or irregularities

such as outliers or "gaps" [7]. The aim of the NN5 competition is to obtain
the most accurate forecast possible with a horizon of 56 days for OSA using
computational intelligence techniques. Each time series consists of 2 years of
daily cash withdrawals at ATM [8].

All series include 3 types of "Gaps" or singularities.

- Observations equal to 0, indicating that no withdrawals have taken place
  due to "cash out" of the ATM.
- "Missing Values" indicating that on that day the client's transaction was
  not recorded.
- Outliers, indicating which data is above or below the normal behavior of
  withdrawals at the ATM.

This research addresses the 3 types of abnormalities, detecting outliers, missing
values and values equal to 0.

To detect outliers the boxplot method by quartiles is used with k = 1.5 where
the lowest quartile is $Q_1 = x_f$ with the f-th ordered observation. f is defined as:

$$f = \frac{\frac{n+1}{2} + 1}{2} \tag{1}$$

If f involves a fraction, Q_1 is the average of x_f and x_{f+1} . For obtaining Q_3, the
f observations are counted from the beginning, e.g $Q_3 = x_{n+1-f}$ [9]. Then an
outlier is one that meets the following condition:

$$x < Q_1 - k(Q_3 - Q_1) \tag{2}$$

$$x > Q_3 + k(Q_3 - Q_1) \tag{3}$$

On the other hand, once each of the anomalous data is identified (a total of
870) it is replaced by cubic spline interpolation with a polynomial form $P(x) =
ax^3 + bx^2 + cx + d$. Fig. 1. shows the amount of outlier identified by each ATM.

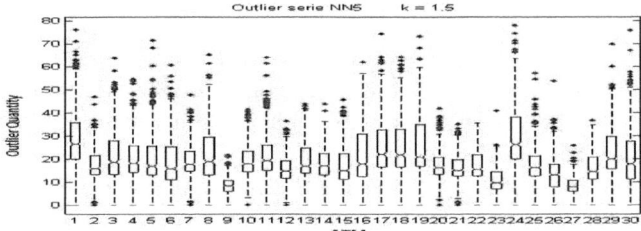

Fig. 1. Identification of outliers by the boxplot method. (*): Outlier data. In the X-
axis 30 ATM are shown while in the Y-axis the amount earned by each ATM can be
observed. All Outlier along the series were replaced by cubic spline interpolation.

3   Methodology

A total of 13 experiments for each series predicted separately (30 initial plus 11 reduced-series ATM) are performed with the following architectures: MLP-NARX [10]; MLP-NARMAX [11]; RBF-NARX; RBF-NARMAX [12] and LS-SVM-NARX [13]. Each structure is used for OSA and MPO predictions. 691 data coming from the set consisting of 30 ATM's are used for training while 100 data are used for testing (prediction purposes). On the other hand, for comparison reasons the NN5 reduced series, consisting of 11 ATM's will be used, under the rules of the competition, i.e. 735 data will be used for training and 56 for OSA predictions.

The quality indices used to measure the performance of each architecture are:

$$SMAPE = \frac{1}{n} \sum_{i=1}^{n} \frac{|\hat{y}_i - y_i|}{\frac{|\hat{y}_i| + |y_i|}{2}} * 100 \tag{4}$$

Symmetric mean absolute percentage error (SMAPE) used in the NN5 competition to determine the winner [14] and the Index of Agreement (IA) [15]:

$$IA = 1 - \frac{\sum_{i=1}^{n}(y_i - \hat{y}_i)^2}{\sum_{i=1}^{n}(|y_i'| + |\hat{y}_i'|)^2} \tag{5}$$

with

$$y_i' = y_i - y_m$$

$$\hat{y}_i' = \hat{y}_i - y_m$$

To determine the amount of autoregressors the system needs a *Lipschitz* function is used [16]. The necessary amount of regressors is 4. Data were normalized in the range [0 1] using the following formula:

$$y = \frac{(y_{max} - y_{min}) * (x - x_{min})}{(x_{max} - x_{min}) + y_{min}} \tag{6}$$

Regarding the variables of the system they could be affected by the number of working days, the day of the week, the week of the month and other calendar effects such as festivals and religious events [17].

In NN5 series a strong daily component is present with a transactional peak on Wednesday, Thursday and Friday. On the other hand, a strong seasonal component is present depending on the week of the year.

Finally the day of the month (u1), day of week (u2), week (u3), month (u4) and a dummy variable (u5) to indicate special dates such as month-end, holidays and other calendar effects of interest are considered as inputs to the system. Given this the considered prediction function is as follows:

$$y_t = f(y_{t-1}, y_{t-2}, y_{t-3}, y_{t-4}, u1_{t-1}, u2_{t-1}, u3_{t-1}, u4_{t-1}, u5_{t-1}) + \varrho_t \qquad (7)$$

With the following associated predictor:

$$\hat{y}(t|\Theta) = \hat{y}(t|t-1, \Theta) = g(\varphi(t), \Theta) \qquad (8)$$

$\varphi(t)$ is a vector containing the regressors, Θ is a vector containg the weights and g is the function realized by the neural network.

In the case of MPO NARMAX predictors:

$$\hat{y}_{MPO}(k) = f[\hat{y}(k-1), ., \hat{y}(k-4), u1(k-1), .., u5(k-1), 0, 0] \qquad (9)$$

The presence of both 0 is because, for prediction, the future values of the error are not known [18].

On the other hand, to find the parameters of LS-SVM tunelssvm toolbox with simplex method and 20-folds cross validation is used, while for the MLP network 9 input neurons, 4 hidden neurons and 1 output neuron is used. Finally for designing the RBF network the NEWRB Matlab Toolbox is used with 9 input neurons and 1 output, the hidden layer is configured at runtime by the Toolbox.

4   Results

The results will be compared based on the best, worst and average results of the experiments using the two quality indices presented in Section 3.

Table 1. Results for all predictive structures and for a prediction horizon of 100 days

System		IA			SMAPE		
		Mean	Best	Worst	Mean	Best	Worst
MLP	NARX-OSA	0.87	0.93	0.70	21.37	15.42	32.50
	NARX-MPO	0.85	0.91	0.69	22.71	14.54	35.84
	NARMAX-OSA	0.87	0.92	0.67	21.56	14.93	28.99
	NARMAX-MPO	0.86	0.92	0.72	22.65	16.80	35.21
RBF	NARX-OSA	0.82	0.92	0.62	25.82	16.05	43.80
	NARX-MPO	0.82	0.92	0.61	25.50	16.05	43.80
	NARMAX-OSA	0.82	0.92	0.62	26.71	15.25	43.16
	NARMAX-MPO	0.83	0.92	0.63	25.91	14.26	51.66
LS-SVM	NARX-OSA	0.78	0.92	0.46	25.48	14.87	39.04
	NARX-MPO	0.70	0.93	0.28	29.70	14.54	53.53

The results show that MLP networks were those that performed better averaging IA=0.87 and IA=0.85 for OSA and MPO predictions respectively. On the other hand, RBF networks also have a good IA= 0.82 for both cases. LS-SVM had the worst results with IA=0.78 (OSA) and IA=0.70 (MPO). Regarding the index SMAPE, MLP again has the better results with 22%, followed by RBF with 26% and LS-SVM with approximately 27%.

These results also show that the difference between NARX and NARMAX models is not significant. In many cases they get the same value. It also shows the great capacity of the MLP to perform MPO predictions (horizon=100 days) with an IA=0.86.

Figure 2 shows MLP performance NARX-OSA and NARX-MPO for ATM 22.

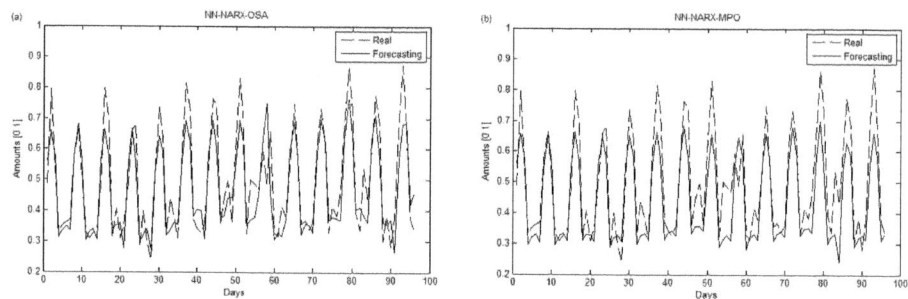

Fig. 2. (a) MLP-NARX-OSA and (b) NARX-MPO predictions for the ATM 22. The quality indexes for OSA are IA = 0.9348 and SMAPE 12.53%. For MPO predictions, IA = 0.9241 and SMAPE = 14.93%.

Table 2 show our results and ranking for reduced dataset NN5.

Table 2. Results obtained with the reduced set NN5

Model		Ranking		
		SMAPE	General	NN & CI methods
MLP	NARX-OSA	19.80%	$3°$	$2°$
	NARMAX-OSA	20.55%	$4°$	$3°$
RBF	NARX-OSA	25.63%	$22°$	$14°$
	NARMAX-OSA	26.03%	$23°$	$15°$
LS-SVM	NARX-OSA	24.35%	$18°$	$12°$

According to the results shown in Table 2, the MLP system, NARX-OSA would have won in the 2nd place the NN5 competition and would have obtained the 3nd place in the overall ranking of all methods.

5   Conclusions

The results show that MLP-NARX model developed here allows to make predictions with a high degree of quality over 85% for long-term predictions. On the other hand, the NARMAX model shows no significant advantage over NARX, therefore NARX is better, aiming to simplicity considerations. Regarding the RBF networks they are also considered as a reliable alternative to tackle these problems, while LS-SVM has poorer results. In the future, new prediction methods will be studied about LS-SVM to improve the obtained results.

Acknowledgement. The authors like to acknowledge partial funding of this work by FONDECYT project 1090316.

References

1. Simutis, R., Dilijonas, D., Bastina, L.: Cash demand forecasting for ATM using neural Networks and support vector regresin algorithms. In: 20th EURO Mini Conference, Vilnius, pp. 416–421 (2008)
2. Simutis, R., Dilijonas, D., Bastina, L., Friman, J., Drobinov, P.: Optimization of Cash Management for ATM Network. Information Technology and Control 36(1A) (2007) ISSN 1392 124x
3. Justine, P.: ATMs and Cash Demand Forecasting: A Study of Two Commercial Bank. Nagoya University of Commerce and Business, 1-20-1, Nishiki, Naka-Ku, Nagoya City, JAPAN- 460 0003 (2007)
4. Velasquez, E.R.: Redes neuronales para sistemas dinmicos tipo NOE y Narmax. Tesis de magster, Universidad de Santiago de Chile. Departamento de Informtica (2007)
5. Ljung, L.: System Identification: Theory for the User. Prentice Hall, Englewood Cliffs (1987)
6. NN5, Forecasting Competition for Artificial Neural Networks & Computational Intelligence (2008), http://www.neural-forecastingcompetition.com/NN5
7. Jorg, D., Wichard: Forecasting the NN5 time series with hybrid models. Leibniz-Institut für Molekulare Pharmakologie (FMP), Molecular Modeling Group, Robert-Roessle-Str. 10, 13125, Berlin, Germany (2010)
8. Teddy, S.D.: Forecasting ATM Cash Demand using a local learning model of a cerebellar associative memory network. Data Mining Department, Institute for Infocomm Research Singapore 138632, Singapore (2010)
9. Tukey, J.W.: Exploratory Data Analisis. Addison Wesley (1977)
10. Bouchachia, A., Bouchachia, S.: Ensemble Learning for Time Series Prediction. In: First International Workshop on Nonlinear Dynamics Synchronization, Austria, INDS (2008)
11. Gao, Y., Joo Er, M.: NARMAX time series model prediction: feedfoward and recurrent fuzzy neural network approaches. Fuzzy Sets and Systems 150, 331–350 (2005)
12. Zemouri, R., Racoceanu, D., Zerhouni, N.: Recurrent radial basis function network for time-series prediction. In: Engineering Applications of Artificial Intelligence, pp. 453–463 (2003)
13. Espinoza, M., Falck, T., Suykens, J., De Moor, B.: Time Series Prediction using LS-SVMs. Kasteelpark Arenberg 10, B-3001 Leuven, Heverlee, Belgium (2008)
14. Garcia-Pedrero, A., Gomez-Gil, P.: Time Series Forecasting using Recurrent Neural Networks and Wavelet Reconstructed Signals. In: 20th International Conference on Electronics, Communications and Computer (CONIELECOMP) (2010)

15. Rode, M., Suhr, U.: Multi-Objective Calibration of a River Water Quality Model For The Elbe River, Germany, UFZ Centre for Environmental Research Leipzig Halle, Department of Hydrological Modelling, Brckstrae 3a, D-39114 Magdeburg, Germany
16. Norgaard, M.: Neural Networks for Modelling and Control of Dynamic Systems: A Practitioner's Handbook (Advanced Textbooks in Control and Signal Processing). Springer, Heidelberg (2006)
17. Soares, P., Rodriguez, P.: Calendar Effects in Daily ATM Withdrawals. Economics and Research Department. Banco de Portugal (2010)
18. Chen, P.-H., Lee, Y.-W., Chang, T.-L.: Predicting thermal instability in a closed loop pulsating heat pipe system. Applied Thermal Engineering (2008)

Deep Learning Networks for Off-Line Handwritten Signature Recognition

Bernardete Ribeiro[1], Ivo Gonçalves[1], and Sérgio Santos[1],
and Alexander Kovacec[2]

[1] CISUC, Department of Informatics Engineering
[2] Department of Mathematics,
University of Coimbra, Portugal
{bribeiro,icpg,sdsantos}@dei.uc.pt, kovacec@mat.uc.pt

Abstract. Reliable identification and verification of off-line handwritten signatures from images is a difficult problem with many practical applications. This task is a difficult vision problem within the field of biometrics because a signature may change depending on psychological factors of the individual. Motivated by advances in brain science which describe how objects are represented in the visual cortex, advanced research on deep neural networks has been shown to work reliably on large image data sets. In this paper, we present a deep learning model for off-line handwritten signature recognition which is able to extract high-level representations. We also propose a two-step hybrid model for signature identification and verification improving the misclassification rate in the well-known GPDS database.

Keywords: Deep Learning, Generative Models, Signature Recognition.

1 Introduction

The robustness and efficiency by which humans can recognize objects has since ever been intriguing for researchers and a trigger challenge in computational intelligence. Motivated by the extreme efficiency of the visual recognition system recent studies in brain science fields show that this is largely due to the expressive deep architecture employed by human visual cortex systems [15]. Research in brain science has recently traced the respective roles of the perceptual and visuo-motor skills on letter shape learning and handwriting movement execution [12]. In the scope of biometric analysis, an important problem is to distinguish between genuine and forged signature which is a hard task. The continued motivation to investigate this problem may be attributed in part to its challenging nature which depends on various factors such as behavioral characteristics like mood, fatigue, energy, etc.. Feature extraction and pattern recognition undoubtedly constitute essential components of a signature verification system. Research has been very intensive in the last years and many approaches have been devised mainly using discriminative techniques [2,6,5,7]. This kind of solutions plays an important role, with many applications in different fields, namely

C. San Martin and S.-W. Kim (Eds.): CIARP 2011, LNCS 7042, pp. 523–532, 2011.

in many official documents, such as detecting whether a person is misusing a citizen ID, or to verify if a bank check was really signed by the owner, or even accelerating the legal process of authenticating documents.

In this paper, we use instead a generative model broadly construed on a deep neural architecture trained by the contrastive divergence method introduced by Hinton [10]. The dataset is the GPDS("Grupo de Procesado Digital de Senales") signatures image database[1] which provided 300 signatures folders, 24 genuine and 30 faked for each folder. First, the feature extraction is performed implementing the algorithms described in literature [2] yet novel features were extracted. Second, we propose a two-step hybrid model, for signatures identification and verification, with good performance for all the dataset. For the sake of results comparison [2], one important part of the tests considered 39 and 44 folders of signatures. Third, we put forward a deep learning architecture which made possible to set up a model with representational layers working out as the human mental representation ability.

The paper is organized as follows. Section 2 describes both the Restricted Boltzmann Machine (RBM) model and the deep learning algorithm. We introduce the signature verification problem in Section 3 starting by describing the GPDS database, and proceeding with the preprocessing and the feature extraction stages. In Section 4 we introduce the experimental setup, present the results, and discuss the proposal regarding the two-step hybrid identification and verification model and the deep learning methodology. Finally, in Section 5, we summarize the conclusions and point out further lines for future work.

2   Deep Learning

Theoretical results suggest that deep learning architectures with multiple levels of non-linear operations provide high-level abstractions for object recognition similar to those found in the human brain. Deep Belief Networks have recently been proposed with notable success excelling the state-of-the-art in visual recognition and AI areas. Bengio [3] gives an overview of the learning algorithms for deep architectures, in particular those exploiting Restricted Boltzmann Machines, which are used to construct deeper models such as Deep Belief Networks.

2.1   Restricted Boltzmann Machine

A Restricted Boltzmann Machine (RBM) is an energy-based generative model that consists of a layer of binary visible units ($\mathbf{v}$, whose states are observed) and a layer of binary hidden units ($\mathbf{h}$, whose states cannot be observed)(Hintom, 2006 [10]), [11]. The hidden units with no pairwise connections act as latent variables (features) that allow the RBM to model distributions over state vectors (see Figure 1). With these restrictions, the hidden units are conditionally independent given visible units (i.e. a visible vector). Given an energy function

----
[1] Offline GPDS signature database http://www.gpds.ulpgc.es/download/

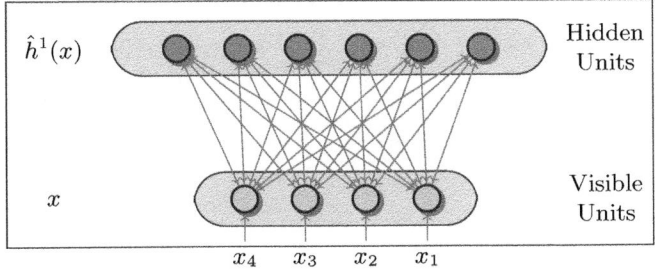

Fig. 1. Restricted Boltzmann Machine (RBM) with ($V = 4$, $H = 6$)

$E(\mathbf{v}, \mathbf{h})$ on the whole set of visible and hidden units, the joint probability is given by:

$$p(\mathbf{v}, \mathbf{h}) = \frac{e^{-E(\mathbf{v}, \mathbf{h})}}{Z} \qquad (1)$$

where Z is a normalizing partition function i.e., ensures that $p(\mathbf{v}, \mathbf{h})$ is a valid distribution.

For the binary units $h_i \in \{0, 1\}$ and $v_i \in \{0, 1\}$ the energy function of the whole network is:

$$E(\mathbf{v}, \mathbf{h}) = -\mathbf{h}^T \mathbf{W} \mathbf{v} - c^T \mathbf{v} - b\mathbf{h}^T$$
$$= -\sum_{jk} W_{jk} v_k h_j - \sum_k c_k v_k - \sum_j b_j h_j \qquad (2)$$

The marginal distribution over $\mathbf{v}$ is:

$$p(\mathbf{v}) = \sum_h p(\mathbf{v}, \mathbf{h}) = \sum_h p(\mathbf{v}|\mathbf{h}) p(\mathbf{h}) \qquad (3)$$

With H hidden units the hidden vector $\mathbf{h}$ can take 2^H possible values, thus 2^H distributions $p(\mathbf{v}|\mathbf{h})$. Therefore, computing the marginal for a large H is impractical. A good estimator of the log-likelihood gradient is the Contrastive Divergence (CD) algorithm ([10]).

A good property of the RBM is that the posterior of one layer given the other is easy to compute.

$$p(\mathbf{v}|\mathbf{h}) = \prod_k p(v_k|\mathbf{h}) \text{ where } p(v_k = 1|\mathbf{h}) = sigm(c_k + \sum_j W_{jk} h_j)$$
$$p(\mathbf{h}|\mathbf{v}) = \prod_j p(h_j|\mathbf{v}) \text{ where } p(h_j = 1|\mathbf{v}) = sigm(b_j + \sum_k W_{jk} v_k) \qquad (4)$$

where $sigm$ is the sigmoid function $\frac{1}{(1+e^{-z_i})}$ with $z_i = b_i + \sum_j W_{ji} s_j$ where s is the state of the unit i and b the bias. Inference of hidden factor $\mathbf{h}$ given the observed $\mathbf{v}$ can be done easily because $\mathbf{h}$ are conditionally independent given $\mathbf{v}$.

2.2   Learning in Deep Neural Networks

Definition 1. *Deep Neural Network: A deep neural network contains an input layer and an output layer, separated by l layers of hidden units.*

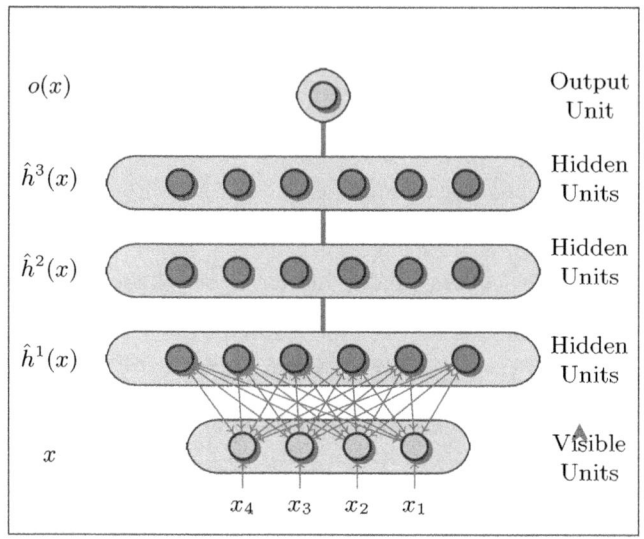

Fig. 2. Deep Belief Network with three hidden layers

The learning algorithm in Boltzmann Machines [1] allows to discover interesting features that may represent complex regularities in the training data. The algorithm can be very slow in networks with many layers, but it is fast in an RBM that has a single layer of feature detectors. The composed neural network can efficiently be trained by composing RBMs using the feature activations of one layer as the training data for the next (see Figure 2). The rationale is that the whole network can be viewed as a single, multilayer generative model and each additional layer improves a lower bound on the probability that the multilayer model would generate the training data (Hinton, 2006 [9]). Learning one hidden layer at a time is much more effective given their size which can be very large (MM of weights). Besides, highest level features are much more useful for classification (or dimension reduction) than raw data vectors.

An energy-based model of RBMs can be learnt by performing (stochastic) gradient descent on the empirical negative log-likelihood of the training data with respect to the RBM parameters.

$$\frac{\partial}{\partial \theta}(-\log p(\mathbf{v}_0)) = E_{p(\mathbf{h}|\mathbf{v}_0)}\left[\frac{\partial E(\mathbf{v}_0, \mathbf{h})}{\partial \theta}\right] - E_{p(\mathbf{v},\mathbf{h})}\left[\frac{\partial E(\mathbf{v}, \mathbf{h})}{\partial \theta}\right] \qquad (5)$$

where θ are the model parameters. This gradient is difficult to compute analytically. Markov Chain Monte Carlo methods are well-suited for RBM models. One iteration of the Markov Chain works well in practice.

$$\mathbf{v}_0 \xrightarrow{p(\mathbf{h}_0|\mathbf{v}_0)} \mathbf{h}_0 \xrightarrow{p(\mathbf{v}_1|\mathbf{h}_0)} \mathbf{v}_1 \xrightarrow{p(\mathbf{h}_1|\mathbf{v}_1)} \mathbf{h}_1 \tag{6}$$

where the operations of sampling are schematically indicated. Estimation of the gradient using the above procedure is denoted by CD-1, where CD-k represents the Contrastive Divergence algorithm [10,4] for performing k iterations of the Markov Chain up to $\mathbf{v}_k$.

Given a training set of state vectors (data) learning consists of finding weights and bias that define a Boltzmann distribution in which the training vectors have high probability.

3   Signature Verification: Problem Statement

Our main task is to develop an off-line signature verification system able to distinguish faked signatures from genuine ones. To achieve this goal, the images pre-processing, feature extraction and classifiers design steps need to be performed in the GPDS database of digitalized signatures.

3.1   GPDS Signature Data Base

The GPDS database was downloaded from http://www.gpds.ulpgc.es/downlo ad/ under a license agreement. The database contains data from 300 individuals: 24 genuine signatures for each individual plus 30 forgeries of his/her signature. Detailed information on how the GPDS dataset was built is given in [6] where it is also described how the data images were acquired (and pre-processed) prior to its completion (and organization) in the dataset. In [14] an interesting discussion on the different types of existing forgeries can be found.

3.2   Feature Extraction for the GPDS Signature Data Base

Feature extraction from image signatures is a crucial component of the verification rate system. Generally, an image feature is a distinctive primitive characteristic of a particular signature. More specifically, certain features are defined by the visual appearance of an image, while other result from image specific manipulations. The challenge is to find the optimal set of features able to perform forgery detection since it is not feasible to use the whole raw image. By using adequate algorithms one can extract features able to isolate characteristic regions within an image (image segmentation) and subsequent identification or labeling of such regions (image classification).

Fourteen different features have been extracted from the GPDS database to allow for signature classification using the methods described in the literature. The features (Width, Height, Tri-Surface, Six-Fold Surface, Best Fit) were described in [2]; the features (Geometric Parameters (Polar and Cartesian)) in [6] and the Modified Direction Feature (MDF) in [5]. The remaining four novel extracted features (K-Means, Histogram of frequencies, Discrete Cosine Transform and Wavelet Transform) are briefly described next.

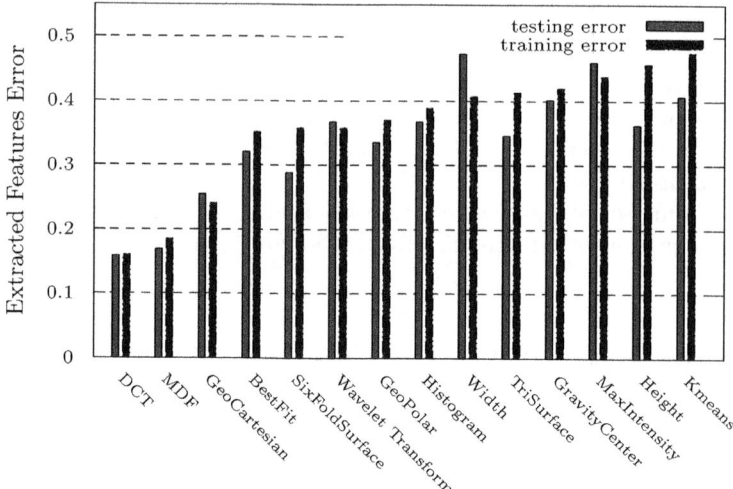

Fig. 3. Feature Ranking Analysis

1. **K-Means:** The k-means clustering algorithm was applied to the images pixels with the goal to identify the positions of the signature's main elements. The algorithm was applied to each image individually, with k set to 5 by empirical experimentation. The clusters' centroids Cartesian coordinates are the feature's values.

2. **Histogram Frequencies:** In order to evaluate signatures' intensity variations along the perpendicular axes, the frequencies of each image's horizontal and vertical histogram were calculated. The histogram frequencies are obtained using the Discrete Fourier Transform. To characterize the frequencies obtained, the three distribution quartiles values were saved.

3. **Discrete Cosine Transform Frequencies (DCT):** This feature evaluates the crispness of the signatures, whether specific frequency intervals occur more along the vertical (or the horizontal) axes. The two-dimensional Discrete Cosine Transform was applied to each image individually. The resultant frequencies are divided into N frequency intervals with the same length, N=5 by empirical experimentation. Each frequency band is separated by a diagonal axis, in order to compare frequencies with mainly a vertical orientation from those with mainly an horizontal orientation. For each interval, the proportion of the frequency amplitudes between the vertical and horizontal regions is calculated and used as a feature value.

4. **Discrete Wavelet Transform Frequencies (DWT):** A space-frequency analysis using the two-dimensional Discrete Wavelet Transform (DWT) is applied to the signatures, to evaluate the horizontal, vertical and diagonal pixels variations. The DWT is recurrently applied, with the *haar* wavelet, to inferior frequency levels. For each orientation (and each level of decomposition), the gravity centers of the frequency amplitudes are calculated. Those values represent the signatures' regions where those frequency intervals are most present.

A global analysis of their discriminative power is illustrated in Figure 3 where MDF and DCT features show the strongest influence on the classifier's performance. An example of the MDF feature extraction is given in Figure 4. Several values of max transitions from black to white were used in the picture and the

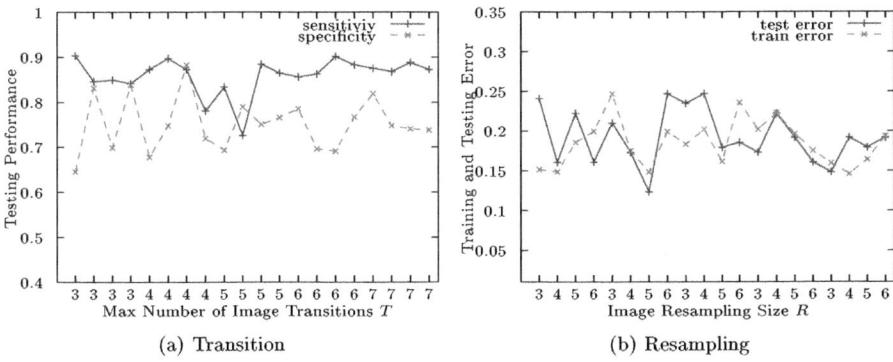

Fig. 4. Performance and Error for (a) Transition (T)/ (b) Resampling (R) for MDF Feature. Best pair found($T = 4; R = 5$)

image resampling. The best results w.r.t. error performance were found with the pair $(T = 4, R = 5)$.

4 Experimental Setup and Results

The database was split in two parts for training and testing. We followed the procedure in [2] i.e., for each signature we used from the genuine set, 20 samples for training and 4 for testing. As for the forged set, 25 samples were used for training and 5 for testing. Overall we come up with 658 attribute values for the whole set of extracted features. We tested out a number of configurations [8] with variable size in number of features' combinations (and corresponding attributes).

4.1 Two-Step Signature Verification Model

We put forward a hybrid model consisting of two steps, the first, identifies the owners of the signatures while, the second, determines its authenticity, i.e., accepts or rejects a signature. This architecture could mostly be used to verify the signature of a check or a signed document. This approach requires a classifier that can identify any signature (*identification classifier*) and several classifiers that given signatures of only one individual can determine its authenticity (*specific classifiers*). This entails the existence of a multi-class classifier for the identification classifier and N binary specific classifiers, one for each individual. The identification classifier will be trained with all the signatures in a standard way. Each specific classifier will be trained with both authentic and forged signatures from only one individual. The specific classifiers are expected to achieve higher accuracy than a *general classifier*, i.e. a binary classifier trained with signatures from different individuals. Intuitively, this originates from the idea that it is easier to find an authentic/forged pattern from a single individual than it is to find the same pattern for every individual possible. The generic classifier is used

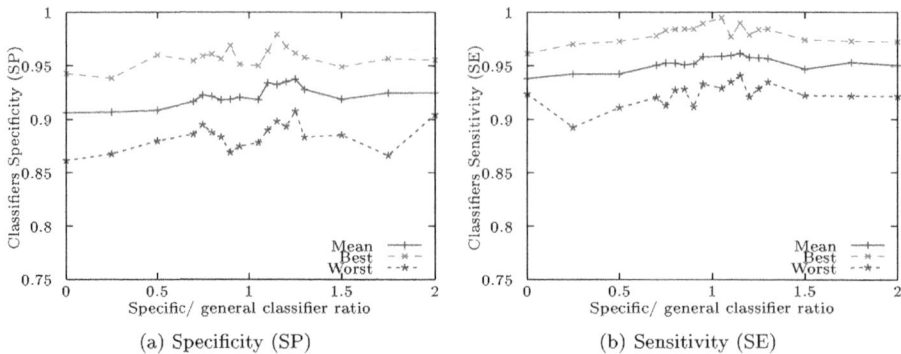

(a) Specificity (SP)   (b) Sensitivity (SE)

Fig. 5. Specific and (Generic) Classifiers Performance versus the Ratio threshold

whenever its predicted accuracy (based on the cross-validation error) is higher than that of the specific classifier. To fine tune the approach we included a prevalence *ratio* threshold that explicitly favors the specific (or generic) classifier if it is greater (or smaller) than 1, respectively. As an example, if we want to choose the specific classifier even if its predicted accuracy is up to 5% lower than the general classifier, a ratio of 1.05 should be set. The results illustrated in Figure 5 show how this works out with changing values of the ratio. It is also observed a higher value of sensitivity than specificity since the number of forged signatures is greater than the genuine ones.

We tried out several algorithms for the design of the classifiers, namely,(Fisher Linear Discriminant, Feed Forward Neural Network, Radial Basis Neural Network, Naive Bayes and Support Vector Machines (SVMs)) whose study is available elsewhere [8]. We choose SVMs to present the results (see Table 1) of an experimental analysis of the performance of the specific classifier with the number of folders varying from 10 to 300. The best feature configuration attained (MDF, Width, Six-Fold Surface and Wavelet Transform) consisting of 179 values for the images signatures was used. Moreover, we perform 30 runs for each number of folders in the Table 1 and averaged the results (including standard deviations). The metrics for performance evaluation were evaluated from the confusion matrix with True Positive (TP), True Negative (TN), False Positive (FP) and False Negative and are indicated as follows: Recall, Precision, Training Accuracy, Testing Accuracy and F1 measure. The latter measures the trade-off between the Recall and Precision and is a good indicator in skewed distributions as in the case of the GPDS database. In Biometrics, the error of type I (i.e. False Positive Rate) is the False Reject Rate (FRR). It means a false alarm of the positive class (forged signature). The error type II (i.e. False Negative Rate) is the False Accept Rate (FAR) which relates to missing to detect a forged signature. The results compare well with those presented in [2] and [13] in particular w.r.t the FAR, which has the lowest value for 44 folders and is a good indicator for the system's performance in the case of 300 folders which contain 16200 signatures.

Table 1. Signature Verification Performance (%)

Folders	Recall	Precision	FRR	FAR	Trn Acc	Test Acc	F1
10	86.67 ± 23.46	84.09 ± 15.31	28.33	13.33	91.26 ± 8.19	80.00 ± 16.22	82.75 ± 16.34
20	84.86 ± 19.85	85.42 ± 13.83	22.86	15.14	95.30 ± 4.20	81.43 ± 14.27	83.65 ± 13.29
39	87.28 ± 9.77	89.01 ± 15.30	17.82	12.72	97.36 ± 3.70	85.01 ± 14.30	85.97 ± 10.32
44	90.76 ± 16.17	84.58 ± 14.78	26.42	**9.24**	93.21 ± 5.88	83.12 ± 14.45	**86.15** ± 12.32
60	80.17 ± 21.99	91.32 ± 12.57	11.77	19.83	97.64 ± 2.54	83.75 ± 13.66	83.19 ± 15.74
120	80.22 ± 22.99	90.45 ± 14.26	11.94	19.78	98.12 ± 1.85	83.70 ± 14.51	83.18 ± 16.86
200	82.25 ± 21.64	91.25 ± 13.56	11.50	17.75	99.46 ± 1.10	85.03 ± 14.25	84.63 ± 16.29
240	82.83 ± 21.14	90.54 ± 14.28	12.71	17.17	99.86 ± 0.56	84.81 ± 14.72	84.75 ± 16.10
300	85.33 ± 20.67	86.23 ± 15.79	20.25	**14.67**	94.10 ± 5.10	82.85 ± 15.11	**84.37** ± 15.05

4.2 Deep Learning Model for Signature Recognition

Figure 6 shows the learned weights of two signatures of different owners, where the white dots appear as noise. The deep neural network architecture with 100 visible units and two layers with 100 hidden units each was able to extract layer-by-layer high-level representations of the images. The learning rate is $\eta = 0.08$ and the momentum $\alpha = 0.4$. The number of epochs was varied from 100, 500, 1000 and 5000. We clamped into the network 10 signature folders after cropping the images to the reasonable size of (144×225). The cost of training was very high increasing with the number of epochs and with the number of hidden units. Therefore it was only possible to test with 10 folders of signatures although there is room for improvements. We show that the architecture learns the relevant features at hand given very limited prior knowledge.

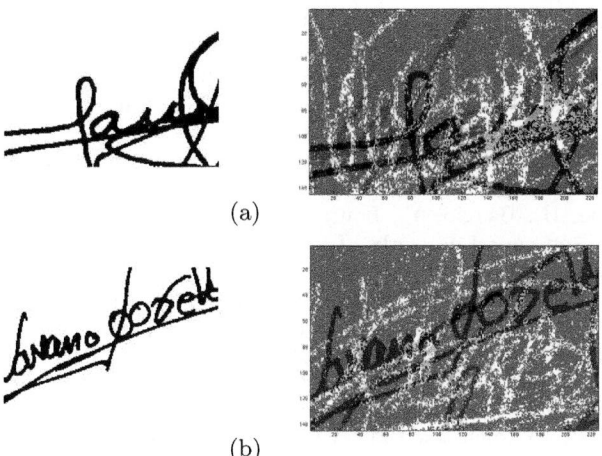

(a)

(b)

Fig. 6. Signature (a) original (b) learning weights

5   Conclusions and Future Work

We presented a verification system for off-line signature recognition proposing a two-step hybrid classifier system with overall good performance in the GPDS database. In addition, the preliminary results with a deep learning architecture are promising and raise interest regarding the application of this kind of models in this problem. We were able to extract a high-representation of the signature images through multi-layers in a deep hierarchical structure that allows non-local generalization and comprehensibility in this specific domain. Despite the great prospect of deep learning technologies future work will perform an extensive study to cope with the millions of parameters that need to be adjusted, in particular, with the use of Graphics Processing Units (GPU).

References

1. Ackley, D., Hinton, G., Sejnowski, T.: A learning algorithm for Boltzmann Machines. Science 9(1), 147–169 (1985)
2. Armand, S., Blumenstein, M., Muthukkumarasamy, V.: Off-line signature verification using an enhanced modified direction feature with single and multi-classifier approaches. IEEE Computational Intelligence Magazine 2(2), 18–25 (2007)
3. Bengio, Y.: Learning deep architectures for AI. Foundations and Trends in Machine Learning 2(1), 1–127 (2009)
4. Bengio, Y., Delalleau, O.: Justifying and generalizing contrastive divergence. Neural Computation 21(6), 1601–1621 (2009)
5. Bluemenstein, M., Liu, X.Y.: A modified direction feature for cursive character recognition. In: IEEE-IJCNN, pp. 2983–2987 (2004)
6. Ferrer, M.A., Alonso, J.B., Travieso, C.M.: Off-line geometric parameters for automatic signature verification using fixed-point arithmetic. IEEE Trans. on Pattern Analysis and Intelligence 27(6), 993–997 (2005)
7. Gader, P.D., Mohamed, M., Chiang, J.H.: Handwritten word recognition with character and inter-character neural networks. IEEE Trans. on Sys., Man and Cyber. - Part B: Cybernetics 27(1), 158–164 (1997)
8. Gonçalves, I., Santos, S.: Off-line signatures verification system. Tech. Rep. trp-#10/11, University of Coimbra, Portugal (2011)
9. Hinton, G.E.: Learning multiple layers of representation. Trends in Cognitive Sciences 11, 428–434 (2007)
10. Hinton, G.E., Osindero, S., Teh, Y.: A fast learning algorithm for deep belief nets. Neural Computation 18, 1527–1554 (2006)
11. Larochelle, H., Bengio, Y., Louradour, J., Lamblin, P.: Exploring strategies for training deep neural networks. J. of Machine Learning Research 10, 1–40 (2009)
12. Longcamp, M., Boucard, C., Gilhodes, J.C., Anton, J.L., Roth, M., Nazarian, B., Velav, J.L.: Learning through hand- or typewriting influences visual recognition of new graphic shapes: Behavioral and functional imaging evidence. Science Journal of Cognitive Neuroscience 20, 802–815 (2008)
13. Lv, H., Wang, W., Wang, C., Zhuo, Q.: Off-line chinese signature verification based on support vector machines. Pattern Recognition Letters 26, 2390–2399 (2005)
14. Nguyen, V., Blumenstein, M., Vallipuram, M., Leedham, G.: Off-line signature verification using enhanced modified direction features in conjunction with neural classifiers and support vector machines. In: IEEE-ICDAR, pp. 1300–1304 (2009)
15. Yu, K., Xu, W., Gong, Y.: Deep learning with kernel regularization for visual recognition. In: Neural Information Processing Systems, NIPS (2009)

A Study on Automatic Methods Based on Mathematical Morphology for Martian Dust Devil Tracks Detection

Thiago Statella[1], Pedro Pina[2], and Erivaldo Antônio da Silva[3]

[1] Instituto Federal de Educação, Ciência e Tecnologia de Mato Grosso - IFMT
95 Zulmira Canavarro 780025-200, Cuiabá, Brazil
thiago.statella@cba.ifmt.edu.br
[2] Centro de Recursos Naturais e Ambiente, Instituto Superior Técnico - IST
Av. Rovisco Pais 1049-001, Lisboa, Portugal
ppina@ist.utl.pt
[3] Universidade Estadual Paulista, Faculdade de Ciências e Tecnologia – FCT
305 Roberto Simonsen 19060-900, Presidente Prudente, Brazil
erivaldo@fct.unesp.br

Abstract. This paper presents three methods for automatic detection of dust devils tracks in images of Mars. The methods are mainly based on Mathematical Morphology and results of their performance are analyzed and compared. A dataset of 21 images from the surface of Mars representative of the diversity of those track features were considered for developing, testing and evaluating our methods, confronting their outputs with ground truth images made manually. Methods 1 and 3, based on closing top-hat and path closing top-hat, respectively, showed similar mean accuracies around 90% but the time of processing was much greater for method 1 than for method 3. Method 2, based on radial closing, was the fastest but showed worse mean accuracy. Thus, this was the tiebreak factor.

Keywords: Mars, Dust Devils Tracks, Mathematical Morphology, Feature Detection.

1 Introduction

Dust devils are vortexes caused by unstable wind convection processes near the planetary surfaces, due to solar heat. They have been studied on Earth for more than a century and were first observed on Mars in orbital images taken by the Viking program in the 1970s. These phenomena can achieve miles in width and height, and knowledge about their activity contributes to the understanding of Martian climate, geology and surface modification which is essential to plan future manned missions [1, 2]. According to [3], air circulation is one of the currently active processes which model the surface of Mars and some researches show that these vortexes are responsible for most of the linear and curvilinear surface features of the planet. Moreover, the inference of the wind direction based on dust devils tracks detection is one of the few techniques for verifying circulation models of the atmosphere. This fact suggests that more research on aeolian processes is needed. The direction of dust devils tracks can be used to get information on wind circulation, and it can be done by image analysis [3].

C. San Martin and S.-W. Kim (Eds.): CIARP 2011, LNCS 7042, pp. 533–540, 2011.
© Springer-Verlag Berlin Heidelberg 2011

Many researchers have being studying dust devils in an attempt to better understand the phenomena. Generally, the research fields comprise mechanic and numerical simulation of dust devils in laboratories [4-6], methodologies for direct recognition of dust devils plumes from rovers on Mars surface [7-9], detection of plumes [10-12] and tracks [1, 3, 13, 14] from orbital images. Despite the number of papers regarding the subject, none of them addresses the automatic detection of dust devils tracks. All those works regarding identification, counting and analysis of dust devils tracks use a manual method and nothing is said about the tracks counting and marking process. As the number of well succeed missions launched to study Mars rises, so does the number of orbital images and their resolutions. There are hundreds of high resolution images depicting Martian surface, providing important data for, among others, researches in Geology, Cartography and Aeolian processes monitoring, at a level of detail never achieved before [15]. The amount of images taken (and therefore the amount of information on them) grew at a rate greater than the human capability to analyze and extract relevant information from these products to characterize the planet under study [16]. As examples of the difficulty in analyzing manually so many images, [1, 3, 13, 14, 17] had to search for tracks in (1,700), (3,000), (6,002), (167,254) and (1,238) MOC images, respectively; [10] searched in (23) HRSC images and [18] did that in (3,079) THEMIS images.

Regarding the amount of images to be analyzed and the importance of detecting dust devils tracks, this paper presents, analyses and compares three automatic methods for detecting dust devils tracks in Mars Global Surveyor (MGS) Mars Orbiter Camera (MOC) and Mars Reconnaissance Orbiter (MRO) High Resolution Imaging Science Experiment (HiRISE) images. All three methods are mainly based on Mathematical Morphology.

2   Image Datasets

Based on some evidences [1, 3, 14] that dust devils are more likely to occur in the southern hemisphere and on the fact that they form during spring and summer, a search for MOC narrow angle (http://www.msss.com/msss_images/) and HiRISE (http://www.hirise.lpl.arizona.edu/) images with solar longitudes ranging between 180° and 360° containing tracks of dust devils was performed in the regions Aeolis, Noachis and Argyre.

A total of 16 images from those regions (12 MOC narrow angle and 4 HiRISE) showing dark dust devils tracks were considered. The albedo of the tracks varies significantly from scene to scene as does the morphology and landform. Based on that, the choice for these 16 images was driven by the attempt to represent as much as possible the high albedo variability of the tracks. In order to decrease time of processing and discard irrelevant information (like areas with no tracks) some of the images were cut, making a set of 21 images. Fig. 1 shows these images and Table 1 summarizes their characteristics. The MOC images are panchromatic and can have up to 1.4 m/pixel of spatial resolution and the HiRISE images were taken in the red band with a spatial resolution as good as 0.25 m/pixel.

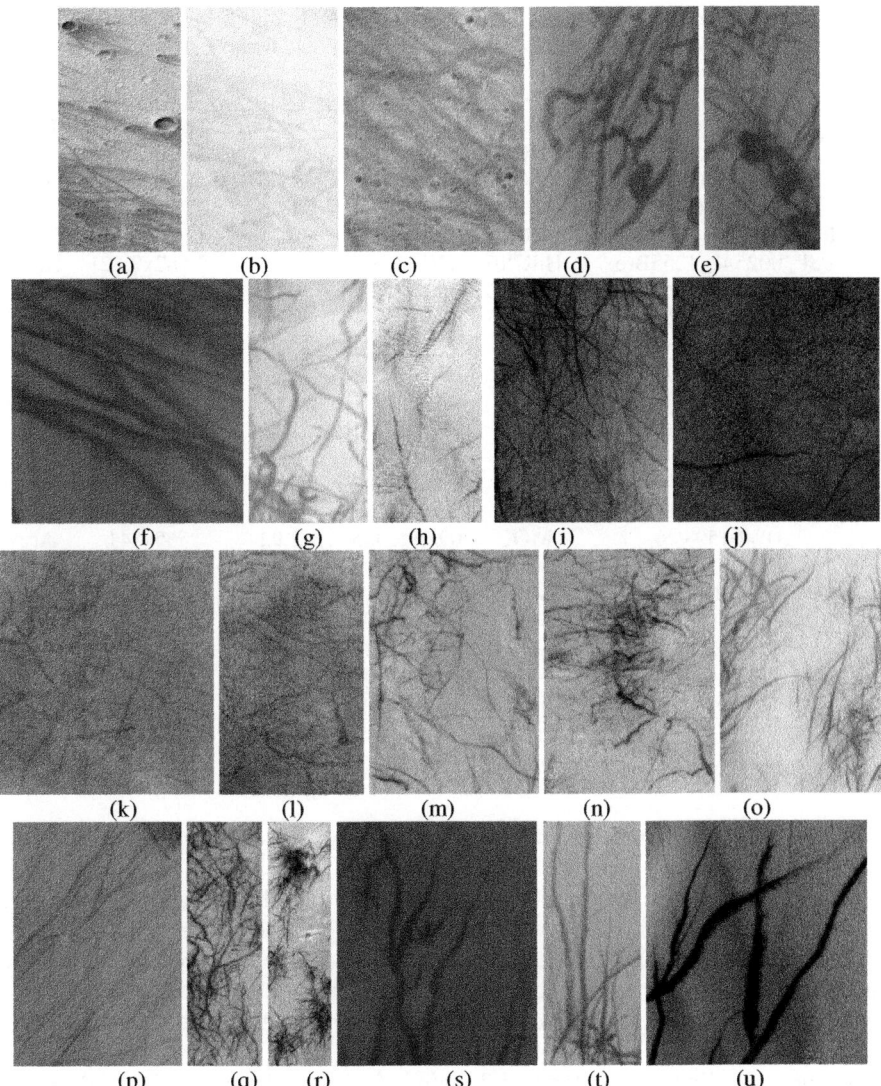

Fig. 1. Diversity of Martian dust devils tracks on MOC and HiRISE images. Table 1 shows information about each of them.

Table 1. Summarized information about the images shown in Fig. 1. In the Table, "Res." stands for "Spatial Resolution" and letters (a) through (u) in the field "Name" correspond to the images shown in Fig. 1.

Name	Sensor	Date	Res. (m)	Size (pixels)	Region
R02-00357(a)	MOC	02/07/2003	2.98	1,024x2,052	Aeolis
R08-02402(b)	MOC	08/27/2003	1.50	1,856x3,017	Aeolis
R13-01467(c)	MOC	01/10/2004	1.43	2,077x2,855	Aeolis
PSP_002548_1255A(d)	HiRISE	02/10/2007	0.25	4,069x2,779	Noachis
PSP_002548_1255B(e)	HiRISE	02/10/2007	0.25	5,582x2,621	Noachis
PSP_002548_1255C(f)	HiRISE	02/10/2007	0.25	2,840x3,011	Noachis
PSP_005528_1255(g)	HiRISE	10/01/2007	0.25	3,000x1,432	Noachis
M10-01206(h)	MOC	12/11/1999	5.55	363x829	Argyre
S08-02952(i)	MOC	07/27/2005	5.95	443x529	Argyre
R13-02691(j)	MOC	01/17/2004	5.81	414x590	Argyre
R08-02621A(k)	MOC	08/30/2003	4.40	564x632	Argyre
R08-02621B(l)	MOC	08/30/2003	4.40	500x856	Argyre
E13-00271A(m)	MOC	02/03/2002	5.83	462x316	Argyre
E13-00271B(n)	MOC	02/03/2002	5.83	420x606	Argyre
S10-01598(o)	MOC	09/29/2005	2.92	565x841	Argyre
S08-03151(p)	MOC	07/30/2005	4.46	233x339	Argyre
M14-00175A(q)	MOC	04/03/2000	5.53	349x1,144	Argyre
M14-00175B(r)	MOC	04/03/2000	5.53	454x1,795	Argyre
M12-02214(s)	MOC	02/21/2000	2.77	482x598	Argyre
PSP_005596_1245(t)	HiRISE	10/06/2007	0.50	2,196x864	Argyre
PSP_006163_1345(u)	HiRISE	11/19/2007	0.25	2,345x2,606	Argyre

3   Methods

Aiming to detect dust devils tracks automatically, three methods were developed, each one being an improvement of the predecessor, until a high level of accuracy was reached. The methods we are proposing are mainly based on morphological operators and their construction in sequence intended to improve some aspects not solved with a high degree of robustness by the preceding method. The main feature characterizing the dust devil tracks is their elongated linear shape, that is, thin shapes of long extensions, normally darker than the surrounding terrain. Method 1 uses the classic top-hat transform for extracting the tracks and morphological granulometries to define their thickness dimensions. Method 2 intends to search directly in every direction for those structures, by integrating information provided by a radial closing transform with linear structuring elements. Finally, Method 3, based on path closings, intends to recover all the regions of those thin structures, that is, not only their more linear (straight) segments but also their curvilinear components.

3.1   Method 1: *Closing Top-Hat*

The first method starts with an initial filtering by median (3x3 mask) and a morphological area opening γ_λ, which is equivalent to the union of all openings γ with the connected Structuring Elements (SE) B whose size in number of pixels equals λ, that is $\gamma_\lambda = \bigvee_i \{\gamma_{Bi} \mid B_i \text{ with } Area(B_i) = \lambda\}$, where $\vee$ is the supremum operator.

The size of the area was set empirically and varies with the image spatial resolution. Next, an initial binarization by Otsu's method [19] is applied and a morphological granulometric analysis with a SE disk is carried out. A granulometry can be defined as the family $\Gamma = (\phi_\lambda)_{\lambda \geq 0}$ of closings by scales $\lambda B = \{\lambda b \mid b \in B\}$ with $\lambda \geq 0$, and B convex. The granulometric analysis is used to infer the radius of the SE to be applied in the filtering by the top-hat $\mu_B(f) = \phi_B(f) - f$, where $\phi_B(f)$ is the closing of f. The radius is chosen so that all dark components in the image do not fit the SE. Finally a binarization by Otsu is carried out to detect the features. The detection is based on the width of the tracks.

3.2 Method 2: *Radial Closing*

The second method starts with an initial filtering by a median operator (3x3 mask) and then applies a morphological radial closing [18]. This is the intersection of the closings performed with linear SEs aligned in every direction, that is $\psi(f) = \wedge_i \phi_{Bi}(f)$. The angles considered vary from $i = 0°$ to $360°$ in steps of $5°$. The length of the SE was empirically chosen and varies with the spatial resolution of the images. Finally, a binarization by Otsu method is performed. The length of tracks is the feature considered in the detection.

3.3 Method 3: *Path Closing Top-Hat*

This third method starts with an initial filtering by morphological surface area opening and closing. The definition of surface area closing is obtained by duality from area opening. Next, a morphological path closing is applied. They can be defined by duality from de definition of path openings given by [20] as follows. Let E be the image domain endowed with a binary adjacency relation $x \rightarrow y$. We call x a predecessor of y and y a successor of x. Using the adjacency relation it is possible to define a dilation by writing $\delta(\{x\}) = \{y \in E \mid x \rightarrow y\}$. The L-tuple $\boldsymbol{a} = (a_1, a_2, ..., a_L)$ is called a δ-path of length L if $a_k \rightarrow a_{k+1}$. The set of all δ-path of length L contained in a subset X of E is denoted by $\Pi_L(X)$. Then the path opening γ_L is the union of all paths of length L contained in X, and we can write $\gamma_L(X) = \bigcup \{\boldsymbol{a} \mid \boldsymbol{a} \in \Pi_L(X)\}$.

This equation can be extended to gray level images by the principle of threshold decomposition [18]. The search for the paths is done in four directions ($0°$, $45°$, $90°$ and $135°$) of the grid according to the rules defined by [20] . The lengths of the paths are defined by the diagonal length of the images times two (although the path closings being used are the constrained ones defined by [20], they still may zig-zag a little so the biggest possible path in the worse case would be the image diagonal times two). Next, the resulting images are binarized by Otsu method to detect the tracks. The detection is mainly driven by the length of the tracks.

4 Results and Discussion

The methods discussed in the previous section were applied to the images shown in Fig. 1. The results for two different spatial resolutions with the images

PSP_002548_1255A and E13-00271(Figs. 1(d) and 1(m)) are shown in Figs. 2(a) to (c) and 3(a) to (c) for all three methods. The analysis of the results was made accordingly to the procedure proposed in [21] and is based on the following measurement $Accuracy = (TP + TN) / (m \times n)$, where TP stands for *true positives* and TN for *true negatives*. TP and TN are defined relative to a ground truth or reference image. For a processed image PI and a ground truth image GT, TP and TN are calculated as $TP = Area(GT \cap PI)$ and $TN = Area(\sim GT \cap \sim PI)$, where $\cap$ and $\sim$ are the operators *intersection* and *negation*, respectively. For each of the 21 images processed, a ground truth image was made manually by an expert on a computer screen. As examples, the ground truth made for image PSP_002548_1255A is shown in Fig. 2(d) and the one made for image E13-00271is shown in Fig. 3(d). For image PSP_002548_1255A the accuracies were 0.7866 for method 1, 0.8369 for method 2 and 0.9414 for method 3.

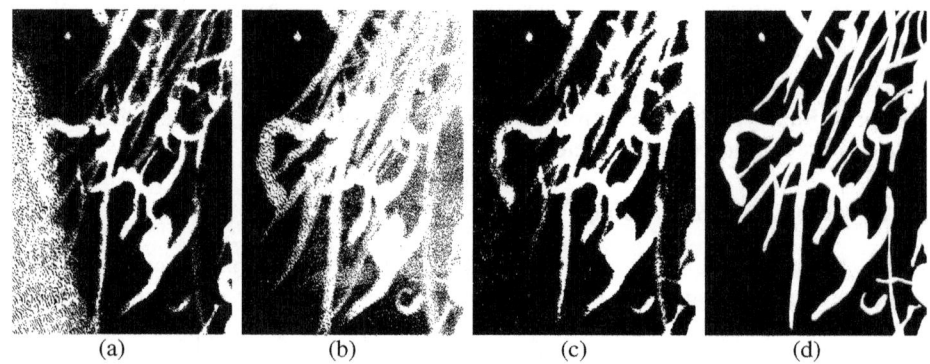

(a)   (b)   (c)   (d)

Fig. 2. Tracks detection in the image PSP_002548_1255A: (a) method 1, (b) method 2, (c) method 3 and (d) ground truth

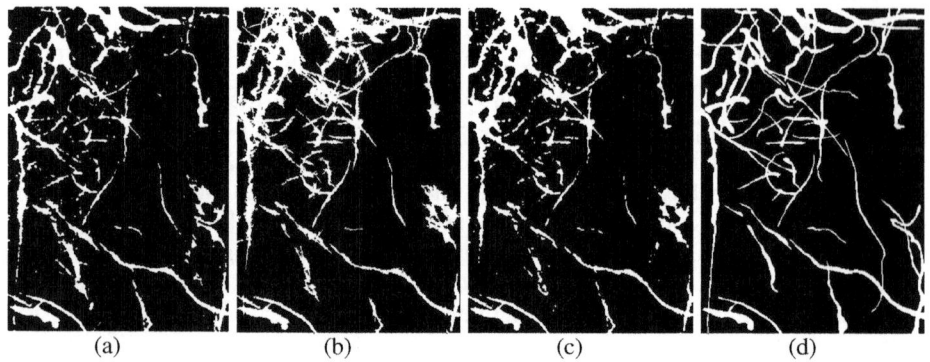

(a)   (b)   (c)   (d)

Fig. 3. Tracks detection in MOC image E13-00271: (a) method 1, (b) method 2, (c) method 3 and (d) ground truth

And for image E13-00271 the accuracies were 0.9638, 0.9669 and 0.9612 for methods 1, 2 and 3, respectively. Table 2 summarizes statistics of the analysis for the whole set of images. Method 2 was the worse one with mean accuracy 0.8230 ± 0.1196. Besides, it is the one by which the smallest accuracy was reached (0.5955 for image M10-01206 (Fig. 1(h)). Methods 1 and 3 presented mean accuracies 0.8857 ± 0.0660 and 0.8960 ± 0.0770, respectively. Considering their standard deviations there is no reason to believe that method 3 is better than method 1. Although, when it comes to the time of processing, method 3 is far faster (mean time of processing 96.27 s ± 140.03 s per image against the 3,566.24 s ± 7,625.67 s of method 1). Speed is an important factor to be considered, especially when working with larger files like those of the HiRISE images. Some of them may have hundreds of thousands of lines and in such cases method 3 would be the preferable for processing. This is why we assume it is the best method from the three presented here.

Table 2. Summary of the results obtained with the three methods

	Accuracy Method 1	Accuracy Method 2	Accuracy Method 3	Time (s) Method 1	Time (s) Method 2	Time (s) Method 3
Mean	0.8857	0.8230	0.8960	3,566.24	21.99	96.27
Stdev	0.0660	0.1196	0.0770	7,625.67	29.80	140.03
Min	0.7567	0.5955	0.7099	6.93	0.68	4.1
Max	0.9781	0.9715	0.9732	30,461.22	105.13	440.75

5   Conclusion

The importance of studying Martian dust devils to get a better understanding of, for instance, low atmosphere and regolith characteristics, may be asserted by the huge amount of papers being published about the subject. But none of them proposes an automatic method for the detection of dust devils tracks. This has been done manually until now and is a time-consuming task. This paper presented three methods for detecting Martian dust devils tracks automatically. Each one is an improvement of its predecessor. All three are based on Mathematical Morphology. Method 3 was considered to be the best, not only for the high mean accuracy it produced but also for being the fastest, which is a crucial factor when processing HiRISE images that may have hundreds of thousands of lines. It succeeds in detecting tracks despite the variation in size and in spatial resolution of the images, and works for a great range of albedo variation as seen in Fig. 1, and can be a very useful tool for intensive mapping and largely increasing our understanding of these aeolion features. In particular, quantitative measures like width, length, number of tracks and their directions, among many others, can be carried out from the resulting binary images of our approach.

References

1. Balme, M.R., Whelley, P.L., Greeley, R.: Mars: Dust Devil Track Survey in Argyre Planitia and Hellas Basin. Journal of Geophysical Research 108 (2003)
2. Balme, M.R., Greeley, R.: Dust Devils on Earth and Mars. Reviews of Geophysics 44 (2006)

3. Örmo, J., Komatsu, G.: Mars Orbiter Camera Observation of Linear and Curvilinear Features in the Hellas Basin: Indications for Multiple Processes of Formation. Journal of Geophysical Research 108 (2003)
4. Rennó, N.O.: A Thermodynamically General Theory for Convective Vortices. Tellus 60, 688–699 (2008)
5. Spiga, A., Forget, F., Lewis, S.R., Hinson, D.P.: Structure and Dynamics of the Convective Boundary Layer on Mars as Inferred from Large-Eddy Simulations and Remote Sensing Measurements. Quarterly Journal of the Royal Meteorological Society 136, 414–428 (2010)
6. Babak, T.G., Taylor, P.A.: Large Eddy Simulation of Typical Dust Devil-Like Vortices in Highly Convective Martian Boundary Layers at the Phoenix Lander Site. Planetary and Space Science 59, 43–50 (2011)
7. Lorenz, R.D., Jackson, B., Barnes, J.W.: Inexpensive Time-Lapse Digital Cameras for Studying Transient Meteorological Phenomena: Dust Devils and Playa Flooding. Journal of Atmospheric and Oceanic Technology 27, 246–256 (2009)
8. Hall, N.W., Lemmon, M.T.: Mass Ejected from Martian Dust Devils as a Function of Heigh and Dust Devil Morphology. In: XL Lunar and Planetary Sciences Conference, Texas, pp. 23–27 (2009)
9. Lorenz, R.D.: Experiments in Time-Lapse Camera Observations of Dust Devil Activity at Eldorado Playa, Nevada. In: XLII Lunar and Planetary Sciences Conference, Texas (2011)
10. Stanzel, C., et al.: Dust Devils Speeds, Directions of Motion and General Characteristics Observed by the Mars Express High Resolution Stereo Camera. Icarus 197, 39–51 (2008)
11. Lorenz, R.D.: Power Law of Dust Devil Diameters on Mars and Earth. Icarus 203, 684–684 (2009)
12. Pathare, A.V., et al.: Assessing the Power Law Hypothesis for the Size–Frequency Distribution of Terrestrial and Martian Dust Devils. Icarus 209, 851–853 (2010)
13. Cantor, B.A., Kanak, K.M., Edgett, K.S.: Mars Orbiter Camera Observations of Martian Dust Devils and their Tracks (September 1997 to January 2006) and Evaluation of Theoretical Vortex Models. Journal of Geophysical Research 111, 1–49 (2006)
14. Whelley, P.L., Greeley, R.: The Distribution of Dust Devil Activity on Mars. Journal of Geophysical Research 113, 1–12 (2008)
15. Bridges, N.T., et al.: Aeolian Studies from HIRISE. In: XXXVIII Lunar and Planetary Science Conference, Texas (2007)
16. Bandeira, L., Saraiva, J., Pina, P.: Impact Crater Recognition on Mars Based on a Probability Volume Created by Template Matching. IEEE Transactions on Geoscience and Remote Sensing 45, 4008–4015 (2007)
17. Whelley, P.L., Greeley, R.: Latitudinal Dependency in Dust Devil Activity on Mars. Journal of Geophysical Research 111, 1–5 (2006)
18. Dougherty, E.R., Lotufo, R.A.: Hands-on Morphological Image Processing. SPIE, Washington (2003)
19. Otsu, N.: A Threshold Selection Method from Gray-Level Histograms. IEEE Transactions on Systems, Man and Cybernetics 9 (1979)
20. Hendriks, C.L.L.: Constrained and Dimensionality-Independent Path Openings. IEEE Transactions on Image Processing 19, 1587–1595 (2010)
21. Bandeira, L., Marques, J.S., Saraiva, J., Pina, P.: Automated Detection of Martian Dune Fields. IEEE Geoscience and Remote Sensing Letters 8, 626–630 (2011)

An Ensemble Method for Incremental Classification in Stationary and Non-stationary Environments[*]

Ricardo Ñanculef, Erick López, Héctor Allende, and Héctor Allende-Cid

Department of Informatics,
Federico Santa María University, Chile
{jnancu,elopez,hallende,vector}@inf.utfsm.cl

Abstract. We present a model based on ensemble of base classifiers, that are combined using weighted majority voting, for the task of incremental classification. Definition of such voting weights becomes even more critical in non-stationary environments where the patterns underlying the observations change over time. Given an instance to classify, we propose to define each voting weight as a function that will take into account the location of an instance to classify in the different class-specific feature spaces and also the prior probability of such classes given the knowledge represented by the classifier as well as its overall performance in learning its training examples. This approach can improve the generalization performance and ability to control the stability/plasticity trade-off, in stationary and non-stationary environments. Experiments were carried out using several real classification problems already introduced to test incremental algorithms in stationary as well as non-stationary environments.

Keywords: Incremental Learning, Dynamic Environments, Ensemble Methods, Concept Drift.

1 Introduction

It is important that machine learning systems be capable of dealing with new observations. Moreover, for large scale applications, it is unrealistic to think that a complete set of representative examples is available from the start, and hence algorithms able to learn from the observation of a sequence of examples delayed in time is crucial. A simple approach consists in using past and current observations to build a new model every time that new observations become available. However this solution is usually impractical or infeasible. An additional problem appears when the patterns underlying the observations change over time, that is the environment is not stationary. For example, in a document filtering problem, it is possible that the features defining a category are no longer valid because the preferences of user have changed. Ensemble methods are based on the idea

---

[*] This work was supported in part Research Grant DGIP-UTFSM (Chile).

C. San Martin and S.-W. Kim (Eds.): CIARP 2011, LNCS 7042, pp. 541–548, 2011.

of combining a set of simple predictors instead of using only one [4,7,16]. An interesting point is that with an appropriate design, the expected performance of the combined predictor can be better than the average performance of the individual predictors. This flexibility makes them particularly suitable for learning in changing environments. There are ensemble methods that have been proposed to address the problem of incremental learning such as in [2,5,10,11,13,15]. Originally these methods were proposed for stationary environments, but today have been extended for non-stationary ones. In this paper, we propose a strategy (based on [9,5,12,15]) for incremental learning in non-stationary environments that consist in using a set of base classifiers, combined using weighted majority voting, where voting weights of each hypothesis h will be a function that depends on the sample used to train classifier h.

2   Problem Definition

To obtain a formal definition of the incremental learning problem we follow a statistical approach. Throughout this work we suppose that observations z live in a space Z and are all drawn according to a probability measure $P(z)$. The observations are of the form $z = (x, y)$ where x represents some information about z and y a desired response or action. Given a sample of the form $S = z_1...z_n$, obtained sampling the distribution P, we are asked to recover a model h representing the relation between x and y. The problem in learning from examples is that instead of the measure P, we only have a finite sample of examples S. We select h such that it minimizes the so called *empirical risk*:

$$R_S(h) = \frac{1}{n} \sum_{i=1}^{n} Q(h(x_i), y_i) \tag{1}$$

Instead of a single sample, in incremental scenarios, we have to deal with a sequence of samples or batches of observations $S_1, S_2, ..., S_t$ which arrive continuously over time and possibly have different size. An exact definition of the learning task in such incremental scenarios is hence not straightforward.

A learning algorithm is called incremental if it is capable to generate hypotheses in steps, where each step starts with certain working hypothesis and a set of new data and ends with an appropriate updated hypothesis. Given a sequence of training sets $S_1, ..., S_t$ such algorithm is hence capable to generate a sequence of hypotheses $h_1, ..., h_t$, where h_t is obtained from h_{t-1} and S_t. We distinguish two possible objectives for the learning tasks: (a) **Stationary Environments**, the goal at time t is to obtain a hypothesis as close as the one obtained by training with a sample $S = S_1 \bigcup ... \bigcup S_t$. If $S_1, ..., S_t$ were drawn according to a distribution P, future cases (S_{t+1}) also appear according to the distribution given by P, so we can measure the performance of the algorithm by using a test set and also any of the partial samples $S_1, ..., S_t$. (b) **Non-Stationary Environments**, the underlying distribution of the new examples changes over time. The goal at time t is to obtain a hypothesis capable to decide well the next batch of observations, that is S_{t+1}.

3   An Ensemble Based System for Learning in Dynamic Environments

The overall structure of Ensemble Methods consist in generating a new hypothesis h_t when a new set of observations S_t becomes available. An updated model is obtained combining the individual hypotheses using majority voting.

The Learn++ algorithm proposed in [13] is based on AdaBoost [3]. The main steps of Learn++ (modified in [10] and [5]), are sketched as algorithm (1). When a new set S_j of observations becomes available, a training sample X_t is generated from S_j, sampling with weights given by a distribution d. A new set of classifiers is then created to learn X_t and stacked with the classifiers generated previously to update the current ensemble H_t.

Algorithm 1. Structure of the Learn++ Algorithm

1: Initialize $T = 0$
2: **for** each batch of observations S_j of size m_j **do**
3:     Initialize the sampling weights $d_0(i)$ of each example $i = 1, \ldots, m_j$
4:     **for** $t = T + 1, \ldots, T + T_j$ **do**
5:         Set the sampling distribution to $D_t = d_t(i)/\sum_{j=1}^{m} d_t(j)$.
6:         Generate a set of examples X_t sampling S_j according to D_t.
7:         **while** $\epsilon_t < 1/2$ **do**
8:             Train a base classifier with X_t to obtain h_t.
9:             Compute the weighted error of h_t on S_j, $\epsilon_t = \sum_{i:h_t(x_i) \neq y_i} D_t(i)$.
10:        **end while**
11:        Compute the ensemble hypothesis $H_t(x)$ using an aggregation algorithm $\oplus$ over the set of classifiers $h_1, h_2, \ldots, h_t$.
12:        Compute the weighted error of H_t on S_j, $E_t = \sum_{i:H_t(x_i) \neq y_i} D_t(i)$
13:        Compute the confidence of H_t, $\alpha_t = \log((1 - E_t)/E_t)$
14:        Update the sampling weights

$$d_{t+1}(i) = d_t(i) \times \begin{cases} e^{-\alpha_t} & \text{, if } H_t(x_i) = y_i \\ 1 & \text{,} \quad \text{otherwise} \end{cases} \quad (2)$$

15:    **end for**
16:        Recall the current number of classifiers $T = \sum_{i=1}^{j} T_i$.
17: **end for**
18: For any x, compute the final ensemble decision $H_T(x)$ applying an aggregation algorithm $\oplus$ over the complete set of classifiers $h_1, h_2, \ldots, h_T$.

The KBS-Stream algorithm proposed in [15] is similar to Learn++ but it is based on a sampling strategy named KBS (Knowledge-Based Sampling) [14]. Instead of using the error on the new observations to define the sampling weights d_t, KBS defines the concept of *Lift*, which measures the correlation (according to a given distribution) between a specific prediction and a specified true label.

4   An Aggregation Framework of Classifiers for Dynamic Environments

We define a majority voting aggregation mechanism appropriate for incremental classification based on algorithm (1). In these approach each classifier h_t votes with a weight w_t on the class it predicts for a given instance x. The final decision is the class that cumulates the highest total weight from all the classifiers [8]. Defining ω_{tj} as 1 if the prediction of h_t corresponds to class j and 0 otherwise, the final decision can be expressed as

$$\widehat{\text{class}}(x) = \arg\max_j \sum_t w_t \omega_{tj}(x) \tag{3}$$

The preservation of previous knowledge and the accommodation of novel information, strongly depends on the relative importance of each classifier. In [13], Polikar et al. proposed the AdaBoost aggregation strategy [3] for algorithm (1). Voting weights are computed as $w_t = \log((1 - \eta_t)/\eta_t)$ where η_t is the training error of h_t . In incremental environments this rule becomes not optimal, since classifiers corresponding to different batches might be model different patterns and hence the performances of these classifiers are not directly comparable. For example, it is possible that the batch S_t contains only instances of one class, say 1, so it is not difficult for a classifier to achieve a high accuracy, let say $\eta_t \sim 0$. If new classes appear in the next batch, the accuracy of the corresponding classifier could be significantly lower than say $\eta_t > 0$. The first classifier however is really not better than the second because it represents an incomplete knowledge of the environment.

An idea to overcome this problem is to use instance-dependent weights. In [5], Gangardiwala et al. proposed to obtain $w_t(x)$ as $\min_k 1/\delta_{tk}(x)$, where δ_{tk} is the class-specific Mahalanobis distance of the test instance to the data used to train the classifier. If X_t is the set of input instances used to train the classifier h_t and X_{tk} is the subset of X corresponding to the instances of class k, with $k = 1, ..., K$, the k-th class-specific distance of an input instance x to X_{tk} is computed as

$$\delta_{tk}(x) = (x - \mu_{tk})' \cdot \mathbf{C}_{tk}^{-1} \cdot (x - \mu_{tk}) \tag{4}$$

where μ_{tk} is the mean and $\mathbf{C}_{tk}$ the covariance matrix of X_{tk}.

We propose to define the voting weight $w_t(x)$ of the classifier h_t, for predicting label x, as a function that depends on the Mahalanobis distance between the instance x and each class-specific subset X_{tk}. If Mahalanobis distance between x and class-specific subset is zero, hypothesis should have greater weighting, otherwise, the weight decreases, penalizing divergence:

$$\widehat{w}_t(x) = \sum_{k=1}^{K} \exp(-(x - \mu_{tk})' \cdot \mathbf{C}_{tk}^{-1} \cdot (x - \mu_{tk})) = \sum_{k=1}^{K} \exp(-\delta_{tk}) \tag{5}$$

In addition, the coverage that the classifier for each class has, is considered. Suppose that classifier h_t has been trained with instances X_{tk} of a given class k very similar to the instance to classify x_{test} but this has not been trained with enough examples of the class k to generalize well. Consider the event $A_k = $ "x is of class k", then $P(k|h_t)$ corresponds to the prior probability of the event A_k given the classifier h_t. Since the knowledge acquired depends on the data, it seems reasonable to use as the prior $P(k|h_t)$ the fraction of such data that belongs to the class k.

$$\widehat{w}_t(x) = \sum_{k=1}^{K} \exp(-\delta_{tk}) \times P(k|h_t) = \sum_{k=1}^{K} \exp(-\delta_{tk}) \times \frac{|X_{tk}|}{|X_t|} \qquad (6)$$

where $|\cdot|$ denotes cardinality, X_t is set of input used to train h_t and X_{tk} the subset of X corresponding to the instances of class k.

Finally, it should be mentioned that knowledge represented by a classifier depends on the classes it was able to learn, that is, the proposed framework should consider how reliable is the knowledge it represents. Then we will use $P(h_t)$ as the probability how much good is the classifier h_t.

$$\widehat{w}_t(x) = \left(\sum_{k=1}^{K} \exp(-\delta_{tk}) \times \frac{|X_{tk}|}{|X_t|} \right) \times P(h_t) \qquad (7)$$

The determination of this probability may be through the classifier accuracy, even in literature, the accuracy is used for determining the weight of h_t, but it is not the only strategy possible. If suppose, we take a uniform distribution for $P(h_t)$, weight $w_t(x)$ is equal (6). If we consider $P(h_t)$ proportional to accuracy, $P(h_y)$ can be defined as $P(h_y) = \log((1 - \eta_t)/\eta_t)$ where η_t is the training error of h_t with S_t. It should be noted that the whole set of classifiers originated after a new batch of observations that arrive to the system are generated to learn the new information contained in these observations. Resampling steps after the first one, make that different classifiers work with partially different data sets.

Hence it makes sense to compute the weight $w_t(x)$ only once per batch, immediately after the first resampling of the data, that has the task of identifying the observations that presumably contain new information. In this approach, which we call *Global Probabilistic*, all the classifiers created for a given batch of data S_k receive the same weight, that is computed using the equation (7) with the set of observations X_t obtained after step 14 of algorithm (1) has been applied for the first time with the current batch.

In non-stationary environments, Scholz [15] used an aggregation strategy capable to follow the dynamic of the drifting observations. Just like the instance selection methods based on sliding windows or example weighting [6,18], where aggregation strategy is biased towards the last observations, our voting strategy can be adapted similarly. Instead of computing the accuracy of the classifier h_j in S_j, we can use the last batch of observations as a better approximation of the distribution of future observations. Then, $P(h_t)$ is recomputed immediately after a new batch of observations become available as $\log((1 - \eta_t)/\eta_t)$, but now η_t is the training error of h_t on the most recent sample of examples.

Since a particular batch of observations could be an incomplete description of a stationary frame in the dynamics of the environment, this strategy could be improved if we were able to detect the step in which a drift takes place and if we use the performance of the classifiers in the set of batches after the drift to compute the prior $P(h_t)$. The effect however is attenuated because our aggregation strategy remains sensitive to the location of the instances to classify in the feature space.

5   Experiments

In [17] we provided comparative results, for problems already studied in [10] and [5] for incremental learning, between our algorithm and the Learn++ algorithm as defined in [5]. Here, we study the behavior of our algorithm in non-stationary environments using one classification problem and three different concept drift scenarios proposed in [15].

The benchmark used to test our algorithm in non-stationary environments consist in the Satellite Image Data obtained from the UCI library [1]. Since it does not contain a known concept drift and in order to allow a comparison, we used the experimental setup proposed in [15]: the data was randomly ordered into a stream and split in 20 batches of equal size (321 examples per batch). Since the KBS-Stream algorithm [15] is designed to deal with binary classification, 2 of the original 6 classes were marked as relevant (class 1) and the other as non-relevant (class 2). The same three concept drift scenarios proposed in [15] were simulated:

1. Scenario A corresponds to an abrupt drift from the first to the second class in batch 10. That is, after the batch 10 examples marked as relevant become not-relevant and viceversa.
2. Scenario B corresponds to a gradual drift from the first to the second class between batches 8 and 12. That is, a linearly increasing fraction of the examples of class 1 becomes of class 2 and viceversa, beginning with 0 in batch 8 and finishing with 1 in batch 12.
3. In Scenario C, an abrupt drift occurs in batch 9, as in scenario A, but it is abruptly reversed in batch 11.

Table (1) shows the best results obtained in the scenarios A, B and C with our framework (7) using accuracy of the classifier without considering concept drift (named *Static Priors*) and using the framework designed for concept drift (named *Adaptive Priors*). The base classifier used is the same on [17]. Tables include the mean and variance of the classification error computed after 20 experimental runs with different random permutations of the examples. Rows of the table correspond to different parameter configurations: number of classifiers per batch (C) and number of neurons (N).

From the results reported above we can conclude that the voting strategy defined to deal with concept drift introduces significant improvements with respect to our original static accuracy based strategy to define the priors over the classifiers. In Scenario A we reduce the misclassification error around 4%, in Scenario B around 3% and in Scenario C, which represents a more complex type of drift, around 2%. Improvements seem independent of the parameter configuration of the algorithms, that is number of classifiers and the number of neurons in the base learners. Moreover, an important reduction of variance is observed

Table 1. Best Results in Non-Stationary Environments

Results in Scenario A				
	Static Priors		Adaptive Priors	
Combinations	Mean Error	Variance	Mean Error	Variance
20N-2C	14.819315	5.788040	9.581776	3.440245
20N-6C	13.628505	5.689071	9.853583	3.193592

Results in Scenario B				
	Static Priors		Adaptive Priors	
Combinations	Mean Error	Variance	Mean Error	Variance
10N-2C	15.162773	4.416926	11.483645	3.030324
20N-6C	14.123832	3.654565	11.693925	2.787356

Results in Scenario C				
	Static Priors		Adaptive Priors	
Combinations	Mean Error	Variance	Mean Error	Variance
10N-2C	11.746885	4.834248	9.409657	6.536859
20N-4C	12.666667	4.659173	9.326324	6.640003

in scenarios A and B (around the half of the original variance). The curves representing the behavior of the algorithm as new batches of observations become available, also show that the algorithm designed for changing environments has a stronger ability to recover for an abrupt or gradual drift. This occurs because the static algorithm can only recover from a drift creating more classifiers representing the new knowledge than the classifiers representing the old knowledge. The dynamic algorithm, on the other hand, is capable to rapidly and selectively reuse old knowledge structures and hence can respond more quickly. This observation, in fact, explains the closer difference between the algorithms in Scenario C.

6   Conclusions

In this paper we have introduced a new voting strategy to incremental learning using an ensemble of classifiers. This strategy identifies a voting weight with two fundamental pieces: (1) a function which depends on the instance to classify and the knowledge represented by the classifier and (2) a prior which represents an instance-independent belief about the ability of the classifier to deal with the environment. By defining both pieces we can obtain an aggregation mechanism with different properties. This paper has examined a model which explores the knowledge cumulated by the classifier in the different class-specific feature spaces and different types of priors. Using priors depending on the overall performance of the classifier in its training set we have obtained an algorithm capable to accommodate new knowledge without compromising previously acquired knowledge and capable to detect the most suitable knowledge substructures to predict a given instance. Experiments in well-known benchmarks show that this algorithm can introduce important improvements or at least competitive results with respect to similar algorithms. Introducing a simple modification on the priors again, we can obtain a new version of the algorithm capable to deal with non-stationary environments. Further improvements could probably be obtained if we were able to detect the specific step in which a drift takes place, and if we use the performance of the classifiers in the set of batches after the drift to recompute the prior.

References

1. Blake, C.L., Merz, C.J.: UCI repository of machine learning databases (1998)
2. Fern, A., Givan, R.: Online ensemble learning: An empirical study. Machine Learning 53(1-2), 71–109 (2003)
3. Freud, Y., Schapire, R.: A short introduction to boosting. Journal of Japanese Society for Artificial Intelligence 14(5), 771–780 (1999)
4. Fumera, G., Roli, F.: A theoretical and experimental analysis of linear combiners for multiple classifier systems. IEEE Transactions on Pattern Analysis and Machine Intelligence 27(6), 942–956 (2005)
5. Gangardiwala, A., Polikar, R.: Dynamically weighted majority voting for incremental learning and comparison of three boosting based approaches. In: Joint Conf. on Neural Networks (IJCNN 2005), pp. 1131–1136 (2005)
6. Klinkenberg, R.: Learning drifting concepts: Example selection vs. example weighting. Intelligent Data Analysis 8(3), 281–300 (2004)
7. Kuncheva, L.I., Bezdek, J.C., Duin, R.P.W.: Decision templates for multiple classifier fusion: An experimental comparison. Pattern Recognition 34(2), 299–314 (2001)
8. Kuncheva, L.: Combining pattern classifiers: Methods and algorithms. Wiley InterScience (2004)
9. Littlestone, N., Warmuth, M.: The weighted majority algorithm. Information and Computation 108(2), 212–261 (1994)
10. Muhlbaier, M., Topalis, A., Polikar, R.: Learn++.MT: A new approach to incremental learning. In: Roli, F., Kittler, J., Windeatt, T. (eds.) MCS 2004. LNCS, vol. 3077, pp. 52–61. Springer, Heidelberg (2004)
11. Oza, N.C.: Online bagging and boosting. In: IEEE International Conference on Systems, Man and Cybernetics, vol. 3, pp. 2340–2345 (2005)
12. Polikar, R.: Ensemble based systems in decision making. IEEE Circuits and Systems 24(4), 21–45 (2006)
13. Polikar, R., Udpa, L., Udpa, S., Honavar, V.: Learn++: An incremental learning algorithm for supervised neural networks. IEEE Transactions on Systems, Man, and Cybernetics Part C: Applications and Reviews 31(4), 497–508 (2001)
14. Scholz, M.: Knowledge-based sampling for subgroup discovery. In: Morik, K., Boulicaut, J.-F., Siebes, A. (eds.) Local Pattern Detection. LNCS (LNAI), vol. 3539, pp. 171–189. Springer, Heidelberg (2005)
15. Scholz, M., Klinkenberg, R.: Boosting classifiers for drifting concepts. Intelligent Data Analysis, Special Issue on Knowledge Discovery from Data Streams 11(1), 3–28 (2007)
16. Todorovski, L., Dzeroski, L.: Combining classifiers with meta decision trees. Machine Learning 50(223), 249 (2003)
17. Trejo, P., Ñanculef, R., Allende, H., Moraga, C.: Probabilistic aggregation of classifiers for incremental learning. In: Sandoval, F., Prieto, A.G., Cabestany, J., Graña, M. (eds.) IWANN 2007. LNCS, vol. 4507, pp. 135–143. Springer, Heidelberg (2007)
18. Widmer, K., Kubat, M.: Learning in the presence of concept drift and hidden contexts. Machine Learning 23, 69–101 (1996)

Teaching a Robot to Perform Task through Imitation and On-line Feedback

Adrián León, Eduardo F. Morales, Leopoldo Altamirano, and Jaime R. Ruiz

National Institute of Astrophysics, Optics and Electronics,
Luis Enrique Erro No. 1, 72840 Tonantzintla, México
{enthe,emorales,robles,jrruiz}@inaoep.mx

Abstract. Service robots are becoming increasingly available and it is expected that they will be part of many human activities in the near future. It is desirable for these robots to adapt themselves to the user's needs, so non-expert users will have to teach them how to perform new tasks in natural ways. In this paper a new teaching by demonstration algorithm is described. It uses a Kinect® sensor to track the movements of a user, eliminating the need of special sensors or environment conditions, it represents the tasks with a relational representation to facilitate the correspondence problem between the user and robot arm and to learn how to perform tasks in a more general description, it uses reinforcement learning to improve over the initial sequences provided by the user, and it incorporates on-line feedback from the user during the learning process creating a novel dynamic reward shaping mechanism to converge faster to an optimal policy. We demonstrate the approach by learning simple manipulation tasks of a robot arm and show its superiority over more traditional reinforcement learning algorithms.

Keywords: robot learning, reinforcement learning, programming by demonstration, reward shaping.

1 Introduction

The area of robotics is rapidly changing from controlled industrial environments into dynamic environments with human interaction. To personalize service robots to the user's needs, robots will need to have the capability of acquiring new tasks according to the preferences of the users and non-expert users will have to be able to program new robot tasks in natural and accessible ways. One option is to show the robot the task and to let the robot imitate the user's movements in what is called Programming by Demonstration (PbD) [4]. This approach, however, normally uses sophisticated hardware and can only reproduce the traces provided by the user, so the performance of the robot depends on the performance of the user in the task. An alternative approach is to use reinforcement learning (RL) and let the robot explore the environment to learn the task [12]. This, however, normally results in long training times.

In this paper, the user shows the robot how to perform a task. To capture the user's demonstration, rather than using a sophisticated arrangement of sensors or

C. San Martin and S.-W. Kim (Eds.): CIARP 2011, LNCS 7042, pp. 549–556, 2011.

special purpose environments, we use a Kinect® sensor to capture the depth information of obstacles and to detect the movements follow by the arm when showing how to perform a particular task. Instead of trying to reproduce exactly the same task, we use reinforcement learning to refine the traces produced by the user. Rather than waiting for the RL algorithm to converge, the user can provide, during the learning process, on-line feedback using voice commands that are translated into additional rewards. We demonstrate the approach in a simple manipulation task.

The rest of the paper is organized as follows. Section 2 reviews the most closely related work. Section 3 describes the proposed method. In Section 4 the experimental set-up is described and the main results presented. Finally Section 5 gives conclusions and future research directions.

2   Background and Related Work

Programing by Demonstration (PbD), Learning from Demonstration (LfD) or Learning by Imitation (LbI), is a mechanism that combines machine learning techniques with human-robot interaction. The idea is to derive control policies of a particular task from traces of tasks performed by a user [3]. One of the advantages of this approach is that the search space is significantly reduced as it is limited to the space used in the demonstration [4]. Several approaches have been used for PbD, however, in most cases the user needs to wear special equipment under particular conditions, limiting its applicability to restricted environments. In this paper, we use a Kinect® sensor which is relatively cheap and robust to changes in illumination conditions. Also, in most of these developments the performance of the system strongly depends on the quality of the user's demonstrations. In this paper, we couple the user's demonstration with a reinforcement learning algorithm to improve over the demonstrations given by the users.

Reinforcement Learning (RL) is a technique used to learn in an autonomous way a control policy in a sequential decision process. The general goal is to learn a control policy that produces the maximum total expected reward for an agent (robot) [12]. Learning an optimal control policy normally requires the exploration of the whole search space and very large training time. Different approaches have been suggested to produce faster convergence times, such as the use of abstractions, hierarchies, function approximation, and more recently reward shaping [11,9,10,1,8,5]. In reward shaping, most of these methods require domain knowledge to design an adequate reward shaping function, or try to learn the reward functions with experience, which can take long training times. In our case, the user can provide feedback to the robot and change the reward function. Some authors also have provided feedback from the user and incorporated it into the reinforcement learning algorithm [6,2,7]. In [2] the robot first derives a control policy from user's demonstrations and the teacher modifies the policy through a critiquing process. A similar approach is taken in [6], however the user's critique is incorporated into the optimization function used to learn the policy. In [7], the authors combine TAMER, an algorithm that models a hypothetical human reward function, with eight different reward shaping functions. Contrary to these approaches, in our work the user can provide, through voice commands, feedback that can be given at any time during the learning process and that directly affects the reward function (see also [13]). We extend this last work with traces given by the user and observed by the robot, and with a more powerful representation language to create more general policies, as explained in the next section.

3   Method and System Design

Our approach, illustrated in Figure 1, has three main modules: 1) demonstration, perception and representation of the task, 2) reproduction and refinement, and 3) on-line user feedback.

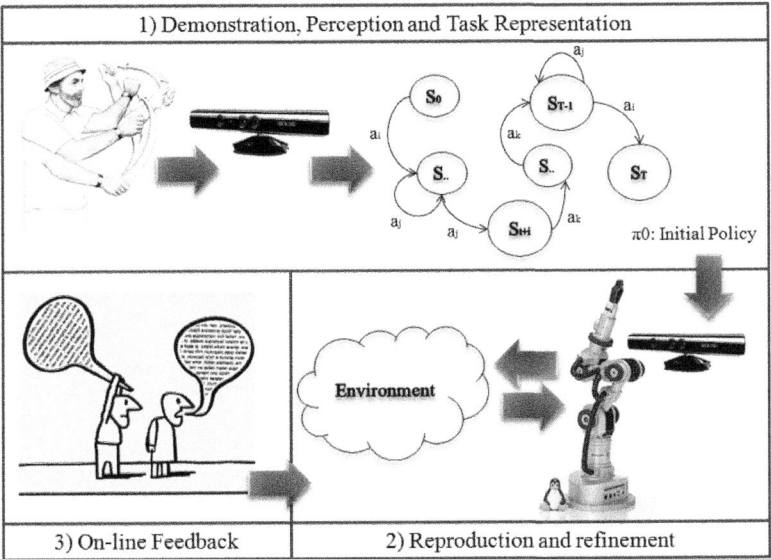

Fig. 1. The imitation and feedback learning

The interaction between the different components of the system is shown in Figure 2, where the initial demonstrations are used to seed the initial Q-values and the system follows a process where the user can intervene during the RL process.

3.1   Demonstration, Perception and Task Representation

In the demonstrations, the instructor shows the robot the task to learn with his/her arm movements. The 3D positions of the hand and of the objects in the environment are tracked using the Kinect® sensor. These 3D coordinates sequences are obtain from a previously calibrated working area that includes all the arm movements. The sequences are processed to obtain relational state-action pairs. Each state $s \in S$ is described by a six-term tuple with the following elements: $s = (H, W, D, dH, dW, dD)$, where:

- H = Height: $\{Up, Down\}$
- W = Width: $\{Right, Left\}$
- D = Depth: $\{Front, Back\}$

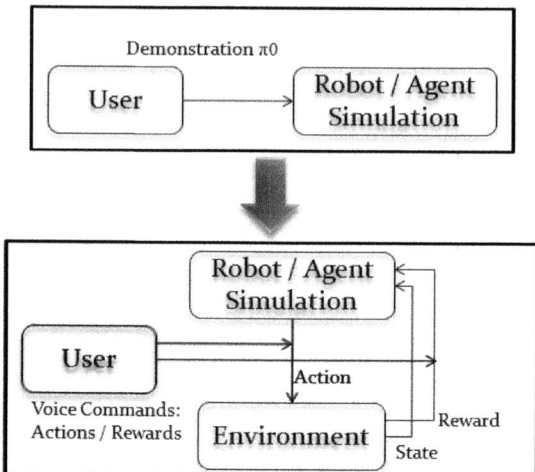

Fig. 2. Training phases of the proposed approach

- dH = Height distance to target: $\{VeryFar, Far, Close, VeryClose, Over\}$
- dW = Width distance to target: $\{VeryFar, Far, Close, VeryClose, Over\}$
- dD = Depth distance to target: $\{VeryFar, Far, Close, VeryClose, Over\}$

Each action $a \in A$ is described as a movement in one direction with information of how much to move the manipulator, $a = (D, pD)$, where:

- D : Direction $\{Up, Down, Right, Left, Front, Back\}$
- pD : a real value that defines the magnitude of the movement performed by the robot according to how close it is from an object. For example, a *right* movement will have a greater displacement to the right when it is far from the target object than a *right* movement when it is close to the target object.

The main advantage of this representation is that, since it is a relative position between the human or robotic arm with the target place or object, it does not need to have any special transformation between the traces shown by the user and the traces used by the robot. On the other hand, the states and the learned policies, as it will be shown later, are consequently relative to the target object so the initial position of the robot arm and the initial and final position of the target object or place can be completely different from the positions shown by the user, and the learned policy is still suitable for the task.

3.2 Reproduction and Refinement

The goal of this stage is to improve over the traces performed by the user. Given a set of initial traces by the user, these are transformed into the state-action pairs with the previously described representation and directly used by the robot to initialize the Q-values of the visited state-action pairs. The robot then follows a normal RL algorithm using Q-learning to improve over the initial policy. During the exploration moves, the robot can reach previously unvisited states that are incrementally added to the state space.

Also, during the execution of actions it is possible to produce continuous actions by combining the discrete actions of the current policy. This is performed as a lineal combination of the discrete actions with the larger Q-values. The lineal combination is proportional to the magnitude of the used Q-values. The updating function over the Q-values is also proportionally performed over all the involved discrete actions.

3.3 On-line Feedback

While the robot is exploring the environment to improve over its current policy, the user can provide on-line voice feedback to the robot. We build over the work described in [13], where a fixed vocabulary was defined for the user's commands. The user feedback can be in the form of action commands or as qualifiers over particular states that are transformed into rewards and added to the current reward function.

Our reward function is defined as: $R = R_{RL} + R_{user}$ where R_{RL} is the normal reward function and R_{user} is the reward obtained from the voice commands given by the user. The main difference with previous reward shaping functions is that in our case the rewards can be given sporadically and can be contrary to what it is needed for achieving a goal. Nevertheless, we assume that when they are given correctly they reinforce the movements where the agent is moving towards the goal and satisfy a potential-based shaping framework. So even with noisy feedback from the user we can still guarantee convergence towards an adequate policy as long as the agent receives in average correct rewards (see [13] for more details).

4   Experiments and Results

We used a 6 DOF robot manipulator, named Armonic Arm 6M (see Figure 3 right), in our experiments and the task was to pick-up an object and place it in a new position.

Fig. 3. Robot Katana Armonic Arm 6M

In front of the Kinect sensor, the user simply picks up an object from a spatial position and places it in a different location. The sensor is responsible for identifying the 3D location of the user hand and object and track the hand movements. From the Kinects tracking system we get a sequence of 3D coordinates to define distances and locations with respect to the object and to determine relational states to characterize the task. Figure 4 shows a human demonstration used to pick-up a object and place it in a different location (up) and the information obtained by the Kinect sensor (down).

Figure 3 shows to the left a sequence performed by the robot after learning this task.

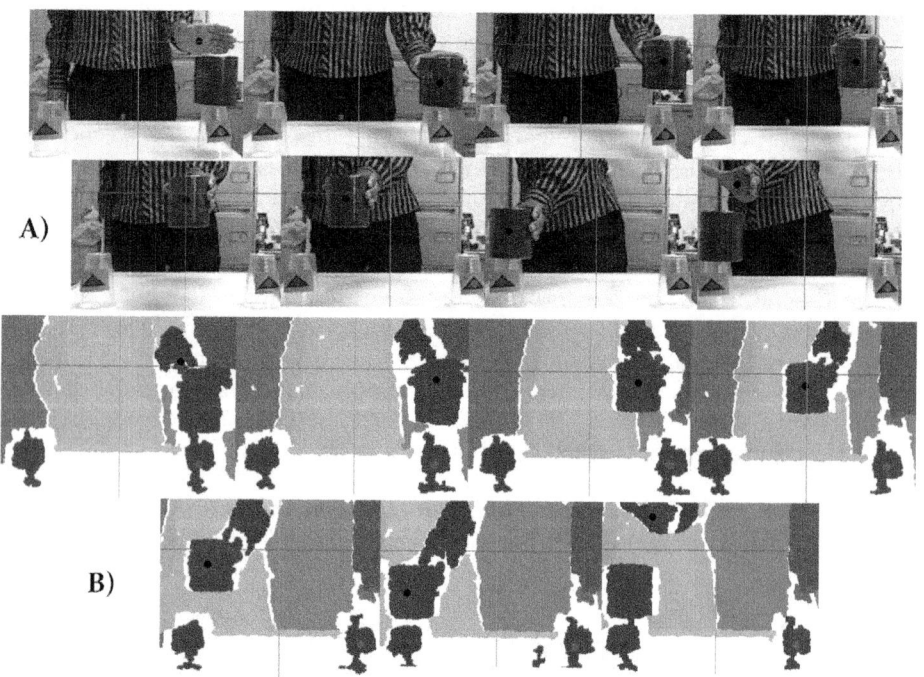

Fig. 4. Human demonstration for picking-up and placing a particular object

For the experiments, we designed different conditions to test the individual parts of the proposed system including a simulator for training during 50 episodes:

1. Using only Reinforcement Learning (RL)
2. Reinforcement Learning + Human demonstration (HD)
3. Reinforcement Learning + Simulation (S) + Human demonstration
4. Reinforcement Learning + Simulation + Human demonstration + User's Feedback (FB)

Figure 5 shows the performance of the different experiments and table 4 shows the total computer times. As can be seen, using human demonstration and user's feedback during the learning process can significantly reduced the convergence times for the RL algorithm. It should be noted that each episode shown in the figure started from random initial positions and ended in random (reachable) object positions.

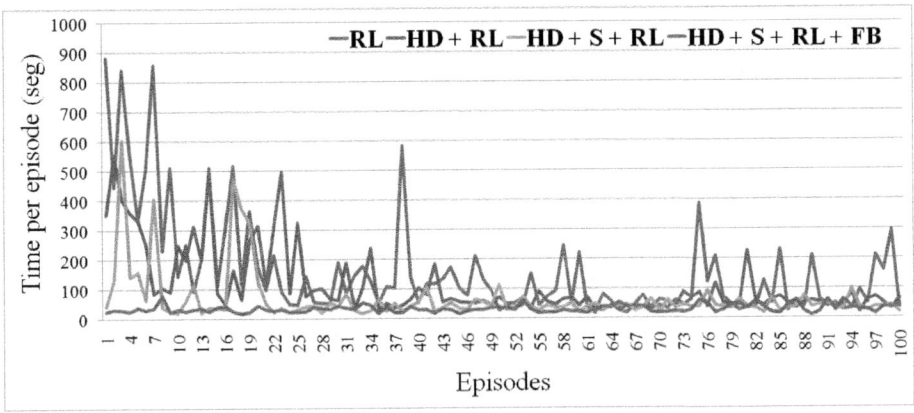

Fig. 5. Performance of the different experimental conditions. (i) RL = reinforcement learning, (ii) $HD + RL$ = RL + human demonstration, (iii) $HD + S + RL$ = RL + simulation traces + human demonstrations, and (iv) $HD + S + RL + FB$ = RL + simulation traces + human demonstrations + user's feedback.

Table 1. Total computing times: The second row shows the time of HD ($~$5 min) and the time of RL. The third and fourth rows show the time of HD, S, and RL respectively in each column; FB does not require additional time. The last column shows the total time spent for each experimental condition.

	Time (s)			Total time (s)
RL			16168.896	16168.896
HD + RL	~300		11056.56	11356.56
HD + S + RL	~300	25.628	6729.399	7055.027
HD + S + RL + FB	~300	19.348	3242.273	3561.621

5 Conclusions and Future Work

Teaching a robot how to perform new tasks will soon become a very relevant topic with the advent of service robots. We want non-expert users to be able to teach robots in natural ways how to perform a new task. In this paper, we have described how to teach a robot to perform a task by combining demonstration performed by the user with voice feedback over the performance of the robot during its learning phase. Our main contributions are: the simple PbD setup with Kinect sensor, the representation used for the demonstration which is used also in RL and the incorporation of on-line voice feedback from the user during the learning process.

There are several research directions that we would like to pursue. So far we have focused our approach in the displacement of the hand and of the end effector. This is suitable in environment; without obstacles or in static environments. As future work, we would like to incorporate information from the movements of all the articulations. We would also like to enrich the vocabulary for other stages in the learning process, like assigning particular names to learned sub-tasks and then re-using them for learning more complex tasks. Finally we would like to test our approach in other maniplation tasks and with different objects.

References

1. Abbeel, P., Ng, A.Y.: Apprenticeship learning via inverse reinforcement learning. In: Proceedings of the Twenty-first International Conference on Machine Learning. ACM Press (2004)
2. Argall, B., Browning, B., Veloso, M.: Learning by demonstration with critique from a human teacher. In: 2nd Conf. on Human-Robot Interaction (HRI), pp. 57–64 (2007)
3. Argall, B.D., Chernova, S., Veloso, M., Browning, B.: A survey of robot learning from demonstration (2009)
4. Billard, A.G., Calinon, S., Dillmann, R., Schaal, S.: Robot programming by demonstration. In: Siciliano, B., Khatib, O. (eds.) Handbook of Robotics, ch. 59. Springer, New York (2008)
5. Grzes, M., Kudenko, D.: Learning shaping rewards in model-based reinforcement learning (2009)
6. Judah, K., Roy, S., Fern, A., Dietterich, T.G.: Reinforcement learning via practice and critique advice. In: AAAI (2010)
7. Bradley Knox, W., Stone, P.: Combining manual feedback with subsequent mdp reward signals for reinforcement learning (2010)
8. Konidaris, G., Barto, A.: Autonomous shaping: knowledge transfer in reinforcement learning. In: Proceedings of the 23rd International Conference on Machine Learning, pp. 489–496 (2006)
9. Laud, A.: Theory and application of reward shaping in reinforcement learning (2004)
10. Mataric, M.J.: Reward functions for accelerated learning. In: Proceedings of the Eleventh International Conference on Machine Learning, pp. 181–189. Morgan Kaufmann (1994)
11. Ng, A.Y., Harada, D., Russell, S.: Policy invariance under reward transformations: Theory and application to reward shaping. In: Proceedings of the Sixteenth International Conference on Machine Learning, pp. 278–287. Morgan Kaufmann (1999)
12. Sutton, R.S., Barto, A.G.: Reinforcement learning: An introduction. The MIT Press, Cambridge (1998)
13. Tenorio-Gonzalez, A.C., Morales, E.F., Villaseñor-Pineda, L.: Dynamic Reward Shaping: Training a Robot by Voice. In: Kuri-Morales, A., Simari, G.R. (eds.) IBERAMIA 2010. LNCS, vol. 6433, pp. 483–492. Springer, Heidelberg (2010)

Improvements on Automatic Speech Segmentation at the Phonetic Level

Jon Ander Gómez and Marcos Calvo

Departament de Sistemes Informàtics i Computació,
Universitat Politècnica de València, Spain
{jon,mcalvo}@dsic.upv.es
http://elirf.dsic.upv.es/

Abstract. In this paper, we present some recent improvements in our automatic speech segmentation system, which only needs the speech signal and the phonetic sequence of each sentence of a corpus to be trained. It estimates a GMM by using all the sentences of the training subcorpus, where each Gaussian distribution represents an acoustic class, which probability densities are combined with a set of conditional probabilities in order to estimate the probability densities of the states of each phonetic unit. The initial values of the conditional probabilities are obtained by using a segmentation of each sentence assigning the same number of frames to each phonetic unit. A DTW algorithm fixes the phonetic boundaries using the known phonetic sequence. This DTW is a step inside an iterative process which aims to segment the corpus and re-estimate the conditional probabilities. The results presented here demonstrate that the system has a good capacity to learn how to identify the phonetic boundaries.

Keywords: automatic speech segmentation, phoneme boundaries detection, phoneme alignment.

1 Introduction

The two main applications of speech segmentation at the phonetic level are text-to-speech synthesis and acoustic models training. For both purposes it is useful to have available as many labelled sentences as possible. Doing this labelling task by hand implies a great and very expensive effort. Additionally, as some authors point out, manual segmentations of a single corpus carried out by different experts can differ significantly, thus it is reasonable to use automatic segmentations in the previous applications. As an example, some researchers gave the same speech database to different human experts to segment it. Then, they evaluated the differences between the manual segmentations obtained. In [1], 97% of the boundaries within a tolerance interval of 20 ms were found, and 93% in [2].

There are some different approaches for performing automatic segmentation of speech corpora when the phonetic sequence of each sentence is available. Most

C. San Martin and S.-W. Kim (Eds.): CIARP 2011, LNCS 7042, pp. 557–564, 2011.

of them are systems that operate in two stages: the first one is done by a phonetic recognizer based on Hidden Markov Models (HMM), which fixes the phonetic boundaries by using the Viterbi algorithm with forced alignment, and the
second stage adjusts the phonetic boundaries. In [1,3,4] different pattern recognition approaches are proposed for local adjustment of boundaries. [5] presents
an HMM-based approach where pronunciation variation rules are applied and
a recognition network is generated for each sentence. Then a Viterbi search determines the most likely path and obtains an adapted phonetic transcription for
each sentence. This process is repeated until the adapted phonetic transcriptions do not change any more. Initial phone HMMs are generated with flat-start
training using the canonical transcriptions of the sentences.

A Dynamic Time Warping (DTW) based method that aligns the spoken utte-
rance with a reference synthetic signal produced by waveform concatenation is
proposed in [6]. The known phonetic sequence of each sentence is used to generate
the synthetic signal. The alignment cost function depends on the pair of phonetic
segment classes being aligned, and is computed taking a combination of acoustic
features. In [7] a set of automatic segmentation machines are simultaneously
applied to draw the final boundary time marks from the multiple segmentation
results. Then, a candidate selector trained over a manually-segmented speech
database is applied to identify the best time marks. In [8] several linear and nonlinear regression methods are used for combining multiple phonetic boundary
predictions which are obtained through various segmentation engines.

An approach inspired in the minimum phone error training algorithm for automatic speech recognition [9] is presented in [10]. The objective of this approach
is to minimize the expected boundary errors over a set of phonetic alignments
represented as a phonetic lattice. A quite different approach, which is presented
in [11], uses an extension of the Baum-Welch algorithm for training HMMs that
use explicit phoneme segmentation to constrain the forward-backward lattice.
This approach improves the accuracy of automatic phoneme segmentation and
is even more computationally efficient than the original Baum-Welch.

A technique that modifies the topology of the HMMs in order to control the
duration of the phonetic boundaries is presented in [12]. The prototype for all the
phones is defined as a 5-state left-to-right topology with duration control states
at each end. This topology improves the segmentation accuracy by reducing
the probability of looping at the beginning and end states, as these model the
boundaries between phonetic units. The acoustic vectors within the transition
from one phonetic unit to the other are clustered at these states.

In this paper we present a technique for automatic speech segmentation at
the phonetic level based on the same idea of altering the topology of the HMMs.
Nevertheless, three differences should be noted: (a) we calculate the emission
probabilities in a different way, (b) the forced alignment is performed by a DTW
algorithm, and (c) we do not use manually segmented sentences for training.
Emission probabilities are computed by combining acoustic probabilities with
conditional probabilities estimated *ad hoc* [13,14]. The conditional probabilities
reflect the relation between the acoustic and the phonetic probability densities.

The estimation of these conditional probabilities is done by means of a progressive refinement iterative process which segments all the sentences of the training set at every step. The initial values of the conditional probabilities are obtained by using a segmentation into equal parts, i.e., the segments assigned to each phonetic unit within a sentence are equally long. The acoustic probability densities are computed using a GMM (Gaussian Mixture Model), obtained as a result of a clustering process.

Next, we describe in Section 2 the recent improvements on the automatic speech segmentation system. Then, in Section 3, we show and comment the experimental results. Finally, we conclude in Section 4.

2   System Improvements

The previous version of our system operated in three stages: (1) a coarse segmentation based on acoustic-phonetic rules was used to estimate the initial conditional probabilities, (2) the refinement of these conditional probabilities by means of an iterative procedure, and (3) a local adjustment of phonetic boundaries considering distinct criteria depending on the pair of consecutive phonetic units [14]. In this work, we present two improvements to this strategy. The first one consists in using HMMs with a little variation in the topology based on the idea presented in [12]. The topology is modified by having states without loops at each end to control the duration of the transitions between phonetic units. This improvement avoids the need for the coarse segmentation. The other improvement consists in the use of transitions between phonetic units as additional units.

The iterative procedure for progressive refinement is based on a DTW algorithm that automatically segments each sentence. This algorithm aligns the sequence of states with respect to the sequence of acoustic frames. The sequence of states of each sentence is obtained by concatenating the model of each phonetic unit according to the given phonetic sequence. There are two relevant features in the topology of the models: the total number of states and the number of duration control states. Figure 1 shows a model with 8 emitting states and 3 duration control states at both sides. It is important to highlight that each phonetic unit can have a different number of states according to its nature.

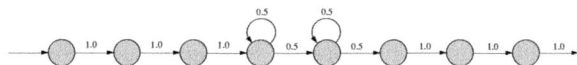

Fig. 1. An 8 emitting states HMM with 3 duration control states at each side

Figure 2 shows the allowed movements inside the DTW matrix in an example of transition between two phonetic units, with one duration control state at each end. We can observe that horizontal movements are forbidden for duration control states, i.e., no loops are permitted. The diagonal movements are the only ones allowed for these states, as these movements represent the transition from

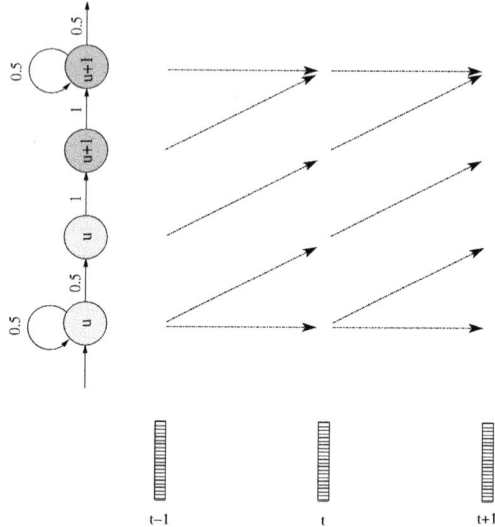

Fig. 2. Example of possible movements in our DTW focused on the join between two phonetic units

one state to the next one. Vertical movements are always forbidden since it is inconsistent to assign one acoustic frame to more than one state.

The alignment cost function used in the DTW algorithm takes $p(x_t|e_i^u)$ as the emission probability, which represents the phonetic class-conditional probability density function of observing the acoustic frame x_t given e_i^u, the i-th state of the phonetic unit u. This phonetic class-conditional probability density function is computed using the following formula

$$p(x_t|e_i^u) = \sum_{a \in A} p(x_t|a) \cdot \Pr(a|e_i^u) \tag{1}$$

where a is an acoustic class modelled by a Gaussian distribution, A is the set of Gaussian distributions in the GMM which contains all the acoustic classes, $p(x_t|a)$ is the acoustic class-conditional probability density function of observing the acoustic frame x_t given the acoustic class a, and $\Pr(a|e_i^u)$ is the conditional probability of the acoustic class a given the state e_i^u [13,14]. The GMM is computed as the first step of the training process using all the acoustic frames of all the sentences of the training subcorpus. This acoustical clustering is performed by using the maximum likelihood estimation.

The initial values of the conditional probabilities are obtained from a segmentation of each sentence into equal parts. The progressive refinement stops when no variations are observed between the segmentations resulting from two consecutive iterations. As a further step, the transitions between each pair of phonetic units are added as new phonetic units, and new conditional probabilities are computed for the new set of units (original units plus transitions). The segmentation obtained in the last iteration of the previous progressive refinement process is used as the starting point for the estimation of the new set of conditional probabilities.

3   Experimentation

3.1   Speech Corpora

In order to carry out experiments for both Spanish and English, we chose two speech databases: *Albayzin* [15] and TIMIT [16]. The phonetic corpus from the *Albayzin* database was used for the Spanish experiments: 6,800 utterances (around six hours of speech) which we split into 1,200 sentences manually segmented and labelled that were used for testing and the remaining 5,600 sentences for training. No speakers appear in both subsets. The TIMIT database was used for the English experiments, which contains 6,300 utterances (approximately five hours of speech). In this case we used the suggested training/test subdivision.

The same acoustic parameters were used on both databases. Each acoustic frame was formed by a 39-dimensional vector composed by the normalized energy, the first 12 Mel frequency cepstral coefficients, and their first and second time derivatives. Each acoustic frame was obtained using a 20 ms Hamming window every 5 ms.

3.2   Evaluation Criteria

The most widely used evaluation criterion to measure the accuracy of an automatic segmentation with respect to a manual one is the percentage of boundaries which error is within a tolerance. Usually, it is calculated for a range of tolerances [1,2,8].

As discussed in the introduction, some researchers have wondered if a manual segmentation could be a valid reference [1,2]. To evaluate this, they gave the same speech corpus to different human experts asking them to annotate it, and then evaluated the differences among the manual segmentations. In the study presented in [1], 97% of the boundaries were found within a tolerance of 20 ms and in [2] 93%. Thus, we can interpret these results as an upper bound for the accuracy of automatic segmentations, since a system that reaches 100% compared with a manual segmentation will at least differ around 5% from another manual segmentation for the same speech database.

3.3   Experimental Results

Our system has been evaluated using different combinations of the number of emitting states (E) and duration control states (B). Table 1 presents the results obtained using different $E \times B$ topologies. Results show that the use of duration control states lead to a significant improvement when the tolerance ranges from 5 to 20 ms. This improvement is bigger when the tolerance interval is more

Table 1. Percentage of correctly fixed phonetic boundaries for a range of tolerances

Topology	*Albayzin*						TIMIT					
	Tolerance in ms						Tolerance in ms					
$E \times B$	5	10	15	20	30	50	5	10	15	20	30	50
5x1	33.0	58.5	74.9	85.3	94.6	98.7	25.5	46.6	62.0	72.7	88.0	97.7
5x2	36.8	62.6	78.6	87.5	94.7	98.5	22.4	43.7	61.9	74.8	89.6	97.8
6x2	37.1	64.4	80.0	87.9	95.2	98.8	**29.5**	**53.6**	69.9	80.3	91.6	97.9
7x0	31.7	58.5	75.5	85.2	94.1	98.3	24.4	44.9	60.8	72.3	88.0	97.9
7x1	33.6	61.0	77.3	85.8	94.4	98.5	24.4	45.2	62.3	74.3	89.5	98.1
7x2	36.2	63.0	78.6	86.9	95.1	98.7	28.5	52.1	68.9	79.8	91.8	98.2
7x3	40.9	67.8	82.1	89.1	95.6	98.9	24.7	47.8	66.6	78.6	91.2	98.1
8x3	40.5	67.5	82.1	**89.5**	**96.2**	**99.2**	27.8	51.9	70.7	**82.7**	93.6	98.5
9x2	39.8	66.8	81.1	88.5	95.7	98.9	28.6	52.2	69.0	79.8	91.6	97.7
9x3	38.1	66.0	81.5	89.0	96.1	99.2	28.2	52.0	**70.8**	82.6	**93.8**	**98.6**
9x4	**44.0**	**70.3**	**82.8**	89.4	95.8	99.0	25.4	49.9	69.3	81.5	92.7	98.2
10x4	42.5	68.9	82.2	88.9	95.8	99.0	26.3	50.1	68.2	79.9	91.6	98.1

restrictive. For example, using the *Albayzin* corpus, if $E = 7$ then the segmentation accuracy improves from 58.5% to 67.8% for a tolerance error of 10 ms as B increases, and from 85.2% to 89.1% for 20 ms.

As mentioned above, our system does not use any manual segmentation for bootstraping. Starting from a blind segmentation of the sentences into equal parts, the learning process converges in less than 20 iterations for all the topologies considered.

We used a subsampling rate of 200 Hz, so, an HMM with 8 emitting states implies a minimum duration for each phonetic unit of 40 ms, which is longer than usual for some of them. Thus, different topologies were used for voiced plosives /b/, /d/ and /g/ when the topology of the remaining phonetic units is larger than 5 states. In the experiments performed with the *Albayzin* corpus, a 5×2 topology was used for these units. The results improved significantly thanks to this shorter topology. The structure of voiceless plosives /p/, /t/ and /k/ was not different from the topologies used for the rest of units, since their preceding silence is properly clustered by the HMM states. Silences were considered a special case and were always modelled with a 3×0 topology.

Since in the TIMIT corpus the voiceless plosives are preceded by a unit representing the closure, a shorter topology was needed for these units. A 3×1 topology was used for /b/, /d/, /g/, /p/, /t/, and /k/.

Additionally, we also considered adding the transitions between pairs of consecutive phonetic units as extra ones. Table 2 shows the results obtained when a 6×2 topology was used for all units except plosives, which were modelled with 4×1 for *Albayzin* and 3×1 for TIMIT. The silences were modelled with a 3×0 topology for both corpora. In the case of the *Albayzin* corpus no significant improvements are observed. However, experiments with the TIMIT corpus show small improvements for tolerances of 5 and 10 ms. Also, a significant improvement can be observed when using the manually segmented sentences of the training subcorpus to initialize the conditional probabilities.

Table 2. Percentage of correctly fixed phonetic boundaries when transitions were used. For the TIMIT corpus results when using the manual segmentation for training are also presented. No manual segmentation for training is available in the *Albayzin* corpus.

Using	*Albayzin*						TIMIT					
	Tolerance in ms						Tolerance in ms					
manual	5	10	15	20	30	50	5	10	15	20	30	50
No	40.6	68.7	83.2	90.5	96.4	99.3	31.5	55.8	71.0	81.1	92.3	98.2
Yes							44.1	70.3	81.9	88.2	94.8	98.7

4 Conclusions

We have presented here an automatic segmentation technique that combines three ideas. The first one consists in using duration control states at each end of every HMM as well as increasing the number of emitting states. The second, detailed in Section 2, deals with the way emission probabilities are calculated. The third idea consists in using a DTW algorithm to align the sequence of states against the sequence of acoustic frames.

The goal of our approach is to automatically segment speech corpora that can be useful to train acoustic models without the need for manually segmented and labelled sentences. The obtained segmentation accuracy for the *Albayzin* corpus in both kinds of experiments is around 90% within a tolerance of 20 ms. This enables our system to be used for the planned purposes, namely, acoustic models training and concatenative text-to-speech synthesis.

The results achieved with the TIMIT corpus without using the manually segmented sentences for training are similar to the ones obtained by other researchers referenced above using standard HMM and the manually segmented sentences. When our system is trained using the manually segmented sentences the results are even better. We have also used the transitions between phonetic units, but this only improves the segmentation accuracy for tolerances of 5 and 10 ms.

Acknowledgments. This work was supported by the Spanish MICINN under contract TIN2008-06856-C05-02.

References

1. Toledano, D.T., Hernández Gómez, L., Villarrubia Grande, L.: Automatic Phonetic Segmentation. IEEE Transactions on Speech and Audio Processing 11(6), 617–625 (2003)
2. Kipp, A., Wesenick, M.B., Schiel, F.: Pronunciation modelling applied to automatic segmentation of spontaneous speech. In: Proceedings of Eurospeech, Rhodes, Greece, pp. 2013–2026 (1997)
3. Sethy, A., Narayanan, S.: Refined Speech Segmentation for Concatenative Speech Synthesis. In: Proceedings of ICSLP, Denver, Colorado, USA, pp. 149–152 (2002)

4. Jarify, S., Pastor, D., Rosec, O.: Cooperation between global and local methods for the automatic segmentation of speech synthesis corpora. In: Proceedings of Interspeech, Pittsburgh, Pennsylvania, USA, pp. 1666–1669 (2006)
5. Romsdorfer, H., Pfister, B.: Phonetic Labeling and Segmentation of Mixed-Lingual Prosody Databases. In: Proceedings of Interspeech, Lisbon, Portual, pp. 3281–3284 (2005)
6. Paulo, S., Oliveira, L.C.: DTW-based Phonetic Alignment Using Multiple Acoustic Features. In: Proceedings of Eurospeech, Geneva, Switzerland, pp. 309–312 (2003)
7. Park, S.S., Shin, J.W., Kim, N.S.: Automatic Speech Segmentation with Multiple Statistical Models. In: Proceedings of Interspeech, Pittsburgh, Pennsylvania, USA, pp. 2066–2069 (2006)
8. Mporas, I., Ganchev, T., Fakotakis, N.: Speech segmentation using regression fusion of boundary predictions. Computer Speech and Language 24, 273–288 (2010)
9. Povey, D., Woodland, P.C.: Minimum Phone Error and I-smoothing for improved discriminative training. In: Proceedings of ICASSP, Orlando, Florida, USA, pp. 105–108 (2002)
10. Kuo, J.W., Wang, H.M.: Minimum Boundary Error Training for Automatic Phonetic Segmentation. In: Proceedings of Interspeech, Pittsburgh, Pennsylvania, USA, pp. 1217–1220 (2006)
11. Huggins-Daines, D., Rudnicky, A.I.: A Constrained Baum-Welch Algorithm for Improved Phoneme Segmentation and Efficient Training. In: Proceedings of Interspeech, Pittsburgh, Pennsylvania, USA, pp. 1205–1208 (2006)
12. Ogbureke, K.U., Carson-Berndsen, J.: Improving initial boundary estimation for HMM-based automatic phonetic segmentation. In: Proceedings of Interspeech, Brighton, UK, pp. 884–887 (2009)
13. Gómez, J.A., Castro, M.J.: Automatic Segmentation of Speech at the Phonetic Level. In: Caelli, T.M., Amin, A., Duin, R.P.W., Kamel, M.S., de Ridder, D. (eds.) SPR 2002 and SSPR 2002. LNCS, vol. 2396, pp. 672–680. Springer, Heidelberg (2002)
14. Gómez, J.A., Sanchis, E., Castro-Bleda, M.J.: Automatic Speech Segmentation Based on Acoustical Clustering. In: Hancock, E.R., Wilson, R.C., Windeatt, T., Ulusoy, I., Escolano, F. (eds.) SSPR&SPR 2010. LNCS, vol. 6218, pp. 540–548. Springer, Heidelberg (2010)
15. Moreno, A., Poch, D., Bonafonte, A., Lleida, E., Llisterri, J., Mariño, J.B., Nadeu, C.: Albayzin Speech Database: Design of the Phonetic Corpus. In: Proceedings of Eurospeech, Berlin, Germany, vol. 1, pp. 653–656 (September 1993)
16. TIMIT Acoustic-Phonetic Continuous Speech Corpus, National Institute of Standards and Technology Speech Disc 1-1.1, NTIS Order No. PB91-5050651996 (October 1990)

An Active Learning Approach for Statistical Spoken Language Understanding

Fernando García, Lluís-F. Hurtado, Emilio Sanchis, and Encarna Segarra

Grup d'Enginyeria del Llenguatge Natural i Reconeixement de Formes,
Department de Sistemes Informàtics i Computació,
Universitat Politècnica de València, València, Spain
{fgarcia,lhurtado,esanchis,esegarra}@dsic.upv.es
http://dsic.upv.es/users/elirf

Abstract. In general, large amount of segmented and labeled data is needed to estimate statistical language understanding systems. In recent years, different approaches have been proposed to reduce the segmentation and labeling effort by means of unsupervised o semi-supervised learning techniques. We propose an active learning approach to the estimation of statistical language understanding models that involves the transcription, labeling and segmentation of a small amount of data, along with the use of raw data. We use this approach to learn the understanding component of a Spoken Dialog System. Some experiments that show the appropriateness of our approach are also presented.

Keywords: active learning, unaligned corpus, spoken language understanding, spoken dialog systems.

1 Introduction

One of the most important drawbacks in almost all the corpus-based approaches to the development of Spoken Language Understanding (SLU) systems is the effort that is necessary to manually transcribe, segment and label a training corpus, process that is essential in this kind of approaches. Manual segmentation and labeling, apart from the time-consuming work, has the disadvantage that sometimes it is difficult to decide a-priori which limits of the segments are more accurate to represent a specific semantic label and to better discriminate from other semantic labels. Despite of this laborious and time-consuming process of preparation of training data, statistical models have been widely used in recent years in the Spoken Language Understanding (SLU) area, mainly in the framework of spoken dialog systems, and they have shown good performances [8], [5], [1], and [4].

Moreover, automatically training an understanding model from a segmented and labeled corpus is a static learning process and it is not possible to adapt the model to new kinds of interactions or to new ways to express the concepts. This is why in recent years different techniques have been proposed to reduce the labeling effort by means of unsupervised o semi-supervised learning techniques

C. San Martin and S.-W. Kim (Eds.): CIARP 2011, LNCS 7042, pp. 565–572, 2011.

and to have the possibility of dynamically adapt the models when the system is interacting with the users in order to allow for an active learning process [7], [9] and [3]. Active learning aims at reducing the number of training examples to be labeled by selectively sampling a subset of the unlabeled data. This is done by inspecting the unlabeled examples and selecting the most informative ones, with respect to a given cost function. Active learning is well-motivated in many modern machine-learning problems, where unlabeled data may be abundant or easily obtained; however, the labeling process is difficult, time-consuming, and expensive.

In this paper we present an approach to SLU that is based on automatic learning of statistical models. In previous versions of our SLU system [8], all the transcribed training corpus was manually segmented and labeled in terms of semantic labels. In the present approach we propose to apply an active learning process to estimate a SLU system which requires only the transcription, segmentation and labeling of a small set of training user utterances.

We propose a two-step approach to the estimation of statistical language understanding models that involves the transcription, segmentation and labeling of a small amount of data (recognized user utterances), along with the use of raw (untranscribed, unsegmented and unlabeled) recognized user utterances. In the first step, from a small corpus of unaligned pairs of recognized sentences and their corresponding semantic representation (frames), we have applied a semi-supervised process [6] obtaining an automatic segmentation of the corpus. From the segmented and labeled sentences of that small corpus, a baseline statistical language understanding model is estimated using an automatic method [8]. In the second step, we incrementally update this baseline language understanding model with more segmented and labeled sentences following an active learning process. A set of new recognized user utterances is automatically segmented and labeled with the baseline statistical language understanding model. According to a confidence measure criterium obtained during the understanding process, a small number of these new sentences (the least reliable ones) are manually transcribed, segmented and labeled by an expert, and together with the automatically segmented and labeled sentences, are used to retrain the baseline statistical language understanding model. This process is repeated for another set of raw sentences, but, this time, the retrained statistical language understanding model is used.

The SLU model used [8] is based on a two-level statistical model, in which both the probabilities of sequences of semantic labels and the lexical realization (that is, the sequences of words associated) of each semantic label are represented. Some confidence measures generated in this decoding process are used to automatically detect sentences that can be candidates for manual labeling. This way only a few of the new sentences are manually labeled, while the sentences that are decoded with high confidence are automatically included in the new training corpus.

Some experiments were performed over a task of information about train timetables and prices in Spanish. The experiments show the accuracy of the proposed learning methods that provides similar results to those obtained from a completely segmented and labeled training corpus. Thus we have the possibility of having a system that can be dynamically adapted while it is used by real users, whereas the effort employed to obtain the models is not comparable with the effort of manually transcribing, segmenting and labeling the full training corpus.

This paper is organized as follows, Section 2 describes the SLU process using the two-level statistical model. Section 3 describes the initial automatic semi-supervised segmentation process and the process of incrementally updating the SLU model through an active learning approach. Section 4 presents the evaluation of our proposal on the Corpus of Dihana, a Spoken Dialog System to access a railway information system using Spontaneous Speech in Spanish. And finally, Section 5 presents the conclusions.

2   Speech Understanding

We have proposed a method for speech understanding based on the use of stochastic models automatically learned from data. The main characteristic of our method is the integration of syntactic and semantic restrictions into one finite-state automaton. To learn syntactic and semantic models a corpus of segmented and labeled sentences is required. Each sentence in the corpus must be segmented and a label (from a set of semantic labels V defined for the task) must be assigned to each segment. The label assigned to each segment represents the semantic information provided by this segment.

From the segmented and labeled corpus two types of finite-state models are learned. A model A_s for the *semantic language* is estimated from the sequences of semantic labels associated to the input sentences. A set of models, *syntactic models* A_{v_i} (one for each semantic label $v_i \in V$), is estimated from all the segments of words assigned to this semantic label.

In order to perform the understanding process, a global automaton A_t is generated by combining the semantic model with the syntactic ones. The states of the semantic automaton A_s are substituted by their corresponding stochastic automata A_{v_i}.

Given the input sentence $w = w_1 w_2 \ldots w_n \in W^*$, the understanding process consists of finding the sequence of semantic labels $v = v_1 v_2 \ldots v_k \in V^*$ which maximizes the probability:

$$\widehat{v} = \underset{v}{\operatorname{argmax}}\, P(w|v)P(v)$$

Where, $P(v)$ is the probability of the sequence of semantic labels v and $P(w|v)$ is the probability of the sequence of words w given the sequence of semantic labels v. We approach this latter probability as the maximum for all possible segmentations of w in $|v|$ segments.

$$P(w|v) = \underset{\forall l_1, l_2, \ldots l_{k-1}}{\max}\, \{P(w_1, \ldots, w_{l_1}|v_1) \cdot P(w_{l_1+1}, \ldots, w_{l_2}|v_2) \cdot \ldots \cdot P(w_{l_{k-1}+1}, \ldots, w_n|v_k)\}$$

The understanding process is performed using the Viterbi algorithm, which supplies the best path through A_t that is able to produce the input sentence w. From this path the sequence of semantic labels and the most likely segmentation of the input sentence associated to it can be easily obtained. More details of our approach to speech understanding can we found in [8].

2.1   Semantic Representation for the DIHANA Task

Although our method is generic, a specific set of semantic labels must be defined for each task. In addition, once the segmentation of the sentence is performed a second phase is required. This second phase is devoted to reordering the semantic labels following a canonical order and instantiating some values, mostly related to hours and dates.

During the DIHANA project a corpus of 900 dialogs was acquired using the Wizard of Oz technique [2]. Four dialogs were acquired for each of the 225 users who cooperated in the acquisition process. The chosen task was the access to an information system using spontaneous speech. The information system provided information about railway timetables, fares, and services. The system was accessed by telephone in Spanish. The number of user turns acquired was 6 280 and the vocabulary size was 823 different words.

The semantic representation chosen for the task was based on frames. The understanding module takes the sentence supplied by the automatic speech recognizer as input and generates one or more frames (which are concepts with their corresponding attributes) as output. The frames are obtained after reordering the semantic labels from the best segmentation of the sentence and instantiating certain values as stated above. A total amount of 25 semantic labels were defined for DIHANA task. In order to label segments without semantic, a *null* label was also added the the label set.

Ten labels related to frame concepts, divided in two different types, were defined:

1. *Task-independent concepts*: *(ACCEPTANCE)*, *(REJECTION)*, and *(NOT-UNDERSTOOD)*.
2. *Task-dependent concepts*: *(HOUR)*, *(DEPARTURE-HOUR)*, *(ARRIVAL-HOUR)*, *(PRICE)*, *(TRAIN-TYPE)*, *(SERVICES)*, and *(TRIP-DURATION)*.

The task-independent concepts represent generic interaction acts which could be used for any task. The task-dependent concepts represent the information the user can ask for. In an user turn, each task-dependent concept can include one or more attributes from a set of fifteen. These attributes represent the constraints that the user can place on his query.

The fifteen attributes defined for the DIHANA task are: *City, Origin-City, Destination-City, Class, Train-Type, Num-Relative-Order, Price, Services, Date, Arrival-Date, Departure-Date, Hour, Departure-Hour, Arrival-Hour,* and *Trip-Type*.

Two examples of the semantic representation, translated from the original Spanish DIHANA corpus, are shown below:

"I want to know the timetable on Friday to Barcelona, on June 18th"
(HOUR)
Destination: Barcelona
Departure-Date: (Friday)[18-06]

"yes, the fares from Valencia"
(ACCEPTANCE)
(PRICE)
Origin: Valencia

3   The Active Learning Process

The goal of the active learning process is to obtain good models by labeling only a small part of the training samples. It also permits the models be dynamically adapted when real users interact with the system. As this process is a kind of bootstrapping process we need to start from an initial model that must be learned using a small set of labeled training samples. Even in this preliminary step of the learning process we avoid the effort of the manual segmentation of the corpus, that is, we only need the pair (sentence, semantic representation in terms of frames) without the explicit association of semantic labels to the segments of the sentence. To do this, we have developed a semi-supervised learning algorithm [6] that associates to each semantic label a set of segments of different lengths based on the co-occurrences of segments and semantic labels. That is, given a fixed length l, $P(v_k|u_l)$ is calculated for every segment of length l, u_l, and every semantic label, v_k, in the training corpus. Then, those segments with $P(v_k|u_l) > theshold$ are considered to belong to v_k.

As the training corpus is small, it is necessary to increase the coverage in order to include more linguistic variability that it is not present in the corpus. To do so, a procedure of categorization, lematization, and semantic generalization based on dictionaries is applied. This is the case for example of the segment *"quiero ir a"* (*I want to go to*) that is generalized to *"querer ir a"* (*to want to go to*) that includes the Spanish conditional form *"querría ir a"* (*I would want to go to*).

Increasing the length of segments, we can better discriminate between words that are semantically ambiguous by adding context to the segment. For example the word *"Valencia"* in an isolated way can not be associated to a semantic label, while the bigram *"to Valencia"* can easily be associated to the semantic label "destination-city". In our experiments, we have considered segments until length 3.

After applying this semi-supervised algorithm, a first segmented and labeled corpus is obtained. From this training corpus we can learn the semantic models as explained in Section 2, and start the active learning process. This process is based on detecting what new samples are not well represented in our models, and only these samples will be manually transcribed, analyzed and, if it is necessary, relabeled. That is, by using our current semantic models we analyze a new set of sentences from the automatic speech recognizer and those sentences that are selected by considering a confidence score will be manually corrected.

The confidence measure we have used is based on the probability of the appearance of sequences of words when a semantic label is found. For each pair (u_i, v_i), a linear combination of two measures is used to determine if the assignment of the semantic label v_i to the segment u_i has been done properly during the decoding process:

- $\frac{logP(u_i|v_i)}{|u_i|}$ is the probability of the segment u_i within the semantic label v_i normalized according to the number of words in the segment. This measure is more sensitive to syntactic variations.
- $\frac{log\prod_{w_j \in u_i} P(u_i|v_i)}{|u_i|}$ is the same probability but considering only the unigram probability. This measure is more sensitive to out-of-vocabulary words.

Sentences containing one or more segments with a low value for the linear combination of these measures are manually revised.

4   Experiments

Some experiments were carried out in order to evaluate the appropriateness of the described technique. We used the 80% of the corpus as training and development set and the 20% as test set. In all the experiments, the output of the recognition module of the test sentences was used as the input of the understanding process. The speech recognizer used in the experimentation had a 74% of word accuracy.

We defined two measures to evaluate the performance of the understanding module:

- %CF, is the percentage of correct frames, i.e. the percentage of obtained frames that are exactly the same as the corresponding reference frame.
- %CFS, is the percentage of correct frame units (concepts and attributes).

Two different experiments were done. In the first experiment, using the manually transcribed, segmented, and labeled corpus we trained an understanding model (Section 2). This experiment gives an upper bound of our understanding technique to compare with the results of subsequent experiments. The second experiment measures the behavior of the semi-supervised algorithm and the active learning process (Section 3).

For the second experimentation, four subsets were created splitting the training corpus in order to apply the active learning technique (T25_1, T25_2, T25_3, and T25_4), each one of them contained the 25% of the training corpus. The models learned in each step were stochastic finite-state automata. The process was as follows:

1. We considered the sentences supplied by the speech recognizer for the first training subset and the semantic representation (in terms of frames) associated to each one of them. An automatic segmentation and labeling process was made using the semi-supervised algorithm. With this labeled data, the first understanding model was trained (T25_1).
2. Using this understanding model, a process of segmentation and labeling of the second training subset was performed.
3. Considering the confidence scores generated in the understanding process, a part of the sentences in the second subset was selected in order to be manually transcribed, segmented, and labeled. Instead of finding a threshold of the confidence scores, we selected the 20% of the segments with the lower confidence score.
4. After the last step a new training corpus was generated. This new corpus consists of the first training subset, the sentences in the second subset that were automatically labeled by the understanding process, and the small part of the second subset (20%) that were manually corrected. With this new corpus a new understanding model was learned (T25_2).
5. We repeated the process for the third and the fourth training subsets (T25_3, T25_4).

The results of the first experiment were 63.8% for the %CF measure and 78.2% for the %CFS measure. The %CFS value is higher than the %CF value. That is because the %CF measure is more strict: an error in one frame unit produces an error in the whole sentence.

Table 1 shows the results of the active learning process. As we can see both measures improve with the increase of training data. The results are slightly worse than the results in the reference experiment (Ref column), but the effort of manual segmentation and labeling is much smaller.

Table 1. Results of the active learning process

	T25_1	T25_2	T25_3	T25_4	Ref
%CF	53.1	54.8	56.9	57.9	63.8
%CFS	70.5	73.1	74.5	75.3	78.2

From a training corpus of 5,024 user turns, 1,256 were semantically labeled for the initial semi-supervised process, and 750 additional turns were transcribed, segmented and labeled during the active learning process. This implies a transcription and segmentation of 15% of the training corpus, and semantic labeling of the 40% of the training corpus. System performance has been reduced by less than 3% compared to models using the entire transcribed, segmented, and labeled training corpus.

5 Conclusions

In this paper, we have presented an active learning approach to the estimation of statistical language understanding models which involves the transcription, labeling, and segmentation of only a small amount of data, along with the use of raw data. We have used this approach to learn the understanding component of a Spoken Dialog System for railway information retrieval in Spanish. Experiments show that the results obtained with the proposed method are quite similar to those obtained from a completely segmented and labeled corpus. However, the effort employed to obtain the models is much lower than the effort required for completely transcribing, segmenting, and labeling the training corpus.

Acknowledgements. Work partially supported by the Spanish MICINN under contract TIN2008-06856-C05-02, and by the Vicerrectorat d'Investigació, Desenvolupament i Innovació of the Universitat Politècnica de València under contract 20100982.

References

1. De Mori, R., Bechet, F., Hakkani-Tur, D., McTear, M., Riccardi, G., Tur, G.: Spoken language understanding: A survey. IEEE Signal Processing Magazine 25(3), 50–58 (2008)
2. Fraser, M., Gilbert, G.: Simulating speech systems. Computer Speech and Language 5, 81–99 (1991)
3. Gotab, P., Bechet, F., Damnati, G.: Active learning for rule-based and corpus-based spoken labguage understanding moldes. In: IEEE Workshop Automatic Speech Recognition and Understanding (ASRU 2009), pp. 444–449 (2009)
4. Gotab, P., Damnati, G., Becher, F., Delphin-Poulat, L.: Online slu model adaptation with a partial oracle. In: Proc. of InterSpeech 2010, Makuhari, Chiba, Japan, pp. 2862–2865 (2010)
5. He, Y., Young, S.: Spoken language understanding using the hidden vector state model. Speech Communication 48, 262–275 (2006)
6. Ortega, L., Galiano, I., Hurtado, L.F., Sanchis, E., Segarra, E.: A statistical segment-based approach for spoken language understanding. In: Proc. of InterSpeech 2010, Makuhari, Chiba, Japan, pp. 1836–1839 (2010)
7. Riccardi, G., Hakkani-Tur, D.: Active learning: theory and applications to automatic speech recognition. IEEE Transactions on Speech and Audio Processing 13(4), 504–511 (2005)
8. Segarra, E., Sanchis, E., Galiano, M., García, F., Hurtado, L.: Extracting Semantic Information Through Automatic Learning Techniques. International Journal of Pattern Recognition and Artificial Intelligence 16(3), 301–307 (2002)
9. Tur, G., Hakkani-Tr, D., Schapire, R.E.: Combining active and semi-supervised learning for spoken language understanding. Speech Communication 45, 171–186 (2005)

Virus Texture Analysis Using Local Binary Patterns and Radial Density Profiles

Gustaf Kylberg[1], Mats Uppström[2], and Ida-Maria Sintorn[1]

[1] Centre for Image Analysis, Lägerhyddsvägen 2, SE-751 05 Uppsala, Sweden
{gustaf.kylberg,ida.sintorn}@cb.uu.se
[2] Vironova AB, Gävlegatan 22, SE-113 30 Stockholm, Sweden
mats.uppstrom@vironova.com

Abstract. We investigate the discriminant power of two local and two global texture measures on virus images. The viruses are imaged using negative stain transmission electron microscopy. Local binary patterns and a multi scale extension are compared to radial density profiles in the spatial domain and in the Fourier domain. To assess the discriminant potential of the texture measures a Random Forest classifier is used. Our analysis shows that the multi scale extension performs better than the standard local binary patterns and that radial density profiles in comparison is a rather poor virus texture discriminating measure. Furthermore, we show that the multi scale extension and the profiles in Fourier domain are both good texture measures and that they complement each other well, that is, they seem to detect different texture properties. Combining the two, hence, improves the discrimination between virus textures.

Keywords: virus morphology, texture analysis, local binary patterns, radial density profiles.

1 Introduction

To image viruses using negative stain transmission electron microscopy (TEM) has proven to be an invaluable tool in early virus diagnostics, [1,2]. Viruses show different surface texture when imaged using TEM. This fact has been utilized from the very beginning of virology when the advances in TEM technology walked hand in hand with the discovery of new viruses and the creation of a virus taxonomy.

The analysis of a virus sample using TEM typically means an visual inspection performed at the microscope. The main problems with this procedure are the need for an expert to perform the analysis at the microscope and that the result is highly dependent on the expert's skill and experience. To make virus diagnostic using TEM more useful, automatic analysis would hence be desirable. The analysis presented in this paper is part of a project with the aim to develop a fully automatic system for virus diagnostics based on TEM in combination with automatic image analysis.

Viruses vary in shape from icosahedral to highly pleomorphic particles and different virus types have different sizes. The appearance of virus particles in

C. San Martin and S.-W. Kim (Eds.): CIARP 2011, LNCS 7042, pp. 573–580, 2011.

TEM images can be divided into properties like size, shape and texture. While size and shape can be used to exclude some virus types they can not, by themselves, confirm a specific virus type. Many viruses show a distinct and recurring texture making it an interesting property to analyse and use to discriminate between different virus types.

Very little work has been reported on analysing virus texture in TEM images. In [3] ring filters in the Fourier power spectrum are used as features to discriminate between four icosahedral viruses. In [4] higher order spectral features are utilized to differentiate between the same four icosahedral viruses. There is no consensus definition of what texture is, but the general opinion often include some repetitive intensity variation. The definition of a good texture measure is hence highly dependent on the problem at hand. When a measure is used in a classification procedure it becomes possible to assess its capabilities and qualities.

Local binary patterns (LBP) emerged in the mid '90s as a local texture measure [5,6]. LBP has along with several extensions become a popular texture measure in several real-world applications, see e.g., [7,8]. The thesis by Mäenpää [9] gives a good overview of LBP and some of it extensions.

Another way of describing the intensity variations in an object is to compute a radial or density profile (RDP). In [10] radial density profiles are used to discriminate between three maturation stages of human cytomegalovirus capsids in TEM images of cell sections. [11,12] are examples of their use in cyro-electron microscopy where DNA packing is compared between two virus types and attachment sites on Simian Cytomegalovirus capsids are analysed, respectively.

In this paper the basic concepts of LBP and RDP, along with some variations, are investigated for the problem of discriminating between virus textures. We use Random Forest [13], an ensemble classifier based on decision trees, to enable a quantitative comparison of how the different texture measures can discriminate between 15 virus types.

2   Material

The data set consists of 15 different virus types represented with 100 TEM image patches each. The virus types are of different sizes and shape. However, the diameter (most common cross section for non spherical viruses) is relatively constant within a virus type. The virus types range from 25 to 270 nm in diameter and their shapes vary from icosahedral to highly pleomorphic (for example like boiled spaghetti). The image patches are disk shaped cutouts centred on automatically segmented virus particles using the segmentation method presented in [14]. The viruses have been imaged at different magnifications in the TEM with a pixel size ranging from 0.5 to 5 nm. To get comparable texture samples we resample the images to two specific scales using bilinear interpolation. In the first, which we call *fixed scale*, the size of a pixel is 1 nanometer. In the second, which we call *object scale*, the radius of a virus particle is represented by 20 pixels. In Fig. 1 an image patch of each virus type in the object scale is shown along with the virus name and diameter.

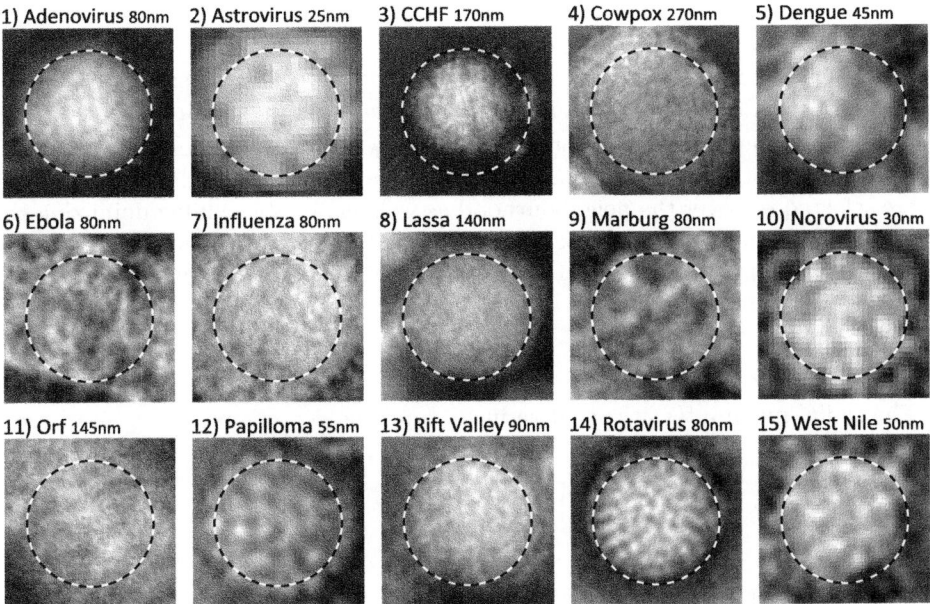

Fig. 1. Example images of the 15 virus types in the data set resampled to object scale. Following the virus name is the approximate particle diameter of each virus type. The dashed circle marks the texture patch used in the analysis.

3 Methods

3.1 LBP

The local binary pattern (LBP) at a pixel q_c with the position (x_c, y_c) in an image I is computed by thresholding a number, N, of neighbour points, p, evenly distributed at a radius R around q_c. The position of the neighbour point p where $p \in [0, \ldots, N - 1]$, is given by: $(x_c + R\cos(2\pi p/N),\ y_c - R\sin(2\pi p/N))$.

The LBP code is then the sequence of zeros and ones from the thresholded values in the neighbour points. If a point p does not coincide with a pixel centre, bilinear interpolation is used to compute the gray value in p. The LBP code can be made rotational invariant, LBP^{ri}, by circularly shifting the binary number until the minimum value is obtained. Furthermore we can restrict our binary codes, considering only uniform binary patterns, LBP^{riu}, further limiting the number of possible codes. Uniform binary patterns are patterns with at the most two spatial transitions between 0 and 1 or 1 and 0. Detailed definitions of LBP, rotational invariance and uniformity can be found in [9]. The rotational invariant and uniform (allowing ≤ 2 transitions) LBP using N samples at the radius R is denoted $\text{LBP}^{\text{riu2}}_{N,R}$. The LBP measure of a set of pixels is then the histogram of occurring LBP codes.

3.2   LBPF

Extending LBP to multiple scales opens up many design options, whereof several alternatives are presented in [9]. A straight forward extension of LBP is to compute several $\text{LBP}^{\text{ri}}_{N,R}$ with increasing R where the points are sampled using Gaussian kernels. This is denoted $\text{LBPF}^{\text{ri}}_{N,R}$, where the additional F stands for filtered. The standard deviation of the Gaussian kernels and the sample points are selected to cover the neighbourhood as well as possible while minimizing the overlap of kernels. We have used an exponentially growing radius R and Gaussian kernels computed as described in [9]. The LBPF codes are then concatenated into one feature vector.

3.3   RDP

The radial mean intensity, f, at radius r from the center pixel q_c in an image I is defined as:

$$f(q_c, r) = \frac{1}{|N|} \sum_{q \in N} I(q), \tag{1}$$

$$N = \{q \, : \, \|q - q_c\|_2 \in (r - 0.5, r + 0.5]\}, \tag{2}$$

where q is a pixel at radius r from q_c and N is the set of pixels at radius r from q_c. $|N|$ is the number of pixels in the set N. The radial density profile with n radii, RDP_n, computed for the pixel q_c is:

$$\text{RDP}_n = [\, f(q_c, 1) - \overline{f}_{q_c} \quad f(q_c, 2) - \overline{f}_{q_c} \quad \cdots \quad f(q_c, n) - \overline{f}_{q_c} \,], \tag{3}$$

where $\overline{f}_{q_c}$ is the mean value of all $f(q_c, r)$, $r \in [1, 2, \ldots, n]$.

3.4   FRDP

The FRDP is computed in the same way as the RDP but using the Fourier magnitude spectra in a $\log_e$ scale as the input image. In this way, the FRDP shows a profile of frequencies occurring in the input image I. FRDP can be interpreted as a generalization of the spectral rings used in [3].

3.5   Classification

To get objective measures of the performances of the investigated texture measures we use the Random Forest classifier. That is an example of an ensemble classifier based on bagged decision trees introduced by Breiman in [13]. When the ensemble is created a new bootstrap sample is drawn for each new tree. When a tree is grown only a random subset of the feature values are used, increasing the diversity among trees even further. The error rate of the built ensemble classifier can be estimated through the samples left out of the bootstrap samples, called "out-of-bag" data by Breiman. We grew 200 trees and the increase in performance per added tree levelled out between 100 and 200 trees meaning that 100 trees is a large enough ensemble. The number of feature values to select at random for each decision split is set to the square root of the number of feature values, proposed by Breiman as a rule of thumb.

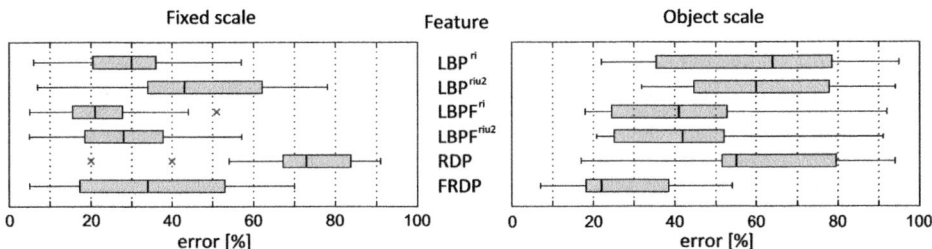

Fig. 2. Estimated classification errors for the Random Forest classifier for the different texture measures. The boxes stretch from the lower to the upper quartile and the line marks the median. The whiskers show min and max in the data excluding outliers. Outliers ($\times$) are data points at least 1.5 times the size of the box away from the box.

4 Results

For the investigation in this paper we have compared i) $\text{LBP}^{\text{ri}}_{8,2}$, ii) $\text{LBP}^{\text{riu2}}_{8,2}$, iii) a multi scale LBPF composed of $\text{LBPF}^{\text{ri}}_{8,1} + {}^{\text{ri}}_{8,2.4} + {}^{\text{ri}}_{8,5.4}$, iv) the uniform variant $\text{LBPF}^{\text{riu2}}_{8,1} + {}^{\text{riu2}}_{8,2.4} + {}^{\text{riu2}}_{8,5.4}$, v) RDP_{20} and vi) FRDP_{20}. The latter two measures are of global character while the LBP variations are of local character. Figure 2 shows the result. We found that the LBPF^{ri} in fixed scale and the FRDP in object scale are the two most promising texture measures investigated.

For $\text{LBP}_{N,R}$ a range of parameter values were tested: $N \in [4, 8, 16]$, $R \in [1, 2, 3, 4]$. For LBPF the following sets of N were tested: $N_1 = [4, 8, 8]$, $N_2 = [4, 8, 16]$, $N_3 = [8, 8, 8]$, $N_4 = [8, 8, 16]$ were tested together with R calculated according to [9]. Many parameter combination resulted in similar discriminant power and the values selected were the best performing options.

The result shows that LBP and its variations generally performed better in the fixed scale. From Fig. 2 it is clear that applying the uniformity restriction results in a poorer discrimination between the virus types in the fixed scale. Among the 1,500 texture patches in the data set, $\text{LBP}^{\text{riu2}}_{8,2}$ resulted in 263 more samples being wrongly classified in the fixed scale compared to using $\text{LBP}^{\text{ri}}_{8,2}$. Applying the uniformity restriction in the LBPF also resulted in a poorer classification result in the fixed scale, but only with 93 more samples incorrectly classified. Most prominent, removing the uniformity restriction for samples of the Cowpox virus the error decreased from 54% to 26% showing that for certain virus textures important discriminant information is found in the non uniform patterns.

Figure 3 shows the confusion matrices for the classification using LBP, LBPF, RDP and FRPD for the fixed scale (a), and the object scale (b). These matrices display the information constituting the boxes for these texture measures in Fig. 2. From the figures it is clear that RDP discriminates between the virus textures rather poorly (week diagonal and relatively high values everywhere in the matrix). It is also easy to see that both LBP and LBPF perform better in the fixed scale (generally lower off-diagonal values), and that the opposite is true for RDPF. Both Fig. 3 and Fig. 2 show that the texture measures best discriminating the virus textures are LBPF in the fixed scale and RDPF in the object scale. By carefully analysing their confusion matrices one can see that LBPF clearly perform better for certain virus textures e.g. 4, 6 and 12, whereas RDPF perform better for 15. Combining these two measures would probably give an even better discrimination. That is in fact the case which is shown in Fig. 4. In the confusion matrix, Fig. 4. a), the off-diagonal values are lower, and the values on the diagonal are much higher compared to the confusion matrices for each of the two texture measures. It is also

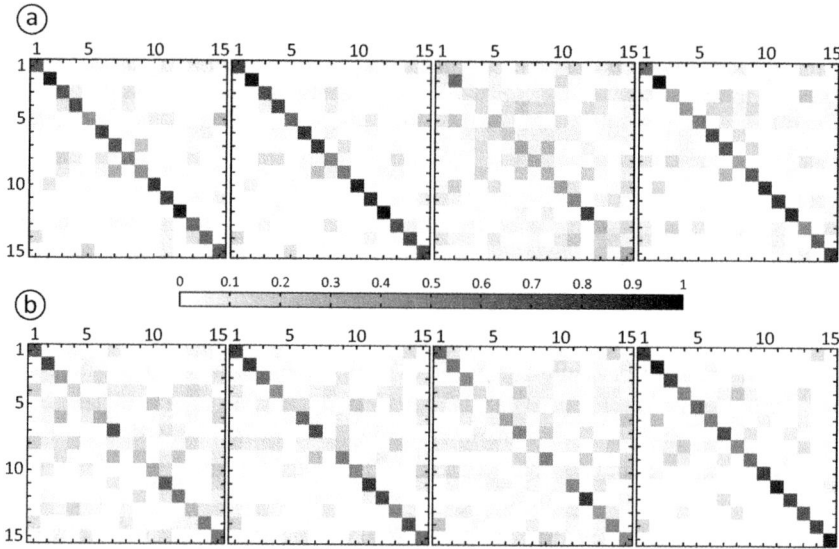

Fig. 3. Resulting confusion matrices, i.e., from the Random Forest classification for the texture measures, from left to right: LBP^{ri}, LBPF^{ri}, RDP, FRDP for a) image patches in fixed scale and b) object scale

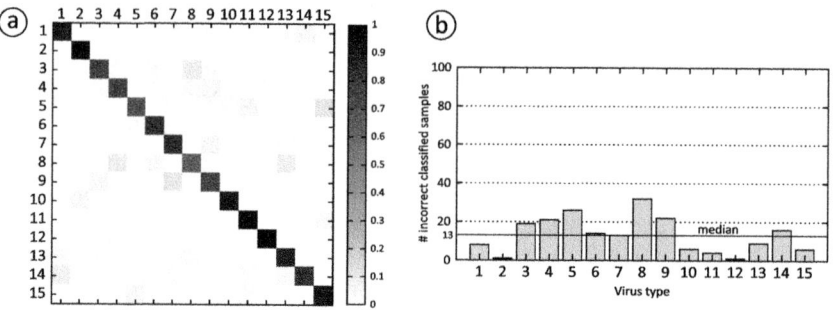

Fig. 4. a) Resulting confusion matrix after combining the LBPF^{ri} measure in the fixed scale with the FRDP in the object scale. b) Total error in classification for each virus type. The median value is marked with a horizontal line.

clear that the two measures provide complementary information for many of the virus textures as using both in the classification results in better discrimination than using the best of the two for each virus class, see e.g. virus 5, 8, 9, and 13. Figure 4 b) shows the classification result from using the combination of the two measures for each of the virus classes. The median classification error rate is 13 % which should be compared to 21% for LBPF in the fixed scale and 22% for RDPF in the object scale.

5 Discussion

When the uniformity restriction was introduced in [15] the authors show that the discriminant power was mainly made up by the uniform patterns. This restriction is commonly regarded as an improvement upon the basic LBP when applied. However, our results show that the non uniform patterns contribute to the discriminant power of LBP and LBPF for the virus texture data.

The approach to handle the different sizes of the viruses was to resample the images into a fixed scale and into an object scale. From Fig. 2 we can conclude that the global measures generally score better in the object scale while the opposite can be observed for the two LBP-based measures.

The choice of classifier can of course be discussed and with a different classifier, e.g., SVM, NN or AdaBoost, the result would most likely have looked slightly different. We have selected the Random Forest classifier based on previous positive experiences using similar measures and on a comparison of classifiers (Random Forest, SVM, GMM, AdaBoost) on a similar problem. However, this paper is not about selecting the best suited classifier but rather using a classifier as a tool to evaluate our texture measures.

Future work includes exploring some of the many possibilities within the LBP framework to make a local texture descriptor that is more robust to noise. Further, combinations of texture measures and size and shape descriptors as well as other *a priori* knowledge about the virus sample type will be used in the discrimination problem present in our intended real-world application. For example haemorrhagic fever viruses such as CCHF, Dengue and Ebola are rarely found in fecal samples. Moreover, many virus particles will be analysed and classified in each patient sample and therefore a certain degree of incorrect classifications do not pose a problem.

Acknowledgement. Thanks to: Ali Mirazimi and Kjell-Olof Hedlund at SMI for preparing the virus samples; Tobias Bergroth and Lars Haag at Vironova for acquiring the images; Erik Wernersson and Gunilla Borgefors for valuable comments regarding the manuscript. The work presented in this paper is part of a project funded by the Swedish Agency for Innovation Systems (VINNOVA), Swedish Defence Materiel Administration (FMV), and the Swedish Civil Contingencies Agency (MSB).

References

1. Goldsmith, C.S., Miller, S.E.: Modern uses of electron microscopy for detection of viruses. Clin. Microbiol. Rev. 22(4), 552–563 (2009)
2. Biel, S.S., Madeley, D.: Diagnostic virology – the need for electron microscopy: a discussion paper. J. Clin. Virol. 22(1), 1–9 (2001)
3. Matuszewski, B.J., Shark, L.K.: Hierarchical iterative bayesian approach to automatic recognition of biological viruses in electron microscope images. In: Proc. of 2001 International Conference on Image Processing (ICIP), vol. 2, pp. 347–350 (2001)
4. Ong, H.C.L.: Virus recognition in electron microscope images using higher order spectral features. PhD thesis, Queensland University of Technology (2006)
5. Harwood, D., Ojala, T., Pietikäinen, M., Kelman, S., Davis, L.: Texture classification by center-symmetric auto-correlation, using kullback discrimination of distributions. Pattern. Recogn. Lett. 16(1), 1–10 (1995)
6. Ojala, T., Pietikäinen, M., Harwood, D.: A comparative study of texture measures with classification based on featured distributions. Pattern. Recogn. 29(1), 51–59 (1996)
7. Hervé, N., Servais, A., Thervet, E., Olivo-Marin, J.C., Meas-Yedid, V.: Statistical color texture descriptors for histological images analysis. In: Proc. of IEEE International Symposium on Biomedical Imaging (ISBI), pp. 724–727 (2011)
8. Zhang, B.: Classification of subcellular phenotype images by decision templates for classifier ensemble. In: Pham, T., Zhou, X. (eds.) Proc. of 2009 International Conference on Computational Models for Life Sciences (CMLS), pp. 13–22 (2010)
9. Mäenpää, T.: The local binary pattern approach to texture analysis - extensions and applications. PhD thesis, University of Oulu (2003)
10. Sintorn, I.M., Homman-Loudiyi, M., Söderberg-Nauclér, C., Borgefors, G.: A refined circular template matching method for classification of human cytomegalovirus capsids in TEM images. Comput. Meth. Prog. Bio. 76, 95–102 (2004)
11. Bhella, D., Rixon, F.J., Dargan, D.J.: Cryomicroscopy of human cytomegalovirus virions reveals more densely packed genomic DNA than in herpes simplex virus type 1. J. Mol. Biol. 295, 155–161 (2000)
12. Trus, B.S., Gibson, W., Cheng, N., Steven, A.C.: Capsid structure of Simian cytomegalovirus from cryoelectron microscopy: Evidence for tegument attachment sites. J. Virol. 73(3), 2181–2192 (1999)
13. Breiman, L.: Random forests. Machine Learning 45, 5–32 (2001)
14. Kylberg, G., Uppström, M., Hedlund, K.O., Borgefors, G., Sintorn, I.M.: Segmentation of virus particle candidates in transmission electron microscopy images (manuscript, 2011)
15. Mäenpää, T., Ojala, T., Pietikäinen, M., Soriano, M.: Robust texture classification by subsets of local binary patterns. In: Proc. of International Conference on Pattern Recognition (ICPR), pp. 3947–3950 (2000)

A Markov Random Field Model for Combining Optimum-Path Forest Classifiers Using Decision Graphs and Game Strategy Approach

Moacir P. Ponti-Jr.[1], João Paulo Papa[2], and Alexandre L.M. Levada[3]

[1] Institute of Mathematical and Computer Sciences
University of São Paulo (ICMC/USP) at São Carlos, SP, Brazil
moacir@icmc.usp.br
http://www.icmc.usp.br/~moacir
[2] Department of Computing, UNESP — Univ Estadual Paulista at Bauru, SP, Brazil
papa@fc.unesp.br
http://wwwp.fc.unesp.br/~papa
[3] Computing Department, Federal University of São Carlos (DC/UFSCar) at
São Carlos, SP, Brazil
alexandre@dc.ufscar.br
http://www.dc.ufscar.br/~alexandre

Abstract. The research on multiple classifiers systems includes the creation of an ensemble of classifiers and the proper combination of the decisions. In order to combine the decisions given by classifiers, methods related to fixed rules and decision templates are often used. Therefore, the influence and relationship between classifier decisions are often not considered in the combination schemes. In this paper we propose a framework to combine classifiers using a decision graph under a random field model and a game strategy approach to obtain the final decision. The results of combining Optimum-Path Forest (OPF) classifiers using the proposed model are reported, obtaining good performance in experiments using simulated and real data sets. The results encourage the combination of OPF ensembles and the framework to design multiple classifier systems.

1 Introduction

The research on multiple classifiers systems comprises the creation of an ensemble of classifiers and also the combination of the decisions. The classifier ensembles are often produced through techniques such as bagging [1], boosting [4] and random subspace methods [6], producing classifiers using different subsets of samples and features. The combination (or fusion) of all decisions is often addressed using fixed rules [8] and also more complex methods.

If the classifiers to be combined provide only class labels as output, the majority voting is the approach commonly used to combine them. The limits of such schemes were investigated and the diversity aspect is currently under discussion, with the study of patterns of failure and success, and "good" and "bad" diversity [2].

C. San Martin and S.-W. Kim (Eds.): CIARP 2011, LNCS 7042, pp. 581–590, 2011.
© Springer-Verlag Berlin Heidelberg 2011

In this study, we propose a framework for the combination of classifiers by creating a decision graph under a Markov Random Field (MRF) model. In order to compute the final decision we explored a majority voting scheme and a game strategy approach (GSA). This should not be confused with fusion of graphs or combination of structural pattern recognition classifiers. We rathers developed a framework to combine classifiers using a random field model constructed from a graph of classifier decisions, as a way to capture the dependency between their outputs. Although another study used game theory to generalize rules for support-vector classifiers combination [5], the GSA combination algorithm proposed here is different, designed so that each classifier is seen as a player and each classifier decision (class label) is seen as a strategy.

This paper aims to combine ensembles of Optimum-Path Forest (OPF) classifiers [12], although the proposed model is general an can be used with a variety of other classifiers. The OPF technique models the feature space as a graph, using optimum-path algorithms to perform training and classification, and it outputs only class labels. The proposed combination is performed by training classifiers with distributed disjoint subsets and it is designed to improve accuracy and reduce running time. To improve speed, the method was developed so that it could be processed using parallel or distributed processors. Therefore, this paper presents contributions both on the study of a new model for combination of classifiers and on the development of a combination algorithm for the OPF classifier.

The paper is organized as follows. Section 2 introduces the OPF classifier used as basis for the ensembles. Section 3 describes the proposed combination framework, including the graph-based MRF model, the GSA combination algorithm and how the ensembles are created. Section 4 and 5 describe the experiments, results and discussion, respectively. Finally, the conclusions are presented in Section 6.

2   Optimum-Path Forest Classifier (OPF)

Papa et al. [12] introduced the idea of designing pattern classifiers based on optimum-path forest. The training samples are interpreted as the vertices of a graph, whose edges are defined by a given adjacency relation and weighted by some distance function. It is expected that samples from a same class are connected by a path of nearby samples. Therefore, the degree of connectedness for any given path is measured by a connectivity (path-value) function, which exploits the distances along the path. Since the true label of the training samples is known, key samples (prototypes) are identified in each class. Optimum paths are computed from the prototypes to each training sample, such that each prototype becomes the root of an optimum-path tree (OPT) composed by its most strongly connected samples. The labels of these samples are assumed to be the same of their root.

The training phase of OPF consists, basically, in finding prototypes and execute OPF algorithm to determine the OPTs rooted at them. Further, the test phase essentially evaluates, for each test sample, which training vertex offered the optimum-path to its. The classification of each new sample t from test set O is performed based on the distance $d(s,t)$ between t and each training vertex $s \in T$ and on the evaluation of the following equation:

$$C_2(t) = \min\{\max\left[C_1(s), d(s,t)\right]\}, \ \forall s \in T. \tag{1}$$

Let $s^* \in T$ be the vertex s that satisfies this equation. It essentially considers all possible paths from S in the training graph T extended to t by an edge (s,t), and label t with the class of s^*.

The OPF classifier has been demonstrated to have similar results to the ones obtained by Support Vector Machines, but running training much faster.

2.1   Learning Algorithm

Large datasets usually present redundancy, so it should be possible to estimate a reduced training set with the most relevant patterns for classification. The use of a training and an evaluation set has allowed OPF to learn relevant training samples from the classification errors in the evaluating, by swapping misclassified samples of the evaluating set and non-prototype samples of the training one during a few iterations. In this learning strategy, the training set remains with the same size and the classifier instance with the highest accuracy is selected to be tested in the unseen test set.

3   Random Field Model for Combination of Classifier Decisions

A classifier that outputs only class labels, for example OPF, allows only abstract-level methods for combination. In such cases, the most common approach is to apply a majority voting rule to obtain the final decision.

In this context, we propose a model similar to a Bayesian Network, using a directed graph of decisions for each object to be classified, where the vertices represent each classifier decision (class label), and the edges denote how each classifier influences the decision of the other ones. At first, this graph can assume any topology. To simplify the model, we are going to avoid cycles and use a tree with inverted directions in this paper. An example of such model is depicted in Figure 1(a), where the final decision is obtained through the propagation of the decisions through the graph, from the source vertices to the sink vertex.

This framework allows the definition of a more general model for combination of decisions. It can be specially useful when there is knowledge about how the decisions must influence each other. One can also use it at random, choosing different levels of vertices and edges.

One of the advantages of this framework is that it can be modeled through a Markov Random Field (MRF). Consider, for example, the situation depicted in Figure 1(a). In this case, we want to model the final decision, provided here by

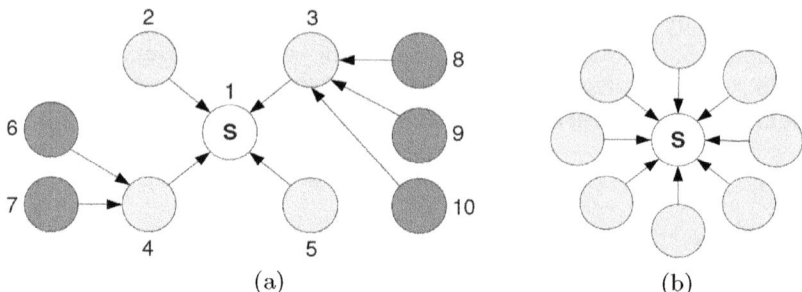

Fig. 1. Examples a graph modelling the decision of classifiers, where the final decision is obtained at the "sink" (S) vertex: (a) 10 classifiers and arcs with different weights, (b) star graph for 9 classifiers

the base classifier "S", in terms of the partial decisions given by other classifiers (competitors). In other words, we want to analize how individual elements (classifiers) modify their behavior to conform to the behavior of other individuals in their vicinity. This is the typical scenario found in MRF models, used to study collective effects based on consequences of local interactions.

Since here each classifier gives as output a hard label (i.e., a discrete number that indicates the class of that sample) a suitable choice is the Potts MRF model.

3.1 The Potts MRF Model

The dependency structure between the classifiers output can be well modeled by a Potts MRF pairwise interaction. This model is both isotropic and stationary, which means that the spatial dependency parameter is the same for all directions and does not change as we move from one vertex to another. According to the Hammersley and Clifford theorem, a MRF model can be equivalently defined by a joint Gibbs distribution (global model) or by a set of local conditional density functions (LCDF). Due to mathematical and computational tractability, we will adopt a local description of the probability model by means of a set of LCDF's. According to [14], the Potts model LCDF for a single observation is given by:

$$p\left(v_i = m | \eta_i, \beta\right) = \frac{exp\left\{\beta U_i\left(m\right)\right\}}{\sum_{\ell=1}^{M} exp\left\{\beta U_i\left(\ell\right)\right\}}, \tag{2}$$

where m is the label of the current vertex, $U_i\left(\ell\right)$ is the number of neighbors of the i-th vertex having label equal to ℓ, $\beta \in \Re$ is the spatial dependency parameter that controls how strong is the influence of the neighboring vertices, and $\ell \in G$, with $G = \{1, 2, \ldots, M\}$, where M represents the number of classes of the decision problem.

3.2 A Game Strategy Approach to Compute the Final Decision

It has been shown that MAP-MRF problems — where MAP stands for Maximum a Posteriori — do not allow closed-form solutions and, in order to approximate the MAP estimator, combinatorial optimization algorithms are required to iteratively improve an initial solution [9]. In this study, we propose a combination scheme (GSAc) based on the Game Strategy Approach (GSA) algorithm [15], a non-cooperative game-theoretic algorithm that has been proved to approximate the MAP-MRF estimator by, given an initial solution, converging to the Nash Equilibrium.

In a n-person game, $I = \{1, 2, \ldots, n\}$ denotes the set of players. Here, each player is a classifier, represented by a vertex in the graph. The idea is to build a decision graph where each vertex is given by a decision of an OPF classifier. The iterative process begins at the source vertices, propagating the labels to the sinc, where the final decision will take place.

Each player has a set of pure strategies S_i. In this case, the set S_i is the same for all players, being defined as $S_i = \{1, 2, \ldots, C\}$, where C is the number of classes. The game process consists of, at a given instant, each player choosing a strategy $s_i \in S_i$ in a way that a play $\mathbf{s} = (s_1, s_2, \ldots, s_n)$ is yielded, and a payoff $H_i(\mathbf{s})$ is assigned to each player.

Algorithm 1 – GSAc: COMBINATION OF CLASSIFIER DECISIONS

INPUT: A labeled cooperation graph G = (V, E) with $|E| = |V| - 1$ (tree) and $|V| = D$ where D is the number of classifiers, and $\alpha \in [0, 1]$

OUTPUT: Set of labels after final decision, L

AUXILIARY: The base classifier is the sinc vertex and the labels of each vertex is the output of the respective classifier.

1.   *For $k = 1$ to D, do*
2.   *Choose the strategy $l_i' \neq l_i^{(k)}$ that maximizes the payoff, i.e., $H_i\left(l_i^{(k)}||l_i'\right) = max_{l_i} H\left(l_i^{(k)}||l_i'\right)$*
3.   *If $H_i\left(l_i^{(k)}||l_i'\right) \leq H_i\left(l_i^{(k)}\right)$*
4. $l_i^{(k+1)} = l_i^{(k)}$
5.   *Else*
6. $l_i^{(k+1)} = l_i'$ *with probability α*
7. $l_i^{(k+1)} = l_i^{(k)}$ *with probability $1 - \alpha$*
8.   *Stop if the labeled graph is a Nash point, or repeat the iteration using the current play.*
9.   *Return the final decision (the result of the combination of the classifiers).*

Two fundamental hypothesis are assumed in GSA: first, the payoff of a player depends only on its own strategy and the strategies of its neighbors, and second, it is supposed that each player knows all possible strategies and the payoff given by each one of them. As GSA is based on non-cooperative game theory, each player selects independently his own strategy to maximize the local payoff. The solutions of a non-cooperative game are the *Nash points*, a condition achieved when none of the players can improve his expected payoff by unilaterally changing his strategy. In mathematical terms, a play $\mathbf{t}^* = (t_1^*, t_2^*, \ldots, t_n^*)$ satisfies the Nash Equilibrium if [11]:

$$\forall i : H_i(\mathbf{t}^*) = max_{s_i \in S_i} H_i(\mathbf{t}^*||\mathbf{t}) \tag{3}$$

where $\mathbf{t}^*||\mathbf{t}$ is the play obtained by replacing $\mathbf{t}^*$ by $\mathbf{t}$. It has been shown that Nash points always exist in non-cooperative games with pure or mixed strategies [11]. The GSA fundamentals are based on a major result derived by [15] which states that given a initial play, the GSA algorithm converges to a *Nash point* in a finite number of steps.

The proposed GSAc algorithm for combining classifiers is given by Algorithm 1. Some considerations must be provided. First, the local payoff is calculated as the local energy, that is, $H_i(l_i) = \beta U(l_i)$, which is directly proportional to the probability value $p(v_i = l_i | \eta_i, \beta)$. Another issue is regarding the $\alpha \in [0, 1]$ parameter existing in GSAc, which controls the probability of acceptance of new strategies. If $\alpha = 1$, we always accept a better strategy (the algorithm becomes deterministic), otherwise even if there is an improved strategy, we might not accept it in that iteration (non-deterministic behavior).

3.3 Building an OPF Classifier Ensemble

To create an ensemble of OPF classifiers, we used disjoint training subsets [13]. Given a fixed number D of subsets, the algorithm chooses random samples, without replacement, from the original training set T until D subsets are created. The samples are taken so that each subset will contain approximately the same number of objects per class. Each subset is then used to train a classifier. The procedure is described in Algorithm 2, where *OPF_learn* and *OPF_classify* corresponds to OPF learning and classification procedures, respectively.

As described in Section 2, the OPF has a fast learning algorithm to rebuild training set using an evaluation set in order to improve accuracy of each classifier, and, therefore, is expected to improve accuracy of the final decision. It has a behavior similar to a boosting algorithm. Moreover, the OPF training algorithm has computational complexity of $\Theta(N^2)$, in which N denotes the training set size, and therefore, it is expected to run faster for k training sets of size X then for a larger one with size $N = k \times X$.

Algorithm 2 – OPFCD: OPF COMBINATION OF DISTRIBUTED DISJOINT SETS

INPUT: Training data set T of size N with correct labels $\omega_j \in \Omega$, $j = \{1, .., C\}$ for C classes, the
          evaluation set V, the set of objects to be classified O (test set), the number of disjoint subsets
          D, the number of samples of each class $P = \{p_1, .., p_C\}$, and the OPF algorithm *OPF_learn* and
          OPF_classify
OUTPUT: Set of labels after final decision, L
AUXILIARY: The number of objects on each subset M, training subsets K_i, classifiers E_i, and objects labeled
          by each classifier I_i, where $i = \{1, .., D\}$

1. $M \leftarrow \lfloor N/D \rfloor$
2.   For each subset $i, (\forall i = 1..D)$, do
3. | For each class $j, (\forall j = 1..C)$, do
4. | $\vdash$ Select randomly $(p_j/D) \times M$ samples of class j from T without replacement and store them in K_i
5. | $E_i \leftarrow OPF\_learn(K_i, V)$
6. $\llcorner$ $I_i \leftarrow OPF\_classify(O, E_i)$
7. $L \leftarrow Vote(I_i)$
8.   Return L

4   Experiments

4.1   Data

The experiments were carried out using four simulated and five real data sets. The simulated data sets were built so that the classes were partially overlapped.

Table 1. Simulated data sets characteristics, where C is the number of classes and F is the number of features

Name	Size	C	F	Type
B2-2D	1,000	2	2	Banana-shape
B2-3D	2,000	4	2	Banana-shape
G4-2D	1,000	2	4	Gaussian
G4-3D	2,000	4	4	Gaussian

Table 2. Real data sets characteristics, where C is the number of classes and F is the number of features

Name	Size	C	F
NTL	8,067	2	4
COREL	1,000	10	150
Wine	178	3	13
KDD-1999	380,271	3	9
Activity	164,860	11	6

The Gaussian data sets have classes with different covariance matrices. The banaha-shape data set with 3 features was generated with a higher variance when compared to the one with 2 features. The project web page[1] contains the code to generate the simulated data using PRTools[2] and an implementation of GSAc. Table 1 shows the characteristics of simulated data sets and Table 2 of real data sets.

NTL is a dataset of an electric power company for identification of legal and illegal profiles of industrial costumers. *COREL* is a subset of an image database including 10 classes with SIFT features [10]. *Wine* is a small data set with results of chemical analysis of wines of three different cultivars [3]. *KDD-1999* models a network intrusion detector, capable of distinguishing intrusions or attacks, and normal connections [3]. *Activity* is the "Localization Data for Person Activity Data Set" to identify what is the current activity of a person based on sensors [7].

4.2   Settings and Implementation

We conducted the experiments as follows: the data sets were partitioned in three sets, 10% for training, 5% for evaluating and 85% for testing.

There are three exceptions in the settings due to the number of samples per class and the size of some real data sets. The exceptions are: i) *COREL* data set with 15% for training and 5% for evaluating, ii) *Wine* data set with 30% for training and 15% for evaluating, and iii) *KDD-1999* data set with 1% for training and 0.5% for evaluating.

---

[1] http://sites.google.com/site/projectensembles/

[2] http://www.prtools.org/

The whole training set was used to train the OPF "single classifier", and the subsets obtained from the training set were used to train several classifiers and build the ensembles. We performed experiments using from 3 to 9 training set partitions (disjoint training subsets) obtained by the OPFcd (Algorithm 2).

In these series of experiments, the decision graph was modeled using a directed star graph, since it is the simplest possible model and can show the robustness of our proposed schema for classifier combination. Figure 1(b) shows an example of the model for an ensemble of 9 classifiers. On each experiment, the sink vertex was randomly chosen from the ensemble and all the other classifiers were conected to the sink node to create the decision graph. No other relations were specified. The GSAc algorithm (Algorithm 1) was then applied to obtain the final decision. We also report the results of a simple majority vote applied to the classifier ensemble in order to compare with the proposed method.

The parameters for the GSAc algorithm was experimentally obtained and defined as $\beta = 0.8$ (spatial dependency parameter) and $\alpha = 0.9$ (probability of acceptance of new strategies).

All experiments were repeated 10 times on different training sets and partitions. The average and standard deviation results are presented. In order to verify the significant differences between groups of results, we performed a two-tailed t-test for samples with unequal variances.

5   Results and Discussion

The main results are shown in Table 3. It displays the classification errors for the data sets using the naive OPF in the first column, and the errors for ensembles of 3, 5, 7, 9 and 42 OPF classifiers using Vote and GSA algorithms to compute the final decision. The results for the ensembles with 4, 6 and 8 classifiers were omitted due to space limitations, since the results were similar to the displayed ones. The ensemble with 42 classifiers was created using the outputs of all classifiers produced by the number of partitions from 3 to 9.

The combination approach using disjoint data sets improved the results for all data sets except for the *Activity*. It was due to a high decrease in performance as less samples are used for training in this data set — a bad scenario for combination of classifiers. However, the combination of all 42 decisions improved the results of all data sets. An improvement on the results was observed for both simulated and real problems in which the single classifier obtained higher error rates, for example *Wine* and *G4-2D*, and also for those with a lower error, for example *KDD-1999* and *B2-2D*. By using an ensemble of 42 OPF classifiers it was possible to achieve an accuracy of 99.95% for the *KDD-1999* data set.

The GSAc results were similar to the Vote method. It is possibly due to the characteristics of the GSAc algorithm under a star graph model, in which the final decision will be dominated by the mode of the classes in the neighborhood. It works as a majority vote rule using a random approach for tie-breaking when the parameters are defined as $\alpha = 1$ and $\beta = 1$. The proposed method is, however, more flexible, allowing the design of different graph topologies and an adjustment on the parameters α and β, as performed in this study.

Although the differences between the proposed and competing method were not significant for all data sets, the GSAc was able to improve the performance using different sizes of classifier ensembles, and, therefore, different number of training set partitions. It also showed a slightly better performance when using the graph with all 42 decisions. We expect that more complex systems can take advantage of the GSAc characteristics.

Table 3. Classification errors for naive OPF and combination of classifiers using Vote and GSA. Results in boldface represents significant improvement for a $p < 0.05$. ∗ the ensemble with 42 classifiers represents the decisions of all classifiers trained with number of partitions from 3 to 9.

DATA SET / NAIVE OPF	COMB. METHOD	NUMBER OF CLASSIFIERS IN THE ENSEMBLE				
		3	5	7	9	42*
B2-2D	VOTE	**5.5±1.0**	**5.5±1.0**	**6.0±0.7**	**4.4±0.7**	**1.4±0.4**
7.1±0.9	GSA	**5.6±0.9**	**5.4±0.8**	**5.6±0.9**	**4.4±0.9**	**1.1±0.5**
B2-3D	VOTE	21.2±1.5	**17.1±1.7**	18.4±2.4	16.4±2.1	**5.6±1.1**
21.6±1.5	GSA	**20.6±1.7**	**17.0±1.5**	18.3±2.4	16.4±2.2	**4.5±0.7**
G4-2D	VOTE	25.3±3.5	**21.5±2.7**	23.7±3.7	**19.5±1.8**	**6.3±0.3**
26.4±2.5	GSA	**23.6±2.2**	**21.6±2.8**	**22.0±3.1**	**19.5±1.9**	**6.0±0.2**
G4-3D	VOTE	14.4±1.3	14.2±1.1	13.5±0.9	**12.3±1.0**	**9.6±1.2**
14.2±1.0	GSA	14.2±1.5	**13.0±0.7**	**12.6±1.0**	**12.3±0.9**	**9.5±1.1**
NTL	VOTE	**8.2±1.4**	**8.4±1.2**	9.1±2.9	9.5±3.5	**5.4±0.2**
10.1±0.4	GSA	**7.7±1.1**	**8.2±1.2**	**8.9±1.7**	10.2±3.3	**5.3±0.1**
COREL	VOTE	**16.4±1.0**	**15.9±0.8**	**15.5±1.6**	16.3±2.0	**12.3±0.3**
18.1±0.6	GSA	**16.4±1.2**	**15.1±0.8**	**15.0±1.2**	**15.3±1.3**	**12.2±0.5**
WINE	VOTE	28.6±2.0	**28.0±1.5**	29.2±2.0	31.1±2.0	**17.7±3.6**
30.4±1.8	GSA	27.8±3.0	**27.1±1.6**	**27.0±1.7**	30.1±2.6	**15.6±3.3**
KDD-1999	VOTE	0.16±0.02	0.25±0.03	0.24±0.04	**0.14±0.02**	**0.04±0.01**
0.21±0.05	GSA	0.17±0.02	0.21±0.02	0.19±0.02	**0.15±0.03**	**0.05±0.01**
ACTIVITY	VOTE	30.9±2.0	31.1±1.6	31.4±0.7	31.8±1.7	**22.1±1.6**
30.0±1.2	GSA	30.8±1.9	30.9±1.2	31.4±1.1	29.8±1.4	**21.3±1.9**

6   Conclusions

Using a simple star graph to model the classifier system, the results showed to decrease the classification error. It was interesting to observe such results even with the combination of few classifiers obtained with the OPFcd method, encouraging the use of OPF classifiers to build ensembles. Since the OPF training algorithm is $\Theta(N^2)$ as discussed in Section 3.3, the combination of OPF ensembles is also a faster procedure when compared with the single OPF, specially when it is carried out with few classifiers, as proposed in this paper using disjoint training subsets.

The behavior of the proposed combination framework was similar to the behavior of known methods for combination of ensemble of classifiers. We believe it is a consequence of the simple star graph model used in the experiments, and that it can change when a more complex model with several levels of decisions are used to model the multiple classifier system. The proposed model allow the design of complex combination schemes, allowing the use of many known methods for MRF and optimization to solve the classification problem. Therefore it has the potential to overcome difficult problems when there is knowledge about how the classifiers decisions should influence each other. A more detailed analysis of how the decision graphs can be designed for different machine learning problems is a point left for future studies.

References

1. Breiman, L.: Bagging predictors. Machine Learning Journal 2(24), 123–140 (1996)
2. Brown, G., Kuncheva, L.I.: "Good" and "Bad" diversity in majority vote ensembles. In: El Gayar, N., Kittler, J., Roli, F. (eds.) MCS 2010. LNCS, vol. 5997, pp. 124–133. Springer, Heidelberg (2010)
3. Frank, A., Asuncion, A.: UCI machine learning repository (2010),
   http://archive.ics.uci.edu/ml
4. Freund, T.: Boosting: a weak learning algorithm by majority. Information and Computation 121(2), 256–285 (1995)
5. Georgiou, H., Mavroforakis, M., Theodoridis, S.: A game-theoretic approach to weighted majority voting for combining SVM classifiers. In: Kollias, S.D., Stafylopatis, A., Duch, W., Oja, E. (eds.) ICANN 2006. LNCS, vol. 4131, pp. 284–292. Springer, Heidelberg (2006)
6. Ho, T.: The random subspace method for constructing decision forests. IEEE Trans. Pattern Analysis and Machine Intelligence 20(8), 832–844 (1998)
7. Kaluza, B., Mirchevska, V., Dovgan, E., Lustrek, M., Gams, M.: An agent-based approach to care in independent living. In: Int. Joint Conf. on Ambient Intelligence (AML 2010), Malaga, Spain (2010)
8. Kittler, J., Hatef, M., Duin, R., Matas, J.: On combining classifiers. IEEE Trans. Pattern Analysis and Machine Intelligence 20(3), 226–239 (1998)
9. Levada, A.L.M., Mascarenhas, N.D.A., Tannús, A.: A novel MAP-MRF approach for multispectral image contextual classification using combination of suboptimal iterative algorithms. Pattern Recognition Letters 31(13), 1795–1808 (2010)
10. Li, J., Wang, J.Z.: Automatic linguistic indexing of pictures by a statistical modeling approach. IEEE Trans. Pattern Analysis and Machine Intelligence 25(9), 1075–1088 (2003)
11. Nash, J.F.: Equilibrium points in n-person games. Proceedings of the National Academy of Sciences 36(1), 48–49 (1950)
12. Papa, J., Falcão, A.X., Suzuki, C.T.N.: Supervised pattern classification based on optimum-path forest. Int. J. Imaging Systems and Technology 19(2), 120–131 (2009)
13. Ponti Jr., M.P., Papa, J.P.: Improving accuracy and speed of optimum-path forest classifier using combination of disjoint training subsets. In: Sansone, C. (ed.) MCS 2011. LNCS, vol. 6713, pp. 237–248. Springer, Heidelberg (2011)
14. Yamazaki, T., Gingras, D.: Image classification using spectral and spatial information based on mrf models. IEEE Trans. on Image Processing 4(9), 1333–1339 (1995)
15. Yu, S., Berthod, M.: A game strategy approach for image labelling. Computer Vision and Image Understanding 61(1), 32–37 (1995)

A New Approach for Wet Blue Leather Defect Segmentation

Patricio Villar, Marco Mora, and Paulo Gonzalez

Les Fous du Pixel
Image Processing Research Group
Department of Computer Science
Catholic University of Maule
Talca-Chile
pvillar@visionlabs.cl, {mora,pgonzalez}@spock.ucm.cl
http://www.ganimides.ucm.cl/mmora

Abstract. In the process plants where beef skin is processed, leather classification is done manually. An expert visually inspects the leather sheet and classifies them based on the different types of defects found on the surface, among other factors. In this study, an automatic method for defect classification of the Wet Blue leather is proposed [1]. A considerable number of descriptors are computerized from the Gray Scale image and the RGB and HSV color model. Features were chosen based on the Sequential Forward Selection method, which allows a high reduction of the numbers of descriptors. Finally, the classification is implemented by using a Supervised Neural Network. The problem formulation is adequate, allowing a high rate of success, obtaining a method with wide range of possibilities for implementation.

1 Introduction

Leather is a raw material for producing a big amount of products from clothes to furniture. Products made of leather are highly appreciated for buyers because in many cases they are hand-made pieces with a high price.

The goal of leather processing plants is to transform the fresh skin (hide), just taken from the animal, in leather sheet to be used in the production of end goods. In figure 1, the main stages in the leather fabrication process are shown. Figure 1(a) shows a stage named Ribera, in which the cow skin is clean from hair and it is hydrated with chemical products to avoid decomposition. At the end of this stage, the sheets are humid and with a blue tone. The hide at this stage is named Wet Blue. Figure 1(b) shows the pre-classification stage, where the Wet Blue leather sheets are manually separated in two categories: good and bad quality. Figure 1(c) shows the draining phase, where the sheets are introduced into a machine to eliminate the humidity excess. Finally, figure 1(d) shows a leather lot already dried.

---

[1] This work is partially supported by VisionLabs S.A. (http://www.visionlabs.cl).

C. San Martin and S.-W. Kim (Eds.): CIARP 2011, LNCS 7042, pp. 591–598, 2011.

Fig. 1. Leather processing: (a) Ribera (b) Pre-classification (c) Drying (d) Wet Blue leather lot

After the drying stage, an expert visually inspects the leather lot and proceeds to classify it based on the amount of surface defects, zone and area affected by the defect, thickness of the sheet, among other factors. The more defects a sheet has the lower the price. Hence, the classification is a critical task for the economical value of the product. The classification process is exposed to human error because of operator fatigue, his mood, etc. An error in the classification devaluates the product on the eyes of the buyer, sometimes producing 15% return rates [1], implying considerable monetary losses for the leather plants.

The rest of the paper is organized as follow: Section 2 presents related studies and research contribution to the topic. Section 3 presents the proposed method. Section 4 analyzes the results. Finally section 5 displays the conclusions for the study.

2   Related Studies

The proposal presented in [1] is a pioneer study for the leather classification problem. A semi-automatic method is introduced, detecting defects and classifying the leather sheet based on the area affected by the defects. This work requires human intervention for the defect detection.

In [2] a method is proposed based on the use of geometric and statistic descriptors, in addition to the use of decision trees for the classification of the leather surface. The leather classification is done on finished leather stages past the Wet Blue, hence a classification error means the irrevocable loss of the leather piece.

In [3] an identification method is proposed which analyze histogram of the image, using the chi-square criteria. This method compares the distance between the histogram for the analyzed area and the histogram of the areas with defects.

The following studies are a series of recent research for the Project DT-COURO[2], whose goal is to detect defects in Raw Hide leather and Wet blue leather. In [4] software is implemented for the extraction and labeling of samples from the areas with defects, all manually. In [5] a comparison of the performance for several classifiers using first order descriptors from the Concurrence Matrix is performed. The study in [6] adopts as a classifier the Support Vector Machine, focusing on properly tuning the parameters of the classifier by using a stochastic method. Finally, in [7,8] the classification scheme is improved by having a stage selecting features, reducing the amount of descriptors used to 90.

This study presents an automatic method for classifying defects on the Wet Blue leather. The most common defects in Chilean leather plants are considered: Open Cut, Closed Cut, and Fly Bite. Computing a big amount of descriptors is proposed as well as the implementation of a selection stage for features based on the Sequential Forward Selection method, allowing approaching the problem with a much reduced amount of descriptors. For the classification, a Multi-layer Perceptron, trained with a method allowing an adequate generalization is adopted. The proposed innovations provided a robust method with a high rate of success, obtaining a method with wide range of possibilities for implementation.

3   Method for Classifying Defects

In this section the different stages of the proposed defect classification method are described. All the stages of a system for pattern recognition are considered, from the sampling to the pattern classification. Four classes for the problem are defined: three of them related to the defects, and one associated to a zero-defect leather.

3.1   Capture

To capture the images, a camera with high sensitivity sensor Exview HAD CCD for visual inspection was used [3]. The camera was installed at the top of a hollow cylinder, 30 cms over the leather sheet. Inside the cylinder, an artificial LED lighting was implemented with the goal of keeping always the same lighting conditions and to avoid light flashes on the leather surface.

159 1000x960-píxel images of Wet Blue leather were taken, from which a dataset of 1769 40x40 pixel samples of normal and defective leather pieces was

---

[2] DTCOURO : http://www.gpec.ucdb.br/dtcouro
[3] PointGrey Chameleon: http://www.ptgrey.com

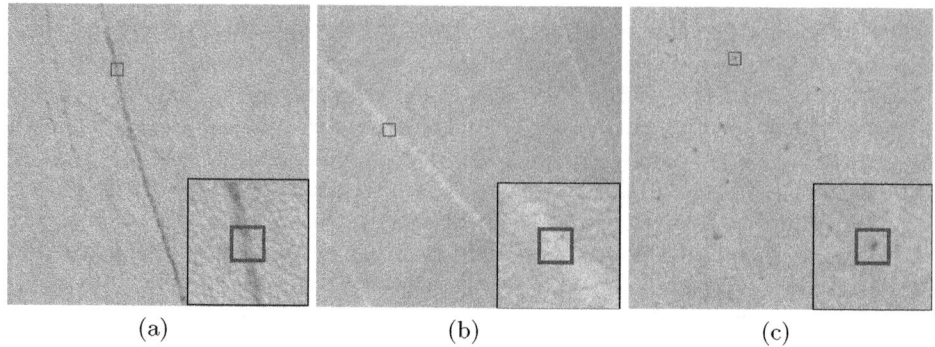

(a)   (b)   (c)

Fig. 2. Leather Defects: (a) Open Cut (b) Close Cut (c) Bite Fly

built. The dataset has 341 samples of Open Cut, 336 Closed Cut, 374 Fly Bite, and 718 normal leather pieces (without defects). Figure 2 presents 3 of the captured samples, each one showing one of the defects.

3.2   Extraction of Features

Following the principle of "The More The Better", a pattern classification problem can be approached by computing a wide amount of descriptors and then using a technique to select features in order to obtain only the relevant descriptors. A big number of features were calculated. Such characteristics were extracted from the Gray Scale image, and from the RGB and HSV channels, for a total of 2002 characteristics. The descriptors extracted can be classified in seven groups: (i) First order statistics, (ii) Contrast characteristics, (iii) Haralick descriptors , (iv) Fourier and Cosine transform, (v) Hu moments with information about intensity, (vi) Local binary patterns, y (vii) Gabor features. Details of the method and the adopted can be found in [9].

3.3   Selection of Features

In this stage the Sequential Forward Selection method (SFS) [10] is adopted. This method allows to rank descriptors based on their contribution to the classification. In order to determine the number of features required to classify the following procedure is followed: a classifier is linked to each class of interest. Classifiers are trained with a determined number of features and the percentage of success in the classification is calculated. Successive trainings of the classifiers are performed, incrementing the number of features based on the ranking provided by SFS.

The result of the process above is presented in figure 3(a). Each curve in the figure shows the percentage of success for each one of the 4 classifiers used. It is clearly noticeable that after a determined number of features, the percentage of success does not improve substantially. This behavior allows to determine the number of features. By analyzing the curves, it is determined that only 10 characteristics, from the universe of 2002 initially computed, are required.

3.4 Design for a Robust Neural Classifier

A Multilayer Perceptron was adopted to design the classifiers because this network belongs to a Universal Converger of Functions [11]. For training the Neural Network the Bayesian Regularization algorithm is used because offer a better training speed and a method to determine the number of neurons in the hidden layer, based on the computing the effective parameters of the network. The procedure for training of the neuronal network is described on [12].

The classifier proposed for the problem is composed by 4 Multilayer Perceptron, 3 networks for recognizing defects and another one for identifying the zero-defect leather sheets. A scheme for classification is presented in figure 3(b), where it can be observed that for each window analyzed, 10 descriptors are finally computed. Considering that all the neural networks give and answer, the class for the network which output value is the closest to 1 is chosen.

For the training of the neural classifiers, the set of available samples was divided in a training set and a test set as is shown in the left zone in table 1. The goal is to have a set to train the classifiers and another set to validate the training with samples that haven't been part of the training.

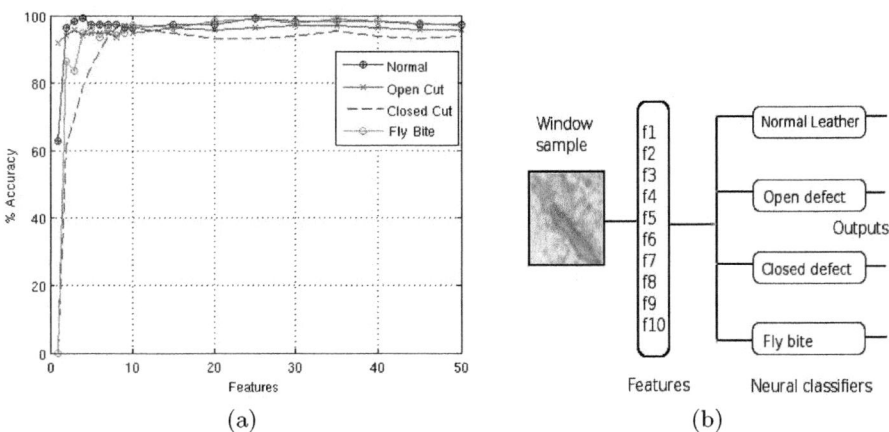

(a)   (b)

Fig. 3. (a) Selection of features (b) Classification scheme

4 Results

In this section results from the method and experiments executed are presented. From table 1 it can be seen that the method provided very good results for classifying the training set as well as the test set. The percentage of success is above 95%, number that is comparable to the studies quoted but by using

Table 1. Classification Performance

Type of Sample	Samples of Training Set	Samples of Test Set	Training Set Hit (%)	Test Set Hit (%)
Open Cut (OC)	200	141	99.5	94.9
Closed Cut (CC)	200	136	94.5	96.4
Fly Bite (FB)	200	174	95.5	96.4
Without Defect (WD)	600	118	97.3	98.2

a significantly reduced number of descriptors. The importance of having few features is that the classifier has less parameters to adjust and, hence, the times for training and classification are reduced considerably.

In figure 4 results from processing images with defects are shown. The top row in the figure shows the images with defects and the bottom row gives the results after classification. In the images resulting from the classification, the baby blue color represents a leather sheet without defects, the blue represents Open Cut (OC), White represents Closed Cut (CC), and red represents Fly Bite. The classified images have a high percentage of success, with low presence

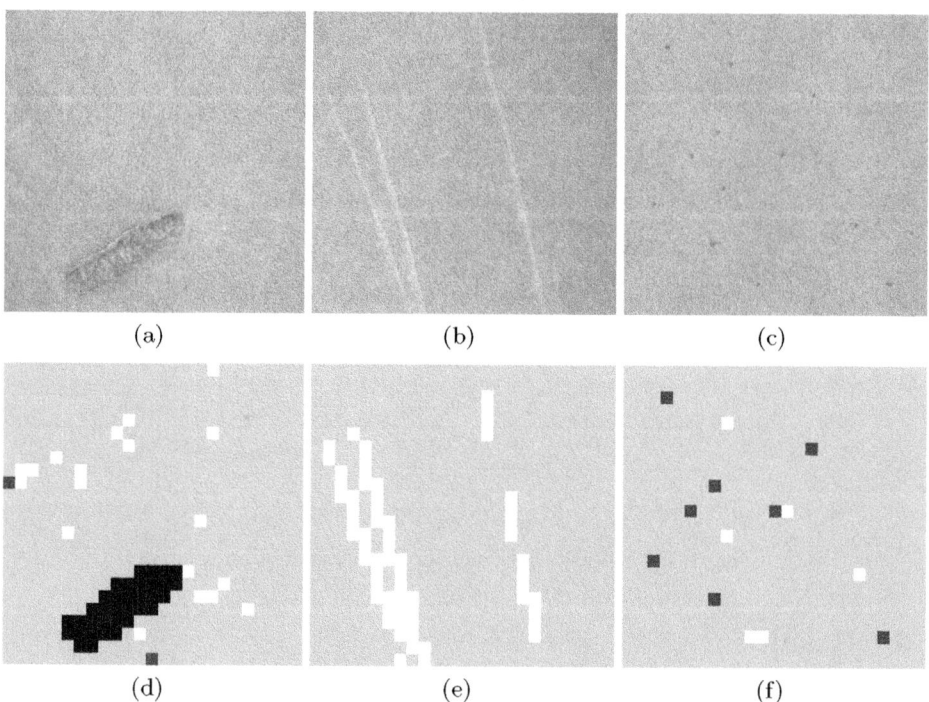

(a)   (b)   (c)

(d)   (e)   (f)

Fig. 4. Results, Top Row: (a) Open Cut (OC) (b) Closed Cut (CC) (c) Bite Fly (BF) Bottom Row: (d) OC Classification (e) CC Classification (f) BF Classification

of errors, which shows the good quality of the discrimination for the selected descriptors and the good training of the classifiers.

5 Conclusions and Future Works

This study has presented an automatic method for classifying defects in Wet Blue leather. Computation for a large set of features is proposed, and then a quite reduced set is selected by using the Sequential Fordward Selection method. The Multilayer Perceptron was selected as a classifier and it was trained by following a procedure that ensures an adequate generalization.

The proposed method contributes to the solution of the defect detection problem in Wet Blue leather, by using new descriptors, applying the Sequential Forward Selection method in the feature selection stage, and with an adequate procedure to train the neural network. Based on all the innovations above, the method has a high reliability detecting defects on leather areas.

Current studies are dealing with a fast stage for finding defects with the goal of recognizing the type of defect in a restricted area, which will allow to improve the speed of the analysis of the leather sheets. Besides the previous goal, the behavior of algorithms with new defects is being studied.

References

1. Yeh, C., Perng, D.: Establishing a Demerit Count Reference Standard for the Classification and Grading of Leather Hides. International Journal of Advanced Manufacturing 22, 731–738 (2001)
2. Kwak, C., Ventura, J., Tofang-Sazi, K.: Automated Defect Inspection and Classification of Leather Fabric. Intelligent Data Analysis 5, 355–370 (2001)
3. Georgieva, L., Krastev, K., Angelov, N.: Identification of Surface Leather Defects. In: Proceedings of the 4th International Conference on Computer Systems and Technologies, pp. 303–307 (2003)
4. Amorim, W., Viana, R., Rodrigues, R., Pistori, H.: Desenvolvimento de um Software de Processamento e Geracao de Imagens para Classificacao de Couro Bovino. In: Workshop de Iniciação Científica - SIBGRAPI 2006 (2006)
5. Pistori, H., Paraguassu, W., Martins, P., Conti, M., Pereira, M., Jacinto, M.: Defect Detection in Raw Hide and Wet Blue Leather. In: Proceedings of the International Symposium on Computational Modelling of Objects Represented in Images 2006, CompIMAGE 2006 (2006)
6. Viana, R., Rodrigues, R.B., Alvarez, M.A., Pistori, H.: SVM with Stochastic Parameter Selection for Bovine Leather Defect Classification. In: Mery, D., Rueda, L. (eds.) PSIVT 2007. LNCS, vol. 4872, pp. 600–612. Springer, Heidelberg (2007)
7. Nara, L., Pistori, H.: Selecao de Atributos para a Segmentacao do Couro Bovino. In: Anais do IV Workshop de Visao Computational (2008)
8. Nara, L., Pistori, H.: A Comparative Analysis of Attribute Reduction Algorithms Applied to Wet-Blue Leather Defects Classification. In: Proceedings of the XXII Brazilian Symposium on Computer Graphics and Image Processing, SIBGRAPI 2009 (2009)

9. Mery, D., Soto, A.: Features: The more the better. In: Proceedings of the 8th Conference on Signal Processing, Computational Geometry and Artificial Vision (ISCGAV 2008), pp. 46–51 (2008)
10. Jain, A., Robert, P., Duin, M.J.: Statistical Pattern Recognition: A Review. Intelligent Data Analysis 22, 4–34 (1999)
11. Funahashi, K.: On the Approximate Realization of Continuous Mappings by Neural Networks. Neural Networks 2, 183–192 (1989)
12. Forensee, F., Hagan, M.: Gauss-Newton Approximation to Bayesian Learning. In: Proceedings of the International Joint Conference on Neuronal Networks, vol. 3, pp. 1930–1935 (1997)

Objective Comparison of Contour Detection in Noisy Images

Rodrigo Pavez, Marco Mora, and Paulo Gonzalez

Les Fous du Pixel
Image Processing Research Group
Department of Computer Science
Catholic University of Maule
Talca-Chile
rpavez@lfdp.org {mora,pgonzalez}@spock.ucm.cl
http://www.ganimides.ucm.cl/mmora

Abstract. The constant appearance of new contour detection methods makes it necessary to have accurate ways of assessing the performance of these methods. This paper proposes an evaluation method of contour detectors for noisy images. The method considers the computation of the optimal threshold that produces a greater approximation to the ground truth and the effect produced by the noise. Both analyzed dimensions allow objective comparisons of the performance of contour detectors.

1 Introduction

The contour detection is one of the most important problems in image processing. New operators and methods are constantly proposed with the aim of detecting contours in complex situations, for example: low contrast images, images in which objects have not precise and incomplete contours, images with high presence of noise, among others. The existence of different approaches to address the contour detection generates the need of evaluating such methods objectively and the need of comparing the performance of them.

To know the results of a contour detection method, a synthetic image from which the contours are known is considered. A human expert manually traces the contours, establishing what is known as a ground truth. This image is used as a benchmark to assess the outcome of a contour detection method.

To carry out the evaluation of a contour detector a performance function (PF) is required. This function is generally an expression that involves the amount of hits and errors on the ground truth. The performance function is usually normalized (values within a range), so it can be compared with the results of different methods.

When applying a contour detector, a dark image where the contours correspond to the lighter pixels is got. To assess the PF, it is necessary to threshold the image resulting from the application of the detector. Thus, we obtain a binary image, where the detected contour pixels differ completely from the background of the image. The number of hits and errors regarding the ground truth depends

C. San Martin and S.-W. Kim (Eds.): CIARP 2011, LNCS 7042, pp. 599–606, 2011.

on the threshold value. Thus, the validity of the comparison depends on the correct computation of the threshold. The works from literature have varying degrees of depth to the computation of the threshold. There are proposals which compare results from different detectors with a determined threshold [1,2], where the validity of results is highly opened to criticism because they can change dramatically by choosing different thresholds. Other works compute the PF with a small set of thresholds [3,4,5,6], which does not permit to figure out if it is in the set where the threshold that produces the grater approximation to the ground truth is found. There are other works like [7], which considering the dependence of the PF on the threshold, perform a search process of the optimal threshold, thus allowing a more objective comparison.

The focus of this paper is the comparison of contour detection in noisy images. The approximation of previous works which were mentioned is enriched when studying the influence of noise in the computation of the appropriate threshold. A procedure to determine the optimal threshold considering different noise situations is proposed. The method enables to objectively compare the performance of contour detectors in images with high noise content.

The rest of the paper is organized as follows: Section 2 presents a new contour detector derived from the coefficient of variation (CV), and the reasons why it is speculated that the new operator detects the contours better than the CV are outlined. Section 3 presents the objective method for evaluating contour detection. The procedure is applied to the detectors discussed in the preceding section, being clear the error in the conclusions. The final section presents the conclusions of the work.

2   A New Contour Detector for Images with Multiplicative Noise

The Coefficient of Variation is a value proposed as a contour detector in images with multiplicative noise [8,9,10,11]. The CV is the ratio between the square root of standard deviation and the mean of a set of data, as shown in the following expression:

$$CV = \frac{\sqrt{\sigma(W)}}{\overline{X}(W)} \tag{1}$$

where W corresponds to a sample of data coming from the image. If the image has a high noise content, the analyzed window will define a population with a significant presence of outliers. A well-known fact is that the mean is not a good predictor of central tendencies when outliers are present. This means that the CV will not be a good contour detector if the images have a high noise content.

To address the above problem, the median can be used in populations with outliers. Following the above observation, the numerator and the denominator of the CV are modified based on the median in the following way: as a measure of deviation the Median Absolute Deviation (MAD) will be adopted, and as measure of central tendency the same median will be occupied. The new operator is called Modified Coefficient of Variation (MCV), and according to the previous reasoning, it should be robust than the CV for detecting contours in images with high content of multiplicative noise. The expressions of MAD and the MCV are presented in (2) and (3), respectively:

$$MAD(X) = median(|(X - median(X))|) \tag{2}$$

$$MCV = \frac{MAD(W)}{median(W)} \tag{3}$$

To generate an image that is contaminated with multiplicative noise a model widely accepted in literature will be used [12]. The expression of this model is:

$$I_n = I_{wn} \times n \tag{4}$$

where I_n corresponds to the noisy image, I_{wn} is the image without noise, and n is the noise. It is noted that n corresponds to a set of random numbers that follow a particular probability distribution. In this case, a Gaussian distribution of mean 1 and a standard deviation σ is used. The value of σ should be very little not to alter the original image significantly.

To compare the results of both detectors on the noisy image, a performance function that considers the hits and errors with respect to the ground truth is adopted [3]. The expression of the performance function is as follows:

$$\rho = \frac{card(PT)}{card(PT) + card(FP) + card(FN)} \tag{5}$$

where ρ is the function of performance, $card(X)$ is the cardinal of a set X, PT is the set of true positives, FP is the set of false positives, and FN is the set of false negatives. The performance function ρ is close to 1 if there are many hits and few errors, and it is close to 0 if there are few hits and many errors.

An interesting approach for contour detection is to consider the contours as outliers of the image resulting from the application of a detector [13]. This implies that contour detection is reduced to establish the values that are distant from the central tendency of the image. In this work, a simple but effective criterion has been adopted in order to determine the threshold, which separates the contour pixels from the rest of the image. The criterion is based on the median of the data as shown in the following expression:

$$th = k \times median(I_c) \tag{6}$$

where th corresponds to the computed threshold, k a constant that indicates the distance of the outlier in relation to a measure of central tendency, and I_c the image resulting from the application of a contour detector.

Figure 1 shows the results of contour detection for the CV and the MCV. A synthetic image has been contaminated with multiplicative noise that follows a gaussian distribution with μ=0 and $\sigma = 0.125$. The threshold has been computed considering $k = 2.5$ for the expression (6). From figures 1(e) and 1(h), it can be

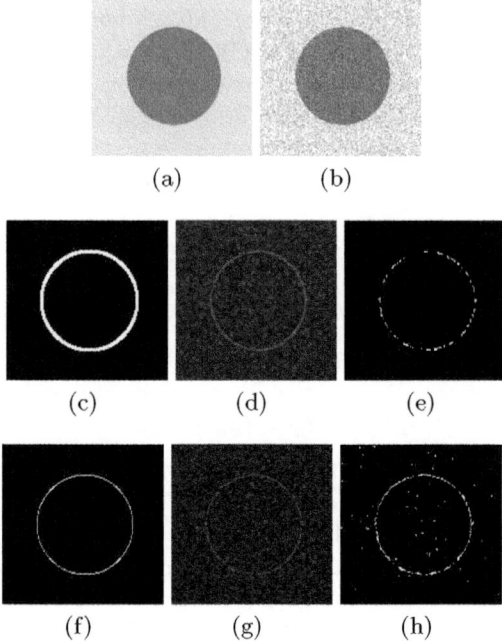

Fig. 1. Results of Contour Detection. Top row: (a) Original image (b) Noisy image with Gaussian distribution of the Noise. Middle row: (c) Original image contour with CV (d) Noisy image contour detection with CV (e) CV detected contours by thresholding. Down row: (f) Original image contour with MCV (g) Noisy image contour detection with MCV (h) MCV detected contours by thresholding.

visually seen that the MCV has a better performance than the CV. Numerically, the result is consistent since $\rho_{CV} < \rho_{MCV}$ (ρ_{CV}=0.1393, y ρ_{MCV}=0.3618).

Figure 2 shows performance curves of the function (ρ) for the CV and MCV, when varying the noise intensity. It starts from an image without noise (σ=0), until an image with high level of noise is reached (σ=0.2). The threshold that determines

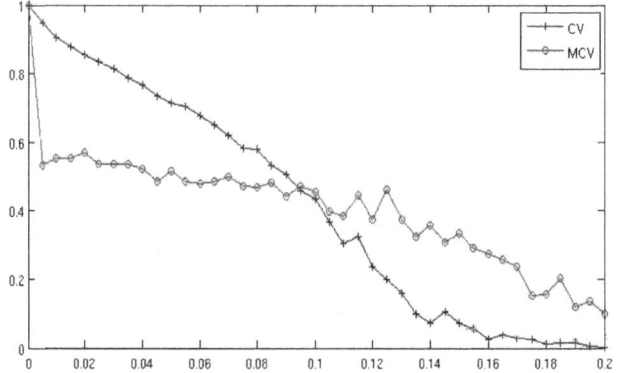

Fig. 2. Performance Function (ρ) versus Noise Deviation (σ)

the detected contours is computed as $th = 2.5 \times median(I_c)$. It is noted that as the noise grows, the PF of both detectors decreases. In the area of most intense noise, the PF of the MCV is higher than the PF of the CV, so it can be concluded that the MCV performs better than the CV on highly noisy images.

3 Objective Comparison of Contour Detection in Noisy Images

In the previous section, the benefits of the MCV as contour detector in images with multiplicative noise were shown. It was determined that for images with high noise level, the MCV performs better than the CV. Unfortunately, the conclusion has been obtained by performing a partial analysis of the variables that influence the performance of the detector.

In this paper, the effect that the threshold value has on the performance of the detector is analyzed as well as the fact of subjecting the image to different

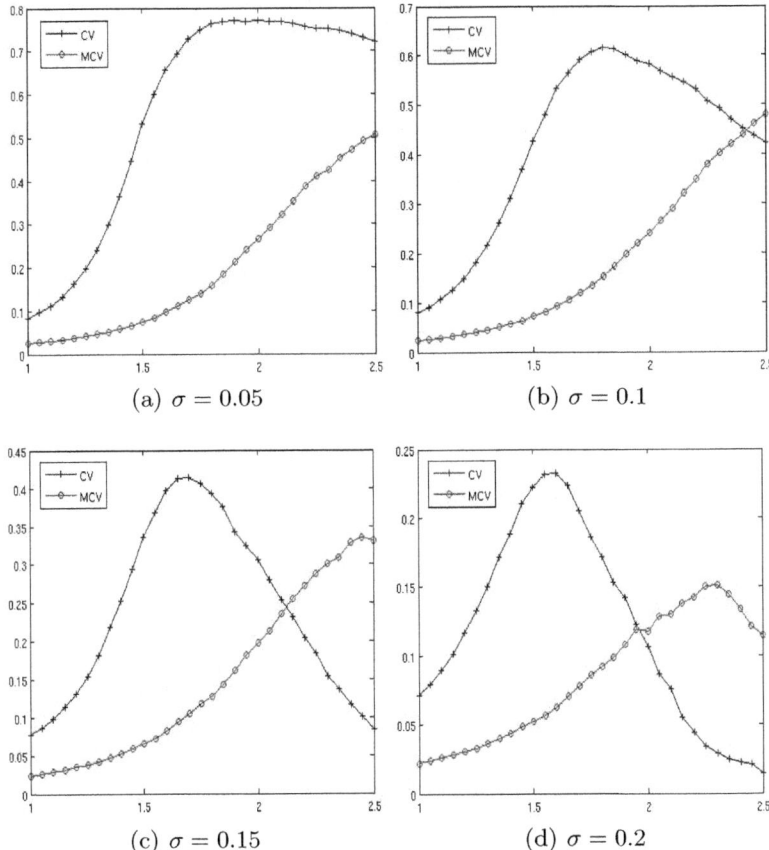

(a) $\sigma = 0.05$ (b) $\sigma = 0.1$

(c) $\sigma = 0.15$ (d) $\sigma = 0.2$

Fig. 3. Behavior of performance function with variable threshold $(1 < k < 2.5)$ in 4 noise intensity cases

intensities of noise. The objective analysis of the performance of a contour detector consists of finding the threshold that maximizes the performance function (optimal threshold) for different noise situations.

Figure 3 shows the value of the performance function of the CV and MCV for a variable threshold variable in 4 different noise situations. The threshold is determined by the constant k, and the noise is defined by the standard deviation σ of the noise distribution. It is clearly observed that, in case of noise, the higher value of the performance function always corresponds to the CV. This figure shows that for these 4 cases of noise, the CV detects the contours better than the MCV, information which contrasts with the results of the previous section.

In order to generalize the previous result, figure 4 presents the curve of the higher value of performance function for a continuous flow of noise case, both for the CV and MCV. From the figure, it can be seen that the value of the performance function associated to the optimal threshold is always higher for the CV (the curve for the CV is always above the curve of the MCV). This figure is an objective test to evaluate and compare the performance of the detectors in question. This allows us to conclude that the CV is a contour detector stronger than the MCV for images with multiplicative noise.

Figure 5 shows the contours detected for 3 levels of noise with CV and MCV. The top row corresponds to a low noise level ($\sigma = 0.1$), the central line to a medium noise level ($\sigma = 0.15$), the bottom row to a high noise level ($\sigma = 0.2$). The columns of the figure show the noisy images, the contours detected by the CV and MCV, respectively. In the caption of noisy images, the noise standard deviation is σ. In the caption of the detected contour images, the optimal threshold is indicated by the constant k, and the maximum value of the performance function by ρ. First, the figure shows that when the noise increases, the errors in the detected contours increase

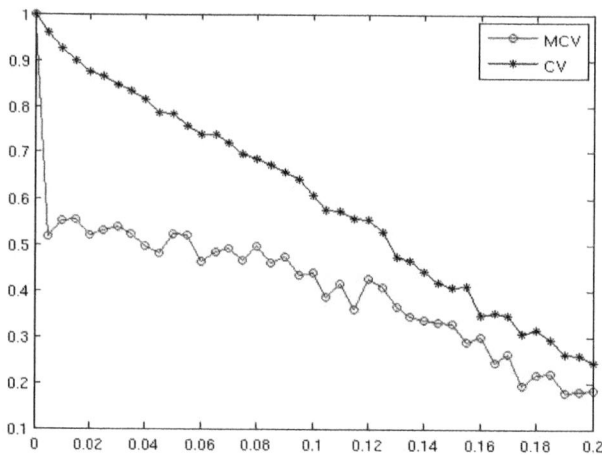

Fig. 4. Maximum values of the performance function computed with variable noise ($0 < \sigma < 0.2$)

as well, what explains the decline of the curve with maximum value of the performance function. Secondly, when observing the numerical indicators, it is confirmed that the CV has a higher value for the performance function ρ than the MCV, no matter the level of noise of the image. Finally, the figure shows that by visual inspection, it is very difficult to decide which method has closer results on the ground truth. This underscores the importance of an objective and numerical comparison of the results of contour detection.

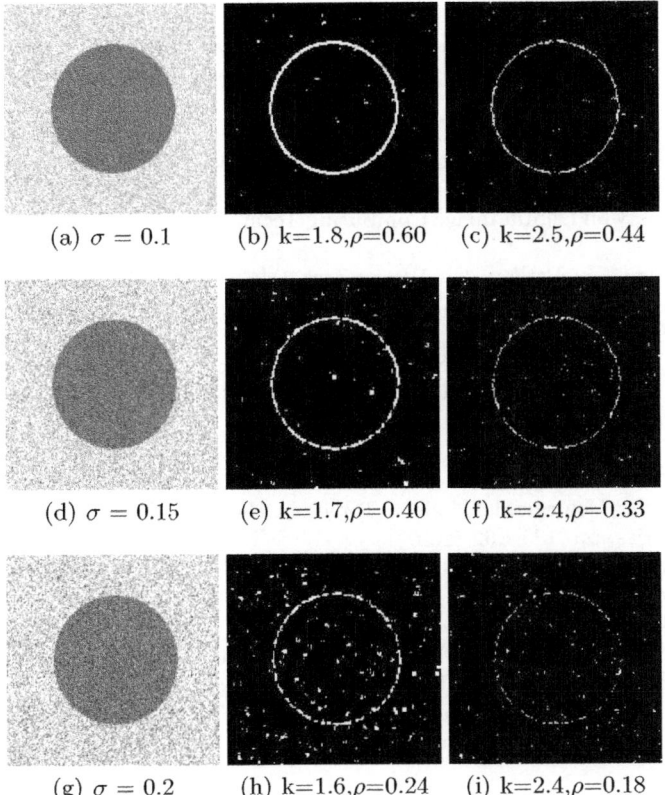

(a) $\sigma = 0.1$ (b) k=1.8,ρ=0.60   (c) k=2.5,ρ=0.44

(d) $\sigma = 0.15$ (e) k=1.7,ρ=0.40   (f) k=2.4,ρ=0.33

(g) $\sigma = 0.2$ (h) k=1.6,ρ=0.24   (i) k=2.4,ρ=0.18

Fig. 5. Results of CV and MCV detected contours with three levels of noise. Top row: Low level of noise (a) Noisy image (b) CV detected contours (c) MCV detected contours. Middle row: Medium level of noise (d) Noisy image (e) CV detected contours (f) MCV detected contours. Down row: High level of noise (g) Noisy image (h) CV detected contours (i) MCV detected contours.

4   Conclusions

A method to compare the result of contour detection in noisy images in an objective way has been presented in this article. The method considers the influence of the threshold that determines the contours which have been detected, and the noise level of the image. As an example, the comparison between two detectors (CV and MCV) for images with multiplicative noise has been developed.

Initially, the CV and MCV were compared by a method with partial information, which led to erroneous conclusions. It is shown that with the proposed method an objective comparison can be made, what permits to draw accurate conclusions when evaluating the performance of contour detectors.

References

1. Pagador, J., Moreno, J., Masero, V., León-Rojas, J.: Active Contour on the Basis of Inertia. In: Proceedings of the 2004 ACM Symposium on Applied Computing, pp. 307–308 (2004)
2. Yu, L., Ma, F., Jayasuriya, A., Sigelle, M., Perreau, S.: A New Contour Detection Approach in Mammogram using Rational Wavelet Filtering and MRF Smoothing. In: Proceedings of the 9th Biennial Conference of the Australian Pattern Recognition Society on Digital Image Computing Techniques and Applications, pp. 106–111 (2007)
3. Grigorescu, C., Petkov, N., Westenberg, M.: Contour Detection based on Non-classical Receptive Field Inhibition. IEEE Transactions on Image Processing 12, 729–739 (2003)
4. Joshi, G., Sivaswamy, J.: A Simple Scheme for Contour Detection. In: International Conference on Computer Vision Theory and Applications (VISAPP 2006), pp. 236–242 (2006)
5. Farag, A., Suri, J., Ferrari, R., Rangayyan, R., Desautels, J., Frère, A., Borges, R.: Detection of the Breast Contour in Mammograms by Using Active Contour Models. In: Deformable Models. Topics in Biomedical Engineering International Book Series, pp. 133–162 (2007)
6. Chabrier, S., Laurent, H., Rosenberger, C., Emile, B.: Comparative Study of Contour Detection Evaluation Criteria based on Dissimilarity Measures. EURASIP Journal on Image and Video Processing (2008)
7. Wang, S., Ge, F., Liu, T.: Evaluating Edge Detection Through Boundary Detection. EURASIP Journal on Applied Signal Processing, 1–15 (2006)
8. Lee, J.: Digital Image Enhancement and Noise Filtering by Using Local Statistic. IEEE Transactions on Pattern Analysis and Machine Intelligence PAMI-2, 165–168 (1980)
9. Frost, V., Stiles, J., Shanmugan, K., Holtzman, J.: A Model for Radar Images and its Application to Adaptive Digital Filtering of Multiplicative Noise. IEEE Transactions on Pattern Analysis and Machine Intelligence PAMI-4, 157–166 (1982)
10. Kuan, D., Sawchuk, A., Strand, T., Chavel, P.: Adaptive Restoration of Images with Speckle. IEEE Transaction on Acoustics, Speech and Signal Processing 35, 373–383 (1987)
11. Lopes, A., Touzi, R., Nezry, E.: Adaptive Speckle Filters and Scene Heterogeneity. IEEE Transactions on Geoscience and Remote Sensing 28, 992–1000 (1990)
12. Krissian, K., Westin, C.F., Kikinis, R., Vosburgh, K.: Oriented Speckle Reducing Anisotropic Diffusion. IEEE Transaction on Image Processing 16, 1412–1424 (2007)
13. Black, M., Sapiro, G.: Edges as Outliers: Anisotropic Smoothing Using Local Image Statistics. In: Nielsen, M., Johansen, P., Fogh Olsen, O., Weickert, J. (eds.) Scale-Space 1999. LNCS, vol. 1682, pp. 259–270. Springer, Heidelberg (1999)

Automatic Search of Nursing Diagnoses

Matías A. Morales[1], Rosa L. Figueroa[1], and Jael E. Cabrera[2]

[1] Electrical Engineering Department, University of Concepción, Chile
[2] Cardiac Surgery Department, Guillermo Grant Benavente Hospital,
Cardiac Surgery ICU, Chile

Abstract. Nursing documentation is all the information that nurses register regarding the clinical assessment and care of a patient. Currently, these records are manually written in a narrative style; consequently, their quality and completeness largely depends on the nurse's expertise. This paper presents an algorithm based on standardized nursing language that searches and sorts nursing diagnoses by its relevance through a ranking. Diagnoses identification is performed by searching and matching patterns among a set of patient needs or symptoms and the international standard of nursing diagnoses NANDA. Three sorting methods were evaluated using 6 utility cases. The results suggest that TF-IDF (83.43% accuracy) and assignment of weights by hit (80.73% accuracy) are the two best alternatives to implement the ranking of diagnoses.

Keywords: NANDA, Nursing documentation, Pattern Matching, Diagnosis retrieval, Decision Support, TF, TF-IDF.

1 Introduction

In nursing all information concerning the care and management of patients is documented in the form of patient records. In many places this information is stored manually in paper records, so its quality and completeness is determined by the nurse's expertise. Currently, there are standards and terminology available that could be used to facilitate the transition to electronic records. Among them we find the terminology established by the North American Nursing Diagnosis Association (NANDA) [1]. This terminology has a total of 188 nursing diagnoses including label, code, definition, defining characteristics, risk factors, and related factors.

In this paper, we present an algorithm that was developed and implemented as part of a nursing care software prototype. The system identifies and retrieves diagnoses from a set of needs that are identified in the clinical assessment of the patient according to the nursing model of Virginia Henderson [2].

2 Materials and Methods

2.1 Data Set

Two data sources were used by our algorithm: NANDA databases and a patient assessment chart. NANDA databases in Spanish were created and are being populated

C. San Martin and S.-W. Kim (Eds.): CIARP 2011, LNCS 7042, pp. 607–612, 2011.

by nurses of the Complejo Hospitalario de Jaén[1]. The patient assessment chart used in this work was created by the researchers in the first stage of the project and is based on Virginia Henderson's model. It contains a set of needs and symptoms commonly used by nurses in the cardio-surgery intensive care unit (ICU) to evaluate their patients.

2.2 Search and Identification of Nursing Diagnoses Algorithm

We implemented a pattern matching algorithm that searches for similarities between a set of needs or symptoms that are obtained from the clinical assessment of the patient and the available information in the NANDA database. Every need is searched among the information that describes each NANDA diagnosis (defining characteristics, related factors and risk factors). In order to improve the search and identification of patterns a tailored medical synonym dictionary was created and used within the search. Abbreviations were expanded and all the texts were normalized, i.e. letters were converted to lower case and accent marks and other diacritics were removed. Some special characters were not eliminated since they were thought to be important for the search (example: temperature is commonly referred as T °).

From pattern matching we obtained a co-occurrence matrix where the columns corresponded to the needs or symptoms of the patient and the rows to the NANDA diagnoses. Then, each diagnosis d_j can be represented by a weight vector $d_j = <w_{j1},...,w_{jn}>$, where n is the total number of different needs across the whole assessment chart, and w_{jk} indicates the importance of the t_k need in d_j [3]. This matrix is used for the next step which will define the relevance ranking of the retrieved list of diagnoses.

2.3 Diagnoses Relevance Ranking

We studied and compared three methods to create a diagnoses relevance ranking. These methods worked by assigning weights to each diagnosis according to the information contained on the co-occurrence matrix.

Frequency of the Terms (T.F.). This method assigns weights based on the frequency of co-occurrence of symptoms or needs in the defining characteristics, related factors and risk factors for each diagnosis. Frequencies of all the different symptoms considered in the search are added and the resulting score is assigned to that diagnosis. Once scores are assigned, diagnoses are sorted in a descending order.

Assignment of Weights by Hit or Coincidence. Each time one of the searched symptoms appears in the information related to the diagnoses ($f_{jk} > 0$) a hit or match is marked [4]. Once the hits for each diagnosis are detected, scores are assigned by adding the hits of those symptoms. Unlike the previous method, this one identifies the presence or absence of the search words, thus the score given to the diagnosis will depend of the presence or absence of the symptom and not on the number of times that this symptom shows in a given diagnosis.

---

[1] Nursing Jaen, http://www.gratisweb.com/enferjoja/

Weights Assignment Using TF-IDF. The I.D.F. method [5] calculates the weight of every need or symptom according to the inverse value of its frequency in the set of diagnoses. Thus, the IDF factor of a need or symptom t_k is given by:

$$idf(t_k) = \log\left(\frac{N}{df(t_k)}\right) . \tag{1}$$

Where, N is the total number of diagnoses and $df(t_k)$ is the number of diagnoses that contain t_k.

TF-IDF calculates the weight of every need or symptom in the vector that represents the diagnosis by taking into account the inverse frequency of the term in the diagnosis, combining it with the frequency of the term within each document (Eq. 2):

$$w_{jk} = tf(t_k, d_j) \cdot idf(t_k) . \tag{2}$$

In order to solve the equation above, we first calculate the frequency of the need or symptom t_k in the diagnosis d_j (TF). Then, we calculate the inverted frequency of the diagnosis d_j using Eq.1. Finally, both measures are combined using Eq.2. Scores for every considered symptom are added to obtain the score for the diagnosis.

Table 1 shows an example for two conditions: "arrhythmias" and "edema". As the arrhythmias is only present in the diagnosis 1 and 3, the df of arrhythmias is $df_a = 2$, and as there are in total 188 NANDA diagnoses, $N = 188$, the inverse frequency of the arrhythmia diagnosis is $idf_a=log(188/2)=1.97$; "Edema" is present in the 3 diagnoses, thus its $df_a = 3$, then inverse frequency of the edema diagnosis is $idf_e=log(188/3)=1.79$. Once TF and IDF values are obtained, the weight of each symptom within each diagnosis is determined by multiplying the frequency of the symptom by its inverse frequency resulting in the weight of the symptom. Finally, a general score for a given diagnosis is determined as the sum of the weights obtained by each symptom. In Table 1 the given order is: diagnosis 2, diagnosis 1, diagnosis 3.

Table 1. Scores calculation examples of Weight assignment by Hit

Diagnostics	Arrhythmias	Edema	Score
Diagnosis 1	2	1	1.97*2+1.79*1=5.73
Diagnosis 2	0	7	1.97*0+1.79*7=12.53
Diagnosis 3	1	1	1.97*1+1.79*1=3.76

2.4 Diagnosis Ranking Assessment

Evaluation of the algorithm was performed in 6 examples of use. These examples were reviewed by a nurse who determined which diagnoses would be expected given a certain set of symptoms and needs. To evaluate the ranking of retrieved diagnoses we compared the list of diagnoses given by the nurse with the results obtained by the three methods described in Section 2.3.

To estimate effectiveness of document retrieval tools, two measures are usually used [6]: Precision and Recall. The Recall measures the proportion of documents - in this case relevant diagnoses - that the system is able to retrieve. Precision measures the proportion of the recovered diagnoses that are relevant to the query. In this case the metric we used to evaluate and compare the rankings is the mean average precision (MAP) which is based on the metrics discussed earlier.

MAP is the average of the non-interpolated average precision over all queries [6]:

$$MAP(Q) = \frac{1}{|Q|} \sum_{j=1}^{|Q|} \frac{1}{m_j} \sum_{k=1}^{m_j} Precision(R_{jk}) \ . \tag{3}$$

Where,

Q	: Total number of consultations.
j	: Index of consultation.
m	: Total number of relevant documents.
k	: Top k of documents.
R	: Documents retrieved.

MAP is suitable for the evaluation of rankings because it rewards methods that provide high scores to the relevant documents; that is, sorted into the top places in the list.

Since the system can retrieve up to the top15 of diagnoses for each of the 6 cases, the assessment was made with the Top-5, Top-10 and Top-15. Only the first 15 diagnoses were evaluated, as it is expected that the algorithm delivers the relevant diagnoses within the first listed.

3   Results

Table 2 presents MAP score results. It is observed that the MAP score tends to decrease as the number of documents to be evaluated increase; that is, going from Top-5 to Top-15. It can be noted that for each case both "Assignment of Weights by Hit" and "TF-IDF" have higher MAP values than the "TF" method.

The method "TF-IDF" has a better response in finding the first documents (MAP = 0.9625), which makes it a very efficient method compared to the "TF" method (MAP = 0.7366). The second best method is the "Assigning Weight by Hit" (MAP = 0.95). In fact, MAP values for "TF-IDF" are very similar to the MAP values obtained by the "Assignment of Weights by Hit". This can be explained by the way in which both methods retrieve the diagnoses. For instance, with "TF-IDF" for each of the 6 queries the first two diagnoses corresponded to those expected by the nurse. In the case of the "Assignment of Weights by Hit", 4 of the 6 queries retrieved relevant diagnoses within the first two positions of the list. In the 2 remaining consultations the expected results were within the Top-5, but not necessarily in the first or second position.

Table 2. MAP comparison for different number of documents

Number of Documents	MAP TF	MAP Weight by Hit	MAP TF-IDF
5	0.7366	0.95	0.9625
10	0.7121	0.85	0.8769
15	0.6995	0.8073	0.8343

4 Conclusions

This article presents a nursing diagnoses search algorithm that uses a set of needs and symptoms from the clinical assessment of a patient. Six use cases were taken as base for the evaluation of the search algorithm and the relevance ranking of diagnoses.

Results suggest a reasonable performance of the algorithm for the identification and recovery of diagnoses (83.43% accuracy Top-15 for TF-IDF, 80.73% accuracy Top 15 for "Assignment of Weight by Hit"). We noted that the performance of the algorithm may have been affected by the lack of data on the Spanish version of the NANDA databases used but even with the available data the results are reasonable and promising for future developments that consider a more extensive evaluation of both usability and accuracy. Because of its simplicity, relevance ranking of diagnoses based on "Assignment of Weights by Hit" was chosen to implement the software prototype for the nursing care process.

The methods shown in this paper allow for automatically retrieving a list of nursing diagnoses. This system constitutes a support tool for the nursing process that assists in the assessment and/or evaluation of the patient and suggests possible diagnoses, but the final decision of the diagnosis is left to the nurse or care giver.

5 Future Work

We propose to implement manual search of NANDA diagnosis by name or code that will allow the nurse to find diagnoses directly. Also, since this is just a preliminary study we plan to perform an extended evaluation involving more use cases. Finally, an interesting future work will be to evaluate the impact of the system in a clinical environment.

Acknowledgments. The authors would like to thank the professional nurse José Jaen of the Jaén Hospital Complex for facilitating the NANDA databases in Spanish.

References

1. NANDA International. Diagnósticos Enfermeros: Definiciones y Clasificación (2008)
2. Caballero, M.E., Becerra, S.R., Hullin, L.C.: Proceso de Enfermería e Informática (2010)

3. Zuñiga Cuevas, R.E.: Codificación de Diagnósticos Médicos utilizando técnicas de aprendizaje automático (2010)
4. Grossman, D.A., Frieder, O.: Information Retrieval, Algorithms and Heuristics (2004)
5. Manning, C.D., Raghavan, P., Schütze, H.: An Introduction to Information Retrieval (2009)
6. Tolosa, G.H., Bordignon, F.: Introduction to Information Retrieval: Concepts, models and basic algorithms

"De-Ghosting" Artifact in Scene-Based Nonuniformity Correction of Infrared Image Sequences

Anselmo Jara and Flavio Torres

Department of Electrical Engineering University of The Frontera,
Casilla 54-D. Temuco, Chile
ftorres@ufro.cl
www.ufro.cl

Abstract. In this paper we present a new technique to improve the convergence and to reduce the ghosting artifacts based on constant statistics (CS) method. We propose to reduce ghosting artifacts and to speed up the convergence by using enhanced constant statistics method with the motion threshold. The key advantage of the method is based in its capacity for estimate detectors parameters, and then compensate for fixed-pattern noise in a frame by frame basics. The ability of the method to compensate for nonuniformity and reducing ghosting artifacts is demonstrated by employing video sequences of simulated and several infrared video sequences obtained using two infrared cameras.

Keywords: Infrared detectors, focal-plane array, non-uniformity correction, fixed-pattern noise, ghosting artifact.

1 Introduction

Infrared imaging systems are employed in several applications such as defense, astronomy and medical science. In general, those systems are based on the infrared focal-plane array IRFPA technology. An IRFPA is a die composed of a group of photodetectors placed in a focal plane forming a matrix of X×Y pixels, which gives the sensor the ability to collect the IR information.

It is well known that nonuniformity noise in IR imaging sensors, which is due to pixel-to-pixel variation in the detectors responses, can considerably degrade the quality of IR images since it results in a fixed-pattern-noise (FPN) that is superimposed on the true image. Even more, what makes matter worse is that the nonuniformity slowly varies over time, and depending on the technology used, this drift can take from minutes to hours. In order to solve this problem, several scene-based nonuniformity correction (NUC) techniques have been developed [1-6]. Scene-based techniques perform the NUC using only the video sequences that are being imaged, not requiring any kind of laboratory calibration technique.

Our group has been given special attention to NUC methods based on estimation theory [7]. Seeking for more e effectiveness in the reduction of NUC, we

C. San Martin and S.-W. Kim (Eds.): CIARP 2011, LNCS 7042, pp. 613–620, 2011.

propose to improve the previously published Minimizing the Ghosting Artifact to RLS Filter scene-based NUC method [8]. Now, we proposed NUC method based in constant statistics CS. This algorithm exhibits the advantages of desirable for simplicity and low mathematical operations [9, 10]. However, the method has shown the following weakness: the supposition that the input scene is constantly moving, in general, is not valid and ghosting artifacts are generated; the assumption that the best target for the unknown input infrared irradiance is an average over its neighboring pixels is scene dependent generating a poor correction in pixels, which are part of objects boundaries. Then, for improving the performance of the CS-NUC algorithm, we propose to reduce ghosting artifacts adding the effects of to speed up the convergence of the algorithm and motion threshold. Both, mixed effects, are tested with simulated and real IR data.

This paper is organized as follows. In Section 2 the IR-FPA model and the CS-NUC method with the proposed enhancement are presented. In Section 3 the proposed method is tested with video sequences of simulated and real raw IR data captured using two infrared cameras. In Section 4 the conclusions of the paper are summarized.

2   The CS Algorithm for Infrared Video Sequences

In this section, the previously published scene-based NUC method [8] is presented for completeness. We begin reviewing the most common model used for the nonuniformity presented IR-FPA technology, and we finish developing the techniques with the ability of being used to reduce ghosting artifacts and to speed up convergence of such method.

2.1   CS Method

First, we assume that each infrared detector is characterized by a linear model. Then, for the ijth detector in the focal-plane array, the measured readout signal $Y_{ij}(n)$ at a given time n can be expressed as

$$Y_{ij}(n) = a_{ij}(n) \cdot X_{ij}(n) + b_{ij}(n) \tag{1}$$

Where $a_{ij}(n)$ and $bij(n)$ are the gain and the o set of the ijth detector, and $X_{ij}(n)$ is the real incident infrared photon flux collected by the respective detector. Each corrupted data pixel $Y_{ij}(n)$ is the input to one of the linear repressors. Equation (1) is reordered for obtain the inverse model given by:

$$X_{ij}(n) = \frac{Y_{ij}(n) - m_{ij}(n)}{s_{ij}(n)} \tag{2}$$

Mean and mean deviation of $Y_{ij}(n)$ can be calculated by the following recursive equations:

$$m_{ij}(n) = \frac{Y_{ij}(n) + (n-1) \cdot m_{ij}(n-1)}{n} \tag{3}$$

$$s_{ij}(n) = \frac{|Y_{ij}(n) + m_{ij}(n)| + (n-1) \cdot s_{ij}(n-1)}{n} \tag{4}$$

2.2 Performance of the CS-NUC Method

The main problems detected on the performance of the CS-NUC method are originated by two basic constraints used in the development of the method. The first is related to the supposition that the scene is constantly moving with respect to the detector. Then, the problem is that when the scene is not moving for a few frames, this is not valid, and the ghosting effect appears. This consists in a ghost present in the next frames.

The second is related with large uniform areas in the scene. Even when the scene is in constantly moving with respect to the detector, the moving camera ensures no variation of photons on the sensor because may come from uniform areas. This also consists of being ghosts in the next frames.

In the next section, we propose enhanced method CS-NUC to be included in the algorithm to reduce the ghosting.

2.3 Nonuniformity and Proposed Ghosting Correction Algorithm

All scene nonuniformity correction algorithms require that the objects in the image do not remain stationary for too long. This can be accomplished by either periodically moving the camera or else requiring objects in the scene to move. If an object in the image violates this assumption and remains stationary for a large number of iteration, the object will blend into the background. If this stationary object eventually moves from the field of view, it will leave a reverse ghost image in the scene. The de-ghosting technique detects the changes of each pixel and compare them with threshold value. This technique slows down the performance of the algorithm. This effect is minimizing if CS method is modifying the Mean and Mean Deviation as follows:

$$m_{ij}(n) = \frac{Y_{ij}(n) + \ldots + Y_{ij}(n-k) + (n-k-1) \cdot m_{ij}(n-1)}{n} \tag{5}$$

$$s_{ij}(n) = \frac{|Y_{ij}(n) + m_{ij}(n)| + \ldots + |Y_{ij}(n-k) + m_{ij}(n-k)| + (n-k-1) \cdot s_{ij}(n-1)}{n} \tag{6}$$

k can be chosen by trial and error, so that there is a compromise between speed of convergence with an acceptable number of mathematical operations. Note that with k=0 is normal CS-NUC (Eq. (3,4)).

3 Evaluation of the Proposed Methods Upgrades

The main goal of this section is to test the ability of the proposed method to reduce nonuniformity on simulated and real infrared video data. The algorithm is tested with simulated infrared image sequences. As a quantitative measure of performance, we use the Root Mean Square Error (RMSE), which measures the difference between the true infrared image with the corrected image using the proposed method. The RMSE is calculated by:

$$RMSE(n) = \left\{ \frac{1}{pm} \sum_{i=1}^{p} \sum_{j=1}^{m} (\widehat{x}_{ij}(n) - x_{ij}(n))^2 \right\}^{1/2} \tag{7}$$

where p×m is the number of detectors in the FPA. A low value of RMSE means a better correction of the frame data. The evaluation procedure for each set of data is detailed in the following sections. Also, as a quantitative measure of performance, we use the performance parameter ρ, which measures the roughness in an image. More precisely, for any digital image f, we define

$$\rho = \frac{\|h_1 * f\|_1 + \|h_2 * f\|_1}{\|f\|_1} \tag{8}$$

where h_1 is a horizontal mask, $[1,-1]$, $h_2 = h_1^T$ is a vertical mask, the asterisk denotes discrete convolution, and, for any image f, $\|f\|_1$ is its L_1 norm (the L_1 norm is simply the sum of the magnitudes of all pixels). The two terms in the numerator of Eq. (8) measure the pixel-to-pixel roughness in the horizontal and the vertical directions, respectively. Normalization by f_1 in Eq. (8) makes ρ invariant under scaling. Clearly, ρ is zero for a constant image, and it increases with the pixel-to-pixel variation in the image.

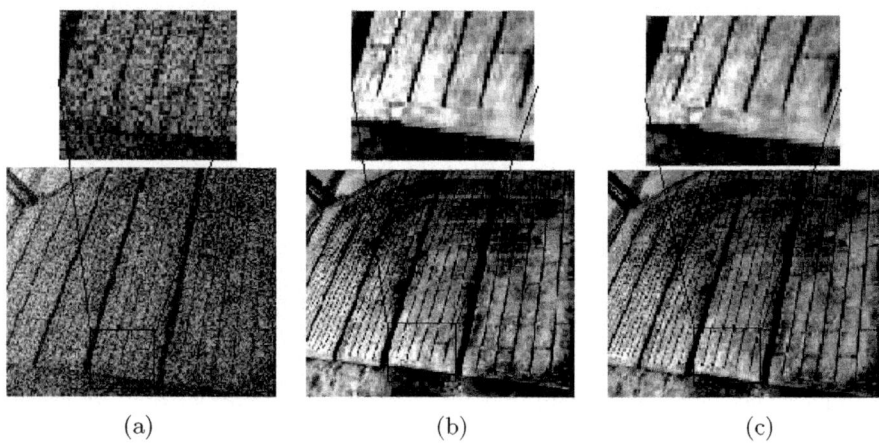

(a)   (b)   (c)

Fig. 1. Results on simulated data with emphasis in ghost artifacts reduction after 700 frame, a) frame with simulated nonuniformity, b) The corresponding frame corrected by the previous CS method [10] and c) The corresponding frame corrected by the enhanced SC method

3.1   Results with Simulated IR Video

The video has been generated using simulated images, where the intensity or gray level indicates the bodies temperature. FPN is added to each image generating the corrupted sequence. As an example, Fig. 1a shows a corrupted data frame.

In Fig. 1b and 1c the corresponding corrected frame by the CS-NUC method and the enhance CS-NUC method with k=1 are presented, respectively. In Fig. 1b and Fig. 1c we have shown a zooming of the corrected image, specifically of the zones indicated by boxes. In them, using only the naked eye is clear that the non-uniformity is better in the proposed method (Fig. 1c) than in the previous published method (Fig. 1b).

Figure 2 shows the calculated RMSE (a) and roughness (b) for the corrupted data, for each frame corrected using CS NUC method [10], and the enhanced CS-NUC method. Further, the average RMSEs computed for the whole infrared sequence are equal to 0.075 and 0.068 for the CS-NUC algorithm and the enhanced CS-NUC algorithm, respectively. It can be seen in Fig. 2a that the RMSE value obtained for the enhanced CS-NUC method has a greater convergence speed, because, for the same number of frame, it reaches a lower RMSE value than other method. It can be seen in Fig. 2b that the roughness parameter associated with the images indicate a reduction of enhanced CS-NUC method in relation to CS-NUC method.

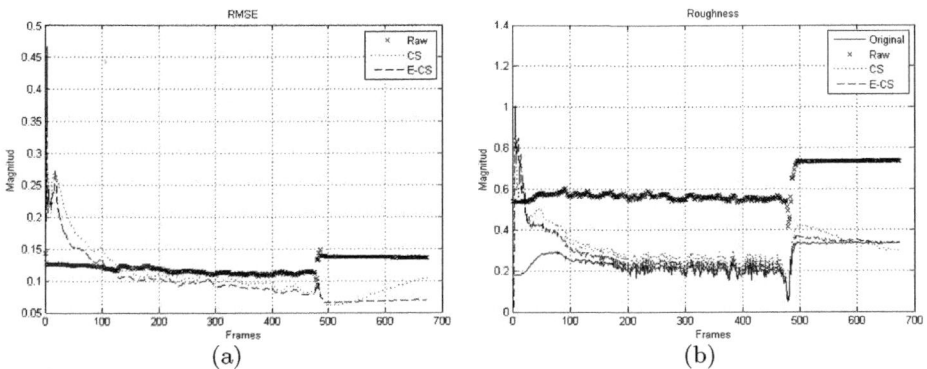

Fig. 2. The performance parameters associated with the images; (a) the evolution of the RMSE between original and the corrected frames; (b) the evolution of the roughness. In both chart, x line represents the corrupted data (Raw); dot line represents the RMSE computed for the CS-NUC method (CS); dashed line represents the RMSE computed for the proposed enhanced CS-NUC method (E-CS); and Solid line represents original frame (Original).

3.2   Results with Two Real Infrared Image Sequences

The first sequence has been collected using a 128×128 InSb FPA cooled camera (Amber Model AE-4128) operating in the 3-5 μm range. As an example, Fig. 3a shows a corrupted readout data frame. In Fig. 3b and 3c the corresponding corrected frame by the CS-NUC method and the enhance CS-NUC method are presented, respectively. In Fig. 3b and Fig. 3c we have shown a zooming of the corrected image, specifically of the zones indicated by boxes. In them, using only the naked eye is clear that the non-uniformity is better in the proposed CS-NUC method (Fig. 3c) than in the previous published method (Fig. 3b).

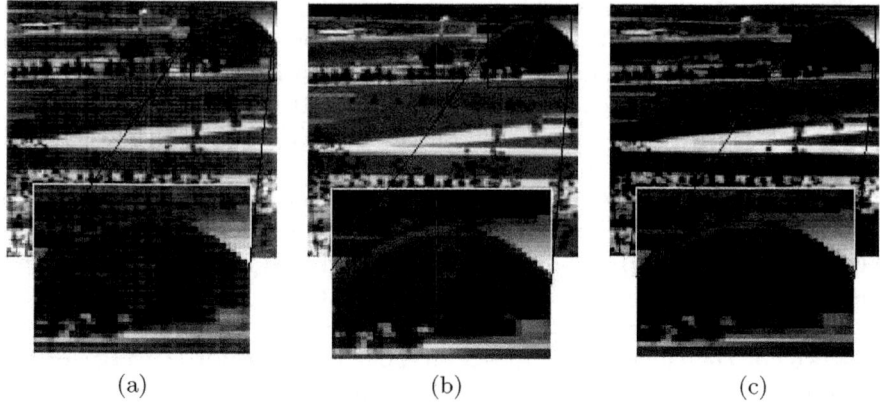

(a)   (b)   (c)

Fig. 3. Results on simulated data with emphasis in ghost artifacts reduction after 915 frame, a) frame with simulated nonuniformity, b) The corresponding frame corrected by the previous CS method [10] and c) The corresponding frame corrected by the enhanced SC method

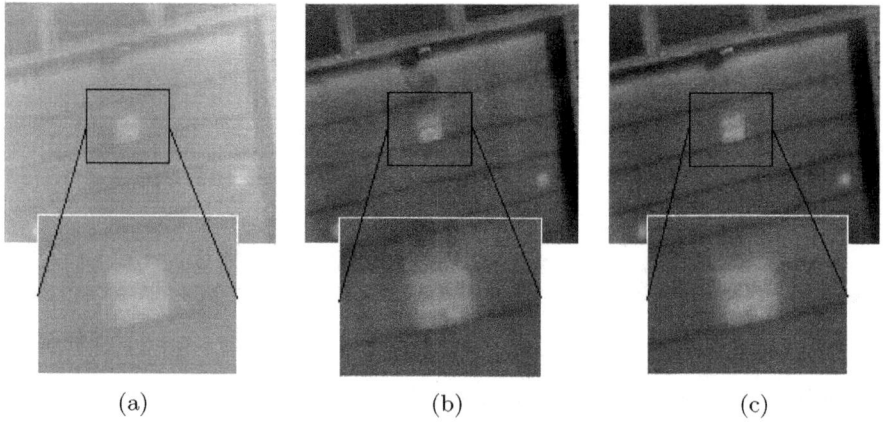

(a)   (b)   (c)

Fig. 4. Performance of the enhanced CS-NUC method under real IR data (Jade model camera), a) The raw corrupted frame, b) The corresponding frame corrected by the CS method and c) The corresponding frame corrected by the proposed enhance method

The second sequence of infrared data has been recorded using a 320×240 HgCdTe FPA cooled camera (CEDIP Jade Model) operating in the 8-12 μm range. As an example, Fig. 4a shows the corrupted readout data. In Fig. 4b, and Fig. 4c the corresponding corrected frames by the previous published method CS and the NUC method proposed in this paper are shown, respectively. The non-uniformity, visually presented in the raw frame, has been notably reduced by the proposed method; in Fig. 4b and Fig. 4c this is specially noticed in the marked region. In Fig. 4b it is possible to appreciate the ghosting present. This ghost effect disappears when we used the enhance method with nonuniformity and ghosting correction algorithm, as it is shown in Fig. 4c. Note that the star in the extended zone is better visually in the Fig. 4c. Thus, we have shown experimentally with real IR data that the proposed scene- based CS-NUC method with ghost correction has the ability of notably reduce both the non-uniformity noise presented in IRFPA sensors and the ghosting generated by lack of motion in the recorded IR data.

The second sequence of infrared data has been recorded using a 320×240 HgCdTe FPA cooled camera (CEDIP Jade Model) operating in the 8-12 μm range. As an example, Fig. 4a shows the corrupted readout data. In Fig. 4b, and Fig. 4c the corresponding corrected frames by the previous published method CS and the NUC method proposed in this paper are shown, respectively. The non-uniformity, visually presented in the raw frame, has been notably reduced by the proposed method; in Fig. 4b and Fig. 4c this is specially noticed in the marked region. In Fig. 4b it is possible to appreciate the ghosting present. Thus, we have shown experimentally with real IR data that the proposed scene based enhanced CS-NUC method has the ability of notably reduce both the non-uniformity noise presented in IRFPA sensors and the ghosting generated by lack of motion in the recorded IR data.

4   Conclusions

In this paper an enhanced version of our previously published NUC method, based in a constant statistics method is presented. The new algorithm has the ability to improve the nonuniformity correction and to eliminate ghosting artifacts more efficiently than the previous method. This is obtained by means adding the effects of to speed up the convergence of the algorithm and motion threshold. Furthermore, the evaluation with simulated and real data has demonstrated that the proposed method reduces ghosting artifacts and improves the RMSE parameter when compared with the previous published method. Using read-out data taken from cameras of two different technologies we were able to observe that the method is capable to reduce nonuniformity, minimizing ghosting, with fast convergence and low RMSE.

Acknowledgments. This work was supported by DIUFRO DI10-0049 Proyect of the Universidad de La Frontera, Temuco, Chile.

References

1. Torres, S., Hayat, M.: Kalman Filtering for Adaptive Nonuniformity Correction in Infrared Focal Plane Arrays. The JOSA-A Opt. Soc. of America 20, 470–480 (2003)
2. Torres, S., Pezoa, J., Hayat, M.: Scene-based Nonuniformity Correction for Focal Plane Arrays Using the Method of the Inverse Covariance Form. OSA App. Opt. Inf. Proc. 42, 5872–5881 (2003)

3. Scribner, D., Sarkady, K., Kruer, M.: Adaptive Nonuniformity Correction for Infrared Focal Plane Arrays using Neural Networks. In: Proceeding of SPIE, vol. 1541, pp. 100–109 (1991)
4. Scribner, D., Sarkady, K., Kruer, M.: Adaptive Retina-like Preprocessing for Imaging Detector Arrays. In: Proceeding of the IEEE International Conference on Neural Networks, vol. 3, pp. 1955–1960 (1993)
5. Torres, S., Vera, E., Reeves, R., Sobarzo, S.: Adaptive Scene-Based Nonuniformity Correction Method for Infrared Focal Plane Arrays. In: Proceeding of SPIE, vol. 5076, pp. 130–139 (2003)
6. Vera, E., Torres, S.: Fast Adaptive Nonuniformity Correction for Infrared Focal Plane Arrays. EURASIP Journal on Applied Signal Processing (2005)
7. Torres, F., Torres, S.N., Martín, C.S.: A Recursive Least Square Adaptive Filter for Nonuniformity Correction of Infrared Image Sequences. In: Sanfeliu, A., Cortés, M.L. (eds.) CIARP 2005. LNCS, vol. 3773, pp. 540–546. Springer, Heidelberg (2005)
8. Torres, F., Martin, C.S., Torres, S.N.: A RLS Filter for Nonuniformity and Ghosting Correction of Infrared Image Sequences. In: Martínez-Trinidad, J.F., Carrasco Ochoa, J.A., Kittler, J. (eds.) CIARP 2006. LNCS, vol. 4225, pp. 446–454. Springer, Heidelberg (2006)
9. Harris, J.G., Chiang, Y.M.: Nonuniformity correction of infrared image sequences using the constant-statistics constraint. IEEE Trans. Image Process 8(8), 1148–1151 (1999)
10. Harris, J.G., Chiang, Y.M.: Nonuniformity correction of infrared image sequences using the constant-statistics constraint. IEEE Transactions on Image Processing 8(8), 1148–1151 (1999)

Reliable Atrial Activity Extraction from ECG Atrial Fibrillation Signals

Felipe Donoso[1], Eduardo Lecannelier[2], Esteban Pino[1], and Alejandro Rojas[1]

[1] Department of Electrical Engineering, University of Concepcion, Concepcion, Chile
{felipedonoso,estebanpino,arojasn}@udec.cl
[2] Department of Internal Medicine, University of Concepcion, Concepcion, Chile
elecanne@udec.cl

Abstract. Atrial fibrillation (AF) is the most common arrhythmia encountered in clinical research, with a prevalence of 0.4% to 1% of the population. Therefore, the study of AF is an important research field that can provide great treatment improvements. In this paper we apply independent component analysis to a 12-lead electrocardiogram, for which we obtain a 12-source set. We apply to this set three different atrial activity (AA) selection methods based on: kurtosis, correlation of the sources with lead V1, and spectral analysis. We then propose a reliable AA extraction based on the consensus between the three methods in order to reduce the effect of anatomical and physiological variabilities. The extracted AA signal will be used in a future stage for AF classification.

Keywords: atrial fibrillation, atrial activity, ECG, ICA, kurtosis, correlation, power spectral density.

1 Introduction

Atrial fibrillation (AF) is the most common arrhythmia encountered in clinic research, with a prevalence of 0.4% to 1% of the population. This prevalence increases with age, reaching up to 8% in population over 80 years old [1,2]. Therefore, the study of AF is an important research field that can provide great treatment improvements, such as lower morbidity and mortality, better life quality, and lower costs for the health care provider.

AF is characterized by uncoordinated atrial activation with consequent deterioration of atrial mechanical function [1]. From a clinical point of view, the analysis of these activities using non-invasive measures is highly desirable. To this end, the standard 12-lead electrocardiogram (ECG) can be used. Unfortunately, atrial activity (AA) is coupled with ventricular activity (VA), represented by the QRST complex, in all the 12-lead measures. Furthermore, AA presents much lower amplitude than VA, sometimes with amplitudes near the noise level. Additionally, both activities have spectral distributions that overlap, making linear filtering solutions not useful. Hence, one of the most important tasks for an appropriate AF analysis is the dissociation of AA from VA. When using 12-lead ECG the challenge we face for the dissociation of both activities is to

C. San Martin and S.-W. Kim (Eds.): CIARP 2011, LNCS 7042, pp. 621–629, 2011.
© Springer-Verlag Berlin Heidelberg 2011

find a representative waveform that estimates the AA, starting from the 12-lead ECG. Some of the algorithms used for AA extraction include spatio-temporal QRST cancellation [3,4], principal components analysis (PCA) [5] and independent component analysis (ICA) [6,7,8].

In this work we apply ICA together with three methods to select the best representation of AA. The goal is to characterize the AA in AF, in order to find patterns that can be recognized as different ECG-based AF classes, in the hope that classes will give complementary information to improve the different treatments currently applied to restore sinus rhythm to patients with this cardiac alteration.

2   Methods

2.1   Data

Real 12-lead ECG recordings were used from four patients with diagnosed AF. Records were 60 s long, sampled at 1200 Hz. A pre-processing consisting in a bandpass filtering and an amplitude normalization were applied. This filtering stage is basically to reduce baseline wandering below 0.5 Hz and high frequency noise above 50 Hz. Amplitude normalization is optional, but helps visually compare signals from different patients.

2.2   Independent Component Analysis

ICA is one of the techniques that solves the blind source separation (BSS) problem [9,10,11]. BSS recovers a set of source signals from the observation of linear mixtures of the sources. These source signals are not directly accessible and have to be extracted or separated from the set of measurable signals or observations. As neither the source signals nor the mixing structure are known, this is referred to as the BSS problem. This problem can be written in a matrix form as

$$X(t) = A \cdot S(t) . \tag{1}$$

$X(t)$ is the vector of acquired signals $X_1(t),...,X_n(t)$ and $S(t)$ is the vector of source signals $S_1(t),...,S_n(t)$. A is called the mixing matrix. The goal of BSS is to estimate $S(t)$ and A from the observations $X(t)$.

The ICA solution to the BSS problem assumes that the sources must be statistically independent and the restriction that the sources must have non-gaussian distributions [11]. The assumption of statistical independence has already been established [6] since during an AF there is an uncoordinated operation of AA and VA [1,12].

2.3   Source Selection for AA

As a result of applying ICA over a 12-lead ECG, a 12-source set is obtained. From this set we have to choose the most representative signal for AA. For this search, three complementary methods will be applied: kurtosis-based extraction, correlation of the sources to lead V1 of the ECG, and spectral features.

The first method is based on the non-gaussianity of the sources, specially for those with considerable contents of VA. It is not difficult to observe that VA presents a super-gaussian behavior, while the AA behaves as a sub-gaussian random process [6,11]. This non-gaussianity of the sources can be measured by the fourth-order marginal cumulant or kurtosis, that gives a high value, typically above 10 for the VA or super-gaussian distributions and negative values for the AA or sub-gaussian distributions. Thus, the best candidate for AA signal is the source with the lowest kurtosis.

In the second method, a 12 by 12 correlation matrix between ECG leads and sources is generated. In this matrix the column for lead V1 is of particular interest. It is generally accepted that lead V1 captures more atrial activity [12,13]. Thus, the first approach to this method is to correlate lead V1 with all the sources and selects the one with higher correlation index. However, it would be wrong to choose directly the highest value, since the sources with high VA components have high correlation with lead V1, hiding the correlation in the non-QRST segments. To avoid this problem, only the sources with low kurtosis are correlated, obtaining a relatively high correlation in the source that has more similarity with the non-QRST segments of lead V1. Then, the most representative source of AA is chosen when the correlation with lead V1 is greater than the correlation with all the other leads.

However, the fact that lead V1 captures more atrial activity is only a general rule, dependent on both physiological and anatomical variability among patients. That is why it is necessary to have redundant tools for an effective AA extraction. The third method is based in this spectral properties of the fibrillatory waves, which has a distinct peak between 4 and 9 Hz [5,6,14,15]. To indentify this feature, the power spectral density (PSD) is estimated using Welch's averaged modified periodogram method [16]. Then, we have to evaluate a spectral parameter that give us infomation about the relative amount of energy of the spectra in the range between 4 and 9 Hz. This parameter is called spectral concentration (SC) [8] and is defined by

$$SC = \frac{\sum_{f=4}^{9} P(f)}{\sum_{f=0.5}^{50} P(f)} \cdot 100\% . \tag{2}$$

$P(f)$ is the PSD of the signal and f the frequency in Hertz. Since we filtered the signals in the band of 0.5 to 50 Hz, the denominator represents the total energy of the signal, while the numerator represents only the energy in the range between 4 and 9 Hz. The criterion applied is that we choose the source with the higher value of SC in the set of 12 sources.

The source chosen by at least two of these three methods is finally selected as the AA signal.

3 Results

With all the 12-lead ECG's signals pre-processed as mentioned in the previous section, FastICA algorithm was applied [17]. For the resulting set of sources the kurtosis method was applied, obtaining in all cases at least 4 sources with kurtosis above 10. This means that those sources have considerable components of VA, represented by a high amplitude QRS complex, as seen in Fig. 1. Table 1 shows the kurtosis found for all sources in all patients studied. We mentioned that AA should have negative kurtosis. For example, in Patient 1, Source 9 is the best candidate for AA signal because it is the source with the lowest kurtosis.

In correlation method, Table 2 shows the selected sources for every patient and the corresponding correlations with the leads. Fig. 2 shows the source selected with this method in Patient 1, with the corresponding segment of lead V1.

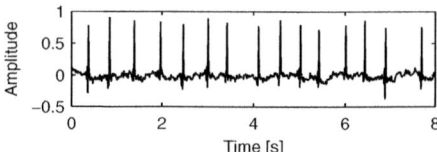

Fig. 1. Source 1 in Patient 1, signal with high kurtosis value. QRS complexes are clearly visible.

Table 1. Kurtosis for all the sources in every patient

Source	Patient 1	2	3	4
1	24.5156	21.9675	113.8125	21.5941
2	26.3407	23.4926	20.8175	19.9526
3	30.555	19.9116	28.0697	34.0353
4	9.249	10.9939	18.0115	11.7974
5	23.5282	7.9972	7.9839	17.5561
6	1.8372	2.74	15.5995	2.5687
7	1.3795	**-0.6597**	1.7316	1.9107
8	1.3427	1.265	2.0633	1.583
9	**-0.5966**	0.8024	1.2774	**-0.3756**
10	-0.4317	0.4478	0.7189	0.6692
11	0.2128	-0.1481	0.4896	-0.1498
12	-0.0792	0.1545	**0.079**	-0.0366

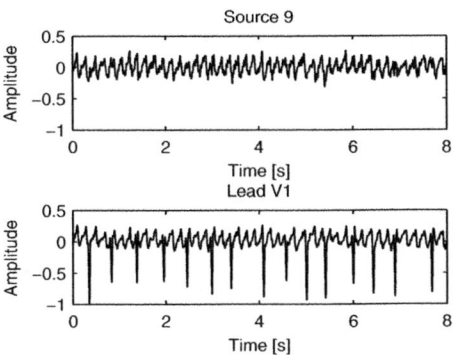

Fig. 2. Comparison between Source 9 and lead V1 in Patient 1. Source 9 has the highest correlation coefficient with this lead.

Table 3 shows the SC parameter for all the sources in the four patients. Fig. 3 shows the PSD of Source 9 (left) in Patient 1, with a SC of 63.2%, and the PSD of Source 1 (right) in the same patient, with a lower SC of only 18.03%. Clearly, Source 9 satisfy the hypothesis mentioned above, with a main peak frequency of 5.86 Hz.

Summarizing, Table 4 shows the results of the three methods for the most representative source of the AA. In this table we see that only in Patient 1 the three methods match. In the other patients one of the methods does not agree. The possible causes for this will be discussed in the next section.

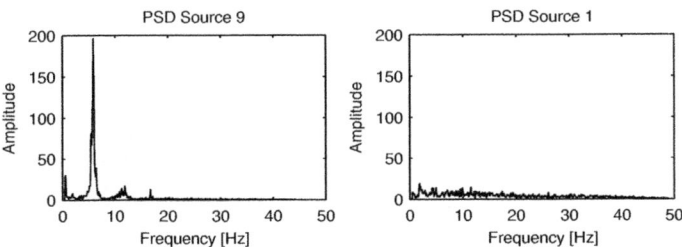

Fig. 3. PSD for Source 9 (left) and Source 1 (right) in Patient 1

4   Discussion

AF is a cardiac alteration that is characterized by uncoordinated atrial activation. On the ECG, AF is seen as the replacement of consistent P waves by rapid oscillations, known as fibrillatory waves, that vary in amplitude and frequency components. Furthermore, anatomical differences between patients give us a source of variabilities in the measurements. This is due to slight variations

Table 2. Correlation coefficients for the selected sources

Leads	Patient/Source			
	1/9	2/12	3/12	4/8
I	-0.041	0.247	0.044	-0.100
II	-0.129	0.118	0.066	-0.023
III	-0.125	0.040	0.017	0.038
aVR	0.114	-0.139	-0.054	0.085
aVL	0.076	0.131	0.031	-0.067
aVF	-0.074	0.095	0.082	0.011
V1	**0.439**	**-0.256**	**0.103**	**-0.385**
V2	0.115	0.114	0.002	-0.062
V3	0.067	0.150	0.011	-0.016
V4	0.008	0.174	0.035	-0.001
V5	0.023	0.167	0.026	0.003
V6	0.023	0.141	0.016	0.009

Table 3. Spectral concentration (SC) in percentage for every source in all patients

Source	Patient			
	1	2	3	4
1	18.03	25.45	10.04	14.36
2	16.80	27.76	22.50	23.65
3	16.06	27.35	15.56	14.25
4	10.62	26.32	13.14	14.39
5	11.47	10.13	9.68	21.25
6	12.35	18.03	22.45	9.49
7	57.14	9.86	6.32	32.41
8	18.10	16.46	25.88	26.29
9	**63.20**	13.72	**27.14**	**60.99**
10	19.81	28.86	11.68	16.30
11	24.60	16.13	26.17	11.07
12	14.86	**44.98**	9.65	17.32

Table 4. Summary of results for the three methods. Sources shown are those selected for each method.

Patient	Method		
	Kurtosis	corr V1	PSD
1	**Source 9**	**Source 9**	**Source 9**
2	Source 7	**Source 12**	**Source 12**
3	**Source 12**	**Source 12**	Source 9
4	**Source 9**	Source 8	**Source 9**

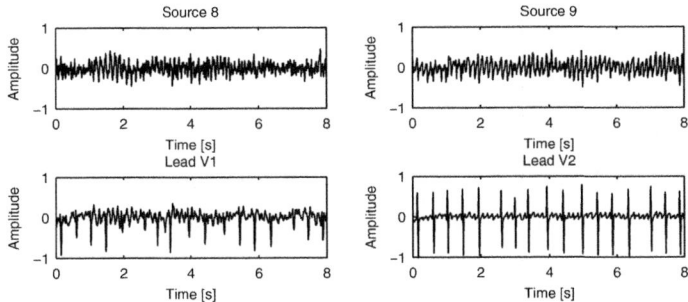

Fig. 4. Comparison between Source 8 and lead V1 (left) and between Source 9 and lead V2 (right). Sources selected by correlation for Patient 4.

in the position of the electrodes in relation to the anatomy of the cardiovascular system of the patient. All these variabilities directly influence the results from the proposed methods, thus we use a consensus between these three selection approaches for AA extraction.

The kurtosis method is an statistical measure, so it is expected that for these fibri-llatory waves we can have variabilities in the estimation of the kurtosis due to the potentially non-stationary nature of the physiological process. For Patient 2 we choose Source 7 due to its lower kurtosis, however, Source 12 (chosen by the other methods) also has a relatively low kurtosis. Although this value is positive, it is relatively close to Source 7 kurtosis, and still far from values of kurtosis from VA. Hence, we can conclude that kurtosis is an effective method to discard the sources that represent the VA, but it is not so accurate to find the source that represents the AA, due to the intrinsic variablities of this activity.

For the correlation method, the hypothesis we use is that lead V1 is the one with more visible AA. As we mentioned, it is possible to have variabilities in anatomical characteristics, resulting in changes of the direction of the electrical vector, projecting lower or higher AA components to the different leads. Lead V1 is not the exception to this problem, so the visibility of AA in this lead will vary for different patients. In Patient 4, Source 8 has the higher correlation with V1, however, the other methods indicate that Source 9 is the most representative source for AA. From the analysis, we found that in this patient, Source 9 has the higher correlation with lead V2. From the above reasoning, we can argue that in this case lead V2 has more visible components of AA. In Figure 4 we show both cases, where clearly lead V2 meets this argument. Also, Source 9 presents a noiseless fibrillatory waves, with a frequency of approximately 7 Hz, matching with the PSD results.

The PSD method is specially sensitive to variabilities in frequency, so it is logical to expect variabilities in the PSD for different cases of AF. However, it is well known that the spectrum of the AA during AF is concentrated between 4 and 9 Hz. In Patient 3 we observe that the SC values for all the sources are under 28%. This means that we have a scattered spectrum, giving lower SC for the range between 4 and 9 Hz. Figure 5 shows the PSD for sources 9 (left)

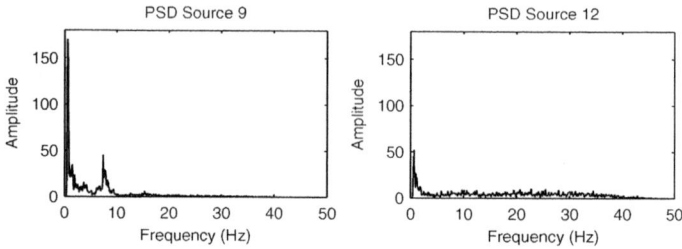

Fig. 5. PSD for sources 9 (left) and 12 (right) in Patient 3. Source 9 have a peak at a frequency of 0.6 Hz, and a secondary peak at 7.4 Hz. Source 12 presents a peak at 0.6 Hz and a scattered distribution in the rest of the spectrum.

and 12 (right) in Patient 3. Source 9 is the one selected by the PSD method, whilst Source 12 is the choice for the kurtosis and correlation methods. It is clear that Source 9 is not the correct signal for AA, since it has a considerable low frequency peak that can not be a component of AA. Aditionally, Source 12 was chosen with a kurtosis value that is not conclusive for the selection, and with correlation method ocurrs the same, where its greatest value is 0.103. Therefore, we have a complicated case for AA extraction, that can easily lead in a complete disagreement of the three methods.

5   Conclusion

In this paper we proposed a reliable extraction of AA during AF. This reliability is based on the use of a consensus between three selection approaches which reduces the effect of the expected variabilities.

The results obtained in this paper are the beginning of a research work which aims to classify AF signals into well-defined subgroups or classes. For the design of a succesful classifier, we need reliable data, from which feature extraction can be done. In that sense, if for a certain AF signal we have a complete disagreement in the results for the three methods proposed, that signal should be discarded.

We trust that the proposed approach will allow for a consistent AA extraction, thus permiting us to move to the next stage of AF classification.

References

1. Fuster, V., Rydén, L.E., Cannom, D.S., et al.: ACC/AHA/ESC 2006 Guidelines for the management of patients with atrial fibrillation. Europace 8(9), 651–745 (2006)
2. Go, A.S., Hylek, E.M., Phillips, K.A., Chang, Y., Henault, L.E., Selby, J.V., Singer, D.E.: Prevalence of diagnosed atrial fibrillation in adults: national implications for rhythm management and stroke prevention: the anticoagulation and risk factors in atrial fibrillation (atria) study. Journal of the American Medical Association 285(18), 2370–2375 (2001)

3. Stridh, M., Sornmo, L.: Spatiotemporal qrst cancellation techniques for analysis of atrial fibrillation. IEEE Transactions on Biomedical Engineering 48(1), 105–111 (2001)
4. Rieta, J.J., Zarzoso, V., Millet-Roig, J., Garcia-Civera, R., Ruiz-Granell, R.: Atrial activity extraction based on blind source separation as an alternative to qrst cancellation for atrial fibrillation analysis. In: Proc. Computers in Cardiology 2000, pp. 69–72 (2000)
5. Langley, P., Bourke, J.P., Murray, A.: Frequency analysis of atrial fibrillation. In: Proc. Computers in Cardiology 2000. pp. 65–68 (2000)
6. Rieta, J.J., Castells, F., Sanchez, C., Zarzoso, V., Millet, J.: Atrial activity extraction for atrial fibrillation analysis using blind source separation. IEEE Transactions on Biomedical Engineering 51(7), 1176–1186 (2004)
7. Phlypo, R., D'Asseler, Y., Lemahieu, I., Zarzoso, V.: Extraction of the atrial activity from the ecg based on independent component analysis with prior knowledge of the source kurtosis signs. In: Proc. 29th Annual Int. Conf. of the IEEE Engineering in Medicine and Biology Society EMBS 2007, pp. 6499–6502 (2007)
8. Xiao, J., Chen, Z., Huang, Z.: Atrial activity extraction for atrial fibrillation analysis using mutual information minimization. In: Proc. 1st Int. Conf. Bioinformatics and Biomedical Engineering ICBBE 2007, pp. 916–919 (2007)
9. Cardoso, J.F.: Source separation using higher order moments. In: Proc. Int. Acoustics, Speech, and Signal Processing ICASSP 1989. Conf., pp. 2109–2112 (1989)
10. Comon, P.: Independent component analysis, a new concept? Signal Processing 36, 287–314 (1994)
11. Hyvärinen, A., Karhunen, J., Oja, E.: Independent Component Analysis. John Wiley & Sons, Inc. (2001)
12. Bollmann, A., Husser, D., Mainardi, L., Lombardi, F., Langley, P., Murray, A., Rieta, J.J., Millet, J., Olsson, S.B., Stridh, M., Sörnmo, L.: Analysis of surface electrocardiograms in atrial fibrillation: techniques, research, and clinical applications. Europace 8(11), 911–926 (2006), http://dx.doi.org/10.1093/europace/eul113
13. Thurmann, M., Janney, J.G.: The diagnostic importance of fibrillatory wave size. Circulation 25, 991–994 (1962)
14. Bollmann, A., Kanuru, N.K., McTeague, K.K., Walter, P.F., DeLurgio, D.B., Langberg, J.J.: Frequency analysis of human atrial fibrillation using the surface electrocardiogram and its response to ibutilide. American Journal of Cardiology 81(12), 1439–1445 (1998)
15. Langley, P., Stridh, M., Rieta, J.J., Sornmo, L., Millet-Roig, J., Murray, A.: Comparison of atrial rhythm extraction techniques for the estimation of the main atrial frequency from the 12-lead electrocardiogram in atrial fibrillation. In: Proc. Computers in Cardiology, pp. 29–32 (2002)
16. Welch, P.: The use of fast fourier transform for the estimation of power spectra: A method based on time averaging over short, modified periodograms. IEEE Transactions on Audio and Electroacoustics 15(2), 70–73 (1967)
17. Hyvärinen, A., Oja, E.: Independent component analysis: algorithms and applications. Neural Networks 13(4-5), 411–430 (2000)

Gray Box Model with an SVM to Represent the Influence of PaCO$_2$ on the Cerebral Blood Flow Autoregulation

Max Chacón[1], Mariela Severino[1], and Ronney Panerai[2]

[1] Departamento de Ingeniería Informática, Universidad de Santiago de Chile,
Av. Ecuador 3659,
Casilla 10233, Santiago, Chile
max.chacon@usach.cl, mariela.severino@gmail.com
[2] Medical Physics Group, Department of Cardiovascular Sciences, Faculty of Medicine,
University of Leicester, Leicester LE1 5WW, UK
rp9@le.ac.uk

Abstract. Since the appearance of methods based on machine learning, they have been presented as an alternative to classical phenomenological modeling and there are few initiatives that attempt to integrate them. This paper presents a hybrid paradigm called *gray box* that blends a phenomenological description (differential equation) and a Support Vector Machine (SVM) to model a relevant problem in the field of cerebral hemodynamic. The results show that with this type of paradigm it is possible to exceed the results obtained with phenomenological models and also with the models based on learning, in addition to contributing to the description of the modelled phenomenon.

Keywords: Gray Box Model, Support Vector Machine, Cerebral hemodynamic, PaCO$_2$.

1 Introduction

In many fields of science and engineering one has partial knowledge of the phenomenon that it is desired to model, having available some equation that describes it partially (deterministic model) –this problem appears more often when the phenomenon is nonlinear–. On the other hand, there are methods based on learning, such as artificial neural networks (random model), which allow modeling nonlinear phenomena but do not describe adequately the principles of the phenomena.

In the 1990s, Psichogios and Ungar [1] proposed the methods called *gray box*, which involve a hybrid strategy that mixes the phenomenological knowledge of an equation, usually differential (*white box*), and an automatic learning method like neural networks (*black box*) to make a more accurate description of the phenomenon (*gray box*). Thompson and Kramer [2] classified these methods into basically two structures. The so-called "*series configuration*", where the neural network participates by adjusting parameters of the differential equation with the purpose of incorporating the data variations in the deterministic model, and the other alternative is the "*parallel configuration*", where the neural network adjusts the results of the differential equation

C. San Martin and S.-W. Kim (Eds.): CIARP 2011, LNCS 7042, pp. 630–637, 2011.

to the data, estimating the residues between both. Representative applications of these methods are found in the fields of chemistry and bioprocesses [3-5].

In this paper we propose the use of the *gray box* method, specifically the series configuration, to model a relevant problem in the field of cerebral hemodynamic; it requires modeling the influence of CO$_2$ pressure (PaCO$_2$) on the system that regulates the cerebral blood flow. An increase of PaCO$_2$ in the body causes a state of hypercapnia, producing dilation of the blood vessels, deteriorating autoregulation, and increasing Cerebral Blood Flow Velocity (CBFV) [6]. The most widely used technique to measure the reactivity of the blood vessels of an individual to PaCO$_2$, consists in measuring the change produced in the CBFV by breathing a mixture of air and 5% PaCO$_2$ [7] to estimate the percent change in CBFV with respect to the change in PaCO$_2$ (the measurement of this ratio is known as the reactivity to PaCO$_2$). The blood flow velocity is measured with Transcranial Doppler Ultrasonography.

Since the CBFV variations depend also on the variations of Arterial Blood Pressure (ABP), the model is completed by measuring ABP in a noninvasive way on the middle finger with a Finapres instantaneous pressure gauge.

At present there are phenomenological models that approximately represent CBFV variation when there are changes in the levels of inspiration of PaCO$_2$ [8]. This model will be used as our *white box* model, to be part of the *gray box* method. Linear [7] and nonlinear nondeterministic models of the autoregulation phenomenon and the influence of PaCO$_2$ on this system have also been made [9-10]. In particular, the work that we have done [10] has shown that Support Vector Machines (SVM) represent an adequate paradigm for modeling (like a *black box*) the cerebral autoregulation system, under normal conditions and when PaCO$_2$ changes.

The hypothesis that we will prove in what follows has to do with a *gray box* model using the model of Poulin et al. [8] as *white box* and an SVM as *black box*, and it will allow a better representation of the phenomenon, both under normal conditions and under conditions of aspiration of 5% PaCO$_2$.

2 Methods

2.1 Data Collection

Sixteen healthy subjects aged 31.8±8.5 years were studied in a temperature controlled laboratory. None of them had a history of hypertension, diabetes, migraine, epilepsy, or any other cardiovascular or neurologic disease. The study was approved by the Leicestershire Research Ethics Committee and informed consent was obtained in all cases.

The subjects were asked to refrain from ingesting alcohol or caffeinated products in the 12 hours preceding the study. Measurements were made in the supine position. CBFV was recorded in the middle cerebral artery with transcranial Doppler (Scimed QVL-120) using a 2 MHz transducer. ABP was measured noninvasively using arterial volume clamping of the digital artery (Finapres 2300 Ohmeda). An infrared capnograph (Datex Normocap 200) with a face mask was used to measure end-tidal CO$_2$ (EtCO$_2$). The face mask was kept in place for the duration of the complete study including the PaCO$_2$ reactivity test with a mixture of 5% PaCO$_2$ in air administered with a Douglas bag and elephant tubing connected to the face mask through a one-way valve.

Baseline values of CBFV, ABP and EtCO$_2$ were recorded for an initial period of 5 min with subjects breathing normal air, after all variables were stable for at least 15 min. This was followed by a 5 min. recording with each subject breathing a mixture of 5% PaCO$_2$ in air.

2.2 Pre-processing

All the signals were collected and saved on a digital audio tape using an 8-channel recording instrument (*Sony PC108M*), and they were then transferred to a microcomputer in real time. The fast Fourier transform was used to extract the maximum frequency of the CBFV signal, with a 5-ms time window. The signals were digitized and sampled at 200 samples/s, and then processed through an 8th order zero-phase Butterworth low-pass filter with a cut-off frequency of 20 Hz.

The beginning and end of each cardiac cycle were detected in the arterial pressure signal, and the mean values of ABP and CBFV were calculated for each heart beat. Spline interpolation, followed by re-sampling every 0.2 s produced time series with a uniform time base. The EtCO$_2$ signal was interpolated linearly between successive end-tidal values and was also re-sampled at 0.2 s intervals. For the purpose of implementing SVM models, the signals were sub-sampled at 0.6 s intervals, resulting in approximately 500 data points for each of the two different segments of data.

2.3 White Box Model

The differential equation proposed by Poulin [8], which represents our *white box* model, is shown in Equation 1.

$$\frac{d(CBFV(t))}{dt} = \frac{1}{\tau}\left[g \bullet u(t-T_d)+CBFV*-CBFV(t)\right] \qquad (1)$$

where the input $u(t\text{-}T_d)=[EtCO_2(t\text{-}T_d)\text{-}EtCO_2*]$, and $EtCO_2*$ is the control period. The three parameters g, τ, $CBFV*$, are obtained using the least squares technique. In the case of constant T_d, a *grid* search is used that minimizes the sum of the squares of the other parameters. This equation is solved using separable variables to obtain the $CBFV(n)$ in discrete times n which correspond to each heart beat.

2.4 Black Box Model

The adopted SVM algorithm was the v-SVM, introduced by Vapnik in 1995 [11]. It is based on the statistical theory of learning, which introduced regression as the fitting of a tube of radius ε to the data. The decision boundary for determining the radius of the tube is given by a small subset of training examples called Support Vectors.

Assuming that $\vec{x}$ represents the input data vector, the output value $f(\vec{x})$ is given by the SVM regression using a weight vector $\vec{w}$, according to equation 2.

$$f(\vec{x}) = (\vec{w} \cdot \vec{x}) + b, \quad \vec{w}, \vec{x} \in \mathbf{R}^N, b \in \mathbf{R}, \tag{2}$$

where b is a constant obtained from $\vec{w}$.

The variation of the v-SVM introduced by Schölkopf et al. [12] consists in adding ε to the minimization problem, weighted by a variable v that adjusts the contribution of ε between 0 and 1.

$$\text{minimize} \quad \theta(\vec{w}, \xi) = \frac{1}{2}\|\vec{w}\| + C\left(lv\varepsilon + \sum_{i=1}^{l}\xi_i\right) \tag{3}$$

In equation 3, l represents the total dimension of the data (number of cases), C is a model parameter determining the trade-off between the complexity of the model, expressed by $\vec{w}$, and the points that remain outside the tube. Slack variables ξ depend on the distance of the data points from the regression line. We used the ε-insensitive loss function.

The solution of this minimization problem for obtaining the weight vectors $\vec{w}$ is found by the standard optimization procedure for a problem with inequality restrictions when applying the conditions of Kuhn-Tuker to the dual problem. The main advantage of introducing parameter $v \in [0\ 1]$ is to make it possible to control the error fraction and the number (or fraction) of Support Vectors with only one normalized parameter.

To solve a nonlinear regression problem it is sufficient to substitute the inner product between two independent original variables $\vec{x}_i \cdot \vec{x}_j$ (Eq. 2) by a kernel function gaussian radial base function (RBF), given by equation 4:

$$k(\vec{x}_i, \vec{x}_j) = \exp(-\|\vec{x}_i - \vec{x}_j\|^2 / (2\sigma^2)) \tag{4}$$

The implementation of the *black box* model for the case of a differential equation must correspond to a dynamic model in time. We have chosen a model of the AutoRegressive with Exogenous input (ARX) type that can consider one (ABP) or two (ABP and EtCO$_2$) inputs to model a parameter ($\theta = \tau$, g or *CBFV**) of Poulin's differential equation [8]. The *black box* model presents two options, as shown in equations 5 and 6.

$$\theta(t) = f(\theta(t-1),..., \theta(t-n_\theta), p(t),..., p(t-n_p)) \tag{5}$$

$$\theta(t) = f(\theta(t-1),..., \theta(t-n_\theta), p(t),..., p(t-n_p),..., c(t),..., c(t-n_c)) \tag{6}$$

where $p(t)$=ABP(t), $c(t)$=EtCO$_2$(t) and $\theta(t)$ is one of the parameters τ, g or *CBFV**.

Function $f()$ can be a linear function when Eq. 2 is used, or a nonlinear one when using the kernel RBF function shown in Eq. 4.

2.5 Gray Box Model

The *gray box* model is implemented using Poulin's differential equation as *white box*, for which some of the parameters τ, g or *CVFB** are estimated by means of an SVM as *black box*, as shown in Figure 1. When Eq. 5 is used, the dotted line from $c(t)$ does not exist, and in the case of Eq. 6 the SVM has two inputs ($p(t)$ and $c(t)$).

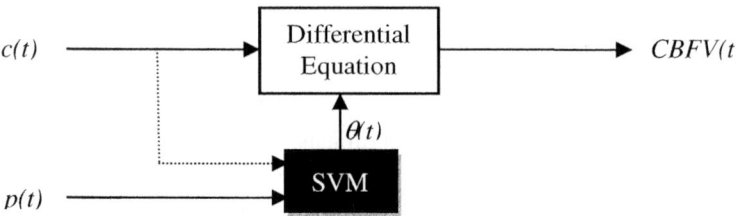

Fig. 1. *Gray box* model; the dotted line indicates if the *black box* model is univariate or multivariate

3   Results

Good quality recordings were obtained for all subjects with both the baseline and the 5% $PaCO_2$ test. Representative fluctuations in ABP, $EtCO_2$ and CBFV are shown in Figure 2 for one subject (#13) for the baseline and 5% $PaCO_2$ data segments.

To train and evaluate the different proposed models two states are chosen, one during the baseline period and the other during the aspiration of 5% de $PaCO_2$ in air. In each state one half of each period is chosen to train and the other half to evaluate. Since the output variables correspond to signals, we chose Pearson's correlation (r) between the real and the estimated CBFV signals, as an index to evaluate the precision of the models.

To estimate each of the three parameters, τ, g and *CBFV**, each of them is isolated from the solution of Eq. 1, and then the SVM models are trained and evaluated using one these parameters as output signals. The best results are obtained by modifying the *CBFV** parameter. The models are applied to each of the 16 subjects.

The results were calculated for the baseline and changes to 5% $PaCO_2$ conditions. In the baseline, for the univariate model of the SVM, only the nonlinear case is calculated. For multivariate 5% $PaCO_2$ changes only the nonlinear case is calculated (the linear cases that were not calculated are not significant under these conditions). The results of the average correlations for the 16 subjects are shown in Table 1.

Figure 3 shows the reactivity curves to $EtCO_2$ for the linear and nonlinear models under the 5% $PaCO_2$ change condition. It is also important to obtain the reactivity indices for these models, which are calculated as the ratio of the change between the CBFV values and the $EtCO_2$ changes. The average values for linear univariate 5% $PaCO_2$ is 4.8 (mm Hg/%), and 4.4 (mm Hg/%) for the nonlinear model.

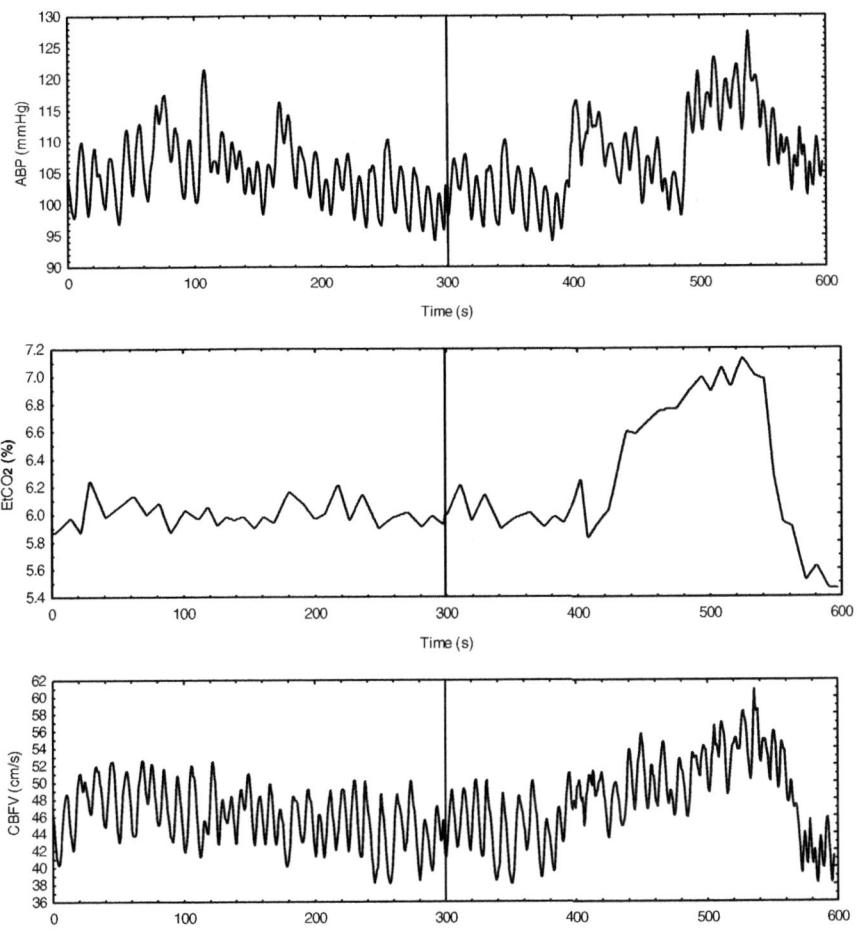

Fig. 2. Representative time-series of ABP, EtCO$_2$ and CBFV showing spontaneous fluctuations during baseline (left) and breathing 5% PaCO$_2$ in air (right)

Table 1. Average correlations for the baseline and 5% PaCO$_2$ change conditions for univariate and multivariate SVM models

	Baseline			**Changes** 5% CO$_2$	
Model	Training	Test	**Model**	Training	Test
SVM Univariate			**SVM Univariate**		
Linear	-	-	Linear	0.989	0.948†
Nonlinear	0.967	0.769#	Nonlinear	0.986	*0.962*†‡
SVM Multivariate			**SVM Multivariate**		
Linear	0.968	0.727*	Linear	-	-
Nonlinear	0.967	0.801#*	Nonlinear	0.987	0.951‡

When the Wilcoxon test was applied to establish if the differences were significant ($p<0.05$), the following values were obtained for p: #0.026, *0.002, †0.501, ‡0.535.

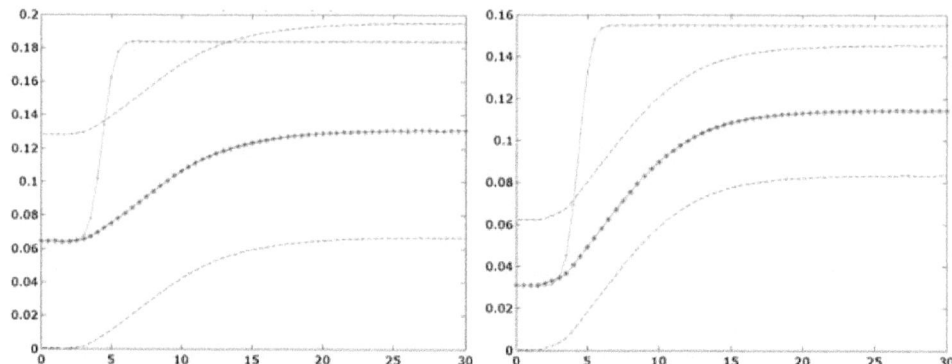

Fig. 3. Normalized CBFV time response (asterisks line) and its standard deviations (dashed line) to a change of EtCO₂ (dotted line). For the nonlinear multivariate model during baseline (left) and response for the nonlinear univariate model for breathing 5% PaCO₂ in air (right).

4   Discussion and Conclusions

When the selection of parameters of the differential equation to estimate them with the SVM is examined, the advantages of a *gray box* model can already be seen, because of the three parameters, the one that can have the largest variation is precisely the baseline of the CVBF*. It is this parameter the one that represents the output of the basic model of the Cerebral Blood Flow Autoregulation phenomenon, when the ABP is the input signal [6,13]. It is also interesting to note that it is the univariate model of the SVM (ABP→CBFV*) the one that achieves the best results, and there are no significant differences with the multivariate model of the SVM (ABP, EtCO2→CBFV*). This can be explained when it is considered that Poulin's equation [8] already considers the contribution of EtCO₂ on the variation of CBFV, so including it in the SVM is redundant.

The average reactivity curves shown in Fig. 3 as well as the calculated reactivity indices coincide with the values of normal subjects like those studied.

The excellent results obtained with the correlation index show that they are significantly better than the *white box* ($r= 0.805$) as well as the *black box* models presented in [10], (nonlinear: $r=0.707$ for baseline and $r=0.909$ for 5% PaCO₂), which were obtained with the same set of data.

The results shown in this *gray box* application with SVM to a problem of cerebral hemodynamic bring up the potential of the method in terms of precision as well as of the valuable contribution that can be obtained from the description of the phenomenon.

In future work it will be important to evaluate the contribution of the SVMs compared to Artificial Neural Networks, and the application to another field of science and engineering.

Acknowledgments. This work was supported by DICYT/USACH Project 061119CP.

References

1. Psichogios, D., Ungar, L.: A Hybrid Neural Networks First Principles Approach to Process Modeling. AIChE J. 38, 1499–1511 (1992)
2. Thompson, M., Kramer, M.: Modeling Chemical Processes Using Prior Knowledge and Neural Networks. AIChE J. 40, 1328–1340 (1994)
3. Anderson, J., McAvoy, T., Hao, O.: Use of Hybrid Models in Wastewater Systems. Ind. Eng. Chem. Res. 39, 94–1704 (2000)
4. Thibault, J., Acuña, G., Pérez-Correa, R., Jorquera, R., Molin, P., Agosin, E.: A hybrid representation approach for modelling complex dynamic bioprocesses. Bioprocess Engineering 22(6), 547–556 (2000)
5. Acuña, G., Cubillos, F., Thibault, J., Latrille, E.: Comparison of Methods for Training Grey- box Neural Models. Computers. Chem. Engng. 23, S561–S564 (1999)
6. Panerai, R.B.: Assesment of cerebral pressure autoregulation in humans - a review of measurement methods. Physiological Measurement 9, 305–338 (1998)
7. Simpson, D., Panerai, R., Evans, D., Garnham, J., Naylor, A., Bell, P.: Estimating normal and pathological flow velocity to step changes in end-tidal PCO2. Medical & Biological Engineering & Computing 38, 535–539 (2000)
8. Poulin, M., Liang, P., Robbins, P.: Dynamics of the cerebral blood flow response to step changes in end-tidal PCO2 and PO2 in humans. Journal of Applied Physiology 81, 1084–1095 (1996)
9. Mitsis, G., Poulin, M., Robbins, P., Marmarelis, V.: Nonlinear modeling of the dynamic effects of arterial pressure and CO2 variations on cerebral blood flow in healthy humans. IEEE Transactions on Biomedical Engineering 51, 1932–1943 (2004)
10. Chacón, M., Araya, C., Panerai, R.B.: Non-linear multivariate modeling of cerebral hemodynamics with autoregressive Support Vector Machines. Medical Engineering & Physics 33(2), 180–187 (2011)
11. Vapnik, V.: The Nature of Statistical Learning Theory. Springer, New York (1995)
12. Schölkopf, B., Smola, A., Williamson, R., Bartlett, P.: New support vector algorithms. Neural Computation 2, 1083–1121 (1998)
13. Tiecks, F., Lam, A., Aaslid, R., Newell, D.: Comparison of static and dynamic cerebral autoregulation measurements. Stroke 26, 1014–1019 (1995)

A New Clustering Algorithm Based on K-Means Using a Line Segment as Prototype

Juan Carlos Rojas Thomas

Universidad de Atacama, Copiapó, Chile
juancarlos.rojas@uda.cl

Abstract. This project shows the development of a new clustering algorithm, based on *k-means*, which faces its problems with clusters of differences variances. This new algorithm uses a line segment as prototype which captures the axis that presents the biggest variance of the cluster. The line segment adjusts iteratively its long and direction as the data are classified. To perform the classification, a border region that determines approximately the limit on the cluster is built based on geometric model, which depends on the central line segment. The data are classified later according to their proximity to the different border regions. The process is repeated until the parameters of the all border regions associated with each cluster remain constant.

Keywords: Clustering, Kmeans, Variance, Central Line Segment, Border Region.

1 Introduction

The process of clustering consists on classifying in an unsupervised way a set of patterns (observations or data) into groups (clusters) [1]. There are many types of clustering algorithms. One of these is the center based algorithms. Compared with the others types of clustering algorithms, the center based algorithms are very efficient with big data bases and with high dimensional data. Usually, these algorithms try to minimize an objective function, which defines how good is the solution obtained [2].

1.1 K-Means

The *k-means* is a clustering algorithm which is considered a center based algorithm. This algorithm tries to find the k partitions that minimize the objective function. The objective function used by this algorithm is the mean square error [3]. This criterion, where m_i corresponds to the mean of the cluster C_i, n to the total number of objects, and k to the total number of clusters, is defined as [4]:

$$E = \frac{1}{n} \sum_{i=1}^{k} \sum_{x \in c_i} \|x - m_i\|^2 \tag{1}$$

In general the *k-means* algorithm performs the classification of the data according to a measure of distance to certain points considered the centers of the clusters in a

C. San Martin and S.-W. Kim (Eds.): CIARP 2011, LNCS 7042, pp. 638–645, 2011.
© Springer-Verlag Berlin Heidelberg 2011

specific space of features. These points, called centroids, are initialized at the beginning of the algorithm, as well as the measure of distance, and the subsequent classification is performed according to proximity to those. Then, after the classification process is completed, the centroids are recalculated as the means of each cluster. Then, the data are reclassified, and the process is repeated until the centroids remain constant [5] [6].

1.2 Advantages and Disadvantages

The advantages of *k-means* are its velocity and its easy application in high dimensional spaces. However it has some disadvantages: the algorithm is applicable only if the mean is defined, the *k* number of clusters has to be estimated, often converges to a local optimum, and the final result depends on the initial values assigned to the centroids [3]. On the other hand, the criterion of the mean square error works well when the clusters are compact clouds well separated. However, when the differences in size of the geometry of the clusters are very big, the use of this criterion could divide the larger clusters [4].

2 Related Works

A lot of works have been made trying to overcome the disadvantages of this algorithm. However, the most of them are focused to resolve the estimation of the parameter *k* (the number of clusters) [7] [8], optimize the convergence speed to the solution [9] [10], the extension of the algorithm to ordinals sets [11], and to determine the initials coordinates of the centroids [12] [13].

Concerning the treatment of clusters of different sizes, the only work founded in the literature is [3]. This algorithm is a modification of *k-means*, whose objective is only to detect clusters with circular shapes.

3 Proposal

The algorithm proposed in this document confronts the limitation of k-means when it is used over clusters of very dissimilar variances, using a line segment as prototype. This new algorithm, as well as the original, can be used in space of high dimensions.

3.1 General Scheme

The inputs that the algorithm receives are the data set, the initial centroids and the number of clusters to detect. Then, the algorithm starts to adjust iteratively the parameters that determine the border regions associated with each cluster and used to capture their variances. This process consists on classifying the data according to their proximity to the different border regions, and then update their parameters. The process is repeated until the parameters of the all border regions associated with each cluster remain constants.

3.2 General Algorithm

```
Input: dataset, number of clusters, initial centroids
Begin
  Repeat
    Classify Data
    Calculate the Parameters of each Border Region
  Until the Parameters of the Regions Associated Remain
  Constant
End
```

3.3 Geometric Model

The geometric model which this algorithm uses is defined by geometrics shapes which border region is made by all points that are equidistant from the same central line segment. This distance is called "radius". Then, the parameters that determine the border region are the direction and length of the central line segment (specified by the coordinates of its extremes) and the radius of the figure. In two dimensions this model generates a rectangle with semicircles in its extremes, in three dimensions generates a cylinder with semispherical caps in its extremes. For simplicity the shape generated will be called "cylinder", independent of the dimensions considered. The figure 1 shows this concept.

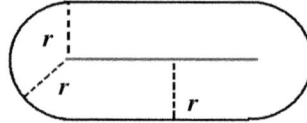

Fig. 1. The figure shows the geometric shape that is built in two dimensions according to the geometric model used by the algorithm. It is possible to note the central segment and the points that localized to a distance r (radius) made the border region.

3.4 Classification

This algorithm performs the classification founded the "cylinders" that best represent the data distribution of the data detected. The parameters that specify a cylinder are the direction and length of the central line segment and its radius. At the beginning of the process the radius are established to zero, and the central axis of each cylinders corresponds to the centroids of the clusters given as initial input to the algorithm, so in the first iteration the classification is performed according to the proximity of the data to the initials centroids. Then, the direction and length of each central line segment associated with the clusters are calculated, with the centroid as the midpoint, and finally the values of the radius of each figure are obtained. Once the values of parameters have been obtained, the data are reclassified. This classification depends on which of the following three situations is each datum, as the figure 2 illustrates:

a)   The datum is not contained inside any cylinder: then the data is assigned to the cluster associated with the nearest cylinder.
b)   The datum is contained inside only one cylinder: then the datum is assigned to the cluster associated with this cylinder.
c)   The datum is contained inside more than one cylinder: then the datum is assigned to the cluster associated with the cylinder whose central segment is the nearest, among the cylinders that contain the datum.

Then, the process to calculate the central segments and radius is repeated, with the subsequence reclassification, until these remain constant.

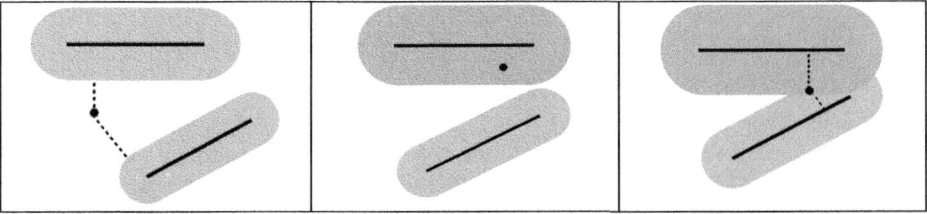

Fig. 2. The images show, from left to right, the situation of a datum extern from two cylinders, with the distances to both marked with dotted lines, the situation of a datum localized inside one cylinder, and the situation of a datum located inside two cylinders that intersects, with the distances to the central segments of both marked with dotted lines.

3.5   Obtaining the Central Line Segment

The generation of the cylinder is based on obtaining a line segment which corresponds to its central axis. It is obtained using the principal component analysis over the data set associated with the cluster, and extracting the vector that represents the component which captures the biggest variance of the data set. Then, a line segment is built, which corresponds to the central axis of the cylinder. This axis is aligned with the direction of the vector just calculated, centered in the centroid of the cluster. The length of this central axis is obtained calculating first the absolute magnitudes of the vectors projections associated to each datum, considering the centroid as the origin, over the line determined by the vector of biggest variance and the centroid. Then, the mean of these values is calculated, and the central axis length is specified, finally, as the double of the mean just calculated. This process is illustrated by the figure 3. Let d_{ij} be the vector associated with the $i\text{-}th$ datum of the cluster j, v_j the principal component with biggest variance of cluster j (assumed with unitary magnitude), n_j the quantity of data of cluster j. Then, the length of central axis of cluster j, l_j, is given by the next formula (the black circle represents the inner product):

$$l_j = 2 * \frac{\sum_{i=1}^{n_j} \left| \vec{d}_{ij} \bullet \vec{v}_j \right|}{n_j} \tag{2}$$

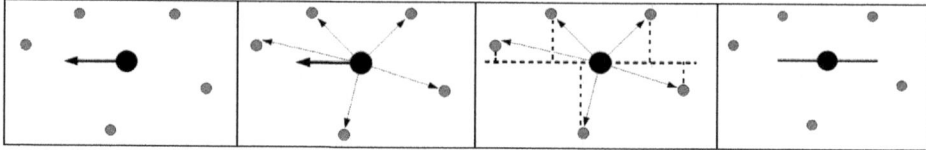

Fig. 3. The images show, from left to right, the generation of the central segment of one cluster (the gray circles correspond to data and the black circle to the centroid). First it is determined the principal component of the biggest variance (black arrow), and then the vectors associated with each datum, their projections over the line, and finally the building of the segment with the centroid as the midpoint.

3.6   The Calculus of the Radio

The radio of a cylinder is obtained calculating the mean of the distances of data to the central segment. Let x_{ij} be the i-th datum of the cluster j, s_j the central segment of the cluster j, $d(x_{ij}, s_j)$ the distance between the i-th datum and the segment of the cluster j, n_j the quantity of data of cluster j. Then, the radio associated with cluster j, r_j, is given by the next formula:

$$r_j = \frac{\sum_{i=1}^{n_j} d\left(x_{ij}, s_j\right)}{n_j} \tag{3}$$

3.7   Distance between a Datum and a Central Segment

This distance is defined as the length of the shortest line segment that connects a datum with some point of the cylinder central segment. To allow the algorithm be extensible to high dimensions the theorem of cosine is used to obtain these distances, to bring the calculation to a two dimensional plane. This procedure consists in generating a triangle whose vertices are the initial and final points of the cylinder central segment, and the datum. Then, the angles of the triangle are calculated using the cosine theorem. If all angles of the triangle are less than 90 degrees, then the distance between the datum and the central segment corresponds to the height of the triangle, which can be easily calculated. If one of the angles is greater than 90, then the distance between the datum and the two extremes points of the cylinder central axis. The lower value corresponds to the distance between the datum and the axis. Both situations are illustrated by the figure 4.

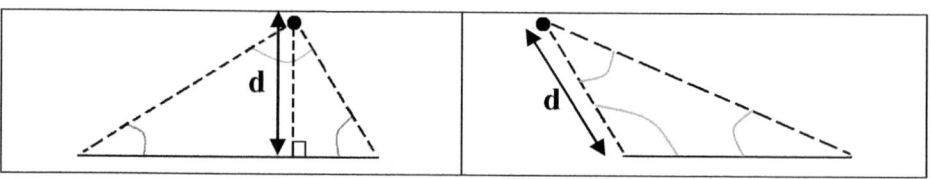

Fig. 4. The images show the two different types of triangulations that can be formed with a datum (black circle) and the line segment (continuous line), and how these are used to obtain the distance between them

3.8 Calculating the Distance between a Datum and a Cylinder

Previous to calculate the distance between a datum and a cylinder, distance between the datum and the cylinder's central segment is calculated. If this distance is less than the cylinder radius, then the datum is considered contained inside the inner space of the cylinder. If this distance is greater than the radius, the datum is considered extern to the cylinder, and then the distance is calculated as the difference between the distance to the central segment just calculated and the cylinder radius. The figure 5 shows this situation. Let x be a datum, v a cylinder, r the cylinder radius, s the cylinder central segment, and d the Euclidian distance, then the distance between a datum and a cylinder is specified as:

$$d(x,v)=d(x,s)-r \tag{4}$$

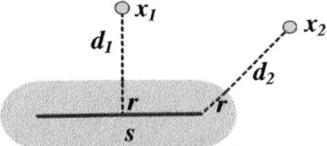

Fig. 5. The figure shows how the distances are obtained from two points (small circles) and a cylinder. The dotted lines which run from each point to the central segment s of the cylinder represent the distances from them to the segment. By subtracting the magnitude of the cylinder radius r the distances from the points to the cylinder border, d_1 and d_2, are obtained.

4 Experimental Results

The performance of the algorithm proposed was compared with the *k-means* in a series of tests. The data were generated artificially with Gaussian distribution. These tests were designed so that, from an initial configuration of clusters with similar variances, it was increasing gradually the ration between the clusters variances along one axis, as the figure 6 illustrates. To evaluate the performance of both algorithm the Rand index was used, which allows to   measure the level of similitude between two partitions, with values ranging from zero (minimal similitude) to one (maximal similitude) [2].

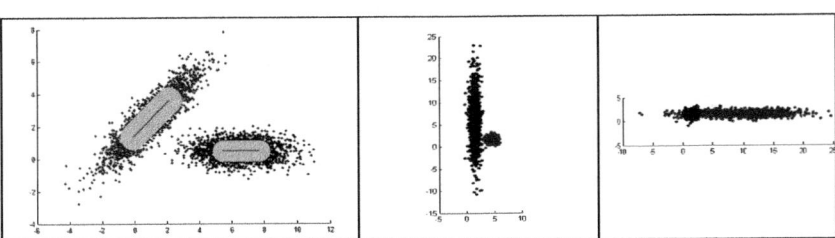

Fig. 6. The image of the left shows, superimposed on two clusters, the cylinders and their central axes after having been applied the algorithm. The next images show the most extremes configurations used in the tests, with a ratio of 1/10 between the variances along y axis (central image) and x axis (right image).

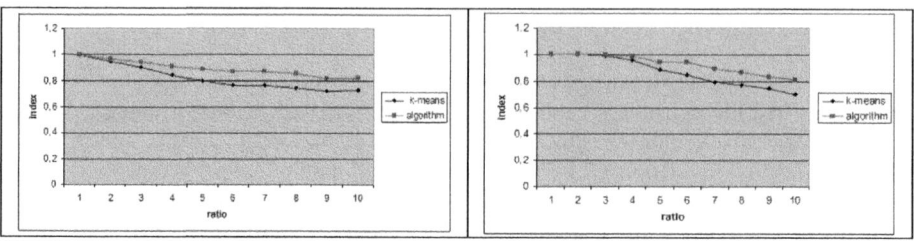

Fig. 7. The graphics illustrate the comparative performance when the ratio between the variances of the two clusters is gradually increased, indicating the values delivered by the Rand index v/s the ratio between variances. The left graphic shows the test series where the ratio is increased along the "y" axis, and the right shows the test series where the ratio is increased along the "x" axis.

The results show that, as the differences between the variances increase, the performance of the algorithm begins to overcome the *k-means*, as the graphics of the figure 7 illustrate.

5   Conclusions and Future Works

The algorithm demonstrated that it improved remarkably the performance of the *k-means* in the situations where the clusters have many different variances. In the situations where the variances are not so different, the performance is similar to *k-means*. However, it is still required a later research, so adding another criteria, or improving the ones that have been used, in the process of building the border region. It is also an option to define other border regions that allow a more accurate capture of the variances.

References

1. Jain, A.K., Murty, M.N., Flynn, O.J.: Data Clustering: a review. ACM Computing Surveys 31(3) (September 1999)
2. Gan, G., Ma, C., Wu, J.: Data Clustering Theory, algorithms and applications. SIAM, Society for Industrial and Applied Mathematics (May 30, 2007)
3. Fahim, M., Saake, G., Salem, A.M., Torkey, F.A., Ramadan, M.A.: K-Means for Spherical Clusters with Large Variance in Sizes. In: Proceedings of World Academy of Science, Engineering and Technology, Paris, vol. 35, pp. 177–182 (November 2008) ISSN 2070-3740
4. Guha, S., Rastogi, R., Shim, K.: CURE: An Efficient Clustering Algorithms for Large Databases. In: Proc. ACM SIGMOD Int. Conf. on Management of Data, Seattle, WA, pp. 73–84 (1998)
5. Bishop, C.M.: Pattern Recognition and Machine Learning. Springer, Heidelberg (2006)
6. Theodoridis, S., Koutroumbas, K.: Pattern Recognition, 3rd edn. (2006)
7. Pham, D.T., Dimov, S.S., Nguyen, C.D.: Selection of k in K-means clustering. Mechanical Engineering Science 219, 103–119 (2004)

8. Pelleg, D., Moore, A.: x-means: Extending k-means with efficient estimation of the number of clusters. In: Proceedings of Seventeenth International Conference on Machine Learning, pp. 727–734. Morgan Kaufmann, San Francisco (2000)
9. Faber, V.: Clustering and the continuous k-means algorithm. Los Alamos Science 22, 138–144 (1994)
10. Phillips, S.: Acceleration of K-means and Related Clustering Algorithms. In: Mount, D.M., Stein, C. (eds.) ALENEX 2002. LNCS, vol. 2409, pp. 166–177. Springer, Heidelberg (2002)
11. Huang, Z.: Extensions to the k-Means Algorithm for Clustering Large Data Sets with Categorical Values. Data Minig and Knowledge Discovery 2(3), 283–304 (1998)
12. Bradley, P.S., Fayyad, U.M.: Refining initial points for k-means clustering. In: Proceedings of the 15th International Conference on Machine Learning, pp. 91–99. Morgan Kaufmann, San Francisco (1998)
13. Deelers, S., Auwatanamongkol, S.: Enhancing K-Means Algorithm with Initial Cluster Centers Derived from Data Partitioning along the Data Axis with the Highest Variance. PWASET 26, 323–328 (2007)

A New Method for Olive Fruits Recognition

C. Gabriel Gatica[1,2], S. Stanley Best[2], José Ceroni[3], and Gaston Lefranc[1]

[1] Pontificia Universidad Católica de Valparaíso, Chile,
Escuela de Ingeniería Eléctrica
gabriel.gatica@hotmail.com, glefranc@gmail.com
[2] Instituto de Investigaciones Agropecuarias,
INIA, PROGAP, Chillán, Chile
sbest@inia.cl
[3] Pontificia Universidad Católica de Valparaíso, Chile,
Escuela de Ingeniería Industrial
jceroni@ucv.cl

Abstract. A model for the recognition of the diameter of olives is presented. The information regarding size of olive fruits is intended for estimating the best harvesting time of olive trees. The recognition is performed by analyzing the RGB images obtained from olive tree pictures

Keywords: image processing, pattern recognition, RGB model, CIELAB color space, olive harvesting.

1 Introduction

One of the important aspects in olive cultivation is being able to estimate when the harvest should take place, trying to obtain the best yielding from the land. Based on this information, it is possible to make the right decisions both financially and agriculturally. The problem of estimating the optimal plantation yield consists on determining the largest fruit size based on its equatorial and polar diameters.

Literature review for the past 30 years shows that there are no publications relating to the count of olives (olive fruit) but only to the identification of olive trees (trees). Most of the publications found in the identification field refer to particular objects. Therefore, we propose to use simultaneously identification and caliber tools to identify the best harvesting time.

Saito et al. [11] used a method of classification of eggplants by using neural networks in the RGB color model and color space CIELAB. The method described by Martinez-Uso et al. [1], uses an algorithm for the minimization of energy for active contours, in order to distinguish the different areas of the fruit, which is the main criterion for image segmentation. This algorithm tends to achieve a similar result to that obtained by clustering.

Unay and Gosselin [2] compare different types of classifiers for the recognition of defective blocks. SVM algorithm achieved the best results, increasing by around 90% of correct classification. Cornelius et al. [4] showed that object

C. San Martin and S.-W. Kim (Eds.): CIARP 2011, LNCS 7042, pp. 646–653, 2011.

recognition can be achieved by correlating the shape and contours of each shape. In many cases, achieved satisfactory results.

Zhao et al. [6] use color and texture properties for the recognition of red and green apples. This analysis proved successful by including the properties of the co-occurrence matrix jointly with the levels of red, performing segmentation using an analysis of "clustering".

Wijethunga et al. [8], proposed a technique for counting kiwis, based on the segmentation of images using the CIELAB color model and the "Watershed" transformation to count the number of fruits in each image. A more simple method was developed by Li et al. [10], proposed the identification of tomatoes using grayscale image, obtaining a 75% of correct classification.

Another technique that refers to the invariability of objects with respect to size and rotation is SIFT (Scale Invariant Feature Transform) used by Wan-Gan et al. [9]. They proposed an algorithm based on this transformation in order to solve the problem of fruit identification. The results were developed into a pilot, as it performed well; using test scenarios.

According to Mirisaee and Woo [17], by taking a greater amount of information with both, physical and color parameters of the RGB color model, a k-NN (k-Nearest Neighbors) based on Euclidean distance, classifier can be obtained for fruit classification. Classification results reached 90% of correct classification. In classification of mature fruits and greens, Jamil et al. [7] used a neuro-fuzzy based classification by taking intensity of the red, green, and blue as a parameter they reached an accuracy level of 73.3% in the classification of ripe and green.

Alternatively, similarly to the study by Unay and Gosselin [2], Wang et al. [5] present a comparison between artificial neural networks (ANN) and Support Vector Machines (SVP) for apple classification. SVP presented a better result in classification apples, yielding almost 90% of correct classification for the apple harvest. In detection and classification of fruits, Mohamad et al. [3] performed a study based on the classification of ripe and green based on the histogram feature of the red, green, and blue, and the gray scale. Previous studies about recognition and classification of fruits has been done by team of this paper [12], [16].

The biggest difference between the objectives of the studies cited and the work presented here, is that most of the reviewed research is concerned primarily with the identification of specific fruits, leaving a large margin of slack when developing classification models. In this paper, we propose a model to characterize olive fruits in the tree and measuring the caliber of each specimen.

2   Background Extraction

From an olive tree picture, histogram analysis is used to verify the possibility of separation of strata and check the data set under analysis for normality. The strata chosen for analysis are: 1) Olive, 2) Leaf type 1 (dark green), 3) Leaf type 2 (light green), and 4) Stem. Fig. 1.a shows the layers corresponding to each stratum with the background turned white for improved perception.

Stratification of the data is improved due to the color reference standard; otherwise, the visual differences between the strata would have been slightly noticeable in the case of leaves and olives. Fig. 1.b shows data sets used in the statistical analysis described next. Top left is olive fruit, top right is leaf type 1, bottom left is leaf type 2, and bottom right is stem. By visual inspection, it could be inferred that in some images there is some overlap of color in the layers, i.e., some olives (or a part of them) have very similar color.

Analyzing the spectral behavior of all 4 layers for the channels red, green, and blue color of RGB model, hue, saturation, value color of model HSV, L, a, b, a/b of CIELAB color space, respectively, it is concluded that the layer segmentation opportunity for olives is more feasible in the matrix $a*$. Fig. 1.c shows the spectrum analysis of channel data to the color space for the four strata (olives, leaves types 1 and 2, and stem). The ideal normal distributions for each stratum were plotted along the empirical curve (thicker line) while keeping the same color for each stratum. Then, a statistical analysis verifies the normality of the data in each stratum because of the data or for each stratum are random variables in the first instance under a normal distribution of data. The probability density function of a normal distributed variable x_k is defined as:

$$\varphi_{\mu_i,\sigma_i{}^2}(x) = \frac{1}{\sigma_i\sqrt{2\pi}}e^{-\frac{1}{2}\left(\frac{x-\mu_i}{\sigma_i}\right)^2} , \tag{1}$$

where:

$\varphi_{\mu_i,\sigma_i{}^2}(x)$: probability density function of the i-th stratum
μ_i : arithmetic mean of the i-th stratum
σ_i : standard deviation of the i-th stratum
x_i : discrete random variable

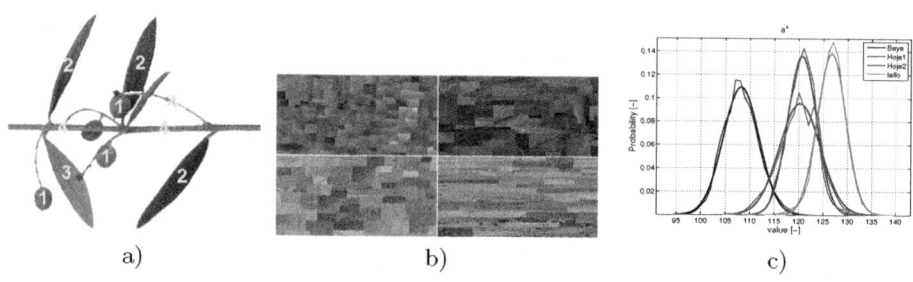

a)   b)   c)

Fig. 1. a) Stratification of the data; b) Set of data used for analysis; c) Spectrum analysis of data

To know the relationship of the data with respect to a normal distribution curve, the random variable is plotted against the probability density curve (normal strata). In this case, the curves obtained have a squared correlation coefficient R^2 between 0.972 and 0.994, therefore they could be considered as excellent correlations. To calculate the amount of accumulated data to each point cut in the normal distribution curves, it is necessary to integrate the probability density function to that point. The distribution function of a normal distribution is:

$$\Phi_{\mu_i,\sigma_i^2}(x_c) = \int_{-\infty}^{x_c} \Phi_{\mu_i,\sigma_i^2}(t)dt = \int_{-\infty}^{x_c} \frac{1}{\sigma_i\sqrt{2\pi}} e^{-\frac{1}{2}\left(\frac{x-\mu_i}{\sigma_i}\right)^2} dt \qquad (2)$$

The main idea of this evaluation is to minimize the amount of probability of occurrence data for the layers leaf type 1 and type two stem leaves, and turn to get as much information as possible for the olives. It is possible to find a good theoretical cutting height, but the data are discrete integer random variables. To resolve this limitation, all distribution functions are evaluated to a closed interval between 112 and 116 to verify their probability of occurrence, Table 1 shows the results.

Table 1. Distribution functions of four strata for closed interval between 112 to 116

Cutoff value		Distribution Function			
x_c	$x_c = f(\mu_1,\sigma 1)$	Olive	Leaf 1	Leaf 2	Stem
112	$\mu_1+1.0441\sigma_1$	85.1771	2.4738	0.1620	0
113	$\mu_1+1.3176\sigma_1$	90.6169	4.2190	0.4604	0
114	$\mu_1+1.5911\sigma_1$	94.4198	6.8484	1.1771	0.0008
115	$\mu_1+1.8645\sigma_1$	96.8873	10.5917	2.7126	0.0030
116	$\mu_1+2.1380\sigma_1$	98.3739	15.6276	5.6462	0.0114

Based on results in Table 1, cutoff value is made equal to 112. This is because layers of leaf type 1, leaf type 2, and stem together do not exceed 3% incidence, while stratum corresponding to olives have an incidence of over 85%, having an average cut equal to the mean plus 1.0441 standard deviations.

In order to represent the ideal olive shape, the Principal Components (PCA) method is used. This means to find the best projection that represents our goal (ready to harvest olives) by statistical representation of least squares. The core of this method is to find the eigenvectors or fundamental components of the data sets that shape all possible combinations of olives.

3   The Model

Our proposed solution consists in creating three matrices R_{eigen}, G_{eigen}, and B_{eigen} respectively, which contain the underlying factors described or as close to it as possible, the data of the stratum or random variables for olives. Having obtained the fundamental matrices linearly independent, theoretically, it is possible to build any olive on the basis of the linear combination of underlying factors represented in the fundamental matrices previously described.

A way to obtain these vectors is by using of PCA method, this method basically find a set of uncorrelated variables to describe the set of observations. In our case, we took a combination of those uncorrelated variables to generate one

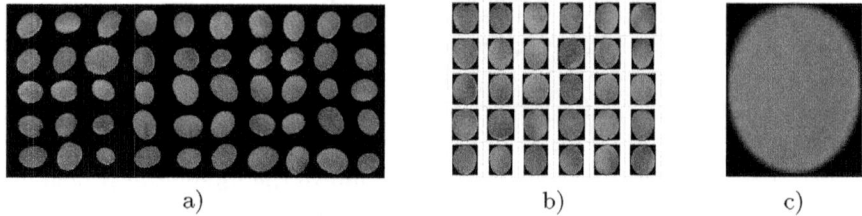

Fig. 2. a) Selected data for analysis; b) Sample of 30 specimens; c) Eigen-image

eigen matrix for each RGB channel. To apply this method, it is necessary to have a data set collected as indicated next. In order to achieve representativeness and also to include variability, samples of various sizes, colors, brightness, contrast, and a number of 50 replications of the random data sets.

Fig. 2.a shows the data set chosen for analysis of principal components. Because olives are of different sizes and their pictures captured at different angles of inclination, a routine to find its rotation angle with respect to a reference point considering the polar and equatorial diameters of the olives was devised. Once found these angles, the median longitudinal, and equatorial diameters, data normalization was applied. Note that the computation of median (or 50 percentile of the data) is independent of presence of extreme data (Fig. 2.b).

After analyzing the 50 standardized samples, for simplicity the eigenvectors were restricted to one dimension for channel, and then this restriction proceeded to merge these three matrices themselves in one of three layers red, green, and blue. Fig. 2.c shows the eigen-image obtained with the PCA analysis.

The cross-correlation index can be used for identifying patterns or correlation between two datasets. An advantage of this index is its utilization with discrete values as well as with continuous functions. It is known that within the CIELAB color space segments of the olives, leaves, and stem are markedly distinct and well defined, as well as with the eigen-image obtained after the PCA process. These two sets of data can also be correlated. The cross-correlation can quickly find sites that correlate better. Figure 3 shows the cross-correlation results.

Regarding olive counting, the need to estimate olives size makes the process not yet complete (contour estimation). Estimation can be achieved by using centroids of figures with greater correlation to the olive's shape, however the

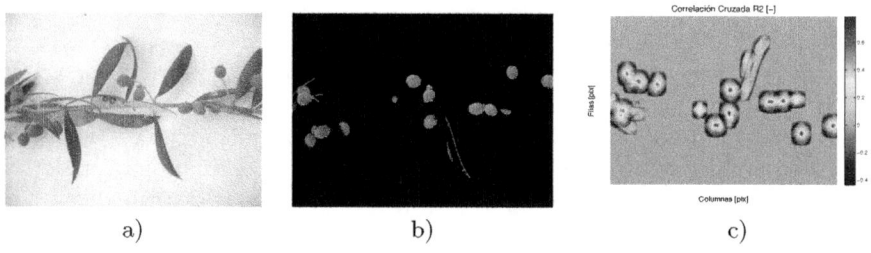

Fig. 3. a) Cross-correlation test; b) filter LAB color space; c) Cross correlation

olive shapes are variable and not complete. Problems arise when there are: two or more overlapped olives. The solution proposed to this problem is an iterative expansion of the object, starting from the centroid to a boundary that minimizes the energy function. Then, splitting separates contiguous specimens by Euclidean distance transformations, for eliminating possible random seams.

By minimizing the Euclidean distance between the candidate's contours, it is possible to reformulate the problem due to boundary estimation assuming presence of active rather than passive or constant contours (Active Contours Chan-Vese method). This last consideration makes possible to vary the image and also allows us to calculate the gradient. The importance of the gradient is critical because it is a normal vector to the surface under study. The gradient gives a significant value where changes or variations occur, which in consequence is very helpful to finding the contours.

On the other hand, the centroids of the potential candidates were identified by the cross-correlation function. However, the problem is the extent to which adjacent olives overlap among them. According to Stokes theorem [15], it can be assumed that the closed integral, limiting the area of the vector field generated by the gradient, equals the surface integral of the curl of the vector field on an open surface. The value of this integral corresponds to the dot product of the vector field with respect to a differential arc length.

The solution proposed by Chan and Vese [13], is to minimize the energy function required to form a region. This solution was described for solving the Mumford-Shah paradigm [14] [15], resulting in an active solution that iteratively finds the point when the energy function phi is zero. It is the same for both regions, as described also by the Continuity theorem. The energy formula is defined by equation (3), where the terms corresponds to the calculated surface energy a and b, respectively.

$$\phi = \int_{\Omega_a} \left(\hat{I} - \overline{X_a} \right)^2 dA + \int_{\Omega_b} \left(\hat{I} - \overline{X_b} \right)^2 dA \qquad (3)$$

Figure Fig. 4.a show the mask generated using the contour search algorithm. One aspect to be emphasized is the starting point of the process of energy minimization. The initial mask of active contours is nothing more than the centroids obtained by the correlation (Fig. 4.b). Note that if iterations tend to infinity or a very large number, it only would slow the overall process, and it also may be incurred in returning to the image with the adjacent samples.

The propused method was programed on MatLab R2007b and our test images (5.0 MPix each) were taken from test-olive-fields in Chile, performing very well with noisy pictures. About the computational complexity of the model, we run at an AMD Athlon(tm)X2 DualCore QL-66, 2.20GHz, 2,74 GB RAM that took just 83.3368 sec each in a batch process. Moreover, dividing the model in three parts: segmentation, correlation and active contourns process they take 8.932%, 3.088 and 87.980% of the average time respectivebly.

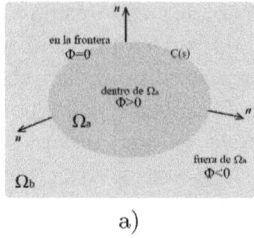
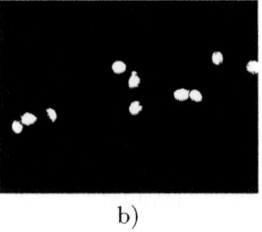

a)   b)

Fig. 4. a) Chan-Vese Diagram; b) Result of active contours after 80 iterations

4   Conclusions

A model for the recognition of the diameter of olives has been presented. This
allows estimating the best harvesting time for an olive tree. Recognition is performed by analyzing the RGB images obtained from olive tree pictures. By reviewing the related literature, all techniques used by many authors from around
the world in the field were summarized. Review of past 30 years of publications
show that there were no publications relating to the count of olives (olive fruits),
only relating to the identification of olive trees (trees).

The proposed model allows not only to identify correctly the olives but also
to measure millimeter caliber of each specimen. The idea of stratified data was
used to investigate the possibility of utilizing stratification as the fundamental
premise to identify that the CIELAB color space, specifically in the channel "a",
could visually identify the possibility of a separation of layers and display a clear
trend data normally.

Validation of data normality was performed by conducting a simple test of
normality based on quadratic correlation between random variables and idealized
normal density curves data, with excellent correlation of 0.9860. Since the data
is discrete and in set Z, height of cut for the separation of strata is analyzed
in terms of the distribution function, leaving the average height of cut 1.0441
standard deviations over the layer of olives. This theoretically ensures that the
non-olive strata ought not to exceed 3% of incidence and an 85% for the layer
of olives, leaving a random error of less than 3%.

The success achieved in contour estimation was due largely to the proper
choice of the number of iterations of the energy minimization algorithm. This
selection was made empirically, concluding that for a great number of iterations the algorithm tends to re-assemble the contiguous contours, while for less
iteration, the algorithm tends to underestimate the area of the olives.

References

1. Martinez-Uso, A., Pla, F., Garcia-Sevilla, P.: A Novel Energy Minimization Criterion for Color Image Segmentation. In: 17th Int. Conference on Pattern Recognition
(ICPR 2004), vol. 3, pp. 206–209 (2004)

2. Unay, D., Gosselin, B.: Artificial Neural Network-Based Segmentation And Apple Grading By Machine Vision. In: IEEE Int. Conference on Image Processing (ICIP 2005), vol. II-630-3 (2005)
3. Mohamad, F.S., Manaf, A.A., Chuprat, S.: Histogram Matching For Color Detection A Preliminary Study. In: Int. Symposium in Information Technology (ITSim), Kuala Lumpur, pp. 1679–1684 (2010)
4. Cornelius, H., Kragic, D., Eklundh, J.: Object and Pose Recognition Using Contour and Shape Information. In: Proc. 12th Int. Conference on Advanced Robotics (ICAR 2005), Seatle, WA, pp. 613–620 (2005)
5. Jin-jing, W., De-an, Z., Wei, J., Jun-jun, T., Ying, Z.: Application of Support Vector Machine to Apple Recognition using in Apple Harvesting Robot. In: IEEE Int. Conference on Information and Automation (ICIA 2009), Zuhuhai, Macau, pp. 1110–1115 (2009)
6. Zhao, J., Tow, J., Katupitiya, J.: On-tree Fruit Recognition Using Texture Properties and Color Data. In: IEEE/RSJ Int. Conference on Intelligent Robots and Systems (IROS 2005), pp. 263–268 (2005)
7. Jamil, N., Mohamed, A., Abdullah, S.: Automated Grading of Palm Oil Fresh Fruit Bunches (FFB) using Neuro-Fuzzy Technique. In: Int. Conference of Soft Computing and Pattern Recognition (SOCPAR 2009), Malaca, pp. 245–249 (2009)
8. Wijethunga, P., Samarasinghe, S., Kulasiri, D., Woodhead, I.: Digital Image Analysis Based Automated Kiwifruit Counting Technique. In: 23rd Int. Conference Image and Vision Computing New Zealand (IVCNZ 2008), Christchurch, pp. 1–6 (2008)
9. Song, W.-g., Guo, H.-x., Wang, Y.: A Method of Fruits Recognition Based on SIFT Characteristics Matching. In: Int. Conference on Artificial Intelligence and Computational Intelligence (AICI 2009), Shanghai, pp. 119–122 (2009)
10. Yinqing, L., Xiaodong, Z., Xiaojie, W.: Fruit Discrimination on Region Feature. In: Fifth International Conference on Fuzzy Systems and Knowledge Discovery (FSKD 2008), Shandong, pp. 590–594 (2008)
11. Saito, Y., Hatanaka, T., Uosaki, K., Shigeto, K.: Eggplant Classification Using Artificial Neural Network. In: Proc. of the International Joint Conference on Neural Networks, vol. 2, pp. 1013–1018 (2003)
12. Gatica, G.: A novel method for detection and counting of flower initiation in pear trees by hyperspectral and digital image analysis. Report at KU Leuven, Biosystems department, Belgium (2010)
13. Chan, T., Vese, L.: Active Contours Without Edges. IEEE Transactions on Image Processing 10(2) (2001)
14. Mumford, D., Shah, J.: Optimal approximations by piecewise smooth functions and associated variational problems. Comm. Pure Appl. Math. 42(5), 577–685 (1989)
15. Chan, T., Esedoglu, S.: A Multiscale Algorithm for Mumford-Shah Image Segmentation, Mathematics Department, UCLA (December 17, 2003)
16. Mery, M., Lefranc, G.: Computer Vision for Fruits Classification by Color and Size (in spanish). In: XVIII Congreso de la Asociación Chilena de Control Automático, Chile (December 2008)
17. Seng, W.C., Mirisaee, S.H.: A New Method for Fruits Recognition System. In: International Conference on Electrical Engineering and Informatics (ICEEI 2009), Selangor, vol. 1, pp. 130–134 (2009)

Wavelet Autoregressive Model for Monthly Sardines Catches Forecasting Off Central Southern Chile

Nibaldo Rodriguez, Jose Rubio, and Eleuterio Yañez

Pontificia Universidad Católica de Valparaíso, Chile
nibaldo.rodriguez@ucv.cl

Abstract. In this paper, we use multi-scale stationary wavelet decomposition technique combined with a linear autoregressive model for one-month-ahead monthly sardine catches forecasting off central southern Chile.The monthly sardine catches data were collected from the database of the National Marine Fisheries Service for the period between 1 January 1964 and 30 December 2008. The proposed forecasting strategy is to decompose the raw sardine catches data set into trend component and residual component by using multi-scale stationary wavelet transform. In wavelet domain, both the trend component and the residual component are independently predicted using a linear autoregressive model. Hence, proposed forecaster is the co-addition of two predicted components. We find that the proposed forecasting method achieves a 99% of the explained variance with a reduced parsimonious and high accuracy.

Keywords: forecasting, wavelet decomposition, autoregression.

1 Introduction

Common sardine is an important fish resource for industrial in the central southern area off Chile. In order to develop sustainable exploitation policies, forecasting the stock and catches of sardines in Chile is one of the main goals of the fishery industry and the government. However, fluctuations in the environmental variables complicate this task. To the best of our knowledge, few publications exist on forecasting models for pelagic species. In recent years, linear regression models [1,2] and artificial neuronal networks (ANN) [3,4] have been proposed for forecasting models. The disadvantage of models based on linear regressions is the supposition of stationarity and linearity of the time series of pelagic species catches. Although ANN allow modeling the non-linear behavior of a time series, they also have some disadvantages such as slow convergence speed and the stagnancy of local minima due to the steepest descent learning method. To improve the convergence speed and forecasting precision of anchovy catches off northern Chile, Gutierrez [3] proposed a hybrid model based on a multilayer perceptron (MLP) combined with an autoregressive integrated moving average model. The architecture of the MLP consists of an input layer with 6 nodes, two hidden layers

C. San Martin and S.-W. Kim (Eds.): CIARP 2011, LNCS 7042, pp. 654–663, 2011.
© Springer-Verlag Berlin Heidelberg 2011

of 15 nodes each, and an output layer with one node; the Levenberg Maquardt (LM) method was used as the learning method. This forecaster obtained a coefficient of determination R^2 of 82%, which improved slightly when combining the MLP model with the ARIMA model, reaching an R^2 of 87%. One of the disadvantages of this hybrid model is its high parsimony (230 parameters) and low forecasting precision. In this paper, the proposed forecasting model is based on multi-scale wavelet decomposition combined with autoregressive models. The multi-scale wavelet decomposition technique was selected due to its popularity in hydrological [5,6], electricity market [7], financial market [8] and smoothing methods [9,10,11]. This wavelet technique is based on the discreet wavelet transform (DWT) or the stationary wavelet transform (SWT) [12]. The advantage of these wavelet transforms in non-stationary time series analysis is their capacity to separate low frequency (LF) from high frequency (HF) components. Whereas the LF component reveals long-term trends, the HF component describes short-term fluctuations in the time series. Being able to separate these components is a key advantage in proposed forecasting strategies since the behavior of each frequency component is more regular than the raw time series.

Therefore, an one-month-ahead monthly sardines catches forecasting scheme is proposed. The forecasting strategy is to decompose the raw sardine catches data set into trend component and residual component by using multi-scale stationary wavelet transform (SWT). In wavelet domain, both the trend component and residual component are independently predicted using a linear autoregressive model.

This paper is organized as follows. In the next section, we briefly describe the multi-scale stationary wavelet transform and the proposed multi-scale wavelet autoregressive forecasting model. The simulation results and performance evaluation are presented in Section 3 followed by conclusions in Section 4.

2   Proposed Forecasting Model

This section presents the proposed forecasting model for one-month-ahead sardines catches off central-southern Chile. Moreover, instead of using the raw data set of past observations to predict the future value $x(n+1)$, we use its wavelet coefficients.

2.1   Stationary Wavelet Decomposition

A signal $x(n)$ can be represented at multiple resolutions by decomposing the signal on a family of wavelets and scaling functions [9,10,11]. The approximation (scaled) signals are computed by projecting the original signal on a set of orthogonal scaling functions of the form:

$$\phi_{jk}(t) = \sqrt{2^{-j}}\phi(2^{-j}t - k) \tag{1}$$

or equivalently by filtering the signal using a low pass filter of length r, $h = [h_1, h_2, ..., h_r]$, derived from the scaling functions. On the other hand, the detail signals are computed by projecting the signal on a set of wavelet basis functions of the form

$$\psi_{jk}(t) = \sqrt{2^{-j}}\psi(2^{-j}t - k) \tag{2}$$

or equivalently by filtering the signal using a high pass filter of length r, $g = [g_1, g_2, ..., g_r]$, derived from the wavelet basis functions. Finally, repeating the decomposing process on any scale J, the original signal can be represented as the sum of all detail coefficients and the last approximation coefficient.

In time series analysis, discrete wavelet transform (DWT) often suffers from a lack of translation invariance. This problem can be tackled by means of the un-decimated stationary wavelet transform (SWT). The SWT is similar to the DWT in that the high-pass and low-pass filters are applied to the input signal at each level, but the output signal is never decimated. Instead, the filters are up-sampled at each level.

Consider the following discrete signal $x(n)$ of length N where $N = 2^J$ for some integer J. At the first level of SWT, the input signal $x(n)$ is convolved with the $h_1(n)$ filter to obtain the approximation coefficients $a_1(n)$ and with the $g_1(n)$ filter to obtain the detail coefficients $d_1(n)$, so that:

$$a_1(n) = \sum_k h_1(n - k)x(k) \tag{3a}$$

$$d_1(n) = \sum_k g_1(n - k)x(k) \tag{3b}$$

because no sub-sampling is performed, $a_1(n)$ and $d_1(n)$ are of length N instead of $N/2$ as in the DWT case. At the next level of the SWT, $a_1(n)$ is split into two parts by using the same scheme, but with modified filters h_2 and g_2 obtained by dyadically up-sampling h_1 and g_1.

The general process of the SWT is continued recursively for $j = 1, ..., J$ and is given as:

$$a_{j+1}(n) = \sum_k h_{j+1}(n - k)a_j(k) \tag{4a}$$

$$d_{j+1}(n) = \sum_k g_{j+1}(n - k)a_j(k) \tag{4b}$$

where h_{j+1} and g_{j+1} are obtained by the up-sampling operator inserts a zero between every adjacent pair of elements of h_j and g_j; respectively.

Therefore, the output of the SWT is then the approximation coefficients a_J and the detail coefficients $d_1, d_2, ..., d_J$, whereas the original signal $x(n)$ is represented as a superposition of the form:

$$x(n) = a_J(n) + \sum_{j=1}^{J} d_j(n) \tag{5}$$

The wavelet decomposition method is fully defined by the choice of a pair of low and high pass filters and the number of decomposition steps J. Hence, in this study we choose a pair of haar wavelet filters [12]:

$$h = \left[\frac{1}{\sqrt{2}} \quad \frac{1}{\sqrt{2}}\right] \tag{6a}$$

$$g = \left[\frac{-1}{\sqrt{2}} \quad \frac{1}{\sqrt{2}}\right] \tag{6b}$$

On the other hand, a key issue for the success of any wavelet forecasting model is suitable selection of the J level decomposition. At higher J, the variability of a large number of predicted data is lower, so their prediction is easier and accurate. In our proposed model, we determine the value of J using a stopping criterion that is given as:

$$\rho = \frac{Pd_j}{P_x} < \epsilon \tag{7}$$

where Pd_j and P_x represents the average power of the detail component $d_j(n)$ and the original data $x(n)$, respectively.

We stop the decomposition on the level for which the ρ ratio is substantially less than a threshold ϵ. The choice of the value of ϵ is not clear from a physical point of view and different sets of approximation coefficients will be produced by the wavelet decomposition method for different values of ϵ. In order to obtain accurate and parsimonious forecasting results, the value of ϵ was set to 0.0 in this work.

Finally, wavelet scales are such that times are separated by multiples of $2^j, j = 1, ..., J$. Our data set involves monthly observations so that the wavelet scales are such that scale 1 is associated with $1 - 2$ month dynamics, scale 2 with $2 - 4$ month dynamics, scale 3 with $4 - 8$ month dynamics, scale 4 with $8 - 16$ month dynamics, and so on.

2.2   Wavelet Autoregressive Model

In order to predict the future signal $x(n+1)$, we can separate the original signal $x(n)$ into two components. The first component presents the trend $t(n)$ of the series and is characterized by slow dynamics, whereas the second component presents the residue $r(n)$ of the series and is characterized by fast dynamics. Therefore, our forecasting model will be the co-addition of two predicted values given as:

$$x(n + 1) = t(n + 1) + r(n + 1) \tag{8}$$

On the one hand, the residual component is estimated using a linear autoregressive (AR) model given as:

$$r(n+1) = \sum_{j=1}^{J} \sum_{i=1}^{m} \alpha_{ji} d_j [n-i+1] \tag{9a}$$

where the J value denotes the level of stationary wavelet decomposition and the m value represents the autoregressive order of the detail coefficients.

On the other hand, the trend component is estimated using a linear AR model given as:

$$t(n+1) = \sum_{i=1}^{m} \beta_i a_J [n-i+1] \tag{10}$$

We propose estimating the linear parameters $\theta = \{\alpha_i, \beta_i\}$ using the least squares method based on the Moore-Penrose pseudo-inverse. If we suppose a set of N_s training input-output samples, then we can perform N_s equations of the form of (9) and (10) as follows:

$$\Re = \alpha \Phi \tag{11a}$$
$$\Gamma = \beta \Psi \tag{11b}$$

where

$$\Phi = [d_1(n), \cdots, d_1(n-m+1), \cdots, d_J(n-m+1)] \tag{12a}$$
$$\Psi = [a_J(n), a_J(n-1), \cdots, a_J(n-m+1)] \tag{12b}$$

The optimal values of the linear parameters α_i and β_i are obtained using the following residual sum of squares (RSS) function defined as:

$$RSS(\alpha) = \sum_{n=1}^{N_s} \left[R(n+1) - r(n+1) \right]^2 \tag{13a}$$

$$R(n+1) = x(n+1) - a_J(n+1) \tag{13b}$$

$$RSS(\beta) = \sum_{n=1}^{N_s} \left[a_J(n+1) - t(n+1) \right]^2 \tag{13c}$$

The result of minimizing the RSS objective function is:

$$\alpha = (\Phi^T \Phi)^\dagger \Phi^T \Re \tag{14a}$$
$$\beta = (\Psi^T \Psi)^\dagger \Psi^T \Gamma \tag{14b}$$

where $(\cdot)^\dagger$ denotes the Moore-Penrose pseudo-inverse [13].

Once we have decided upon a forecasting structure to use, the next task is to determine the autoregressive order on the different scales. This can be done using the criterion given by the ration of the mean absolute deviation to the mean of the time series (MADM) versus lagged values of the predictor variables, where the MADM value is defined as [14]:

$$MADM = \frac{\sum_{i=1}^{N_s} |A_i - F_i|}{\bar{A}} \tag{15}$$

where A_i is the actual value at time i , F_i is the forecasted value at time i, $\bar{A}$ is the mean value of observed monthly catches, and N_s is the number of samples.

3   Experiments and Results

In this section, we apply the proposed strategy for 1-month-ahead forecasting of the monthly catches of sardines. The data set used corresponded to sardine landings off central southern area Chile. These samples were collected monthly from 1 January 1964 to 30 December 2008 by the National Fishery Service of Chile (www.sernapesca.cl).

The proposed linear wavelet autoregressive (WAR) forecasting model basically involves three stages. In the first stage, the original data set is decomposed into different wavelet scales by using stopping criterion given in (7) to separate both the trend component (approximation component) and the residual component (difference between original data and trend component). In the second stage, the trend component and residual component are independently forecasted by using an linear autoregressive model. In the third stage, the next sample is predicted by the co-addition of two predicted components.

The raw sardines data set have been normalized to the range from 0 to 1 by simply dividing the real value by the maximum of the appropriate set. On the other hand, the original data set was also divided into two subsets as shown in Fig.1. In the first subset, the data from 1 January 1964 to 30 December 2003 were chosen for the training phase ($N_s = 480$ months), whereas the remaining data

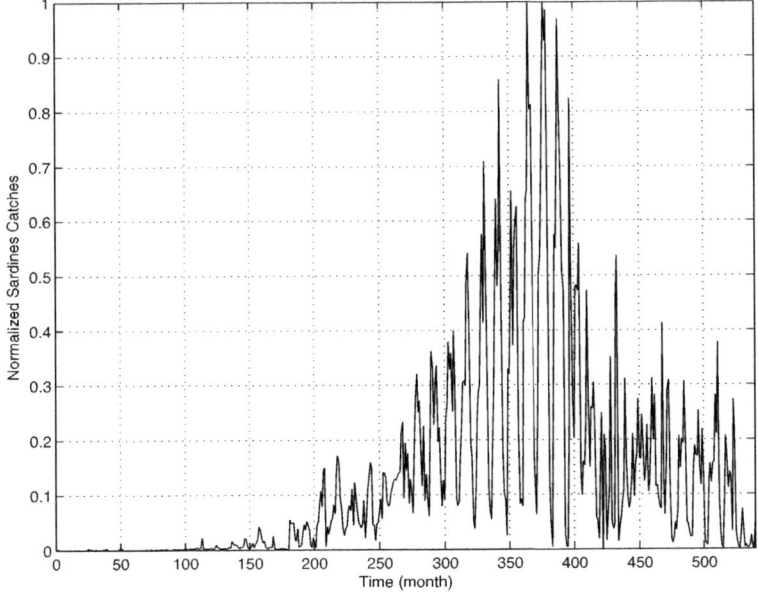

Fig. 1. Observed monthly sardine catches data from 1964 to 2008

were used for the validation phase. This normalized data set, when subjected to the stopping criterion (7), yielded a 5 level wavelet decomposition. The low frequency component a_5 represents the trend of the observed sardines catches data set. On the other hand, detail components $\{d_1, d_2, d_3, d_4, d_5\}$ contain high frequency components of the original data such that d_1 the highest frequency component and d_1 is considered to be more related to the noisy part of the observed data, whereas d_5 contains lower frequency information than $\{d_4, d_3, d_2\}$.

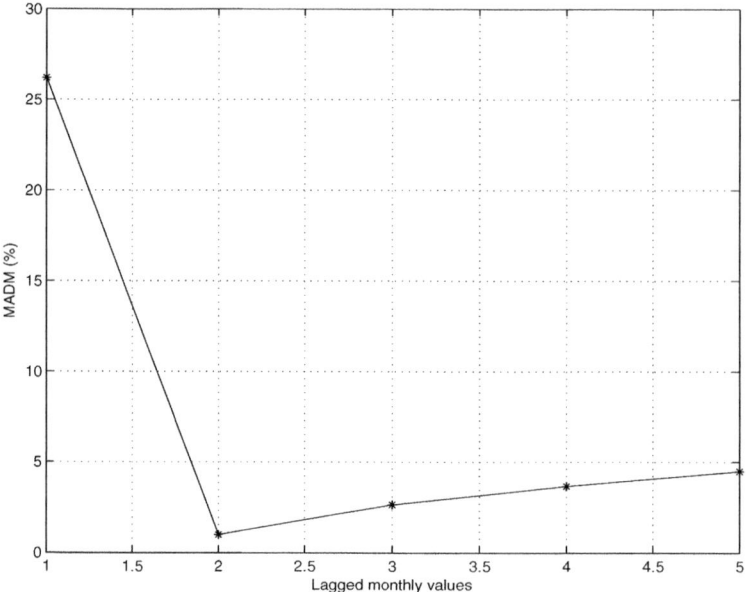

Fig. 2. Model order selection criteria

Hence, residual component forecasting is based on a linear AR model, whereas predicting the trend component also is done with a linear AR model. Once we chose the multi-scale autoregressive forecasting structure to use, the next task was to determine the autoregressive order by using the method given in (14) and (15). After we applied the least squares method and the MADM, we decided to use two lagged values on each level wavelet decomposition due to the parsimony principle and precision of the proposed WAR(J,m) model with $J = 5$ and $m = 2$ as shown in Fig.2. In this study, two criteria of forecasting accuracy were used to evaluate the forecasting capabilities of the WAR model. The first measurement is the coefficient determination (R^2) given as:

$$R^2 = 1 - \frac{\sum_{i=1}^{N_s}(A_i - F_i)^2}{\sum_{i=1}^{N_s}(A_i - \bar{A})^2} \tag{16}$$

where A_i is the actual value at time i, F_i is the forecasted value at time i, $\bar{A}$ is the mean value of observed monthly catches, and N_s is the number of forecasts.

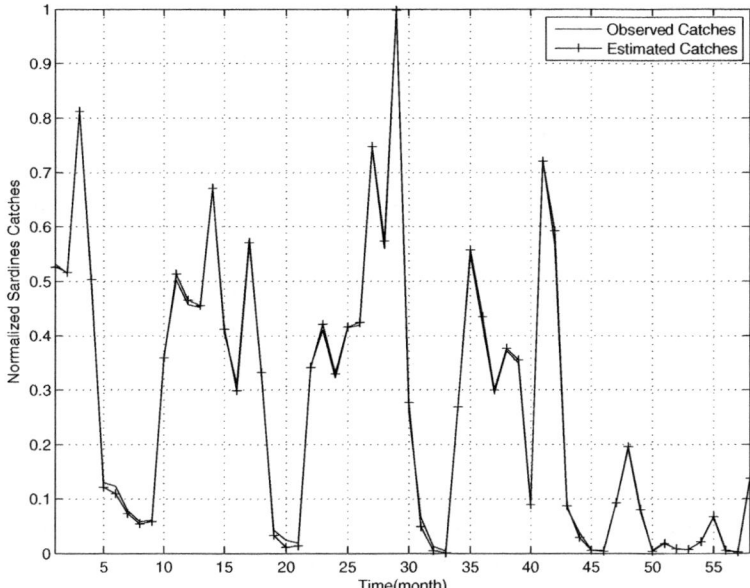

Fig. 3. Observed sardine catches vs estimated sardine catches from 2004 to 2008

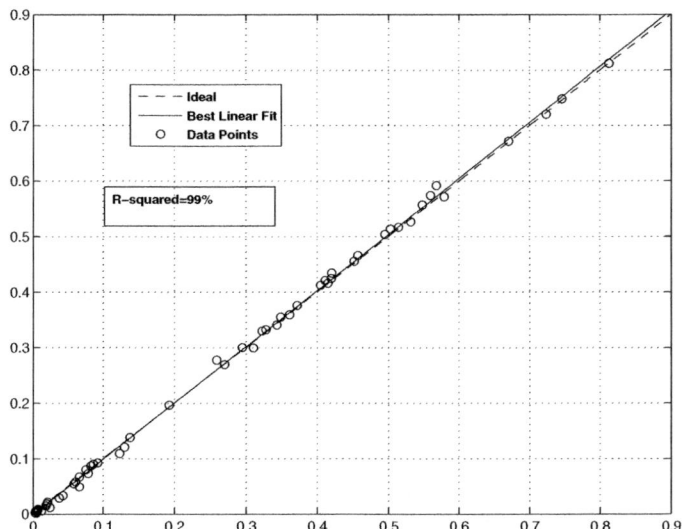

Fig. 4. Scatter for estimates monthly sardines catches

If R-square is large, then the model is good. Conversely, if R-square is small, then the model is bad.

The second criterion is the mean absolute percentage error (MAPE) given as:

$$MAPE(\%) = \frac{1}{N_s} \sum_{i=1}^{N_s} \left| \frac{A_i - F_i}{F_i} \right| \times 100 \qquad (17)$$

Figures 3 and 4 show the results obtained with the best WAR(5,2) forecasting model during the testing phase. Fig. 3 provides data on observed monthly sardine catches versus forecasted catches; this forecasting behavior is very accurate for testing data with a MAPE below 9.4%. Fig. 4 shows the regression between observed and estimated monthly sardine catches. The good fit of the data to line 1 : 1 and 99% of the explained variance can be seen in Fig.4. This level of explained variance was achieved due to use of multi-scale stationary wavelet decomposition.

4   Conclusions

In this paper was proposed a one-month-ahead monthly sardine catches forecasting strategy to improve prediction accuracy. The reason of the improvement in forecasting accuracy was due to use stationary haar wavelet decomposition to separate both the trend and residual components of the raw time series, since the behavior of each component is more smoothing than raw data set. It was show that the proposed forecaster achieves a MAPE value of 9.4% and a R-squared of 99%. Besides, proposed forecasting results showed that the 32 previous months contain valuable information to explicate a highest variance level for sardines catches forecasting. These months can be related with ocean-atmospheric aspects, which have a great influence on pelagic fish fisheries in Chile. Finally, wavelet-autoregressive forecasting strategy can be suitable as a very promising methodology to any other pelagic specie.

References

1. Stergiou, K.I.: Prediction of the Mullidae fishery in the easterm Mediterranean 24 months in advance. Fish. Res. 9, 67–74 (1996)
2. Stergiou, K.I., Christou, E.D.: Modelling and forecasting annual fisheries catches: comparison of regression, univariate and multivariate time series methods. Fish. Res. 25, 105–138 (1996)
3. Gutierrez, J.C., Silva, C., Yaez, E., Rodriguez, N., Pulido, I.: Monthly catch forecasting of anchovy engraulis ringens in the north area of Chile: Nonlinear univariate approach. Fisheries Research 86, 188–200 (2007)
4. Garcia, S.P., DeLancey, L.B., Almeida, J.S., Chapman, R.W.: Ecoforecasting in real time for commercial fisheries:the Atlantic white shrimp as a case study. Marine Biology 152, 15–24 (2007)
5. Adamowski, J.F.: Development of a short-term river flood forecasting method for snowmelt driven floods based on wavelet and cross-wavelet analysis. Journal of Hydrology 353(3-4), 247–266 (2008)

6. Kisi, O.: Stream flow forecasting using neuro-wavelet technique. Hydrological Processes 22(20), 4142–4152 (2008)
7. Amjady, N., Keyniaa, F.: Day ahead price forecasting of electricity markets by a mixed data model and hybrid forecast method. International Journal of Electrical Power Energy Systems 30, 533–546 (2008)
8. Bai-Ling, Z., Richard, C., Marwan, A.J., Dominik, D., Barry, F.: Multiresolution Forecasting for Futures Trading Using Wavelet Decompositions. IEEE Trans. on Neural Networks 12(4) (2001)
9. Coifman, R.R., Donoho, D.L.: Translation-invariant denoising, Wavelets and Statistics. Springer Lecture Notes in Statistics, vol. 103, pp. 125–150. Springer, Heidelberg (1995)
10. Nason, G., Silverman, B.: The stationary wavelet transform and some statistical applications, Wavelets and Statistics. Springer Lecture Notes in Statistics, vol. 103, pp. 281–300. Springer, Heidelberg (1995)
11. Pesquet, J.-C., Krim, H., Carfantan, H.: Time-invariant orthonormal wavelet representations. IEEE Trans. on Signal Processing 44(8), 1964–1970 (1996)
12. Percival, D.B., Walden, A.T.: Wavelet Methods for Time Series Analysis. Cambridge University Press, Cambridge (2000)
13. Serre, D.: Matrices: Theory and applications. Springer, New York (2002)
14. Kolassa, S., W, S.: Advantages of the mad/mean ratio over the mape. The International Journal of Applied Forecasting (6), 40–43 (2007)

A Multi-level Thresholding-Based Method to Learn Fuzzy Membership Functions from Data Warehouse

Dario Rojas[1], Carolina Zambrano[1], Marcela Varas[2], and Angelica Urrutia[3]

[1] Depto. de Ingeniería Informática y Ciencias de la Computación,
Universidad de Atacama, Copiapó, Chile
{dario.rojas,carolina.zambrano}@uda.cl
[2] Depto. de Ingeniería Informática y Ciencias de la Computación,
Universidad de Concepción, Concepción, Chile
mvaras@udec.cl
[3] Depto. de Computación e Informática. Universidad Católica del Maule,
Talca, Chile
aurrutia@spock.ucm.cl

Abstract. Learn fuzzy membership functions automatically for characterization and operation of fuzzy measures in Data Warehouse is a problem of recent concern. This paper presents a new method to learn membership functions of linguistic labels of fuzzy measures from Data Warehouse. We proposed a multilevel thresholding based method with clustering validation indices in order to obtain optimal number of labels and parameters of membership functions. Validation is performed by comparing the proposal against a supervised learning approach based on clustering and genetic algorithms, including the application in response to queries in a Data Warehouse with fuzzy measures.

Keywords: Fuzzy Logic, Data Warehouse, Multi-Level Thresholding, Clustering, Clustering Validation Indices.

1 Introduction

Most events are vague or uncertain, ie, they imply on its characteristics a certain degree of imprecision (*fuzzyness*). This imprecision may be associated with any type of data as shape, position, time, color, texture, or even the semantics to describe what they are. In many cases, the same concept can have different meanings in different contexts or moments. A warm day in winter is not exactly the same as a warm day in spring, the exact definition of when the temperature goes from warm to temperate is imprecise and context-dependent. It is difficult to associate a specific and unique value with warm or temperate, it can be 24°C, but 25°C could be warm too. This kind of imprecision or *fuzzyness* is constantly linked to phenomena, and is common in every field of study: sociology, physics, biology, finance, engineering, and so on.

C. San Martin and S.-W. Kim (Eds.): CIARP 2011, LNCS 7042, pp. 664–674, 2011.

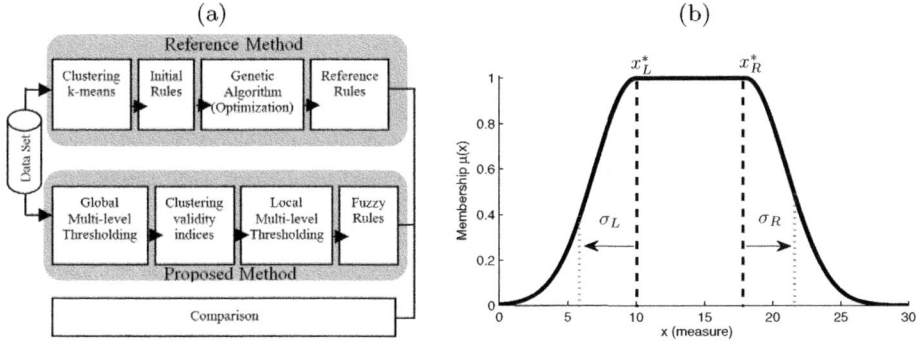

Fig. 1. (a) General scheme for definition and validation of rules generated through proposed method, (b) Example of two-sided Gaussian function

A formalization to express and operates this kind of data, is fuzzy set theory, introduced by L. A. Zadeh [3] in 1965. His proposal considers that each element has a degree of belonging to a set, and this degree is usually a value from 1 (completely belonging) and 0 (not belonging).

Majority of data (precise and imprecise) actually is stored in transactional databases. In order to manage the uncertainty in transactional data bases there are proposals on Fuzzy Databases (FDB), which aim to apply the theory of fuzzy sets to the database, usually as an extension to relational database technology. FDB has been studied at modeling level in [4,13], and in term of design and implementation in [4,9,10,11,12]. One factor to note about the fuzzy management in databases is that they have allowed the management of qualitative information. On the other hand, Data Warehouse (DW) is a repository of data from different sources and usually these sources are transactional databases that collect information over time. DW processes this information and uses it to perform data analysis at the strategic and support decision-making levels in an organization [8].

Fuzzy Data Warehouse (FDW) is defined for purposes of this research as: *A DW that can store data and operate fuzzy measures of a cube.* In addition, one of the main characteristics of FDW is that it can provide qualitative information through fuzzy measures enriched with linguistic labels that are assigned to each indicator according to its value and set of membership function based on the principles of fuzzy logic.

On the other hand, fuzzy multidimensional models, syntax and semantics for answering fuzzy queries have been proposed [1,2]. In this context, an area that has been little explored is the development of rules that explain the nature of data, ie, to obtain the parameters of membership functions from data analysis. This implies that a membership function which defines a linguistic label of an attribute, gets its parameters from context, given from a historical set of data. For the above techniques you can use machine learning and pattern recognition in general. In [16] clustering algorithms and optimization techniques such as hill-climbing is performed in order to obtain classification rules of fuzzy logic, however, this method is a supervised learning approach, which implies the use of a set of training data to obtain the membership functions, and this is not possible directly in the context of Data Warehouse. On the other hand, in [4] we can find an approach that uses fuzzy clustering to obtain the rules, but this approach only generates triangular membership rules that can be locally optimal [10], because it defines the degree of membership of a cluster based on the distance to its center. In this context, in [14,15] multi-level thresholding techniques are used in order to perform a segmentation of irregular histograms over biofilm images, where the algorithms used are efficient at runtime and optimal, a nice feature, allowing direct and objective comparison of results.

This article proposes a new method in order to obtain membership functions to perform labeling of fuzzy measures in a Data Warehouse using an optimal and efficient unsupervised learning approach, which is organized as follow: In section 2 we present methodology to obtain and validate the new method for obtaining fuzzy rules. In section 3 the application of the proposed method for automatic labeling of fuzzy measures in a Data Warehouse is shown, presenting the results of two common fuzzy queries in such systems. Finally, in section 4 we present the conclusion, comments and future works.

2   Methodology

The proposed method mainly consists in the application of multi-level thresholding and clustering validity indices algorithms in order to obtain the amount and parameters of fuzzy membership functions (two-sided Gaussian functions). In our proposed approach, member functions that are obtained are results of an automatic, unsupervised, optimal and efficient process, and therefore no-subjective and comparable.

In order to validate proposed method, a reference method is developed based on clustering techniques and genetic algorithms (supervised learning approach) in order to ensure high precision of classification through membership functions (also called rules in classification process). Then, results are compared between the proposed method and reference method. In Fig. 1(a), the general scheme for definition and validation of proposed method is depicted.

2.1   Data Set

In order to validate rules obtained from our proposed method, a classical benchmark problem in pattern classification (Fisher's Iris Data Set) is used [5]. The iris data set consists of a set of 150 data samples that map four input features values (sepal length, petal width, petal length y sepal width) into one of three species of iris flowers: Iris-setosa, Iris-versicolor, Iris-virginica.

A DW measure is a quantitative attribute which is mapped in a multidimensional space through dimension hierarchies (qualitative attributes). However, a DW measure is a one-dimensional attribute under pattern recognition approach. Therefore, in order to obtain fuzzy rules and compare results between proposed method and reference method, a Principal Component Analysis (PCA) is performed in order to project the four-dimensional space into a one-dimensional space and transform iris data set into a DW measure.

2.2   Reference Method

In order to obtain initial fuzzy rules, k-means clustering algorithm is applied in reduced feature space. Fig. 2(a) shows cluster results where symbol • represents Iris-Setosa class, symbol * represents Iris Virginica and symbol + represents Iris Versicolor. For each cluster c_i the mean m_i and standard deviations σ_i are obtained, where $i \in [1, k]$, and $k = 3$ for each flower class. For each cluster, a rule of classification is generated, where each m_i represents the values of data set which have associated a degree of membership equals to 1. On the other hand, each standard deviation are used as right and left parameters for the two-sided Gaussian functions. In Fig. 1(b) is depicted a typical Gaussian functions and the four parameters used: two standard deviations and two mean.

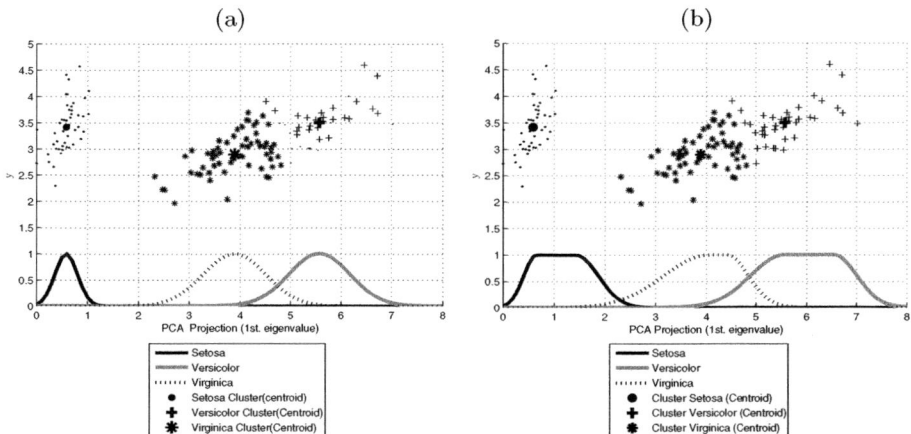

Fig. 2. (a) Two-sided Gaussian Membership Functions obtained through k-means clustering without optimization, (b) Two-sided Gaussian membership functions optimized through genetic algorithm (projection in y is only for visualization purposes)

Initially, each rule is generated from each cluster c_i with $m_i = x^*_{L_i} = x^*_{R_i}$ and $\sigma_i = \sigma_{L_i} = \sigma_{R_i}$. For reference method, three initials rules are generated trough this method, where each rule defines the degree of the values projected by PCA to each class of flowers. The initial rules without optimization are depicted in Fig. 2(a), which have a 79% of precision in classification.

In a second process, a genetic algorithm optimization process is performed in order to optimize initials m_i and σ_i parameters. The chromosomes are a feature vector of four parameters for the three rules (12 chromosomes in total). The fitness function to minimize is normalized error of classification $error =$

$1 - precision$. The rules obtained after optimization process is depicted in Fig. 2(b), where precision of classification is 98%.

2.3   Proposed Method

After of dimensional reduction process (PCA), a relative frequency histogram h is obtained. Then, three multi-level threshold algorithms [18] are applied to h: Entropy-Based thresholding (ENTROPY), Otsu's thresholding (OTSU) and Minimun Error thresholding (MINERROR). In this context, a multi-level thresholding process with $k-1$ thresholds, have a direct relationship with the number of classes k, in which a histogram is partitioned [14]. Viewing thresholding as a problem of clustering frequency histogram h, clustering validity indices [17] can be used in order to obtain the best number of classes k in which the histogram can be clustered, and hence the best number of membership functions or labels can be obtained. In this work, four clustering validity indices are used to determine the best number of thresholds and select the best thresholding technique: Davies-Bouldin Index (DB), Dunn's Index (DN), Index I (IndexI), Calinski Harabasz Index (CH), Xie-Beni Index (XB).

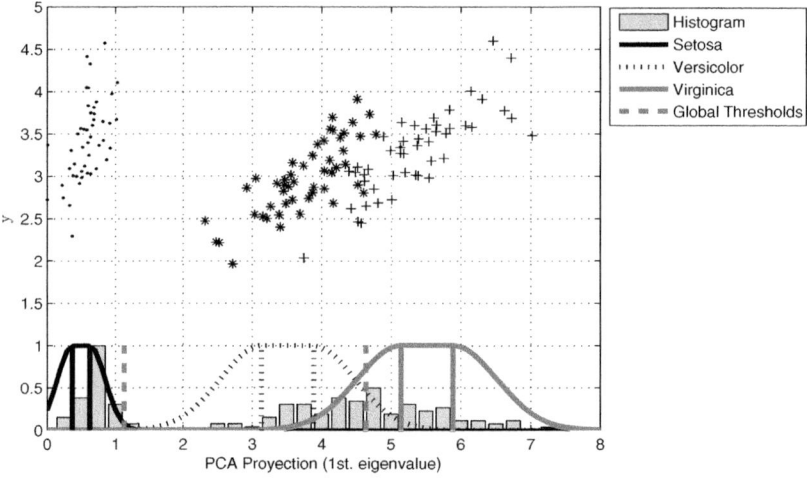

Fig. 3. Two-sided Gaussian membership functions defined through multi-level thresholding techniques (projection in y is only for visualization purposes)

The Fig. 3 shows the resulting rules of multi-level thresholding process. The dotted gray lines represent the global thresholds T_g^G with $g \in [1, k-1]$, which divide the histogram into k initial clusters c_i with $i \in [1, k]$. The solid black lines, dotted black lines and solid gray lines represent the local thresholds T_l^L with $l \in [1, 2]$ for each cluster c_i. Each membership function μ_i for each cluster is defined by:

$$\mu_i = f(T_1^L, T_2^L, \sigma_i), \tag{1}$$

where, f is a two-sided Gaussians function (see Fig. 1(b)), $T_1^L = x_{L_i}^*$, $T_2^L = x_{R_i}^*$ and $\sigma_i = \sigma_{L_i} = \sigma_{R_i}$. As can be see the interval between T_1^L and T_2^L always have a membership degree equal to 1, and the values belonging to the right and left intervals have lower degrees of membership according to the variance of each cluster σ_i.

The classification process carried out with this approach achieves the best accuracy of classification with the MINERROR and OTSU criteria, using an unsupervised technique and obtained objective results, since for the same data always get the same results in an optimal way. Table 1 shows the results of classification precision of the three thresholding criteria using $k = 3$.

Table 1. Precision for each multilevel thresholding criteria, best values are showed in boldface

Thresholding Criteria	ENTROPY	MINERROR	OTSU
Precision	0.5667	**0.9333**	**0.9333**

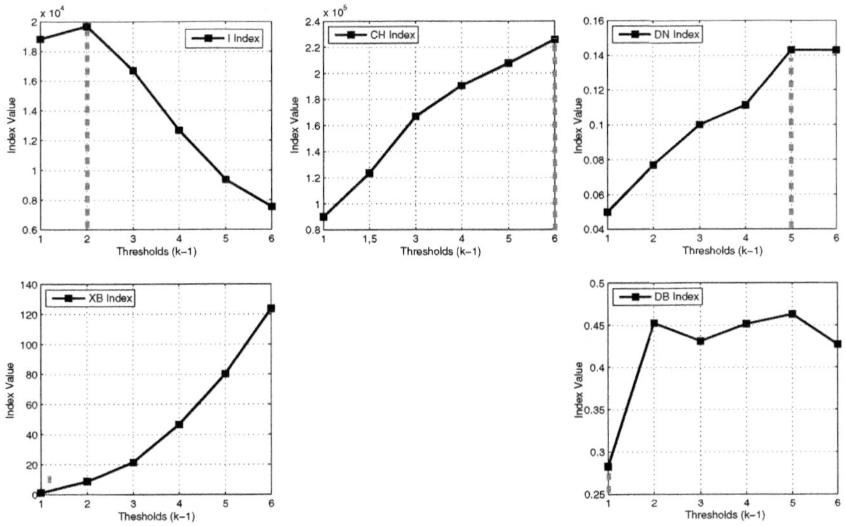

Fig. 4. I, CH, DN, XB and DB cluster validity indices applied after OTSU thresholding. The gray dotted line show the optimal number of clusters obtained by each index.

According to the behavior of cluster validation indices shown in Fig. 4 and Table 2, we can see that CH, XB and DN indices increase monotonically as it increases the numbers of $k - 1$ thresholds used. From the above, the selection criteria that obtain the numbers of thresholds and hence also the number of labels, can be defined by the next expression:

$$k = min(I_j^*, DB_j^*) + 1, \tag{2}$$

where $i \in [1, K]$, I_j^* is the number of thresholds defined by I index, DB_j^* is the optimal number of thresholds obtained by DB index, and K is maximum number of thresholds to find in data set (parameter defined by user).

In summary, the proposed method involves the application of multi-level thresholding algorithm (OTSU) to obtain k membership functions, with k given by Equation 2 through applying clustering validation indices, each membership function μ_i, is obtained by the definition given in Equation 1 through applying global and local thresholding criteria in order to perform the parameterization of a two-sided Gaussian distribution function. We should note that the proposed method is not comparable to other classification techniques directly, because the process itself is for the membership functions and the classification is only for validation purposes, because is not possible to determine classes on measures of a Data Warehouse directly.

Table 2. I, CH, DN, XB and DB cluster validity indices applied with OTSU thresholding. Values shown in boldface represent optimal number of clusters for each index.

# Thresholds	I	CH	DB	DN	XB
1	18822	90066	**0.283**	0.050	**1.10**
2	**19682**	123331	0.452	0.077	8.70
3	16695	166604	0.431	0.100	21.4
4	12672	190410	0.451	0.111	46.4
5	9355	207642	0.463	**0.143**	80.0
6	7549	**225759**	0.427	0.143	123.7

3   Fuzzy Queries in Data Warehouse

In order to perform fuzzy queries using the automatic fuzzy functions proposed, cube depicted in Figure 5 was developed over a subset from a data warehouse system implemented for research at the University of Atacama, Chile [7]. This figure shows part of a conceptual scheme of a DW with fuzzy measures [4]. This schema has been modeled through an instance of the Fuzzy CWM OLAP Meta Model [2]. The cube has six fuzzy measures: marks, age, mathematics, history, science and language, where the last four measures are score of student in a set of tests performed in the admission process of student to the university. In the same context, the dimensions of analysis are: Courses, Time, Students, Cohort and Undergraduate Program.

3.1   Case Study: Automatics Fuzzy Rules from Data Warehouse

Fuzzy rules for the six fuzzy measures obtained through method proposed are depicted in Fig. 6. According the conceptual model, labels are defined according

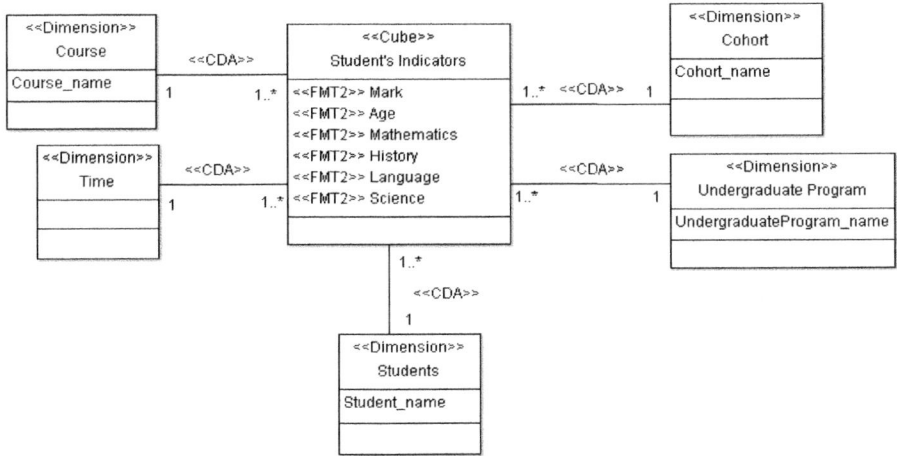

Fig. 5. Conceptual scheme of DW with fuzzy measures. The label $<< FMT2 >>$ is stereotype of Fuzzy Measure (type 2) defined in [2].

the number of rules determined for each measure as: low, medium-low, medium-high, and high. In order to show the use of rules obtained through this method a set of typical queries are performed in the DW using fuzzy approach proposed in [6]:

Query 1 - Average High Marks by Cohort: Table 3 presents the results of query 1, where you can see that all cohorts with high marks have the maximum possibility around 5.9. However, we can appreciate that other values are possible, ie, the 2010 cohort has an average of 5.43 with possibility 84.9%.

Table 3. Results of Query 1: *Average High Marks by Cohort*

Possibility	2003	2004	2005	2006	2007	2008	2009	2010
84.9%	5.69	5.54	5.48	5.52	5.54	5.56	5.49	5.43
93.0%	5.83	5.93	5.80	5.75	5.67	5.65	5.59	5.50
98.2%	5.76	5.67	5.79	5.76	5.76	5.55	5.80	5.73
100%	5.91	5.90	5.90	5.89	5.89	5.87	5.92	5.85

Query 2 - Average High Age by Undergraduate Program: Table 4 presents the results of query 2, where you can see that all undergraduate programs have 24 years as the most possible high age, except Geological Engineering and Business that have values slightly lower.

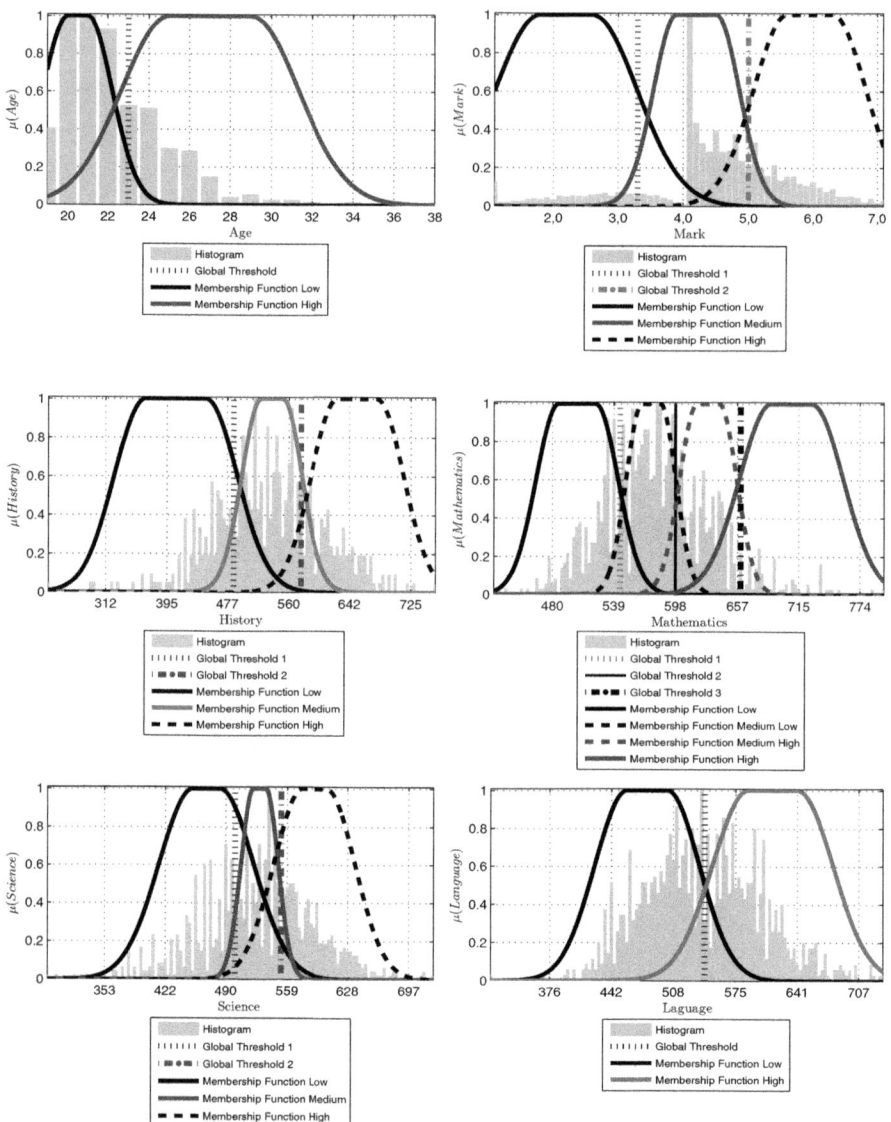

Fig. 6. Fuzzy membership functions DW obtained through multi-level thresholding based method from six measures

Table 4. Results of query *Average High Age by Undergraduate Program.*

Possibility	Business	Computere Science	Geological Engineering	Industrial Engineering	Metallurgical Engineering	Mining Engineering
71.0%	21.0	24.3	21.5	24.7	24.5	22.5
91.8%	22.0	24.3	22.2	24.3	24.5	24.2
100%	23.5	24.0	23.3	24.2	24.0	24.1

4 Conclusion

This work has presented a multi-level thresholding method for obtaining membership functions from fuzzy measures in a Data Warehouse. The proposal has been validated by external criteria (classification rules) and relative criteria (Index Validation) and applied to a real database.

From the results, you can see the great potential of this approach. Undoubtedly, the automation of obtaining the membership functions is one of the least covered issues in fuzzy logic and data warehouse, since it is a process that has not been fully automated.

It is important to add that defining membership functions in fuzzy measures regardless of the context of data, could lead to obtain membership functions with parameters that do not reflect the reality of the domain or organization. For example, the parameters that define the membership function for the high marks label are not the same at a university or another, but should be directly related to the data from each of the universities.

As future works, this method can be appliied to fuzzy levels and extending method to other types of fuzzy data in DW considering the efficiency and objectivity of the proposed approach.

Acknowledgments. This work has been partially supported by MIDAL, Machine Learning and Data Analysis Laboratory and the University of Atacama (University Grant for Research and Artistic Creativity (Projects: *Data Warehouse Difuso Para Análisis Con Jerarquías Difusas* and *Un nuevo algoritmo óptimo de multilevel thresholding para la segmentación de datos e imágenes con determinacin automática de la cantidad de umbrales en tiempo eficiente*)).

References

1. Delgado, M., Molina, C., Sánchez, D., Vila, A., Rodr'iguez-Ariza, L.: A Fuzzy Multidimensional Model for Supporting Imprecision in OLAP. In: Proceedings of IEEE International Conference on Fuzzy Systems (2004)
2. Carrera, S., Varas, M., Urrutia, A.: Transformación de Esquemas Multidimensionales Difusos desde el Nivel Conceptual al Nivel Lógico. Ingeniare. Revista Chilena de Ingenier'ia 18, 165–175 (2010)
3. Zadeh, L.A.: Fuzzy Sets. Information and Control 8, 338–353 (1965)
4. Galindo, J., Urrutia, A., Piatinni, M.: Fuzzy Databases: Modeling, Design and Implementation. Idea Group Inc. (2006)

5. Xu, D.: Clustering. IEEE Press Series on Computational Intelligence. A John Wiley & Sons (2009)
6. Rundensteiner, E., Bic, L.: Aggregates in posibilistic databases. In: Proceeding of the 15th Conference in Very Large Databases (VLDB 1989), Amsterdam, Holland, pp. 287–295 (1989)
7. Zambrano C., Rojas D.: Data Warehouse para analizar el comportamiento académico, In: XXIV Congreso de la Sociedad Chilena de Educación en Ingeniería, SOCHEDI 2010, Valdivia, Chile (2010)
8. Inmon, W.: Building the Data Warehouse. John Wiley & Sons (2002)
9. Galindo, J., Urrutia, A., Carrasco, R., Piattini, M.: Relaxing Constraints in Enhanced Entity-Relationship Models Using Fuzzy Quantifiers. IEEE Transactions on Fuzzy Systems 12, 780–796 (2004)
10. Galindo, J., Urrutia, A., Piatinni, M.: Handbook of Research on Fuzzy Information Processing in Databases, Universidad de Málaga, Spain (2008)
11. Galindo, J., Urrutia, A., Carrasco, R., Piattini, M.: Fuzzy Constraints using the Enhanced Entity-Relationship Model. In: XXI International Conference of the Chilean Computer Science Society, Chile, pp. 86–94 (2001)
12. Galindo, J., Urrutia, A., Carrasco, R., Piattini, M.: Relaxing Constraints in Enhanced Entity-Relationship Models Using Fuzzy Quantifiers. IEEE Transactions on Fuzzy Systems 12, 780–796 (2004)
13. Urrutia, A.: Definición de un Modelo Conceptual para Bases de Datos Difusas. Doctoral Thesis (2003)
14. Rojas, D., Rueda, L., Urrutia, H., Ngom A., Carcamo G.: Automatic Segmentation Methods and Applications to Biofilm Image Analysis. In: Data Mining in Biomedical Signaling, Imaging and Systems. CRC Press (2011)
15. Rojas, D., Rueda, L., Urrutia, H., Ngom, A., Carcamo, G.: Image Segmentation of Biofilm Structures Using Optimal Multi-Level Thresholding. International Journal of Data Mining and Bioinformatics 5, 266–286 (2011)
16. Dubois, D., Prade, H., Yager, R.: Fuzzy Information Engineering. Wiley Computer Publishing (1997)
17. Maulik, U., Bandyopadhyay, S.: Performance evaluation of some clustering algorithms and validity indices. IEEE Transactions on Pattern Analysis and Machine Intelligence 24, 1650–1655 (2002)
18. Rueda, L.: An Efficient Algorithm for Optimal Multilevel Thresholding of Irregularly Sampled Histograms. In: da Vitoria Lobo, N., Kasparis, T., Roli, F., Kwok, J.T., Georgiopoulos, M., Anagnostopoulos, G.C., Loog, M. (eds.) S+SSPR 2008. LNCS, vol. 5342, pp. 602–611. Springer, Heidelberg (2008)

A Probabilistic Iterative Local Search Algorithm Applied to Full Model Selection

Esteban Cortazar and Domingo Mery

Department of Computer Science,
School of Engineering,
Pontificia Universidad Católica de Chile
Vicuña Mackenna 4860, Santiago, Chile
ecortaza@puc.cl, dmery@ing.puc.cl

Abstract. Currently, there is no solution, which does not require a high runtime, to the problem of choosing preprocessing methods, feature selection algorithms and classifiers for a supervised learning problem. In this paper we present a method for efficiently finding a combination of algorithms and parameters that effectively describes a dataset. Furthermore, we present an optimization technique, based on ParamILS, which can be used in other contexts where each evaluation of the objective function is highly time consuming, but an estimate of this function is possible. In this paper, we present our algorithm and initial validation of it over real and synthetic data. In said validation, our proposal demonstrates a significant reduction in runtime, compared to ParamILS, while solving problems with these characteristics.

Keywords: Full Model Selection, FMS, Machine learning Challenge, Iterative Local Search, ILS.

1 Introduction

The Model Selection task can be described as choosing the model that best describes a data set [2]. In the machine learning context, this problem may be interpreted in several different ways, from feature selection to parameter tuning. In this paper we will use a broader interpretation, based on the definition of *Full Model Selection* (FMS) as described by [4]. The FMS problem is defined as: given a pool of preprocessing methods, feature selection and classification algorithms, select the combination of these that obtains the lowest classification error for a given data set. This task also includes the selection of the hyperparameters for the considered methods.

In today's practice, the supervised learning problem is usually solved by applying conventions (e.g. the number of neighbors considered in KNN should be relatively low), ad hoc choices (SVM has worked well in the past, why not apply it now), and experimental comparisons on a limited scale (testing three different classifiers with their default settings and comparing performances). The problem with this approach is that, while it may return acceptable results, it does not truly consider the particularities of the problem at hand. The advantages of using a more specific

C. San Martin and S.-W. Kim (Eds.): CIARP 2011, LNCS 7042, pp. 675–682, 2011.

solution over the generalized approach have been shown in several studies [6]. An explanation for this improvement is given in the *No Free Lunch Theorems for Optimization* [1]. In a nutshell, this theorem says that any improvement in the performance of a model over one class of problems is offset by a lower performance over another class. Therefore, in order to obtain the best possible performance over a certain data set, the generalist approach should be discarded and replaced by the search for a specific model for the problem at hand.

As mentioned before, the FMS problem explores different combinations of algorithms and their hyperparameters, resulting in a vast search space. Furthermore, in order to accurately evaluate each candidate model, training and testing using some validation technique (like Cross Validation) can take a long time, especially over large data sets, which are not uncommon in this field. This combination of a large search space with a long evaluation time, generates a problem well suited for stochastic optimization techniques.

The proposed approach is to use an *Iterative Local Search* (ILS) algorithm, which are well suited for combinatorial optimization problems like this one. Specifically, an implementation ParamILS [5] was adjusted to solve the FMS problem. ParamILS is a parameter tuning algorithm designed with runtime optimization of algorithms in mind, but can be easily modified to fit the needs of the FMS problem. In this paper we present a new algorithm, called PILS (*Probabilistic Iterative Local Search*), which is specifically designed for combinatorial optimization problems with long evaluation time.

This paper is organized as follows: Section 1 gives an overview of the problem. Section 2 describes the basic operators of ParamILS. Section 3 describes our proposed method, PILS. Section 4 reviews our technique for validating this algorithm and the initial results. Finally, Section 5 is a brief conclusion.

2   Iterative Local Search (ILS)

Iterated local search [5] (ILS) is a general meta-heuristic with two basic operators for generating new solutions. The first is the Local Search Operator, which attempts to find the local optimum in the neighborhood of a solution. The second is the Perturbation Operator, which is applied to the local optimum in order to generate a new starting point for a local search.

A general overview of the ILS algorithm is presented in Algorithm 1:

```
Algorithm 1: Iterative Local Search
loop
          x'  = Perturbation(x*);
          x'' = LocalSearch(x');
          if better(x'',x*)
            x* = x'';
```

2.1   ParamILS

ParamILS [5], is the ILS on which our algorithm is based. This is a simple, but powerful, algorithm designed for parameter tuning that relies on the following definitions:

Solution. As was mentioned before, ParamILS is a parameter tuning algorithm. Therefore, it defines each solution as an array of values, where each position in the array represents a specific parameter. At some point during the algorithm execution, depending on the values of the solution, some of the parameters may become inactive. An inactive parameter is a parameter that, if changed, has no effect on the cost function. The relation between parameters that defines when they become inactive must be defined beforehand and is used to describe conditional relationships among parameters.

Local Search. All ILS algorithms must define the way in which they look for a local optimum in the neighborhood surrounding a particular solution. ParamILS starts by defining a neighbor as a solution that differs from the initial one by only one parameter, as long as that parameter is active. Subsequently, it follows an *Iterative First Improvement* technique for finding a local optimum. This technique takes all the neighbors of an initial solution, in randomized order, and compares them to the initial solution. As soon as a solution is found to be better than the initial one, the process restarts using the new solution as a starting point. This will continue until a solution that is better than all of its neighbors is found (local optimum).

Perturbation. ILS algorithms jump from local optimum to local optimum. In order to do this, they must define an operator that allows them to escape from the optimum they are currently in and restart the local search. This operator is defined as the Perturbation Operator. In the case of ParamILS, a very straightforward technique is used to find a new starting point. The Perturbation Operator is defined as a number of jumps from neighbor to neighbor, starting from the current optimum. The number of jumps will define how different one solution is from its predecessor. A small number will increase the likelihood or falling back on the same local optimum, while a large number of jumps will end up with a completely random starting point.

Better. Any ILS algorithm requires a way of defining if one solution is better that another. ParamILS proposes two options for defining the Better Function. The first is BasicILS, which simply compares an each solution with a user defined cost function. The second is FocusedILS, which uses a variable number of training instances in each evaluation in order obtain results with a lower computational cost. The Better Function is precisely what is modified by our algorithm (PILS), so the implementation made by ParamILS is not explained in great depth here. For a more comprehensive understanding of the Better Functions and the ParamILS algorithm, please refer to [5].

3 Our Approach (PILS)

ParamILS proves to be an effective way of moving along the search space finding local optimums. The problem that arises is that, with large datasets, the training and testing time necessary to accurately validate each candidate solution is too long. In turn, this means that, even though only a small portion of the search space is evaluated, a very long time is necessary to do it. In response to this problem we propose a new algorithm based on ParamILS, which redefines the Better Function in order to diminish its runtime. Because of its probabilistic approach, we called it *Probabilistic Iterative Local Search* (PILS)[1].

Definitions. Considering the optimization problem being solved by ParamILS, we define a function which is an estimate of the original objective function, but with a considerably smaller runtime. In exchange for the reduction in runtime, we allow this estimate to be noisy. We model this estimation as shown in (1), where it is described as the objective function $f(x)$ plus a random variable e_x representing noise. Finally, the estimate function is defined so that the mean of several evaluations converges to the objective function, as represented in (2) and (3).

$$\hat{f}(x) = f(x) + e_x .$$ (1)

$$\overline{\hat{f}(x)} \rightarrow f(x) .$$ (2)

$$\overline{e_x} \rightarrow 0 .$$ (3)

Assumptions. We assume that independent evaluations of the estimation function produce independent and identically distributed random noise variables. This powerful assumption allows us to use the *Central Limit Theorem*, with regards to the distribution of the noise mean. After analyzing empirical results from the problem at hand, this assumption has proven to be reasonable. Furthermore, we were able to observe that, even though, the noise variance for different candidate solutions (x) were not the same, they were very similar. This fact is integrated into the PILS algorithm and is, therefore, a necessary requirement for a correct use of this tool.

Algorithm. As before mentioned, PILS uses the same search strategy as ParamILS, but it redefines the function responsible for comparing two candidate solutions. The goal behind the formulation of this algorithm is to decrease the uncertainty only on candidate solutions that could be optimums, in order to waste as little runtime as possible on bad candidate solutions. The way in which it decreases the uncertainty of a candidate solution is by evaluating it several times and averaging the results, which should eventually converge to the objective function. Thanks to the *Central Limit Theorem*, we can model the average noise of several evaluations as a random variable with mean zero, and a variance dependant on the number of evaluations and the variance of these evaluations.

$$\overline{e_x} \sim N(0, \frac{\sigma^2}{N})$$ (4)

Thus, we can easily define a function that, given several evaluations of two candidate solutions, calculates the probability that one is better than the other. Afterwards, the algorithm decides, based on this probability, which of three possible courses to

---

[1] The MatLab code for this algorithm can be downloaded from http://dl.dropbox.com/u/3304215/PILS.zip (Note for reviewers: if the paper is published, this code will be linked from our webpage)

follow. First, if the calculated probability is either very high or very low, then there is enough certainty to simply compare the two means directly. Second, if the probability is very close to 0.5 then the algorithm assumes that there is not a significant difference between the two candidate solutions and defines the one with the lowest variance as the best. This will, probably, save runtime in future comparisons. Third, if neither of the options mentioned is satisfied, the algorithm calculates a new evaluation of the estimation function for the candidate solution that has the lowest number of evaluations, and begins again.

In order to ensure that this function ends, a maximum number of evaluations parameter was added. In case the maximum number of parameters is reached by both candidate solutions, the two means are compared directly.

Our proposed Better Function can be seen bellow in Algorithm 2.

```
Algorithm 2: PILS Better Function
// x1, x2: Candidate Solutions that are being compared.
// mu1, mu2: Mean of x1 and x2 respectively.
// var1, var2: Variance of mu1 and mu2 respectively.
// N1, N2: Number of evaluations of x1 and x2.
better (x1, x2)
{
        loop
        {
          p = ProbabilityBetter (x1, x2);
          d = |0.5 - p|;
          if d>=Us
            return mu1>mu2;
          if d<=Ui
            return var1<var2;
          if min(N1, N2) >= Nmax
            return mu1>mu2;
          if N1<N2
            evaluate (x1);
          else
            evaluate (x2);
        }
}
```

Variance Estimation. The algorithm described in the previous section requires an estimation of the variance associated with each candidate solution.

$$var\left(\overline{\hat{f}(x)}\right) = \frac{var(\hat{f}(x))}{N} \qquad (5)$$

The problem that arises is that we now require, at least, two evaluations of the estimation function, in order to calculate its unbiased variance. Empirical testing showed that the problem went further, because the variance calculated for only two samples was still a very poor estimation. Based on the assumption that the variances of different candidate solutions are similar, the calculation is formulated to consider a Global Variance variable.

$$varEstimate = \frac{GlobalVar * (Nmax - N) + var\left(\hat{f}(x)\right) * (N - 1)}{Nmax - 1} \tag{6}$$

$$var\left(\overline{\hat{f}(x)}\right) = \frac{varEstimate}{N} \tag{7}$$

The Global Variance strongly depends on the way the estimation function is formulated and the dataset at hand. Moreover, it would require extensive experimentation in order to estimate this variable a priori. For these reasons, a way of approximate this variable in real time is necessary. Our implementation considers a user-defined estimation (prior) and its weight, associated with the level of confidence in this estimation. Throughout the algorithms execution, the Global Variance is a weighted mean that considers the user-defined prior and all the sample variances calculated for different candidate solutions, as shown in (8). Empirical experimentation has shown that the Global Variance variable converges quickly, and is a good estimation of the variance mean.

$$GlobalVar = \frac{prior * weight + \sum_i var\left(\hat{f}(x_i)\right) * (N_i - 1)}{weight + \sum_i (N_i - 1)} \tag{8}$$

4   Experimentation

When validating a supervised learning model, 10-fold Cross Validation is usually considered an accurate estimation of its prediction abilities. Its downside is that it requires a long time for training and testing each subset. In our experimentation, we compare the use of ParamILS with 10-fold Cross Validation against PILS using a simple Hold Out Validation technique, which should take one tenth of the time but, on average, should converge to the same result.

Using different machine learning toolboxes, like Balu[2] and CLOP[3], and several small datasets for testing purposes, the assumptions listed for the PILS algorithm were found to be adequately satisfied. But, in order to accurately show the advantages of PILS over the ParamILS algorithm, a very large number of tests under different conditions were necessary. For this purpose, we developed an artificial objective function that mimicked the conditions observed in our testing of real datasets.

4.1   Real Data Set

In our initial approach, we ran PILS, using Hold Out Validation, against ParamILS, using Cross Validation 10-fold over the Fishbone Dataset presented in [7]. Even though the results looked very promising, where ParamILS took up to ten times

---

[2] Machine Learning toolbox available at http://dmery.ing.puc.cl/
[3] Machine Learning toolbox available at http://www.modelselect.inf.ethz.ch/

longer than PILS to obtain the same classification performance, this was not a very effective way of testing our proposal for several reasons. First, the time required by different candidate models was very uneven, which meant that the result from one execution depended on the search trajectory, more than on the optimization algorithm itself. Second, running either PILS or ParamILS was still a rather long task, which meant that extensive testing, in order to obtain more general results or analyze the relevance of certain parameters, was extremely time consuming. Finally, even though this test allowed us to observe the characteristics of this problem, it did not give us much control over the scenarios we wanted to evaluate.

4.2 Artificial Objective Function

The artificial objective function used for these results was constructed using a mixture of five n-dimensional Gaussian functions. Also, random, but similar, variances were assigned to each point in this search space, in order to emulate the estimation function. Using this artificial data, two functions where created. The first is a simple evaluation of the Gaussian mix, representing the real objective function, equivalent to Cross Validation in the Model Selection problem. The second is an evaluation of the Gaussian mix plus a normally distributed noise, representing the estimation function, equivalent to Hold Out Validation in the Model Selection problem.

Table 1. Number of evaluations necesary for similar performance levels. The time column represents the persentaje of time that PILS would of needed, based on ParamILS.

ParamILS		PILS		Time
Performance	N. of Evaluations	Performance	N. of Evaluations	
82	628.962	83.5	1203.278	19.13
90.8	838.871	90	1685.198	20.09
99	1419.927	97	2867.64	20.20

One thousand tests were performed using ParamILS with the objective function and PILS with the estimation function. Table 1 shows the average number of evaluations necessary for each algorithm to obtain similar performance levels. As shown in this table PILS requires approximately twice as many evaluations as ParamILS to obtain similar results. But, considering that this data was mimicking a situation where each evaluation by ParamILS should take ten times longer, it's easy to see the advantages offered by our proposal.

5   Conclusions

Even though further testing is necessary to fully validate our method, the initial results show that our proposal could be very useful in helping to solve the FMS problem. Still, a more in depth analysis of the algorithms parameters is necessary, in order to completely understand their impact on the output and find and adequate configuration for solving this particular problem. In addition to the FMS problem, the proposed algorithm could prove to be useful in solving other optimization problems where the definitions and assumptions listed in section 2.2 are valid.

Acknowledgments. We thank Alvaro Soto, Karim Pichara and Jorge Baier for many helpful discussions regarding this work.

References

1. Wolpert, D.H., Macready, W.G.: No Free Lunch Theorems for Optimization. IEEE Transactions on evolutionary computation 1(1) (1997)
2. Hastie, T., Tibshirani, R., Friedman, J.: The Elements of Statistical Learning. In: Data Mining, Inference, and Prediction. Springer, Heidelberg (2001)
3. Zhang, Q., Sun, J.: Iterated Local Search with Guided Mutation. IEEE Congress on Evolutionary Computation (2006)
4. Escalante, H.J., Montes, M., Sucar, L.E.: Particle Swarm Model Selection. Journal of Machine Learning Research 10 (2009)
5. Hutter, F., Hoos, H.H., Leyton-Brown, K.: ParamILS: An Automatic Algorithm Configuration Framework. Journal of Artificial Intelligence Research 36, 267–306 (2009)
6. Smit, S., Eiben, A.: Parameter Tuning of Evolutionary Algorithms: Generalist vs. Specialist. In: Di Chio, C., Cagnoni, S., Cotta, C., Ebner, M., Ekárt, A., Esparcia-Alcazar, A.I., Goh, C.-K., Merelo, J.J., Neri, F., Preuß, M., Togelius, J., Yannakakis, G.N. (eds.) EvoApplicatons 2010. LNCS, vol. 6024, pp. 542–551. Springer, Heidelberg (2010)
7. Mery, D., Lillo, I., Loebel, H., Riffo, V., Soto, A., Cipriano, A., Aguilera, J.: Automated Fish Bone Detection using X-ray Testing. Journal of Food Engineering 105, 485–492 (2011)

Face Recognition Using TOF, LBP and SVM in Thermal Infrared Images*

Ramiro Donoso Floody[1,2], César San Martín[1,2], and Heydi Méndez-Vázquez[3]

[1] Center for Optics and Photonics, University of La Frontera, Chile
[2] Information Processing Laboratory, DIE, University of La Frontera, Chile
[3] Advanced Technologies Application Center, CENATAV, Cuba

Abstract. In this work, Binary Local Patterns (LBP), Support Vector Machine (SVM) and Trade-off (TOF) correlation filter are evaluated in face recognition tasks using thermal infrared imagery. The infrared technology has a particular kind of noise called non-uniformity and correspond to a fixed pattern noise superimposed at the input image, degrading the quality of the scene. Non-uniformity varies over time very slowly, and in many applications, depending of the technology used, can be assumed constant for at least several hours. Additionally, additive Gaussian noise (variable over time) is generated by the associated electronics. Both kind of noise affect the performance of classifiers in face recognition applications using infrared technology and must be considered. The comparison of performance of each method considering fixed and variable over time noise leads allow to conclude that SVM is more robust under both kind of noise.

Keywords: Face Recognition, Infrared Thermal Imaging, SVM, LBP and TOF.

1 Introduction

Actually, there are many works on face recognition [7], which mainly uses the visible spectral range, although there are some works like Ghiass et al. [3], that present a state of art in terms of facial recognition in the infrared spectral range. Additionally, the work of Kong et al [4] presents a comparison between the advantages and disadvantages of the techniques used in both spectral ranges. In face recognition problem, the efficiency of classification process in visible range depends principally of the face angle view, occluding objects, distance between face and camera, facial expressions, and mostly the light or existing lighting in the environment. In this work, an evaluation between TOF classification methods [9], LBP [6,1] and SVM [11] using infrared imagery is presented. The infrared thermal images correspond to the range $8 - 14\mu m$, i.e., infrared emission being independent of any light source. In particular, human skin has an emissivity close to 1 (see [8]), which represents a unique thermal signature for each subject.

Infrared technology present a non-uniformity in the output scene when a flat-image is captured. This effect is know as fixed pattern noise, i.e., remains

---

* This work was partial supported by *Center for Optics and Photonics* FB0824/2008.

C. San Martin and S.-W. Kim (Eds.): CIARP 2011, LNCS 7042, pp. 683–691, 2011.

constant in time. For example, Figure 1a shows a capture without noise and in Figure 1b a capture with fixed pattern noise using CEDIP JADE UC camera is presented. In effect, the original capture is represented in Figure 1b while the Figure 1a is obtained by correcting the non-uniformity at the scene using a black body at two different temperatures (two-point calibration). This correction requires stopping the capture process and the use of black bodies as a reference. The aim of this work is to recognize individuals using images as Figure 1b without the need to correct or eliminate the fixed pattern noise.

(a)   (b)

Fig. 1. Infrared images captured using the CEDIP JADE camera, a) free noise image and b) image with fixed pattern noise. The goal is to recognize the subject in an image as b).

This work is organized as follows. In section 2 the algorithms TOF and LBP are reviewed, and what is a support vector machine (SVM) is briefly explained. In section 3 the used comparison methods for the algorithms mentioned above is presented. In section 4 the experiment and results is presented. Finally, some discussions and conclusions are reported in section 5 and 6, respectively.

2   Methodology

In this section, three traditional methods of face recognition are presented: Trade-Off (TOF) correlation filter, Local Binary Patterns (LBP) based, and Support Vector Machine (SVM).

2.1   Correlation Filter

Correlation is a measure commonly used to characterize the similarities between a reference pattern and a test pattern. This concept is used frequently in recognition applications, presenting a greater importance degree on the use of cross-correlation for get the relative position of the object. The cross-correlation is given by:

$$c(\tau_x, \tau_y) = \int \int T(f_x, f_y) R^*(f_x, f_y) \exp^{j2\pi(f_x, f_y) + f_y \tau_y} df_x df_y, \tag{1}$$

$$= IFT \left\{ T(f_x, f_y) R^*(f_x, f_y) \right\}, \tag{2}$$

Where $R(f_x, f_y)$ and $T(f_x, f_y)$ are the 2D Fourier transforms of the reference pattern and the test pattern, respectively. In general, the use of a correlation filter for face recognition, as shown in Figure 2. Consists in to apply a filter (in particular, in this work we used the filter TOF 2.1) on subject image under study, and observe which is the highest amplitude (high peak (equation 1)) of the resulting image cross-correlation, and then calculate a similarity measure (PSR or PCE [5]) to classify a subject as valid or not.

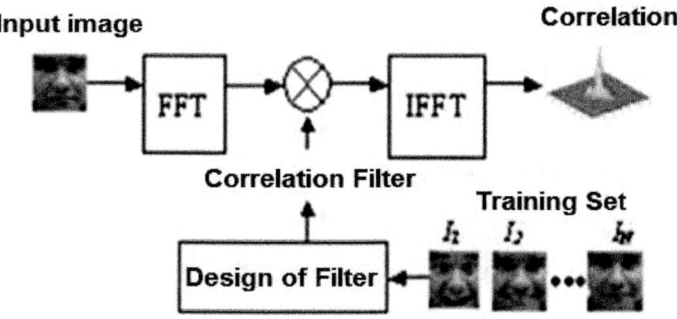

Fig. 2. Correlation filters in face classification

Optimal Tradeoff Filter (TOF). TOF algorithm (3) [9] provides a compromise between the MACE filter characteristics [2], which increases the peak of positive results, and the NTC filter, which aims to reduce the output noise variance. In this case it is necessary to assume the presence of white noise in order to approximate the matrix C to identity matrix, and the commitment between the two is defined by α in the form:

$$\textbf{TOF filter: } h = T^{-1}X(X * T^{-1}X)^{-1}u, \tag{3}$$

$$\textbf{Trade-off: } T = \alpha MACE + (1 - \alpha)NTC. \tag{4}$$

2.2   Local Binary Patterns-(LBP)

The use of LBP in face recognition was introduced by Ahonen et al. in their work [1] and different variations have appeared after Marcel et al. (2007) [6]. The work of Socolinsky et al. [10] shows good results using methods based on appearance. By the above, we were decided to explore the LBP algorithm, which is a texture descriptor based on appearance, which is rather robust and less influenced by possible alignment problems of infrared images.

As shown in Figure 3, the original LBP, each neighborhood (of 3x3) is thresholding according to the central pixel (g_c) thereof, and the result is considered as a binary number called LBP code. Then, the image is divided into rectangular regions, and for each region is calculated the histogram of the LBP code. Finally, the histogram of each region is concatenated into one that represents the image of the face. The Chi-square similarity measure [1] is used to compare the histograms of two different images, and thereby discriminate whether a subject is considered valid or impostor. The method of nearest neighbor was used to make the classification (identification). The TEER (Threshold of Equal Error Rate) was found to verification problem, and the value (obtained by means of training set, that corresponding to the comparison with the measure Chi-square similarity) was used as a threshold in the test set.

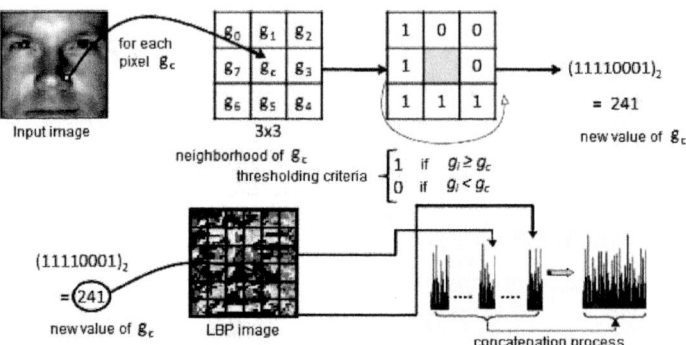

Fig. 3. Original Local-Binary Patterns [8]

2.3   Support Vector Machine (SVM)

Support Vector Machines [11] allow to solve classification problems. In its original form were made to solve classification problems with only two classes, although there are different methods for use in multiclass problems. In this work we chose the original version, due to it adapts to the verification problem, where the first class represents a subject, and the second class represents the other subjects (impostors). A support vector machine assumes that if we have a set of data not linearly separable of n dimension (which belong to two classes), then they are linearly separable in the $(n + 1)$ dimension. The SVM can use different types of kernels, which greatly promotes the search for solutions to problems of classification. These kernels can be: linear, polynomial, RBF, sigmoid, etc. In particular, this paper each image was represented as a column vector where each element contains the intensity of the pixel, which can be classified as a method of appearance.

3   Evaluation Methods

To measure the fixed and variable noise tolerance, the following evaluation methods are used (see [7]):

False Accepted Rate (FAR). The false accepted rate is calculated by the relation between the number of accepted impostor subjects and the total number of impostor subjects, i.e.:

$$FAR = \left(\frac{\text{impostors accepted as valid subjects}}{\text{total number of impostor subjects}} \right) \tag{5}$$

False Rejected Rate (FRR). The false rejected rate is calculated by the relation between the number of rejected valid subjects and the total number of valid subjects, i.e.:

$$FRR = \left(\frac{\text{valid subjects rejected}}{\text{total number of valid subjects}} \right) \tag{6}$$

Equal Error Rate (EER). As shown in Figure 4, the EER value is obtained when $FRR = FAR$. Note that while more smaller is this value, better is the system to classify.

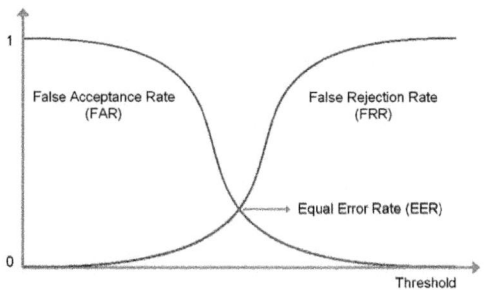

Fig. 4. EER as the intersection of FAR and FRR curves [7]

Note that these three indicators (EER, FAR and FRR) are proportional inversely to the performance of facial recognition methods, i.e., while more closer to zero are these indicators, the methods obtain a better classification.

4 Experimentation and Results

4.1 Experiment Description

To evaluate the noise tolerance of the three methods mentioned in section 2, we performed the following experiment. A training set and test set from a database was created, which contains two separate sets of faces, the expression set E (joy, anger, surprise, etc.) and vocalization set V (vowels or words). The database has 102 subjects, 6 images per subject (subdivided into two sets: 3 images for the set E and 3 for the set V). The training set was of 34 subjects, i.e., 68 subjects will be impostors for the system. For each subject belonging to training set, a training subset was defined, which consists of 3 images of a set (E or V) as hits and 1 image (the same set) of each one of the other subjects in the training set (as rejections). As test subset to this subject was considered the 3 images in the group (E or V) that weren't considered in the training set (as hits) and all images of impostor subjects (as rejections).

To train the system, the complete and original images were used, i.e., free noise and the original size (320x240px). And then, case-by-case the noise tolerance (fixed and variable pattern) was evaluated, adding to the original image a Gaussian noise simulated by a normal distribution with mean 0 and variance $t\%$ of 2^8, where $t = \{10, 20, 30, 40, 50, 80\}$ for fixed noise, and $t = \{1, 5, 10\}$ for temporal noise. Recall that in each case were used two training subsets (one E and one with V) and two test subsets for each subject belonging to the training set. Moreover, 5 exercises for each combination to obtain better statistics were performed.

4.2   Results

Below, the Table 1 is presented, which contains the performance of the methods with images in their original condition, i.e., free noise. Following, the tables show the results of the experiment described above. Remember that the images are classified into two sets (E and V), so the results are given separately for each one. In Tables 2, 3 and 4 are presented the results of classification with fixed pattern noise. Moreover, in Tables 5, 6 and 7 is shown the results considering the variable white noise.

Table 1. Performance, EER, FAR y FRR for original images

Method	Set E Accuracy	EER	FAR	FRR	Set V Accuracy	EER	FAR	FRR
TOF	94.77	5.88	6.39	8.33	98.69	3.92	3.70	10.78
LBP	97.71	1.96	2.15	3.27	99.35	1.96	2.15	3.27
SVM	97.69	2.28	2.29	5.88	97.19	2.70	2.75	9.80

Table 2. Performance of TOF method with fixed pattern noise

exercise	Set E var 10%	var 20%	var 30%	Set V var 10%	var 20%	var 30%
1	74.5098	64.7059	60.4575	85.9477	82.0261	78.1046
2	65.0327	56.8627	52.2876	84.9673	81.6993	76.7974
3	59.8039	49.3464	49.0196	83.3333	82.0261	76.7974
4	56.8627	47.3856	47.7124	82.0261	80.3922	76.1438
5	52.2876	45.4248	45.7516	84.3137	79.7386	74.5098
Mean	61.6993	52.7451	51.0457	84.1176	81.1765	76.4706

Table 3. Performance of LBP method with fixed pattern noise

	Set E			Set V		
exercise	var 10%	var 20%	var 30%	var 10%	var 20%	var 30%
1	96.7320	96.0784	96.0784	97.0588	97.0588	98.0392
2	97.0588	96.7320	96.0784	97.7124	97.0588	97.3856
3	96.7320	96.7320	96.0784	97.7124	97.3856	97.0588
4	96.7320	96.0784	96.0784	97.3856	97.3856	97.0588
5	97.3856	96.4052	95.7516	96.7320	97.0588	98.0392
Mean	96.9281	96.4052	96.0130	97.3202	97.1895	97.5163

Table 4. Performance of SVM method with fixed pattern noise

	Set E			Set V		
exercise	var 10%	var 20%	var 30%	var 10%	var 20%	var 30%
1	98.1466	98.0034	97.3952	98.1466	98.3970	98.3469
2	98.1895	97.9748	97.7601	98.2038	98.4901	98.4901
3	98.1394	97.9963	97.8174	98.1823	98.5258	98.5616
4	98.1752	98.0034	97.9176	98.1609	98.4471	98.4686
5	98.2038	98.0893	97.7315	98.1537	98.4686	98.5187
Mean	98.1709	98.0135	97.7243	98.1695	98.4657	98.4772

Table 5. Performance of TOF method with variable white noise

	Set E			Set V		
exercise	var 1%	var 5%	var 10%	var 1%	var 5%	var 10%
1	94.7712	93.4641	88.2353	97.3856	94.4444	91.5033
2	94.4444	91.1765	86.9281	97.3856	95.4248	89.2157
3	94.1176	92.1569	88.2353	97.0588	96.0784	88.8889
4	94.7712	93.4641	88.2353	97.0588	95.7516	88.5621
5	94.1176	93.7908	89.2157	97.3856	94.7712	89.8693
Mean	94.4444	92.8105	88.1699	97.2549	95.2941	89.6079

Table 6. Performance of LBP method with variable white noise

	Set E			Set V		
exercise	var 1%	var 5%	var 10%	var 1%	var 5%	var 10%
1	96.7320	96.7320	95.0980	98.0392	97.7124	97.0588
2	97.0588	96.4052	95.4248	98.6928	97.3856	96.7320
3	96.7320	97.0588	95.0980	97.7124	97.0588	97.0588
4	96.7320	96.7320	95.4248	98.3660	96.4052	96.7320
5	97.0588	97.0588	95.0980	99.0196	96.7320	97.0588
Mean	96.8627	96.7974	95.2287	98.3660	97.0588	96.9281

Table 7. Performance of SVM method with variable white noise

exercise	Set E			Set V		
	var 1%	var 5%	var 10%	var 1%	var 5%	var 10%
1	97.8317	98.0607	98.1466	97.5097	97.9891	98.2038
2	97.8102	98.0750	98.1967	97.4524	98.0106	98.1967
3	97.8460	98.0321	98.1895	97.4882	97.9963	98.2181
4	97.8818	98.0249	98.2110	97.5025	98.0106	98.1609
5	97.8603	97.9963	98.1466	97.4667	97.9677	98.1251
Mean	97.8460	98.0378	98.1780	97.4839	97.9948	98.1809

5   Discussion

As shown in Table 1 the LBP method succeeds in obtaining the best performance for face recognition with free noise images in E set, obtaining a performance of 97.71%, closely followed by SVM with 97.69%. As is expected, the LBP method also gets the lowest values for the indexes EER (1.96%), FAR (2.15%) and FRR (3.27%). When is considered the V set of images, again the Table 1 shows that the LBP method gets the best performance with 99.35% followed by TOF correlation filter with 98.69%. Note that despite the TOF filter gets a better performance than SVM, the SVM gets the lowest value to EER, FAR and FRR.

As shown in Tables 2, 3 and 4, the performance of classifiers in general is better for set V than for set E, with differences exceeding 20% in accuracy comparing to the same noise (in the case of TOFF correlation filter) and minor variations in accuracy 0.0014% in case of SVM. Therefore, and according to the averages shown in Table 4, the SVM is more stable when classifying both sets of images, i.e. the accuracy obtained for the set E is very similar to that obtained for the set V.

As shown in Table 2, the TOF correlation filter obtains the worst results for the two sets (E and V) obtaining a minimum accuracy of 51.05% when considering a 30% of fixed noise. Moreover, the best accuracy to the same noise is achieved by the SVM (97.72%).

As shown in Tables 5, 6 and 7 the TOF correlation filter gets the worst performance, and the SVM gets the best performance again. Note that, the results obtained by SVM are usually slightly higher by about 1% to those obtained by LBP, except in the training set V, with variable noise of 1%, where LBP is higher than SVM at 0.8%.

For all the above and Table 1, we recommend the use of LBP method in faces recognition with free or very little noise; on the other hand we recommended the use of SVM for noisy images, due to SVM is robust to fixed and variable noise. Also, SVM gets low values for the indexes EER, FAR and FRR.

Finally, we note that in some cases to increase the percentage of noise, is produced a slight increase in accuracy, which could be considered as a possible inconsistency in the results, it's logical to think that while more noise the analyzed image has, worse will be the performance of classification. But this behavior can be explained if is considered that with a slight noise added randomly to the image, will be incorporated a differentiation element between them, which is the responsible for the slight increase in accuracy obtained.

6 Conclusions

Due to the main factor of face recognition problem is the lighting, in this work was used infrared thermal imaging to make a comparison between the TOF method, LBP and SVM applied to this problem. In the previous section recommends the use of one method over another in certain cases. They also concluded that SVM is usually the most robust against noise from fixed and variable pattern over time.

Further work is needed to incorporate other methods in the study of face recognition in infrared images, it is also possible to extend the experiment and increasing the percentage of noise to see that finally the algorithms performance drops when this increase, and thus give more consistency to the data presented.

References

1. Ahonen, T., Hadid, A., Pietikäinen, M.: Face Recognition With Local Binary Patterns. In: Pajdla, T., Matas, J(G.) (eds.) ECCV 2004. LNCS, vol. 3021, pp. 469–481. Springer, Heidelberg (2004)
2. Casasent, D., Ravichandran, G.: Advanced distortion-invariant minimum average correlation energy (MACE) filters. Applied Optics 31, 1109–1116 (1992)
3. Ghiass, R.S., Bendada, A., Maldague, X.: Infrared Face Recognition: A Review of the State of the Art. In: 10th International Conference on Quantitative InfraRed Thermography (July 2010)
4. Kong, S.G., Heo, J., Abidi, B.R., Paik, J., Abidi, M.A.: Recent advances in visual and infrared face recognition - a review. Computer Vision and Image Understanding 97, 103–135 (2005)
5. Vijaya Kumar, B.V.K., Hassebrook, L.: Performance measures for correlation filters. Applied Optics 29(20), 2997–3006 (1990)
6. Marcel, S., Rodriguez, Y., Heusch, G.: On the Recent Use of Local Binary Patterns for Face Authentication. International Journal on Image and Video Processing Special Issue on Facial Image Processing (2007)
7. San Martin, C., Carrillo, R., Meza, P., Mendez, H., Plasencia, Y., García-Reyes, E., Hermosilla, G.: Recent Advances on Face Recognition using Thermal Infrared Images. InTech (2011)
8. Méndez, H., Martín, C.S., Kittler, J., Plasencia, Y., García-Reyes, E.: Face Recognition with LWIR Imagery Using Local Binary Patterns. In: Tistarelli, M., Nixon, M.S. (eds.) ICB 2009. LNCS, vol. 5558, pp. 327–336. Springer, Heidelberg (2009)
9. Refregier, R.: Optimal trade-off filter for noise robustness, sharpness of the correlation peaks, and horner efficiency. Optics Letters 32, 1933–1935 (1993)
10. Socolinsky, D., Selinger, A., Neuheisel, J.: Face recognition with visible and thermal infrared imagery. Comput. Vis. Image Und. 91, 72–114 (2003)
11. Theodoridis, S., Koutroumbas, K.: Pattern Recognition (2006)

Hybrid Algorithm for Fingerprint Matching Using Delaunay Triangulation and Local Binary Patterns

Alejandro Chau Chau and Carlos Pon Soto

Departamento de Ingeniería de Sistemas y Computación
Universidad Católica del Norte, Chile
{achau2,cpon}@ucn.cl

Abstract. This paper proposes a hybrid algorithm for fingerprint matching using geometric structures with Delaunay triangle´s based formed by the minutiae. For those minutiae triangles candidates for fingerprint matching, the texture information is extracted from the original raw image localized inside the triangle using Local Binary Patterns techniques (LBP). The preliminary results have shown that the merging technique is fairly robust for genuine fingerprint matching discrimination, reducing thus the error rate for FRR and FAR and the time comparison between fingerprint in the verification and/or identification process. The experimental results have shown that the proposed algorithm is effective and reliable. Tests were conducted from the database BD1 and BD2 of FVC2002 competition, obtaining an EER of 6.18% and 3.17% respectively.

Keywords: Fingerprint Matching, Delaunay Triangles, Local Binary Pattern.

1 Introduction

Fingerprint matching provides a matching score that quantifies the similarity between the recognition feature set and the enrollment template. Fingerprint matching applications are concerned with two types of systems: the verification and identification systems. A verification system authenticates a person´s identity by comparing the captured fingerpring characteristics with her enrolled template fingerprint. It conducts a one-to-one comparison to confirm whether the claim of identity by the individual is true. In a identification system this recognizes an individual by searching the entire enrollment template database for a match. It conducts one-to-many comparisons to establish if the individual is present in the database.

A categorization of fingerprints matching approaches are divided in three groups [1]: Correlation-based-matching, is the superposition of two fingerprint images and the correlation between corresponding pixels is computed for different alignments (e.g., various displacements and rotations). Minutiae-based-matching, is based on the minutiae extraction on both fingerprints and stored as sets of points in the two-dimensional plane. This type of matching can be classified as local and global matching. The global matching consists of finding the alignment between the template and the input minutiae sets that result in the maximum number of minutiae pairings. The local matching algorithms try to match a subset of minutiaes that are

C. San Martin and S.-W. Kim (Eds.): CIARP 2011, LNCS 7042, pp. 692–700, 2011.

closed related based on geometric structures formed by local minutiae neigborhood. The atributes of these geometric structures provides a matching invariant to rotation and displacement of fingerprints. The Dealunay triangulation has been used in the last few years as an approach of geometrical structures [3-5]. One problem with Delaunay triangulation is its sensitivity to the false minutiae, producing different local structures. However, the inclusion of a new point in the triangulation only affect the topology around the new point, keeping the other areas of the topology undisturbed [5]. The third category of fingerprint matching is a non-minutiae feature-based. The aproach belonging to this family compare fingerprints in terms of features extracted from the ridge pattern. The most popular technique for comparing fingerprint texture is based on the method used by FingerCode [6], obtaining information using a Gabor filterbank around the core of the fingerprint. The most critical approach is to align the FingerCode using the area around the core. Some fingerprints do not have a core or are very difficult to determine their position accurately. In other case, the core is very close to the edges of the image, which cause the FingerCode to be incomplete or incompatible with the image of the fingerprint. In [7, 8] they propose a hybrid variant in which the images are aligned using information from the minutiae and then extract the information based on the texture of the fingerprint using Gabor filters on the entire image. In [9] it is presented another hybrid approach where the fingerprints are aligned using the minutiae and then the texture-based features are extracted from the full image using the local binary patterns (LBP) operator [10] with Gabor filters. A problem with methods based on comparison of fingerprint features is a high computational cost to calculate the vectors [7-9].

This paper propose a hybrid approach combining fingerprint triangle structures, where the minutiae are vertices of the triangle using Delaunay triangulation techniques, merged with textural characteristics of the fingerprint extracted locally on the center of each triangle candidate for matching using the LBP operator. For each pair of feature vectors obtained from the Delaunay triangle candidates for matching, a difference of the LBP histogram is calculated from the center of the triangle which offer better discrimination between fingerprints.

Section 2 describes the implementation details of the hybrid algorithm. Section 3 shows the experiments and results. Finally, in section 4 presents conclusions and future work.

2   Comparison of Fingerprints

The system is to compare fingerprints with Delaunay minutiae triangles structures. For each triangle, geometric features invariant to rotation and translation are obtained to avoid a previous step of alignment. Once the similarity between triangles are calculated, they are confirmed by comparing the LBP operator histogram obtained locally on the center of the structures, which contain information about the texture of the triangle image.

2.1   Delaunay Triangulation

By applying the Delaunay triangulation on the set of minutiae, each fingerprint is represented as a set of triangles. The Delaunay triangles have certain properties that are desirable for the application [5, 11, 12]: 1) The Delaunay triangulation of a non-degenerated set of N minutiaes is unique and can be computed in $O(NlogN)$, producing $O(N)$ triangles. 2) The inclusion or absence of a triangulation point only affects the neighboring triangles, keeping the topology in unaffected areas. 3) The Delaunay triangulation guarantees the connectivity of each point, with about 2.6 segments per point. This representation of the minutiae triangle structures is used to find similarity between fingerprints.

2.2 Local Binary Patterns

The LBP operator is a descriptor of texture images and has been used widely in face recognition applications [13, 14]. It has been proven to be highly discriminative and its main advantage is its invariance to changes to the gray scale and computational efficiency. The basic idea for the calculation of LBP is that the binary code is described using a pattern of local texture, constructed by the central value pixel used as a threshold and its neighbour pixels (Fig. 1).

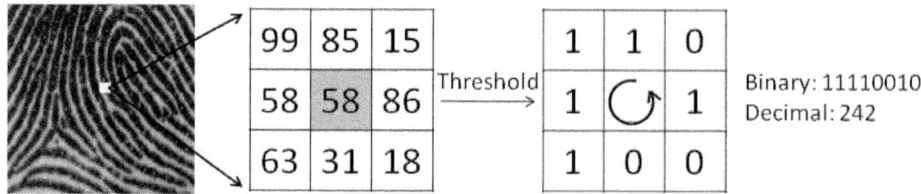

Fig. 1. Calculation of the LBP operator

Then a histogram formed by the values obtained for each pixel of the image is used as a texture descriptor. To deal with textures at different sizes, the LBP operator defines the local neighborhood as a set of equally spaced sampled points on a circle centered at the tagged pixel, allowing the LBP define any kind of radio r and p sample points, whose notation is $LBP_{(p,r)}$. Another extension for the LBP is the definition of uniform patterns, whose notation is $LBP_{(p,r)}^{u2}$. A LBP is called uniform if the binary pattern contains at most two transitions 0 to 1 or viceversa. To calculate the LBP histogram, each uniform pattern is stored in a separated bin and all non-uniform patterns are asigned to a single common bin [10].

2.3 Algorithm

The proposed method uses two different types of information in the fingerprint image: The minutiae and texture based features on the image of the fingerprint. The minutiae extraction stage is performed by applying the NFIS Mindtct [15]. Thus, there are two sets of minutiae, one for the input fingerprint and another for the template fingerprint. By applying the Delaunay triangulation on both minutiae sets, it obtaining two sets of triangles, computed for both the feature vector set invariant to rotation and translation, used for comparing the structures between the two fingerprints. The vector of local characteristics of a triangle is given by $Vi = [dij, djk, dki, ang\alpha, ang\beta, ang\gamma, difiSij,$

difjSij, difjSjk, difkSjk, difkSki, difiSki], where *dij* represents the distance between the minutiae *i* and *j*, *angα* correspond to the inner angle of the triangle with respect to the minutiae *i*, *difiSij* is the angle between the direction of the minutiae *i* with respect to the segment formed between the minutiae *i* and *j* in clockwise direction. (Fig. 2).

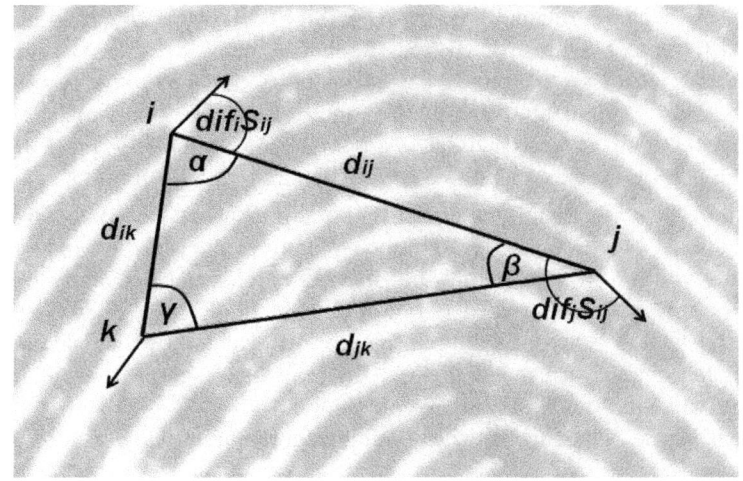

Fig. 2. Delaunay minutiae triangle and their features

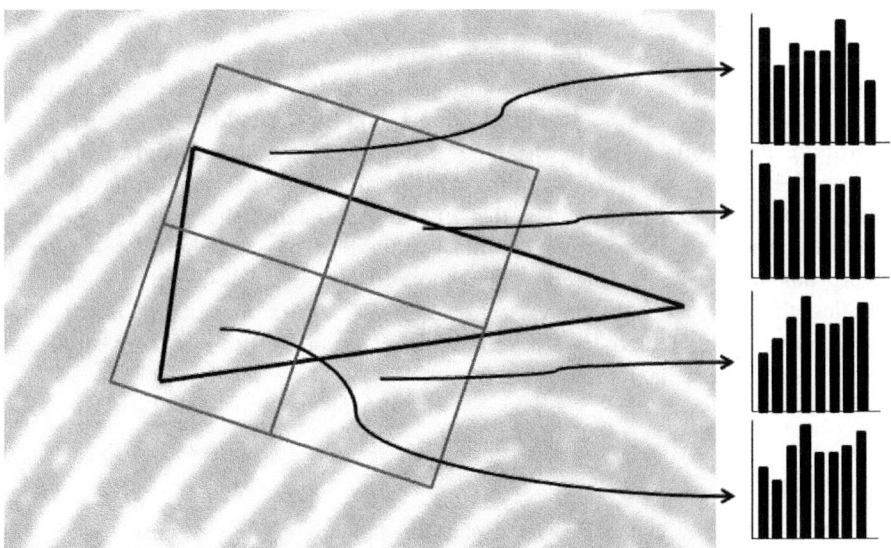

Fig. 3. LBP operator applied on a Delaunay minutiae triangle

The Delaunay triangulation tends to avoid triangles with obtuse angles, but this is not guaranteed. To avoid these triangles, the system rejects those who have interior angles greater than 168° and below 10°. The comparison is to find matches between vectors of the triangles of the input fingerprint and the template fingerprint. For each of the comparisons between the feature vectors of fingerprints, the feature vector of the input fingerprint is rotated three times, one for each side of the triangle, using the smallest difference between the vectors, this being the best similarity to be found. If the difference of these vectors is below a define threshold, the two vectors are considered a possible match, being marked and stored as candidate matched triangles. Following, for each pair of candidates, a comparison is made by the LBP operator. This approach uses the operator $LBP_{(8,2)}^{u2}$ which is used by [13, 14] for face recognition. The way of applying the LBP operator is through a window $w \times w$ whose midpoint coincides with the centroid of the structure analyzed. The window is divided into 4 sub-windows, by computing the LBP histograms independently in each. The four histograms are concatenated into a single vector (Fig. 3). Before applying the LBP operator, the window of the input fingerprint is rotated by the angular difference with one side common of the triangle of the template fingerprint. Thus, the LBP is applied in both windows with the same orientation.

To measure the difference between both histograms, it uses the chi-square distance χ^2 [13]:

$$\chi^2(T,E) = \sum_{i=1}^{n} \frac{(T_i - E_i)^2}{(T_i + E_i)} \tag{1}$$

where T and E are histograms of the template fingerprint and input fingerprint, respectively, n is the length of the histogram. If the difference between the two histograms does not exceed a defined threshold, the LBP histograms are similar, confirming the similarity of the triangle at the level of minutiae and texture of the fingerprint image. Finally, to determine whether these sets of triangles have a similar spatial distribution, it determines the Euclidean distance between each centroid structure, removing those triangles that vary in distance. Figure 4 shows two fingerprints of the same finger, which shows triangles that match (in white) and triangles that does not complied with the LBP operator neither in the spatial distribution (in segmented lines). We define the score of comparison between the input fingerprint and the template fingerprint as:

$$sc = \frac{e}{min(e1, e2)} \tag{2}$$

where e is the number of structure pairs that match, $e1$ and $e2$ corresponds to the structure numbers that are formed by Delaunay triangulation of the input fingerprint and the template fingerprint respectively.

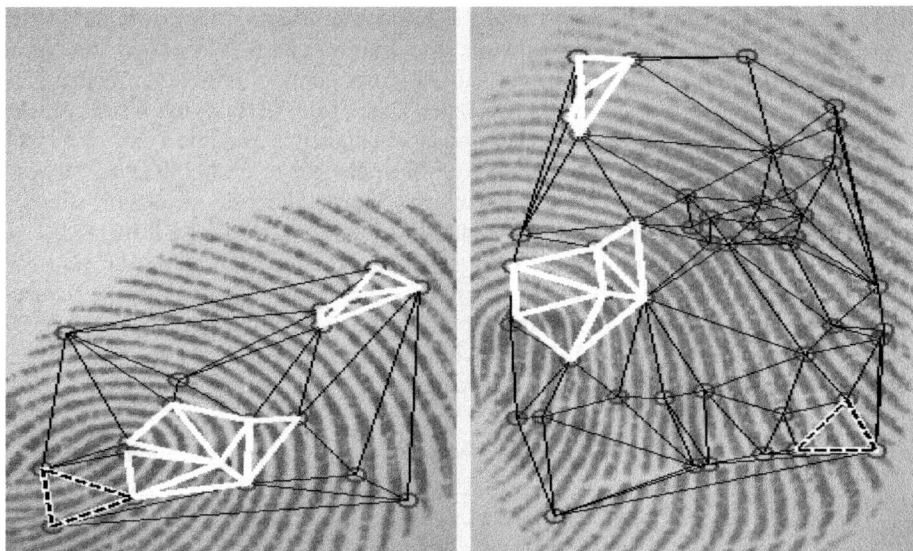

Fig. 4. Delaunay triangle structures for two fingerprints of the same finger taken from DB2 for the FVC2002 competition

3 Experiments and Results

3.1 Data Set and Evaluation Methodology

To obtain the results and determine the performance of the algorithm, it used fingerprint database DB1 and DB2 from FVC2002 competition [16]. Each database contains 800 images, 8 prints of the same finger for each of 100 individuals. The images of DB1 are 388x374 acquired with an optical sensor "TouchView II" by Identix. The images of DB2 are 296x560 using an optical sensor "FX2000" by Biometrika.

The performance of the algorithm is measured by the Equal Error Rate (EER), parameter given by [16]. The EER occurs when the FRR (percent of comparisons when there is a false rejection) and FAR (percent of comparisons when there is a false acceptance) have the same value. The lower EER, the better is the comparison system.

The algorithm was implemented in Matlab. The implementation of the algorithms was done in a laptop with Windows 7, Intel Core i5 (2.27 GHz), under normal working session.

3.2 Experimental Results

The first experiment is to estímate the parameters to be used in the LBP operator $LBP_{(8,2)}^{u2}$. We use two configurations and two sizes of windows. One configuration use a single window of w x w and the other configuration use the same window size divided en four sub-windows, to obtain four LBP histograms that are concatenated to get a single histogram. The purpose of the last configuration arises from the fact that you can get better results by dividing a window into sub-windows for greater discrimination. A histogram with four sub-windows contain more texture information locally that one with a single window. Table 1 and Table 2 show the results obtained with DB1 and DB2 respectively. It is observed that the execution time between a complete window and four sub-windows of the same size (1 of 80x80 and 4 of 40x40) shows no difference between the execution times. The best results of EER are obtained when it uses a set of 4 sub-windows in an area. In the LBP of DB1 4 sub-windows of 20x20, performs better with respect to other configurations due to the size of the image being used. When larger windows size is used (80x80), the performance drops, because it captures areas that fall outside the zone of interest. By contrast, DB2 obtain better performance with bigger window size because the images are larger (4 sub-windows of 40x40) and these windows capture more texture information.

Table 1. EER and times associated with different parameters for LBP in DB1

N° of windows	window size	EER	Avg. FAR	Avg. FRR
1	80x80	9.19%	0.18seg	0.39seg
4	40x40	7.48%	0.19seg	0.47seg
1	40x40	6.67%	0.17seg	0.32seg
4	20x20	6.18%	0.19seg	0.39seg

Table 2. EER and times associated with different parameters for LBP in DB2

N° of windows	window size	EER	Avg. FAR	Avg. FRR
1	80x80	4.59%	0.28seg	0.71seg
4	40x40	3.27%	0.32seg	0.75seg
1	40x40	5.58%	0.25seg	0.43seg
4	20x20	5.24%	0.28seg	0.51seg

Table 3. EER and times associated with different configurations for LBP in DB1

Configuration	EER	AVG
(+LBP +DIST)	6.18%	0.26seg
(+LBP -DIST)	7.17%	0.22seg
(-LBP +DIST)	7.33%	0.14seg
(-LBP -DIST)	8.39%	0.12seg

The second experiment is to validate the behavior of the hybrid algorithm. Different tests are performed using the LBP operator in different configurations with the Euclidan distance between structures. The EER and time associated with each of the configurations are shown in Table 3 and Table 4 for DB1 and DB2 respectively. The lowest EER is obtained when combining the comparison of Delaunay triangles in conjunction with the LBP operator and the Euclidan distance between structures (+LBP + DIST). The highest execution times were obtained for those configurations where EER was less, mainly because of the increased number of calculations of LBP operator when fingerprints have more common structures.

Table 4. EER and times associated with different configurations for LBP in DB2

Configuration	EER	AVG
(+LBP +DIST)	3.27%	0.47seg
(+LBP -DIST)	4.07%	0.40seg
(-LBP +DIST)	4.30%	0.36seg
(-LBP -DIST)	7.30%	0.33seg

4 Conclusions and Future Work

This paper presents a hybrid approach using Delaunay triangulation in conjunction with the LBP texture based operator. The triangle structures proved to have sufficient discriminatory features for comparison. The execution times are relatively low because the LBP operator is calculated only on those triangles that are candidate for comparison. The fusion of the Delaunay and LBP operator generates a structure with additional discriminatory features in the comparison for fingerprint matching. As future work we intend to use the ridge count between minutiae as another parameter for discrimination in the triangles, and generate more tests with the new addition to the algorithm with other databases. One problem with Delaunay triangulation is its sensitivity to false minutiae, affecting the formation of false structures, thus worsening the system performance. For this problem it is proposed the use of another minutia extractor and use enhanced fingerprint images.

References

1. Maltoni, D., Maio, D., Jain, A.K., Prabhakar, S.: Handbook of Fingerprint Recognition, 2nd edn. Springer, New York (2009)
2. Bazen, A., Verwaaijen, G., Gerez, S., Veelenturf, L., Zwaag, B.: A correlation-based fingerprint verification system. In: Proceedings of the Program for Research on Integrated Systems and Circuits, pp. 205–213 (2000)
3. Wang, C., Gavrilova, M.L.: Delaunay triangulation algorithm for fingerprint matching. In: Proceedings of the 3rd IEEE International Symposium on Voronoi Diagrams in Science and Engineering (ISVD 2006), pp. 208–216 (2006)
4. Parziale, G., Niel, A.: A Fingerprint Matching Using Minutiae Triangulation. In: Zhang, D., Jain, A.K. (eds.) ICBA 2004. LNCS, vol. 3072, pp. 241–248. Springer, Heidelberg (2004)
5. Bebis, G., Deaconu, T., Georgiopoulos, M.: Fingerprint Identification Using Delaunay Triangulation. In: Proc. IEEE International Conference on Intelligence, Information, and Systems (ICIIS), pp. 452–459 (1999)
6. Jain, A.K., Prabhakar, S., Hong, L., Pankanti, S.: Filterbank-based fingerprint matching. IEEE Transactions on Image Processing 9, 846–859 (2000)
7. Ross, A., Jain, A.K., Reisman, J.: A hybrid fingerprint matcher. Pattern Recognition 36, 1661–1673 (2003)
8. Jain, A.K., Ross, A., Prabhakar, S.: Fingerprint Matching Using Minutiae and Texture Features. In: Proc. Int. Conf. on Image Processing, pp. 282–285 (2001)
9. Nanni, L., Lumini, A.: Local Binary Patterns for a Hybrid Fingerprint Matcher. Pattern Recognition 41(11), 3461–3466 (2008)

10. Ojala, T., Pietikäinen, M., Mäenpää, T.: Multiresolution gray-scale and rotation invariant texture classification with local binary patterns. IEEE Transactions on Pattern Analysis and Machine Intelligence 24(7), 971–987 (2002)
11. Deng, H., Huo, Q.: Minutiae Matching Based Fingerprint Verification Using Delaunay Triangulation and Aligned-Edge-Guided Triangle Matching. In: Kanade, T., Jain, A., Ratha, N.K. (eds.) AVBPA 2005. LNCS, vol. 3546, pp. 270–278. Springer, Heidelberg (2005)
12. Ham, M.I., Pereira, Y.B., Reyes, E.B.G.: A Multiple Substructure Matching Algorithm for Fingerprint Verification. In: Rueda, L., Mery, D., Kittler, J. (eds.) CIARP 2007. LNCS, vol. 4756, pp. 172–181. Springer, Heidelberg (2007)
13. Ahonen, T., Hadid, A., Pietikäinen, M.: Face description with local binary patterns: Application to face recognition. IEEE Transactions on Pattern Analysis and Machine Intelligence 28(12), 2037–2041 (2006)
14. Maturana, D., Mery, D., Soto, A.: Face Recognition with Local Binary Patterns, Spatial Pyramid Histograms and Naive Bayes Nearest Neighbor classification. In: I Workshop Chileno Sobre Reconocimiento de Patrones: Teoría y Aplicaciones, pp. 125–132 (2009)
15. User's Guide to NIST Fingerprint Image Software (NFIS), NISTIR 6813, National Institute of Standards and Technology
16. Maio, D., Maltoni, D., Capelli, R., Wayman, J.L., Jain, A.K.: FVC 2002: Second Fingerprint Verification Competition. In: 16th International Conference on Pattern Recognition, Quebec City, QC, Canada, pp. 30811–30814 (2002)

Segmentation of Short Association Bundles in Massive Tractography Datasets Using a Multi-subject Bundle Atlas

Pamela Guevara[1,2,3], Delphine Duclap[1,2], Cyril Poupon[1,2],
Linda Marrakchi-Kacem[1,2], Josselin Houenou[1,2,4],
Marion Leboyer[4], and Jean-François Mangin[1,2]

[1] Neurospin, CEA, Gif-sur-Yvette, France
[2] Institut Fédératif de Recherche 49, Gif-sur-Yvette, France
[3] University of Concepción, Concepción, Chile
[4] AP-HP, University Paris-East, Department of Psychiatry, INSERM, U955 Unit

Abstract. This paper presents a method for automatic segmentation of some short association fiber bundles from massive dMRI tractography datasets. The method is based on a multi-subject bundle atlas derived from a two-level intra-subject and inter-subject clustering strategy. Each atlas bundle corresponds to one or more inter-subject clusters, presenting similar shapes. An atlas bundle is represented by the multi-subject list of the centroids of all intra-subject clusters in order to get a good sampling of the shape and localization variability. An atlas of 47 bundles is inferred from a first database of 12 brains, and used to segment the same bundles in a second database of 10 brains.

1 Introduction

Diffusion MRI allows noninvasive study of brain white matter (WM) structure through the measurement of the restricted diffusion of water. The fiber orientation can be inferred from this data and fiber bundles can be reconstructed using tractography algorithms [1]. Until now, several WM bundle atlases have been proposed [2,3] for the bundles belonging to deep white matter (DWM). However, short fibers of superficial white matter (SWM) have been barely considered, probably because these are more variable across sujects. Furthermore, the partial volume effect in subcortical regions prevents accurate delineation of small fiber bundles. The continuous improvement of DW-MRI acquisition schemes, diffusion models and tractography algorithms leads to increasingly complex and large tractography datasets, with known DWM tracts composed by various fiber fascicles of different shapes and lengths, and a big amount of short SWM association bundles. This improvement allows deeper analyses of WM bundles, but, at the same time, increases the requirements of tractography datasets analysis and segmentation techniques. The segmentation of human brain WM fiber bundles is therefore a complex and not completely solved problem. In particular, the cartography of fiber bundles of SWM is still an unachieved task. In [4], the authors

C. San Martin and S.-W. Kim (Eds.): CIARP 2011, LNCS 7042, pp. 701–708, 2011.
© Springer-Verlag Berlin Heidelberg 2011

performed a group analysis to study SWM using a voxel-based approach relying on linear brain normalization. They could identify only four U-fiber bundles because of the blurring occurring with such a normalization. Most recently, this method was improved using non-linear normalization, and was able to detect 29 short association bundles in 20 subjects [5]. These results are very interesting but as a ROI (region of interest) based approach was used, there is no guarantee that the fibers present the same shape across subjects.

The usual strategies proposed for the segmentation of fiber bundles follow two complementary ideas. The first approach is based on ROIs used to select or exclude tracts [3,5]. The second strategy is based on tract clustering using pairwise similarity measures [6]. This last approach requires less interaction than manual approaches and integrates fiber shape and position information in the analysis, which is not the case of most ROI-based segmentation approaches. It can also embed a priori knowledge represented by a bundle template [7]. However, the clustering-based methods commonly present a limitation on the number of fibers that can be analyzed. In spite of two recent works that describe the analysis of huge datasets (120,000 [8] and 480,000 fibers [9]), the segmentation of huge tractography datasets, presenting more than one million tracts, is still a challenge.

Hence, this paper presents a method for the segmentation of SWM fiber bundles from massive tractography datasets using a priori information embedded in a multi-subject (MS) fiber bundle atlas. The method builds upon a multiresolution intra-subject clustering that can compress millions of tracts into a few thousand consistent bundles, described in [10]. A second level of clustering is performed across subjects in order to infer a list of generic bundles with consistent shape and localization in a normalized space [11]. The most reproducible inter-subject (IS) clusters computed from a database of 12 brains were manually labeled to build the atlas. This MS strategy, embedding the shape and localization variability, has been shown recently to be more efficient than the usual single template approach for brain structure recognition because of weaknesses of the spatial normalization paradigm [12]. New tractography datasets are first compressed with the same intra-subject clustering. The resulting clusters are then labeled using pairwise distances to the centroids representing the MS atlas bundles. To the best of our knowledge, this is the first SWM clustering-based segmentation method.

2   Material and Method

2.1   Diffusion and Tractography Datasets

The atlas was constructed from 12 subjects of a High Angular Resolution Diffusion Imaging (HARDI) adult database (DB1). This database provides high quality T1-weighted images and diffusion-weighted (DW) data acquired with a GE Healthcare Signa 1.5 T Excite scanner. The diffusion data presents a high angular resolution based on 200 directions and a b-value of 3000s/mm^2 (voxel size of $1.875 \times 1.875 \times 2$ mm).

Ten subjects of another adult HARDI database (DB2), were used to test the segmentation method. This database provides high quality T1-weighted images and DW data acquired with a Siemens 3.0 T Tim Trio system. The DW data is based on 41 directions and a b-value of $1000 \, \text{s/mm}^2$ (voxel size of $2 \times 2 \times 2 \, \text{mm}$).

DW data were acquired using a twice refocusing spin echo technique compensating Eddy currents to the first order. Geometrical distortions linked to susceptibility artifacts were corrected using a phase map acquisition. T1 and DW data were automatically realigned using a rigid 3D transform. The diffusion Orientation Distribution Function (ODF) was reconstructed in each voxel. For subjects from DB1, a spherical deconvolution (SD) of the fiber ODF was used. It is a SD transform reconstructed from q-ball imaging with a constrained regularization [13], using a maximum spherical harmonic order $SH_{max} = 8$ and a Laplace-Beltrami regularization factor $\lambda_{LB} = 0.006$. For subjects from DB2, an analytical solution of the q-ball model was determined [14], using a $SH_{max} = 6$ and a $\lambda_{LB} = 0.006$. Whole-brain tractography was performed using an improved tractography propagation mask (using T1 data rather than FA) and a regularized deterministic tractography algorithm. Tractography was initiated from two seeds in each voxel of the mask (with T1 resolution), in both retrograde and anterograde directions, according to the maximal direction of the underlying ODF. Tracking parameters included a maximum curvature angle of $30°$ and a minimum and maximum fiber length of $20 \, \text{mm}$ and $250 \, \text{mm}$, respectively, leading to a set of about 1.5 millions tracts per subject.

2.2 HARDI Multi-subject Fiber Bundle Atlas

The two-level clustering was performed using the method described in [11] applied on database DB1, with some improvements. First, intra-subject clustering [10] was applied to each dataset. This **intra-subject clustering** reduces the tractography dataset information from more than one million of tracts to a few thousand fiber bundles. The obtained bundles are thin and regular fiber fascicles composed by fibers presenting similar length and shape. In addition, during the analysis most of noise fibers are discarded, leading to a cleaner fiber dataset. Due to its regular shape, each resulting fiber bundle can be represented by a single fiber, called a bundle centroid. This compressed representation of a tractography dataset allows the application of further processing steps that could not be applied to the whole fiber dataset.

The second clustering level aimed at matching the putative bundles produced by the previous level across the population of subjects. In this **inter-subject clustering**, fiber centroids from all the subjects were aligned by an affine transformation to the Talairach space (TS), estimated from the T1-weighted image. Then, the centroids were clustered using pairwise distance measures [15] in order to match bundles with similar shapes and positions in TS. In order to get population representative clusters, only clusters composed by centroids from at least half of the subjects were selected. The final addition of closest centroids described in [11] was not performed with the aim of keeping very tight clusters.

Region	Abbrev.	Region	Abbrev.
Superior frontal gyrus	SFG	Superior temporal gyrus	STG
Middle frontal gyrus	MFG	Middle temporal gyrus	MTG
Inferior frontal gyrus	IFG	Inferior temporal gyrus	ITG
Medial fronto-orbital gyrus	MFOG	Cuneus	Cu
Lateral fronto-orbital gyrus	LFOG	Pre-cuneus	PrCu
Precentral gyrus	PrCG	Cingulate gyrus	CG
Postcentral gyrus	PoCG	Paracentral gyrus	PaCG
Supramarginal gyrus	SMG	Fusiform gyrus	FuG
Angular gyrus	AG	Lingual gyrus	LG
Superior parietal gyrus	SPG	Insular	Ins
Middle occipital gyrus	MOG		

Fig. 1. Cortical surface anatomical regions used to identify the atlas short association bundles. Images where adapted from *http://www.bartleby.com/107/* and *http://www.netterimages.com/*.

The inter-subject clusters belonging to SWM were manually labeled by an expert using gyral parcellation of cortical surfaces, in order to give an anatomical name to each reproducible bundle (see Fig. 1). Each atlas bundle is then represented by the complete set of individual centroids belonging to the underlying intra-subject clusters. A last visual inspection led to discard a few artefactual centroids clearly including spurious parts like loops. The resulting multi-subject representation provides a good sampling of the inter-subject variability of the bundle trajectory after affine normalization. The atlas inference was done for the bundles of the left hemisphere (LH), with a length between 35 and 110 mm. The bundles of the right hemisphere (RH) were obtained using the symmetric of those of the LH with respect to Talairach inter-hemispheric plane. The goal is to get a symmetric atlas for the validation described in this paper. Ongoing work aims at performing the same inference for the RH in order to remove any bias. The current atlas includes a total of 47 SWM bundles; see details in Fig. 2.

2.3   WM Tracts Segmentation

The segmentation of a new tractography dataset begins with a compression into a few thousand bundles equivalent to the compression used during the atlas inference, described in [10]. Then, the resulting bundles are labeled using a supervised classification based on the fiber bundle atlas. The bundle centroids are normalized to the TS using an affine transformation. Then pairwise distances are computed between each centroid of the new subject and all the centroids of the atlas. The distance measure used is the maximum of the Euclidean distances between corresponding points (dM), defined for two fibers A and B, described by N_p points, as

$$d_M(A, B) = \min\left(\max_i \| \mathbf{a}_i - \mathbf{b}_i \|, \max_i \| \mathbf{a}_i - \mathbf{b}_{N_p - i} \|\right), \quad (1)$$

where $\mathbf{a}_i$ and $\mathbf{b}_i$ are the position of the points of fibers A and B respectively, for $i = 0..N_p - 1$. This distance is a good representation of the similarity between two

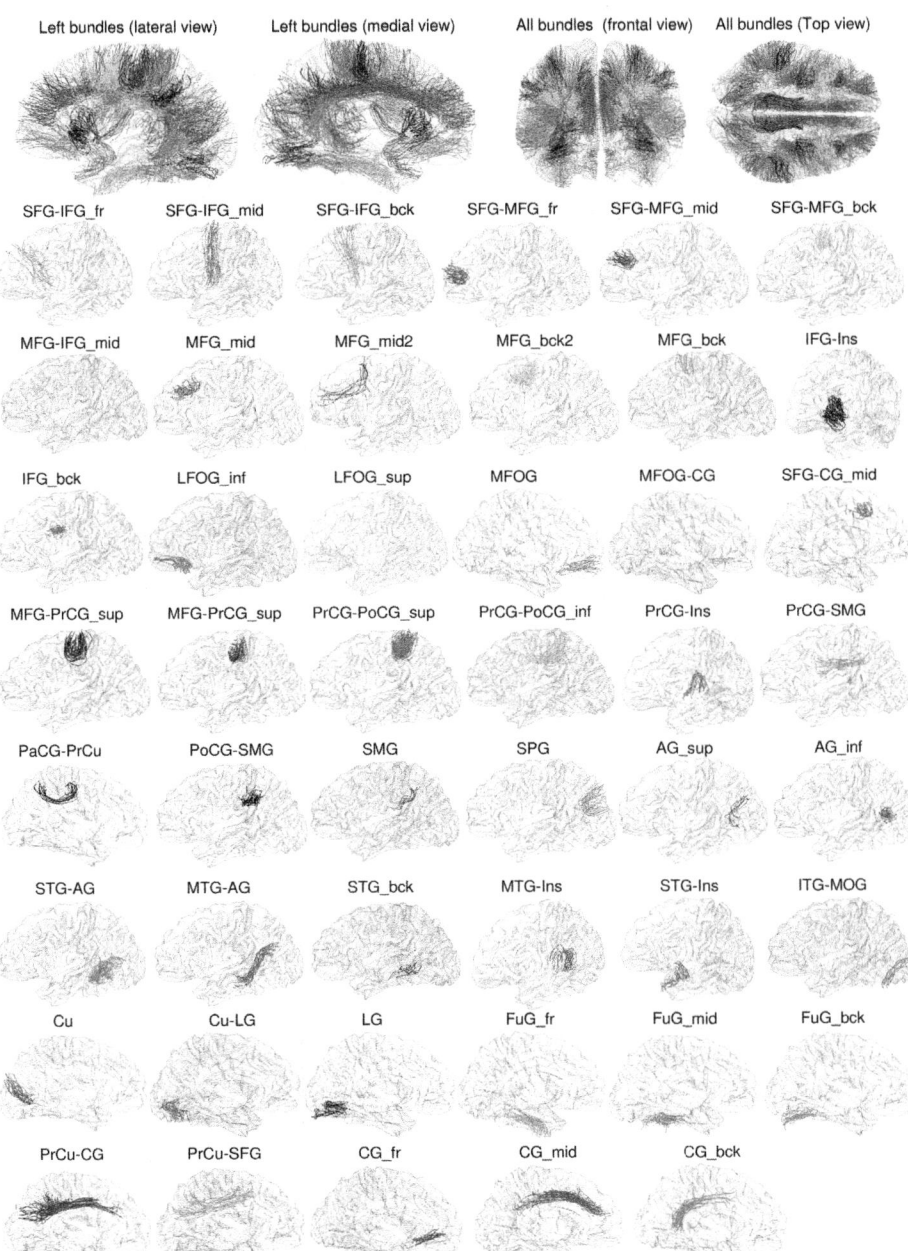

Fig. 2. Short association bundle atlas (47 bundles per hemisphere). The first row shows all the atlas bundles. The remaining rows show each bundle in a separated figure. Bundle names were assigned in function of the regions that the bundles connect, following the names illustrated in Fig. 1. In some cases, an additional spatial specification was used: fr (frontal), mid (middle), bck (back), sup (superior), inf (inferior).

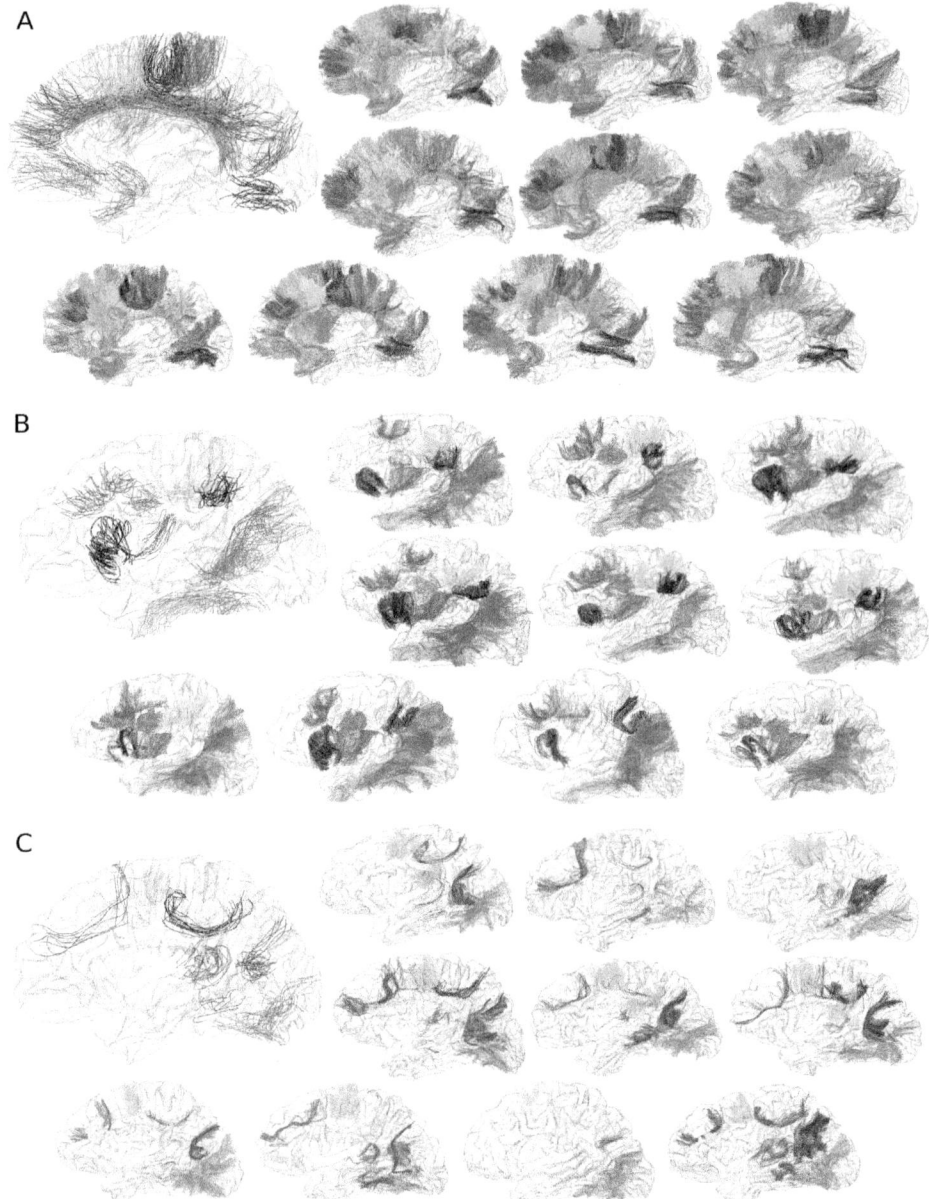

Fig. 3. Automatic fiber bundle segmentation results. Only left hemisphere bundles are shown. Colors are the same as for the bundle atlas (Fig. 2). The bundles were divided into three groups, in function of their reproducibility. Atlas bundles are shown in the upper-left corner of each image. **A**: Fiber bundles found in all the subjects (21 bundles). **B**: Fiber bundles found in 9 of the 10 subjects (12 bundles). **C**: Fiber bundles found in 5 to 8 subjects (14 bundles).

fibers, as it takes into account the fiber positions and shapes. It is more restrictive than distances based on the closest points [15,6]. For the calculation, the atlas fibers and the individual centroids are resampled using 21 equally distributed points. The whole set of pairwise distances is obtained in a few minutes.

Each individual centroid is labeled by the closest atlas bundle, provided that the distance to this bundle, namely the smallest pairwise distance to the centroids representing this bundle, is lower than a threshold. This threshold was empirically adapted to each atlas bundle (between 8–14 mm) taking into account the bundle mean fiber length and the proximity to other atlas bundles, leading to higher thresholds for long and isolated bundles. A leave-one-out strategy for the determination of the thresholds could be implemented in the future.

3   Results

A general problem for evaluating WM bundle segmentation is the lack of gold standard. This is even more complex for SWM, which cartography is still largely unknown and to the best of our knowledge, no atlas describing the shape of these bundles has been proposed. We evaluate our approach using a second database (DB2). The results for the ten subjects are presented in Fig. 3. All the bundles were found in at least half of the subjects, which is consistent with our atlas construction requirements. Twenty-one bundles were found in all the subjects. Twelve bundles were found in nine subjects and fourteen bundles were found in between five to eight subjects. The segmentations were validated by the expert who defined the atlas. To get an insight of the quality of the results, the bundles were visually compared with those obtained using larger distance thresholds. It was found that the chosen thresholds were close to optimal for most of the bundles. Long and isolated bundles were in general well segmented, when these existed, but some classifications errors were found in short bundles localized very close to other atlas bundles.

4   Discussion and Conclusion

The proposed method shows that it is possible to segment the most reproducible SWM bundles using a clustering-based approach in a population of subjects. The use of a multi-subject representation of bundles and shape information could lead to cleaner bundles than when using a ROI-based strategy, which may improve the sensitivity of morphometric studies. Furthermore, this new atlas and the possibility to manipulate massive tractography datasets allow finer decompositions of the bundles, for instance, we proposed two subdivisions of the bundle connecting the pre- and post-central gyri. Our atlas is bound to be refined with more of such subdivisions in the near future.

However, the proposed method is far from be perfect. This is due in part to the high inter-subject variability of short association SWM bundles and the current limitations of dMRI techniques. Our results depend strongly on the quality of the

tractography results: bundles that are not tracked in individuals can not be segmented, a problem that particularly affects SWM due to the partial volume effect.

But an important improvement will be obtained by the use of non-linear
normalization [16]. First, the atlas construction will be performed using this
kind of normalization, leading to a better multi-subject representation of the
variability of the atlas bundles. Furthermore, the recognition of the bundles
should be also improved if non-linear normalization is used between the subjects
and the atlas, reducing the classification errors produced in bundles presenting
very similar shapes and close positions.

References

1. Mori, S., van Zijl, P.C.M.: Fiber tracking: principles and strategies - a technical review. NMR Biomed. 15(7-8), 468–480 (2002)
2. Mori, S., Wakana, S., van Zijl, P.C.M., Nagae-Poetscher, L.M.: MRI Atlas of Human White Matter, 1st edn. Elsevier Science (August 2005)
3. Catani, M., Thiebaut de Schotten, M.: A diffusion tensor imaging tractography atlas for virtual in vivo dissections. Cortex 44(8), 1105–1132 (2008)
4. Oishi, K., Zilles, K., Amunts, K., et al.: Human brain white matter atlas: Identification and assignment of common anatomical structures in superficial white matter. Neuroimage 43(3), 447–457 (2008)
5. Zhang, Y., Zhang, J., Oishi, K., et al.: Atlas-guided tract reconstruction for automated and comprehensive examination of the white matter anatomy. NeuroImage 52(4), 1289–1301 (2010)
6. O'Donnell, L.J., Kubicki, M., Shenton, M.E., et al.: A method for clustering white matter fiber tracts. AJNR 27(5), 1032–1036 (2006)
7. O'Donnell, L., Westin, C.F.: Automatic tractography segmentation using a high-dimensional white matter atlas. IEEE Transactions on Medical Imaging 26(11), 1562–1575 (2007)
8. Wang, X., Grimson, W.E.L., Westin, C.F.: Tractography segmentation using a hierarchical dirichlet processes mixture model. Neuroimage 54(1), 290–302 (2011)
9. Visser, E., Nijhuis, E.H.J., Buitelaar, J.K., Zwiers, M.P.: Partition-based mass clustering of tractography streamlines. Neuroimage 54(1), 303–312 (2011)
10. Guevara, P., Poupon, C., Rivière, D., et al.: Robust clustering of massive tractography datasets. NeuroImage 54(3), 1975–1993 (2011)
11. Guevara, P., Poupon, C., Rivière, D., et al.: Inference of a HARDI Fiber Bundle Atlas Using a Two-Level Clustering Strategy. In: Jiang, T., Navab, N., Pluim, J.P.W., Viergever, M.A. (eds.) MICCAI 2010. LNCS, vol. 6361, pp. 550–557. Springer, Heidelberg (2010)
12. Lyu, I., Seong, J.K., Shin, S.Y., et al.: Spectral-based automatic labeling and refining of human cortical sulcal curves using expert-provided examples. Neuroimage 52(1), 142–157 (2010)
13. Tournier, J.D., Calamante, F., Connelly, A.: Robust determination of the fibre orientation distribution in diffusion MRI: non-negativity constrained super-resolved spherical deconvolution. Neuroimage 35(4), 1459–1472 (2007)
14. Descoteaux, M.E., Fitzgibbons, S., Deriche, R.: Regularized, fast and robust analytical q-ball imaging. Magn. Reson. Med. 58, 497–510 (2007)
15. Corouge, I., Gouttard, S., Gerig, G.: Towards a shape model of white matter fiber bundles using diffusion tensor MRI. In: ISBI 2004 (2004)
16. Auzias, G., Colliot, O., Glaunes, et al: Diffeomorphic brain registration under exhaustive sulcal constraints. IEEE Transactions on Medical Imaging 99 (2011)

Classifying Execution Times in Parallel Computing Systems: A Classical Hypothesis Testing Approach

Hugo Pacheco, Jonathan Pino, Julio Santana, Pablo Ulloa, and Jorge E. Pezoa[*]

Departamento de Ingeniería Eléctrica and Center for Optics and Photonics (CEFOP)
Universidad de Concepción, Concepción, Chile
{hpacheco,jopino,juliosantana,pulloag,jpezoa}@udec.cl

Abstract. In this paper two classifiers have been derived in order to determine if identical computer tasks have been executed at different processors. The classifiers have been developed analytically following a classical hypothesis testing approach. The main assumption of this work is that the probability distribution function (pdf) of the random times taken by the processors to serve tasks are known. This assumption has been fulfilled by empirically characterizing the pdf of such random times. The performance of the classifiers developed here has been assessed using traces from real processors. Further, the performance of the classifiers is compared to heuristic classifiers, linear discriminants, and non-linear discriminants among other classifiers.

1 Introduction

Pattern recognition is a well-established research area that, in brief, takes groups of known patterns and abstracts their fundamental characteristics in terms of classes or clusters of data. Technically speaking, the stage where information is abstracted from the known-patterns is termed as the training process, and the known-patterns are called the training classes from the data sets. Based upon the information obtained during the training process, classifiers are next mathematically devised with the goal of determining, as accurate as possible, the class of a given sample data. This stage is called the classification process [1]. Lately, classification as well as pattern recognition techniques have been employed in new application areas, such as parallel data processing, distributed data processing, network analysis, intrusion detection, customer analysis at communication service providers, etc. The common factor in all these areas is that it becomes mandatory to classify either the execution time of the applications executed on the system or the sojourn time of customers in the system, [2, 3, 4, 5, 6].

For instance, in computer networks' intrusion detection, it becomes necessary to monitor the processing time taken by a packet-analyzer to break down the

---

[*] The authors thank Professors Rosa L. Figueroa and Mario R. Medina with Universidad de Concepción for their valuable comments and suggestions. J. E. Pezoa acknowledges support of CEFOP and Grant CONICYT PFB-0824.

C. San Martin and S.-W. Kim (Eds.): CIARP 2011, LNCS 7042, pp. 709–717, 2011.

data packets present in the computer network. If an accurate estimate of such processing time is at hand, the behavior of normal as well as abnormal packets flowing in the network can be understood, and more importantly for classification and pattern recognition purposes, such behavior can be abstracted in a mathematical fashion [2, 3, 5]. In parallel computing systems where servers are not homogeneous, as in the case of distributed computing clusters, tasks assigned to such systems must be smartly mapped onto servers so that a balanced allocation of the computing resources can be achieved. It is know that an efficient allocation of the computing resources in parallel and distributed computing systems depends vitally on an accurate knowledge about the execution time of the individual tasks forming an application [4, 7]. For instance, Zhang and Figuereido employed in [4] a principal component analysis and k-NN classifiers to categorize the execution time of tasks being processed on a cluster of computers. In [6], Yang *et al.* proposed a classifier, based on the maximum-likelihood principle, to determine if the customers of a telecommunications service-provider are switching or not between different companies. To do so, they trained classifiers to learn the waiting time that different service providers offer to their customers.

In this paper, two classifiers have been developed in order to distinguish if identical tasks, which have been assigned to processors in a parallel computing system, are executed or not on different processors. The classifiers have been developed analytically using a classical hypothesis testing approach and the Bayesian as well as the Neyman-Pearson design criteria. Using traces taken from a real distributed system, a training process was conducted in order to characterize the *a priori* probability distribution functions (pdfs) of the random times taken by the processors to a serve task. As a result of the training process, the pdfs of the execution times were fitted and mathematically modeled. The performance of the classifiers developed here has been evaluated by categorizing real data. Further, the performance of our classifiers was compared to generic classifiers such as heuristic classifiers, linear discriminants, quadratic discriminants, and classifiers based on the Mahalanobis distance. Results have shown that the classifiers developed in this work consistently outperform those generic classifiers. At last, we comment that the motivation of this work is to implement the classifiers developed here in the distributed system shown in [7] with the goal of enhancing the load balancing algorithms of the system.

The rest of this paper is organized as follows. In Section 2 the empirical characterization of the pdf of the execution times is carried out as part of the training process. In Section 3 a Bayesian and a Neyman-Pearson classifiers are developed, and their performance in classifying the execution time of tasks is evaluated in Section 4. Our conclusions and future work are presented in Section 5.

2   Problem Definition and Training Stage

2.1   Problem Definition

Consider a parallel computing system based on two classes of processors. Suppose that atomic identical tasks are assigned to the processors in the system for their concurrent execution. Due to the nature computing systems, executing such tasks on any processor takes a random execution time, which depends solely on the processor where they are executed. This paper addresses the problem of (i) characterizing, for the purpose of designing classifiers, the processing times of these atomic tasks; and (ii) classifying a series of samples of the execution time of tasks in one out of the two classes of processors that are known to exist in the parallel computing system.

2.2   Training Stage and Characterization of the Execution Times

Statistical classification theory assumes that the pdf of the hypotheses are known it a priori. In order to obtain the pdf of processing times of the tasks forming the application being executed on the parallel computing system, we have conducted an experimental characterization of these random times by means of training data-sets of each class of processor in the system. First, we describe the classes of processors employed in the system. The first class of machines corresponds to tablet computers equipped with Crusoe processors. We name this class as it Crusoe and we also associate such machines, in the classification problem, with the null hypothesis, H_0. The second class of machines corresponds to laptop computers equipped with a Pentium 4 Mobile processors. We name this second class as $P4m$ and associate them with the alternative hypothesis, H_1. For training purposes, a total of 22026 samples of the execution times were used in the case of the $Crusoe$ class, while 9805 samples of the execution time were used during the characterization of the execution time of the $P4m$ class.

During the training process, different probability distributions were fitted for the execution times. In order to determine the best fit, the minimum total square error criterion was employed. As a result, the Log-Normal distribution was selected as the best model for the pdf of the execution time of both machines. Fitted pdfs for different distribution functions can be observed in Fig. 1, while in Table 1 the total minimum square errors for each fitted pdf are listed. From these results, the pdf of the random variable T_i, $i = \{0, 1\}$, which denotes the execution time of ith hypothesis H_i, $i = \{0, 1\}$, is mathematically described by the function:

$$f_{T_i}(t; \mu_i, \sigma_i) = \frac{1}{t\sigma_i\sqrt{2\pi}} \exp\left(\frac{-(\ln(t) - \mu_i)^2}{2\sigma_i^2}\right). \tag{1}$$

The parameters of each pdf estimated from the training data sets are: $\mu_0 = 0.7203$, $\sigma_0 = 0.5459$ for the $Crusoe$ class and $\mu_1 = 0.9760$, $\sigma_1 = 0.4599$ for the $P4m$ class.

3   Classifiers Design

3.1   Bayesian Classifier

To design a Bayesian classifier, first we must define both the costs associated to all the different classification errors and the rewards associated to correct

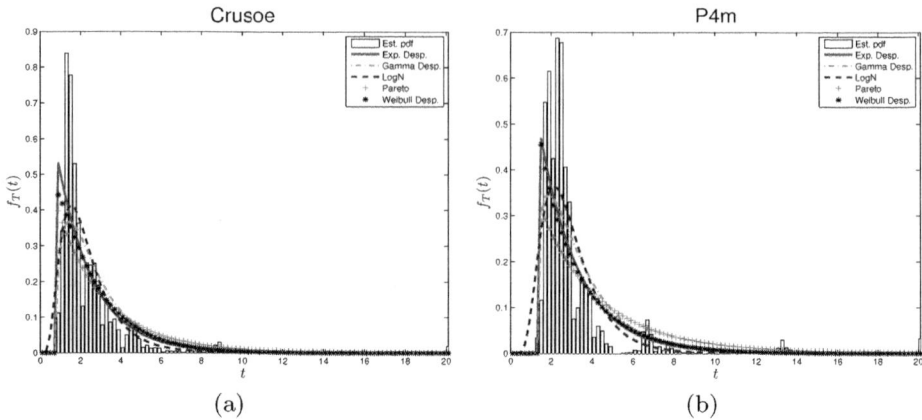

Fig. 1. Fitted pdfs for the execution time in: (a) *Crusoe*; and (b) *P4m* processors

Tabla 1. Total square error between the fitted and the empirical pdfs of the execution time of tasks in the *Crusoe* class and in the *P4m* class of processors

Machine	Total square error				
	Exponential	Gamma	Log-normal	Pareto	Weibull
Crusoe	0.612	0.524	0.466	0.698	0.603
P4m	0.610	0.566	0.524	0.826	0.656

classifications. It has been assumed here that the cost of making a mistake are symmetrical and unitary for the type I and type II errors and for both hypotheses, that is $c_{ij} = 1$, $i, j = \{0, 1\}$, $i \neq j$, while the rewards associated to correct classifications were assumed here to be zero, $c_{ij} = 0$, $i, j = \{0, 1\}$, $i = j$. In addition, it has been assumed here that the it a priori probabilities of the hypotheses H_0 and H_1 are identical and, as traditionally assumed, equal to 0.5. With this set-up defined, the classifier is designed after partitioning the sample set $\Omega = \Omega_0 \cup \Omega_1$ by means of one or more threshold values, which must be determined in some optimal fashion with the goal of reducing the average classification risk that is denoted here as $\delta(\cdot)$. The minimal classification risk, $r^*(\delta)$, can be expressed as [8]:

$$r^*(\delta) = \min_{\Omega_1}\{r(\delta)\} = \{t \in \Omega : \sum_{j=0}^{1} \pi_j(c_{1j} - c_{0j})f_T^j(t) \leq 0\}. \tag{2}$$

Once the probability distributions of the hypotheses, $f_T^j(t)$, the cost associated to each mistaken classificaion,c_{ij}, and the *a priori* probabilities, π_j, are known, the likelihood ratio test (LRT) $L(t) = \frac{f_T^1(t)}{f_T^0(t)} = \frac{\sigma_0}{\sigma_1} \exp\left(\frac{(\ln(t)-\mu_0)^2}{2\sigma_0^2} - \frac{(\ln(t)-\mu_1)^2}{2\sigma_1^2}\right)$ can be used to find the threshold values defining the classification regions.

The threshold values are obtained from the LRT by solving the second-order equation in the variable $z = \ln(t)$:

$$\left(\frac{\sigma_1^2 - \sigma_0^2}{\sigma_1^2 \sigma_0^2}\right) z^2 + 2\left(\frac{\mu_1 \sigma_0^2 - \mu_0 \sigma_1^2}{\sigma_1^2 \sigma_0^2}\right) z + \left(\frac{\mu_0^2}{\sigma_0^2} - \frac{\mu_1^2}{\sigma_1^2} - 2\ln\frac{\sigma_1}{\sigma_0}\right) = 0, \quad (3)$$

whose solutions are $t_a = 2.027$ and $t_b = 12.143$. These solutions uniquely define the following two classification regions: $\Omega_0 = (0, 2.027) \cup (12.143, \infty)$ and $\Omega_1 = [2.027, 12.143]$.

3.2 Neyman-Pearson Classifier

The Neyman-Pearson criterion consists in maximizing the probability of true positive $P_D = P_1\{\Omega_1\}$, i.e, the probability of effectively announcing that the alternative hypothesis is observed when such hypothesis has truly occurred. The Neyman-Pearson criterion also states that the probability of true positive is maximized under the constraint of allowing a false positive or false alarm probability of $P_{FA} = P_0\{\Omega_1\} = \alpha$. To fulfill these requirements a partition Ω_1 of Ω must be determined such that:

$$\left(\frac{\sigma_1^2 - \sigma_0^2}{\sigma_1^2 \sigma_0^2}\right) \ln^2(t) + 2\left(\frac{\mu_1 \sigma_0^2 - \mu_0 \sigma_1^2}{\sigma_1^2 \sigma_0^2}\right) \ln(t) + \left(\frac{\mu_0^2}{\sigma_0^2} - \frac{\mu_1^2}{\sigma_1^2} - 2\ln\frac{\sigma_1}{\sigma_0}\right) \geq \ln\gamma \quad (4)$$

$$\int_{\{t : L(t) \geq \gamma\}} f_T^0(t)dt = \alpha \quad (5)$$

where γ is the threshold value associated to the LRT. Solving the system of non-linear inequalities (4) and (5) is a non trivial task, and to the best of our knowledge, it is not possible to solve for analytically. We have developed here an algorithm to solve numerically for this system of inequalities. The algorithm must execute the following steps:

1. An initial threshold value is set, say to γ_0.
2. Equation (4) is solved for to find the values $t_a(\gamma_0)$ and $t_b(\gamma_0)$. These solutions, which are parameterized by the initial threshold value, satisfy the LRT.
3. The false positive in the classification region $\Omega_1(\gamma_0)$ is calculated by means of the equation $\alpha(\gamma_0) = F_0(t_b(\gamma_0)) - F_0(t_a(\gamma_0))$, where $F_0(\cdot)$ is the cummulative distribution function (CDF) of the null hypothesis.
4. If the relationship $\alpha(\gamma_0) \approx \alpha$ holds, then the classification region, Ω_1, has been accurately defined, otherwise the algorithm must be executed from step 1 using a different threshold value.

In Fig. 2(a) the inequality (4) is shown. Note that if the false positive probability is fixed to $\alpha = 0.5$, the values $t_a(\gamma)$ y $t_b(\gamma)$ satisfying the system of inequalities are $t_a(\gamma) = 2.056$ and $t_b(\gamma) = 11.97$. These values define the following classification regions: $\Omega_0 = (0, 2.056) \cup (11.97, \infty)$ and $\Omega_1 = [2.056, 11.97]$.

Note that by inspection of Figs. 2(a) and (b) a simple classification rule can be proposed. We propose here the boundary $t_u = 2.0$, which approximately balances the areas under the pdfs of the execution times. This boundary and its classification regions, which have been determined in a qualitative and intuitive manner, are jointly termed here as the heuristic classifier.

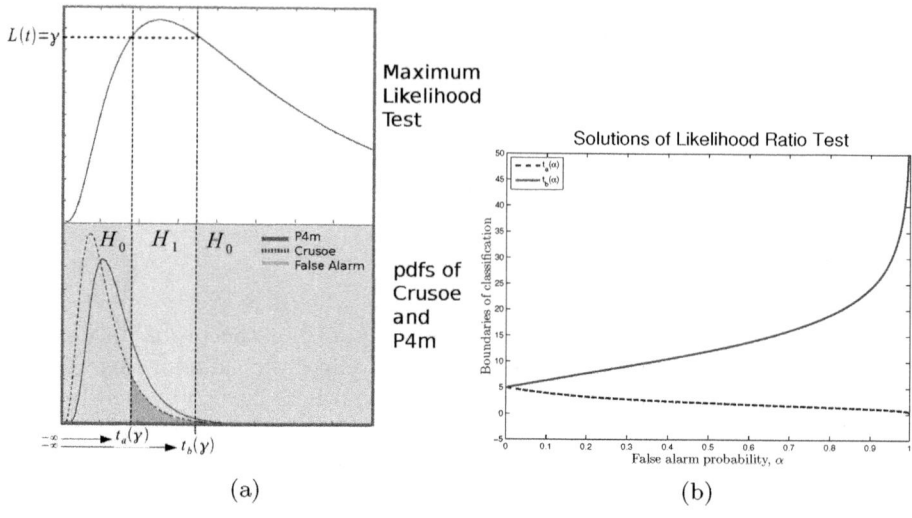

Fig. 2. (a) False positive probability α, the LRT $L(t)$, and the pdfs of the execution times which represent the hypotheses of the problem. Solutions t_a and t_b of the LRT.

4   Results

To assess the performance of the classifiers devised here we have employed the following metrics: the percentage of hits, the percentage of positive classifications, the percentage of misclassification, the percentage of false positives, and classification error (in percentage). The metrics are mathematically defined as:

$$\% \text{ Hits} = 100 \left(\frac{Q\{H_0 : H_0\}}{2Q\{H_0\}} + \frac{Q\{H_1 : H_1\}}{2Q\{H_1\}} \right), \tag{6}$$

$$\% \text{ Positive hits} = 100 \frac{Q\{H_1 : H_1\}}{Q\{H_1\}}, \tag{7}$$

$$\% \text{ False negative} = 100 \frac{Q\{H_0 : H_1\}}{Q\{H_1\}}, \tag{8}$$

$$\% \text{ False positives} = 100 \frac{Q\{H_1 : H_0\}}{Q\{H_0\}}, \tag{9}$$

$$\% \text{ Errors} = 1 - \% \text{ Hits}, \tag{10}$$

where $Q\{H_i\}$ is the number of times that the ith class happen to occur during the assessment of the classifier, and $Q\{H_i : H_j\}$ is the number of times that the ith class was announced as true, when actually the jth class was the true class from which the sample under analysis was drawn.

The results of the classifiers developed in this paper are listed in Table 2. For comparison, we have employed the tool `classify` from Matlab's statistics toolbox®, and we have trained (using the same data employed to characterize the distributions) classifiers based on linear discriminants, diag-linear discriminants, quadratic discriminants, diag-quadratic discriminants, and classifiers based on the Mahalanobis distance. The performance results of these Matalab based classifiers are listed in Table 3.

From Table 2 we can observe that the Bayesian and the Neyman-Pearson classifiers achieve a fairly good percentage of hits. We note, however, that the Neyman-Pearson classifier offers some versatility over the Bayesian classifier through the false alarm parameter. The designer, or even the user, of a Neyman-Pearson classifier may adjust the false alarm probability to control the size of the classification regions. From Tables 2 and 3 it can be observed that the classifiers designed in this paper clearly outperform the classification methods implemented in Matlab's statistics toolbox in both metrics percentage classification hits and percentage of classification errors.

Figure 3(a) shows the percentage of hits of the Neyman-Pearson classifier as a function of the probability of false alarm. From the figure it can be observed the existence of a point where the percentage of classification hits is the same for both processors. At this point, the probability of false alarm is approximately 0.45. From Fig. 3(a) it can also be observed that the point where the percentage of classification hits is maximized corresponds to approximately to a probability of false alarm of 0.7. Figure 3(b) shows the receiver operating curve of the Neyman-Pearson classifier. From such figure we can observe that the marginal increment in the probability of classification is higher for values of the probability of false alarm below 0.5, as compared with the marginal increment observed for probabilities of false alarm larger than 0.6. In a more theoretical matter, it can be noticed that the receiver operating curve shown in Fig. 3(b), which was calculated numerically, indeed exhibits the property of concavity expected from any receiver operating curve [8].

Tabla 2. Performance of the classifiers designed in this paper

	Heuristic	Bayes	Neyman-Pearson		
			$\alpha = 0.2$	$\alpha = 0.5$	$\alpha = 0.7$
Hits	58.84%	66.05%	52.80%	66.04%	67.57%
Errors	41.15%	33.95%	47.20%	33.95%	32.43%
False alarm	39.83%	39.57%	14.37%	39.57%	63.14%
Positive hits	74.71%	71.67%	19.98%	71.67%	98.28%
False negative	25.28%	28.33%	80.02%	28.33%	1.72%

Tabla 3. Performance of generic classifiers

	Linear	Diag-linear	Quadratic	Diag-quadratic	Mahalanobis
Hits	57.08%	57.08%	58.25%	58.25%	32.58%
Errors	42.92%	42.92%	41.75%	41.75%	67.41%
False alarm	20.83%	20.83%	2.92%	2.92%	83.74%
Positive hits	25.49%	25.49%	2.72%	2.72%	55.93%
False negative	74.51%	74.51%	97.28%	97.28%	44.06%

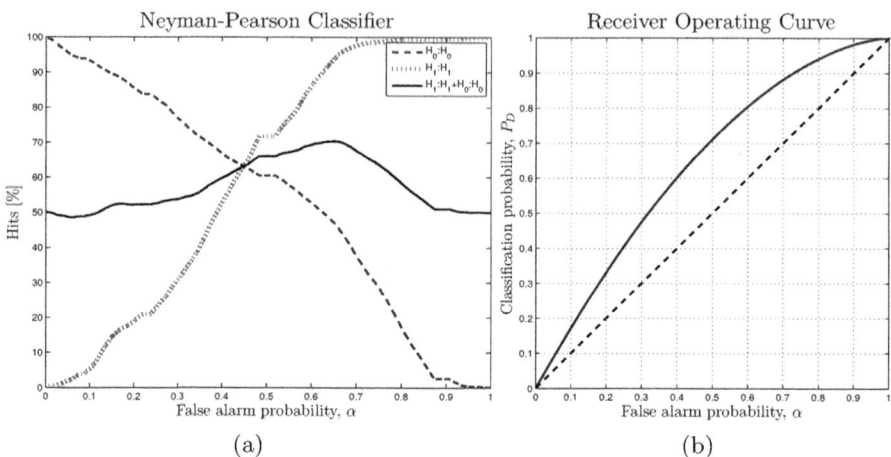

Fig. 3. Performance metrics of the Neyman-Pearson classifier: (a) Percentage of hits in classifying H_0 and H_1. (b) The receiver operating curve.

5   Conclusions

In this paper we have devised two classifiers for determining whether identical tasks have been executed or not in different processors. Since the Bayesiand and the Neyman-Pearson classifiers devised here have been developed for a specific application, their performance is indeed superior, as confirmed by our results, to the performance of generic classifiers which have been devised for classifying a wide class of applications. From our results we have observed also that the classification regions of Neyman-Pearson classifiers, with a probability of false alarm of 0.5, are similar to those obtained by the Bayesian classifier. This result is expected because a false alarm probability of 0.5 implies that the misclassification costs are symmetrical and unitary for both the null and the alternative hypothesis, and these costs are equal to the costs of the Bayesian classifier.

As a future work we will attempt to implement the classifiers developed here in a distributed system to improve its resource allocation algorithms.

References

1. Duda, R.O., Hart, P.E., Stork, D.G.: Pattern Classification, 2nd edn. Wiley-Interscience (November 2001)
2. Vasiliadis, G., Antonatos, S., Polychronakis, M., Markatos, E.P., Ioannidis, S.: Gnort: High Performance Network Intrusion Detection Using Graphics Processors. In: Lippmann, R., Kirda, E., Trachtenberg, A. (eds.) RAID 2008. LNCS, vol. 5230, pp. 116–134. Springer, Heidelberg (2008)
3. Dickinson, W., Leon, D., Podgurski, A.: Pursuing failure: the distribution of program failures in a profile space. In: FSE Conference Proceedings, pp. 246–255 (2001)

4. Zhang, J., Figueiredo, R.J.: Application classification through monitoring and learning of resource consumption patterns. In: Proceedings of the 20th International Conference on Parallel and Distributed Processing, IPDPS 2006, Washington, DC, USA, p. 144 (2006)
5. Cabrera, J.B.D., Gosar, J., Lee, W., Mehra, R.K.: On the statistical distribution of processing times in network intrusion detection. In: Proc. 43rd IEEE Conference on Decision and Control (2004)
6. Yang, Y., Yang, Q., Lu, W., Pan, J., Pan, R., Lu, C., Li, L., Qin, Z.: Preprocessing Time Series Data for Classification With Application to CRM. In: Zhang, S., Jarvis, R.A. (eds.) AI 2005. LNCS (LNAI), vol. 3809, pp. 133–142. Springer, Heidelberg (2005)
7. Pezoa, J.E., Dhakal, S., Hayat, M.M.: Maximizing service reliability in distributed computing systems with random failures: Theory and implementation. IEEE Trans. Parallel and Dist. Systems 21(10), 1531–1544 (2010)
8. Kay, S.M.: Fundamentals of statistical signal processing: estimation theory. Prentice-Hall, Inc., Upper Saddle River (1993)

Author Index

Batch number: 09490866

Printed by Printforce, the Netherlands